WORLD RACISM
AND
RELATED INHUMANITIES

**Recent Titles in
Bibliographies and Indexes in World History**

Foreign Policy of the French Second Empire: A Bibliography
William E. Echard, compiler and editor

The Anglo-American Relationship: An Annotated Bibliography of Scholarship, 1945-1985
David A. Lincove and Gary R. Treadway, compilers

Glimpses of India: An Annotated Bibliography of Published Personal Writings by Englishmen, 1583-1947
John F. Riddick, compiler

The American Field Service Archives of World War I, 1914-1917
L. D. Geller, compiler

An Annotated Bibliography of Latin American Sport: Pre-Conquest to the Present
Joseph L. Arbena, compiler

Modern Italian History: An Annotated Bibliography
Frank J. Coppa and William Roberts, compilers

Colonial British Caribbean Newspapers: A Bibliography and Directory
Howard S. Pactor, compiler

France under the German Occupation, 1940-1944: An Annotated Bibliography
Donna Evleth, compiler

A World In Turmoil: An Integrated Chronology of the Holocaust and World War II
Hershel Edelheit and Abraham J. Edelheit

First-Person Accounts of Genocidal Acts Committed in the Twentieth Century: An Annotated Bibliography
Samuel Totten

A Catalogue of Audio and Video Collections of Holocaust Testimony—Second Edition
Joan Ringelheim, compiler

A Guide to East Asian Collections in North America
Thomas H. Lee, compiler

WORLD RACISM AND RELATED INHUMANITIES

A Country-by-Country Bibliography

COMPILED BY
MEYER WEINBERG

Bibliographies and Indexes in World History, Number 26

GREENWOOD PRESS
New York • Westport, Connecticut • London

Z
7164
.R12
W5
1992

Library of Congress Cataloging-in-Publication Data

Weinberg, Meyer.
  World racism and related inhumanities : a country-by-country
bibliography / compiled by Meyer Weinberg.
      p. cm.—(Bibliographies and indexes in world history, ISSN
0742-6852 ; no. 26)
   Includes bibliographical references and indexes.
   ISBN 0-313-28109-2 (alk. paper)
   1. Racism—Bibliography. 2. Human rights—Bibliography.
3. Discrimination—Bibliography. I. Title. II. Series.
Z7164.R12W5   1992
[HT1521]
016.3058—dc20   92-4094

British Library Cataloguing in Publication Data is available.

Copyright © 1992 by Meyer Weinberg

All rights reserved. No portion of this book may be
reproduced, by any process or technique, without the
express written consent of the publisher.

Library of Congress Catalog Card Number: 92-4094
ISBN: 0-313-28109-2
ISSN: 0742-6852

First published in 1992

Greenwood Press, 88 Post Road West, Westport, CT 06881
An imprint of Greenwood Publishing Group, Inc.

Printed in the United States of America

The paper used in this book complies with the
Permanent Paper Standard issued by the National
Information Standards Organization (Z39.48-1984).

10 9 8 7 6 5 4 3 2 1

To
my colleagues in the W.E.B. DuBois
Department of Afro-American Studies,
University of Massachusetts, Amherst

CONTENTS

Introduction	xi
Afghanistan	1
Albania	3
Algeria	4
Angola	8
Argentina	10
Australia	16
Austria	39
Bangladesh	48
Belgium	51
Belize	55
Benin	56
Bolivia	57
Botswana	59
Brazil	61
Bulgaria	73
Burkina Faso	77
Burundi	78
Cambodia	79
Cameroon	81
Canada	83
Cape Verde Islands	123
Central African Republic	124
Chad	125
Chile	126
China	129
Colombia	144
Congo	147
Costa Rica	148
Cuba	150
Cyprus	158
Czechoslovakia	159

viii CONTENTS

Denmark	167
Dominican Republic	170
Ecuador	172
Egypt	174
El Salvador	181
Ethiopia	183
Finland	188
France	191
Gabon	218
Germany	219
Ghana	252
Great Britain	254
Greece	331
Guatemala	334
Guinea-Bissau	338
Guyana	340
Haiti	342
Honduras	346
Hungary	347
Iceland	354
India	355
Indonesia	381
Iran	386
Iraq	390
Ireland	393
Israel	396
Italy	443
Ivory Coast	452
Japan	454
Jordan	463
Kenya	464
Korea	469
Kuwait	472
Laos	473
Lebanon	474
Liberia	476
Libya	479
Madagascar	481
Malawi	482
Malaysia	484
Mali	490
Mauritania	491
Mauritius	492
Mexico	494
Mongolian People's Republic	504
Morocco	506
Mozambique	509
Myanmar	511
Namibia	513
Nepal	517

Netherlands	518
New Zealand	528
Nicaragua	536
Nigeria	549
Norway	557
Pakistan	559
Panama	562
Papua - New Guinea	565
Paraguay	568
Peru	570
Philippines	575
Poland	585
Portugal	594
Rumania	596
Rwanda	603
Saudi Arabia	604
Senegal	605
Sierra Leone	607
Singapore	609
Somalia	611
South Africa	612
Spain	637
Sri Lanka	645
Sudan	652
Suriname	656
Swaziland	658
Sweden	659
Switzerland	665
Syria	668
Tanzania	670
Thailand	673
Togo	676
Tunisia	677
Turkey	679
Uganda	686
Uruguay	688
U.S.S.R.	690
USA	724
Venezuela	745
Vietnam	747
Yemen	750
Yugoslavia	752
Zaire	760
Zambia	763
Zimbabwe	765
Africa	770
Asia	788
Caribbean	792
Europe	803

CONTENTS

Latin America	830
Middle East	845
Oceania	852
Elsewhere	865
Ancient History	896
Bibliography	903
Author Index	915
Subject Index	1021

INTRODUCTION

This is the first comprehensive, worldwide bibliography of racism. It contains references on some 135 countries and extends from ancient times to the present. The last set of entries directs the reader's attention to still other bibliographies for more material. Ending the volume are two indexes, one of authors and the other of subjects. Each of the more than 12,000 entries is separately numbered for ease of consultation. The following numbers, however, were not used: 1743, 3539, 3603, 3726, 3780, 3792, 4210, 4261, 5234, 5355, 6809, 7019, 7208, 7350, 7499, 7950, and 10399.

The word "racism" did not come into wide usage in the English-speaking world until after World War II. As recently as 1933 the word did not appear in the Oxford English Dictionary. For years racism was viewed as simple racial prejudice, then as discrimination; racism was either a personal attitude or an individual action against another person. The treatment of Blacks and others in South Africa and the United States as well as of Jews in Nazi Germany suggested that racism could be more properly regarded as a social system of actions. In time - in fact, quite recently - racism came to be seen to rest on a view of group superiority over a supposedly inferior group as purported justification for privileging the "superiors" and penalizing the "inferiors." Thus, the unequal distribution of wealth and income, housing, education, and much else is portrayed by racists as an inevitable consequence of some vaguely defined racial condition.

More likely, however, these inequalities of treatment are in part products of still other inequalities. A class structure, for example, that apportions goods and services by a standard of privilege and penalty helps create the basis for a "racist" apportionment as well. Similarly, a society that treats women as inferiors thereby prepares the way for racism, and helps sustain it once under way.

This system of interacting, mutually supportive forces leads to the concept of the "inhumanities." *By this term is meant all the ways that present-day societies have*

xii   INTRODUCTION

of denying systematically the equal worth of some groups of people in the interest of others. It is thus artificial to treat racism in isolation from additional inhumanities. A glance at the subject - index of this volume indicates the social, economic, and political complexity of racism.

The inhumanities dealt with here include the following:

1. Racism. A belief in the inherent superiority of some groups of people and the inherent inferiority of others, and the distribution of goods and services - let alone respect - in accordance with such judgment of unequal worth.

2. Slavery. The ownership of human beings by other humans and denial of access to family life and common social rights.

3. Class domination. Highly unequal distribution of wealth and income and deprivation of material living standards.

4. Sexism. Discrimination against women in education, employment, political rights, and collective self-organization.

5. National oppression. Denials of the right of national self-determination and acts of compulsory assimilation. Also covers xenophobia or fear of foreigners.

6. Imperialism. Domination of other countries by economic, political, and military means.

7. Colonialism. The occupation of a foreign area, suppression of its indigenous culture, and exploitation of its resources, including low-paid labor, along with a thoroughgoing racism toward the indigenous people.

8. Antisemitism. Denial of religious, civil, and cultural rights of Jews, and portrayal of Jews as an evil, secretive presence. Jews are punished for being Jews.

References to movements aimed at countering and eliminating the inhumanities are included both in the interest of completeness and encouragement.

The first part of the bibliography (1-10028) consists of references dealing with single countries. The second part contains references to areas or regions that cover entire areas or large parts of them but do not duplicate any references in the first part. For the "Caribbean" and "Oceania," however, areas and single countries which did not appear in the first part, are listed. Under "Elsewhere" are listed world-wide surveys, conglomerate groups of countries, geographically wide-ranging general works, and highly - specialized works that study single racism - related elements over a large geographical range. The section "Ancient History" is included to accommodate historical examples of countries which cannot be considered direct precursors of later nation-states (ancient Greece in relation to present day Greece, ancient Rome in relation to modern Italy). The final subject heading, "Bibliography," is broadly inclusive except for works on single countries.

INTRODUCTION   xiii

   This work was completed while the U.S.S.R. and Yugoslavia were still in existence. While the book was being published some successor states were granted international diplomatic recognition and others not. Accordingly, the entries remain as originally compiled.

   This bibliography has many references to material published or otherwise competed during the 1980s; including some in 1990. Besides English language items, a number in German, French, and Spanish are included; a scattering of items in other languages are also to be found. Whenever English language abstracts are appended to non-English articles, this fact is noted in brackets.

   I wish to thank Anita Weigel for her indispensable work with the computer. She designed the format of the bibliography and labored indefatigably to create a readable and reliable version of it. I greatly appreciate her devoted and untiring contribution. Elise Young performed with dispatch and competence the data entry. I am grateful for her aid. For help in various other ways, I appreciate the contributions of Ann Prosten, Donna Goodleaf, and Curtis Haynes. The reference librarians at the University of Massachusetts, Amherst, were, as usual, obliging and helpful.

AFGHANISTAN

1. Ahmad, Eqbal and Richard J. Barnet. "Bloody Games." New Yorker (April 11, 1988): 44-86.

2. Anwar, Raja. The Tragedy of Afghanistan: A First-Hand Account. Translated by Khalid Hasan. New York: Verso, 1989.

3. Bradsher, Henry S. "Stagnation and Change in Afghanistan." Journal of South Asian and Middle Eastern Studies 10 (Fall 1986): 3-35.

4. Gankovsky, Yu V. and others. A History of Afghanistan. Translated by Vitaly Baskakov. Moskow: Progress Publishers, 1985.

5. Halliday, Fred. "Revolution in Afghanistan." New Left Review 112 (November-December 1978): 3-44.

6. Hyman, Anthony. Afghanistan Under Soviet Domination, 1964-1983. London: Macmillan, 1984.

7. Laber, Jeri. "Afghanistan's Other War." New York Review of Books (December 18, 1986) [Educators of Afghanistani children.]

8. Moghadam, Val. "Afghanistan at the Crossroads." Against the Current 3 (November-December 1988): 8-16.

9. Newell, Richard S. "Post-Soviet Afghanistan: The Positions of the Minorities." Asian Survey 29 (November 1989): 1090-1108.

10. Orywal, Erwin. "Baluch Ethnicity in Afghanistan." Newsletter of Baluchistan Studies 2 (1985): 40-53.

11. Ross, David. "Beyond the Soviet Invasion: Afghanistan and the Concept of Self-determination." University of Toronto Faculty of Law Review 48 (Winter 1990): 92-116.

12. San Gupta, Bhabani. *Afghanistan: Politics, Economics and Society*. Boulder, CO: Lynne Rienner Publishers, Inc., 1986.

13. Vercellin, Giorio. *Crime de silence et crime de tapage: panorama des lectures sur l'Afghanistan contemporain*. Naples: Institutio Universitario Orientale, 1985.

14. Yehoshua, Benzion D. "Germans, Nazis, and Anti-Semitism in Afghanistan." *Forum on the Jewish People, Zionism and Israel* 62 (Winter-Spring 1989): 85-99. [Afghanistan.]

ALBANIA

15. Biberaj, Elez. Albania. Boulder, CO: Westview, 1989.

16. Bowers, Stephen R. "Stalinism in Albania: Domestic Affairs under Enver Hoxha." East European Quarterly 22 (1988): 441-457.

17. Ellman, Michael. "Albania's Economy Today and Tomorrow." World Economy 7 (September 1984)

18. Elsie, Robert. Dictionary of Albanian Literature. Westport, CT: Greenwood, 1986.

19. Holliday, Jon, ed. The Artful Albanian: The Memoirs of Enver Hoxha. London: Chatto & Windus, 1986.

20. Howe, Marvine. "No Hint of Change in Albania Where Liberalization Has Long Been Suspect." New York Times (November 12, 1989)

21. Pipa, Arshi. Albanian Stalinism, Ideo-political Aspects Boulder, CO: East European Monograph, 1990.

22. Pipa, Arshi. "The Other Albania: A Balkan Perspective." S. Slav Journal 8 (1985): 20-31.

23. Prifiti, Peter. Socialist Albania since 1944. Cambridge, MA: MIT Press, 1978.

24. Stamm, Christoph. "Zur Deutschen Besatzung Albaniens 1943-1944." Militargeschich. Mitt. 30 (1981): 99-120.

ALGERIA

25. Abitol, Michel. "Algeria." In Encyclopedia of the Holocaust I. 18-22. New York: Macmillan, 1990.

26. Aloula, Malek. The Colonial Harem. Minneapolis: University of Minnesota Press, 1986.

27. Amipaz-silber, Gitta. La resistance juive en Algérie, 1940-1942. Jerusalem: R. Mass, 1986.

28. Amtouche, Fadhma A. M. My Life Story: The Autobiography of a Berber Woman. Translated by Dorothy S. Blair. New Brunswick N.J.: Rutgers University Press, 1989.

29. Ansky, Michel. Les juifs d'Algérie, du Décret Crémieux à la libération. Paris: 1950.

30. Ayoun, Richard. "Les juifs d'Algerie." Les Temps Modernes 394 (1979): 146-161

31. Benhassine, M. L. "Formation et développement de la classe ouvière en Algérie." Su. Sociales Panorama (May 1982): 35-56.

32. Bennoune, Mahfoud. "Algeria's Facade of Democracy." Middle East Report 163 (March-April 1990): 9-13.

33. Bennoune, Mahfoud. The Making of Contemporary Algeria, 1830- 1987. New York: Cambridge University Press, 1988.

34. Blin, Louis. "Les noires dans l'Algérie contemporaine." Pol. Afric. (June 1988): 22-31.

35. Bourdieu, Pierre. "The Algerian Subproletariat." In Man, State, and Society in the Contemporary Maghrib edited by William Zartman. (NY, 1973)

36. Braun, Sidney D. "Benjamin Cremieux: Jew and Frenchman." Judaism 36 (Fall 1987): 451-459.

37. Brett, Michael. "Legislating for Inequality in Algeria: The Senatus-Consulte of 14 July 1865." Bulletin of the School of Oriental and African Studies 51 (1988): 440-461.

38. Chouraqui, André. A Man in Three Worlds. Lanham, MD: Translated by Kenton Kilmer. University Press of America, 1984.

39. Christelow, Allan. Muslim Law Courts and the French Colonial State in Algeria. Princeton, NJ: Princeton University Press, 1985.

40. Cohen, J. "Colonialism and Racism in Algeria." In Readings in Racial and Ethnic Relations, edited by Anthony H. Richmond. Oxford: Pergamon Press, 1972.

41. Colonna, Fanny. "Cultural Resistance and Religious Legitimacy in Colonial Algeria." Economy and Society 3 (1974): 233-252.

42. Colonna, Fanny. "Language, Social Relations and Intellectual Production in Algeria." Review of Middle East Studies 4 (1988)

43. Cooke, James L. "The Colonial Origins of Colon and Muslim Nationalism in Algeria, 1880-1920." Indian Political Science Review 10 (1976): 19-36.

44. Dermenjian, Geneviève. La crise antijuive oranaise 1895-1905: L'antisemitisme dans l'Algérie coloniale. Paris: L'Harmattan, 1986.

45. Dermenjian, Geneviève. Juifs et Européens d'Algérie: l'antisemitisme oranais (1892-1905). Jerusalem: Institut Ben-Zvi, 1983.

46. Dersa (pseud.). L'Algérie en debat: luttes et développment. Paris: Francois Maspero, 1981.

47. El Tayeb, Salah El Din El Zein. "The Europeanized Algerians and the Emancipation of Algeria." Middle Eastern Studies 22 (April 1986): 206-235.

48. Entelis, John P. Algeria: the Revolutions Institutionalized. Boulder, CO: Westview Press, 1986.

49. Friedman, E. Colonialism & After: An Algerian Jewish Community. South Hadley, MA: Bergin & Garvey, 1988.

50. Gallissot, Rene. "Precolonial Algeria." Economy and Society 4 (November 1975): 418-445.

51. Gellner, Ernest and Charles Micaud, eds. Arabs and Berbers: From Tribes to Nation in North Africa. London: Duckworth, 1973.

52. Gordon, David C. *Women of Algeria: An Essay on Change*. Cambridge, MA: Harvard University Press, 1968.

53. Green, Elliot A. "Jewish Anti-Nazi Resistance in Wartime Algeria." *Midstream* 35 (January 1989): 46-49.

54. Hamoumou, Mohand. "Le relations parent-enfants dans les familles algérienne immigrées." *An. Ec. Soc Civil* 41 (July-August 1986): 771-788.

55. Harik, Elsa M. and Donald G. Schilling. *The Politics of Education in Colonial Algeria and Kenya*. Athens, OH: Ohio University Monographs in International Studies, 1984.

56. Heffernan, Michael J. "The Parisian Poor and the Colonization of Algeria during the Second Republic." *French History* 3 (December 1989): 377-403.

57. Heggoy, Alf A. "Cultural Disrespect: European and Algerian Views on Women in Colonial and Independent Algeria." *Muslim World* 62 (1972): 323-334.

58. Heggoy, Alf A. "The Evolution of Algerian Women." *African Studies Review* 17 (1974): 449-456.

59. Heggoy, Alf A. *The French Conquest of Algiers, 1830: An Algerian Oral Tradition*. Athens, OH: Center for International Studies, Ohio University, 1986.

60. Henouda, A. *Agrarian Policy and Social Transformation in Algeria since Pre-colonial Times*. Master's thesis: University of Keele, 1988.

61. Holsinger, Donald. "Muslim Response to French Imperialism: An Algerian Saharan Case Study." *Int. Jn. Afric. Hist. Stud.* 19 (1986): 1-16.

62. Knauss, Peter R. *The Persistence of Patriarchy: Class, Gender, and Ideology in Twentieth Century Algeria*. New York: Praeger, 1987.

63. Laacher, Smain. *Algérie: réalités sociales et pouvoir*. Paris: Editions d'Harmattan, 1985.

64. Lustick, Ian. *State-building Failure in British Ireland & French Algeria*. Berkeley: Institute of International Studies, University of California, 1986.

65. Maran, Rita R. *Torture during the French-Algerian War The Role of the "Mission Civilisatrice"*. Doctoral Dissertation. Santa Cruz: University of California, 1987.

66. Maran, Rita R. *Torture, the Role of Ideology in the French-Algerian War*. New York: Praeger, 1989.

ALGERIA 7

67. Melasuo, Tuomo. "Culture and Minorities in the Arab-Islamic Identity of Algeria." In Islam: State and Society, edited by Klaus Ferdinand and Mehdi Mozaffari. Riverdale, MD: Riverdale, 1988.

68. Murphey, Elizabeth H. "Colonial Propaganda: Jacques Soustelle in Defense of French Algeria, 1955-1962." Proc. Fr. Colonial Hist. Soc. 6-7 (1982): 76-85.

69. Oshane, R. K. Land Expropriation and Assimilation: A Comparative Study of French Policy in Algeria and Federal Indian Policy in the United States during the Nineteenth Century. Doctoral dissertation. University of Keele, 1988.

70. Pfeifer, Karen. Agrarian Reform Under State Capitalism in Algeria. Boulder, CO: Westview Press, 1985.

71. Powers, David S. "Orientalism, Colonialism, and Legal History: The Attack on Muslim Family Endowments in Algeria and India." Comparative Studies in Society and History 31 (Autumn 1989): 535-571.

72. Prochaska, David. Making Algeria French: Colonialism in Bone, 1870-1920. New York: Cambridge University Press, 1990.

73. Roberts, Hugh J. R. "The Economics of Berberism: The Kabyle Question in Contemporary Algeria." Government and Opposition 18 (Spring 1983): 218-235.

74. Rouanet, Gustave. L'antisemitisme algérien. Paris: "La Petite Republique", 1899.

75. Tabory, Mala and Ephraim Tabory. "Berber Demands for Linguistic Rights in Algeria." Plural Society 16 (1986): 126-160.

76. Tlemcani, Rachid. State and Revolution in Algeria. London: Zed Press, 1986.

77. Trautmann, Wolfgang. "The Nomads of Algeria under French Rule: A Study of Social and Economic Change." Journal of Historical Geography 15 (April 1989): 126-138.

78. Vatin, Jean Claude. "Conditions et formes de la domination coloniale en Algérie (1919-1945)." Revue algérienne des science juridiques, politiques et économiques 9 (December 1972): 873-906.

79. Zouiche, Farida. Women and the Process of Educational Democratization in the Arab World: The Case of Algeria. Doctoral dissertation: Boston University, 1987. UMO # 8722597.

ANGOLA

80. Bender, Gerald J. Angola Under the Portuguese: The Myth and the Reality. Berkeley: University of California Press, 1978.

81. Bhagawan, M. R. Angola's Political Economy 1975-1985. Uppsala, Sweden: Scandinavian Institute of African Studies, 1986.

82. Clarence-Smith, W. Gervase. "Business Empire in Angola Under Salazar, 1930-1961." African Economic History 14 (1985): 1-13.

83. Clarence-Smith, W. Gervase. "Class Structure and Class Struggle in Angola in the 1970's." Journal of Southern African Studies 7 (October 1980)

84. Clarence-Smith, W. Gervase. "Slavery in coastal southern Angola, 1875-1913." Journal of Southern African Studies 2 (1976): 214-223.

85. Clarence-Smith, W. Gervase. The Third Portuguese Empire, 1925-1975. Dover, NH: Manchester University Press, 1984.

86. Dias, J. R. "Famine and Disease in the History of Angola c. 1830-1930." Journal of African History 22 (1981): 340-596.

87. Diogo, Junior Alfredo. Angola perante a escravatura. Luanda: Editora Quissanje, [s/d.]

88. Falola, Toyin. "Colonialism & Exploitation: The Case of Portugal in Africa." Lusophone Areas Stud. Journal 1 (January 1983): 41-66.

89. Heywood, Linda M. "UNITA and Ethnic Nationalism in Angola." Journal of Modern Africa 27 (March 1989): 47-66.

90. Miller, Joseph C. Way of Deaths: Merchant Capitalism and the Angolan Slave Trade, 1730-1830. Madison: University of Wisconsin Press, 1989.

91. Neumann, Gerd. "Some Issues in the Social and Economic Development of Angola." Economic Quarterly 17 (1982): 3-17.

92. Pélissier, René. "Conquête coloniale et résistance in Angola (1845-1926)." Mois Afrique 22 (October-November 1986): 140-153.

ARGENTINA

93. Altimir, O. "Estimaciones de la distribucion del ingreso en la Argentina, 1953-1980." Desarrollo Económico 25 (January-March 1986) [English summary.]

94. Ander Egg, Ezequil and others. Opresión y marginalidad de la mujer en el orden social machista. Buenos Aires: Edit. Humanitas, 1972.

95. Andrews, George R. The Afro-Argentines of Buenos Aires, 1800-1900. Madison: University of Wisconsin Press, 1980.

96. "Anti-discrimination Law Adopted [in Argentina]." Patterns of Prejudice 22 (Autumn 1988): 47-49.

97. Argentina. Comision Nacional sobre la Desaparicion de Personas. Nunca mas: The Report of the Argentine National Commission on the Disappeared. New York: Farrar, Straus, & Giroux, 1986.

98. Avni, Jaim. "Antisemitismo estatl en la Argentina? (A proposito de los sucesos de la semana tragica-enero de 1919)." Coloquio 4 (1982): 49-67.

99. Bartolomé, Miguel A. "La desindianizacion de la Argentina." Boletín de Antropologia Americana (Mexico) 11 (1985): 39-50.

100. Bellardi, Marta and Aldo de Paula. Villas miseria: origen, erradicación y respuestas populares. Buenos Aires: Centro Editor de América Latina, 1986.

101. Ben-Dror, Graciela. "Argentina." Encyclopedia of the Holocaust,I, 81-83. New York: Macmillan, 1990.

102. Blum, Leonor. "Anti-Semitism in Argentina." Canadian Zionist 49 (1979)

103. Braslavsky, Cecilia. La discriminación educativa en Argentina. Buenos Aires: Grupo Editor Latinamericano, 1985.

104. Braslavsky, Cecilia. "Youth in Argentina: Between the Legacy of the Past and the Construction of the Future." CEPAL Review 29 (August 1986): 41-54.

105. Brooke, James. "A Weary Buenos Aires Family Wonders How to Keep Afloat." New York Times (June 18, 1989):

106. Carlson, Marifran. Feminismo: The Women's Movement in Argentinia from its Beginning to Eva Peron. Chicago: Acad. Chicago, 1988.

107. Carrera, Nicolás. "Violence as an Economic Force: The Process of Proletarianisation among the Indigenous People of the Argentinian Chaco, 1884-1930." IWGIA Document 46 (1982): 1-50.

108. Castell, Pablo. "Entre capitanes y coroneles." Realidad Ecónomica (1987): 11-25.

109. Castillo, Hugo P. and Joseph S. Tulchin. "Développement capitaliste et structures sociales des régions en Argentine (1880-1930)." An : Éc., Soc., Civil. 41 (November-December 1986): 1359-1384.

110. Castro, Donald S. "El Negro del acordeón: The Image of the Black Argentina." Afro-Hispanic Review 7 (January-September 1988): 11-18.

111. Centro de Documentation e Informacion sobre Judaismo Argentino 'Marc Turcow' comp. Bibliografia tematica sobre Judaismo Argentino. Vol. 3: Antisemitosmo en la Argentina 1909-1929. Buenos Aires: 1985.

112. Conklin, Margaret and Daphne Davidson. "The IMF and Economic and Social Human Rights: A Case Study of Argentina, 1958- 1985." Human Rights Quarterly 8 (May 1986): 227-269.

113. Cony, Stella. La Mujer avanza. Buenos Aires: Ediciones Agon, 1985. [Discrimination against women.]

114. Corradi, Juan E. "Argentina today: The Cultural Mood." Dissent 34 (Winter, 1987): 23-26.

115. Corradi, Juan E. The Fitful Republic: Economy, Society, and Politics in Argentina. Boulder, CO: Westview Press, 1985.

116. Corradi, Juan E. "Terror in Argentina." Telos 54 (Winter, 1982-83)

117. Deutsch, Sandra M. "The Argentina Right and the Jews, 1919-1933." Journal of Latin American Studies 18 (May 1986): 113-134.

12 WORLD RACISM AND RELATED INHUMANITIES

118. Deutsch, Sandra M. *Counterrevolution in Argentina, 1900-1932: The Argentine Patriotic League*. Lincoln: University of Nebraska Press, 1986.

119. Eloy Martinez, Tomas. *Peron and the Nazi War Criminals*. Washington, D.C.: Wilson Center, 1984. [Working Papers, no. 144.]

120. Gil, Germán R. *La izquierda peronista: para una interpretación ideologica (1955-1974)*. Buenos Aires: Centro Editor de América Latina, 1989.

121. González Arzac, Alberto Ricardo. *La esclavitud en la Argentina*. Buenos Aires: 1974.

122. Gudmundson, Lowell. "De 'negro' a 'blanco' en la Hispano-america del siglo xix: la asimilacion afroamericans en Argentina y Costa Rica." *Mesoamerica* 7 (1986): 309-329.

123. Hebert, John R. *The Tragic Week of January 1919 in Buenos Aires: Background, Events, Aftermath*. Doctoral dissertation: Georgetown University, 1972.

124. Hernández, Isabel. *Derechos humanos y aborigenes: el pueblo Mapuche*. Buenos Aires: Ediciones Busqueda, 1985.

125. Hernández, Isabel. "Identidad indigena y educación." *Desarrollo Económico* 28 (April-June 1988): 121-137.

126. Hintze, Susana. *Estrategias alimentarias de sobrevivencia (un astudio de caso en el Gran Buenos Aires)* 2 vols. Buenos Aires: Centro Editor de América Latina, 1989.

127. Hodge, John E. "The Formation of the Argentine Public Primary and Secondary School System." *The Americas* 44 (July 1987): 45-66.

128. Inigo Carrera, Nicolos. *Violence as an Economic Force: the Process of Proletarianization among the Indigenous People of the Argentinian Chaco*. Copenhagen: IWGIA, 1982.

129. Johnson, Lyman L. "The Racial Limits of Guild Solidarity: An Example from Colonial Buenos Aires." *R. Hist. Am.* 99 (January-June 1985): 7-26.

130. Knudson, Jerry W. "Antisemitism in Latin America (2): Social Change in Argentina." *Patterns of Prejudice* 6 (1972): 22-30.

131. Lattuado, Mario J. *Politica agraria del liberalismo-conservador, 1946-1985*. Buenos Aires: Centro Editor de América Latina, 1987. [Defense of large-scale landowners.]

132. Leis, Héctor R. *El movimento por los derechos humanos y la politica argentina* 2 vols. Buenos Aires: Centro Editor de América Latina, 1989.

133. Lewis, Paul H. The Crisis of Argentine Capitalism. Chapel Hill: University of North Carolina Press, 1989.

134. Marshall, Adriana. Politicas sociales: el modelo neoliberal Argentina (1976-1983). Buenos Aires: Editorial Legasa, 1988.

135. McGee Deutsch, Sandra M. "The Argentina Right and the Jews, 1919-1933." Journal of Latin American Studies 18 (May 1986): 113-134.

136. McGee Deutsch, Sandra F. "Right-Wing Female Activists in Buenos Aires, 1900-1932." In Women and the Social Structure, edited by Barbara J. Harris and Jo Ann McNamara, 85-97. Durham, NC: Duke University Press, 1983.

137. Mignone, Emilio F. Witness to the Truth: the Complicity of Church and Dictatorship in Argentina. Orbis Books, 1987.

138. Mirelman, Victor A. Jewish Buenos Aires, 1800-1930: In Search of An Identity. Detroit: Wayne State University Press, 1989.

139. Mirelman, Victor A. "The Semána Trágica of 1919 and the Jews of Argentina." Jewish Social Studies 37 (January 1975): 61-73.

140. Munck, Ronaldo. "Cycles of Class Struggle and the Making of the Working Class in Argentina, 1890-1920." Journal of Latin American Studies 19 (May 1987): 19-39.

141. Nunca Mas. The Report of the Argentine National Commission on the Disappeared. New York: Farrar, Straus & Giroux, 1986.

142. O'Donnell, Guillermo. "State and Alliances in Argentina 1956-1976." 1978 15, 3-33

143. Partnoy, Alicia. The Little School: Tales of Disappearance and Survival in Argentina. Translated by Alicia Partnoy, Lois Athey, and Sandra Braunstein. P.O. Box 8933, Pittsburgh, PA: Cleis Press, 1986.

144. Potter, Anne L. "The Failure of Democracy in Argentina, 1916-1930: An Institutional Perspective." Journal of Latin American Studies 13 (1981): 83-109.

145. Quiroga, Hugo. Estado, crisis económica y poder militar (1880-1981). Buenos Aires: Centro Editor de América Latina, 1985.

146. Recabarron, Maria E. La Mujer y el feminismo la Argentina. Buenos Aires: Centro Editor de la Mujer, 1980.

147. Rock, David. Argentina, 1516-1982: From Spanish Colonization to the Falklands War. Berkeley: University of California Press, 1986.

148. Rock, David. "Intellectual Precursors of Conservative Nationalism in Argentina, 1900-1927." Hispanic American Historical Review 67 (May 1987): 271-300.

149. Rodriquez, Nemesio J. Oppression in Argentina: The Mataco Case. Copenhagen: International Work Group for Indigenous Affairs, 1975.

150. Rouquié, Alain. "Hegemonia Militar, Estado y Dominacion Social." In Argentina Hoy, edited by Rouquié, 11-50. Mexico: Siglio xxi, 1982.

151. Salvatore, Ricardo D. "Labor Control and Discrimination: The Contratista System in Mendoza, Argentina, 1880-1920." Agricultural History 60 (Summer 1986): 52-80.

152. Schvarzer, Jorge and others. "Argentina and the Future." Telos 18 (Summer 1985): 124-133.

153. Schwartz, Kessel. "Anti-Semitism in Modern Argentina Fiction." Jewish Social Studies 40 (Spring, 1978): 131-140.

154. Senkman, Leonardo, ed. El antisemitismo en la Argentina. 3 vols. Buenos Aires: Centro Editor de America Latina, 1986. [1959-1983.]

155. Simonovich, Javier. "Desparecidos y antisemitismo en la Argentia (1976-1983)." Nueva Sión (October 19, 1985)

156. Smith, Peter H. "The Breakdown of Democracy in Argentina, 1916-1930." In The Breakdown of Democratic regimes: Latin America, edited by Juan Linz and Alfred Stepan, 3-27. Baltimore, MD: John Hopkins University Press, 1978.

157. Spitta, Arnold. "Corrientes antisemitos y politica de immigración en la Argentina de los años treinta y cuarenta." Estudios Migratorios Latinamericanos 4 (1989): 19-26.

158. Stroganov, A. I. "Distinctive Features of the Development of Capitalism in Argentina." Sov. Stud. Hist. 26 (Spring 1988): 41-55.

159. Turkovic, Robert J. Race Relations in the Province of Cordoba, Argentina, 1800-1853. Doctoral dissertation: University of Florida, 1981. UMO # 8213708.

160. Waisman, Carlos H. "The Ideology of Right-wing Nationalism in Argentina: Capitalism, Socialism and the Jews." World Congress Jewish Studies 9 (1986): 337-344.

161. Weisbrot, Robert. "Anti-Semitism in Argentina." Midstream 24 (May 1978): 12-23.

162. White, Elizabeth B. German Influence in the Argentine Army, 1900 to 1945. Doctoral dissertation: University of Virginia, 1986. UMO # 8716985.

AUSTRALIA

163. Aarons, Mark. <u>Nazi Fugitives in Australia</u>. Port Melbourne: Wm. Heinemann Australia, 1989.

164. Albinski, Henry S. "Australia." In <u>International Handbook on Race and Race Relations</u>, edited by Jay A. Sigler. Westport, CT: Greenwood, 1987.

165. Alderman, Geoffrey. "The Jew as a Scapegoat? The Settlement and Reception of Jews in South Wales before 1914." <u>Jewish Hist. Soc. Engl. Trans.</u> 26 (1974-1978): 62-70.

166. Aman, Reinhold. "Offensive Words in Dictionaries, IV: Ethnic, Racial, Religious and Sexual Slurs in an American and Australian Dictionary." <u>Maledicta</u>, 10 (1988-1989): 126-135.

167. Anderson, Don S. and A. E. Vervoorn. <u>Access to Privilege: Patterns of Participations in australian Post-Secondary Education</u>. Miami, FL: Australian National University Press, 1984.

168. "Antisemitic Anti-Communism in Australia." <u>Patterns of Prejudice</u> 18 (July 1984): 43-44.

169. <u>Asia in Australian Education</u>. 3 vols. Canberra, Australia: Asian Studies Association of Australia, 1980.

170. Austin, Diane J. <u>Australian Sociologies</u>. Boston, MA: G. Allen & Unwin, 1984.

171. Australia. <u>Review of Material Relating to the Entry of suspected War Criminals</u>. Canberra: Australian Government Printing Service, 1987.

172. "Australian Attitudes toward the Jews, Antisemitism and the Middle East." <u>Patterns of Prejudice</u> 21 (Summer 1987): 50-51.

173. Barbara, Susan B. "Conceptualizations of Women within Australian Egalitarian Thought." Comparative Studies in Society and History 30 (July 1988): 483-510.

174. Baxter, J. H. and others. "The Australian Class Structure: Some Preliminary Results from the Australian Class Project." Australia and New Zealand Journal of Sociology 25 (May 1989): 100-120.

175. Bell, J. H. and U.S. Pandey. "The Exclusion of women from Australian Post-Secondary Agricultural Education and Training 1880-1969." Australian Journal of Politics and History 36 (1990)

176. Birrell, R. and A. Seitz. "The Myth of Ethnic Inequality in Australian Education." Journal of the Australain Population Association 3 (1986): 52-74.

177. Blackbeney, Michael. Australia and the Jewish Refugees 1933- 1948. Sydney: Croom Helm Australia, 1985.

178. Blackmore, Jillian A. Schooling for Work: Vocationalism in Secondary Education in Victoria, Australia, 1930-60. Doctoral dissertation, Stanford University, 1986. UMO # 8700729.

179. Bottomley, Gill. "Ethnicity, Race and Nationalism in Australia: Some Critical Perspectives." Australian Journal of Social Issues 23 (August 1988): 169-183.

180. Bradbury, Bruce and others. "Housing and Poverty in Australia." Urban Studies 24 (April 1987): 95-102.

181. Bryson, Lois. "The Proletarianization of Women: Gender Justice in Australia." Social Justice 16 (Fall 1989): 87-102.

182. Buckley, Ken and Ted Wheelwright. No Paradise for Workers, Capitalism and the Common People in Australia 1788-1914. New York: Oxford University Press, 1988.

183. Butlin, N. G. "Contours of the Australian Economy 1788- 1860." Australian Economic History Review 26 (September 1986): 1986.

184. Carter, M. and R. Maddock. "Leisure and Australian Wellbeing 1911-1981." Australian Economic History Review 27 (March 1987)

185. Castles, S. and others. Mistaken Identity: Multiculturalism and the Demise of Nationalism in Australia. Sydney: Pluto, 1988.

186. Catley, R. and B. McFarlane. Australian Capitalism in Boom and Depression. Chippendale: Alternative Publishing Cooperative, 1981.

187. Clark, C. M. H. *A History of Australia*. 6 vols. Melbourne: Melbourne University Press, 1962-1987.

188. Connell, R. W. *Class Structure in Australian History: Documents, Narrative, and Argument*. Melbourne: Longman Cheshire, 1980.

189. Connell, R. W. *Ruling Class, Ruling Culture, Studies in Conflict, Power and Hegemony in Australian Life*. New York: Cambridge University Press, 1977.

190. Cowlishaw, Gillian. *Black, White or Brindle: Race in Rural Australia*. New York: Cambridge University Press, 1988.

191. Cresciani, Gianfranco. "Italian Fascism in Australia 1922-1945." *Studi Emigrazione* 25 (1988): 237-246.

192. Crockett, G. "Socio-economic Background of Students in Tertiary Education in Australia: Some Additional Evidence." *Australian Bulletin of Labour* 13 (March 1987)

193. Crowley, F. K. *Working-Class Conditions in Australia, 1788- 1851*. Doctoral dissertation: University of Melbourne, 1949.

194. Curthoys, Ann. *For and Against Feminism: A Personal Journey into Feminist Theory and History*. Allen and Unwin, 1988.

195. Curthoys, Ann and Andrew Markus, eds. *Who Are Our Enemies? Racism and the Australian Working Class*. Canberra: Australian Society for the Study of Labour History, 1978.

196. De Lepervanche, Marie M. *Indians in a White Australia*. Winchester, MA: Allen and Unwin, 1984.

197. Dilnot, A. W. "The Distribution and Composition of Personal Sector Wealth in Australia." *Australian Economic Review* 90 (Winter 1990)

198. Doobov, A. L. "Racism in School Books." *Australian Quarterly* 46 (1974)

199. Drago, R. "The Extent of Wage Discrimination in Australia." *Australian Bulletin of Labour* 15 (September 1989)

200. Duffield, Ian. "The Life and Death of 'Black' John Goff: Aspects of the Black Convict Contribution to Resistance Patterns during the Transportation Era in Eastern Australia." *Australian Journal of Politics and History* 33 (1987): 30-44.

201. Dwight, Alan. "The Chinese in New South Wales Law Courts, 1848-1854." *Journal of the Royal Australian Historical Society* 73 (1987): 75-93.

AUSTRALIA 19

202. Edyvean, Janine E. Australian Impressions of the Pacific, 1860-1914: An Aspect of Australian Racism. B.A.(Hons.) thesis: University of Adelaide, 1973.

203. Ellis, C. J. Why Does the ALP Support the White Australian Policy? 1855-1940. Master's thesis: University of Melbourne, 1950.

204. Encel, Sol. "Antisemitism and Prejudice in Australia." Patterns of Prejudice 23 (Spring 1989): 16-27.

205. Encel, Sol. Equality and Authority, a Study of Class, Status and Power in Australia. Melbourne: Cheshire, 1970.

206. Encel, Sol. "The FitzGerald Report on Australia's Immigration Policies." Patterns of Prejudice 22 (Winter 1988): 48-49.

207. Encel, Sol. Women and Society: An Australian Study. Melbourne: Cheshire, 1971.

208. Evans, M. D. R. and J. Kelley. "Immigrants' Work: Equality and Discrimination in the Australian Labour Market." Australia and New Zealand Journal of Sociology 22 (July 1986): 187-207.

209. Evans, R. and others Exclusion, Exploitation and Extermination: Race Relations in Colonial Queensland. Sydney: ANZ Book Co, 1975.

210. Fabian, Suzanne and Jeanette Morag Loh. Australian Children through 200 Years. Kangaroo Press, 1985.

211. Fitzpatrick, Brian. The British Empire in Australia. Melbourne: Macmillan, 1941.

212. Fletcher, Frank. "The Victorian Jewish Community, 1891-1901: Its Interrelationship with the Majority Gentile society." Australian Jewish Historical Society 8 (1978): 221-271.

213. Fry, E. C. The Condition of the Wage-earning Class in Australia in the 1880s. Doctoral dissertation: Australian National University, 1956.

214. Gardner, John. "Sex Discrimination in Employment." Law Quarterly Review 106 (July 1990): 361-365.

215. Getzler, Israel. Neither Toleration Nor Favour: The Struggle of the Jewish Communities in the Australian Colonies for Equal Religious Rights in the 1840s and 1850s. Master thesis: University of Melbourne, 1960.

216. Getzler, Israel. Neither Toleration Nor Favor, Australian Chapter of Jewish Emancipation. Melbourne, Australia: University Press, 1970.

217. Gibson, John and David Allen. "The Issue of Racial Vilification." Law Institute Journal 64 (August 1990)

218. Giddings, Jeff and others. "Justice and Equity v. Cost Cutting." Legal Service Bulletin 14 (February 1989): 13-15.

219. Goldlust, J. "Jewish Reactions to Prejudice in Australia." Patterns of Prejudice 4 (March-April 1970): 11-14.

220. Gott, K. D. Voices of Hate: a Study of the Australian League of Rights and Its Director, Eric D. Butler. Melbourne: Dissent Pub. Assoc., 1965.

221. Graetz, Brian. "The Reproduction of Privilege in Australian Education." British Journal of Sociology 39 (September 1988): 358-376.

222. Grassby, Albert J. The Tyranny of Prejudice. Melbourne: AE Press, 1984.

223. Harcourt, David. Everyone Wants to be Fuehrer: National Socialism in Australia and New Zealand. Cremorne, NSW: Angus and Robertson, 1972.

224. Hartwig, M. C. "The Theory of Internal Colonialism: the Australian Case." In Essays in the Political Economy of Australian Capitalism, edited by E.L. Wheelwright and Ken Buckley. Sydney: Australian and New Zealand Book Co., 1978.

225. Hawthorne, Lasleeyanne, ed. Refugee: The Vietnamese Experience. New York: Oxford University Press, 1982.

226. Higley, John and others. Elites in Australia. London: Routledge and Kegan Paul, 1979.

227. Hirst, John. "Egalitarianism." Australian Cultural History 5 (1986): 12-31.

228. Hollingsworth, P. Two Worlds: School and the Migrant Family. Melbourne: Stockland Press, 1970.

229. Hooper, Beverley J. Australian Reactions to German Persecution of the Jews and Refugee Immigration, 1933-1947. Master's thesis, Australian National University, 1972.

230. Indochinese Refugee Resettlement - Australian Involvement. Canberra: Australian Government Publishing Service, 1982.

231. Inglis, C. B. The Darwin Chinese: A Study of Assimilation. Master's thesis, Australian National University, 1968.

232. Iredale, R. R. The Occupational Adjustment of Indo-Chinese Refugees in Australia. Canberra: The Australian National University, 1983.

233. Jakubowicz, A. M. and others. Ethnicity, Class and Social Policy in Australia. Kensington, New South Wales: Social Welfare Centre, University of New South Wales, 1984.

234. Jakubowicz, Andrew. "Racism, Multiculturalism and the Immigration Debate in Australia: A Bibliographic Essay." Sage Race Relations Abstracts 10 (August 1985): 1-15.

235. Johnson, D. "The Measurement of Poverty in Australia: 1981- 82 and 1985-86." Australian Economic Review 83 (Spring 1988)

236. Johnston, Gerald L. "The Sociocultural Schism in Australian Schooling." Australian Journal of Education 34 (April 1990)

237. Jones, Frank L. and Peter Davis. "Class Structuration and Patterns of Social closure in Australia and New Zealand." Sociology 22 (May 1988): 271-291.

238. Jones, Frank L. "Sources of Gender Inequality in Income: What the Australian Census Says." Social Forces 62 (1983): 134-152.

239. Kakwani, Nanak. Analyzing Redistribution Policies: A Study Using Australian Data. New York: Cambridge University Press, 1986.

240. Kalantzis, Mary and other. "Pluralism and Social Reform: A Review of Multiculturalism in Australian Education." Thesis Eleven 10-11 (1984/85): 195-215.

241. Karmel, Peter, ed. Education, Change and Society. 1981.

242. Karmel, Peter. "Quality and Equality in Education." Australian Journal of Education 29 (1985): 279-293.

243. Kelley, Jonathan and Ian McAllister. "Immigrants, Socio- Economic Attainment, and Politics in Australia." British Journal of Sociology 35 (September 1984): 387-405.

244. Knibbs, G. H. The Private Wealth of Australia and Its Growth. Melbourne: 1918.

245. Kwiet, K. and O. Reinhardt. "A Nazi Assessment of Australian Racial Policy from 1935." Australian Journal of Politics and History 34 (1988)

246. Lepervanche, Marie M. de. Indians in a White Australia. Boston, MA: George Allen & Unwin, 1984.

247. Lewis, Milton and Roy A. MacLeod. "A Workingman's Paradise? Reflections on Urban Mortality in ColonialAustralia, 1860-1900." Medical Hist. 31 (October 1987): 387-402.

22 WORLD RACISM AND RELATED INHUMANITIES

248. Linke, R. D. and others. "Participation and Equity in Higher Education: A Preliminary Report on the Socioeconomic Profile of Higher Education Students in south Australia, 1974-1984." Australian Bulletin of Labour 11 (June 1985)

249. Lippman, Lorna. The Functions of Racism in Australian Educational Literature. Melbourne: Office of the Commissioner for Community Relations, 1979.

250. Lippman, Lorna. Words or Blows: Racial Attitudes in Australia. Harmondsworth: Penguin, 1973.

251. Manne, Robert, ed. The New Conservatism in Australia. New York: Oxford University Press, 1982.

252. Marks, Gary N. and others. "Class and Income in Australia." Australia and New Zealand Journal of Sociology 25 (November 1989): 410-427.

253. Markus, A. and R. Rasmussen, eds. Prejudice in the Public Arena: Racism. Victoria, Australia: Monash University, Centre for Migrant and Intercultural Studies, 1987.

254. Matthews, P. W., comp. Prejudice and Discrimination: A Bibliography. Carlton: Department of Education, Melbourne State College, 1974.

255. McGill, Stuart C. The Australian Social Wage. Doctoral dissertation, New School for Social Research, 1990. UMO # 9031850.

256. McLean, Jan and Sue Richardson. "More or Less Equal? Australian Income Distributions in 1933 and 1980." Economic Record 62 (March 1986): 67-81.

257. McMichael, A. J. "Social Class as Estimated by Occupational Prestige and Mortality in Australian Wales in the 1970s." Community Health Studies 9 (1985): 220-230.

258. McMichael, Philip. "Class Formation in a World-Historical Perspective: Lessons from Australian History." Review 9 (Fall 1985): 275-303.

259. McMichael, Philip. "Settlers and Primitive Accumulation: Foundations of Capitalism in Australia." Review 49 (1980): 307-334.

260. McMichael, Philip. Settlers and the Agrarian Question: foundations of Capitalism in Colonial Australia. New York: Cambridge University Press, 1984.

261. Mcqueen, Humphrey. State's Rights as Class Interests in Gallipoli To Petrov: Arguing with Australian History. Boston, MA: George Allen and Unwin, 1984.

262. McQueen, Humphrey. "The Sustenance of Silence: Racism in the 20th Century Australia." Meanjin 2 (1971):

263. Meagher, G. A. and Peter B. Dixon. "Analyzing Income Distribution in Australia." Economic Record 62 (December 1986): 427-441.

264. Melbourne Institute of Jewish Affairs. Attitudes and Opinions toward Australian Jews and Jewish Affairs. 1986. The Institute, 4th floor, 550 Bourke Street, Melbourne, Victoria 3000, Australia.

265. Mendelsohn, Ronald. The Conditions of the People: Social Welfare in Australia, 1900-1975. Boston, Ma: Allen and Unwin, 1979.

266. Menzies, A. C. C. Review of Material Relating To the Entry of Suspected War Criminals into Australia. Canberra: Australian Government Publishing Service, 1987.

267. Mercer, Patricia M. An Analysis of Racial Attitudes Towards Melanesians Expressed in the Queensland Legislative Assembly and Newspapers, 1877-92. B.A.(Hons.) thesis: James Cook University of North Queensland, 1972.

268. Mercer, Patricia M. and C.R. Moore. "Australia's Pacific Islanders, 1906-1977." Journal of Pacific History 13 (1978): 90-101.

269. Miller, Paul W. and Paul A. Volker. "Economic Progress in Australia: An Analysis of Occupational Mobility." Economic Record 61 (March 1985): 463-475.

270. Miller, Paula. "Efficiency, Stupidity, and Class Conflict in South Australian Schools, 1875-1900." History of Education Quarterly 24 (Fall 1984): 393-409.

271. Molesworth, B. H. The History of Kanaaka Labour in Queensland. Master's thesis, University of Queensland, 1979.

272. Moore, Andrew. The Secret Army and the Premier. Conservative Paramilitary Organizations in New South Wales. Kensington: New South Wales University Press, 1989.

273. Moore, Clive. Kanaka: A History of Melanesian Mackay. Port Moresby: University of Paua New Guinea Press, 1985.

274. Morton, John. "Rednecks, Roos and Racism: Kangaroo Shooting And the Australian Way." Social Analysis (August 1990)

275. Mungawa Fasl, Eve and others. "Race and Racism [in Australia]." Social Justice 16 (Autumn 1989)

276. Murray, Davis. "Changes in Income Inequality: Australia 1968-69 to 1973-74." Review of Income and Wealth 25 (September 1979): 309-325.

277. Nedale, A. R. Ethnic Stereotypes and Children. Richmond, Victoria: Clearing House on Migration Issues, 1987.

278. Nevile, J. W. and N.A. Warren. "How Much Do We Know About Wealth Distribution in Australia." Australian Economic Review 68 (4th Quarter 1984):

279. Nichols, Stephen, ed. Convict Workers, Reinterpreting Australia's Past. New York: Cambridge University Press, 1989.

280. O'Brien, Anne. Poverty's Prison: The Poor in New South Wales, 1880-1914. Melbourne: Melbourne University Press, 1988.

281. O'Farrell, Patrick. The Irish in Australia. Notre Dame, IN: University of Notre Dame Press, 1989.

282. Oddie, G. A. The Chinese in Victoria, 1870-1890. Master's thesis, University of Melbourne, 1959.

283. Parker, R. S. "Power in Australia." A.N.Z. Journal of Sociology 1 (1965): 85-96.

284. Pettman, J. "Whose Country Is It Anyway? Cultural Politics, Racism and Construction of Being Australian." Journal of Intercultural Studies 9 (1988): 1-24.

285. Piggott, John. "The Distribution of Wealth in Australia- A Survey." Economic Record (September 1974): 60.

286. Piggott, John. "The Distribution of Wealth: What Is It, What Does It Mean, and Is It Important?" Australian Economic Review (Spring 1988): 83.

287. Piggott, John. "The Nation's Private Wealth - Some New Calculations for Australia." Economic Record 63 (March 1987): 61-79.

288. Pittock, Barrie A. "Politics and Race in Australia." In Politics of Race - Comparative Studies, edited by Donald G. Baker, 163-190. Saxon House, D.C. Heath, 1975.

289. Pittock, Barrie A. Racism in Australia: An Introductory Perspective. Melbourne: Division of Christian Education, Australian Council of Churches: 1971.

290. Playford, J. "Who Rules Australia?" In Australian Capitalism, edited by Playford and D. Kirsner, 108-155. Ringwood: Penguin, 1972.

291. Podder, N. and N. Kakwani. "Distribution of Wealth in Australia." Review of Income and Wealth 22 (March 1976): 75-92.

292. Poer, C. and F. Robertson. "Participation and Equity in Higher Education: socio-economic Profiles of Higher Education Students Revisited." Australian Bulletin of Labour 13 (March 1987)

293. Ramsland, John. "The Development of the Ragged School Movement in Nineteenth century Hobart." Journal of the Royal Australian Historical Society 73 (1987): 126-137.

294. Ray, John J. "Antisemitic Types in Australia." Patterns of Prejudice 7 (January-February 1973): 6-16.

295. Ray, John J. "Is Anti-Semitism a Cognitive Simplification? Some Observations on Australian Neo-Nazis." Jewish Journal of Sociology 14 (1972): 207-213.

296. Rendell, M. P. The Chinese in South Australia and the Northern Territory in the Nineteenth Century: A Study of the Social, Economic and Legislative Attitudes Adopted towards the Chinese in the Colony. Master's thesis, University of Adelaide, 1952.

297. Rubenstein, W. D. Australian Attitudes to Jews and Antisemitism. Melbourne: Australian Institute of Jewish Affairs, 1986.

298. Rubenstein, W. D. "The Distribution of Personal Wealth in Victoria, 1860-1974." Australian Economic History Review 19 (March 1979)

299. Rutland, Suzanne D. "Australian Responses to Jewish Refugee Migration before and after World War II." Australian Journal of Politics and History 31 (1985): 29-48.

300. Saunders, K. Workers in Bondage: The Origins and Bases of Unfree Labour in Queensland, 1824-1916. St. Lucia: University of Queensland Press, 1981.

301. Shaver, Sheila. "Gender, Class and the Welfare State: Income Security in Australia." Socialism and Democracy 8 (May 1989)

302. Shoemaker, A. "A Checklist of Black Australian Literature." Australian Literary Studies 11 (October 1983): 255-262.

303. Sinclair, Keith, ed. Tasman Relations: New Zealand and Australia, 1788-1988. Auckland: Auckland University Press, 1987.

304. Smolicz, J. J. "Multiculturalism in Australia: Rhetoric or Reality." New Community 12 (Winter 1985): 450-463.

26 WORLD RACISM AND RELATED INHUMANITIES

305. Soltow, Lee. "The Censuses of Wealth of Men in Australia in 1915 and in the United States in 1860 and 1870." Australian Economic History Review (September 1972)

306. Spurr, Russell. "Australia Goes Asian." New York Times Magazine (December 4, 1988)

307. Starke, J. S. "The High Cost of Justice." Australian Law Journal 64 (April 1990): 167-168.

308. Stone, J. O. "Youth Unemployment in Australia." National Westminster Bank Quarterly Review (May 1985)

309. Trigger, David S. "Racial Ideologies in Australia's Gulf Country." Ethnic and Racial Studies 12 (April 1989): 208-232.

310. Troy, Patrick N., ed. A Just Society? Essays on Equity in Australia. Boston, Ma: Allen and Unwin, 1981.

311. Tsokhes, Kosmas. A Class Apart? Businessmen and Australian Politics, 1960-1980. New York: Oxford University Press, 1984.

312. Vick, Malcolm. "Individuals and Social Structure: Recent Writings in the History of Education in Australia." History of Education Quarterly 27 (Spring 1987): 63-74.

313. Vickers, Adrian. "Racism and Colonialism in Early Australian Novels About Southeast Asia." ASAA Review 12 (July 1988): 7-12.

314. Victorian Ethnic Affairs Commission. Indochinese Refugees in Victoria: AnAnalysis of Informal Social Support Networks. East Melbourne: Victorian Ethnic Affairs Commission, Division of Research and Policy.

315. Victorian Ethnic Affairs Commission. Racism in the 1980s: A Response. East Melbourne: Office of the Minister for Ethnic Affairs, 1984.

316. Viviani, Nancy. The Long Journey: Vietnamese Migration and Settlement in Australia. Melbourne: Melbourne University Press, 1984.

317. Wallace-Crabbe, Chris. "Struggling with an Imperial Language." Southerly 3 (September 1989): 409-420.

318. Waterhouse, Richard. "Minstrel Show and Vaudeville House: The Australian Popular Stage, 1838-1914." Australian Historical Studies 23 (October 1989): 366-385.

319. Watson, Betty L. "Past a Joke: A Century of Australian Literary Attitudes to Chinese Sojourners." Armidale and District Historical Society 14 (1971): 33-43.

320. Waysman, Dvora. "Unwelcome Warning." Jerusalem Post (December 30, 1982)

321. Wesern, J. S. Social Inequality in Australian Society. Melbourne: Macmillan, 1983.

322. Wheelwright, E. L. and Ken Buckley, eds. Essays in the Political Economy of Australian Capitalism. Vol.5 Sydney: ANZ, 1983.

323. Wheelwright, E. L. and K. Buckley, eds. Political Economy of Australian Capitalism. 3 vols. Sydney: ANZ, 1978.

324. Willard, M. History of the White Australia Policy to 1920. Melbourne University Press, 1967.

325. Williams, Alan W. "Colonial Origins of Land Acquisitions in New South Wales and Queensland." Journal of Legal History

326. Williams, Ross A. "The Economic Determinants of Private Schooling in Australia." Economic Record 61 (September 1985): 622-628.

327. Windschuttle, Elizabeth, ed. Women, Class, and History: Feminist Perspective on Australia 1788-1978. Auckland, N.J.: Fontana, 1980.

328. Wood, David. "Positive Discrimination and the High Court." University of Western Australia Law Review 17 (June 1987): 128-149.

329. Wynne, Edward C. Racial Discrimination in the Attitude of Australia towards the Japanese. 2 vols. Doctoral dissertation, Harvard University, 1927.

330. Yan, Chung-Ming. A Wakening Conscience: Racism in Australia. Hong Kong: Lung Men Press, 1983.

331. Yarwood, A. T., ed. Attitude to Non-European Immigration. Cassell, Australia: 1968.

332. Yuval-Davies, Nira. "Ethnic/Racial Divisions and the Nation in Britain and Australia." Capital & Class 28 (Spring 1986): 87-103.

333. Zubrzycki, Jerzy. "Multiculturalism and Beyond: The Australian Experience in Retrospect and Prospect." New Community 13 (Autumn 1986): 167-176.

AUSTRALIA - ABORIGINES

334. Alexander, Christian. "Aboriginals in Capitalist Australia: What It Means to Become Civilized." Australia and New Zealand Journal of Sociology 20 (July 1984): 233-242.

335. Allen, Harry. "History Matters: A Commentary on Divergent Interpretations of Australian History." Australian Aboriginal Studies 2 (1988): 79-89.

336. Altman, Jon C. and John P. Nieuwenhuysen. The Economic Status of Australian Aborigines. New York: Cambridge University Press, 1979.

337. Atkinson, Alan. "Ethics of Conquest, 1786." Aboriginal History 6 (1982): 82-91.

338. Barta, Tony. "After the Holocaust: Consciousness of Genocide in Australia." Australian Journal of Politics and History 31 (1985): 154-161.

339. Beckett, Jeremy R., ed. Past and Present: The Construction of Aboriginality. Canbera: Aboriginal Studies Press, 1988.

340. Bell, D. and P. Ditton. Law, the Old and the New. Aboriginal History for Central Australian Legal Service, 1980.

341. Bennett, Scott C. Aborigines and Political Power. Boston, MA: Allen & Unwin, 1989.

342. Berndt, Ronald M. and Robert Tonkinson, eds. Social Anthropology and Australian Aboriginal Studies: A Contemporary Overview. Canberra: Aboriginal Studies Press, 1988.

343. Biles, D. and others. "Aboriginal and Non-Aboriginal Deaths in Custody." Australia and New Zealand Journal of Criminalogy 23 (March 1990)

AUSTRALIA - ABORIGINES

344. Bin-Sallik, Mary Ann. <u>Aboriginal Tertiary Education in Australia: How Well Is It Serving the Needs of Aborigines?</u> Doctoral dissertation, Harvard University, 1989. UMO # 9000855.

345. Biskup, Peter. "Aboriginal History." in <u>New History: Studying Australia Today</u> G. Osborne and W. F. Mardle (eds.) Boston, MA: Allen & Unwin, 1982.

346. Biskup, Peter. <u>Native Administration and Welfare in Western Australia, 1897-1954</u>. Master's thesis, University of Western Australia, 1965.

347. Biskup, Peter. "White Aboriginal Relations in Western Australia: An Overview." <u>Comparative Studies in Society and History</u> (July 1968)

348. Boast, R. P. "Treaty Rights or Aboriginal Rights?" <u>New Zealand Law Journal</u> (January 1990): 32-36.

349. Bradley, Carol. "A Change in Status for Aboriginal Women? Aboriginal Women in the Australian Workforce." <u>Aboriginal History</u> 11, part 2 (1987):

350. Broome, Richard. <u>Aboriginal Australians: Black Response to White Dominance, 1788-1980</u>. Boston, MA: Allen & Unwin, 1982.

351. Brown, Kevin M. "'Racial' Referents: Images of European- Aboriginal Relations in Australian Feature Films, 1955-1984." <u>Sociological Review</u> 36 (August 1988): 474-502.

352. Burger, Julian. <u>Aborigines Today, Lands and Justice</u>. London: Anti-Slavery Society, 1988.

353. Butlin, N. G. "The Paleoeconomic History of Aboriginal Migration." <u>Australian Economic History Review</u> 29 (September 1989):

354. Campbell, Judy. "Smallpox in Aboriginal Australia, the Early 1830s." <u>Historical Studies</u> 21 (April 1985): 336-358.

355. Cassidy, Julie. "A Reappraisal of Aboriginal Policy in Colonial Australia: Imperial and Colonial Instruments and Legislation Recognizing the Special rights and Status of the Australian Aboriginals." <u>Journal of Legal History</u> 10 (December 1989): 365-379.

356. Cassidy, Julie. "Significance of the Classifications of a Colonial Acquisition: The Conquered/Settled Distinction." <u>Australian Aboriginal Studies</u> 1 (1988): 2-17.

357. Cole, Mike. "The Aboriginal Struggle: An Interview with Helen Boyle." <u>Race and Class</u> 27 (Spring 1986): 21-33.

30 WORLD RACISM AND RELATED INHUMANITIES

358. "The Colonization of Australia's Aboriginal People." Akwesasne Notes 14 (Late Fall 1982): 26,34.

359. Coombs, H. C. Aboriginal Australians 1967-76: A Decade of Progress? Perth: Murdock University, 1976.

360. Coombs, H. C. Australia's Policy Towards Aborigines, 1967- 1977. London: Minority Rights Group, 1978.

361. Coombs, H. C. Kulinma: Listening to Aboriginal Australians. Canberra: Australian National University Press, 1978.

362. Cousins, David and J. Nieuwenhuysen. Aboriginals and Ore Mining Industry: Case Studies of the Australian Experience. London: Allen & Unwin, 1984.

363. Crawford, James. "The Aboriginal Legal Heritage: Aboriginal Public Law and the Treaty Proposal." Australian Law Journal 63 (June 1989): 392-403.

364. Davies, Susanne. "Aborigines, Murder and the Criminal Law in Early Port Phillip, 1841-1851." Historical Studies 22 (1987): 313-335.

365. Dawson, James. Australian Aborigines. Atlantic Highlands, NJ: Humanities Press, 1981.

366. Duguid, Charles. Doctor and the Aborigines. Rigby, 1973.

367. Eckermann, Anne-Katrin and Lynette Toni Dowd. "Structural Violence and Aboriginal Organisations in Rural-Urban Australia." Journal of Legal Pluralism and Unofficial Law (1988): 55-77.

368. Edwards, N. R. Native Education in the Northern Territory of Australia: A Critical Account of Its Aims, Development and Present Position. Master's thesis, University of Sydney, 1962.

369. Ellis, S. "Racism in Australia: A Contribution to the Debate." Australian Quarterly (September 1972): 58-66.

370. Fien, John. "Structural Silence: Aborigines in Australian Geography Textbooks." Contemporary Issues in Geography and Education 1 (Spring 1984): 22-25.

371. Fisk, E. K. The Aboriginal Economy in Town and Country. Sydney: Allen & Unwin, 1985.

372. Folds, R. "Aboriginals and School: A Resistance Hypothesis and Its Implication for Educational Change." Curriculum Perspectives 5 (1985): 33-38.

373. Franklin, A. E. Black and White Australians - An Interracial History 1788-1975. Melbourne: Heinemann Educational, 1976.

374. Fraser, Stewart E. "Australian Aborigines: A Growing or Contracting Minority?" Immigrants & Minorities 5 (July 1986): 204-217.

375. Gale, Fay and J. Wundersitz. "Aboriginal Visibility in the 'System'." Australian Social Work 39 (1986): 21-27.

376. Gale, Fay. "Aboriginal Youth: A History of Inequity in the Delivery of Australian Justice." Aboriginal History 11, part 1 (1987)

377. Gale, Fay and others. Aboriginal Youth and the Criminal Justice System. New York: Cambridge University Press, 1990.

378. Gale, Fay and J. Wundersitz. "The Operation of Hidden Prejudice in Pre-court Procedures: The Case of Australian Aboriginal Youth." Australian and New Zealand Journal of Criminology 22 (March 1986): 1-21.

379. Gale, Fay. "The Participation of Australian Aboriginal Women in a Changing Political Environment." Political Geography Quarterly 9 (October 1990)

380. Gale, Fay and J. Wundersitz. "Police and Black Minorities: The Case of Australian Aboriginal Youth in South Australia." Australian and New Zealand Journal of Criminology 20 (June 1987): 78-94.

381. Gale, Fay and Alison Brookman, eds. Race Relations in Australia: The Aborigines. Sydney: McGraw Hill, 1975.

382. Gale, Fay, ed. We Are Bosses Ourselves: The Status and Role of Aboriginal Women Today. Canberra: Australian Insitute of Aboriginal Studies, 1983.

383. Goldie, Terry. Fear and Temptation: The Image of the Indigene in Canadain, Australian, and New Zealand Literatures. Knighton: McGill-Queens University Press, 1989.

384. Grabosky, Peter N. "Aboriginal Deaths in Custody: The Case of John Pat." Race and Class (Winter 1988)

385. Grassby, A. J. "Linguistic Genocide." In Language Problems and Aboriginal Education, edited by E. Brumby and E. Vaszolyi. Mt. Lawley: College of Advanced Education, 1977.

386. Grassby, A. J. and M. Hill. Six Australian Battlefields: The Black Resistance to Invasion and the White Struggle Against Colonial Oppression. Sydney: Angus and Robertson, 1988.

387. Gumbert, Marc. Neither Justice Nor Reason: A Legal and Anthropological Analysis of Aboriginal Land Rights. New York: University of Queensland Press, 1985.

388. Gurr, Ted Robert. "Outcomes of Public Protest Among Australia's Aborigines." American Behavioral Science 26 (January-February 1983): 353-373.

389. Gurr, Ted Robert. "The Politics of Aboriginal Land Rights and their Effects on Australian Resource Development." Australian Journal of Politics and History 31 (1985): 474-489.

390. Haas, Sandra K. "An Outward Sign of an Inward Struggle: The Fight for Human Rights of the Australian Aborigine." Florida International Law Journal 5 (Fall 1989): 81-109.

391. Hanks, Peter and Bryan Keon-Cohen, eds. Aborigines and the Law: Essays in Memory of Elizabeth Eggleston. Boston, MA: Allen & Unwin, 1984.

392. Hassell, K. L. The Relations Between the Settlers and Aborigines in South Australia, 1836-1860. Master's thesis, University of Adelaide, 1927.

393. Hastie, R. M. and D.F. Treagust. "Helping Aboriginal Students to Understand Mathematics and Science Concepts." Aboriginal Child at School 13 (1985): 8-15.

394. Healy, John J. Literature and the Aborigine in Australia, 1770-1975. New York St. Martin's Press: 1979.

395. Heppell, M. "Introduction: Past and Present Approaches and Future Trends in Aboriginal Housing." AIAS New series, 6 (1979): 1-64.

396. Hercus, Luise and Peter Sutton, eds. This Is What Happened: Historical Narratives by Aborigines. Canberra: Australian Institute of Aboriginal Studies, 1986.

397. Hollows, Fred. "An Analysis of the Situation of Aboriginal Society in Australia and Some Suggestions for Change." Australian Journal of Forensic Sciences 20 (December- February 1987): 235-240.

398. Howard, Michael C. Aboriginal Politics in Southwestern Australia. Nedlands, Australia: University of Western Australia Press, 1982.

399. Howard, Michael C., ed. Aboriginal Power in Australian Society. Honolulu: University of Hawaii Press, 1982.

400. Howe, K. R. "On Aborigines and Maoris in Australian and New Zealand Historiography." Int. Hist. Review 10 (November 1988): 594-610.

401. Huttenback, Robert A. Racism and Empire, White Settlers and Colored Immigrants in the British Self-governing Colonies, 1830-1910. Ithaca, NY: Cornell University Press, 1976.

402. Imhoff, Arthur E. "Der Vorzeitige Tod in Australien und Neuseeland: kein Mysterium, sondern ein Anlass zum Nachdenken." Zeitschrift fur die Bevolkerungswissenschaft: Demographie 12 (1986): 53-97.

403. Jones, Peter D. "Australian Aborigines Refuse to Celebrate Oppression." Guardian (NYC) (December 7, 1988)

404. Jordan, Deirdre F. "Aboriginal Identity: The Management of a Minority Group by the Mainstream Society." Canadian Journal of Native Studies 6 (1986): 271-311.

405. Jordan, Deirdre F. "The Social Construction of Identity: The Aboriginal Problem." Australian Journal of Education 28 (1984): 274-290.

406. Jurich, Marilyn. "A Critical Exploration of the Image of the Aborigine in Australian Books for Children." In Webs and Wardrobes: Humanist and Religious World Views in Children's Literature, edited by Joseph O. Milner and Lucy F. Morrock, pp. 79-97. Lanham, MD: University Press of America, 1987.

407. Kaberry, P. M. The Position of Women in Australian Aboriginal Society. Doctoral dissertation, London School of Economics, 1938.

408. Keeffe, Kevin. "Aboriginality: Resistance and Persistance." Australian Aboriginal Studies 1 (1988): 67-81.

409. Keen, Ian, ed. Being Black: Aboriginal Cultures in 'Settled' Australia. Canberra: Aboriginal Studies Press, 1988.

410. Kirkby, Dianne. "Colonial Policy and Native Depopulation in California and New South Wales 1770-1840." Ethnohistory 31 (1984): 1-16.

411. Koolmatrie, Janis. "Aboriginal Women in Education." AIAS new series, 41 (1983): 124-125.

412. Labumore, Elsie R. An Aboriginal Mother Tells of the Old and the New. Edited by Paul Memmot and Robyn Horsman. New York: Penguin, 1984.

413. Larsen, K. and others. Discrimination Against Aborigines and Islanders in North Queensland - The Case of Townsville. Canberra: 1977.

414. Lattas, Andrew. "Aborigines and Contemporary Australian Nationalism." Social Analysis (August 1990):

415. Layton, Robert. Uluru - An Aboriginal History. Australian Insitute of Aboriginal Studies, 1986.

416. Liberman, Kenneth. Understanding Interactions in Central Australia: An Ethnomethodological Study of Australian Aboriginal People. Boston, MA: Routledge & Kegan Paul, 1985.

417. Lippman, Lorna. Generations of Resistance: The Aboriginal Struggle for Justice. Melbourne: 1981.

418. Lippman, Lorna. Words or Blows: Racial Attitudes in Australia. Victoria, Australia: Penguin Book Australia, 1973.

419. Malin, Merridy A. Invisibility in Success, Visibility in Transgression for the Aboriginal Child in the Urban Classroom: Case Studies at Home and At School in Adelaide. 2 vols. Doctoral dissertation, University of Minnesota, 1989. UMO # 9003009.

420. Marjoribanks, Kevin and D.F. Jordan. "Ethnic Stereotyping in Secondary Schools: A Further Analysis." Educational Studies 11 (1985): 181-187.

421. Mattingley, Christobel and Ken Hampton, eds. Survival in Our Own Land: 'Aboriginal' Experiences in 'South Australia' since 1836. Adelaide: Wakefield Press, 1988.

422. McQueen, Humphrey. Australia Connexions - Aborigines, Race and Racism. Ringwood, Victoria: Penguin Books Australia, 1974.

423. McQueen, Humphrey. "The Sustenance of Silence: Racism in Twentieth Century Australia." Meanjin Qaurterly 30 (June 1971)

424. Meagher, G. A. and P.B. Dixon. "Analyzing Income Distributions in Australia." Economic Record 62 (December 1986)

425. Mercer, David. "Patterns of Protest: Native Land Rights and Claims in Australia." Political Geography Quarterly 6 (1987): 171-194.

426. Merlan, Francesca. "Land, Language and Social Identity in Aboriginal Australia." Mankind 13 (1982): 133-148.

427. Middleton, Hannah. But Now We Want the Land Back, A History of the Australian Aboriginal People. Sydney: New Age Publishers, 1977.

428. Miller, Charles. "The Aboriginal Image." New Society (December 5, 1986)

429. Miller, P. W. "The Structure of Aboriginal and Non- aboriginal Youth Unemployment." Australain Economic Papers 28 (June 1989)

430. Moeckel, Margot J. "Aboriginal Women's Role Today in Early Childhood School Education." AIAS new series 41 (1983): 104-121.

431. Morgan, Sally. My Place. New York: Holt, 1989.

432. Morris, Barry. "From Unemployment to Unemployment: The Changing Role of Aborigines in a Rural Economy." Mankind 13 (1983): 499-516.

433. Nettheim, Garth. "Australian Aborigines and the Law." Law and Anthroplogy 2 (1987): 371-403.

434. Nettheim, Garth. "Developing Aboriginal Rights." Victoria University of Wellington Law Review 19 (November 1989): 403-419.

435. Nettheim, Garth. Victims of the Law: Black Queenslanders Today. Boston, MA: Allen & Unwin, 1982.

436. O'Neil, Bernard J. "Beyond Trinkets and Beads: South Australia's Aboriginal Legal Rights Movement, 1971-1978." Aboriginal History 6 (1982): 28-38.

437. Osborne, P. D. The Other Australia: The Crisis in Aboriginal Health. Hobart, Tasmania: Dept. of Political Science, University of Tasmania, 1982.

438. Palmer, Ian. Buying Back the Land: Organizational Struggle and the Aboriginal Land Fund Commissions. Canberra: Aboriginal Studies Press, Australian Insitute of Aboriginal Studies, 1988.

439. Pattman, Jan. "Learning about Power and Powerlessness: Aborigines and White Australia's Bicentenary." Race and Class 29 (Winter 1988): 69-86.

440. Peterson, Nicolas and Marcia Langton, eds. Aborigines, Land, and Land Rights. Canberra: Australian Insitute of Aboriginal Studies, 1983.

441. Pilger, John. The Secret Country. London: Jonathan Cape, 1989.

442. Pittock, Barrie A. Australian Aborigines: The Common Struggle for Humanity. Copenhagen: International Work Group for Indigenous Affairs.

443. Pollard, David. Give and Take: The Losing Partnership in Aboriginal Poverty. Sydney: Hale & Ironmonger, 1989.

444. Pope, Alan. "Aboriginal Adaptations to Early Colonial Labour Markets: The South Australian Experience." Labour History No. 54 (1988): 1-15.

445. Rangiah, Darryl. "Batons for Blacks." Legal Service Bulletin 12 (April 1987): 76-77.

446. Ray, John J. "Explaining Australian Attitudes towards Aborigines." Ethnic and Racial Studies 4 (July 1981): 348-352.

447. Read, Peter. "Cheeky, Insolent and Anti-White. The Split in the Federal Council for the Advancement of Aboriginal and Tones Strait Islanders - Easter 1970." Australian Journal of Politics and History 36 (1990)

448. Read, Peter. *A Hundred Years War: The Wiradjuri People and the State*. Sydney: Australian National University Press, 1988.

449. Reynolds, Henry. *Frontier: Aborigines, Settlers and Land*. Sydney: Allen & Unwin, 1987.

450. Reynolds, Henry. *The Other Side of the Frontier: Aboriginal Resistance to the European Invasion of Australia*. Melbourne: Penguin, 1982.

451. Reynolds, Henry. "Racial Thought in Early Colonial Australia." *Australian Journal of Politics and History* 20 (1974)

452. Rowley, C. D. *The Destination of Aboriginal Society*. Canbera: National University Press, 1970.

453. Rowley, C. D. *Outcasts in White Australia: Aboriginal Policy and Practice*. Canbera: Australian National University Press, 1971.

454. Rowse, Tim. "Aborigines as Historical Actors: Evidence and Inference." *Historical Studies* 22 (October 1986): 176-198.

455. Russo, C. and R. B. Baldouf, Jr. "Language Development without Planning: A Case Study of Tribal Aborigines in the Northern Territory, Australia." *Journal of Multilingual and Multicultural Development* 7 (1986): 301-317.

456. Ryan, Lyndall. *The Aboriginal Tasmanians*. Vancouver: University of British Columbia Press, 1982.

457. Sawer, Marian. "Two Steps Backwards: Equal Opportunity Policy under Howard and Hawke." *Politics* (Australia), 22 (1987): 92-96.

458. Shoemaker, Adam. *Black Words, White Page: Aboriginal Literature 1929-1988*. St. Lucia: University of Queensland Press, 1989.

459. Smith, Arthur Richard. *A Retrospective Description and Analysis of an Aboriginal Teacher Education Development, The University of Wollongong, 1982-1985*. 2 vols. Doctoral dissertation, Ohio State University, 1985. UMO # 8603055.

460. Spalding, I. "Elements in the Australian Racist Syndrome." *Historian* 25 (October 1973)

461. Stanner, William E. H. "Aboriginal Humor." *Aboriginal History* 6 (1982): 39-48.

462. Stevens, Frank S. "Aboriginal Labour." *Australian Quarterly* 43 (1971): 70-78.

463. Stevens, Frank S. *Black Australia*. Sydney: Alternative Pub. Co-operative, 1981.

AUSTRALIA - ABORIGINES

464. Stevens, Frank S., ed. Racism: The Australian Experience A Study of Race Prejudice in Australia. 3 vols. Sydney: Australia and New Zealand Book Co., 1971-1972.

465. Sullivan, Sharon. "The Custodianship of Aboriginal Sites in Southeastern Australia." In Who Owns the Past?, edited by Isabel McBryde. New York: Oxford University Press, 1985.

466. Suter, Keith and Kaye Sterman. Aboriginal Australians. London: Minority Rights Group, 1982.

467. Tatz, Colin M., ed. Black Viewpoints: The Aboriginal Experience. Sydney: ANZ Book Co., 1975.

468. Tatz, Colin M. Race Politics in Australia: Aborigines, Politics and Law. Armidale: University of New England Publishing Unit, 1979.

469. Tatz, Colin M. "Racism, Responsibility, and Reparation: South Africa, Germany, and Australia." Australian Journal of Politics and History 31 (1985): 162-172.

470. Treadgold, M. L. "Intercensal Change in Aboriginal Incomes, 1976-1986." Australian Bulletin of Labour 14 (September 1988)

471. Turnbull, Clive. Black War: The Extermination of the Tasmanian Aborigines. Melbourne: F. W. Cheshire, 1948.

472. Turner, Graeme. "Breaking the Frame: The Representation of Aborigines in Australian Film." Kunapipi 10 (1988): 135-145.

473. Tyler, William. "Aboriginality and Socioeconomic Attainment in Australia's Northern Territory." Australian and New Zealand Journal of Sociology 26 (March 26): 68-86.

474. "Violence in Aboriginal Communities." Australian Journal of Social Issues 25 (November 1990): three articles.

475. Weaver, Sally M. "Australian Aboriginal Policy: Aboriginal Pressure Groups or Government Advisory Bodies?" Oceana 54 (1983): 1-22, 85-108.

476. Webb, Andrew. "Down and Out, Down Under." In These Times (April 13, 1988)

477. White, Isabel and others, eds. Fighters and Singers: The Lives of Some Australian Aboriginal Women. Boston, MA: Allen & Unwin, 1985.

478. Whittaker, Alan. Aborigines Today - Land and Justice. London: Anti-Slavery Society, February 1988.

479. Wieneke, Christine E. <u>Destruction and Survival: Articulation of Aboriginal and Capitalist Modes of Production in Three Specific Areas of Colonial and Contemporary Australia</u>. Doctoral dissertation, University of New South Wales, 1983.

480. Williams, Nancy A. <u>The yoluna and Their Land: A System of Land Tenure and the Fight for Its Recognition</u>. Stanford, CA: Stanford University Press, 1986.

481. Woolmington, Jean. "Missionary Attitudes to the Baptism of Australian Aborigines before 1850." <u>Journal of Religious History</u> 13 (June 1985): 283-293.

482. Wright, Judith. <u>The Cry for the Dead</u>. New York: Oxford University Press, 1982.

483. Yarwood, A. T. <u>Growing Up in Macquarie's Sydney</u>. Portland, OR: Kangaroo Press, 1985.

AUSTRIA

484. Andics, Hellmut. Die Juden in Wien. Vienna: Kremayr & Scheriau, 1988.

485. Austria - Lingering Shadows: An Examination of the Ultra- Rightist and Antisemitic Tendencies in the Republic of Austria. New York: American Jewish Congress, 1966.

486. Barker, Thomas M. "The Ethnic Evolution of Austria's Carinthian Slovenes in Recent Years." Canadian Review of Studies in Nationalism 16 (1989): 189-196.

487. Barker, Thomas M. The Slovene Minority of Carinthia. Boulder, Co: East European Monographs, 1984.

488. Bauböck, Rainer and others, eds. Und raus bist Du! Ethnische Minderheiten in der Politik. Vienna: Verlag für Gesellschaftskritik, 1988.

489. Baum, R. C. "Die Bürde der Wahrheit. Juden und Nichtjuden in Österreich und der Bundesrepublik Deutschland nach dem Krieg." Kölner Zeitschrift für Soziologie und Sozialpsychologie (1989)

490. Beller, Steven. Vienna and the Jews, 1867-1938. A Cultural History. New York: Cambridge University Press, 1989.

491. Benard, Cheryl and Edit Schlaffer. "Austria: Benevolent Despotism Versus the Contemporary Feminist Movement." In Sisterhood is Global, edited by Robin Morgan, 72-76. Garden City, NY: Anchor Press, Doubleday, 1984.

492. Benziger, Marguerite M. Austria Nazified. Years of Terror, 1938-1955. 1986.

493. Bister, Feliks J. "Die slowenische ethnische Gruppe in Wien." Eur. Ethnica 43 (1986): 169-179.

40 WORLD RACISM AND RELATED INHUMANITIES

494. Boshyk, Yury. "Repatriation and Resistance: Ukrainian Refugees and Displaced Persons in Occupied Germany and Austria." In <u>Refugees in the Age of Total War</u>, edited by Anna C. Bramwell. Boston, MA: Unwin Hyman, 1988.

495. Botz, Gerhard. "Austro-Marxist Interpretation of Fascism." <u>Journal of Contemporary History</u> 11 (1976): 129-156.

496. Botz, Gerhard. "National Socialist Vienna: Antisemitism as a Housing Policy."<u>Wiener Library Bulletin</u> 29 (1976): 47-55.

497. Boyer, John W. <u>Political Radicalism in Late Imperial Vienna. Origins of the Christian Social Movement 1848-1897</u>. Chicago,IL: University of Chicago Press, 1984.

498. Brousek, Karl M. <u>Wien und seine Tschechen: Integration und Assimilation einer Minderheit im 20. Jahrhundert</u>. Vienna: Verlag für Geschichte und Politik, 1980.

499. Bunzl, John and Bernd Marin. <u>Antisemitismus in Österreich. Social-historische und soziologische Studien</u>. Innsbruck: Inn-Verlag, 1983.

500. Bunzl, John. "Austrian Identity and Antisemitism." <u>Patterns of Prejudice</u> 21 (1987): 3-8.

501. Burder, Dieter A. "Der 'reiche Jude'. Zur sozialdemokratischen Kapitalismuskritik und zu deren antisemitischen Feindbildern in der Ersten Republik." <u>Geschichte und Gegenwart</u> 4 (1985): 43-53.

502. Burrian, Peter. "The State Language Problem in Old Austria." <u>Austrian History Yearbook</u> 6-7 (1970-1971): 81-103.

503. Carsten, Francis L. <u>Fascist Movements in Austria: From Schönerer to Hitler</u>. Beverly Hills, CA: Sage, 1977.

504. Delapina, Thomas. "Die Verteilung des österreichischen Volkeinkommens, 1976-1986." <u>Wirtschaft und Gesellschaft</u> 13 (1987): 431-447.

505. Diamant, Alfred. <u>Prototypes of Austro-German Fascism</u>. Doctoral Dissertation, Yale University, 1957.

506. Diekmann, Andreas. <u>Sozialindikatoren der Ungleichheit, Chanceungleichheit und Diskriminierung: Anwendungen einfacher mathematischer Hilfsmittel in der Ungleichheitsforschung</u>. Vienna: Fachverlag für Wirtschaft und Technik, 1981.

507. Dor, Milo, ed. <u>Die Leiche im Keller. Dokumente des Widerstandes gegen Dr. Kurt Waldheim</u>. Vienna: Picus Verlag, 1988.

508. Dostal, W. "Die Zigeuner in Österreich." Archiv für Völkerkunde 10 (1955): 1-15.

509. Drabek, Anna M. and others. Das Österreichische Judentum. Vienna: Jugend und Volk, 1974.

510. Edmondson, C. Earl. The Heimwehr and Austrian Politics 1918- 1936. Athens: University of Georgia Press, 1978.

511. Fellner, Gunther. Antisemitismus in Salzburg 1918-1938. Vienna: Geyer, 1979.

512. Fischer-Kowalski, Marina and Josef Bucek, eds. Ungleichheit in Österreich: ein Sozialbericht. Vienna: Jugend und Volk Verlagsgesellschaft, 1980.

513. Fischer, R. "The Bilingual School of the Slovenes in Austria." Journal of Multilingual and Multicultural Development 7 (1986): 187-197.

514. Fraenkel, Josef, ed. The Jews of Austria. Essays on their Life, History and Destruction. London: Vallentine, Mitchell and Co., 1967.

515. Freidenreich, Harriet P. Jewish Politics in Vienna, 1918- 1938. Bloomington: Indiana University Press, 1991.

516. Friedman, I. "The Austro-Hungarian Government and Zionism, 1897-1918." Jewish Social Studies 27 (1965): 147-167, 236-249.

517. Glettler, Monika. "The Acculturation of the Czechs in Vienna." In Labor Migration in the Atlantic Economies, edited by Dirk Hoerder. Westport, CT: Greenwood Press, 1985.

518. Glettler, Monika. Die Wiener Tschechen um 1900. Strukturanalyse einer nationalen Minderheit in der Grosstadt. Munich: 1971.

519. Grothaus, M. Der Erbfeind christlicher Nahmens. Studien zum Türkenfeinde in der Kultur de Habsburger Monarchie zwischen 16 und 18 Jahrhundert. Doctoral dissertation, University of Graz, 1986.

520. Gruber, Helmut and Rudolf de Cillia. "Menschenfresser aller Lander, vereinigt euch! Antisemitische Stereotype in den österreichischen Medien seit 1986." Journal für Sozialforschung 29 (1989): 215-242.

521. Haddock, Mike. "20th Century Austrian Minority Problems." Kansas Geographer 14 (1979): 5-12.

522. Haller, Max and others. Klassenbildung und soziale Schichtung in Österreich: Analysen zur Sozialstruktur, sozialen Ungleichheit und Mobilität. Frankfurt: Canysus Verlag, 1982.

523. Hamish, Ernst. "The Image of the Jew in Austrian Literature." Patterns of Prejudice 7 (1973): 23-33.

524. Haslinger, M. Rom heisst Mensch - zur Geschichte des 'geschichtslosen Zigeunervolkes' in der Steirmark (1850- 1938). Doctoral dissertation, University Press of Graz, 1986.

525. Hellwing, I. A. Der konfessionelle Antisemitismus im 19. Jahrhundert in Österreich. Salzburg: Institut für Kirchliche Zeitgeschichte, 1972.

526. Henker, Reinhold, ed. Leben lassen ist nicht genug. Minderheiten in Österreich. Vienna: Kremayer & Scherriau, 1988.

527. Himka, John-Paul. Galician Villagers and the Ukrainian Movement in the Nineteenth Century. New York: St. Martin's Press, 1988.

528. Hitchins, Keith. The Nationality Problem in Austria-Hungary. Leiden: Brill, 1974.

529. Holzer, Willibald. Im Schatten des Faschismus. Der österreichische Widerstand gegen den Nationalsozialismus (1938-1945). Vienna: Dr. Karl Renner Institut, 1978.

530. Hwaletz, Otto. "Antisemitismus - eine abendlandische und österrreichische Tradition." Aufrisse 4 (1983): 33-45.

531. Insdorf, Annette. "Alex Corti's Films Explore World War II's Impact." New York Times (July 24, 1988)

532. Institut fur Hohere Studien, ed. Struktur der sozialen Ungerechtigkeit in Österreich. 3 vols. Vienna: 1978,

533. Jahoda, Marie. "Antisemitism in Austria." Patterns of Prejudice 17 (October 1983): 46-48.

534. Jedlicka, Ludwig. "Die Anfänge des Rechtsradikalismus in Österreich (1919-1925)." Wissenschaft und Weltbild 24 (1971): 96-110.

535. Kann, Robert A. "Trends toward Colonialism in the Habsburg Empire, 1878-1918: The Case of Bosnia-Herzegovina, 1878-1914." In Russian and Slavic History, edited by D. and G.E. Orchard Rowney. Columbus, OH: Slavica Publishers, 1977.

536. Kann, Robert A. and Zdenek V. David. The Peoples of the Eastern Habsburg Lands, 1526-1918. Seattle: University of Washington Press, 1984.

537. Karbach, Oskar. "The Liquidation of the Jewish Community of Vienna." Jewish Social Studies 2 (1940): 255-278.

538. Kein einig Volk von Brudern: Studien zum Mehrheiten-/ Minderheitensproblem am Beispiel Kärntens. Vienna, Verlag für Gesellschaftskritik, 1982.

539. Keyserlink, Robert H. Austria in World War II: An Anglo- American Dilemma. Kingston, Ontario: McGill-Queen's University Press, 1988.

540. Kitchen, Martin. The Coming of Austrian Fascism. London: Croom Helm, 1980.

541. Klemperer, Klemens von. "On Austrofascism." Central European History 11 (September 1978): 313-317.

542. Koltringer, Richard and Ernst Gehmacher. "Antisemitismus und die 'Waldheim-diskussion' während des österreichischen Bundespräsidentschaftswahlkampfes." Kölner Zeitschrift für Soziologie und Sozialpsychologie 41 (1989): 555-562.

543. Kondert, Reinhard. The Rise and Early History of the Austrian Heimwehr Movement. Doctoral dissertation, Rice University, 1972.

544. Konrad, Helmut and Wolfgang Neugebauer, eds. Arbeiterbewegung, Faschismus, Nationalbewusstsein. Vienna: Europa-Verlag, 1983.

545. Kozenski, Jerzy. "The Discredit of the Idea of Anschluss in the Years 1938-1945." Polish Western Affairs 9 (1968): 225-257.

546. Kozig, Jan. The Ukrainian National Movement in Galicia, 1815-1849. Translated by Lawrence D. Orton and Andrew Gorski. Edmonton: Canadian Institute of Ukrainian Studies, University of Alberta, 1986.

547. Lador-Lederer, J. J. "Jews in Austrian Law." East European Quarterly 12 (Spring-Summer 1978): 27-41, 129-142.

548. Lewis, Jill. Fascism and the Working Class in Austria, 1918- 1934. Berg: 1991.

549. Lichtenberger, Elizabeth. Gastarbeiter: Leben in zwei Gesellschaften. Vienna: Verlag Hermann Bohlaus, 1984.

550. Liebmann, Maximilian. "Die 'Antifaschistische Freiheitsbewegung Österreichs'." Geschichte und Gegenwart 4 (1985): 255-281.

551. Liebmann, Maximilian. "Die kirchliche Hierarchie in Österreich und das Dritte Reich." In Religion und Kultur an Zeitenwenden. Auf Gottes Spuren in Österreich, edited Norbert Leser, 274-293. Vienna: Herold, 1984.

552. Lohmann, Klaus, ed. 1000 Jahre österreichisches Judentum. Eisenstadt: Edition Rotzer, 1982.

553. Luza, Radomir V. The Resistance in Austria,1938-1945. Minneapolis: University of Minnesota Press, 1984.

554. Marin, Bernd. "Ein Historisch neuartiger 'Antisemitismus ohne Antisemiten'? Beobachtungen und Thesen am Beispiel Österreichs nach 1945." Geschichte und Gegenwart 5 (1979): 545-569.

555. Markovits, Andrie S. The Austrian Student Right: A Study in Political Continuity. Doctoral dissertation, Columbia University, 1975.

556. Moderegger, Silvia. Die Juden im österreichischen Standesstaat 1934-1938. Vienna: Geyer, 1973.

557. Molden, Fritz. Fires in the Night: The Sacrifices and Significance of the Austrian Resistance, 1938-1945. Boulder, CO: Westview Press, 1989.

558. Mulley, Klaus-Dieter. "Die NSDAP in Niederösterreich 1918 bis 1938: ein Beitrag zur vorgeschichte des 'Anschlusses'." Österreich Gesch. Lit. 33 (May-August 1989): 169-191.

559. "The Nationality Problem in the Habsburg Monarchy in the Nineteenth Century: A Critical Appraisal." Austrian History Yearbook. Houston, TX: Rice University, 1968.

560. "Neo-Nazis in Austria." Patterns of Prejudice 16 (January 1982): 13-18.

561. Neugebauer, Wolfgang and others, eds. Rechtsextremismus in Österreich nach 1945. Vienna: Österreichischer Bundesverlag, 1979.

562. Oxaal, Ivar and others, eds. Jews, Antisemitism and Culture in Vienna. New York: Routledge & Kegan Paul, 1987.

563. Pauley, Bruce F. "A Case Study in Fascism: The Styrian Heimatschutz and Austrian National Socialism." Austrian History Yearbook 12-13 (1976-1977): 251-273.

564. Pauley, Bruce F. Hitler and the Forgotten Nazis: A History of Austrian National Socialism. Chapel Hill: University of North Carolina Press, 1981.

565. Pelinka, Anton. "The Great Austrian Taboo: The Repression of the Civil War." New German Critique No. 43 (1988): 69-82.

566. Pototsching, Franz and others, eds. Semitismus und Antisemitismus in Österreich: Ein Unterrichtsversuch. 2d ed. München: Roman Kovar, 1988.

567. Prantner, Robert. "Christliche Frauen im Widerstand gegen Hitler in Österreich." Christliche Demokratie 2 (1984): 264-292.

568. Pronay, Inge. "Denk-und Merkwürdigkeiten zum Bild der Frau in österreichischen Schulbüchern." In Das ewige Klischee, zum Rollenbild und Selbstverständniss bei Männern und Frauen. 276-304. Vienna: Hermann Bohlaus, 1981.

569. Pulzer, Peter. The Rise of Political Anti-Semitism in Germany & Austria. 2d ed. London: Peter Halban, 1988.

570. Rathkolb, Oliver. "U.S. - Entnazifizierung in Österreich zwischen kontrollierter Revolution und Elitenrestauration (1945-1949)." Zeitgeschichte 11 (1983-84): 302-325.

571. Reichhold, Ludwig. Kampf um Österreich: die vaterlandische Front und ihr Widerstand gegen den Anschluss, 1933-1938. Vienna: Österreichischer Bundesverlag, 1984.

572. Riedlsperger, Max E. The Lingering Shadow of Nazism: The Austrian Independent Party Movement since 1945. Boulder, CO: East European Quarterly, 1978.

573. Rosenaft, Menachem Z. "Jews and Antisemites in Austria at the End of the Nineteenth Century." Leo Baeck Inst. Yrbk. 21 (1976): 57-86.

574. Rosenkranz, Herbert. "Austria." In Encyclopedia of the Holocaust. 126-132. New York: Macmillan, 1990.

575. Rosenkranz, Herbert. "Vienna." In Encyclopedia of the Holocaust. 1564-1571. New York: Macmillan, 1990.

576. Rowley, A. R. "Minority Schools in the South Tyrol and in the Austrian Burgenland: A Comparison of Two Models." Journal of Multilingual and Multicultural Development 7 (1986): 229-251.

577. Saltman, Jack. Kurt Waldheim: A Case to Answer? London: Robson Books, 1990.

578. Schumann, Wolfgang and Ludwig Nestler, eds. Nacht uber Europa. Die Okkupationspolitik des deutschen Faschismus (1938-1945). Achtbändige Dokumenten editon Vol.I: Die faschistische Okkupationspolitik in Österreich und der Tschechoslowakei (1938-1945). Cologne: Pahl-Rugenstein, 1988.

579. Schwarz, Robert. "Antisemitism and Socialism in Austria 1918-1962." In The Jews of Austria, edited by Josef Fraenkel, 445-466. London: Vallentine, Mitchell and Co., 1967.

580. Schwarz, Robert. "Nazism in Austria." Syracuse Scholar 3 (Spring 1982): 17-25.

581. Shedel, James. "Austria and its Polish Subjects, 1866-1914: A Relationship of Interests." Austrian History Yearbook 19-20, part 2 (1983-1984): 23-41.

582. Simon, Walter B. Die verirrte Erste Republik: Eine Korrektur österreichischer Geschichtsbilder. Vienna: Multiplex Media Verlag, 1988.

583. Slapnicka, Harry. "Zum Antisemitismus - Problem in Oberösterreich." Zeitgeschichte 1 (1974): 264-267.

584. Spiegel, Tilly. Frauen und Mädchen im österreichischen Widerstand. Vienna: Europa-Verlag, 1967.

585. Spira, Leopold. Feindbild 'Jud'. 100 Jahre politisches Antisemitismus in Österreich. Vienna: Locker Verlag, 1981.

586. Spitzer, Leo. Lives in Between Assimilation and Marginality in Austria, Brazil, and West Africa, 1780-1945. New York: Cambridge University Press, 1989.

587. Stadler, Karl R. "Austria." In Fascism in Europe, edited by S. J. Woolf. London: Methuen, 1982.

588. Stadler, Karl R. "Fifty Troubled Years: The Story of the Burgenland." Austrian History Yearbook 8 (1972): 59-79.

589. Steinmetz, Selma. Österreichs Zigeuner in NS-Staat. Vienna: Europa-Verlag, 1966.

590. Stiefel, Dieter. Entnazifizierung in Österreich. Vienna: Europa-Verlag, 1981.

591. Stranzinger, Ernst. "Neo-Nazis in Austria." Patterns of Prejudice 16 (1982): 13-18.

592. Suppan, Arnold. Die österreichischen Volksgruppen: Tendenzen ihrer gesellschaftlichen Entwicklungen im 20. Jahrhundert. Munich: R. Oldenbourg Verlag, 1983.

593. Talos, Emmerich and others, eds. NS-Herrschaft in Österreich 1938-1945. Vienna: Verlag für Gesellschaftskritik, 1988.

594. Thurner, Erika. Nationalsozialismus und Zigeuner in Österreich. Vienna: Geyer, 1983.

595. Van Arkel, Dirk. Anti-Semitism in Austria. Doctoral dissertation: University of Leiden, 1966.

596. Veiter, Theodor. Das Recht der Volksgruppen und Sprachminderheiten in Österreich. Vienna: Wilhelm Braumüller, 1970.

597. Verdery, Katherine. "Internal Colonialism in Austria- Hungary." Ethnic and Racial Studies 2 (July 1979): 378-399.

598. Weinzierl, Erika. "Austrian Catholics and the Jews." In Judaism and Christianity under the Impact of National Socialism, 1919-1945, eds. Otto Dov Kulka and Paul R. Mendes-Flohr. Jerusalem: Historical Society of Israel, 1987.

599. Weinzierl, Erika. Emanzipation? Oesterreichische Frauen im 20. Jahrhundert. Vienna: Jugend und Volk, 1975.

600. Weinzierl, Erika. Zu wenig Gerechte: Österreicher und Judenverfolgung. Vienna: Verlag Styria, 1985.

601. Weiss, Hilde. Antisemitische Vorurteile in Österreich: Theoretische und empirische Analysen. Vienna: Braumuller, 1984.

602. Whiteside, Arthur G. Austrian National Socialism before 1918. The Hague: Martinus Nijhoff, 1962.

603. Whiteside, Arthur G. The Socialism of Fools. Berkeley: University of California Press, 1976.

604. Wiesenthal, Simon. Justice Not Vengeance: Recollections. New York: Grove Weidenfeld, 1989.

605. Williams, Maurice. "Delusions of Grandeur: The Austrian National Socialists." Canadian Journal of History 14 (December 1979): 415-436.

606. Wiltschegg, Walter. Die Heimwehr. Vienna: Verlag für Geschichte und Politik, 1985.

607. Wistrich, Robert S. "Karl Lueger and the Ambiguities of Viennese Antisemitism." Jewish Social Studies 45 (Summer-Fall 1983): 251-262.

608. Wistrich, Robert S. "Liberalism, Deutschtum and Assimilation." Jerusalem Quarterly no.42 (1987): 100-118.

BANGLADESH

609. Ahmed, Nahleen. *Pluralism and Genocide: Case Study of the Genocide in Bangladesh, 1971*. Master's thesis: College of William and Mary, 1987.

610. Alam, Sultana. "Women and Poverty in Bangladesh." *Women's Studies International Forum* 8 (1985): 361-371.

611. Bairagi, R. "Food Crisis, Nutrition, and Female Children in Rural Bangladesh." *Population and Development Review* 12 (June 1986):

612. Begum, S. "Infant Mortality in Bangladesh: Trends and Differentials." *Bangladesh Development Studies* 11 (December 1983):

613. Chaudhury, R. H. "The Effect of Mother's Work on Child Care, Dietary Intake, and Dietary Adequacy of Pre-School Children." *Bangladesh Development Studies* 10 (December 1982)

614. Chen, Lincoln C. and others. "Sex Bias in the Family Allocation of Food and Health Care in Rural Bangladesh." *Population and Development Review* 7 (1981):

615. Chen, Martha A. *A Quiet Revolution: Women in Transition in Rural Bangladesh*. Cambridge, MA: Schenkman, 1983.

616. Chowdhury, Bazlul M. *A Sociological Study of the Development of Social Classes and Social Structure of Bangladesh*. Doctoral dissertation, University of Aberdeen, 1982. Order No. BRDX90022.

617. Ennals, David. "Biharis in Bangladesh: The Third Great Migration?" *Jr. Inst. Muslim Minority Affairs* 8 (July 1987): 238-245.

618. *From Isolation to Exile. Refugees from the Chittagong Hill Tracts of Bangladesh*. U.S. Committee for Refugees: 1988,

619. Hashemi, Syed. Class Structure and Surplus Flows in the Economy of Bangladesh. Doctoral dissertation: University of California, 1984.

620. Islam, J. and H. Khan. "Income Inequality, Poverty and Socio-economic Development in Bangladesh: An Empirical Investigation." Bangladesh Development Studies 14 (June 1986)

621. Islam, Rizwanul and M. Muqtada, eds. Bangladesh: Selected Issues in Employment and Development. New Delhi, India: International Labour Organization, Asian Employment Programme, 1986.

622. Kabeer, Naila. "Subordination and Struggle: Women in Bangladesh." New Left Review No. 168 (March-April 1988): 95-121.

623. Kabir, Muhammad G. Minority Politics in Bangladesh, 1947- 1971. Master's thesis: University of British Columbia, 1977.

624. Kabir, Muhammad G. Minority Politics in Bangladesh. New Delphi: Vikas, 1980.

625. Kabir, Muhammad G. "Religion, Language and Nationalism in Bangladesh." Journal of Contemporary Asia 17 (1987): 473-487.

626. Khan, A. A. "Analyzing Spatial Disparities in Access to Health Care: A Methodology with Application in Bangladesh." GeoJournal 10, #1 (1985):

627. Lifschultz, Lawrence. Bangladesh: The Unfinished Revolution. London: Zed Press, 1979.

628. Mey, Wolfgang, ed. Genocide in the Chittagong Hill Tracts, Bangladesh. Copenhagen, Denmark: International Work Group for Indigenous Affairs, December, 1984.

629. Mukherjee, R. "Nation-building and State Formation in Bangladesh. A Retrospective Study." South Asian Studies 7 (July 1972): 137-162.

630. O'Donnell, Charles P. Bangladesh: Biography of a Muslim Nation. Boulder, CO.: Westview Press, 1984.

631. Rahim, Aminur. Nationalism, Class and Education in Bangladesh. Doctoral dissertation, University of Toronto, 1986.

632. Rahman, Atiur. "Land Concentration and Dispossession in Two Villages of Bangladesh." Bangladesh Development Studies 10 (June 1982)

633. Rahman, Atiur. Peasants and Classes. A Study in Differentiation in Bangladesh. London: Zed Press, 1986.

634. Rahman, Atiur. "Poverty Alleviation and the Most Disadvantaged Groups in Bangladesh Agriculture." Bangladesh Development Studies 14 (March 1986)

635. Rahman, P. M. M. "Some Aspects of Income Distribution in Rural Bangladesh." Applied Economics 20 (August 1988)

636. Smock, Audrey C. "Bangladesh: A Struggle with Tradition and Poverty." in Women: Roles and Status in Eight Countries, edited by Janet Z. Giele and A.C. Smock. New York: Wiley, 1977.

637. "We Want the Land and Not the People: Genocide in the Chittagong Hill Tracts." Survival International Review (1984): 7-25.

638. Whitaker, Ben and others. The Biharis in Bangladesh. London: Minority Rights Group, 1982. [4th revised edition.]

639. Wood, Geoffrey D. "Rural Class Formation in Bangladesh, 1940-1980." Bulletin of Concerned Asian Scholars 13 (October-December 1981): 2-15.

BELGIUM

640. Aubenos-Bastie, Jaqueline. "68-78: Dix ans de feminisme en Belgique." In *Les femmes et leur maitres*, edited by Maria-Antonietta Macciocchi, 309-330. Paris: C. Bourgeois, 1979.

641. Aubert, Roger and others. *L'Immigration Italienne en Belgique: histoire, langues, identite. Bibliographie 1945-1985*. Brussels, Belgium: Instituto Italiano di Cultura and Universite Catholique de Louvain, 1985.

642. Bastenier, Albert and Felice Dasseto. "Organisations musulmanes de Belgique et insertion sociale des populations immigrées." *R. eur. migrations int.* 1 (1985): 9-21.

643. Bastenier, Albert and Felice Dassetto. "Les Particularités d'un Jeune Prolétariat non fixé: Les Jeunes Issus de l'Immigration Italienne en Belgique." *Studi Emigrazione* 23 (Jan. March 1986): 37-50.

644. Belgium, Ministry of National Education. "Education in the Dutch-speaking Area of Belgium." *Western European Education* 18 (1986): 3-24.

645. Blaupain, Roger and others. "Unlawful Employment Discrimination: A Discussion of Belgian Law and Related Issues." *Georgia Journal of International and Comparative Law* 20 (Spring 1990): 123-132.

646. Braeckman, C. *Les étrangers en Belgique*. Brussels: 1973.

647. Briey, Philippe de. *Le Comité de Défense des Juifs de Belgique (1940-1945) Bel exemple de résistance civile et populaire*. Brussels: MIR-IRG, 1981.

648. Brustein, William. "The Political Geography of Belgian Fascism: The Case of Rexism." *American Sociological Review* 53 (1988): 69-80.

649. Carpinelli, Giovanni. "Belgium." In *Fascism in Europe*. edited by S. J. Woolf. London: Methuen, 1982.

52 WORLD RACISM AND RELATED INHUMANITIES

650. Carpinelli, Giovanni. "The Flemish Variant in Belgian Fascism." Wiener Library Bulletin 26 (1972/73): 20-27.

651. Clark, Samuel. "Nobility, Bourgeoisie and the Industrial Revolution in Belgium." Past and Present 105 (November 1984): 140-175.

652. Covell, Maureen. "Ethnic Conflict, Representation and the State in Belgium." in Ethnic Groups and the State, edited by Paul Bross. Totawa, NJ: Barnes & Noble, 1985.

653. Deleeck, Herman. "The Adequacy of the Social Security System in Belgium, 1976-1985." Journal of Social Policy 18 (1989): 91-117.

654. Diviser pour règner: racisme comme stratégie. Brussels: Editions Vie Ouvriere, n.d.

655. Edwards, John and Clare Ahearn. "Language and Identity in Belgium: Perceptions of French and Flemish Students." Ethnic and Racial Studies 10 (1987): 135-148.

656. Erdmann-Degenhardt, Dan. "La deportation des Juifs de Belgique." Monde Juif 109 (1983): 1-24.

657. Garfinkels, B. Les Belges face à la persécution raciale 1940-1944. Brussels: 1965.

658. Gotovitch, Jose. "L'antisémitisme en Belgique." R. Nouvelle 78, No. 10 (1983): 291-296.

659. Groote, Jacqueline de and M-C Lefebvre. "Discrimination in Classified Advertisements for Jobs." Memo from Belgium (1979): 129-131.

660. Havelange, Pierre. Racisme à Bruxelles. Brussels: Louis Musin Editeur, 1981.

661. Irving, Ronald E. M. The Flemings and Walloons of Belgium. London: Minority Rights Group, 1980.

662. Jacquemin, J-M. "La loi du 30 juillet 1981 tendant a reprimer certains actes inspires par le racisme ou la xenophobie: chronique d'une loi mal appliquee." L'Annee Sociale (May-August 1987): 119-130.

663. Jacquemyns, J. La Société Belge sous l'Occupation Allemande 2 vols. Brussels: 1950.

664. Keunings, Lue. "The Secret Police in Nineteenth-century Brussels." Intelligence and National Security 4 (1989): 59-85.

665. Kless, Schlomo. "The Rescue of Jewish Children in Belgium during the Holocaust." Holocaust & Genocide Studies 3 (1988): 275-287.

666. Krajzman, Maurice. "L'Image des Juifs et du Judaïsme dans les manuels d'histoire belges." Rev. de l'Inst. de Sociologie (Belgium) No.1 (1974): 103-132.

667. Liebman, Marcel. Né Juif, une famille juive pendant la guerre. Paris: Duculot, 1975. [Belgium, 1941-1945.]

668. Lis, Catharina. Social Change and the Labouring Poor, Antwerp, 1776-1860. New Haven, Ct: Yale University Press, 1986.

669. Lorwin, Val R. "Belgium: Religion, Class, and Language in National Politics." In Political Oppositions in Western Democracies, edited by Robert Dahl. New Haven, CT: Yale University Press, 1966.

670. Lorwin, Val R. "Linguistic Pluralism and Political Tension in Modern Belgium." Canadian Journal of History 5 (1970): 1-23.

671. Maguran, H. C. Integration, Political Behavior and Attitude Change: A Comparative Study of 100 Southern Spanish and 100 Sicilian Migrants in Charleroi, Belgium. Doctoral dissertation, University of Kent, 1985.

672. Mandel, Ernest. "The Dialectic of Class and Region in Belgium." New Left Review 20 (1963): 5-31.

673. Michman, Dan. "Antwerp." in Encyclopedia of the Holocaust, I. pp. 77-80. New York: Macmillan, 1990.

674. Michman, Dan. "Belgium." in Encyclopedia of the Holocaust, I. pp. 160-169. New York: Macmillan, 1990.

675. Michman, Dan. "Brussels." in Encyclopedia of the Holocaust, I. pp. 249-252. New York: Macmillan, 1990.

676. Ministere de la Justice, Commission des Crimes de Guerre. La persecution antisemitique en Belgique. Liege: 1947.

677. Morelli, Anne. "Les diplomates italiens en Belgique et la 'question juive' 1938-1943." Bulletin de l'Institut Historique Belge de Rome 53-54 (1983-84): 357-407.

678. Nielsen, F. "Structural Conduciveness and Ethnic Mobilization: The Flemish Movment in Belgium." In Competitive Ethnic Relations, edited by Susan Olzak and Joane Nagel. Orlando, FL: Academic Press, 1986.

679. Passelecq, G. and M. H. Fournier. "L'antisémitisme en Belgique." Rencontre Chretienes et Juifs 42 (1975): 161-164.

680. Roosens, Eugeen. "Desavantages et discrimination: la question des immigres en Belgique." Studi Emigrazione 16 (June 1979): 229-303.

681. Roosens, Eugeen. "Migration and Caste Formation in Europe: The Belgian Case." Ethnic and Racial Studies 11 (April 1988): 207-217. [Immigrant workers.]

682. Samuels, S. "'Kristallmorgen' in Antwerp." ADL Bulletin 39 (January 1982): 10-11.

683. Sternberg, Maxime. Dossier Bruxelles Auschwitz: la police SS et l'extermination des Juifs de Belgique. Brussels: Comite Belge de Soutien a la partie civile dans le proces des officiers SS, 1980.

684. Sternberg, Maxime. L'etoile et le fusile: la question juive 1940-1942. Brussels: Vie Ouvriere, 1983. [Treatment of Jews in Belgium.]

685. Velimsky, Vitezslav. "Belgium of the Eighties: Unitary, Bi- cultural or Made Up of Three Regions?" Europa Ethnica 40 (1983): 1-14.

686. Willequet, Jacques. La Belgique sous la botte: Résistances et collaborations 1940-1945. Paris: Editions Universitaires, 1986.

687. Willequet, Jacques. "Les fascismes belge et la seconde guerre mondiale." R. d'Histoire de la Deuxième Guerre Mondiale 17 (1967): 85-109.

688. Zolberg, Aristide. "The Making of Flemings and Walloons: Belgium, 1830-1914." Journal of Interdisciplinary History 5 (1974): 179-235.

BELIZE

689. Bolland, O. Nigel. <u>The Formation of a Colonial Society: Belize, from Conquest to Crown Colony</u>. Baltimore, MD: Johns Hopkins University Press, 1977.

690. Bolland, O. Nigel. "Labour Control and Resistance in Belize in the Century After 1838." <u>Slavery & Abolition</u> 7 (1986): 173-187.

691. Everitt, J. C. "The Torch is Passed: Neocolonialism in Belize." <u>Caribbean Quarterly</u> 33 (1987): 42-59.

692. Medina, Laurie K. "Creating and Manipulating Power within Dependency." <u>Belizean Studies</u> 16 (1988): 2-13.

693. Naylor, Robert A. <u>Penny Ante Imperialism: The Mosquito Shore and the Bay of Honduras, 1600-1914: A Case Study in British Informal Empire</u>. Rutherford, NJ: Fairleigh Dickinson University Press, 1989.

BENIN

694. Cornevin, Robert. <u>La Republique Populaire du Benin des origines dahomeennes a nos jours</u>. Paris: Editions G.P. Maisonneuve et Larose, 1981.

695. Garcia, Luc. <u>Le royaume du Dahome face a la penetration coloniale</u>. Paris: 1988.

696. Hounkpatin, Philippe. <u>Der Sozialismus als Überwindungsstrategie der Unterentwicklung am Fall Benin</u>. Giessen: Focus-Verlag, 1987.

697. Krasnowolski, Andrzej. "Independence or Equality of Rights: The Movement of Protest in Colonial Dahomey between 1894 and 1946." <u>African Bulletin</u> 34 (1987): 121-131.

698. Law, Robin. "History and Legitimacy: Aspects of the Use of the Past in Precolonial Dahomey." <u>Africa</u> 15 (1988): 431-456.

699. Law, Robin. "Slave-raiders and Middlemen, Monopolists and Face-traders: The Supply of Slaves for the Atlantic Trade in Dahomey, c. 1715-1850." <u>Journal of African History</u> 30 (1989): 45-68.

700. Obichere, Boniface I. "Women and Slavery in the Kingdom of Dahoumey." <u>R. fr. hist. outre-mer</u> 62 (1978): 5-20.

701. Ronen, Dov. "The Colonial Elite in Dahomey." <u>African Studies Review</u> 17 (1974): 55-76.

BOLIVIA

702. Barrios de Chungara, Domitila. Let Me Speak! Testimony of Domitila, a Woman of the Bolivian Mines. NY: Monthly Review Press, 1978.

703. Cole, Jeffrey A. The Potosi Mita, 1573-1700: Compulsory Indian Labor in the Andes. Stanford, CA: Stanford University Press, 1985.

704. Dunkerley, James and Rolando Morales. "The Crisis in Bolivia." New Left Review 155 (January-February 1986): 86-106.

705. Grieshaber, Erwin P. "Survival of Indian Communities in Nineteenth-Century Bolivia: A Regional Comparison." Journal of Latin American Studies 12 (1980): 223-269.

706. Kelley, Jonathan. "Class Conflict or Ethnic Oppression? The Cost of Being Indian in Rural Bolivia." Rural Sociology 53 (1988): 399-420.

707. Kelley, Jonathan and Herbert S. Klein. "Revolution and the Rebirth of Inequality: The Bolivian National Revolution." ERIC ED 155 073 (1977)

708. Knudsen, Jerry W. "The Bolivian Immigration Bill of 1942: A Case Study in Latin American Anti-Semitism." American Jewish Archives 22 (Nov. 1970): 138-158.

709. Larson, Brooke. Colonialism and Agrarian Transformation in Bolivia, Cochabamba, 1550-1900. Princeton, NJ: Princeton University Press, 1988.

710. Morales Anaya, Rolando. Desarrollo y pobreza en Bolivia: La situacion del niño y la mujer. La Paz: Mundy, 1984.

711. Nash, June. We Eat the Mines and the Mines Eat Us: Dependency and Exploitation in Bolivian Tin Mines. NY: Columbia University Press, 1979.

712. Saignes, Thierry. "Politicas etnicas en Bolivia colonial, siglos XVI-XIX." Historia Boliviana 3 (1983): 1-30.

713. Simon, Brigette and others. I Sold Myself: I was Bought: A Socio-Economic Analysis Based on Interviews with Sugar-Cane Harvesters in Santa Cruz de la Sierra, Boliva. Copenhagen: IWGIA, 1980.

714. Thompson, Stephen I. "Separate but Superior: Japanese in Bolivia." In Ethnic Encounters: Identities and Contexts, edited by George L. Hicks and Philip E. Leis, pp. 89-101. North Scituate, MA: Duxbury Press, 1977.

715. Urioste Fernández de Cordova, Miguel. El Estado anticampesino. Quito: Instituto Latinoamericano de Investigaciones Sociales, 1984.

BOTSWANA

716. Chernichovsky, Dov and others. The Household Economy of Rural Botswana: An African Case. Washington, D.C.: World Bank, 1985.

717. Chernichovsky, Dov. "Socioeconomic and Demographic Aspects of School Enrollment and Attendance in Rural Botswana." Ec. Dev. Cult. Change 33 (January 1985): 319-332.

718. Crowder, Michael. The Flogging of Phinehas McIntosh: A Tale of Colonial Folly and Injustice: Bechuanaland 1933. New Haven, CT: Yale University Press, 1988.

719. Curry, R. L., Jr. "Mineral-based Growth and Development- generated Socioeconomic Problems in Botswana: Rural Inequality, Water Scarcity, Food Insecurity, and Foreign Dependence Challenge New Governing Class." American Journal of Economics and Sociology 44 (July 1985)

720. Curry, R. L., Jr. "Poverty and Mass Unemployment in Mineral-Rich Botswana." American Journal of Economics and Sociology 46 (January 1987): 71-88.

721. Dixey, R. A. Education and Inequality in Botswana. Doctoral dissertation: University of Liverpool, 1987.

722. Duncan, Wendy A. "Schooling for Girls in Botswana: Patterns of Enrolment and Performance." Botswana Educational Research Journal 4 (1986): 52-61.

723. Egner, E. B. and A. Klausen. Poverty in Botswana. Gaborone: University College of Botswana, 1980.

724. Leepile, M. "The Impact of Migrant Labour on the Economy of Kweneng, 1940-1980." Botswana Notes Rec. 13 (1981): 33-34.

725. Mantle, Goontatlhe. "Changes in Botswana Primary School Curriculum: 1966-1982." Boleswa Educational Res. Journal 3 (1985): 69-78.

726. Mgadla, Part T. Missionary and Colonial Education among the Bangwato: 1862-1948. Doctoral dissertation, Boston University, 1986. UMO # 8601366.

727. Molamu, Louis. "Alcoholism in Botswana: A Historical Overview." Contemporary Drug Problems 16 (Spring 1989): 3-42.

728. Molutsi, Patrick P. Social Stratification and Inequality in Botswana: Issues in Development, 1950-1985. Doctoral dissertation: University of Oxford, 1986. Order No. BRD-87816.

729. Parson, J. D. The Political Economy of Botswana. Doctoral dissertation: University of Sussex, 1979.

730. Picard, Louis A. The Politics of Development in Botswana. Boulder, CO: 1987.

BRAZIL

731. Abu-El-Haj, Jawdat Ahed. The Transition to Capitalism in Northeast Brazil: Proletarianization and Working Class Formation. Doctoral dissertation, University of California, Riverside, 1987. UMO # 8729398.

732. Adamo, Sam C. The Broken Promise: Race, Health, and Justice in Rio De Janeiro, 1890-1940. Doctoral dissertation, University of New Mexico, 1983. UMO # 8424825.

733. Adriance, Madelaine. Opting for the Poor: Brazilian Catholicism in Transition. Kansas City, Mo: Sheed & Ward, 1989.

734. Alden, Dauril and Joseph C. Miller. "Out of Africa: The Slave Trade and the Transmission of Smallpox to Brazil." Journal of Interdisciplinary History 18 (Autumn 1987): 195-224.

735. Algranti, Leila M. "Slave Crimes: The Use of Police Power to Control the Slave Population of Rio de Janeiro." Luso- Brazilian Review 25 (1988): 27-48.

736. Alvarez, Sonia E. Engendering Democracy in Brazil. Women's Movements in Transition Politics. Princeton, NJ: Princeton University Press, 1990.

737. Andrews, George R. "Black and White Workers: Sao Paulo, Brazil, 1888-1928." Hispanic American Historical Review 68 (August 1988): 491-524.

738. Arns, Paulo Evaristo. Torture in Brazil. Brasil: Nunca Mais.

739. Azevedo, Aluisio. Mulatto. Translated by Murray G. MacNicoll. Cranbury, NJ: Fairleigh Dickinson University, 1990. [Brazilian novel first published in 1881.]

740. Bacchus, Wilfred A. *Mission in Mufti. Brazil's Military Regimes, 1964-1985*. Westport, CT: Greenwood, 1990.

741. Baiocchi, Mari de Nasare. *Negros de Cedro*. Sao Paulo: Editora Atica, 1983.

742. Barbe, Dominique. *Grace and Power: Base Communities and Nonviolence in Brazil*. Orbis, 1987.

743. Barbosa, Luiz C. "Manumission in Brazil and Surinam: The Role of Dutch Hegemony and Decline in the Capitalist World-Economy." *Ethnic and Racial Studies* 10 (1987): 349-65.

744. Bastide, Roger. "Race Relations in Brazil." *International Social Science Bulletin* 4 (1957): 495-512.

745. Bianco, Janis R. *A Learning Community: A Study of a Brazilian Favela*. Doctoral dissertation: Columbia University, 1986. UMO # 8620336.

746. Bills, David B. and A. O. Haller. "Socioeconomic Development and Social Stratification: Reassessing the Brazilian Case." *J. Dev. Areas* 19 (October 1984): 59-70.

747. Birdsell, Nancy. "Public Inputs and Child Schooling in Brazil." *Jr. Dev. Ec.* 18 (May-June 1985): 67-86.

748. Bresser Pereira, Luiz. *Development and Crisis in Brazil, 1930-1983*. Boulder, Co.: Westview Press, 1984.

749. Bunker, Stephen G. *Underdeveloping the Amazon: Extraction, Unequal Exchange, and the Failure of the Modern State*. Champaign: University of Illinois Press, 1985.

750. Cardoso, Gerald. *Negro Slavery in the Sugar Plantations of Veracruz and Pernambuco, 1550-1680: A Comparative Study*. Wash., D.C.: University Press of America, 1983.

751. Carneiro, Maria L. T. *O Anti-Semitismo no Era Vargas. Fantasmas de una Geracao (1930-1945)*. Sao Paulo: Editora Brasiliense, 1988.

752. Chilcote, Ronald H. *Power and Ruling Classes in Northeast Brazil Juazeiro and Petrolina in Transition*. NY: Cambridge University Press, 1990.

753. Cleary, David. *Anatomy of the Amazon Gold Rush*. Iowa City: University of Iowa Press, 1990.

754. Cohen, Youssef. *The Manipulation of Consent. The State and Working-Class Consciousness in Brazil*. Pittsburg, PA: University of Pittsburgh Press, 1989.

BRAZIL 63

755. Conniff, Michael L. "The National Elite." In Modern Brazil: Elites and Masses in Historical Perspective, edited by Conniff and Frank D. McCann. Lincoln: University of Nebraska Press, 1989.

756. Conniff, Michael L. and Frank D. McCann, eds. Modern Brazil: Elites and Masses in Historical Perspective. Lincoln: University of Nebraska Press, 1989.

757. Conrad, Robert E. "The Brazilian Slave." In History of Latin American Civilization: Sources and Interpretations, II, edited by Lewis Hanke, 155-213. 1967.

758. Conrad, Robert E. Children of God's Fire. A Documentary History of Black Slavery in Brazil. Princeton, NJ: Princeton University Press, 1983.

759. Conrad, Robert E. The Destruction of Brazilian Slavery 1850- 1888. Berkeley: University of California Press, 1972.

760. Corwin, Arthur F. "Afro-Brazilians: Myths and Realities." In Slavery and Race Relations in Latin America, edited by Robert B. Toplin. Westport, CT: Greenwood, 1974.

761. Dantas Júnior, Altino, ed. Lula sem censura: "e ai a peãozada partiu pro pau". Petropolis, Brazil: Editora Vozes, 1981. [Luis Ignacio da Silva.]

762. Dassin, Joan, ed. Torture in Brazil: A Report by the Archdiocese of Sao Paulo. Translated by Jaime Wright. New York: Vintage Books, 1988.

763. Denslow, D. Jr and W. Tyler. "Perspectives on Poverty and Income Inequality in Brazil." World Development 12 (Oct. 1984)

764. Do Nascimento, Abdias. Brazil: Mixture or Massacre? Essays in the Genocide of a Black People. Translated by Elisa Larkin Nascimento. 2nd edition Dover, MA: Majority, 1989.

765. Do Nascimento, Abdias. Combate ao racismo. Brasilia: Carvara dos Deputados, 1983.

766. Dos Santos, Eliana P. L. "'Indigenous Peoples Speak Your History'." PCR Information (World Council of Churches) 24 (1987): 14-18.

767. Dos Santos, Pe A. F. "Eu, Negro". Discriminação racial no Brasil. Existe? São Paulo, Brazil: Edicoes Loyola, 1986.

768. Dreifuss, Rene A. O jogo da direita: na Nova Republica. Petropolis, Brazil: Editora Vozes, 1989. [Political influence of businessmen and landowners during the 1980s.]

769. Drescher, Seymour. "Brazilian Abolition in Comparative Perspective." Hispanic American Historical Review 68 (August 1988): 429-460.

770. Dzidzienyo, Anani. "Brazil." In International Handbook on Race and Race Relations, edited by Jay A. Sigler. Westport, CT: Greenwood, 1987.

771. Dzidzienyo, Anani. The Position of Blacks in Brazilian and Cuban Society. New edition London: Minority Rights Group, 1979.

772. Eakin, Marshall C. "Race and Identity: Silvio Romero, Science, and Social Thought in Late 19th Century Brazil." Luso-Braz Rev. 22 (Winter 1985): 151-174.

773. Fernandes, Florestan. O desafio educacional. Sao Paulo: Cortez Editora, 1989.

774. Fernandes, Florestan. "Reflections on the Brazilian Counterrevolution." International Journal of Sociology 11 (1981): 3-185.

775. Ferrer, Ada. "Gilberto Freyre: A Problem in the Historiography of Brazilian Slavery." Inter-American Review of Bibliography 38 (1988): 196-211.

776. Flory, Thomas. "Fugitive Slaves and Free Society: The Case of Brazil." Journal of Negro History 64, 2 (1979): 116-130.

777. Fontaine, Pierre-Michel. "Race and Class in Brazil: New Issues and New Approaches." CAAS Newsletter 4, 2 (May 1980): 2.

778. Fontaine, Pierre-Michel. Race, Class and Power in Brazil. Los Angeles, CA: UCLA Center for Afro-American Studies, 1989.

779. Fontaine, Pierre-Michel. "Transnational Relations and Racial Mobilization: Emerging Black Movements in Brazil." In Ethnic Minorities in a Transnatinal World Jr ed. John F. Stack. Westport, CT: Greenwood, 1981.

780. Fontaine, Pierre-Michel, ed. Race, Class, and Power in Brazil. Los Angeles: Center for Afro-American Studies, University of California, 1986.

781. Foracchi, Marialice M. A participacão social dos excluidos. Sao Paulo: Editora de Humanismo, Ciencia e Tecnologia, 1982.

782. Foweraker, Joe. The Struggle for Land: A Political Economy of the Pioneer Frontier in Brazil from 1930 to the Present Day. N.Y.: Cambridge University Press, 1981.

783. Giacomini, Sonia Maria. Mulher e escrava: uma introducão historica ao estudo da mulher negra no Brasil. Petropolis: Vozes, 1988.

784. Godfrey, Brian J. "Boom Towns of the Amazon." Geographical Review 30 (April 1990):

785. Goldenberg, Paulette. Repensando a desnutricao como questao social. Campinas: Editora da Universidade Estadual de Campinas, 1988. [Deals especially with São Paulo.]

786. Gomes, Gustavo M. The Roots of State Intervention in the Brazilian Economy. NY: Praeger, 1986.

787. Gomes, Mercio P. Os Indios e o Brasil: ensaio sobre um holocaust e sobre uma nova possibilidade de convivencia. Petropolis: Editora Vozes, 1988. [Since colonial times.]

788. Green, Duncan, ed. Fight for the Forest: Chico Mendes in His Own Words. London: Latin America Bureau, 1989.

789. Greenbaum, Linda. "Plundering the Timber on Brazilian Indian Reservations." Cultural Survival Quarterly 12 (1989): 23-26.

790. Gross, R. and others. "The Influence of Economic Deterioration in Brazil on the Nutritional Status of Children in Rio de Janeiro." Ecology Food and Nutrition 19 (1987): 265-280.

791. Haberly, David. "Abolitionism in Brazil, Anti-Slavery, and Anti-Slave." Luso-Brasilian Review 9, 2 (1972): 30-46.

792. Hahner, June E. Poverty and Politics: The Urban Poor in Brazil, 1970-1920. Albuquerque: University of New Mexico Press, 1986.

793. Hasenblag, Carlos A. and Nelson da Valle Silva. Estrutura social, mobilidade e raça. São Paulo: Edicões Vertice, 1988.

794. Hasenblag, Carlos A. and Guellen Huntington. "Brazilian Racial Democracy: Reality or Myth?" Humboldt Journal of Social Relations 10 (Fall-Winter 1982-83): 129-42.

795. Hell, Jürgen. "Der brasilianische Plantagen-Komplex (1532- 1808): Ein Beitrag zur Charakteristik der Sklaverei in Amerika." Asien-Afrika-Latein-Amerika 6 (1978): 117-38.

796. Heller, Milton I. Resisténcia democrática: a repressão no Parana. Rio de Janeiro, Brazil: Editora Paz e Terra, 1988. [The 1964 military coup and after.]

797. Hellwig, David J. "A New Frontier in a Racial Paradise: Robert S. Abbott's Brazilian Dream." Luso-Braz. Review 25 (Summer 1988): 59-68.

798. Hemming, John. Amazon Frontier. The Defeat of the Brazilian Indians. Cambridge, MA: Harvard University Press, 1988. [1760-1810.]

799. Hemming, John, ed. Changes in the Amazon Basin. 2 vols. Manchester: Manchester University Press, 1985.

800. Hemming, John. Red Gold: The Conquest of the Brazilian Indians, 1500-1760. Cambridge, MA: Howard University Press, 1978.

801. Hewitt, W. E. "The Preferential Option for the Poor in the Archdiocese of Sao Paulo." Canadian Journal of Latin American and Caribbean Studies 12 (1987): 75-88.

802. Hewitt, W. E. "Religion and the Consolidation of Democracy in Brazil--The Role of the Communidades-Ecclesiaisde-Base (CEBs)." Sociological Analysis 51 (Summer 1990)

803. Hilton, Stanley E. "Acao integralista brasileira: Fascism in Brazil, 1932-1938." Luso-Brazilian Review 9 (1972): 3-29.

804. Hodges-Betts, Bobbie. "Recomposing the Samba: A Look at the Contemporary Black Movement in Post-Abolition Brazil." Sage 6 (Summer 1989)

805. Huggins, Martha K. From Slavery to Vagrancy in Brazil: Crime and Social Control in the Third World. New Brunswick, NJ: Rutgers University Press, 1985.

806. José, Oiliam. Racismo em Minas Gerais. Belo Horizonte: Impr. Oficial de Minas Gerais, 1981.

807. Karasch, Mary C. Slave Life and Culture in Rio de Janeiro, 1808-1850. Princeton, NJ: Princeton University Press, 1985.

808. Kennedy, James H. "Political Liberalization, Black Consciousness, and Recent Afro-Brazilian Literature." Phylon 47 (September 1986): 199-209.

809. Kiple, Dalila de S. Darwin and Medical Perceptions of the Black: A Comparative Study of the United States and Brazil, 1871-1918. Doctoral dissertation, Bowling Green State University, 1987. UMO # 8720070.

810. Kramer, Jane. "Letter from the Elysian Fields." New Yorker (March 2, 1987) [The liberation church in Campos Eliseos, Rio de Janeiro, Brazil.]

811. Leacock, Ruth. Requiem for Revolution. The United States and Brazil, 1961-1969. Kent, Ohio: Kent State University Press, 1990.

812. Leitman, Spencer L. "The Black Ragamuffins: Racial Hypocrisy in Nineteenth Century Southern Brazil." Americas 33 (January 1977): 504-518.

813. Lesser, Jeff H. "Continuity and Change within an Immigrant Community: The Jews of Sao Paulo, 1924-1945." Luso-Brazilian Review 25 (1988): 45-58.

814. Lesser, Jeffrey H. Pawns of the Powerful: Jewish Immigration to Brazil, 1904-1945. Doctoral dissertation, New York University, 1989. UMO # 9004217.

815. Levine, Robert M. "'Turning On the Lights': Brazilian Slavery Reconsidered One Hundred Years After Abolition." Latin American Research Review 24 (1989): 201-217.

816. Lopes, Jorge E. G. Secondary Education under Authoritarian Governance: The Case of Brazil, 1930-1945. Doctoral dissertation, University of Miami, 1986. UMO # 8619505.

817. Lovell, Peggy Ann. Racial Inequality and the Brazilian Labor Market. Doctoral dissertation, University of Florida, 1989. UMO # 9021944.

818. Luebke, Frederick C. Germans in Brazil: A Comparative History of Cultural Conflict during World War I. Baton Rouge: Louisiana State University Press, 1987.

819. MacDonald, Neil. Brazil. An Oxfam Report. Oxford, England: Oxfam Publications, 1991.

820. Maclachlan, Colin. "Slavery, Ideology and Institutional Change: The Impact of the Enlightenment on Slavery in Late Eighteenth-Century Uranaishao." Journal of Latin American Studies 2 (May 1979): 1-17.

821. Maestri Filho, M. J. Quilombos e quilombolas em terras gaúchas. Porto Alegre: Escola superior de Teologia São Lourenco de Brindes, Caias do Sul: Universidade de Caxias, 1979.

822. Mafei, Maristela. Sangue na terra: a luta des mulheres. São Paulo: Icone Editore Ltda., 1985. [Terror against peasants demanding land.]

823. Mantegra, G. and M. Moraes. "A Critique of Brazilian Political Economy." Capital and Class 10 (Spring 1980): 125-54.

824. Marchant, Alexander. From Barter to Slavery: The Economic Relations of Portugal & Indians in the Settlement of Brazil, 1500-1580. 1942.

825. Martin, Phillip. "Racial Inequalities Are Now Being Challenged in Brazil." Boston Globe (September 3, 1987)

826. Martnis, José de Souza. A reforma agrária e os limites da democracia na Nova Republica. Sao Paulo: Editora de Humanismo, Ciencia e Tecnologia, 1986.

827. Mattoso, Katia M. de Iueros. To Be a Slave in Brazil: 1550- 1888. Translated by Arthur Goldhammer. New Brunswick, NJ: University Press, 1986.

828. May, Laurie J. The Returns to Schooling and the Demand for Education in Brazil. Doctoral dissertation, University of Pennsylvania, 1985. UMO # 8523438.

829. Meade, Teresa and G. A. Pirio. "In Search of the Afro- American 'Eldorado': Attempts by North American Blacks to Enter Brazil in the 1920s." Luso-Braz. Review 25 (Summer 1988): 85-110.

830. Minayo, Maria C. de Souza, ed. A saudé em estado de choque. Rio de Janeiro: Editora Espaco e Tempo, 1986.

831. Moore, Zelbert L. "Out of the Shadows: Black and Brown Struggles for Recognition and Dignity in Brazil, 1964-1985." Journal of Black Studies 19 (June 1989): 394-410.

832. Moore, Zelbert L. "Reflections on Blacks in Contemporary Brazilian Popular Culture in the 1980s." Studies in Latin American Popular Culture 7 (1988): 213-226.

833. Moraes, Evaristo de. A escravidão africana no Brasil (das origens à extincção). Sao Paulo: 1933.

834. Moreira Alves, Maria H. "Building Democratic Socialism: The Partido Dos Trabalhadores in Brazil." Monthly Review 42 (September 1990): 1-16.

835. Moscatelli, Luigi. Politica da repressão: força e poder de uma justiça de classe. Rio de Janeiro: Ediçoes Achiame, 1982.

836. Moura, Clóvis. Brasil: raizes do protesto negro. Sao Paulo: Global Editora, 1983.

837. Moura, Clóvis. Rebeliões da senzala: Quilombos, insurreiçoes, guerrilhas. Rio: 1972.

838. Nascimento, Abdias do. "Racial Democracy" in Brazil, Myth or Reality? A Dossier of Brazilian Racism. Translated by Elisa Larkin do Nascimento. 2nd edition revised and augmented. Ibadan: Sketch Publishing, 1977.

839. Nascimento, Elisa Larkin. "Aspects of Afro-Brazilian Experience." Journal of Black Studies 10 (December 1980): 195-216.

840. Niani. "Black Consciousness vs. Racism in Brazil." Black Scholar 11 (January 1980): 59-70.

841. O genocidio do Nordeste, 1979-1983. Edicoes Mandocaru, 1987.

842. Pallemaerte, Marc. "Development, Conservation, and Indigenous Rights in Brazil." Human Rights Quarterly 8 (August 1986): 374-400.

843. Pastore, Jose. Inequality and Social Mobility in Brazil. Translated by Robert M. Oxley. Madison: University of Wisconsin Press, 1982.

844. Pfefferman, Guy and Richard Webb. "Pobreza e distribuicão de renda no Brazil, 1960-1980." Revista Brasileira de Economia 37 (1983): 147-175.

BRAZIL 69

845. Pierson, Donald. Negroes in Brazil: A Study of Race Contact at Bahia. 2nd edition. Carbondale: Southern Illinois University Press, 1967.

846. Pinto Vallejos, Julio. "Slave Control and Slave Resistance in Colonial Minas Gerais, 1700-1750." Journal of Latin American Studies 17 (May 1985): 1-34.

847. Plant, D. N. "State Action and the Distribution of School Enrollments in Brazil, 1970." Economics of Education Review 5 (1986)

848. Poskonina, L. S. "Brazilian Radical Left Historiography on the Problems of the Development of Latin American Capitalism." Soc. Stud. Hist. 26 (Spring 1988): 84-102.

849. "Prejudice against Jews in Brazil." In the Dispersion 5 (1968): 65-72.

850. Price, David. Before the Bulldozer: The Nabiquara Indians and the World Bank. Seven Locks Press, 1989.

851. Pucci, Bruno. A nova praxis educacional da Igria (1968- 1979). São Paulo: Edicões Paulinas, 1985. [Base communities and the Catholic church.]

852. Queirós Mattoso, Katia M. De. "Slave, Free and Freed Family Structures in Nineteenth-Centruy Salvador, Brazil." Luso-Braz. Review 25 (Summer 1988): 69-84.

853. Queiroz, S. R. R. de. "El origen de los negros brasileños." Revista de la Universidad de México (1970)

854. Ramos, Artur. A aculturação negra no Brasil. São Paulo: Editora Nacional, 1942.

855. Reicher Madeira, Felicia. "Youth in Brazil: Old Assumptions and New Approaches." CEPAL Review 29 (August 1986): 55-78.

856. Reis, Elisa P. "Brazil: One Hundred Years of the Agrarian Question." International Statistical Review 42 (May 1990)

857. Reis, João José. "Slave Resistance in Brazil: Bahia, 1807- 1835." Luso-Braz. Review 25 (Summer 1988): 111-144.

858. Reis, João José and P. F. Moraes Farias. "Islam and Slave Resistance in Bahia, Brazil." Islam Soc. Sud. Sahara 3 (1989): 41-66.

859. Riding, Alan. "Improving Brazilian Social Welfare Proves Far Easier Said Than Done." New York Times, (August 9, 1988)

860. Rios, Jose A. "Linchamentos: do arcaico ao moderno." Revista de Informaçao Legislativa 25 (October-December 1988): 207-238. [Lynching in Brazil.]

861. Rivers, Richard. "Brazil: How the Right Retained Power." Z Magazine 3 (March, 1990): 37-46.

862. Rout, Leslie B., Jr. "Sleight of Hand: Brazilian and American Authors Manipulate the Brazilian Racial Situation, 1910-1951." Americas 29 (April 1973): 471-488.

863. Russell-Wood, A. J. R. The Black Man in Slavery and Freedom in Colonial Brazil. NY: St. Martin's Press, 1982.

864. Santos, Paula. "Brazil: Women's Issues-Women's Activism." African Commentary (August 1990): 20-22. [Black women in Brazil.]

865. Santos, Silvio C. dos and others, eds. Sociedades indigenas direito: uma questão de direitos humanos; ensaios. Florianopolis: Editora da Universidade Federal de Santa Catrina, 1985.

866. Schwartz, Stuart B. "Free Labor in a Slave Economy: The Lavradores de cana of Colonial Bahia." In Colonial Roots of Modern Brazil, edited by Dauril Alden, 147-197. Berkeley: 1973.

867. Schwartz, Stuart B. "Patterns of Slaveholding in the Americas: New Evidence from Brazil." American Historical Review April 1973, 29 (Americas):

868. Schwartz, Stuart B. "Recent Trends in the Study of Slavery in Brazil." Luso-Brazilian Review 25 (Summer 1988): 1-25.

869. Schwartz, Stuart B. "Resistance and Accommodation in Eighteenth-Century Brazil: The Slaves' View of Slavery." Hisp. Am. Hist. R. 57 (Feb. 1977): 69-81.

870. Scott, Rebecca and others. The Abolition of Slavery and the Aftermath of Emancipation in Brazil. Durham, NC: Duke University Press, 1989.

871. Serbia, Ken. "Brazilian 'Gold Rush' Threatens Amazon Indians." National Catholic Reporter (October 28, 1988):

872. Serbia, Ken. "Pastoral Agents Movement Raises Fledgling Black Awareness in Brazil." National Catholic Reporter (April 20, 1990):

873. Shidlo, Gil. Social Policy in a Non-democratic Regime: The Case of Public Housing in Brazil. Boulder, Co.: Westview, 1990.

874. Silva, Aracy Lopes da, ed. A questão da educacão indigena. Sao Paulo: Editora Brasiliense, 1981.

875. Silva, Martiniano Jose da. Racismo à brasileira: raizes historicas. Brasil: Thesaurus Editora, 1987.

876. Silveira, Ricardo A. R. The Distribution of Wealth in Brazil - The Case of Rio de Janeiro : 1870s to 1980s. Doctoral dissertation, University of California, Berkeley, 1985. UMO # 8610215.

877. Simons, Marlise. "Brazil's Blacks Feel Prejudice 100 years After Slavery's End." New York Times (May 14, 1988):

878. Simons, Marlise. "Japanese Gone Brazilian: Unhurried Workaholics." New York Times (May 8, 1988):

879. Singer, Paul. Dominação e desigualdade: estrutura de clases e repartição da renda no Brasil. Rio de Janeiro: Editôra Paz e Terra, 1981.

880. Skidmore, Thomas E. Black Into White. Race and Nationality in Brazilian Thought. NY: Oxford Unviersity Press, 1974.

881. Skidmore, Thomas E. "Race and Class in Brazil: Historical Perspectives." Luso-Braz. Review 20 (Summer 1983): 104-118.

882. Soares, Glaucio and Nelson do Valle Silva. "Urbanization, Race, and Class in Brazilian Politics." Latin American Research Review 22 (1987): 177-191.

883. Sobrinho, Jose A. The Economic and the Political in the Brazilian Educational System - 1956-1982. Doctoral dissertation, Stanford University, 1985. UMO # 8602542.

884. Southgate, D. and C. Runge. "Toward an Economic Model of Deforestation and Social Change in Amazonia." Ricerche Economiche 39 (October-December 1985)

885. Sundiata, I. K. "Late Twentieth Century Patterns of Race Relations in Brazil and the United States." Phylon 48, 62-76 (March 1987)

886. Tanner, Christopher. "Malnutrition and the Development of Rural Households in the Agreste of Paraiba State, North-East Brazil." J. Dev. Studies 23 (January 1987): 242-264.

887. Taylor, Quintard. "Frente Negra Brasileira: The Afro- American Civil Rights Movement, 1924-1937." Umoja: A Scholarly Journal of Black Studies 2 (1978): 25-40.

888. Thomas, V. "Differences in Income and Poverty within Brazil." World Development 15 (February 1987): 263-274.

889. Toplin, Robert B. "Brazil: Racial Polarization in the Developing Giant." Black World 22 (November 1972): 15-22.

890. Toplin, Robert B. Freedom and Prejudice: The Legacy of Slavery in the United States and Brazil. Westport, Ct.: Greenwood, 1981.

891. Trochim, Michael. "The Brazilian Black Guard: Racial Conflict in Post-Abolition Brazil." The Americas 44 (January 1988): 285-300.

892. Urban, Greg. "Developments in the Situation of Brazilian Tribal Populations from 1976-1982." Latin Am. Res. R. 20 (1985): 7-26.

893. Valle Silva, Nelson do. "Updating the Cost of Not Being White in Brazil." In Race, Class, and Power in Brazil, edited by Pierre-Michel Fontaine. Los Angeles, CA: Center for Afro-American Studies, University of California, 1985.

894. Victora, Cesar G. and others. "Child Malnutrition and Land Ownership in Southern Brazil." Ecology Food Nutrition 18 (1986): 265-276.

895. Victora, Cesar G. and others. Epidemiologia da desigualdade... São Paulo: Editora de Humanismo, Ciencia e Technologia, 1988.

896. Viotti da Costa, Emilia. The Brazilian Empire: Myths and Histories. Chicago, IL: University of Chicago Press, 1985. [Includes essay on anti-black discrimination in Brazilian history.]

897. Webster, Peggy L. and Jeffrey W. Dwyer. "The Cost of Being Nonwhite in Brazil." Sociology and Social Research 72 (1988): 136-142.

898. Wellen, Aloys I. Indianische Rechte in Brasilien: die Rechtssituation der Indianer Brasiliens unter besonderer Berücksichtigung ihres Rechtes auf Boden. Mettingen: BKV- Brasilienkinde Verlag, 1986.

899. Whitaker, Dulce C. A. A seleção dos privilegidos : um estudo sobre a educação brasileira. São Paulo: Editora Semente, 1981. [Universities.]

900. Willeke, Venantius. "Kirche und Negersklaven in Brasilien, 1550-1888." Neue Zeitschrift für Missionswissenschaft 32 (1976): 15-26.

901. Williams, Mary M. "The Treatment of Negro Slaves in the Brazilian Empire: A Comparison with the US." Journal of Negro History 15 (1930): 313-336.

902. Wolff, Egon and Frieda. "Os judeus e seus escravos negros." Shalom, Sao Paulo 177 (1980): 4-5.

903. Wood, Charles H. and Jose Magno de Carvalho. The Demography of Inequality in Brazil. NY: Cambridge University Press, 1988.

BULGARIA

904. Amnesty International. *Bulgaria: Imprisonment of Ethnic Turks: Human Rights Abuse During the Forced Assimilation of the Ethnic Turkish Minority*. London: Amnesty International, 1986.

905. Amnesty International. *Bulgaria: Continuing Human Rights Abuses against Ethnic Turks*. New York: Amnesty International, July 1987.

906. Amnesty International. *Imprisonment of Ethnic Turks and Human Rights Activists*. New York: Amnesty International, February 1989.

907. Bachmaier, Peter. "Assimilation oder Kulturautonomie. Das Schulwesen der nationalen Minderheiten in Bulgarien nach dem 9. September 1944." *Osterr. Osth.*, 26 (1984): 391-404.

908. Baest, Torsten F. "Bulgaria's War at Home. The People's Republic and Its Turkish Minority (1944-1985)." Translated by A. Winton Jackson. *Across Frontiers* 2 (Winter 1985): 18-26.

909. Ben, Eyal. "Jews and the Anti-Nazi Resistance in Bulgaria." *International Problems (Tel Aviv)* 25 (1986)

910. Ben-Yakov, Avraham. "Bulgaria." in *Encyclopedia of the Holocaust*. New York: Macmillan, 1990.

911. Benvenisty, David. "The Struggle of the Bulgarian Communist Party for Internationalism against Anti-semitism in Bulgaria (1891-1903)." in *Social, Cultural and Educational Association of the Jews in the People's Republic of Bulgaria. Annual*. 29-79. 1975.

912. Benvenisty, David. "The Unfavorable Conditions for the Dissemination of Antisemitic Propaganda in Bulgaria (1891- 1903)." *Social, Cultural and Educational Association of the Jews in the People's Republic of Bulgaria. Annual* 15 (1980)

913. Binder, David. "Going Back: Bulgaria, 20 Years Later." New York Times Magazine (December 8, 1985) [Anti-Turkish policy inside Bulgaria.]

914. Boyadjjieff, Christo. Saving the Bulgarian Jews in World War II. Ottawa: Free Bulgarian Center, 1989.

915. Bozhinov, Voin. "The Public Opinion in Bulgaria and the Salvation of the Bulgarian Jews from the Death Camps." Social, Cultural and Educational Association of the Jews in Bulgaria Annual 19 (1984): 99-107.

916. Champion, Marc. "Return to Bulgaria Is No Homecoming for Turkish Minority." Boston Globe (March 26, 1990):

917. Chary, Frederick B. Bulgaria and the Jews: The Final Solution, 1940-1944. Doctoral dissertation, University of Pittsburgh, 1968. UMO #69-12,825.

918. Cohen, Albert and Anri Assa. Saving of the Jews of Bulgaria, 1941-1944. Sofia Translated by Ljudmila Dimova: State Publishing House, Septemvri, 1977.

919. Dramaliev, K. "The Theory and Practice of Greater Bulgarian Chauvinism." Macedonian Review (Yugoslavia) 16 (1986): 68-76.

920. Georgeoff, John. "Ethnic Minorities in the People's Republic of Bulgaria." in The Politics of Ethnicity in Eastern Europe, edited by George Klein and Milan J. Reban. New York: Columbia University Press, 1981.

921. Girard, Andre. Les minorites nationales, ethnique et religieuses en Bulgaria. Doctoral dissertation: University of Paris, 1932.

922. Haberman, Clyde. "Bulgaria Forces Turkish Exodus of Thousands." New York Times (June 22, 1989):

923. Haberman, Clyde. "Flow of Turks Leaving Bulgaria Swells to Hundreds of Thousands." New York Times (August 15, 1989):

924. Hofwiler, R. "Turken auf der Flucht." Pogrom 150 (1989): 19-23.

925. Hopken, Wolfgang. "Die Emigration von Türken aus Bulgarien: historisches und gegenwärtiges: Teil I, Die Emigration 1878 bis 1951." Südosteuropa 36 (1989): 608-637.

926. Hopken, Wolfgang. "Im Schatten der nationalen Frage: die bulgarisch-türkischen Beziehungen." Südosteuropa 36 (1987): 178-194. [Turkish minority in Bulgaria.]

927. Hopken, Wolfgang. "Modernisierung und Nationalismus: Sozialgeschichtliche Aspekte der bulgarischen Minderheitenpolitik gegenüber den Türken." Südost-Europa Nos. 7/8 (1986): 437-457.

928. Karasapan, Omer. "Bulgarian Govenment Brutally Supresses Turkish Minority." Guardian (NYC) (June 21, 1989):

929. Laber, Jeri. "The Bulgarian Difference." New York Review of Books (May 17, 1990) [Treatment of Turks in Bulgaria.]

930. Ludzev, Ditimar. "The Petty Bourgeoisie in Bulgaria in Historical Perspective." Bulgarian Hist. Review 15 (1987): 21-33.

931. Mango, A. "Turkish Exodus from Bulgaria." The World Today 45 (October 1989):

932. Matkovski, A. "The Destruction of Macedonian Jews." Yad Vashem Studies 3 (1959): 203-260.

933. Miller, M. L. Bulgaria during the Second World War. Stanford: 1975.

934. Minev, D. and others. "The Bulgarian Country Profile: The Dynamics of Some Inequalities in Health." Social Science & Medicine 31 (1990)

935. Monnesland, Svein. "The Turkish Minority in Bulgaria." Nordic Journal of Soviet and East European Studies (Sweden) 4 (1987): 53-63.

936. Oliver, Haim D. We Were Saved. How the Jews in Bulgaria Were Kept from the Death Camps. 2d ed. Translated by Vesselin Izmirliev. Sofia: Sofia Press, 1978.

937. Oren, N. "The Bulgarian Exception: A Reassessment of the Salvation of the Jewish Community." Yad Vashem Studies 7 (1968): 83-106.

938. Oschlies, Wolf. Bulgarien-Land ohne Antisemitismus. Erlangen: 1976.

939. "Pomaks of Bulgaria." In World Directory of Minorities, edited by Minority Rights Group. Harlow: Longman, 1990.

940. Popovic, Alexandre. "The Turks of Bulgaria (1878-1985)." Central Asian Survey 5 (1986): 1-32.

941. Silverman, Carol. "Bulgarian Gypsies: Adaptation in a Socialist Context." Nomadic Peoples 21 (1986): 51-62.

942. Todorova, Maria. "Language As Cultural Unifier in a Multilingual Setting: The Bulgarian Case during the 19th Century." Eastern European Politics and Societies 4 (Autumn 1990)

943. Todorova, Maria. "The Reactions of the Poor to Poverty: The Case of Bulgaria (Fifteenth-Nineteenth Centuries." In Les reactions des pauvres a la pauvrete: Etudes d'histoire sociale et urbaine, edited by Thomas Riis. Odense: Odense University Press, 1989.

944. Troebst, S. "Partei, Staat und Türkische Minderheit in Bulgarien: Kontinuität und Wandel (1956-1986)." Europäische Rundschau No. 2 (1986)

945. "[Turks in Bulgaria]." International Commission of Jurists Review (June 1987): 1-3.

946. "Turks of Bulgaria." In World Directory of Minorities, edited by Minority Rights Group. 124-127. Harlow: Longman, 1990.

947. Zang, Ted Jr. Destroying Ethnic Identity: The Expulsion of the Bulgarian Turks. New York: Helsinki Watch, 1989.

BURKINA FASO

948. Cordell, Dennis D. "Labor Reservoirs and Populations: French Colonial Strategies in Koudougou, Upper Volta, 1914-1939." Journal of African History 23 (1982): 205-224.

949. Dubuch, Claude. "Langage du pouvoir, pouvoir du langage." Pol. Afric. (December 1985): 44-53.

950. Oyatek, René. "The Revolutionary Process in Burkina Faso: Breaks and Continuities." Journal of Communist Studies 1 (1985): 82-100.

951. Sharp, Robin. Burkina Faso: New Life for the Sahel? Oxford, England: Oxfam Publications, 1990.

952. Thomas Sankara Speaks. The Burkina Faso Revolution, 1983- 1987. New York: Pathfinder Press, 1988.

953. Traore, Fathié. Memoires d'autres temps. Ougadougou: Presses Africaines, 1984. [Colonization]

954. Wilkins, M. "The Death of Thomas Sankara and the Rectification of the People's Revolution in Burkina-Faso." African Affairs 88 (July 1989):

BURUNDI

955. Kay, Reginald. Burundi Since the Genocide. London: Minority Rights Group, 1987.

956. Lemarchand, René. "Burundi: The Killing Fields Revisited." Issue 18 (1989): 22-28.

957. Lemarchand, René. "Ethnic Genocide." Society 12 (January- February 1975): 50-60.

958. Lemarchand, René and David Martin. Selective Genocide in Burundi. London: Minority Rights Group, 1974.

959. Loft, Frances. "Massacres in Burundi." R. Afric. Pol. Economy 43 (1988): 88-93.

960. Perlez, Jane. "The Bloody Hills of Burundi." New York Times Magazine (November 6, 1988):

961. Watson, Catherine. "Classes, Not Tribes, Cause Civil War." Guardian (NYC, September 28, 1988)

962. Weinstein, Warren and Robert Schire. Political Conflict and Ethnic Strategies: A Case Study of Burundi. New York: Maxwell School of Citizenship and Public Affairs, Syracuse University, 1976.

CAMBODIA

963. Association of Kampuchean Women. "Education in Kampuchea. A New Beginning from Nothing." People's Daily World (October 16, 1986)

964. Bunheang Ung. The Murderous Revolution: Life and Death in Pol Pot's Kampuchea. Chippendale, Australia: Alternative Publishing Cooperative Limited, 1985.

965. Chandler, David P. and Ben Kiernan, eds. Revolution and Aftermath in Kampuchea: Eight Essays. New Haven, CT: Southeast Asian Studies, Yale University, 1983.

966. Fenton, James, ed. Cambodian Witness: The Autobiography of Someth May. London: Faber, 1986.

967. Frieson, Kate. "The Political Nature of Democratic Kampuchea." Pacific Affairs 61 (Fall 1988): 405-427.

968. Hannum, Hurst. "International Law and Cambodian Genocide: The Sounds of Silence." Human Rights Quarterly 11 (February 1989): 82-138.

969. Jackson, Karl D., ed. Cambodia, 1975-1978, Rendezvous with Death. Princeton, NJ: Princeton University Press, 1989.

970. Kamm, Henry. "A Broken Country." New York Times Magazine (September 20, 1987)

971. Kiernan, Ben. "The Genocide in Cambodia, 1975-79." Bulletin of Concerned Asian Scholars 22 (April-June 1990)

972. Kiernan, Ben. "Kampuchea's Ethnic Chinese under Pol Pot: A Case of Systematic Social Discrimination." Journal of Contemporary Asia 16 (1986): 18-29.

973. Kiljunen, Kimmo, ed. <u>Kampuchea: Decade of the Genocide. Report of a Finnish Inquiry Commission</u>. London: Zed Press, 1984.

974. McCormack, Gavan. "The Kampuchean Revolution 1975-1978: The Problem of Knowing the Truth." <u>Journal of Contemporary Asia</u> 10 (1980): 75-118.

975. Mysliwiec, Eva. <u>Punishing the Poor. The International Isolation of Kampuchea</u>. Oxford: Oxfam Publications, 1988.

976. Osborne, Milton E. <u>The French Preserve in Cochin China and Cambodia: Rule and Response (1859-1905)</u>. Ithaca, NY: Cornell University Press, 1969.

977. Reid, Anthony and Jennifer Brewster, eds. <u>Slavery, Bondage, and Dependency</u>. New York: St. Martin's Press, 1984.

978. Silber, Irwin. <u>Kampuchea: The Revolution Rescued</u>. Oakland, CA: Line of March Publication, 1986.

979. Swank, Emory. "Cambodia: The Rebirth of a Nation." <u>Far Eastern Economic Review</u> (March 17, 1983)

980. Szymusiak, Molyda. <u>The Stones Cry Out: A Cambodian Childhood, 1975-1980</u>. Translated by Linda Coverdale. New York: Hill and Wang, 1986.

CAMEROON

981. Abega, Prosper. "Le système éducatif camerounais: auto-colonisation o authenticité?" California Dept. Lang. Afric. Ling. No.1 (1981): 1-6.

982. Beauvilain, Alain. Nord-Cameroun: crises et peuplement. 2 vols. University of Rouen: Doctoral dissertation, 1989. [Since early 1900's]

983. DeLancey, Mark W. Cameroon: Dependence and Independence. Aldershot: Gower, 1989.

984. Elango, Lovett Z. "Councils of Notables and the Politics of Control in Cameroon under French Rule, 1925-1949." Transafrica Journal of History 16 (1987): 24-46.

985. Engo, P. D. "Social Protection in the United Republic of Cameroon." International Social Security Review No. 3(1984): 265-278.

986. Epale, Simon J. Plantations and Development in Western Cameroon, 1885-1975: A Study in Agrarian Capitalism. NewYork: Vantage Press, 1985.

987. Eteki-Otabela, Marie-Louise. Misère et grandeur de la démocratie au Cameroun. Paris: 1987.

988. Flambeau Ngayap, Pierre. Cameroun: qui gouverne? Paris: Editions l'Harmattan, 1983.

989. Gardinier, David E. "Education in the Cameroon under French Trusteeship." French Colonial Studies 3 (1979, published 1986): 21-49.

990. Green, December. Reassessing the Sacred Trust: Health in the Cameroons during the Period of Mandate and Trusteeship. University of South Carolina: Doctoral dissertation, 1988.

991. Kivo, E. M. "Community Education and Community Development in Cameroon: the British Colonial Experience, 1922-1961." Community Development Journal 19 (October 1984): 204-213.

992. Mbu, A. N. T. Mill of Justice. Yaounde, Cameroon: 1986.

993. Myeng, Ayi M. Colonial Rebellions in South-Central Cameroon, 1887-1907. University of London: 1985. Doctoral dissertation.

994. Nana-Fabu, Stella. Status of Women in Cameroon: A Historical Perspective. Milwaukee: Univeristy of Wisconsin, 1987.

995. Ndongko, W. A. "Political Economy of Development in Cameroon: Relations between the State, Indigenous Businessmen and Foreign Investors." Development Peace (Autumn 1986): 146-170.

996. Ntoko, Samuel N. Effects of Social Origins and Education on Socio-economic Achievement in Africa: A Cameroon Case. University of Pettsburgh, 1985. Doctoral dissertation.

997. Paulin, Adjai. La revolte des esclaves mercenaires: Doula 1893. Bayreuth, West Germany: Bayreuth University, 1987.

998. Quinn, Frederick. "German and French Rule in the Cameroon." Tarikh 4 (1974): 55-69.

999. Schatzberg, Michael G. and I. William Zartman, eds. Political Economy of Cameroon. New York: Praeger, 1986.

1000. Tala, Kashim I. "Ten Years of Cameroon Literature." New Horizons 2 (1982): 4-26.

1001. Thomas, Ajamah Asa-Ah. One Hundred Years of Cameroonian History, 1884-1984. Nkwen: Victory Press, 1985.

1002. Todd, Loreto. "E Pluribus Unum? The Language for a National Literature in a Multilingual Community." Ariel 15 (1984): 69-82.

1003. Um Nyobé, Ruben. Le probleme national kamerunais. Paris: Editions l'Harmattan, 1984.

1004. Van Beek, Wouter. "L'Etat ce n'est pay nous! Cultural Proletarianization in Cameroon." Cah. CEDAF (July 1986): 65-88.

CANADA

ANTI-SEMITISM

1005. Abella, Irving. "Anti-Semitism in Canada in the Interwar Years." In Jews of North America, edited by Moses Rischin. Detroit, MI: Wayne State University Press, 1987.

1006. Abella, Irving. "Canada and the Jewish Refugee Crisis 1933- 1939." Michael 10 (1986): 9-30.

1007. Abella, Irving and Harold Troper. None Is Too Many: Canada and the Jews of Europe 1933-1948. Toronto: Lester and Orpen Dennys, 1982.

1008. Anctil, Pierre. Le Devoir, les Juifs et l'Immigration. Montreal: Inst. Quebecois de Recherche sur la Culture, 1988.

1009. Anctil, Pierre. Le Rendezvous Manque: les Juifs de Montreal Face au Quebec de l'entre-deux-guerres. Montreal: Inst. Quebecois de Recherche sur la Culture, 1988.

1010. Angenot, Marc. Ce que l'on dit des Juifs en 1889: semitisme et discours social. Inveruniversity Centre for European Studies, 1984.

1011. Aster, Howard. Jewish-Ukrainian Relations: Two Solitudes. (Revised edition). Mosaic Press: 1987.

1012. Aster, Howard. "Jews and Ukrainians in the Aftermath of the Deschenes Commission: An Opinion." Canadian Ethnic Studies 19 (1987): 117-123.

1013. Barrett, Stanley R. "Fascism in Canada." Contemporary Crises 8 (1984): 345-377.

1014. Bercuson, David Jay and D. Wertheimer. Trust Betrayed: the Story of Jim Keegstra. Garden City, New York: Doubleday, 1985.

1015. Betcherman, Lita-Rose. *Swastika and the Maple Leaf: Fascist Movements in Canada in the Thirties*. Toronto: Fitzhenry and Whiteside, 1975.

1016. Brenner, Rachel F. "A.M. Klein and Mordecai Richler: Canadian Responses to the Holocaust." *Journal of Canadian Studies* 24 (1989): 65-77.

1017. Brown, Michael. *Jew or Juif? Jews, French Canadians, and Anglo Canadians, 1759-1914*. Philadelphia, PA: Jewish Publication Society, 1987.

1018. "Canadian Nationalism and the Jews." *Chronicle Review* (1972): 7-59.

1019. Chalk, Frank, ed. *Review of Anti-Semitism in Canada: 1987*. Montreal: League of Human Rights, B'nai B'rith Canada, 1987.

1020. Cohn, Werner. "English and French Canadian Public Opinion on Jews and Israel: Some Poll Data." *Canadian Ethnic Studies* 11 (1979): 31-48.

1021. Davies, Alan. "Keegstra in Red Deer." *Touchstone* 5 (January 1987): 33-39.

1022. Davies, Alan. "Tale of Two Trials - Antisemitism in Canada 1985." *Holocaust and Genocide Studies* 4 (1989)

1023. Elliot, D. R. "Anti-Semitism and the Social Credit Movement: The Intellectual Roots of the Keegstra Affair." *Canadian Ethnic Studies* 17 (1985): 78-89.

1024. Elman, Bruce P. "Promotion of Hatred and the Canadian Charter of Rights and Freedoms: A Review of "Keegstra v. The Queen"." *Canadian Public Policy* 15 (1989): 72-83.

1025. Heinrichs, Terry. "Free Speech and the Zundel Trial." *Queen's Quarterly* 95 (1988): 837-854.

1026. Hill, Leonides E. "Trial of Ernst Zundel." *Simon Wiesenthal Center Annual* 6 (1989): 165-219.

1027. Hoffman, G. H. "Canadian Fascist Movements in the '30's." *Jewish Frontier* 43 (January 1976): 26-29.

1028. Horowitz, Aron. *Striking Roots: Reflections on Five Decades of Jewish Life in Canada*. Mosaic Press, 1979.

1029. Jedwab, Jack. "Uniting Uptowners and Downtowners: the Jewish Electorate and Quebec Provincial Politics, 1927-1939." *Canadian Ethnic Studies* 18 (1986): 7-19.

1030. Kayfetz, Ben. "Neo-Nazis in Canada." *Patterns of Prejudice* 13 (January-February 1979): 29-31, 34.

1031. Koch, Erich. *Deemed Suspect: a Wartime Blunder*. Toronto: Methuen, 1980. [Internment of Jewish refugees from Nazi Germany.]

1032. Langlais, Jacques and David Rose. *Juifs et Quebecois francais: 200 ans d'histoire commune*. Montreal: Fides, 1986.

1033. Laponce, J. A. "Left or Centre? the Canadian Jewish Electorate, 1953-1983." *Canadian Journal of Political Science* 21 (December 1988): 691-714.

1034. Levitt, Cyril and W. Shaffir. "Swastika as Dramatic Symbol: a Case-Study of Ethnic Violence in Canada." *Jewish Journal of Sociology* 31 (June 1989): 5-24.

1035. Lupul, Manoly R. "Ukrainian-Jewish Relations in Canada." In *Ukrainian-Jewish Relations in Historical Perspective*, edited by Peter J. Potichnyj and Howard Aster. Edmonton, Alberta: Canadian Institute of Ukrainian Studies, 1988.

1036. Quenneville, Ginette. *Le nationalistes Quebecois et les juifs*. Master's thesis. University of Montreal, 1986.

1037. *Report of the Special Committee on Hate Propaganda in Canada 1966*. Ottawa: Queen's Printer, 1966.

1038. Rome, David. *Anti-Semitism I: the Plamondon Case and S.W. Jacobs*. 2 vols. Canadian Jewish Congress, 1982.

1039. Rome, David. *Anti-Semitism III: Early Anti-Semitism: Threats to Equality*. Canadian Jewish Congress, 1983.

1040. Rome, David. *Anti-Semitism IV: Early Anti-Semitism: Across the Dominion*. Canadian Jewish Congress, 1983.

1041. Rome, David. *Anti-Semitism V: Early Anti-Semitism: the Voice of the Media*. Canadian Jewish Congress, 1984.

1042. Rome, David. *Anti-Semitism VI: Early Anti-Semitism: the Holy Land: Tardivel*. Canadian Jewish Congress, 1985.

1043. Rome, David. *Anti-Semitism VIII: Early Anti-Semitism: the Imprint of Drumont*. Canadian Jewish Congress, 1985.

1044. Rome, David. *Clouds in the Thirties: Antisemitism in Canada, 1929-1939*. 13 vols. Canadian Jewish Congress, 1977-1981.

1045. Ross, Malcolm. *Web of Deceit*. Moncton, N.B.: Stronghold Publishing Co., 1978. [Antisemitic views on Canada.]

1046. Schreter, S. M. "French-Canadian Anti-Semitism." *Strobe* 3 (1969): 73-110. [McGill University Hillel Foundation.]

1047. Silverberg, M. "Six Percent Solution: An Analysis of Hate Legislation in Canada." *Journal of Jewish Communal Service* 61 (Fall 1984): 54-63.

1048. Trachtenberg, Henry M. "Old Co" Move: Anti-Semitism, Politics, and the Jews of Winnipeg, 1882-1921. York University, 1984. Doctoral dissertation.

1049. Trachtenberg, Henry M. "Winnipeg Jewish Community in the Interwar Period 1919-1939: Anti-Semitism and Politics." Canadian Jewish Historical Society 4 (Spring 1980): 44-70.

1050. Troper, Harold. "Canada and Jewish Displaced Persons, 1945- 1948." Michael 10 (1986): 181-225.

1051. Troper, Harold. "Canada." in Encyclopedia of the Holocaust, I. New York: Macmillan, 1990.

1052. Troper, Harold. "James Keegstra, Teacher of Hate." Congress Monthly 53 (February 1986): 6-8.

1053. Troper, Harold and Morton Weinfeld. Old Wounds: Jews, Ukrainians and the Hunt for Nazi War Criminals in Canada. Chapel Hill: University of North Carolina Press, 1989.

1054. Troper, Harold. "Queen v. Zundel: Holocaust Trial in Toronto." Congress Monthly 52 (July-August 1985): 7-10.

1055. Usiskin, Roz. "'Alien' and the 'Bolshevik': the 1919 Winnipeg General Strike." Canadian Jewish Outlook 21 (1983)

1056. Wagner, Jonathan F. Brothers Beyond the Sea: National Socialism in Canada. Waterloo, Canada: Wilfred Laurier University Press, 1981.

1057. Wagner, Jonathan F. "Deutscher Bund Canada 1934-1939." Canadian Historical Review 58 (June 1977): 176-200.

1058. Wagner, Jonathan F. "Die NS-Bewegung in Kanada." Vierteljahrsch. Zeitgesch. 29 (April 1981): 246-268.

1059. Weimann, Gabriel and Conrad Winn. "Misperception of Public Opinion: the Canadian Nazi Trials and their Implications." PS 19 (1986): 641-645.

1060. Weinfeld, Morton. "Jews of Quebec: Perceived Antisemitism, Segregation, and Emigration." Jewish Journal of Sociology 22 (June 1980): 5-20.

1061. Weinmann, Gabriel and Conrad Winn. Hate on Trial: the Zundel Affair, the Media and Public Opinion in Canada. Oakville, Ontario: Mosaic Press, 1986.

CANADA - ASIANS

1062. Ahmed, Abu I. M.U. Class and Ethnic Consciousness among the Bangladeshis in Toronto: Historical Bases and Current Patterns. York University, 1985. Doctoral dissertation.

1063. Aiken, Rebecca B. Montreal Chinese Property Ownership and Occupational Change, 1881-1981. McGill University, 1985. Doctoral dissertation.

1064. Anderson, Kay J. "Community Formation in Official Context: Residential Segregation and the 'Chinese' in Early Vancouver." Canadian Geographer 32 (Winter 1988): 354-356.

1065. Anderson, Kay J. "Cultural Hegemony and the Race-Definition Process in Chinatown, Vancouver: 1880-1980." Society and Space 6 (June 1988): 127-250.

1066. Basavarajappa, K. G. and R.B.P. Verma. "Asian Immigrants in Canada: Some Finding from 1981 Census." International Migration 23 (March 1985): 97-121.

1067. Baureiss, Gunter. "Ethnic Resilience and Discrimination: Two Chinese Communities in Canada." Journal of Ethnic Studies 10 (Spring 1982): 69-87.

1068. Broadfoot, Barry. Years of Sorrow, Years of Shame. Toronto: Doubleday Canada, 1977. [Evacuation of Japanese Canadians during World War II.]

1069. Chan, Kwok and Lawrence Lam. "Chinese in Timmins, Canada, 1915-1950: a Study of Ethnic Stereotypes in the Press." Asian Profile 14 (1986): 169-183.

1070. Chan, Kwok B. and Denise Helly, eds. "Coping with Racism: the Chinese Experience in Canada." Canadian Ethnic Studies 19 (1987): entire issue.

1071. Chan, Kwok B. Racism and Human Rights: the Experience of Asians in Montreal. Montreal: Center for Research Action on Race Relations, 1987.

1072. Chan, Kwok B. and D.M. Indra, eds. Uprooting, Loss and Adaption: the Resettlement of Indochinese Refugees in Canada. Ottawa: Canadian Public Health Association, 1987.

1073. Chandra, Kanamur V. Racial Discrimination in Canada: Asian Minorities. San Francisco: R and E Research Associates, 1973.

1074. Chandrasekhar, S. "History of Canadian Legislation with Respect to Immigration from India." Plural Societies 16 (October 1986): 254-280.

1075. Chandresekhar, S., ed. From India to Canada: a Brief History of Immigration. La Jolla, CA: Population Review, 1986.

1076. Con, Harry and others. From China to Canada: a History of the Chinese Communities in Canada. Toronto: McClelland and Stewart, 1982.

1077. Daniels, Roger. "Japanese in the United States and Canada: an Essay in Comparative Racism." In Japanese Experience in North America, edited by N. Brian Winchester and others. Lethbridge: Department of Political Science, University of Lethbridge.

1078. Dorais, Louis-Jacques and others. "Survival of the Vietnamese Language in Quebec." Vitnam Forum 6 (1985): 220-238.

1079. Faustino-Santos, Ronald. "Race of Cuckoos: Chinese Migration, Anti-Chinese Legislation, and the Canadian Pacific Railway." Alternate Routes 8 (1988): 42-73.

1080. Ferguson, Ted. White Man's Country: an Exercise in Canadian Prejudice. Garden City, NY: Doubleday, 1975. [Asians in Vancouver.]

1081. Henry, Franklin J. Experience of Discrimination: a Case Study Approach. San Francisco: R and E Research Associates, 1974. [Anti-Japanese discrimination in Canada.]

1082. Ijaz, Mian A. Ethnic Attitudes of Elementary School Children Toward Blacks and East Indians and the Effect of a Cultural Program on These Attitudes. University of Toronto, 1980.

1083. Indra, D. M. "South Asian Stereotypes in the Vancouver Press." Ethnic and Racial Studies 2 (April 1979): 166-189.

1084. Itani, Francis. No Other Lodging. Fredericton, Canada: Fiddlehead Poetry Books, 1978. [Poetry relating to expulsion of Japanese Canadians from British Columbia during World War II.]

CANADA - ASIANS

1085. Iwaasa, David B. "Japanese in Southern Alberta, 1941-1945." Alberta History 24 (1976): 5-19.

1086. Johnson, Phyllis J. "Impact of Ethnic Communities on the Employment of Southeast Asian Refugees." Amerasia Journal 14 (1988): 1-22. [British Columbia.]

1087. Johnston, Hugh J. M. Voyage of the Komagata Maru: the Sikh Challenge to Canada's Colour Bar. Vancouver: University of British Columbia Press, 1989 (org. 1979).

1088. Kobayashi, Cassandra. Spirit of Redress: Japanese Canadians in Conference. Japanese Canadian Studies Society, 1989.

1089. Lee, W. M. "But, Do You Have Canadian Experience?" Asianadian 1 (1979): 14-19. [Employment discrimination.]

1090. Li, Peter S. "Economic Cost of Racism to Chinese Canadians." Canadian Ethnic Studies 19 (1987): 102-113.

1091. Li, Peter S. "Prejudice against Asians in a Canadian City." Canadian Ehtnic Studies 11 (1979): 70-77.

1092. Mababe, Tomoko. "Canadian Evacuation and Nisei Identity." Phylon 41 (Summer 1986): 116-125.

1093. Malik, Iftikhar H. "Early South Asian Immigrants in North America." Pakistan Journal of American Studies 4 (March 1986): 79-111.

1094. Marie, Gillian. Development of Prejudice toward Chinese Immigrants to British Columbia, 1858-1978. Simon Fraser University, 1978. [Master's thesis.]

1095. Masson, Jack K. "Conflict and Tragedy: Canada's East Indian Community." Amerasia Journal 15 (1989): 27-48.

1096. McEvoy, F. J. "Symbol of Racial Discrimination: the Chinese Immigration Act and Canada's Relations with China, 1942- 1947." Canadian Ethnic Studies 14 (1982): 24-42.

1097. Naidoo, Josephine C. Canadian Perspectives on East Indian Immigrants. May 26, 1978.

1098. Naidoo, Josephine C. "Contemporary South Asian Women in the Canadian Mosaic." International Journal of Women's Studies 8 (September-October 1985): 338-350.

1099. Nakano, Takeo Uyo with Leatrice Nakano. Within the Barbed Wire Fence: a Japanese Man's Account of His Internment in Canada. Seattle: University of Washington Press, 1981.

1100. National Association of Japanese Canadians. Economic Losses of Japanese Canadians after 1941. Vancouver: Association, 1986.

1101. O'Neil, Daniel J. "Canadian and American Policies toward their Japanese Minorities during the Second World War." In Comparative Social Research, edited by Richard F. Tomasson. Greenwich, CT: JAI Press, 1981.

1102. Ono, Dawn K. "White Male Supremacy and the 'Oriental Doll'." Asianadian (Fall-Winter 1978): 24-25.

1103. Palmer, H. "Pattern of Racism: Attitudes towards Chinese and Japanese in Alberta, 1920-1950." Histoire Sociale 13 (May 1980): 137-160.

1104. Paupst, K. "Note on Anti-Chinese Sentiment in Toronto before the First World War." Candian Ethnic Studies 9 (1977): 54-59.

1105. Roy, Patricia E. "The Oriental 'Menace' in British Columbia." In Historical Essays on British Columbia, edited by J. Friesen and H.K. Ralaton. Toronto: McClelland and Stewart, 1976.

1106. Roy, Patricia E. "Protecting their Pocketbooks and Preserving their Race: White Merchants and Oriental Competition." In Cities in the West, edited by A. R. McCormack and Dan McPherson. Ottawa: National Museum of Man, 1975.

1107. Roy, Patricia E. "Soldiers Canada Didn't Want: Her Chinese and Japanese Citizens." Canadian Historical Review 59 (September, 1978): 341-358.

1108. Roy, Patricia E. White Man's Province: British Columbia Politicians and Chinese and Japanese Immigrants, 1858-1914. University of British Columbia Press, 1989.

1109. Roy, Sudipta. "Occupational Segregation of Asian Male Labour Force in Canada, 1921,1941,1961." Journal of the Indian Anthropological Society (Calcutta) 17 (1982): 245-252.

1110. Sandhu, K. S. "Indian Immigration and Racial Prejudice in British Columbia: Some Preliminary Observations." In Peoples of the Living Land: Geography of Cultural Diversity in British Columbia, edite by Julian V. Minghi. Vancouver: Tantalus Research, Ltd., 1972.

1111. Satzewich, Vic. "Racisms: the Reactions to Chinese Migrants in Canada at the Turn of the Century." International Sociology 4 (September 1989): 311-327.

1112. Sunahara, Ann G. Politics of Racism: the Uprooting of Japanese Canadians during the Second World War. Toronto: Lorimer, 1981.

1113. Takashima, Shizuya. Child in Prison Camp. Tundra, 1971.

1114. Takata, Toyo. *Nikkei Legacy: the Story of Japanese Canadians from Settlement to Today*. Toronto: NC Press, 1983.

1115. Ujimoto, K. Victor, ed. *Asian Canadians: Regional Perspectives*. Guelph: Department of Sociology and Anthropology, University of Guelph, 1989.

1116. Ward, W. Peter. "B.C. and the Japanese Evacuation." *Canadian Historical Review* 57 (September 1976): 289-308.

1117. Ward, W. Peter. *White Canada Forever: British Columbia's Response to Orientals, 1858-1914*. Queen's University, 1972. Doctoral dissertation.

1118. Ward, W. Peter. *White Canada Forever: Popular Attitudes and Public Policy toward Orientals in British Columbia*. Montreal: McGill-Queen's University Press, 1978.

1119. Yee, May. "Chinese Canadian Women: Our Common Struggle." *Canadian Ethnic Studies* 19 (1987): 174-184. [Discrimination.]

BLACKS IN CANADA

1120. Abucar, Mohmed. *Struggle for Development: the Black Communities of North and East Preston and Cherry Brook, Nova Scotia 1784-1987*. Black Cultural Centre of Nova Scotia, 1987.

1121. Alexander, E. *Caribbean Seasonal Workers in Canada*. Carleton University (Canada), 1984. Master's thesis.

1122. Bearden, Jim and Linda Jean Butler. *Life and Times of Mary Shadd Cary*. NC Press, Ltd., 1977.

1123. Bertley, Leo W. *Universal Negro Improvement Association of Montreal, 1917-1979*. Concordia University (Canada), 1980. Doctoral dissertation.

1124. Boyd, Herb. "Canada." *Crisis* 93 (1986): 46-48,50,54.

1125. Bramble, Linda. *Black Fugitive Slaves in Early Canada*. St. Catherines, Ontario: 1988.

1126. Burns, John F. "City's Black's, No Longer Merely Les Invisibles." *New York Times* (December 10, 1987) [Montreal.]

1127. Calliste, Agnes. "Blacks [Working] on Canadian Railways." *Journal of Ethnic Studies* 20 (1988): 36-52.

1128. Calliste, Agnes. "Sleeping Car Porters in Canada: an Ethnically Submerged Split Labor Market." *Canadian Ethnic Studies* 19 (1987): 1-20.

1129. Carter, Velma. *Black Canadians: their History and Contributions*. Edmonton: Reidmore Publishing, 1989.

1130. Clarimont, Donald H. and Dennis Magill. *Nova Scotia Blacks: an Historical and Structural Overview*. Henson College, 1970.

1131. D'Oyley, Vincent, ed. Black Presence in Multi-ethnic Canada. University of British Columbia: Centre for the Study of Curriculum & Instruction, Faculty of Education, 1982.

1132. Dubuisson, Wilfrid. Immigration et integration sociale des Haitiens au Quebec. Sherbrooke, Quebec: Editions Naaman, 1988.

1133. Fells, Kenneth. Voices from the Past Reaching for the Future: the Blacks of Southwestern Nova Scotia. Acadia University (Canada), 1989. Master's thesis.

1134. Forsythe, Dennis, ed. Let the Niggers Burn! the Sir George Williams University Affair and Its Caribbean Aftermath. Montreal: Black Rose Books, 1971. [See Tunteng, below.]

1135. Head, Wilson A. and Jeri Lee. "Black Presence in the Canadian Mosic: Discrimination in Education." Interchange 9 (1979): 85-93.

1136. Henry, Frances. Forgotten Canadians: the Blacks of Nova Scotia. Harcourt Brace Jovanovich, Canada, 1973.

1137. Henry, Keith S. Black Politics in Toronto Since World War I. Multicultural History, 1981.

1138. Hill, Daniel G. Blacks in Early Canada: the Freedom Seekers. Irwin, 1981.

1139. Hill, Donna, ed. Black Man's Toronto, 1914-1918: the Reminiscences of Harry Gairey. Toronto: Multicultural History Society of Ontario, 1981.

1140. Hill, J. S. Alberta's Black Settlers: a Study of Canadian Immigration Policy and Practice. University of Alberta, 1981.

1141. Kasozi, A. B. K. Integration of Black African Immigrants in Canadian Society: a Case Study of Toronto CMA. Toronto: CANACT, 1986.

1142. Kilian, Crawford. Go Do Some Great Thing: the Black Pioneers of British Columbia. Douglas & McIntyre, 1978.

1143. Laferiere, M. "Blacks in Quebec: Minorities among Minorities." Canadian and International Education 14 (1985): 59-82.

1144. Law, Howard. "Self-Reliance Is the True Road to Independence: Ideology and the Ex-slaves in Buxton and Chatham." Ontario History 77 (June 1985): 107-121.

1145. Mannette, Joy Anne. Making Something Happen: Nova Scotia's Black Renaissance, 1968-1986. Carleton University, 1988. Doctoral dissertation.

1146. Pachai, Bridglal. Beneath the Clouds of the Promised Land: the Survival of Nova Scotia's Blacks. Black Educators Association, 1987.

94 WORLD RACISM AND RELATED INHUMANITIES

1147. Pachai, Bridglal. Blacks. Tantallon, Nova Scotia: 1987.

1148. Pachai, Bridglal. My Africa, My Canada. Hantsport, Nova Scotia: Lancelot Press, 1989.

1149. Potter, Harold H. "Negroes in Canada." Race 3 (1961): 39- 56.

1150. Riddell, William R. "Slave in Canada." Journal of Negro History 5 (1920): 261-377.

1151. Riendeau, Roger. Enduring Heritage: Black Contributions to Early Ontario. Dundurn, 1985.

1152. Ruck, Calvin W. Canada's Black Batallion: No.2 Construction Batallion 1916-1920. Black Cultural Centre of Nova Scotia, 1986.

1153. Ruck, Calvin W. Canada's Black Batallion. Nimbus, 1987. [Revised edition.]

1154. Satzewich, Vic. "Canadian State and the Racialization of Caribbean Migrant Farm Labor, 1947-1966." Ethnic and Racial Studies 11 (1988): 282-304.

1155. Schultz, John. "White Man's Country: Canada and the West Indian Immigrant, 1900-1965." in Canada and the Commonwealth Caribbean Brian D. Tennyson, ed. Lanham, MD: University Press of America, 1988.

1156. Scott, Nobert P. Jr. "Black Peoples of Canada." In Politics of Race-Comparative Studies Donald G. Baker. Heath: Saxon House, 1975.

1157. Scott, Nobert P., Jr. Perception of Racial Discrimination by Neroes in Metropolitan Winnipeg, Manitoba, Canada. Doctoral dissertation, Pennsylvania State University, 1971.

1158. Shepard, R. Bruce. "Little 'White' Schoolhouse: Racism in a Saskatchewan Rural School." Saskatchewan History 39 (1986): 81-93.

1159. Shepard, R. Bruce. "North to the Promised Land: Black Migration to the Canadian Plains." Chronicles of Oklahoma 66 (1988): 306-327.

1160. Shepard, R. Bruce. "Plain Racism: the Reaction against Oklahoma Black Immigration to the Canadian Plains." Prairie Forum 10 (1985): 365-382.

1161. Silverman, Jason H. Unwelcome Guests: American Fugitive Slaves in Canada, 1830-1860. University of Kentucky, 1981. Doctoral dissertation.

1162. Silverman, Jason H. Unwelcome Guests: Canada West's Response to American Fugitive Slaves, 1800-1865. Millwood, NY: Associated Faculty Press, 1985.

1163. Silverman, Jason H. and Donna A. Gillie. "Pursuit of Knowledge Under Difficulties: Education and the Fugitive Slave in Canada." Ontario History 74 (June 1982): 75-112.

1164. Solomon, Rovell P. Creation of Separation: the Lived Culture of West Indian Boys in a Toronto High School. State University of New York at Buffalo, 1987. Doctoral dissertation.

1165. Stouffer, Allen P. "Black Abolitionists in Britain and Canada." Canadian Review of American Studies 19 (Summer 1988): 249-255.

1166. Sullivan, Veronica. Gem: Discovering Black Scientists and Inventors. Carib-Can, 1987.

1167. Talbot, Carol. Growing Up Black in Canada. Williams-Wallace, 1984.

1168. Thomson, Colin A. Blacks in Deep Snow: Black Pioneers in Canada. Dent, 1978.

1169. Troper, Harold M. "Creek-Negroes of Oklahoma and Canadian Immigration, 1909-1911." Canadian Historical Review 53 (1972): 272-288.

1170. Tunteng, P. Kiven. "Racism and the Montreal Computer Incident of 1969." Race 14 (January 1973): 229-240. [See Forsythe, above.]

1171. Walton, Jonathan W. Blacks in Buxton and Chatham, Ontario, 1830-1890: Did the 49th Parallel Make a Difference? Princeton University, 1979. Doctoral dissertation.

1172. Williams, Dorothy W. Blacks in Montreal 1628-1986: an Urban Demography. Cowansville: Les Editions Yvon Blais, 1989.

1173. Winks, Robin. Blacks in Canada: a History. New Haven, CT: Yale University Press, 1971.

CANADA - FIRST NATIONS

1174. Adams, Howard. Prison of Grass: Canadian History from a Native Point of View. (Revised edition). Fifth House, 1989.

1175. Archer, John H. "Anglican Church and the Indian in the Northwest." Journal of Canadian Church History 28 (April 1986): 19-30.

1176. Asche, Michael. Home and Native Land - Aboriginal Rights and the Canadian Constitution. Nelson, 1984.

1177. Assu, Harry. Assu of Cape Mudge: Recollections of a Coastal Indian Chief. Vancouver: University of British Columbia Press, 1989.

1178. Badcock, William T. Who Owns Canada? Aboriginal Title and the Canadian Courts. C.A.S.N.P., 1976.

1179. Baker, Marilyn. Indian Infant Mortality in British Columbia. University of British Columbia, 1981. Master's thesis.

1180. Barlett, Richard H. "Indian and Native Law." Ottawa Law Review 15 (Spring 1983): 431-502.

1181. Barman, Jean and others, eds. Indian Education in Canada. Vol I: The Legacy. Vancouver: University of British Columbia Press, 1985.

1182. Barman, Jean and others, eds. Indian Education in Canada. Vol. 2: The Challenge. Vancouver: University of British Columbia Press, 1987. [Since 1972.]

1183. Barrett, Stanley R. Is God a Racist? The Right Wing in Canada. Toronto: University of Toronto Press, 1988.

1184. Boisvert, David and Keith Turnbull. "Who Are the Metis." Studies in Political Economy 18 (Fall 1985): 107-147.

1185. Boldt, Menno and J. Anthony Long in association with Leroy Little Bear, eds. Quest for Justice: Aboriginal Peoples and Aboriginal Rights. Toronto: University of Toronto Press, 1985.

1186. Bolshevik Union of Canada. Nationhood or Genocide: the Struggle of the Native People Against Canadian and American Imperialism. Montreal: Lines of Communication Press, 1979.

1187. Boshyk, Yury, ed. Ukraine during World War II: History and Its Aftermath: A Symposium. Edmonton: Canadian Institute of Ukrainian Studies, University of Alberta, 1986. [Part II: War Criminals in Canada.]

1188. Bottos, Dino. "Keegstra and Andrews: a Commentary on Hate Propaganda and the Freedom of Expression." Alberta Law Review 27 (Spring 1989): 461-475.

1189. Bourgeault, Ron. "Development of Capitalism and the Subjugation of Native Women in Northern Canada." Alternate Routes 6 (1983)

1190. Bourgeois, Donald J. "Six Nations: A Neglected Aspect of Canadian Legal History." Canadian Journal of Native Studies 6 (1986): 253-270.

1191. Brodribb, Somer. "Traditional Roles of Native Women in Canada and the Impact of Colonization." Canadian Journal of Native Studies 4 (1984): 85-103.

1192. Canada Commission of Inquiry on War Criminals. Report. Part 1: Public. Ottawa: Canadian Government Publishing Centre, 1986.

1193. Carey, Miriam R. New Ideology of Aboriginal Rights. University of Calgary, 1981. [Master's thesis.]

1194. Cassidy, Frank. Indian Government: Its Meaning in Practice. Lantzville, B.C.: Oolieham Books, 1989.

1195. Chatworthy, Stewart J. and Jeremy Hull. Native Economic Conditions in Regina and Saskatoon. University of Winnepeg, 1983.

1196. Churchill, Ward. "Last Stand at Lubicon Lake." Zeta Magazine 2 (September 1989): 92-100. [The landbase of the Lubicon Lake Band of Cree, Northern Alberta, Canada.]

1197. Clark, B. A. Right of Indian Self-Government in Canada. University of Aberdeen, 1988. Doctoral dissertation.

1198. Coates, Kenneth S. Best Left as Indians: Native-White Relations in the Yukon Territory, 1840-1950. University of British Columbia, 1984. Doctoral dissertation.

1199. Coates, Kenneth S. "Best Left as Indians: The Federal Government and the Indians of the Yukon, 1894-1950." Canadian Journal of Native Studies 4 (1984): 174-204.

1200. Costisella, Joseph. Racisme et discrimination au Gouvernement du Quebec.... Montreal: Ligue Internationale contre de Racism, 1981.

1201. Cox, Bruce A., ed. Native People, Native Lands: Canadian Indians, Inuit and Metis. New York: Oxford University Press, 1988.

1202. Creery, Ian. Inuit (Eskimo) of Canada. London: Minority Rights Group, 1983.

1203. Crossley, John E. Making of Canadian Indian Policy to 1946. University of Toronto, 1987. Doctoral dissertation.

1204. Daniels, Harry, Forgotten People: Metis and the Non- Status Indian Land Claims. Ottawa: Native Council of Canada, 1979.

1205. Davis, Robert and Mark Zannis. Genocide Machine in Canada: the Pacification of the North. Montreal: Black Rose Press, 1973.

1206. Devens, Carol. "Separate Confrontations: Gender As a Factor in Indian Adaptation to European Colonization in New France." American Quarterly 38 (1986): 461-480.

1207. Dickason, Olive P. Myth of the Savage: and the Beginnings of French Colonialism in the Americas. University of Alberta Press, 1984.

1208. Donad, Patrick C. "Canadian Metis Identity: A Pattern of Evolution." Anthropos 78 (1983): 71-88.

1209. Drake-Terry, Joanne. Same as Yesterday: the Lillooet Chronicle the Theft of Their Lands and Resources. Lillooet: Lillooet Tribal Council, 1989.

1210. Ens, Gerhard J. Kinship, Ethnicity, Class and the Red River Metis: the Parishes of St. Francois Zavier and St. Andrews. University of Alberta, 1989. 1835-1890, Doctoral dissertation.

1211. Faith, K. and others. "Native Women in Canada: A Quest for Justice." Social Justice 17 (Autumn 1990)

1212. Fish, Arthur. "Hate Promotion and Freedom of Expression: Truth and Consequences." Canadian Journal of Law and Jurisprudence 2 (July 1989): 111-137.

1213. Fisher, Robin. Contact and Conflict: Indian-European Relations in British Columbia. University of British Columbia Press, 1979.

1214. Flanagan, Thomas, ed. Riel and the Metis. Winnepeg: Monitoba Metis Federation, 1979.

1215. Flanagan, Thomas. Riel and the Rebellion 1885 Reconsidered. Saskatoon, 1983.

1216. Fleras, Augie. "Race Relations as Collective Definition: Renegotiating Aboriginal-Government Relations in Canada." Symbolic Interaction 13 (Spring 1990)

1217. Franks, C. E. S. "Aboriginal Self-government in Canada." Queen's Quarterly 94 (1987): 666-679.

1218. Frideres, James S. Native Peoples in Canada: Contemporary Conflicts. 3d ed. Scarborough: Prentice-Hall Canada, 1988.

1219. Ghostkeeper, Elmer. Metism: a Canadian Identity. Edmonton: Alberta Federation of Metis Settlement Associations, June, 1982.

1220. Giraud, M. Le Metis canadien. Paris: Institut d'Ethnologie, 1945.

1221. Glaser, Kurt and Bernard T.K. Joei. "Canada's Native Minorities and their Status." Plural Societies 17 (September 1987): 52-74.

1222. Goldie, Terry. Fear and Temptation: the Image of the Indigene in Canadian, Australian, and New Zealand Literature. Kingston: McGill-Queen's University Press, 1989.

1223. Gormley, Daniel J. "Aboriginal Rights As Natural Rights." Canadian Journal of Native Studies 4 (1984): 29-49.

1224. Green, Leslie C. Law of Nations and the New World. Edmonton: University of Alberta Press, 1989.

1225. Griffiths, Curt T. "Native Indians and the Police: The Canadian Experience." Police Studies 11 (Winter 1988): 155-160.

1226. Haig-Brown, Celia. Resistance and Renewal: Surviving the Indian Residential School. Vancouver, B.C.: Tillacum Library, 1988.

1227. Hall, Anthony J. Red Man's Burden: Land, Law and the Lord in the Indian Affairs of Upper Canada, 1791-1858. University of Toronto, 1984. Doctoral dissertation.

1228. Hall, D. J. "Serene Atmosphere? Treaty 1 Revisited." Canadian Journal of Native Studies 4 (1984): 321-358.

1229. Harding, Jim. Aboriginal Rights and Government Wrongs: Uranium Mining and Neocolonialism in Northern Saskatchewan. Regina: University of Regina - Prairie Justice Research, 1988.

1230. Harrison, J. Metis People between Two Worlds. Vancouver: Douglas and McIntyre, 1985.

1231. Heinemann, L. Investigation into the Origins and Development of the Metis Nation, the Rights of the Metis as an Aboriginal People, and their Relationship and Dealings with the Government of Canada. Regina: Gabriel Dumon Institute, 1984.

1232. Hobart, Charles W. "Impact of Resource Development on the Health of Native People in the Northwest Territories." Canadian Journal of Native Studies 4 (1984): 257-278.

1233. Ivanitz, M. J. Questionable Efficiency of Acculturation: the Case of the Candian North. University of Alberta, 1985. Master's thesis.

1234. Jackson, Michael. "Locking Up Natives in Canada." University of British Columbia Law Review 23 (Summer 1989): 215-300.

1235. Johnston, Darlene. Taking of Indian Lands in Canada: Consent or Coercion? Saskatoon: University of Saskatchewan Native Law Centre, 1989.

1236. Johnston, Eric and Diane Longboat. "Sovereignty, Jurisdiction and Guiding Principles in Aboriginal Education in Canada." Canadian Journal of Native Studies 6 (1986): 173-179.

1237. Judd, Carol. "Native Labour and Social Stratification in the Hudson's Bay Company's Northern Department 1770-1870." Canadian Review of Sociology and Anthropology 17

1238. Kato, Hiroaki. Group Rights, Democracy and the Plural Society: the Case of Canada's Aboriginal Peoples. Carleton University, 1986. Doctoral dissertation.

1239. Katzer, Bruce. "Caughnawaga Mohawks: the Other Side of Ironwork." Journal of Ethnic Studies 15 (Winter 1988): 39-55.

1240. Kelly, David D. Bilingual/Multicultural Education in Canada: Interpretation and Bibliography. Buffalo: Comparative Education Center, State University of New York, 1986.

1241. Krotz, Larry. Indian Country: Inside Another Canada. Toronto: McClelland & Stewart, 1990.

1242. LaPrairie, Carol. "La justice penale chez les autochtones du Canada. Principes et pratiques." Anthropologie et Societes 13 (1989)

1243. LaPrairie, Carol. "Role of Sentencing in the Over- representation of Aboriginal People in Correctional Institutions." Canadian Journal Criminology 32 (July 1990): 429-440.

1244. Legros, D. "Wealth, Poverty, and Slavery among the XIXth Century Tutchone Athapaskans." Research in Economic Anthropology 7 (1985): 37-64.

1245. Lewis, Paul. "Canada about to Sign Major Land Agreement with Eskimos." New York Times (August 21, 1989)

1246. Long, J. Anthony, ed. Government in Conflict? Provinces and Indian Nations in Canada. Toronto: University of Toronto Press, 1988.

1247. Long, J. Anthony and Menno Boldt. "Self-Determination and Extra-Legal Action: The Foundations of Native Indian Protest." Canadian Review of Studies of Nationalism 15 (1988): 111-119.

1248. "Louis Riel's Petition of Rights, 1884." Saskatchewan History 12 (Winter 1970): 16-26.

1249. Lucas, Martin. "TV on Ice." New Society (January 9, 1987) [Inuit Broadcasting Corporation, Canada.]

1250. Lussier, Antoine S. and D. Bruce Sealey. The Other Natives: the les Metis. Winnepeg: Manitoba Metis Federation, 1978.

1251. MacDonald, John A. "Child Welfare and the Native Indian Peoples of Canada." Windsor Yearbook of Access to Justice 5 (1985): 284-305.

1252. Macgregor, Roy. Chief: the Fearless Vision of Billy Diamond. Markham: Viking, 1989. [Leader of James Bay Cree.]

1253. MacLaine, Craig S. and Michael S. Baxendale. This Land Is Our Land: the Mohawk Revolt at Oka. Montreal: Optimum Publishing International, 1990.

1254. Mawhiney, Anne-Marie. Hegemony and Counter-hegemony: a Study of Relations between Status Indian Peoples and the Government of Canada. York University, 1990. Doctoral dissertation.

1255. McCandless, Robert. Yukon Wildlife: a Social History. Edmonton: University of Alberta Press, 1985.

1256. McLean, Donald G. Metis in Western Canada: a Study of Structural Unemployment. University of Regina, 1981. Master's thesis.

1257. McMillan, Alan D. Native Peoples and Cultures of Canada: an Anthropological Overview. Vancouver: Douglas & McIntyre, 1988.

1258. Miller, James Rodger. "From Riel to the Metis." Canadian Historical Review 69 (March 1988): 1-20.

1259. Miller, James Rodger. Skyscrapers Hide the Heavens: a History of Indian-White Relations in Canada. Toronto: University of Toronto Press, 1989.

1260. Monture, Patricia A. "Ka-nin-geh-heh-gah-e-sa-nonh-yah- gah." <u>Canadian Journal of Women and the Law</u> 2 (Winter-Spring 1986): 159-171. [Conflicts between feminists and native women in Canada's law schools.]

1261. Morrison, William R. <u>Showing the Flag: the Mounted Police and Canadian Sovereignty in the North, 1894-1925</u>. Vancouver, B.C.: University of British Columbia, 1985.

1262. Nakatsuru, Shaun. "Constitutional Right of Indian Self- Government." <u>University of Toronto Faculty of Law Review</u> 43 (Fall 1985): 72-99.

1263. Nichols, Roger L. "United States, Canada, and the Indians: 1865-1876." <u>Social Science Journal</u> 26 (1989): 249-263.

1264. Opekokew, Delia. <u>Political and Legal Inequities among Aboriginal Peoples in Canada</u>. Queen's University, 1987.

1265. Palmer, Howard. <u>Patterns of Prejudice: a History of Nativism in Alberta</u>. Toronto: McClelland and Stewart, 1982.

1266. Peterson, Jacqueline and Jennifer S. H. Brown, ed. <u>New Peoples: Being and Becoming Metis in North America</u>. Lincoln: University of nebraska Press.

1267. Petrone, Penny , <u>First People, First Voices</u>. Toronto: University of Toronto Press, 1982. [Native writing, 1630-1980.]

1268. Ponting, J. Rick. <u>Arduous Journey: Canadian Indians and Decolonization</u>. McClelland, 1986.

1269. Prattis, J. Ian and J.P. Chartrand. "Cultural Division of Labour in the Canadian North: A Statistical Study of the Inuit." <u>Canadian Review of Sociology and Anthropology</u> 27 (February 1990)

1270. Ray, Arthur J. "Reflections on Fur Trade Social History and Metis History in Canada." <u>American Indian Culture and Research Journal</u> 6 (1982): 91-107.

1271. Redford, James W. <u>Attendance at Indian Residential Schools in British Columbia, 1890-1920</u>. University of British Columbia, 1978. Master's thesis.

1272. Regular, William K. <u>Red Backs and White Burdens: a Study of White Attitudes toward Indians in Southern Alberta 1896-1911</u>. University of Calgary, 1985.

1273. Riel, Louis. <u>Collected Writings of Louis Riel, 5 vols.</u> University of Alberta Press.

1274. Sawchuk, Joe and others. <u>Metis Land Rights in Alberta</u>. Edmonton: Metis Association of Alberta, 1981.

CANADA - FIRST NATIONS 103

1275. Schmalz, Peter S. Ojibwa of Southern Ontario. University of Waterloo, 1985. [Appendix on education.]

1276. Scott-Brown, Joan. "Calgary Indian Industrial School, 1896- 1907." Canadian Journal of Native Education 14 (1987): 41-49.

1277. Shawana, Perry. "Indian Health Care: Sociology Perspectives in Law." Canadian Journal of Native Education 15 (1988): 39-65.

1278. Shkilmyk, Anastasia M. Poison Stronger than Love: the Destruction of an Ojibwa Community. New Haven, CT: Yale University Press, 1985.

1279. Shocking Truth about Indians in Textbooks. Winnipeg: Manitoba Indian Brotherhood, 1974.

1280. Sprague, D. N. Canada and the Metis, 1869-1885. Waterloo, Ontario: Wilfrid Laurier University Press, 1988.

1281. Sprenger, George H. Analysis of Selected Aspects of Metis Society, 1810-1870. University of Manitoba, 1972.

1282. St.Onge, Nicole J. M. "Dissolution of a Metis Community: Pointe a Grouette, 1860-1885." Studies in Political Economy 18 (Fall 1985): 149-172.

1283. Sterling, Robert and Yvonne M. Hebert. "Non-Authority in Nicola Valley Indian Culture and Implications for Education." Canadian Journal of Native Studies 4 (1984): 193-301.

1284. Stone, Thomas. "Mounties as Vigilantes: Perceptions of Community and the Transformation of Law in the Yukon, 1885-1897." Law and Society Review 14 (1979-1980)

1285. Stuckey, Naneen E. Tsimshian Testimony before the Royal Commission on Indian Affairs for the Province of British Columbia (1913-1916). University of Victoria, 1981.

1286. Tanner, Adrian , Politics of Indianness: Case studies in Native Ethnopolitics in Canada. ISER Books, 1983.

1287. Taylor, John Leonard. Canadian Indian Policy during the Inter-War Years, 1918-1939. Ottawa: Treaties and Historical Research Centre, 1984.

1288. Tennant, Paul. Aboriginal Peoples and Politics: the Indian Land Question in British Columbia, 1849-1989. Vancouver: University of British Columbia Press, 1990.

1289. Thomson, Duncan D. History of the Okanagan: Indians and Whites in the Settlement Era, 1860-1920. University of British Columbia, 1985. Doctoral dissertation.

1290. Tobias, John L. "Canada's Subjugation of the Plains Cree, 1879-1885." Canadian Historical Review 64 (1983)

1291. Toohey, K. "English as a Second Language for Native Canadians." Canadian Journal of Education 10 (1985): 275-292.

1292. Tough, Frank J. Native People and the Regional Economy of Northern Manitoba: 1870-1930's. York University, 1987. Doctoral dissertation.

1293. Trigger, Bruce G. "Historians' Indian: Native Americans in Canadian Historical Writing from Charevoix to the Present." Canadian Historical Review 67 (1986): 315-342.

1294. Trigger, Bruce G. Natives and Newcomers: Canada's "Heroic Age" Reconsidered. Buffalo, NY: McGill-Queen's University Press, 1986.

1295. Tynan, James. Inside Out: an Autobiography by a Native Canadian. Saskatoon: Fifth House, 1989.

1296. Vallerand, Robert J. and Larry Menard. "Increasing the School Attendance of Native Students: An Application of Cognitive Evolution Theory." Canadian Journal of Native Studies 4 (1984): 241-255.

1297. Wagner, Jonathan F. Brothers Beyond the Sea: National Socialism in Canada. Waterloo, Ontario: Wilfrid Laurier University Press, 1981.

1298. Wahn, M. B. Economic Development and Native Health in the Northwest Territories. University of Alberta, 1980.

1299. Wall, Denis V. Internal Colonialism and Northland School Division #61: a Context for Decision-Making. University of Alberta, 1987. [98 percent Native students, Doctoral dissertation.]

1300. Watkins, Mel, ed. Dene Nation, Colony Within. Buffalo, NY: University of Toronto Press, 1977.

1301. Wilson, James. Canada's Indians. London: Minority Rights Group, 1982. Revised edition.

1302. Wood, Dean. "Schools in a Multi-ethnic Society: Responding to Prejudice and Discrimination." Canadian Ethnic Studies 15 (1983): 125-129.

1303. Wyatt, J. D. "Mt. Currie Indian Community School: Innovation and Endurance." Canadian Journal of Education 10 (1985): 250-274. [British Columbia.]

1304. York, Geoffrey. Dispossessed: Life and Death in Native Canada. Toronto: Lester and Orpen Dennys, 1989.

1305. Young, John. "How Our Schools Are Teaching Indians to Become Failures." Vancouver Sun (March 17, 1973):

CANADA - FRENCH

1306. Beaude, H. La déportation des Acadiens. Montreal: Bibliotheque de l'Action-francaise, 1918.

1307. Bienvenue, Rita M. "Language Politics and Social Divisions in Manitoba." American Review of Canadian Studies 19 (Summer 1989): 187-202.

1308. Boucher, Michel. "Les Canadiens francais dans la Ligue nationale de Hockey: une analyse statistique." Actualite Economique 60 (1984): 308-325.

1309. Caldwell, Gary. Les études ethniques au Québec: bilan et perspectives. Québec: Institut Quebécois de Recherche sur la culture, 1983.

1310. Candau, Pierre and Roger Guir. "Affinité et clivage ethnique dans la direction des grande enterprises." Rélations Industrielles 35 (1980): 231-250.

1311. Caraffe, Marc de. "Difficult Beginnings of a Public Education System in Quebec (1801-1876)." Research Bulletin National Historic Parks and Sites Branch 188 (1983): 1-14.

1312. Caraffe, Marc de. "Fate of Quebec Public Schools between 1876 and 1930." Research Bulletin - National Historic Parks and Sites Brach 189 (1983): 1-22.

1313. Coleman, William D. Independence Movement in Quebec, 1945- 1980. Toronto: University of Toronto Press, 1984.

1314. Copp, T. Anatomy of Poverty: the Condition of the Working Class in Montreal, 1897-1919. Toronto: 1974.

1315. Dofny, Jacques. "Ethnic Cleavages, Labor Aristocracy, and Nationalism in Quebec." In New Nationalisms in the Developed West: toward Explanation, edited by Edward A. Tiryakian and Ronald Rogowski. Boston: Allen & Unwin, 1985.

1316. Dumont, Fernand and others, eds. Ideologies au Canada Francais, vol. 4. Sainte Foy, Quebec: Presses de l'Université Laval, 1981.

1317. Green, Leslie. "Are Language Rights Fundamental?" Osgoode Hall Law Journal 25 (Winter 1987): 639-669.

1318. Legendre, Camille. French Canada in Crisis: a New Society in the Making? London: Minority Rights Group, 1982. Revised edition.

1319. Levine, Marc V. Reconquest of Montreal: Language Policy and Social Change in a Bilingual City. Philadepphia, PA: Temple University Press, 1990.

1320. Marcil-Lacoste, Louise, comp. La thématique contemporaine l'egalité: repertoire, résumés, typologie. Montreal: Les Presses del'Université de Montreal, 1984.

1321. McCaffrey, Vivian E. Stanley B. Ryerson: Marxist Intellectuals and the French-Canadian National Question. University of Ottawa, 1981. Master's thesis.

1322. McRoberts, Kenneth. "Internal Colonialism: the Case of Quebec." Ethnic and Racial STudies 2 (July 1979): 293-318.

1323. Milner, Sheilagh H. and Henry Milner. Decolonization of Quebec. Toronto: McClelland and Stewart, 1973.

1324. Shapiro, D. M. and M. Stekner. "Earnings Disparities among Linguistic Groups in Quebec, 1970-1980." Canadian Public Policy 13 (March 1987)

CANADA - GENERAL

1325. Abele, F. and D. Stariulis. "Canada as a 'White Settler Colony': What about Natives and Immigrants." in The New Canadian Political Economy W. Clement and G. Williams. Kingston: McGill-Queens University Press, 1989.

1326. Abowitz, Deborah A. Class and Status: Determinants of Income in Canada. Master's thesis: Brown University, 1982.

1327. Acheson, T. W. "Changing Social Origins of the Canadian Industrial Elite, 1880-1910." Business History Review, 47 (Summer 1973)

1328. Actes du forum immigration, racisme et pluralisme. Montreal: Mouvement Quebecois pour Combattre le Racisme, 1987.

1329. Adamson, Nancy and others. Feminist Organizing for Change: The Contemporary Women's Movement in Canada. Toronto: Oxford University Press, 1988.

1330. Adolphe, Robin W. Roots of Discontent: Early Causes of Labour Unrest in British Columbia 1850-1914. Master's thesis: Western Washington University, 1978.

1331. Agocs, Carol. "Affirmative Action, Canadian Style: A Reconnaissance." Canadian Public Policy 12 (1986): 148-162.

1332. Akbari, A. H. "The Benefits of Immigrants to Canada: Evidence on Tax and Public Services." Canadian Public Policy 15 (December 1989):

1333. Alibhai, Yasmin. "Canadian Club." New Statesman & Society (September 2, 1988) [Countering racism in Canada.]

1334. Anderson, Ellen M. The Role of the Reader in the Curriculum: The Second Report. North York, Ont.: North York Board of Education, Curriculum and Staff Development Services, 1986.

1335. Andiappan, Palaniappan and others. "Racial Discrimination in Employment in Canada." Relations Ind. 44 (Autumn 1989): 827-849.

1336. Antler, Steven. "The Capitalist Underdevelopment of Nineteenth Century Newfoundland." In Underdevelopment and Social Movements in Atlantic Canada, edited by R.J. Bryn and R.J. Socouman. Toronto: 1979.

1337. Apps, Eric P. "Minority Language Education Rights." University of Toronto Faculty of Law Review 43 (Fall 1985): 45-71.

1338. Archibald, Bruce P. "Sentencing and Visible Minorities: Equality and Affirmative Action in the Criminal Justice System." Dalhousie Law Journal 12 (November 1989): 377-411.

1339. Armitage, Peter and John C. Kennedy. "Redbaiting and Racism On Our Frontier: Military Expansion in Labrador and Quebec." Canadian Review of Sociology and Anthropology 20 (November 1988)

1340. Avery, D. Dangerous Foreigners: European Immigrant Workers and Labour Radicalism in Canada, 1896-1932. Toronto: McClelland and Stewart, 1979.

1341. Bacher, John C. and J. David Hulchanski. "Keeping Warm and Dry: The Policy Response to the Struggle for Shelter Among Canada's Homeless, 1900-1960." Urban History Review 16 (October 1987): 147-163.

1342. Baer, Douglas E. Social Class, Legitimacy and the Canadian State. Doctoral dissertation: Univerity of Waterloo (Canada), 1987. [1977 and 1984 data.]

1343. Bakker, Isabella. The Reproduction of the Working Population in Canada, 1945 to 1983: A Theoretical and Empirical Contribution. Doctoral dissertation: New School for Social Research, 1986. UMO # 8700549.

1344. Banting, Keith. "The Welfare State and Inequality in the 1980's." Canadian Review of Sociology and Anthropology 24 (August 1987): 309-338.

1345. Barrett, Stanley R. Is God a Racist? The Right Wing in Canada. Toronto: University of Toronto Press, 1987.

1346. Barrett, Stanley R. "White Supremacists and Neo-Fascists: Laboratories for the Analysis of Racism in Wider Society." Canadian Ethnic Studies 16 (1984): 1-15.

1347. Bartlett, Eleanor A. Real Wages and the Standard of Living in Vancouver, 1901-1929. Master's thesis: University of British Columbia, 1980.

1348. Basran, G. S. "Canadian Immigration Policy and Theories of Racism." In *Racial Minorities in Multicultural Canada*, edited by Peter S. Li and B. Singh. Toronto: Garamond, 1983.

1349. Bedford, Judith B. *Social Justice in Calgary: A Study of Urban Poverty and Welfare Development in the 1920's*. Master's thesis: University of Calgary, 1981.

1350. Bickenbach, Jerome E. "Lawyers, Law Professors, and Racism in Ontario." *Queen's Quarterly* 96 (Autumn 1989): 385-398.

1351. Bickerton, James. "Underdevelopment and Social Movements in Atlantic Canada: A Critique." *Studies in Political Economy* No. 9 (Fall 1982): 191-202.

1352. Boivin, Michelle and others eds. *Canadian Human Rights Yearbook*. Cumberland, Ottawa: University of Ottowa Press, 1990.

1353. Bolaria, B. Singh. *Racial Oppression in Canada* (2nd revised edition). Toronto: Garamond Press, 1988.

1354. Breton, Raymond. "Class Bias in Toronto Schools." *This Magazine Is About Schools* 5 (Fall-Winter 1971): 7-35.

1355. Brodie, Janine. *Crisis, Challenge and Change: Party and Class in Canada Revisited*. Ottawa: Carleton University Press, 1988.

1356. Brym, Robert J. with Bonnie J. Fox. *From Culture to Power: The Sociology of English Canada*. New York: Oxford University Press, 1989.

1357. Brym, Robert J. "Social Stratification: Class and Ethnic Dimensions." *Current Sociology* 34 (Spring 1986): 74-101.

1358. Brym, Robert J. *The Structure of the Canadian Capitalist Class*. Toronto: 1985.

1359. Buchignani, Norman. *Perceptions of Racial Discrimination in Calgary: A Situation Report*. Multiculturalism Directorate: Department of the Secretary of State, 1982.

1360. Buchignani, Norman. "Some Comments on the Elimination of Racism in Canada." *Canadian Ethnic Studies* 15 (1983): 118-124.

1361. Bullen, John. "Hidden Workers: Child Labour and the Family Economy in Late Nineteenth-century Urban Ontario." *Labour* 18 (Autumn 1986): 163-187.

1362. Burrell, Leon F. and Carole P. Christensen. "Minority Students' Perceptions of High School: Implications for Canadian School Personnel." *Journal of Multicultural Counseling & Development* 15 (January 1987): 3-15.

CANADA - GENERAL 111

1363. Calderwood, William. "Pulpit, Press, and Political Reactions to the Ku Klux Klan Saskatchewan." In The Twenties in Western Canada: Papers of the Western Canadian Studies Conference, edited by S.M. Trofiurenkoff. Ottawa: History Division, National Museum of Man, 1972.

1364. Calderwood, William. "Religious Reactions to the Ku Klux Klan in Saskatchewan." Saskatchewan History 26 (1973): 103-114.

1365. Calderwood, William. The Rise and Fall of the Ku Klux Klan in Saskatchewan. Master' thesis: University of Saskatchewan, 1968.

1366. Canada, Government of. Participation of Visible Minorities in Canadian Society. Ottawa: Queens Printer, 1984.

1367. Canadian Human Rights Commission. Discrimination in Canada: A Survey of Knowledge, Attitudes and Pratices Concerned with Discrimination. September 1979. ERIC ED 202 749.

1368. Carney, Robert. "Teacher Education in the Northwest Territories: Cultural Inclusion, Cultural Imperialism and Teacher Autonomy." History of Education Review 17 (1988): 18-26.

1369. Carroll, William K. "The Canadian Corporate Elite: Financiers or Finance Capitalist?" Studies in Political Economy, No. 8 (Summer 1982): 89-114.

1370. Carroll, William K. Capital Accumulation and Corporate Interlocking in Post-War Canada. Doctoral dissertation: York University, 1981.

1371. Carroll, William K. Corporate Power and Canadian Capitalism. Vancouver: University of British Columbia Press, 1986.

1372. Carroll, William K. "The Individual, Class and Corporate Power in Canada." Canadian Journal of Sociology 9 (Summer 1984): 245-268.

1373. Case, Frederic I. Racism and National Consciousness. Toronto: Plowshare Press, 1980.

1374. Clark, Peter and Anthony Davis. "The Power of Dirt: An Exploration of Secular Defilement in Anglo-Canadian Culture." Canadian Review of Sociology and Anthropology 26 (1989): 650-673.

1375. Clement, W. Class, Power and Property: Essays on Canadian Society. Toronto: Methuen, 1983.

1376. Clow, Michael. "Politics and Uneven Capitalist Development." Studies in Political Economy 14 (Summer 1984)

1377. Coates, Kenneth S. The Modern North: People, Politics and the Rejection of Colonialism. Toronto: James Lorimer, 1989.

1378. Connelly, M. Patricia and Martha MacDonald. "Women's Work: Domestic and Wage Labour in a Nova Scotia Community." Studies in Political Economy No. 10 (Winter 1983): 45-72. ["Big Harbour"; population ca. 300.]

1379. Cook, Ramsey and Wendy Mitchinson, eds. The Proper Sphere: Women's Place in Canadian Society. Toronto, Canada: Oxford University Press, 1976.

1380. Craig, Terrence. Racial Attitudes in English Canadian Fiction 1905-1980.

1381. Creese, Gillian L. Working-class Politics, Racism and Sexism: The Making of a Politically Divided Working Class in Vancouver, 1900-1939. Doctoral dissertation: Carleton University, 1986.

1382. Cummins, Jim. "From Multiculturalism to Anti-Racist Education: An Analysis of Programs and Policies in Ontario." In Minority Eduction: From Shame to Struggle, edited by T. Skutnabb-Kangas and Jim Cummins. Philadelphia, PA: Multilingual Matters, 1988.

1383. Cuneo, Carl J. "Class Exploitation in Canada." Canadian Review of Sociology and Anthropology 15 (1979): 284-300.

1384. Curtis, Bruce. The Political Economy of Elementary Educational Development: Comparative Perspectives on State Schooling in Upper Canada. Doctoral dissertation: University of Toronto, 1980.

1385. Curtis, Bruce. "Preconditions of the Canadian State: Educational Reform and the Construction of a Public in Upper Canada, 1837-1846." Studies in Political Economy No. 10 (Winter 1983): 99-121.

1386. D'Orsay, John V. The Economic Determination of Social Classes in the Canadian Social Formation: A Provisional Analysis. Master's thesis: Dalhousie University, 1983.

1387. Dahlie, Jorgen and Tissa Fernando, eds. Ethnicity, Power and Politics in Canada. Toronto: Methuen, 1981.

1388. Davies, J. B. "On the Size Distribution of Wealth in Canada." Review of Income and Wealth 25 (September 1979): 237-259.

1389. Denis, Ann B. "Adaptation to Multiple Subordination? Women in the Vertical Mosaic." Canadian Ethnic Studies 18 (1986): 61-74.

1390. Donovan, Kenneth. "Tattered Clothes and Powdered Wigs: Case Studies of the Poor and Well-to-Do in Eighteenth-Century Louisbourg." In Cape Breton at 200... edited by Donovan. Sydney, Nova Scotia: University College of Cape Breton Press, 1985.

CANADA - GENERAL   113

1391. Dooley, Martin D. "The Overeducated Canadian? Changes in the Relationship among Earnings, Education, and Age for Canadian Men: 1971-1981." Canadian Journal of Economics 19 (February 1986): 142-159.

1392. Drache, Daniel. "Staple-ization: A Theory of Canadian Capitalist Development." In Imperialism, Nationalism and Canada, edited by John Saul and Craig Heron. Toronto: 1977.

1393. Les droits des minorités. Quebec: Laval University, Faculty of Law, 1986.

1394. Dugas, Clermont. Disparites socio-economiques au Canada. Silery: Presses de l'Universitaires du Quebec, 1988.

1395. Dutton, Alan. Capitalism, the State and Minority Ethnic Relations in British Columbia. Master's thesis: University of Victoria, Canada, 1985.

1396. Fairley, Bryant D. "The Struggle for Capitalism in the Fishing Industry in Newfoundland." Studies in Political Economy No. 17 (Summer 1985): 33-69.

1397. Fallick, ARthur L. Homelessness and the Homeless in Canada: A Geographic Perspective. Doctoral dissertation: University of British Columbia, 1988.

1398. Ferguson, Ted. A White Man's Country. An Exercise in Canadian Prejudice. Garden City, New York: Doubleday, 1976. [The Komagata Mary incident of 1914.]

1399. Finkel, Alvin. "Canadian Immigration Policy and the Cold War, 1945-1960." Journal of Canadian Studies 21 (1986): 53-70.

1400. Finlay, John L. The Structure of Canadian History. Scarborough: Prentice-Hall, Canada, 1989.

1401. Fraser, David. "Racism and the Law: It's Alright, Ma. I'm Only Bleeding. Is it Possible to Achieve a Legal Solution to Racism." Legal Service Bulletin 14 (April 1989): 69-71.

1402. Frideres, James S. and William J. Reeves. "The Ability to Implement Human Rights Legislation in Canada." Canadian Review of Sociology and Anthropology 26 (1989): 311-332.

1403. Frideres, James S. "Discrimination in Western Canada." Race 15 (October 1973): 213-222.

1404. Gagnon, Nathaly. Un vol organisé: la discrimination des femmes. Hull, Que: Les Editions Asticou, 1989. [Province of Québec.]

1405. Grayson, J. Paul, Class, State, Ideology and Change: Marxist Perspectives on Canada. Toronto: Holt, Rinehart and Winston of Canada, 1980.

1406. Greer, Allan. "Wage Labour and the Transition to Capitalism: A Critique of Pentland." Labour 15 (Spring 1985): 7-22.

1407. Gupta, Dipankar. "Racism Without Colour: The Catholic Ethnic and Ethnicity in Quebec." Race and Class 25 (Summer 1983): 23-44.

1408. Hale, C. A. "Publicly Funded Schools in Nova Scotia, pre- 1930." Research Bulletin-National Historic Parks and Sites Branch No. 210 (1983): 1-24.

1409. Hamilton, Roberta. Feudal Society and Colonization: The Historiography of New France. Gananoque, Ontario: Langdale, 1988.

1410. Henry, Frances. The Dynamics of Racism in Toronto: A Preliminary Report. Downsview, Ontario: Department of Anthropology, York University, 1977.

1411. Herberg, Edward N. Ethnic Groups in Canada: Adaptations and Transitions. Scarborough: Nelson Canada, 1989.

1412. Hertzog, Stephen and Robert D. Lewis. "A City of Tenants: Homeownership and Social CLass in MOntreal, 1847-1881." Canadian Geographer 30 (Winter 1986): 316-323.

1413. Hughes, David R. and Evelyn Kallen. The Anatomy of Racism: Canadian Dimensions. Montreal: Harvest House, 1974.

1414. Jabbra, Nancy W. and Ronald L. Casper. "Ethnicity in Atlantic Canada: A Survey." Canadian Ethnic Studies 20 (1988): 6-27.

1415. Jain, Harish C. "Affirmative Action/Employment Equity Programs in Canada: Issues and Policies." Labor Law Journal 41 (August 1990): 487-492.

1416. Jain, Harish C. and Rick D. Hackett. "Measuring Effectiveness of Employment Equity Programs in Canada: Public Policy and a Survey." Canadian Public Policy 15 (1989): 189-204.

1417. Jain, Harish C. "Racial Minorities and Affirmative Action/ Employment Equity Legislation in Canada." Ind. Relations 44 (Summer 1989): 593-613.

1418. Johnson, Dana. "For the Privileged Few: The Private and Specialist Schools at Ontario, 1800-1930." Research Bulletin-National Historic Parks and Sites Branch No. 215 (1984): 1-30.

1419. Johnson, Leo. "The Development of Class in Canada in the 20th Century." in Capitalism and the National Question in Canada, edited by Gary Teeple. Toronto: University of Toronto Press, 1972.

1420. Johnson, Leo. Poverty in Wealth: The Capitalist Labour Market and Income Distribution in Canada. Toronto: 1974.

1421. Johnson, Thomas. "Color Prejudice in Canada." Anthropological Journal of Canada 16 (1978): 2-11.

1422. Jones, Frank E. "Age at Immigration and Education: Further Explorations." International Migration Review 21 (Spring 1987): 70-85.

1423. Kallen, Evelyn. Label Me Human: Minority Rights of Stigmatized Canadians. Toronto: University of Toronto Press, 1989.

1424. Kallen, Evelyn. "The Meech Lake Accord: Entrenching a Pecking Order of Minority Rights." Canadian Public Policy 14 (1988)

1425. Kealey, Gregory S. "Looking Backward: Reflections on the Study of Class in Canada." History and Social Science Teacher 16 (Summer 1981): 213-222.

1426. Kealey, Gregory S. "The Structure of Canadian Working-Class History." In Lectures in Canadian Labour and Working-Class History, edited by W.J.C. Cherwinski and Gregory S. Kealey. St. John's, Newfoundland: Committee on Canadian Labour History and New Hogtown Press, 1985.

1427. Kobayashi, A. "Racism and Law in Canada: A Geographical Perspective." Urban Geography 11 (September-October 1990):

1428. Kyba, Patrick. "Ballots and Burning Crosses-The Election of 1919." In Politics of Saskatchewan, edited by Norman Ward and Duff Spafford. Don Mills: Longmans Canada, 1968.

1429. Laferriere, M. "Language and Cultural Programs for Ethnic Minorities in Quebec: A Critical View." Canadian and International Education 14 (1985): 49-58.

1430. Laferriere, M. "Languages, Ideologies, and Multicultural Education in Canada: Some Historical and Sociological Perspectives." Canadian and International Education 14 (1985): 5-15.

1431. Lai, David C. "The Issue of Discrimination in Education." Canadian Ethnic Studies 19 (1987): 47-67.

1432. Leadbeater, David T. L. Impoverishment in Canada, 1929- 1981. Doctoral dissertation: University of Toronto, 1990.

1433. Levitt, Cyril and William Shaffer. The Riot of Christie Pitts. Lester & Orpen Dennys: 1987.

1434. Lewis, Debra J. Just Give Us the Money: A Discussion of Wage Discrimination and Pay Equity. Vancouver: Women's Research Centre, 1988.

1435. Ley, David. "Social Upgrading in Six Canadian Inner Cities." Canadian Geographer 32 (Spring 1988): 31-45.

1436. Li, Peter S. Ethnic Inequality in a Class Society. Toronto: Wall & Thomspon, 1988.

1437. Little, John Irvine. Nationalism, Capitalism, and Colonization in Nineteenth-Century Quebec: The Upper St. Francis District. Kingston: McGill-Queen's University Press, 1989.

1438. Lucas, Rex A. Minetown, Milltown, Railtown: Life in Canadian Communities of Single Industry. Toronto: 1971,

1439. Luciuk, Lubomyr Y. A Time for Atonement: Canada's First National Internment Operations and the Ukrainian Canadians, 1914-1920. Kingston: Limestone Press, 1988.

1440. Luciuk, Lubomyr Y. "Ukrainians and Internment Operations in Ontario during the First World War." Polyphony (Canada) 10 (1988): 27-31.

1441. MacKinnon, Catharine A. "Sex Equality and Nation-building in Canada: The Meech Lake Accord." Tulsa Law Journal 25 (Summer 1990): 735-757.

1442. MacKintosh, Gordon H. Federal Anti-discrimination Policy: A Study of the Canadian Human Rights Act, 1977. Master's thesis: University of Manitoba, 1981.

1443. Macpherson, C. B. Democracy in Alberta: Social Credit and the Party System. Toronto: 1962.

1444. Manitoba Human Rights Commission. Report to the Manitoba Human Rights Commission on Racism in Winnipeg School Division No. 1 Schools. Winnipeg: The Commission, 1982.

1445. Matheson, Gwen, Women in the Canadian Mosaic. Toronto, Canada: Peter Martin, 1976.

1446. McCallum, Margaret C. "Keeping Women in Their Place: Minimum Wage in Canada, 1910-1925." Labour 17 (Spring 1986): 29-56.

1447. McDermott, Patricia C. "Pay Equity in Ontario: A Critical Legal Analysis." Osgoode Hall Law Journal 28 (Summer 1990): 381-407.

1448. McDougall, David. "The Reduction of Prejudice through Education: Strategies for Action in Canada and Implications for Research." Canadian Ethnic Studies 17 (1985): 81-90.

1449. Mealing, Stanley R. "The Concept of Social Class and the Interpretation of Canadian History." Canadian Historical Review 46 (1965): 201-218.

1450. Meghji, Alnasir. "Canada's Policy of Multiculturalism- An Illusion of Belonging." Reconstruction 1 (Winter 1990)

1451. Messinger, Hans. "The Size and Distribution of the Poverty Gap in Canada: A MicroAnalysis of Variations Among Demographic Groups." Review of Income and Wealth 34 (September 1988): 275-288.

1452. Miles, Angela and Geraldine Finn. Feminism in Canada. From Pressure to Politics. Montreal: Black RoseBooks, 1983.

1453. Miller, David and Barbara Roberts. "Minorities and Exploitation: A Canadian Tradition." Integrateducation 19 (May-December 1981): 98-108.

1454. Mock, Karen R. Implementing Race and Ethnocultural Equity Policy in Ontario School Boards. Toronto: Ontario Ministry of Education, 1989.

1455. Morrow, A. M. M. "The Measurement of Inflation Experienced by the Poor, 1970-1980." Canadian Public Policy 12 (March 1986):

1456. Moscovitch, Allan and G. Drover, eds. Inequality: Essays on the Political Economy of Social Welfare. Toronto: University of Toronto Press, 1981.

1457. Moscovitch, Allan. "The Welfare State since 1975." Journal of Canadian Studies 21 (Summer 1986): 77-95.

1458. Murphy, P. L. Social Characteristics of Edmonton's Elite 1951-1974: An Exploratory Study. Master's thesis: University of Alberta, 1983.

1459. Myers, Gustavus. A History of Canadian Wealth. Chicago: 1914.

1460. Neary, Peter, The Political Economy of Newfoundland, 1929-1972. Vancouver: 1973.

1461. Neatby, Hilda. "Racism in the Old Province of Quebec." In Racism in the Eighteenth Century, edited by Harold E. Pagliaro. Cleveland, Ohio: Press of Case Western Reserve University, 1973.

1462. Neis, Barbara. "Competitive Merchants and Class Struggle in Newfoundland." Studies in Political Economy No. 5 (Spring 1981): 127-143.

1463. Newman, Peter C. The Canadian Establishment, 2 vols. Toronto: McClelland and Stewart, 1981.

1464. Niosi, Jorge. Canadian Capitalism: A Study of Power in the Canadian Business Establishment. Toronto: 1981.

1465. Noisi, Jorge. "The Canadian Bourgeoisie: Towards a Synthetical Approach." Canadian Journal of Political and Social Theory 7 (1983): 128-149.

1466. Normandeau, Andre. "Le systeme de justice est-il raciste?" Canadian Journal of Criminology 31 (October 1989): 591- 603.

1467. Oiwa, K. "The Structure of Dispersal: The Japanese-Canadian Community of Montreal 1942-1952." Canadian Ethnic Studies 18 (1986): 20-37.

1468. Ontario Human Rights Commission. Working Together: Strategy for Race Relations in Ontario. April 1982. ERIC ED 230 661.

1469. Oriedger, Leo and Richard Mezoff. "Ethnic Prejudice and Discrimination in Winnipeg High Schools." Canadian Journal of Sociology 6 (1981): 1-18.

1470. Ornstein, Michael. "The Development of Class in Canada." In Introduction to Sociology: An Alternate Approach, edited by J. Paul Grayson, 216-259. Toronto: Sage, 1983.

1471. Ornstein, Michael. "Social Organization of the Canadian Capitalist Class in Comparative Perspective." Canadian Review of Sociology and Anthropology 26 (1989): 151-177.

1472. Palmer, Bryan. "Working-Class Canada: Recent Historical Writing." Queen's Quarterly 86 (1979): 594-616.

1473. Palmer, Howard. Patterns of Prejudice: A History of Nativism in Alberta. Toronto: McClelland and Stewart, 1982.

1474. Paton, L. and J. Deverell, eds. Prejudice in Social Studies Textbooks: A Content Analysis of Social Studies Textbooks Used in Saskatchewan Schools. Saskatoon: Saskatchewan Human Rights Commission, 1974.

1475. Peitchinis, Stephen G. Women at Work: Discrimination and Response. Toronto: McClelland & Stewart, 1989.

1476. Pentland, H. Clare. "The Development of a Capitalist Labour Market in Canada." Candian Journal of Economics and Political Science 25 (1959): 450-461.

1477. Pentland, H. Clare. Labour and Capital in Canada, 1650- 1860. Toronto: 1981. [Ed. by Paul Phillips.]

1478. Podoluk, J. R. "The Size Distribution of Personal Wealth in Canada." Review of Income and Wealth 20 (June 1974): 203-216.

1479. Polyzoi, E. "Psychologists' Perceptions of the Canadian Immigrant before World War II." Canadian Ethnic Studies 18 (1986): 52-65.

1480. Pratt, Geraldine. "Housing Tenure and Social Cleavages in Urban Canada." Annals of the Association of American Geographics 76 (September 1986): 366-380.

1481. Prentice, Alison and others. Canadian Women: A History. Toronto: Harcourt Brace Jovanovich, 1988.

1482. Progress Towards Equality: Proceedings of the National Symposium Held on 16-18 September 1988. Vancouver: Committee for Racial Justice, 1989.

1483. Pugh, Terry. "Fear and Loathing in the Heartland." Canadian Dimension 20 (1986): 4-7. [Rightist extremist groups in Canadian farm areas.]

1484. Racial and Ethnic Discrimination in Employment. Toronto: Social Planning Council of Metro Toronto, February 1982.

1485. Rahim, Aminur. "Multiculturalism or Ethnic Hegemony: A Critique of Multicultural Education in Toronto." Journal of Ethnic Studies 18 (Fall 1990): 29-46.

1486. Ramcharan, Subhar. Racism: Nonwhites in Canada. Toronto: Butterworths, 1982.

1487. Reitz, J. G. "Less Racial Discrimination in Canada or Simply Less Racial Conflict? Implications of Comparisons with Britain." Canadian Public Policy 14 (December 1988)

1488. Renaud, L. A Study in the Persistence of Poor Working Conditions and Low Status: Immigrant Domestic Workers in Canada. Master's thesis: Carleton University, 1984.

1489. Richards, John and L.R. Pratt. Prairie Capitalism: Power and Influence in the New West. Toronto: 1979.

1490. Roberts, B. "Shovelling Out the Mutinous': Political Deportation from Canada before 1936." Labour 18 (1986)

1491. Rosenbluth, David. Economic Inequality in Canada: The Effects of Region, Ethnicity and Gender on Earnings. Doctoral dissertation: York University (Canada), 1985.

1492. Ross, David P. The Canadian Fact Book on Poverty, 1989. Ottawa: Canadian Council on Social Development, 1989.

1493. Russell, Bob. "The Politics of Labour-Force Reproduction Funding Canada's Social Wage, 1917-1946." Studies in Political Economy No. 14 (Summer 1984): 43-73.

1494. Ryerson, Stanley B. and others. 150 Ans de Lutte: Histoire du mouvement ouvrier au Québec, 1825-1976. Montreal: Confédération des syndicats nationaux- Corporation des enseignants du Québec, 1979.

1495. Ryerson, Stanley B. 1837: The Birth of Canadian Democracy. Toronto: Francis White, 1937.

1496. Ryerson, Stanley B. *Le Capitalisme et la Confédération: Aux sources du conflit, Canada-Québec, 1760-1873*. Montreal: Parti Pris, 1978.

1497. Ryerson, Stanley B. *The Founding of Canada: Beginnings to 1815*. Toronto: Progress, 1975.

1498. Ryerson, Stanley B. *French Canada: A Study in Canadian Democracy* (New edition). Toronto: 1980.

1499. Ryerson, Stanley B. *Unequal Union: Confederation and the Roots of Conflict in the Canadas, 1815-1873*. Toronto: Progress, 1975.

1500. Sacouman, R. James. "Semi-Proletarianization and Rural Underdevelopment in the Maritimes." *Canadian Review of Sociology and Anthropology* 17 (August 1980)

1501. Sangster, Joan. *Dreams of Equality: Women on the Canadian Left, 1920-1950*. Toronto: McClelland & Steward, 1989.

1502. Satzewich, Vic. "Racism and Canadian Immigration Policy: The Government's View of Caribbean Migration, 1962-1966." *Canadian Ethnic Studies* 21 (1989): 77-97.

1503. Schecter, Stephen. "Capitalism, Class and Educational Reform in Canada." in *The Canadian State: Political Economy and Political Power* Leo Panitch (ed.), pp. 373-416. Toronto: 1977.

1504. Sears, Alan. "Immigration Controls as Social Policy: The Case of Canadian Medical Inspection 1900-1920." *Studies in Political Economy* No. 33 (Autumn 1990): 91-112.

1505. Shaw, R. P. "The Burden of Unemployment in Canada." *Canadian Public Policy* 11 (June 1985)

1506. Shaw, R. P. "Unemployment and Low Family Incomes in Canada." *Canadian Public Policy* 12 (June 1986)

1507. Siddiq, Fazley. "The Size Distribution of Probate Wealthholdings in Nova Scotia in the Late 19th Century." *Acadiensis* 18 (1988): 136-147.

1508. Sider, Gerald M. *Culture and Class in Anthropology and History: A Newfoundland Illustration*. New York: Cambridge University Press, 1986.

1509. Smiley, D. V. *Canada in Question: Federalism in the Seventies*. Toronto: Mc-Graw-Hill Ryerson, 1976.

1510. Stasiulis, Daiva K. "Minority Resistance in the Local State: Toronto in the 1970s and 1980s." *Ethnic and Racial Studies* 12 (1989): 63-83.

CANADA - GENERAL   121

1511. Stasiulis, Daiva K. Race Ethnicity and the State: The Political Structuring of South Asian and West Indian Communal Action in Combatting Racism. Doctoral dissertation: University of Toronto, 1982.

1512. Stasiulis, Daviva K. "Racism and the Canadian State." Explorations in Ethnic Studies 8 (January 1985): 13-31.

1513. Stevenson, Paul. "Capital and State in Canada: Some Critical Questions on Carroll's Finance Capitalists." Studies in Political Economy No. 12 (Fall 1983): 163-167.

1514. Sunahara, Ann. The Politics of Racism. Toronto: James Lorimec and Co., 1981.

1515. Tarnopolsky, W. S. "Le controle de la discrimination." Les Cahiers de Droit 18 (December 1977): 663-689.

1516. Trainor, Catherine H. The Development of Affirmative Action in Canada 1960-1985. Master's thesis: Dalhousie University, 1986.

1517. Trudel, Marcel. L'Esclavage au Canada francais... 1960.

1518. Veltman, Calvin. "The Interpretation of the Language Questions of the Canadian Census." Canadain Review of Sociology & Anthropology 23 (August 1986): 412-422.

1519. Vipond, Mary. "Nationalism and Nativism: The Native Sons of Canada in the 1920's." Can. Rev. Stud. Nationalism 9 (Spring 1982): 81-95.

1520. Vorst, Jesse and others, eds. Race, Class, Gender: Bonds and Barriers. Toronto: Between the Lines, 1990.

1521. Wanner, Richard A. "Educational Inequality: Trends in Twentieth-Century Canada and the United States." Comparative Social Research 9 (1986): 47-66.

1522. Ward, Jim. Organizing for the Homeless. Ottawa: Canadian Council on Social Development, 1989.

1523. Ward, W. Peter. "Class and Race in the Social Structure of British Columbia, 1870-1939." B.C. Studies 45 (Spring 1980): 17-35.

1524. Weiermair, Klaus. "Secular Changes in Youth Labour Markets and Youth Unemployment in Canada." Relations Ind. 41 (1986): 469-490.

1525. Weinfeld, Morton. "The Development of Affirmative Action in Canada." Canadian Ethnic Studies 13 (1981): 23-39.

1526. Whitaker, R. Double Standard: The Secret History of Canadian Immigration. Toronto: Lester and Orpen Denys, 1987.

1527. Wilkinson, B. W. "Elementary and Secondary Education Policy in Canada: A Survey." Canadian Public Policy 12 (December 1986)

1528. Wilson, J. Donald. An Imperfect Past: Education and Society in Canadian History. Vancouver: 1984.

1529. Winn, C. "Affirmative Action and Visible Minorities: Eight Premises in Quest of Evidence." Canadian Public Policy 11 (December 1985)

1530. Woehrling, Jose. "Minority Cultural and Linguistic Rights and Equality Rights in the Canadian Charter of Rights and Freedoms." McGill Law Journal 31 (December 1985): 50-92.

1531. Wolfson, Michael C. "Stasis Amid Change. Income Inequality in Canada, 1965-1983." Review of Income and Wealth 32 (December 1986): 337-369.

1532. Wolfson, Michael C. "Wealth and the Distribution of Income, Canada 1969-1970." Review of Income and Wealth 25 (June 1979): 129-140.

1533. Wotherspoon, T. , The Political Economy of Canadian Schooling. Toronto: 1987.

1534. Zaffaroni, Irene G. The Great Chain of Being: Racism and Imperialism in Colonial Victoria, 1858-1871. Master's thesis: University of Victoria, Canada, 1987.

CAPE VERDE ISLANDS

1535. Carreira, Antonio. The People of the Cape Verde Islands: Exploitation and Emigration. London Translated by Christopher Ryfe: Hurst, 1983.

1536. Davidson, Basil. The Fortunate Isles: A Study in African Transformation. Trenton, NJ: Africa World Press, 1989.

1537. Foy, Colm. Cape Verde: Politics, Economics and Society. New York: Pinter, 1988.

1538. Meintel, Deidre. Race, Culture, and Portuguese Colonialism. Syracuse, New York: Maxwell School of Citizenship and Public Affairs, Syracuse University, 1984.

CENTRAL AFRICAN REPUBLIC

1539. Caprile, Jean. "French and African Languages in Central African Republic and Chad." <u>West Africa Journal of Modern Languages</u> (June 1978): 98-105.

1540. O'Toole, Thomas. <u>The Central African Republic: The Continent's Hidden Heart</u>. Boulder, CO.: Westview, 1986.

1541. Samarin, William J. "A Colonial Heritage of the Central African Republic: A Linguistic Perspective." <u>International Journal of African Historical Studies</u> 22 (1989): 697-712.

CHAD

1542. D'Azevedo, Mario. "Power and Slavery in Central Africa: Chad (1890-1925)." Journal of Negro History 68 (Fall 1982): 198-211.

1543. Gardinier, David E. "L'enseignement colonial français au Tchad (1900-1960)." Afrique Asie Mod. 161 (Summer 1989): 59-71.

1544. Orobator, S. E. "Civil Strife and International Involvement: The Case of Chad (1964-1983)." Africa (Italy) 39 (1984): 300-316.

1545. Reyna, S. P. Wars Without End: The Political Economy of a Precolonial African State. Hanover, NH: University Press of New England, 1990.

1546. Whiteman, Kaye. Chad. London: MInority Rights Group, 1988.

CHILE

1547. Bulnes A., Gonzalo. Los Mapuches y la tierra: politica y legislacion chilena respecto al pueblo mapuche (2nd revised edition). Santiago de Chile: PAS, n.d.

1548. "Chile Indigena." America indigena 48 (1988): entire issue.

1549. Chuchryk, Patricia. Protest, Politics and Personal Life: The Emergence of Feminism in a Military Dictatorship, Chile, 1973-1983. Doctoral dissertation: University of Toronto, 1984.

1550. Constable, Pamela. "Children Bear Scars of Repression." Boston Globe, (December 22, 1985) [In Pinochet's Chile, the PIDEE School (For Youth Damaged by the States of Emergency).]

1551. Dubet, Francois and others. Pobladores: luttes sociales et democratie au Chili. Paris: Editions l'Harmattan, 1989.

1552. Echeverria, Rafael. "Politica educacional y transformacion an del sistema de educacion en Chile a partir de 1973." Revista mexicana de sociologia 44 (1982): 529-557.

1553. Farrell, Joseph P. The National Unified School in Allende's Chile: The Role of Education in the Destruction of a Revolution. Vancouver: University of British Columbia Press, 1986.

1554. Flushe, Della M. and Eugene H. Korth. Forgotten Females: Women of African and Indian Descent in Colonial Chile, 1535-1800. Detroit, MI: Blaine Ethridge Books, 1982.

1555. Foxley Rioseco, Felipe and Jorge Rodriquez Grossi. Los derechos economico-sociales del hombre. Santiago de Chile: Instituto Chileno de Estudios Humanisticos, 1986.

1556. Fruhling Ehrlich, Hugo , Represion politica y defensa de los derechos humanos. Santiago de Chile: Centro de Estudios Sociales Ltda.: 1986.

1557. Garcia H., Alvaro and John Wells. "Chile: A Laboratory for Failed Experiments in Capitalist Political Economy." Cambridge Economic Journal 7 (September-December 1983): 287-304.

1558. Grugel, Jean. "Nationalist Movements and Fascist Ideology in Chile." Bulletin of Latin American Research 4 (1985): 109-122.

1559. Labarca, Guillermo. Educacion y sociedad: Chile, 1964-1984. Amsterdam: Centro de Estudios y Documentacion Latinoamericanos, 1985.

1560. Labarca Huberston, Amanda. Feminismo Contemporaneo. Santiago: Zig Zag, 1947. [Esp. Chile.]

1561. Loveman, Brian. Chile. The Legacy of Hispanic Capitalism. 2d ed. New York: Oxford University Press, 1988.

1562. Martinez, Javier and Eduardo Valenzuela. "Chilean Youth and Social Exclsuion." CEPAL Review No. 29 (August 1986): 93-106.

1563. Mattelart, Armand and Michele Mattelart. La mujer chilena en una nueva sociedad: un estudio exploratorio acerca de la situacion e imagen de la mujer en Chile. Translated by J. Budge de Ducci: Santiago Edit. del Pacifico, 1968.

1564. Mellafe, Rollando. La introduccion de la esclavitud negra en Chile: trafico y rutas. Santiago: 1959.

1565. Mihovilovic Eterovic, Milenko. 1000 datos: 15 anos de retroceso para el trabajador y su organizacion. Santiago de Chile: Editorial Ariete, 1989. [During period of Pinochet rule.]

1566. Moran, Theordore H. Multinational Corporations and the Politics of Dependence. Princeton, NJ: Princeton University Press, 1974.

1567. Notle, Detlef. Zwischen Rebellion und Integration: Gewerkschaften in der chilenischen Politik. Fort Lauderdale, FL: Verlag Breitenbach Publishers, 1986.

1568. O'Brien, T. F. "'Rich Beyond the Dreams of Avarice': The Guggenheims in Chile." Business History Review 63 (Spring 1989)

1569. Pizzaro, C. La huelga obrera en Chile, 1890-1970. Santiago de Chile: Ediciones Sur, 1986.

1570. Przeworski, Joanne F. The Decline of the Copper Industry in Chile and the Entrance of North American Capital, 1870-1916. New York: Arno Press, 1980.

1571. Rodriquez, Jorge. El papel redistributivo del gasto social: Chile. Santiago de Chile: Centro de Estudios Publicos, 1983.

1572. Rodriquez Grossi, Jorge. Distribution del ingreso y el gasto social en Chile. Santiago de Chile: Editorial Salesiana, 1983.

1573. Rosenberg, Tina. "Pinochet's Chile: Order and Chaos." Present Tense 15 (November-December 1987): 16-22. [Jews in Chile.]

1574. Stever, Tammie L. National Integration and Marginality among the Mapuche Indians of Chile. Master's thesis: University of Kansas, Lawrence, 1987.

1575. Tirono Barrios, Eugenio. Los silencios de la revolucion: Chile: la otra cara de la modernizacion. Puerta Abierta: 1988. [Standard of living for workers, poor, and others.]

1576. U. S. Congress, 99th 1st session, Committee on Foreign Affairs, Subcommittee on Human Rights and International Organizations. Human Rights in Chile: Hearing... Washington, D.C.: GPO, 1985.

1577. Urzua F., Raul and Patricio Dooner D., eds. La opcion preferencial por los pobres: de la teoria a la practica. Santiago de Chile: Centro de Investigaciones Socioculturales Roberto Bellarmino, 1987.

1578. Valdes, Juan G. La Escuela de Chicago: operacion Chile. Buenos Aires, Argentina: Grupo Editorial Zeta S.A., 1989.

1579. Valdes Bunstr, Gustavo. El Poder Economico de los Jesuitas en Chile (1593-1767). Santiago: Imprenta Pucara, 1985.

1580. Vidal, Virginia. La emacipacion de la mujer. Santiago: Ed. Nacional Quinantu, 1972.

1581. Winn, Peter. Weavers of Revolution: The Yarur Workers and Chile's Road to Socialism. New York: Oxford University Press, 1986.

CHINA

NATIONAL MINORITIES

1582. Avedon, John. <u>In Exile From the Land of Snows</u>. New York: Knopf, 1984. [Touches on role of CIA in Tibet.]

1583. Beckwith, Christopher I. <u>Tibetan Empire</u>. Princeton, NJ: Princeton University Press, 1987.

1584. Benson, Linda. <u>The Ili Rebellion: A Study of Chinese Policy on Xinjiang (1944-1949)</u>. Armonk, New York: Sharpe, 1989.

1585. Birnbaum, Norman. <u>Communist China's Policy Toward Her Minority Nationalities: 1950-1965</u>. Doctoral dissertation: St. John's University, 1970. UMO # 7025590.

1586. Butterfield, Fox. "Moslems Prospering in Rugged Chinese Border Area." <u>New York Times</u>, (October 29, 1980) [Turpan, Xinjiang.]

1587. Chae-Jin Lae. <u>China's Korean Minority: The Politics of Ethnic Education</u>. Boulder, CO: Westview Press, 1986.

1588. Chang, Hajji Yusuf. "The Hui (Muslim) Minority in China: An Historical Overview." <u>Journal (Institute of Muslim Minority Affairs)</u> 8 (1987): 62-78.

1589. Chao, Wei Wang. <u>Evolutionary Theory and Cultural Diversity: A Study of the Ethnology of China's National Minorities</u>. Doctoral dissertation: University of California, Berkeley, 1986. UMO # 8624729.

1590. Chiao, Chien and Nicholas Tapp, eds. <u>Ethnicity and Ethnic Groups in China</u>. Hong Kong: Chinese University of Hong Kong, New Asia College, 1989.

1591. <u>China's Minority Nationalities (1)</u>. Beijing: China Reconstructs, 1984.

1592. "China's National Minorities." Beijing Review (May 23, 1983) [1982 statistics of population, economy, and education.]

1593. Clark, Paul. "Ethnic Minorities in Chinese Films: Cinema and the Exotic." East-West Film Journal 1 (June 1987): 15-31.

1594. Clothing and Ornaments of China's Miao People. Beijing: Nationality Press, 1987.

1595. Crook, David. "Tibet: Need for Balanced Presentation." Beijing Review (October 12, 1987)

1596. Davis, Horace B. "Nationalism and the Chinese Revolution." In Toward a Marxist Theory of Nationalism Horace B. Davis. New York: Monthly Review Press, 1978.

1597. Deal, David. "'The Question of Nationalities' in Twentieth Century China." Journal of Ethnic Studies 12 (Fall 1984): 23-53.

1598. Diamond, Norma. "The Miao and Poison: Interactions on China's Southwest Frontier." Ethnology 27 (1988): 1-25. [Han-Miao interaction.]

1599. Diao, Richard. "The National Minorities of China and their Relation with the Chinese Communist Regime." In Southeast Asian Tribes, Minorities, and Nations, edited by Peter Kunstadter. Princeton, NJ: Princeton University Press, 1967.

1600. Dowdle, Nancy B. The Dai People: A National Minority in the Chinese Revolution. Master's thesis: University of Hawaii, 1979.

1601. Dreyer, June T. China's Forty Millions: Minority Nationality and National Integration in the People's Republic of China. Cambridge, MA: Harvard University Press, 1976.

1602. Fan Wenlan. "Problems of Conflict and Fusion of Nationalities in Chinese History." Social Sciences in China 1 (March 1980): 71-82.

1603. Fei Hsiao Tung. "On the Social Transformation of China's National Minorities." in Towards a People's Anthropology. Beijing: New World Press, 1981.

1604. Forbes, Andrew D. W. Warlords and Muslims in Chinese Central Asia: A Political History of Republican Sinkiang, 1911-1949. New York: Cambridge University Press, 1986.

1605. Gargan, Edward A. "A 1,000-Year-Old Culture with Few Tomorrows." New York Times, (May 25, 1987) [Miao minority in Hunan province.]

1606. Goldstein, Melvyn C. A History of Modern Tibet, 1913-1951. The Demise of the Lamaist State. Berkeley: University of California Press, 1989.

CHINA - NATIONAL MINORITIES

1607. Grunfeld, A. Tom. The Making of Modern Tibet. London: Zed Press, 1987.

1608. Heaton, William R., Jr. "The Minorities and the Military in China." Armed Forces and Society 3 (Winter 1977): 325-346.

1609. Heberer, Thomas. Bremer Beitrage zur Geographie und Raumsplanung. Bremen: Universitat Bremen, Druckschriftenlager, 1984.

1610. Heberer, Thomas. China and Its National Minorities: Autonomy or Assimilation? Armonk, New York: Sharpe, 1989.

1611. Heberer, Thomas. "Die Bevolkerungspolitik gegenuber den ethnischen Minoritaten in der Volksrepublik China." Zeitschrift fur die Bevolkerungswissenschaft 9 (1983): 259-273.

1612. Helly, Denise. "Mouvements nationalitaires en Republique Populaire de Chine: Le cas des Muslinans du Xinjiang (1949-1963)." Pluriel Nos. 32-33 (1982-1983): 87-100.

1613. Honig, Emile. "Invisible Inequalities. The Status of Sutei People in Contemporary Shanghai." China Quarterly No. 122 (June 1990)

1614. Honig, Emile. "The Politics of Prejudice: Sutei People in Republican Era Shanghai." Modern China 15 (July 1989): 243-274.

1615. Huang Shoubao and Liu Zonghe. Ethnic Costume from Guihou. Clothing Designs and Decorations from Minority Ethnic Groups in Southwest China. Beijing: Foreign Languages Press, 1987.

1616. Klatt, W. "The Staff of Life: Living Standards in China, 1977-1981." China Quarterly 93 (March 1983)

1617. Kwong, J. and H. Xiao. "Educational Equality Among China's Minorities." Comparative Education 25 (1989)

1618. Kwong, J. "Theoretical Basis of China's Politics Toward Her Minority Nationalities." Ethnicity 7 (June 1980): 203-217.

1619. Lee, Chae-Jin. China's Korean Minority: The Politics of Ethnic Education. Boulder, CO: Westview Press, 1986.

1620. Leong, S. T. "The Hakka Chinese of Lingnan: Ethnicity and Social Change in Modern Times." In Ideal and Reality: Social and Political Change in Modern China, 1860-1949, edited by David Pong and Edmund S.K. Fung. Lanham, MD: University Press of America, 1985.

1621. Liao, H. S. "Growing Unrest among Sinkiang's Ethnic Minorities." Issues and Studies 26 (May 1990)

1622. Llata, Richard and Mario Barrera. "The Chinese National Minorities Policy." Aztlan 6 (Fall 1975): 379-408.

1623. Lu Yun. "Expediting Development in Minority Areas." Beijing Review (March 27, 1989):

1624. Lu Yun. "Inner Mongolia Scores Historic Progress." Beijing Review (September 7, 1987):

1625. Ma Yin and others. Questions and Answers about China's Minority Nationalities. Beijing, China: New World Press, 1985.

1626. McKenzie, Eric F. Chinese Communist Policy toward Minority Nationalities in the Xinjiang-Uighur Autonomous Region in the Context of the Sino-Soviet Dispute, 1956-1965. Doctoral dissertation: University of Virginia, 1986. UMO # 8700695.

1627. McMillen, Donald H. Chinese Communist Power and Policy in Xinjiang, 1949-1977. Boulder, CO: Westview Press, 1979.

1628. Meserve, Walter J. and Ruth I. Meserve. "Theater for Assimilation: China's National Minorities." Journal of Asian History 13 (1979): 95-120.

1629. Ming Yin. United and Equal- The Progress of China's Minority Nationalities. Peking: Foreign Language Press, 1977.

1630. Moseley, George Van Horn, III, The Party and the National Question in China. Cambridge, MA: MIT Press, 1966.

1631. Mullin, Chris and Phuntsog Wangyal. The Tibetans: Two Perspectives on Tibetan-Chinese Relations. (New edition). London: Minority Rights Group, 1983.

1632. Nam, Jung H. Korean Minority Nationality in China: A Case Study of China's Minority Nationalities Policy. Doctoral dissertation: University of Connecticut, 1989. UMO # 9003822.

1633. Newby, Laura J. The Rise of Nationalism in Eastern Turkestan, 1930-1950. Doctoral dissertation: University of Oxford, 1986. Order No. BRD-90101.

1634. Norbu, Dawa. Red Star Over Tibet. New York: Envoy Press/Apt Books, 1988.

1635. Norbu, Dawa. "The Tibetan Response to Chinese 'Liberation'." Asian Affairs 2 (1975): 264-274.

1636. Parkins, Geoffrey. "China Aids Illiterate Minorities." Times Higher Education Supplement, (June 13, 1986):

1637. "Party Members and Muslims." Beijing Review, (March 7, 1988) [Ningxia Hvi Autonomous Region.]

1638. Pien, F. K. "The Population of Chinese Minority Nationalities." Issues and Studies 26 (April 1990):

1639. Pillsbury, Barbara L. K. Chronology of Muslim History in China. London: Institute of Muslim Minority Affairs, 1985.

1640. Posten, D. L., Jr. and J. Shu. "The Demographic and Socioeconomic Composition of China's Ethnic Minorities." Population and Development Review 13 (December 1987)

1641. "Questions and Answers on the Lhasa Riots." Beijing Review, (November 21, 1988) [Interview on events of Sept.-Oct. 1987 and March 1988.]

1642. Sanjorj, M. Manchu Chinese Colonial Rule in Northern Mongolia. New York Translated by Urgunge Ovon: St. Martin's Press, 1980.

1643. Schermerhorn, R. S. The Muslim Minority in China. London: Institute of Muslim Minority Affairs, 1985.

1644. Schwartz, Ronald D. "Reform and Repression in Tibet." Telos No. 80 (Summer 1989): 7-25.

1645. Schwarz, Henry G. Chinese Policies Towards Minorities. An Essay and Documents. Bellingham: Program in East Asian Studies, Western Washington State College, 1971.

1646. Schwarz, Henry G. The Minorities of Northern China: A Survey. Bellingham: Western Washington University, 1984.

1647. Schwarz, Henry G. "The Treatment of Minorities." In Developmental Experience, edited by Michael Oksenburg. New York: Praeger, 1973.

1648. Shen Che. Life among the Minority Nationalities. Beijing: Foreign Languages Press, 1987.

1649. Shifu, Z. and D.Y.H. Wu. "Ethnic Conflict Management in Yunnan, China." In Ethnic Conflict. International Perspectives, edited by Jerry Boucher and others. Newbury Park, CA: Sage, 1987.

1650. Shu, Jing. Minority Nationalities in China: Their Social Formation, Geographical Location, and Differential from the Han Majority. Doctoral dissertation: University of Texas, 1989. UMO # 8920841.

1651. Tam, Sui-Mi and David Y.H. Wu. "Minorities Policy in the People's Republic of China: Its Implications in Southeast Asia." South East Asia Journal of Social Science 16 (1988): 78-95.

134 WORLD RACISM AND RELATED INHUMANITIES

1652. Thaxton, Ralph. "The Peasants of Yaocun: Memories of Exploitation, Injustice, and Liberation in a Chinese Village." Journal of Peasant Studies 9 (1981): 3-46.

1653. Tibetans on Tibet. Beijing: China Reconstructs, 1988.

1654. Tsepon W.D. Shakabpa. Tibet: A Political History. New York: Potala Publications, 1984.

1655. Wang, Livia A. The Development of Minorities Nationalities Policy in the People's Republic of China to 1965. Master's thesis: University of California, Berkeley, 1978.

1656. Wu, D. Y. H. "Chinese Minority Policy and the Meaning of Minority Culture: The Example of Bai in Yunnan, China." Human Organization 49 (Spring 1990)

1657. Wu, Michael R. The Mongolian Autonomous Movement of the 1930's. Master's thesis: Brigham Young University, 1978.

1658. Wu Naitao. "Tibet Opens to the Outside World." Beijing Review (October 19, 1987)

1659. Zhang, Tianlu. "Tibet's Population Develops." Beijing Review (August 17, 1987)

1660. Zhu Li. "The Tibet Myth vs. Reality." Beijing Review (October 12, 1987)

CHINA - GENERAL

1661. Andors, Phyllis. The Unfinished Liberation of Chinese Women, 1949-1980. Bloomington: Indiana University Press, 1983.

1662. Ashbrook, Tom. "Chinese Puzzle: How to Loosen Lid but Hang on to Best and Brightest." Boston Globe, (October 12, 1987) [Reluctance of Chinese students in U.S. universities to return to China.]

1663. "Attitude Survey of City Dwellers." Beijing Review, (February 1, 1988) [Fall 1987, in 324 cities.]

1664. Bettelheim, Charles. "Economic Reform in China." Journal of Development Studies 24 (1988): 15-49.

1665. Bix, Herbert. "Japanese Imperialism and the Manchurian Economy 1900-1931." China Quarterly, No. 51 (1972): 425-443.

1666. Blecher, Marc. "Inequality and Socialism in Rural China: A Conceptual Note." World Development 13 (January 1985)

1667. Blecher, Marc. "Peasant Labor for Urban Industry: Temporary Contract Labor, Urben-Rural Balance and Class Relations in a Chinese Rural County." World Development 11 (1983): 731-745.

1668. Burns, John F. "A Bit of Vietnam Is Planted in China." New York Times, (December 31, 1985) [Ethnic Chinese formerly of Vietnam, now residing in China.]

1669. Burton, Margaret Ernestine. The Education of Women in China. New York: Fleming H. Revell Co., 1911.

1670. Chaffee, John W. The Thorny Gates of Learning in Sung China: A Social History of Examinations. New York: Cambridge University Press, 1985.

1671. Chen, Ching-chi. "Impact of Japanese Colonial Rule on Taiwanese Elites." Journal of Asian History 22 (1988): 25- 51.

1672. Chen Qiuping. "School Dropouts a Major Problem." Beijing Review, (October 19, 1987)

1673. Chen Xiao. "Causes Given for Income Unfairness." Beijing Review, (November 14, 1988)

1674. Chiang, Yung-Chen. Social Engineering and the Social Sciences in China, 1898-1949. Doctoral dissertation: Harvard University, 1986. UMO # 8704472.

1675. Chien Lin, Sharon. "Historical Development of a Library Education in China." Journal of Library History 20 (1985): 368-386.

1676. Chossudovsky, Michel. "China and the International Division of Labour." Studies in Political Economy No. 10 (Winter 1983): 73-97.

1677. Copper, John F. and others. Human Rights in Post-Mao China. Boulder, CO: Westview Press, 1985.

1678. Croll, Elisabeth. Chinese Women Since Mao. M.E. Sharpe, 1984.

1679. Crossley, Pamela Kyle. "The Qianlong Retrospect on the Chinese-Martial Banners." Late Imperial China , 10 (June 1989): 62-107.

1680. Crossley, Pamela Kyle. "Thinking about Ethnicity in Early Modern China." Late Imperial China (Summer 1990):

1681. Curran, Thomas D. Education and Society in Republican China. Doctoral dissertation: Columbia University, 1986. UMO # 8610752.

1682. Dai Yannian. "Dealing With Unfair Income Gaps." Beijing Review (August 15, 1988):

1683. Davis, Deborah. "Chinese Social Welfare: Policies and Outcomes." China Quarterly , No. 119 (September 1989)

1684. Davis-Friedman, Deborah. "Intergenerational Inequalities and the Chinese Revolution: The Importance of Age-Specific Inequalities for the Creation and Maintenance of Social Strata Within a State-Socialist Society." Modern China 11 (April 1985)

1685. De Francis, John. The Chinese Language: Fact and Fantasy. Honolulu: University of Hawaii Press, 1984.

1686. Deane, Hugh. "Mao's Rural Policies Revisited." Monthly Review 40 (March 1989): 1-9. [See William H. Hinton, below.]

CHINA - GENERAL 137

1687. Dikotter, F. "Group Definition and the Idea of Race in Modern China (1793-1949)." Ethnic and Racial Studies 13 (July 1990)

1688. Duus, Peter. "Japan's Informal Empire in China 1895-1937." In The Japanese Informal Empire in China, 1895-1937, edited by Duus and others. Princeton, NJ: Princeton University Press, 1989.

1689. Edwards, R. Randle and others. Human Rights in Contemporary China. New York: Columbia University Press, 1986.

1690. Erkes, E. Das Problem der Sklaverei in China. Berlin: 1954.

1691. Feuchtwang, Stephen and Athar Hussain, eds. The Chinese Economic Reforms. New York: 1983.

1692. Feuerwerker, Albert. "Japanese Imperialism in China: A Commentary." In The Japanese Informal Empire in China, 1895- 1937, edited by Peter Duus and others. Princeton, N.J.: Princeton University Press, 1989.

1693. Gao Yuan. "In China, Black Isn't Beautiful." New York Times, (January 25, 1989):

1694. Gargan, Edward A. "China's Unhappy Chosen." New York Times, (December 26, 1986) [Demonstrations by university students.]

1695. Gaskell, A. The Colonization and Settlement of Manchuria. Master's thesis: University of Liverpool, 1932.

1696. Gergere, Marie-Claire. The Golden Age of the Chinese Bourgeoisie, 1911-1937. New York: Cambridge University Press, 1990.

1697. Gipoulon, Catherine. "The Emergence of Women in Politics in China, 1898-1927." Chinese Studies in History 23 (Winter 1989-1990): 46-67.

1698. Griggin, Keith , Institutional Reform and Economic Development in the Chinese Countryside. Armonk, New York: Sharpe, 1985.

1699. Guan, Shijie. "Chartism and the First Opium War." History Workshop No. 24 (1987): 17-31.

1700. Guisso, Richard W. and Stanley Johannesen, eds. Women in China: Current Directions in Historical Scholarship. Youngstown, New York: Philo Press, 1981.

1701. Hager, Mark M. "Law and the Political Economy of Repression in Deng's China." American University Journal of International Law and Policy , 5 (Spring 1990): 773-834.

1702. He Dougchang. "Campus Unrest: Result of 'Liberalization'." Beijing Review (February 23, 1987)

1703. Hermann-Pillath, Carsten. Lebenskrisen, soziale Sicherung und Krise der Reformspolitik der VR China. Cologne: Bundesinstitut fur Ostwissenschaftliche und Internationale Studien, 1990.

1704. Hershatter, Gail. The Workers of Tianjin, 1900-1949. Stanford, CA: Stanford University Press, 1986.

1705. Hinton, William H. "Dazhai Revisited." Monthly Review 39 (March 1988): 34-50. [Economic reform and standards of living.]

1706. Hinton, William H. The Great Reversal. The Privatization of China 1978-1989. New York: Monthly Review Press, 1990.

1707. Hinton, William H. "A Response to Hugh Deane." Montly Review 40 (March 1989): 10-36. [See Hugh Deane, above.]

1708. Honig, Emily. Sisters and Strangers: Women in the Shanghai Cotton Mills, 1919-1949. Stanford, CA: Stanford University Press, 1986.

1709. Hooper, Beverley. Youth in China. Penguin, 1985.

1710. Howard, Pat. Breaking the Iron Rice Bowl: Prospects for Socialism in China's Countryside. Armonk, New York: Sharpe, 1987.

1711. Howard, Pat and Roger Howard. "China's Workers: Prospects for Self Management." Studies in Political Economy No. 18 (Fall 1985): 69-106.

1712. Hsiao, Wey. Changes in Class Structure and Reward Distribution in Postwar Taiwan. Doctoral dissertation: Indiana University, 1987. UMO # 8717801.

1713. Hu Jimkai and Zhao Yining. "University Students and Higher Education." Beijing Review (February 23, 1987)

1714. Hussain, Athar and Nicholas Stern. On the Recent Increase in Death Rate in China. London: STICERD: London School of Economics, 1990. [China Paper #8.]

1715. Jamison, D. T. "Child Malnutrition and School Performance." Journal of Development Economics 20 (March 1986)

1716. Johnson, Kay Ann. Women, the Family and Peasant Revolution in China. Chicago, IL: 1983.

1717. Kuo Mo-jo. "La societe esclavagiste chinoise." Recherches internationales a la lumiere du marxisme 2 (1957): 153-164.

1718. Lamontagne, Jacques. "Educational Development in the PRC: Regional and Ethnic Disparities." Issues and Studies 22 (1986): 73-94.

CHINA - GENERAL

1719. Lamontagne, Jacques. "Educational Disparities in Mainland China-Characteristics and Trends." Issues and Studies 25 (December 1989)

1720. Lee, Robert Stuart. France and the Exploitation of China: A Study in Economic Imperialism, 1885-1901. New York: Oxford University Press, 1989.

1721. Lee, Stephen B. S. La iglesia catolica en la Republica Popular de China: Las relaciones iglesia-estado durante 1948- 1988. Doctoral dissertation: University of Navarrone (Spain), 1989.

1722. Leung, Trini. Smashing the Iron Rice Pot: Workers and Unions in China's Market Socialism. Hong Kong: Asia Monitor Resource Center, 1988.

1723. Levey, Richard. "The Chinese Student Demontrations." Monthly Review 39 (September 1987): 31-43.

1724. Li Maoguan. "Why 'Laws Go Unenforced'." Beijing Review (September 11, 1989) [In China.]

1725. Lin Wei and Arnold Chao, eds. China's Economic Reforms. Philadelphia: 1982.

1726. Liu Chia-yi. "The Treatment of Aliens As Viewed from the Chinese Legal Thought, Treaties and Legislation." Journal of Social Science (Taiwan) 22 (1973): 197-262.

1727. Liu Jianjun. "The Privatization of Urban Housing." Beijing Review (November 14, 1988)

1728. Liu Suinian and Wu Lungan, eds. The Outline History of China's Socialist Economy (1949-1984). Beijing: Beijing Review, 1985.

1729. Liu Xiaojun. "Politics, Law and Culture: Historical Difference Between China and West." Beijing Review (July 10, 1989)

1730. Losang Chenlei. "Government Functionary Discusses Religion." Beijing Review (August 14, 1989) [Interview.]

1731. Mackerras, Colin. "Education in the Guomindang Period, 1928-1949." In Ideal and Reality: Social and Political Change in Modern China, 1860-1949, edited by David Pong and Edmund S. K. Fung. Lanham, MD: University Press of America, 1985.

1732. Martin, Michael F. "Bias and Inequality in Rural Incomes in Post-Reform." Journal of Peasant Studies 17 (January 1990)

1733. McDermott, Joseph P. "Bondservants in the T'ai-hu Basin During the Late Ming: A Case of Mistaken Identities." Journal of Asian Studies 40 (1981): 675-701.

1734. Meijer, Marinus J. "Slavery at the End of the Ch'ing Dynasty." In Essays on China's Legal Tradition, edited by Jerome Alan Cohen and others. 327-358. Princeton, N.J.: Printeton University Press, 1980.

1735. Moser, Leo J. "Racial, Ethnic, and Subethnic Conflict among the Chinese." International Journal of Group Tensions 19 (1989): 8-27, 97-116.

1736. Nathan, Andrew. Chinese Democracy. New York: Knopf, 1985.

1737. Ono Kazuko. Chinese Women in a Century of Revolution, 1850- 1950. Stanford, CA: Stanford University Press, 1989.

1738. Park, Henry. The Political Economy of Counterrevolution in China: 1976-1984. Cambridge, MA: MIM Distributors, 1985.

1739. Piazza, Alan L. Food Consumption and Nutritional Status. Boulder, CO.: Westview, 1986. [People's Republic of China.]

1740. Pokora, Timoteus. "Existierte in China eine Sklavenhaltergesellschaft?" Archivo orientalni 31 (1963): 353-363.

1741. Pulleyblank, E. G. "The Origins and Nature of Chattel Slavery in China." Journal of the Economic and Social History of the Orient 1 (1958): 201-205.

1742. Riskin, Carl. China's Political Economy: The Quest for Development Since 1949. New York: Oxford University Press, 1987.

1743. No entry

1744. Robinson, Jean C. "Decentralization, Money, and Power: The Case of People-Run Schools in China." Comparative Education Review 30 (February 1986): 73-88.

1745. Rofel, Lisa B. Eating Out of One Big Pot: Hegemony and Resistance in a Chinese Factory. Doctoral dissertation: Stanford University, 1989. UMO # 8925939.

1746. Rosen, Stanley. "Prosperity, Privatization, and China's Youth." Problems of Communism 34 (March-April 1985): 1-28.

1747. Rosen, Stanley. "Recentraliztion, Decentralization, and Rationalization: Deng Xiaoping's Bifurcated Educational Policy." Modern China 11 (July 1985): 301-346.

1748. Salzman, Mark. "Of Confucius, 'E.T.' and Happiness Candy." New York Times Magazine (December 21, 1986): [Foreign teacher in China, August 1982-July 1984.]

1749. Scitovsky, Tibor. "Economic Development in Taiwan and South Korea: 1965-1981." Food Research Institute Studies 19 (1985)

CHINA - GENERAL 141

1750. Snow, Helen Foster. Women in Modern China. The Hague: The Netherlands: Mouton and Co., 1967.

1751. Snow, Philip. The Star Raft: China's Encounter with Africa. Ithaca, New York: Cornell University Press, 1988.

1752. Spence, Jonathan D. Ts'ao Yin and the K'ang-hsi Emperor, Bondservant and Master. New Haven, CT: Yale University Press, 1966.

1753. Stacey, Judith. Patriarchy and Socialist Revolution in China. Berkeley: University of California Press, 1983.

1754. Stacey, Judith. "When Patriarchy Kowtows: The Significance of the Chinese Family Revolution for Feminist Theory." Feminist Studies 2 (1975): 64-112.

1755. State Statistical Bureau. "Changes in the Life-Style of Urban Residents." Beijing Review (November 14, 1988):

1756. State Statistical Bureau. "Education in Present Day China." Beijing Review (July 17, 1989)

1757. "Student Upheaval: What's It All About?" Beijing Review (February 23, 1987)

1758. Sudama, Trevor. "Analysis of Classes by Mao Tse Tung 1923-1939." Journal of Contemporary Asia 8 (1978): 355-373.

1759. Suryadinata, Leo. China and the Asian States. The Ethnic Chinese Dimension. Athens: Ohio University Press, 1987.

1760. Thogersen, Stig. "Through the Sheep's Intestines-Selection and Elitism in Chinese Schools." Australian Journal of Chinese Affairs 21 (1989): 29-56.

1761. Tian, Jujian. "When Did Feudalism Begin in China?" Social Sciences in China 1 (June 1980): 5-20.

1762. Tokei, F. "Die Formen der chinesischen patriarchalischen Sklaverei in der Chou-Zeit." Opuscula ethnologia memoriae Ludovici Biro Sacra (1959) [Budapest.]

1763. van Ginneken, W. K. "Employment and Labour Incomes in China, 1978-1986." Labour and Society 13 (1988): 55-78.

1764. Walder, Andrew. "The Remaking of the Chinese Working Class, 1949-1981." Modern China 10 (January 1984)

1765. Wang, I-t'ung. "Slaves and Other Comparable Social Groups During the Northern Dynasties, (386-618)." Harvard Journal of Asiatic Studies 16 (December 1953): 293-364.

1766. Warren, C. "Women in China and Southeast Asia: A Course Outline and Bibliography." Bulletin of Concerned Asian Scholars 22 (April-June 1990)

1767. Wasserstrom, Jeffrey and Xinyong Liu. "Student Protest and Student Life: Shanghai 1919-1949." Social History 14 (January 1989): 1-29.

1768. Watson, James L. "Chattel Slavery in Chinese Peasant Society: A Comparative Analysis." Ethnology 15 (1976): 361- 375.

1769. White, Lynn T., III. Policies of Chaos: the Organizational Causes of Violence in China's Cultural Revolution. Princeton, NJ: Princeton University Press, 1989.

1770. Wiens, Mi Chu. "The Origins of Modern Chinese Land-lordism." In Festschrift in Honor of the Eightieth Birthday of Professor Shen Kang-po, edited by Wang Pi-ch'eng, 289-344. Taipei: Lien-ying ch'u-pan shih-yeh King-ssu, 1976.

1771. Wiu, H. T. The Treatment of Europe in Chinese School Textbooks. Master's thesis: University of London, Institute of Education, 1949.

1772. Wolf, Margery and Roxanne Witke, eds. Women in Chinese Society. Stanford, CA: Stanford University Press, 1975.

1773. Wong, Kang-Kau B. Economics, Ideology and Education in China after Mao. Doctoral dissertation: University of Toronto, 1986.

1774. Wortzel, Larry M. Class in China: Stratification in a Classless Society. Westport, Ct: Greenwood, 1987.

1775. Xia Zhi. "Campus Incident in Nanjing." Beijing Review (January 23, 1989) [Racial factors in conflict involving African students.]

1776. Yahuda, Michael , New Directions in the Social Sciences and Humanities in China. New York: St, Martin's Press, 1986.

1777. Yoshinami, Takashi. "Patriarchal Domestic Slavery in Ancient China." Rebishigaku Kenkiju 462 (November 1978): 13-23.   [In Japanese.]

1778. Young, Lung-chang. "Regional Stereotypes in China." Chinese Studies in History 21 (1988): 32-57.

1779. Young, Marilyn Blatt, ed. Women in China: Studies in Social Change and Feminism. Ann Arbor: University of Michigan Center for Chinese Studies, 1973.

1780. Yue Daikun and Carolyn Wakeman. To the Storm, The Odyssey of a Revolutionary Chinese Woman. Berkeley: University of California Press, 1985. [Student leader inside and outside communist movement.]

1781. Zhang, X. "On the Contradiction between the Economic Growth Rate and Improvement of People's Well-Being." Chinese Economic Studies , 21 (Spring 1988):

1782. Zhang Shaowen and Wei Liming. "Combating Illiteracy in China." Beijung Review (February 16, 1987):

1783. Zhang Xinxin and Sang Ye. Chinese Lives. An Oral History of Contemporary China. New York Translated by W.J.F. Jenner andothers: Pantheon Press, 1987.

1784. Zhuang, Jiaying. Education and Social-class Structures: The Case of the People's Republic of China. Doctoral dissertation: University of California, Santa Barbara, 1989.

COLOMBIA

1785. Aguilera Peña, Mario. Los comuneros: Guerra Social y Lucha Anticolonial. Bogota: U. Nac. de Colombia, 1985.

1786. Arango M., Francisco. "Tribus indigenas de Colombia." R. Acad. Colombiana Hist. Ecles. No. 38 (1980): 146-153.

1787. Bejarano, Jesús A. "Empleo y distribucion de ingreso en el sector rural." Revista de Planeación y Desarrollo 21 (January-June 1989): 39-85.[Sine 1950's.]

1788. Berry, A. "Changing Income Distribution under Development: Colombia." Review of Income and Wealth 20 (September 1974): 289-316.

1789. Bierck, Harold A., Jr. "The Struggle for Abolition in Gran Colombia." Hispanic American Historical Review 33 (August 1953): 365-386.

1790. Buenaventura-Posso, Elisa and Susan E. Brown. "Forced Transition from Egalitarianism to Male Dominance: the Bari of Colombia." In Women and Colonization: Anthropological Perspectives, edited by Mona Etienne and Eleanor Leacock. New York: J.F.Bergin, 1980.

1791. Caicedo, Edgar. Militares y militarismo (un análisis historico-politico). Bogota, Colombia: Ediciones FondoEditorial Suramerica, 1989.

1792. Castillo-Cardenas, Gonzalo. Liberation Theology from Below: The Life and Thought of Manuel Quintin Lame. Maryknoll, New York: Orbis Books, 1987. [Manuel Quintin Lame Chantre: Indians of Colombia.]

1793. Chandler, David L. "Slave over Master in Colonial Colombia and Ecuador." The Americas 38 (January 1982): 315-326.

1794. Colombia. Departamento Administrativo Nacional de Estadistica. La pobreza en Colombia, 2 vols. Bogota: División de Edición, 1989.

1795. Cortes, Pedro. Indian Social Movements: A Case Study in Cauca, Colombia, from a Marxist Perspective. Doctoral dissertation: Ohio State University, 1988. UMO # 88122239.

1796. Desir, Lucia M. Between Loyalties: Racial, Ethnic and "National" Identity in Providencia, Colombia. Doctoral dissertation: Johns Hopkins University, 1990. UMO # 9018574.

1797. Friedmann, Nina S. de and Jaime Arocha. De sol a sol: génesis, transformación y presencia de los negros en Colombia. Bogotá: Planeta, 1986.

1798. Hobsbawm, Eric J. "Murderous Colombia." New York Review of Books, (November 20, 1986)

1799. Jaramillo Uribe, Jaime. "Esclavo y señores en la sociedad colombiana del siglo XVIII." Anurario Colombiano de HistoriaSocial y de la Cultura 1 (1963): 3-62.

1800. Jimenez, E. and J.P. Tan. "Selecting the Brightest for Post-secondary Education in Colombia: The Impact on Equity." Economics of Education Review 6 (1987)

1801. Kalmanovitz, Salomón. Economia y nación: una breve historiade Colombia. Bogota: Siglo Veintiuno Editores, 1985.

1802. Leal Buitrago, Francisco. Estado y politica en Colombia. Bogota: Siglo Veintiuno Editores, 1984.

1803. León de Leal, Magdalena. La realidad colombiana. Bogota: Asociación Colombiana para el Estudio de Población,1982.

1804. León de Leal, Magdalena. Sociedad, subordinación y feminismo. Bogota: Asociacion Colombiana para el Estudio de Población, 1982.

1805. Lloyd-Jones, Robin. "The Lost Boys." Times Educational Supplement, (September 19, 1986):[Street boys in Bogota.]

1806. Neira de Fonseca, Cristina and Carlos Fuentes. "Situación nutricional de la población colombiana." Revista de Planeación y Desarrollo 15 (1983): 107-121.

1807. Parra Sandoval, Rodrigo. "The Missing Future: Colombian Youth." CEPAL Review 29 (August 1986): 79-92.

1808. Pavy, David. "The Provenience of Colombian Negroes." Journal of Negro History 52 (January 1967): 35-58.

1809. Paz Gomez, Enelia. Black in Colombia. Mexico City: Costa-Amic Editores, 1985. [English version by Muriel Laycock and author.]

146 WORLD RACISM AND RELATED INHUMANITIES

1810. Rappaport, Joanne. The Politics of Memory: Native Historical Interpretation in the Colombian Andes. New York:Cambridge University Press, 1990.

1811. Reyes Posada, Alvaro. "Evolución de la distribución del ingreso en Colombia." Desarrollo y Sociedad (March 1988): 39-51.

1812. Rivera Sierra, Jairo. "El resguardo indigena en la republica: una politica y unas perspectivas." Boletin de Historia y Antiguedades 72 (1985): 803-856. [Indian land rights in Colombia.]

1813. Rubbo, Anna. "The Spread of Capitalism in Rural Colombia: Effects on Poor Women." In Toward and Anthropology of Women, edited by Rayna R. Reiter, pp. 333-357. New York: Monthly Review Press, 1975.

1814. Sharp, William J. Slavery on the Spanish Frontier. The Colombian Chocó, 1680-1810. Norman: University of OklahomaPress, 1976.

1815. Solaún, Mauricio and others. "Claro, Trigueño, Moreno. Testing for Race in Cartagena." Caribbean Review 15 (Winter 1987): 18-19.

1816. Torres Giraldo, Ignacio. Los inconformes: historia de la rebeldía de las masas en Colombia, 3 vols. Bogotá: 1972.

1817. Torres Sanchez, Jaime. Colombia represión, 1970-1981, 2 vols. Bogotá: Centro de Investigacion y Educacion Popular, 1982.

1818. Urrutia, Miguel. Winners and Losers in Colombia's Economic Growth of the 1970's. New York: Oxford University Press,1985.

1819. Wade, Peter. "Patterns of Race in Colombia." Bulletin of Latin American Research 5 (1986): 1-20.

1820. Wade, Peter. "Racial Discrimination in Colombia: Guises and Disguises." Cambridge Anthropology 10 (1985): 15-28.

1821. Wörthmuller, Angelika. Patientern zweiter Klasse: Gesundheitspolitik und pharmazeutische Industrie in Kolumbien. Ft. Lauderdale, FL: Verlag Breitenbach Publishers, 1986.

CONGO

1822. Daninos, Guy. "Le racisme colonial a travers la litterature congolaise." Mois Afrique 16 (April-May 1981): 120-126.

1823. Mampouya, Joseph. Le tribalisme au Congo. Paris: Le Pensee Universelle, 1983.

1824. Mboukou, Alexandre. "Neo-Colonialism and the Politics of Oil in Africa: The Case of France and the People's Republic of the Congo." Africa Quarterly 24 (1984): 1-12.

1825. N'Gakegni, Prosper. Problèmes actuels d'education en République Populaire du Congo. Eppelheim, Germany: Prosper Kivouvou Verlag, 1985.

1826. Sanders, Margaret. "Measurement of Levels of Living in the People's Republic of the Congo Since 1950." Journal of Economic History 43 (March 1983): 243-250.

COSTA RICA

1827. Achio, Mayra. "Crisis y reproduccion de la fuerza de trabajo industrial en Costa Rica." Revista de Ciencias Sociales (Costa Rica) (September-December 1987): 81-89.

1828. Acuña de Chacon, Angela. La mujer costarricense a través de cuatro siglos, 2 vols. San Jose, Costa Rica: Imprenta Nacional, 1969-1970.

1829. Ameringer, Charles D. Democracy in Costa Rica. New York: Praeger, 1982.

1830. Brumbaugh, Charles S. Costa Rica: The Making of a Livable Society. Doctoral dissertation: University of Wisconsin, 1985. UMO # 8601529.

1831. Carvajal, M. J. and D.T. Geithman. "Income, Human Capital and Sex Discrimination: Some Evidence from Costa Rica, 1963 and 1973." Journal of Economic Development 10 (July 1985):

1832. Denton, C. "Nationalism in Costa Rica: A Preliminary Analysis." Can. R. Stud. Nationalism 13 (Fall 1986): 199-209.

1833. Espinoza Esquivel, Juan R. La democracia costarricense. Heredia: Editorial de la Universidad Nacional, 1986.

1834. Fernandez, Gabriela T. and others, eds. Case Studies of Educational Needs among Refugees: I. Mexico and Costa Rica. Cambridge, England: International Extension College, 1984.

1835. Gonzalez-Suarez, Mirta. "Barriers to Female Achievement: Gender Stereotypes in Costa Rican Textbooks." Women's Studies International Forum 11 (1988): 599-609.

1836. Gudmundson, Lowell. "Aspects sociales, politcos y económicos del antisemitismo en C.R., 1900-1960." In El Judio en Costa Rica Jacobo

Schifter Sikora and others. San Jose: Editorial Universidad Estatal a Distancia, 1979.

1837. Gudmundson, Lowell. "De 'negro' a 'blanco' en la Hispanico-america del siglo XIX: la asimilacion afroamericana en Argentina y Costa Rica." Mesoamerica 7 (1986): 309-329.

1838. Irwin, Philippe B. "Etnicidad y lucha de clases en la subsidiaria de la United Fruit Company en Costa Rica y Panama." Boletin de Antropologia Americana (Mexico) No. 8(1983): 63-74.

1839. Krisjjanson, Lowell G. Estratificacion socio-racial y economica de Costa Rica: 1700-1850. San Jose: Editorial Universidad Estatal a Distancia, 1978.

1840. Mendiola, Haydee M. "Reform of Higher Education in Costa Rica: Effects on Social Stratification and Labor Markets." Comparative Education Review 33 (August 1989): 334-356.

1841. Mesa-Lago, Carmelo. "Health Care in Costa Rica: Boom and Crisis." Social Science Medicine 21 (1985): 13-22.

1842. Miron, Louis F. The National Plan for Educational Development in Costa Rica: Theoretical and Historical Perspectives. Doctoral dissertation: Tulane University, 1986. UMO # 8624423.

1843. Paniagua, Carlos G. The State and Higher Education in Costa Rica. Doctoral dissertation: Stanford University, 1988. UMO # 8815035.

1844. Soto Acosta, Willy A. "Crisis económica y dominación ideológica: el papel del medio difusor en la articulactión de la clase dominante costarricense." Revista de Ciencias Sociales 30 (December 1985): 77-88.

1845. Stone, Samuel. La dinastía de los conquistadores: la crisis del poder en la Costa Rico contemporeanea. 3rd edition. San Jose: Editorial Universitaria Centro-Americana, 1983.

1846. Wignal, Guillermo J. "Black Liberation Struggle in Costa Rica." Militant (October 14, 1977) [Interview.]

CUBA

1847. "Afro-Cubans." In World Directory of Minorities, edited by Minority Rights Group, pp. 44-45. Harlow: Longman, 1990.

1848. Aimes, Hubert H. S. A History of Slavery in Cuba, 1511-1868. New York: Octagon, 1967. [orig. 1907.]

1849. Arrabal, Fernando. "Le 'nouveau racisme' de Cuba." Politique Internationale 25 (1984): 47-51.

1850. Azicri, Max. Cuba. Politics, Economics, and Society. Pinter, 1987.

1851. Barreda, Pedro. The Black Protagonist in the Cuban Novel. Translated by Page Bancroft. Amherst: University of Massachusetts, 1979.

1852. Bejarano, Margalit. "Antisemitism in Cuba under Democratic, Military and Revolutionary Regimes 1944-1963." Patterns of Prejudice 24 (Summer 1990): 32-46.

1853. Bejarano, Margalit. "The Deproletarization of Cuban Jewry." World Congress of Jewish Studies 9 (1986): 233-240.

1854. Bejarano, Margalit. "Deproletarization of Cuban Jews." In Judaica Latinoamericana, edited by Amilat. Jerusalem: 1988.

1855. Bengelsdorf, Carollee. "On the Problem of Studying Women in Cuba." Race and Class 27 (Autumn 1985): 35-50.

1856. Bergad, Laird W. "Land Tenure, Slave Ownership, and Income Distribution in Nineteenth Century Cuba: Colon and Cardenas, 1859-1876." Social and Economic Studies 37 (March-June1988):

1857. Bergman, Arlene E. "Red and Black in Cuba." The Movement (January 1969):

1858. Betancourt Bencomo, Juan René. "Castro and the Cuban Negro." Crisis 68 (1961)

1859. Betancourt Bencomo, Juan René. Doctrina Negra. La unica teoria certera contra la discriminacion racial en Cuba. Havana: P. Fernandez, 1958.

1860. Betancourt Bencomo, Juan René. El Negro: Ciudadano del futuro. Havana: Talleres Tipograficos de Cardenas, 1959.

1861. Betancourt Bencomo, Juan René. Preludios de la libertad. La tragedia del negro y la tactica del partido comunista. Havana: 1950.

1862. Black, George. "[Cuba:] Toward Victory Always, But When?" Nation (October 24, 1988): 373-386.

1863. Blum, Leonor. "Fidel's Other Revolution." Times Educational Supplement, (November 22, 1985) [Education in Cuba.]

1864. Booth, David. "Cuba, Color and the Revolution." Science &Society, 40 (Summer 1976): 129-172.

1865. Bueno, Salvador. "Esclavitud y relaciones interraciales en Cecilia Valdes." Revista de la Biblioteca Nacional José Marti 28 (1986): 43-67. [Novel by Cirilo Villaverde (1812-1894).]

1866. Cannon, Terry and Johnnetta Cole. Free and Equal. The End of Racial Discrimination in Cuba. New York: The Venceremos Brigade, 1978.

1867. Carneado, José F. "La discriminación racial en Cuba no volvera jamas." Cuba Socialista 2 (1962): 54-67.

1868. Casal, L. Revolution and Race: Blacks in Contemporary Cuba. Washington, D.C.: Woodrow Wilson International Center for Scholars, 1980.

1869. Castellanos, Jorge and Isabel Castellanos. Cultura afrocubana. Vol. 1: El Negro en Cuba, 1492-1844. Miami: Ediciones Universal, 1988.

1870. Castellanos, Jorge and Isabel Castellanos. "The Geographic, Ethnologic, and Linguistic Roots of Cuban Blacks." Cuban Studies 17 (1987): 95-110.

1871. Chrisman, Robert , "Roundtable on the History of Racial Prejudice in Cuba." Black Scholar 16 (January-February 1985): 36-44.

1872. Clytus, John. Black Man in Cuba. Coral Gables, FL: University of Miami Press, 1970.

1873. Coker, Olumide. "Racism in Cuba: A Personal Viewpoint." Cuba Si No. 13 (March-April 1988): 7-8.

1874. Cole, Johnnetta B. Race Toward Equality. Havana: 1986.

1875. Corbitt, Duvon C. The Chinese in Cuba 1847-1947. Lexington: University of Kentucky Press, 1971.

1876. Dixon, Heriberto. "Cuban-American Counterpoint: Black Cubans in the United States." Dialectical Anthropology 13 (1988): 227-239.

1877. Dominguez, Jorge J. "Racial and Ethnic Relations in the Cuban Armed Forces: A Non Topic." Armed Forces and Society 2 (February 1976)

1878. Dzidzienyo, Anani and L. Casal. The Position of Blacks in Brazilian and Cuban Society. London: Minority Rights Group, 1979.

1879. Eckstein, Susan. "Restratification after Revolution: The Cuban Experience." In Crises in the Caribbean Basin, edited by Richard Tardanieo. Sage, 1987.

1880. Epstein, Erwin H. "The Peril of Paternalism: The Imposition of Education on Cuba by the United States." American Journal of Education 96 (1987): 1-23.

1881. Epstein, Erwin H. "Social Structure, Race Relations and Political Stability in Cuba Under U.S. Administration." R. Interam 8 (Summer 1979): 192-203.

1882. La esclavitud en Cuba. Havana: Editorial Academia, 1986.

1883. Feinsilver, Julie M. Symbolic Politics and Health Policy: Cuba as a "World Medical Power". Doctoral dissertation: Yale University, 1989. UMO # 9010652.

1884. Fermoselle, Rafael. Politica y color en Cuba. Montevideo: 1974.

1885. Fermoselle-Lopez, Rafael. Black Politics in Cuba: The Race War of 1912. Doctoral dissertation: American University, 1972.

1886. Fox, Geoffrey E. "Cuban Racism." In Cuban Communism, edited by Irving Louis Horowitz. Edison, NJ: Transaction Books, 1972.

1887. Fox, Geoffrey E. "Race and Class in Contemporary Cuba." In Cuban Communism. 3d ed. edited by Irving Louis Horowitz. New Brunswick, NJ: Transaction Books, 1977.

1888. Gendler, Everett. "Holy Days in Havana." Conservative Judaism 23 (Winter 1969): 15-24.

1889. Griffith, Albert R. "Cuba from a Black Perspective." Crisis 87 (May 1980): 181-183.

1890. Grillo Saez, David. El Problema del Negro Cubano. Havana: 1953.

1891. Hillson, Jon. "'Cuban Racism' Charge Sparks Harlem Debate." Militant (March 16, 1990) [Carlos Moore, Castro, the Blacks, and Africa.]

1892. Holt-Seeland, Inger. Women of Cuba. Westport, CT: Lawrence Hill, 1982.

1893. Hopkins, Dwight N. "A Black Student's Journal: Trip to Communist Cuba." Harvard Crimson (January 13, 1975)

1894. Horne, Gerald C. "Black Youth in Cuba." Freedomways 15 (Third Quarter 1975): 215-220.

1895. Iatridis, Demetrius S. "Cuba's Health Care Policy: Prevention and Active Community Participation." Social Work 35 (January 1990): 29-35.

1896. Jackson, Sandra C. Women in Development: A Study of Access to Education and Work in Tanzania and Cuba, 1960-1980. Doctoral dissertation: University of California, Berkeley, 1987. UMO # 8726242.

1897. Jimenez Pastrana, Juan. Los chinos en la historia de Cuba, 1847-1930. Havana: Ed. Ciencias Sociales, 1983.

1898. Johnson, Herschel. "Inside Report on Black Congressman's Visit to Castro's Cuba." Jet (July 7, 1977):

1899. Jorge, Antonio. "Growth with Equity: The Failure of the Cuban Case." Inter-Am. R. Bibliography 35 (1985): 48-62.

1900. Kashif, Lonnie. "Cuba Tackles Problem of Wiping Out Effects of Imperialist Racism." Muhammad Speaks (April 9, 1971)

1901. Kiple, Kenneth F. Blacks in Colonial Cuba, 1774-1899. Gainesville: University Presses of Florida, 1975.

1902. Knight, Franklin. "Slavery, Race, and Social Structure in Cuba During the Nineteenth Century." In Slavery and Race Relations in Latin America, edited by Robert B. Toplin. Westport, CT: Greenwood Press, 1974.

1903. Krauss, Clifford. "Blacks Praise Cuban Revolution's Benefits." Wall Street Journal (July 9, 1986)

1904. Kubayanda, Joseph B. "Hispanic Humanism and Nineteenth-century Cuban Blacks: An Historico-Literary Perspective." Plantation Soc. Americas 1 (October 1981): 343-363.

1905. Kukovecz, Gyorgy. "The Racial Question in the Social and Political Conflict during the Neocolonial Republic in Cuba." Szazdok 118 (1984): 730-758. [In Hungarian.]

1906. Lachantanere, Romulo. "Some Aspects of the Color Problem in Cuba." Negro Quarterly 2 (Summer 1942): 145-154.

1907. Lamore, Jean. "La obra antiracista de Fernando Ortiz: el caso de las revista Ultra." Santiago (Cuba) 58 (1985): 45-62.

1908. Langley, Lester D. "Slavery, Reform, and American Policy in Cuba, 1823-1878." Revista de historia de America 65-6(1968): 71-84.

1909. Leal, Juan F. "Las clases sociales en Cuba en visperas de la revolución." Rev. Mexicana de Ciencia Pol. 19 (1973): 99-109.

1910. Liss, Sheldon B. Roots of Revolution. Radical Thought in Cuba. Lincoln: University of Nebraska Press, 1987. [18402-1950s.]

1911. Lopez Valdez, Rafael. Racial Discrimination from Colonial Times to the Revolution. Havana: Instituto Cubano de Amistad con los Pueblos, 1971.

1912. Lopez Valdez, Rafael. "Racial Discrimination in Cuba." Cuba Resource Center Newsletter 2 (January 1973): 6-14.

1913. Luis, William. Literary Bondage: Slavery in Cuban Narrative. Austin: University of Texas Press, 1990.

1914. Luzon, Jose L. "Housing in Socialist Cuba." Cuban Studies 18 (1988): 65-86.

1915. Madden, Richard R. La Isla de Cuba. Havana: Consejo Nacional de Cultura, 1964. [Slavery: pp. 131-272.]

1916. Marquez, Robert. Racismo, cultura y revolucion. Havana: 1980.

1917. Marti, Jorge L. "La cuestión racial en la evolución constitucional cubana." Politica (Caracas) 33 (April 1964)

1918. Martin, Juan Luis. El Crimen de Jabin. Disquisiciones sobre el moderno antisemitismo. Havana: 1945.

1919. [Martinez] Elizabeth Sutherland. "Colony Within the Colony." In The Youngest Revolution: A Personal Report on Cuba Elizabeth Sutherland [Martinez]. New York: Dial Press, 1969.

1920. Martinez Heredia, Fernando. "Christianity and Liberation. A Cuban Study of Latin American Liberation Theology." Social Compass (Belgium) 35 (1988)

1921. Masferrer, Marianne and Carmelo Mesa-Lago. "The Gradual Integration of the Black in Cuba: Under the Colony, the Republic, and the Revolution." in Slavery and Race Relations in Latin America Robert B. Toplin (ed.), pp. 348-384. Westport, CT: Greenwood Press, 1974.

1922. McGrath, Tom. "Robert Williams: Racism in Cuba?" Los Angeles Free Press (February 17, 1967)

1923. Montejo, Esteban. The Autobiography of a Runaway Slave. New York: 1968.

1924. Moore, Carlos. Castro, the Blacks, and Africa. Los Angeles: Center for Afro-American Studies, University of California, 1988.

1925. Moore, Carlos. "Congo or Carabili: Race Relations in Socialist Cuba." Caribbean Review 15 (1986): 12-15, 43.

1926. Moore, Carlos. "Le peuple noir a-t-il sa place dans la revolutión cubaine?" Presence Africaine 52 (1964): 177-230.

1927. Moreno Fraginals, Manuel. "Africa in Cuba: A Quantitative Analysis of the African Population in the Island of Cuba." Annals of the New York Academy of Sciences 292 (1977): 187-201.

1928. Naranjo, Consuelo. "Análisis histórico de la emigración española a Cuba, 1900-1959." R. Indias 174 (1984): 507-529.

1929. Nazzari, Muriel. "The Woman Question in Cuba: An Analysis of Material Constraints on Its Solution." Signs 9 (Winter1983): 246-263.

1930. Nodal, Roberto. "The Black Man in Cuban Society: From Colonial Times to the Revolution." Journal of Black Studies 16 (1986): 251-267.

1931. Nordheimer, Jon. "Black Cubans: Apart in Two Worlds." New York Times, (December 2, 1987)

1932. North, Joseph. "Negro and White in Cuba." Political Affairs (July 1963)

1933. Olliz-Boyd, Antonio. "Race Relations in Cuba: A Literary Perspective." Rev. Interamericana 8 (1978): 225-233.

1934. Ortiz, Fernando. "Por la Integracion Cubana de Blancos y Negros." Revista Bimestre Cubana (March-April 1943)

1935. Padula, Alfred. The Fall of the Bourgeoisie, Cuba, 1959-1961. Doctoral dissertation: University of Mexico, 1974.

1936. Paquette, Robert L. Sugar Is Made With Blood: The Conspiracy of La Escalera and the Conflict between Empires over Slavery in Cuba. Middletown, CT: Wesleyan University Press, 1989.

1937. Perez, Louis A., Jr. "Aspects of Hegemony: Labor, State, and Capital in Plattist Cuba." Cuban Studies 16 (1986): 49-69.

1938. Perez, Louis A., Jr. Cuba under the Platt Amendment, 1902-1934. Pittsburgh, PA: University of Pittsburgh Press, 1986.

1939. Perez, Louis A., Jr. "Vagrants, Beggars, and Bandits: Social Origins of Cuban Separatism, 1878-1895." American Historical Review 90 (December 1985): 1092-1121.

1940. Pérez de la Riva, Juan. El Barracón. Esclavitud y capitalismo en Cuba. Barcelona: Ed. Critica, 1978.

1941. Phillips, W. M., Jr. "Race Relations in Cuba: Some Reflections." Review of Black Political Economy 8 (Winter 1978): 173-183.

1942. Ralston, Richard D. "Cuba in Africa and Africa in Cuba." In Revolution in Southern Africa, edited by Marlene Dixon and Rod Bush. San Francisco, CA: Synthesis Publications, 1983.

1943. Ring, Harvey. How Cuba Uprooted Race Discrimination. (2nd edition). New York: Pioneer Publishers, 1969.

1944. Rivas Munoz, Mercedes. La narrativa antiesclavista cubana (1838-1882). Doctoral dissertation: University of Seville (Spain), 1989.

1945. Rodriquez, Jose L. "Los efectos de la reforma agraria sobre el campesinado en Cuba." Economia y Desarrollo (March-April 1986): 144-173. [1959-1984.]

1946. Rose Green-Williams, C. "Re-writing the History of the Afro-Cuban Woman: Nancy Morejon's Mujer Negra." Afro-Hispanic Review 8 (September 1989): 7-13.

1947. Rowbotham, Sheila. "Colony Within the Colony." in Women, Resistance and Revolution Sheila Rowbotham. New York: Random House, 1974.

1948. Sánchez, Juan. "Aspectos de la discriminación racial: Un mal del pasado." Bohemia 65 (May 25, 1973): 100-106.

1949. Santana, S. M. "The Cuban health Care System: Responsiveness to Changing Population Needs and Demands." World Development 15 (January 1987)

1950. Schwartz, Rosalie. The Displaced and the Disappointed: Cultural Nationalists and Black Activists in Cuba in the 1920s. Doctoral dissertation: University of California, San Diego, 1977. UMO # 7805756.

1951. Scott, Rebecca J. "Class Relations in Sugar and Political Mobilization in Cuba, 1868-1899." Cuban Studies/Estudios Cubanos 15 (1985)

1952. Scott, Rebecca J. "Explaining Abolition: Contradiction, Adaptation, and Challenge in Cuban Slave Society, 1860-1886." Comparative Studies in Society and History 26 (January 1984): 83-111.

1953. Scott, Rebecca J. Slave Emancipation and the Transition to Free Labor in Cuba, 1868-1895. Doctoral dissertation: Princeton University, 1982. UMO # 8206944.

1954. Scott, Rebecca J. Slave Emancipation in Cuba. The Transition to Free Labour, 1860-1899. Princeton, NJ: Princeton University Press, 1985.

1955. Serviat, Pedro. "La discriminacion en Cuba, su origen, desarrollo y terminacion definitiva." Islas (La Habana) 66 (May-August 1980)

1956. Shakur, Assata. Assata, An Autobiography. Westport, Ct: Lawrence Hill & Co., 1987. [On the issue of racism in Cuba.]

1957. Stolcke, Varena Martinez-Alier. Marriage, Class, and Colour in Nineteenth Century Cuba: A Study of Racial Attitudes and Sexual Values in a Slave Society. 2d ed. Ann Arbor: University of Michigan Press, 1989.

1958. Taylor, Frank F. "Revolution, Race, and Some Aspects of Foreign Relations in Cuba Since 1959." Cuban Studies 18 (1988): 19-44.

1959. Terris, Milton. "The Health Status of Cuba..." Journal of Public Health Policy 10 (Spring 1989): 78-87.

1960. Thomas, Hugh. "Black Cuba." in Cuba: The Pursuit of Freedom. Chapter 91. New York: Harper & Row, 1971.

1961. Urrútia, Gustavo E. "El prejudicio en Cuba." In Negro Anthology, edited by Nancy Cunard. London: Nancy Cunard at Wishart & Co., 1934.

1962. Valdex-Cruz, Rosa. "The Black Man's Contribution to Cuban Culture." Americas 34 (October 1977): 244-251.

1963. Van Ness, Carol. Sugar, Railroads and Dollar Diplomats: Railroad Construction in Eastern Cuba, 1898-1923. Master's thesis: University of Florida, 1985.

1964. Yglesias, Jose. In the Fist of the Revolution: Life in a Cuban Town. New York: Random House, 1968. [Deals with women, among other topics.]

1965. Zimbalist, Andrew , Cuba's Socialist Economy Toward the 1990s. Boulder, CO: Lynne Rienner Publishers, 1987.

1966. Zimbalist, Andrew , Cuban Political Economy: Controversies in Cubanology. Boulder, CO: Westview Press, 1988.

CYPRUS

1967. Athnias, Floya and Ron Ayres. "Ethnicity and Class in Cyprus." Race and Class (Summer 1983): 59-76.

1968. Jennings, Ronald C. "Black Slaves and Free Blacks in Ottoman Cyprus, 1590-1640." Journal of the Economic and Social History of the Orient 30 (1987): 286-302.

1969. Karageorghis, Vassos. Blacks in Ancient Cypriot Art. Houston, TX: Meril Foundation, 1988.

1970. Kelling, George H. Countdown to Rebellion: British Policy in Cyprus, 1939-1955. New York: Greenwood, 1990.

1971. Kyle, Keith. Cyprus (new edition). London: Minority Rights Group, 1984.

1972. Sant Cassia, Paul. "Religion, Politics and Ethnicity in Cyprus during the Turkocratia (1571-1878)." European Journal of Sociology 27 (1986): 3-28.

CZECHOSLOVAKIA

1973. Adam, Magda. "The Hungarian Minority of Czechoslovakia and Its Press." Hungarian Studies Review 26 (1989): 47-56.

1974. Baker, Stephanie. "Slovaks Speak Language of Nationalism." Guardian (NYC) (December 26, 1990)

1975. Baum, Karl. "Nazi Anti-Jewish Legislation in the Czech Protectorate: A Documentary Note." Soviet Jewish Affairs No. 3 (1972): 116-128.

1976. Berney, Louis. "East of Equality." Boston Globe Magazine, (December 30, 1990) [Women in Czechoslovakia and Hungary.]

1977. Boder, Menachem. Sad Missions. Hakibbutz Haartzi Hashomer Hatzair: Sefriat Poalim, 1979. [Slovakia.]

1978. Bondyova, J. and V. Petraskova. "The Standard of Living in Czechoslovakia." Czechoslovak Economic Digest No. 4 (June 1987)

1979. Campion, Joan. In the Lion's Mouth. Gisi Fleichmann and the Jewish Fight for Survival. Lanham, MD: University Press of America, 1987.

1980. Cervinka, Frantisek. "The Hilsner Affair." in Year Book XIII Leo Baeck Institute. London: East and West Library, 1968.

1981. Cohen, Cary B. "Jews in German Society: Prague, 1860-1914." Central European History 10 (March 1977): 28-54.

1982. Conway, John S. "The Churches, the Slovak State and the Jews, 1939-1945." Slavonic and East European Review 52 (1974): 85-112.

1983. Cotic, Meir. The Prague Trial. The First Anti-Zionist Show Trial in the Communist Bloc. New York: Herzl Press, 1987.

1984. Daschke, John W. Nationalism, Communism and Federalism: The Politics of Ethnic Development in Czechoslovakia. Doctoral dissertation: Indiana University, 1985. UMO # 8525354.

1985. Davidova, Eva and D.E. Guy. "Czechoslovakia Solves Its Gypsy Problem." Race Today 4 (March 1972): 82-84.

1986. Duff, S. G. German Protectorate: The Czechs under Nazi Rule. London: 1970.

1987. Durica, Milan S. Aussenpolitische Beziehungen der Slovakischen Republik. Munich: Schriftenreihe des Slowakischen Matus Cernak-Instituts, 1983.

1988. Felak, James R. At the Price of the Republic: Hlinka's Slovak People's Party, 1929-1938. Doctoral dissertation: Indiana University, 1989. UMO # 9020713.

1989. Fuchs, Abraham. The Unheeded Cry: The Life of Rabbi Michael Weissmandel. Torah Umesorah, 1984. [Slovakia.]

1990. Hahn, Fred. "The Dilemma of the Jews in the Historic Lands of Czechoslovakia, 1918-1938." East Central Europe 10 (1983): 24-39.

1991. Hajda, Jan. "Class Structure in Czechoslovakia in 1930 and 1967." Kosmos 6 (1987): 43-59.

1992. Herman, Karel. "The Czechoslovak National Liberation Movement in the Nineteenth and Beginning of the Twentieth Centuries." East European Quarterly 24 (June 1990): 219-226.

1993. Hochmaulova, D. "Education of Young People in Czechoslovakia." Czechoslovak Economic Digest No. 8 (December 1985)

1994. Hodos, George H. Show Trials, Stalinist Purges in Eastern Europe. Westport, CT: Praeger, 1987.

1995. Hradilek, Tomas and others. "The Tragedy of the Jews in Post-War Czechoslovakia." Soviet Jewish Affairs 20 (Spring 1990): 58-65.

1996. Iggers, Wilma , Die Juden in Böhmen und Mähren: Ein historisches Lesebuch. Munich: C.H. Beck, 1986.

1997. Iggers, Wilma. "The Flexible National Identities of Bohemian Jewry." East Central Europe/l'Europe du Centre-Est 7, part 1 (1980): 39-48.

1998. Janics, Kalman. Czechoslovak Policy and the Hungarian Minority, 1945-1948. Translated by Stephen Borsody. New York: Social Science Monographs, 1982.

1999. Janics, Kalman. "Czechoslovakia's Magyar Minority: An Example of Diaspora Nationalism." Canadian R. Stud. Nationaliam 3 (Fall 1975): 34-44.

2000. Janics, Kalman. "The Hungarians of Slovakia: From Czechoslovak to Slovak Rule." In The Hungarians: A Divided Nation, edited by Stephen Borsody. New Haven, CT: Yale Center for International and Area Studies, 1988.

2001. Jelinek, Yeshayahu A. "Bratislava." in Encyclopedia of the Holocaust, I. 240-241. New York: Macmillian, 1990.

2002. Jelinek, Yeshayahu A. "The Communist Party of Slovakia and the Jews: Ten Years (1938-1948)." East Central Europe 5 (1978): 186-202.

2003. Jelinek, Yeshayahu A. "The Holocaust of Slovakian Jewry." East Central Europe/l'Europe du Centre-Est 10 (1983): 14-23.

2004. Jelinek, Yeshayahu A. "The Jews in Slovakia, 1945-1949." Soviet Jewish Affairs 8 (Autumn 1978)

2005. Jelinek, Yeshayahu A. The Lust for Power: Nationalism, Slovakia, and the Communists, 1918-1948. New York: Columbia University Press, 1983.

2006. Jelinek, Yeshayahu A. The Pariah Republic: Hlinka's Slovak People's Party, 1939-1945. New York: Columbia University Press, 1976.

2007. Jelinek, Yeshayahu A. "The Role of the Jews in Slovakian Resistance." Jahrbuch für Geschichte Osteuropas 15 (September 1967): 415-422.

2008. Jelinek, Yeshayahu A. "Slovakia and Its Minorities 1939-1945: People With and Without National Protection." Nationalities Papers 4 (Spring 1976): 1-15.

2009. Jelinek, Yeshayahu A. "Slovaks and the Holocaust: Attempts at Reconciliation." Soviet Jewish Affairs 19 (Spring 1989): 57-68.

2010. Jelinek, Yeshayahu A. and Robert Rozett. "Slovakia." In Encyclopedia of the Holocaust, IV. New York: Macmillan, 1990.

2011. "The Jewish Question and Other Aspects of Modern Czechoslovakia." East Central Europe 10 (1983): entire issue.

2012. Jirava, M. "Raising the Living Standard- the Aim and Prerequisite for Building an Advanced Socialist Society." Czechoslovak Economic Digest No. 5 (August 1985)

2013. Johnson, Owen V. Slovakia 1918-1938. Education and the Making of a Nation. New York: East European Monographs, 1985.

2014. Kalvoda, Josef. The Genesis of Czechoslovakia. New York: Columbia University Press, 1986.

2015. Kamenec, Ivan. "Slovak Society and Antifascist Resistance during World War II up to the Year 1943." Studia Historica Slovaca 14 (1985): 71-105.

2016. Kaplan, Karel. Report on the Murder of the General Secretary. Translated by Karel Kovanda. Columbus: Ohio State University Press, 1990. [The staged trial of Rudolf Slansky in Czechoslovakia.]

2017. Kestenberg-Gladstein, Ruth. Neuere Geschichte der Juden in den bohmischen Ländern. Part I. Das Zeitalter der Aufklarung 1780-1830. Tubingen: J.C.B. Mohr, 1969.

2018. Kieval, Hillel J. The Making of Czech Jewry: National Conflict and Jewish Society in Bohemia 1870-1918. New York: Oxford University Press, 1988.

2019. Kirschbaum, Stanislav J. "The Slovak Republic, 1939-1945." In Reflections on Slovak History, edited by Kirschbaum and Anne C.R. Roman. Toronto, Canada: Slovak World Congress, 1987.

2020. Kirschbaum, Stanislav J. "Slovak Nationalism in the First Czechoslovak Republic, 1918-1939." Canadian R. Stud. Nationalism 16 (1989): 169-187.

2021. Klassen, John. "The Disadvantaged and the Hussite Revolution." International Review of Social History 35 (1990): 249-272.

2022. Komarek, V. "Conditions and Limits of Economic and Social Advancement in the Czechoslovak Socialist Republic (2parts)." Czechoslovak Economic Digest No. 8 (December1988)

2023. Kostelancik, D. J. "The Gypsies of Czechoslovakia-Political and Ideological Considerations in the Development of Policy." Studies in Comparative Communism 22 (Winter 1989)

2024. Kovaly, Heda. Under a Cruel Star: A Life in Prague, 1941-1968. Translated by Franci Epstein, Helen Epstein, and Heda Kovaly. New York: Penguin Books, 1989.

2025. Krejci, Jaroslav. "Classes and Elites in Socialist Czechoslovakia." In The Social Structure of Eastern Europe, edited by Bernard L.Faber. New York: Praeger, 1976.

2026. Kulka, Erich. "The Jews in Czechoslovakia between 1918 and 1968." In Czechoslovakia: Crossroads and Crises, 1918-1988, edited by Norman Stone and Eduard Strouhal. New York: St. Martin's, 1989.

2027. Kwasnik-Rabinowiez, Kurt A. M. Die juedische Minderheit in der Tsechoslowakei. Eine rechtsgeschichtliche Analyse, 1918-1939. Doctoral dissertation: University of Amsterdam, 1966.

2028. Langer, Jo. *Convictions, Memories of a Life Shared with a Good Communist*. London: Andre Deutsch, 1979. [Anti-semitism in Czechoslovakia.]

2029. Lazer, Arnold. "Reminiscences from Fascist Slovakia." *Yad Vashem Bulletin* No. 18 (1966): 17-25.

2030. Lazniekova, A. "Overcoming Social Disparities between the Urban and Rural Population in Socialist Society." *Czechoslovak Economic Digest* No. 5 (August 1985)

2031. Leff, Carol S. *National Conflict in Czechoslovakia. The Making and Remaking of the State. 1918-1937*. Princeton, NJ: Princeton University Press, 1988.

2032. Lipscher, Ladislav. *Die Juden im slowakischen Staat, 1939-1945*. Munich: R. Oldenbourg, 1980.

2033. Loebl, Eugene. *Sentenced and Tried. The Stalinist Purges in Czechoslovakia*. London: Elek Books, 1969.

2034. Machann, Clinton. "The 'Ethnic Situation' in Czechoslovakia after the Revolution of November 1989." *Journal of Ethnic Studies* 18 (Winter 1991): 135-141. [Minorities and majorities in Czechoslovakia.]

2035. Macu, Pavel. "The Present State of National Consciousness among the Rusyns of Czechoslovakia." *Europa Ethnica* 31 (1974): 98-111.

2036. Magocsi, Paul R. *The Rusyn-Ukrainians of Czechoslovakia. An Historical Survey*. Vienne: Braumuller, 1983.

2037. Martinka, K. "The 40th Anniversary of the Slovak Uprising and the Socio-economic Development of Slovakia." *Czechoslovak Economic Digest* No. 8 (December 1984)

2038. Mastuy, V. *The Czechs under Nazi Rule: The Failure of National Resistance, 1939-1942*. New York: 1971,

2039. Mikus, Joseph A. *Slovakia and the Slovaks*. Washington, D.C.: Three Continents Press, 1977.

2040. Mlynar, Zdenek , *Der "Prager Frühling": ein Wissenschaftliches Symposion*. Cologne: Bund-Verlag, 1983.

2041. Moskowitz, Moses. "The Jewish Situation in the Protectorate of Bohemia-Moravia." *Jewish Social Studies* 4 (1942): 17-44.

2042. Nagy, Karoly. "Hungarian Minority Education in Czechoslovakia: A Struggle for Ethnic Survival." *Hungarian Studies Review* 26 (1989): 57-65.

2043. Neumann, Kurt K. "The Slovak Republic: A Lived Experience." In Reflections on Slovak History, edited by Stanislav J. Kirschbaum and Anne C.R. Roman. Toronto, Canada: Slovak World Congress, 1987.

2044. Neumann, Yermeyahu Oscar. Gisi Fleischmann: The Story of a Heroic Woman. Tel Aviv Translated and enlarged by Karen Gershon: World Wizo, 1970. [Slovakia.]

2045. Newman, A. "The Expulsion of the Jews from Prague in 1745." Jewish Historical Society of England 22 (1970): 30-41.

2046. Pavlat, Leo and others. "Open Letter to the Leadership of the Council of Jewish Communities in the Czech Lands." Soviet Jewish Affairs 20 (Spring 1990): 66-68.

2047. Peek, M. "Czech Jewry after Dubcek." Congress Weekly 36 (September 13, 1969): 13-15.

2048. Peterson, James W. "Representation of Ethnic Groups Within the Czechoslovak Political System, 1918-1982." East Central Europe/l'Europe du Centre-Est 10 (1983): 92-114.

2049. Purs, Jaroslav. Changes in the Standard of Living and Nutrition of the Working Class in the Czech Lands, 1849-1859. Prague: Institute of Czechoslovak and World History of the Czechoslovak Academy of Sciences, 1986.

2050. Reinfeld, Barbara. "The Question of Moravia's Special Position and Identity 1848-1918." Kosmos 4 (1985): 63-69.

2051. Riff, Michael A. The Assimilation of the Jews of Bohemia and the Rise of Political Anti-Semitism, 1848-1918. Doctoral dissertation: University of London, School of Slavonic and East European Studies.

2052. Riff, Michael A. "Czech Antisemitism and the Jewish Response before 1914." Wiener Library Bulletin 29 (1976): 8-20.

2053. Rothkirchen, Livia. "Bohemia and Moravia, Protectorate of." in Encyclopedia of the Holocaust I. 227-230. New York: Macmillan, 1990.

2054. Rothkirchen, Livia. "The Churches and the 'Final Solution'in Slovakia." In Judaism and Christianity under the Impact of National Socialism, 1919-1945, edited by Otto Dov Kulka and Paul R.Mendes-Flohr. Jerusalem: Historical Society of Israel, 1987.

2055. Rothkirchen, Livia. "Czech Attitude towards the Jews during the Nazi Regime." Yad Vashem Studies, Vol. XIII, edited by Rothkirchen. New York: KTAV Publishing House, 1979.

2056. Rothkirchen, Livia. The Destruction of Slovakian Jewry. Jerusalem: Yad Vashem, 1961.

2057. Rothkirchen, Livia. "The Stand of the Churches vis-a-vis the Persecution of the Jews of Slovakia." in Judaism and Christianity under the Impact of National Socialism, International Symposium. 273-286. Jerusalem: Historical Society of Israel, 1982.

2058. Rothkirchen, Livia. "Vatican Policy and the 'Jewish Problem' in Independent Slovakia (1939-1945)." Yad Vashem Studies 6 (1967): 22-54.

2059. Ruzickova, Z. and V. Seidl. "Economic Aspects of Health and Sickness." Czechoslovak Economic Digest No. 7 (November 1985)

2060. Sabak, Constantine. Carpatho-Russian Autonomy under the Czechoslovak Republic, 1918-1938. Master's thesis: Florida Atlantic University, 1980.

2061. Salzmann, Zdenek. "Interethnic Relations in a Multinational State: The Czech-Slovak Case." Research Report-Department of Anthropology, University of Massachusetts, Amherst No. 22 (1983): 101-143.

2062. Salzmann, Zdenek. "Portrayal of Gender Relations in Contemporary Czech Mass Media." East European Quarterly 23(January 1990): 399-407.

2063. Schmidt, Maria. "Margit Slachta's Activities in Support of Slovakian Jewry, 1942-1943." Holocaust and Genocide Studies 5 (1990): 67-72.

2064. Schumann, Wolfgang and Ludwig Nestler, eds. Nacht über Europa. Die Okkupationspolitik des deutschen Faschismus (1939-1945). Acht-bändige Dokumentenedition. Vol. I: Die faschistische Okkupationspolitik in Österreich und der Tschechoslowakei (1938-1945). Cologne: Pahl-Rugenstein, 1988.

2065. Seidl, V. and L. Prasa. "Changes in the Social Security System in 1970-1985." Czechoslovak Economic Digest No. 6 (September 1985)

2066. Skalnik Leff, Carol. National Conflict in Czechoslovakia: The Making and Remaking of the State, 1918-1987. Princeton, NJ: Princeton University Press, 1988. [Czechs and Slovaks.]

2067. Skilling, H. Gordon. The German-Czech National Conflict in Bohemia, 1879-1893. Doctoral dissertation: University of London, School of Slavonic and East European Studies, 1940.

2068. Skilling, H. Gordon. "Masaryk: Permanent Dissenter: The Hilsner Case and Anti-Semitism." Cross Currents 8 (1989): 243-260.

2069. Szarka, Laszlo. "The Slovak Separation in 1918: An Indirect Form of Self-Determination." Danubian Historical Studies 1(1987): 23-33.

2070. Teichova, Alice. The Czechoslovak Economy, 1918-1980. London: Routledge, 1988.

2071. Tiso, Joseph. "President Tiso's Defense of Statehood." Jednota Ann. Furdek 17 (1978): 10-12.

2072. Tomasek, P. "Egalitarianism is Harmful." Czechoslovak Economic Digest No.4 (June 1984)

2073. Ulc, Otto. "Gypsies in Czechoslovakia: A Case of Unfinished Integration." Eastern European Politics and Societies 2 (1988): 306-332.

2074. Vachel, J. "Czechoslovakia's Economic and Social Development." Czechoslovak Economic Digest No.7 (November1985)

2075. Vardy, Steven Bela. "The Hungarians of the Carpatho-Ukraine: From Czechoslovak to Soviet Rule." In The Hungarians: A Divided Nation, edited by Stephen Borsody. New Haven, CT: Yale Center for International and Area Studies, 1988.

2076. Weiss, John. "Fascism in Czechoslovakia, 1919-1939." East Central Europe 4 No. 1 (1977): 35-43.

2077. Wyatt, Jiri. Against Capitulation. London: Quartet, 1984. [A Jew in Slovakia.]

2078. Zorach, Jonathan. "The Nationality Problem in the Czechoslovak Army between the Two World Wars." East Central Europe 5 (1978): 169-185.

DENMARK

2079. Bamberger, Ib Nathan. <u>A Cultural History of the Jews of Denmark, 1622-1900</u>. Doctoral dissertation: Yeshiva University, 1974. UMO # 75-20586.

2080. Bamberger, Ib Nathan. <u>Jews in Denmark, 1913-1943</u>. Master's thesis: Yeshiva University, 1967.

2081. Bjerke, Kjeld and Soren Brodersen. "Studies of Income Redistribution in Denmark for 1963 and 1971." <u>Review of Income and Wealth</u> 24 (June 1978): 137-159.

2082. Boje, Per. "The Standard of Living in Denmark 1750-1914." <u>Scandanvian Econmic Historical Review</u> 34 (1986): 171-179.

2083. Borchsensius, Paul. "Aspects of the Rescue of Danish Jews." <u>Wiener Library Bulletin</u> 22 (Autumn 1968): 36-40.

2084. Byram, Michael. <u>Minority Education and Ethnic Survival</u>. Clevedon, Avon: Multilingual Matters, 1986. [German minority in Denmark.]

2085. Dern, Ann L. <u>In the Shadow of the Swastika: Prelude to the German Occupation of Denmark, 1930-1939</u>. Master's thesis: University of San Diego, 1980.

2086. Djursaa, Malene. "Denmark." In <u>Fascism in Europe</u>, edited by S.J. Woolf. London: Methuen, 1982.

2087. Flender, Harold. <u>Rescue in Denmark</u>. New York: Holocaust Library, 1981.

2088. Goldberger, Leo, ed. <u>The Rescue of the Danish Jews. Moral Courage Under Stress</u>. New York: New York University Press, 1987.

2089. Haestrup, Jorgen. Secret Alliance. A Study of the Danish Resistance Movement, 1940-1945. New York: New York University Press, 1985.

2090. Hoff, Jens and J. G. Anderson. "The Danish Class Structure." Acta Sociologica 32 (1989): 23-52.

2091. Johansen, Hans C. The Danish Economy in the Twentieth Century. New York: St. Martin's Press.

2092. Jones, W. Glyn. Denmark: A Modern History. London: Croom Helm, 1986.

2093. Kaarsted, Tage. "De tyske flygtninge i Danmark 1945-1949." Historie 17 (1987): 254-277. [Debate.]

2094. Lindstrom, Ulf. Fascism in Scandanavia, 1920-1940. Stockholm: Almquist and Wiksell, 1985.

2095. Lofton, Joseph Evans, Jr. The Abolition of the Danish Atlantic Slave Trade. PhD dissertation: The Louisiana State University and Agricultural and Mechanical College, 1977.

2096. Lund, Jens. "The Legend of the King and the Star." Indiana Folklore 8 (1975): 1-37. [King Christian X and the Jews of Denmark during World War II.]

2097. Mathiesen, Anders. "Polarization of the Qualification Structure of the Danish Labour Force: The Role of the Educational System in Post-War Denmark." Acta Sociologica 23 (1980): 157-172.

2098. Nellemann, George. Polske Landarbejdere i Danmark og dere eftemkommere 1893-1929. Copenhagen: 1981. [Polish farm workers and their children.]

2099. Petrow, R. The Bitter Years: The Invasion and Occupation of Denmark and Norway, April 1940-1945. New York: 1974.

2100. Roslyng-Jensen, Palle. "The Military and Danish Democracy. Civil-Military Relations in Denmark during the German Occupation, 1940-1945." Scandanavian Journal of History 11 (1986): 243-263.

2101. Schwartz, Jonathan M. Reluctant Hosts: Denmark's Reception of Guest Workers. Copenhagen: Akademisk Forlag, 1985.

2102. Secher, Knud. Kampf ohne Waffen. Dänemark unter deutscher Besatzung. Zurich: Europa-Verlag, 1945.

2103. Sojndergaard, B. and Michael Byram. "Pedagogical Problems and Symbolic Values in the Language Curriculum- the Case of the German Minority in Denmark." Journal of Multilingual and Multicultural Development 7 (1986): 147-167.

2104. Voorhis, Jerry L. "Germany and Denmark 1940-1943." Scandanavian Studies 44 (1972): 171-185.

2105. Wylie, Jonathan. The Faroe Islands: Social Change and Cultural Continuity. Lexington: University Press of Kentucky, 1986.

2106. Yahil, Leni. "Denmark", in Encyclopedia of the Holocaust, I. pp. 362-365. New York: Macmillan, 1990.

2107. Yahil, Leni. "Methods of Persecution: A Comparison of the 'Final Solution' in Holland and Denmark." Scripta Hierosolymitana 23 (1972): 279-300.

2108. Yahil, Leni. The Rescue of Danish Jewry: Test of a Democracy. Philadelphia, PA. Translated by Morris Gradel: Jewish Publication Society of America, 1969.

DOMINICAN REPUBLIC

2109. Alcantara Almanzar, José. "Black Images in Dominican Literature." Nieve West-Indische Gids 61 (1987): 161-173.

2110. Báez Evertsz, Franc. Braceros haitianos en la Republica Dominicana. Santo Domingo: 1986

2111. Betarces Medina, Emelio K. The Political Process in the Dominican Republic: The Making of the Dominican Capitalist State, 1844-1924. Doctoral dissertation: Rutgers University, 1989. UMO # 9013391.

2112. Brown, Susan E. Coping with Poverty in the Dominican Republic: Women and their Mates. Doctoral dissertation: University of Michigan, 1972.

2113. Cassá, Roberto. Capitalismo y dictadura. Santo Domingo: Editora de la Universidad Autonoma de Santo Domingo, 1982.

2114. Castro, Max J. Dominican Journey: Patterns, Context, and Consequences of Migration from the Dominican Republic to United States. Doctoral dissertation: University of North Carolina, 1985. UMO # 8605583.

2115. Del Castillo, José and Martin F. Murphy. "Migration, National Identity and Cultural Policy in the Dominican Republic." Journal of Ethnic Studies 15 (Fall 1987): 49-69.

2116. Doré y Cabral, Carlos. "Reforma agraria y luchas sociales en la República Dominicana, 1966-1978." Estudios Sociales Centroamericanos 9 (January-April, May-August 1980): 91-123, 9-36.

2117. Espinal, R. F. Classes, Power, and Political Change in the Dominican Republic. Doctoral dissertation: Washington University, 1985. UMO # 8608315.

2118. Fennema, Meindert and Troetje Loewenthal. La construcción de raza y nación en la Republica Dominicana. Santo Domingo: Editora Universitaria, 1987.

2119. Hoetink, Harry. The Dominican People, 1850-1900: Notes for a Historical Sociology. Baltimore, MD Translated by Stephen K. Ault: Johns Hopkins University Press, 1982.

2120. Kurkansky, Mark. "In the Land of the Blind Caudillo." New York Times Magazine, (August 6, 1989): [Touches on the subject of racism in the Dominican Republic.]

2121. Latortue, Paul. "Haitians in the Dominican Republic." Caribbean Review 14 (Fall 1985): 18-20.

2122. Lemoine, Maurice. Bitter Sugar: Slaves Today in the Caribbean. Chicago, IL Translated by Andrea Johnston: Banner Press, 1985.

2123. Mariñez, Pablo A. Resistencia campesina, imperialismo y reforma agraria en Republica Dominicana (1899-1978). Santo Domingo: Centro de Planificación y Acción Ecuménica, 1984.

2124. Pierre-Charles, Gérard and others. Problemas dominico- haitianos y del Caribe. Mexico City: Universidad Nacional Autónomos de México, 1973.

2125. Plant, Roger. Sugar and Modern Slavery: A Tale of Two Countries. Atlantic Highlands, NJ: Zed Books, 1987. [Dominican Republic and Haiti.]

2126. Rosario, Esteban. Los dueños de la Republica. Santo Domingo: Editoria Buho, 1988. [The Dominican Republic's wealthiest and most powerful families.]

2127. Tolentino, H. "El fenómeno racial en Haiti y en la Republica Dominicana." In Problemas dominico-haitianos y del Caribe, edited by Gérard Pierre-Charles and others. México City: Universidad Nacional Autonomos de Mexico, 1973.

2128. Vargas-Lundius, Rosemary. Peasants in Distress: Poverty and Unemployment in the Dominican REpublic. Boulder, Co: Westview, 1990. 2129. Veras, Ramon A. Migracion caribena y un capitulo haitano. Santo Domingo: Editora Taller, 1985.

2129. Veras, Ramon A. Migracion caribeña y un capitulo haitano. Santo Domingo: Editora Taller, 1985.

ECUADOR

2130. Aulestia, Juan A. From the Voices of the Oppressed: Cultural and Educational Experiences of Indigenous People in the Andean Region of Ecuador. Doctoral dissertation: University of Massachusetts, 1990. UMO # 9022663.

2131. Brooke, James. "Newly Militant Indians in Ecuador Unnerve Propertied Class." New York Times, (January 20, 1991):

2132. Chandler, David L. "Slave over Master in Colonial Colombia and Ecuador." The Americas 38 (January 1982): 315-326.

2133. Cueva, Agustin. The Process of Political Domination in Ecuador. New Brunswick, NJ Translated by Danielle Salti: Transition Books, 1981.

2134. Ehrenreich, Jeffrey D. Contact and Conflict: An Ethnographic Study of the Impact of Acculturation, Racism and Benevolent Ethnocide on the Egalitarian Coaiquer Indians of Ecuador. Doctoral dissertation: New School for Social Research, 1985. UMO # 8607153.

2135. Hurtado, Oswaldo. Political Power in Ecuador. Albuquerque Translated by Nick D. Mills, Jr.: University of New Mexico Press, 1980.

2136. Ibarra Illannez, Alicia. Los indígenas y el Estado en el Ecuador. Quito: Ediciones Abya-yala, 1987.

2137. Lesser, M. "Capital and Urban Poor in Quito." In Research in Political Economy vol. 8, edited by Paul Zarembka. Greenwich, CT: JAI Press, 1985.

2138. Los derechos humanos en Ecuador. Quito: Fundacíon Ecuatoriana de Estudios Sociales, 1987.

2139. Martinez, Luciano. De campesinos a proletarios: cambios en la mano de obra rural en la Sierra central del Ecuador. Quito: Editorial El Conejo, 1984.

2140. Miño Grijalva, Manuel. La Economia Colonial: Relaciones Socio-Ecónomicas de la Real Audiencia de Quito. Quito: Corporación Editora Nac., 1984.

2141. Peek, Peter. "Pobreza urbana, migración y reforma agraria en el Ecuador." Notas de Población 8 (August 1980): 47-91.

2142. Politica estatal y población indigena. Quito: Ediciones Abya-yala, 1984.

2143. Santana, Roberto. "La cuestion etnica y la democracia en Ecuador." R. Mex. Sociol. 49 (April-June 1987): 127-144.

2144. Santos, E. "Poverty in Ecuador." CEPAL Review, No. 38 (December 1989):

2145. Schubert, Grace. "To Be Black is Offensive: Racist Attitudes in San Lorenzo." In Cultural Transformations and Ethnicity in Modern Ecuador, edited by Norman E. Whitten, Jr. Urbana: University of Illinois Press, 1981.

2146. Verdesota, Luis, ed. Movimientos sociales en la Ecuador. Quito: Instituto Latinoamericana de Investigaciones Sociales, 1986.

2147. Weismantel, M. J. Food, Gender and Poverty in the Ecuadorian Andes. Philadelphia: University of Pennsylvania Press, 1988.

2148. Whitten, Norman E., Jr. Bicuanga Runa: The Other Side of Development in Amazonian Ecuador. Urbana: University of Illinois Press, 1985.

2149. Whitten, Norman E., Jr. "Ecuadorian Ethocide and Indigenous Ethnogenesis: Amazonian Resurgence Amidst Andean Colonialism." Journal of Ethnic Studies 4 (Summer 1976): 1-22.

2150. Wray, Natalia. "La constitución del movimiento étnico- nacional indio en Ecuador." América Indigena 49 (1989): 77-99.

EGYPT

2151. Abdalla, Ahmed. *The Student Movement and National Politics in Egypt*. London: Al Saqi Books, 1985.

2152. Abdel Kadel, Soha. *The Status of Egyptian Women, 1900-1973*. Cairo: Ford Foundation, 1973.

2153. Abdel-Khalek, Gouda and Robert Tignor. *The Political Economy of Income Distribution in Egypt*. New York: Holmes and Meier, 1982.

2154. Abel, E. L. "The Myth of Jewish Slavery in Ptolemaic Egypt." *Revue des etudes Juives* 127 (1968): 253-258.

2155. Adams, Richard H., Jr. "Development and Structural Change in Rural Egypt, 1952-1982." *World Development* 13 (June 1985)

2156. Adams, Richard H., Jr. *Development and Social Change in Rural Egypt*. Syracuse, NY: Syracuse University Press, 1986.

2157. Albert, Robert. "Qui est grec? La nationalite comme enjeu en Egypte (1830-1930)." *Relations Internationales* No.54 (1988): 139-160.

2158. Amayo, Gershom N. "The Birthplace of the Ancient Blacks' Education and Culture." *Transafrican Journal of History* 10 (1981): 1-10.

2159. An-Na'M, A. "Religious Freedom in Egypt: Under the Shadow of the Islamic dhimma System." *Copts: Christians Egypt* 14 (January 1987): 2-6.

2160. Anawati, George C. "Christians of Egypt." *Pro mundi vita: dossiers* 2-31 (April 1982): [Copts.]

2161. Ansari, Hamried. *Egypt: The Stalled Society, 1863-1984*. Albany: State University of New York Press, 1986.

2162. Assad, Maurice. "Christian Education in Egypt: Past, Present, and Future." Near East School Theol. Review 7 (1986): 44-61.

2163. Ayalon, Ami. "Egyptian Intellectuals versus Fascism and Nazism in the 1930s." In The Great Powers in the Middle East, 1919-1939, edited by Uriel Dann. New York: Holmes and Meier, 1988.

2164. Baer, Gabriel. "Slavery in Nineteenth Century Egypt." Journal of African History (1967): 417-441.

2165. Baer, Gabriel. Studies in the Social History of Modern Egypt. Chicago: University of Chicago Press, 1969.

2166. Beinin, Joel and Zachery Lockman. Workers on the Nile. Nationalism, Communism, Islam, and the Egyptian Working Class, 1882-1954. Princeton, NJ: Princeton University Press, 1987.

2167. Botman, Selma. "The Ethnic Origins of the Egyptian Communist Movement." Immigrants and Minorities 5 (1986): 193-203.

2168. Botman, Selma. "The Rise and Experience of Egyptian Communism: 1919-1952." Studies in Comparative Communism 18 (Spring 1985): 49-66.

2169. Carter, Barbara Lynn. The Copts in Egyptian Politics. Dover, NH: Croom Helm, 1986.

2170. Chitham, E. J. The Coptic Community in Egypt: Spatial and Social Change. Durham: Centre for Middle Eastern and Islamic Studies, University of Durham, 1986.

2171. Cochran, Judith. Education in Egypt. Dover, NH: Croom Helm, 1986.

2172. Cole, Juan Ricardo I. "Feminism, Class, and Islam in Turn- of-the-Century Egypt." International Journal of Middle East Studies 13 (1981): 387-407.

2173. Collins, Jeffrey G. The Egyptian Elite Under Cromer, 1882- 1907. Doctoral dissertation: University of California, Los Angeles, 1981. UMO # 8120934.

2174. Cooper, Mark. "Egyptian State Capitalism in Crisis: Economic Policies & Political Interests, 1967-1971." International Journal of Middle East Studies 10 (November 1979): 481-516.

2175. Daus, Timothy D. The Coptic Community in 19th Century Egypt. Master's thesis: University of Calgary, 1985.

2176. Davis, S. Race Relations in Ancient Egypt. London: Methuen, 1951.

2177. Deeb, Marius. "The Socioeconomic Role of the Local Foreign Minorities in Modern Egypt, 1805-1961." International Journal of Middle Eastern Studies 9 (February 1978): 11-22.

2178. Diop, Cheikh Anta. "Origin of the Ancient Egyptians." Journal of African Civilizations 8 (June 1986): 35-63.

2179. Egger, Vernon. A Fabian in Egypt: Salamah Musa and the Rise of the Professional Classes in Egypt, 1909-1939. Lanham, MD: University Press of America, 1986.

2180. El Batrawi, A. M. The Racial History of Egypt and Nubia from Predynastic to Present Times. Doctoral dissertation: University of London, University College, 1940.

2181. El-Sayed, Mustapha. "Egyptian Popular Attitudes toward the Palestinians since 1977." Journal of Palestine Studies 18 (Summer 1989): 37-51.

2182. Eliraz, Giora. "Tradition and Change: Egyptian Intellectuals and African Studies 20 (July 1986): 233-262.

2183. Eskandaramy, Ya'acoub D. "Egyptian Jewry-Why It Declined." Khamsin 5 (1978)

2184. Farah, Nadia R. Religious Strife in Egypt: Crisis and Ideological Conflict in the Seventies. New York: Gordon & Breach, 1986.

2185. Fernea, Robert. Nubians in Egypt, Peaceful People. Austin: University of Texas Press, 1977.

2186. Gershoni, Israel and James P. Jankowski. Egypt, Islam, and the Arabs. The Search for Egyptian Nationhood, 1900-1930. New York: Oxford University Press, 1986.

2187. Gershoni, Israel. "Egyptian Intellectual History and Egyptian Intellectuals in the Interwar Period." Asian & African Studies 19 (November 1985): 133-164.

2188. Goddard, H. P. "Contemporary Egyptian Muslim Views of Christianity." Renaissance Mod. Stud. , 31 (1987): 74-86.

2189. Goldberg, Ellis. Tinker, Tailor, and Textile Worker. Class and Politics in Egypt, 1930-1954. Berkeley: California Press, 1986.

2190. Goldschmidt, Arthur Jr. Modern Egypt: The Formation of a Nation-State. Boulder, Co: Westview Press, 1988.

2191. Grabowski, R. and D. Swan. "The Price of Food, Labor Scarcity and the Real Wage: Egypt, 1950 to 1974." Pakistan Journal of Applied Economics 4 (Winter 1985)

2192. Gran, Peter. Islamic Roots of Capitalism: Egypt, 1760-1840. Austin: University of Texas Press, 1979.

2193. Haarman, Ulrich W. "Ideology and History, Identity and Alterity: The Arab Image of the Turk from the 'Abbasids to Modern Egypt." International Journal of Middle East Studies 20 (1988): 175-196. [800-1952.]

2194. Hatem, Michael. "Egypt's Middle Class in Crisis: The Sexual Division of Labor." Mid. E. Jr. 42 (Summer 1988): 407-422.

2195. Hinnebusch, R. "From Nasir to Sadat: Elite Transformation in Egypt." Journal of South Asian and Middle Eastern Studies 7 (Fall 1983): 24-49.

2196. Holt, A. E. The Non-Muslim Communities in Cairo, 969-1517 A.D. Master's thesis: University of Hull, 1973-1974.

2197. Holter, Age. "The Copts in the Egypt of Today. A Camouflaged Minority (1973): 129-146.

2198. Hourani, Albert. "The Middlemen in a Changing Society: Syrians in Egypt in the Eighteenth and Nineteenth Centuries." in Emergence of the Modern Middle East. 124-142. London: Macmillan, 1981.

2199. Ibrahim, Fouad N. "The Growing Islamization in Egypt and the Situation of the Copts." British Proc. Int. Conference 70-79 (1989)

2200. Junker, H. "The First Appearance of the Negroes in History." Journal of Egyptian Archeology 7 (1921): 1-132.

2201. Kamil, Jill. Coptic Egypt: A History and Guide. Cairo, Egypt: American University of Cairo Press, 1985.

2202. Kifner, John. "Mubarak Fights a Fundamentalist Tide on Campus." New York Times, (October 5, 1986) [Asyut University.]

2203. Kitroeff, Alexander. The Greeks in Egypt: Ethnicity and Class. St. Anthony's Middle East Monographs. No. 21.

2204. Kourvetaris, Yorgos A. "The Greeks of Asia Minor and Egypt as Middlemen: Economic Minorities during the Late 19th and 20th Centuries." Ethnic Groups 7 (1988): 85-112.

2205. Kramer, Gudrun. The Jews in Modern Egypt, 1914-1952. Seattle: University of Washington Press, 1989.

2206. Kuhuke, La Verne. Lives at Risk. Public Health in Nineteenth-Century Egypt. Berkeley: University of California Press, 1990.

2207. Laskier, Michael. "From War to War: The Jews of Egypt from 1948 to 1970." Studies in Zionism 7 (Spring 1986): 111-147.

2208. Levy, Victor. "The Distributional Impact of Economic Growth and Decline in Egypt." Mid. E. Stud. 22 (January 1986): 89-103.

2209. Lockman, Zachery. "British Policy Toward Egyptian Labor Activism, 1882-1936." International Journal of Middle East Studies 20 (1988): 265-285.

2210. Majjar, Fauzi M. "Egypt's Laws of Personal Status." Arab Studies Quarterly (Summer 1988):

2211. Mayerson, Philip. "Anti-Black Sentiment in the Vitae Patrum." Harvard Theological Review 71 (1978): 304-311. [Anti-black prejudice, 3rd-5th centuries, in Egyptian monastic communities.]

2212. Mitchell, Timothy. Colonising Egypt. New York: Cambridge University Press, 1988.

2213. Mizrahi, Maurice. "La lutte anti-nazie en Egypte." Nahar Misraim 2 (1981)

2214. Mokhtar, Hermine. The Upper Economic Class in Egypt. Master's thesis: American University in Cairo, 1980.

2215. Murphy, Robert T. The Minorities of Egypt. Doctoral dissertation: Harvard University, 1959.

2216. Nelson, Cynthia. "Changing Roles of Men and women: Illustrations from Egypt." Anthropological Quarterly 41 (1968): 57-77.

2217. Papanek, Hannah. "Class and Gender in Education-Employment Linkages." Comparative Education Review 29 (August 1985): 317-346.

2218. Parkinson, Dilworth B. "Egyptian Arabic Abuse." Maledicta 10 (1988-1989): 145-161.

2219. Parveen Shaukat Ali. Status of Women in the Muslim World: A Study in the Feminist Movements in Turkey, Egypt, Iran, and Pakistan. Lahore: Aziz Publishers, 1975.

2220. Pawelka, Peter. Herrschaft und Entwicklung im Nahen Osten: Ägypten. Heidelberg: C.F. Müller Juristischen Verlag, 1985.

2221. Pennington, J. D. "The Copts in Modern Egypt." Middle Eastern Studies 18 (April 1982): 158-179.

2222. Philipp, Thomas. The Syrians in Egypt, 1725-1975. Stuttgart: Franz Steiner, 1985.

2223. Radwan, Samir M. and Eddy Lee. Agrarian Change in Egypt: An Anatomy of Rural Poverty. Dover, NH: Croom Helm, 1985.

2224. Richards, Alan R. "Primitive Accumulation in Egypt, 1798-1822." Review 1 (Fall 1977): 3-49.

2225. Sattin, Anthony. Lifting the Veil: British Society in Egypt, 1768-1956. London: J. M. Dent, 1988.

2226. Saul, Amir. "Y a-t-il une question des minorites en Egypte? Analyses eyptiennes et contexte historique." Guerres Mondiales et Conflits Contemporains 38 (1988): 9-34.

2227. Scarantino, Anna. "La comunita ebraica in egitto fra le due guerre mondiali." Storia Contemporanea 17 (1986): 1033-1082. [Egyptian Jewry in the interwar years.]

2228. Schlicht, Alfred. "Muslime und Kopten im heutigen Agypten: zum Minoritaten Problem im Zeitalter der Resilamisierung." Orient 24 (1983): 226-234.

2229. Sidhom, Samcha. "Emancipation of Women as a Social Movement in Egypt." National Review of Social Sciences 3 (January 1966): 95-135.

2230. Soliman, Ahmed M. "Housing the Urban Poor in Egypt: A Critique of Present Policies." International Journal of Urban and Regional Research 12 (1988): 65-86.

2231. Soliman, Ahmed M. The Poor in Search of Shelter: An Examination of Squatter Settlements in Alexandria, Egypt. Doctoral dissertation: University of Liverpool (England), 1985. UMO # 8614623.

2232. Soliman, Ahmed M. "Informal Land Acquisition and the Urban Poor in Alexandria." Third World Planning Review (February 1987): 21-40.

2233. Strouhal, Eugen. "Evidence of the Early Penetration of Negroes into the Prehistoric Egypt." Journal of African History 12 (1971): 1-9.

2234. Tadros, H. "Social Security and the Family in Egypt." Cairo Papers in Social Science 7 (1984): 1-87.

2235. Tignor, Robert. "The Economic Activities of Foreigners in Egypt, 1920-1950: From Millet to Haute Bourgeoisie." Comparative Studies in Society and History 22 (July 1980): 416-449.

2236. Toledano, Ehud R. "Slave Dealers, Women, Pregnancy, and Abortion: The Story of a Circassian Slave-Girl in Mid-Nineteenth Century Cairo." Slavery and Abolition 2 (May 1981): 52-68. [Racial factors.]

2237. Toledano, Ehud R. State and Society in Mid-Nineteenth- Century Egypt. New York: Cambridge University Press, 1990.

2238. Tucker, Judith. Women in 19th Century Egypt. New York: Cambridge University Press, 1985.

2239. Van Vleck, Michael R. British Educational Policy in Egypt Relative to British Imperialism in Egypt, 1882-1922. Doctoral dissertation: University of Wisconsin, 1990. UMO # 9025736.

2240. Wakin, Edward. A Lonely Minority. New York: Morrow, 1963.

2241. Welch, William M., Jr. No Country For a Gentleman. British Rule in Egypt, 1883-1907. Westport, CT: Greenwood, 1988.

2242. Wikan, Unni. Life Among the Poor in Cairo. London: Tavistock, 1980.

2243. Wikan, Unni. "Living Conditions among Cairo's Poor: A View from Below." Middle East Journal 39 (Winter 1985): 7-26.

2244. Wilson, Keith M., ed. Imperialism and Nationalism in the Middle East: The Anglo-Egyptian Experience 1882-1982. London: Mansell, 1983.

2245. Wipzycka, Ewa. "Le degre d'alphabetisation en Egypte byzantine." R. Et. Augustiniennes 30 (1984): 279-296.

2246. Yadlin, Ricka. An Arrogant Oppressive Spirit: Anti-Zionism as Anti-Judaism in Egypt. Oxford: Pergamon Press, 1989.

2247. Yurco, Frank J. "Were the Ancient Egyptians Black or White? " Biblical Archaeology Review 15 (1989): 24-29, 58.

2248. Zaalouk, Malak. Power, Class and Foreign Capital in Egypt. The Rise of the New Bourgeoisie. London: Zed Press, 1987.

2249. Zenie-Ziegler, Wedad. La face voilee des femmes d'Egypte. Paris: Mercure de France, 1985.

EL SALVADOR

2250. Anderson, Ken and Richard Anderson. "Limitations of the Liberal-Legal Model of International Human Rights: Six Lessons from El Salvador." Telos 18 (Summer 1985): 91-104.

2251. Figueroa Salazar, Amilcar. El Salvador: elementos de su historia y sus luchas (1932-1985). Caracas, Venezuela: Fondo Editorial Tropykos, 1987.

2252. Goldstein, James and Jerema Rone. A Decade of Terror. El Salvador Since the Assassination of Archbishop Romero. New Haven, CT: Yale University Press, 1991.

2253. Gruson, Lindsey. "Land for Salvador's Poor: To Many, Bitter Victory." New York Times, (September 28, 1987)

2254. Gruson, Lindsey. "Salvador's Poverty Is Called Worst of Century." New York Times, (October 16, 1988)

2255. Hard Lessons: Report of NUT/WUS Delegation to El Salvador. London: World University Service, 1986.

2256. Klawiter, Richard F. "La Tierra es Nuestra! The Campesino Struggle in El Salvador and a Vision of Community-based Lawyering." Stanford Law Review 42 (July 1990): 1625-1689.

2257. Lindo-Fuentes, Hector. Weak Foundations. The Economy of El Salvador in the Nineteenth Century 1821-1898. Berkeley: University of California Press, 1991.

2258. Lungo U., Mario. La lucha de las masas en El Salvador. San Salvador: UCA Editores, 1987. [Since the 19th century.]

182 WORLD RACISM AND RELATED INHUMANITIES

2259. Mason, T. David and Dale A. Krane. "The Political Economy of Death Squads: Toward a Theory of the Impact of State- sanctioned Terror." International Studies Quarterly 33 (1989): 175-198.

2260. Menjivar, Rafael. Formación y lucha del proletariado industrial salvadoreno. San José: Editorial Universitaria Centro-americana, 1981.

2261. North, Lusa L. "El Salvador: The Historical Roots of the Civil War." Studies in Political Economy No. 8 (Summer 1982): 59-87.

2262. Schoonover, Thomas. "A U.S. Dilemma: Economic Opportunity and Anti-Americanism in El Salvador, 1901-1911." Pacific Historical Review 58 (1989): 403-428.

2263. Tapia, Gabriel G. "Crisis y politizacion empresarial en Centroamerica." Presencia (El Salvador) 2 (July-September 1989): 99-109. [El Salvador and Guatemala.]

2264. Thomson, Marilyn. Women of El Salvador: The Price of Freedom. Philadelphia, PA: Institute for the Study of Human Issues, 1986.

2265. White, A. T. The Social Structure of the Lower Classes in San Salvador, Central America: A Case Study of the Social Consequences of Economic Change. Doctoral dissertation: University of Cambridge, 1966.

ETHIOPIA

2266. Abacchi, Alberto. Ethiopia under Mussolini: Fascism and the Colonial Experience. London: Zed Press, 1985.

2267. Abbink, G. Jon. "A Socio-Structural Analysis of the Beta Esra'el as an 'Infamous Group' in Traditional Ethiopia." Sociologus 37 (1987): 140-154.

2268. Abouchar, A. "The Firm in Abyssinia: Capitalism, Socialism, and Economic Development in Ethiopia." ACES Bulletin 26 (Winter 1984) [Association for Comparative Economic Studies.]

2269. Ahmad, Abdussamod H. "The Gondar Muslim Minority in Ethiopia: The Story Up to 1935." Jr. Inst. Muslim Minority Affairs 8 (Jan. 1988): 76-85.

2270. Alschuler, Alfred. "Fervent Advocates of Education." Valley Advocate (September 12, 1988) [Eritrea.]

2271. Antonelli, Judith. "Plight of Ethiopian Jews." Cultural Survival 7 (1983): 8-10.

2272. Araya, M. "The Eritrean Question- An Alternative Explanation." Journal of Modern African Studies 28 (March 1990):

2273. Barie, Ottavio. "Italian Imperialism: The First Stage." Journal of Italian History 2 (Winter 1979): 531-565.

2274. Birkbeck, Rosie. "Fighting Drought With new Ways of Schooling." Times Educational Supplement, (November 1, 1985) [Tigrayan People's Liberation.]

2275. Brooke, James. "Under Marxism, Ethiopia's Christians Abide." New York Times, (March 9, 1987)

184 WORLD RACISM AND RELATED INHUMANITIES

2276. Cliffe, Lionel. "Forging a Nation: The Eritrean Experience." Third World Quarterly 11 (October 1989): 131-147.

2277. Cohen, John M. Research on Socioeconomic Development in Ethiopia: Past Problems and Future Issues in Rural-Urban Studies. Ithaca, N.Y.: Cornell University, 1977.

2278. Corrett, J. A. Despised Occupational Groups in Ethiopia. B. Litt. thesis: University of Oxford, 1974.

2279. Davidson, Basil and others. Behind the War in Eritrea. London: Spokesman Books, 1980.

2280. El Bushra, Judy. Case Studies of Educational Needs among Refugees: II. Eritrean and Ethiopian Refugees in the Sudan. Cambridge, England: International Extension College, 1985.

2281. Ellingson, Lloyd S. Eritrea: Separation and Irredentism, 1941-1985. Doctoral dissertation: Michigan State University, 1986. UMO # 8707119.

2282. Ensuring the Rights of Nationalities. Addis Ababa: Preparatory Committee for the Founding of the People's Democratic Republic of Ethiopia, 1987.

2283. Erlich, Haggai. The Struggle over Eritrea, 1962-1978. Stanford, CA: 1983.

2284. "The Fascist Italian Invasion and the Ethiopian People's Struggle for Liberation." Meskerem (March 1981): 66-89.

2285. Gebru Tareke. "Preliminary History of Resistance in Tigrai (Ethiopia)." Africa (Italy) 39 (1984): 201-226.

2286. Ghose, A. K. "Transforming Feudal Agriculture: Agrarian Change in Ethiopia since 1974." Journal of Development Studies 22 (October 1985)

2287. Gruber, Ruth. Rescue: The Exodus of the Ethiopian Jews. New York: Athaneum, 1988.

2288. Gudeta, Mammo. "Ethiopie: La Campagne Nationale d'Alphabetisation." Perspectives 12 (1982): 205-212.

2289. Halliday, Fred and Maxine Molyneux. The Ethiopian Revolution. London: Verso, 1981.

2290. Hasselblatt, Gunnar. Nächstes Jahr in Oromoland: von der eklatanten Verletzung der Menschenrechte durch den abessinisch-amharischen Rassismus in Athiopien: ein Bericht. Stuttgart: Radius-Verlag, 1982.

2291. Hassen, Mohammed. The Oromo of Ethiopia: A History, 1570- 1860. New York: Cambridge University Press, 1990.

2292. Henze, Paul. Rebels and Separatists in Ethiopia-Regional Resistance to a Marxist Regime. Santa Monica, CA: Rand, December 1985.

2293. Jalata, Asafa. The Question of Oromia: Euro-Ethiopian Colonialism, Global Hegemonism and Nationalism, 1870s-1980s. Doctoral dissertation: State University of New York at Binghamton, 1990. UMO # 9022075.

2294. Keller, Edmond J. "Ethiopia: Revolution, Class and the National Question." African Affairs (London) 80 (October 1981): 519-550.

2295. Keller, Edmond J. Revolutionary Ethiopia. From Empire to People's Republic. Bloomington: Indiana University Press, 1988.

2296. Keller, Edmond J. "State, Party, and Revolution in Ethiopia." African Studies Review 28 (March 1985): 1-18.

2297. Keneally, Thomas. "In Eritrea." New York Times Magazine, (September 27, 1987)

2298. Kessler, David. The Falashas: The Forgotten Jews of Ethiopia. New York: Schocken, 1985. [With new preface.]

2299. Kessler, David and Tudor Parfitt. The Falashas: The Jews of Ethiopia. London: Minority Rights Group, 1985.

2300. Kushner, Arlene and Shmuel Avraham. Treacherous Journey: My Escape from Ethiopia. New York: Shapolsky Publishers, 1986. [The latter author's escape from Ethiopia via Sudan to Israel.]

2301. Legum, Colin and James Finebrace. Eritrea and Tigray. new ed. London: Minority Rights Group, 1983.

2302. Lencho, Tumtu. "The Question of Nationalities and Class Struggle in Ethiopia." Challenge 11 (July): 1-66.

2303. Lewis, J. M., ed. Nationalism and Self-Determination in the Horn of Africa. London: Ithaca Press, 1981.

2304. Marcus, Harold G. Haile Selassie I: The Formative Years, 1892-1936. Berkeley: University of California Press, 1987.

2305. Markakis, John. "The Nationalist Revolution in Eritrea." Journal of Modern African Studies 26 (March 1988): 51-70.

2306. McCann, James. From Poverty to Famine in Northeast Ethiopia: A Rural History, 1900-1935. Philadelphia, PA: University of Pennsylvania Press, 1986.

2307. Mesghenna, Yemane. "Italian Colonialism in Eritrea, 1882- 1941." Scandanavian Economic History Review 37 (1989): 65-72. [Review article.]

2308. Mulat, T. "Education Policy and the Regional Distribution of Schools in Ethiopia." Eastern Africa Economic Review 4 (December 1988)

2309. Negash, Lemlem and Julie Rothenberg. "Trying to Live by Eritrean and U.S. Rules." Sojourner (July 1986) [Growing up in war-torn Eritrea.]

2310. Negash, Tekeste. Italian Colonialism in Eritrea, 1882-1941. Stockholm: Almquist & Wiksell, 1987.

2311. Ottaway, Marina, ed. The Political Economy of Ethiopia. Westport, CT: Praeger, 1990.

2312. Pankhurst, Richard. "Economic Verdict on the Italian Occupation of Ethiopia (1936-1941)." Ethiopia Observer 14 (1971): 68-82.

2313. Pankhurst, Richard. "Ethiopian Slave Reminicences of the Nineteenth Century." Transafric. J. Hist 5, No. 1 (1976): 98-110.

2314. Pankhurst, Richard. "The Medical History of Ethiopia during the Italian Fascist Invasion and Occupation." Ethiopian Observer 16 (1973): 108-117.

2315. Pankhurst, Richard. "The Secret History of Italian Fascism." Africa Quarterly 16 (April 1977): 35-86.

2316. Pankhurst, Rita. "Women in Ethiopia Today." Africa Today 28 (1981): 49-52.

2317. Parfitt, Tudor and David Kessler. The Falashas. London: Minority Rights Group, 1985.

2318. Parfitt, Tudor. Operation Moses. The Story of the Exodus of the Falasha Jews from Ethiopia. London: Weidenfeld and Nicolson, 1985.

2319. Pateman, R. "Liberte, Egalite, Fraternite: Aspects of the Eritrean Revolution." Journal of Modern African Studies 28 (September 1990)

2320. Rahmato, Dessalegn. Agrarian Reform in Ethiopian. Trenton, NJ: Red Sea Press, 1985.

2321. Rapaport, Louis. Redemption Song. The Story of Operation Moses. San Diego, CA: Harcourt Brace Jovanovich, 1986.

2322. Saith, Ashwani. "The Distributional Dimensions of Revolutionary Transition: Ethiopia." Journal of Development Studies 22 (October 1985): 150-179.

2323. Sbacchi, Alberto. Italian Colonialism in Ethiopia, 1936- 1940. Doctoral dissertation: University of Illinois, Chicago, 1975. UMO # 75523364.

2324. Shehim, Kassim. "Ethiopia, Revolution, and the Question of Nationalities: The Case of the Afar." Journal of Modern African Studies 23 (June 1985): 331-348.

2325. Sherman, Richard. Eritrea, the Unfinished Revolution. New York: Praeger, 1980.

2326. Sweeter than Honey: Testimonies of Tigrayan Women. London: Links, 1989.

2327. Ta'a, Tesema. The Political Economy of Western Central Ethiopia: From the Mid-16th to the Early 20th Centuries. Doctoral dissertation: Michigan State University, 1986. UMO # 8700528.

2328. Tibebu, Teshale. The Making of Modern Ethiopia, 1900-1975: An Inquiry in Historical Sociology. Doctoral dissertation: State University of New York at Binghamton, 1990. UMO # 9012655.

2329. Todd, Dave. "The Origins of Outcastes in Ethiopia: Reflections on an Evolutionary Theory." Abbay 9 (1978): 145-158.

2330. Waldman, Menachem. The Jews of Ethiopia: The Beta Israel Community. Translated by Naftali Greenwood. Jerusalem: JDC- Israel, 1985.

2331. Winston, Diane. "The Falashas: History and Analysis of Policy towards a Beleaguered Community." Perspectives (April 1980): 1-24.

2332. Yimer, Erku. Literacy Programs in Ethiopia: A Comparative Study of Pre- and Post February, 1974 Revolution Periods. Doctoral dissertation: University of Wisconsin, Madison, 1987. UMO # 8703862.

2333. Yohannes, Okbazghi. "The Eritrean Question: A Colonial Case?" Journal of Modern African Studies 25 (December 1987): 643-668.

2334. Zewde, Bahru. "Economic Origins of the Absolutist State in Ethiopia (1916-1935)." Jr. Ethiopian Studies 17 (November 1984): 1-29.

2335. Zewde, Bahru. A History of Modern Ethiopia, 1855-1974. Athens: Ohio University Press, 1990.

FINLAND

2336. Alestalo, M. Structural Change, Classes and the State. Finland in an Historical and Comparative Perspective. Helsinki, Finland: Research Group for Comparative Sociology, 1986.

2337. Asp, Erkki. The Finnicization of the Lapps. Turku, Finland: Turku University, 1966.

2338. Astrom, Sven-Erik. "The Role of Finland in the Swedish National and War Economies during Sweden's Period as a Great Power." Scandanavian Journal of History 11 (1986): 135-147.

2339. Dempster, Carolyn. "Unfrozen Assets." Times Higher Education Supplement, (August 1, 1986) [Higher education in Finland.]

2340. Eidheim, Harold. Aspects of the Lappish Minority Situation. Oslo, Norway: Universitetsforlaget, 1971.

2341. Gadolin, Axel von. "Die schwedische Volksgruppe in Finnland." Europa Ethnica 25 (1968): 1-12.

2342. Gambier, Yves. La Finlande bilingue: histoire, droit et realites. Chrest, Quebec: Editeur Officiel du Quebec, 1986.

2343. Gustaffson, B. and H. Uusitalo. "The Welfare State and Poverty in Finland and Sweden from the Mid-1960s to the Mid- 1980s." Review of Income and Wealth (September 1990)

2344. Harviainen, Tapani. "Die Juden in Finnland." Europa Ethnica 46 (1989): 73-80.

2345. Heikkinen, Sakari. "On Private Consumption and the Standard of Living in Finland, 1860-1912." Scandanavian Economic Historical Review 34 (1986): 122-134.

2346. Hill, R. G. P., ed. The Lapps Today in Finland, Norway and Sweden, I. Paris: Mouton, 1960.

2347. Hill, R. G. P. and K. Nickul, eds. The Lapps Today in Finland, Norway and Sweden, II. Oslo-Bergen-Tromso, Norway: Universitetsvorlaget, 1969.

2348. Hoapala, Pertti. "How Was the Working Class Formed? The Case of Finland, 1850-1920." Scandanavian Journal of History 12 (1987): 179-197.

2349. Jauhianen, Marjatta. "The Sins of Women in Finnish Belief Legends." In Folk Narrative, 210-220. Helsinki: Suomalaisen Kirjallisuuden Seura, 1989.

2350. Jutikkala, Eino. "The Distribution of Wealth in Finland in 1800." Scandanavian Economic History Review 1 (1953)

2351. Kalela, Jorma. "Right-wing Radicalism in Finland during the Inter-war Period: Pespectives from and an Appraisal of Recent Literature." Scandanavian Journal of History 1 (1976): 105- 124.

2352. Klinge, Matti. "Sprache oder Klasse?" Europa Ethnica 44 (1987): 121-130. [The Swedish language in Finland.]

2353. Kujala, Antti V. Revolution and the Right to National Self- determination: Russian Socialist Parties and Finiish Radicalism at the Beginning of the Twentieth Century. Helsinke: Finnish Historical Society, 1989. [In Finnish.]

2354. Lauren, C. "Bilingual Finland." Language and Society 3 (Autumn 1980): 7-11. [Finnish and Swedish.]

2355. Lethtinen, Erkki. "Nations of a Finnish National Identity during the Period of Swedish Rule." Scandanavian Journal of History 6 (1981): 277-295.

2356. Liebkind, Karmela. Minority Identity and Identification Processes: A Social Psychological Study. Helsinki: Societas Scientiarum Fennica, 1984.

2357. Lohr, Steve. "Developing Finnish Lapland." New York Times, (August 18, 1986)

2358. Lonnqvist, Bo. "Social Ideals and Cultural Patterns in Twentieth-Century Finland." Etnol. Scand. 18-32 (1986)

2359. Luostarinen, Heikki. "Finnish Russophobia: The Story of an Enemy Image." Journal of Peace Research 26 (1989): 123-137.

2360. Mohamed-Salih, M. A. The Position of Gypsies in Finnish Society. Doctoral dissertation: University of Manchester, 1985.

2361. Nickul, Kar. The Sami as People and Citizens. Helsinki: Society of Finnish Literature, 1970.

2362. Paasivirta, Juhani. *Finland and Europe. International Crises in the Period of Autonomy, 1808-1914*. Edited by D.G. Kirby. Translated by Anthony F. Lipton and Sirkka R. Upton. Minneapolis: University of Minneapolis Press, 1982.

2363. Penrose, Janet M. *The Relationship between Economic Integration and Cultural Transition: The Case of the Finnish Sami*. Master's thesis: McGill University, 1981.

2364. Rautkallio, Hannu. *Finland and the Holocaust: The Rescue of Finland's Jews*. New York: 1987,

2365. Singleton, Fred. *The Economy of Finland in the Twentieth Century*. Bradford, England: University of Bradford, 1986.

2366. Siruainen, Eino and Pekka Aikio. *The Lapps in Finland*. Helsinki: Society for the Promotion of Lapp Culture, 1977.

2367. Soikkanen, Hannu. "Finnish Research on Changes in the Standard of Living." *Scandanavian Economic Historical Review* 34 (1986): 167-170.

2368. Sundberg, J. *The Dilemma of Ethnicity in Finland. Cooperation and Cleavage within the Swedish Finnish Community during the Twentieth Century*. Helsingfors, Finland: The Finnish Society of Sciences and Letter, Sudlmansgatan 9-11 00170, 1985. [In Swedish.]

2369. Thaden, Edmund C. "Finland and the Baltic Provinces: Elite Roles and Social and Economic Conditions and Structures." *Journal of Baltic Studies* 15 (1984): 216-227.

2370. Upton, A. F. "Finland." In *Fascism in Europe*, edited by S.J. Woolf. London: Methuen, 1982.

2371. Vaisanen, Maija, ed. *Nationality and Nationalism in Italy and Finland from the Mid-Nineteenth Century to 1918*. Helsinki: Suomen Historiallinen Seura, 1984.

FRANCE

2372. Aballea, Francois. "Besoin de santé et classes sociales." Recherche Sociale (January-March 1982): 3-80.

2373. Abanime, Emeka P. "The Anti-Negro French Law of 1777." Journal of Negro History 64 (1979): 21-29.

2374. Abray, Jane. "Feminism in the French Revolution." American Historical Review 80 (Fall 1975): 43-62.

2375. Adler, Jacques. The Jews of Paris and the Final Solution. Response and Internal Conflicts, 1940-1944. New York: Oxford University Press, 1987.

2376. Adler, Karen. "The Extreme Right and Anti-Immigrant Opinion in France." Research Report (Institute of Jewish Affairs, London) No. 1 (1990

2377. Ageron, Charles-Robert. Les Algériens musulmanes et la France (1871-1919). 2 vols. Paris: 1968.

2378. Ageron, Charles-Robert. "L'Association des Étudiants Musulmans Nord-Africains en France Durant l'Entre-deux- guerres. Contribution a l'Etude des Nationalismes Maghrébins." R. fr. histr. outre-mer 70 (1983): 25-56.

2379. Albistur, Maité and Daniel Armogathe, eds. Histoire de féminisme francais du Moyen Age à nos jours. Paris: Editions des femmes, 1977.

2380. Algazy, Joseph. L'extrême-droite en France de 1965 à 1984. Paris: Editions l'Harmattan, 1989.

2381. Algazy, Joseph. La tentation neo-fasciste en France de 1944 a 1965. Paris: Librairie Artheme Fayard, 1984.

192   WORLD RACISM AND RELATED INHUMANITIES

2382. Allen, Robert B. *Selected French Press Relations to Antisemitism 1933-1939*. Master's thesis: Southern Methodist University, 1983.

2383. Anne Frank Stichting. *Racisme in Frankrijk: Le Pen in het land van Vrijheid, Gelijkheit en Brolderschap*. Amsterdam: De Balie, 1988.

2384. Antweiler, Phillip L. *The Search for Welsh and Breton Ethnic Autonomy: Toward a Political Sociology of Nations without States*. 3 vols. Doctoral dissertation: Boston University, 1986. UMO # 8606838.

2385. Arnal, Oscar L. *Ambivalent Alliance: The Catholic Church and the Action Francaise, 1899-1939*. Pittsburgh, PA: University of Pittsburgh Press, 1985.

2386. Aron, Raymond. *Essais sur la condition juive contemporaine*. Paris: Editions de Fallois, 1989.

2387. Austin, Roger. "Political Surveillance and Ideological Control in Vichy France: A Study of Teachers in the Midi, 1940-1944." In *Vichy France and the Resistance: Culture and Ideology*, edited by Roderick Kedward and Roger Austin. Totowa, NJ: Barnes and Noble, 1985.

2388. Aziz, Philippe. *Le livre noir de la trahison: histoires de la Gestapo en France*. Paris: Editions Ramsay, 1984.

2389. Balinska, Maria. "French Public Opinion and the Front National." *Patterns of Prejudice* 23 (Spring 1989): 53-54.

2390. Balinska, Maria. "SOS-Racisme." *Patterns of Prejudice* 22 (Winter 1988): 46-48.

2391. Barnes, Ian R. "Intellectual Processes on the French Far Right." *Patterns of Prejudice* 16 (January 1982): 3-12.

2392. Barnes, Ian R. "The Pedigree of GREC." *Patterns of Prejudice* 14 (July and October 1980): 14-24, 29-39.

2393. Barontini, C. "Les travailleurs immigrés et les luttes de classe en France." *Cahiers du Communisme* 5 (May 1973): 35- 44.

2394. Barou, Pierre. "In the Aftermath of Colonization: Black African Immigrants in France." In *Migrants in Europe: The Role of Family, Labor, and Politics*, edited by Hans Christian and Judith Maria Buechler. Westport, Ct: Greenwood, 1987.

2395. Barouh, Ida S. "Minorités en France: Populations originaires, des pays de l'Asie du Sud-Est." *Pluriel* Nos. 32-33 (1982-1983): 59-70.

2396. Barthe, Marie-Annick. "Les formes de la pauvreté dans la société française." *Revue Française de Science Politique* 41 (April-June 1987): 113-125.

2397. Beaud, Paul. La société de connivence: media, médiations et classes sociales. Paris: Editions Aubier-Montaigne, 1984.

2398. Becker, Jean-Jacques and S. Berstein. "L'anticommunisme en France." XXe Siecle. R. Hist. 15 (1987): 17-27.

2399. Beer, William R. "Ethnic Activists in Contemporary France: Social Class and Social Mobility." Europa Ethnica 35 (1978): 50-60.

2400. Beer, William R. The Unexpected Rebellion: Ethnic Activism in Contemporary France. New York: New York University Press, 1980.

2401. Begag, Azouz. "The 'Beurs': Children of North-African Immigrants in France: The Issue of Integration." Journal of Ethnic Studies 18 (Spring 1990)

2402. Bejin, A. and J. Freund, eds. Racismes-Anti-racismes. Paris: Meridiens/Klinchsieck, 1986.

2403. Belbahri, Abdelkader. Immigration et situations postcoloniales: le cas des Maghrebins en France. Paris: Editions l'Harmattan, 1987.

2404. Belorgey, Jean-Michel. La gauche et les pauvres. Paris: Editions Syros/Alternatives, 1988.

2405. Ben Jelloun, Tahar. Hospitalité français: racisme et immigration maghrébine. Paris: Editions du Seuil, 1984.

2406. Bensimon, Doris. Les grandes rafles: Juifs en France, 1940- 1944. Toulouse: Editions Edouard Privat, 1987.

2407. Bensimon, Doris and Benjamin Pinkus, eds. Les Juifs de France, le sionisme et l'Etat d'Israel. 2 vols. Paris: Institut national des langues et civilisations orientales, 1989.

2408. Bergen, Barry H. Molding Citizens: Ideology, Class and Primary Education in Nineteenth-century France. Doctoral dissertation: University of Pennsylvania, 1987. UMO # 8725139.

2409. Berlanstein, Lenard R. "Managers and Engineers in French Big Business of the Nineteenth Century." Journal of Social History 22 (Winter 1988) 211-236.

2410. Bernard, Rene. "Des gitans, du racisme et de la société." Études 338 (1973): 189-196.

2411. Bernstein, Richard. "France's Bitter Brand of Ethnic Politics." New York Times, (December 22, 1985

2412. Bernstein, Richard. "In Tense French Town, the Melting Pot Boils Over." New York Times, (September 3, 1986): [Right-wing racists in Toulon.]

2413. Betts, Raymond F. "The French Colonial Empire and the French World-View." In Racism and Colonialism, edited by Robert Ross. The Hague: Martinus Nyhoff, 1982.

2414. Beyer, Lisa. "Issues of Color And of Creed." Trine (May 28, 1990)

2415. Biarnes, Jean and Michele Surhomme. L'enfant antillais en France. Paris: Editions l'Harmattan, 1982.

2416. Bidouze, Henriette and others. Les Femmes dans la Résistance. Monaco: Editions de Rocher, 1977.

2417. Bloch-Michel, Jean. "Anti-Semitism and the French 'New Right'." Dissent 27 (1980): 291-298.

2418. Boisvert, Collette C. "Working-class Portuguese Families in a French Provincial Town: Adaptive Strategies." In Migrants in Europe: The Role of Family, Labor, and Politics, edited by Hans Christian and Judith Maria Buechler. Westport, CT: Greenwood, 1987.

2419. Bolle, Pierre. "Les Protestants et leurs Églises devant la persecution des Juifs en France." Ét. théol. relig. 57 (1982): 185-208.

2420. Boulle, Pierre. "In Defense of Slavery: Eighteenth Century Opposition to Abolition and the origins of a Racist Ideology in France." in History from Below Frederick Krantz. 219-246. Oxford: 1988.

2421. Boulot, Serge and Danielle Boyzon-Fradet. Les immigrés et l'école: une course d'obstacles. L'Harmattan: CIEMI, 1988.

2422. Bower, Tom. Klaus Barbie: Butcher of Lyons. London: M. Joseph Ltd., 1984.

2423. Brock, Colin, ed. The Caribbean in Europe: Aspects of the West Indian Experience in Britain, France and the Netherlands. Totowa, NJ: Frank Cass, 1987.

2424. Brubaker, W. R. "Immigration, Citizenship, and the Nation State in France and Germany: A Comparative Historical Analysis." International Sociology 5 (December 1990)

2425. Brustein, William. The Social Origins of Political Regionalism: France, 1849-1981. Berkeley: University of California Press, 1988.

2426. Busi, Frederick. "The Jew in 20th Century French Thinking: The Impact of Fascism." Patterns of Prejudice 8 (1974): 9- 16.

2427. Busi, Frederick. The Pope of Antisemitism: The Career and Legacy of Edouard-Adolphe Drumont. Lanham, MD: University Press of America, 1986.

2428. Byrnes, Robert F. Antisemitism in Modern France. Vol.I; The Prologue to the Dreyfus Affair. New Brunswick, N.J.: Rutgers University Press, 1950.

2429. Cantan, M. Maurice. La Condition des Etrangers en France. Paris: Secours Catholique, 1985.

2430. Cardinal, Linda and Alan Fennal. "La republique des 'potes': S.O.S. Racisme and the Politics of Youth in France Today." Canadian Dimension 19 (1986): 29-31,34.

2431. Carr-Hill, Ray A. "'O Bring Me Your Poor': Immigrants in the French System of Criminal Justice." Howard Journal of Criminal Justice 26 (November 1987): 287-302.

2432. Cassilly, Thomas A. The Anticolonial Tradition in France: The Eighteenth Century to the Fifth Republic. Doctoral dissertation: Columbia University, 1975.

2433. Castor, Elie and Georges Othily. La région Guyane, 1960- 1983. Paris: Editions l'Harmattan, 1984.

2434. Catrice, Paul. "L'antisémitisme social francais au miroir de la littérature des XIXe et XXe siecles." Revue de Psychologie des Peuples 22 (1967): 248-281.

2435. Chairoff, P. Dossier Néo-Nazisme. Paris: 1977.

2436. Charlot, Monica. "L'emergence du Front national." Revue Francaise de Science Politique 36 (1986): 30-45.

2437. Chatain, Jean. Les Affaires de M. Le Pen. Paris: Messidor, 1987.

2438. Chatel, Nicole. Les Femmes dans la Résistance. Paris: Juillard, 1972.

2439. Chebel d'Appollonia, Ariane. L'Extrême-droite en France: De Maurras à Le Pen. Brussels: Editions Complexe, 1988.

2440. Chisick, Harvey. "French Charity Schools in the Seventeenth and Eighteenth Centuries, with Special Reference to the Case of Amiens." Hist. sociale 16 (1983): 241-277.

2441. Chisick, Harvey. The Limits of Reform in the Enlightenment: Attitudes to the Education of the Lower Classes in France, 1762-1789. Princeton, NJ: Princeton University Press, 1981.

2442. Christophe, Marc A. "Changing Image of Blacks in Eighteenth Century French Literature." Phylon 48 (Fall 1987): 183-189.

2443. Clark, Linda L. "The Primary Education of French Girls: Pedagogical Prescriptions and Social Realities, 1880-1940." History of Education Quarterly 21 (Winter 1981): 411-428.

2444. Clark, Linda L. Social Darwinism in France. University of Alabama Press, 1984.

2445. Clary, Norman J. French Antisemitism During the Years of Drumont and Dreyfus, 1886-1906. Doctoral dissertation: Ohio State University, 1970. UMO # 70-26265.

2446. Closets, Francois de. Toujours plus! Paris: Société d'Editions Grasset et Fasquelle, 1982. [Wealth and income.]

2447. Cohen, Jim. "For Whom Does SOS Speak?" Socialist Review 19 (January-March 1989): 5-7, 161-162. [See response by Susan Ossman, pp.162-164.]

2448. Cohen, R. J. The Burden of Conscience: French Jewish Leadership during the Holocaust. Bloomington, IN: 1987.

2449. Cohen, William B. The French Encounter with Africans: White Response to Blacks, 1530-1880. Bloomington: Indiana University Press, 1980. [See Mpuyi-Buatu, below.]

2450. Cohen, William B. "Literature and Race: Nineteenth Century French Fiction, Blacks and Africa." Race and Class 16 (October 1974): 181-205.

2451. Coleman, William. Death Is a Social Disease: Public Health and Political Economy in Early Industrial France. Madison, WI: 1982.

2452. Cooper, Anna Julia. Slavery and the French Revolutionists, 1788-1805. Lewiston Translated by Frances R. Keller: E. Mellen Press, 1988.

2453. Costa-Lascoux, Jacqueline. "De l'immigré au citoyen." Notes et Etudes Documentaires No. 11 (1989): 1-160.

2454. Costa-Lascoux, Jacqueline and Emile Termine. Les Algériens en France: genese et devinir d'une migration. Paris: Editors PubliSud, 1986.

2455. Coulet, N. "Juifs et justice en Provence au 15e siècle: un procès et un pogrom à Aix (1425-1430)." Michael 4 (1976): 9-26.

2456. Council of Europe. "France: Towards Greater Democracy in Lower Secondary Schools." Western European Education 18 (Fall 1986): 31-53.

2457. Courtois, Stephane and Gilles Kepel. "Musulmans et proletaires." R. fr. sci. pol. 37 (December 1987): 782-793.

2458. Cox, Donald and John V. Nye. "Male-Female Wage Discrimination in Nineteenth-century France." Journal of Economic History 49 (December 1989): 903-920.

2459. Daumard, Adeline. Les Fortunes Françaises au XIXe Siecle. Paris: 1973.

2460. Daumard, Adeline. Histoire économique et sociale de la France. 5 vols. Paris: 1979. [See, esp., vols. 2 and 4.]

2461. Daumard, Adeline. "Wealth and Affluence in France Since the Beginning of the Nineteenth Century." In Wealth and the Wealthy in the Modern World, edited by W.D. Rubenstein. London: Croom Helm, 1980.

2462. Davies, Alan T. "Religion and Racism: The Case of French Anti-Semitism." Journal of Church and State 20 (Spring 1978): 273-286.

2463. De Comarmond, P. and C. Duchet, eds. Racisme et Société. Paris: Maspéro, 1969.

2464. DeConchy, Jean P. and others. "Effects of Social Categorization (Religious and National) among Guinean Workers in France." Journal of Social Psychology 128 (June 1988): 325-332.

2465. Dennis, John A. The René Maran Story: The Life and Times of a Black Frenchman, Colonial Administrator, Novelist and Social Critic, 1887-1960. Doctoral dissertation: Stanford University, 1987. UMO# 8707653.

2466. Désert, Gabriel. "Réflexions sur les progrès de l'alphabétisation dans la France du XIXe siecle." Hist. Social Research 34 (1985): 44-59.

2467. Désir, Harlem. Touche pas à mon pote. Paris: 1985.

2468. Dewald, Jonathan. Port-St.-Pierre, 1398-1789. Lordship, Community, and Capitalism in Early Modern France. Berkeley: University of California Press, 1987.

2469. Dewitte, Philippe. Les mouvements nègres en France, 1919- 1939. Paris: Editions L'Harmattan, 1985.

2470. Dhoquois, Régine. "De l'étranger au naturalisé. Ou comment passe-t-on des droits de l'homme aux droits du citoyen?" Cahiers de recherche sociologique 13 (Fall 1989): 119-137.

2471. Diefendorf, Barbara. "Prologue to a Massacre: Popular Unrest in Paris, 1557-1572." American Historical Review 90 (December 1985): 1067-1091.

2472. "Discriminations." Actes 51 (September 1985): 1-76.

198 WORLD RACISM AND RELATED INHUMANITIES

2473. Dray, Julien. SOS Génération: l'histoire du mouvement des jeunes de novembre-décembre 1986. Paris: Ramsay, 1987.

2474. Dreyfus, François-Georges. "Antisemitismus in Frankreich von 1935 bis heute: mehr Eigengewächs als Importware." Dokumente 38 (1982): 229-235.

2475. Drumont, Edouard. Le testament d'un antisémite. Paris: Dentu, 1891.

2476. Duchen, Calire. Feminism in France from May 68 to Mitterand. London: Routledge & Kegan Paul, 1986.

2477. Dumont, Serge and others. Le systeme Le Pen. Paris: Les Editions Ouvrieres, 1985.

2478. Echenberg, Myron. "Morts pour la France: The African Soldier in France during the Second World War." Journal of African History 26 (1985): 363-380.

2479. Enriquez, Eugène. "Le retour des forces obscures: le racisme comme symptôme." Connexions No. 45 (1985): 217-229. [Racism in France.]

2480. Epstein, Simon. L'antisemitisme français aujourd'hui et demain. Paris: Editions Pierre Belfond, 1984.

2481. Espaces 89. L'Identité française. Paris: Tierce, 1985. [North Africans in France.]

2482. Estebe, Jean. "Les Gouvernants de la III Republique et leur Fortunes, 1871-1914." Revue d'Histoire Economique et Sociale 54 (1976)

2483. Fanoudh-Siefer, Leon. Le Mythe du nègre et de l'Afrique noire dans la littérature française de 1800 à la 2e guerre mondiale. Paris: 1968.

2484. Fenet, Alain and Gerard Soulier, eds. Les minorites et leurs droits depuis 1789. Paris: Éditions l'Harmattan, 1989.

2485. Flamand, Jean-Paul. Loger le peuple: essai sur l'histoire du logement social en France. Paris: Editions La Découverte, 1989. [Since 1830.]

2486. Flem, Lydia. Le racisme. Paris: MA Edition, 1985.

2487. Forrest, Alan. The French Revolution and the Poor. Oxford: Blackwell, 1981.

2488. Forster, Robert. "Who Is a Citizen? The Boundaries of 'La Patrie': The French Revolution and the People of Color, 1789- 1791." Fr. Pol. & Soc. 7 (Summer 1989): 50-64.

2489. Fouquet, A. and D. Strauss-Kohn. "The Size Distribution of Personal Wealth." Review of Income and Wealth 30 (December 1984)

2490. La France au pluriel? Paris: Editions l'Harmattan, 1984.

2491. "La France avec les immigrés." Project (Paris) No. 199 (May-June 1986)

2492. "France's Le Pen Movement: Neo-Nazi, Racist, and Anti- Semitic Factions, 1972-1987." ADL International Report-Europe 1-9 (April 1988)

2493. Freeman, Gary P. British and French Policies on Immigration and Race Relations, 1945-1974. Doctoral dissertation: University of Wisconsin, 1975. UMO # 7529809.

2494. Fresco, Nadine. "The Denial of the Dead: On the Faurisson Affair." Dissent (Fall 1981): 467-483.

2495. Friedlander, Judith. Vilna on the Seine: Jewish Intellectuals in France Since 1968. New Haven, CT: Yale University Press, 1990.

2496. Friedman, Gerald. "Capitalism, Republicanism, Socialism, and the State: France, 1871-1914." Social Science History 14 (Summer 1990)

2497. Friedman, Jean-Pierre. Au coeur du racisme. Paris: Pierre- Marcel Favre, 1984.

2498. "The 'Front National' in France: Nazi, Neo-Nazi and Anti- Semitic Connections." ADL European Report 1-6 (December 1985)

2499. Fuchs, Rachel G. "Morality and Poverty: Public Welfare for Mothers in Paris, 1870-1900." Fr. Hist. 2 (September 1988): 288-311.

2500. Furet, F. and J. Ozouf. Lire et écrire: L'alphabetisation des Français de Calvin à Jules Ferry. Paris: Ed. de Minuit, 1977.

2501. Gallie, Duncan. Social Inequality and Class Radicalism in France and Britain. New York: Cambridge University Press, 1983.

2502. Le Gallou, J. Y. La Preference Nationale: reponse a l'immigration. 1985. [On the supposedly unassimilable Muslims and Arabs in France.]

2503. Garaud, X. and A. Courbet. "The Book Trade on the French Far Right." Patterns of Prejudice 16 (July 1982): 41-45.

2504. Geggus, David. "Racial Equality, Slavery and Colonial Secession during the Constituent Assembly." American Historical Review 94 (December 1989): 1290-1308.

2505. Geoffroy, Claude. "The Community Divided." Inside Asia No. 6 (November-December 1985): 25-26. [Cambodians in Paris.]

2506. Giblin, Beatrice. "Le Front national dans une région de gauche: le Nord-Pas-de-Calais." Hérodote 50-51 (July- December 1988): 50-65.

2507. Giblin, Beatrice. "Le Front national, un vote raciste?" Hérodote 50-51 (July-December 1988): 11-21.

2508. Giraud, Michel. "Le Regard égaré: ethnocentrisme, xénophobie ou racisme?" Les Temps Modernes No. 459 (October 1984): 737-750.

2509. Giraud, Michel and Jean-Luc Jamard. "Contre l'economisme: le cas antillais." Critiques de l'Économie Politique n.s. (July-September 1982): 110-142.

2510. Giudice, Fausto. Têtes de Turcs en France. Paris: Editions la Découverte, 1989. [Foreign workers in France.]

2511. Giullon, Michelle and Isabelle T. Leonetti. Le Triangle de Choisy: Un Quartier Chinois a Paris. Paris: CIEMI, Editions L'Harmattan, 1986.

2512. Golb, Norman. "New Light on the Persecution of French Jews at the Time of the First Crusade." American Academy for Jewish Research Proceedings 34 (1966)

2513. Goldkorn, Isaac. "Renan and Racism." Midstream 32 (1986): 40-42.

2514. Gordon, Bertram M. Collaborationism in France During the Second World War. Ithaca, New York: Cornell University Press, 1980.

2515. GRECO 13 CNRS. Les Algériens en France. Genèse et Devenir d'une Migration. Paris: 1985.

2516. Green, Mary Jean. "Fascists on Film: The Brasillach and Bardèche Histoire du cinéma." South Central Review 6 (Summer 1989): 32-47.

2517. Green, Nancy. The Pletzl of Paris: Jewish Immigrant Workers in the Belle Epoque. New York: Holmes & Meier, 1986. [Late 19th and early 20th centuries.]

2518. Grew, Raymond and others. "The Availability of Schooling in Nineteenth-century France." Journal of Interdisciplinary History 14 (1983): 25-63.

2519. Grew, Raymond and others. "La scolarisation en France, 1829-1906." Annales 39 (1984): 116-157.

2520. Grew, Raymond and Patrick Harrigan. "The Catholic Contribution to Universal Schooling in France, 1840-1906." Journal of Modern History 57 (June 1985): 211-247.

2521. Griffiths, Richard. "Anticapitalism and the French Extra- parliamentary Right, 1870-1940." Journal of Contemporary History 13 (1978): 721-740.

2522. Grillo, R. D. Dominant Languages: Language and Hierarchy in Britain and France. New York: Cambridge University Press, 1989.

2523. Grillo, R. D. Ideologies and Institutions in Urban France: The Representation of Immigrants. New York: Cambridge University Press, 1985. [North Africans in Lyons.]

2524. Gritti, Jules. Déraciner les racismes. Paris: Editions S.O.S., 1982.

2525. Gucht, A.-M. van der. "La rélégation culturelle et linguistique des élèves issus des classes dominées dans l'institution scolaire et ses conséquences psychoaffectives." Recherches Sociologiques 11 (1980): 179- 194.

2526. Guillaumin, Colette. "Je sais bien mais quand même ou les avatars de la notion de 'race'." Le Genre Humain No. 1 (1981)

2527. Guillaumin, Colette. "The Popular Press and Ethnic Pluralism: The Situation in France." International Social Science Journal 23 (1971): 576-593.

2528. Guiral, Pierre and Émile Temine, eds. L'idee de race dans la pensée politique française contemporaine. Paris: Editions du Centre National de la Recherche Scientifique, 1977.

2529. Hainsworth, Paul. "The Triumph of the Outsider: Jean-Marie le Pen and the 1988 Presidential Election." In Contemporary France, Vol.3, A Review of Interdisciplinary Studies, edited by Jolyon Howorth and George Ross. New York: Pinter, 1989.

2530. Hamoumou, Mohand. "L'Honneur perdu; relations parents- enfants dans les familles d'immigrés algériens." An., Ec., Soc., Civil 41 (July 1986): 771-788.

2531. Hanna, Martha T. Intellectuals and the Action française: The Appeal of an Adversative Idiom for Jacques Maritain, André Gide, and Georges Bernanos. Doctoral dissertation: Georgetown University, 1989. UMO # 9004735.

2532. Hannoun, Michel. L'Homme est l'espérance de l'Homme. Rapport sur le racisme et les discriminations en France au secrétaire d'État auprés du Premier ministre chargé des Droits de l'Homme. Paris: 1987.

2533. Harouel, Jean-Louis. Essai sur l'inégalité. Paris: Presses Universitaires de France, 1984.

2534. Hause, Steven C. and Anne R. Kenney. Women's Suffrage and Social Politics in the French Third Republic. Princeton, NJ: Princeton University Press, 1984.

2535. Hémery, Daniel. "De patriotisme au marxisme: l'immigration vietnamienne en France de 1926 à 1930." Mouvement Social 90 (1975): 3-54.

2536. Hersch, J. "Sur la notion de race." Diogène No. 59 (1967): 125-142.

2537. Herte, Robert de. "Avec les immigrés contre le nouvel esclavage." Eléments pour la civilisation européenne No. 45 (Spring 1983)

2538. Herzstein, Robert Edwin. "Le nazisme et la France (1939- 1942): population et racisme." R. hist. deux. guerre mond. 29 (July 1979): 1-25.

2539. Heywood, Colin. "The Market for Child Labour in Nineteenth Century France." History 66 (1981): 34-49.

2540. Hifi, Belkacem. L'Immigration Algérienne en France: Origins et perspectives de non-retour. Paris: L'Harmattan/CIEM, 1985.

2541. Hirschfeld, Gerhard and Patrick Marsh, eds. Collaboration in France: Politics and Culture during the Nazi Occupation, 1940-1944. New York: Berg, 1989.

2542. Hoberman, J. M. "Defining the Post-War French Ultra-Right 1929-1955." In Proceedings of the Annual Meeting of the Western Society for French History. Las Cruces: University of New Mexico Press, 1978.

2543. Hoch, Marie-Therese. "A Survey of Jewish-Christian Relations in France in Recent Years." Journal of Ecumenical Studies 22-23 (Fall-Winter 1985-1986): 869-875; 185-193.

2544. Hollifield, James F. "Immigration and the French State: Problems of Policy Implementation." Comparative Political Studies 23 (April 1990)

2545. Hollifield, James F. The Political Economy of Immigration: The French Case, 1945-1981. Doctoral dissertation: Duke University, 1985. UMO # 8608923.

2546. Horne, John. "Immigrant Workers in France during World War I." French Historical Studies 14 (Spring 1985): 57-88.

2547. Howe, Darcus. "Black Workers Break the French Mould." Race Today 15 (April-May 1984): 9-15.

2548. Howorth, Jolyon and Philip G. Cerny, eds. Elites in France: Formation and Continuity. New York: St. Martin's Press, 1981.

2549. Hunt, David. "Working People of France and their Historians." Radical History Review Nos. 28-30 (1984): 45- 68.

2550. Hunting, Claudine. "The philosophes and the Question of Black Slavery." Journal of the History of Ideas 39 (July 1978): 405-419.

2551. "Les Immigrés." Communio (Paris) (March-April 1986)

2552. Les immigrés et la participation a la vie locale. Paris: Editions Syros/Alternatives, 1989.

FRANCE 203

2553. Ivorra, Pierre. "Portrait de groupe des 100,000 français le plus riches." Cahiers du Communisme 59 (1983): 32-45.

2554. Jacob, James B. "Ethnic Conflict in Contemporary France." Contemporary French Civilization 5 (1980): 23-42.

2555. Jacquard, A. "A la recherche d'un contenu pour le mot 'race'. La Reponse du généticien." In La Racisme, Mythes et Sciences. Brussels: Editions Complexe, 1981.

2556. Jazouli, Adil. L'Action Collective des Jeunes Maghrébins de France. Paris: L'Harmattan, 1986.

2557. Jenson, Jane. "Le feminisme en France depuis mai 68." Vingtieme Siecle No. 24 (1989): 55-67.

2558. Join-Lambert, P. "Discriminations raciales et tsiganes." Revue des Droits de l'Homme 5 (1972)

2559. Jolivet, Marie-José. La question créole: essai de sociologie sur la Guyane Francaise. Bondy, France: Office de la recherche scientifique et technique outre-mer, 1982.

2560. Jordan, William. The French Monarchy and the Jews, From Philip Augustus to the Last Capetians. Philadelphia: University of Pennsylvania, 1989.

2561. Jordan, William C. From Servitude to Freedom: Manumission in the Senonais in the Thirteenth Century. Philadelphia: University of Pennsylvania Press, 1986.

2562. Josephs, J. Swastika over Paris: The State of the French Jews. London: Bloomsbury, 1989.

2563. Jouanna, Arlette. L'idée de race en France au XVIème siècle et au début du XVIIème siècle (1498-1614) 3 vols. Paris: Librairie Honoré Champion, 1976.

2564. Kalla, Moise. Les français sont-ils racistes? Loi contraraciste du 1er Juillet 1972. Paris: La Pense Universelle, 1979.

2565. Kaplan, Alice Y. Reproductions of Banality: Fascism, Literature and French Intellectual Life. Minneapolis: University of Minnesota Press, 1986.

2566. Kaplan, Steve L. and Cynthia J. Koepp, eds. Work in France: Representations, Meaning, Organization, and Practice. Ithaca, New York: Cornell University Press, 1986.

2567. Kastoryano, Riva. Être turc en France, Reflexions sur familles et Communautes. Paris: Ed. CIEMI/L'Harmattan, 1986.

2568. Khandriche, Mohammed. "Les Enfants d'Émigrés Algériens en France: Eléments d'Analyse." R. algérienne sci. jur. éc. pol. 20 (December 1983): 457-496.

2569. Kingston, Paul J. Anti-Semitism in France during the 1930's: Organizations, Personalities, and Propoganda. Hull, England: University of Hull Press, 1983.

2570. Klarsfeld, Serge. "Corrected Record." Jerusalem Post Magazine, (December 16, 1983): [Accounts in French textbooks dealing with French responsibility for killing of Jews during World War II.]

2571. Klarsfeld, Serge. Vichy-Auschwitz: le rôle de Vichy dans la solution finale de la question juive en France, 1942. Paris: Librairie Artheme Fayard, 1983.

2572. Klaus-Erich, Gerth. "Latest Developments in Early Bilingual Education in France and Southern Europe." Journal of Multilingual and Multicultural Development 9 (1988): 193- 202.

2573. Kramer, Jane. "Letter from Europe." New Yorker (January 30, 1989): [Algeria and Algerians in France.]

2574. Krieger-Krynicki, Anne. Les Musulmans en France: Religion et culture. Paris: 1985.

2575. Kupferman, Fred. "L'évolution du sentiment xenophobe en France du debut du siecle à nos jours." AMIF 28 (1980): 1455-1459.

2576. Kutschera, C. "Betrayed: North Africans in France." Mid. E. No. 120 (1984): 15-19.

2577. "L'Autre, L'Etranger: presence et exclusion dans le discours." MOTS 8 (March 1984): entire issue.

2578. "L'Islam en France." Les Cahiers de l'Orient 3 (1986): 15-94.

2579. Ladurie, Emmanuel Le Roy. The French Peasantry, 1450-1660. Berkeley: University of California Press, 1986.

2580. Laffey, John F. "Racism and Imperialism: French Views of the Yellow Peril, 1894-1914." Third Republic 1 (May 1976): 1-52.

2581. Landau, Lazare. De l'aversion à l'estime: Juifs et catholiques en France de 1919 à 1939. Paris: Le Centurion, 1980.

2582. Langdon, John W. "Social Appeals of Jesuit Education in Provincial France, 1675-1901." Md. Historian 14 (1983): 11- 22.

2583. Lehmann, André. Le Rôle de la femme française au milieu du XXeme siècle. Paris: Ligue française pour le droit des femmes, 1965.

2584. Leon, P. Géographie de la Fortunes et Structures Sociales à Lyon au XIXe Siècle (1815-1914). 1974.

2585. Levy, Deborah R. "Women of the French National Front." Parliamentary Affairs 42 (January 1989): 102-111.

2586. Lewis, Flora. "Harlem Désir's Message." New York Times, (September 25, 1987): [Racism in France.]

2587. Lion, Antoine and Pierre Maclouf, eds. L'insecurité sociale: pauperisation et solidarité. Paris: Les Editions Ouvrieres, 1982.

2588. Lloyd, Cathie. "What Is the French CP Up To?" Race & Class 22 (Spring 1981): 403-407. [Racism in the French Communist Party.]

2589. Lottman, Herbert R. "Rumor in Chalon: The Jew as Outsider." Present Tense 2 (1975): 41-47. [Antisemitism in Chalon.]

2590. Lubac, Henri de. Christian Resistance to Anti-Semitism: Memories from 1940-1944. Translated by Elizabeth Englund. San Francisco, CA: Ignatius Press, 1990.

2591. Mack-Kit, Samuel. Le Problème des Noirs et la Révolution de 1789. Paris: Épinay-sous-Sénart, 1989.

2592. MacShane, Denis. "Awaking Racism." New Statesman 106 (September 30, 1983): 20-21.

2593. Madrian, Jean and others. "Le soi-disant anti-racisme. Une technique d'assassinat juridique et moral." Itinéraires (December 1983): [Critique of anti-racism.]

2594. Majewska-Peyre, U., ed. Socialisation et déviance des jeunes immigrés. Vaucresson: Centre de Recherche Interdisciplinaire, 1984.

2595. Malausséna, Paul-Louis. "Maîtres et esclaves en Provence au moyen âge." Melanges Roger Aubenas (Montpellier) (1974): 527- 544.

2596. Malinvaud, E. "The Rise of Unemployment in France." Economica 53 (1986): Supplement.

2597. Manchuelle, Edouard F. Background to Black African Emigration to France: The Labor Migration of the Soninke, 1848-1987. Doctoral dissertation: University of California, Santa Barbara, 1987. UMO # 8729678.

2598. Mancorps, P. H. and others. Les Français et le racisme. Paris: Payot, 1965.

2599. Manor, Yohanan. "L'antisionisme." Revue Française de Science Politique (1984): 295-323.

2600. Markham, James M. "Blight of Hate Creeps Over a Political Landscape." New York Times, (October 12, 1987): [Anti-Arab movement in Aix-en-Provence.]

2601. Markham, James M. "If the Racism Tastes Sour, How Sweet Is Success." New York Times, (November 16, 1988)

2602. Markoff, John. "Literacy and Revolt: Some Empirical Notes on 1789 in France." American Journal of Sociology 92 (Summer 1986): 323-349.

2603. Markoff, John. "Some Effects of Literacy in Eighteenth- century France." Journal of Interdisciplinary History 17 (Autumn 1986): 311-334.

2604. Marks, Elaine and Isabelle de Courtvon, eds. New French Feminism: An Anthology. New York: Schocken, 1981.

2605. Marrus, Michael R. "Are the French Antisemitic?" Jerusalem Quarterly No. 32 (Summer 1984): 81-97.

2606. Marrus, Michael R. "French Antisemitism in the 1980s." Patterns of Prejudice 17 (April 1983): 3-20.

2607. Marrus, Michael R. "French Churches and the Persecution of Jews in France, 1940-1944." In Judaism and Christianity under the Impact of National Socialism (1919-1945). Historical Society of Israel, 1982.

2608. Marrus, Michael R. "Vichy before Vichy: Antisemitic Currents in France during the 1930s." Wiener Library Bulletin 33 (1980): 13-20.

2609. Marrus, Michael R. and Robert O. Paxton. Vichy France and the Jews. New York: Schocken, 1983.

2610. Marseille, Jacques. Empire colonial et capitalisme français: Histoire d'un divorce. Paris: Albin Michel, 1984.

2611. Martin, Benjamin F. Crime and Criminal Justice under the Third Republic: The Shame of Marianne. Baton Rouge: Louisiana State University Press, 1990.

2612. Martos, Fernando. "L'évolution des classes sociales en France: 1954-1975." Revue d'Économique Politique 88 (November-December 1978): 1020-1039.

2613. Matza, Michael. "Love Thy Neighbors?" Boston Globe Magazine, (May 25, 1986): [Anti-Arab racism in France.]

2614. Mauco, Georges. Les étrangers en France et le problème du racisme. Paris: Pensée Universelle, 1984.

2615. Mayer, Nonna and Pascal Perrineaux, eds. Le Front National à découvert. Paris: Presses de la Fondation Nationale des Sciences Politiques, 1989.

2616. McCloy, Shelby T. The Negro in France. Lexington: University of Kentucky Press, 1961.

2617. McConnell, Bernie Scott. Leftward Journey: The Education of Vietnamese Students in France, 1919-1939. New Brunswick, NJ: Transaction, 1989.

2618. McConnell, Bernie Scott. Not Collaborators But Rebels: The Education of Vietnamese Students in France, 1919-1939. Doctoral dissertation: Columbia University, 1987. UMO # 8724062.

2619. McDonald, J. R. "Labour Immigration in France, 1946-1965." Annals of the Association of American Geographers 59 (1969): 116-134.

2620. McDonald, Maryon. We Are Not French! Language, Culture, and Identity in Britanny. New York: Routledge, 1989.

2621. McMillan, James. Housewife or Harlot: The Woman Question in France under the Third Republic. New York: Martin's, 1980.

2622. Mehlman, Jeffrey. Legacies of anti-semitism in France. Minneapolis: University of Minnesota Press, 1983.

2623. Mettam, Roger. "Language and Society: 1500-1800. Conflict in Continuity in Seventeenth Century France." History Today 37 (February 1987): 30-35.

2624. Milano, Serge. La pauvreté absolue. Paris: Editions Hachette, 1988.

2625. Milano, Serge. La pauvreté en France. Paris: Editions Le Sycomore, 1982.

2626. Milza, Pierre. Francais et italiens àla fin du XIXe siècle. Turin: 1981.

2627. Milza, Pierre. "Y-a-il un 'melting pot' français?" Revue des Sciences Morales et Politique 141 (1986): 235-250.

2628. Minc, R. L'enfer des innocents-Les enfants juifs dans la tourmente nazie: Recits. Paris: 1966.

2629. "Minorités nationales en France." Les Temps Modernes Nos. 324-326 (August-September 1973)

2630. Mitchell, Allan. "The German Influence on Subversion and Repression in France during the Early Third Republic." Francia 13 (1985): 409-433.

2631. Mitra, Subrata. "The National Front in France- A Single- Issue Movement?" West European Politics 11 (1988): 47-64.

2632. Moncan, Patrice de. Who Owns Paris? Paris: SEESAM, 1990.

2633. Montagnon, Pierre. *La France coloniale: La Gloire de l'Empire*. Paris: Pygmalion, 1988.

2634. Morel, Bernard and Philippe Sanmarco. "Marseille sous la menace." *Herodote* 50-51 (July-December 1988): 66-95. [National Front.]

2635. Moser, Mary Theresa. *The Evolution of the Option for the Poor in France, 1880-1965*. Lanham, MD: University Press of America, 1985.

2636. Mosse, George L. "Fascism and the French Revolution." *Journal of Contemporary History* 24 (January 1989): 5-26.

2637. Motley, Mark E. *Becoming a French Aristocrat: The Education of the Court Nobility, 1580-1715*. Princeton, NJ: Princeton University Press, 1990.

2638. Mpuyi-Buatu, Th. "William B. Cohen et le racisme français anti-noir." *Peuples Noirs, Peuples Afric.* 5 (May-June 1982): 71-112. [See Cohen, above.]

2639. Muchembled, Robert. *Popular Culture and Elite Culture in France, 1400-1750*. Baton Rouge Translated by Lydia Cochrane: Louisiana State University Press, 1985.

2640. Muller, Detlef K. and others, eds. *The Rise of the Modern Educational System, Structural Change and Social Reproduction, 1870-1920*. New York: Cambridge University Press, 1987.

2641. Murati, Antoine. "Impérialisme en Corse depuis 1789, responsabilités." *Contrasti* 1 (1983): 27-45.

2642. "Les Musulmans dans la société française." *Revue Française de Science Politique* 37 (December 1987): 765-890.

2643. Nasse, Simone and others. *L'emigration Maghrébine de 1962 a 1985*. Aix-en-Provence: Universités d'aix-Marseille, 1986.

2644. Neto, Felix. *Jovens Portugueses em Franca: Aspectos da sua Adaptacao Psico-Social*. Portugal: Journal de Psicologia, 1985.

2645. Neveux, Hugues. "Alphabétisation et ségrégation sociale à Caen en 1606." *Congrès Soc. Savantes, Sect. Hist. Mod.* 105 (1984): 10-14.

2646. Noirel, Gérard. *Le creuset français*. Paris: Seuil, 1988. [History of immigration into France.]

2647. Noirel, Gérard. *Longwy: Immigrés et prolétaires, 1880-1980*. Paris: Presses Univérsitaires de France, 1984. [Italian immigrant workers.]

2648. Norberg, Kathryn. *Rich and Poor in Grenoble, 1600-1814*. Berkeley: University of California Press, 1986.

2649. Nouschi, André. "Notes on French Expansion in the Mediterranean during the Nineteenth and Twentieth Centuries." Mediterr. Hist. Review 1 (1986): 86-99.

2650. Numa, Guy. Avenir des Antilles-Guyane: des solutions existent: projetéconomique et politique. Paris: Editions l'Harmattan, 1986.

2651. Offen, Karen M. "The 'Woman Question' as a Social Issue in Nineteenth-Century France." Third Republic 3-4 (Spring-Fall 1977): 238-299.

2652. Ogden, P. "France: Recession, Politics and Migration." Geography 70 (April 1985): 158-162.

2653. Oriol, Paul. Les immigrés: métèques ou citoyens? Paris: Editions Syros, 1985.

2654. Ory, Pascal. "L'université française face à la persécution antisemite." In La France et la Question Juive 1940-1944 Georges Wellers and others. Paris: Éditions Sylvie Messinger, 1981.

2655. Ossman-Dorent, Susan. "SOS Racisme: Studied Disorder in France." Socialist Review 18 (April-June 1988): 39-53.

2656. Paraf, Pierre. "L'humanisme français contre le racisme." Historia 402 (May 1980): 133-138.

2657. "Pauvreté et pauperisation: la situation de la France." Recherche Sociale (1982): 3-72,75-136.

2658. Perville, Guy. Les étudiants algériens de l'université français, 1880-1962: populisme et nationalisme chez les étudiants et intellectuels musulman algériens de formation française. Paris: Editions du Centre National de la Recherche, 1984.

2659. Peters, Annie. The Breton Case for Regional Autonomy: Centuries of struggle in Brittany, France. Master's thesis: University of Nebraska, 1985.

2660. La Peyronnie, Didier. "Marginalite et lutte sociale chez les jeunes de la seconde generation de l'immigration maghrebine en France." In Jugendprotest und Generationenkonflikt, edited by Dieter Dowe. Bonn: Neue Gesellschaft, 1986.

2661. Phlipponneau, Michel. Géopolitique de la Bretagne. Rennes: Editions Ouest-France, 1985.

2662. Pinto, Antonio C. "Fascist Ideology Revisited: Zeev Sternhell and His Critics." European History Quarterly 16 (1986): 465-483.

2663. Plenel, E. and Alain Rollat. L'effet Le Pen. Paris: La Découverte/Le Monde, 1984.

2664. Pluchon, Pierre. Nègres et Juifs au XVIIIe siècle: le racisme au siècle des lumieres. Paris: Tallandier, 1984.

2665. Poliakov, Leon. "An Opinion Poll on Anti-Jewish measures in Vichy France." Jewish Social Studies 15 (1953): 135-150.

2666. Policar, Alain. "Racism and Its Mirror Images." Telos No. 83 (Spring 1990): 99-108. Translated by Eleni Mahaira-Odoni. [Discussion of Pierre-Andre Taquieff, La Force du prejuge.]

2667. Poznanski, Renee. "A Mythological Approach to the Study of Jewish Resistance in France." Yad Vashem Studies 18 (1987): 1-39.

2668. Price, Roger. A Social History of Nineteenth Century France. New York: Holmes and Meier, 1988.

2669. Le procès d'un peuple. Bastia, Corsica: A Ricossa, 1980. [Trial of Corsican nationalists.]

2670. Prost, Antoine. L'enseignement s'est-il démocratisé? Les élèves des lycées et collèges de l'agglomération d'Orleans de 1945 a 1980. Paris: Presses Universitaires de France, 1986.

2671. Przeworski, Adam and others. "The Evolution of the Class Struggle of France, 1901-1968." Economic Development and Cultural Change 28 (1980): 725-752.

2672. Quinney, Valerie. "Decisions on Slavery, the Slave Trade, and Civil Rights for Negroes in the Early French Revolution." Journal of Negro History 55, 2 (1970): 117-130.

2673. "Racism and Immigration in France." Race and Immigration No. 170 (1984): 8-15.

2674. Rasson, Lue. "Vichy and French Fascism: On a Recent Controversy." Contemporary French Civilization 11 (1987): 53-65.

2675. Rebatet, Lucien. Les memoires d'un fasciste. reprint. 2 vols. Paris: Pauvert, 1976.

2676. Reddy, William M. "Money and Liberty in the Old Regime." Proc. W. Soc. Fr. Hist. 14 (1987): 31-36.

2677. Ricoeur, Paul. "Tolérance, intolérance, intolérable." Bulletin Soc. Hist. Prot. fr. 134 (April-June 1988): 435- 450.

2678. Riding, Alan. "France Seeks a Way to Cope With New Upsurge in Racism." New York Times, (May 27, 1990)

2679. Robinson, Walter S. Jr. Colonel François de la Rocque: His Croix de Feu and Parti Social Français. Doctoral dissertation: Texas Christian University, 1990. UMO # 9026877.

2680. Roche, Daniel. The People of Paris. Berkeley: University of California Press, 1987. [19th century.]

2681. Rollat, Alain. Les hommes de l'extrême droite: Le Pen, Marie, Ortiz et les autres. Paris: Calmann-Levy Editions, 1985.

2682. Rosenfield, Leonora C. "The Rights of Women in the French Revolution." Studies in Eighteenth Century Culture 7 (1978): 117-138.

2683. Rossiter, Margaret L. Women in the Resistance. Westport, CT: Greenwood, 1985.

2684. Roussel, Eric. Le cas le Pen: les nouvelles droites en France. Paris: Editions Jean-Claude Lattès, 1985.

2685. Rousso, Henri. Le syndrome de Vichy (1944-198...). Paris: Editions de Seuil, 1987.

2686. Rovan, Joseph. "Des Français contre les immigrés." Histoire 57 (1983): 6-17.

2687. Roy, Olivier. "Dreux: de l'immigration au ghetto ethnique." Espirit 2 (February 1990): 5-10.

2688. Ruscio, Alain. La décolonization tragique: une histoire de la décolonisation française, 1945-1962. Paris: Messidor/ Editions Sociales, 1987.

2689. Rustant, Maurice. Inegalités, solidarité. Lyons: Chronique Sociales de France, 1982.

2690. Rutkoff, Peter M. Revanche and Revision: The Ligue des Patriotes and the Origins of the Radical Right in France, 1882-1900. Athens: Ohio University Press, 1981.

2691. Ryan, Donna F. Vichy and the Jews: The Example of Marseille, 1939-1944. 2 vols. Doctoral dissertation: Georgetown University, 1984. UMO # 8602366

2692. Sadoun, Marc. Les socialistes sous l'occupation: résistance et collaboration. Paris: Presses de la Fondation Nationale des Sciences Politiques, 1982.

2693. Safran, William. "The French Left and Ethnic Pluralism." Ethnic and Racial Studies 7 (October 1984): 447-461.

2694. Safran, William. "Minorities, Ethnics, and Aliens: Pluralist Politics in the Fifth Republic." In Policy-Making in France: From de Gaulle to Mitterand, edited by Paul Godt. New York: Pinter, 1989.

2695. Sala-Molins, Louis. Le Code noir, ou, Le calvaire de Canaan. Paris: Presses universitaries de France, 1987.

2696. Samuel, M. Le proletariat afrique noir en France. Paris: Maspero, 1978.

2697. Sanderson, Barbara M. "The Encyclopedia and Colonial Slavery." British Journal of Eighteenth-Century Studies 7 (Spring 1984): 15-38.

2698. Schain, Martin A. "The National Front in France and the Construction of Political Legitimacy." Western Europe Politics 10 (April 1987): 229-252.

2699. Schain, Martin A. "Racial Politics in France: The National Front and the Construction of Political Legitimacy." In The French Socialists in Power 1981-1986, edited by Patrick McCarthy. Westport, Ct: Greenwood Press.

2700. Scham, Alan M. "Emile Zola and French Anti-Semitism." Midstream 30 (December 1984): 52-55.

2701. Schiff, Michel. L'intelligence gaspillee: inegalite sociale, injustice scolaire. Paris: Seuil, 1982.

2702. Schnapper, Dominique and Sylvie Strudel. "Le 'vote juif' en France." Revue Française de Science Politique 33 (1983): 933-961.

2703. Schneider, William. "Toward the Improvement of the Human Race: The History of Eugenics in France." Journal of Modern History 54 (June 1982): 268-291.

2704. Schor, Ralph. L'opinion française et les etrangers 1919- 1939. Paris: Publications de la Sorbonne, 1986.

2705. Schwartz, Robert M. Policing the Poor in Eighteenth-Century France. Chapel Hill: University of North Carolina Press, 1989.

2706. Sewell, William H. Structure and Mobility: The Men and Women of Marseille, 1820-1870. New York: Cambridge University Press, 1985.

2707. Shapiro, Ann-Louise. Housing the Poor of Paris, 1850-1902. Madison: University of Wisconsin Press, 1985.

2708. Shields, James G. "Politics and Populism: The French Far Right in the Ascendant." Contemporary French Civilization 11 (1987): 39-52.

2709. Siddle, D. J. "Cultural Prejudice and the Geography of Ignorance- Peasant Literacy in South-Eastern France, 1550- 1790." Trans. Inst. Brit. Geographers 12 (1987): 19028.

2710. Simoni, Pierre. "Science anthropologique et racisme à la époque de l'expansion coloniale: le cas du Grand dictionnaire universel du XIXe siècle de Pierre Larousse." Hist. Pap. 167-184 (1980)

2711. Simons, Marlise. "Anti-racism Group Aids 'New French'." New York Times, (December 26, 1990): [SOS Racisme, founded in 1984.]

2712. Singer, Daniel. "France, Racism and the Left." Nation (September 28, 1985)

2713. Smith, Richard L. The Images of West Africa in the French Mass Press, 1876-1909. Doctoral dissertation: Rutgers University, 1972. UMO # 7304782.

2714. "Société face au racisme." Genre Humain No. 11 (November 1984): 1-278.

2715. Sofres. "Quel Raciste Etes-Vous?" Le Nouvel Observateur (November 7, 1967)

2716. Sorlin, Pierre. "Jewish Images in the French Cinema of the 1930s." Hist. J. Film, Radio & TV 1 (October 1981): 139- 150.

2717. Soucy, Robert J. "The Nature of Fascism in France." Journal of Contemporary History 1 (1966)

2718. Spillmann, Georges. "L'anticolonialisme en France de XVIIe siècle a nos jours." Afrique et l'Asie No. 101 (1974): 3- 20.

2719. Spivak, Gayatri C. "French Feminism in an International Framework." Yale French Studies 62 (1981): 154-184.

2720. Steinberg, Jonathan. All or Nothing: The Axis and the Holocaust. Routledge: 1990. [Jews under Italian and German occupation in Yugoslavia, Greece, and France, 1941-1943.]

2721. Steins, M. "Les mouvements negres a Paris, 1919-1939." Bulletin des Séances de l'Academie Royale des Sciences d'Outre-Mer 29 (1983): 267-277.

2722. Sternhell, Zeev. Antisemitism and the Right in France. Jerusalem: Shazar Library, Institute of Contemporary Jewry, the Hebrew University, 1988.

2723. Sternhell, Zeev. Neither Right Nor Left: Fascist Ideology in France. Berkeley Translated by David Maisel: University of California Press, 1986.

2724. Sternhell, Zeev. "Les origines intellectuelles du racisme en France." Histoire 106-114 (1979)

2725. Sternhell, Zeev. "Sur le fascisme et sa variante française." Debat 32 (1984): 28-51.

2726. Sternhell, Zeev and others. Naissance de l'idéologie fasciste. Paris: Fayard, 1989.

2727. Stovall, Tyler. "Sous Les Toits de Paris: The Working Class and the Paris Housing Crisis, 1914-1924." In Proceedings of the Annual Meeting of the

Western Society for French History, 1986, edited by William Roosen. Flagstaff: Northern Arizona University, 1987.

2728. Strumingher, Laura S. "Square Pegs into Round Holes: Rural Parents, Children and Primary Schools: France 1830-1880." In Popular Traditions and Learned Culture in France: From the Sixteenth to the Twentieth Century, edited by Marc Bertrand. Saratoga, CA: Anma Libri, 1985.

2729. Strumingher, Laura S. What Were Little Girls/Boys Made of. Primary Education in Rural France, 1830-1880. Edison, N.J.: State University of New York Press, 1982.

2730. Sweets, John F. Choices in Vichy France: The French Under Nazi Occupation. New York: Oxford University Press, 1986. [Clermont-Ferrand.]

2731. Szajkowski, Zosa. Anti-semitism in the French Labor Movement. New York: 1948.

2732. Taguieff, Pierre-André. "La Démagogie à visage républicain." Revue Politique et Parlementaire No. 915 (March-April 1985)

2733. Taguieff, Pierre-André. "La doctrine du national - populisme en France ." Etudes 364 (January 1986): 27-46.

2734. Taguieff, Pierre-André. "Les droites radicales en France." Les Temps Modernes No. 465 (April 1985)

2735. Taguieff, Pierre-André. La Force du préjugé. Paris: Editions la Découverte, 1988.

2736. Taguieff, Pierre-André. "L'Identité insécurisée. Genèses d'un mythe politique." Cahiers Bernard Lazare Nos. 115-116 (November 1986): 15-63.

2737. Taguieff, Pierre-André. "L'identité nationale saisie pour les logiques de racisation." Mots No. 12 (March 1986): 89- 126.

2738. Taguieff, Pierre-André. "Le Néo-Racisme differentialiste." Langage et societé No. 34 (December 1985): 69-98.

2739. Taguieff, Pierre-André. "The New Cultural Racism in France." Telos No. 83 (Spring 1990): 109-122.

2740. Taguieff, Pierre-André. "La nouvelle judéophobie: antisionisme, antiracisme, anti-imperialisme." Temps. mod. 520 (November 1989): 1-80.

2741. Taguieff, Pierre-André. "Racisme et anti-racismes: modèles et paradoxes." In Racismes-Anti-racismes, edited by A. Bejin and J. Freund. Paris: Méridiens/Klincksieck, 1986.

2742. Taguieff, Pierre-André. "La Rhétorique du national- populisme." Mots No. 9 (October 1984)

2743. Taguieff, Pierre-André. "La stratégie culturelle de la 'Nouvelle Droite' en France (1968-1983)." In Vous avez dit fascismes? Paris: Arthaud/Montalba, 1984.

2744. Taguieff, Pierre-André. "Typologies, racisations, antisemitismes." Traces Nos. 9-10 (1984): 137-154.

2745. Taleb, A. The Algerian Emigration to France: A Sociological Study of the Background, Origin and Present Difficultires. Doctoral dissertation: University of Essex, 1987.

2746. Tea in the Harem. 1985. [French film about Arab-French working-class teenager in Paris area.]

2747. Terrel, H. "L'Islam arabe en France." Cah. Orient (1986): 15-42.

2748. Tesse, Richard. "Private Schools in France." Comparative Education Review 80 (May 1986): 247-259.

2749. Thomas-Chevallier, Hubert. Le Racisme Français. Nancy: Impr. Thomas, 1943.

2750. Tilly, Louise A. "Women's Collective Action and Feminism in France, 1870-1914." In Class Conflict and Collective Action, edited by Tilly and Charles Tilly. Louise A. Beverly Hills, CA: Sage, 1981.

2751. Touraine, Alain. "Sociological Intervention and the Internal Dynamics of the Occitanist Movement." In New Nationalisms of the Developed West: Toward Explanation, edited by Edward A. Tiryakian and Ronald Rogowski. Boston: Allen and Unwin, 1985.

2752. Touraine, Alain and others. Le pays contre l'Etat: luttes occitanes. Paris: Seuil, 1981.

2753. Trenard, Louis. "Les fondements de l'idée de race au XVIIIe siècle." Information hist. 43 (1981): 165-173.

2754. Turner, C. J. The Discourse of the Extreme Right in France in the Inter-War Years. Doctoral dissertation: University of Sussex, 1986.

2755. Ugochukwu, Françoise. "La pauvreté en France-quelques données." Contemp. Fr. Civil 9 (1985): 76-90.

2756. Vélis, Jean-Pierre. La France illetrée. Paris: Editions du Seuil, 1988.

2757. Verhaeren, Raphael-Emmanuel. "The Role of Foreign Workers in the Seasonal Fluctuations of the French Economy." International Migration Review 20 (Winter 1986): 856-874.

2758. Verlinden, Charles. "Esclavage noir en France méridionale et courante de traite en Afrique." Annals du Midi 28 (1966): 335-443.

2759. Vouin, R. "Répression de la discrimination raciale en France." Revue des Droits de l'Homme 5 (1972)

2760. Warner, G. "France." In Fascism in Europe, edited by S.J. Woolf. London: Methuen, 1982.

2761. Webb, Bill. "Socialists Put the Boot In." Socialist Review 53 (April 1983): 9-11. [Racism in France.]

2762. Weber, Eugen. Action Française: Royalism and Reaction in Twentieth-Century France. Stanford, CA: Stanford University Press, 1962.

2763. Weber, Eugen. "Of Stereotypes and of the French." Journal of Contemporary History 25 (May-June 1990): 169-203.

2764. Weinberg, David H. A Community on Trial. The Jews of Paris in the 1930s. Chicago: University of Chicago Press, 1977.

2765. Weinberg, David H. "The French Jewish Community After World War II: The Struggle for Survival and Self-Definition." Forum on the Jewish People, Zionism and Israel No. 45 (Summer 1982): 45-54.

2766. Weinberg, Henry H. "Facing the Left and the Right in France." Midstream 31 (March 1985): 3-6.

2767. Weinberg, Henry H. "The Image of the Jews in Late Nineteenth-Century French Literature." Jewish Social Studies 45 (Summer-Fall 1983): 241-250.

2768. Weinberg, Henry H. The Myth of the Jew in France, 1967- 1982. Oakville: Mosaic Press, 1987.

2769. Weitz, Margaret C. "The Status of Women in France Today." Contemporary French Civilization 3 (Fall 1978): 29-46.

2770. Weitz, Margaret C. "The Status of Women in France Today: A Reassessment." Contemporary French Civilization 6 (Fall- Winter 1981-1982): 203-218.

2771. White, Paul and others. "South-East Asian Refugees in Paris: The Evolution of a Minority Community." Ethnic & Racial Studies 10 (January 1987): 48-61.

2772. Wihtol de Wenden, Catherine. Les immigrés et la politique: cent cinquante ans d'évolution. Paris: Presses de la Fondation Naitonale des Sciences, 1988. [1850-1986.]

2773. Williams, Patrick. "Ethnologue face aux racismes: l'exemple tsigane." Ethnologie française 18 (1988): 173-176.

2774. Wilson, Nelly. Bernard Lazare, Antisemitism and the Problem of Jewish Identity in Late Nineteenth-Century France. New York: Cambridge University Press, 1978.

2775. Wilson, Stephen. Ideology and Experience: Antisemitism in France at the Time of the Dreyfus Affair. London: Associated University Press, 1982.

2776. Winock, Michel. "Le Fascisme en France." L'Histoire 28 (November 1980): 40-49. [Pre-World War II.]

GABON

2777. Akelaguelo, A. "Esquisse d'Histoire Ethnique du Gabon." Presence afric. No.4 (1984): 3-32.

2778. Biffot, Laurent. "Genese des classes sociales au Gabon." An. Ecole Not. Adm. No.1, No.2 (1978): 31-48, 17-32.

2779. Gruat, J. V. "The Extension of Social Protection in the Gabonese Republic: Consolidating the Development Process." Int. Labour Review 123 (1984): 457-472.

2780. Gruat, J. V. "The Social Guarantee in the Gabonese Republic; A New Kind of Social Protection in Africa." International Social Security Review (1985): 157-171.

2781. Reed, Michael C. "Gabon: A Neo-Colonial Enclave of Enduring French Interest." Journal of Modern African Studies 25 (1987): 283-320.

GERMANY

2782. Adolphs, Lotte. Die Beteiligung der Frauen an der Wissenschaft. Duisburg: Walter Braun Verlag, 1981.

2783. Adorno, Theodor W. "Zur Bekämpfung des Antisemitismus heute." Das Argument 29 (1964)

2784. Albrecht, Richard. "Was ist der Unterschied zwischen Türken und Juden?" Zeitschrift für Volkskunde 78 (1982): 220-229.

2785. Altner, Günter. "Zur Geschichte des Rassenbegriffs in Deutschland." In Rasse, Kirche und Humanum, edited by Klaus-Martin Beckmann, 95-111. Güterloh: 1969.

2786. Aly, G. and others. Aussonderung und Tod. Die Klinische Hinrichtung der Unbrauchbaren. Berlin: 1985.

2787. Aly, G. and others. Reform und Gewissen. 'Euthanasie' im Dienst des Fortschritts. Berlin: 1985.

2788. Andereggen, Anton. "The Turkish 'Lumpenproletariat': West Germany's Industrial Reserve Army." German Life and Letters 39 (July 1986): 314-321.

2789. Angress, Ruth K. "A 'Jewish Problem' in German Postwar Fiction." Modern Judaism 5 (1985): 215-233.

2790. Angress, Werner T. Between Fear and Hope. Jewish Youth in the Third Reich. Translated by Angress and Christine Granger. New York: Columbia University Press, 1988.

2791. Ansbach, Tatjana and Hans-Joachim Heintze. Selbstbestimmung und Verbot der Rassendiskriminierung im Völkerrecht. East Berlin: Staatsverlag der Deutschen Demokratischen Republik, 1987.

2792. Antifaschismus-Kommission Kommunistischer Bund. Wer mit wem? Braunzonene zwischen CDU/CSU und Neonazis: ein Nachschlagewehr für Antifaschisten. 1981.

2793. Arendt, Hans-Jurgen. "Mädchenerziehung im faschistischen Deutschland, unter besonderer Berücksichtigung des BDM." Jb. Erziehungs.-u. Schulgeschichte 23 (1983): 107-127.

2794. Arndt, Ino. Rechtsextremismus in der Bundesrepublik Deutschland. Frankfurt/M.: 1984.

2795. Arnold, B. "The Past as Propaganda: Totalitarian Archeology in Nazi Germany." Antiquity 64 (September 1990)

2796. Aronsfeld, C. C. "'Perish Judah'. Nazi Extermination Propaganda 1920-1945." Patterns of Prejudice 12 (September- October, 1978): 17-26.

2797. Aronsfeld, C. C. The Text of the Holocaust: A Study of Nazi Extermination Propaganda, 1919-1945. Marblehead, MA: Micah Publications, 1985.

2798. "Ausländerfeindlichkeit, Ausländerpolitik." Gewerkschaftliche Monatshefte 33 (1982): 393-464.

2799. Backes, Uwe. Politischer Extremismus im demokratischen Verfassungsstaaten. Opladen: 1989.

2800. Backes, Uwe. "The West German Republikaner: Profile of a Nationalist, Populist Party of Protest." Patterns of Prejudice 24 (Summer 1990): 3-18.

2801. Backes, Uwe and Eckhard Jesse, eds. Extremismus und Demokratie. Bonn: 1989.

2802. Backes, Uwe and Eckhard Jesse. Politischer Extremismus in der Bundesrepublik Deutschland. 4 vols. Koln: Verlag Wissenschaft & Politik, 1989.

2803. Backes, Uwe and Eckhard Jesse. Totalitarismus, Extremismus, Terrorismus: Ein Literaturfuhrer und Wegweiser zur Extremismusforschung in der Bundesrepublik Deutschland. 2d ed. Opladen: Leske und Budrich, 1985.

2804. Backes-Gellner, Uschi and Bernd Frick. "Discrimination in Employment in the Federal Republic of Germany." Georgia Journal of International and Comparative Law 20 (Spring 1990): 105-121.

2805. Bade, Klaus J., ed. Auswanderer-Wanderarbeiter- Gastarbeiter: Bevölkerung, Arbeitsmarkt und Wanderung in Deutschland seit der Mitte des 19. Jahrunderts. 2 vols. 2d ed. Ostfildem: Scripta Mercatureae Verlag, 1984.

2806. Bade, Klaus J. Gastarbeiter zwischen Arbeitswanderung und Einwanderung. Tutzing: 1983.

GERMANY 221

2807. Bade, Klaus J. Imperialismus und Kolonialmission im Kaiserliches Deutschland und koloniales Imperium. 2d ed. Stuttgart: 1984.

2808. Baker, D. P. and others. "Effects of Immigrant Workers on Educational Stratification in Germany." Sociology of Education 58 (1985): 213-227.

2809. Bankiers, David. "The German Communist Party and Nazi Antisemitism, 1933-1938." Leo Baeck Institute Yearbook 32 (1987): 325-340.

2810. Barfuss, Karl M. 'Gastarbeiter' in Nordwestdeutschland 1884-1918. Bremen: The Archive, 1986.

2811. Barkai, Abraham. From Boycott to Annihilation: The Economic Struggle of German Jews, 1933-1943. Hanover, NH: University Press of New England, 1989.

2812. Barkin, Kenneth. "Germany and England: Economic Inequality." Tel Aviver deutsche Geschichte 16 (1987): 200-211.

2813. Barnouw, Dagmar. Visible Spaces: Hannah Arendt and the German-Jewish Experience. Baltimore, MD: John Hopkins University Press, 1990.

2814. Bärsch, Claus-E. "Antijudaismus, Apokalyptik und Satanologie: Die religiösen Elemente des nationalsozialistischen Antisemitismus." Zeitschrift für Religions- und Geistesgeschichte 40 (1988): 112-133.

2815. Bartov, Owen. The Eastern Front, 1941-1945: German Troops and the Barbarization of Warfare. New York: St. Martin's Press, 1986.

2816. Becker, Jorg. "Anti-Semitism in German Children's Materials." Interracial Books for Children Bulletin 1-2 (1979): 11-12.

2817. Becker, Jorg. "Racism in West German Children's Books." Interracial Books for Children Bulletin 4 (Winter, 1972-1973): 3.

2818. Beckman, Evelyn T. "Sexism, Racism, and Class Bias in German Utopias of the Twentieth Century." Soundings 58 (Spring 1975): 112-129.

2819. Behnken, Renate. Soziale Gerechtigkeit und Wohnungspolitik: eine empirische Verteilungsanalyse für die Bundesrepublik Deutschlands. W. Berlin: Duncker & Humblot, 1982.

2820. Beiträge zur National Sozialistischen Gesundheits- und Sozialpolitik. 1. Aussonderung und Tod. Die Klinische Hinrichtung der Unbrauchbaren. Berlin: 1985.

2821. Ben, Gershom E. "From Haubel to Hackenthal: Lessons from Nazi Medicine for Students and Practitioners of Medicine." Holocaust and Genocide Studies 5 (1990): 73-87.

222 WORLD RACISM AND RELATED INHUMANITIES

2822. Bendelow, Paul. "Anti-semitic Undercurrents Surface in Secondary Survey." Times Educational Supplement (December 12, 1986): 17.

2823. Berentsen, William H. "German Infant Mortality 1960-1980." Geographical Review 77 (April 1987): 157-170.

2824. Berghahn, Volker R. and Hanna Schissler, eds. Perceptions of History: International Textbook Research on Britain, Germany, and the United States. New York: Berg, 1987.

2825. Bergmann, Werner. "Public Beliefs about Anti-Jewish Attitudes in West Germany: A Case of 'Pluralistic Ignorance'." Patterns of Prejudice 22, 15-21 (Autumn 1988)

2826. Bering, Dietz. Der Name als Stigma. Antisemitismus im deutschen Alltag 1812-1933. Stuttgart: Klett-Cotta, 1987.

2827. Berkin, A. G. K. A Structural Analysis of the Gastarbeiter Phenomenon in the Federal Republic of Germany and Its Implications for Turkey with Special Reference to the Social Position of Women. Doctoral dissertation: Boston University, 1990. UMO # 9023984.

2828. Betz, Hans-Georg. "Deutschpolitik on the Margins: On the Evolution of Contemporary New Right Nationalism in the Federal Republic." New German Critique 44 (1988): 127-157.

2829. Betz, Hans-Georg. "Politics of Resentment: Right-wing Radicalism in West Germany." Comparative Politics 23 (October, 1990)

2830. Beyerchen, A. D. Scientists Under Hitler: Politics and the Physics Community in the Third Reich. New Haven, CT: 1977.

2831. Bhagwati, J. N. and others. "The West German Gastarbeiter System of Immigration." European Economic Review 26 (December 1984)

2832. Bier, Jean-Paul. "The Holocaust and West Germany: Strategies of Oblivion 1947-1979." New German Critique 19 (Winter 1980): 9-29.

2833. Binder-Wehberg, Friedelind. Ungleichbehandlung von Mann und Frau. Berlin: Duncker & Humblot, 1970.

2834. Blackbourn, David. "The Mittelstand in German Society and Politics 1871-1914." Social History 2 (1977): 409-433.

2835. Blackburn, Gilmer W. Education in the Third Reich. Race and History in Nazi Textbooks. Albany: State University of New York Press, 1984.

2836. Bock, Gisela. "Racism and Sexism in Nazi Germany: Motherhood, Compulsory Sterilization, and the State." Signs 8 (Spring 1983): 400-421.

2837. Booth, H. Guestworkers or Immigrants? A Demographic Analysis of the Status of Migrants in West Germany. Birmingham, England: ESRC Research Unit on Ethnic Relations, 1984.

2838. Bower, Tom. Blind Eye to Murder. Britain, America and the Purging of Nazi Germany - A Pledge Betrayed. London: 1981.

2839. Brachmann, Hans-Jurgen. "Research into the Early History of the Slav Populations in the Territory of the German Democratic Republic." Med. Archaeol. 27 (1983): 89-106.

2840. Brankack, Jan and Frido Metsk. Geschichte der Sorben, Vol.I: Von den Anfangen 1789. Bautzen, DDR: VEB Domowina- Verlag, 1977.

2841. Brehmer, Ilse, ed. Sexismus in der Schule der heimliche Lehrplan der Frauendiskriminierung. Weinheim, Germany: Beltz Verlag, 1982.

2842. Britschgi-Schimmer, I. Die Wirtschaftliche und soziale Lage der italienischen Arbeiter in Deutschland. Karlsruhe: 1916.

2843. Brubaker, W. R. "Immigration, Citizenship, and the Nation- State in France and Germany: A Comparative Historical Analysis." International Sociology 5 (December 1990)

2844. Brumlich, Micha and others, eds. Jüdisches Leben in Deutschland seit 1945. Konigstein/Ts: Judischer Verlag bei Athenaum, 1986.

2845. Bryson, Philip J. and others. "Economy and Society in the German Democratic Republic." E. Central Europe 11 (1984): 1-128.

2846. Burleigh, Michael. Germany Turns Eastwards: A Study of Ostforschung in the Third Reich. New York: Cambridge University Press, 1988.

2847. Buscher, Frank M. The U.S. War Crimes Trial Program in Germany, 1946-1955. Westport, CT: Greenwood, 1989.

2848. Buszko, Jozef. "Auschwitz." In Encyclopedia of the Holocaust. I, 107-119. New York: Macmillan, 1990.

2849. Calvert, Hildegund M. Germany's Nazi Past: A Critical Analysis of the Period in West German High School History Textbooks. Doctoral dissertation: Ball State University, 1987. UMO # 8713551.

2850. Carlebach, Emil and Kurt Bachmann. Kauf' Dir einen Minister: Flick in Weimar, im Dritten Reich und in Bonn. Frankfurt: Verlag Marxistische Blatter, 1985.

2851. Casey, B. "The Dual Apprenticeship System and the Recruitment and Retention of Young Persons in West Germany." British Journal of Industrial Relations 24 (March 1986)

2852. Castles, S. "The Guests Who Stayed - The Debate on 'Foreigners Policy' in the German Federal Republic." International Migration Review 19 (Fall 1985): 517-534.

2853. Castles, S. "Racism and Politics in West Germany." Race and Class 25 (Winter 1983): 37-51.

2854. Clemens, Bärbel and others, eds. Töchter der Alma Mater: Frauen in der Berufs- und Hochschulforschung. Frankfurt: Campus Verlag, 1986.

2855. Cohen, Nava. "Medical Experiments." In Encyclopedia of the Holocaust, III. 957-966. New York: Macmillan, 1990. [September 1939 - April 1945, conducted in Nazi concentration camps.]

2856. Collatz, Jürgen and others, eds. Gesundheit für alle: die medizinische Versorgung türkischer Familien in der Bundesrepublik. Hamburg: Verlag fur Erwachsenbildung, 1985.

2857. Conrad, Christoph. "Die Entstehung des modernen Ruhestandes: Deutschland im Internationalen Vergleich 1850- 1960." Geschichte und Gesellschaft 14 (1988): 417-447.

2858. Conway, John S. "The Political Theology of Martin Niemoller." German Studies Review 9 (1986): 521-546.

2859. Costelloe, Kevin. "Gypsies Want Reparation for Slave Labor under Nazis." Minneopolis Star and Tribune, March 25, 1986.

2860. Craig, Gordon A. "Women." In his The Germans. Chapter 7. New York: Putnam's, 1981.

2861. Cyz, Beno. Die DDR und die Sorben. Bautzen: VEB Domowina- Verlag, n.d.

2862. Dagis, Janis. "Die Lettischen Bildungsanstalten in Deutschland." Acta Balt. 23 (1984): 203-258.

2863. Davies, Alan T. "Racism and German Protestant Theology: A Prelude to the Holocaust." Annals 450 (July 1980): 20-34.

2864. Die Volkssozialistische Bewegung Deutschlands. Sammelbecken migranter Rechtsradikaler. Munich: Pressedienst Demokratische Initiative, 1981.

2865. Dietrich, Donald J. "Modern German Catholic Anti-Semitism." Face to Face. An International Bulletin 12 (Winter 1985): 4-10.

2866. Dippmann, Klaus J. "The Legal Position of the Lusatian Sorbs Since the Second World War." Slavonic and East European Review 53 (1975): 62-77.

2867. Dohse, Knuth. Ausländische Arbeiter und bürgerlicher Staat. Königstein: Hain, 1981.

2868. Dohse, Knuth. "Ausländerpolitik und betriebene Ausländerdiskriminierung." Leviathan (1981): 499-526.

2869. Dohse, Knuth. Foreign Workers in the Federal Republic of Germany: Government Policy and Discrimination in Employment. Berlin: International Institute for Comparative Social Research, 1982.

2870. Doring, J. J. Die Zigeuner in NS-Staat. Hamburg: 1964.

2871. Dörner, K. and others. Der Krieg gegen die Psychisch Kranken. Rehburg-Loccum: 1980.

2872. Doskow, Ambrose and Sidney B. Jacoby. "Anti-Semitism and the Law in Pre-Nazi Germany." Contemporary Jewish Record 3 (1940): 498-509.

2873. Dudek, Peter. Jugendliche Rechtsextremisten zwischen Hakenkreuz und Odalsrune, 1945 bis heute. Cologne: Bund- Verlag, 1985.

2874. Dundes, Alan and Thomas Hauschild. "Auschwitz Jokes." Western Folklore 42 (1983): 249-260. [[See also Linke and Dundes, below].]

2875. Dundes, Alan and Thomas Hauschild. "Kennt der Witz kein Tabu? Zynische Erzählformen als Versuch der Bewaltigung Nationalsozialistischen Verbrechen." Zeitschrift fur Volkskunde 83 (1987): 21-31.

2876. Edwards, G. E. GDR Society and Social Institutions: Facts and Figures. London: Macmillan, 1986.

2877. Ehrlich, Konrad, ed. Sprache im Faschismus. Frankfurt am Main: Suhrkamp, 1989.

2878. Einhorn, Barbara. "Socialist Emancipation: The Women's Movement in the GDR." In Promissory Notes, edited by Sonia Kruks and others. New York: 1989.

2879. Eley, Geoff. "Capitalism and the Wilhelmine State: Industrial Growth and Political Backwardness." In Eley From Unification to Nazism: Reinterpreting the German Past. London: 1986.

2880. Eley, Geoff. "Educating the Bourgeoisie: Students and the Culture of 'Illiberalism' in Imperial Germany." History of Education Quarterly 26 (Summer 1986): 287-300.

2881. Eley, Geoff. "Nazism, Politics and the Image of the Past: Thoughts on the West German Historikerstreit 1986-1987." Past & Present 121 (November 1988): 171-208.

2882. Eley, Geoff. Reshaping the German Right. Radical Nationalism and Political Change after Bismarck. Ann Arbor: University of Michigan Press, 1990.

2883. Elling, Hanna. Frauen im deutschen Widerstand: 1933-45. Frankfurt am Main: Roderberg-Verlag, 1978.

2884. Elsehans, Theodor. Kants Rassentheorie und ihre bleibende Bedeutung. Leipzig: Engelmann, 1904.

2885. Elsner, Eva-Maria and Lothar. "Nachbemerkungen zum Thema: Ausländerfeindschaft in der DDR." Ausländerfeindschaft im 19. und 20. Jahrhundert - Ursachen, Erscheinungen, Konsequenzen. pp. 1-6. Rostock: Wilhelm Pieck - Universität Rostock, sektion Geschichte, 1989. [separately available with "Gedanken zum Thema".]

2886. Elsner, Lothar. "Foreign Workers and Forced Labor in Germany during the First World War." In Labor Migration in the Atlantic Economies, edited by Dirk Hoerder. Westport, CT: Greenwood, 1985.

2887. Endruweit, Gunter. "Gastarbeiter zwischen Türkischer Identität und deutscher Integration." Zeitschrift fur Ausländerrecht und Ausländerpolitik 2 (1982): 139-148.

2888. Engelmann, Bernt. In Hitler's Germany: Daily Life under the Nazis, 1933-1945. Translated by Krishna Winston. New York: Pantheon, 1987.

2889. Enssle, Manfred J. "The Harsh Discipline of Food Scarcity in Postwar Stuttgart, 1945-1948." German Studies Review 10 (October 1987): 481-502.

2890. Erbslöh, Barbara and others. "Klassenstruktur und Klassenbewusstsein in der Bundesrepublik Deutschland." Kölner Zeitschrift für Soziologie und Sozialpsychologie 40 (1988): 245-261.

2891. Eschwege, H., ed. Kennzeichen, J. Bilder, dokumente, Berichte zur Geschichte der Verbrechen des Hitlerfaschismus an den deutschen Juden 1933-1945. East Berlin: 1981.

2892. Esh, S. "Words and their Meaning: Twenty-five Examples of Nazi Idiom." Yad Vashem Studies 5 (1961): 133-167.

2893. Esser, H. "The Integration of Second Generation Immigrants in Germany." In Education for Democratic Citizenship. A Challenge for Multi-Ethnic Societies, edited by Roberta S. Sigel and Marilyn Hoskin. Hilldale, NJ: Lawrence Erlbaum Associates, 1990.

2894. Evans, Richard J. The Feminist Movement in Germany 1894- 1933. London: Sage, 1976.

2895. Faller, Kurt. "Damals Juden - heute Ausländer?" Marxistische Blätter für Probleme der Gesellschaft, Wirtschaft und Politik (1983): 36-42.

2896. Faller, Kurt and Heinz Siebold, eds. Neofaschismus: dulden? verbieten? ignorieren? bekämpfen? Frankfurt: Roderberg-Verlag, 1986.

2897. Faschismus in Deutschland, Faschismus in der Gegenwart. Cologne: Pahl-Rugenstein, 1980.

2898. Faschismus in Deutschland: Ursachen und Folgen, Verfolgung und Widerstand, und neonazistische Gefahren. Cologne: Bund- Verlag, 1985.

2899. Feil, C. "Migrant Children in the German Kindergarten: Data, Problems, and Pedagogical Models." International Migration 23 (December 1985): 473-494.

2900. Feit, Margret. Die 'Neue Rechte' in der Bundesrepublik: Organisation Ideologie Strategie. Frankfurt am Main: Campus Verlag, 1987.

2901. Felden, Klemens. Die Ubernahme des antisemitischen Stereotyps also soziale Norm durch die burgerliche Gesellschaft Deutschlands (1875-1900). Doctoral dissertation: University of Heidelberg, 1965.

2902. Ferencz, Benjamin. Less than Slaves, Jewish Forced Labor and the Quest for Compensation. Cambridge, MA: 1979.

2903. Fetscher, Irving, ed. Marxisten gegen Antisemitismus. Hamburg: 1974.

2904. Field, Geoffrey G. Evangelist of Race: The Germanic Vision of Houston Stewart Chamberlain. New York: Columbia University Press, 1981.

2905. Fijalkowski, Jürgen. "Gastarbeiter als industrielle Reservearmee? Zur Bedeutung der Arbeitsimmigranten für die wirtschaftliche und gesellschaftliche Entwicklung der Bundesrepublik Deutschland." Arch. Sozialgeschichte 24 (1984): 399-456.

2906. Filmer, Werner and Heribert Schwan, eds. Was von Hitler blieb: 50 Jahre nach der Machtergreifung. Vienna: Verlag Ullstein, 1982.

2907. Fink, Carole K. "Defender of Minorities: Germany in the League of Nations, 1926-1933." Central European History. December 1972.

2908. Fischer, C. Stormtroopers: A Social, Economic, and Ideological Analysis, 1929-1935. London: 1983.

2909. Fischer, Fritz. From Kaiserreich to Third Reich. Winchester, MA: Allen & Unwin, 1986.

2910. Fishman, Sterling and Lothar Martin. Estranged Twins: Education and Society in the Two Germanies. New York: Praeger, 1986.

2911. Forycki, P. Edmund. "Die polnische Minderheit in der Bundesrepublik Deutschland." Eur. Ethnica 41 (1984): 193- 198. [English summary, p. 198]

2912. Freese, C. Zur Geschichte und Gegenwart der Zigeuner und Landesfahrer in Deutschland. Doctoral dissertation: University of Erlangen-Nuremberg, 1980.

2913. Fremgen, Gisela. Und wenn du dazu noch schwarz bist: Berichte schwarzer Frauen in der Bundesrepublik. Bremen: Edition CON, 1984.

2914. Frevert, Ute. Women in German History. Berg: 1990, [Translated by Stuart McKinnon-Evans, Terry Bond, and Barbara Norden.]

2915. Friedlander, Henry. "The Judiciary and Nazi Crimes in Postwar Germany." Simon Wiesenthal Center Annual 1 (1984): 27-49.

2916. Friedman, Regine M. L'image et son Juif: le Juif dans le cinema. Paris: Payot, 1983.

2917. Funcke, L. Daten Fakten zur Ausländersituation. Bonn: Der Beauftragte der Bundesregierung für Ausländerfragen, 1985.

2918. Funke, Hajo. "The Unorthodox Approach to Jewish History in the German Democratic Republic: An Interview with Eschwege." New German Critique 38 (Spring/Summer 1986): 88-104. [Edited and translated by Robin Ostow.]

2919. Galanis, Georgios N. Migranten - kriminalitat in der Presse: eine inhaltsanalytische Untersuchung dargestellt am Beispiel der Zeitschriften Stern und Quick von 1960-1982. Berlin: Express Edition GmbH, 1987.

2920. Gallin, Alice. Midwives to Nazism: University Professors in Weimar Germany, 1925-1933. Macon, GA: Mercer University Press, 1986.

2921. Gatz, Karen L. East Prussian and Sudeten German Expellees in West Germany, 1945-1960: A Comparison of their Social and Cultural Integration. Doctoral dissertation: Indiana University, 1989. UMO # 8925140.

2922. Geissler, Rainer. "Bildungschancen und Statusvererbung in der DDR." Kölner Zeitschrift für Soziologie und Sozialpsychologie 35 (1983): 755-770.

2923. Geissler, Rainer, ed. Soziale Schichtung und Lebenschancen in der Bundesrepublik Deutschland. Stuttgart: Ferdinand Enke Verlag, 1987.

2924. Gelber, Mark H. "Thomas Mann and Antisemitism." Patterns of Prejudice 17 (October 1983): 31-40.

2925. Gellately, Robert. "The Gestapo and German Society: Political Denunciation in the Gestapo Case Files." Journal of Modern History 60 (1988): 654-694.

2926. Gellately, Robert. The Gestapo and German Society: Enforcing Racial Policy, 1935-1945. New York: Oxford University Press, 1990.

2927. The German Worker. Working-class Autobiographies from the Age of Industrialization. Translated and edited by Alfred Kelly. Berkeley: University of California Press, 1987. [13 men and 6 women.]

2928. Geuter, Ulfried. Die Professionalisierung der deutschen Psychologie im Nationalsozialismus. Frankfurt: 1984.

2929. Geuter, Ulfried. "German Psychology during the Nazi Period." In Psychology in Twentieth-Century Thought and Society, edited by Mitchell G. Ash and William R. Woodward. New York: Cambridge University Press, 1987.

2930. Giles, Geoffrey J. "German Students and Higher Education Policy in the Second World War." Central European History 17 (December 1984): 330-354.

2931. Giles, Geoffrey J. Students and National Socialism in Germany. Princeton, NJ: Princeton University Press, 1986.

2932. Gilman, Sander L. "Jewish Writers in Contemporary Germany: The Dead Author Speaks." Studies in Twentieth Century Literature 13 (Summer 1989): 215-243.

2933. Gilman, Sander L. On Blackness without Blacks: Essays on the Image of the Black in Germany. Boston, MA: Hall, 1982.

2934. Gimbel, John. Science, Technology, and Reparations. Exploitation and Plunder in Postwar Germany. Stanford, CA: Stanford University Press, 1990.

2935. Glass, Bentley. "A Hidden Chapter of German Eugenics Between the Two World Wars." Proc. Am. Phil. Soc. 125 (1981): 357-367.

2936. Goschler, Constantin. "Controversy about a Pittance: The Compensation of Forced Laborers from Concentration Camps by Germany's Post-War Industry." Dachau Review 1 (1988): 157- 176.

2937. Great Britain. Her Majesty's Inspectorate. Education in the Federal Republic of Germany - Aspects of Curriculum and Assessment. London: HMSO, 1986.

2938. Grebing, Helga, ed. Lehnstucke in Solidaritat: Briefe und Biographen deutscher Sozialisten 1945-1949. Stuttgart: Deutsche Verlags-Anstalt, 1983.

2939. Greiner, C. "The Defence of Western Europe and the Rearmament of West Germany, 1947-1950." In Western Security: The Formative Years: European and Atlantic Defence, 1947- 1953, edited by Olav Riste. New York: Columbia University Press, 1985.

2940. Gress, Franz and Hans Gerd Jaschke. Rechtsextremismus in der Bundesrepublik nach 1960... Munich: Pressedienst Demokratische Initiative, 1982.

2941. Grimm, Reinhold and Jost Herman, eds. Blacks and German Culture. Madison: University of Wisconsin Press, 1986.

2942. Grove, Lloyd. "Lament of the Gypsies: 40 Years after Auschwitz, Petitioning for a Place." Washington Post (July 21, 1984)

2943. Gutteridge, Richard J. Open Thy Mouth for the Dumb! The German Evangelical Church and the Jews: 1879-1950. New York: Barnes & Noble, 1976.

2944. Habbe, Christian, ed. Ausländer - Die Verfemten Gäste. Reinbeck bei Hamburg: Rowohlt, 1983.

2945. Habermas, Jürgen. The New Conservatism: Cultural Criticism and the Historians Debate. Cambridge, MA: MIT Press, 1990.

2946. Hagen, William W. "Working for the Junker: The Standard of Living of Manorial Laborers in Brandenburg, 1584-1810." Journal of Modern History 58 (March 1986): 143-158.

2947. Haller, Max. "Positional and Sectorial Differences in Income: The Federal Republic, France and the United States." International Journal of Sociology 17 (Spring-Summer 1987): 172-190.

2948. Halperin, Jean and Anne Sovik, eds. Luther, Lutheranism and the Jews. Geneva: Department of Studies, Lutheran World Federation, 1984.

2949. Hancock, Ian F. "Gypsies in Germany: The Fate of Romany." Michigan Germanic Studies 6 (Fall 1980): 247-264.

2950. Hancock, Ian F. The Pariah Syndrome: An Account of Gypsy Slavery and Persecution. Ann Arbor, MI: Karoma, Inc., 1986.

2951. Hardach, Karl. The Political Economy of Germany in the Twentieth Century. Berkeley: University of California Press, 1980.

2952. Harris-Schenz, B. Black Images in Eighteenth Century German Literature. Stuttgart: Heinz, 1984.

2953. Hartung, Gunter. "Notizen zur Judendarstellung in der deutschen Literatur." Weimarer Beiträge 35 (1989): 868-876.

2954. Harvey, Ruth A. "Equal Treatment of Men and Women in the Work Place: The Implementation of European Community's Equal Treatment Legislation in the Federal Republic of Germany." American Journal of Comparative Law 38 (Winter 1990): 31- 71.

2955. Hausmann, Bernd. "Die Ausländer und die Ängste der Deutschen." Zeitschrift für Ausländerrecht und Ausländerpolitik 2 (1982): 97-100.

2956. Hayes, Peter. Industry and Ideology, I.G. Farben in the Nazi Era. New York: Cambridge University Press, 1989.

2957. Hedrich, Kurt. Der Rassengedanke im deutschen Kolonialrecht. Schramber: Gatzer und Hahn, 1941. [Doctoral dissertation, University of Tubingen.]

2958. Heinemann, M. "Die Assimilation fremdsprachiger Schulkinder durch die Volksschule in Preussen seit 1880." Bildung und Erziehung 28 (1975)

2959. Heller, Peter. "Nietzsche and the Jews." In Nietzsche Heute: Die Rezeption seines Werkes nach 1968, edited by Sigrid Bauschinger and others, 149-160. Bern: Francke, 1988.

2960. Hellfeld, Matthias von. Im Schatten der Krise: Rechtsextremismus, Neofaschismus und Ausländerfeindlichkeit in der Bundesrepublik. Cologne: Pahl-Rugenstein Verlag, 1986.

2961. Henke, Klaus-Dietmar. Politische Sauberung unter französischer Besatzung: die Entnazifierung in Württemberg- Hohenzollern. Stuttgart: Deutsche Verlags-Anstalt, 1981.

2962. Hennig, Eike. Bürgerliche Gesellschaft und Faschismus in Deutschland: Ein Forschungsbericht. Frankfurt am Main: 1977.

2963. Henningsen, Manfred. "The Politics of Memory: Holocaust and Legitimacy in Post-Nazi Germany." Holocaust and Genocide Studies 4 (1989)

2964. Herbert, Ulrich. A History of Foreign Labor in Germany, 1880-1990: Seasonal Workers, Forced Laborers, Guest Workers. Ann Arbor: University of Michigan Press, 1990. [Translated by William Templer.]

2965. Herbert, Ulrich. "Zwangsarbeit als Lernprozess: Zur Beschäftigung ausländischer Arbeiter in der Westdeutschen Industrie im Ersten Weltkrieg." Arch. Sozialgesch. 24 (1984): 285-304.

2966. Herde, Georg. 40 Jahre Bundesrepublik Deutschland: 40 Jahre Staatlich geförderte Revanchistenverbände: Vorschau auf die revanchistischen

Grossveranstaltungen. Frankfurt am Main: Vereinigung der Verfolgten des Naziregimes (VVN): Bund der Antifaschisten Bundesvorstand, 1989.

2967. Herzig, Arno. "The Role of Antisemitism in the Early Years of the German Workers' Movement." Leo Baeck Institute Yearbook 26 (1981): 243-259.

2968. Heye, Uwe-Karsten. "Lehrer für Hanus und Hassan: Alltag in einer Kölner Hauptschule." Die Zeit (overseas edition), Nr.2 (January 7, 1983)

2969. Hill, Arlette C. "Democratic Education in West Germany: The Effects of the New Minorities." Comparative Education Review 31 (May 1987): 273-290.

2970. Hirsch, Kurt. Rechts von der Union: Personen, Organisationen, Parteien seit 1945; ein Lexikon. Munich: Knesebeek und Schuler, 1989. [Ultra-rightist parties.]

2971. Histor, Manfred. Willy Brandts vergessene Opfer: Geschichte und Statistik der politisch motivierten Berufsverbote in Westdeutschland 1971-1988. Freiburg: Ahriman-Verlag, 1989.

2972. Hockenos, Paul. "Fascism in the Antifascist State." Z Magazine (March 1990): 105-109. [German Democratic Republic.]

2973. Hockenos, Paul. "Violence Begets Violence in East Berlin Youth Culture." In These Times (May 23, 1990)

2974. Hoffmann, Barbara and others. Graue Wölfe, Koranschulen, Idealistenvereine: Türkische Faschisten in der Bundesrepublik. Cologne: Pahl-Rugenstein, 1981.

2975. Hoffmann, Lutz and Herbert Even. Soziologie der Ausländerfeindlichkeit: zwischen nationaler Identität und multikultureller Gesellschaft. Basel: Beltz Verlag, 1984.

2976. Hohmann, Joachim S. Geschichte der Zigeunerverfolgung in Deutschland. Frankfurt: Campus Verlag, 1981.

2977. Hohmann, Joachim S. Zigeuner und Zigeunerwissenschaft: ein Beitrag zur Grundlagenforschung und Dokumentation des Volkermords im 'Dritten Reich'. Marburg/Lahn: Guttandin und Hoppe, 1980.

2978. Hollstein, Dorothea. Antisemitische Filmpropaganda. Die Darstellung der Juden im Nationalsozialistischen Spielfilm. München-Pullach: Verlag Dokumentation, 1971.

2979. Holtfrerich, Carl-Ludwig. The German Inflation, 1914-1923: Causes and Effects in International Perspective. New York: De Gruyter, 1986.

GERMANY 233

2980. Holzner, Lutz. "West Germany." In International Handbook on Race and Race Relations, Jay A. Sigler. Westport, Ct: Greenwood, 1987.

2981. Horchem, Hans Josef. "Rightist Extremism in the Federal Republic of Germany, 1977." Conflict 1 (1979): 171-190.

2982. Hsia, R. Po-chia. The Myth of Ritual Murder. Jews and Magic in Reformation Germany. New Haven: Yale University Press, 1988.

2983. Huhn, Anne and Alwin Meyer. "Einst kommt der Tag der Rache": die rechtsextreme Herausforderung 1945 bis heute. Freiburg/Breisgau: Dreisam-Verlag, 1986.

2984. "ILO Inquiry's Findings on Discrimination in Public Employment in Federal Republic of Germany." International Commission on Jurists Review (June 1987): 26-30.

2985. "In Ernster Sorge vor Gefahr von rechts." Neues Deutschland (November 11, 1989)

2986. Iram, Yaacov. "Higher Education Traditions of Germany, England, the USA, and Israel: A Historical Perspective." Paedagog Hist. 22 (1982): 93-118.

2987. Italaander, Rolf, ed. "Fremde Raus?" Fremdenangst und Ausländerfeindlichkeit: Gefahren für jede Gemeinschaft. Frankfurt: Fischer Taschenbuch Verlag, 1983.

2988. Jackson, James H. "Die sozialen konsequenzen der Wohnungskrise in Duisburg im spaten 19. Jahrhundert." Duisburger Forschung 31 (1985): 34-81.

2989. Jarausch, Konrad H. Students, Society, and Politics in Imperial Germany: The Rise of Academic Illiberalism. Princeton, NJ: Princeton University Press, 1982.

2990. Jay, Martin. "Anti-semitism and the Weimar Left." Midstream 20 (1974): 42-50.

2991. Jay, Martin. "The Jews and the Frankfurt School: Critical Theory's Analysis of Anti-semitism." New German Critique No. 19 (Winter 1980): 137-149.

2992. Jenks, Manfred. Verschworung von rechts? Ein Bericht uber den Rechtsradikalismus in Deutschland nach 1945. Berlin: Colloquium Verlag, 1961.

2993. Jersch-Wenzel, Stefi. "The Jews as a 'Classic' Minority in Eighteenth- and Nineteenth Century Prussia." Leo Baeck Institute Yearbook 27 (1982): 37-49.

2994. Jochmann, W. Gesellschaftskrise und Judenfeindschaft in Deutschland 1870-1945. Hamburg: H. Christians, 1988.

2995. John, Michael. "The Peculiarities of the German State: Bourgeois Law and Society in the Imperial Era." Past & Present 119 (May 1988): 105-131.

2996. Johnson-Krojzal, Clare. The Social Institutions of Turkish Migrant Workers in West Berlin. Doctoral dissertation: University of Oxford (U.K.), 1987. Order No. BRD-85468.

2997. Jones, P. N. "West Germany's Declining Guestworker Population: Spatial Change and Economic Trends in the 1980s." Regional Studies 24 (June 1990)

2998. Jürgensen, Kurt. "The Concept and Practice of 'Re-education' in Germany, 1945-50." In The Political Re-education of Germany and Her Allies after World War II, edited by Nicholas Pronay and Keith Wilson. Totawa, NJ: Barnes & Noble, 1985.

2999. Kahn, Siegbert. Dokumente des Kampfes der revolutionären deutschen Arbeiterbewegung gegen Antisemitismus und Judenverfolgung. East Berlin: Dietz, 1960.

3000. Kampe, Norbert. "Jews and Antisemites at Universities in Imperial Germany [part 2] : the Friedrich-Wilhelms- Universität of Berlin: A Case Study on the Students' 'Jewish Questions'." Leo Baeck Institute Yearbook 32 (1987): 43-101.

3001. Kang, Chong-Sook. "Institutioneller Rassismus und auslandische Frauen." Beitrage zur Feministischen Theorie und Praxis 13 (1990): 120-126. [West Germany.]

3002. Kaplan, M. A. "Jewish Women in Nazi Germany: Daily Life, Daily Struggles, 1933-1939." Feminist Studies 16 (Autumn 1990)

3003. Karasek, Erika and others. Grosstadtproletariat: Zur Lebensweise einer Klasse. Berlin: Museum für Deutsche Volkskunde, 1983.

3004. Kasper, Martin. Geschichte der Sorben. Vol. 3: Von 1917 bis 1945. Bautzen: VEB Domowina-Verlag, 1976.

3005. Kater, Michael H. "Anti-Fascist Intellectuals in the Third Reich." Canadian Journal of History 16 (August 1981): 263- 277.

3006. Kater, Michael H. "Problems of Political Reeducation in West Germany, 1945-1960." Simon Wiesenthal Center Annual 4 (1987): 99-123.

3007. Katz, Jacob. The Darker Side of Genius: Richard Wagner's Anti-Semitism. Translated by Allan Arkush. Hanover, NH: University Press of New England, 1986.

3008. Kaya, Ural and I. Strutz. "Türken in Deutschland-Deutschland in der Türkei." Int. Schulbuchforsch. 10 (1988): 71-86.

3009. Kennedy, Paul and Anthony Nicholls, eds. Nationalist and Racialist Movements in Britain and Germany Before 1914. London: Macmillan, 1982.

3010. Kenrick, Donald and Grattan Puxon. Sinti und Roma. Die Vernichtung eines Volkes im NS-Staat. Gottingen: Gesellschaft für bedrohte Volker, 1981.

3011. Kent, Bruce. The Spoils of War. The Politics, Economic, and Diplomacy of Reparations 1918-1932. Oxford University Press, 1989.

3012. Kershaw, Ian. "The Persecution of the Jews and German Popular Opinion in the Third Reich." Leo Baeck Institute Yearbook 26 (1981): 261-189.

3013. Kisch, Guido. The Jews in Medieval Germany: A Study of their Legal and Social Status. 2d ed. Chicago, IL: University of Chicago Press, 1970, orig. 1949.

3014. Klanberg, Frank. Armut und Ökonomische Ungleichheit in der Bundesrepublik Deutschland. Doctoral dissertation: University of Frankfurt, 1978.

3015. Klarsfeld, Serge, ed. The Holocaust and the Neo-Nazi Mythomania. New York: Beate Klarsfeld Foundation, 1979.

3016. Kleber, Wolfgang. "Labor Force Change in Germany Since 1882: A Life Cycle Perspective." Exploration in Economic History 22 (January 1985): 97-126.

3017. Klee, Ernst. "Euthanasia" im NS-Staat: Die "Vernichtung lebensunwerten Lebens". Frankfurt a/M: S. Fischer, 1983.

3018. Klee, Ernst. Was sie taten - was sie wurden. Arzte, Juristen und andere Beteiligte am Kranken oder Judenmord. Frankfurt: 1986,

3019. Kleff, Hans-Gunter. Vom Bauern zum Industriearbeiter: Aus Kollektiven Lebensgeschichte der Arbeitsimigranten aus der Turkei. Mainz, Germany: Werkmeister Uranthano, 1985.

3020. Klessmann, Christoph. "Polish Miners in the Ruhr District: their Social Situation and Trade Union Activity." In Labor Migration in the Atlantic Economies, Dirk Hoerder. Westport, CT: Greenwood, 1985.

3021. Klessmann, Christoph. Polnische Bergarbeiter im Ruhrgebiet 1870-1945. soziale Integration und nationale Subkultur einer Minderheit in der deutschen Industriegesellschaft. Göttingen: 1978.

3022. Klier, John D. "German Antisemitism and Russian Judeo phobia in the 1880s: Brothers and Strangers." Jb. Gesch. Osteur. 37 (1989): 524-540.

3023. Klönne, Arno. Jugend im Dritten Reich: die Hitler-Jugend und ihre Gegner. Dokumente und Analysen. Düsseldorf: Eugen Diedrichs Verlag, 1982.

3024. Knutter, Hans-Helmuth. Die Juden und die deutsche Linke in der Weimarer Republik 1918-1933. Dusseldorf: 1971.

3025. Kocka, Jürgen, ed. Das Bürgertum im 19. Jahrhundert. Deutschland im europäischen Vergleich. 3 vols. Munich: DTV, 1988.

3026. Kolinsky, Martin and Eva Kolinsky. "The Treatment of the Holocaust in West German Textbooks." Yad Vashem Studies on the European Jewish Catastrophe and Resistance 10 (1974): 149-216.

3027. "Kommen jetzt die Neonazis auf Uns zu?" Neues Deutschland (November 25, 1989)

3028. Kraus, Birgitta. "Die Schulsituation der türkischen Kinder." Deutsch-Türkische Gesellschaft Mitteilungen Heft 105 (1982)

3029. Kuczynski, Jürgen. "Die Entwicklung der Sozialstruktur und Produktivität seit 1850." Jb. Wirtschaftsgesch. No. 2 (1988): 9-22.

3030. Kuczynski, Jurgen. Studien zur Geschichte der Lage der Arbeiterin in Deutschland von 1700 bis zur Gegenwart. Berlin: Akademie Verlag, 1965.

3031. Kuhlmann, Michael and Alwin Meyer, eds. Ayse und Devrim - Wo Gehören wir hin? Bornheim: Lamuv Verlag, 1983.

3032. Kuhnert, Hanno. "Rassistische Klange." Die Zeit (overseas edition) 6 (February, 1982)

3033. Kuhnrich, Heinz. Die KPD im Kampf gegen die faschistische Diktatur, 1933 bis 1945. E. Berlin: Dietz Verlag, 1983.

3034. Kulczycki, John J. "Nationalism over Class Solidarity: The German Trade Unions and Polish Coal Miners in the Ruhr to 1902." Canadian Review of Studies in Nationalism 14 (Fall 1987): 261-276.

3035. Kulczycki, John J. School Strikes in Prussian Poland, 1901- 1907: The Struggle Over Bilingual Education. New York: Columbia University Press, 1981.

3036. Kulka, Otto Dov. "Major Trends and Tendencies in German Historiography on National Socialism and the Jewish Question (1924-1984)." Leo Baeck Institute Yearbook 30 (1985): 215-242.

3037. Kulka, Otto Dov. "Popular Christian Attitudes in the Third Reich to National Socialist Policies toward Jews." In Judaism and Christianity under the Impact of National Socialism (1919-1945). Historical Society of Israel, 1982.

3038. Kulka, Otto Dov. "'Public Opinion' in Nazi Germany and the 'Jewish Question'." Jerusalem Quarterly No. 25 (Fall 1982): 121-144.

3039. Kulka, Otto Dov and Esriel Holdesheimer. "Germany." In Encyclopedia of the Holocaust. II New York: Macmillan, 1990.

3040. Kwaniewski, K. and others. "Ethnic Stereotypes and Polish- German Relations." Polish Western Affairs 19 (1979): 165-305.

3041. L'Allemagne nazie et le genocide juif. Paris: Editions du Seuil, 1985.

3042. Langenmayr, Arnold. Diskriminierung von Mädchen in Erziehungsberatungsstellen. New York: Campus Verlag, 1980.

3043. Large, David C. "Reckoning without the Past: The HIAG of the Waffen-SS and the Politics of Rehabilitation in the Bonn Republic, 1950-61." Journal of Modern History 59 (1987): 79- 113.

3044. Lautmann, Rudiger and others. The Persecution of Homosexuals in Nazi Germany: Sexual Politics in a Fascist State. Lewiston, NY: E. Mellen Press, 1990.

3045. Lee, W. R. "Economic Development and the State in Nineteenth-Century Germany." Economic History Review 41 (August 1988): 346-367.

3046. Leggewie, Claus. Die Republikaner: Phantombild der Neuen Rechten. Berlin: Rotbuch Verlag, 1989.

3047. Leibfried, Stephan and Florian Tennstedt, eds. Politik der Armut und die Spaltung des Sozialstaats. Frankfurt: Suhrkamp, 1985.

3048. Leiser, E. Nazi Cinema. New York: 1975.

3049. Lepsius, M. Ranier. "Development of Sociology in Germany after World War II (1945-1968)." International Journal of Sociology 13 (1983): 1-88.

3050. Lersch, Paul, ed. Die verkannte Gefahr: Rechtsradikalismus in der Bundesrepublik. Hamburg: Rowohlt, 1981.

3051. Leschinski, Achim and others. "Türkische Schüler in der Bundesrepublik Deutschland." Z. Padagog. 35 (May 1989): 313- 397.

3052. Levine, H. S. "A Jewish Collaborator in Nazi Germany: The Strange Career of George Kareski, 1933-37." Central European History 8 (1975): 251-281.

3053. Levy, Richard Simon. Anti-Semitic Political Parties in the German Empire. Doctoral dissertation: Yale University, 1969. UMO # 70-02762.

3054. Lewis, Rand C. Right-wing Extremism in West Germany, 1945-1989: A Nazi Legacy. Doctoral dissertation: University of Idaho, 1990. UMO # 9024746.

3055. Lewy, Guenter. "The Jewish Question." In The Catholic Church and Nazi Germany. 268-308. New York: McGraw Hill, 1964.

3056. Liang, Hsi-Huey. "Lower-class Immigrants in Wilhelmine Berlin." Central European History 3 (1970): 94-111.

3057. Lifton, R. J. The Nazi Doctors: Medical Killing and the Psychology of Genocide. New York: 1986.

3058. Lilienthal, Georg. "Anthropology and National Socialism." In Encyclopedia of the Holocaust, I. pp. 48-52. New York: Macmillan, 1990.

3059. Linke, Uli H. "Caste and Class in Germany: A Study of the Power Politics of Labor Migration from 1955-1980." Kroeber Anthropological Society Papers Nos. 61-62 (1982): 78-87.

3060. Linke, Uli H. and Alan Dundes. "More on Auschwitz Jokes." Folklore 99 (1988): 3-10. [See also Dundes and Hauschild, above.]

3061. Loewenstein, Kurt. "Thomas Mann zur jüdischen Frage." Bull. des Leo Baeck Institute 10 (1967): 1-59.

3062. Lüdtke, Alf. "Hunger in der Grossen Depression: Hungererfahrungen und Hungerpolitik am Ende der Weimarer Republik." Arch. Sozialgesch. 27 (1987): 145-176.

3063. Lundgreen, P., ed. Wissenschaft im Dritten Reich. Frankfurt: 1985.

3064. Lyotard, Jean-Francois. Heidegger and "the Jews". Minneapolis: University of Minnesota Press, 1990.

3065. Maier, Charles S., ed. The Marshall Plan and Germany: West German Development within the Framework of the European Recovery Program. New York: Berg, 1990.

3066. Malhotra, M. K. "The Educational Problems of Foreign Children of Different Nationalities in West Germany." Ethnic and Racial Studies 8 (April 1985): 291-309.

3067. Marcuse, Peter. "Social, Political and Urban Change in the GDR: Scarcely-existing Socialism." International Journal of Urban and Regional Research 14 (September 1990)

3068. Maretzki, T. W. "The Documentation of Nazi Medicine by German Medical Sociologists: A Review Article." Social Science and Medicine 29 (1989): 1319-1332.

3069. Markham, James M. "Third World Refugees Flooding West Berlin." New York Times (July 25, 1986).

3070. Marks, Sally. "Black Watch on the Rhine: A Study in Propaganda, Prejudice and Prurience." European Studies Review 13 (1983): 297-334.

3071. Martins-Heuss, Kirsten. "Reflections on the Collective Identity of Germa Roma and Sinti (Gypsies) after National Socialism." Holocaust and Genocide Studies 4 (1989): 193-211.

3072. Mason, Tim. "Women in Nazi Germany." History Workshop 1 (1976): 74-113.

3073. Mason, Tim. "Women in Nazi Germany." History Workshop 2 (1976): 5-32.

3074. Massing, Paul W. Rehearsal for Destruction: A Study of Political Anti-semitism. New York: Harper, 1949.

3075. McClelland, Charles E. "Structural Change and Social Reproduction in German Universities, 1870-1920." History of Education 15 (September 1986): 177-193.

3076. McLaughlin, B. and P. Graf. "Bilingual Education in West Germany: Recent Development." Comparative Education 21 (1985): 241-255.

3077. Meinhardt, Rolf, ed. Türken raus? oder: Verteidigt den sozialen Frieden. Beiträge gegen Ausländerfeindlichkeit. Hamburg: Rowohlt, 1984.

3078. Meinicke, Wolfgang. "Die Entnazifizierung in der sowetischen Besatzungszone 1945 bis 1948." Zeitschrift für Geschichtswissenschaft 32 (1984): 968-979.

3079. Merhav, Meir. "Lingering Guilt." Jerusalem Post (November 28, 1982): [Reflections on failure of Germans to confront failure to punish those responsible for the Holocaust.]

3080. Michael, Robert. "Luther, Luther Scholars and the Jews." Encounter 46 (1985): 339-356.

3081. Mieder, Wolfgang. "Proverbs in Nazi Germany: The Promulgation of Anti-Semitism and Stereotypes through Folklore." Journal of American Folklore 95 (Oct-Dec 1982): 435-464.

3082. Milton, Sybil. "Women and the Holocaust: The Case of German and German-Jewish Women." In When Biology Became Destiny. Women in Weimar and Nazi Germany, edited by Renate Bridenthal and others. pp. 297-333. New York: Monthly Review Press, 1984.

3083. Mosse, W. E. Jews in the German Economy: The German-Jewish Economic Elite, 1820-1935. New York: Oxford University Press, 1987.

240 WORLD RACISM AND RELATED INHUMANITIES

3084. Mucke, Karl-Heinz. Die Darstellung des Hitler-faschismus in Schulgeschichtsbüchern der BRD. Doctoral dissertation: Pädagogische Hochschule, Erfurt-Muhlhausen, 1978.

3085. Müller, Detlef K. and others, eds. The Rise of the Modern Educational System. Structural Change and Social Reproduction, 1870-1920. New York: Cambridge University Press, 1987.

3086. Müller, Hermann. Rassen und Völker im Denken der Jugend. Stuttgart: Ernst Klett Verlag, 1967.

3087. Müller, Ingo. Hitler's Justice. The Courts of the Third Reich. Translated by Deborah L. Schneider. Cambridge, Ma: Harvard University Press, 1991.

3088. Müller-Hill, Berno. Murderous Science: Elimination by Scientific Selection of Jews, Gypsies and Others, Germany, 1933-45. Translated by George R. Fraser. New York: Oxford University Press, 1988.

3089. Naumann, Uwe, ed. Sammlung Nr. 4: Jahrbuch für antifaschistische Literatur und Kunst. Frankfurt: Roderberg- Verlag, 1981.

3090. Nebe, J. M. "Residential Segregation of Ethnic Groups in West German Cities." Cities 5 (August 1988): 235-244.

3091. Neumann, Franz. Behemoth: The Structure and Practice of National Socialism, 1933-1944. New York: Harper & Row, 1944.

3092. Nicosia, Francis R. and Lawrence D. Stokes. Germans Against Nazism. Nonconformity Opposition and Resistance in the Third Reich. Berg: 1991.

3093. Niemöller, Martin. Exile in the Fatherland: Martin Niemöller's Letters from the Moabit Prison. Translated by Ernst Kaemke, Kathy Elias, and Jacklyn Wilfred and edited by Hubert G. Locke. Grand Rapids, MI: Erdmans, 1986.

3094. Noakes, Jeremy. "Social Outcasts in Nazi Germany." History Today 35 (1985): 15-19. [Gypsies.]

3095. Nolan, Mary. "The Historikerstreit and Social History." New German Critique 44 (1988): 51-80.

3096. Noll, Hans. "Früchte des Schweigens: jüdische Selbstverleugnung und Antisemitismus in der DDR." Deutschland Archiv 22 (July 1989): 769-778.

3097. O'Loughlin, J. "The Geographical Distribution of Foreigners in West Germany." Regional Studies 19 (August 1985)

3098. Oertel, Joachim. Die DDR-Mafia: Gangster, Maoisten und Neonazis im SED-Staat. Boblingen: Anita Tykve Verlag, 1988.

GERMANY 241

3099. Oppolzer, Alfred. Wenn du arm bist, musst du früher sterben: soziale Unterschiede in Gesundheit und Sterblichkeit. Hamburg: Verlag für das Studium der Arbeiterbewegung, 1986.

3100. Ostow, Robin. Jews in Contemporary East Germany. The Children of Moses in the Land of Marx. New York: St. Martin's Press, 1989.

3101. Panahi, Bodi. Rassismus, Antisemitismus, Nationalismus in der Bundesrepublik heute; eine empirische Untersuchung. Frankfurt: S. Fischer Verlag, 1980.

3102. Patzold, Kurt. "Zur innen-und aussenpolitischen Funktion des Rassismus im faschistischen Deutschland." Jenaer Beitrage zur Parteiengeschichte 37-38 (1976): 125-147.

3103. Paucker, Arnold, ed. Die Juden im Nationalsozialistischen Deutschland/The Jews in Nazi Germany 1933-1945. Tubingen: J.C.B. Mohr, 1986.

3104. Pehle, Walter H. November 1938. From the Reichskristallnacht to Genocide. Translated by William Templer. Berg: 1991.

3105. Peterson, Brian. "The Politics of Working-class Women in the Weimar Republic." Central European History 10 (June 1977): 87-111.

3106. Peukert, Detlev J. K. Inside Nazi Germany: Conformity, Opposition, and Racism in Everyday Life. Translated by Richard Deveson. New Haven, CT: Yale University Press, 1987.

3107. Peukert, Detlev J. K. and Frank Bajohr. Rechtsradikalismus in Deutschland: zwei historische Beiträge. Hamburg: Ergebnisse Verlag, 1990.

3108. Pfarr, Heide M. and Klaus Bertelsmann. Diskriminierung im Erwerbsleben: Ungleichbehandlungen von Frauen und Männern in der Bundesrepublik Deutschland. Baden-Baden: Nomos Verlagsgesellschaft, 1989.

3109. Pierenkemper, Toni. "The Standard of Living and Employment in Germany, 1850-1980. An Overview." Journal of European Economic History 16 (Spring 1987): 51-73.

3110. Pinn, Irmgard. "Die 'Verwissenschaftlichung' völkischen und rassistischen Gedankenguts am Beispiel der Zeitschrift 'Volk und Rasse'." 1999 2 (October 1987): 80-95.

3111. Pommerin, Reiner. "The Fate of Mixed Blood Children in Germany." German Studies Review 5 (October 1982): 315-324.

3112. Pommerin, Reiner. Sterilisierung der Rheinlandbastarde. Das Schicksal einer farbigen Minderheit. Dusseldorf: 1979.

3113. Pritchard, Rosalind M. O. The End of Elitism? The Democratisation of the West German University System. New York: Berg, 1990.

3114. Proctor, Robert N. Racial Hygiene. Medicine Under the Nazis. Cambridge, MA: Harvard University Press, 1988.

3115. Pulzer, Peter. The Rise of Political Anti-Semitism in Germany and 'Austria. Essays in Comparative History. London: Peter Halban, 1988.

3116. Pusch, Luise F., ed. Feminismus: Inspektion der Herrenkultur: ein Handbuch. Frankfurt: Suhrkamp, 1983.

3117. Puxon, Grattan. "Gypsies Seek Reparations." Patterns of Prejudice 15 (January 1981): 21-25.

3118. Rabofsky, Eduard and Gerhard Oberkofler. Verbirgene Wurzeln der NS-Justiz: Strafrechtliche Rüstung für zwei Weltkriege. Vienna: Europa-Verlag, 1985.

3119. Rajewsky, Christiane and Adelheid Schmitz, eds. Nationalsozialismus und Neonazismus: ein Reader für Jugendarbeit und Schule. Düsseldorf: Informations-und Pressestelle, Fachhochschule Düsseldorf, 1988.

3120. Ray, J. J. "Racism and Personal Adjustments: Testing the Bagley Hypothesis in Germany and South Africa." Personality & Individual Differences 9, 685-686 (1988)

3121. Reinders, Robert. "Racialism on the Left: E. D. Morel and the 'Black Horror on the Rhine'." International Review of Social History 13 (1968): 1-28.

3122. Reinharz, Jehuda. "The Zionist Response to Antisemitism in Germany." Leo Baeck Institute Yearbook 30 (1985): 105-140.

3123. Renn, Walter F. "Confronting Genocide: The Depiction of the Persecution of the Jews and the Holocaust in West German History Textbooks." In Contemporary Views of the Holocaust, R. L. Braham. pp. 157-180. Boston, MA: 1983.

3124. Renn, Walter F. and others. The Treatment of the Holocaust in Textbooks. The Federal Republic of Germany, Israel, and the United States. New York: Columbia University Press, 1987.

3125. Retallack, James N. "Anti-Semitism, Conservative Propaganda, and Regional Politics in Late Nineteenth Century Germany." German Studies Review 11 (October 1988): 377-403.

3126. Retallack, James N. Notables of the Right: The Conservative Party and Political Mobilization in Germany, 1876-1918. Winchester, MA: Allen & Unwin, 1988.

GERMANY 243

3127. Rhoades, Robert E. "Foreign Labor and German Industrial Capitalism 1871-1978: The Evolution of a Migratory System." American Ethnologist 5 (1978): 553-573.

3128. Richarz, Monika, ed. Jewish Life in Germany. Memoirs from Three Centuries. Translated by Stella P. Rosenfeld and Sidney Rosenfeld. Bloomington: Indiana University Press, 1991.

3129. Rinser, Luise. Wer wirft den Stein? Zigeuner sein in Deutschland. Eine Anklage. Suttgart: Eds. Weitbrecht, 1985.

3130. Roggenkamp, Gerhard H. W. Germans and Gastarbeiter: A Study of Prejudice. Doctoral dissertation: Syracuse University, 1982. UMO # 8229011.

3131. Roggenkamp, Gerhard H. W. Germans and Gastarbeiter: A Study of Prejudice. New York: AMS Press, 1989.

3132. Rose, Paul L. Revolutionary Antisemitism in Germany from Kant to Wagner. Princeton, NJ: Princeton University Press, 1990.

3133. Rosenberg, Dorothy. "The Emancipation of Women in Fact and Fiction: Changing Roles in GDR Society and Literature." In Women, State, and Party in Eastern Europe, edited by Sharon L. Wolchik and Alfred G. Meyer. pp. 433-361. Durham, NC: Duke University Press, 1985.

3134. Rosenhaft, Eve. Beating the Fascists? The German Communists and Political Violence, 1929-1933. New York: Cambridge University Press, 1983.

3135. Rotermundt, Rainer. Verkehrte Utopien: Nationalsozialismus, Neonazismus, neue Barbarei: Argumente und Materialien. Frankfurt: Verlag Neue Kritik, 1980.

3136. Roth, Jürgen. Zeitbombe Armut: soziale Wirklichkeit in der Bundesrepublik. Hamburg: Rasch und Rohring Verlag, 1985.

3137. Rothbarth, Maria. "Die Bemühungen des Europäischen Minderheitskongresses um die Durchsetzung der imperialistischen deutschen Minderheitenforderungen in der internationalen Arena (1925-1929)." Jb. Gesch. sozial. Lander Eur. 29, 177-198 (1985)

3138. Rothenhöfer, D. Untersuchungen zur Sklaverei in den ostgermanischen Nachfolgestaaten des Romischen Reiches. Doctoral dissertation: Tubingen, 1967.

3139. Rowe, David E. "'Jewish Mathematics' at Göttingen in the Era of Felix Klein." Isis 77 (1986): 422-449.

3140. Rürüp, Reinhard. "The Tortuous and Thorny Path to Legal Equality: 'Jew Laws' and Emancipatory Legislation in Germany from the Late Eighteenth Century." Leo Baeck Institute Yearbook 31 (1986): 3-33.

3141. Sadji, Uta. Die Negermythos am Ende des 18. Jahrunderts in Deutschland: e. Analyses d. Rezeption von Reiseliteratur uber Schwarzafrika. Doctoral dissertation: Free University of Berlin, 1979.

3142. Saller, K. Die Rassenlehre des Nationalsozialismus in Wissenschaft und Propaganda. Darmstadt: 1961.

3143. Salt, J. "West German Dilemma: Little Turks or Young Germans." Geography 70 (April 1985): 162-168.

3144. Sayler, Wilhelmine M. Wider die Xenophobie! Ausländer zwischen Ablehnung und Integration am Beispiel spanischer Migranten in Deutschland. Fort Lauderdale, FL: Verlag Breitenbach Publishers, 1987.

3145. Schaeffer, Herman. "Les ouvriers italiens en Allemagne, 1890-1914." Risorgimento (Belgium) 4 (1983): 21-39.

3146. Schaller, Helmut W. "Die Entwicklung der Sorabistik in Deutschland." Z. Ostforschung 32 (1983): 368-380.

3147. Scheuch, Erwin K. "Politischer Extremismus in der Bundesrepublik." In Die zweite Republik, edited by Richard Lowenthal and Hans-Peter Schwarz. pp. 433-469. Stuttgart: 1974.

3148. Schleunes, Karl A. Schooling and Society: The Politics of Education in Prussia and Bavaria, 1750-1900. New York: Berg, 1989.

3149. Schleunes, Karl A. The Twisted Road to Auschwitz. Nazi Policy toward German Jews, 1933-1939. Urbana, IL: University of Illinois Press, 1971.

3150. Schlotzhauer, Inge. "Ideologie und Organisation des politischen Antisemitismus in Frankfurt am Main 1880-1914." Frankf. Geschichte 28 (1989): 1-327.

3151. Schmerl, Christiane. Das Frauen-und Madchenbild in den Medien. Leverkusen, W. Germany: Leske Verlag & Budrich, 1984.

3152. Schmitter, B. "Immigrant Minorities in West Germany: Some Theoretical Concerns." Ethnic and Racial Studies 6 (1983): 308-319.

3153. Schneider, Rudolf. Die SS ist ihr Vorbild: neonazistische Kampfgruppen und Aktionskreise in der Bundesrepublik. Frankfurt: Roderberg-Verlag, 1981.

3154. Schneider, Ullrich. "Berlin, der Kalte Krieg und die Grundung der Freien Universitat 1945-1949." Jb. Gesch. Mittel - u. Ostdeutschlands 34 (1985): 37-101.

3155. Schneider, Ullrich. "Zur Entnazifizierung der Hochschullehrer in Niedersachsen 1945-1949." Niedersachs. Jb. Landesgesch. 61 (1989): 325-346.

3156. Schober-Brinkmann, K. "The Crisis of Youth Employment and Training in West Germany: Public Intervention and the Response of Employers and Trade Unions." Economia e Lavoro 20 (October-December 1986)

3157. Schoenberg, Ulrike. "Participation in Ethnic Associations: The Case of Immigrants in West Germany." International Migration Review 19 (Fall 1985): 416-437.

3158. Scholder, Klaus. The Churches and the Third Reich. 2 vols. Translated by John Bowden. London: SCM Press, 1987-1988.

3159. Scholtz-Klink, Gertrud. Die Frau im Dritten Reich. Tubingen: Grabert, 1978.

3160. Schröder, Hannelore, ed. Die Frau is frei geboren. 2 vols. Munich: C. H. Beck, 1979, 1981.

3161. Schröder, Hans-Jürgen. "The Economic Reconstruction of West Germany in the Context of International Relations, 1945- 1949." In Power in Europe: Great Britain, France, Italy, and Germany in a Postwar World, edited by Josef Becker and Franz Knipping. Berlin: Walter De Gruyter, 1986.

3162. Schuler, Hans. "Die Angst vor den Fremden." Die Zeit 1 (January 1982)

3163. Schulte, Axel and others, eds. Ausländer in der Bundesrepublik: Integration, Marginalisierung, Identität. Frankfurt: Materialis Verlag, 1985.

3164. Schutt, Peter. Der Mohr hat seine Schuldigkeit getan: Gibt es Rassismus in der Bundesrepublik? Dortmund: Weltkrieg- Verlag, 1981.

3165. Schütte, Wolfgang and Waldemar Süss. Armut in Hamburg: eine Dokumentation zur Arbeitslosigkeit und Sozialhilfebedurftigkeit. Hamburg: VSA-Verlag, 1988.

3166. Schwartz, Thomas A. America's Germany. John J. McCloy and the Federal Republic of Germany. Cambridge, MA: Harvard University Press, 1991.

3167. Seidel, Gill. The Holocaust Denial, Antisemitism, Racism & the New Right. Leeds, England: Beyond the Pale Collective, 1986. [Box 6, Cookridge Street, Leeds LS2 3aw, England.]

3168. Seydewitz, R. and M. Seydewitz. Anti-Semitism in West Germany. Berlin: Committee for German Unity, 1956.

3169. Seyhan, Azade and others. "[Special Issue on Minorities in German Culture]." New German Critique 46 (Winter 1989): 3- 208.

246 WORLD RACISM AND RELATED INHUMANITIES

3170. Shaffer, Harry. Women in the Two Germanies: A Comparative Study of a Socialist and a Non-socialist Society. New York: Pergamon Press, 1981.

3171. Sharfman, Glenn R. The Jewish Youth Movement in Germany, 1900-1936: A Study in Ideology and Organization. doctoral dissertation: University of North Carolina, 1989. UMO # 9033031.

3172. Sichrovsky, Peter. Born Guilt. Children of Nazi Families. Translated by Jean Steinberg: New York, Basic Books.

3173. Silbermann, Alphons and H. A. Sallen. "Latenter Antisemitismus in der Bundesrepublik Deutschland." Kölner Zeitschrift für Soziologie und Sozialpsychologie 28 (1976): 706-723.

3174. Silbermann, Alphons and Julius H. Schoeps, eds. Antisemitismus nach dem Holocaust: Bestandsaufnahme und Erscheinungsformen in deutschsprachigen Landern. Cologne: Verlag Wissenschaft & Politik, 1986.

3175. Silberner, Edmund. "Die Kommunistische Partei Deutschlands zur Judenfrage." Jahrbuch des Instituts für Deutsche Geschichte 8 (1979): 283-334.

3176. Silberner, Edmund. "Rosa Luxemburg, ihre Partei und die Judenfrage." Jahrbuch des Instituts für Deutsche Geschichte 7 (1978): 299-337.

3177. Smith, Woodruff D. The Ideology of German Colonialism: 1840-1918. Doctoral dissertation: University of Chicago, 1972.

3178. Smith, Woodruff D. "The Ideology of German Colonialism, 1840-1906." Journal of Modern History 46 (December 1974): 641-662.

3179. Sochatzky, Klaus and others. Parole: rechts! Jugend, wohin? Neofaschismus im Schulerurteil. Eine empirische Studie. Frankfurt am Main: 1981.

3180. Sohn-Rethel, Alfred. Economy and Class Structure of German Fascism. London: CSE Books, 1978.

3181. Solta, Jan and others. Geschichte der Sorben. Vol. 2: Von 1789 bis 1917. Bautzen: VEB Domowina-Verlag, 1974.

3182. Sorensen, A. B. and H. P. Blossfeld. "Socioeconomic Opportunities in Germany in the Post-War Period." In Research in Social Stratification and Mobility, vol. 8, edited by A. L. Kalleberg. Greenwich, CT: JAI Press, 1989.

3183. Spangenthal, Max. "The Jewish Question and the German Resistance Movement." Yad Vashem Bulletin No. 19 (1966): 60-63.

3184. Spencer, Elaine. Management and Labor in Imperial Germany. Ruhr Industrialists as Employers, 1896-1914. New Brunswick, NJ: Rutgers University Press, 1984.

3185. Spoo, Eckart. "Freund-und Feinbilder in der Presse." Blatter für Deutsche und Internationale Politik 27 (1982): 995-1007.

3186. Spree, Reinhard. Health and Social Class in Imperial Germany: A Social History of Mortality, Morbidity, and Inequality. Translated by Stuart McKinnon-Evans. New York: Berg, 1988.

3187. Staeck, Klaus and Inge Karst, eds. Macht Ali deutsches Volk Kaputt. Gottingen: Seidl, 1982.

3188. Stephenson, Jill. The Nazi Organization of Women. Totowa, NJ: Barnes & Noble, 1981.

3189. Stiller, Michael. Die Republikaner: Franz Schonhuber und seine rechtsradikale Partei. Munich: 1989.

3190. Stilley, Susan A. The "Sponsored" Mode of Social Reproduction and the Primary School Classroom in the Federal Republic of Germany. Doctoral dissertation: University of Houston, 1986. UMO # 8709919.

3191. Stokes, Raymond G. "German Energy in the U.S. Post-War Economic Order, 1945-1951." Journal of European Economic History 17 (Winter 1988): 621-639.

3192. Stone, Gerald. The Smallest Slavonic Nation: The Sorbs of Lusatia. New York: Oxford University Press, 1972.

3193. Stöss, Richard. Die extreme Rechte in der Bundesrepublik: Entwicklung, Ursachen, Gegenmassnahmen. Wiesbaden: Westdeutscher Verlag, 1989.

3194. Stöss, Richard. "The Problem of Right-Wing Extremism in West Germany." W. Eur. Pol. 11 (April 1988): 34-46.

3195. Stöss, Richard. Die 'Republikaner': Woher sie kommen-was sie wollen-wer sie Wählt-was zu tun ist. Cologne: 1990.

3196. Strauss, Herbert A. "Hostage of 'World Jewry': On the Origin of the Idea of Genocide in German History." Holocaust and Genocide Studies 3 (1988): 125-136.

3197. Suhr, Heidrun. "Ausländerliteratur: Minority Literature in the Federal Republic of Germany." New German Critique 46 (Winter 1989): 71-103.

3198. Suhr, Heidrun. "Fremde in Berlin: The Outsider's View from the Inside." In Berlin, Culture and Metropolis, edited by Charles W. Haxthausen and Heidrun Suhr. Minneapolis: University of Minnesota Press, 1990.

3199. Tagliabue, John. "Sorbs of Germany Say Long Live the Difference." New York Times (December 26, 1990).

3200. Tenorth, Heinz-Elmar. "Deutsche Erziehungswissenschaft 1930 bis 1945." Z. Padagogik 32 (June 1986): 299-321.

3201. Teraoka, Arlene A. "'Gastarbeiterliteratur': The Other Speaks Back." Cultural Critique No. 7 (Fall 1987)

3202. Thalmann, Rita. Être femme sous le IIIe Reich. Paris: Editions Robert Laffont, 1982.

3203. Théolleyre, Jean-Marc. Les Néo-nazis. Paris: Temps actuels- Messidor, 1982.

3204. Thompson, E. A. "Slavery in Early Germany." Hermathena 89 (1957): 17-29.

3205. Tournier, Michelle. "Women and Access to University in France and Germany (1861-1967)." Comparative Education 9 (Ocotober 1973): 107-117.

3206. Tsiakolos, Georgios. Ausländerfeindlichkeit: Tatsachen und Erklärungsversuche. Munich: C.H. Beck, 1983.

3207. Tübingen Projektgruppe Frauenhandel. Frauenhandel in Deutschland. Bonn: Verlag J.H.W. Dietz Nachf., 1989.

3208. Turner, Ian D. "Denazification in the British Zone." In Reconstruction in Post-war Germany: British Occupation Policy and the Western Zones, 1945-55, edited by Turner. New York: Berg, 1989.

3209. Tworuschka, Monika. Der Islam in den Schulbüchern der Bundesrepublik Deutschland. 2 vols. Braunschweig, FRG: Georg-Eckert-Institut, 1986.

3210. Tyrnauer, Gabrielle. The Fate of the Gypsies during the Holocaust. Special Report. Washington, D.C.: U.S. Holocaust Memorial Council, 1985.

3211. Vittori, Jean-Pierre. Eux,les STO. Paris: Temps actuels- Messidor, 1982. [Forced French labor in Nazi Germany.]

3212. Voigt, Dieter and others. Sozialstruktur der DDR: Eine Einfuhrung. Darmstadt: Wissenschaftliche Buchgesellschaft, 1987.

3213. Volberg, Heinrich. Ausländsdeutschtum und Drittes Reich: der Fall Argentinien. Cologne: Bohlau-Verlag, 1981.

3214. Von Hitler zu Bürger? zur Geschichte, Ideologie und Rechtssituation der NDP. [Nationaldemokratische Partei] Vienna: Junge Generation in der Sozialistischen Partei Oesterreichs, 1981.

3215. Wagner, Ulrich and others. "Contact and Prejudice between Germans and Turks: A Correlational Study." Human Relations 42 (July 1989): 561-574.

3216. Waldorf, Brigitte. Segregation, Mobility and Residential Location of Foreign Workers in Dusseldorf, West Germany. Doctoral dissertation: University of Illinois, 1988. UMO # 8908883.

3217. Wallraff, Günter. "Lowest of the Low: The Turkish Worker in West Germany." Race and Class (Autumn 1986)

3218. Wallraff, Günter. Lowest of the Low. London: Methuen, 1988. [German journalist lives in guise of illegal Turkish worker.]

3219. Warmbold, Joachim. Germania in Africa: Germany's Colonial Literature. New York: Peter Lang, 1989.

3220. Webber, Douglas. "A Relationship of 'Critical Partnership'? Capital and the Social-Liberal Coalition in West Germany." In Capital and Politics in Western Europe, David Marsh. pp. 61-86. London: 1983.

3221. Weber, Eva. In Zwei Welten: Migration und Kunst. Frankfurt am Main: Verlag Neue Kritik, 1988. [Painting and sculpture of migrants in West Germany.]

3222. Weber, R. G. S. The German Student Corps in the Third Reich. London: Macmillan, 1986.

3223. Weckbecker, Arno. Judenverfolgung in Heidelberg 1933-1945. Doctoral dissertation: University of Mannheim, 1985.

3224. Wegner, G. P. "Germany's Past Contested - The Soviet- American Conflict in Berlin over History Curriculum Reform, 1945-48." History of Education Quarterly 30 (Spring 1990)

3225. Wehling, Hans-Georg, ed. Die Türkei und die Türken in Deutschland. Stuttgart: Kohlkammer Taschenbücher, 1982.

3226. Weidig, Rudi and others. Sozialstruktur der DDR. East Berlin: Dietz Verlag Berlin, 1988.

3227. Weil, Frederick. "The Imperfectly Mastered Past: Anti-Semitism in West Germany Since the Holocaust." New German Critique No. 20 (Spring/Summer 1980): 135-153.

3228. Weindling, Paul. Health, Race, and German Politics Between National Unification and Nazism, 1870-1945. New York: Cambridge University Press, 1989.

3229. Weindling, Paul. "Weimar Eugenics: The Kaiser Wilhelm Institute for Anthropology, Human Heredity and Eugenics in Social Context." Annals of Science 42 (May 1985): 303-318.

3230. Weingarter, J. J. "The SS Race and Resettlement Main Office: Toward an Order of Blood and Soil." Historian 34 (November 1971): 62-77.

3231. Weingart, Peter. "German Eugenics between Science and Politics." Osiris 5 (1989)

3232. Weische, Alexa. Sozial-kulturelle Probleme junger Turkinnen in der BRD. Bamberg: Dissertationschuck M. SchADEL, 1978.

3233. Weiss, Sheila F. "The Race Hygiene Movement in Germany." Osiris 3 (1987): 193-236. [1890-1920s.]

3234. Weiss, Sheila F. Race Hygiene and National Efficiency. The Eugenics of Wilhelm Schallmayer. Berkeley: University of California Press, 1987.

3235. Weitz, Bernard O. Sprache und Berufswahl als zentrale Probleme türkischer Schüler in der beruflichen Grundbildung. Verlag Anton Hain, 1986.

3236. Welch, David. "Priming the Pump of German Democracy: British 'Re-education' Policy in Germany after the Second World War." In Reconstruction in Postwar Germany: British Occupation Policy and the Western Zones, 1945-55, edited by Ian D. Turner. New York: Berg, 1989.

3237. Westmüller, Horst, ed. Frauen zwischen zwei Kulturen: Frauen aus der Türkei in der Bundesrepublik Deutschland. Loccum: Evangelische Akademie Loccum, 1985.

3238. Wiggershaus, Renate. Geschichte der Frauen und der Frauenbewegung. In der Bundesrepublik Deutschland und in der DDR nach 1945. Wuppertal: Hammer, 1979.

3239. Winkler, Arno. Neofaschismus in der BRD: Erscheinungen, Hintergrunde, Gefahren. E. Berlin: Dietz Verlag Berlin, 1980.

3240. Winrow, Gareth. "East Germany, Israel and the Reparations Issue." Soviet Jewish Affairs 20 (Spring 1990): 31-46.

3241. Wohlwill, Joachim F. "German Psychological Journals under National Socialism: A History of Contrasting Paths." Journal of the History of the Behavioral Sciences 23 (1987): 169-185.

3242. Woods, W. Wilson. The American Race Issue as a Factor in "The Black Horror on the Rhine" Controversy (1919-1922). Master's thesis: Western Michigan University, 1982.

3243. Wrzesinski, Wojciech. "Die polnische Minderheit in der Weimarer Republik." Schriftenreihe Georg-Eckert-Inst. int. Schulbuchforsch. 22 (1985): 89-95.

3244. Wülfing, Svea. Türkische Vorschulkinder in Köln. Köln: 1978.

3245. Wynot, Edward D., Jr. "The Polish Germans, 1919-1939: National Minority in a Multinational State." Polish Review 27 (Winter 1972): 23-64.

3246. Yücel, A. Ersan. "Turkish Migrant Workers in the Federal Republic of Germany." In Migrants in Europe: The Role of Family, Labor, and Politics, edited by Hans Christian Buechler and Judith Maria Buechler. Westport, CT: Greenwood, 1987.

3247. Yurochko, William P. German High School History Textbooks: How Well Do They Deal With the Rise and Fall of the Third Reich? Doctoral dissertation: Virginia Polytechnic Institute and State University, 1988. UMO # 8817429.

3248. Zapf, Wolfgang and others. "German Social Report: Living Conditions and Subjective Well-Being, 1978-1984." Social Indicator research 19 (February 1987): 1-171.

3249. Zimmermann, Mosche. Wilhelm Marr. The Patriarch of Anti-Semitism. New York: Oxford University Press, 1986.

3250. Zorn, Gerda and Gertrud Meyer. Frauen gegen Hitler. Frankfurt am Main: Roderberg-Verlag, 1974.

3251. Zur Muhlen, Patrik von and Richard Löwenthal, eds. Widerstand und Verweigerung in Deutschland, 1933 bis 1945. Bonn: Dietz Nachf., 1982.

GHANA

3252. Aidoo, Agnes A. "Women in the History and Culture of Ghana." Research Review 1 (1985): 14-51.

3253. Ansah-Koi, K. "A Note on Police Violence in Post-Colonial Ghana." Research Review 2 (1986): 39-59.

3254. Arbim, Kwame. "A Note on the Asante akonkofo: A Non-literate sub-elite, 1900-1930." Africa (London) 56 (1986): 25-32.

3255. Asamoa, Anoa. Classes and Tribalism in Ghana. Accra: Information Services Dept., 1982.

3256. "Autobiographical Reminiscences of an Asante Slave, 'Mose'." Asantesem (June 1975): 19-20.

3257. Bennell, Paul. "Industrial Clan Formation in Ghana: Some Empirical Observations." Development and Change 15 (October 1984): 593-612.

3258. Brown, David. "The Political Response to Immiseration: A Case Study of Rural Ghana." Geneve-Afrique 18 (1980): 55- 74.

3259. Darko, Samuel F. A Historical Inquiry into the Development of Higher Education in Ghana, 1948-1984: A Study of the Major Factors that have Controlled and Inhibited the Development of the Universities of Ghana. North Texas State University, 1985. Doctoral dissertation.

3260. Ekoko, A. E. "British Colonial Interests and Imperial Defence in the Gold Coast and Nigeria, 1885-1898." Journal, Historical Society of Nigeria 12 (1984-1985): 61-75.

3261. Hadjor, Kofi B. Nkrumah and Ghana: The Dilemma of Post- colonial Power. New York: Kegan Paul International, 1988.

3262. Johan, Kwesi. "Imperialism, the State and the Indigenization of the Ghanian Economy." Africa Development 10 (1985): 63-99.

3263. McCaskie, T. C. "Accumulation, Wealth and Belief in Asante History. Part II: The Twentieth Century." Africa (London) 56 (1986): 3-24.

3264. Mikell, Gwendolyn. "Expansion and Contraction in Economic Acess for Rural Women in Ghana." Rural Africa (Winter 1985): 13-30.

3265. Patton, Adell. "Dr. John Farrell Easmon: Medical Professionalism and Colonial Racism in the Gold Coast, 1856- 1900." International Journal of African Historical Studies 22 (1989): 601-636.

3266. Pellow, Deborah. Women in Accra: Options for Autonomy. Algonac, MI: Reference Publications, 1977.

3267. Sutton, Inez. "Colonial Agricultural Policy: The Non- Development of the Northern Territories of the Gold Coast." International Journal of African Historical Studies 22 (1989): 637-670.

3268. Tettey, Charles. "Medical Practitioners of African Descent in Colonial Ghana." International Journal of African Historical Studies 18 (1985): 139-144.

3269. Van Hear, Nick. "Child Labour and the Development of Capitalist Agriculture in Ghana." Development and Change 13 (1982): 499-513.

GREAT BRITAIN

ANTI-SEMITISM

3270. Alderman, Geoffrey. "Anglo-Jewry: The Unspoken Fears." Forum 37 (1980): 53-60.

3271. Alderman, Geoffrey. "Antisemitism in Britain." Jewish Journal of Sociology 31 (1989): 125-130.

3272. Almog, Shmuel. "Antisemitism as a Dynamic Phenomenon: The Jewish Question in England at the End of the First World War." Patterns of Prejudice 21 (1987): 3-18.

3273. Aronsfeld, C. C. "The Anti-Semitism of Appeasement." Jewish Frontier 39 (1972): 34-35.

3274. Bayme, Steven Gilbert. Jewish Leadership and Anti-Semitism in Britain, 1898-1918. Doctoral dissertation, Columbia University, 1977. UMO # 77-14778.

3275. Blume, H. S. B. A Study of Anti-Semitic Groups in Britain, 1918-1940. M. Phil. thesis, University of Sussex, 1971.

3276. Bolchover, R. L. Anglo-Jewish Response to the Holocaust, 1942-1946. M. Litt. thesis, University of Oxford: 1987.

3277. Brewer, John D. "The British Union of Facists and Anti- Semitism in Birmingham." Midland History 9 (1984): 109-122.

3278. Brown, Malcolm. "The Jews of Hackney before 1840." Transaction. Jewish Historical Society of England. 30 (1987-1988): 71-89.

3279. Cesarani, David. "Anti-Alienism in England after the First World War." Immigrants and Minorities 6 (March 1987): 5-29.

3280. Cesarani, David. "The Anti-Jewish Career of Sir William Joynson-Hicks, Calvinist Minister." Journal of Contemporary History 24 (1989): 411-435.

3281. Cesarani, David. "Anti-Zionist Politics and Political Anti-semitism in Britain, 1920-1924." Patterns of Prejudice 23 (Spring 1989): 28-45.

3282. Cohen, M. J. "Churchill and the Jews: the Holocaust." Modern Judaism 6 (February 1989): 27-49.

3283. Cohen, Steve. "Anti-semitism, Immigration Controls and the Welfare State." Critical Social Policy No.13 (Summer 1985): 73-92.

3284. Cohen, Steve. From the Jews to the Tamils: Britain's Mistreatment of Refugees. Manchester, UK: South Manchester Law Centre, 1988.

3285. Colbenson, Peter D. British Socialism and Anti-Semitism. Doctoral dissertation, Georgia State University, 1977.

3286. Dobson, R. B. "The Decline and Expulsion of the Medieval Jews of York." Jewish Historical Society of England 26 (1979): 62-70.

3287. Endelman, Todd M. Radical Assimilation in English Jewish History, 1656-1945. Bloomington: Indiana University Press, 1990.

3288. Field, Geoffrey G. "Anti-Semitism with the Boots Off: Recent Research on England." Wiener Library Bulletin (1983): 25-46.

3289. Finestein, Israel. "A Modern Examination of Macauley's Case for the Civil Emancipation of the Jews." Jewish Historical Society of England, Transactions 28 (1981-1982): 39-59.

3290. Finestein, Israel. "Religious Minorities and Civil Rights in 19th Century England." Jewish Life and Times (1983): 146- 154.

3291. Gelber, Mark H. "Pedagogical Guidelines for Literary Antisemitism." Patterns of Prejudice 20 (January 1986): 34- 44.

3292. Gilam, Abraham. "The Leeds Anti-Jewish Riots, 1917." Jewish Quarterly 29 (1981): 34-37.

3293. Glassman, Bernard. Anti-Semitic Stereotypes Without Jews: Images of the Jews in England, 1290-1700. Detroit: Wayne State University Press, 1975.

3294. Goldman, A. "The Resurgence of Anti-Semitism in Britain during World War II." Jewish Social Studies 46 (Winter, 1984): 37-50.

3295. Green, Geoffrey. "Anglo-Jewish Trading Connections with Officers and Seamen of the Royal Navy, 1740-1820." Jewish Historical Studies 29 (1982-1986): 97-133.

3296. Henriques, U. R. G. "The Jewish Emancipation Controversy in 19th Century Britain." Past and Present No.40 (1968): 126- 146.

3297. Holmes, Colin. Anti-Semitism and British Society. New York: Holmes and Meier, 1979.

3298. Holmes, Colin. "The Ritual Murder Accusation in Britain." Ethnic and Racial Studies 4 (1981): 265-288.

3299. Janner, Greville. "Black-Jewish Controversies in Britain." Patterns of Prejudice 20 (1986): 3-12.

3300. Klein, C. L. "English Antisemitism in the 1920's." Patterns of Prejudice 16 (March-April 1972): 23-28.

3301. Kosmin, Barry A. "Localism and Pluralism in British Jewry 1900-1980." Jewish Historical Society of England Transactions 28 (1981-1982): 111-125.

3302. Kushner, Tony. British Anti-Semitism in the Second World War. Doctoral dissertation, University of Sheffield, 1986.

3303. Kushner, Tony. "Horns and Dilemmas: Jewish Evacuees in Britain during the Second World War." Immigrants and Minorities 7 (1988): 273-291.

3304. Lebzelter, Gisela C. Political Anti-Semitism in England, 1918-1939. London: Macmillan, 1979.

3305. Lebzelter, Gisela C. "The Protocols in England." Wiener Library Bulletin 31 (1978): 111-117. [The Protocols of the Elders of Zion]

3306. Levy, E. D. "Antisemitism in England at War, 1914-1916." Patterns of Prejudice 4 (September-October 1970): 27-30.

3307. Lipman, Vivian D. "The Anatomy of Medieval Anglo-Jewry." Jewish Historical Society of England 21 (1968): 64-77.

3308. Lipman, Vivian D. A History of the Jews in Britain since 1858. New York: Holmes and Meier, 1990.

3309. Matar, N. J. "The Controversy Over the Restoration of the Jews in English Protestant Thought:1701-1753." Durham University Journal 80 (1988): 241-256.

3310. Menache, Sophia. "Faith, Myth and Politics: The Stereotype of the Jews and their Expulsion from England and France." Jewish Quarterly Review 75 (April 1985): 351-374.

3311. Newman, Aubrey, ed. The Jewish East End, 1840-1939. London: 1981,

GREAT BRITAIN - ANTI-SEMITISM   257

3312. Orwell, George. "Anti-Semitism in Britain." Contemporary Jewish Record 8 (1945): 163-171. [See also Walton, below.]

3313. Ovrut, Barnett D. "Edward I and the Expulsion of the Jews." Jewish Quarterly Review 67 (1977): 224-235.

3314. Pollins, Harold. Economic History of the Jews in England. London: Associated University Press, 1983.

3315. Polonsky, Antony. "Political Anti-Semitism in Britain before the First World War." Studia nad Faszyzmen i Zbrodniami Hitlerowskimi 9 (1985): 67-87.

3316. Rothschild, Walter. "Report on the Commemoration of the Eight Hundreth Anniversary of the Massacre at Clifford's Tower, York of 16 March 1190." Christian Jewish Relations 23 (Summer 1990): 32-34.

3317. Rubenstein, W. D. "Jews among Top British Wealth Holders, 1857-1969: Decline of the Golden Age." Jewish Social Studies 34 (1972): 73-84.

3318. Seidel, Gill. The Holocaust Denial: Anti-Semitism, Racism and the New Right. Leeds: Beyond the Pale Collective, 1986.

3319. Simpson, William W. "Jewish-Christian Relations Since the Inception of the Council of Christians and Jews." Jewish Historical Society of England. Transactions 28 (1981-1982): 89--101.

3320. Spector, David. "Brighton Jewry Reconsidered." Transactions. Jewish Historical Society of England 30 (1987-1988): 91-124.

3321. Steinberg, Bernard. "Anglo-Jewry and the 1944 Education Act." Jewish Journal of Sociology 31 (December 1989): 81- 108.

3322. Thurlow, Richard C. "The Jew-Wise: Dimensions of British Political Anti-Semitism." Immigrants and Minorities 6 (March 1987): 44-65.

3323. Walton, David. "George Orwell and Antisemitism." Patterns of Prejudice 16 (January 1982): 19-34. [See also Orwell, above.]

3324. Wasserstein, Bernard. Britain and the Jews of Europe 1939- 1945. London: Oxford University Press, 1979.

3325. Zweig, Ronald W. Britain and Palestine during the Second World War. England: Woodbridge, 1986.

3326. Zweig, Ronald W., Hedva Ben-Israel, Colin Holmes, and others. "Great Britain." Encyclopedia of the Holocaust, Macmillian, New York (1990): 600-610.

GREAT BRITAIN - BLACKS

3327. Acer. Racism and the Black Child. London: Afro-Caribbean Education, 1982.

3328. Ahmed, Sharma and others, eds. Social Work with Black Children and their Families. London: Batsford, 1986.

3329. Akhtar, Shabnaz and Stronach, Ian. "They Call Me Blacky." Times Educational Supplement (September 19, 1986)

3330. Aldrich, Howard and others. "From Periphery to Peripheral: The South Asian Petite Bourgeoisie in England." In Research in the Sociology of Work, edited by Ida H. and Richard Simpson. Greenwich, CT.: JAI Press, 1983.

3331. Alibhai, Yasmin. "Black Nightingales." New Statesman and Society 1 (October 1988): 26-27.

3332. Alibhai, Yasmin. "Criminal Injustice: How the Legal System Treats Blacks." New Statesmen and Society (July 29, 1988)

3333. Alladina, S. "South Asian Language in Britain: Criteria for Description and Definition." Journal of Multilingual and Multicultural Development 6 (1985): 449-466.

3334. Amos, Valerie. "Black Women in Britain: A Bibliographic Essay." Sage Race Relations Abstracts 7 (February 1972): 1- 11.

3335. "The Attainment of Black Pupils Undermined by Racial Prejudice and Stereotyping." New Equals No.27 (Autumn 1987): 9.

3336. Badawi, Z. Islam in Britain. London: Taha Publishers, 1981.

3337. Baker, Nick. "A School Apart." Times Educational Supplement (November 22, 1985)

3338. Barthelemy, Anthony S. Black Face, Maligned Race: The Representation of Blacks in English Drama from Shakespeare to Southerne. Baton Rouge: Louisiana State University Press, 1987.

3339. Berridge, Virginia. "East End Opium Dens and Narcotic Use in Britain." London Journal 4 (1978): 3-28.

3340. Bhachu, Parminder. Parental Educational Strategies: The Case of Punjabi Sikhs in Britain. Coventry cv4 7AL: Centre for Research in Ethnic Relations, University of Warwick, 1986.

3341. Bhachu, Parminder. Twice Migrants: East African Sikh Settlers in Britain. New York: Tavistock, 1986.

3342. Bhat, Ashok and others, eds. Britain's Black Population: A New Perspective. Brookfield, VT: Gower, 1988.

3343. Black People and the Criminal Justice System. London: NACRO, 1986.

3344. Black People in Brent-Explorations in Coping Strategies. London: Hansib Publishing Ltd., 1987.

3345. Black Youth Futures; Ethnic Minorities and the Youth Training Scheme. Leicester: National Youth Bureau, 1987.

3346. Bogues, Tony. "Black Youth in Revolt." International Socialism No. 102 (October 1977): 12-15.

3347. Braham, P. and others. Discrimination and Disadvantage in Employment:The Experience of Black Work. London: Harper and Row, 1981.

3348. Brixton Black Women's Group. "Black Politics: Black Feminism." Off Our Backs 14 (1984): 14-15, 28.

3349. Brock, Colin, ed. The Caribbean in Europe: Aspects of the West Indian Experience in Britain,. London: Frank Cass, 1986.

3350. Bryan, Beverley and others. The Heart of the Race. London: Virago, 1985.

3351. Campaign Against Racism and Fascism. Southall: The British of a Black Community. London: Institute of Race Relations, 1981.

3352. Carey, Sean. "Anatomy of Racial Violence." New Society (April 11, 1986)

3353. Carey, Sean and Abdus Shukur. "A Profile of the Bangladeshi Community in East London." New Community 14 (Winter 1985): 405-417.

3354. Carmichael, Kay. "Tibet in Scotland." New Society (April 25, 1986)

3355. Carrington, Bruce and Edward Wood. "Black Youth and Sport in the United Kingdom." In The Caribbean in Europe, by Colin Brock. London: Frank Cass, 1986.

3356. Carrington, Bruce. "Social Mobility, Ethnicity and Sport." British Journal of Sociology of Education 7 (1986): 3-18.

3357. Carter, Bob and others. "The 1951-1955 Conservative Government and the Racialization of Black Immigrants." Immigrants and Minorities 6 (1987): 335-347.

3358. Carter, Trevor. Shattering Illusions: West Indians in British Politics. London: Lawrence and Wishart, 1986.

3359. Caudrey, Adriana. "The West Indian Robin Hood." New Society (June 27, 1986)

3360. The Chinese Community in Britain: The Home Affairs Committee Report in Context. London: Runnymede Trust, 1986.

3361. Coronary Prevention Group. Coronary Heart Disease and Asians in Britain. London: The Coronary Prevention Group for the Confederation of Indian Organizations, May, 1986.

3362. Crow, Gain. "Black People and Criminal Justice in the UK." Howard Journal of Criminal Justice 26 (November 1987): 303-314.

3363. Dabydeen, D., ed. The Black Presence in English Literature. Manchester University Press, 1985,

3364. Dabydeen, D. Hogarth's Blacks: Images of Blacks in Eighteenth Century English Art. Athens: University of Georgia Press, 1987.

3365. Daniels, Therese and Jane Gerson, eds. The Colour Black. Bloomington: Indiana University Press, 1990.

3366. Davosta, Cornel. Ideology and Practice within the Black Supplementary School Movement. Doctoral dissertation, University of Surrey, 1987. Oder NO. BRDX 81122.

3367. Daye, S. G. Middle-class Afro-Caribbeans: A Racial Fraction of the British Middle Class or a Class Fraction of a Racial Group? Doctoral dissertation, University of Aston, 1988.

3368. Dean, D. W. "Coping with Colonial Immigration, the Cold War and Colonial Policy: The Labour Government and Black Communities in Great Britain 1945-1951." Immigrants and Minorities 6 (1987): 305-334.

3369. Dennis, Ferdinand. *Behind the Frontlines: Journey into Afro-Britain*. London: Gollance, 1988.

3370. Dex, Shirley. "Earnings Differentials of Second Generation West Indian and White School Learners in Britain." *Manchester School of Economic and Social Studies* 54 (June, 1986)

3371. Dex, Shirley. "A Note on Discrimination in Employment and Its Effects on Black Youths." *Journal of Social Policy* 8 (1979): 357-369.

3372. Dex, Shirley. "The Second Generation: West Indian Female School-learners." In *One Way Ticket*, edited by Annie Phizacklea. London: Routledge and Kegan Paul, 1983.

3373. *The Different Reality*. West Midlands County Council, 1986.

3374. Donovan, Jenny. *We Don't Buy Sickness, It Just Comes: Health, Illness, and Health Care in the Lives of Black People in London*. Brookfield, CT: Gower, 1986.

3375. Drew, D. and Gray, J. "The 5th-Year Examination Achievements of Black Young People in England and Wales." *Educational Research* 32 (Summer 1990)

3376. Eade, John. *The Politics of Community: The Bangladeshi Community in East London*. Brookfield, VT: Gower, 1989.

3377. Edwards, Viv. "Black British English. A Bibliographical Essay on the Language of Children of West Indian Origin." *Sage Race Relations Abstracts* 5 (September 1980): 1-25.

3378. Edwards, Viv. *Language in a Black Community*. Clevedon, Avon: Multilingual Matters, 1986.

3379. Evans, Neil. "Regulating the Reserve Army: Arabs, Blacks and the Local State in Cardiff, 1919-1945." *Immigrants and Minorities* 4 (July 1985): 68-115.

3380. Faizi, Ghazala. *A History of the Black Presence in London*. London: Greater London Council, 1986.

3381. Farrar, Max. "Chaos of Carnival." *New Statesman and Society* (August 5, 1988)

3382. *The Fight Against Racism. A Pictorial History of Asians and Afro-Caribbeans*. London: Institute of Race Relations, 1986.

3383. Figueroa, John J. "The Relevancy of West Indian Literature to Caribbean Heritage People Living in Britain." In *The Caribbean in Europe*, edited by Colin Brock. London: Frank Cass, 1986.

3384. Figueroa, Peter M. E. "Educational Inequality of Children of Caribbean Background in Britain." In Dependence and Interdependence in Education: International perspective, edited by K. Watson London: Croom Helm, 1984.

3385. File, N. and C. Power. Black Settlers in Britain 1555-1958. London: Heinemann Educational, 1981.

3386. Fiscian, C. E. Minority Group Prejudice: A Study of Some Sociological and Psychological Correlates of Anti-English Prejudice among West Indian Immigrants in London. Doctoral dissertation, University of London, 1955/56.

3387. Fitzgerald, Marian. Black People and Party Politics in Britain. London: Runnymede Trust, 1987.

3388. FitzHerbert, K. West Indian Children in London. London: G. Bell, 1967.

3389. Forster, Imogen. "Nature's Outcast Child: Black People in Children's Books." Race and Class 31 (July-September, 1989): 59-77.

3390. Foster-Carter, Olivia. "Black Women/White Feminism in Britain." Sage Race Relations Abstracts 13 (February 1988): 3-16.

3391. Gates, Henry Louis, Jr. "Black London." Antioch Review 34 (Spring 1976): 301-337.

3392. Gibson, Ashton with Jocelyn Barrow. The Unequal Struggle. London: Centre for Caribbean Studies, 1986.

3393. Gibson, Margaret A. and Bhachu, Parminder. "Community Forces and School Performances: Punjabi Sikhs in Rural California and Urban Britain." New Community 13 (1986): 27- 39.

3394. Gordon, Paul. "Black People and the British Criminal Justice System: A Bibliographic Essay." Sage Race Relations Abstracts 11 (1986)

3395. Gordon, Paul. "Black People and the Criminal Law: Rhetoric and Reality." International Journal of the Sociology of the Law 16 (August 1988): 295-313.

3396. Gordon, Paul. "Police and Black People in Britain: A Bibliograhic Essay." Sage Race Relations Abstracts 16 (May 1985): 3-33.

3397. Gordon, Paul and Rosenberg, David. Daily Racism: The Press and Black People in Britain. London: Runnymede Trust, May 1989.

3398. Goulbourne, Harry, ed. Black Politics in Britain. Brookfield, VT: Avebury, 1990.

3399. Great Britain Commission for Racial Equality. *Teaching English as a Second Language: Report of a Formal Investigation in Calderdale Local Education Authority*. London: CRE, 1986.

3400. Green, Jeffrey P. "A Black Community?- London, 1919." *Immigrants and Minorities* 5 (1986): 107-116.

3401. Halstead, J. M. *The Case for Muslim Voluntary-aided Schools: Some Philosophical Reflections*. Cambridge, England: Islamic Academy, 1986.

3402. Hatch, S. "Coloured People in School Textbooks." *Race* 4 (1962)

3403. Haynes, Aaron. *The State of Black Britain*. London: 1983.

3404. Holton, J. E. "The Status of the Coloured in Britain." *Phylon* 22 (1961)

3405. Howe, Darcus. *From Bobby to Babylon: Blacks and the British Police*. London: Race Today Publications, 1988.

3406. *Islam and the GCSE Examination in Religious Studies: Areas of agreement*. Cambridge, England: The Islamic Academy, 1986.

3407. Jacobs, Brian E. *Black Politics and Urban Crisis in Britain*. New York: Cambridge University Press, 1986.

3408. James, Winston. "A Long Way from Home: On Black Identity in Britain." *Immigrants and Minorities* 5 (1986): 258-284.

3409. Jenkinson, Jacqueline. "The Black Community of Salford and Hull 1919-1921." *Immigrants and Minorities* 7 (July 1988): 166-183.

3410. Jenkins, Richard and Solomos, John. *Racism, Equal Opportunity Policies in the 1980's*. New York: Cambridge University Press, 1987.

3411. John, Gus. *In the Service of Black Youth: a Study of the Political Culture of Youth and Community Work with Black People in English Cities*. Leicester: National Association of Youth Clubs, 1981.

3412. Johnson, Linton Kwesi. "Black Culture and Politics in Britain." *Forward Motion (Jamaica Plain, MA)* 6 (March-April 1987): 13-20.

3413. Joly, Daniele S. "Ethnic Minorities and Education in Britain: Interaction between the Muslim Community and Birmingham Schools." *Research Papers- Centre for the Study of Islam and Christian-Muslim Relations* 41 (March 1989): 1-28.

3414. Joly, Daniele S. *Making a Place for Islam in British Society: Muslims in Birmingham*. Coventry: Centre for Research in Ethnic Relations, University of Warwick, 1987.

3415. Lamming, George. The Pleasures of Exile. London: Allison and Busby, 1984.

3416. Lashley, Horace. "Prospects and Problems of Afro-Caribbeans in the British Education System." In The Caribbean in Europe, edited by Colin Brock. London: Frank Cass, 1986.

3417. Layton-Henry, Zig and Studlar, Donley T. "The Electoral Participation of Black and Asian Britons: Integration or Alienation?" Parliamentary Affairs 38 (Summer 1985): 307-318.

3418. Leech, Kenneth. Brick Land 1978: The Events and Their Significance. Birmingham: AFFOR, 1980.

3419. Lotz, Rainer E. "The Negro Operetta Company and the Foreign Office-1913." New Community 13 (Autumn 1986): 204-207.

3420. Mabey, Christine. "Black Pupils' Achievement in Inner London." Educational Research 28 (November 1986): 163-173.

3421. Mac an Ghaill, Mairtin. "Coming-of-Age in 1980's England: Reconceptualizing Black Students' Schooling Experience." British Journal of Sociology of Education 10 (1989)

3422. Mawby, R. L. and Batta, L.D. Asians and Crime: the Bradford Experience. London: Scope Communication for National Association of Asian Youth, 1980.

3423. Melville, Joy and Israel, Rosha. "The Small World of the Bangladeshi." New Society (August 22, 1986)

3424. Mirza, Z. and Morsbach, G. "The Home Background and English-Language Comprehension of Punjabi-speaking Children." New Community 12 (Winter 1985): 430-435.

3425. Mitter, Swasti. "Rise of a Semi-Proletariat: Bangladeshi Female Homeworkers in the London Rag Trade." Homeworking on a World Scale. Newsletter of International Labour Studies, The Hague (April 1984)

3426. Mohanti, Prafulla. Through Brown Eyes. New York: Oxford University Press, 1985.

3427. Monroe, Sylvester. "Blacks in Britain: Grim Lives, Grimmer Prospects." Newsweek (January 4, 1987)

3428. Nazar, Ek. "From the Asian Ethnic Press." New Community 13 (Autumn 1986): 282-285.

3429. Newnham, Anne. Employment, Unemployment and Black People. London: Runneymede Trust, 1986.

GREAT BRITAIN - BLACKS

3430. Nielsen, Jorgen S. A Survey of British Local Authority Responses to Muslim Needs. Birmingham: Centre for the Study of Islam and Christian-Muslim Relations, 1986.

3431. Nqcobo, Lauretta, ed. Let It Be Told: Essays by Black Women in Britain. London: Pluto Press, 1987.

3432. Oldham, James. "New Light on Mansfield and Slavery." Journal of British Studies 27 (1988): 45-68.

3433. Owusu, Kwesi and Ross, Jacobi. Behind the Masquerade. London: Arts Media Group, 1988.

3434. Owusu, Kwesi, ed. Storms of the Heart. London: Camden Press, 1988.

3435. Policing Against Black People. London: Institute of Race Relations, 1988.

3436. Poulter, Sebastina M. Asian Traditions and English Law: A Handbook. London: Runnymede Trust and Trentham Books, 1990.

3437. Prashar, U. and Nicholas, S. Routes or Roadblocks? London: Runneymede Trust, 1986.

3438. Prince, Graham J. The Yellow Peril in Britain, 1890-1920. Master's thesis, University of Lethbridge, 1987.

3439. Pryce, Ken. The Black Experience in Britain: A Study of the Life-styles of West Indians in Bristol. St. Augustine, Trinidad: Institute of Social and Economic Research, University of the West Indies, 1977.

3440. The Race Today Collective. The Servants, A Pictorial Essay on Blacks in Britain. London: Race Today Publications, March 1987.

3441. Ramdin, Ron. The Making of the Black Working Class in Britain. Aldershot: Wildwood House, 1987.

3442. Reeves, Frank and Chevannes, Mel. "The Political Education of Young Blacks in Britain." Educational Review 36 (1984): 175-185.

3443. Rich, Paul B. "The Black Diaspora in Britain: Afro- Caribbean Students and the Struggle for a Political Identity, 1900-1950." Immigrants and Minorities 16 (July 1987): 151- 173.

3444. Rich, Paul B. "Blacks in Britain: Responses and Reaction, 1945-1962." History Today 36 (1986): 14-20.

3445. Robinson, Vaughan. "Roots to Mobility: The Social Mobility of Britain's Black Population." Ethnic and Racial Studies 13 (April 1990)

3446. Robinson, Vaughn. Transients, Settlers, and Refugees: Asians in Britain. New York: Oxford University Press, 1986.

3447. Russell, Emily, ed. Black People and the Criminal Justice System. London: Howard League for Penal Reform, 1989.

3448. Saggar, Shamit. "The 1983 Labour Force Survey and Britain's Asian Population: A Research Note." New Community 12 (Winter 1985): 418-429.

3449. Saunders, D. The West Indians in Britain. London: Batsford, 1985.

3450. Sawh, Roy. From Where I Stand. London: Hansib Publishing Ltd., 1987.

3451. Sivanandan, A. "Fighting Tory Racism." Race and Class 21 (Winter 1980): 291-296.

3452. Solomos, John. "Black Youth, Economic Marginalisation and the State in Britain." In Cultural Identity and Structural Marginalisation of Migrant Workers, edited by H. Korte. Strasbourg: European Science Foundation, 1982.

3453. Solomos, John. The Politics of Black Youth Unemployment: A Critical Asnalysis of Official Ideologies and Policies. Aston: SSRC Research Unit on Ethnic Relations, 1983.

3454. Stapleton, M. Education and Racism: A Study of the Teachers' and the Pupils' Relations in the Schooling of Black Boys. Doctoral dissertation, University of Aston in Birmingham, 1985.

3455. Stone, Maureen. The Education of the Black Child in Britain. The Myth of Multicultural Education. London: Fontana, 1981.

3456. Stopes-Roe, Mary and Raymond Cochrane. "Is There an Indianist View on Education? A Comment on Bhachu's Affirmation." New Community 12 (Winter 1985): 436-438.

3457. Stopes-Roe, Mary and Raymond Cochrane. "Prejudice: Asian and British Views on its Present Occurrence." New Community 13 (Autumn 1986): 235-249.

3458. Sutcliffe, David and Wong Ansel, eds. The Language of the Black Experience. Cultural Expression through Word and Sound in the Caribbean and Black Britain. New York: Blackwell, 1986.

3459. Taylor, Monica J. with Hegarty, Seamus. The Best of Both Worlds? A Review of Research into the Education of Pupils of South Asian Origin. NFER-Nelson, 1986.

3460. Taylor, Monica J. Caught Between: A Review of Research Into the Education of Pupils of West Indian Origin. NFER-Nelson, 1986.

3461. Taylor, Monica J. Chinese Pupils in Britain. NFER-Nelson, 1986.

3462. Thomas, David. "The Job Bias Against Blacks." New Society 70 (November 1, 1984): 167-170.

3463. "Unemployment and Black People." Race and Immigration No. 159 (September 1983): 6-11.

3464. Venner, Mary. "West Indian Families in Britain: A Research Note." New Community 12 (Winter 1985): 504-514.

3465. Verma, Gajendra. Ethnicity and Educational Achievement in British Schools. London: Macmillan, 1986.

3466. Visram, Rozina. Ayahs, Loscars and Princes: Indians in Britain. London: Pluto Press, 1986.

3467. Walkowisk, Adam. Rastafarians in London: Between Religion and Youth Counterculture. Master's thesis, University of Toronto, 1986.

3468. Walton, Heather and others. A Tree God Planted: Black People in British Methodism. London: Ethnic Minorities in Methodism Working Group, N.D.

3469. Wilson-Tagoe, Dabydeen David and Nana. Reader's Guide to West Indian and Black British Literature. Chingaroo Press, 1987.

3470. Wright, C. Y. "The Influence of School Processes on the Educational Opportunities of Children of West Indian Origin." Multicultural Teaching 4 (1985)

3471. Wright, C. Y. The School Experience of Pupils of West Indian Background. Doctoral dissertation, University of Keele, 1988.

3472. Yekwai, Dimela. British Racism, Miseducation and the Afrikan Child. London: Karmak House, 1988.

GREAT BRITAIN - HIGHER EDUCATION

3473. Collier, J. and A. Burke. "Racial and Sexual Discrimination in the Selection of Students for London Medical Schools." Medical Education 20 (1986): 86-90.

3474. Heyck, Thomas W. "The Idea of a University in Britain, 1870-1970." History of European Ideas 8 (1987): 205-220.

3475. Neave, Guy R. "Elite and Mass Higher Education in Britain: A REgressive Model?" Comparative Education Review 29 (August 1985): 347-361.

3476. Parekh, Bhikhu. "Without Prejudice." New Statesman & Society (November 11, 1988). [Does allowing freedom of speech at universities mean giving a platform to racists, fascists, and other partisan speakers who will add nothing to academic discourse?]

3477. Racism and Freedom of Speech on the Campus. London: Commission for Racial Equality, 1988.

3478. Reeves, F. and M. Chevannes. "Multicultural, Antiracist, and Equal Opportunity Policy in English Tertiary Education- The Consequences of Student Choice in the Face of the Logic of the Labor Market." In Affirmative Action and Positive Policies in the Education of Ethnic Minorities, edited by A. Yogev and S. Tomlinson. Greenwith, CT: JAI Press, 1989.

3479. Rudd, E. "The Educational Qualifications and Social Class of the Parents of Undergraduates Entering British Universities in 1984." Journal of the Royal Statistical Society, Series A 150 (1987)

3480. Symonds, Richard. Oxford and Empire: The Last Lost Cause? London: Macmillan, 1986.

GREAT BRITAIN - HONG KONG

3481. Bond, H. M. "Intergroup Relations in Hong Kong: The Tao of Stability." In Ethnic Conflict, International Perspectives, edited by Jerry Boucher and others. Sage, 1987.

3482. Cheng, Joseph Y. S. "The Democracy Movement in Hong Kong." International Affairs 65 (1989): 443-462.

3483. Davis, Michael C. Constitutional Confrontation in Hong King: Issues and Implications of the Basic Law. New York: St. Martin's Press, 1990.

3484. Kwan, Chan Wai. The Making of Hong Kong Society: A Sociological Study of Class Formation in Hong Kong, 1841- 1922. Doctoral dissertation: University of Essex, 1989. Order No. BRD-88380.

3485. Leung, Benjamin K. P., ed. Social Issues in Hong Kong. New York: Oxford University Press, 1990.

3486. Lin, T-b. "Growth, Equity, and Income Distribution Policies in Hong Kong." Developing Economics 23 (December 1985)

3487. Lo, S. H. "Democratization in Hong-Kong. Reasons, Phases, and Limits." Issues & Studies 20 (May 1990)

3488. Ming Chan and Michael Kirst. "Hong Kong: The Political Economy of Education." In Education, Recession and the World Village, edited by Frederick M. Wirt and Grant Harman. Philadelphia, PA: Falmer Press, 1986.

3489. Parlin, Timothy B. "The Nationality Crisis of Hong Kong's Non-Chinese Residents-Scholarly Myth or Harsh Reality?" Brooklyn Journal of International Law 12 (March 1986): 369-388.

GREAT BRITAIN - HOUSING

3490. Benson, John, ed. The Working Class in England, 1875-1914. Dover, NH: Croom Helm, 1985.

3491. Benthan, G. "Socio-Tenurial Polarization in the United Kingdom 1953-1983: The Income Evidence." Urban Studies 23 (April 1986)

3492. Bridges, Lee. "Racism and the Crisis in Public Housing." Race and Class 30 (April-June 1989): 67-76.

3493. Burnett, John. A Social History of Housing 1815-1985. 2d ed. London: Tavistock, 1986.

3494. Coleman, Alice. Utopia on Trial. London: Hilary Shipman, 1985. [Critique of large housing estate.]

3495. Commission for Racial Equality. Living in Terror: A Report of Racial Violence and Harassment in Housing. London: Commission for Racial Equality, 1987.

3496. Cooper, Stephanie. Public Housing and Private Property, 1970-1984. Brookfield: Gower 1985,

3497. Daunton, M. J. House and Home in the Victorian City: Working-class Housing, 1850-1914. Baltimore, MD: Edward Arnold, 1983.

3498. Dennis, Richard. English Industrial Cities of the Nineteenth Century: A Social Geography. New York: Cambridge University Press, 1984. [Development of housing segregation.]

3499. Hamnett, C. "Housing the Two Nations: Socio-Tenurial Polarization in England and Wales, 1961-1981." Urban Studies 21 (Nov. 1984)

3500. Harriman, Ed. "Racial Politics and the Housing Shortage." Patterns of Prejudice 7 (1973): 1-6.

3501. Hopkins, Eric. "Working-class Housing in Birminghan during the Industrial Revolution." Internatioanl Review of Social History 31 (1986): 80-94.

3502. Institute of Race Relations. Policing Against Black People. London: IRR, 1987. [1979-1987.]

3503. Maclennan, D. and A.J. O'Sullivan. "Housing Policy in the U.K.: Efficient or Equitable?" In Housing Markets and Policies under Fiscal Austerity Wilhem van Vliet. Westport, CT: Greenwood, 1987.

3504. Pooley, C. G. "Housing for the Poorest Poor: Slum-clearance and Rehousing in Liverpool, 1890-1918." Journal of Historical Geography 11 (January 1985): 70-88.

3505. "Racism in Housing." Labour Research (July 1987): 10-12.

3506. Rodger, Richard. Housing in Urban Britain, 1780-1914: Class, Capitalism, and Construction. London: Macmillan, 1989.

3507. Rodger, Richard. "Political Economy, Ideology and the Persistence of Working-Class Housing Problems in Britain, 1850-1914." International Review of Social History 32 (1987): 109-143.

3508. Schwartz, Nathan H. "Race and the Allocation of Public Housing in Great Britain: The Autonomy of the Local State." Comparative Politics 16 (January 1984): 205-222.

3509. Shah, A. and H. Rees. "The Distribution of Housing Tenure in Britain." Manchester School of Economics and Social Studies 53 (September 1985)

3510. Shaw, Frederick. The Homes and Homeless of Post-War Britain. Totwa, NJ: Barnes and Noble, 1985.

3511. Slater, J. R. "Income, Location and Housing in Greater London." Urban Studies 23 (August 1986)

3512. Swenarton, Mark and Sandra Taylor. "The Scale and Nature of the Growth of Owner-Occupation in Britain between the Wars." Economic History Review 38 (August 1985): 373-392.

3513. Ward, Colin. Housing: An Anarchist Approach. London: Freedom Press,

3514. Webster, Charles. "Health, Welfare and Unemployment during the Depression." Past & Present 109 (November 1985): 204- 230.

3515. Welch, Susan and D.T. Studlar. "The Impact of Race on Political Behavior in Britain." British Journal of Political Science 15 (October 1985): 528-539.

3516. Yelling, J. A. *Slums and Slum Clearance in Victorian London*. London: Allen & Unwin, 1986.

IRISH IN GREAT BRITAIN

3517. Barber, Sarah. "Irish Migrant Agricultural Labourers in Nineteenth Century Lincolnshire." Saothar. Journal of the Irish Labour History Society 8 (1982): 10-23.

3518. Clapham, John H. "Irish Immigration into Great Britain in the Nineteenth Century." Bulletin of the International Committee of Historical Sciences 20, Vol. 5, part 3 (July 1933): 596-605.

3519. Curtis, Liz. Nothing But the Same Old Story: The Roots of Anti-Irish Racism. London: Information on Ireland, 1984.

3520. Feheney, J. Matthew. "Toward Religious Equality for Catholic Pauper Children, 1861-1868." British Journal of Educational Studies 31 (June 1983): 141-153.

3521. Gilley, Sheridan. "English Attitudes to the Irish in England, 1789-1900." In Immigrants and Minorities in British Society Colin Homes. London: 1978.

3522. Holmes, Colin and others. "Immigration into Britain: The Irish." History Today 35 (June 1985): 16-23.

3523. Hornsby-Smith, Michael P. and A. Dale. "The Assimilation of Irish Immigrants in England." British Journal of Sociology 39 (December 1988): 519-544.

3524. Lees, Lynn H. "Patterns of Lower-Class Life: Irish Slum Communities in Nineteenth-Century London." In Nineteenth- Century Cities: Essays in the New Urban Histories, edited by S. Thernstrom and R. Sennett. New Have, CT: Yale University Press, 1969.

3525. Lowe, W. J. The Irish in Mid-Victorian Lancashire: The Shaping of a Working-class Community. New York: P. Land, 1989.

3526. Noonan, Kathleen M. Brethern Only to a Degree: Irish Immigration to London in the Mid-Seventeenth Century, 1640- 1660. Doctoral dissertation: University of California, Santa Barbara, 1989. UMO # 9029569.

3527. Paz, D. G. "Anti-Catholicism, Anti-Irish Stereotpying, and Anti-Catholic Racism in Mid-Victorian Working-Class Periodicals." Albion 18 (Winter 1986): 601-616.

3528. Swift, Roger. "The Outcast Irish in the British Victorian City: Problems and Perspectives." Irish Historical Studies 25 (1987): 264-276.

3529. Swift, Roger and Sheridan Gilley, eds. The Irish in Britain, 1815-1939. Savage, MD: Barnes & Noble, 1989.

3530. Swift, Roger and Sheridan Gilley, eds. The Irish in the Victorian City. Dover, NH: Croom Helm, 1985.

3531. Tuathaigh, M. O. O. "The Irish in Nineteenth-century Britain: Problems of Integration." Transactions of the Royal Historical Society 31 (1981): 149-173.

3532. Williamson, Jeffrey G. "The Impact of the Irish on British Labor Markets during the Industrial Revolution." Journal of Economic History 46 (September 1986): 693-720.

GREAT BRITAIN - NORTHERN IRELAND

3533. Applebey, G. "Religious Equality of Opportunity in Northern Ireland." Civil Justice Quarterly 7 (1988): 18-23.

3534. Blackman, Trin and others. "Housing and Health: A Case Study of Two Areas in West Belfast." Journal of Social Policy 18 (January 1989): 1-26.

3535. Cairns, Edmund. Caught in Crossfire: Children in Northern Ireland. Syracuse, NY: Syracuse University Press, 1987.

3536. Cairns, Edmund. "The Development of Ethnic Discrimination in Young Children in Northern Ireland." In Children and Young People in a Society under Stress, edited by J. and J. Harbison. Somerset, England: Open Books, 1980.

3537. Cairns, Edmund. "Intergroup Conflict in Northern Ireland." In Group Identity and Intergroup Attitudes Henri Tajfel. New York: Cambridge University Press, 1982.

3538. Cairns, Edmund and B. Duriez. "The Influence of Accent on the Recall of Catholic and Protestant Children in Northern Ireland." British Journal of Social and Clinical Psychology 15 (1976): 441-442.

3539. No entry

3540. Carswell, L. and others. "Health and Social Services in Northern Ireland." Social Policy and Administration 24 (May 1990)

3541. Clines, Francis X. "In U.S. Scant Note of Model Belfast School." New York Times, (March 28, 1988): [Forge Integrated Primary School, Belfast.]

3542. Conway, A. G. and P. O'Hara. "Education of Farm Children." Economic and Social Review 17 (July 1986)

3543. Cullen, Kevin. "Inequities in Education, Hiring Plague Ulster." Boston Globe, (May 29, 1989)

3544. Curran, P. S. and W. Gregg. "Psychiatric Aspects of Terrorist Violence in Northern Irland 1969 to 1989." Medico- Legal Journal 58 (Spring 1990): 83-96.

3545. Darby, John. "Circles of Deprivation: Young People in Northern Ireland." In Children and Conflict in Sweden and Northern Ireland M. Gray. Stockholm: Radda Barnen, 1982.

3546. Darby, John. Dressed to Kill: Cartoonists and the Northern Irish Conflict. Belfast: Appletree, 1983.

3547. Darby, John. "History in the Schools: a Review Article." Community Forum. Journal of the Communist Relations Commission 4 (1974): 37-42.

3548. Darby, John. Intimidation and the Controls on Conflict. Syracuse, NY: Syracuse University Press, 1986.

3549. Darby, John. "Out and Down: School-leavers in Londonderry and Strabane." In Employment in Northern Ireland, edited by R.J. Cormack and R.D. Osborne. Belfast: Appletree, 1982.

3550. Darby, John and Seamus Dunn. "Segregated Schools and the Research Evidence." In Education and Policy in Northern Ireland, edited by R.D. Osborne and others. Belfast: Policy Research Institute, 1987.

3551. Davies, Janet. Hilden: Some Social and Historical Perspectives on an Integrated Mill School. Mater's thesis: Queens University Belfast, 1981.

3552. Dunn, Seamus. "Cooperation between Segregated Schools." Fortnight 4 (February 17, 1985)

3553. Dunn, Seamus and others. "Education and Community in Northern Ireland: Schools Apart?" CORE 2 (1978)

3554. Dunn, Seamus. Education and Conflict in Northern Ireland: A Guide to the Literature. Centre for the Study of Conflict: University of Ulster, 1986.

3555. Dunn, Seamus. "The Education Debate in Northern Ireland: the Integrated Option." Studies 75 (1986): 308-317.

3556. Dunn, Seamus. "Education, Religion and Cultural Change in Ireland." In Religion, Educational Provision and National Identity, edited by Witold Tulasiewicz and Colin Brock. London: Croom Helm, 1987.

3557. Dunn, Seamus. "Integrated Schools in Northern Ireland." Oxford Review of Education 15 (1989)

3558. Dunn, Seamus. "Northern Ireland Schools: Isolation, Communication or Integration." l'Irlande Politique et Sociale 2 (1987)

3559. Dunn, Seamus. "The Role of Education in the Northern Ireland Conflict." Oxford Review of Education 12 (1986): 233-242.

3560. Dunn, Seamus and others. "Schools Together." In Collected Original Resources in Education. June 1985.

3561. Ellis, Evelyn. "The Fair Employment Legislation of 1989." Public Law 161-172 (Summer 1990)

3562. Fields, Rona M. "Psychological Genocide: The Children of Northern Ireland." History of Childhood Quarterly 3 (1975): 201-224.

3563. Gray, M., ed. Children amid Conflict in Sweden and Northern Ireland. Stockholm: Radda Barmen, 1982.

3564. Green, John and others. "The Project on 'Religion in Ireland'; An Experiment in Reconstructionism." Lumen Vitae 39 (1984): 331-342.

3565. Greer, John. A Questioning Generation. Belfast: Church of Ireland Board of Education, 1972.

3566. Harbison, J. and J., eds. A Society under Stress: Children and Young People in Northern Ireland. Somerset: Open Books, 1980.

3567. Harkness, David. Northern Ireland since 1920. Dublin: Helicon, 1983.

3568. Hayes, M. "Your Good Health: Access to Health and Health Care in Northern Ireland." Regional Studies 20 (October 1986)

3569. Hepburn, A. C. "The Belfast Riots of 1935." Social History 15 (January 1990): 75-96.

3570. Hepple, Bob. "Discrimination and Equality of Opportunity- Northern Irish Lessons." Oxford Journal of Legal Studies 10 (Autumn 1990): 408-421.

3571. Hosin, A. and E. Cairns. "The Impact of Conflict on Children's Ideas about their Country." Journal of Psychology 118 (1984): 161-168.

3572. Houston, J. E. and others. "The Assessment of Ethnic Sensitivity among Northern Ireland Schoolchildren." British Journal of Development Psychology 8 (November 1990)

3573. Hout, Michael. "Opportunity and the Minority Middle Class: A Comparison of Blacks in the United States and Catholics in Northern Ireland." American Sociological Review 51 (1986): 214-223.

3574. Jackson, Harold. The Two Irelands: The Problem of the Double Minority. London: Minority Rights Group, 1984. [3rd revised edition.]

3575. Keane, M. Ethnic Residential Change in Belfast, 1969-1977: The Impact of Public Housing Policy in a Plural Society. Doctoral dissertation: Queen's University of Belfast, 1985.

3576. Kelby, J. and I. McAllister. "The Genesis of Conflict: Religion and Status Attainment in Ulster, 1968." Sociology 18 (1984): 171-190.

3577. Kenneally, Christopher. "Children Begin to Bridge Ulster Rift in Integrated School." Boston Globe, (January 17, 1988): [Mill Strand Primary School in Coleraine, Northern Ireland.]

3578. Kennedy, Liasm and Philip Ollerenshaw, eds. An Economic History of Ulster, 1820-1940. Dover, NH: Manchester University Press, 1985.

3579. Kovalcheck, Kassian A. "Catholic Grievances in Northern Ireland: Appraisal and Judgment." British Journal of Sociology 38 (March 1987): 77-87.

3580. Lohr, Steve. "Push on Hiring Bias in Ulster." New York Times, (September 4, 1986)

3581. Loughran, Maria C. The Origins and Development of Feminist Groups in Northern Ireland. Doctoral dissertation: Queen's University, 1987.

3582. Malone, John. School Projects in Community Relations. Belfast: Northern Ireland Relations Commission, 1973.

3583. McAuley, P. On the Fringes of Society: Adults and Children in a Disadvantaged Belfast Community. Doctoral dissertation: Queen's University, Belfast, 1988.

3584. Munck, Ronald. "Class and Religion in Belfast: A Historical Perspective." Journal of Contemporary History 20 (April 1985): 241-260.

3585. Murray, Dominic. Worlds Apart: Segregated Schools in Northern Ireland. Belfast: Appletree Press, 1985.

3586. Osborne, R. D. Religion and Educational Qualifications in Northern Ireland. Belfast: Fair Employment Agency, 1985.

3587. Osborne, R. D. "Segregated Schools and Examination Results in Northern Ireland: Some Preliminary Research." Educational Research 28 (February 1986)

3588. Osborne, R. D. and R.J. Cormack. "Fair Employment: Towards Reform in Northern Ireland." Policy and Politics 17 (October 1989)

3589. Osborne, R. D. and R. J. Cormack. "Unemployment and Religion in Northern Ireland." Economic and Social Review 17 (April 1986)

3590. Osborne, R. D. and others, eds. *Education and Policy in Northern Ireland*. Belfast: Policy Research Institute, 1987.

3591. Osborne, R. D. and others. "Trends in Higher Education Participation in Northern Ireland." *Economic and Social Review* 19 (July 1988)

3592. Raines, Howell. "British Plan Laws to End Ulster Bias." *New York Times*, (March 3, 1988)

3593. Robinson, ALan. "Education and Sectarian Conflict in Northern Ireland." *New Era* 52 (1971)

3594. Robinson, Alan. *The Schools Cultural Studies Project: A Contribution to Peace in Northern Ireland*. New York University of Ulster, 1981.

3595. Rolsten, Bill. "Mothers, Whores and Villains: Images of Women in Novels of the Northern Ireland Conflict." *Race and Class* 31 (July-September 1989): 41-57.

3596. Russell, J. *Some Aspects of the Civic Education of Secondary Schoolboys in Northern Ireland*. Belfast: Northern Ireland Community Relations Commission, 1972.

3597. Russell, J. "The Sources of Conflict." *Northern Teacher* 11 (1974): 3-11.

3598. See, K. O. "For God and Crown: Class, Ethnicity, and Protestant Politics in Northern Ireland." In *Competitive Ethnic Relations*, edited by Susan Olzark and Joane Nagel. Orlando, FL: Academic Press, 1986.

3599. Shannon, Elizabeth. "Growing Up Catholic and Protestant in Northern Ireland." *Boston Globe*, (May 9, 1988)

3600. Skilbeck, Malcolm. "The School and Cultural Development." *Northern Teacher* 11 (1973)

3601. Smyth, W. *Irish History in Secondary Intermediate Schools in Northern Ireland. A Survey of the Extent, Teaching Methods, Qualifications of Teachers and Pupil Attitudes*. Master's thesis: Queen's University Belfast, 1974.

3602. Stringer, M. and Edmund Cairns. "Catholic and Protestant Young People's Ratings of Stereotyped Protestant and Catholic Faces." *British Journal of Social Psychology* 23 (1983): 241-246.

3603. No entry

3604. Sutherland, A. E. and others. *Curriculum Projects in Post-primary Schools*. Northern Ireland Council for Educational Research, 1983.

3605. Taylor, Rupert L. *The Queen's University of Belfast and Its Relationship to the "Troubles": The Limits of Liberalism*. Doctoral dissertation: University of Kent, 1986.

3606. Taylor, Rupert L. "Social Scientific Research on the 'Troubles' in Northern Ireland: The Problem of Objectivity." Economic and Social Review 19 (1988): 123-145.

3607. Waddell, N. and Edmund Cairns. "Situational Ethnicity in Northern Ireland." British Journal of Social Psychology 25 (1986): 25-31.

3608. Walker, Clive. "Police and Community in Northern Ireland." Northern Ireland Legal Quarterly 41 (Summer 1990): 105- 142.

3609. Weinraub, Bernard. "Poverty, Fear and Strife Add Up to Fewer Jobs for Catholics in Ulster." New York Times, (August 4, 1988)

3610. Wilson, J. A. Environment and Primary Education in Northern Ireland. Northern Ireland Council for Educational Research, 1971.

3611. Wilson, J. A. Transfer and the Structure of Secondary Education. Belfast: Northern Ireland Council for Educational Research, 1986.

GREAT BRITAIN - SCOTLAND

3612. Anderson, Robert D. "Education and Society in Modern Scotland: A Comparative Perspective." History of Education Quarterly 25 (Winter 1985): 459-481.

3613. Anderson, Robert D. "School Attendance in Nineteenth- Century Scotland: A Reply." Economic History Review 38 (May 1985): 282-286. [See Mason, below.]

3614. Anderson, Robert D. "Secondary Schools and Scottish Society in the Nineteenth Century." Past & Present 109 (November 1985): 176-203.

3615. Bowes, A. M. and others. "The Changing Nature of Glasgow's Ethnic Minority Community." Scottish Geographical Magazine 106 (September 1990)

3616. Bowes, A. M. and others. "Racism and Harassment of Asians in Glasgow." Ethnic and Racial Studies 13 (January 1990)

3617. Brand, Jack A. "Nationalism and the Neocolonial Periphery: A Discussion of Scotland and Catalonia." In New Nationalisms of the Developed West: Toward Explanation, edited by Edward A. Tiryakian and Ronald Ragowski. Boston: Allan & Unwin, 1985.

3618. Cage, R. A., ed. The Working Class in Glasgow 1750-1914. Beekenham, England: Croom Helm, 1987.

3619. Callinicos, Alex. "Should Scotland Separate?" Socialist Worker (July 11, 1987)

3620. Davies, R. R. Domination and Conquest: The Experience of Ireland, Scotland, and Wales, 1100-1300. New York: Cambridge University Press, 1990.

3621. Devine, T. M., ed. Farm Servants and Labour in Lowland Scotland, 1770-1914. Edinburgh: J. Donald, 1984.

3622. Devine, T. M. The Great Highland Famine: Hunger, Emigration, and the Scottish Highlands in the Nineteenth Century. Edinburgh: J. Donald, 1988.

3623. Dickinson, Tony. "Marxism, Nationalism and Scottish History." Journal of Contemporary History 20 (April 1985): 323-336.

3624. Dickinson, Tony, ed. Scottish Capitalism: Class, State and Nation from Before the Union to the Present. London: Lawrence & Wishart, 1980.

3625. Eagles, Munroe. "The Neglected Regional Dimension in Scottish Ethnic Nationalism." Canadian Review of Studies in Nationalism 12 (Spring 1985): 81-98.

3626. Harris, A. H. and others. "Who Gains from Structural Change? The Distribution of the Benefits of Oil in Aberdeen." Urban Studies 23 (August 1986)

3627. Henderson, Toni. "Helping Women to Get Equal Rights." Scottish Legal Action Group 129-131 (September 1990)

3628. Houston, R. A. Scottish Literary and Scottish Identity: Illiteracy and Society in Scotland and Northern Ireland, 1600-1800. New York: Cambridge University Press, 1985.

3629. Houston, R. A. and I. D. Whyte, eds. Scottish Society, 1500-1800. New York: Cambridge University Press, 1988.

3630. Humes, Walter M. The Leadership Class in Scottish Education. Edinburgh: J. Donald, 1986.

3631. Insh, G. P. Scottish Colonial Schemes Prior to the Union. Doctoral dissertation: University of Glasgow, 1922.

3632. Leruez, Jacques. L'Ecosse: une nation sans Etat. Lille: Presses Universitaires de Lille, 1983.

3633. Lever, William and Chris Moore, eds. The City in Transition: Policies and Agencies for the Economic Regeneration of Clydeside. New York: Oxford University Press, 1986.

3634. MacLaren, A. Allan. Social Class in Scotland: Past and Present. Edinburgh: John Donald, 1976.

3635. Mason, D. M. "School Attendance in Nineteenth-Century Scotland." Economic History Review 38 (May 1985): 276-281. [See Anderson, above.]

3636. Miles, Robert and Anne Dunlop. "The Racialization of Politics in Britain: Why Scotland is Different." Patterns of Prejudice 20 (January 1986): 23-33.

3637. Mitchison, Rosalind. "Who Were the Poor in Scotland, 1690- 1830." In Economy and Scociety in Scotland and Ireland, 1500- 1939 Mitchison and Peter Roebuck, eds. Edinburgh: John Donald, 1988.

3638. Pacione, M. "The Urban Crisis, Poverty and Deprivation in the Scottish City." Scottish Geographical Magazine 105 (September 1989)

3639. Rice, Francis J. "Class and the Treatment of the Insane in Mid-nineteenth Century Scotland." Journal of the Scottish Labour History Society No. 20 (1985): 43-58.

3640. Ritchie, Harry. "Edinburgh's Elitism." New Society (May 27, 1988) [Middle and upper-class English entrants in Scottish universities.]

3641. Saville, Richard, ed. The Economic Development of Modern Scotland, 1950-1980. Edinburgh: J. Donald, 1985.

3642. Scottish Anti-Racist Teacher Education Network. Learning in Terror in Scotland. Glasgow: Jordanhill College of Education, 1989.

3643. Scottish Ethnic Minorities Research Unit. Racial Harassment in Glasgow. 1986.

3644. Smout, T. C. A Century of the Scottish People, 1830-1950. New Haven, CT: Yale Univerity Press, 1986.

3645. Soltow, Lee. "An Index of the Poor and Rich of Scotland, 1861-1961." Scottish Journal of Political Economy 18 (1971)

3646. Thomson, Frank. "The Gaelic Dimension in Scotland." Europa Ethnica 45 (1988)

3647. Treble, J. H. "The Standard of Living of the Working Class." In People and Society in Scotland. Vol.I, 1760-1830, edited by T.M. Devine and Rosalind Mitchison. Edinburgh: John Donald, 1988.

3648. Walsh, Dave. Racial Harassment in Glasgow. Glasgow: Scottish Ethnic Minorities Research Unit, 1987.

3649. West, Patrick and others. "Social Class and Health in Youth: Findings from the West of Scotland Twenty-07 Study." Social Science & Medicine 30 (1990)

3650. Whatley, Christoper A. "Economic Causes and Consequences of the Union of 1707: A Survey." Scottish Hist. Rev. 68 (October 1989): 150-181.

3651. Young, James D. The Rousing of the Scottish Working Class. Montreal: McGill-Queen's University Press, 1979.

GREAT BRITAIN - WALES

3652. Aitchison, J. W. and H. Carter. "The Welsh Language in Cardiff: A Quiet Revolution." Trans. Inst. Brit. Geographers 12 (1987): 482-506.

3653. Aitchison, J. W. and others. "The Welsh Language at the 1981 Census." Area 17 (1985)

3654. Antweiler, Phillip L. The Search for Welsh and Breton Ethnic Autonomy: Toward a Political Sociology of Nations without States. 3 vols. Doctoral dissertation: Boston University, 1986. UMO # 8606838.

3655. Astroff, Roberta J. Cultural Nationalism in the Age of Mass Media: Television and the Struggle over Meaning in Wales. Doctoral dissertation: University of Illinois, 1987. UMO # 8721577.

3656. Baker, C. Aspects of Bilingualism in Wales. Clevedon: Multilingual Matters Ltd, 1985.

3657. Boyns, T. "Work and Death in the South Wales Coalfield, 1874-1914." Welsh Hist. Review 12 (Dec. 1985): 514-537.

3658. Brourberg, E. J. "Wales & the Medieval Slave Trade." Speculum 17 (April 1942)

3659. Davies, C. "Ethnic Jokes and Social Change: The Case of Welsh." Immigrants & Minorities 4 (March 1985): 46-63.

3660. Davies, R. R. Domination and Conquest: The Experience of Ireland, Scotland, and Wales, 1100-1300. New York: Cambridge University Press, 1990.

3661. Evans, Neil. "The Welsh Victorian City: The Middle Class and Civic and National Consciousness in Cardiff, 1850-1914." Welsh Hist. Review 12 (June 1985): 350-387.

3662. Harris, C. C. Redundancy and Recession in South Wales. New York: Blackwell, 1987. [Margam plant near Port Talbot.]

3663. McGlyne, John. "Racial Discrimination and the Welsh Language." New Law Journal 139 (October 13, 1989)

3664. Myers, Charles R. Nationalism and Cultural Conflict in Wales: A Structuralist Perspective. Doctoral dissertation: Temple University, 1985. UMO # 8521118.

3665. Philip, Alan Butt. The Welsh Question. Nationalism in Welsh Politics 1945-1970. Cardiff: University of Wales Press, 1975.

3666. Rawkins, Phillip. "Living in the House of Power: Welsh Nationalism and the Dilemma of Anti-system Politics." In New Nationalisms of the Developed West: Toward Explanations Edward A. Tiryakian and Ronald Ragowski. Boston: Allen & Unwin, 1985.

3667. Rees, Alwyn D. Life in a Welsh Countryside. Cardiff: University of Wales Press, 1968, orig. 1951.

3668. Roderick, Gordon W. "Education, Culture and Industry in Wales in the Nineteenth Century." Welsh Hist. Rev. 13 (December 1987): 438-452.

3669. Stevens, Meic, ed. The Oxford Companion to the Literature of Wales. New York: Oxford University Press, 1986.

3670. Thomas, B. "Schools in Ethnic Minorities: Wales." Journal of Multilingual and Multicultural Development 7 (1986): 169-186.

3671. Walker, David. Medieval Wales. New York: Cambridge University Press, 1990.

3672. Wilks, Ivor. South Wales and the Rising of 1839: Class Struggle as Armed Struggle. Urbana: University of Illinois Press, 1984.

3673. Williams, D. G. Bilingual Education in Cardiganshire, 1904- 1974. Doctoral dissertation: Open University, 1984.

3674. Williams, Glyn. "The Political Economy of Contemporary Nationalism in Wales." In New Nationalisms in the Developed West: Toward Explanation, edited by Edward A. Tiryakian and Ronald Ragowski. Boston: Allen & Unwin, 1985.

GREAT BRITAIN - GENERAL

3675. Aaronvitch, S. and others. The Political Economy of British Capitalism. New York: McGraw-Hill, 1981.

3676. Adam, Ruth. A Woman's Place 1910-1975. London: Chatto and Windus, 1975.

3677. Adler, M. "Race Relations in Britain, 1965." Wiener Library Bulletin 20 (1966)

3678. Akhtar, S. "A Case Study of Education for Ethnic Minority Children in Norwich." Master's thesis, University of East Angkia (1986)

3679. Alderman, Geoffrey. "Explaining Racism." Political Studies 23 (March, 1985): 129-135.

3680. Alexander, Peter. "Racism: A Parliamentary Pawn." Socialist Review No. 52 (March 1983)

3681. Allen, S. and Macey M. "Race and Ethnicity in the European Context." British Journal of Sociology 41 (September 1990)

3682. Allied Technicians. Patterns of Discrimination against Women in the Film and Television Industries: A Special Report. London: ACTT, 1975.

3683. Allsobrook, David. Schools for the Shires. The Reform of Middle-Class Education in Mid-Victorian. Manchester: Manchester University Press, 1986.

3684. Anand, V. S. and Ridley, F. The Emergence of Enoch Powell. London: Medusa Press, 1969.

3685. Anglicans and Racism. London: Race, Plurality and Community Group, Church of England, 1986.

3686. Anwar, Muhammad. Ethnic Minority Broadcasting: A Research Report. London: Commission for Racial Equality, 1983.

3687. Anwar, Muhammad. Race and Politics, Ethnic Minorities and the British Political System. London: Tavistock, 1986.

3688. Appleby, Andrew B. "Nutrition and Disease: The Case of London, 1550-1750." Journal of Interdisciplinary History 6 (1975): 1-22.

3689. Aronsfeld, C. C. "Challenge to Socialist Brotherhood: British Dockers and Coloured Immigrants." Patterns of Prejudice 2 (July-August 1968)

3690. Artingstoll, Trevor. "Letter: Ethnic Rights." Freedom 47 (April 1986): 19.

3691. Atkinson, A. B. and Harrison A.J. The Distribution of Personal Wealth. Cambridge: 1978.

3692. Atkinson, A. B. Unequal Shares- The Distribution of Wealth in Britain. London: 1974.

3693. Atkinson, A. B. and Harrison, A.J. "Wealth Distribution and Investment Income in Britain." Review of Income and Wealth 20 (June 1974): 125-142.

3694. Atkinson, A. B. and others. "Trends in the Shares of Top Wealth-Holders in Britain, 1923-1981." Oxford Bulletin of Economics and Statistics 51 (August 1989)

3695. Aurora, G. S. Indian Workers in England. Master's thesis, University of London (1960)

3696. Babington, Anthony. Military Intervention in Britain: From the Gordon Riots to the Gibraltar Killings. New York: Routledge, 1990.

3697. Bailey, Susan F. Women and the British Empire. New York: Garland, 1983.

3698. Balinska, Maria. "Anti-racist Policies in British Schools Criticized." Patterns of Prejudice 22 (Summer 1988): 45-46.

3699. Balinska, Maria. "Racism and the Press in Britain." Patterns of Prejudice 23 (Summer 1989): 44-45.

3700. Banton, Michael. "The Influence of Colonial Status upon Black-White Relations in England, 1948-1958." Sociology 17 (1983): 546-549.

3701. Banton, Michael. "Optimism and Pessimism about Racial Relations." Patterns of Prejudice 22 (1988): 3-13.

3702. Barker, M. and Breezer, A. "The Language of Racism- and Examination of Lord Scarman's Report on the British Riots." International Socialism No.18 (1982): 108-125.

3703. Barnett, John. Plenty and Want: A Social History of Diet in England from 1815 to the Present Day. London: 1966.

3704. Barrett, Michele. Women's Oppression Today. London: 1980,

3705. Barron, R. D. and Morris, G.M. "Sexual Divisions and the Dual Labour Market" In Dependence and Exploitation in Work and Marriage, edited by Diana L. Barber and Sheila Allen. New York: Longman, 1976.

3706. Baxter, Carol and Baxter, David. "Racial Inequalities in Health: A Challenge to the British National Health Service." International Journal of Health Service 18 (1989)

3707. Beckett, J. V. The Aristocracy in England 1660-1914. New York: Blackwell, 1986.

3708. Bee, M. and Dolton, P.J. "Educational Production in Independent Secondary Schools." Bulletin of Economic Research 37 (Janaury 1985)

3709. Behlmer, George K. "The Gypsy Problem in Victorian England." Victorian Studies 28 (Winter 1985): 231-253.

3710. Beier, A. L. Masterless Men: The Vagrancy Problem in England 1560-1640. New York: Methuen, 1985.

3711. Bellamy, Joan. "The Struggle against Racism in Britain." World Marxist Review 17 (1974): 97-105.

3712. Ben-Tovim, Gideon and Gabriel, John. "The Politics of Race in Britain 1962 to 1979: A Review of the Major Trends and of the Recent Literature." Sage Race Relations Abstracts 4 (November 1979): 1-56.

3713. Ben-Tovin, Gideon and others. "A Political Analysis of Race in the 1980's." In Race in Britain, edited by Charles Husband. London: Hutchinson, 1983.

3714. Ben-Tovim, Gideon and others. "Race, Left Strategies and the State." Politics and Power 3 (1981)

3715. Benson, John, ed. The Working Class in England, 1875-1914. London: Croom Helm, 1985.

3716. Benson, John, ed. Scarman and After: Essays Reflecting on Lord Scarman's Report, The Riots and Their Aftermath. Oxford: Pergamon,

3717. Bercusson, Brian. "Discrimination in Employment: Reflections on the European Community Experience with Particular Reference to the United Kingdom." Georgia Journal of International and Comparative Law 20 (Spring 1990): 133- 184.

3718. Berghahn, Volker R. and Schissler, Hanna, eds. Perceptions of History: International Textbook Research on Britain, Germany, and the United States. New York: Berg, 1987.

3719. Bidwell, Sydney J. Red, White and Black: Race Relations in Britain. London: Gordon and Cremonesi, 1976.

3720. Big Flame. The Past Against Our Future: Fighting Racism and Fascism. Liverpool: Big Flame Anti-Fascist/Anti-Racist Commission, 1980.

3721. Billig, Michael and Bell, Andrew. "Fascist Parties in Post- War Britain." Sage Race Relations Abstracts 5 (February 1980): 1-30.

3722. Billig, Michael. "Rhetoric of the Conspiracy Theory: Arguments in National Front Propaganda." Patterns of Prejudice 22 (1988): 23-34.

3723. Black, JOhn. The New Pediatrics: Child Health in Ethnic Minorities. London: British Medical Journal, 1985.

3724. Blackaby, D. H. "An Analysis of the Male Racial Earnings Differential in the UK, Using the General Household Survey." Applied Economics 18 (November 1986)

3725. Blewett, Neal. "The Franchise in the United Kingdom." Past and Present 32 (December 1965): 27-56.

3726. No entry

3727. Bolin-Hoit, Per. Work, Family and the State: Child Labour and the Organization of Production in the British Cotton Industry, 1780-1920. Lund: Lund University Press, 1990.

3728. Bonnett, A. "Anti-Racism as a Radical Educational Ideology in London and Tyneside." Oxford Review of Education 16 (1990)

3729. Booker, Roger and others. "Struggling Towards Better Practice: A Psychological Service Team and Anti-racism." Educational Psychology in Practice 5 (October 1989): 123- 129.

3730. Borooah, V. K. and Sharpe D.R. "Household Income, Consumption and Savings in the United Kingdom, 1966-1982." Scottish Journal of Political Economy 32 (November 1985)

3731. Bosanguet, N. and Doeringer, P.B. "Is There a Dual Labour Market in Britain?" Economic Journal 83 (1973)

3732. Bourne, Jenny. "Towards an Anti-Racist Feminism." Race and Class 25 (Summer 1983): 1-22.

3733. Bowling, B. "Conceptual and Methodological Problems in Measuring Race Differences in Delinquency: Reply." British Journal of Criminology 30 (Autumn 1990)

3734. Boyce, Robert. British Capitalism at the Crossroads 1918-1932. New York: Cambridge University Press, 1987.

3735. Boyer, George R. An Economic History of the English Poor Law, 1750-1850. New York: Cambridge University Press, 1990.

3736. Brake, Mike. "The Skinheads: An English Working Class Subculture." Youth and Society 6 (1974): 179-200.

3737. Bratton, J. S. "English Ethiopians, British Audiences and Black-Face Acts, 1835-1865." Yearbook of British Studies 2 (1981): 127-142.

3738. "Breaking Down the Barriers." New Law Journal 139 (March 3, 1989): 281.

3739. Breen, Richard. "Status Attainment or Job Attainment? The Effects of Sex and Class on Youth Unemployment." British Journal of Sociology 35 (September 1984): 363-386.

3740. Breen, Richard and Whelan, Christopher T. "Vertical Mobility and Class Inheritance in the British Isles." British Journal of Sociology 36 (June 1985): 175-192.

3741. Brennan, Tim. "Cosmopolitans and Celebrities." Race and Class 31 (July-September, 1989): 1-19.

3742. Brewer, John D. "Looking Back at Fascism: A Phenomenological Analysis of BUF Membership." Sociological Review 32 (1984): 742-760.

3743. Brewer, R. J. and Haslum. "Ethnicity: The Experience of Socio-economic Disadvantage and Educational Attainment." British Journal of Sociology of Education 7 (1986): 19-34.

3744. Broadfoot, P. "Assessment Policy and Inequality: The United Kingdom Experience." British Journal of Sociology of Education 7 (1986): 205-224.

3745. "The Broadwater Farm Inquiry." Report of the Independent Inquiry into Disturbances of October 1985 at the Broadwater Farm Estate, Tottenham (1986): Civic Centre, Wood Green, London N22, England.

3746. Brown, Andrew. Trials of Honeyford, Problems in Multicultural Education. London: Centre for Policy Studies, 1985.

3747. Brown, C. V. and others. "Tax Evasion and Avoidance on Earned Income: Some Survey Evidence." Fiscal Studies 5 (August 1984)

3748. Brown, Colin. Black and White: The Third PSI Survey. London: Heinemann, 1984.

3749. Brown, Colin and Gray, Pat. Racial Discrimination: Seventeen Years After the Act. London: Policy Studies Institute, 1985.

3750. Brown, Kevin M. "Turning a Blind Eye: Racial Oppression and the Unintended Consequences of White 'Non-racism'." Sociological Review 33 (November 1985): 67-90.

3751. Bruegel, Irene. "Sex and Race in the Labour Market." Feminist Review 32 (1989): 49-68.

3752. Buchanan, Keith. "Planned Ruination: Thatcher's Britain." Monthly Review 39 (February 1988): 1-9.

3753. Bunyan, Tony. The Political Police in Britain. London: Julian Friedman, 1976.

3754. Burstyn, Joan N. "Education and Sex: The Medical Case against Higher Education for Women in England, 1870-1900." Proceedings of the American Philosophical Society 117 (April, 1973): 79-89.

3755. Burt, R. A. Colour Prejudice in Great Britain. Princeton, NJ: Author, 1960.

3756. Burtonwood, Neil. The Culture Concept in Educational Studies. Philadelphia, PA: NFER-Nelson, 1986.

3757. Cain, P. J. and Hopkins A.G. "Gentlemanly Capitalism and British Expansion Overseas: I. The Old Colonial System, 1688- 1850." Economic History Review 39 (1986): 501-525.

3758. Cain, P. J. and Hopkins, A.G. "Gentlemanly Capitalism and British Expansion Overseas II: New Imperialism 1850-1945." Economic History Review 40 (February 1987): 1-26.

3759. Callinicos, Alex and Harman, Chris. The Changing Working Class: Essays on Class Structure. London: Bookmarks, 1987.

3760. Campaign Against Racism and Fascism. "Racism and Criminal Statistics." Searchlight No. 83 (1982)

3761. Campbell, Mike. Capitalism in the UK: A Perspective from Marxist Political Economy. London: Croom Helm, 1981.

3762. Campbell, Tom and others, eds. Human Rights: From Rhetoric to Reality. London: Blackwell, 1986.

3763. CARF. "1985- The Assault on Anti-Racism." Searchlight No. 127 (January 1986): 16-18.

3764. Carrington, Bruce and Short, Geoffrey. "Policy Presentation? The Psychology of Anti-racist Education." New Community 15 (January 1989): 227-240.

3765. Cashmore, Ernest Ellis. The Logic of Racism. Boston, MA: Allen and Unwin, 1987.

3766. Cashmore, Ernest Ellis. United Kingdom? Class, Race and Gender Since the War. London: Unwin Hyman, 1989.

3767. Cashmore, Ernest Ellis. "Who Are the Real Racists?" New Society (June 13, 1986)

3768. Centre for Research in Ethnic Relations. The Opinions of Mirpuri Parents in Saltley, Birmingham, about their Children's Schooling. Coventry, England: The Centre, University of Warwick, 1986.

3769. Chape, A. "Urban Poverty and Economic Decline: A Liverpool Perspective." Regional Studies 19 (February 1985)

3770. Chater, A. Race Relations in Britain. London: Lawrence and Wishart, 1966.

3771. Child Poverty Action Group, Leicester Branch. Double Discrimination: A Report on Racism in Social Security. CPAG, 1984.

3772. Children Today 1986. London N510D, England, 85 Highbury Park: National Children's Home,

3773. Chinn, Carl. They Worked All Their Lives: Women of the Urban Poor in England, 1880-1939. New York: Manchester University Press, 1988.

3774. Chiplin, Brian and Sloane, P.J. Sex Discrimination in the Labour Market. London: Macmillan, 1976.

3775. Claiborne, Louis and others. Race and Law in Britain and the United States, 3rd edition. London: Minority Rights Group, 1983.

3776. Coates, David and others, eds. A Socialist Anatomy of Britain. London: Policy Press, 1985.

3777. Cohen, David and Gosschalk, Brian. "Divided Britains." New Statesman 107 (June 29, 1984): 12.

3778. Cohen, Paul. "The Police, the Home Office and Surveillance of the British Union of Fascists." Intelligence and National Security 1 (1986): 416-434.

3779. Cohen, Philip and Bains, H.S. Multi-Racist Britain. Basingstoke: Macmillan Education, 1988.

3780. No entry

3781. Cole, Mike, ed. The Social Contexts of Schooling. New York: Falmer Press, 1989.

3782. Colley, Linda. "Whose Nation? Class and National Consciousness in Britain 1750-1830." Past and Present 113 (November 1986): 97-117.

3783. Compton, R. and others. "Gender Relations and Employment." British Journal of Sociology 41 (September, 1990)

3784. Connock, Michael. "Reform and Rebellion in a System under Siege." Times Higher Education Supplement (January 9, 1987)

3785. Constantine, L. Colour Bar. London: Stanley Paul, 1964.

3786. Cook, J. and Watt, S. "Racism, Women and Poverty." in C. Glendinning and J. Muller (eds.) Women and Poverty in Britain (1987): 53-70. [Brighton, Wheatsheaf.]

3787. Coombe, Vivienne and Little, Alan, eds. Race and Social Work. A Guide to Training. London: Tavistock, 1986.

3788. Cooper, Richard. "Race and the Social Origins of Disease." Radical Community Medicine No. 16 (Winter 1983/1984): 5- 19.

3789. Cowburn, Will. Class Ideology and Community Education. London: Croom Helm, 1986.

3790. Coyle, Angela. Work, Women and the Labour Market. London: Routledge and Kegan Paul, 1982.

3791. Crabtree, Michael F. Strategies against Racism: A Comparison of a Social Movement and Case Studies of Anti-racist Policy and Practice in the Local State. 2 vols. Doctoral dissertation: University of Aston, 1988. Order No. BRDX 89645.

3792. No entry

3793. Crompton, R. and Mann, J., eds. Gender and Stratification. London: Polity, 1986.

3794. Cross, Colin. "Britain's Racialists." New Society 5 (June 1965)

3795. Cross, Colin. The Fascists in Britain. London: Barrie and Rockliff, 1961.

3796. Cross, Malcolm. "Migration and Exclusion: Caribbean Echoes and British Realities." In The Caribbean in Europe, edited by Colin Brook. London: Frank Cass, 1986.

3797. Crossick, Geoffrey. "Classes and the Masses in Victorian England." History Today 37 (March 1987): 29-35.

3798. Crossick, Geoffrey. "The Petite Bourgeoisie in Nineteenth Century Britain." In *Essays in Social History*, edited by Pat Thane and Anthony Sutcliffe. Oxford, Clarendon Press: 1986.

3799. Croucher, Richard. *We Refuse to Starve in Silence: A History of the National Unemployed Workers' Movement, 1920- 1946*. London: Lawrence and Wishart, 1988.

3800. Cullen, Stephen. "The Development of the Ideas and Policy of the British Union of Fascists, 1932-1940." *Journal of Contemporary History* 22 (1987): 115-136.

3801. Cunningham, Hugh. "The Employment and Unemployment of Children in England, c. 1680-1851." *Past and Present* No. 126 (February 1990): 115-150.

3802. Dale, Angela and Bamford, Calire. "Social Polarization in Britain 1973-1982- Evidence from the General Household Survey: A Comment on Pahl's Hypothesis." *International Journal of Urban and Regional Research* 13 (September 1989)

3803. Dashwood, A. "Juries in a Multi-racial Society." *Criminal Law Review* (1972)

3804. Davies, Bernard. *Threatening Youth: Towards a National Youth Policy*. Milton Keynes: Open University Press, 1986.

3805. Davis, Jennifer. "From 'Rookeries' to 'Communities': Race, Poverty and Policing in London, 1." *History Workshop* No. 27 (Spring 1989): 66-85.

3806. Deakin, S. *Liberal Values and New Commonwealth Immigration: 1961-1981*. Doctoral dissertation: University of Warwick, 1987,

3807. Debrunner, H. W., comp. *Presence and Prestige: Africans in Europe*. Basel: Basler Afrika Bibliographien, 1979.

3808. Delamont, Sara and Maurice, Galton. *Inside the Secondary Classroom*. London: Routledge and kegan Paul, 1986.

3809. Dench, Geoff. *Minorities in Open Society: Prisoners of Ambivalence*. New York: Routledge and Kegan Paul, 1986.

3810. Dhesi, A. "Some Economic Consequences of Discrimination." *IRR Newsletter* (March 1969)

3811. Digby, Anne and Bosanquet, Nick. "Doctors and Patients in an Era of National Health Insurance and Private Practice, 1913-1938." *Economic History Review* 41 (February 1988): 74-94.

3812. Dilnot, A. W. and Stark G.K. "The Distributional Consequences of Mrs. Thatcher." *Fiscal Studies* 7 (May 1986)

3813. Dilnot, A. W. and others. "The UK Tax System, Structure and Progressivity, 1948-1982." Scandanavian Journal of Economics 86 (1984)

3814. Dominelli, Lena. Anti-Racist Social Work. Basingstoke: Macmillan, 1988.

3815. Dominelli, Lena. "An Uncaring Profession: An Examination of Racism in Social Work." New Community 15 (April 1989): 391- 403.

3816. Doughan, David. Lobbying for Liberation: British Feminism 1918-1968. London: City of London Polytechnic, 1980.

3817. Drake, St. Clair, J. G. "The Colour Problem in Britain: A Study in Social Definitions." Sociological Review 3 (December 1955)

3818. Duke, Vic and Edgell, Stephen. "The Operationalisation of Class in British Sociology: Theoretical and Empirical Considerations." British Journal of Sociology 38 (December 1987): 445-463.

3819. Dummett, Ann and Nicol, Andrew. Subjects, Citizens, Aliens and Others: Nationality and Immigration Law. London: Weidenfeld & Nicolson, 1990.

3820. Dummett, Ann, ed. Towards a Just Immigration Policy. London: Cobden Trust, 1986.

3821. Dures, A. and K. Poverty. London: Blanford, 1985.

3822. Dwork, Deborah. "The Mild Option: An Aspect of the History of the Infant Welfare Movement in England 1898-1908." Medical History 31 (January 1987): 51-69.

3823. The Education of Bilingual Learners. SEO/SO, Inner London Educational Authority Divisional Office 2, 3 Picton Place, London WIM 5DD, England.

3824. "Educational Provision and Sex Discrimination." Local Government Review 152 (July 30, 1988): 605-608.

3825. Edwards, Judith and others. "Street Life, Ethnicity and Social Policy." In The Crowd in Contemporary Britain, edited by George Gaskell and Robert Benewick. Newbury Park, CA: Sage, 1987.

3826. Edwards, Judith. Working Class Adult Education in Liverpool: A Radical Approach. Manchester: Haigh and Hochland Ltd., 1986.

3827. Edwards, Susan. Female Sexuality and the Law. Oxford: Robertson, 1981.

3828. Eggleston, John and others. Education for Some. The Educational and Vocational Experiences of 15-18 year-old Members of Minority Ethnic Groups. Trentham Books, 1986.

3829. Ellain, Judith and Triggs, Pat. The Books for Keeps Guide to Children's Books for a Multi-Cultural Society. 1 Effingham Road, London SE12 8NZ, London: Books for Keeps, 1986.

3830. Ellis, Alex. Educating Our Masters. Influences on the Growth of Literacy in Victorian Working Class Children. Brookfield, VT.: Gower, 1985.

3831. Esedebe, P. O. A History of the Pan African Movement in Britain, 1900-1948. Doctoral dissertation: University of London, 1968-1969.

3832. Evans, Neil. "The South Wales Race Riots of 1919." Journal of the Society for the Study of Welsh Labour History (Spring 1980)

3833. Everitt, Alan. "Social Mobility in Early Modern England." Past and Present 33 (1966): 56-73.

3834. Eyles, John. The Geography of the National Health: An Essay in Welfare Geography. Wolfeboro, New Hampshire: Croom Helm, 1987.

3835. Eyles, John and Donovan, Jenny. "Making Sense of Sickness and Care: An Ethnography of Health in a West Midlands Town." Trans. Institute British Geographers 11 (1986): 415-427.

3836. Racism and the Press in Thatcher's Britain. London: Institute of Race Relations, 1989.

3837. Faith in the City: A Report of the Archbishop of Canterbury's Commission on Urban Priority Areas. London: Church House Publishing Company, 1985.

3838. "Fascism in Leicester." International Socialism No. 93 (November/December 1976): 16-19.

3839. Fekete, Liz. "Europe for the Europeans: East End for the East Enders." Race & Class 32 (July-September 1990): 66-76. [British National Party.]

3840. Fekete, Liz. "Racist Violence: Meeting the New Challenge." Race & Class 30 (October- December 1988): 71-76.

3841. Field, Frank. Losing Out: The Emergence of Britain's Underclass. London: Basil Blackwell, 1989.

3842. Field, S. "Trends in Racial Inequality." Social Studies Review 1 (March 1986)

3843. Fitz, J. Childhood and the Law. Doctoral dissertation: Open University, 1986,

3844. Fitzpatrick, Peter. "Racism and the Innocence of Law." Journal of Law and Society 14 (Spring 1987): 119-132.

3845. Flint, James. "Must God Go Fascist? English Catholic Opinion and the Spanish Civil War." Church History 56 (September 1987): 364-374.

3846. Foot, Paul. The Rise of Enoch Powell. London: Haymarket, 1969.

3847. Fossett, Mark. "Community-level Analysis of Racial Socioeconomic Inequality: A Cautionary Note." Sociological Methods and REsearch 16 (May 1988): 454-491.

3848. Foster, Margaret. Significant Sisters: The Grassroots of Active Feminism, 1839-1939. New York: Knopf, 1985.

3849. Foster, Peter M. Policy and Practice in Multicultural and Anti-Racist Education: A Case Study of a Multiethnic Comprehensive School. Doctoral dissertation: Open University, 1988. Order # BRDX87526.

3850. Foster-Carter, Olivia. "Insiders, Outsiders and Anomalies: A Review of Studies of Identity." New Community 13 (Autumn 1986): 224-234.

3851. Foster-Carter, Olivia. "Racial Bias in Children's Literature: A Review of the Research on Africa." Sage Race Relations Abstracts 9 (November 1984): 1-12.

3852. Fox, Alan. History and Heritage: The Social Origins of the British Industrial Relations System. Boston, MA: Allen & Unwin, 1985.

3853. Fox, Irene. Private Schools and Public Issues: The Parents' View. London: Macmillan, 1985.

3854. Framar, Lindsay. "The Politics of Legal Signification: Press Coverage of Urban Disorder in 1985." Liverpool Law Review 9 (Winter 1987): 3-22.

3855. Franklin, Bob, ed. The Rights of Children. New York: Blackwell, 1986.

3856. Friedman, Alice T. "The Influence of Humanism on the Education of Girls and Boys in Tudor England." History of Education Quarterly 25 (Spring-Summer 1985): 57-70.

3857. From Ballots to Bombs: The Inside Story of the National Front's Political Soldiers. London: Searchlight, 1989.

3858. From the Dole Line to the Sweatshop. London: Law Pay Unit, 1984.

3859. Fry, V. C. "Inequality in Family Earnings." Fiscal Studies 5 (August 1984)

3860. Fullerton, Madeline. "Jobs for Blacks." New Society (June 20, 1986)

3861. Furnham, Adrian. "Some Explanations for Immigration to and Emigration from, Britain." New Community 13 (Spring-Summer 1983): 65-78.

3862. Gaffney, John. Interpretation of Violence: The Handsworth Riots of 1985. Coventry: Centre for Research in Ethnic Relations, 1987.

GREAT BRITAIN - GENERAL 299

3863. Gagnier, Regina. "Social Atoms: Working-class Autobiography, Subjectivity, and Gender." Victorian Studies 30 (Spring 1987): 335-363.

3864. Gaine, Chris. No Problems Here. A Practical Approach to Education and "Race" in White Schools. London: Hutchinson, 1987.

3865. Gardner, John. "Racial Discrimination and Statistics." Law Quarterly Review 105 (April 1989): 183-186.

3866. Garside, W. R. "Youth Unemployment in 20th Century Britain: Protest, Conflict and the Labour Market." In Jugendprotest und Generationenkonflikt in Europa in 20. Jahrhundert, edited by Dieter Dowe. Bonn: Neue Gesellschaft, 1986.

3867. Gearing, Brian. "The Convergence of Race and Crime News." Sage Race Relations Abstracts 10 (August 1985): 16-32.

3868. Genders, Elaine and Player, Elaine. Race Relations in Prisons. Oxford: Clarendon Press, 1989.

3869. Gifford, Lord and others. Loosen the Shackles: First Report of the Liverpool 8 Inquiry Into Race Relations in Liverpool. London: Karia Press, 1989.

3870. Gilbert, V. F. "Race and Labour in Britain: A Bibliography." In Race and Labour in Twentieth-Century Britain, edited by Kenneth Lunn. Totowa, New Jersey, Frank Cass, 1985.

3871. Gilliat, Penelope. "Flares." Grand Street 8 (Autumn 1988): 167-181.

3872. Gilroy, Paul. There Ain't No Black in the Union Jack: The Cultural Politics of "Race" and Nation. London: Hutchinson, 1987.

3873. Goldstrom, J. M. "The Content of Education and the Socialization of the Working-Class Child, 1830-1860." In Popular Education and Socialization in the Nineteenth Century, edited by Phillip McCann, 93-109. London, 1977.

3874. Goldthorpe, J. H. "Women and Class Analysis: In Defense of the Conventional View." Sociology 17 (1983)

3875. Gordon, Paul. "Bibliographic Essay: Inquiring into the 'Riots': A Review of Reports on the 1985 Urban Disorders." Sage Race Relations Abstracts 12 (August 1987): 3-22.

3876. Gordon, Paul. Citizenship for Some? Race and Government Policy 1979-1989. London: Runnymede Trust, 1989.

3877. Gordon, Paul. "The New Right, Race and Education." Race & Class (Winter 1988)

300 WORLD RACISM AND RELATED INHUMANITIES

3878. Gordon, Paul. Policing Immigration. London: Pluto Press, 1985.

3879. Gordon, Paul. Race in Britain: A Research and Information Guide. London: Runneymede Trust, 1988.

3880. Gordon, Paul. Racial Violence and Harassment. London: Runnymede Trust, 1986.

3881. Gordon, Paul. White Law: Racism in the Police, Courts and Prisons. London: Pluto Press, 1983.

3882. Gordon, Paul and Klug, Francesca. New Right, New Racism. London: Searchlight, 1986.

3883. Gordon, Paul and Newham, Anne. Different Worlds. 2d ed. London: Runneymede Trust, 1986.

3884. Graces, Pamela M. Women in British Working Class Politics, 1883-1939. Doctoral dissertation: University of Pittsburgh, 1989. UMO # 9019778.

3885. Grassby, Richard. "English Merchant Capitalism in the Late Seventeenth Century. The Composition of Business Fortunes." Past and Present No. 46 (1970)

3886. Grassby, Richard. "The Personal Wealth of the Business Community in Seventeenth Century England." Economic History Review 23 (1970)

3887. Gray, Nigel, ed. The Worst of Times: An Oral History. Totowa, New Jersey: Barnes and Noble, 1986.

3888. Gray, R. "Race Relations and the Church in Britain." Dublin Review (Winter 1958-59)

3889. Great Britain Commission for Racial Equality. The Nature and Extent of Racial Harassment in the London Borough of Hounslow. London: CRC, 1986.

3890. Great Britain, Home Affairs Committee. Racial Attacks and Harassment. London: HMSO, 1986.

3891. Great Britain, Home Office Research Unit. "Statistics of Those Arrested in Connection with the Serious Instances of Public Disorder September-October 1985." Home Office Statistical Bulletin (October 1986)

3892. Great Britain, Secretary of State for Education, May 21, 1986. "Without Prejudice: Education for an Ethnically Mixed Society." New Community 13 (Autumn 1986): 200-203.

3893. Greater London Council. Racism Within Trade Unions. London: Anti-Racist Trade Union Working Group, London GLC, November 1984.

3894. Green, A. E. "The Likelihood of Becoming and Remaining Unemployed in Great Britain, 1984." Trans. Institute British Geographers 11 (1986): 37-56.

3895. Griggs, Clive. The Trade Union Congress and the Struggle for Education 1868-1925. Basingstoke, Harts: Falmer Press, 1983.

3896. Gurnah, Ahmed. "The Politics of Racism Awareness Training." Critical Social Policy No. 11 (Winter 1984): 6-20.

3897. Haggis, Jane. "Gendering Colonialism or Colonising Gender? Recent Women's Studies Approaches to White Women and the History of British Colonialism." Women's Studies International Forum 13 (1990): 105-115.

3898. Hall, Stuart. "Racism and Reaction." In Five Views of Multi-racial Britain, edited by Commission for Racial Equality. London, 1978.

3899. Hall, Stuart. "The Whites of Their Eyes: Racist Ideologies and the Media." In Silver Linings: Some Strategies for the Eighties, edited by George Bridges and Rosalind Brunt. London: Lawrence and Wishart, 1981.

3900. Halsey, A. H., ed. British Social Trends Since 1900: A Guide to the Changing Social Structure of Britain. London: Macmillan, 1988. [2nd edition.]

3901. Halstead, Mark. Education, Justice and Cultural Diversity. London: Falmer Press, 1988.

3902. Hamnett, C. "A Tale of Two Cities: Sociotenurial Polarisation in London and the South East, 1966-1981." Environment and Planning 19 (April 1987)

3903. Hanawalt, Barbara A. The Ties that Bound: Peasant Families in Medieval England. New York: Oxford University Press, 1986. [Late 14th and 15th centuries.]

3904. Harbury, C. D. "Inheritance and the Distribution of Personal Wealth in Britain." Economic Journal 72 (1962): 845-868.

3905. Harper, Carol A. Social Order in Tudor and Stuart England: Statutory Implications of Rank and Wealth. Doctoral dissertation: University of Oregon, 1982.

3906. Harris, Sydney. "Spearhead of British Racialism." Patterns of Prejudice 7 (1973): 15-19,33. [British National Front.]

3907. Harrison, Brian. Separate Spheres: The Opposition to Woman Suffrage in Britain, 1867-1928. New York: Holmes & Meier, 1978.

3908. Harrison, Paul. Inside the Inner City: Life under the Cutting Edge. New York: Penguin, 1985. [Revised edition, Hackney, London.]

3909. Hart, Nicky. "Gender and the Rise and Fall of Class Politics." New Left Review No. 175 (May-June 1989): 19-47.

3910. Hartmann, P. and Husband, C. Racism and the Mass Media. London: Davis Poynter, 1974.

3911. Hasley, A. H. Change in British Society. London: Oxford University Press, 1986.

3912. Hawkins, Alun. Poor Labouring Men: Rural Radicalism in Norfolk, 1872-1923. Boston, MA: Routledge & Kegan Paul, 1985.

3913. Hearn, Francis. Domination, Legitimation, and Resistance: The Incorporation of the Nineteenth- Century English Working Class. Westport, CT: Greenwood, 1978.

3914. Heath, A. F. and Clifford P. "Class Inequalities in Education in the Twentieth Century." Journal of the Royal Statistical Society, Series A 153 (1990)

3915. Hepple, B. Race, Jobs and the Law in Britain. London: Allen Lane & Penguin, 1968.

3916. Hewitt, Roger. White Talk Black Talk. Inter-racial Friendship and Communication amongst Adolescents. New York: Cambridge University Press, 1986. ["London Jamaican" creole in South London.]

3917. Hewton, Eric. Education in Recession. Crisis in County Hall and Classroom. Winchester, MA: Allen & Unwin, 1986.

3918. Hill, C. and Matthews, D., eds. Race: A Christian Symposium. London: Gollancz, 1968.

3919. Hill, Dave. Out of His Skin: The John Barnes Phenomenon. London: Faber &Faber, 1989.

3920. Hind, Robert J. "The Loss of English Working-Class Parents' Control Over Their Children's Education: The Role of Property-Holders." Historical Reflections 12 (Spring 1985): 77-108.

3921. Hobsbawm, Eric. Labouring Men. New York: Basic Books, 1964.

3922. Hobson, Dorothy. Women Take Issue: Aspects of Women's Subordination. London: Hutchinson, 1978.

3923. Hogan, J. and Palloni A. "The Social Reproduction of a Criminal Class in Working-class London, circa 1950-1980." American Journal of Sociology 96 (September 1990)

3924. Hoggart, Keith and Kofman, Eleonore, eds. Politics, Geography, and Social Stratification. Dover, NH: Croom Helm, 1986.

3925. Holgate, Geoff. "Race Discrimination and Compliance with Statutory Requirements." Local Government Review 154 (August 18, 1990)

3926. Holmes, Colin. "Immigration into Britain: The Myth of Fairness: Racial Violence in Britain, 1911-1919." History Today 35 (1985): 41-45.

3927. Holmes, Colin, ed. Immigrants and Minorities in British Society. Winchester, MA: Allen & Unwin,

3928. Holmes, Colin. "Violence and Race Relations in Britain, 1953-1968." Phylon 36 (1975): 113-124.

3929. Horsman, Reginald. "Origins of Racial Anglo-Saxonism in Great Britain before 1850." Journal of the History of Ideas (July-September 1973): 387-410.

3930. Houlton, David. Cultural Diversity in Primary School. London: Batsford, 1986.

3931. How Racism Came to Britain. London: Institute of Race Relations, 1985.

3932. Howarth, Janet and Curthoys, M. "The Political Economy of Women's Higher Education in Late Nineteenth and Early Twentieth-Century Britain." Historical Research 60 (June 1987): 208-231.

3933. Hudson, Kenneth. Men and Women: Feminism and Anti-Feminism Today. Newton Abbott: David Charles, 1968.

3934. Hugill, Barry. "Rotten Borough or Champion of Racial Equality?" Times Educational Supplement (November 21, 1986): [Complaints of racism against primary school head teachers.]

3935. Humphrey, D. Police Power and Black People. London: Panther, 1972.

3936. Humphries, Jane. "Class Struggle and the Persistence of the Working Class Family." Cambridge Journal of Economics 1 (1977): 241-258.

3937. Husband, Charles. "Racism in Social Work." Community Care 29 (November 1978): 39-40.

3938. Husband, Charles. White Media and Black Britain. London: Arrow, 1975.

3939. Husbands, Christopher T. "Extreme Right-wing Politics in Great Britain: the Recent Marginalisation of the National Front." West European Politics 11 (1988): 65-79.

3940. Husbands, Christopher T. "Regional Change in a Pre-Industrial Economy: Wealth and Population in England in the Sixteenth and Seventeenth Centuries." Journal of Historical Geography 13 (October 1987): 345-359.

3941. Inikori, Joseph E. "Slavery and the Development of Industrial Capitalism in England." Journal of Interdisciplinary History 17 (1987): 771-793.

3942. Inikori, Joseph E. "Slavery and the Revolution in Cotton Textile Production in England." Social Science History 13 (Winter 1989): 343-379.

3943. Inter-Departmental Racial Attacks Group. The Response to Racial Attacks and Harassment: Guidance for the Statutory Agencies. London: Home Office, 1989.

3944. Isherwood, H. B. Race and Politics: The Myth of Racial Equality. Southampton, England: Racial Preservation Society: 1978, [Antagonistic to racial equality.]

3945. Jacobs, Brian D. Black Politics and Urban Crisis in Britain. New York: Cambridge University Press, 1986.

3946. James, C. L. R. CLR James's 80th Birthday Lectures, edited by Margaret Busby and Darcus Howe. London: Race Today Publications, 1984.

3947. James, John A. "Personal Wealth Distribution in Late Eighteenth-Century Britain." Economic History Review 41 (November 1988): 543-565.

3948. Jefferson, Tony. "Race, Crime and Policing: Empirical, Theoretical and Methodological Issues." International Journal of the Sociology of the Law 16 (November 1988): 521-539.

3949. Jenkins, Richard. "Intervening Against 'Racial' Disadvantage: Educational Policy and Labor-Unit Market Outcomes in the United Kingdom." Comparative Education Review 32 (February 1988): 1-19.

3950. Jenkins, Richard. Racism and Recruitment: Managers, Organisations and Equal Opportunity in the Labour Market. New York: Cambridge University Press, 1986.

3951. Jenkinson, Jacqueline. The 1919 Race Riots in Britain: Their Background and Consequences. Doctoral dissertation: University of Edinburgh, 1987. Order No. BRD-86171.

3952. Jenkinson, Jacqueline. "The Glasgow Race Disturbances of 1919." Immigrants & Minorities 4 (1985): 43-67.

3953. John, Angela V., ed. Unequal Opportunities. Women's Employment in England 1800-1918. Oxford: Basil Blackwell, 1986.

3954. Johnson, Mark. "The Spirit Still Moves in the Inner City: The Churches and Race." Ethnic and Racial Studies 11 (1988): 366-373.

3955. Johnson, P. and Stark, G. "Ten Years of Mrs. Thatcher: The Distributional Consequences." Fiscal Studies 10 (May 1989)

GREAT BRITAIN - GENERAL 305

3956. Johnson, Paul. Saving and Spending: The Working-Class Economy in Britain, 1870-1939. New York: Oxford University Press, 1985.

3957. Jones, C. and others. Race and the Press. London: Runnymede Trust, 1971.

3958. Jones, Gareth Stedman. Outcast London: A Study in the Relationship between Classes in Victorian Society. New York: Oxford University Press, 1971.

3959. Jones, Greta. Social Hygiene in Twentieth Century Britain. Wolfeboro, NH: Croom Helm, 1986.

3960. Jones, Jack. Union Man: The Autobiography of Jack Jones. London: Collins, 1986.

3961. Jordan, Ellen. "The Exclusion of Women From Industry in Nineteenth-Century Britain." Comparative Studies in Society and History 31 (April 1989): 273-296.

3962. Jordan, Thomas E. "'Stay and Starve, or Go and Prosper!' Juvenile Emigration from Great Britain in the Nineteenth Century." Social Science History 9 (Spring 1985): 145-166.

3963. Joshi, S. and Carter, B. "The Role of Labour in the Creation of a Racist Britain." Race and Class 25 (Winter 1984): 53-70.

3964. Jowell, Roger and Witherspoon, Sharon, eds. British Social Attitudes: the 1985 Report. Aldershot: Gower, 1985.

3965. Jubb, Michael. "Income, Class and the Taxman: A Note on the Distribution of Wealth in Nineteenth-century Britain." Bulletin Institute of Historical Research 60 (February 1987): 118-124.

3966. Junger, M. "Studying Ethnic Minorities in relation to Crime and Police Discrimination: Answer to Bowling." British Journal of Criminology 30 (Autumn 1990)

3967. Jupp, Peter J. "The Landed Elite and Political Authority in Britain, ca. 1760-1850." Journal of British Studies 29 (January 1990): 53-79.

3968. Kadish, A. "University Extension and the Working Classes: The Case of the Northumberland Miners." Historical Research 60 (June 1987): 188-207.

3969. Karn, Valerie. "Race and Housing in Britain: The Role of the Major Institutions." In Ethnic Pluralism and Public Policy: Achieving Equality in the United States and Britain, edited by Nathan Glazer and Ken Young, 162-183. London: Heinemann, 1983.

3970. Katz, Wendy R. Rider Haggard and the Fiction of Empire: A Critical Study of British Imperial Fiction. New York: Cambridge University Press, 1988.

3971. Kavale, Kenneth A. and Sink, Christopher A. "Sir Cyril Burt in Review: An Empiricist in the Dock." Revista de Historia de la Psicologia (Spain) 6 (1985): 287-316.

3972. Kay, J. A. "Changes in Tax Progressivity, 1951-1985." Fiscal Studies 6 (May 1985)

3973. Kennedy, Paul and O'Brien Patrick K. "The Costs and Benefits of British Imperialism 1846-1914." Past & Present No. 125 (November 1989): 186-199. [Debate.]

3974. Kennedy, Paul and Anthony Nicholls, eds. Nationalist and Racialist Movements in Britain and Germany Before 1914. London: Macmillan, 1982.

3975. Kenny, Jamie. "Out of the Frying Pan." New Society (May 27, 1988): [The Chinese in Britain.]

3976. Kent, Susan K. "The Politics of Sexual Difference: World War I and the Demise of British Feminism." Journal of British Studies 27 (1988): 232-253.

3977. Killingray, David. "Race and Rank in the British Army in the Twentieth Century." Ethnic and Racial Studies 10 (1987): 276-290.

3978. King, Ronald. "Sex and Social Class Inequalities in Education: A Re-examination." British Journal of Sociology of Education 8 (September 1987): 287-303.

3979. Kirk, Neville. "In Defence of Class. A Critique of Recent Revisionist Writing upon the Nineteenth Cenury English Working Class." International Review of Social History 32 (1987): 2-47.

3980. Klug, Francesca and Gordon, Paul. Different Worlds: Racism and Discrimination in Britain. London: Runnymede Trust, May 1983.

3981. Kushner, Tony and Lunn, Kenneth, eds. Traditions of Intolerance. Historical Perspectives on Fascism and Race Discourse in Britain. Manchester: Manchester University Press, 1989.

3982. Kushnick, Louis. "Creeping Racism in England." Liberator 9 (August 1969)

3983. Kushnick, Louis. "Racism, the National Health Service and the Health of Black People." International Journal of Health Services 18 (1988)

3984. Kwamdela, Odimumba (formerly J. Ashton Brathwaite). Black British Soldier. Brooklyn, New York: Kibo Books, 1986.

3985. Laing, Stuart. Representations of Working Class Life 1957- 1964. London: Macmillan, 1986.

3986. Landau, Nick. Statistics of London's Ethnic Minorities, 1979-1981. London: Greater London Council Intelligence Unit, 1986.

3987. Laqueur, Thomas. "Working-class Demand and the Growth of English Elementary Education." In Schooling and Society, edited by Lawrence Stone, 192-205. Baltimore, MD., 1976.

3988. Lashley, Horace. "Politics of One Black One Vote." Times Higher Education Supplement (July 11, 1986): [Blacks in British politics.]

3989. Law, I. and Henfrey, J. A History of Racism in Liverpool, 1660-1950. Liverpool: Merseyside Community Relations Council, 1981.

3990. Lawrence, Anne. "The Cradle to the Grave: English Observations of Irish Social Customs in the Seventeenth Century." Seventeenth Century 3 (1988): 63-84.

3991. Lawrence, Daniel. "Racial Violence in Britain: Trends and a Perspective." New Community 14 (Autumn 1988): 151-160.

3992. Layton-Henry, Zig. "Immigration into Britain: The New Commonwealth Migrants, 1945-1962." History Today 35 (December 1985): 27-32.

3993. Layton-Hentry, Zig and Rich, Paul B., eds. Race, Government and Politics in Britain. London: Macmillan, 1986.

3994. Learning in Terror: A Survey of Racial Harassment in Schools and Colleges. London: Commission for Racial Equality, 1988.

3995. Lee, A. M. "Mass Media Mythmaking in the United Kindgdom's Interethnic Struggles." Ethnicity 8 (1981): 18-30.

3996. Leech, Kenneth. Struggle in Babylon: Racism in the Cities and Churches of Britain. London: Sheldon Press, 1988.

3997. Leigh, L. H. "Keeping the Public Order- II." Solicitors' Journal 131 (January 30, 1987): [Racism in Britain.]

3998. Levine, David. "Industrialization and the Proletarian Family in England." Past and Present 107 (May 1985): 168- 203.

3999. Levine, Kenneth. The Social Content of Literacy. Boston, MA: Routledge & Kegan Paul, 1986,

4000. Lewis, D. S. Illusions of Grandeur. Mosley, Fascism and British Society, 1931-1981. New York: St. Martin's Press, 1990.

4001. Lewis, G. and others. "Are British Psychiatrists Racist?" British Journal of Psychiatry 157 (September 1990)

4002. Lewis, J. Women in England, 1870-1950. Brighton: Wheatsheaf, 1984.

4003. Lindert, Peter H. "Unequal English Wealth Since 1670." Journal of Political Economy 94 (1986): 1127-1162.

4004. Lindert, Peter H. "Who Owned Victorian England? The Debate Over Landed Wealth and Inequality." Agricultural History 61 (Fall 1987): 25-51.

4005. Linguistic Minorities Project. The Other Languages of England. London: Routledge & Kegan Paul, 1985.

4006. Lipsey, David. "Rich Get Richer- Official." New Society (November 21, 1986)

4007. Lister, I. "Civic Education for Positive Pluralism in Britain." In Education for Democratic Citizenship. A Challenge for Multi-Ethnic Societies, edited by Roberta S. Sigel and Marilyn Hoskan. Hillsdale, NJ: Lawrence Erlbaum Associates, 1990.

4008. Lister, Ruth. The Exclusive Society: Citizenship and the Poor. London: Child Poverty Action Group, 1989.

4009. Little, Alan and Diana Robbins. Loading the Law: A Study of Transmitted Deprivation, Ethnic Minorities and Affirmative Action. London: Commission for Racial Equality, 1982.

4010. Little, Kenneth L. "The Anthropology of Some Coloured Communities in Great Britain with Comparative Material on Colour Prejudice." London School of Economics, 1945.

4011. Littlewood, R. "Racism, Diagnosis and Treatment." British Journal of Psychiatry 157 (September 1990)

4012. Loomba, Amia. Race, Gender, Renaissance Drama. New York: Manchester University Press, 1989.

4013. Lorimer, Douglas A. Colour, Class and the Victorians: English Attitudes to the Negro in the Mid-Nineteenth Century. Leicester: 1978.

4014. Lorimer, Douglas A. "Theoretical Racism in Late-Victorian Anthropology, 1870-1900." Victorian Studies 31 (Spring 1988): 405-430.

4015. Low, Frances. "How Poor Ladies Live." Nineteenth Century 41,42 (March 1897, July 1897): 405-417, 161-168.

4016. Lunn, Kenneth. "Immigrants and British Labour's Response, 1870-1950." History Today 35 (November 1985): 48-52.

4017. Lunn, Kenneth, ed. Race and Labour in Twentieth-Century Britain. London: Frank Cass, 1985.

4018. Lunn, Kenneth. "Race Relations or Industrial Relations?" Immigrants and Minorities 4 (July 1985): 1-29.

4019. Lustgarten, Laurence. "Racial Inequality and the Limits of Law." Modern Law Review 49 (January 1986)

4020. Macdonald, J. "The Capitalist Way to Curb Discrimination." Race Today (August 1973)

4021. MacDougall, Hugh A. Racial Myth in English History: Trojans, Trentons, and Anglo-Saxons. Harvest House, 1982.

4022. Macfarlane, Alan. The Family Life of Ralph Josselin... New York: Cambridge University Press, 1970.

4023. Macintyre, S. "The Patterning of Health by Social Position in Contemporary Britain: Directions for Social Research." Social Science and Medicine 23 (1986): 393-415.

4024. MacKenzie, John M. Propaganda and Empire: The Manipulation of British Public Opinion, 1880-1960. Manchester, 1984.

4025. MacKenzie, John M., ed. Imperialism and Popular Culture. Manchester University Press, 1986.

4026. Macnicol, John. "Eugenics and the Campaign for Voluntary Sterilization in Britain Between the Wars." Social History of Medicine 2 (August 1989): 147-170.

4027. Macnicol, John. "Going to the Country." Times Higher Education Supplement (April 18, 1986): [Evaluation of inner city working class children to reception areas during World War II.]

4028. MacRitchie, David. Ancient and Modern Britons: A Retrospect. Los Angeles, CA: W. Preston, 1985-1986, orig. 1884.

4029. Male George A. "England." Education and Urban Society 18 (August 1986): 477-486. [Education of minority children.]

4030. Male, George A. Issues in the Education of Minorities, England and the United States. Wolfeboro, NH: Longwood Publishing Group, 1989.

4031. Male, George A. "Problems in the Education of Minorities in England." Review Journal of Philosophy and Social Science 6 (1981): 4-36.

4032. Manchester City Council. Poverty in Manchester. Manchester, England: The Council, 1986.

4033. Mangan, J. A., ed. Making Imperial Mentalities. Manchester: Manchester University Press, 1990.

4034. Marke, Ernest. *In Troubled Waters: Memoirs of My Seventy Years in England*. London: Karia Press, 1986.

4035. Marriott, Stuart. *Primary Education and Society*. Basingstoke, Hants: Falmer Press, 1985.

4036. Marsden, William E. "Residential Segregation and the Hierarchy of Elementary Schooling from Charles Booth's Surveys." *London Journal* 11 (1985): 127-146.

4037. Marsden, William E. *Unequal Educational Provision in England and Wales: The Nineteenth-century Roots*. Totowa, NJ: Woburn Press, 1986.

4038. Marsh, Alan. "Who Hates the Blacks." *New Society* 37 (September 23, 1976): 649-652.

4039. Marsh, David and Gareth Locksley. "Capital in Britain: Its Structural Power and Influence over Policy." In *Capital and Politics in Western Europe*, edited by Marsh, 36-60. London, 1983.

4040. Marshall, Gordon and others. "Class, Citizenship, and Distributional Conflict in Modern Britain." *British Journal of Sociology* 36 (June 1985): 259-284.

4041. Marshall, Gordon and others. *Social Class in Modern Britain*. London: Hutchinson, 1988.

4042. Marshall, Gordon and Rose, David. "Proletarianization in the British Class Structure?" *British Journal of Sociology* 39 (December 1988): 498-518.

4043. Martin, J. "Racism and Immigration." *New Society* 71 (February 1985): 261-262.

4044. Martin, John E. *Feudalism to Capitalism: Peasant and Landlord in English Agrarian Development*. Atlantic Highlands, NJ: Humanities, 1983.

4045. Martin, Ron. "The Political Economy of Britain's North- South Divide." *Trans. Institute British Geographers* 13 (1988): 389-418.

4046. Matthews, Glen. "The Search for a Cure for Vagrancy in Worcestershire, 1870-1920." *Midland History* 11 (1986): 100-116.

4047. Mayall, David. *Gypsy-Travellers in Nineteenth-Century Society*. New York: Cambridge University Press, 1988.

4048. Mayled, John. *Let's Discuss Racism*. Hove, East Sussex, England: Wayland, 1986. [Written for use in British upper junior schools.]

4049. McCarthy, M. *Campaigning for the Poor*. London: Croom Helm, 1986.

4050. McCormick, B. "Employment Opportunities, Earnings and the Journey to Work of Minority Workers in Great Britain." Economic Journal 96 (June 1986): 375-397.

4051. McCormick, B. "Evidence about the Comparative Earnings of Asian and West Indian Workers in Great Britain." Scottish Journal of Political Economy 33 (May 1986)

4052. McGrady, Richard. "Joseph Emidy: An African in Cornwall." Musical Times 127 (October 1986): 119-123.

4053. McIvor, A. J. "Manual Work, Technology, and Industrial Health, 1918-1939." Medical History 31 (April 1987): 160- 189.

4054. McKibbin, Rose. The Ideologies of Class: Social Relations in Britain, 1880-1950. New York: Oxford University Press, 1990.

4055. McLean, M. "Education and Cultural Diversity in Britain: Recent Immigrant Groups." Comparative Education 19 (1983): 179-191.

4056. Meacham, Standish. A Life Apart: The English Working Class, 1890-1914. Cambridge, MA: Harvard University Press, 1977.

4057. Mentor, Ian. "Teaching Practice Stasis: Racism, Sexism and School Experience in Initial Teacher Education." British Journal of Sociology of Education 10 (1989): 459-473.

4058. Merseyside Action Against Racial Terrorism. Racial Terrorism in Merseyside, 1987. Liverpool: Merseyside Community Relations Council, 1987.

4059. Messina, Anthony M. "Anti-Immigrant Illiberalism and the 'New' Ethnic and Racial Minorities in Western Europe." Patterns of Prejudice 23 (Autumn 1989): 17-31.

4060. Messina, Anthony M. "Ethnic Minority Representation and Party Competition in Britain: The Case of Earling Borough." Political Studies 35 (June 1987): 224-238.

4061. Messina, Anthony M. "Mediating Race Relations: British Community Relations Councils Revisited." Ethnic and Racial Studies 10 (1987): 186-202.

4062. Messina, Anthony M. "Race and Party Competition in Britain: Policy Formation in the Post-Consensus Period." Parliamentary Affairs 38 (Autumn 1985): 423-436.

4063. Messina, Anthony M. Race and Party Competition in Britain. Oxford, 1989.

4064. Miles, Robert. "Between Two Cultures: United Kingdom, the Struggle Against Discrimination." UNESCO Courier 38 (September 1985): 21-23.

4065. Miles, Robert. "Nationality, Citizenship, and Migration to Britain, 1949-1951." Journal of Law and Society 16 (Winter 1989): 426-442.

4066. Miles, Robert. "The Racialization of British Politics." Political Studies 38 (June 1990)

4067. Miles, Robert. "Racism and Nationalism in Britain." Race in Britain, edited by C. Husbands. London: Hutchinson, 1982.

4068. Miles, Robert. "Recent Marxist Theories of Nationalism and the Issue of Racism." British Journal of Sociology 38 (1987): 24-43.

4069. Miles, Robert. The Relative Autonomy of Ideology: Racism and the Migration of Labour to Britain since 1945. Paris: Grami, Document de Travail 7: 1985.

4070. Miles, Robert and Phizacklea, A. Labour and Racism. London: Routledge & Kegan Paul, 1980.

4071. Miles, Robert and Phizacklea, eds. Racism and Political Action in Britain. London: Routledge & Kegan Paul, 1979.

4072. Millner, R. "Racism and the Law." Labour Monthly (July 1965)

4073. Mills, Dennis R. and Short, Brian M. "Social Change and Social Conflict in Nineteenth-Century England." Journal of Peasant Studies 10 (July 1984): 253-262.

4074. Milman, David and de Gama Katherine. "Sexual Discrimination in Education: One Step Forward, Two Steps Back?" Journal of Social Welfare Law 1 (1989): 4-22.

4075. Miner, Kathleen N. "The Politics of Educational Racism: A Case Study of Educational Policy and Politics in Wolverhampton." Council for National Academic Awards, 1987. Order # BRDX84086.

4076. Mitch, David F. "The Impact of Subsidies to Elementary Schooling on Enrollment Rates in Nineteenth-century England." Economic History Review 39 (1986): 371-391.

4077. Mitter, Swasti. "Industrial Restructuring and Manufacturing Homework: Immigrant Women in the UK Clothing Industry." Capital and Class No. 27 (Winter 1986): 37-80.

4078. Mohanty, S. P. "Kipling's Children and the Colour Line." Race and Class 31 (July-September 1989): 21-40.

4079. Mokyr, Joel, ed. The Economics of the Industrial Revolution. Totowa, NJ: Rowman & Allanheld, 1985. [Great Britain, 1760-1860.]

4080. Mokyr, Joel. "Is There Still Life in the Pessimist Case? Consumption during the Industrial Revolution, 1790-1850." Journal of Economic History 48 (March 1988): 69-92.

4081. Moodley, Ronnie. "Theology and Practice for the '90's." Race and Class 32 (July- September 1990): 76-83.

4082. Moore, Robert. "Labour and Colour, 1945-1968." Venture (September 1968)

4083. Morton, James. "Black Injustice." New Law Journal 138 (October 14, 1988): [Discrimination in criminal justice in Great Britain.]

4084. Morton, James and Harvie, Dominique. "Racial Discrimination amongst Solicitors." New Law Journal 140 (August 10, 1990)

4085. Morton, James and Harvie, Dominique. "Racial Discrimination in the Legal Profession." New Law Journal 140 (August 3, 1990)

4086. Mullard, Chris. Race, Power and Resistance. London: Routledge & Kegan Paul, 1986.

4087. Mullard, Chris. "The Three R's: Rampton, Racism and Research." In Race, Educacation, and Research. Centre for Multicultural Education, 12-23. London: University of London Institute of Education, 1984.

4088. Muller, Detlef K. and others, eds. The Rise of the Modern Educational System, Structural Change and Social Reproduction 1870-1920. New York: Cambridge University Press, 1987.

4089. Munn, G. H. Thought on Race as Part of the Ideology of British Imperialism, 1894-1904. British Litt. thesis. Oxford University, 1976.

4090. Murder in the Playground: The Report of the Macdonald Inquiry into Racism and Racial Violence in Manchester Schools. London: Longsight Press, 1989.

4091. Murphy, J. "A Most Respectable Prejudice: Inequality in Educational Research and Policy." British Journal of Sociology 1 (1990): 29-54.

4092. Murray, Charles. "The British Underclass." Public Interest No.99 (Spring 1990)

4093. Murray, Nancy. "Anti-Racists and Other Demons: The Press and Ideology in Thatcher's Britain." Race and Class 27 (Winter 1986): 1-20.

4094. Narendranathan, W. and others. "An Investigation into the Incidence and Dynamic Structure of Sickness and Unemployment in Britain, 1965-1975." Journal of the Royal Statistical Society 148, Series A, part 2 (1985): 254-267.

4095. Neild, N. The Social and Economic Condition of the Unfree Classes in England, from the Twelfth to the Fourteenth Century, with special Reference to the Eastern Countries. Doctoral dissertation: University of London, 1908.

4096. Nelson, Wade W. Cheap or Efficient: An Examination of English Elementary Education during the Era of Payment by Results, 1863-1890. Doctoral dissertation, University of Iowa, 1987. UMO # 8729496.

4097. Newton, K. and Karran T.J. The Politics of Local Expenditure. London: Macmillan, 1986.

4098. Nicholas, Joe. "British Language Diversity Surveys (1977- 1987): A Critical Examination." Language and Education 2 (1988): 15-33.

4099. Northam, Gerry. Shooting in the Dark: Riot Police in Britain. London: Faber, 1988.

4100. O'Brien, Patrick K. "British Incomes and Property in the Early Nineteenth Century." Economic History Review (1959)

4101. O'Brien, Patrick K. "The Costs and Benefits of British Imperialism 1846-1914." Past and Present No. 120 (August 1988): 163-200.

4102. O'Brien, Patrick K. "The Political Economy of British Taxation, 1660-1815." Economic History Review 41 (February 1988): 1-32.

4103. O'Donnell, Mike. "Racial Discrimination." New Society (May 27, 1988)

4104. O'Driscoll, E. "The Poor in English Literature." National University of Ireland, 1917.

4105. O'Higgins, Michael. "Inequality, Redistribution and Recession: The British Experience, 1976-1982." Journal of Social Policy 14 (July 1985): 279-312.

4106. Oakley, Robin and Carey, Sean. "Street Life, Youth and Ethnicity in Inner City Areas." New Community 13 (Autumn 1986): 214-223.

4107. Okely, Judith. "Twentieth Century English Gypsy Women: Models in Conflict." Perceiving Women, edited by Shirley Aredener, 55-86. London: Malaby Press, 1975.

4108. Osman, Arthur. Neglected Britain. London: Building Employers Confederates, 1986. [Disrepair of school buildings.]

4109. "An Outline of the Grievances of Women." Metropolitan Magazine 22 (1838): 16-27.

4110. Pahl, Jan and Vaile, Michael. Health and Health Care Among Travellers. Canterbury, Kent: Health Services Research Unit, University of Kent, 1986.

4111. Palmer, Frank, ed. Anti-Racism: An Assault on Education. London: Sherwood Press, 1986. [Attacks on multicultural education.]

4112. Palmer, Stanley. Police and Protest in England and Ireland, 1780-1850. New York: Cambridge University Press, 1988.

4113. Pamuk, Elsie R. "Social Class Inequality in Mortality from 1921 to 1972 in England and Wales." Population Studies 35 (March 1985)

4114. Pamuk, Elsie R. "Social Class Inequality in Infant Mortality in England and Wales: 1925-1984." University of Pennsylvania, 1989. UMO # 8922580.

4115. Parekh, Bhikhu. "Educational Opportunity in Multi-Ethnic Britain." In Ethnic Pluralism and Public Policy, edited by Nathan Glazer and K. Young. London: Heinemann, 1983.

4116. Parekh, Bhikhu. "Legacy of the Empire." New Statesman & Society (September 9, 1988): [Critical review of Russell Lewis, Anti-Racism A Mania Exposed.]

4117. Parker, Sara. "Caught in the Cross-fire." Times Educational Supplement (November 15, 1985): [Clashing loyalties of youth workers in poor areas.]

4118. Parkinson, Michael. Liverpool on the Brink: One City's Struggle Against Government Cuts. London: Policy Journals, 1986.

4119. Payen, Geoff and others. "Trends in Female Social Mobility." In Gender, Class and Work, edited by Eva Gamarnikow and others, 61-76. London: Heinemann, 1983.

4120. Peach, Ceri. "The Muslim Population of Great Britain." Ethnic and Racial Studies 13 (July 1990)

4121. Pearson, Karl and N. Moul. "The Problem of Alien Immigration into Great Britain: Illustrated by an Examination of Russian and Polish Jewish Children." Annals of Eugenics 1 (1925- 1926): 5-127.

4122. Pelteret, David A. E. "Late Anglo-Saxon Slavery: An Inter- disciplinary Approach to the Various Forms of Evidence." University of Toronto, 1976.

4123. Perkin, Harold. The Origins of Modern English Society, 1780-1880. London: Routledge and Kegan Paul, 1969.

4124. Perrott, Roy. The Aristocrats: A Portrait of Britain's Nobility and their Way of Life Today. New York: Macmillan, 1968.

4125. Phillipps, K. C. Language and Class in Victorian England. New York: Blackwell, 1986.

4126. Phillips, R. Education for Racial Domination. London: Pan African Institute, 1979.

4127. Piachaud, David. "Poverty in Britain 1899 to 1963." Journal of Social Policy 17 (July 1988): 335-350.

4128. Pilkington, Edward. Beyond the Mother Country: West Indians and the Notting Hill White Riots. London: I.B. Tauris, 1988.

4129. Platt, Steve. "Investigating Racial Attacks." New Society (August 15, 1986): [Racial violence in Tower Hamlets, a London borough.]

4130. Platt, Steve. "Is Brent Barmy?" New Society (November 28, 1986): [Complaints of racism against primary school head teachers.]

4131. Plewis, G. "Assessing and Understanding the Educational Progress of Children from Different Ethnic Groups." Journal of Royal Statistical Society, Series A 151 (1988)

4132. Pollard, Sidney and Crossley, David W. The Wealth of Britain, 1085-1966. London: 1968,

4133. Pope, Rex and others, eds. Social Welfare in Britain, 1885-1985. Dover, NH: Croom Helm, 1986.

4134. Popkess, A. "The Racial Disturbances in Nottingham." Criminal Law Review (October 1969)

4135. Popplewell, Richard. "The Surveillance of Indian Revolutionaries in Great Britain and On the Continent, 1903- 1914." Intelligence and National Security 3 (1988): 56-76.

4136. Porter, Bernard. Plots and Paranoia: A History of Political Espionage in Britain, 1790-1988. Boston, MA: Unwin Hyman, 1989.

4137. Poulter, Sebastian M. English Law and Ethnic Minority Customs. London: Butterworth, 1986.

4138. Power, C. and others. "Health in Childhood and Social Inequalities in Health in Young Adults." Journal of the Royal Statistical Society, Series A 153 (1990)

4139. Prest, Mike. "Black Youth and the White Left." Leveller 15 (November 1977)

4140. Preston, Barbara. "Statistics of Inequality." Sociological Review 22 (1974): 103-118. [Mortality rates by social class in Britain.]

GREAT BRITAIN - GENERAL 317

4141. "Race and the Legal Profession." New Law Journal 139 (April 28, 1989)

4142. Racial Harassment Project. Because the Skin Is Black. Sheffield: Sheffield City Council, 1989.

4143. Racial Attacks: A Survey in Eight Areas. London: Commission for Racial Equality, 1987.

4144. Racial Harassment in Leeds 1985-1986: A Report of the Independent Commission of Enquiry into Racial Harassment. Leeds: Leeds Community Relations Council, 1987.

4145. Racial Justice in Magistrates' Courts. London: Commission for Racial Equality, 1989.

4146. The Racial Politics of Militants in Liverpool. London: Runnymede Trust, 1986.

4147. Racial Violence and Harassment. London: Runnymede Trust, 1986.

4148. Rainger, Ronald. "Philanthropy and Science in the 1830's: The British and Foreign Aborigines Protection Society." Man 15 (1980): 702-717.

4149. Randall, Steve. "Bibliographic Essay: The New Right, Racism and Education in Thatcher's Britain." Sage Race Relations Abstracts 13 (August 1988): 3-17.

4150. Rappaport, Steve. "Social Structure and Mobility in Sixteenth-Century London: Part II." London Journal 10 (Winter 1984): 107-134.

4151. Ratcliffe, Peter. Racism and Reaction: A Profile of Handsworth. London: Routledge and Kegan Paul, 1981.

4152. Rathwell, Thomas and Phillips, David, eds. Health, Race and Ethnicity. London: Croom Helm, 1986.

4153. Ray, John J. and Furnham, Adrian. "Authoritarianism, Conservatism and Racism." Ethnic & Racial Studies 7 (July 1984): 406-412.

4154. Ray, R. "Prices, Children and Inequality: Further Evidence for the U.K., 1965-1982." Economic Journal 95 (December 1985): 1069-1077.

4155. Reed, Mike. "Social Change and Social Conflict in Nineteenth-Century England: A Comment." Journal of Peasant Studies 12 (October 1984): 109-123.

4156. Reed, Mike and Wells, Roger, eds. Class, Conflict, and Protest in the English Countryside, 1700-1880. Savage, MD: Frank Cass, 1990.

4157. Reeves, Frank W. Race and Borough Politics. Brookfield, VT: Gower, 1989.

4158. Rendall, Jane. Women and Industrialization in England, 1750-1880. Cambridge, MA: Blackwell, 1990.

4159. Revell, J. R. S. The Wealth of the Nation. Cambridge, 1967.

4160. Rex, John. "The Heritage of Slavery and Social Disadvantage." In The Caribbean in Europe, edited by Colin Brock. London: Frank Cass, 1986.

4161. Rice, P. G. "Juvenile Unemployment, Relative Wages and Social Security in Great Britain." Economic Journal 96 (June 1986): 352-374.

4162. Rich, Paul B. "The Dusty Road to Disaster." Times Higher Education Supplement (August 1, 1986): [Racism in the Commonwealth.]

4163. Rich, Paul B. Elixir of Empire: The English Public Schools Ritualism, Freemasonry, and Imperialsim. London: Regency Press, 1989.

4164. Rich, Paul B. "The Impact of South African Segregationist and Apartheid Ideology on British Racial Thought: 1939-1960." New Community 13 (Spring-Summer 1980): 1-17.

4165. Rich, Paul B. "The Politics of 'Surplus Colonial Labour': Black Immigration to Britain and Governmental Responses, 1940-1962." In The Carribean in Europe, edited by Colin Brock. London: Frank Cass, 1986.

4166. Rich, Paul B. Race and Empire in British Politics. New York: Cambridge University Press, 1986.

4167. Rich, Paul B. "T. H. Green, Lord Scarman and the Issue of Ethnic Minority Rights in English Liberal Thought." Ethnic and Racial Studies 10 (1987): 149-168.

4168. "The Rich in Britain." New Society (August 22, 1986): [special section.]

4169. Richards, Eric. "Women in the British Economy since about 1700: An Interpretation." History 59 (October 1974): 337- 357.

4170. Richards, Jeffrey, ed. Imperialism and Juvenile Literature. Manchester: Manchester University Press, 1989.

4171. Richards, Thomas. The Commodity Culture of Victorian England, Advertising and Spectacle, 1851-1914. Stanford, CA: Stanford University Press, 1990.

4172. Richardson, John and Lambert, John. The Sociology of Race. Ormsbirk: Causeway Press, 1985.

4173. Richardson, Ruth. Death, Dissection and the Destitute. New York: Routledge & Kegan Paul, 1987. [Anatomy Act of 1832.]

4174. Roberts, Elizabeth. A Woman's Place. An Oral History of Working-class Women 1890-1940. New York: Blackwell, 1986.

4175. Roberts, Elizabeth. "Working-class Standards of Living in Barrow and Lancaster, 1890-1914." in Pat Thane and Anthony Sutcliffe (eds.) Essays in Social History, II (1986): [New York: Clarendon Press.]

4176. Robson, A. H. "The Education of Children Engaged in Industry in England, 1833-1876." University of London, King's College, 1930.

4177. Robson, M. "Unemployment and Real Wages in Britain, 1967-1983." Oxford Economic Papers 41 (October 1989)

4178. Roderick, Gordon W. and Michael Stephens, eds. Where Did We Go Wrong? Industry, Education and Economy of Victorian Britain. Basingstoke, Hants: Falmer Press, 1981.

4179. Rogers, Rick, ed. Education and Social Class. Philadelphia, PA: Falmer Press, 1986.

4180. Rooney, Barney. Racism and Resistance to Change: A Study of the Black Social Workers Project-Liverpool Social Servives Department, 1975-1985. Liverpool: Merseyside Area Profile Groups Department of Sociology, University of Liverpool, 1987.

4181. Rose, Lionel. The Massacre of the Innocents: Infanticide in Britain, 1800-1939. Boston, MA: Routledge & Kegan Paul, 1968.

4182. Rose, Michael E., ed. The Poor and the City: The English Poor Law in Its Urban Context, 1834-1914. New York: St. Martin's Press, 1985.

4183. Rose, Michael E. The Relief of Poverty, 1834-1914. Atlantic Highlands, New Jersey: Humanities Press, 1982.

4184. Rothwell, Tom and David Phillips, eds. Health, Race, & Ethnicity. Dover, NH: Croom Helm, 1986.

4185. Rubenstein, W. D. "British Millionaires, 1809-1949." Bulletin of the Institute of Historical Research 48 (1974)

4186. Rubenstein, W. D. "Education and the Social Origins of British Elites 1880-1970." Past & Present 112 (August 1986): 163-207.

4187. Rubenstein, W. D. Elites and the Wealthy in Modern British History: Essays in Social and Economic History. New York: St. Martin's Press, 1987.

4188. Rubenstein, W. D. "Men of Property: Some Aspects of Occupation, Inheritance and Power Among Top British Wealthholders." In Elites and Power in British Society, edited by P. Stanworth and A. Giddens. Cambridge University Press, 1974.

4189. Rubenstein, W. D. "Men of Property: The Wealthy in Britain 1809-1939." Johns Hopkins University, 1975.

4190. Rubenstein, W. D. "Modern Britain." In Wealth and the Wealthy in the Modern World, edited by W.D. Rubenstein. London: Croom Helm, 1980.

4191. Rubenstein, W. D. "Occupations Among British Millionaires, 1857-1969." Review of Income and Wealth 17 (December 1971): 371-378.

4192. Rubenstein, W. D. "The Size and Distribution of the English Middle Class in 1860." Historical Research 61 (February 1988): 65-89.

4193. Rubenstein, W. D. "Social Class, Social Attitudes, and British Business Life." Oxford Review of Economic Policy 4 (Spring 1988)

4194. Rubenstein, W. D. "The Victorian Middle Classes: Wealth, Occupation and Geography." Economic History Review 30 (1977)

4195. Rubenstein, W. D. Wealth and Inequality in Britain. London: Faber, 1986.

4196. Rubenstein, W. D. "Wealth, Elites and the Class Structure of Modern Britain." Past and Present No. 76 (August 1977)

4197. Rubin, Miri. Charity and Community in Medieval Cambridge. New York: Cambridge University Press, 1987.

4198. Rule, John. The Labouring Classes in Early Industrial England, 1750-1850. New York: Longman, 1986.

4199. Runciman, W. G. "How Many Classes Are There in Contemporary British Society?" Sociology 24 (August 1990)

4200. Sachs, Albert L. and Wilson, Joan H. Sexism and the Law: A Study of Male Beliefs and Legal Bias in Britain and the United States. New York: Free Press, 1979.

4201. Salter, Brian and Tapper, Ted. Power and Policy in Education: The Case of Independent Schooling. Basingstoke, Hants: Falmer Press, 1985.

4202. Sanderson, M. "Education and Economic Decline, 1890-1980." Oxford Review of Economic Policy 4 (Spring 1988)

4203. Santamaria, U. and Couper K. "The Making of the Multiracial Society in the United Kingdon: Strategies and Perspectives." Social Sciences Information 24 (March 1985): 145-159.

4204. Sarre, P. "Race and the Class structure." In Restructuring Britain: The Changing Social Structure, edited by C. Hammett and others. London: Sage, 1989.

4205. Sauners, Barbara. Homeless Young People in Britain. London: Bedford Square Press, 1986.

4206. Scarman, Lord. "Injustice in the Cities." New Society (February 14, 1986)

4207. Schifferes, Steve. "The Rich in Britain." New Society (August 22, 1986)

4208. Schwarz, L. D. "The Standard of Living in the Long Run: London, 1770-1860." Economic History Review 38 (February 1985): 24-41.

4209. Scott, Hilda. Working Your Way to the Bottom: The Feminization of Poverty. London: Pandora Press, 1984.

4210. No entry

4211. Scouloudi, I. "Alien Immigration into and Alien Communities in London, 1558-1640." London School of Economics, 1936.

4212. Scraton, Phil. The State of the Police. London: Pluto Press, 1985.

4213. Seabrook, Jeremy. "Waging War on the Poor." New Society (May 20, 1988)

4214. Searle, Chris. All Our Words. London: Young World books, 1986. [Minorities and the English language.]

4215. Searle, Chris. "Race before Wicket: Cricket, Empire, and the White Race." Race & Class 31 (January-March 1990): 31- 48.

4216. Searle, Chris. "Reclaiming Our Words." Race & Class 30 (October-December 1988): 41-59.

4217. Searle, Chris. "Your Daily Dose: Racism and the Sun." Race & Class 29 (Summer 1987): 55-71.

4218. "Sex, Race and the Law Lords." Solicitors Journal 134 (July 6, 1990): 763.

4219. Sexton, Robert D. "Travelling People in the United Kingdom in the First Half of the Twentieth Century." Doctoral dissertation: University of Southampton, 1989. Order Number BRDX86453.

4220. Shah, A. "Does Education Act as a Screening Device for Certain British Occupations?" Oxford Economic Papers 37 (March 1985)

4221. Shah, A. "Education and Earnings Inequality across British Labour Markets." Applied Economics 18 (February 1986)

4222. Shah, Sneh. "History and Inter-cultural Education: The Relevant Issues." Teaching History No. 48 (1987): 3-7.

4223. Shapiro, Shelby. Unions and Racism. Oldham, England: Industrial Workers of the World, British Section, 1980.

4224. Sharpe, L. J. "Devolution and Celtic Nationalism in the UK." W. Eur. Pol. 8 (July 1985): 82-100.

4225. Sherwood, Marika. "'It Is Not a Case of Numbers': A Case Study of Institutional Racism in Britain, 1941-1943." Immigrants and Minorities 4 (July 1985): 116-141.

4226. Shipley, Peter. "The National Front: Racialism and Neo- Fascism in Britain." Conflict Studies No. 97 (July 1978): 1-16.

4227. Short, Geoffrey. "Unfair Discrimination: Age-related Differences in Children's Understanding of 'Race,' Gender and Social Class." Doctoral dissertation: University of Newcastle Upon Tyne, 1989. Order Number BRDX 89948.

4228. Sibley, D. "Urban Change and the Exclusion of Minority Groups in British Cities." Geoforum 21 (1990)

4229. Sim, Joe. "Scarman: the Police Counter-attack." Socialist Register. London: Merlin, 1982.

4230. Sivanandan, A. "All That Melts Into Air Is Solid: The Hokum of New Times." Race & Class 31 (January-March 1990): 1-31. [Contemporary British society and politics.]

4231. Sivanandan, A. "Challenging Racism: Strategies for the '8o's." Race & Class 25 (Autumn 1983)

4232. Sivanandan, A. "The Enigma of the Colonised: Reflections on Naipaul's Arrival." Race & Class 32 (July-September 1990): 33-43.

4233. Sivanandan, A. "Extending Views: Challenging Racism: Strategies for the '80's." Sage Race Relations Abstracts 9 (February 1984): 15-26.

4234. Sivanandan, A. "The New Racism." New Statesman and Society 1 (November 1988): 8-9.

4235. Slack, Paul A. "The Reactions of the Poor to Poverty in England c. 1500-1750." In Les reactions des pauvres a la pauvrete: Etudes d'histoire sociale et urbaine, edited by Thomas Ries. Odense: Odense University Press, 1986.

4236. Slaney, Robert A. Reports of the House of Commons on the Education and Health of the Poorer Classes. New York: Garland, 1985 (orig.1840).

4237. Small, Stephen. Police and People in London: A Group of Young Black People. London: Policy Studies Institute, 1983.

4238. Smith, David J. and Tomlinson, Sally. The School Edict: A Study of Multi-racial Comprehensives. London: Policy Studies Insitute, 1989.

4239. Smith, F. B. The Retreat of Tuberculosis, 1850-1950. New York: Croom Helm, 1988.

4240. Smith, Stephen. Britain's Shadow Economy. New york: Oxford University Press, 1986.

4241. Smith, Stephen. "The Other Economy." New Society (October 17, 1986): Unofficial, untaxed economy.]

4242. Smith, Stephen and Wied-Nebbeling, Suzanne. The Shadow Economy in Britain and Germany. London: Anglo-German Foundation, 1986.

4243. Smith, Susan J. The Politics of Race and Residence. Citizenship, Segregation and White Supremacy in Britain. Cambridge, MA: Basil Blackwell, 1989.

4244. Smithies, B. and Fiddick, P., eds. Enoch Powell on Immigration. London: Sphere, 1969.

4245. Smyth, Rosaleen. "The British Colonial film Unit and Sub- Saharan Africa, 1939-1945." Historical Journal Film, Radio & TV 8 (1988): 285-298.

4246. Snell, K. D. M. Annals of the Labouring Poor: Social Change and Agrarian England, 1660-1900. New York: Cambridge University Press, 1985.

4247. Sobchack, Thomas. "Gypsies, Children and Criminals: Anti-authority Themes in Early British Silent Film." Journal of Popular Film and Television 17 (Spring 1989): 15-19.

4248. Solomos, John. Race and Racism in Contemporary Britain. London: Macmillan, 1989.

4249. Solomos, John. "Trends in the Political Analysis of Racism." Political Studies 34 (June 1986): 313-324.

4250. Sparks, Colin. "Fascism in Britain." International Socialism No. 71 (September 1974): 13-29.

4251. Sparks, Colin. "Fascism and the Working Class. Part Two: the National Front Party." International Socialism 2 (Winter 1978): 17-38.

4252. Spenceley, G. F. R. "The Health and Disciplining of Children in the Pillow Lace Industry in the Nineteenth Century." Textile Industry 7 (1976): 166-169.

4253. Spender, Dale, ed. The Education Papers. Women's Quest for Equality in Britain 1850-1912. New York: Methuen, 1987.

4254. Spidle, Jake W. "Victorian Juvenilia and the Image of the Black African." Journal of Popular Culture 9 (1975)

4255. Spindley, B. "'Race' and Education in Birmingham, 1960-1985: A Case Study of Multiculturalism and Anti-racism." Doctoral dissertation, Ashton University, 1985.

4256. Squires, P. "Studies in the Criminalisation of Poverty: Pauperism, Pathology and Policing." Doctoral dissertation, University of Bristol, 1985.

4257. Stallabrass, Julian. "The Idea of the Primitive: British Art and Anthropology 1918-1930." New Left Review No. 183 (September-October 1990): 95-115.

4258. Stark, Thomas. A New A-Z Income & Wealth. London: Fabian Society, 1988.

4259. Stephens, W. B. Education, Literacy, and Society, 1830- 1870: The Geography of Diversity in Provincial England. Dover, NH: Manchester University Press, 1987.

4260. Stephenson, James. "Distribution of Income {in Britain}." New Society cover 4 (April 1, 1988)

4261. No entry

4262. Stillman, Andy, ed. The Balancing Act of 1980. Parent Politics and Education. Upton Park, Slough, Berbs: NFER, 1986.

4263. Stone, John. Racial Conflict in Contemporary Society. London: Collins and Fontana, 1986.

4264. Stone, Lawrence. "Social Mobility in England, 1500-1700." Past and Present 33 (1966)

4265. Stromquist, N. P. "Gender Inequalities in Education. Accounting for Women's Subordination." British Journal of Sociology of Education 11 (1990)

4266. Stubbs, Paul. "The Reproduction of Racism in State Social Work: A Cast Study of Child Care Structures in Two "Progressive" Social Service Departments." Doctoral dissertation, University of Bath, 1988. Order No. BRDX 86887.

4267. Swart, L. Thomas. "The Educational Achievement of Ethnic Minority Pupils: A Case Study of an Inner-City Comprehensive School." Doctoral dissertation, University of Southampton, 1983.

4268. Tabili, Laura E. "Black Workers in Imperial Britain, 1914- 1945." Doctoral dissertation, Rutgers University, 1988. UMO # 8914253.

4269. Tabili, Laura E. "A Compansion and Analysis of Race and Youth as Factors in Twentieth Century Violence in Britain." University of Wisconsin, 1982.

4270. Taylor, Monica J. "'Education for All': Some Ethical Dimensions of the Swann Report." Journal of Moral Education 15 (January 1986): 68-80.

GREAT BRITAIN - GENERAL

4271. Taylor, Monica J. and Seamus Hegarty. The Best of Both Worlds? NFER-Taylor, 1986. [Review of British research on race, inequality, and schools.]

4272. Taylor, Richard and Ward, Kevin. Adult Education and the Working Clas: Education for the Missing Millions. London: Croom Helm, 1986.

4273. "Teachers' Racism Shown in N.F.E.R. Probe." Education 148 (July 1976)

4274. "Television Notes." New Community 13 (Autumn 1986): 286- 290. [Black issues on British TV.]

4275. Terror On Our Terraces: The National Front Football Violence and Leeds United. Leeds: Leeds Trades Union Council and Leeds Anti-Fascist Action, March 1988.

4276. Thane, Pat. "Women and the Poor Law in Victorian and Edwardian England." History Workshops 6 (Autumn 1978): 29- 51.

4277. Thomas, Barb and Novogrodsky, Charles. Combatting Racism in the Workplace, A Course for Workers. Toronto: Cross Cultural Communication Centre, 1983.

4278. Thomas, David N. White Bolts, Black Locks: Participation in the Inner City. London: Allen & Unwin, 1986.

4279. Thurlow, Richard C. "British Fascism and State Surveillance, 1934-1945." Intelligence and National Security 3 (1988): 77-99.

4280. Thurlow, Richard C. "Racial Population in England." Patterns of Prejudice 10 (July-August 1976): 27-32.

4281. Thurlow, Richard C. "Satan and Sambo: The Image of the Immigrant in English Racial Populist Thought since the First World War." In Hosts, Immigrants and Minorities..3490.1870-1914, edited by Kenneth Lunn. Folkestone, Kent, 1980.

4282. Tinker, Hugh. "Race and Neo-Victorianism." Encounter 38 (1972): 47-55.

4283. Titmuss, Richard. Income Distribution and Social Change. London: 1962,

4284. Tizard, Barbara and others. Young Children at School in the Inner City. Hillsdale, NJ: Lawrence Erlbaum Associates, 1988.

4285. Tomlinson, Sally. Ethnic Minority Achievement and Equality of Opportunity. Nottingham: School of Education, University of Nottingham: 1986.

4286. Tomlinson, Sally. "Towards an Efective Multicultural Education for Britain." In Affirmative Action and Positive Policies in the Education of Ethnic

<u>Minorities</u>, edited by A. Yogev and S. Tomlinson. Greenwich, CT: JAI Press, 1989.

4287. Tompson, Keith. <u>Under Seige: Racism and Violence in Britain Today</u>. London: Penguin, 1988.

4288. Torkington, Ntombenhie P. K. <u>The Racial Politics of Health- A Liverpool Profile</u>. Liverpool: Merseyside Area Profile Group, May 1983.

4289. Tosi, Arturo. <u>Immigration and Bilingual Education: A Case of Study of Movement of Population, Language Change, and Education Within the EEC</u>. New York: Pergamon, 1984. [Italians in England.]

4290. Trades Union Congress. <u>TUC Workbook on Racism</u>. London: TUC Education Department, 1983.

4291. Treble, James H. <u>Urban Poverty in Britain, 1830-1914</u>. London: Batsford, 1979.

4292. Tredinnick, D. A. S. "The Police and Ethnic Minorities in Britain since 1945, with Particular Reference to the Metropolitan Police Department." Doctoral dissertation, University of Oxford, 1985.

4293. Trollope, Joanna. <u>Britannia's Daughters: Women of the British Empire</u>. London: Hutchinson, 1983.

4294. Tronrud, Thorold J. "Dispelling the Gloom. The Extent of Poverty in Tudor and Early Stuart Towns: Some Kentish Evidence." <u>Canadian Journal of History</u> 20 (April 1985): 1- 21.

4295. Troyna, Barry and Williams, Jenny. <u>Racism, Education and the State: The Racialisation of Educational Policy</u>. London: Croom Helm, 1986.

4296. Tullock, Gordon. <u>The Economics of Wealth and Poverty</u>. London: Wheatsheaf, 1986.

4297. Turner, Barry. <u>Equality for Some: The Story of Girls' Education</u>. London: Ward Lock Educational, 1974.

4298. Tuttle, Carolyn. "Children at Work in the British Industrial Revolution." Doctoral dissertation, Northwestern University, UMO# 8621879.

4299. Twitchin, John, ed. <u>The Black and White Media Book</u>. Stoke on Trent, 1988.

4300. <u>Unequal Comrades: Trade Unions, Equal Opportunities and Racism</u>. Centre for Research in Ethnic Relations Arts Building: University of Warwick, Coventry, 1986.

4301. Urry, John and Wakeford, John, eds. <u>Power in Britain</u>. London: 1973.

4302. Usker, Graham. "Employment Training: Britain's New Bantustans." Race & Class 32 (July-September 1990): 45-56.

4303. Verma, Gajendra K. and Ashworth Brandon. Ethnicity and Educational Achievement in British Schools. Basingstoke: Macmillan, 1986.

4304. Verma, Gajendra K. "The Swann Report and Ethnic Achievement: A Comment." New Community 12 (Winter 1985): 470-475.

4305. "A Very Conservative Lot: The Social Background of Judges and Magistrates." Christian Action Journal (Autumn, 1986)

4306. Vicinus, Martha, ed. Suffer and Be Still. Women in the Victorian Age. Bloomington: Indiana University Press, 1973.

4307. Walber, Martin. With Extreme Prejudice: An Investigation into Police Vigilantism in Manchester. London: Canary Press, 1986.

4308. Walby, Sylvia. Theorizing Patriarchy. London: 1990.

4309. Walfe, Joel D. "Class Formation and Democracy: The Decline of Working-class Power in Britain." Western European Politics 9 (July 1986): 343-361.

4310. Walkendine, Valene and others, eds. Language, Gender, and Childhood. Boston, Ma: Routledge & Kegan Paul, 1985.

4311. Walker, Monica. "Interpreting Race and Crime Statistics." Journal of the Royal Statistical Society 150, part i (1987): 39-56.

4312. Wallace. C. School, Work and Unemployment: Social and Cultural Reproduction on the Isle of Sheppey. Doctoral dissertation: University of Kent, 1984.

4313. Walvin, James. England, Slaves and Freedom, 1776-1838. Oxford: University Press of Mississippi, 1986.

4314. Walvin, James, ed. Slavery and British Society 1776-1846. London: Macmillan, 1983.

4315. Wandsworth Policing Campaign. Racism in the Police Force Is Now a Disciplinary Offence. London: Wandsworth Policing Campaign, 1986.

4316. Waters, Robert. Ethnic Minorities and the Criminal Justice System. Brookfiled, VT: Gower, 1990.

4317. Watkins, Steve. "Racialism in the National Health Service." Radical Community Medicine No. 16 (Winter 1983): 55-60.

4318. Watson, Ian. *Double Depression: Schooling, Unemployment and Family Life in the Eighties*. Boston, Ma.: G. Allen & Unwin, 1985.

4319. Watson, J. K. P. "From Assimilation to Anti-Racism: Changing Educational Policies in England and Wales." *Journal of Multilingual and Multicultural Development* 9 (1988): 531-532.

4320. Watson, K. and Roberts, R. "Multicultural Education and Teacher Training- The Picture After Swann." *Journal of Multilingual and Multicultural Development* 9 (1988): 339- 352.

4321. Weakliem, David. "Class and Party in Britain, 1964-1983." *Sociology* 23 (May 1989): 285-297.

4322. Webber, G. C. *The Ideology of the British Right, 1918-1959*. New York, 1986.

4323. Weeks, Alan. *Comprehensive Schools: Past, Present and Future*. New York: Methuen, 1986.

4324. Weinter, Merle H. "Fundamental Misconceptions about Fundamental Rights: The Changing Nature of Women's Rights in the EEC and their Application in the United Kingdom." *Harvard International Law Journal* 31 (Spring 1990): 565-610.

4325. Welch, Susan and Donley T. Studlar. "The Impact of Race on Political Behaviour in Britain." *British Journal of Political Science* 15 (1985): 528-539.

4326. Westwood, Sallie and others. *Sadness in My Heart: Racism and Mental Health*. Leicester: Leicester Black Mental Health Group, University of Leicester, 1989.

4327. Whitaker, Ben. *Teaching About Prejudice*. London: Minority Rights Group, 1985.

4328. White, Jeny. *The Worst Street in North London: Campbell Bunk, Islington, between the Wars*. Boston, MA: Routledge & Kegan Paul, 1986.

4329. Whiteley, Paul and Stephen Winyard. *Pressure for the Poor. The Poverty Lobby and Policy Making*. New York: Methuen, 1987.

4330. Widgery, David. *Beating Time: Riot 'N' Race 'N' Rock 'N' Roll*. London: Chatto and Windus, 1986.

4331. Widgery, David. "The Rise of Radical Rock." *New Socialist* (November-December 1981): 35-77.

4332. Widlake, Paul. *Reducing Educational Disadvantage*. Milton Keynes: Open University Press, 1986.

4333. Wilce, Hilary. "Living on a Short Fuse." *Times Educational Supplement*, (November 1, 1985)

4334. Wilkinson, J. P. "Why Magistrates Need Race Relations Training." *New Community* 12 (Winter 1985): 476-484.

4335. Wilkinson, Richard G. "Class Mortality Differentials, Income Distribution and Trends in Poverty, 1921-1981." *Journal of Social Policy* 18 (July 1989): 307-335.

4336. Wilkinson, Richard G. "Income Distribution and Mortality: A Natural Experiment." *Sociology of Health & Illness* 12 (December 1990)

4337. Wilkinson, Richard G., ed. *Class and Health. Research and Longitudinal Data*. London: Tavistock, 1986.

4338. Williams, Fiona. *Social Policy: A Critical Introduction. Issues of Race, Gender and Class*. Cambridge, MA: Basil Blackwell, 1989.

4339. Williamson, Jeffrey S. *Did British Capitalism Breed Inequality?* Boston, MA: Allen & Unwin, 1985.

4340. Williamson, John. "Threat of Racialism in Britain." *Political Affairs* 45 (January 1966)

4341. Williams, Karel. *From Pauperism to Poverty*. London: 1981.

4342. Willis, Paul. "Unemployment: The Final Inequality." *British Journal of Sociology of Education* 7 (1986): 155-169.

4343. Wilson, Elizabeth. *Only Halfway to Paradise: Women in Postwar Britain, 1945-1960*. New York: Tavistock, 1980.

4344. Winchester, Hilary P. M. "Women and Children Last: The Poverty and Marginalization of One-Parent Families." *Transactions, Institute of British Geographers* 15 (1990)

4345. Winks, Robin. "A System of Commands: the Infrastructure of Race Contact." In *Studies in British Imperial History*, edited by Gordon Martel. New York, St. Martin's Press, 1986.

4346. Winter, J. M. *The Great War and the British People*. Cambridge, MA: Harvard University Press, 1986.

4347. Winter, J. H. "The Webbs and the Non-white World: A Case of Socialist Realism." *Journal of Contemporary History* 9 (January 1974)

4348. Wohl, Anthony S. "The Bitter Cry of Outcast London." *International Review of Social History* 13 (1968): 189-245.

4349. Wolfee. W.J. "Values in Conflict: Incitement to Racial Hatred and the Public Order Act 1986." Public Law (Spring 1987): 855-95.

4350. Wood, Deborah A. "Educational Opportunities in Tudor York." Doctoral dissertation, University of Nebraska, 1980.

4351. Woods, P. and Grugeon, E. "Pupils and Race: Integration and Disintegration in Primary Schools." British Journal of Sociology of Education 11 (1990)

4352. Woods, R. I., and others. "The Causes of Rapid Infant Mortality Decline in England and Wales, 1861-1921 (Part II)." Population Studies 43 (March 1989)

4353. Work and the Jobless. School of Environmental Studies, Gloucestershire College of Arts and Technology, Oxstalls Land, Gloucester GLL 9HW, England: 1986. [Racial discrimination in employment.]

4354. Worpole, Ken. "Scholarship Boy: The Poetry of Tony Harrison." New Left Review No. 153 (September-October 1985): 63-74.

4355. Wright, J. F. "Real Wage Resistance: Eighty Years of the British Cost of Living." Oxford Economic Papers 36 (November 1984): supplement.

4356. Yates, L. "Theorizing Inequality Today." British Journal of Sociology of Education 7 (1986): 119-134.

4357. Yelling, J. A. Slums and Slum Clearance in Victorian London. London: Allen & Unwin, 1986.

4358. Yeo, E. and Yeo, S., eds. Popular Culture and Class Conflict 1590-1914. Brighton: 1981.

4359. Yuval-Dravis, Nira. "Ethnic/Racial Divisions and the Nation in Britain and Australia." Capital & CLass No. 28 (Spring 1986): 87-103.

4360. Zabalza, A. and Tzannatos, A. "The Effect of Britain's Anti-discriminatory Legislation on Relative Pay and Employment." Economic Journal 95 (September 1985)

GREECE

4361. Abog Loko, J. "La communaute noire en Grece." Peuples Noirs, Peuples Afri 4 (July-August 1981): 55-84.

4362. Bahcheli, Tozun. "The Muslim-Turkish Community in Greece: Problems and Prospects." Journal (Institute of Muslim Minority Affairs 8 (1987): 109-120.

4363. Ben, Joseph. "Jewish Leadership in Greece during the Holocaust." In Patterns of the Jewish Leadership in Nazi Europe (1977): 335-352. [Yad Vashem.]

4364. Bowman, Steven B. and Kerem Yitzchak. "Greece." In Encyclopedia of the Holocaust (1990): 610-617. [New York: Macmillan.]

4365. Bowman, Steven B. "Jews in Wartime Greece." Jewish Social Studies 48 (Winter 1986): 45-62.

4366. Bowman, Steven B. "Salonika." In Encyclopedia of the Holocaust, IV, 1324-1326. New York: Macmillan, 1990.

4367. Carpi, D. "Notes on the History of the Jews in Greece during the Holocaust Period: The Attitude of the Italians (1941-1943)." In Festschrift in Honor of Dr. George S. Wise, edited by H. Ben-Shahar and others, 25-62. Tel Aviv: 1981.

4368. Colakis, Marianthe. "Images of the Turk in Greek Fiction of the Asia Minor Disaster." Journal of Modern Greek Studies 4 (1986): 99-106.

4369. Eckert, Rainer. "Die Verfolgung der griechischen Juden in deutschen Okkupationsgebiet Saloniki-agais vom April 1941 bis zum Abschluss der Deportationen in August 1943." Bulletin des Arbeitskreises Zweiter Weltkrieg Nos. 1-4 (1986): 41- 69.

4370. Freris, A. F. The Greek Economy in the Twentieth Century. New York: St. Martin's Press, 1986.

4371. Hoffmann, Peter. "Roncalli in the Second World War: Peace Initiatives, the Greek Famine, and the Persecution of the Jews." Journal of Ecclesiastical History 40 (January 1989): 74-99.

4372. Hoppe, Hans-Joachim. "Bulgarian Nationalities Policy in Occupied Thrace and Aegean Macedonia." Nationalities Papers 14 (1986): 89-100.

4373. Kitroeff, Alexandros. "Greek Wartime Attitudes towards the Jews in Athens." Forum on the Jewish People, Zionism and Israel No. 60 (Summer 1987): 41-51.

4374. Kofos, Evangelos. "The Macedonian Question: The Politics of Mutation." Balkan Studies (Greece) 27 (1986): 157-172.

4375. Liakos, Anthony. "Problems on the Formation of the Greek Working Class." Et. balkaniques 24 (1988): 43-54.

4376. Livada, Alexander. "Aspects of Income Inequality in Greece, 1959-1982." Doctoral dissertation, University of Essex, 1988. Order No. BRD-84454.

4377. Molho, Michael and Nelhama, Joseph. The Destruction of Greek Jewry 1941-1944. Jerusalem: Yad Vashem, 1965.

4378. Molho, Rena. "The Jewish Community of Salonika and Its Incorporation into the Greek State, 1912-1919." Middle Eastern Studies 24 (1988): 391-403.

4379. Molho, Rena. "Venizelos and the Jewish Community of Salonika, 1912-1919." Journal of the Hellenic Diaspora 13 (1986): 113-123.

4380. Samatas, Minces. "Greek McCarthyism: A Comparative Assessment of Greek Post-Civil War Repressive Anti-communism and the U.S. Truman-McCarthy Era." Journal of the Hellenic Disapora 13 (1986): 5-75.

4381. Sapounas, G. "Household Expenditure in Greece. The Case of Socioeconomic Groups." Greek Economic Review 6 (August 1984)

4382. Scjaky, Leon. Farewell to Salonica: Portrait of an Era. New York: Current Books, 1946.

4383. Sevillias, Errikos. Athens to Auschwitz. Translated by Nikos Stavroulakis. New York: New York University Press, 1987.

4384. Stavrianos, L. S. "The Jews of Greece." Journal of Central European Affairs 8 (October 1948)

4385. Steinberg, Jonathan. All or Nothing: The Axis and the Holocaust. Routledge & Kegan Paul, 1990. [Jews under Italian and German occupation in Yugoslavia, Greece, and France, 1941-1943.]

4386. Tsakloglou, P. "Aspects of Poverty in Greece." Review of Income and Wealth (December 1990)

GUATEMALA

4387. Adams, Richard N. *Cucifixion by Power: Essays on Guatemalan National Social Structure, 1944-1966*. Austin: University of Texas Press, 1970.

4388. Aguilera Peralta, Gabriel and others. *Dialectic del terror en Guatemala*. San Jose, Costa Rica: Educa Press, 1981.

4389. Anderson, Ken and Simon, Jean-Maries. "Permanent Counterinsurgency in Guatemala." *Telos* No. 73 (Fall 1987): 9-46.

4390. Arias, Arturo. "Cultura popular, culturas indigenas, genocidio y etnocidio en Guatemala." *Boletin de antropologia americana* 7 (1983): 57-77.

4391. Arias, Arturo. "La cultura, la politica y el poder en Guatemala." *Boletin de Antropologia Americana* (Mexico) 13 (1986): 75-105.

4392. Asturias, M. Angel. *El problema social del Indio*. Paris: 1971.

4393. Barillas, Edgar and others. "Formación nacional y realidad étnica en Guatemala." *América Indigena* 49 (January-March 1989): 101-129.

4394. Le Baron, Alan A. "Impaired Democracy in Guatemala, 1949- 1951." Doctoral dissertation, University of Florida, 1988. UMO # 8923991.

4395. Bermudez, Fernando. *Death and Resurrection in Guatemala*. Maryknoll, New York: Orbis, 1986.

4396. Black, George and others. *Garrison Guatemala*. New York: Monthly Review Press, 1985.

4397. Bossen, Laurel. "Plantations and Labor Force Discrimination in Guatemala." *Current Anthropology* 23 (1982): 263-268.

4398. Bunleigh, ELizabeth. "The Pattern of Childhood Malnutrition in San Jose Poaquil, Guatemala." University of California, 1986. UMO # 8621032.

4399. Cambranes, J. C. Coffee and Peasants: The Origins of the Modern Plantation Economy in Guatemala, 1853-1897. South Woodstock, VT: Plumstock Meso-american Studies, 1985.

4400. Carmack, R. "Indians and the Guatemalan Revolution." Cultural Survival Quarterly 7 (1983): 52-54.

4401. Chea Urruela, José Luis. Guatemala: la cruz fragmentada. San Jose: DEI, 1988.

4402. Davis, Shelton H. "The Social Roots of Political Violence in Guatemala." Cultural Survival Quarterly 7 (1983): 4-11.

4403. Eble, Roland H. "When Indians Take Power: Conflict and Consensus in San Juan Ostuncalco." In Harvest of Violence: The Maya Indians and the Guatemalan Crisis, edited by Robert M. Carmack. Norman: University of Oklahoma Press, 1988.

4404. Figueroa Ibarra, Carlos. El proletariado rural en el agro guatemalteco, 3rd ed. Guatemala City: Editorial Universitaria, 1980. [Indians.]

4405. Gleijeses, Piero. "The Agrarian Reform of Jacobo Arbenz." Journal of Latin American Studies 21 (October 1989)

4406. Gleijeses, Piero. Shattered Hope. The Guatemalan Revolution and the United States, 1944-1954. Princeton, NJ: Princeton University Press, 1991.

4407. Guatemala: a Government Program of Political Murder. London: Amnesty International, 1981.

4408. Handy, Jim. Gift of the Devil. A History of Guatemala. Boston: South End Press, 1985.

4409. Handy, Jim. "'A Sea of Indians': Ethnic Conflict and the Guatemalan Revolution, 1944-1952." The Americas 46 (October 1989): 189-204.

4410. Hendrickson, Carol. "Guatemala- Everybody's Indian When the Occasion's Right." Cultural Survival Quarterly 9, #2 (1985): 22-23.

4411. Jones, Grant D. Maya Resistance to Spanish Rule: Time and History on a Colonial Frontier. Alburquerque: University of New Mexico Press, 1989.

4412. Kinzer, Stephen. "Walking the Tightrope in Guatemala." New York Times Magazine (November 11, 1986)

4413. Kunst, J. "Notes on Negroes in Guatemala during the Seventeenth Century." Journal of Negro History 1,4 (1916): 392-398.

4414. Lessmann, R. "500 Jahre Versklavung der Maya: 25 Jahre Krieg gegen die Zivilbevolkerung." Pogrom 150 (1989): 42- 45.

4415. Lovell, William George. Conquest and Survival in Colonial Guatemala: A Hitorical Geography of the Cuchumatan Highlands, 1500-1821. Kingston: McGill-Queen's University Press, 1985.

4416. Lovell, William George. "From Conquest to Counter- Insurgency." Cultural Survival Quarterly 9, #2 (1985): 46- 49. [Guatemalan Indians.]

4417. Lovell, William George. "Surviving Conquest: The Maya of Guatemala in Historical Perspective." Latin American Research Review 23 (1988): 25-58.

4418. Marks, Frederick W., III. "The CIA and Castillo Armas in Guatemala, 1954." Diplomatic History 14 (1990): 67-86.

4419. McCreery, David. "Debt Servitude in Rural Guatemala, 1876- 1936." Hispanic American Historical Review 63 (November 1983): 735-760.

4420. McCreery, David. "Land, Labor and Violence in Highland Guatemala: San Juan Ixcoy (Huehuetenango), 1893-1945." Americas 45 (1988): 237-249.

4421. Montejo, Victor. Testimony: Death of a Guatemalan Village. Willimantie, CT: Curbstone Press, 1988. [Translated by Victor Perera.]

4422. Paul, Benjamin D. and Demarest, William J. "The Operation of a Death Squad in San Pedro La Laguna." In Harvest of Violence: The Maya Indians and the Guatemalan Crisis, edited by Robert M. Carmack. Norman: University of Oklahoma Press, 1988.

4423. Sheean, Edward R. F. "A 'Triangle of Death' for Guatemala's Indians." Boston Globe (November 25, 1986)

4424. Simon, Jean-Marie. Guatemala: Eternal Spring, Eternal Tyranny. New York: Norton, 1987.

4425. Spiegler, S. "Anti-Semitism in the Guatemalan Press." Journal of Jewish Communal Service 59 (Fall 1982): 91.

4426. Vides de Orive, Enna and Schneider, Pablo R. Análisis de la situacion económica de Guatemala, 1965-1984. 2d ed. Guatemala City: Centro de Investigaciones Economicas Nacionales, 1985.

4427. Warren, Kay B. The Symbolism of Subordination: Indian Identity in a Guatemalan Town. Austin: University of Texas Press, 1973.

4428. Wasserstrom, R. "Revolution in Guatemala: Peasants and Politics under the Arbenz Government." Comparative Studies in Society and History 17 (1975): 443-478.

4429. Woodward, R. L. Jr. Class Privilege and Economic Development. Chapel Hill: University of North Carolina Press, 1966.

GUINEA-BISSAU

4430. Barreto, M. A. "Pedagogie africaine-innovation et participation: une experience recente d'education en milieu rural en Guinee-Bissau: les C.E.P.I." Cah. ped. afric. (1983- 1984): 40-79.

4431. Chabal, Patrick. "National Liberation in Portuguese Guinea." African Affairs (London) 80 (January 1981): 75-100.

4432. Chabal, Patrick. "Revolutionary Democracy in Africa: The Case of Guinea-Bissau." In Political Domination in Africa: Reflections on the limits of Power, edited by Chabal. New York: Cambridge University Press, 1986.

4433. Cunningham, James. "The Colonial Period in Guine." Tarikh 6 (1980): 31-46.

4434. Davidson, Basil. "On Revolutionary Nationalism: The Legacy of Cabral." Race & Class 27 (Winter 1986): 21-46.

4435. Forrest, Joshua B. "Guinea-Bissau Since Independence: A Decade of Domestic Power Struggle." Journal of Modern African Studies 25 (March 1987): 95-116.

4436. Galli, Rosemary E. and Jones, Jocelyn. Guinea Bissau: Politics, Economics, and Society. Boulder, CO: L. Rienner, 1987.

4437. Galli, Rosemary E. "The Political Economy of Guinea-Bissau: Second Thoughts." Africa 59 (1989): 371-380.

4438. Gertzel, Cherry. "Guinea-Bissau: Revolution and Development." In Revolution: A History of the Idea, edited by David Close and Carl Bridge. Totowa, NJ: Barnes and Noble, 1985.

4439. Gomes, Joaquim and others. "Malnutricao e mortalidade infantil nas regioes de Tombali, Cacheu, Oio, Biombo e Gabu." Boletim de Informacao Socio-Economica 5 (September 1989): 11-44.

4440. Heimer, Franz-Wilhelm. "Bildung als Praxis der Befreiung: Ansatze alternativer Erziehung in Guinea-Bissau." Bildung Erziehung 33 (1981): 70-85.

4441. Lopes, Carlos. Guinea Bissau: From Liberation Struggle to Independent Statehood. London: Zed Press, 1986. [Translated by Michael Wolfers.]

4442. Lyon, Judson M. "Marxism and Ethno-Nationalism in Guinea- Bissau, 1956-1976." Ethnic and Racial Studies 3 (April 1980): 156-168.

4443. Olaniyan, Richard. Guinea-Bissau in Anglo-Portuguese Relations, 1860-1870: A Study in the Diplomacy of Colonial Acquisition. Ibadan, Nigeria: African Press, 1984.

GUYANA

4444. Bartels, Dennis A. "Class Conflict and Racist Ideology in the Formation of Modern Guyanese Society." Canadian Review of Sociology and Anthropology 14 (1977): 396-405.

4445. Bartels, Dennis A. "Class Conflict and Racist Ideology in the Formation of Modern Guyanese Society." Doctoral dissertation, University of Alberta, 1978.

4446. Bartels, Dennis A. "Ethnicity, Ideology, and Class Struggle in Guyanese Society." Anthropologica 22 (1981): 45-60.

4447. Beaumont, J. The New Slavery: An Account of Indian and Chinese Immigrants in British Guiana. London: W. Ridgway, 1871.

4448. Cross, Malcolm. The East Indians of Guyana and Trinidad. London: Minority Rights Group, 1972.

4449. David, Peggy A. "The Afro-Guyanese People: A Study of Social Organization during the Colonial Period." Doctoral dissertation, Howard University, 1986. UMO # 8807171.

4450. Forte, Janette. "Pueblos indigena de Guyana." America Indigena 48 (1988): 323-352.

4451. Fredericks, Marcel and others. Society and Health in Guyana: The Sociology of Health Care in a Developing Nation. Durham, NC: Carolina Academic Press, 1986.

4452. Glasgow, Roy W. Guyana: Race and Politics Among Africans and East Indians. The Hague: Martinus Nijhoff, 1970.

4453. Hintzer, Percy C. "Ethnicity, Class and Internal Capitalist Penetration in Guyana and Trinidad." Social and Economic Studies 34 (1985): 107-164.

4454. Ho, Christine. "'Hold the Chow Mein, Gimme Soca': Creolization of the Chinese in Guyana, Trinidad and Jamaica." Amerasia 15 (1989): 3-25.

4455. Inamina, Odida T. Mineworkers of Guyana. The Making of a Working Class. London: Zed Press, 1987. [Alcan's Plantation Mackenzie bauxite mine and company town.]

4456. Jain, Prakash C. "Exploitation and Reproduction of Migrant Indian Labour in Colonial Guyana and Malaysia." Journal of Contemporary Asia 18 (1988): 189-206.

4457. Jeffrey, Henry B. and Baber, Colin. Guyana: Politics, Economic, and Society: Beyond the Burnham Era. Boulder, Co: L. Rienner, 1986.

4458. Mangru, Basdeo. "Indian Labour in British Guiana." History Today 36 (April 1986): 43-48.

4459. Menezes, Mary N. British Policy Towards the Amerindians in British Guiana, 1803-1873. New York: Oxford University Press, 1977.

4460. Moore, Brian L. Race, Power, and Social Segmentation in Colonial Society: Guyana after Slavery, 1838-1891. New York: Gordon and Breach, 1987.

4461. Moore, R. J. "East Indians and Negroes in British Guiana, 1838-1880." University of Sussex, 1970.

4462. Rodney, Walter. "Guyana: The Making of the Labour Force." Race & Class 22 (Spring 1981): 231-252.

4463. Rodney, Walter. "Immigrants and Racial Attitudes in Guyanese History." Institute of Commonwealth Studies Seminar Papers (1977)

4464. Sanders, Andrew. "British Colonial Policy and the Role of Amerindians in the Politics of the Nationalist Period in British Guiana, 1945-1968." Social and Economic Studies 36 (1987): 77-98.

HAITI

4465. Aristide, Jean-Bertrand. In the Parish of the Poor: Writings from Haiti. Translated by Amy Wilentz. Orbis Books, 1990.

4466. Baez Evertsz, Franc. Braceros haitianos en la Republica Dominicana. 2d ed. Santo Domingo: Editora Taller, 1986.

4467. Cole, Hubert. Christophe, King of Haiti. London: 1967.

4468. Constable, Pamela. "Seeking Freedom from Prison of Illiteracy." Boston Globe, (November 25, 1986)

4469. Danner, Mark D. "The Struggle for a Democratic Haiti." New York Times Magazine, (June 24, 1987)

4470. Desmangles, L. G. "The Maroon Republics and Religious Diversity in Colonial Haiti." Anthropos 85 (1990)

4471. Diaz Santana Arismendi. "The Role of Haitian Braceros in Dominican Sugar Production." Latin American Perspectives 3 (1972): 12-132.

4472. Dupuy, Alex. Haiti in the World Economy: Class, Race, and Underdevelopment Since 1700. Boulder, Co.: Westview, 1989.

4473. Ferguson, James A. "Le Premier des Noirs: The Nineteenth- Century Image of Toussaint L'Ouverture." Nineteenth-Century French Studies 15 (Summer 1987): 394-407.

4474. Ferguson, James A. A State of Hell. Haiti Under the Duvaliers. New York: Blackwell, 1987.

4475. Fick, Carolyn E. The Making of Haiti. The Saint Dominque Revolution from Below. Knoxville: University of Tennessee Press, 1990.

HAITI

4476. Fiehrer, Thomas. "Political Violence in The Periphery: The Haitian Massacre of 1937." Race & Class 32 (October- December 1990): 1-20.

4477. Garrigus, John. "Between Servitude and Citizenship: Free Coloreds in Pre-Revolutionary Saint Dominique." Doctoral dissertation, John Hopkins University, 1988.

4478. Labelle, Micheline. Idéologie de couleur et classes sociales en Haiti. Montreal: Les Presses de L'Université de Montreal, 1978.

4479. Leyburn, James G. The Haitian People. New Haven, CT: Yale University Press, 1966.

4480. Lobb, John. "Caste and Class in Haiti." American Journal of Sociology 46 (1940): 23-34.

4481. Logan, Rayford. Haiti and the Dominican Republic. London: 1968.

4482. Lundahl, Mats. Peasants and Poverty: A Study of Haiti. New York: St. Martin's Press, 1979.

4483. Massing, Michael. "Haiti: The New Violence." New York Review of Books (December 3, 1987)

4484. McCarthy, Tim. "Haiti: Literacy Under the Gun." National Catholic Reporter (July 15, 1988)

4485. Moreau de Saint-Mery, Mederic L. E. A Civilization that Perished: The Last years of White Colonial Rule in Haiti. Translated by Ivor D. Spencer. University Press of America, 1986.

4486. Ott, Thomas O. The Haitian Revolution, 1789-1804. Knoxville: University of Tennessee Press, 1987.

4487. Pamphile, Léon D. "America's Policy-making in Haitian Education, 1915-1934." Journal of Negro Education 54 (1985): 99-108.

4488. Pamphile, Léon D. L'éducation en Haiti sous l'occupation américaine 1915-1934. Port-au-Prince: 1988.

4489. Pattee, Richard. Jean Jacques Dessalines: Fundador de Haiti. Havana: 1936.

4490. Pierre- Charles, Gerard. "Sobre la problematica actual del hombres negro en las sociedaded dependientes y subdesarrollados; el caso de Haiti." Casa de las Americas 11 (1971): 119-126.

4491. Plant, Roger. Sugar and Modern Slavery: A Tale of Two Countries. Atlantic Highlands, NJ: Zed Books, 1987. [Haiti and the Dominican Republic.]

4492. Plummer, Brenda G. "The Afro American Response to the Occupation of Haiti, 1915-1934." Phylon No. 43 (June 1982)

4493. Plummer, Brenda G. Haiti and the Great Powers. Baton Rouge: Louisiana State University Press, 1988.

4494. Plummer, Brenda G. "Haitian Migrants and Background Imperialism." Race and Class 26 (Spring 1985): 35-44.

4495. Plummer, Brenda G. "The Metropolitan Connection: Foreign and Semi-Foreign Elites in Haiti, 1900-1915." Latin America Research Review 19 (1984): 119-142.

4496. Plummer, Brenda G. "Race, Nationality, and Trade in the Caribbean: The Syrians in Haiti, 1903-1934." International History Review 3 (1981): 517-539.

4497. Rotberg, Robert A. "Haiti's Past Mortgages Its Future." Foreign Affairs 67 (Fall 1988)

4498. Rotberg, Robert A. Haiti: The Politics of Squalor. Boston, MA: Houghton Mifflin, 1971.

4499. Sarigiania, Steven M. A Geographic and Political Analysis of Poverty in Haiti. Master's thesis: Pennsylvania State University, 1985.

4500. Stief, William. "Tens of Thousands of Children in Slavery in Impoverished Haiti." National Catholic Reporter (November 16, 1990)

4501. Thoumi, Francisco E. "Social and Political Obstacles to Economic Development in Haiti." In The Newer Caribbean: Decolonization, Democracy, and Development, edited by P. Henry and C. Stone. Philadelphia, PA: ISHI, 1983.

4502. Tolentino, H. "El Fenómeno racial en Haiti y en la Republica Dominicana." In Problems dominico-haitianos y del Caribe. Gérard Pierre-Charles and others. México City: Universidad National Autonomos de Mexico, 1973.

4503. Trouillot, Michel-Rolph. "Haiti and Neo-colonialism." Monthly Review Newsletter (Summer 1990)

4504. Trouillot, Michel-Rolph. Haiti: State Against Nation. The Origins and Legacy of Duvalierism. New York: Monthly Review Press, 1990.

4505. Trouillot, Michel-Rolph. "Motion in the System: Coffee, Color, and Slavery in Eighteenth-Century Saint-Dominique." Review 5 (1982): 331-388.

4506. Trouillot, Michel-Rolph. Nation, State, and Society in Haiti, 1804-1984. Washington, D.C.: Woodrow Wilson International Center for Scholars, 1985.

4507. U. S. Congress 99th 1st session, House of Representatives, Committee on Foreign Affairs, Subcommittee on Human Rights and International Organization. Human Rights in Haiti: Hearing. Washington, D.C.: GPO, 1985.

4508. Wilentz, Amy. "Bringing Down Baby." Village Voice (April 29, 1986): [Haiti after Jean-Claude Duvalier.]

HONDURAS

4509. Acker, Alison. Honduras: The Making of a Banana Republic. Toronto: Between the Lines, 1988.

4510. Beaucage, P. "Economic Anthropology of the Black Carib of Honduras." Doctoral dissertation, University of London, 1969-70.

4511. Boyer, Jefferson C. "Capitalism, Campesinos and Colonies in Southern Honduras." Urban Anthropology 15 (Spring- Summer 1986): 3-24.

4512. Bueso, Julio A. El Subdesarrollo hondureno. Tegucigalpa e Honduras: Editorial Universitaria, 1987.

4513. Honduras Direccion General de Estadisticas y Censos. Mortalidad infantil: los riesgos de muerte infantil en diferentas contextos sociales y geograficos, 1955-1985. San Jose, Costa Rica: Centro Latinamericano de Demografia, January 2988.

4514. Newson, Linda. The Cost of Conquest: Indian Decline in Honduras under Spanish Rule. Boulder, Co.: Westview, 1986.

HUNGARY

4515. Balogh, Eva S. "The Nationality Policy of the Hungarian Soviet Republic of 1919." Doctoral dissertation, Yale University, 1968.

4516. Barney, Louis. "East of Equality." Boston Globe Magazine, (December 30, 1990): [Women in Hungary and Czechoslovakia.]

4517. Berend, Ivan R. and Ranki, G. The Hungarian Economy in the Twentieth Century. New York: St. Martin's Press, 1985.

4518. Bernat, Tivadar, ed. An Economic Geography of Hungary. Translated by I. Veges. Budapest: Akademiai Kiado, 1985.

4519. Bigler, Robert M. "Heil Hitler and Heil Horthy! The Nature of Hungarian Racist Nationalism and Its Impact on German-Hungarian Relations." East European Quarterly 8 (Fall 1974): 251-272.

4520. Birkas, Maria. "Access to Culture As a Public Service in Hungary: 1948-1978." Doctoral dissertation, University of California, 1985. UMO # 8603932.

4521. Bitton, Livia. "Jewish Nationalism in Hungary." Doctoral dissertation, New York University, 1968.

4522. Borsody, Stephen, ed. The Hungarians: A Divided Nation. New Haven, CT.: Yale Center for International and Area Studies, 1988.

4523. Braham, R.L. The Politics of Genocide: The Holocaust in Hungary. 2 vols. New York: Columbia University Press, 1983.

4524. Braham, R.L., ed. The Tragedy of Hungarian Jewry. New York: Institute for Holocaust Studies, CUNY, 1987.

4525. Cadzow, John F. and others, eds. Transylvania. The Roots of Ethnic Conflict. Kent, Ohio: Kent State University Press, 1984.

4526. Daniel Zauzsa. "Public Housing, Personal Income and Central Redistribution in Hungary." Acta Oeconomica 31 (1983)

4527. Daniel, Zauzsa. "The Effect of Housing Allocation on Social Inequality in Hungary." Journal of Comparative Economics 9 (December 1985): 391-409.

4528. Deak, Istvan. "Collaborationism in Europe, 1940-1945: The Case of Hungary." Austrian History Yearbook 15-16 (1979- 1985): 157-164.

4529. Deak, Istvan. "Hungarian Fascism." In The European Right, edited by Hans Rogger and Eugene Weber. Berkeley: University of California Press, 1965.

4530. Deak, Istvan. "The Peculiarities of Hungarian Fascism." In The Holocaust in Hungary: Forty Years Later, edited by Randolph L. Braham and Bela Vago, 43-51. New York:Institute for Holocaust Studies, 1985.

4531. Don, Yehuda. "The Economic Dimensions of Antisemitism: Anti-Jewish Legislation in Hungary, 1938-1944." East European Quarterly 20 (1986): 447-465.

4532. Eros, J. "Hungary." In Fascism in Europe. rev. ed., edited by S. J. Woolf. London: Methuen, 1982.

4533. Falus-Szikra, K. "Wage and Income Disparities between the First and Second Economies in Hungary." Acta Oeconomica 36 (1986)

4534. Fischer, Rolf. Entwicklungstufen des Antisemitismus in Ungarn, 1867-1939. Die Zerstorung der Magyarisch-judischen Symbiose. Munich: R. Oldenbourg Verlag, 1988.

4535. Flakierski, Henryk. Economic Reform and Income Distribution. A Case Study of Hungary and Poland. Armouk, New York: Sharpe, 1986.

4536. Gacs, E. "Hungary's Social Expenditures in International Comparison." Acta Oeconomica 36 (1986)

4537. Garai, George. "Rakosi and the 'Anti-Zionist' Campaign of 1952-1953." Soviet Jewish Affairs 12 (1982): 19-36.

4538. Hanak, Peter. "Economics, Society, and Sociopolitical Thought in Hungary during the Age of Capitalism." Austrian History Yearbook 11 (1975): 113-135.

4539. Haselsteiner, Horst. "Schulstruktur und nationale Identitat der Serben Ungarns an Beginn des 20. Jahrhunderts." Osterr Osth 26 (1984): 405-416.

4540. Heinrich, Hans-Georg. *Hungary: Politics, Economics, and Society*. Boulder, CO: L. Rienner Publishers, 1986.

4541. Herzog, Ferencz. "National Minorities in Hungary." *New Hungarian Quarterly* 19 (1978): 89-96.

4542. "Is There a 'Jewish Question' in Present-Day Hungary?" *Soviet Jewish Affairs* 18 (Winter 1988): 56-74.

4543. Janos, Andrew C. *The Politics of Backwardness in Hungary, 1825-1945*. Princeton, NJ: Princeton University Press, 1981.

4544. Juhasz, Gyula. "Hungarian Intellectual Life and the 'Jewish Problem' During World War II." In *The Holocaust in Hungary Forty Years Later*, edited by Randolph L. Braham. New York: Institute for Holocaust Studies, 1985.

4545. Kafer, Istvan. "Slovak and Hungarian Culture, Past and Present." *New Hungarian Quarterly* 29 (1988): 150-160.

4546. Kamm, Henry. "Hungary's Germans Reasserting Identity." *New York Times*, (November 12, 1990)

4547. Karady, Victor. "Post-Holocaust Hungarian Jewry, 1945-1948: Class Structure, Re-Stratification and Potential for Social Mobility." *Stud. Contemp. Jewry* 3 (1987): 147-160.

4548. Katzburg, Nathaniel. *Anti-Semitism in Hungary*. Tel-Aviv: Dvir, 1969.

4549. Katzburg, Nathaniel. *Hungary and the Jews: Policy and Legislation, 1920-1943*. Ramat Gan, Israel: 1981,

4550. Katzburg, Nathaniel. "The Tradition of Anti-Semitism in Hungary." In *The Holocaust in Hungary: Forty Years Later*, edited by Randolph L. Braham and Bela Vago. New York: Institute for Holocaust Studies, 1985.

4551. Kende, Pierre. "Communist Hungary and the Hungarian Minorities." In *The Hungarians: A Divided Nation*, edited by Stephen Borsody. New Haven, CT: Yale Center for International and Area Studies, 1988.

4552. Klein, Bernard. "Anti-Jewish Demonstrations in Hungarian Universities, 1932-1936: Istvan Bethlen vs. Gyula Gombos." *Jewish Social Studies* 44 (1982): 113-124.

4553. Kornai, Janos. "The Hungarian Reform Process: Visions, Hopes, and Reality." *Journal of Economic Literature* 24 (December 1986): 1687-1737.

4554. Kovacs, Andras. "The Jewish Question in Contemporary Hungary." *Telos* No. 58 (Winter 1983-1984): 55-74.

4555. Kovacs, I. "The Development of Living Standards in Hungary from 1975-1983." Acta Oeconomica 33 (1984)

4556. Kovago, Laszlo. "Nationalitatenfrage und Nationalitaten politik in Ungarn." Zeitschrift fur Donauraumforschung 25 (1980): 92-104.

4557. Kozminski, Maciej. "National Consciousness and Stereotypes in the Hungarian-Slovakian Borderland Area After the First World War." Acta Poloniae Historica No. 50 (1984): 157-198.

4558. Kroll, Robert E. "Will Hungarian Democracy Include Gypsies? " Guardian (NYC) (May 16, 1990)

4559. Lacko, M. Arrow Cross Men and National Socialists, 1935- 1944. Budapest: 1968.

4560. Ladanyi, Janos. "Changing Patterns of Residential Segregation in Budapest." International Journal of Urban and Regional Research 13 (1989): 555-572.

4561. Laszlo, Leslie. "Nationality and Religion in Hungary, 1867- 1918." Eastern European Quarterly 17 (1983): 41-56.

4562. Levai, E. "The War Crimes Trials Relating to Hungary." Hungarian Jewish Studies 2 (1969): 252-296.

4563. Levai, E. "The War Crimes Trials Relating to Hungary: A Follow-Up." Hungarian Jewish Studies 3 (1973): 251-290.

4564. McCagg, William O. Jr. "Jews and Peasants in Interwar Hungary." Austrian History Yearbook 21 (1985): 59-75.

4565. Miller, Judith. "Out of History." New York Times, Magazine (December 9, 1990): [Jews and antisemitism in contemporary Hungary.]

4566. Nagy, Peter. "The Ideas of the Hungarian Radical Right." East European Quarterly 20 (1986): 215-255.

4567. Nagy-Talavera, Miklos. The Green Shirts and the Others: A History of Fascism in Hungary and Rumania. University of California Press, 1967.

4568. Orosz, E. "The Hungarian Country Profile: Inequalities in Health and Health Care." Social Sciences & Medicine 31 (1990)

4569. Papp, N. S. "The German Minority in Hungary between the Two World Wars: Loyal Subjects or Oppressed Citizens?" East European Quarterly 2 (1988): 495-514.

4570. Paul, David W. "Slovak Nationalism and the Hungarian State, 1870-1910." In Ethnic Groups and the State, edited by Paul Brass. Totowa, NJ: Barnes and Noble, 1985.

4571. Ranki, Gyorgy and Braham, R.L. "Hungary." Encyclopedia of the Holocaust, II (1990): 693-703. [New York: Macmillan.]

4572. Ranki, Gyorgy and Locko Miklos. "The Restoration and Crisis of Capitalism in Hungary, 1919-1944." Austrian History Yearbook 12-13 (1976-1977): 291-311.

4573. Reuveni, Sari. "'After the Holocaust: National Attitudes to Jews': Antisemitism in Hungary 1945-1946." Holocaust and Genocide Studies 4 (1989): 41-62.

4574. Sanborn, Anne F. and de Czege Geza W., eds. Transylvania and the Hungarian-Rumanian Problem: A Symposium. Astor, FL: Danubian Press, 1979.

4575. Sanders, Ivan. "Sequels and Revisions: The Hungarian Jewish Experience in Recent Hungarian Literature." Soviet Jewish Affairs 14 (1984): 31-45.

4576. Schickert, Klaus. "Die Judenfrage in Ungarn. Judische Assimilation und antisemitische Bewegung im 19. und 20. Jahrhundert." Doctoral dissertation, University of Munich, 1937.

4577. Seewann, Gerhard. "Zigeuner in Ungarn." Sudosteuropa 36 (1987): 19-32.

4578. Siklos, Andras. Revolution in Hungary and the Dissolution of the Multinational State, 1918. Budapest: Akademiai Kiado, 1988.

4579. Simkus, Albert and Andorka, Rudolf. "Inequalities in Educational Attainment in Hungary, 1923-1973." American Sociological Review 47 (1982): 740-751.

4580. Sitzler, Kathrin. "Die ungarische Nationalitatenpolitik der letzten Jahre: konstante Prinzipien bei modifizierten Praxis." Sudosteuropa 36 (1987): 33-44.

4581. Spira, Thomas. "Connections between Trianon Hungary and the Weimar Republic, and the Swabian Minority School Problem." Internationales Jahrbuch fur Geschichts und Geographie-unterricht 13 (1970-1971): 164-190.

4582. Spira, Thomas. The German-Hungarian-Swabian Triangle, 1936-1939: The Road to Discord. New York: East European Monographs, 1990.

4583. Spira, Thomas. "Numerus clausus. The Jewish Minority and the League of Nations." Ungarn Jahrbuch 4 (1972): 115-128.

4584. Spira, Thomas. "The Radicalization of Hungary's Swabian Minority after 1935." Hungarian Studies Review 11 (1984): 9-22.

4585. Spira, Thomas. "Worlds Apart: The Swabian Expulsion from Hungary after World War II." Nationalities Papers 13 (1985): 188-197.

4586. Stipac, Boris. "Origins and Development of Croat Nationalism and the Croat-Magyar Controversy." Doctoral dissertation, University of Alberta, 1964.

4587. Szaraz, Gyorgy. "The Jewish Question in Hungary: A Historical Retrospective." In The Holocaust in Hungary: Forty Years Later, edited by Randolph L. Braham and Vago Bela, 13-30. New York: Institute for Holocaust Studies, 1985.

4588. Szelenyi, Ivan. Socialist Enrepreneurs: Embourgeoisement in Rural Hungary. Madison: University of Wisconsin Press, 1988.

4589. Szollosi-Janze, Marget. Die Pfeilkreuzlerbewegung in Ungarn: Historischen Kontext, Entwicklung und Herrschaft. Munich: Oldenbourg, 1989.

4590. Szucs, Ivan K. "Chronology: Hungary's Partition and the Hungarian Minorities since World War I." In The Hungarians: A Divided Nation Stephen, edited by Borsody. New Haven, CT: Yale Center for International and Area Studies, 1988.

4591. Tilkovazky, Lorant. "The Confrontation between the Policy toward National Minorities and the German Ethnic Group Policy in Hungary during the Second World War." Danubian Historical Studies 1 (1987): 33-49.

4592. Turgeon, Lynn. "Aren't You Hungary for Market Socialism?" Guardian (NYC) (January 8, 1966)

4593. Turgeon, Lynn. "Beauty and Brains in the Socialist Market Place." Guardian (NYC) (January 22, 1986): [Touches on education of Gypsies in Hungary.]

4594. Vaga, Raphael. "Nationality Policies in Contemporary Hungary." Hungarian Studies Review 11 (1984): 43-60.

4595. Vekerdi, Jozsef. "The Gypsies and the Gypsy Problem in Hungary." Hungarian Studies Review 15 (1988): 13-26.

4596. Verdery, Katherine. "On the Nationality Problem in Transylvania Until World War I: An Overview." Eastern Europe 2 19 (1985): 15-30.

4597. Versztovsek, R. "The Effect of Price Increases on the Average Food Consumption and on the Nutrition Standards of Social Groups in Hungary." Acta Oeconomica 32 (1984)

4598. Volgyes, Ivan. "The German Question in Hungary." East European Quarterly 23 (June 1989): 145-157.

4599. Wagner, Francis S. "The Gypsy Problem in Postwar Hungary." Hungarian Studies Review 14 (1987): 35-43.

4600. Yahil, Leni. "Raoul Wallenberg: His Mission and His Activities in Hungary." Yad Vashem Studies 15 (1983): 7-54.

4601. Yehuda, Don. "The Economic Effect of Anti-Semitic Discrimination: Hungarian Anti-Jewish Legislation, 1938- 1944." Jewish Social Studies 48 (Winter 1986): 63-82.

4602. Zinoviev, A. The Second Society: The Reduplication of the Social Paradigm in Contemporary Society: The Case of Hungary. Budapest: Institute of Sociology, Hungarian Academy of Sciences, 1985.

ICELAND

4603. Broddason, Thorbjorn and Webb, Keith. "On the Myth of Social Equality in Iceland." Acta Sociologica 18 (1975): 49-61.

4604. Byock, Jesse L. Medieval Iceland. Society, Sagas, and Power. Berkeley: University of California Press, 1988.

4605. Durrenberger, E. Paul. "Stratification without a State: The Collapse of the Icelandic Commonwealth." Ethnos 53 (1988): 239-265.

4606. Durrenberger, E. Paul and Palsson Gisli, eds. Anthropology of Iceland. Iowa City: University of Iowa Press, 1989.

4607. Gislason, Ingolfur V. "Enter the Bourgeoisie- Aspects of the Formation and Organization of Icelandic Employers, 1894- 1934." Lund University, 1990.

4608. Gunnarsson, Thorsteinn V. Controlling Curriculum Knowledge: A Documentary Study of the Icelandic Social Science Curriculum Project (SSCP), 1974-1984. Ohio University, 1990. UMO # 9024120.

4609. Tomasson, Richard F. Iceland: The First New Society. Minneapolis: University of Minnesota Press, 1980.

4610. Williams, C. O. Thraldom in Ancient Iceland. Chicago: 1937.

INDIA

4611. Abbay, Frehiwot. The Problem of Housing Low Income Groups in India. Master's thesis: Queens College, 1981.

4612. Abel, E.L. The Anglo-Indian Community: Survival in India. Columbia, MO: Chanakya, 1988.

4613. Abraham, Margaret. Ethnic Identity and Marginality: A Study of the Jews of India. Doctoral dissertation, Syracuse University, 1989. UMO # 9012738.

4614. Achyuthan, K. R. "The Social Spectrum of Kerala." Journal of Kerala Studies 10 (March-December 1983): 11-62.

4615. Agnew, Vijay. "A Review of the Literature on Women." Journal of Indian History 55 (1977): 307-324.

4616. Ahamed Kutty, E. K. "The Development of Arabic Education in Kerala: A Survey." Journal of Kerala Studies 9 (March- December 1982): 77-92.

4617. Ahmad, Syed Nesar. Hindu-Muslim Conflict in India: A World System Perspective. Doctoral dissertation, State University of New York, Binghamton, 1987. UMO # 8725945.

4618. Ahmad, Syed Nesar. "Origins of the Hindu-Muslim Conflict: Impact of the World Economic Crisis, 1873-96." In Rethinking the Nineteenth Century: Contradictions and Movements, edited by Francisco O. Ramirez. Westport, CT: Greenwood, 1988.

4619. Ahmed, Zaheda. "The Financing of Education in Bengal." Journal Asiatic Society Bangladesh 24-26 (1979-1981): 129- 158.

4620. Alavi, Hamza. "India: Transition from Feudalism to Colonial Capitalism." Journal of Contemporary Asia 10 (1980): 359- 399.

4621. Alexander, K. C. "Study of the Changing Behaviour of An Untouchable Caste: The Pulayas of Kerala." Doctoral dissertation, Poona University, 1966.

4622. Ali, A. K. M. Y. "Education for Muslims under the Bengal Sultanate." Islamic Studies 24 (October-December 1985): 421-444.

4623. Ali, Imran. "Malign Growth? Agricultural Colonization and the Roots of Backwardness in the Punjab." Past & Present No. 114 (1987): 110-132.

4624. Ambedkar, B. R. Untouchables: Who Were They and Why They Became Untouchables. Buddha Shiksha Parishad, 1969.

4625. Amin, Shahid. Sugarcane and Sugar in Gorakhpur: An Inquiry Into Peasant Production for Capitalist Enterprise in Colonial India. New York: Oxford University Press, 1984.

4626. Apana, A. B. "Reservation and Merit." Economic and Political Weekly 25 (September 22, 1990): [Affirmative action.]

4627. Arnold, David. "Cholera and Colonialism in British India." Past & Present No. 113 (1986): 118-151.

4628. Arnold, David. Police Power and Colonial Rule: Madras, 1859-1947. Delhi: Oxford University Press, 1986.

4629. Asthana, Pratima. Women's Movement in India. Delhi: Vikas Publishing House, 1974.

4630. Azariah, M. The Un-Christian Side of the Indian Church, 1985. Dalit Sahitya Akademy, 109/7th Cross, Palace Lower Orchards, Bangalore-560 003, India.

4631. Baig, Tara Ali. India's Woman Power. New Delhi: S. Chand, 1976.

4632. Balachandran, G. "Imperialism: The Auditor's Report: Review Article." Indian Economic and Social History Review 27 (April-June 1990)

4633. Balasubramanuam, V. N. The Economy of India. Boulder, CO: Wetview Press, 1986.

4634. Ballhatchet, Kenneth. Race, Sex and Class Under the Raj. London: Weidenfeld and Nicolson, 1980.

4635. Banaji, D. R. Slavery in British India. Bombay: D. B. Taraporevala, 1933.

4636. Bandyopadhyay, Sekhar. "Towards a Corporate Pluralist Society: Caste and Colonial Policy of Protective Discrimination in Bengal, 1911-1937." Calcutta Historical Journal 11 (July 1986-June 1987): 69-117.

4637. Banerjee, A. C. State and Society in Northern India, 1206-1526. Calcutta: K.P. Bagchi, 1982.

4638. Banerjee, B. and Knight J.B. "Caste Discrimination in the Indian Urban Labour Market." Journal of Development Economics 17 (April 1985)

4639. Banerjee, H. N. "Re-Consideration of the Principles of Social Stratification Viewed Through Class-Caste Distinction- Social Mobility in India- A Sociological Approach." Man in India 69 (December 1989)

4640. Banerjee, Nirmala. Women Workers in the Unorganized Sector: The Calcutta Experience. Hyderabao, India: Sangam Books, 1985.

4641. Banerjee, Sanjoy. Dominant Classes and the State in Development Theory and the Case of India. Boulder, CO: Westview, 1984.

4642. Banerjee, Sumanta. India's Simmering Revolution. The Naxalite Uprising. London: Zed, 1984.

4643. Bardham, Pranab. Land, Labor, and Rural Poverty. New York: Columbia University Press, 1984.

4644. Bardhan, Pranab. The Political Economy of Development in India. New York: Blackwell, 1984.

4645. Baruah, Sanjib. "Minority Policy in the North-East- Achievements and Dangers." Economic and Political Weekly 24 (September 16, 1989)

4646. Baruch, Sanjib. "Immigration, Ethnic Conflict, and Political Turmoil; Assam, 1979-1985." Asian Survey 26 (1986): 1184-1206.

4647. Basu, Alaka. Culture, the Status of Women and Demographic Behavior. New Delhi: National Council of Applied Economic Research, 1988.

4648. Bayly, C. A. The New Cambridge History of India. Vol. 2, part 1, Indian Society and the Making of the British Empire. New York: Cambridge University Press, 1988.

4649. Bayly, C. A. "The Pre-History of 'Communalism'? Religious Conflict in India, 1700-1860." Modern Asian Studies 19 (April 1985): 177-203.

4650. Bayly, C. A. "State and Economy in India over Seven Hundred Years." Economic History Review 38 (November 1985)

4651. Bayly, C. A. and Kolff, D.H.A., eds. Two Colonial Empires: Comparative Essays on the History of India and Indonesia in the Nineteenth Century. Dordrecht, Netherlands: M. Nijhoff, 1986.

4652. Bayly, Susan. Saints, Goddesses, and Kings: Muslims and Christians in South Indian Society, 1700-1900. New York: Cambridge University Press, 1990.

4653. Berhrman, J. R. and Deolalikar, A.B. "Will Developing Country Nutrition Improve with Income? A Case Study for Rural South India." Journal of Political Economy 95 (June 1987)

4654. Beteille, Andre. "Race and Descent as Social Categories in India." Daedalus (Spring 1967)

4655. Bhadra, B. K. "The Mode of Production, Social Classes and the State in Colonial India, 1757-1947: A Case Study of the Process of Dependent Capitalist Development." Doctoral dissertation, McMaster University, 1984.

4656. Bhagawan, M. R. "A Critique of India's Economic Policies and Strategies." Monthly Review 39 (July-August 1987): 56- 79.

4657. Bharti, I. "Paharia Tribals' Plight and Government's Indifference." Economic and Political Weekly 24 (July 8, 1989)

4658. Bhaskar, Manu. "Changing Positions of Harijans in Kerala." Eastern Anthropologist 41 (1988): 313-323.

4659. Bhattacharya, S. "The Colonial Working Class and the Anti- Imperialist Struggle." Indian Historical Review 12 (July 1985-January 1986): 266-280.

4660. Blaise, CLark and Mukherjee, Bharati. Days and Nights in Calcutta. London: Penguin, 1986.

4661. Bonner, Arthur. Averting the Apocalypse: Social Movements in India TOday. Durham, NC: Duke University Press, 1990.

4662. Borale, P. T. Segregation and Desegregation in India. New Delhi: Allied, 1969.

4663. Bose, Nemai S. Racism, Struggle for Equality, and Indian Nationalism. Calcutta: Firina KLM, 1981.

4664. Bowen, Huw V. "Lord Clive and Speculation in East India Company Stock." Historical Journal 30 (1987): 905-920.

4665. Brass, Paul. The Politics of India Since Independence. New York: Cambridge University Press, 1990.

4666. Breman, Jan. "Even Dogs Are Better Off: The Ongoing Battle Between Capital and Labour in the Canefields of Gujarat." Journal of Peasant Studies 17 (July 1990)

4667. Breman, Jan. Of Peasants, Migrants and Paupers: Rural Labour Circulation and Capitalist Production in West India. New York: Oxford University Press, 1986.

4668. Burton, Antoinette M. "The White Woman's Burden: British Feminists and the Indian Woman, 1865-1915." Women's Studies International Forum 13 (1990): 295-308.

4669. Cahndra, Bipan. Communalism in Modern India. New Delhi: Vikas, 1984.

4670. Caldwell, J. C. and others. "Educational Transition in Rural South India." Population and Development Review 11 (March 1985)

4671. Calman, Leslie J. "Congress Confronts Communism: Thana District, 1945-1948." Modern Asian Studies 21 (1987): 329- 348.

4672. Calman, Leslie J. "Women and Movement Politics in India." Asian Survey 29 (1989): 940-958.

4673. Carson, Penelope. "An Imperial Dilemma: The Propagation of Christianity in Early Colonial India." Journal of Imperial Commonwealth History 18 (May 1990): 169-190.

4674. Chakrabarty, Dipesh. "Class Consciousness and the Indian Working Class: Dilemmas of Marxist Historiogrpahy." Journal of Asian African Studies 23 (January- April 1988): 21-31.

4675. Chakrabarti, R. "Pax Britannica and the Nature of Police Control in Bengal c. 1800-1860." Bengal Past & Present 105 (January-December 1986): 78-99.

4676. Chakravarti, Ranabir. Warfare for Wealth: Early Indian Perspective. Calcutta: Firma KLM, 1986.

4677. Chakravarti, U. "The Social Philosophy of Buddhism and the Problem of Inequality." Compass 33 (1986)

4678. Chalam, K. S. "Caste Reservations and Equality of Opportunity in Education." Economic and Political Weekly 25 (October 13, 1990): [Affirmative action.]

4679. Chandra, Nirmal K. The Retarded Economies: Foreign Domination and Class Relations in India and Other Emerging Nations. New York: Oxford University Press, 1989.

4680. Chatterjee, A. K. Slavery in India. Calcutta: L.K. Pandeya, 1959.

4681. Chatterjee, Partha. "The Colonial State and Peasant Resistance in Bengal, 1920-1947." Journal of Social Studies 22 (October 1983): 1-44.

4682. Chatterjee, Partha. "Colonialism, Nationalism, and Colonized Women: The Content in India." American Ethnologist 16 (1989): 622-633.

4683. Chattopadhyay, Amal Kumar. Slavery in India. Calcutta: 1959.

4684. Chattopadhyay, Amal Kumar. Slavery in the Bengal Presidency, 1772-1843. London: Golden Eagle, 1977.

4685. Chattopadhyay, D. K. History of the Assamese Movement since 1947. Doctoral dissertation, State University of New York at Buffalo, 1988. UMO # 8812329.

4686. Chattopadhyay, M. Conditions of Labour in Indian Agriculture: Apparent and Real. Calcutta: K.P. Bagchi, 1985.

4687. Chattopadhyay, M. and others. "Inter and Intra Occupational Differences in Income and Level of Living." Economic and Political Weekly 24 (October 28, 1989)

4688. Chaudhary, N. Socio-Economic History of Mugal India. Delhi: Discovery House, 1987.

4689. Chauduri, Buddhabed, ed. Tribal Development in India- Problems and Prospects, 1982. 105 Anand Nagar, Delhi 110035, India: Inter India Publication,

4690. "Christian Dalits and Caste in Churches." Religion and Society 34 (September 1987): entire issue.

4691. Cooper, Adrienne E. "Sharecroppers and Landlords in Bengal, 1930-50: The Dependency Web and Its Implications." Journal of Peasant Studies 10 (1983): 227-255.

4692. Cooper, Adrienne E. "Sharecropping and Sharecroppers' Struggles in Bengal, 1930-1950." University of Sussex, 1985.

4693. Crossette, Barbara. "Campus Under Fire; Not Just a Crisis of Identity." New York Times, (January 10, 1991). [Aligarh Muslim University.]

4694. Currie, C. "Caste and Class in India: Revolution or Stagnation in Anthropology: A Critical Appraisal." Journal Institute of Asian Studies 4 (1986): 1-20.

4695. Cutler, P. "The Measurement of Poverty: A Review of Attempts to Quantify the Poor, with Special Reference to India." World Development 12 (November-December 1984)

4696. D'Souza, Henry J. De-radicalization of a Social Movement: A Case Study in India. 2 vols. Doctoral dissertation, University of Michigan, 1989. UMO # 9013889.

4697. Dalal, Agit K. and others. "Own-Group Bias in Social Perception: The Role of Caste and Class Membership." Psychologia 31 (March 1988): 42-46.

4698. Danda, A. K. "Tribes in India." Man in India 68 (1988): 313-334.

4699. Dange, Shripad A. *India From Primitive Communism to Slavery*. Bombay: 1949.

4700. Darbari, I. "Socio-economic Factors in the Education of Harijans." Doctoral dissertation, Allahabad University, 1956.

4701. Das, Amal. "The Politics of the Lower Order: Labour Protests in the Jute Mills of Howrah." *Quarterly Review of Historical Studies* 25 (January-March 1986): 36-48.

4702. Das, N. R. "The Problems of Education of the Hill Tribes and Aboriginals of Tripura." Doctoral dissertation, Sayajirao University of Baroda, 1961.

4703. Das, Suranjan. "Communal Riots in Bengal, 1905-1947." Doctoral dissertation, University of Oxford, 1987.

4704. Das Gupta, Monica. "Selective Discrimination against Female Children in Rural Punjab, India." *Population and Development Review* 3 (1987)

4705. Datta, Kalinkar. "Position of Women in Bengal in the Mid- eighteenth Century." *Calcutta Review* 37 (1930): 17-32.

4706. Datta, N. K. *Origin and Growth of Caste in India.* 2 vols. Calcutta: Vidyodya Library, 1965.

4707. Datta, P. and others. "Understanding Communal Violence: Nizamuddin Riots." *Economic and Political Weekly* 25 (November 10, 1990)

4708. Datta, R. C. "Schooling, Experience and Earnings: An Empirical Analysis." *Margin* 17 (January 1985)

4709. Datta-Ray, S. K., ed. *Minorities and the Media in India*. Bombay: Nachiketa Publication, 1982.

4710. Davidson, Andrew P. *Cultural Pluralism Reconsidered: Kerala and Tamilnadu*. Doctoral dissertation, University of Missouri, 1979.

4711. Dayal, E. "Wealth and Poverty in Rural India." *GeoJournal* 11 (1985)

4712. Desai, A. R., ed. *Agrarian Struggles in India After Independence*. Delhi: Oxford University Press, 1986.

4713. Desai, A. R. *Violation of Democratic Rights in India*. Bombay: Popular Prakashan, 1986.

4714. Desai, L. P. *Caste, Caste Conflict, and Reservations*. Delhi: Ajanta, 1985. [Affirmative action.]

4715. Desai, Niera. *Woman in Modern India*, 2d ed. Bombay: Vora and Co., 1977.

4716. Devitt, Richard B. For the Millions Who Surround N's: Company Education Policy in Madras, 1820-1848. Doctoral dissertation, University of Wisconsin, 1977.

4717. Dewey, Clive, ed. Arrested Development in India: The Historical Dimension. Riverdale, MD: Riverdale, 1988.

4718. Dhavan, Rajeev. "Religious Freedom in India." American Journal of Comparative Law 35 (Winter 1987): 209-254.

4719. Dickey, Sara. "Accommodation and Resistance: Expression of Working-class Values through Tamil Cinema." Wide Angle 11 (July 1989): 26-32.

4720. Dogra, B. "Protesting Crimes Against Women." Economic and Political Weekly 25 (November 24, 1990)

4721. "Dominant Castes, Ruling Classes and the State." Economic and Political Weekly 25 (November 10, 1990)

4722. Driver, Edwin D. "Class, Caste, and 'Status Summation' in Urban South India." Contributions to Indian Sociology 16 (1982): 225-253.

4723. Driver, Edwin D. "Social Class in South India: A Cognitive Approach." Journal of Asian and African Studies 16 (1981): 238-260.

4724. Drury, David A. The Iron Schoolmaster: Education, Employment and the Family in Northern India. Doctoral dissertation, University of California, 1985. UMO # 8610002.

4725. Dutt, A. K. and others. "Spatial Pattern of Languages in India: A Culture-Historical Analysis." GeoJournal 10,#1 (1985)

4726. Dutt, Romesh. India in the Victorian Age: An Economic History of the People. New Delhi: Daya Publishing House, 1985.

4727. Engineer, A. A. Indian Muslims: A Study of the Minority Problems in India. Delhi: Ajanta Publications, 1985.

4728. Everett, Jana G. M. Women and Social Change in India. New York: St. Martin's Press, 1979.

4729. Feitag, Sandria B. Collective Action and Community. Public Arenas and the Emergence of Communalism in North India. Berkeley: University of California Press, 1989.

4730. Franke, Richard and Chasin, Barbara. Kerala: Radical Reform as Development in an Indian State. Institute for Food and Development Policy, 1989.

4731. Frykenberg, Robert E. "Education as an Instrument of Imperial Integration During the Company's Raj in South India." Indo-British Review 12 (June 1986): 58-85.

4732. Frykenberg, Robert E. "Elite Groups in a South India District: 1788-1858." Indo-British Review 10 (1983): 42-57.

4733. Frykenberg, Robert E. "Modern Education in South India, 1784-1854: Its Roots and Its Role as a Vehicle of Integration under Company Raj." American Historical Review 91 (February 1986): 37-65.

4734. Gaiha, R. "Inequality, Earnings and Participation among the Poor in Rural India." Journal of Development Studies 23 (July 1987)

4735. Galanter, Marc. Competing Equalities: Law and the Backward Classes in India. Berkeley: University of California Press, 1984.

4736. Galanter, Marc. Law and Society in Modern India. Edited by Rajiev-Dhavan. New York: Oxford University Press, 1990.

4737. Galanter, Marc. "Pursuing Inequality: An Assessment of India's Policy of Compensatory Discrimination for Disadvantaged Groups." In Economic and Social Development in India, edited by Dilip K. Basu and Richard Sisson. Newbury Park, CA: Sage, 1986.

4738. Gandhi, Rajmohan. Eight Lives: A Study of the Hindu-Muslim Encounter. Albany: State University of New York Press, 1986.

4739. Gandhi, Raj S. "India." In International Handbook on Race and Race Relations, edited by Jay A. Sigler. Westport, CT: Greenwood, 1987.

4740. Gauri, Viswanathan. The Ideology of Literary Education in British India, 1813-1880. Doctoral dissertation, Columbia University, 1985. UMO # 8810439.

4741. Gedge, Evelyn S. and Choksi Mithan, eds. Women in Modern India: Fifteen Papers by Indian Women Writers. Bombay: D.B. Taraporewala Sons & Co., 1929.

4742. George, Alexander. Social Ferment in India. Atlantic Highlands, NJ: Humanities Press, 1986.

4743. Gharpure, J. R. Rights of Women under the Hindu Law. Bombay: University of Bombay, 1943.

4744. Ghosh, P. "Communalism and Colonial Labour. Experience of Calcutta Jute Mill Workers, 1880-1930." Economic and Political Weekly 25 (July 28, 1990)

4745. Ghosh, Ratna and Zachariah Matthew, eds. Education and the Process of Change. Newbury Park, CA: Sage, 1987.

4746. Glass, Ruth. "Divided and Degraded: The Downtrodden Peoples of India." Monthly Review 34 (July-August 1982): 101-127. [Critique of affirmative-action approach.]

4747. Goonatilake, S. Crippled Minds: An Exploration Into Colonial Culture. New Delhi: Vikas.

4748. Gordon, Richard K., Jr. and Lindsay, Jonathan M. "Law and the Poor in Rural India: The Prospects for Legal Aid." American University Journal of International Law and Policy 5 (Spring 1990): 655-772.

4749. Gough, Kathleen. Rural Society in Southeast India. New York: Cambridge University Press, 1981.

4750. Gough, Kathleen. "Socio-economic Change in Southeast India, 1950's to 1980's." Journal Contemporary Asia 17 (1987): 276-292.

4751. Gourgey, Perey S. "Indian Jews and the Indian Freedom Struggle." Indo-British Review 15 (1989): 85-90.

4752. Goyal, B. R. Education of the Depressed Classes in India During the British Period. Doctoral dissertation, University of Baroda, 1973.

4753. Greenberger, A. J. British Image of India: A Study in the Literature of Imperialism. Bombay: Oxford University Press, 1966.

4754. Gregory, Robert G. India and East Africa: A History of Race Relations within the British Empire, 1890-1939. Oxford: Clarendon Press, 1972.

4755. Guha, R. and Gadgil Madhav. "State Forestry and Social Conflict in British India." Past & Present No. 123 (May 1989): 141-177.

4756. Gupta, A. R. Women in Hindu Society: A Study of Tradition and Transition. New Delhi: Jyotsna Prakashan, 1976.

4757. Gupta, Devendra B. Urban Housing in India. Washington, D.C.: World Bank, 1985.

4758. Gupta, S. K. The Scheduled Castes in Modern Indian Politics: Their Emergence as a Political Power. New Delhi: Munshirain Manoharlel, 1985.

4759. Habib, Irfan. "Processes of Accumulation in Pre-Colonial and Colonial India." Indian Historical Review 11 (July 1984-January 1985): 65-90.

4760. Habib, Irfan. "Studying a Colonial Economy-without Perceiving Colonialism." Modern Asian Studies 19 (1985): 355-382.

4761. Hampton, Francesca. "Tibetans in India- A New Generation in Exile." Cultural Survival Quarterly 9,#2 (1985): 13-15.

4762. Haq, E. "Open Education and Closed Society- A Study in Social and Educational Inequalities in Contemporary India." In Affirmative Action and Positive Policies in the Education of Ethnic Minorities, edited by A. Yogev and S. Tomlinson. Greenwich, CT. JAI Press, 1989.

4763. Haque, Mozammel. "Impediments Which Delayed Muslim Progress in Education 1900-1911: An Analysis." Islam Modern Age 16 (February 1985): 1-26.

4764. Haque, Mozammel. "Muslim Education in Bengal: Problems and Progress, 1871-1900." Islam Modern Age 14 (August 1983): 161-182.

4765. Haque, S. A. The Education of the Depressed Classes in India. Doctoral dissertation, University of Leeds, 1938.

4766. Harriss, John. Capitalism and Peasant Farming: Agrarian Structure and Ideology in Northern Tamil Nadu. New York: Oxford University Press, 1982.

4767. Hartnaek, Christiane. "British Psychoanalysts in Colonial India." In Psychology in Twentieth-Century Thought and Society, edited by Mitchell G. Ash and William R. Woodward. New York: Cambridge University Press, 1987.

4768. Hasan, Mishirul. "In Search of Integration and Identity: Indian Muslims Since Independence." Islam Modern Age 19 (November 1988): 217-250.

4769. Hashmi, Tajul-Islam. "The Communalisation of Class Struggle: East Bengal Peasantry, 1923-1929." Indian Economic Social Historical Review 25 (April-June 1988): 171-204.

4770. Hassan, M. K. Prejudice in Indian Youth: A Socio- psychological Study. New Delhi: Classical Publications, 1981.

4771. Hate, Chandrakala Anandrao. Changing Status of Women in Post-Independence India. Bombay, India: Allied Publishers, 1969.

4772. Hazarika, Sanjoy. "Delhi's Poor Get 2 Blankets But Little Else." New York Times, (January 4, 1987)

4773. Hiro, Dilip. The Untouchables of India. London: Minority Rights Group, 1982.

4774. Hirway, Inira. Abolition of Poverty in India: with Special Reference to Target Group Approach in Gujarat. New Delhi: Vikas, 1986.

4775. Hjejle, Benedicte. "Slavery and Agricultural Bondage in South India in the 19th Century." Scandanavian Economic History Review 15 (1967): 71-126.

4776. Holmstrom, Mark. Industry and Inequality: The Social Anthropology of Indian Labour. New York: Cambridge University Press, 1984.

4777. Hume, John C., Jr. "Colonialism and Sanitary Medicine: The Development of Preventive Health Policy in the Punjab, 1860-1900." Modern Asian Studies 20 (October 1986): 703-724.

4778. Hussain, Monirul. "The Muslim Question in India." Journal of Contemporary Asia 19 (1989)

4779. Inden, R. "Orientalist Construction of India." Modern Asian Studies No. 20 (1986): 401-446.

4780. Inder, Pal S. Rural Income Distribution: An Analytical Study of Punjab. Delhi: B.R. Publication Corporation, 1986.

4781. India (Republic) Committee on the Status of Women in India. Towards Equality. New Delhi: Department of Social Welfare, Ministry of Education and Social Welfare, Government of India, 1975.

4782. Irschick, Eugene F. "Order and Disorder in Colonial South India." Modern Asian Studies 23 (July 1989): 459-492.

4783. Isenberg, Shirley B. India's Bene Israel: A Comprehensive Inquiry and Sourcebook. Judah Magnes Museum Order Department, 911 Russell Street, Berkeley, Ca 94705: 1990.

4784. Iyengar, N. S. "Recent Studies on Poverty in India: A Survey." Journal of Quantitative Economics 5 (July 1989)

4785. Iyer, V. R. K. Justice in Words and Injustice in Deeds for the Depressed Classes. New Delhi: Indian Social Institute, 1984.

4786. Jain, Devaki, ed. Indian Women. New Delhi: Publications Division, Ministry of Information and Broadcasting, Government of India, 1975.

4787. Jainj, Anrudh K. and Visarea P., eds. Infant Mortality in India. Differentials and Determinants. Newbury Park, CA: Sage, 1988.

4788. Jalali, Rita. The State and the Political Mobilization of the Disadvantaged: The Case of the Scheduled Castes in India. Doctoral dissertation, Stanford University, 1990. UMO # 9017856.

4789. Jayaraman, Raja. Caste and Class: Dynamic of Inequality in Indian Society. Delhi: Hindustan Publication Corporation, 1981.

4790. Jeffery, Roger. The Politics of Health in India. Berkeley: University of California Press, 1988.

4791. Jeffrey, Robin. "Governments and Culture: How Women Made Kerala Literate." Pacific Affairs 60 (1987): 447-472.

4792. Joshi, Barbara, ed. Untouchable! Voices from the Dalit Liberation Movement. London: Zed Press, 1986.

4793. Juergensmeyer, Mark. "What If the Untouchables Don't Believe in Untouchability?" Bulletin of Concerned Asian Scholars 12 (January-March 1980): 23-29.

4794. Kalirajam, K. P. and Shand R.T. "Schooling, Non-Formal Education and Productivity." Indian Economic Journal 31 (April-June 1984)

4795. Kamble, N. D. Deprived Castes and Their Struggle for Equality. Delhi: Ashish, 1983.

4796. Kaplan, Patricia. Class and Gender in India. London: Tavistock, 1985.

4797. Kapoor, B. L. "Labour Market Discrimination against Migrant Workers in an Indian State: The Case of Punjab." Journal of Development Studies 23 (April 1987)

4798. Kapoor, M. P. The Educational Implications of the Problem of Unemployment among the University-Educated of Bihar. Doctoral dissertation, Patna Univerity, 1959.

4799. Karim, Abdul. Social History of the Muslims in Bengal (Down to A.D. 1538), 2nd edition. Chittagong: British Sharaf Islamic Research Institute, 1985.

4800. Karuppaiyan, E. "Alienation of Tribal Lands in Tamil-Nadu." Economic and Political Weekly 25 (June 2, 1990)

4801. Katzenstein, M. F. "Preferential Treatment and Ethnic Conflict." Public Policy 25 (Summer 1977). [Affirmative action.]

4802. Kelker, S. V. Education of the Backward Classes in the State of Bombay (1800-1950). Doctoral dissertation, Bombay University, 1950.

4803. Khare, R. S. "The Bhopal Puzzle: A Failure of Modern Technology, Law and Values." International Social Science Journal 41 (1989): 273-282.

4804. Kly, Y. N. International Law and the Dalits in India. Geneva: Dalit Liberation Education Trust, 1989.

4805. Kohli, Stul. The State and Poverty in India: the Politics of Reform. New York: Cambridge University Press, 1987.

4806. Kosambi, Meere. Bombay in Transition: The Growth and Social Ecology of a Colonial City, 1889-1980. Stockholm: Almquist and Wiksell, 1986.

4807. Krishnam, Prakha and Dighe, Anita. Affirmation and Denial: Construction of Femininity on Indian Television. Newbury Park, CA: Sage, 1990.

4808. Krishna, Raj. "Growth, Investment and Poverty in Midterm Appraisal of Sixth Plan." Economic and Political Weekly (November 19, 1983)

4809. Kuber, Waman N. Critical Study of the Social and Political thought of Dr. B.R. Ambedkar. Doctoral dissertation, Poona University, 1967.

4810. Kumar, Dharma. "Caste and Landlessness in South India." Comparative Studies in Society and History 4 (1961-1962)

4811. Kumar, Dharma and Thorner, Daniel and Alice. Land and Labour in India. Delhi: Asia Publishing House, 1962.

4812. Kumar, Ikram Ali. "Racial Discrimination and Science in Nineteenth Century India." Indian Economic Social Historical Review 19 (January-March 1982): 63-82.

4813. Kumar, Pramod. "Communication in India- Some Theoretical Issues." Man and Development 8 (December 1986): 35-62.

4814. Kumar, Radha. "The Feminist Movement in India." New Politics 1 (Winter 1988): 148-155.

4815. Kundu, A. "Reservationists, Anti-reservationists and Democracy." Economic and Political Weekly 25 (November 10, 1990). [Affirmative action.]

4816. Lal, A. K. Politics of Poverty: A Study of Bonded Labour. New Delhi: Chetana, 1980.

4817. Lal, Deepak. Cultural Stability and Economic Stagnation: India, c. 1500 BC-AD 1980. New York: Oxford University Press, 1988.

4818. Lardinois, Roland. "Les luttes de classement en Inde." Actes de la Recherche en Sciences Sociales No, 59 (1985): 78-84.

4819. Leopold, Joan. "British Applications of the Aryan Theory of Race in India." Economic History Review 89 (July 1974): 578-603.

4820. Liddle, Joanna and Joshi, Rama. Daughters of Independence Gender, Caste and Class in India. London: Zed Press, 1986.

4821. Liddle, Joanne and Joshi, Rama. "Gender and Colonialism: Women's Organization under the Raj." Women's Studies International Forum 8 (1985): 21-29.

4822. Madhok, Balraj. Punjab Problem, the Muslim Consequence. New Delhi: Hindu World Publication, 1985.

4823. Mahajani, Usha. "Slavery, Indian Labour, and British Colonialism." Pacific Affairs 50, 2 (1977): 263-271.

4824. Mahar, J. Michael, ed. The Untouchables of Contemporary India. Tucson: University of Arizona Press, 1972.

4825. Manmohan, Kaur. Role of Women in the Freedom Movement, 1857-1947. New Delhi: Sterling, 1968.

4826. Markova, Dagmar. "On the National Consciousness of Indian Muslims." Archaelogy Orient (Prague) 54 (1986): 1-18.

4827. Markovits, Claude. Indian Business and Nationalist Politics, 1931-1939: The Indigenous Capitalist Class and the Rise of the Congress Party. New York: Cambridge University Press, 1985.

4828. Marshall, P. J. "The Whites of British India, 1780-1830: A Failed Colonial Society." International Historical Review 12 (February 1990): 26-44.

4829. Martin, Gregory. "The Influence of Racial Attitudes on British Policy towards India during the First World War." Journal of Imperial Commonwealth History 14 (January 1986): 91-113.

4830. Maskiell, Michelle. "Social Change and Social Control: College-Educated Punjabi Women 1913-1960." Modern Asian Studies 19 (February 1985): 55-83.

4831. Massey, James. "Dalits." PCR Information No. 27 (1990): 68-79.

4832. Mathew, A. Ministry of Education of the Government of India: An Organizational History. New Delhi: National Institute of Educational Planning and Administration, 1984.

4833. Mathur, S. C. "Rural Poverty and Agricultural Performance in India." Journal of Development Studies 21 (April 1985)

4834. Mathur, S. C. A Sociological Approach to Indian Education. Agra: Vinod Pustak Mandir, 1985.

4835. Mathur, Y. B. Women's Education in India, 1813-1966. Bombay: Asia Publishing House, 1973.

4836. Maxwell, Neville G. A. India and the Nagas. London: Minority Rights Group, 1973.

4837. Mehta, J. L. Medieval Indian Society and Culture. New Delhi: Sterling, 1983.

4838. Metcalf, Thomas R. "Rural Society and British Rule in Nineteenth-Century India." Journal of Asian Studies 39 (1979)

4839. Miller, Barbara. The Endangered Sex: Neglect of Female Children in Rural North India. Ithaca, New York: Cornell University Press, 1981.

4840. Misra, B. B. Government and Bureaucracy in India, 1947- 1976. New York: Oxford University Press, 1986.

4841. Misra, B. B. The Indian Middle Class. Oxford University Press, 1961.

4842. Misra, Sailendra. Police Brutality: An Analysis of Police Behaviour. Delhi: Vikas, 1986.

4843. Mitra, Asok. The Status of Women: Literacy and Employment. New Delhi: Allied, 1979.

4844. Mitra, Subrata. "The Perils of Promoting Equality: The Latent Significance of the Anti-reservation Movement in India." Journal of Commonwealth & Comparative Politics 25 (1987): 292-312. [Affirmative action.]

4845. Mittar, V. "Income Distribution and Poverty in the Urban Informal Sector." Margin 18 (January 1986)

4846. Modi, B. M. Income Patterns and Education. Khampur: Ahmedabad, 1984.

4847. Moore, Robin James. Endgames of Empire: Studies of Britain's Indian Problem. New York: Oxford University Press, 1989.

4848. Mukherjee, Ila. Social Status of North Indian Women, 1526- 1707 A.D. Agra: Shiva Lal Agarwala, 1972.

4849. Mukherji, R. Sociology of Indian Sociology. New Delhi: 1979.

4850. Mukhopadhyay, Maitrayee. Silver Shackles. Women and Development in India. Oxford, England: Oxfam Publications, 1984.

4851. Muraleedharan, V. R. "Rural Health Care in the Madras Presidency: 1919-1939." Indian Economic Social Historical Review 24 (July-September 11987): 323-334.

4852. Muthiah, S., ed. A Social and Economic Atlas of India. Delhi: Oxford University Press, 1988.

4853. The Naga Nation and Its Struggle Against Genocide. Copenhagen: IWGIA, 1986.

4854. Naidir, Mark. "The Abolitionists and Indian Slavery." Journal of Asian History 15, No. 2 (1981): 146-158.

4855. Nair, D. P. "Demand-Supply Imbalance of Higher Education in Kerala." Margin 18 (October 1985)

4856. Nanavati, M. B. and Vakil, C.N. Group Prejudice in India: A Symposium. Bombay: Vora, 1951.

4857. Nandy, Ashis. The Intimate Enemy: Loss and Recovery of Self Under Colonialism. New York: Oxford University Press, 1983.

4858. Narayan, T. "Health Impact of Bhopal Disaster: An Epidemiological Perspective." Economic and Political Weekly 25 (August 18, 1990)

4859. Natsume, Ryo. Left Front Government Policies in West Bengal, India, from 1977 to 1987. Doctoral dissertation, Cornell University, 1988.

4860. Nayak, J. L. "Education among the Harijans of Surat District." Bombay University, 1958.

4861. Niranjana, T. "Class, Caste and Reservations." Economic and Political Weekly 25 (November 17, 1990)

4862. Niranjana, T. "History, Really Beginning: Compulsions of Post-colonial Pedagogy." Economic and Political Weekly 25 (October 20, 1990)

4863. Nossiter, T. J. Marxist State Governments in India: Politics, Economics, and Society. New York: Pinter, 1988.

4864. O'Hanlon, Rosalind. Caste, Conflict, and Ideology: Mahatma Jotirao Phule and Low Caste Protest in Nineteenth- Century India. New York: Cambridge University Press, 1985.

4865. Ommen, T. K. Social Transformation in Rural India: Mobilization and State Intervention. Delhi: Vikas, 1984.

4866. Omvedt, Gail. "Hinduism and Politics." Economic and Political Weekly 25 (April 7, 1990)

4867. Omvedt, Gail. "India's Movements for Democracy." Zeta Magazine 2 (November 1989): 32-37.

4868. Omvedt, Gail. "The Left in India." Journal of Contemporary Asia 15 (1985): 172-182.

4869. Omvedt, Gail. "Women and Rural Revolt in India." South Asia Papers 1 (1977): 1-59.

4870. Oomen, T. K. "Sources of Deprivation and Styles of Protest: The Case of the Dalits in India." Contributions to Indian Sociology 18 (1984)

4871. Ostergaard, Geoffrey. Nonviolent Revolution in India. New Delhi: Gandhi Peace Foundation, 1986.

4872. Padmanabhan, C. B. "Toward a Rational Financial Policy for Indian Education." Education Quarterly 37 (Autumn 1985): 1- 5.

4873. Pakrasi, Kanti B. Female Infanticide in India. Calcutta: Editions Indian, 1970.

4874. Pal, P. and others. "Poverty in Rural India: A Decomposition Analysis." Indian Economic Review 21 (July- December 1986)

4875. Panandikar, S. G. The Wealth and Welfare of the Bengal Delta. Doctoral dissertation, University of London, 1926.

4876. Panda, M. K. "Poverty in Rural Orissa (1960-1983)." Margin 20 (December 1987)

4877. Pandey, R. N. "Women: Status, Employment and Wage Disparity." Indian Labour Journal 17 (1976): 1-18.

4878. Pandey, V. N. "Property Law and Agrarian Relations in Colonial Awodh, 1909-1920." Economic and Political Weekly 25 (November 24, 1990)

4879. Panigrahi, Lalita. British Social Policy and Female Infanticide in India. New Delhi: Munshiram Manoharial, 1972.

4880. Pannikar, K. M. Politics of Racialism. Agra: Shiva Lal, 1967.

4881. Parekh, Bhikhu C. Colonialism, Tradition, and Reform: An Examination of Gandhi's Political Discourse. Newbury Park, CA: Sage, 1989.

4882. Parikh, S. "The Supreme Court, Civil Rights, and Preference Policies: Judicial Decision Making Processes in the United States and India." Teachers College Record 92 (Winter 1990). [Affirmative action.]

4883. Parvathamma, C. Employment Problems of University Graduates. New Delhi: Ashish Publishing House, 1981.

4884. Pathy, Joganath. "Politics of Tribal Welfare: Some Reflections." Eastern Anthropologist 35 (1982): 285-300.

4885. Patnaik, Utsa and Dingwaney, M., eds. Chains of Servitude: Bondage and Slavery in India. Madras, India: Sangam Books, 1985.

4886. Patwardham, S. P. "Study of the Scheduled Castes in An Urban Setting." Poona University, 1965.

4887. Pavier, Barry. "Class Struggle in India." International Socialism No. 2 (Summer 1983)

4888. Pavlov, V. I. *Indian Capitalist Class: A Historical Study*. Delhi: 1964.

4889. Pescatello, Ann M. "The African Presence in Portuguese India." *Journal of Asian History* 11 (1977): 26-48.

4890. Pinto, Marina R. "Reservation Policy in India." *Journal of the University of Bombay* 49-53 (1980-1984): 65-82. [Affirmative action.]

4891. Prabhakar, M. E. "The Indian Christian Dalits." *PCR Information* No. 22 (1986): 33-38.

4892. Prabhakar, N. R. "Patterns of Child Migration and Child Migrant Labor in the Cities of India." *Janasamkhya* 11 (June 1984)

4893. Prakash, Gyan. *Bonded Histories: Genealogies of Labor Servitude in Colonial India*. New York: Cambridge University Press, 1989.

4894. Prakash, Nirupawa. "Perception of Scheduled Castes towards Education." *Journal of Sociological Studies* 9 (January 1990): 109-115.

4895. Radhakrishnan, P. "Backward Classes in Tamil-Nadu: 1872- 1988." *Economic and Political Weekly* 25 (March 10, 1990)

4896. Radhakrishnan, P. "Indigenous Education in British India: A Profile." *Contributions to Indian Sociology* 24 (January- June 1990)

4897. Rahman, Anika. "Religious Rights versus Women's Rights in India: A Test Case for International Human Rights Law." *Columbia Journal of Transnational Law* 28 (Spring 1990): 473-498.

4898. Raizada, Ajit. *Tribal Development in Madhya Pradesh: A Planning Perspective*. New Delhi: Inter-India Publications, 1984.

4899. Raj Chanana, Dev. *Slavery in Ancient India*. New Delhi: People's Publishing House, 1960.

4900. Rajagopal, Indhu. *The Tyranny of Caste: The Non-Brahman Movement and Political Development in South India*. New York: Advent, 1985.

4901. Rajshekar, Shetty V. T. *Dalit, the Black Untouchables of India*. Atlanta, GA: 1987.

4902. Ramachandran, V. K. *Wage Labour and Unfreedom in Agriculture*. New York: Oxford University Press, 1990.

4903. Ramanujam, G. *Indian Labour Movement*. New Delhi: Sterling Publications, 1986.

4904. Ramaswamy, V. "Aspects of Women and Work in Early South India." *Indian Economic and Social History Review* 26 (January-March 1989)

4905. Rav, Shudha. Education and Rural Development. Beverly Hills, CA: Sage, 1986. [Dalena, India.]

4906. Rav, Shudha. "Quality and Its Role in Universalizing Elementary Education." Education Quarterly 37 (Spring 1985): 27-31.

4907. Rav, T. D. "Urban Income and Wealth Distribution by Size in Andhra Pradesh." Margin 18 (April 1986)

4908. Rawson, J. L. State, Society and Economy: The Nature of India's Mass Poverty from the Seventeenth Century. Doctoral dissertation, University of New South Wales, 1988.

4909. Ray, Krishnalal. Education in Medieval India. Delhi: B.R. Publishing Corp., 1984.

4910. Raychaudhury, Rakhi. "Living Conditions of the Female Workers in the Eastern Collieries (Bihar and Bengal) from 1901-1921." Quarterly Review of Historical Studies 24 (1985): 13-19.

4911. Reddy, T. Chandramohan and Kalippan, V.R. "Status of Scheduled Castes in Rural Power Structure: An Analysis." Man in India 67 (1987): 372-382.

4912. "Reservation for Backward Classes: The Real Issues." Economic and Political Weekly 25 (September 15, 1990): [Affirmative action.]

4913. Robb, Peter, ed. Rural India: Land, Power, and Society Under British Rule. London: Curzon Press, 1983.

4914. Roberts, J. P. "The Sociobiology of Ethnocentrism in an Indian City." Ethnology and Sociobiology 11 (November 1990)

4915. Roland, Joan G. Jews in British India: Identity in a Colonial Era. Hanover, NH: University Press of New England, 1989.

4916. Rose, Madhuri. In Pawn for Life: Debt Bondage in Rural India. London: Anti-Slavery Society, 1983.

4917. Roy, M. N. "The Ideal of Indian Womanhood." In Crime and Karma, Cats and Women: Fragments from a Prisoner's Diary, by M.N. Roy, 101-176. Calcutta: Renaissance Publishers, 1957.

4918. Rudra, A. "Emergence of the Intelligentsia as a Ruling Class in India." Indian Economic Review 24 (July-December 1989)

4919. Rudra, Ashok Utsa Patnaik and others. Studies in the Development of Capitalism in India. Lahore: Vanguard Books, 1978.

4920. Ruhela, Satya Pal. The Children of Indian Nomads. New Delhi: Sterling Publishers, 1984. [Kalandars, Geduliya Lohars, Bhat Puppeteers, and Nadibuts.]

4921. Saha, Suranjit K. "Historical Premises of India's Tribal Problem." Journal of Contemporary Asia 16 (1986): 274-319.

4922. Saini, Krishan G. "The Growth of the Indian Economy: 1860- 1960." Review of Income and Wealth 15 (September 1969): 247-263.

4923. Sangari, Kumkum and Vaid, Gudesh, eds. Recasting Women in India: Essays in Colonial History. New Brunswick, NJ: Rutgers University Press, 1990.

4924. Sangwan, Satparl. "Science Education in India under Colonial Constraints, 1792-1857." Oxford Review of Education 16 (1990)

4925. Saradamoni, K. "Abolition of Slavery in Kerala in the 19th Century." Journal of Kerala Studies 2 (June 1975): 217-236.

4926. Sarasivathi, S. Minorities in Madras State: Group Interests in Modern Politics. Delhi: Impex India, 1974.

4927. Sarasivathi, S. and Dutta, Ranjana, comps. Developmental Psychology in India, 1975-1986. Newbury Park, CA: Sage, 1987. [Bibliography on development and psychology of Indian children.]

4928. Sarkar, B. N. "Enrollment and Primary Education Force in Rural India." Margin 18 (April 1986)

4929. Sarkar, S. Critique of Colonial India. Calcutta: Papyrus, 1985.

4930. Sebstad, Jennefer and others. Women and Self-Reliance in India. The Sewa Story. London: Zed Press, 1986. [SEWA, Self- Employed Women's Association, city of Ahmedabad.]

4931. Seetharamu, A. S. and Ushadevi, M.D. Education in Rural Areas. New Delhi, India: Ashish, 1985.

4932. Sen, Amartya and Jocelyn Lynch. "Indian Women: Well-being and Survival." Cambridge Journal of Economics 7 (1983)

4933. Sen, Jahar. "Slave Trends on the Indo-Nepal Border in the Nineteenth Century." Kailash 1, No.2 (1973): 159-166.

4934. Sen, R. "Influence of Caste on Achievement." Lucknow University, 1961.

4935. Sen, Sunil K. The Working Women and Popular Movements in Bengal: From the Ghandi Era to the Present Day. Calcutta: K.P.Bagehi, 1986.

4936. Seshadari, K. Social Unrest in India. New Delhi: Intellectual Publishing House, 1983.

4937. Sethi, Harsh and Kothari, Sunitu, eds. People's Politics. Community Struggles in India Today. London: Zed Press, 1987.

4938. Shah, Mohammad. "Communalism in Indian Historiography." Journal of Asiatic Society of Bangladesh 31 (December 1986): 85-101.

4939. Shah, S. Shamim. Muslim Managed Schools and Colleges in India. New Delhi: Hamdard Education Society, Hamdard Nagar.

4940. Shaikh, A. U. "Education of Indian Muslims." Islam Modern Age 15 (August 1984): 193-200.

4941. Shankar, K. "Land Ownership, Asset Structure, and Income Distribution in Eastern Uttar Pradesh." Economic and Political Weekly 25 (October 20, 1990)

4942. Sharma, A. K. "What the Poor Think About Their Poverty." Indian Journal of Social Work 50 (April 1989)

4943. Sharma, Monica. "Caste, Class, and Gender: Production and Reproduction in North India." Journal of Peasant Studies 12 (1985): 57-88.

4944. Sharma, Monica. "Health Profile of India: Problems, Services and Issues." Journal, Indian Anthropological Society 19 (1984): 93-117.

4945. Sharma, Rama. Marginality, Identity and Politicisation of the Bhangi Community, Delhi. 2 vols. Doctoral dissertation, University of Keele, 1987. Order No. BRDX88704.

4946. Sharma, Satish K. The Chamar Artisans: Industrialization, Skills, and Social Mobility. New Delhi: B.R. Publishing Corporation, 1986.

4947. Shashi, S. S. The Tribal Women of India. Delhi: Sundeep Prakashan, 1978.

4948. Shattty, V. T. R. Crocodile Tears Over Harijan Atrocities. Bangalore: Dalit Action Committee, 1978.

4949. Shrivastava, G. Language Controversy and the Minorities. Delhi: Atma Ram, 1982.

4950. Shrivastava, Paul. Bhopal: Anatomy of a Crisis. Cambridge, MA: Ballinger, 1987.

4951. Simmons, Colin. "Industrialization and the Indian Economy, ca. 1850-1947." Modern Asian Studies 19 (July 1985): 593-622.

4952. Singh, Andrea M. and De Souza, Alfred. The Urban Poor: Slum and Pavement Dwellers in the Major Cities of India. New Delhi: Manohav, 1980.

4953. Singh, Anita I. "The Congress and the Hindu-Muslim Problem, 1920-1947." In The Indian National Congress: Centenary Hindsights, edited by D.A. Law. New York: Oxford University Press, 1988.

4954. Singh, Bhawani. Politics of Alienation in Assam. Delhi: Ajanta Publications, 1985.

4955. Singh, Gian. Economic Conditions of Agricultural Labourers and Marginal Farmers. Delhi: B.R. Publication Corporation, 1986.

4956. Singh, H. "Inequality in Labour-Market Rewards and Education in India (A Case Study of Delhi)." Indian Economic Review 18 (July-December 1983)

4957. Singh, J. P. "Conditions for the Rise of Nationalist Movement in India." Asian Profile (Hong Kong) 13 (1985): 45-60.

4958. Singh, J. B. Intelligence of Harijans. Doctoral dissertation, Allahabad University, 1955.

4959. Singh, K. S., ed. Tribal Movements in India. Vol. 1. New Delhi: Manohar, 1983.

4960. Singh, M. "Development, Social Justice and Modernisation." Indian Economic Journal 33 (April-June 1986)

4961. Singh, Rajendra. Land, Power, and People, Rural Elite in Transition, 1801-1970. Newbury Park, CA: Sage, 1988. [Basti district of India.]

4962. Singh, Ram G. The Depressed Classes of India: Problems and Prospects. New Delhi: B.R. Publication Corporation, 1986.

4963. Sinha, Arun. Against the Few: Struggles of India's Rural. Atlantic Highlands, NJ: Zed, 1989.

4964. Sinha, Arun. "Class War, Not 'Atrocities' Against Harijans." Journal of Peasant Studies 9 (1982): 148-152.

4965. Sivaramayya, B. Affirmative Action: The Scheduled Castes and the Scheduled Tribes. May 1984, ERIC ED 249 299.

4966. Srivastava, S. N. Harijans in Indian Society: A Cultural Study of the Status of Harijans and Other Backward Classes. New Delhi: S. Chand, 1987.

4967. Srivastava, Swesh C. "Women In India: Law and Practice." Law Institute Journal 64 (June 1990): 524-526.

4968. State Terrorism in the Punjab. New Delhi: Committee for Information and Initiative on Punjab, 1989. [Indian governmental torture and abuse of Sikhs.]

4969. Subrahmanyam, S. "Adjustmental Problems of Primary School Children: A Survey in Andhra Pradesh." Education Quarterly 37 (Spring 1985): 32-37.

4970. Sundrum, R. M. Growth and Income Distribution in India. Policy and Performance Since Independence. Newbury Park, CA: Sage, 1987.

4971. Suntharalingham, R. Indian Nationalism: An Historical Analysis. New Delhi: Vikas, 1983.

4972. A Survey of Muslim Education-India. Cambridge, England: The Islamic Academy, 1986.

4973. Tendulkar, S. D. and Jain, L. R. "Rural Poverty and Its Alleviation in India: A Critical Scrutiny." Economic and Political Weekly 25 (September 22, 1990).

4974. Teresa, Mother. My Life for the Poor. San Francisco, CA: Harper & Row, 1985. [Edited by Jose L. Gonzalez-Balado and Janet N. Playfoot.]

4975. Thakur, D. S. "Estimation of Poverty in India- An Empirical Investigation." Margin 19 (October 1986)

4976. Thakur, D. S. "A Survey of Literature on Rural Poverty in India." Margin 17 (April 1985)

4977. Thakur, V. K. "Recent Writings on Indian Feudalism: A Historiographical Critique." Bihar Res. Soc. Journal 65-66 (1979-1980): 1-86.

4978. Thapar, Romila. Ancient Indian Social History. New Delhi: Orient Longman, 1984.

4979. Tharamangalam, Joseph. "The Penetration of Capitalism and Agrarian Change in Southwest India, 1901 to 1941: A Preliminary Analysis." Bulletin of Concerned Asian Scholars 16 (January-March 1984): 53-62.

4980. Thorner, Alice. "Contemporary Debate on Class and Modes of Production in India." Political and Economic Weekly 16, Nos. 10-12 (1982)

4981. Tilak, J. B. G. The Economics of Inequality in Education. Newbury Park, CA: Sage, 1987.

4982. Tilak, J. B. G. "Urban Bias and Rural Neglect in Education: A Study of Rural-Urban Disparities in Education in Andhra Pradesh." Margin 17 (October 1984)

4983. Tomlinson, B. R. "The Historical Roots of Indian Poverty: Issues in the Economic and Social History of Modern South Asia: 1880-1960." Modern Asian Studies 22 (February 1988): 123-140.

4984. Toppo, Sita. Dynamics of Educational Development in Tribal India. New Delhi: Classical Publications, 1979.

4985. Torri, M. "Westernised Middle Class Intellectuals and Society in Late Colonial India." Economic and Political Weekly 25 (January 27, 1990)

4986. Trivedi, Harshad R. Scheduled Caste Women: Studies in Exploitation with Reference to Superstition, Ignorance and Poverty. Delhi: Concept Publishing Co., 1977.

4987. Tyabil, Badr-Ud-Din. "Islam in India since Independence." Islam Modern Age 16 (November 1985): 197-204.

4988. Upadhya, Carol B. From Kulak to Capitalist: The Emergence of a New Business Community in Coastal Andhra Pradesh, India. Doctoral dissertation, Yale University, 1988. UMO # 9009431.

4989. Vakil, A. K. Reservation Policy and Scheduled Castes in India. New Delhi: Ashish, 1985. [Affirmative action.]

4990. van de Walle, D. "Population Growth and Poverty: Another Look at the Indian Time Series Data." Journal of Development Studies 21 (April 1985)

4991. Vanaik, Achin. "The Indian Left." New Left Review No. 159 (September-October 1986): 49-70.

4992. Vanaik, Achin. "The Rajiv Congress in Search of Stability." New Left Review No. 154 (November-December 1985): 55-82.

4993. Verma, Y. M. Problems of Tribal India. New Delhi: Classical, 1986.

4994. Vermani, R. C. British Colonialism in India. Delhi: Authors Guide Publications, 1983.

4995. Vidyadharan, A. "The Enemy Within: India's Separatist Movements." Cultural Survival Quarterly 13 (1989): 43-51.

4996. Vilanilam, J. "Television Advertising and the Indian Poor." Media, Culture & Society 11 (October 1989)

4997. Vincentnatham, Lynn. Harijan Subculture and Self-esteem Management in a South Indian Community. Doctoral dissertation, University of Wisconsin, 1987. UMO # 8800735.

4998. Viswanathan, Gauri. Masks of Conquest, Literary Study and British Rule in India. New York: Columbia University Press, 1990.

4999. Wallerstein, I. "The Incorporation of the Indian Sub- continent into the Capitalist World- economy." In *The Indian Ocean. Explorations in History, Commerce, and Politics*, edited by Satish Chandra. Newbury Park, CA: Sage, 1987.

5000. Weisman, Steven R. "A Corner of India Stirs Hope for Unity." *New York Times*, (Februry 22, 1987)

5001. Weisman, Steven R. "For Some of India's Poorest, the Gift of Self-Help." *New York Times*, (November 22, 1985): [Seva Mandir movement and descendants of aboriginal tribespeople.]

5002. Weisman, Steven R. "India's Old School Tie: Hanow by the Himalayas." (November 12, 1985): [The Doon School, Dehra Dun, India.]

5003. Wilson, K. "The Economic Basis of Casteism." *PCR Information (World Council of Churches)* No. 24 (1987): 24- 27.

5004. Wood, John R. "Reservations in Doubt: The Backlash Against Affirmative Action in Gujarat, India." *Pacific Affairs* 60 (1987): 408-430.

5005. Woodsmall, Ruth F. "Women in India." In *Women and the New East*. Ruth F. Woodsmall. Washington, D.C.: Middle East Institute, 1960.

5006. Yang, Anand A. "Disciplinary 'Natives': Prisons and Prisoners in Early Nineteenth Century India." *South Asia* 10 (December 1987): 29-45.

5007. Yang, Anand A. *The Limited Raj. Agrarian Relations in Colonial India, Saran District, 1793-1920*. Berkeley, CA: University of California Press, 1989.

5008. Yesudas, R. N. *A People's Revolt in Travancore: A Backward Class Movement for Social Freedom*. Trivandrum: Manju Publishing House, 1975.

5009. Younger, Coralie. "Racial Attitudes and the Anglo-Indians Perceptions of a Community Before and After Independence." *South Asia* 6 (November 1983): 34-45.

5010. Zaidi, Grace Lilly. "Status of Dalit Women and the Church." *PCR Information* No. 27 (1990): 80-86.

5011. Zaidi, S. A. "Poverty and Disease: Need for Structural Change." *Indian Economic Journal* 36 (April-June 1989)

5012. Zakaria, R. A. *Muslims in India: A Political Analysis (From 1885-1906)*. Doctoral dissertation, University of London, School of Oriental and African Studies, 1948.

INDONESIA

5013. Aditjondro, George J. "The Irianese Ethnic Minorities in Indonesia. An Issue of National Integration." Impact 17 (1982): 63-67.

5014. Alexander, Jennifer and Paul Alexander. "Shared Poverty as Ideology: Agrarian Relationships in Colonial Java." Man 17 (1982): 597-619.

5015. Anderson, Benedict. "Old State, New Society: Indonesia's New Order in Comparative Historical Perspective." Journal of Asian Studies 42 (May 1983)

5016. Asra, Abuzar. "Inequality Trends in Indonesia, 1969-1981: A Re-examination." Bulletin Indonesian Ec. Studies 25 (August 1989): 100-110.

5017. Australia Parliament, Senate Standing Committee on Foreign Affairs and Defence. The Human Rights and Conditions of the People of East Timor, September 1983. Canberra: AGPS, 1983.

5018. Aziz, M. A. Japan's Colonialism and Indonesia. The Hague: Martinus Nijhoff, 1955.

5019. Bakker, H. "Class Relations in Java in the Nineteenth Century: A Weberian Perspective." Canadian Journal of Development Studies 8 (1987)

5020. Bayly, C. A. and D.H.A. Kolff, eds. Two Colonial Empires: Comparative Essays on the History of India and Indonesia in the Nineteenth Century. Dordrecht, Netherlands: M. Nijhoff, 1986.

5021. Berman, Peter and others. "Equity in Public-Sector Primary Health Care: The Role of Service Organization in Indonesia." Economic Development and Cultural Change 37 (July 1989): 777-803.

5022. Booth, Anne. "Living Standards and the Distribution of Income in Colonial Indonesia: A Review of the Evidence." Journal of Southeast Asian Studies 19 (1988): 310-334.

5023. Budiardjo, Carmel and L.S. Liong. The War against East Timor. London: Zed, 1984.

5024. Chernichovsky, Dov and O.A. Meesook. School Enrollment in Indonesia. Washington, D.C.: World Bank, 1985.

5025. Coppel, Charles A. and others. The Chinese in Indonesia, the Philippines and Malaysia. London: Minority Rights Group, 1982. [Revised edition.]

5026. Coppel, Charles A. Indonesian Chinese in Crisis. Kuala Lumpur: Oxford University Press, 1983.

5027. Dhofier, A. "Transformation of Islamic Education in Indonesia." Prisma 38 (December 1985): 21-27.

5028. Dick, Howard W. "Japan's Economic Expansion in the Netherlands Indies between the First and Second World Wars." Journal of South East Asian Studies 20 (September 1989): 244- 272.

5029. Dick, Howard W. "The Rise of a Middle Class and the Changing Concept of Equity in Indonesia: An Interpretation." Indonesia 39 (April 1985): 71-92.

5030. Dietz, Ton. "The Redevelopment of Dutch Imperialism with Regard to Indonesia Since 1965." In Research in Political Economy. Vol. 2, edited by Paul Zarembka. Greenwich, CT: JAI Press, 1979.

5031. Drake, Christine. National Integration in Indonesia: Patterns and Policies. Honolulu: University of Hawaii Press, 1989.

5032. Dumasy, E. A. H. "The Process of Education in Indonesia." Kabar Seberang 13-14 (1984): 29-61.

5033. Evans, Grant. "Portuguese Timor." New Left Review NO. 91 (1975): 67-79.

5034. Faust, James P. "The Tragic History of East Timor." Cornell University, 1989.

5035. Federspiel, Howard M. "The Political and Social Language of Indonesian Muslims: The Case of Al-Muslimun." Indonesia 38 (October 1984): 55-73.

5036. Gietzelt, Dale. "The Indonesianization of West Papua." Oceania 59 (March 1989): 201-221.

5037. Go, G. T. "Chinese in Indonesia: Past and Present." Kabar Seberang 13-14 (1984): 137-156.

5038. Gordon, Alec. "Some Problems of Analyzing Class Relations in Indonesia." Journal of Contemporary Asia 8 (1978): 210- 218.

5039. Hansen, David O. and others. "Determinants of Access to Higher Education in Indonesia." Comparative Education Review 33 (August 1989): 317-333.

5040. Islam, Iyanatul and H. Khan. "Income Inequality, Poverty and Socio-economic Development in Indonesia: An Empirical Investigation." Asian Profile 13 (April 1985): 139-151.

5041. Islam, Iyanatul and H. Khan. "Spatial Patterns of Inequality and Poverty in Indonesia." Bulletin of Indonesian Economic Studies 22 (August 1986): 80-102.

5042. Jolliffe, Jill. East Timor: Nationalism and Colonialism. St. Lucia, Q.: University of Queensland, 1978.

5043. Kintanar, Thelma B. "Social Class as a Theme in Indonesian Fiction." Solidarity 113 (July-August 1987): 81-86.

5044. Lindblad, J. Thomas. "Economic Aspects of the Dutch Expansion in Indonesia, 1870-1914." Modern Asian Studies 23 (February 1989): 1-24.

5045. Ludwig, Klemens and Korinna Horta. "Ost Timor. Das vergessene Sterben. Indonesischer Völkermord unter Ausschluss der Weltöffentlichkeit." Pogrom 16 (June 1985): 7-147.

5046. Maddison, Angus. "Dutch Income In and From Indonesia: 1700- 1938." Modern Asian Studies 23 (October 1989)

5047. Mangan, James. "The Impact of Schooling on Traditional Societies in Indonesia." Prisma 38 (December 1985): 8-20.

5048. Mohd Aris Hj Othman. "Caste as Manifested in the Indonesian Society." Sari 3 (January 1985): 75-81.

5049. Nawawi, M. A. "Punitive Colonialism: The Dutch and the Indonesian National Integration." Journal of South Eastern Asian Studies (September 1971)

5050. Otten, Mariel. Transmigrasi Indonesian Resettlement Policy 1965-1985. Myths and Realities. Copenhagen: IWGIA, 1987.

5051. Pemberton, John. The Appearance of Order: A Politics of Culture in Colonial and Postcolonial Java. Doctoral dissertation, Cornell University, 1989. UMO # 9001331.

5052. Penders, C. L. M. "Colonial Education Policy and Practice in Indonesia: 1900-1942." Austrian National University, 1968.

5053. Penders, C. L. M., ed. Indonesia: Selected Documents on Colonialism and Nationalism, 1830-1942. University of Queensland Press, 1977.

5054. Penny, David H. Starvation: The Role of the Market System. Canberra, Australia: Australian National University Press, 1986.

5055. Rakindo, Adil. "Chinese Scapegoat Politics in Suharto's 'New Order'." In Ten Years' Military Terror in Indonesia, 135- 138. Nottingham: Spokesman Books, 1975.

5056. Ramos-Horta, Jose. Funu, The Unfinished Saga of East Timor. Trenton, NJ: Red Sea Press, 1986.

5057. Reid, Anthony. "The Pre-colonial Economy of Indonesia." Bulletin of Indonesian Economic Studies 20 (August 1984): 151-167.

5058. Reid, Anthony and Oki Akira, eds. The Japanese Experience in Indonesia: Selected Memoirs of 1942-1945. Athens: Center for International Studies, Ohio University, 1986.

5059. Retboll, Torben. "The East Timor Conflict and Western Repsonse." Bulletin of the Concerned Asian Scholars 19 (January-March 1987): 24-40.

5060. Retboll, Torben, ed. East Timor: The Struggle Continues. Copenhagen: IWGIA, 1984.

5061. Robinson, Kathryn M. Stepchildren of Progress: The Political Economy of Development in an Indonesian Town. Albany: State University of New York Press, 1986. [Soroako.]

5062. Robison, Dick. "Factors Affecting the Structure of Indonesian Capitalism." Prisma 26 (December 1982): 35-45.

5063. Saleh, Abdul A. Determinants of Access to Higher Education in Indonesia. Ohio State University, 1986. UMO # 8618844.

5064. Schiel, Tilman. Despotism and Capitalism: A Historical Comparison of Europe and Indonesia. Saarbrucken: Breitenbach, 1985.

5065. Schulten, C. M. "Tactics of the Dutch Colonial Army in the Netherlands East Indies." Revue Internationale d'Histoire Militaire 70 (1988): 59-67.

5066. Schweizer, Thomas. "Soziale Schichtung im kolonialen Java." Anthropos 80 (1985): 153-183.

5067. Shin, Yoon Hwan. Demystifying the Capitalist State: Political Patronage, Bureaucratic Interests, and Capitalists- in-Formation in Soeharto's Indonesia. Doctoral dissertation: Yale University, 1989.

5068. Siagian, T. P. "Some Notes on Christian Education in Indonesia." Prisma 38 (December 1985): 33-43.

5069. Siegal, James T. Solo in the New Order: Language and Hierarchy in an Indonesian City. Princeton, NJ: Princeton University Press, 1987. [Solo, Indonesia, a Javanese city.]

5070. Sigit, Hananto. "Income Distribution and Household Characteristics." Bulletin of Indonesian Economic Studies 21 (December 1985): 51-68.

5071. Speare, A. Jr. and J. Harris. "Education, Earnings, and Migration in Indonesia." Economic Development and Cultural Change 34 (January 1986)

5072. Stoler, Ann L. Capitalism and Confrontation in Sumatra's Plantation Belt 1870-1979. New Haven, Ct: Yale University Press, 1985.

5073. Supraptong, Seha. "Current Issues in Indonesian Education." South East Asin Journal Education Sstudies 23 (1986): 1-65.

5074. Suter, Keith. East Timor and West Irian. rev. ed. London: Minority Rights Group, 1982.

5075. Tan, Mily G. "The Role of Ethnic Chinese Minority in Development: The Indonesian Case." South East Asin Studies 25 (December 1987): 363-382.

5076. Thee, Kian W. "Japanese and American Direct Investment in Indonesian Manufacturing Compared." Economic Finance Indonesia 32 (March 1984): 89-105.

5077. Uppal, J. S. "Income Distribution, Poverty and Economic Growth in Indonesia." Economic and Finance Indonesia 33 (1985): 319-347.

5078. Uppal, J. S. "Income Distribution and Poverty in Indonesia." Journal of Economic Development 11 (December 1986): 177-196.

5079. West Papua: Plunder in Paradise. London: Anti-Slavery Society, 1986.

5080. Wirahodikusumah, Miftah. The Rise and Development of the Indonesian New Order Regime. Doctoral dissertation: University of Hawaii, 1990. UMO # 9030587.

5081. Yoneda, K. "A Note on Income Distribution in Indonesia." Developing Economies 23 (December 1985)

IRAN

5082. Allen, Paul D. "The Baha'is of Iran: A Proposal for Enforcement of International Human Rights Standards." Cornell International Law Journal 20 (Summer 1987): 337-361.

5083. Amanat, Abbas. Resurrection and Renewal. The Making of the Bahi Movement in Iran, 1844-1850. Ithaca, New York: Cornell University Press, 1989. [Forerunner of Baha'i religion.]

5084. Atash, Farhad. Spatial Disparities in Iran, 1949-1978. Doctoral dissertation: Rutgers University, 1986. UMO # 8620006.

5085. Bakhash, Shaul. "Islam and Social Justice in Iran." In Shi'ism, Resistance, and Revolution, edited by Martin Kramer. Boulder, Co.: Westview Press, 1987.

5086. Bakhash, Shaul. "The Politics of Land, Law, and Social Justice in Iran." Middle East Journal 43 (1989): 186-201.

5087. Bakhash, Shaul. The Reign of the Ayatollahs: Iran and the Islamic Republic. New York: Basic Books, 1984.

5088. Beeman, William O. Language, Status, and Power in Iran. Bloomington: Indiana University Press, 1986.

5089. Bestor, Jane F. The Kurds of Iranian Baluchistan: A Regional Elite. Master's thesis: McGill University, 1979.

5090. Bordewich, Fergus M. "Holy Terror." Atlantic (April 1987): 26, 28-31. [Attacks on Baha'is in Iran.]

5091. Bruinessen, Martin van. "Kurdish Tribes and Iran: The Case of Simbo's Revolt." Stud. Kurdica (Paris) 4 (1986): 6-32.

5092. Bruinessen, Martin van. "The Kurds between Iran and Iraq." Merip Report 16 (July-August 1986): 14-27.

5093. Bruinessen, Martin van. "Nationalismus und religiosen Konflikt: der kurdische Widerstand in Iran." In Religion und Politik in Iran, edited by Kurt Gruessing. Frankfurt am Main: 1981.

5094. Chokay, J. "Zoroastrians in Muslim Iran." Iranian Studies 30 (1987): 17-30.

5095. Cooper, Roger. The Bah'ais of Iran. rev. ed. London: Minority Rights Group, 1985.

5096. Cotton, Richard W. Nationalism in Iran. Pittsburgh, PA: University of Pittsburgh Press, 1964.

5097. Dowty, Alan. "Baha'is of Iran: Trapped in a Genocidal Nightmare." National Catholic Reporter (January 27, 1989)

5098. Entessar, Nader. "Educational Reforms in Iran: Cultural Revolution or Anti-Intellectualism?" Journal of South Asian Middle Eastern Studies 7 (Fall 1984): 47-64.

5099. Esmailzadeh, Nadir and Hazhir Teimourian. "The Unseen War." New Statesman and Society (February 10, 1989): [Iranian government's war against the Kurdish people.]

5100. Fischel, Walter J. "The Jews in Mediaeval Iran from the 16th to the 18th Centuries: Political, Economic and Communal Aspects." Irano-Judaica (1982): 265-291.

5101. Foran, John F. Social Structure and Social Change in Iran from 1500 to 1979. Doctoral dissertation: University of California, Berkeley, 1989. UMO # 8916661.

5102. Gasiorowski, Mark. "The 1953 Coup d'Etat in Iran." International Journal of Middle East Studies 19 (August 1987): 261-286.

5103. Katouzian, Homa. The Political Economy of Modern Iran: Despotism and Pseudo-Modernisn, 1926-1979. London: MacMillan, 1981.

5104. Keddie, Nikki R. "Class Structure and Political Power in Iran Since 1796." Iranian Studies 11 (1978): 305-330.

5105. Kestenberg-Amighi, Janet T. The Zoroastrians: Persistence of a Small Minority Group in Moslem Iran. Doctoral dissertation: University of Missouri, 1984. UMO # 8512224.

5106. Klima, Otakar. "Zur Problematik der Sklaverei im alten Iran." Altorientalische Forschungen 5 (1977): 91-6.

5107. Loeb, Laurence D. "Dhimmi Status and Jewish Roles in Iranian Society." Ethnic Groups 1 (1976): 89-105.

5108. Loeb, Laurence D. Outcaste: Jewish Life in Iran. New York: Gordon and Beach, 1978.

5109. Majid, M. G. "Land Reform Policies in Iran." American Journal of Agricultural Economics 69 (November 1987)

5110. Martin, Douglas. The Persecution of the Baha'is of Iran, 1844-1984. Ottawa, Ontario: Association for Baha'i Studies, 1984.

5111. Martin, Douglas. "The Baha'is of Iran Under the Islamic Republic, 1979-1983." Middle East Focus (Toronto) 17-27, 30-31 (November 1983)

5112. Maslujak, S. "Persian Jewry- Prelude to a Catastrophe." Judaism 29 (Fall 1980): 390-430.

5113. Mohtadi, H. "Rural Stratification, Rural to Urban Migration, and Urban Inequality: Evidence from Iran." World Development 14 (June 1986)

5114. Moreen, Vera B. Iranian Jewry's Hour of Peril and Heroism: A Study of Babai Ibn Lutf's Chronicle, 1617-1662. New York: American Academy for Jewish Research, 1987.

5115. Moreen, Vera B. "The Persecution of Iranian Jews during the Reign of Shah 'Abbas II (1642-1666)." Hebrew Union College Annual 52 (1982): 275-309.

5116. Moreen, Vera B. "The Status of Religious Minorities in Safavid Iran 1617-1661." Journal of Near Eastern Studies 40 (1981): 119-134.

5117. Najmabadi, Afsaneh, ed. Women's Autobiographies in Contemporary Iran. Cambridge, MA: Harvard University Press, 1991.

5118. Nakhaie, Mahmoud R. Development of Capitalism in Iran. Doctoral dissertation: University of Waterloo, 1986.

5119. Nash, Geoffrey. Iran's Secret Pogrom: The Conspiracy to Wipe Out the Baha'is. Sudbury: N. Spearman: 1982,

5120. Nashat, Guity, ed. Women and Revolution in Iran. Boulder, CO.: Westview Press, 1983.

5121. Netzer, Amnon. "The Fate of the Jewish Community of Tabriz." Ayalon (1986): 411-419.

5122. Parveen Shaukat Ali. Status of Women in the Muslim World: A Study in the Feminist Movements in Turkey, Egypt, Iran and Pakistan. Lahore: Aziz Publishers, 1975.

5123. Sabahi, Houshang. British Policy in Persia, 1918-1925. Savage, M.D.: Frank Cass, 1990.

5124. Saber, Mostafa. Situation of the Working Class in Iran. Stockholm: OIS, 1990.

5125. Sanasarian, Eliz. The Women's Rights Movement in Iran: Muting, Appeasement, and Repression from 1900 to Khomeni. New York: Praeger, 1982.

5126. Sears, William. A Cry from the Heart: The Baha'is in Iran. Oxford: G. Ronald, 1982.

5127. Shenker, Barry. "Anti-Zionism and Antisemitism in the Iranian Revolution." Research Report (Institute of Jewish Affairs) No. 2 (February 1980)

5128. Smith, Peter. The Babi and Baha'i Religions: From Messianic Sh'ism to a World Religion. New York: Cambridge University Press, 1987.

5129. Soroudi, Sorour. "Jews in Islamic Iran." Jerusalem Quarterly 21 (1981): 99-114.

5130. Tabari, Azar and Nahid Yeganeh, eds. In the Shadow of Islam: The Women's Movement in Iran. London: Zed Press, 1983.

5131. Vader, John P. "August Forel Defends the Persecuted Persian Baha'is, 1925-1927." Gesnerus 41 (1984): 53-60.

5132. Zabih, Sepehr. The Left in Contemporary Iran. Stanford, CA: Hoover Institution Press, 1986.

IRAQ

5133. Abramski-Bligh, Irit. "Iraq." in Encyclopedia of the Holocaust, II. 716-718. New York: Macmillan, 1990.

5134. Attar, K. A-R. The Minorities of Iraq During the Period of the Mandate, 1920-1932. Doctoral dissertation: Columbia University, 1967. UMO # 6812928.

5135. Axelgard, Frederick W., ed. Iraq in Transition. A Political, Economic, and Strategic Perspective. Boulder, CO: Westview, 1986.

5136. Batatu, Hanna. "Class Analysis and Iraqi Society." Arab Studies Quarterly 1 (Summer 1979)

5137. Bruinessen, M. van. "The Kurds between Iran and Iraq." Middle East Report No. 141 (July-August 1986): 14-27.

5138. Cobbett, Deborah. "Women in Iraq." in Saddam's Iraq. Revolution or Reaction? CARDI. London: Zed Books, 1986.

5139. Cohen, Hayyim J. "Exodus from Iraq." Jerusalem Quarterly No. 9 (Autumn 1978): 124-130.

5140. Cohen, Stuart A. British Policy in Mesopotamia 1903-1914. London: Ithaca Press, 1976.

5141. Committee Against Repression and for Democratic Rights in Iraq. Saddam's Iraq. Revolution or Reaction? London: Zed Books, 1986.

5142. Farouk-Sluglett, Marion. "'Socialist' Iraq 1963-1978- Towards a Reappraisal." Orient 23 (1982)

5143. Farouk-Sluglett, Marion and Peter Sluglett. "The Transformation of Land Tenure and Rural Social Structure in Central and Southern Iraq,

1870-1958." International Journal of Middle Eastern Studies NO. 15 (1983)

5144. Farouk-Sluglett, Marion and Peter Sluglett. "Labour and National Liberation: The Trade Union Movement in Iraq, 1920- 1958." Arab Studies Quarterly 5 (1981)

5145. Feitelson, Dina. "Aspects of the Social Life of Kurdish Jews." Jewish Journal of Sociology 1 (1959): 201-216.

5146. Gat, Moshe. "The Connection between the Bombings in Baghdad and the Emigration of the Jews from Iraq, 1950-1951." Middle Eastern Studies 24 (July 1988): 312-330.

5147. Ghareeb, Edmund A. The Kurdish Question in Iraq. Syracuse, New York: Syracuse University Press, 1981.

5148. Haddad, Subhy. "Rebel Kurds Trouble Iraq." Jerusalem Post (June 3, 1986)

5149. Haim, Sylvia G. "Aspects of Jewish Life in Baghdad under the Monarchy." Middle Eastern Studies 12 (1976): 188-208.

5150. Haj, Samira. "Ba'ath's Bloody Background." Against the Current No. 29 (November-December 1990): 18-21. [Interview.]

5151. Hillel, Shlomo. Operation Babylon: The Story of the Rescue of the Jews of Iraq. Translated by Ira Friedman. New York: Doubleday, 1988.

5152. Ibrahim, Ferhad. Die Kurdische Nationalbewegung im Irak: eine Fallstudie zur Problematik Etnischer Konflikte in der Dritten Welt. Berlin: Schwarz, 1983.

5153. Jawad, Sa'ad N. Iraq and the Kurdish Question. London: Ithaca Press, 1981.

5154. Kedourie, E. "The Jews of Baghdad in 1910." Middle Eastern Studies 3 (1971)

5155. Kelidar, Abbas, ed. The Integration of Modern Iraq. London: Croom Helm, 1979.

5156. Khadduri, W. "The Jews of Iraq in the Nineteenth Century." Journal of the Social Sciences 5 (January 1978): 208-218.

5157. Khazoum, E. "An Arab View of the Jews of Iraq." Middle East Review 9 (1976-1977): 31-36.

5158. Korn, David A. Human Rights in Iraq. New Haven, CT.: Yale University Press, 1991.

5159. Luks, H. P. "Iraqi Jews During World War I." Wiener Library Bulletin 30 (1977): 30-39.

5160. Masliyah, Sadok H. "Zionism in Iraq." Middle Eastern Studies 25 (1989): 216-237.

5161. Morony, Michael G. Iraq After the Muslim Conquest. Princeton, NJ: Princeton University Press, 1984. [The Jews, pp.306-330.]

5162. Nasser, Munir H. "Iraq: Ethnic Minorities and their Impact on Politics." Journal of South Asian and Middle Eastern Studies 8 (Spring 1985): 22-37.

5163. Popovic, Alexandre. La Revolte des esclaves en Iraq au IIIe/IXe siecles. Paris: 1976.

5164. Rejwan, Nissim. The Jews of Iraq: 3000 Years of History and Culture. Boulder, CO: Westview, 1985.

5165. Sargius, Francis and B. Beit-Ishoo. "Assyrians on the Millstone." Nation (May 31, 1975)

5166. Shiblak, Abbas. The Lure of Zion: The Case of the Iraqi Jews. London: Al Saqi Books, 1986.

5167. Sluglett, Peter. Britain in Iraq 1914-1932. London: Ithaca Press, 1976.

5168. Vanly, Ismet S. "Kurdistan in Iraq." In People Without a Country. The Kurds and Kurdistan, edited by Gerard Chaliand. 153- 210. London: Zed Press, 1980.

IRELAND

5169. Aalen, F. H. A. "The Rehousing of Rural Labourers in Ireland under the Labourer (Ireland) Acts, 1883-1919." Journal of Historical Geography 12 (July 1986): 287-306.

5170. Akenson, Donald H. A Mirror to Kathleen's Face: Education in Independent Ireland, 1920-1960. Montreal: McGill-Queen's University Press, 1975.

5171. Bowen, Kurt. Protestants in a Catholic State: Ireland's Privileged Minority. McGill: Queen's University Press, 1983.

5172. Brady, Ciaran and Raymond Gillespie, eds. Natives and Newcomers: The Making of Irish Colonial Society 1534-1641. Irish Academic Press, 1986.

5173. Carlin, Norah. "Ireland and Natural Man in 1649, Vol. 2." In Europe and Its Others, edited by F. Barker and others, 93-117. University of Essex, 1985.

5174. Crawford, E. Margaret, ed. Famine: The Irish Emergence, 900-1900: Subsistence Crises and Famines in Ireland. Edinburgh: J. Donald, 1989.

5175. Crotty, Raymond D. Ireland in Crisis: A Study in Capitalist Colonial Underdevelopment. Dover, NH: Brandon, 1986.

5176. Davies, R. R. Domination and Conquest: The Experience of Ireland, Scotland, and Wales, 1100-1300. New York: Cambridge University Press, 1990.

5177. Finnegan, Richard B. "The Blueshirts of Ireland During the 1930's: Fascism Inverted." Eire-Ireland 24 (Summer 1989): 79-99.

5178. Gillingham, John. "Images of Ireland, 1170-1600: The Origins of English Imperialism." History Today 37 (February 1987): 16-22.

5179. Greaney, V. and T. Kellaghan. "Factors Related to Level of Educational Attainment in Ireland." Economic and Social Review 16 (January 1985)

5180. Hopkins, Sean. "The Two Irelands: On 'Racism' and 'Irishmen for Export'." Freedom at Issue No. 20 (1973): 16-17.

5181. Hout, Michael. Following in Father's Footsteps. Social Mobility in Ireland. Cambridge, MA: Harvard University Press, 1989.

5182. Hyland, Aine. "Schools and Values." Studies (Ireland) 75 (1986): 250-266.

5183. Kelleher, Patricia. "Familism in Irish Capitalism in the 1950's." Economic and Social Review 18 (1987): 75-94. [Wealth in Ireland.]

5184. Lynch, K. "An Analysis of Some Presuppositions Underlying the Concepts of Meritocracy and Ability as Presented in Greaney and Kellaghan's Study." Economic and Social Review 16 (January 1985)

5185. Lyons, Patrick M. "The Size Distribution of Personal Wealth in the Republic of Ireland." Review of Income and Wealth 20 (June 1974): 181-202.

5186. Maccurtain, Margaret and Douncha O'Corrain, eds. Women in Irish Society: The Historical Dimension. Westport, CT: Greenwood, 1979.

5187. Mokyr, Joel. Why Ireland Starved: A Quantitative and Analytical History of the Irish Economy, 1800-1850. Winchester, MA: Allen & Unwin, 1983.

5188. Moore, G. "Socio-Economic Aspects of Anti-Semitism in Ireland, 1880-1905." Economic and Social Review 12 (April 1981)

5189. Moore, Robert. "Race Relations in the Six Countries: Colonialism, Industrialization, and Stratification in Ireland." Race 14 (July 1972): 20-42.

5190. Nadel, Ira Bruce. Joyce and the Jews: Culture and Texts. Iowa City: University of Iowa Press, 1989.

5191. Nolan, B. and T. Callan. "Measuring Trends in Poverty over Time: Some Robust Results for Ireland 1980-1987." Economic and Social Review 20 (July 1989)

5192. Nolan, B. "Socio-economic Mortality Differentials in Ireland." Economic and Social Review 21 (January 1990)

5193. Nordheimer, Jan. "Irish Gypsy: Native as Shamrock, Hated as Plague." New York Times, (February 17, 1983)

5194. O'Brien, Jack. British Brutality in Ireland. Cork: Mereier Press, 1989.

IRELAND 395

5195. O'Connell, John. Education and Partition: A Case Study of Ethnic and Religious Minorities in Twentieth Century Ireland. Doctoral dissertation: University of California, Los Angeles, 1988. UMO # 8906410.

5196. O'Dowd, Anne. The Irish Migrant Farm Worker 1830-1920. Irish Academic Press Book, 1990.

5197. O'Neil, Daniel J. "Enclave Nation-Building: The Irish Experience." Journal of Ethnic Studies 15 (Fall 1987): 1- 25.

5198. O'Riordan, Manus. "Anti-Semitism in Irish Politics." Irish- Jewish Year Book 34 (1984-1985): 15-27.

5199. Proudfoot, Lindsay J. Urban Patronage and Estate Management on the Duke of Devonshire's Irish Estates (1764-1891): A Study in Landlord-Tenant Relationships. Doctoral dissertation: Queen's University of Belfast, 1989.

5200. Pyle, Jean L. The State and Women in the Economy: Lessons from Sex Discrimination in the Republic of Ireland. Albany: State University of New York Press, 1990.

5201. Raftery, A. E. and M. Hout. "Does Irish Education Approach the Meritocratic Ideal? A Logistic Analysis." Economic and Social Review 16 (January 1985)

5202. Roth, Stephen J. "Incitment to Racial and Religious Hatred To Be Banned." Patterns of Prejudice 22 (Winter 1988): 43- 44.

5203. Sheehan, Elizabeth A. The Academics and the Powers: Colonialism, National Development and the Irish University. Doctoral dissertation: City University of New York, 1990. UMO # 9029977.

5204. Smyth, Alibhe. Women's Rights in Ireland. Dublin: Ward River Press, 1983.

ISRAEL

5205. Abbink, G. Jon. "Aspects of the Ethnic Identity of Ethiopian Immigrants in Israel." Plural Societies 16 (June 1986): 102-125.

5206. Abbink, G. Jon. "The Changing Identity of Ethiopian Immigrants (Falashas) in Israel." Anthropological Quarterly 57 (1984): 139-153.

5207. Abbink, G. Jon. "Ethno-cultural Differences and Assimilation: Falashas in an Israeli Immigrant Absorption Center." Bijd. -Tot Taal-, Land- en Volkenk. 141 (1985): 1-18.

5208. Adler, Chaim. "Rescuing Youths from Poor Areas." Jerusalem Post, (June 26, 1986): [Youth Aliya.]

5209. Agursky, Mikhail. "The Political and Social Implications of Soviet Aliya." New Outlook 34 (January 1991): 8-11.

5210. Alexander, Tamar. "A Legend of the Blood Libel in Jerusalem: A Study of a Process of Folk-tale Adaptation." International Folklore Review 5 (1987): 60-74.

5211. Amare, Girma. "Education and Society in Prerevolutionary Ethiopia." N.E. African Studies 6 (1984): 61-80.

5212. Amouyal, Barbara. "Birth Pains." Jerusalem Post, (December 15, 1985): [Differential infant mortality rates in Israel.]

5213. Ashkenazi, Abraham. Nationalism and National Identity in Divided Cities: Jerusalem and Berlin. Berlin: Das Arabische Buch, Ethnizitat und Gesellschaft, 1990.

5214. Ashkenazi, Michael and Weingrod, Alex, eds. Ethiopian Jews and Israel. New Brunswick, NJ: Transaction Publishers, 1987.

5215. Ashkenazi, Michael and Weingrod, A. "From Falasha to Ethiopian Jews." Israel Social Science Research 3 (1985): 3-8.

5216. Atlas, Yedidya. "Rabbinical Perspective." Jerusalem Post, (November 8, 1985). [Defense of Israel's Chief Rabbinate policy on Ethiopian Jewish immigrants.]

5217. Atlas Of Israel, 3rd edition. New York: Macmillan, 1986.

5218. Atran, Scott. "Surrogate Colonization of Palestine, 1917- 1959." American Ethnologist 16 (1989): 719-744.

5219. Ayalon, Hanna and others. "Class Consciousness in Israel." International Journal of Comparative Sociology 28 (September-December 1987): 158-172.

5220. Bahiri, Simcha. "Military and Colonial Aspects of the Israeli Economy since 1967." New Outlook 30 (May-June 1987): 31-33.

5221. Bar-On, Mordechai. "Trends in the Political Psychology of Israeli Jews 1967-1986." Journal of Palestine Studies 17 (Autumn 1987): 21-36.

5222. Bard, Mitchell. "The Unfinished Exodus of Ethiopian Jews." Midstream 34 (January 1988): 8-11.

5223. Barnett, Don S. "Going 'Home': Problems of Deculturation and Identity Experienced by Ethiopian Jews." Journal of Intercultural Studies 8 (1987): 27-37.

5224. Bedein, David S. "Culture within Culture: Ethiopian Jews in Israel." Midstream 33 (March 1987): 38-39.

5225. Beinin, Joel. "Marching Toward Civil War." Merip Reports Nos. 136-137 (October-December 1985): 3-6.

5226. Beit-Hallahmi, Benjamin. "Black Hebrews in the Promised Land." Middle East Report No. 160 (September-October 1989): 36.

5227. Belfer, Ella. "The Jewish People and the Kingdom of Heaven: A Study of Jewish Theocracy." Jewish Political Studies Review 1 (Spring 1989): 7-37.

5228. Ben Shaul, D'vora. "Where Do We Go From Here?" Jerusalem Post, (January 16, 1987): [Problems of Ethiopian Jews in Israel.]

5229. Ben-Ezer, G. "Cross-cultural Misunderstandings: The Case of Ethiopian Immigrant Jews in Israeli Society." Israel Social Science Research 3 (1985): 63-73.

5230. Ben-Porat, Amir. Between Class and Nation: The Formation of the Jewish Working Class in the Period before Israel's Statehood. Westport, CT.: Greenwood, 1986.

5231. Ben-Porat, Amir. Divided We Stand: Class Structure in Israel from 1948-1980's. Westport, CT: Greenwood, 1989.

5232. Ben-Porath, Yoram, ed. The Israeli Economy: Maturing through Crisis. Cambridge, MA: Harvard University Press, 1986.

5233. Ben-Yehuda, Nachman. "Social Meaning of Alternative Systems." In The Israeli State and Society: Boundaries and Frontiers, edited by Baruch Krimmerling. Albany: State University of New York Press, 1989.

5234. No entry

5235. Benvenisti, Meron. Conflicts and Contradictions. New York: Villard, 1986.

5236. Benvenisti, Meron. "Growing Up in Jerusalem." New York Times, (October 16, 1988)

5237. BenShaul, D'vora. "Creation of a Sub-culture." Jerusalem Post (May 24, 1987): [Ethiopian women in Israel.]

5238. Bernstein, Deborah. The Struggle for Equality: Urban Women Workers in Prestate Israeli Society. New York: Praeger, 1986.

5239. Bernstein, Irving. "Reluctant Consensus." Jerusalem Post, (July 1, 1986): [Future of Project Renewal.]

5240. "The Black Hebrew Israelites." ADL Research Report (February 1987): 1-15.

5241. Bookmiller, Robert J. "Rabbi Meir Kahane: His Messianic View and the State of the Jews." Journal of South Asian and Middle Eastern Studies 11 (Summer 1988): 21-37.

5242. Carmi, Shulamit and Rosenfeld, Henry. "The Emergence of Militaristic Nationalism in Israel." International Journal of Politics, Culture and Society 3 (Fall 1989): 5-49.

5243. Chafetz, Gary. "Second Look. 'Operation Moses' Revisited." Boston Globe, (February 15, 1988): [Ethiopian Jews in Israel.]

5244. Cohen, Mitchell J. Palestine and the Great Powers, 1945- 1948. Princeton, NJ: Princeton University Press, 1982.

5245. Dar, Y. and Resh Nura. Classroom Composition and Pupil Achievement: A Study of the Effects of Ability-based Classes. New York: Gordon and Breach, 1986.

5246. David, Helen. "Now for the Hard Part." Baltimore Jewish Times, (September 19, 1986): 69-77. [Ethiopian Jews in Israel.]

5247. Domb, Yocheved and Stanley Schneider. "Group Work With the Ethiopian Community in Israel." Jewish Social Work Forum (Spring 1989): 81-91.

5248. Doron, Abraham. "The Histadrut, Social Policy and Equality." Jerusalem Quarterly No. 47 (Summer 1988): 131- 144.

5249. Dothan, T. "Jewish Children from Ethiopia: Some Observations on their Adaptation Patterns." Israel Social Science Research 3 (1985): 97-103.

5250. Eashman, Green Fay. "Learning to Live Together." Jerusalem Post, (September 20, 1985): [Anti-racism education in Israeli schools.]

5251. Eisenstadt, S. N. The Transformation of Israeli Society. Boulder, CO: Westview Press, 1986.

5252. Eisikovits, R. A. "Children's Institute in Israel as Mirrors of Social and Cultural Change." Child & Youth Services 7 (1985): 21-29.

5253. Freid, Yochanan. "In the Land of the Jews." New Outlook 30 (May-June 1987): 17-19.

5254. Freindly, Alfred and Silver, Eric. Israel's Oriental Immigrants and Druzes. London: Minority Rights Group, 1981.

5255. Frenkel, Shlomo. "Israel's Economic Crisis." Merip Reports Nos. 136-137 (October-December 1985): 20-23.

5256. Friedler, Ya'acov. "Working a Miracle." Jerusalem Post, Magazine (May 17, 1986): [Development towns in Israel.]

5257. Friedmann, D. and Santamaria, U. "Identity and Change: The Example of the Falashas, Between Assimilation in Ethiopia and Integration in Israel." Dialectical Anthropology 15 (1990)

5258. Ginor, Fanny. Analysis of Low Income Groups. Tel Aviv: Horowitz Institute, Tel Aviv University, 1974.

5259. Goldberg, Albert I. and Kirschenbaum, Alan. "Black Newcomers to Israel: Contact Situations and Social Distance." Sociology and Social Research 74 (1989): 52-57.

5260. Goldberg, Giora and Ben-Zadok, Efraim. "Ethnic Rebellion against the Political Machine: The Case of Oriental Jews in Israel." Ethnic Groups 7 (1988): 205-226.

5261. Goldberg, H. E. Greentown's Youth: Disadvantaged Youth in a Developmental Town in Israel. Assen: Van Gorcum, 1984.

5262. Habib, Jack and others. "The Effect on Poverty Status in Israel of Considering Wealth and Variability of Income." Review of Income and Wealth 23 (March 1977): 17-38.

5263. Halper, J. "The Absorption of Ethiopian Immigrants: A Return to the Fifties." Israel Social Science Research 3 (1985): 112-139.

5264. Hever, Hannan. "An Extra Pair of Eyes:Hebrew Poetry under Occupation." Tikkun 2, No. 2 (1987): 84-87.

5265. Hoffman, Charles. "Conditions Worsen at Ethiopian Housing Center." Jerusalem Post, (April 21, 1986)

5266. Hoffman, Charles. "Has the 'Lost Tribe' Been Lost in Red Tape?" Baltimore Jewish Times, (June 19, 1987): 56-63. [Ethiopian Jews in Israel.]

5267. Hoffman, Charles. "Helping Where It Hurts." Jerusalem Post, (March 3, 1986): [Evaluation of Project Renewal.]

5268. Horowitz, Tamar R., ed. Between Two Worlds: Children from the Soviet Union in Israel. New York: University Press of America, 1986.

5269. Ilam, Yigal. "1967- A Reevaluation." New Outlook 30 (May- June 1987): 25-27.

5270. "Israel Reports Least Immigration Since '48 Amid Worry for Future." New York Times, (January 7, 1986)

5271. Jaffe, Eliezer D. "Ethiopian Politics." Jerusalem Post, (October 1, 1985): [Politics of the Ethiopian Jewish Community in Israel.]

5272. Jaffe, Eliezer D. Unequal by Chance: Opportunity Deprived, Disadvantaged Students in Higher Education in Israel. Jerusalem, Israel: Gefer Publishing House, 1988.

5273. Jonas, Serge. "Les classes sociales en Israel." Cahiers Internationaux de Sociologie 38 (1965)

5274. Kahane, Reuven. "Informal Agencies of Socialization and the Integration of Immigrant Youth into Society: An Example from Israel." International Migration Review 20 (Sping 1986): 21-39.

5275. Kaplan, John. "The Case for Absorbing the Black Hebrews." Jerusalem Post, (December 23, 1986)

5276. Karp, Judith. "The Legal Status of Women in Israel Today." Israeli Democracy (Tel Aviv) (Summer 989)

5277. Kass, David. "The Ethiopian Experience [in Israel]." Jerusalem Post, (May 12, 1986)

5278. Katz, Y. J. and others. "Two Different Education Structures in Israel and Social Integration." Educational Research 28 (1986): 141-146.

5279. Kenan, Amos. "Kahaneism." Nation (November 9, 1985)

5280. Kimmerling, Baruch, ed. The Israeli State and Society. Albany: State University of New York Press, 1988.

5281. Kop, Yaakov, ed. Israel's Social Services. Jerusalem, Israel: Center for Social Policy Studies, June 1987.

5282. Kop, Yaakov, ed. Changing Social Policy: Israel, 1985-1986. Jerusalem, Israel: Center for Social Policy Studies, 1986.

5283. Landsberger, Michael. "The Distribution of Net Worth in Israel in 1963-1964." Bank of Israel Bulletin 28 (1967)

5284. Lee, Eric. "Countering Racism in Israel." In These Times (November 13, 1985)

5285. Lerner, Natan. "Israel Adopts Bad Law against Racism." Patterns of Prejudice 20 (October 1986): 52-53.

5286. Levi, Abraham. Attitudes and Stereotypes of Eastern and Western Students in Integrated and Nonintegrated Classes in High Schools in Israel. Fordham University, 1988. UMO # 8821956.

5287. Medding, Peter Y., ed. Israel: State and Society, 1948- 1988. New YOrk: Oxford University Press, 1989.

5288. Miller, Ylana N. Government and Society in Rural Palestine, 1920-1948. Austin: University of Texas Press, 1985.

5289. Moriel, Liora. "Cracking Down on Black Hebrews." Jerusalem Post, (November 9, 1986)

5290. Moskovitch, Wolf. Rising to the Challenge: Israel and the Absorption of Soviet Jews. London: Institute of Jewish Affairs, 1990.

5291. Moskowitz, Stuart B. "The Cochini Transformed: Emerging Ethnic Identity among South Indian Jews in Israel." Catholic University of America, 1986.

5292. Nesvisky, Matthew. "Culture Shock. Thousands of Ethiopian Jews Are Now in Israel. How Are They Doing?" Present Tense 14 (Autumn 1986): 12-19.

5293. Noggo, Y. "Agrarian Reform and Class Struggle." Journal of Social Studies 1-30 (April 1984)

5294. Nundi-Izrael, Dafna. "Israeli Women in the Work Force." Jerusalem Quarterly No. 27 (Spring 1983): 59-80.

5295. Orent, Wendy. In the Panther's Skin: The Politics of Identification among the Georgian Jews of Israel. University of Michigan, 1986. UMO # 8612595.

5296. Orr, Akiva. The UnJewish State: The Politics of Jewish Identity in Israel. London: Ithaca Press, 1983.

5297. Peled, Yoav. "Ethnic Exclusivism in the Periphery: The Case of Oriental Jews in Israel's Development Towns." Ethnic and Racial Studies 13 (July 1990)

5298. Peleg, Yoav and Shapir, Gershon. "Who Votes for Kahane?" Merip Reports Nos. 136-137, 32 (October-December 1985). [Translated from Davar, June 21, 1985.]

5299. Porat, Dina. The Blue and the Yellow Star of David: The Zionist Leadership in Palestine and the Holocaust, 1939-1945. Cambridge, MA: Harvard University Press, 1990.

5300. Raday, Frances. "Equality of Women Under Israeli Law." Jerusalem Quarterly No. 27 (Spring 1983): 81-108.

5301. Rahav, Michael and others. "Distribution of Treated Mental Illness in the Neighborhoods of Jerusalem." American Journal of Psychiatry 143 (October 1986): 1249-1254.

5302. Rapoport, Louis. "Frightening Crisis for Ethiopian Jews [in Israel]." Jerusalem Post, (April 7, 1986)

5303. Rapoport, Louis. "No Longer Strangers." Jerusalem Post, Magazine (November 14, 1986): [Ethiopians in Israel.]

5304. Roumani, Maurice M. "From Immigrant to Citizen." Plural Societies 9 (1978): 1-163. [Oriental Jews in Israel.]

5305. Roumani, Maurice M. "The Sephardi Factor in Israeli Politics." Middle East Journal (Summer 1988): 423-435.

5306. Schneller, R. "Heritage and Changes in the Nonverbal Language of Ethiopian Newcomers." Israel Social Science Research 3 (1985): 33-54.

5307. "Schooling in Israel." Urban Education 25 (January 1991)

5308. Schrag, Carl. "The Case Against Poverty in Israel." Israel Scene (Jerusalem) (July 1989): 6-10.

5309. Schwab, Peter. "Israel and the Ethiopian Jews." Jewish Currents 41 (September 1987): 4-7,28.

5310. Shapira, Amos. "Fighting Racism by Law in Israel." Research Report (Institute of Jewish Affairs) No. 14 (December 1986)

5311. Sharansky, Natan. "A New Struggle for Sharansky (interview)." Jerusalem Post (December 5,1986)

5312. Sharkansky, I. "Who Gets What Amidst High Inflation: Winners and Losers in the Israeli Budget, 1978-1984." Public Budgeting and Finance 5 (Winter 1985)

5313. Simon, Rita J. and others. "Public Support for Civil Liberties in Israel." Middle East Review (Summer 1989): 2-8.

5314. Simon, Rita J. and Landis, Jean M. "Trends in Public Support for Civil Liberties." Social Science Quarterly 71 (March 1990): 93-104.

5315. Sprinzak, Ehud. "The Emergence of the Israeli Radical Right." Comparative Politics 21 (1989): 171-192.

5316. Sprinzak, Ehud. "Kach and Meir Kahane: The Emergence of Jewish Quasi-Fascism. II: Ideology and Politics." Patterns of Prejudice 19 (October 1985): 3-13.

5317. Steinberg, M. B. "Education and Integration in Israel: The First Twenty Years." Jewish Journal of Sociology 30 (1988): 17-36.

5318. Streeter, Allan. "On Black Jews and Israel." Chicago Defender (May 27, 1986)

5319. Strunin, Lee. Ethnicity and Education in Israel: Integration in the Middle School. Brandeis University, 1986. UMO # 8617033.

5320. Swirski, Shlomo. Israel: The Oriental Majority. Translated by Barbara Swirski. London: Zed Books, 1989.

5321. Tabory, Ephraim. "Anti-Democratic Legislation in the Service of Democracy: Anti-Racism in Israel." International Journal of the Sociology of Law 17 (February 1989): 87-102.

5322. Viorst, Milton. Sands of Sorrow, Israel's Journey from Independence. New York: Harper & Row, 1987.

5323. Wagaw, Teshome G. "The Emigration and Settlement of Ethiopian Jews in Israel." Middle East Review 20 (Winter 1987-1988): 41-48.

5324. Wall, Henry. "Kahane, Not Just Israel's Problem." ADL Bulletin 1 (November 1985): 12-14.

5325. Weingrod, Alex, ed. Studies in Israeli Ethnicity. New York: Gordon & Breach, 1986.

5326. Weinstein, Brian. "Ethiopian Jews in Israel: Socialization and Re-education." Journal of Negro Education 54 (Spring 1985): 213-224.

5327. Weisbund, David L. Deviance as a Social Reaction: A Study of the Gush Emunim Settlements in Israel. Doctoral dissertation, Yale University, 1985. UMO # 8600999.

5328. Wieseltier, Leon. "The Demons of the Jews." New Republic 15-21 (November 11, 1985): 24-25. [Meir Kahane.]

5329. Wigoder, Geoffrey. "Interfaith Relations in Israel." Christian Jewish Relations 19 (September 1986): 7-15.

5330. Will, Donald S. "The Impending Polarization of Israeli Society." Arab Studies Quarterly 8 (Summer 1986): 231-252.

5331. Yogev, A. "From School Reform to Ethnic Integration in Israeli Schools-Social Myths and Educational Policy." In Affirmative Action and Positive Policies in the Education of Ethnic Minorities, edited by A. Yogev and S. Tomlinson. Greenwich, CT: JAI Press, 1989.

5332. Yonah, Yossi. "How Right-Wing Are the Sephardim?" Tikkun 5 (May/June 1990): 38-39, 100-102.

5333. Zima, Suellen. "Forty-two Ethiopian Boys: Observations of their First Year in Israel." Social Work 32 (July-August 1987): 359-360.

ISRAEL - PALESTINIANS

5334. A'si, Murad. "Israeli and Palestinian Public Opinion." In Public Opinion and the Palestine Question, edited by Ellia Zureik and Fouad Moughrabi. London: Croom Helm, 1987.

5335. Abdo-Zubi, Nahla. "Colonial Capitalism and Rural Class Formation: An Analsis of the Processes of Social, Economic and Political Change in Palestine, 1920-1947." Doctoral dissertation, University of Toronto, 1989.

5336. Abdulhadi, Rami S. "Land Use Planning in the Occupied Palestinian Territories." Journal of Palestine Studies 19 (Summer 1990): 46-63.

5337. Abed, George T. "The Economic Viability of a Palestinian State." Journal of Palestine Studies 19 (Winter 1990): 3- 28.

5338. Abed, George T., ed. The Palestinian Economy: Studies in Development under Prolonged Occupation. New York: Routledge, 1988.

5339. Abramov, S. Zalman. "Democracy and Demography." Midstream 34 (May 1988): 28-30. [Jews and Arabs in Israel.]

5340. Abu Khalaf, Nader A. M. The Development of Higher Education in the West Bank (1971-1983). Doctoral dissertation, University of Pittsburgh, UMO # 8519468.

5341. Abu Shakrah, Jan. "The 'Iron Fist,' October 1985 to January 1986." Journal of Palestine Studies 15 (Summer 1986): 120- 126. [Occupied territories in Israel.]

5342. Abu Shakrah, Jan. "Occupied Territories: Report. Developments of the First Quarter: February to April 1986." Journal of Palestine Studies 16 (Autumn 1986): 113-119.

5343. Abu-El-Assal, Riah and others. Children in Israeli Military Prisons.

5344. Abu-Lughod, Ibrahim, ed. The Transformation of Palestine, 2nd edition. Evanston, IL: Northwestern University Press, 1987.

5345. Abu-Lughod, Ibrahim and B. Abu-Laban, eds. Settler Regimes in Africa and the Arab World. Wilmette, IL: Medina Press, 1974.

5346. Abu-Lughod, Janet L. Demographic Characteristics of the Palestinian Population: Relevance for Planning the Palestine Open University. Paris: UNESCO, 1980.

5347. Abu-Lughod, Janet L. "The Demographic War for Palestine." The Link 19 (December 1986): 1-14.

5348. Academic Freedom at Birzeit University: 1985-1986. Public Relations Office, Birzeit University, Birzeit, West Bank, via Israel, 1987.

5349. Al-Asmar, Fouzi. "The Portrayal of Arabs in Hebrew Children's Literature." Journal of Palestine Studies 16 (Autumn 1986): 81-94.

5350. Al-Assal, Riah Abu. "Zionism: As It Is in Israel for an Arab." In Judaism or Zionism? What Difference for the Middle East?, edited by EAFORD and AJAZ, 169-175. London: Zed Books, 1986.

5351. al-Haj, Majid. "The ABC's of Arab Education [in Israel]." New Outlook 30 (April 1987): 14-15.

5352. Al-Haj, Majid. "Adjustment Patterns of the Arab Internal Refugees in Israel." International Migration (Geneva) (September 1986): 651-674.

5353. al Haj, Majid. "Blue Collar Intellectuals." New Outlook 33 (March 1990): 8-10.

5354. Al-Haj, Majid. Social Change and Family Processes: Arab Communities in Israel. Boulder, CO.: Westview, 1986.

5355. No entry

5356. Alcalay, Ammiel. "Wounded Kinship's Last Resort." Middle East Report 19 (July-August 1989): 18-23. [Cultural kinship of Arab and Jews in Israel.]

5357. Alnasrawi, Abbas. "The Economics of the Israeli Occupation of the West Bank, Gaza, and South Lebanon." Scandanavian Journal of Development Alternatives 6 (March 1987)

5358. American Public Health Association. West Bank Health Care Assessment. 3 vols. Washington, D.C.: APHA, 1986.

5359. Amitay, Yossi. "The Occupied Fourth Estate, Part 2." New Outlook 28 (December 1985): 11-12. [East Jerusalem newspapers.]

5360. Amnesty International. Israel and the Occupied Territories- Excessive Force: Beatings to Maintain Law and Order. New York: Amnesty International, August 1988.

5361. Amnesty International. "Israel and the Occupied Territories." Journal of Palestine Studies 20 (Autumn 1990): 137-141.

5362. Amun, Hasan and others. Palestinian Arabs in Israel: Two Case Studies. London: Ithaca Press, 1977.

5363. Anabtaw, Samir N. Palestinian Higher Education in the West Bank and Gaza. A Critical Assessment. New York: RKP/KPI, Methuen, 1987.

5364. Aqil, Mahmoud A. The Palestinian Family in the West Bank and Gaza Strip after 1967. Doctoral dissertation, United States International University, 1986. UMO # 8606164.

5365. "Arabs in Israel." New Outllok 5 (March-April 1962)

5366. "Arabs in Israel Respond to the Intifadah." New Outlook 31 (July 1988): 14-29.

5367. Arens, Moshe. "Testing Ground for a Revisionist (interview)." Jerusalem Post, (October 31, 1986): [Minister for Arab affairs.]

5368. Aronson, Dori. "The Politics of Social Welfare: The Case of East Jerusalem." Merip Report No. 146 (May-June 1987): 33- 35.

5369. Aronson, Geoffrey. Creating Facts: Israel, Palestinians and the West Bank. Washington, D.C.: Institute for Palestine Studies, 1987.

5370. Ashkenasi, Abraham. "The International Institutionalization of a Refugee Problem: The Palestinians and UNRWA." Jerusalem Journal of International Relations 12 (January 1990): 45- 75.

5371. Ashmore, Robert B. "Palestinian Universities under Israeli Occupation- A Human Rights Analysis." American-Arab Affairs No. 16 (Spring 1986): 79-92.

5372. Association of Israeli and Palestinian Physicians for Human Rights. Report on the Condition of Health Services in the Gaza Strip. Tel Aviv: AIPPHR, August 1989.

5373. Ata, Ibrahim W. The West Bank Palestinian Family. New York: RKP/KPI, Methuan, 1987.

5374. Atran, Scott. "The Surrogate Colonization of Palestine, 1917-1939." American Ethnologist 16 (November 1989): 719- 744.

5375. Avnery, Uri. My Friend, the Enemy. Westport, CT: Lawrence Hill, 1986. [Arabs and Jews.]

5376. Bahiri, Simcha. Industrialization in the West Bank and Gaza. Jerusalem: West Bank Data Base Project, 1987.

5377. Baker, Ahmed M. "The Psychological Impact of the Intifada on Palestinian Children in the Occupied West Bank and Gaza- An Exploratory Study." American Journal of Orthopsychiatry 60 (October 1990)

5378. Baker, Ahmed M. "Recent M.A. Theses in Education at Birzeit University: A Critical Review." Birzeit Research Review 1, No.1 (1985): 15-24.

5379. Bakri, Muhammad. "I Am Not a Stranger in This Land." New Outlook 30 (April 1987): 16-19. [Palestinian actor in Israel.]

5380. Bandler, Kenneth. "Ezer Weizman and Israeli Arabs: A New Approach to Government Policy." Israel Horizons (September- October 1985)

5381. Bandler, Kenneth. "Givat Haviva Diary." Israel Horizons (November-December 1986): 9-12.

5382. Bar-On, Mordechai. "Israeli Reactions to the Palestinian Uprising." Journal of Palestine Studies 17 (Summer 1988): 46-65.

5383. Baramki, Gabi. "Building Palestinian Universities Under Occupation." Journal of Palestine Studies 17 (Autumn 1987): 12-20.

5384. Barash, Liora. "And the Hands Are the Hands of Dov." New Outlook 129 (November-December 1986): 27-30. [Defense of Sasson Somekh's "The Image of the Arab in Hebrew and Translated Literature as Taught in the Israeli High School".]

5385. Basisu, Mu'in. Descent Into Water: Palestinian Notes from Arab Exile. Wilmette, IL: Medina Press, 1980. [Gazan-born poet.]

5386. Bearfield, Lev. "Taking Kahane Seriously." Hadassah Magazine 37-39 (February 1986)

5387. Bearfield, Lev. "Unsettled Bedouin." Jerusalem Post Magazine, (January 9, 1987): [Galilee.]

5388. Beinin, Joel. "From Land Day to Equality Day." Merip No. 150 (January-February 1988): 24-27. [Political movements among Palestinians in Israel.]

5389. Bellos, Susan. "Stepchild of the Syllabus." Jerusalem Post (February 13, 1986): [Teaching Arabs in Jewish schools.]

5390. Ben Porath, Yoram. The Arab Labor Force in Israel. Jerusalem: 1966,

ISRAEL - PALESTINIANS **409**

5391. Ben-Aharon, Yitzak. "Do We Want to Live by the Sword Forever?" New Outlook 30 (May-June 1987): 20-22.

5392. Benjamin, A. and R. Peleg. Higher Education and the Arabs in Israel. Tel Aviv: 'Am 'Oved, 1977.

5393. Benjamin, Jesse. "The Negev-Bedouin: The Struggle for Equal Rights." New Outlook 33 (August 1990): 17-19.

5394. Benvenisti, Eyal. Legal Dualism: The Absorption of the Occupied Territories into Israel. Boulder, CO.: Westview, 1990.

5395. Benvenisti, Meron. 1987 Report: Demographic, Economic, Legal, Social and Political Developments in the West Bank. Jerusalem: Jerusalem Post, 1987.

5396. Benvenisti, Meron. "Changing the Status Quo: A Long and Complex Process." New Outlook 33 (May-June 1990): 36-37.

5397. Benvenisti, Meron. Conflicts and Contradictions. New York: Villard Books, 1986. [Jewish-Arab relations on West Bank.]

5398. Benvenisti, Meron. "Gaza's Not So Bright Side." Jerusalem Post, (September 10, 1986)

5399. Benvenisti, Meron. Israeli Censorship of Arab Publications: A Survey. Jerusalem: West Bank Data Base Project, 1983.

5400. Benvenisti, Meron. Jerusalem: A Study of a Polarized Community. Jerusalem: West Bank Data Base Project, 1983.

5401. Benvenisti, Meron. "New Act, Old Tragedy." New York Times, (January 3, 1988): [Arabs in Israel.]

5402. Benvenisti, Meron. "The Peace Process and Intercommunal Strife." Journal of Palestine Studies 17 (Autumn 1987): 3- 11.

5403. Benvenisti, Meron. "The Second Republic." Jerusalem Post, (January 7, 1987): [Jews and Arabs, conquerors and conquered.]

5404. Benvenisti, Meron. "A Twilight Zone between War and Peace." New Outlook 30 (May-June 1987): 14-17.

5405. Benvenisti, Meron. The West Bank Data Base Project 1987 Report. Jerusalem: West Bank Data Base Project, 1987,

5406. Benvenisti, Meron. The West Bank: A Generation After. Jerusalem: West Bank Data Base, 1987.

5407. Benvenisti, Meron. "Who Speaks for the Palestinians?" Moment (November 1986): 21-24.

5408. Bilu, Yoram. "The Other as a Nightmare: The Israeli-Arab Encounter as Reflected in Children's Dreams in Israel and the West Bank." Political Psychology 10 (September 1989): 365- 389.

5409. Binur, Yusuf K. My Enemy, My Self. Garden City, New York: Doubleday, 1989. [A Jewish Israeli journalist disguises self as Arab for six months.]

5410. Birzeit University Research Centre. Recent Trends in Palestinian Education: Research Institute in Jerusalem. Birzeit, West Bank: The Centre, 1985.

5411. Bisharat, Carol. "Palestine and Humanitarian Law: Israeli Practice in the West Bank and Gaza." Hastings International and Comparative Law Review 12 (Winter 1989): 325-371.

5412. Bisharat, George E. Palestinian Lawyers and Israeli Rule: Law and Disorder in the West Bank. Austin: University of Texas Press, 1990.

5413. Bisharat, George E. Practicing Law under Occupation: Palestinian Lawyers of the West Bank. Doctoral dissertation, Harvard University, 1987. UMO # 8800870.

5414. Black, Ian. "Peace or No Peace, Israel Will Still Need Cheap Labour." New Statesman 96 (September 29, 1978)

5415. Bourne, Jenny. "The Wrenching Pain of Re-enactment." Race & Class 32 (October-December 1990): 67-72. [Ending Israeli occupation in the Territories.]

5416. Brinkley, Joel. "Pride and Resentment Rising Among Israeli Arabs." New York Times, (June 18, 1989)

5417. Brinner, William H. "The Arabs of Israel: The Past Twenty Years." Middle East Review 20 (Fall 1987): 13-21.

5418. Brinner, William H. and Moses Rischin, eds. Like All the Nations? The Life and Legacy of Judah L. Magnes. Albany: State University of New York Press, 1988.

5419. Budeiri, Musa. "Najati Sidgi and the Arabisation of Palestinian Communism." Birzeit Research Review No. 2 (Winter 1985/1986): 70-76.

5420. Cainkar, Louise. "The Patterns of Institutionalized Exclusivity." In Separate and Unequal. The Dynamics of South African and Israeli Rule, edited by Cainkar. Chicago, IL: Palestine Human Rights Campaign, 1985.

5421. Cainkar, Louise, ed. Separate and Unequal. The Dynamics of South African and Israeli Rule. Chicago, IL: Palestine Human Rights Campaign, 1985.

5422. Caplan, Neil. Futile Diplomacy. 2 vols. London: Frank Cass, 1983,1986. [On pre-1948 Arab-Zionist negotiations] Vol. 1: 1913-1931, Vol. 2: 1932-1947.

5423. The Casualities of Conflict: Medical Care and Human Rights in the West Bank and Gaza Strip. Somerville, MA: Physicians for Human Rights, 1988.

5424. Chafets, Ze'ev. "Arab Rage Inside Israel." New York Times Magazine, (April 3, 1988)

5425. Chagnollaud, Jean-Paul. Israel et les territoires occupees: La confrontation silencieuse. Paris: L'Harrmattan, 1985.

5426. Chomsky, Noam. "Scenes from the [Palestinian] Uprising." Zeta Magazine 1 (July-August 1988): 9-20.

5427. Christison, Kathleen M. "Myths about Palestinians." Foreign Policy No. 66 (Spring 1987)

5428. Cohen, Avraham. "Israeli Arabs: Housing Conditions." New Outlook 29 (July 1986): 15-17.

5429. Cohen, Jack J. The Reunion of Isaac and Ishmael. Mosaic Press and the Reconstructionist Press, 1987. [Arab students on Israeli college campuses.]

5430. Cohen, Stanley. "Education as Crime." Jerusalem Post, (May 18, 1989)

5431. Collins, Frank. Nonviolence and Death at Bir Zeit University: An Investigative Report. Chicago, IL: Palestine Human Rights Campaign, 1987.

5432. Cook, Lindsey. "Learning Under Occupation: The State of Palestinian Education in the Occupied Territories." MTA Today 20 (September 15, 1989)

5433. Court, Andy. "Building Ties." Jerusalem Post, Magazine (June 27, 1986): [Interns for Peace: conducting intercommunal meetings between Jews and Arabs.]

5434. Cowell, Alan. "For Arabs, 'Uprising' Takes an Economic Toll." New York Times, (March 14, 1988)

5435. Cromer, Gerald. The Debate about Kahanism in Israeli Society 1984-1988. New York: Harry Guggenheim Foundation, 1988.

5436. Cromer, Gerald. "Jewish Underground- At the Center or on Periphery of Israeli Society." Terrorism 11 (1988)

5437. Cromer, Gerald. "The Tip of the Iceberg: An Observation on the Reaction to Kahanism in Israeli Society." Patterns of Prejudice 23 (Summer 1989): 29-34.

5438. Curtius, Mary. "Arab and Jew in Love Face Hostility, Anguish." Boston Globe, (February 16, 1988)

5439. Curtius, Mary. "Arabs Find Opportunity in Israel's Democracy." Boston Globe, (February 15, 1988): [Political currents among Israeli Palestinians.]

5440. Curtius, Mary. "Israeli Arabs Still Feeling Like Outsiders." Boston Globe, (February 15, 1988)

5441. Curtius, Mary. "Palestinian Revolt: Amid Bitterness, Pride." Boston Globe, (February 14, 1988)

5442. Dabbak, Ibrahim. "Back to Square One: A Study in the Re-emergence of the Palestinian Identity in the West Bank, 1967-1980." In Palestinians Over the Green Line, edited by Alexander Scholch. London: Ithaca Press, 1983.

5443. Dabbak, Ibrahim. "Development and Control in the West Bank." Arab Studies Quarterly 7 (1985): 74-87.

5444. Dallal, Shaw J. "Israeli Human Rights Violations and Palestinian Violence." Syracuse Journal of International Law and Commerce 14 (Winter 1987): 109-124.

5445. DataBase Project on Palestinian Human Rights. Colonial Pursuits: Settler Violence During the Uprising in the Occupied Territories. Chicago, IL: DataBase Project, 1990.

5446. Davis, Uri. "Israel's Zionist Society: Consequences for Internal Opposition and the Necessity for External Intervention." In Judaism or Zionism? What Difference for the Middle East?, edited by EAFORD and Ajaz. London: Zed Books, 1986.

5447. Davis, Uri. Israel: An Apartheid State. London: Zed Press, 1987.

5448. Davis, Uri and Walter Lehn. The Jewish National Fund. New York: Metheun, 1987.

5449. Dehter, Aaron. How Expensive Are West Bank Settlements? Jerusalem: West Bank Data Base Project, 1987.

5450. Dillman, Jeffrey D. "Water Rights in the Occupied Territories." Journal of Palestine Studies 19 (Autumn 1989): 46-71. [Discrimination against Palestinians in occupied territories.]

5451. Edelman, Martin. "The Druze Courts in the Political System of Israel." Middle East Review 19 (Summer 1987): 54-61.

5452. Efrat, Elisha. "Settlement Pattern and Economic Changes of the Gaza Strip 1947-1977." Middle East Journal 31 (Summer 1977)

5453. El-Asmar, Fouzi. Through the Hebrew Looking-Glass. Arab Stereotypes in Children's Literature. London: Zed Press, 1986.

5454. Elpeleg, Zvi. "West Bank Story." Middle East Review (Summer 1986): 7-16.

5455. Elrazik, Adnan A. and others. The Destiny of Arab Students in Institutions of Higher Education in Israel. An Outline Towards a Discussion of the Prospects for an Arab University in the Galilee. June 1977.

5456. Ennab, Wa'el Rif'at M. Ali. "Population Geography of the Refugee Camps in the West Bank." University of Durham (Great Britain), 1989. [Order No. BRD-89389.]

5457. "An Epidemic of Violence: Medical Rights Abuses in the West Bank and Gaza Strip." Health/PAC Bulletin 19 (Fall 1989): 1-34.

5458. Epstein, Yitzak. "A Zionist Pioneer's Dissent." New Outlook 28 (December 1985): 27-29. [A speech of 1905 to the 7th Zionist Congress calling for cooperation with Arabs.]

5459. Falah, Ghazi. "The Development of the 'Planned Bedouin Settlement' in Israel, 1964-1982: Evaluation and Characteristics." Geoform 14 (1983): 311-323. [See Kliot and Medzini, below.]

5460. Falah, Ghazi. "Israelization of Palestine Human Geography." Progress in Human Geography 13 (1989): 535-550.

5461. Falah, Ghazi. "Israeli State Policy toward Bedouin Sedentarization in the Negev." Journal of Palestine Studies 18 (Winter 1989): 71-91.

5462. Falah, Ghazi. The Processes and Patterns of Sedentarization of the Galilee Bedouin, 1880-1982. Doctoral dissertation, University of Durham, 1982.

5463. Falloon, Virgil. Excessive Secrecy, Lack of Guidelines: A Report on Military Censorship in the West Bank. Ramallah: Law in the Service of Man, 1985.

5464. Farky, Ben-Zion. "Current Legal Trends in the Area Administered by Israel." Military Law Review (Summer 1986): 47-60.

5465. Fasheh, Munir J. "Community Education: To Reclaim and Transform What Has Been Made Invisible." Harvard Educational Review 60 (February 1990): 19-35.

5466. Fasheh, Munir J. Education as Praxis for Liberation: Birzeit University and the Community. Doctoral dissertation, Harvard University, 1988. UMO # 8811791.

5467. Fellah, A. Citizenship in Arab and Druze Elementary Schools. Nazareth: al-Nahadah, 1976.

5468. Flapan, Simha. "The Palestinian Exodus of 1948." Journal of Palestine Studies 16 (Summer 1987): 3-26.

5469. Fletcher, Elaine R. "Concrete Solutions." Jerusalem Post Magazine, (April 24, 1987): [Analysis of Arabs moving into Upper Nazareth.]

5470. Fletcher, Elaine R. "Unsettled Bedouin." Jeruslaem Post Magazine, (January 16, 1987)

5471. Frankel, David and Will Reissner. Israel's War against the Palestinian People. New York: Pathfinder Press,

5472. Friedler, Ya'acov. "Arab Students Drawn to Haifa University's Department of Geodesic Engineering." Jerusalem Post, (June 5, 1987)

5473. Friedman, Robert J. "The Palestinian Refugees." New York Review of Books (March 29, 1990)

5474. Friedman, Thomas L. "A Forecast for Israel: More Arabs than Jews." New York Times, (October 19, 1987)

5475. Friedman, Thomas L. "I Too Am Israeli, One Arab Declares (in Hebrew)." New York Times, (January 21, 1987): [Anton Shammas, in novel, Arabesque.]

5476. Friedman, Thomas L. "An Islamic Revival Is Quickly Gaining Ground in an Unlikely Place: Israel." New York Times, (April 30, 1987)

5477. Friedman, Thomas L. "Israeli Policy in West Bank: Mixed Record." New York Times, (January 5, 1986)

5478. Friedman, Thomas L. "Israeli in Disguise Learns the Anguish of An Arab." New York Times, (May 5, 1986): [Israeli Jewish reporter impersonates an Arab for six weeks.]

5479. Friedman, Thomas L. "My Neighbor, My Enemy." New York Times, (July 5, 1987): [Arabs and Jews in Israel.]

5480. Friedman, Thomas L. "Palestinians under Israel: Bitter Politics." New York Times, (January 12, 1987)

5481. Friedman, Thomas L. "Palestinian Cause Turns to Fury As It Passes from Fathers to Sons." New York Times, December 28, 1987.

5482. Friedman, Thomas. "Road to Power: Do Palestinians Ride Israel's Bus?" New York Times, (August 4, 1987)

5483. Frisch, Hiller and Fraiman, Y. Stagnation and Frontier: Arab and Jewish Industry in the West Bank. Jeusalem: West Bank Data Base Project, 1983.

5484. Gabbai, Sheli. "The 'Palestinianization' of Israel's Arabs." Journal of Palestine Studies 15 (Summer 1986): 182-183. [Excerpts of story in Ma'ariv.]

5485. Gabriel, Judith. "The Economic Side of the Intifadah." Journal of Palestine Studies 18 (Autumn 1988): 198-213.

5486. Gabriel, S. A. and Sabatello E.F. "Palestinian Migration from the West Bank and Gaza: Economic and Demographic Analyses." Economic Development and Cultural Change 34 (January 1986)

5487. Galtung, Johan. Nonviolence and Israel/Palestine. Honolulu: University of Hawaii Institute for Peace, 1989.

5488. Gerner, Deborah J. "Israeli Restrictions on the Palestinian Universities in the Occupied West Bank and Gaza." Journal of Arab Affairs 8 (1989): 74-123.

5489. Geva, Ahron. "The Arab Housing Crunch [in Israel]." New Outlook 30 (March 1987): 27-30.

5490. Giacaman, Rita. Life and Health in Three Palestinian Villages. London: Ithaca Press, 1988.

5491. Giannou, Chris. "The Palestinian Question: Interview.." Studies in Political Economy No. 27 (Autumn 1988): 7-27.

5492. Ginat, Joseph. "The Elections in the Arab Sector; Voting Patterns and Political Behaviour." Jerusalem Quarterly No. 53 (Winter 1990): 27-55.

5493. Ginat, Joseph. "Israeli Arabs: Some Recent Social and Political Trends." Asian and African Studies 23 (1989)

5494. Goell, Yosef. "Close Encounters of Another Kind." Jerusalem Post, (June 12, 1986): [Jews and Arabs at Ulpan Akiva.]

5495. Goell, Yosef. "Garden-variety Prejudice Isn't Racism." Jerusalem Post, (June 6, 1986): [Anti-Arab racism.]

5496. Goell, Yosef. "Histadrut's Failure in the Arab Sector." Jerusalem Post, (January 30, 1987)

5497. Goell, Yosef. "Life Is the Same All Over." Jerusalem Post, (June 25, 1986): [Schooling in Muslim Arab village of Baka el-Gharbieh.]

5498. Goell, Yosef. "Next Step for Israeli Arabs." Jerusalem Post, (January 14, 1987)

5499. Goell, Yosef. "True Unions." Jerusalem Post Magazine, (February 6, 1987): [Israeli Arab men who have completed a medical education in the USSR and elsewhere.]

5500. "The Golan Heights: Twenty Years After." Journal of Palestine Studies 17 (Autumn 1987): 136-143.

5501. Goldstein, Eric. "The Israeli Army and the Intifada." Journal of Palestine Studies 20 (Autumn 1990): 190-195. [Excerpts from report by Middle East Watch, July 25, 1990.]

5502. Goldstein, Eric. Journalism Under Occupation: Israel's Regulation of the Palestinian Press. New York: Committee to Protect Journalists and Article 19, 1988.

5503. Gordon, Haim. "The Lack of Jewish-Arab Dialogue in Israel and the Spirit of Judaism: A Testimony." Journal of Ecumenical Studies (Spring 1986): 266-275.

5504. Gordon, Jean. "Jewish Israelis Seeking Accomodation with Israeli Arabs." Jewish Currents 41 (January 1987): 4-6.

5505. Gorenberg, Gershom. "Israel Arab Women Break Taboo, Hit Books." Jerusalem Post, (August 13, 1986): [Higher Education.]

5506. Gorenberg, Gershom. "Relationships: Jewish Men and Arab Women." Jerusalem Post, (August 6, 1986)

5507. Gorny, Yosef. Zionism and the Arabs 1882-1948: A Study of Ideology. Translated by Chaya Galai. Oxford, England: Clarendon Press, 1987.

5508. Gover, Yerach. "Were You There, Or Was It a Dream? Ideological Imposition on Israeli Literature." Journal of Palestine Studies 16 (Autumn 1986): 56-80.

5509. Government of Israel. "Education and Culture in Judea and Samaria and Gaza Strip from 1967-1981." Report to UNESCO (April 1982)

5510. Gray, M. W. "The Phantom Universities of the West Bank and Gaza." Academe 76 (May-June 1990)

5511. Greenberg, Joel. "Al Fajr's Goal: Experiencing the Palestinian View." Jerusalem Post, (September 10, 1986): [Arab newspaper published in East Jerusalem.]

5512. Greenberg, Joel. "The Body Politic." Jerusalem Post Magazine, (September 26, 1986): [Hospital services on West Bank.]

5513. Greenberg, Joel. "Hebron Diary." Jerusalem Post Magazine, (December 5, 1986): [Jews and Arabs in Hebron.]

5514. Greenberg, Joel. "A House Divided." Jerusalem Post Magazine, (May 2, 1986): [Barta's, an Arab community located in Israeli proper and on West Bank.]

5515. Greenberg, Joel. "Keeping the Faith." Jerusalem Post Magazine, (June 27, 1986): [Islamic University, Gaza.]

5516. Greenberg, Joel. "Mixed Feelings." Jerusalem Post, (March 16, 1986): [Intermarriage of Jewish women and Arab men.]

5517. Greenberg, Susan. "Israel's Racial Double-Act." New Society (August 15, 1986): [Exceedingly weak, confusing law purportedly against racism.]

5518. Grossman, David. Jewish and Arab Settlements in the Tulkarm Subdistrict. Jerusalem: West Bank Data Base Project, 1986.

5519. Grossman, David. "The Yellow Wind-I." New Yorker (February 8, 1988): Translated by Haim Watzman.

5520. Grossman, Edward. "A Man for All Seasons." Jerusalem Post Magazine, (March 28, 1986): [Anwar Nusseibeh, former Jordanian governor of Jerusalem.]

5521. Grossman, Edward. "Village in the City." Jerusalem Post Magazine, (May 22, 1987): [Beit Safafa, an Arab town surrounded by Jerusalem.]

5522. Haberer, Rose B. Status, Power and Influence of Women in an Arab Village in Israel. Doctoral dissertation, Purdue University, 1985. UMO # 8606547.

5523. Habiby, Emile. Saeed, the All-Fated Pessoptimist. New York: Vantage Press, 1982. [Novel of Arab life in Israel.]

5524. Hadawi, Sami. Palestinian Rights and Losses in 1948. A Comprehensive Study. London: Saqi Books, 1987.

5525. Haidar, Aziz. The Palestinians in Israeli Social Science Writings. Washington, D.C.: Near East Cultural and Educational Foundation of Canada and the International Center for Research and Public Policy, 1987.

5526. Haidar, Aziz and Elia Zureik. "The Palestinians Seen through the Israeli Cultural Paradigm." Journal of Palestine Studies 16 (Spring 1987): 68-86.

5527. Haidar, Aziz. Social Welfare Services for Israel's Arab Population. Boulder, CO: Westview Press, 1989.

5528. Haidar, Aziz. Types of Patterns of Economic Entrepreneurship in Arab Villages in Israel. Doctoral dissertation, Hebrew University, 1985.

5529. Haim, Yehoyada. Abandonment of Illusions: Zionist Political Attitudes towards Paletinian Arab Nationalism, 1936-1939. Boulder, CO.: Westview Press, 1983.

5530. Hallaj, Muhammad. "Israel's War on Palestinian Education." The Return 2 (February 1990): 31-34.

5531. Hallaj, Muhammad. "Mission of Palestinian Higher Education." In A Palestinian Agenda for the West Bank and Gaza, edited by Emile Nakhleh, 58-76. Washington, D.C.: American Enterprise Institute, 1980.

5532. Harkabi, Yehoshafat. "Choosing between Bad and Worse." Journal of Palestine Studies 16 (Spring 1987): 43-52. [Interview.]

5533. Harkabi, Yehoshafat. "A Policy for the Moment of Truth." Journal of Palestine Studies 17 (Spring 1988): 80-90. [The Uprising.]

5534. Harlow, Barbara. "Narrative in Prison: Stories from the Palestinian Intifadah." Modern Fiction studies 35 (Spring 1989): 29-46.

5535. Hassan, Amira. "Israeli Arabic Radio and Television: Serving Official Policy." New Outlook 30 (July-August 1987): 17-20.

5536. Hassan, Sana. Enemy in the Promised Land: An Egyptian Woman's Journey into Israel. New York: Pantheon, 1987.

5537. Hassim, Yael. "Jewish and Arab Juvenile Delinquency in Israel: The Problem and Its Remedies." International Journal of Comparative and Applied Criminal Justice 11 (Spring/ Winter 1987): 213-230.

5538. Heacock, Roger and Nassar, Jamal, eds. Intifada: Palestine at a Crossroads. New York: Praeger, 1990.

5539. Hentoff, Nat. "The Killings at Bir Zeit University." Village Voice, (January 6, 1987)

5540. Hentoff, Nat. "The Olive Trees of Iatanna." Village Voice, (December 23, 1986): [Palestinian Center for the Study of Nonviolence, Occupied Territories.]

5541. Hiltermann, Joost R. Before the Uprising: The Organization and Mobilization of Palestinian Workers and Women in the Israeli-occupied West Bank and Gaza Strip. Doctoral dissertation, University of California, 1988. UMO # 8905623.

5542. Hiltermann, Joost R. "The Emerging Trade Union Movement in the West Bank." Merip Reports Nos. 136-137 (October- December 1985): 26-31.

5543. Hiltermann, Joost R. "Human Rights Reports Issued during the Palestinian Uprising." Journal of Palestine Studies 18 (Summer 1989): 122-134.

5544. Hiltermann, Joost R. "Human Rights and the Palestinian Struggle for National Liberation." Journal of Palestine Studies 18 (Winter 1989): 109-118.

5545. Hiltermann, Joost R. Israel's Deportation Policy in the Occupied West Bank and Gaza. Ramallah: Law in the Service of Man, 1986.

5546. Hiltermann, Joost R. "Israel's Golden Rule: Keeping a Grip on the Palestinian Economy." Multinational Monitor 9 (April 1988): 28-30.

5547. Hiltermann, Joost R. "Palestinian Collaborators: The Enemy Inside the Intifada." Nation (September 10, 1990)

5548. Hiltermann, Joost R. "Workers' Rights during the Uprising." Journal of Palestine Studies 19 (Autumn 1989): 83-91.

5549. Hitchens, Christopher. "Minority Report." Nation (August 16, 1986): [Interview with Meir Kahane.]

5550. Hofman, John E. and others. Arab-Jewish Relations in Israel. Bristol, IN: Wyndham Hall Press, 1988.

5551. "Human Rights and Israel's Rule in the Territories." New York University Journal of International Law and Politics 21 (Spring 1989): 439-574.

5552. Hunt, Paul. Justice? The Military Court System in the Israeli-occupied Territories. Ramallah, West Bank: Al-Haq/Law in the Service of Man, 1987.

5553. Husayni, Faysal. "We Want National As Well As Civil Rights." New Outlook 29 (November-December 1986): 9-10.

5554. "In Defense of Settlement: An Interview with Professor Yoseph Ben-Shlomo." Tikkun 2, No. 2 (1987): 72-77.

5555. Index of High Court Judgements: West Bank, Gaza and East Jerusalem. Jerusalem: West Bank Data Base Project, 1983.

5556. Isaac, Jad. "A Socio-economic Study of Administrative Detainees at Ansar 3." Journal of Palestine Studies 18 (Summer 1989): 102-109.

5557. "Israel and the Palestinians: Policy Perspectives for Americans." Church and Society 3-103 (March-April 1987): entire issue.

5558. "Israel Lets Arab Pupils Back in School." New York Times, (July 23, 1989)

5559. Israel's War Against Education in the Occupied West Bank: A Penalty for the Future. Ramallah: Al-Haq/Law in the Service of Man, November 1988.

5560. "Israel's West Bank Policy." Commentary 82 (September 1986): 6-8. [Letters, with response on article by Menahem Milson "How Not to Occupy the West Bank," ibid, April 1986.]

5561. Israeli Socialist Left. The December Uprising. Tel Aviv: March 1988. [Intifada]

5562. Israeli, Rafi. "The Arabs in Israel: A Surging New Identity." Jerusalem Letter/Viewpoints (Jerusalem Center for Public Affairs) (January 1, 1989): 1-4.

5563. "It Is Necessary to Criticize: An Interview with a Young Israeli Arab Man." New Outlook 33 (March 1990): 14-16.

5564. Jaffee Center for Stretegic Studies Study Group. Israel, the West Bank and Gaza: Toward a Solution. Tel Aviv: Jaffee Center for Strategic Studies, Tel Aviv University, 1989.

5565. Jaffee Center for Strategic Studies Study Group. The West Bank and the Gaza Strip: Israel's Options for Peace. Tel Aviv: Jaffee Center for Strategic Studies, Tel Aviv University, 1989.

5566. Jatin. "Sexual Harassment of [Palestinian] Political Prisoners." Marxist Matzpen (April 1989): [Reprinted in From the Hebrew Press. Monthly Translations and Commentaries from Israel. By Dr. Israel Shahak, 1 (July 1989) 14-17.]

5567. Jedlicki, Witold. "Israel and the Palestinians. An Empire at Close Range." Against the Current 2 (March-April 1987): 15-24.

5568. Jerusalem Media and Communications Center. Bitter Harvest: Israeli Sanctions Against Palestinian Agriculture During the Uprising. Jerusalem: JMCC, 1989.

5569. Johnson, Penny. "Occupied Territories: Report. Palestinian Universities under Occupation, June to August 1986." Journal of Palestine Studies 16 (Autumn 1986): 120-127.

5570. Johnson, Penny. "Palestinian Universities under Occupation." Journal of Palestine Studies 15 (Summer 1986): 127-133.

5571. Johnson, Penny. "Palestinian Universities Under Occupation, May-June 1987." Journal of Palestine Studies 17 (Autumn 1987): 129-135.

5572. Johnson, Penny. "Palestinian Universities under Occupation, November 1986-January 1987." Journal of Palestine Studies 16 (Spring 1987): 134-141.

5573. Johnson, Penny. "Palestinian Universities under Occupation, February-April 1987." Journal of Palestine Studies 16 (Summer 1987): 115-121.

5574. Johnson, Penny. "Palestinian Universities Under Occupation, November 1987-January 1988." Journal of Palestine Studies 17 (Spring 1988): 100-105.

5575. Johnson, Penny. "Palestinian Universities Under Occupation, February-May 1988." Journal of Palestine Studies 17 (Summer 1988): 116-122.

5576. Johnson, Penny. "Palestinian Universities under Occupation 15 August- 15 November [1988]." Journal of Palestine Studies 18 (Winter 1989): 92-100.

5577. Johnson, Penny. "The Routine of Repression." Merip No. 150 (January-February 1988): 3-11. [West Bank and Gaza.]

5578. "Jordan's Five-Year Development Plan for the Occupied Territories, Amman, 1986." Journal of Palestine Studies 16 (Autumn 1986): 205-212.

5579. Josephs, Bernard. "Israel's Neglected Arab Schools." Jerusalem Post, (December 7, 1986)

5580. Journard, Ron and Joshua Brilliant. "The Power of Petition." Jerusalem Post, (March 4, 1986): Use of Israeli High Court of Justice by Arabs on West Bank or Gaza Strip.]

5581. "A Judicial System Where Even Kafka Would Be Lost: An Interview with Felicia Langer." Journal of Palestine Studies 20 (Autumn 1990): 24-36.

5582. Kahan, David. Agriculture and Water Resources in the West Bank and Gaza (1967-1987). Jerusalem: West Bank Data Base Project, 1987.

5583. Kamen, Charles S. "After the Catastrophe: The Arabs in Israel, 1948-1951." Middle East Studies 23 (October 1987): 453-495.

5584. Kamen, Charles S. "After the Catastrophe II: The Arabs in Israel, 1948-1951." Middle East Studies 24 (January 1988): 68-109.

5585. Kamen, Charles S. Little Common Ground. Arab Agriculture and Jewish Settlement in Palestine, 1920-1948. Pittsburgh, PA: University of Pittsburgh Press, 1991.

5586. Kapeliouk, Amnon. "New Light on the Israeli-Arab Conflict and the Refugee Problem and Its Origins." Journal of Palestine Studies 16 (Spring 1987): 16-24.

5587. Kassim, Anis F., ed. The Palestine Yearbook of International Law, II (1985). Nicosia, Cyprus: Al-Shaybani Society of International Law Ltd., 1986.

5588. Kaufman, Edy. "The Intifadah and the Peace Camp in Israel: A Critical Introspective." Journal of Palestine Studies 17 (Summer 1988): 66-80.

5589. Kaufman, Edy. "The Intifada's Limited Violence." Journal of Arab Affairs 9 (Autumn 1990)

5590. Khalidi, Raja. The Arab Economy in Israel: The Dynamics of a Region's Development. New York: Croom Helm, 1988.

5591. Khalidi, Raja. "The Economy of the Palestinian Arabs in Israel." In The Palestinian Economy: Studies in Development Under Prolonged Occupation, edited by George T. Abed. New York: Routledge, 1988.

5592. Khalifeh, Sahar. Wild Thorns. Translated by Trevor Le Gassick and Elizabeth Frenea. London: al-Saqi Books, 1985.

5593. Kifner, John. "The Face of Rage in Gaza: Frustrated Youth." New York Times, (December 21, 1987)

5594. Kimche, Jon. "Can Israel Save the Palestinian Arabs?" Midstream 34 (May 1988): 3-6.

5595. Kimmerling, Baruch. The Economic Interrelationship between the Arab and Jewish Communities in Mandatory Palestine. Cambridge, MA: Center for International Studies, Massachusetts Institute of Technology, 1979.

5596. Kliot, N. and A. Medzini. "Bedouin Settlement Policy in Israel, 1964-1982: Another Perspective." Geoform 16 (1985): 428-439. [See Falah, above.]

5597. Kliot, N. and S. Waterman. "The Political Impact on Writing the Geography of Palestine/Israel." Progress in Human Geography 14 (June 1990): 237-260.

5598. Kofman, Ilana. The Bases of Electoral Support for the Communist Party of Israel among the Arabs in Israel, 1948- 1984. Doctoral dissertation, University of California, 1989. UMO # 9005178.

5599. Kolinsky, M. "Premeditation in the Palestine Disturbances of August 1929." Middle Eastern Studies 26 (1990): 18-34.

5600. Kossaifi, G. "Forced Migration of Palestinians from the West Bank and Gaza Strip 1967-1983." Population Bulletin of ESCWA 27 (December 1985): 73-109.

5601. Kraus, Vered and Robert W. Hodge. Promises in the Promised Land. Mobility and Inequality in Israel. Westport, CT: Greenwood Press, 1990.

5602. Kreimer, Sarah. "Entrepreneurism in Israel's Arab Communities." New Outlook 30 (July-August 1987): 9-14.

5603. Kreimer, Sarah and Rogeb Abbas. "Working Together." New Outlook 30 (July-August 1987): 15-16. [Business partnerships of Arabs and Jews.]

5604. Kressel, Gideon M. "The Cultural-Economic Variable in the Use of Disposable Personal Income: Patterns of Consumption on the West Bank and in the Gaza Strip, 1967-1977." Asian and African Studies 20 (November 1986): 281-308.

5605. Kretzmer, David. The Legal Status of the Arabs in Israel. Boulder, CO: Westview Press, 1990.

5606. Krivine, David. "Don't Shun Gaza's Workers." Jerusalem Post, (August 21, 1986)

5607. Krivine, David. "The Gaza Jigsaw-Puzzle." Jerusalem Post, (September 17, 1986)

5608. Kunstel, Marcia and Joseph Albright. Their Promised Land. Arab versus Jew in History's Cauldron-One Valley in the Jerusalem Hills. New York: Crown, 1991. [Valley of Sorek, west of Jerusalem.]

5609. Kupferschmidt, Uri M. The Supreme Muslim Council: Islam Under the British Mandate for Palestine. Leiden: E.J. Brill, 1987.

5610. Kushner, D. "The Ottoman Governors of Palestine, 1864-1914." Middle East Studies 23 (July 1987): 274-291.

5611. Kuttab, Daoud. "The Occupied Territories: Old City Violence." Middle East International No. 289 (December 5, 1986): 14-15.

5612. Kuttab, Daoud. "The Palestinian Uprising: The Second Phase, Self-Sufficiency." Journal of Palestine Studies 17 (Summer 1988): 36-45.

5613. Kuttab, Daoud. "A Profile of the Stonethrowers." Journal of Palestine Studies 17 (Spring 1988): 14-23.

5614. Kuttab, Jonathan. Analysis of Military Order No. 854 and Related Orders Concerning Educational Institutions in the Occupied West Bank. Ramallah: Law in the Service of Man, May 1981.

5615. Kuttab, Jonathan. "The Children's Revolt." Journal of Palestine Studies 17 (Summer 1988): 26-35.

5616. Kuttab, Jonathan. "A Palestinian View of the Israeli Peace Camp." New Outlook 33 (March 1990): 31-32.

5617. Lador-Lederer, J. J. "Minderheiten in Israel." Europa Ethnica 30 (1973): 2-21. [Summary in English, pp.20-21.]

5618. LaMonte, Ruth B. "The Education of Palestine Refugees on the West Bank and Gaza Strip: The Role of the United Nations Relief and Works Agency." Canadian and International Education 17 (1988): 27-35.

5619. Landau, Dov. "And the Voice is the Voice of Sasson." New Outlook 29 (November-December 1986): 25-27. [Attack on Sasson Somekh's "The Image of the Arab in Hebrew and Translated Literature as Taught in the Israeli High School".]

424 WORLD RACISM AND RELATED INHUMANITIES

5620. Langellier, Jean-Pierre. "Palestinian Nationalism and Israeli Society." Journal of Palestine Studies 17 (Autumn 1987): 199-202. [From Manchester Guardian Weekly, June 14, 1987.]

5621. Langer, Felicia. The Death of Ibrahim al-Umtux, or : The Closed File that Remains Open. Tel Aviv: League for Human and Civil Rights, September 1989.

5622. Langer, Felicia. An Image of Stone. London: Quartet, 1988.

5623. Law in the Service of Man. Torture and Intimidation in the West Bank: The Case of Al-Fara'a Prison. Geneva: International Commission of Jurists and Law in the Service of Man, 1984.

5624. Lawrence, Dina and Kamel Nasr. Children of Palestinian Refugees vs. the Israeli Military: Personal Acounts of Arrest, Detention, and Torture. Lafayette, CA: BIP Publications, 1987.

5625. Lee, Eric. "Countering Racism in Israel." In These Times (November 13, 1985): [Arabs in Histadrut.]

5626. Leibel, Aaron. "Talking to Palestinians." Jerusalem Post, (March 3, 1986): [The Palestine Press Service, founded in 1977.]

5627. Lesch, Ann M. Gaza: Heading for a Dead End? UFSI, 620 Union Drive, Indianapolis, In 46202: [1948-early 1980's.]

5628. Lesch, Ann M. "Prelude to the Uprising in the Gaza Strip." Journal of Palestine Studies 20 (Autumn 1990): 1-23.

5629. Levin, Jerry. "'Creeping Transfer' Hits the West Bank." New Outlook 33 (March 1990): 28-30.

5630. Lewando-Hundt, G. A. Health Inequalities and the Articulation of Gender, Ethnicity and Class in the Post Partum Health Care of Negev Bedouin Arab Mothers and their Children. Doctoral dissertation, University of Warwick, 1988.

5631. Lewin-Epstein, Noah. "Labor Market Position and Antagonism Towards Arabs in Israel." In Research in Inequality and Social Conflict, vol. 1, edited by I. Wallimann and M. Dobkowski. Greenwich, CT: JAI Press, 1989.

5632. Lewin-Epstein, Noah and Moshe Semyonov. "Ethnic Group Mobility in the Israeli Labor Market." American Sociological Review (June 1986): 342-352.

5633. Litani, Yehuda. "The Great Divide." Jerusalem Post Magazine,(May 22, 1987): [Western Wall and Temple Mount.]

5634. Litani, Yehuda. "Legacy of Hate." Jerusalem Post Magazine,(June 5, 1987): [Jews and Arabs in Hebron.]

5635. Locke, Richard and Antony Steward. Bantustan Gaza. London: Zed Press, 1985.

5636. Lorch, Netanel. "The Israeli Struggle against Racism." Jerusalem Letter/Viewpoints (May 20, 1986): 1-5.

5637. Lustick, Ian S., ed. Books on Israel. Volume I. Albany: State University of New York, 1988.

5638. Lustick, Ian S. "Changing Rationales for Political Violence in the Arab-Israeli Conflict." Journal of Palestine Studies 20 (Autumn 1990): 54-79.

5639. Lustick, Ian S. For the Land and the Lord. New York: Council on Foreign Relations, 1988. [Jewish fundamentalism in Israel.]

5640. Lustick, Ian S. "Israeli State-building in the West Bank and the Gaza Strip: Theory and Practice." International Organization 41 (Winter 1987): 151-171.

5641. Lynk, Michael. "Vignettes of Nablus." Journal of Palestine Studies 20 (Autumn 1990): 101-114.

5642. Ma'oz, Moshe. Palestinian Leadership on the West Bank. London: Frank Cass, 1984.

5643. Mahameed, Hashem and Yosef Gottman. "Autostereotypes and Heterostereotypes of Jews and Arabs Under Various Conditions of Contact." Israeli Journal of Psychology and Counseling in Education NO. 16 (September 1983)

5644. Mahamid, Muhamid and Yizak Platek, eds. The Mark of Coal. Givat Haviva Institute, 1989. [Interviews with young Arabs in Israel aged 8-14.]

5645. Mahshi, K. and R. Rihan. "Education: Elementary & Secondary." In A Palestinian Agenda for the West Bank and Gaza, edited by Emile Nakleh, 29-57. Washington, D.C.: American Enterprise Institute, 1980.

5646. Makhul, Makram Khuri. "This Is Not a Revolt- This Is a War." Journal of Palestine Studies 17 (Spring 1988): 91-99.

5647. Mallison, W. Thomas and Sally V. Mallison. The Palestine Problem in International Law and World Order. New York: Longman, 1986.

5648. Mandel, Neville J. "Turks, Arabs and Jewish Immigration." Oxford University, 1965.

5649. Mandell, Joan. "Gaza: Israel's Soweto." Merip Reports Nos. 136-137 (October-December 1985): 7-19,58.

5650. Mansour, Atallah. "Fear of War and Faith in Peace." New Outlook 30 (May-June 1987): 36-37. [1967 and Israeli Arabs.]

5651. Mar'i, Mariam Mahmoud. "We Simply Don't Meet Often Enough." New Outlook 30 (July-August 1987): 24-25. [On Arab-Jewish coexistence.]

5652. Mar'i, Miriam Mahmood. "Between Men and Women: Sex Role Perceptions." New Outlook 29 (July 1986): 18-20. [Palestinian society in Israel.]

5653. Mar'i, Sami K. Education, Culture and Identity among Palestinians in Israel. London: Eaford, 1984.

5654. Margalit, Avishai. "The Storm Has Finally Arrived." New Outlook 29 (November-December 1986): 7-9. [On Jewish-Arab relations.]

5655. Marks, Shannee. Where Is Palestine? The Arabs in Israel. London: Pluto Press, 1984.

5656. Maron, S. "Socio-Economic Processes in the Territories Administered by Israel." International Problems (Tel Aviv) 22 (1988)

5657. Marshall, Phil. "Palestinian Nationalism and the Arab Revolution." International Socialism 33 (Autumn 1986)

5658. Masalha, Nur-eldeen. "On Recent Hebrew and Israeli Sources for the Palestinian Exodus, 1947-1949." Journal of Palestine Studies 18 (Autumn 1988): 121-137.

5659. Mawassi, Idris. "Reflections of a Young Arab." Viewpoint (Mapam) (December 1986): [Supplement to Al Hamishmar.]

5660. Mendes-Flohr, Paul. "Martin Buber, Zionism and the Arabs." New Outlook 28 (December 1985): 17-19.

5661. Mergui, Raphael and Philippe Simonnot. Israel's Ayatollahs. Meir Kahane and the Far Right in Israel. London: Al Saqi Books, 1987.

5662. Metzger, Jan. This Land Is Our Land. The West Bank Under Israeli Occupation. London: Zed Press, 1983. [West Bank since 1967.]

5663. Mi'Ari, Mahmoud. "Traditionalism and Political Identity of Arabs in Israel." Journal of Asian and African Studies 22 (January-April 1987): 33-44.

5664. Miari, Samir M. The Arabs in Israel: A National Minority and Cheap Labor Force, a Split Labor Market Analysis. Doctoral dissertation, Loyola University of Chicago, 1987. UMO # 8704852.

ISRAEL - PALESTINIANS 427

5665. Milson, Menahem. "How Not to Occupy the West Bank." Commentary 81 (April 1986): 15-22.

5666. Minns, Amina and Nadia Hijab. Citizens Apart. A Portrait of the Palestinians In Israel. New York: I.B. Tauris, 1990.

5667. Mize, D. and others. An Assessment of Education in the West Bank and Gaza strip (Preliminary Findings). Washington, D.C.: AMIDEAST, 1979.

5668. Moralig, Gilead. "The Arab As 'Other' in Israeli Fiction." Middle East Review 22 (Autumn 1989)

5669. Morris, Benny. The Birth of the Palestinian Refugee Problem, 1947-1949. New York: Cambridge University Press, 1987.

5670. Morris, Benny. "The Causes and Character of the Arab Exodus from Palestine: The Israel Defence Forces Intelligence Branch Analysis of June 1948." Middle Eastern Studies 22 (January 1986): 5-19.

5671. Morris, Benny. "The Crystallization of Israeli Policy Against a Return of the Arab Refugee: April-December, 1948." Studies in Zionism 6 (1985): 85-118.

5672. Morris, Benny. "The Harvest of 1948 and the Creation of the Palestinian Refugee Problem." Middle East Journal 40 (Autumn 1986): 671-685.

5673. Morris, Benny. "Haifa's Arabs: Displacement and Concentration, July 1948." Middle East Journal 42 (Spring 1988): 241-259.

5674. Morris, Benny. "Operation David and the Palestinian Exodus from Lydda and Ramle in 1948." Middle East Journal 40 (Winter 1986): 82-109.

5675. Morris, Benny. "Yosef Weitz and the Transfer Committee, 1948-1949." Middle Eastern Studies 22 (October 1986): 522- 561. [Forced emigration of Arabs.]

5676. Moskin, J. Robert. "A Very Cruel Dilemma." Present Tense 14 (Autumn 1986): 57-58. [Annexation by Israel of the occupied territories.]

5677. Moughrabi, Fouad. "The International Consensus on the Palestine Question." Journal of Palestine Studies 16 (Spring 1987): 115-133. [Jewish and Palestinian opinion on Palestinian rights.]

5678. Moulton, Muriel. "Arabs and Jews in Haifa." Present Tense 14 (Autumn 1986): 54-57.

5679. Muhareb, M. The Israeli Communist Party and the Palestinian Question, 1948-1981: A Critical Study. Doctoral dissertation, University of Reading, 1986.

5680. Mundy, Yosef. "The Governor of Jericho (a play)." New Outlook 30 (May-June 1987): 45-47.

5681. Murray, Nancy. "Living the Intifadah Day by Day: an Interview with Amal Wahdan." Race & Class 30 (1989): 73-79.

5682. Muslih, Muhammad Y. "Arab Politics and the Rise of Palestinian Nationalism." Journal of Palestine Studies 16 (Summer 1987): 77-94.

5683. Muslih, Muhammad Y. The Origins of Palestinian Nationalism. New York: Columbia University Press, 1987.

5684. Nairn, Allan. "The Occupation." Village Voice (March 1, 1988)

5685. Nakleh, Emile A. "The West Bank and Gaza: Twenty Years Later." Middle East Journal 42 (Spring 1988): 209-226.

5686. Nassar, Jamal R. "Apartheid in the Jewish State: The Refugees Who Never Left Home." Scandanavian Journal of Development Alternatives (March 1987)

5687. A Nation Under Siege: Al-Haq's Annual Report on Human Rights in the Occupied Palestinian Territories 1989. Ramallah, West Bank, via Israel: Al-Haq, May 1990.

5688. Nazzal, Nafez. The Palestinian Exodus from Galilee 1948. Beirut: Institute for Palestine Studies, 1978.

5689. Nevo, Ofra. "Humor Diaries of Israeli Jews and Arabs." Journal of Social Psychology 126 (June 1986): 411-413.

5690. Nimrod, Yoram. Meetings at the Crossroads: Jews and Arabs in Palestine during Recent Generations. Haifa: University of Haifa, 1984. [In Hebrew]

5691. Nixon, Anne. The Status of Palestine Children During the Uprising in the Occupied Territories. Jerusalem, Israel: Save the Children Fund, May 1990.

5692. Noble, Allen G. and Elisha Efrat. "Geography of the Intifadah." Geographical Review 80 (July 1990): 288-307.

5693. O'Brien, Lee. "Palestinian Universities under Occupation 15 May- 15 August 1988." Journal of Palestine Studies 18 (Autumn 1988): 191-197.

5694. Occhiogrosso, Paul F. "The Shin Beth Affair: National Security versus the Rule of Law in the State of Israel." Loyola of Los Angeles International and Comparative Law Journal 11 (Winter 1989): 67-116.

5695. Ophir, Adi. "Occupation: A Perspective from the Israeli Left." Tikkun 1, No.2 (1987): 66-71.

5696. Orpaz, Yitzhak. "The Crowd Roars. Who Wouldn't be Afraid?" New Outlook 30 (May-June 1987): 34-35. [1967, 20 years after.]

5697. Oweiss, Ibrahim M. "Economics of the Israeli Settlements in Occupied Arab Territories." Egypte Contemp. (Cairo) 85 (October 1985): 237-260.

5698. Palestine Human Rights Information Center. The Massacre of Palestinians at al-Haraw al-Sharif, October 8, 1990: A Special Investigative Report. Chicago, IL: PHRIC, October 31, 1990.

5699. Palestinian Education: A Threat to Israeli Security? East Jerusalem: The Jerusalem Media and Communication Centre, 1989.

5700. "The Palestinians Fourteen Demands." Journal of Palestine Studies 17 (Spring 1988): 63-65.

5701. Palumbo, Michael. The Palestinian Catastrophe: The 1948 Expulsion of a People from their Homeland. London: Faber and Faber, 1987.

5702. Parmenter, Barbara M. Toward a Geography of Home: Palestinian Literature and the Sense of Place. Master's thesis, University of Texas, 1985.

5703. Patai, Raphael. The Seed of Abraham: Jews and Arabs in Contact and Conflict. Salt Lake City: University of Utah Press, 1986.

5704. Peleg, Ilan and Ofira Seliktar, eds. The Emergence of a Binational Israel: The Second Republic in the Making. Boulder, CO: Westview Press, 1989.

5705. Peres, Yochanan. "Most Israelis are Committed to Democracy." Israeli Democracy (Israel Diaspora Institute, Tel Aviv University) (February 1987): 16-19. [Study by Modi'in Ezrachi.]

5706. Peretz, Don. "Intifadeh: The Palestinian Uprising." Foreign Affairs (Summer 1988)

5707. Peretz, Don. The West Bank: History, Politics, Society, and Economy. Boulder, CO: Westview, 1986.

5708. Perry, Glenn E., ed. Palestine: Continuing Disposession. Belmont, MA: Association of Arab-American University Graduates, 1986.

5709. Pess, Flavia. "Women's Work and Women's Pay: Super Exploitation in the Sewing Industry." Al-Fajr (English edition) (April 19, 1985)

5710. Picadou, Nadine. "Genese des elites politiques Palestiniennes, 1948-1982." Revue Francaise de Science Politique 34 (1984): 3240351.

5711. Playfair, Emma. Administrative Detention in the West Bank. Ramallah: Law in the Service of Man, 1986.

5712. Playfair, Emma. Demolition and Sealing of Houses as a Punitive Measure in the Israeli-Occupied West Bank. Ramallah: al-Haq/Law in the Service of Man, 1987.

5713. Plocker, Sever I. "The Palestinian State in the Territories: An Economic Report." New Outlook 30 (May-June 1987): 28-30.

5714. "Poll in West Bank Finds Palestinians Strongly Favor Arafat." New York Times (September 9, 1986)

5715. Pomerantz, Marsha. "Learning Disabilities." Jerusalem Post Magazine, (April 4, 1986): [Problems of Druse education in Israel.]

5716. Ponger, Anna. "Jewish Settlements in the Gaza Strip." Swiss Review of World Affairs 36 (May 1986): 12-13.

5717. Portugali, J. "Jewish Settlement in the Occupied Territories. Israel's Settlement Structure and the Palestinians." Political Geography Quarterly 10 (January 1991)

5718. Pressburg, Gail. "The Uprising: Causes and Consequences." Journal of Palestine Studies 17 (Spring 1988): 38-50.

5719. Puanamaki, Raija-Leena. "Content of and Factors Affecting Coping Modes among Palestinian Children." Scandanavian Journal of Development Alternatives 6 (March 1987): 86-98.

5720. Punamaki, Raija-Leena. "Experience of Torture, Means of Coping, and Level of Symptoms among Palestinian Political Prisoners." Journal of Palestine Studies 17 (Summer 1988): 81-96.

5721. Punishing a Nation: Human Rights Violations during the Palestinian Uprising, December 1987-1988. Ramallah: Al-Haq/ Law in the Service of Man, December 1988.

5722. Quigley, John. Palestine and Israel: A Challenge to Justice. Durham, NC: Duke University Press, 1990.

5723. Rabbani, Mouin. "Intifada Profile: Narratives of a Small Proprietor and a Fugitive." Journal of Palestine Studies 19 (Spring 1990): 89-100.

5724. Rabin, Roni C. "As Arab Workers Stay Home, the Israeli Economy Suffers." New York Times, (January 15, 1988): [Palestinians from West Bank and Gaza.]

5725. Rabinovich, Abraham. "Stateless in Gaza." Jerusalem Post Magazine (June 20, 1986)

5726. Ramras-Rauch, Gila. The Arab in Israeli Literature. Bloomington: Indiana University Press, 1989.

5727. Randa, Ernest W. Creating Dependency. Palestinian Arab Society 1918-1948. Master's thesis, Western Washington University, 1980.

5728. Rapaport, C. and others. Arab Youth in Israel. Knowledge, Values and Behavior in the Social and Political Spheres. Jerusalem: Henrietta Szold Institute, June 1980.

5729. Rapp, Uri. "Stunning Sobol." Jerusalem Post Magazine, (November 8, 1985): [A play, The Palestinian, by Yehoshua Sobol, about Arab-Jewish relations.]

5730. Ravitsky, Aviezer. The Phenomenon of Kahanism: Consciousness and Political Reality. Jerusalem: 1985.

5731. "Rebel with a Cause: An Interview with a Young Israeli Woman." New Outlook 33 (March 1990): 11-14.

5732. "Recent Trends in Palestinian Education." Birzeit Research Review 1, No. 1 (1985): entire issue.

5733. Reches (Rekhess), Elie. "The Arab Communist Challenge to the Israeli Communist Party (1970-1985)." Studies in Comparative Communism 22 (Winter 1989): 337-350.

5734. Reches (Rekhess), Elie. "Arabs in a Jewish State: Images vs. Realities." Middle East Insight 7 (January-February 1990): 3-9.

5735. Reches (Rekhess), Elie. "The Employment in Israel of Arab Labourers from the Adminstered Areas." Israel Yearbook on Human Rights 5 (1975)

5736. Reches (Rekhess), Elie. "Israeli Arabs and the Arabs of the West Bank and Gaza: Political Affinity and National Solidarity." Asian and African Studies 23 (1989)

5737. Reches (Rekhess), Elie. "Partisan Press." Jerusalem Post, (April 22, 1987): [Arab press in occupied territories.]

5738. Reches (Rekhess), Elie. "Tuition Fees Fan Arab Fires." Jerusalem Post, (May 22, 1987): [Analysis of proposal that Arab students pay higher university tuition than Jews.]

5739. Reches (Rekhess), Elie. "Unemployed of Arab Academies." New Outlook 30 (July-August 1987): 20-21.

5740. "Refugee Interviews." Journal of Palestine Studies 18 (Autumn 1988): 158-171.

5741. Regev, Menachem. "The 'Arab Problem' in Israel Children's Books." Dispersion and Unity No. 9 (1969): 84-110.

5742. Reicin, Cheryl V. "Preventive Detention, Curfews, Demolition of Houses, and Deportations: An Analysis of Measures Employed by Israel in the Administered Territories." Cardozo Law Review 8 (February 1987): 515-558.

5743. Reiss, Nira. "Processes Affecting the Distribution of Public Health Services to the Arabs in Israel." Asian and African Studies 23 (1989)

5744. "Report of the Secretary-General of the United Nations to the Security Council Regarding the Situation in the Occupied Territories." Journal of Palestine Studies 17 (Spring 1988): 66-79.

5745. "A Report on Jewish Settlements in the Occupied Territories." Journal of Palestine Studies 20 (Autumn 1990): 178-179. [Excerpts from Ha'aretz, June 22, 1990.]

5746. Report on the Violations of Human and Civil Rights. Tel Aviv, Israel: Israeli League for Human and Civil Rights, 1988.

5747. Report on the Violations of Human Rights in the Territories During the Uprising 1988. Tel Aviv: Israeli League for Human and Civil Rights, 1988.

5748. "Response of Law in the Service of Man (West Bank affiliate of the International Commission of Jurists) to the Chapter on Israel and the Occupied Territories in the U. S. State Department's 1985 Country Reports on Human Rights Practices for 1984." Journal of Palestine Studies 15 (Summer 1986): 198-206. [Ramallah, West Bank, 1985.]

5749. Ricks, Thomas M. "Education in the West Bank: Research Trends and Directions." Birzeit Research Review 1, No. 1 (1985): 3-14.

5750. Rishmawi, Mona. Planning in Whose Interest? Land-Use Planning as a Strategy for Judaization. Ramallah, West Bank: Al-Haq, 1986.

5751. Roberts, Adam and others. Academic Freedom under Israeli Military Occupation: Report on WUS/ICJ Mission of Enquiry into Higher Education in the West Bank and Gaza. London: World University Service/International Commission of Jurists, 1984.

5752. Roberts, Adam. "Prolonged Military Occupation: The Israeli- Occupied Territories Since 1967." American Journal of International Law 84 (January 1990)

5753. Robins, E. A. "Attitudes, Stereotypes of Prejudice among Arabs and Jews in Israel." New Outlook 15 (1972): 36-48.

5754. Robson, Clive and Cossali, Paul. Stateless in Gaza. London: Zed Press, 1986.

5755. Rodison, Maxine. "Dialogue with the Palestinians." Chpt. 6 In Cult, Ghetto, and State. London: Al Saqi Books, 1983.

5756. Rolef, Susan Hattis. "Israeli Arabs Might Fare Better without [Ezer] Weizman." Jerusalem Post, (October 16, 1986)

5757. Roman, Michael. "Jews and Arabs in Hebron: Between Confrontation and Daily Coexistence." Jerusalem Quarterly 43 (1987): 49-70.

5758. Romann, Michael. Jewish Kiryat Arba versus Arab Hebron. Jerusalem: West Bank Data Base Project, 1985.

5759. Ronel, Eti. "20 Years Later. Walking Between the Raindrops." New Outlook 30 (May-June 1987): 8-12. [Arab and Israeli youth reflect on last 20 years of Israeli military occupation.]

5760. Rosen, Miriam. "Arab Cinema in Exile." Merip Reports No. 136-137 (October-December 1985): 47-50.

5761. Rouhana, Kate. "Children and the Intifadah." Journal of Palestine Studies 18 (Summer 1989): 110-121.

5762. Rouhana, Nadim. "The Collective Identity of Arabs in Israel." New Outlook 30 (July-August 1987): 22-23.

5763. Rouhana, Nadim. "The Intifada and the Palestinians of Israel: Resurrecting the Green Line." Journal of Palestine Studies 19 (Spring 1990): 58-75.

5764. Roy, Sara. "The Gaza Strip: A Case of Economic De-Development." Journal of Palestine Studies 17 (Autumn 1987): 56-88.

5765. Roy, Sara. The Gaza Strip Survey. Boulder, CO.: Westview Press, 1987.

5766. Roy, Sara. "The Gaza Strip: Critical Effects of the Occupation." Arab Studies Quarterly 10 (Winter 1988): 59- 103.

5767. Rubenberg, Cheryl A. "Twenty Years of Israeli Economic Policies in the West Bank and Gaza: Prologue to the Intifada." Journal of Arab Affairs 8 (1989): 28-73.

5768. Rubenstein, Danny. "Reform in Educational Obejectives for the Arab Sector." New Outlook 19 (1976): 70-71.

5769. Rubenstein, Danny. "Student Elections Highlight Great Palestinian Divide." Jerusalem Post, (August 6, 1986): Translated by Joel Greenberg.

5770. Rudge, David. "Acre's Arabs Demand a Better Deal." Jerusalem Post, (June 25, 1986): [Housing problems.]

5771. Rudge, David. "School Gap for Arabs Called 'Wide as Ever'." Jerusalem Post, (September 2, 1986)

5772. Rudge, David. "Unequal Partners." Jerusalem Post Magazine, (April 4, 1986): [Growing questioning by Druse of their traditional role in Israel.]

5773. Rudge, David. "Village at the Barricades." Jerusalem Post, (June 5, 1987): [Charges of discrimination against Druse village, Beit Jann.]

5774. Ruether, Rosemary. "Invisible Palestinians: Ideology and Reality in Israel." Christian Century (July 1, 1987): 587- 591.

5775. Sahliyah, Emile. "The West Bank Pragmatic Elite: The Uncertain Future." Journal of Palestine Studies 15 (Summer 1986): 34-45.

5776. Said, Edward W. After the Last Day: Palestinian Lives. New York: Pantheon, 1986.

5777. Said, Edward. "On Palestinian Identity: A Conversation with Salman Rushdie." New Left Review No. 160 (November-December 1986): 63-80.

5778. Said, Edward. "Spurious Scholarship and the Palestinian Question." Race & Class (Winter 1988)

5779. Said, Edward W. and others. Blaming the Victims. Spurious Scholarship and the Palestinian Question. New York: Verso, 1987.

5780. Saleh, Abdul Jawad. Israel's Policy of De-Institutionalization: A Case Study of Palestinian Local Governments. London: Jerusalem Center for Development Studies, 1987.

5781. Saleh, Abdul Jawad and A.A.S. Salhab. Can It Happen Again:. A Report on Mass Poisoning in the Palestinian Territories Under Israeli Occupation: Amman, Jordan: Jerusalem Center for Development Studies, 1985.

5782. Samara, Adel. Economics of Hunger in the West Bank and Gaza Strip. Tel-Aviv: Dar Miftah, 1979.

5783. Samara, Adel. The Political Economy of the West Bank Peasants under the Israeli Occupation, from Peripherilization to Development. Doctoral dissertation, University of Exeter, 1987.

5784. Samara, Adel. The Political Economy of the West Bank 1967- 1987: From Peripheralization to Development. London: Khamsin, 1988.

5785. Sayigh, Yusif A. "The Palesinian Economy under Occupation: Dependency and Pauperization." Journal of Palestine Studies 15 (Summer 1986): 46-67.

5786. Schenker, Hillel. "Gaza: The Invisible Land." New Outlook 28 (December 1985): 7-10.

5787. Schenker, Hillel and Manny Erez. "Case No. 777- The Akram Haniyyah." New Outlook 29 (November-December 1986): 21-23. [Expulsion from occupied territories.]

5788. Scholch, A., ed. Palestinians Over the Green Line. London: Ithaca Press, 1983.

5789. Segal, Mark. "Expert cites 'Palestinization' Alarm Bells." Jerusalem Post Magazine, (April 25, 1986): [Eli Rekhess on growing ties between Arabs in the territories and in Israel proper.]

5790. Segal, Mark. "Sounding the Alarm." Jerusalem Post, (September 27, 1985): [Elie Rekhess on role of Arabs in Israel and the occupied territories.]

5791. Segev, Tom. 1949. The First Israelis. New York: Free Press, 1985.

5792. Semyonov, Moshe. "Bi-ethnic Labor Markets, Mono-ethnic Labor Markets, and Socio-economic Inequality." American Sociological Review (April 1988): 256-266. [Arabs and Jews in Israel.]

5793. Semyonov, Moshe. "The Socioeconomic Status of Non-citizen Arab Workers in the Israeli Labor Market: Costs and Benefits." Social Science Quarterly 67 (June 1986)

5794. Semyonov, Moshe and Noah Lewin-Epstein. Hewers of Wood and Drawers of Water: Noncitizen Arabs in the Israeli Labor Market. Ithaca, New York: ILR Press, 1987.

5795. Shahak, Israel. From the Hebrew Press. Monthly Translations and Commentaries from Israel. Washington, D.C.: American Educational Trust, 1989+.

5796. Shahak, Israel. "Israeli Apartheid and the Intifadah." Race and CLass 30 (July-September 1988): 1-12.

5797. Shahak, Israel. "Palestinian Life Under Israeli Apartheid." In Separate and Unequal. The Dynamics of South African and Israeli Rule, edited by Louise Cainkar. Chicago, IL: Palestine Human Rights Campaign, 1985.

5798. Shalev, Michael. "Jewish Organized labor and the Palestinians." In The Israeli State and Society: Boundaries and Frontiers, edited by Baruch Kimmerling. Albany: State University of New York Press, 1989.

5799. Shamai, S. "Critical Sociology of Education Theory in Practice: The Druze Education in the Golan." British Journal of Sociology of Education 11 (1990)

5800. Shammas, Anton. "A Stone's Throw." New York Review of Books, (March 31, 1988) [Uprising of Palestinians in occupied areas of Israel.]

5801. Shapiro, Amos. "Confronting Racism by Law in Israel- Promises and Pitfalls." Cardozo Law Review 8 (February 1987): 595-608.

5802. Sharaf, Shamil. Die Palastinenser, Geschichte der Entstehung eines nationalen Bewusztseins. Vienna: Braumuller, 1983.

5803. Sharp, Gene. "Nonviolent Struggle." Journal of Palestine Studies 17 (Autumn 1987): 37-55.

5804. Shavit, Yossi. "Segregation, Tracking and the Educational Attainment of Minorities: Arabs and Oriental Jews in Israel." American Sociological Review 55 (February 1990): 115-126.

5805. Shehadeh, Raja. Occupier's Law: Israel and the West Bank. Washington, D.C.: Institute for Palestine Studies, November 1985.

5806. Shehadeh, Raja. "Occupier's Law and the Uprising." Journal of Palestine Studies 17 (Spring 1988): 24-37.

5807. Shehadeh, Raja. The Third Way: A Journal of Life on the West Bank. London: Quartet,

5808. Shinar, Dov and Danny Rubenstein. Palestinian Press in the West Bank: The Political Dimension. Jerusalem: West Bank Data Base Project, 1987.

5809. Shipler, David. Arab and Jew: Wounded Spirits in a Promised Land. New York: Times Books, 1986.

5810. Shipler, David. Arab and Jew-Wounded Spirits in a Promised Land. Washington, D.C.: Greater Washington Educational Telecommunications Association, 1989. [Teacher's guide.]

5811. Shipler, David K. "Arabs and Jews in Israel." New York Times Magazine, (August 10, 1986)

5812. Shlaim, Avi. "The Rise and Fall of the All-Palestine Government in Gaza." Journal of Palestine Studies 20 (Autumn 1990): 37-53.

5813. Shor, Yitzhak. "Intimate Encounters." Israel Horizons (September-October 1986): 25-27. [Jews and Arabs in Israel.]

5814. Shor, Yitzhak. "There Is Still a Gap Between the Jewish and Arab School Systems." Al Hamishmar (October 15, 1990): [English translation in From the Hebrew Press by Dr. Israel Shahak, 2 (December 1990) 19-22.]

5815. Simon, Rita J. "Assessing Israel's Record of Human Rights." Annals of the American Academy of Political and Social Science No. 506 (November 1989): 115-128.

5816. Siniora, Hanna. "An Analysis of the Current Revolt." Journal of Palestine Studies 17 (Spring 1988): 3-13.

5817. Siniora, Hanna. "It Is Criminal to Remain Silent." New Outlook 30 (July-August 1987): 32-34. [Arab editor who was exploring possibility of running in the Jerusalem municipal elections.]

5818. Smith, Colin and others. The Palestinians, 5th edition. London: Minority Rights Group, 1984.

5819. Smooha, Sammy. Arabs and Jews in Israel. Vol. I: Conflicting and Shared Attitudes in a Divided Society. Boulder, CO.: Westview Press, 1989.

5820. Smooha, Sammy. "Existing and Alternative Policy toward the Arabs in Israel." Ethnic and Racial Studies 5 (January 1982)

5821. Smooha, Sammy. "Minority Status in an Ethnic Democracy: The Status of the Arab Minority in Israel." Ethnic and Racial Studies 13 (July 1990)

5822. Smooha, Sammy. The Orientation and Politicization of the Arab Minority in Israel. Haifa: University of Haifa, Jewish-Arab Center Institute of Middle Eastern Studies, 1984.

5823. Smooha, Sammy. "A Typology of Jewish Orientations toward the Arab Minority in Israel." Asian and African Studies 23 (1989)

5824. Smooha, Sammy and Don Peretz. "The Arabs in Israel." Journal of Conflict Resolution 26 (1982): 451-484.

5825. Soen, Dan and Aharon, Shmuel. "The Israeli Bedouin: Political Organization at the National Level." Middle Eastern Studies 23 (July 1987): 329-347.

5826. Sohlberg, S. C. "Social Desirability Responses in Jewish and Arab Children in Israel." Journal of Cross-cultural Psychology 7 (1976): 301-314.

5827. Spielmann, Miriam. If Peace Comes... Atlantic Highlands, NJ: Humanities Press, 1984. [Jewish and Arab children and youth in Israel.]

5828. Sprinzak, Ehud. "The Emergence of the Israeli Radical Right." Comparative Politics 21 (January 1989): 171-192.

5829. Sprinzak, Ehud. "Kach and Meir Kahane: The Emergence of Jewish Quasi-fascism (2 parts)." Patterns of Prejudice 19 (1985): # 3:15-21;#4:3-13.

5830. Stein, Georg. The Palestinians: Oppression and Resistance of a Disinherited People. Koln: Pahl-Rugenstein, 1988.

5831. Stein, Kenneth W. "The Intifadah and the 1936-39 Uprising; A Comparison." Journal of Palestine Studies 19 (Summer 1990): 64-85.

5832. Steinberg, Bernard. "Education, Judaism and Politics in Israel: A Survey." Jewish Social Studies 48 (Summer-Fall 1986): 235-256.

5833. Stephens, Marc. Taxation in the Occupied West Bank, 1967- 1989. Ramallah, West Bank, via Israel: Al-Haq, 1990.

5834. Sternhell, Zeev and others. "Israeli Roundtable: Facing the Meaning of Conquest." Tikkun 2, No.2 (1987): 61-65.

5835. Stockton, Ronald R. "Intifadah Deaths." Journal of Palestine Studies 18 (Winter 1989): 101-108.

5836. Stockton, Ronald R. "Intifada Deaths." Journal of Palestine Studies 19 (Summer 1990): 86-95.

5837. Students under Fire: A Report on Army Actions at Birzeit University on December 4, 1986. Public Relations Office, Birzeit University, Birzeit, West Bank, via Israel: 1987.

5838. Sullivan, Anthony T. Palestinian Universities Under Occupation. Cairo, Egypt: American University in Cairo Press, 1988.

5839. Sullivan, Anthony T. "Politics and Relevance in Palestinian Higher Education: The Case of Birzeit University." American- Arab Affairs 27 (Winter 1988-1989): 58-69.

5840. Syrkin, Marie. "The Kahane Phenomenon." Middle East Review (Fall 1986): 14-20.

5841. Taggan, Yehuda. The Mufti of Jerusalem and Palestine: Arab Politics, 1930-1937. New York: 1987.

5842. Taggart, Simon. Workers in Struggle-Palestinian Trade Unions in the Occupied West Bank. London: Editpride, 1985.

5843. Talmon, Jacob L. "Self-determination for Palestinian Arabs: An Open Letter by Professor J. L. Talmon." Jewish Liberation Journal (NYC) (November-December 1989)

5844. Tannous, Izzat. The Palestinians: A Detailed Documented Eyewitness History of Palestine under British Mandate. New York: IGT Company, 1988.

5845. Tarbush, S. "PLO and UNESCO Work Towards Palestine Open University." Middle East Education Digest 12-18 (October 12, 1979)

5846. Tarbush, Mohammad A. Reflections of a Palestinian. Washington, D.C.: American-Arab Affairs Council, 1986. [May 1971-October 1985.

5847. Tekiner, Roselle. "Jewish Nationality Status as the Basis for Institutionalized Racial Discrimination in Israel." American Arab Affairs No. 17 (Summer 1986)

5848. Tekiner, Roselle. "On the Inequality of Israeli Citizens." Without Prejudice 1 (Fall 1987): 48-57.

5849. Terry, Janice. Mistaken Identity: Arab Stereotypes in Popular Writing. 1730 M Street, NW, Suite 411, Washington, D.C. 20036: American-Arab Affairs Council, 1985. [Jewish-Arab relations in literature.]

5850. Tessler, Mark. "The Intifada and Political Discourse." Journal of Palestine Studies 19 (Winter 1990): 43-61.

5851. Tibawi, A. Arab Education in Mandatory Palestine. London: Luzac, 1956.

5852. Toledano, Shmuel. "Racism in Schoolclothes." Israel Horizons (September-October 1986): 17-22. [Israeli high school students and anti-Arab racism.]

5853. Totah, Khalil A. "Education in Palestine." Annals of American Academy of Political and Social Science 164 (November 1932): 155-166.

5854. Toukan, Fadwa. "Meeting with Moshe Dayan." Jerusalem Post, (November 5, 1986): [Arab-Jewish issues.]

5855. Tsemel, Lea. "Double Standard Justice in Israel: The Case of the Jewish Terror Organization." In The Palestine Yearbook of International Law. Vol. 2, edited by Anis Kassim. Nicosia, Cyprus: Al-Shaybani Society of International Law Ltd., 1985.

5856. Twenty Years of Israeli Occupation of the West Bank and Gaza. Ramallah, West Bank: Al-Haq/Law in the Service of Man, 1987.

5857. Tzemach, Mina. Attitudes of the Jewish Majority Toward the Arab Minority. Jerusalem: Van Leer Foundation, 1980.

5858. Tzemach, Mina and Ruth Tzin. Attitudes of Adolescents with Regard to Democratic Values. Jerusalem: Dahaf Research Institute and the Van Leer Jerusalem Foundation, September 1984.

5859. United Nations, General Assembly, Economic and Social Council, 38th Session. Living Conditions of the Paletinian People in the Occupied Palestinian Territories: Report of the Secretary General. New YOrk: UN, June 22, 1983.

5860. UNRWA. A Brief History, 1950-1982. Vienna: 1983.

5861. UNRWA, UNESCO Department of Education. Benchmarks in Education. Vienna: 1979.

5862. Uval, Beth. "Arab Women's Problems Begin Even Before They Are Born." Jerusalem Post, (January 18, 1987)

5863. Van der Hardt, Anya A. A Case for the Palestine Liberation Organization: Human Rights Violations in the West Bank and Gaza. Doctoral dissertation, Union for Experimenting Colleges and Universities, 1987. UMO # 9016671.

5864. Vermund, S. H. and others. Health Status and Services in the West Bank and Gaza Strip: Report of Cooperation for Development, a Community-based Health Project. New York: Institute for Middle East Peace and Development, September 1985.

5865. Viorst, Milton. Reaching for the Olive Branch, UNRWA and Peace in the Middle East. Bloomington: Indiana University Press, 1989.

5866. Vitullo, Anita. Israel's War by Bureaucracy: "We'll Blow Your House Down". Chicago, IL: Human Rights Research and Education Foundation, 1988.

5867. Vitullo, Anita. "Palestinian Workers: Enslaved by Israel." Guardian (NYC) (June 21, 1989)

5868. Wallach, John and Janet Wallach. Still Small Voices: The Untold Human Stories Behind the Violence on the West Bank and Gaza. New York: Harcourt Brace Jovanovich, 1989.

5869. Warnock, Kitty. Land Before Honor: Palestinian Women in the Occupied Territories. New York: Monthly Review Press, 1990.

5870. Warshawski, Michel. "The Legitimacy of Solidarity [between the Palestinians and Jews of Israel]." Against the Current 4 (July-August 1989): 20-22.

5871. Warshawski, Michel. "An Assessment of the Intifada." Against the Current 4 (July-August 1989): 23-24.

5872. Weil, Chalva. "Learning within an Uneasy Coexistence." Times Educational Supplement, (July 25, 1986): [Arab village of Beit Safafa, in Israel.]

5873. Weisbund, David. Jewish Settler Violence: Deviance as Social Reaction. University Park: Pennsylvania State University Press, 1989.

5874. West Bank Data Base Project. "Population, Employment and Public Funding on the West Bank, 1985." New Outlook 29 (January-February 1986): 35-37.

5875. White, Patrick. Let Us Be Free: A Narrative Before and During the Intifada. Clifton, NJ: Kingston Press, 1989.

5876. Wilkie, Curtis. "Bedouins Grapple with Shift in Lifestyle." Boston Globe, (June 30, 1986)

5877. Wilkie, Curtis. "Land Without a Country." Boston Globe Magazine, (September 7, 1986): [Gaza Strip.]

5878. Will, Donald and Sheila Ryan. Israel and South Africa: Legal Systems of Settler Dominance. Trenton, NJ: Africa World Press, 1990.

5879. Wolf, Joseph M. "National Security v. the Rights of the Accused: The Israeli Experience." California Western International Law Journal 20 (Winter 1989): 115-151.

5880. Wolfe, Lisa. "The Palestinian Campus." New York Times Magazine, (April 19, 1987): [Bir Zeit University.]

5881. Wolffsohn, Michael. Israel: Polity, Society and Economy 1882-1886. Atlantic Highlands, NJ: Humanities Press, 1987.

5882. "The Work of the Special Committee to Investigate Israeli Practices Affecting the Human Rights of the Population of the Occupied Territories." Journal of Palestine Studies 16 (Autumn 1986): 128-137.

5883. Ya'ari, Arieh. "Meron Benvenisti's 'Communal Myth'." New Outlook 33 (May-June 1990): 37-39.

5884. Yitzhaki, Ahiya. "Milson's Year on the West Bank." Middle East Review (Winter 1985-1986): 37-47. [Menahem Milson.]

5885. Younis, Abdullatif. "Israeli Arabs Not Willing to Be Second-class Citizens." Jerusalem Post, (June 3, 1986): [Long letter.]

5886. Younis, Mona. Community Development versus Personal Prosperity: Israel's Pacification Policy in the Occupied West Bank and Gaza Strip. Center for Hebraic Studies: Yarmouk University, Information Series 2, No. 1, February 1987.

5887. Yuchtman-Yaar, Ephriam. "The Test of Israel's Arab Minority." Israeli Democracy (Tel Aviv) (Spring 1988): 42-46.

5888. Yuval-Davis, Nira. "Woman/Nation/State: The Demographic Race and National Reproduction in Israel." Radical America 21 (November-December 1987)

5889. Zarhi, S. and A. Achiezra. The Economic Condition of the Arab Minority in Israel. Givat Haviva: 1966.

5890. Zayyad, Tawfiq. "[Interview on Palestinians in Israel and Occupied Territories]." People's Daily World (October 30, 1986): [Communist mayor of Nazareth.]

5891. Zayyad, Tawfiq. "People in the News." People's Daily World (October 30, 1986)

5892. Zogby, J. J., ed. Perspectives on Palestinian Arabs and Israeli Jews. Wilmette, IL: Medina Press, 1977.

5893. Zu'bi, E. "The Changing Status of Arab Women in Israel." Kidma 2 (1975): 31-33.

5894. Zureik, Elia. "For Good Reasons, Israeli Arabs Still See Themselves as Palestinians." In These Times (May 25, 1988)

5895. Zureik, Elia. "Palestinians under Israeli Control." Arab Studies Quarterly 7 (1985)

ITALY

5896. Adler, Winfried. Die Minderheitenpolitik des Italienischen Faschismus in Südtirol in Aostatal 1922-1929. Doctoral dissertation, University of Trier, 1979.

5897. Aimi, A. "Gli immigrati dal Terzo Mondo a Milano. Aspetti Quantitativi." Affari Sociali Internazionali 13 (1985)

5898. Alcock, Anthony E. "The History of the South Tyrol Question." University of Geneva, 1970.

5899. Alcock, Anthony E. The History of the South Tyrol Question. London: Michael Joseph, 1970.

5900. Alfieri, Paola and G. Ambrosini. La condizione economica, sociale e giuridica della donna in Italia. Turin: Pavarici, 1970.

5901. Alfieri, Vittorio E. "La resistenza al fascismo nella scuola italiana." Risorgimento (Italy) 38 (October 1986): 157-164.

5902. Algini, Maria L. "Cultura cattolica e oppressione." In Donna, cultura e tradizione, 32-59. Milan: Mazzotta, 1976.

5903. Ammassari, Paolo. "Classes and Class Relationships in Italian Contemporary Society." Politico 44 (March 1979): 70-91.

5904. Arnold, W. Vincent. Fascist War Propoganda, 1939-1943. Miami University, 1990. UMO # 9029371.

5905. Ascoli, G. and others, eds. La Questione femminile in Italia dal '900 ad oggi. Milan: Franco Angeli Editore, 1977.

5906. Aymard, Maurice. "From Feudalism to Capitalism in Italy: The Case That Doesn't Fit." Review (F. Braudel Center) 6 (Fall 1982): 131-208.

5907. Aymard, Maurice and Guiseppi Giarrizzo, eds. La Sicilia. Turin: Giulio Einaudi Editore, 1987.

5908. Baranski, Zygmunt G. and Shirley W. Vinall, eds. Women and Italy. Essays on Gender Culture and History. Berg: 1991.

5909. Bell, Donald H. Sesto San Giovanni: Workers, Culture, and Politics in An Italian Town, 1880-1922. New Brunswick, NJ: Rutgers University Press, 1986.

5910. Bell, Donald H. "Working Class Culture and Fascism in an Italian Industrial Town, 1918-1922." Soc. Hist. 9 (1984): 1-24.

5911. Benedikter, Rudolf and others, eds. Nationalismus und Neofaschismus in Sudtirol: die Erfolge des Movimiento Sociale Italiano..beiden Gemeinderatswahlen vom 12. Mai 1985: Ursachen, Bedingungen, Auswirkungen. Vienna: Wilhelm Braumuller, Universitats-Verlagsbuchhandlung, 1987.

5912. Bernardini, Gene. "The Origins and Development of Racial Anti-Semitism in Fascist Italy." Journal of Modern History 49 (September 1977): 431-453.

5913. Birnbaum, Lucia C. Liberazione della Donna: Feminism in Italy. Middletown, CT: Wesleyan University Press, 1986.

5914. Bocca, Giorgio. Gli italiani sono razzisti? Milan: Garzanti Editore, 1988. [In re: black immigrants.]

5915. Brustein, William and B. Markovsky. "The Rational Fascist: Interwar Fascist Party Membership in Italy and Germany." Journal of Political and Military Sociology 17 (Winter 1989)

5916. Caciagli, Mario. "The Movimento Sociale Italiano-Destra Nazionale and Neo-fascism in Italy." West European Politics 11 (1988): 19-233. [Since 1946.]

5917. Caffaz, Ugo. L'antisemitismo italiano sotto il fascismo. Firenze: La Nuova Italia, 1975.

5918. Canepa, Andrew M. "Emancipation and Jewish Repsonse in Mid-Nineteenth-century Italy." European History Quarterly 16 (1986): 403-439.

5919. Canestrini, Sandro. "Italy's Ethnic Minorities and the Contradictions of Self-Determination." Social Justice 16 (1989): 99-102.

5920. Caputo, G. and others. Il pregiudizio antisemitico in Italia. Roma: Newton Compton, 1984.

5921. Carboni, Carlo. "Elementi per uno studio su stato e classi sociali." Rassegna Italiana di Sociologia 23 (1982): 201-250.

5922. Carboni, Carlo, ed. Classi e movimienti in Italia, 1970-1985. Bari: Giuseppe Laterza & Figli, 1986.

5923. Carpi, D. "Notes on the History of the Jews during the Holocaust Period; the Attitude of the Italians (1941-1943)." Wise (1981): 25-62.

5924. Chianese, Gloria. Storia sociale della donna in Italia. Naples: Guido, 1980.

5925. Chiesi, Antonio M. "L'elite finanziaria italiana." Rassegna Italiana di Sociologia 23 (1982): 572-595.

5926. Clark, Martin. "Italian Squadrism, Contemporary Vigilantism." European History Quarterly 18 (January 1988): 33-49.

5927. Comitato Di Associazoni Femminili Per La Parita Di Retribuzione. L'emancipazione femminile in Italia, un secolo di discussioni: 1861-1961. Florence: Nuova Italia, 1963.

5928. Creveld, M. van. "Beyond the Finzi-Contini Garden: Mussolini's 'Fascist Racism'." Encounter 42 (1974): 42-47.

5929. Davidson, Nicolas. "The Inquisition and the Italian Jews." Inquisition and Society in Early Modern Europe (1987): 19-46.

5930. Der italienische Faschismus: Probleme und Forschungstendenzen. Munich: R. Oldenbourg Verlag, 1983.

5931. Dessart, Francis. "The Albanian Ethnic Groups in the World: An Historical and Cultural Essay on the Albanian Colonies in Italy." East European Quarterly 15 (1981): 469-484.

5932. di Nola, Alfonso M. "Antisemitismo come, oggi." Ponte 34 (1978): 1489-1497. [Antisemitism in contemporary Italy.]

5933. di Nola, Alfonso M. Antisemitismo in Italia, 1962-1972. Florence, Italy: Vallecchi, 1973.

5934. Duggan, Christopher. Fascism and the Mafia. New Haven, CT: Yale University Press, 1989.

5935. Fargion, Libana P. "The Anti-Jewish Policy of the Italian Social Republic (1943-1945)." Yad Vashem Studies 17 (1986): 17-49.

5936. Forgacs, David, ed. Rethinking Italian Facism: Capitalism, Populism, and Culture. London: Lawrence and Wishart, 1986.

5937. Frigessi, Delia. "Alcuni stereotipi nell'Italia di oggi." La Critica Sociologica 89 (1989): 86-93. [Anti-semitic stereotypes in contemporary Italy.]

5938. Gaddi, Giuseppe. "Il razzismo in Italia." Qualestoria 16 (October 1988): 10-38.

5939. Galbo, Joseph. The Social and Cultural Origins of Italian Fascism: A Historical Sociology. Doctoral dissertation, York University, 1988.

5940. Gerhardi Bon, Silvia. La persecuzione anti-ebraica a Trieste (1938-1945). Udine: Del Bianco, 1972.

5941. Giannone, A. "Evaluations of Italian National Wealth in the Last 50 Years." Banca Nazionale del Lavoro Quarterly Review (December 1963)

5942. Gini, Corrado. L'ammontare e la Composizione della Richezza delle Nazioni. 1914.

5943. Giorgetti, G. Capitalismo e agricoltura in Italia. Rome: 1977.

5944. Giura, Vincenzo. "La communita greca a Napoli (1534-1861)." Clio 18 (1982): 524-560.

5945. Goglia, Luigi and Fabio Grassi, eds. Il colonialismo italiano da Adua all'impero. Rome: Guiseppe Laterza & Figli, 1981.

5946. Golden, M. A. "Political Attitudes of Italian Workers: Twenty Years of Survey Evidence." European Journal of Political Research 19 (May 1990)

5947. Grand, Alexander de. "Women under Italian Fascism." Historical Journal 19 (December 1976): 947-968.

5948. Grassi, Corrado. "Deculturalization and Social Degradation of the Linguistic Minorities in Italy." Linguistics 191 (May 24, 1977): 45-54.

5949. Gross, Feliks. Ethnics in a Borderland: An Inquiry Into the Nature of Ethnicity and Reduction of Ethnic Tensions in a One-Time Genocide Area. Westport, CT: Greenwood, 1978. [Trentino-Alto Adige, Italy.]

5950. Gruber, Alfons. Sudtirol unter dem Faschismus. 3d ed. Bozen: Arthesia, 1978.

5951. Guerry, Louis. L'antisemitisme italien. Paris: Societe des Editions des Amis de la Liberte, 1953.

5952. Haas, Hanna. "Sudtirol 1918-1939." Zeitgeschichte 8 (1981): 397-410.

5953. Hunecke, Volker. "Soziale Ungleichheit und Klassen-strukturen in Italien vom Ende des 18. bis zum Anfang des 20. Jahrhunderts." In Klassen in der europaischen Sozialgeschichtes, edited by Hans-Ulrich Wehler. Gottingen: Vandenhoeck und Rupricht, 1979.

5954. Il pregiudizio antisemitico in Italia. Roma: Newton Compton editori, 1984.

5955. Incerti Delmonte, Maria G. "A proposito di salari in eta giolittiana: la disicriminazione femminile." Rivista di Storia Economica 2 (1985): 415-424.

5956. Isenburg, Luisa. Diveti di discriminazione nel rapporto di lavoro. Milan: Dott. Antonino Guiffre Editore, 1984.

5957. Klein, Gabriella. "La politica linguistica nella scuola fascista: Appunti sull' educazione linguistica e sul ruolo della seconde lingue." Movim. operaio socialista 7 (1984): 97-106.

5958. Kuehn, Thomas James. "Emancipation in Late Medieval Florence." University of Chicago, 1977.

5959. Ledeen, Michael A. "The Evolution of Italian Fascist Anti- semitism." Jewish Social Studies 37 (January 1975): 3-17.

5960. Ledeen, Michael A. "Italian Jews and Fascism." Judaism 18 (Summer 1969): 277-298.

5961. Lo Giudice, Maria R. "Razza e giustizia nell'Italia fascista." Rivista di Storia Contemporanea 12 (1983): 70- 90.

5962. Luazza, Guido. "La resistenza al fascismo in Italia." Italia Contemporanea No. 162 (1986): 7-25.

5963. Luraghi, Raimondo. "Slave Labor in the "Rice Belt" of Northern Italy and Slave Labor in the American South- A First Approach." Southern Studies 16, 2 (1977): 109-127.

5964. Lyttelton, Adrian. "Causas y caracticticas de la violencia fascista." Estud. historia social (1987): 81-95.

5965. Mayda, Giuseppe. "La persecuzione antisemita 1943-1945." Ponte 34 (1978): 1428-1439.

5966. Meyer, Donald. Sex and Power: The Rise of Women in America, Russia, Sweden, and Italy. Middletown, CT: Wesleyan University Press, 1987.

5967. Miccoli, Giovanni. "Santa Sede e Chiesa italiana di fronte alle leggi antiebraiche." Studi Storici 4 (1988)

5968. Michaelis, Meir. Mussolini and the Jews. German-Italian Relations and the Jewish Question in Italy, 1922-1945. Oxford: Clarendon Press, 1978.

5969. Michaelis, Meir and D. Carpi. "Italy." In Encyclopedia of the Holocaust, II, 720-730. New York: Macmillan, 1990.

5970. Mori, G. Il capitalismo industriale in Italia. Rome: 1977.

5971. Mozzoni, Anna Maria. La liberazione della donna. Milan: Gabriele Mazzotta, 1975.

5972. Olmi, Massimo. Italiani dimezzati: le minoranze etnico- linguistiche non protette. Naples: Edizione Dehoniane, 1986.

5973. Origo, Iris. "The Domestic Enemy: The Eastern Slaves in Tuscany in the Fourteenth and Fifteenth Centuries." Speculum 30 (1955): 321-366.

5974. Ostenc, Michel. "La conception de la femme fasciste." Resorgimento (Belgium) 4 (1983): 155-174.

5975. Ostenc, Michel. L'education en Italie pendant le fascisme. Paris: Sorbonne, 1980.

5976. Paci, Massimo. "Class Structure in Italian Society." Arch. Eur. Sociology 20 (1979): 40-55.

5977. Paci, Massimo, ed. Capitalismo e classi sociali. Bologna: 1978.

5978. Pankhurst, Richard. "The Development of Racism in Fascist Italy's Colonial Empire (1935-1941)." Ethiopian Journal of African Studies 4 (1987): 31-51.

5979. Passerini, Luisa. Fascism in Popular Memory. The Cultural Experience of the Turin Working Class. Translated by Robert Lumley and Jude Bloomfield. New York: Cambridge University Press, 1987.

5980. Pedatella, R. Anthony. "Italian Attitudes toward Jewry in the Twentieth Century." Jewish Social Studies 47 (1985): 51-62.

5981. Petersen, Jens. "Jugend und Jugendprotest in faschistischen Italien." In Jugendprotest und Generationenkonflikt in Europa im 20. Jahrhundert, edited by Dieter Dowe. Bonn: Neue Gesellschaft, 1986.

5982. Pezzati, Sergio. "Racial Problem in Florence." Italian Journal, (Dobbs Ferry, New York) 4 (1990): 26-27.

5983. Pichetto, Maria Teresa. "L'Antisemitismo nella cultura della destra radicale." Italia Contemporanea No. 165 (1986): 71-84.

5984. Pieroni Bortolotti, Franca. Feminismo e partiti politici in Italia, 1919-1926. Rome: Editori Riuniti, 1978.

5985. Pirrotta, R. A. "Incomes, Savings and Real Wealth of Italian Households in 1977." Economic Conditions in Italy 33 (1979): 19-52.

5986. Piscitelli, E. Storia della resistanza romana. Bari: 1965.

5987. Pittau, Franco and Giuseppe Ulivi. "La tutela giuridica degli stranieri in Italia: problemi e prospettive." Providenza Sociale 40 (1984): 1211-1229. [Immigrants in Italy without protection of law.]

5988. Pivato, Stefano. "Popular and Devotional Press in Italy during Fascism." Kyrkohistorisk Arsskrift 77 (1977): 122-127. [Catholic Church.]

5989. "The Presence of Foreign Immigrants in Italy. New Outlooks." Studi Emigrazione/Etudes Migrations Nos. 82-83 (June- September): 347.

5990. Preti, Luigi. "Fascist Imperialism and Racism." In The Ax Within. Italian Fascism in Action, edited by Roland Sarti. New York: Watts, 1974.

5991. Pristinger, Flavia. "Ethnic Conflict and Modernization in the South Tirol." In Nations Without a State, edited by Charles R. Foster, 153-188. New York: Praeger, 1980.

5992. "Refuge and Persecution in Italy, 1933-1945." Simon Wiesenthal Center Annual 4 (1987): 3-64.

5993. "La ricchezza delle famiglie in Italia (1975-1985)." Banca d'Italia Bol. Econ. (October 1986): 11-23.

5994. Robertson, Esmonde M. "Race as a Factor in Mussolini's Policy in Africa and Europe." Journal of Contemporary History 23 (January 1988): 37-58.

5995. Ross, Robert H., III. Reform Politics and Elite Perceptions in the Italian Transition from "Elite" to Mass" Higher Education. Doctoral dissertation, Yale University, 1987. UMO # 8729138.

5996. Rossi, Amato, ed. La Resistenza italiana: scritti, documenti e testimonianze. Rome: Luciano Lucarini Editore, 1981. [1922-1945.]

5997. Roth, Cecil. The History of the Jews in Italy. Philadelphia, PA: Jewish Publication Society of America, 1946.

5998. Rowley, A. R. "Minority Schools in the South Tyrol and in the Austrian Burgenland: A Comparison of Two Models." Journal of Multilingual and Multicultural Development 7 (1986): 229-251. [Germans in Italy.]

5999. Sarpellon, Giovanni. Rapporto sulla poverta in Italia. Milan: Franco Angeli Editore, 1983.

6000. Sarti, Roland. Fascism and the Industrial Leadership in Italy, 1919-1940. Berkeley: University of California Press, 1971.

6001. Snowden, Frank M. Violence and Great Estates in the South of Italy, Apulia, 1900-1922. New York: Cambridge University Press, 1987.

6002. Sodi, Risa. "The Italian Roots of Racialism." UCLA Historical Journal 8 (1987): 40-70.

6003. Stow, Kenneth R. "Expulsion Italian Style: The Case of Lucio Ferraris." Jewish History 3 (1988): 51-63.

6004. Suro, Roberto. "Gypsies Not Welcome! Romans Say." New York Times, (November 18, 1987)

6005. Tagliabue, John. "Tyrol Isn't Utopia Yet, Just the Little Fatherland." New York Times, (March 10, 1987) [German speaking minority in Italy.]

6006. Tarrow, Sidney and Sonia Stefanizzi. "Protesta e regolazione sociale in Italia: stato e societa nel ciclo 1965-1974." Stato e Mercato (April 1989): 11-47.

6007. Taylor, P. M. "Anthropology and the 'Racial Doctrine' in Italy before 1940." Antropologia Contemporanea 11 (1988): 45-58.

6008. Toscano, Mario. Alto Adige-South Tyrol. Baltimore, MD: John Hopkins University Press, 1975.

6009. Toscano, Mario. "Gli ebrei in Italia dall'emancipazione alle persecuzioni." Storia Contemporanea 17 (1986): 905- 954.

6010. Verlinden, Charles. "Le colonie venitienne de Tana, centre de la traite des esclaves au XIVe et au debut du XVe siecle." Studi in onore di Gino Luzzatto, II (1950): Milan.

6011. Voigt, Klaus. "Refuge and Persecution in Italy, 1935-1945." Simon Wiesenthal Annual 4 (1987): 3-64.

6012. White, Steven F. Italian Popular Education between Fascism and Democracy, 1943-1954: The Work and Legacy of the Allied Control Commission Education Subcommission. University of Virginia, 1985. UMO # 8615594.

6013. Wolff, Richard J. "'Fascistizing' Italian Youth: The Limits of Mussolini's Educational System." History of Education 13 (1984): 287-298.

6014. Woolf, Stuart J. "Italy." In Fascism in Europe, edited by S.J. Woolf. London: Methuen, 1982.

6015. Zamagni, Vera. "The Rich in a Late Industrialiser: The Case of Italy, 1800-1945." In Wealth and the Wealthy in the Modern World, edited by W. D. Rubenstein. 122-166. London: Croom Helm, 1980.

6016. Zucchinali, Monica. A destra in Italia oggi. Milan: Sugar Co. Edizioni, 1986. [Right-wing ideologies.]

6017. Zuccotti, Susan. The Italians and the Holocaust. Persecution, Rescue, Survival. New York: Basic Books, 1987.

IVORY COAST

6018. Ainsworth, Martha and Juan Munoz. The Cote d'Ivoire Living Standards Survey: Design and Implementation. Washington, D.C.: World Bank, 1986.

6019. Amin, Samir. "Capitalism and Development in Ivory Coast." In African Politics and Society, edited by Irving L. Markovitz. New York: Free Press, 1970.

6020. Amondji, Marcel. Cote d'Ivoire: le P.D.C.I. et la vie politique de 1944 a 1985. Paris: Editions l'Harmattan, 1986.

6021. Chauveau, Jean-Pierre and Jean-Pierre Dozon. "Ethnies et Etat en Cote-d'Ivoire." Revue Francaise de Science Politique 38 (October 1988): 732-747.

6022. Diawara, Bakary. "La Formation d'une Elite Nouvelle Ivoirienne: l'Ecole William-Ponty dans l'Isle de Goree, au Large de Dakar." An. U. Abidjan, ser. I; Hist. 10 (1982): 171-182.

6023. Domergue-Cloarec, Camille. Politique coloniale francaise et realites coloniales. 2 vols. Paris: 1986.

6024. Keita, G. "Enseignement du francais et biculturalisme en Cote d'Ivoire." Bulletin Observatoire fr. contemp. Afrique noire (1983): 141-156.

6025. Kozel, Valerie. The Composition and Distribution of Income in Cote d'Ivoire. Washington, D.C.: World Bank, 1990.

6026. Le Pape, Marc. "De l'espace et des races a Abidjan, entre 1903 et 1934." Cahiers d'Etudes Africaines 25 (1985): 295- 307.

6027. Toure, Abdou. La civilisation quotidienne en Cote-d'Ivoire: proces d'occidentalisation. Paris: Editions Kerthala, 1981.

6028. Woods, Dwayne. "State Action and Class Interests in the Ivory Coast." African Studies Review 31 (1988): 93-116.

6029. Yao, Joseph Y. The Redistribution of Earnings in the Ivory Coast: The Role of Higher Education Finance. Doctoral dissertation: Stanford University, 1987. UMO # 8723126.

JAPAN

6030. Abe, Kazuhiro. Japanese Capitalism and the Korean Minority in Japan: Class, Race, and Racism. Doctoral dissertation: University of California, Los Angeles, 1989. UMO # 8922207.

6031. Abe, Kazuhiro. "Race Relations and the Capitalist State: A Case study of Koreans in Japan, 1917 through the Mid-1920's." Korean Studies 7 (1983): 35-60.

6032. Armstrong, Bruce. "Racialization and National Ideology: The Japanese Case." International Sociology 4 (September 1989): 329-343. [Racism in Japan.]

6033. Babu, Yuko. "A Study of Minority-Majority Relations: The Ainu and the Japanese in Hokkkaido." Japan Interpreter 13 (Summer 1980): 60-92.

6034. Buchanan, George. "Koreans in Japan Denied Basic Rights." Militant (February 1, 1991)

6035. Burke, B. Meredith. The Kimono in the Workplace: The Changing Economic Role of Japanese Women (1955-1980). Ann Arbor: Center for Japanese Studies, University of Michigan, 1985.

6036. Burkshardt, William R. "Institutional Barriers, Marginality, and Adaptation among the American Japanese Mixed Bloods in Japan." Journal of Asian Studies 42 (1983): 519- 544.

6037. Chira, Susan. "Rich Man, Poor Man in Japan: Not an Economic Party for All." New York Times, (December 26, 1988)

6038. Chira, Susan. "They Call Japan Home, but Are Hardly Home." New York Times, (February 1, 1988): [Koreans living in Japan.]

6039. Chung, Chin-Sung. Colonial Migration from Korea to Japan. Doctoral dissertation: University of Chicago, 1984.

JAPAN 455

6040. De Vos, George A. and Hiroshi Wagatsuma. Japan's Invisible Race. Caste in Culture and Personality. Berkeley: University of California Press, 1966. [Burakumin.]

6041. De Vos, George A. and William O. Wetherall. Japan's Minorities: Burakumin, Koreans, Aime and Okinawans. new ed. London: Minority Rights Group, 1983.

6042. Dean, Macabee. "The Arab Boycott and the Jewish-Japanese Problem." Jerusalem Post, (June 10, 1986): [Antisemitism in Japan.]

6043. "Distortions Abound on Life of Koreans in Japan." New York Times, (February 26, 1988): [Two letters.]

6044. Forrer, Stephen E. and others. Measuring Japanese Racial Attitudes. ERIC ED 120 593, 1975. [Toward blacks and Koreans.]

6045. Fox, John P. "Japanese Reactions to Nazi Germany's Racial Legislation." Wiener Library Bulletin 23 (1969): 46-50.

6046. Fujiyoshi, Ronald Susumu. "The Fingerprinting Issue in Japan: My Involvement as a Japanese American." Amerasia Journal 15 (1989): 295-298.

6047. Fukuda, Masa-aki. "A Critical Analysis of Juvenile Justice System in Japan: Debasement of the Juvenile Law to Attain Unarticulated Social and Economic Purposes." Hitotsubashi Journal of Law and Politics 18 (February 1990): 1-13.

6048. Geiser, Peter. "The Contemporary Ainu: A People in Search for Society." Human Organization 26 (1971)

6049. Gohl, Gerhard. Die Koreanische Minderheit in Japan als Fall einer "politisch-ethnischen" Minderheitengruppe. Harrassowitz: 1976.

6050. Goldberg, Faye J. "The Question of Skin Color and Its Relation to Japan." Psychologia 16 (1973): 132-146.

6051. Goodman, David. "Reason for Concern in Japanese Anti- Semitism." New York Times, (March 25, 1987) [letter.]

6052. Haberman, Clyde. "For Nakasone, Boos from an Unmelted Minority." New York Times, (November 5, 1986) [The Ainu people.]

6053. Haberman, Clyde. "Japanese Writers Critical of Jews." New York Times, (March 12, 1987)

6054. Hanley, S. B. "How Well Did the Japanese Live in the Tokugawa Period? A Historian's Reappraisal." Economic Studies Quarterly 38 (December 1987)

6055. Haraguchi, Koichi. "The Embassy of Japan Responds (letter)." Moment (January-February 1988) [Reply to charges of antisemitism in Japan.]

6056. Haroda, Tomobiko. "Discrimination Against Buraku." in Long- Suffering Brothers and Sisters Unite. Osaka, 1981.

6057. Harris, David A. "'The Elders of Zion' in Tokyo- What Should We Do About Japanese Anti-Semitism?" Moment (October 1987): 32-37.

6058. Hirasawa, Yasumasa. "The Burakumin: Japan's Minority Population." Integrateducation 20 (November 1983): 3-8.

6059. Hirasawa, Yasumasa. A Policy Study of the Evolution of Dowa Education in Japan. Doctoral dissertation: Harvard University, 1989. [Education of Burakumin.]

6060. Hoston, Germaine A. Marxism and the Crisis of Development in Prewar Japan. Princeton, NJ: Princeton University Press, 1987. [The rise of capitalism in Japan.]

6061. Ichiro, Ono. "The Issue of Buraku Discrimination in Japan Today." PCR Information No. 22 (1986): 12-17. [Pastor and former chairperson of the Kyodan Buraku Liberation Center Committee, 1975-1985.]

6062. Ichiyo, Muto. Class Struggle and Technological Innovation in Japan Since 1945. Amsterdam: International Institute for Research and Education, 1987.

6063. Imonti, Felix. "The Fugu Plan." Midstream 33 (March 1987): 27-28. [Antisemitism in Japan.]

6064. Ishida, Hiroshi. Educational Credentials, Class, and the Labor Market: A Comparative Study of Social Mobility in Japan and the United States. Doctoral dissertation: Harvard University, 1986. UMO # 8704412.

6065. Ishida, Hiroshi and others. Intergenerational Class Mobility in Post-War Japan. Oxford, England: Nissan Occasional Paper Series, NO, 8, 1988.

6066. Iwassawa, Yuji. "Legal Treatment of Koreans in Japan: The Impact of International Human Rights Law on Japanese Law." Human Rights Quarterly 8 (1986): 131-179.

6067. Jacobs, N. "Modern Capitalism and Japanese Development." In Sociology and History: Theory and Research, edited by W. J. Cahnmann and A. Boskoff. London: Free Press of Glencoe, 1964.

6068. "Japan and Anti-Semitism: The Proliferation of Anti-Jewish Literature." ADL International Report (April 1987): 1-9.

6069. Japan's Assimilation and Control Policy. Honolulu: American Friends Service Committee, 1986. [Anti-Korean discrimination in Japan.]

6070. "Japan's Perception of the Jews: A Dialogue." Brotherhood (Chautauqua Society) (May-June 1988): 3-4.

6071. Japan's Subtle Apartheid-The Korean Minority Now, 1990. RAIK, Room 52, 2-3-18 Nishi Waseda, Shinjuku-ku, Tokyo 169, Japan:

6072. "Japanese Anti-Semites and Philo-Semites." Studies on Jewish Life and Culture 7 (1975): 32-49.

6073. Jeong Ho Lee. "One Man's Struggle to Preserve a Bitter Memory." New York Times, (December 5, 1989): [Oppression and exploitation of Koreans in Japan.]

6074. Jo, Moon Hwan. The Problems of the Korean Minority in Japan: Goal Conflict and Assimilation. Doctoral dissertation: New York University, 1974. UMO # 7429998.

6075. Kazuhiro, Tanimoto. "Buraku Discrimination in Japan." PCR Information No. 22 (1986): 9-11. [By a minister who is a Buraku.]

6076. Keitaro, O. "Resident Koreans Are Native Speakers Too." Japan Quarterly 37 (October-December 1990)

6077. Kim, Yoon Shin. "Marriage Pattern of the Korean Population in Japan." Journal of Biosocial Science 17 (October 1985): 445-450.

6078. Kim Dong Hoon. "Korean Residents in Japan." PCR Information No. 22 (1986): 18-20.

6079. Kinzley, W. Dean. "Japan's Discovery of Poverty: Changing Views of Poverty and Social Welfare in the Nineteenth Century." Journal of Asian History 22 (1988): 1-24.

6080. Kitahara, Michio. "The Western Impact on Japanese Racial Self-Image." Journal of Developing Societies 3 (1987): 184- 189. [Inferior self image.]

6081. Kitakamal, Taro. "Ainu Concepts of Social Order and the Law of Japan." Law and Anthropology 2 (1987): 239-254.

6082. Kiyoshige, Naohuro. "The Japanese and the Jews." LWF Studies (1983) [Geneva: Department of Studies, Luthern World Federation.]

6083. Kohno, Testsu. "The Jewish Question in Japan." Jewish Journal of Sociology 29 (1987): 37-54.

6084. Kranzler, David. "Japan." In Encyclopedia of the Holocaust, II. New York: Macmillan, 1990.

6085. Kranzler, David. The Japanese, the Nazis, and the Jews. New York: 1976.

6086. Kranzler, David. "Japanese Policy toward the Jews, 1938- 1941." Japan Interpreter 11 (1977): 493-527.

6087. Kranzler, David. "The Japanese Ideology of Anti-Semitism and the Holocaust." In Contemporary Views on the Holocaust, edited by Randolph L. Braham. Boston, MA: Kluver-Nijhoff, 1983.

6088. Kublin, Hyman. "Star of David and Rising Sun." Jewish Frontier 25 (April 1958): 15-22.

6089. Lee, Changsoo. "Chosoren: An Analysis of the Korean Communist Movement in Japan." Journal of Korean Affairs 3 (1973): 3-32.

6090. Lee, Changsoo. "Ethnic Discrimination and Conflict: The Case of the Korean Minority in Japan." In Case Studies on Human Rights and Fundamental Freedoms: A World Survey, vol 4., edited by A. Veenhoven. The Hague: Martinus Nijhoff, 1976.

6091. Lee, Changsoo. The Politics of the Korean Minority in Japan. Doctoral dissertation: University of Maryland, 1971. UMO # 724141.

6092. Lie, John. "The Discriminated Fingers: The Korean Minority in Japan." Monthly Review 38 (January 1987): 17-23.

6093. Linhart-Fischer, Ruth and Fleur Woss. Japans Frauen heute: vom Stereotyp zur Wirklichkeit. Vienna: Literas- Universitatsverlag, 1988.

6094. Maezuka, Yoshikazu. "The Issues Confronting me As a Member of One of Japan's Minorities (Buraku)." PCR Information No. 27 (1990): 50-55.

6095. Makihara, Kumiko and K.C. Hwang. "No Longer Willing To Be Invisible." Time (May 28, 1990): [Koreans in Japan.]

6096. Manorama, Ruth Austen Brandt, and Soo Hae Oh. "Report on Koreans in Japan." Link No. 3 (1990): [Published by the World Council of Churches Programme to Combat Racism.]

6097. Meyer, Ernie. "A Present for Purim." Jerusalem Post Magazine, (March 12, 1982) [Anti-Semitism in Japan.]

6098. Mitchell, Richard H. The Korean Minority in Japan, 1910- 1963. Berkeley: University of California Press, 1968.

6099. Miyazawa, Masanoti. "Japanese Anti-Semitism in the Thirties." Translated by Harold Solomon and others. Midstream 33 (March 1987): 23-27.

6100. Mizuno, Takaaki. "Ainu: The Invisible Minority." Japan Quarterly 34 (April-June 1987): 143-148.

JAPAN 459

6101. Moris-Suzuki, Tessa and Seiyama Takuro, eds. Japanese Capitalism Since 1945. Armonk, New York: Sharpe, 1990.

6102. Morishima, Michio. "Turning Swords into Shares." Times Higher Education Supplement, (July 20, 1984): ["Samurai Capitalism" in Japan.]

6103. Myers, Ramon H. and Mark R. Peattie, eds. The Japanese Colonial Empire, 1895-1945. Princeton, NJ: Princeton University Press, 1984.

6104. Myung, Park Moon. A Review of Alien Rights Under the Japanese Constitution. Doctoral dissertation: University of Georgia, 1983. UMO # 84055068.

6105. Nickerson, Colin. "Asia's Jobless Turn to Japan for Opportunity." Boston Globe, (August 27, 1988)

6106. Nickerson, Colin. "Blacks in Japan See Racial Sensitivity Lagging." Boston Globe, (August 22, 1988)

6107. Nickerson, Colin. "Japan's Sayonara to Black Sambo." Boston Globe, (January 23, 1989)

6108. Oba, Kaoru Y. A Study of the Implementation of Japanese Equal Employment Opportunity Law and An Analysis of the Effectiveness of a Law Without Sanctions. Master's thesis: Cornell University, 1988.

6109. Ohnuki-Tierney, Emiko. The Ainu of the Northwest Coast of Southern Sakhalin. New York: Holt, 1974.

6110. Ohwae, Kenichi. "Dark Clouds Over Japan's Economy." New York Times, (July 29, 1987)

6111. Park, Philip. "No Change for Koreans [in Japan]." LINK (World Council of Churches) No. 4 (1990)

6112. Park, Soon-chul. The Problem of Korean Residents in Japan. Master's thesis: University of San Francisco, 1977.

6113. Parkinson, Loraine. "Japan's Equal Employment Opportunity Law: An Alternative Approach to Social Change." Columbia Law Review 89 (April 1989): 604-661.

6114. Pharr, Susan J. Losing Face: Status Politics in Japan. Berkeley: Univerity of California Press, 1990.

6115. Rabinovich, Abraham. "Disobedient Diplomat." Jerusalem Post, (November 29, 1985): [Aid to Jews fleeing Nazis by Japanese Consul in Kovno, Lithuania in 1939.]

6116. Radden, Viki. "A Black Woman in Rural Japan." Sage 6 (Summer 1989)

6117. Ruyle, Eugene E. "Conflicting Japanese Interpretations of the Outcaste Problem (buraku Mondei)." American Ethnologist 6 (1979): 55-72.

6118. Ruyle, Eugene E. The Political Economy of the Japanese Ghetto. Doctoral dissertation: Columbia University, 1971. [Burakumin in Kyoto.]

6119. Ryu, Sanghee. "Why Koreans Oppose the Fingerprint Law." Japan Quarterly 32 (1985): 308-311.

6120. Sala, Garry C. "Protest and the Ainu of Hokkaido." Japan Interpreter 10 (Summer 1975): 44-65.

6121. Sato, Kazuo. Economic Development of Japan. New York: Blackwell, 1987.

6122. Schooler, C. "The Individual in Japanese History: Parallels to and Divergences from the European Experience." Sociological Forum 5 (December 1990)

6123. Schudrick, Michael J. "Antisemitism in Japan." Research Report (Institute of Jewish Affairs) No. 12 (December 1987)

6124. Selby, M. "Human Rights and Undocumented Immigrant Workers in Japan." Stanford Journal of International Law 26 (Autumn 1989)

6125. Shillony, Ben Ami. "The Imaginary Devil: Japanese Anti- semitism." In Politics and Culture in Wartime Japan. 156-171. Oxford: Clarendon Press, 1981.

6126. Shimahara, Nobuo. Burakumin: A Japanese Minority and Education. The Hague: Martinus Nijhoff, 1971.

6127. Shinichiro, Tahakura. The Ainu of Northern Japan: A Study in Conquest and Acculturation. Philadelphia, PA: American Philosophical Society, 1960.

6128. Shoji, Tsutomu. "Japanese Religions and Discrimination against Buraki People." Japanese Religion 12 (December 1982): 17-24.

6129. Sklar, Deborah. "Testing Japan's Anti-Korean Laws." Nation (June 25, 1990): [The case of Ron Fujiyoshi.]

6130. Smythe, Hugh. "A Note on Racialism in Japan." American Sociological Review 16 (1951)

6131. Somers, David J. Assimilation, Repatriation or Ethnic Isolation: Choices Confronting the Korean Minority in Japan. Master's thesis: University of Kansas, 1977.

6132. Soo Hae Oh. "Japan's Korean Minority Today." PCR Information No. 27 (1990): 38-41.

6133. Steven, Rob. Classes in Contemporary Japan. New York: Cambridge University Press, 1983.

6134. Steven, Rob. Japan's New Imperialism. Armonk, New York: Sharpe, 1990.

6135. Tachibanaki, T. "Japan's New Policy Agenda: Coping with Unequal Asset Distribution." Journal of Japanese Studies 15 (Summer 1989): 345-369.

6136. Takazato, Suzuyo. "No Sleep for the Women of Okinawa." PCR Information No. 27 (1990): 58-62.

6137. Tokayer, Marien and Swartz, Mary. The Fugu Plan: The Untold Story of the Japanese and the Jews in WWII. New York: Paddington Press, 1979.

6138. Tsurumi, Yoshi. "[Letter on Dowa people (Burakumin) and other aspects of contemporary Japan]." New York Times, (December 25, 1990)

6139. Upham, Frank K. Law and Social Change in Postwar Japan. Cambridge, MA: Harvard University Press, 1987. [Deals with Buraku liberation and other subjects.]

6140. Upham, Frank K. "Ten Years of Affirmative Action for Japanese Burakumin." Law in Japan 13 (1980)

6141. Utangi, Takashi. "The Buraku, the Ainu, and Applied Folklore." Folklore and Mythology Studies 11-12 (1987-1988): 59-66.

6142. Verba, Sidney and others. Elites and the Idea of Equality. A Comparison of Japan, Sweden, and the United States. Cambridge, MA: Harvard University Press, 1987.

6143. Wagner, Edward W. The Korean Minority in Japan: 1904-1950. New York: Institute of Pacific Relations, 1951.

6144. Weiner, Michael A. The Origins and Early Development of the Korean Minority in Japan: 1910-1925, 2 vols. Docotral dissertation: University of Sheffield, 1982. Order No. BRDX 89080.

6145. Weiner, Michael A. The Origins of the Korean Community in Japan, 1910-1923. Atlantic Highlands, NJ: Humanities, 1989.

6146. Weisman, Steven R. "Japan's Homeless: Seen Yet Ignored." New York Times, (January 19, 1991)

6147. Whitehall, William. "The Antisemitic Book Boom." Japan Times, (September 9, 1987)

6148. Whiteside, Larry. "The Agony of Being Black in Japan." Boston Globe, (January 6, 1991)

6149. Williams, Peter and David Wallace. Unit 731: The Japanese Army's Secret of Secrets. London: Hodder and Stoughton, 1989.

6150. Williams, Teresa. "The Japanese and Blacks: Which Direction for the 1990's?" African Commentary 2 (May 1990): 27-29. [Anti-black racism in Japan.]

6151. Wilson, Dick. "A Paler Shade of Yellow." New Society (October 11, 1984): [Color prejudice in Japan.]

6152. Yasuba, Yasukichi. "Standard of Living in Japan Before Industrialization: From What Level Did Japan Begin? A Comment." Journal of Economic History 46 (March 1986): 217- 224.

6153. Yawata, Y. F. and H. Loiskandl. "Race and Ethnic Relations in Japan." Occasional Papers of the Royal Anthropological Institute 11 (1984): 110-119.

6154. Yetes, Ronald E. "In Japan, Expectations Fall or Incomes Rise." Chicago Tribune, (September 20, 1987)

6155. Yoshihisa Moshiko, Asahi Shinbun. "Seeking the Human Rights of the Ainu People." PCR Information No. 27 (1990): 63-67.

6156. Yoshino, I. Roger. "The Buraku Minority of Japan." Patterns of Prejudice 17 (January 1983): 39-47.

6157. Young-Hwan Jo. "Japan." In International Handbook on Race and Race Relations, edited by Jay A. Sigler. Westport, CT: Grenwood, 1987.

JORDAN

6158. Bailey, Clinton. *Jordan's Palestinian Challenge, 1948-1983*. Boulder, CO: Westview Press, 1984.

6159. Hamarneh, Mustafa B. *Social and Economic Transformation of Trans-Jordan, 1921-1946*. Doctoral dissertation: Georgetown University, 1985. UMO # 8613934.

6160. Iutub, Ishaq. "The Rise of the Middle Class in Jordan." *Middle East Forum* (December 1961): 40-44.

6161. Jaber, Kamel Abu and others. *Income Distribution in Jordan*. Boulder: Westview Press, 1990.

6162. Jureidini, Paul A. and R.D. McLaurin. *Jordan: The Impact of Social Change on the Role of the Tribes*. New York: Praeger, 1984.

6163. Lewis, Paul. "Jordan's Christian Arabs, a Small Minority, Play a Major Role." *New York Times*, (January 7, 1987)

6164. Plascov, Avi. *The Palestinian Refugees in Jordan 1948-1957*. London: Cass, 1981.

6165. Salah, Rima Y. *The Changing Roles of Palestinian Women in Refugee Camps in Jordan*. Doctoral dissertation: State University of New York at Binghamton, 1986. UMO # 8616415.

6166. Shoup, John A. *The Bedouins of Jordan: History and Sedentarization*. Master's thesis: University of Utah, 1980.

KENYA

6167. Adebola, A. S. "The Kikuyu Independent Schools Movement and the Mau Mau Uprising." Journal Historical Society Nigeria 10 (June 1981): 53-72.

6168. Amolo, Milcah. Trade Unionism and Colonial Authority. Nairobi: University of Nairobi, Department of History, 1978.

6169. Anyang' Nyong'o P. "Class Struggle in Kenya." Mawazo 5 (December 1983): 25-42.

6170. Atieni-Odhiambo, E. J. "The Colonial Government, the Settlers and the 'Trust' Principle in Kenya 1939." Transafrican Journal of History 2 (1972): 94-113.

6171. Atieni-Odhiambi, E. J. "The Political Economy of the Asian Problem in Kenya, 1888-1939." Transafrican Journal of History 4 (1974): 135-149.

6172. Bigsten, Arne. Income Distribution and Growth in a Dual Economy: Kenya, 1914-1976. Gothenberg: Department of Economics, Gothenburg University, 1987.

6173. Bigsten, Arne. "Race and Inequality in Kenya, 1914-1976." Eastern Africa Economic Review 4 (June 1988): 1-11.

6174. Bigsten, Arne. "Welfare and Economic Growth in Kenya, 1914-1976." World Development 14 (September 1986)

6175. Bogonko, S. N. "Colonial Chiefs and African Development in Kenya with Special Reference to Secular Education." Transafrican Journal of History 14 (1985): 1-20.

6176. Bollig, Michael. "The Imposition of Colonial Rule in North West Kenya: Interethnic Conflicts and Anti-Colonial Resistance." Afrik. Arbeitspap. No. 11 (1987): 5-39.

6177. Bongonki, S. N. "Africans and the Politics of their Education in Kenya, 1910-1934." Journal East African Res. Dev. 14 (1984): 19-38.

6178. Broune, Dallas L. "Race and Class in Kenya." Bulletin of the International Committee on Urgent Anthropological and Ethnological Research 25 (1983): 51-75.

6179. Buch-Hanson, M. and J. Keiler. "The Development of Capitalism and the Transformation of the Peasantry in Kenya." Rural Africana Nos. 15-16 (1983): 13-40.

6180. Buchanan, Keith. "The Gun and the School. Reflections on Ngugi wa Thiong'o's Decolonizing the Mind." Race and Class 30 (October-December 1988): 61-69.

6181. Cheruiyot, Ruth C. A Study of Racial Discrimination in Kenya during the Colonial Period. Master's thesis: Oklahoma State University, 1977.

6182. Clark, Mari H. "Woman-headed Households and Poverty: Insights from Kenya." Signs 10 (Winter 1984): 338-354.

6183. Collier, Paul and Deepak Lal. Labour and Poverty in Kenya, 1900-1980. New York: Oxford University Press, 1986.

6184. Collier, Paul and Deepak, Lal. "Why Poor People Get Rich: Kenya 1960-1979." World Development 12 (October 1984): 1007-1018.

6185. Cooper, Frederick. On the African Waterfront: Urban Disorder and the Transformation of Work in Colonial Mombasa. New Haven: Yale University Press, 1987.

6186. Cooper, Frederick. "The Treatment of Slaves on the Kenya Coast in the Nineteenth Century." Kenya Historical Review 2 (1973): 87-108.

6187. Currie, Kate and Larry Ray. "State and Class in Kenya- Notes on the Cohesion of the Ruling Class." Journal of Modern African Studies 22 (December 1984): 559-594.

6188. Fleuret, Patrick and Anne Fleuret. "Socio-economic Determinants of Child Nutrition in Taita, Kenya: A Call for Discussion." Culture and Agriculture (Tucson) 19 (1983): 8, 16-20.

6189. Frost, Richard A. Race Against Time: Human Relations and Politics in Kenya Before Independence. London: Collings, 1978.

6190. Gould, W. T. S. "Migration and Development in Western Kenya, 1971-1982: A Retrospective Study of Primary School Learners." Africa (London) No. 3 (1985): 262-285.

6191. Gutto, S. B. O. "Constitutional Law and Politics in Kenya since Independence: A Study in Class and Power in a Neo- Colonial State in Africa." Zimbabwe Law Review 5 (1987): 142-171.

6192. Harik, Elsa M. and Donald G. Schilling. The Politics of Education in Colonial Algeria and Kenya. Athens: Ohio University Monographs in International Studies, 1984.

6193. "The Historic Debate. Law, Democracy & Multiparty Politics in Kenya." Nairobi Law Monthly No. 23 (1990)

6194. "In Dependent Kenya. A Class Analysis of Colonial and Neo- Colonial Domination." Ikwezi (October 1982): 3-30.

6195. Kennedy, Dane K. Islands of White: Settler Society and Culture in Kenya and Southern Rhodesia, 1890-1939. Durham, NC: Duke University Press, 1987.

6196. Kitching, G. N. Class and Economic Change in Kenya: The Making of an African Petite Bourgeoisie 1905-1970. New Haven, CT: Yale University Press, 1980.

6197. Lavrijsen, J. S. G. Rural Poverty and Impoverishment in Western Kenya. Utrecht: Department of Geography, University of Utrecht, 1984.

6198. Leo, Christopher. Land and Class in Kenya. Toronto: University of Toronto Press, 1984.

6199. "Looters, Bankrupts and the Begging Bowl: Our Plundered Economy." Race & Class 24 (Winter 1983): 267-286.

6200. Macharia, K. "Housing Policy in Kenya- The View from the Bottom: A Survey of Low-income Residents in Nairobi and Thika." International Journal of Urban Regional Research (September 1985): 405-419.

6201. Mahlmann, Peter. "Sport As a Weapon of Colonialism in Kenya: A Review of the Literature." Transafrican Journal of History 17 (1988): 152-171.

6202. Malova, A. O. A Study into Effectiveness of Schools in Kenya Case Study: Kakamega District. Doctoral dissertation: Ohio University, 1987. UMO # 8715314.

6203. Mambo, Robert M. "Racial Education in Colonial Kenya: The Coastal Experience in the Protectorate Up to 1950." Transafrican Journal of History 12 (1983): 175-193.

6204. Martin, C. J. "Education and Inequality: The Case of Margoli, Kenya." International Journal of Education and Development 4 (1984): 97-112.

KENYA 467

6205. Maughan-Brown, David. Land, Freedom and Fiction: History and Ideology in Kenya. London: Zed Books, 1985.

6206. Maxon, Robert M. Conflict and Accomodation in Western Kenya: The Gusii and the British, 1907-1963. Rutherford, NJ: Fairleigh Dickinson University Press, 1989.

6207. Morton, Rodger Frederic. Slaves, Fugitives, and Freedmen on the Kenya Coast, 1873-1907. Doctoral dissertation: Syracuse University, 1976.

6208. Mukonoweshuro, Eliphas. "Authoritarian Reaction to Economic Crises in kenya." Race & Class 31 (April-June 1990): 39-59.

6209. Mwangi, W. M. and G.M. Mwabu. "Economics of Health and Nutrition in Kenya." Social Science Medicine 22 (1986): 775-780.

6210. Nyasani, Joseph M. The British Massacre of the Gusii Freedom Defenders. Nairoi, Kenya: 1984.

6211. Nzibo, Y. A. "Islam and the Swahili-speaking Community of Nairobi, c. 1895-1963." Journal of the Institute of Muslim Minority Affairs 5 (July 1984): 446-453.

6212. Ochieng, William R. "Autobiography in Kenyan History." Ufahamu 14 (1985): 80-101.

6213. Oculi, Okello. Colonial Capitalism and Malnutrition: Nigeria, Kenya and Jamaica. Doctoral dissertation: University of Wisconsin, 1977.

6214. Overton, John. "The Colonial State and Spatial Differentiation: Kenya, 1895-1920." Journal of Historical Geography 13 (July 1987): 267-282.

6215. Overton, John. "The Origins of the Kikuyu Land Problem: Land Alienation and Land Use in Kiambu, Kenya, 1895-1920." African Studies Review 31 (September 1988): 109-126.

6216. "The Politics of Justice in Kenya." Race & Class 24 (Winter 1983): 245-258.

6217. Rai, Kauleshwar. "British Policy towards Indians in Kenya." Journal of Indian History (1973): 909-914.

6218. Redley, M. G. The White Community in Kenya, 1918-1932. Doctoral dissertation: University of Cambridge, 1976.

6219. Rothchild, Donald. Racial Bargaining in Independent Kenya. A Study of Minorities and Decolonization. New York: Oxford University Press, 1973.

6220. Schatzberg, Michael, ed. The Political Economy of Kenya. New York: Praeger, 1987.

6221. Shati, P. M. A History of Asians in Kenya, 1900-1970. Doctoral dissertation: Howard University, 1976. UMO # 785427.

6222. Sifuna, D. N. "British Colonial Education in Kenya." African Journal of Sociology 2 (May 1982): 29-41.

6223. Standt, Kathleen A. "Sex, Ethnic, and Class Consciousness in Western Kenya." Comparative Politics 14 (January 1982): 149-168.

6224. Swainson, Nicola. The Development of Corporate Capitalism in Kenya, 1918-1977. Berkeley: University of California Press, 1980.

6225. Throup, David. Economic & Social Origins of Mau Mau, 1945- 1953. London: Athens, 1987.

6226. Vorlaufer, Karl. "Ethnozentrismus, Tribalismus und Urbanisierung in Kenya: das Wanderungs-und Segregationsverhalten ethnischen Gruppen am Beispiel Nairobi." In Studien zur regionalen Wirtschaftsgeographie. 107-157. 1985.

6227. Wa. Thiong'O, Ngugi. "The Tension between National and Imperialist Culture." World Lit. Written Eng. 24 (1984): 3- 9.

6228. Youe, Christopher P. "Settler Capital and the Assault on the Squatter Peasantry in Kenya's Uasin Gishu District, 1942- 1963." African Affairs (London) 87 (July 1988): 393-418.

6229. Zwanenberg, R. van. "The Background to White Racialism in Kenya." Kenya Historical Review (1974): 5-12.

KOREA

6230. Barringer, H. R. "Social Differentiation, Stratification and Mobility." In Korea: A Decade of Development, edited by Chang-Yun- Shik. Seoul: Seoul National University Press, 1980.

6231. Brudnoy, David. "Japan's Experiment in Korea." Monumenta Nipponica 25 (1970): 155-195.

6232. Cha, Jongchun. Social Stratification and Group Formation in Contemporary Korea. Doctoral dissertation: University of Wisconsin, 1987. UMO # 8708077.

6233. Chira, Susan. "Koreans Ask, Is the Society Fair to Labor?" New York Times, (December 26, 1986)

6234. Choe, Won Hyung. Curricular Reform in Korea during the American Military Government, 1945-1948. Doctoral dissertation: University of Wisconsin, 1986. UMO # 8618264.

6235. Dong, Wonmo. Japanese Colonial Policy and Practice in Korea, 1905-1945: A Study in Assimilation. Doctoral dissertation: Georgetown University, 1965.

6236. Eckert, Carter J. The Colonial Origins of Korean Capitalism: The Koch'Ang Kims and the Kyongsong Spinning and Weaving Company, 1876-1945. Doctoral dissertation: University of Washington, 1986. UMO # 8706543.

6237. Eto, Skinkichi. "Asianism and the Duality of Japanese Colonialism, 1879-1945." In History and Underdevelopment, edited by L. Blusse and others. Pairs: 1980.

6238. Halliday, Jon. "The North Korean Enigma." New Left Review No. 127 (May-June 1981): 18-52.

6239. Halliday, Jon. "Women in North Korea: An Interview with the Korean Democratic Women's Union." Bulletin of Concerned Asian Scholars 17 (July-September 1985): 46-56.

6240. Hamilton, Clive. Capitalist Industrialization in Korea. Boulder, CO: Westview Press, 1986.

6241. Human Rights in Korea. New York: Asia Watch Committee, 1986.

6242. Jones, Randall S. The Economic Development of Colonial Korea. Doctoral dissertation: University of Michigan, 1984. UMO # 8502852.

6243. Kil, Jeong Woo. The Development of Authoritarian Capitalism- A Case Study of South Korea. Doctoral dissertation: Yale University, 1986. UMO # 8628047.

6244. Kim, S. K. Business Concentration and Government Policy: A Study of the Phenomenon of Business Groups in Korea, 1945- 1985. Doctoral dissertation: Harvard Business School, 1987.

6245. Kimura, Mitsuhiko. "Public Finance in Korea under Japanese Rule: Deficit in the Colonial Account and Colonial Taxation." Explorations in Economic History 26 (1989): 285-310.

6246. Koo, Hagen. "The Political Economy of Income Distribution in South Korea: The Impact of the State's Industrialization Policy." World Development 12 (October 1984)

6247. Koo, Hagen and D.S. Hong. "Class and Income Inequality in Korea." American Sociological Review 45 (August 1980): 610- 626. [Seoul.]

6248. Kwon, Manhak. Capitalist Growth and Political Change in South Korea. Doctoral dissertation: University of Texas, 1988. UMO # 8901357.

6249. Lee, Gil Sang. Ideological Context of American Educational Policy in Occupied Korea, 1945-1948. Doctoral dissertation: University of Illinois at Urbana-Champaign, 1989. UMO # 9010926.

6250. Lee, Mi-Na. Education Effects on Earnings in the Korean Labor Market: Education as a Policy Device for Mobility of the Disadvantaged. Doctoral dissertation: Harvard University, 1986. UMO # 8704576.

6251. Lim, Byung O. The Effect of an Unbalanced Growth Pattern on Inflation and the Distribution of Income in Korea. Doctoral dissertation: University of Utah, 1986. UMO # 8622415.

6252. McNamara, Dennis L. The Colonial Origins of Korean Enterprise 1910-1945. New York: Cambridge University Press, 1990.

6253. Nahm, Andrew C., ed. Korea Under Japanese Colonial Rule: Studies of the Policy and Techniques of Japanese Colonialism. Kalamazoo, MI: Center for Korean Studies, Western Michigan University, 1973.

6254. Nickerson, Colin. "Leaving the Poor Behind in Korea." Boston Globe, (August 23, 1987)

6255. Rabenau, Kurt con. Struktur, Entwicklung and Ursachen der sudkoreanischen Einkommensverteilung von 1963-1979. Saarbrucken: Verlag Breitenbach Publishers, 1982.

6256. Rhee, Ma-Ji. Moral Education in Korea under Japanese Colonialism during 1910-1945. Doctoral dissertation: Rutgers University, 1989. UMO # 9008013.

6257. Scitovsky, Tibor. "Economic Development in Taiwan and South Korea: 1965-1981." Food Research Institute Studies 19 (1985)

6258. Shaw, William, ed. Human Rights in Korea: Historical and Policy Perspectives. Cambridge, MA: East Asian Legal Studies Program of the Harvard Law School, 1990.

6259. Sklar, Deborah. "Testing Japan's Anti-Korean Laws." Nation (June 25, 1990)

6260. "Slavery in Korea." Korea Review 2 (1902): 149-155.

6261. Song, K. S. The Impact of U. S. Military Occupation on the Social Development of Decolonized South Korea, 1945-1949. Doctoral dissertation: University of California, 1989. UMO # 8910303.

6262. Suh, Jae J. Capitalist Class Formation and the Limits of Class Power in Korea. Doctoral dissertation: University of Hawaii, 1988. UMO # 8821366.

6263. Suh, Sun-Hee. Women's Work in Korea: Colonial Industrialization and Its Impact, 1910-1945. Doctoral dissertation: Pennsylvania State University, 1988. UMO # 8826825.

6264. Vacante, Russell A. Japanese Colonial Education in Korea, 1910-1945: An Oral History. Doctoral dissertation: State University of New York at Buffalo, 1987. UMO # 8718577.

6265. Yoo, Jong Goo. An Empirical Investigation of the Individual Welfare Inequality in Korea: 1965-1983. Doctoral dissertation: Northern Illinois University, 1985. UMO # 8518711.

6266. Yoo, Jong Goo and J. K. Kwon. "Welfare Inequality among Urban Households in South Korea: 1965-1983." Applied Economics 19 (April 1987)

KUWAIT

6267. Al-Ostad, Ameer B. An Ethnic Geography of Kuwait: A Study of Eight Ethnic Groups. Doctoral dissertation: Kent State University, 1986. UMO # 8617072.

6268. Ishow, Habib. Le Koweit: evolution politique, economique et sociale. Paris: Editions l'Harmattan, 1989.

6269. Ismael, Jacqueline S. Kuwait: Social Change in Historical Perspective. Syracuse, New York: Syracuse University Press, 1982.

6270. Ismael, Jaqueline S. "The Conditions of Egyptian Labor in the Gulf: A Profile of Kuwait." Arab Studies 8 (1986): 390- 403.

6271. Lawson, Fred. "Class and State in Kuwait." Merip Reports No. 132 (May 1985): 16-21, 32.

6272. Shah, Nasra M. "Foreign Workers in Kuwait: Implications for the Kuwaiti Labor Force." International Migration Review 20 (Winter 1986): 815-832.

6273. Viorst, Milton. "Out of the Desert." New Yorker (May 16, 1988)

LAOS

6274. Evans, Grant. Lao Peasants under Socialism. New Haven, CT: Yale University Press, 1990.

6275. Gunn, Geoffrey C. "Shamans and Rebels: The Batchai (Meo) Rebellion of Northern Laos and North-West Vietnam (1918- 1921)." Journal Siam Society 74 (1986): 107-121.

6276. Promuihane, K. Revolution in Laos: Practice and Prospects. Moscow: Progress Publishers, 1981.

6277. Rumpf, Roger. "A 10-year Journey From Pain Toward Peace." Guardian (May 7, 1986)

6278. Stuart-Fox, Martin. Laos: Politics, Economics, and Society. Boulder, CO: L. Rienner, 1986.

6279. Tapp, Nicholas. "The Impact of Missionary Christianity Upon Marginalized Ethnic Minorities: The Case of the Hmong." Journal of South East Asian Studies 20 (March 1989): 70- 95.

6280. Yia Lee, Gary. "Ethnic Minorities and Nation-Building in Laos: the Hmong in the Lao State." Peninsule 16-17 (1985- 1986): 215-232.

LEBANON

6281. Al-Azmeh, Aziz. "The Progressive Forces." In <u>Essays on the Crisis in Lebanon</u>, edited by R. Owen. London: 1976.

6282. Bar, Luc-Henri de. <u>Les communautes confessionelles du Liban</u>. Paris: Recherche sur les civilisations, 1983.

6283. Barakat, Halim. <u>Lebanon in Strife. Student Prelude to the Civil War</u>. Austin: University of Texas Press, 1977.

6284. Bashour, Munir. "The Deterioration of the Educational System in Lebanon." in <u>The Lebanese Crisis: Social and Economic Dimensions</u>. Amman: Arab Thought Forum, 1988.

6285. Bayoudh, Edma and Rose Ghorayyib. <u>Status of Women in Lebanon</u>. Beirut: National Young Women's Christian Association, 1951.

6286. Bryce, Jennifer W. and Hartoune K. Armenian, eds. <u>In Wartime: The State of Children in Lebanon</u>. Beirut: American University of Beirut, 1986.

6287. Chamie, J. "The Lebanese Civil War: an Investigation into the Causes." <u>World Affairs</u> 139 (1976-1977): 171-188.

6288. Dham, Najwa S. <u>Schooling and National Development: The Role of Schooling in Building a Sense of Social Integration</u>. Doctoral dissertation: State University of New York at Buffalo, 1988. UMO # 8727689.

6289. Dubar, Claude. "Structure confessionelle et classes sociales au Liban." <u>Revue francaise de Sociologie</u> 15 (1974): 301-328.

6290. El-Khazen, Farid E. <u>The Disintegration of the Lebanese Confessional System, 1967-1976</u>. Doctoral dissertation: John Hopkins University, 1987. UMO # 8716622.

LEBANON 475

6291. Frangieh, Rizk T. "Sectarianism and Class Division in Lebanon." *Plural Societies* 11 (1980): 71-79.

6292. Frayha, Nemer M. *Religious Conflict and the Role of Social Studies for Citizenship Education in the Lebanese Schools between 1920 and 1983*. Doctoral dissertation: Stanford University, 1985. UMO # 8522144.

6293. Hares, Abdullatif K. *Education and National Integration in Lebanon*. Doctoral dissertation: Columbia University, 1985. UMO # 8611680.

6294. Harfouche, Jamal K. *Social Structure of Low-income Families in Lebanon*. Beirut: Khavat, 1965.

6295. Joby, Gertrude. "The Women of the Lebanon." *Royal Central Asian Society Journal* 38 (April-July 1951): 177-184.

6296. Krayem, Hassan H. *Class and Social Change: The Civil War and the Structural Crisis of the Lebanese System*. Doctoral dissertation: University of Southern California, 1989.

6297. Mannock, Robin. "Inflation Puts Squeeze on Lebanon's Education." *Boston Globe*, (October 11, 1987)

6298. McDonall, David. *Lebanon: A Conflict of Minorities*. London: Minority Rights Group, 1983.

6299. Olmert, Yossi. "The Resurgence of the Shi'ites in Lebanon: Causes and Implications." *Research Report (Institute of Jewish Affairs)* No. 7 (October 1985)

6300. Randal, Jonathan C. *Going All the Way: Christian Warlords, Israel Adventurers, and the War in Lebanon*. New York: Viking, 1983.

6301. Zamir, Meir. *The Formation of Modern Lebanon*. Dover, NH: Croom Helm, 1985.

LIBERIA

6302. Akpa, E. K. "The Size Distribution of Income in Liberia." Review of Income and Wealth 27 (December 1981): 387-400.

6303. Akpan, Monday B. African Resistance in Liberia: The Vai and the Gola-Bandi. Bremen: Liberia Working Group, 1988.

6304. Akpan, Monday B. "Black Imperialism: America-Liberian Rule Over the African People of Liberia." Canadian Journal of African Studies 7 (1973): 217-236.

6305. Barrows, Carl P. The Americo-Liberian Ruling Class and Other Myths: A Critique of Political Science in the Liberian Context. Philadelphia, PA: Dept. of African Studies, Temple University, 1989.

6306. Berkeley, Bill. Liberia: A Promise Betrayed. New York: Lawyers Committee for Human Rights, 1986.

6307. Beyan, Amos J. The American Colonization Society and the Formation of Political, Economic and Religious Institutions in Liberia, 1822-1900. Doctoral dissertation: West Virginia University, 1985.

6308. Bonaparte, T. H. "Multinational Corporations and Culture in Liberia." American Journal of Economics and Sociology (July 1979): 236-251.

6309. Burrowes, Carl P. "Economic Relations Within Pre-Liberian Societies." Liberian Studies Journal 13 (1988): 76-103.

6310. Chalk, Frank. "Du Bois and Garvey Confront Liberia." Canadian Journal of African Studies 1 (November 1967)

6311. Davis, Lenwood. "Black American Images of Liberia." Liberian Studies Journal 6 (1975)

6312. Gershoni, Yekutiel. Black Colonialism: The Americo-Liberian Scramble for the Hinterland. Boulder, CO: Westview, 1984.

6313. Gershoni, Yekutiel. "An Historical Examination of Liberia's Economic Policies, 1900-1944." Liberian Studies Journal 11 (1986): 20-34.

6314. Gray, Beverly Ann. Liberia during the Tolbert Era. Washington, D.C.: 1983.

6315. Harris, John. "Liberian Slavery: The Essentials." Contemporary Review 1 (1931): 303-309.

6316. Hlophe, S. S. "Ruling Families and Power Struggles in Liberia." Journal of African Studies 6 (1979): 75-82.

6317. Johnson, Charles S. Bitter Canaan. The Story of the Negro Republic. 2d ed. New Brunswick, NJ: Transaction Publishers, 1987(orig. 1948).

6318. Kappel, Robert and others, eds. Liberia: Underdevelopment and Political Rule in a Peripheral Society. Hamburg: Institut fur Afrika-Kunde, 1986. [English and German.]

6319. Khafre, Kadallah. "Towards a Political Economy of Liberia." Review of African Political Economy 12 (May-August 1978): 105-113.

6320. Liberia, a Promise Betrayed: A Report on Human Rights. New York: Lawyers Committee for Human Rights, 1986.

6321. Oldfield, John R. Alexander Crummell (1819-1898) and the Creation of an African-American Church in Liberia. Lewiston, New York: Mellen, 1990.

6322. Robinson, Cedric. "Du Bois and Black Sovereignty: The Case of Liberia." Race & Class 32 (October-December 1990): 39- 50.

6323. Rosenberg, Emily S. "The Invisible Protectorate: The United States, Liberia, and the Evolution of Neo-Colonialism, 1909- 1940." Diplomatic History 9 (1985): 191-214.

6324. Sawyer, Amos. "Effective Immediately: Dictatorship in Liberia, 1980-1986: A Personal Perspective." Liberia Working Group Papers No. 5 (1987): 1-41.

6325. Seyon, Patrick L. N. "Liberia's Second Republic: Superpower Geopolitics in Africa." Liberian Studies Journal 12 (1987): 56-82.

6326. Shick, Tom W. Behold the Promised Land: A History of Afro- American Settler Society in Nineteenth-Century Liberia. Baltimore, MD: Johns Hopkins University Press, 1980.

6327. Shick, Tom W. The Social and Economic History of Afro- American Settlers in Liberia, 1820-1900. Doctoral dissertation: University of Wisconsin, 1976.

478 WORLD RACISM AND RELATED INHUMANITIES

6328. Spivey, Donald. The Politics of Miseducation: The Booker Washington Institute of Liberia, 1929-1984. Lexington:University of Kentucky, 1986.

6329. Sundiata, I. K. Black Scandal, American and the Liberian Labor Crisis, 1929-1936. Philadelphia, PA: Institute for the Study of Human Issues, 1980.

6330. Taryor, Nya K., Jr., ed. Justice, Justice: A Cry of My People: Speeches, Papers, and Important Documents by Some of the Makers of the Liberian Revolution (Yet to Come) in the Movement for Justice in Africa. 2003W. 67th Place, Chicago, Il 60636: Strugglers' Community Press, 1985.

LIBYA

6331. Abitbol, Michel and Irit Abramski-Bligh. "Libya." In Encyclopedia of the Holocaust, III. New York: Macmillan, 1990.

6332. Anderson, Lisa. The State and Social Transformation in Tunisia and Libya, 1830-1980. Princeton, NJ: Princeton University Press, 1986.

6333. Bah, Khalifah S. el-. Fascist Colonial Schooling of Libyan Muslim Arab Children (1922-1942): A Political System Analysis. Doctoral dissertation: University of California, Los Angeles, 1985. UMO # 8513109.

6334. Bearman, Jonathan. Qadhafi's Libya. London: Zed Press, 1986.

6335. Deeb, Marius K. and Mary Jane Deeb. Libya Since the Revolution: Aspects of Social and Political Development. New York: Praeger, 1982.

6336. DeFelice, Renzo. Jews in an Arab Land: Libya, 1835-1970. Translated by Judith Roumani. Austin: University of Texas Press, 1985.

6337. El-Garid, El. Social Mobility Orientations in Libya. Master's thesis: University of Utah, 1982.

6338. El-Khawas, M. A. "Quaddafism, Theory & Practice." Search 7 (Winter 1986): 44-76.

6339. First, Ruth. Libya: The Elusive Revolution. New York: Holmes and Meier, 1973.

6340. Folayan, Kola. "The Resistance Movement in Libya." Tarikh 4 (1973): 46-56. [Italian intervention.]

6341. Folayan, Kola. "Italian Colonial Rule in Libya." Tarikh 4 (1974): 1-10.

6342. Goldberg, Harvey E. The Book of Mordechai. A Study of the Jews of Libya. Philadelphia: Institute for the Study of Human Issues.

6343. Goldberg, Harvey E. Jewish Life in Muslim Libya: Rivals and Relatives. Chicago, IL: University of Chicago Press, 1990.

6344. Joffe, E. G. H. and K.S. McLachlan, eds. Social and Economic Development of Libya. Boulder, CO: Westview Press, 1983.

6345. Mattes, Hanspeter. "Die gesellschaftliche Transformation Libyens (1951-1984): Aufsteig und Fall der Bourgeoisie." Orient 26 (1985): 27-47.

6346. Mead, Richard and Alan George. "The Women of Libya." Middle East International No. 25 (July 1973): 18-20.

6347. Roumani, Maurice M. "Zionism and Social Change in Libya at the Turn of the Century." Studies in Zionism 8 (1987): 1- 24.

6348. Segre, Claudio G. Fourth Shore. The Italian Colonization of Libya. Chicago, IL: University of Chicago Press, 1974.

6349. Souriau, C. "La societe feminine en Libya." Revue de l'Occident Musulman et de la Mediterranee 6 ((1st and 2nd trimesters 1969): 127-155.

MADAGASCAR

6350. Bouillon, Antoine. Madagascar: le colonisé et son 'âme': essai sur le discours psychologique colonial. Paris: Editions l'Harmattan, 1981.

6351. Campbell, Gwyn. "Slavery and fanompoana: The Structure of Forced Labour in Imerina (Madagascar), 1790-1861." Journal of African History 29 (1988): 463-486.

6352. Deleris, Ferdinand. Ratsiraka: socialisme et misere à Madagascar. Paris: Editions l'Harmattan, 1986.

6353. Fremigacci, Jean. "L'administration coloniale: les aspects oppressifs." Omaly Sy Anio (January-December 1978): 209-238.

6354. Gintzburder, Alphonse. "Accomodation to Poverty: The Case of the Malagasy Peasant Communities." Cah. Et. Afric. 23 (1983): 419-442.

6355. Kottak, Conrad P. and others. Madagascar: Society and History. Durham, NC: Carolina Academic Press, 1986.

6356. Molet, Louis. "Quarante ans d'histoire de Madagascar." R. fr. Hist. Outre-Mer 75 (1988): 89-102.

6357. Mosca, Liliana. "Questione etnica ed integrazione nazionale a Madagascar." Africa (Italy) 42 (1987): 485-501.

6358. Razafimahatratra, F. Y. Evolution des nationalismes malagaches. Doctoral dissertation: Paris-EHESS, 1979.

MALAWI

6359. Bone, David S. "The Muslim Minority in Malawi and Western Education." Jr. Inst. Muslim Minority Aff. 6 (1985): 412- 419.

6360. Kalinga, Owen J. M. "Colonial Rule, Missionaries, and Ethnicity in the North Nyasa District, 1891-1938." African Studies Review 28 (March 1985): 57-72.

6361. Lamba, I. C. "African Women's Education in Malawi, 1875- 1952." Journal of Education Administration 14 (January 1982): 46-54.

6362. Mandala, Elias. "Capitalism, Kinship, and Gender in the Lower Tchiri (Shire) Valley of Malawi 1860-1960: An Alternative Theoretical Framework." African Economic History No. 13 (1984): 137-170.

6363. Mpakati, Attati. "Malawi: The Birth of a Neocolonial State." African Review 3 (1973): 33-68.

6364. Needham, D. E. From Iron Age to Independence. Harlow, Essex, England: 1984.

6365. Ng'Ong'Ola, Clement. "The Political Economy of Land in Nyasaland." African Social Research (December 1983): 493-514.

6366. Pachai, B. "African Politics in Twentieth Century Colonial Malawi." Kleio 6 (1974): 31-59.

6367. Pennant, Thomas. "Housing in Urban Labor Force in Malawi: An Historical Overview, 1930-1980." African Urban Studies (Spring 1983): 1-22.

6368. Vaughn, Megan. "Poverty and Famine: 1949 in Nyasaland." Journal of Social Science, University of Malawi 11 (1984): 46-72.

6369. White, Landeg. "'Tribes' and the Aftermath of the Chilembwe Rising [in 1915 in Nyasaland]." African Affairs 83 (1984): 511-541.

MALAYSIA

6370. Abraham, C. E. R. "Malaysia." In International Handbook on Race and Race Relations, edited by Jay A. Sigler. Westport, CT: Greenwood, 1987.

6371. Abraham, C. E. R. "Racial and Ethnic Manipulation in Colonial Malaya." Ethnic and Racial Studies 6 (1983): 18- 32.

6372. Ali, Ameer. "Phases of Capitalism in Malaysia: A Profile of Her Political Economy." Asian Thought Soc. 9 (July-November 1984): 207-216.

6373. Amin, Mohammad and Malcolm Caldwell, eds. Malaya: The Making of a Neo-colony. Nottingham: Spokesman Books, 1977.

6374. Anand, Sudhir. "Aspects of Poverty in Malaysia." Review of Income and Wealth 23 (March 1977): 1-26.

6375. Ayab, Ahmad Y. Ethnic Occupational Differentials in Peninsular Malaysia from 1957-1975. Master's thesis: Brown University, 1985.

6376. Azizah, Kassim. "The Unwelcome Guests: Indonesian Immigrants and Malayan Public Responses." South East Asian Studies 25 (September 1987): 265-278.

6377. Bajumid, Ibrahim A. "Challenges and Changes in Malaysian Education." South East Asian Journal Education Studies 25 (1988): 1-46.

6378. Basham, Richard D. "National Racial Policies and University Education in Malaysia." In Culture, Ethnicity, and Identity, edited by WilliaM C. McCready. New York: Academic Press, 1983.

6379. Beeman, Mark A. The Migrant Labor System: The Case of Malaysian Rubber Workers. Doctoral dissertation: University of Illinois, 1985. UMO # 8600123.

6380. Blust, Robert. "The Linguistic Study of Indonesia." Archipel 34 (1987): 27-47.

6381. Brennan, Martin. "Class, Politics and Race in Modern Malaysia." Journal of Contemporary Asia 12 (1982): 188-215.

6382. Butcher, John G. The British in Malaya, 1880-1914: The Social History of a European Community in Colonial South-East Asia. New York: Oxford University Press, 1979.

6383. Carey, Iskandar. "The Kensiu Negritos of Baling, Kedah." Journal of the Malaysian Branch of the Royal Asiatic Society 43 (1970): 143-154.

6384. Cham, B. N. "Colonialism and Communalism in Malaysia." Journal of Contemporary Asia 7 (1977): 178-199.

6385. Chua, Yee Yen. "Wage Discrimination by Sex in Malaysia." Journal Ekonomi Malaysia 1 (1984): 57-77.

6386. Colletta, N. J. "Malaysia's Forgotten People: Education, Cultural Identity, and Socio-Economic Mobility among South Indian Plantation Workers." Contributions to Asian Studies 7 (1975): 87-182.

6387. Corner, Lorraine. "The Persistence of Poverty: Rural Development Policy in Malaysia." Kajian Malaysia 1 (June 1983): 38-61.

6388. Daud, Fatimah. "Some Patterns of Ethnic Relations in Malaysia." Asian Profile 13 (April 1985): 117-128.

6389. DeVanzo, J. and J. P. Habicht. "Infant Mortality Decline in Malaysia, 1946-1975..." Demography 23 (May 1986)

6390. Fan Yew Teng. The UMNO Drama: Power Struggles in Malaysia. Kuala Lumpur: Egret Books, 1989.

6391. Fisk, E. K. and H. Osman-Rani, eds. The Political Economy of Malaysia. Kuala Lumpur: Oxford University Press, 1982.

6392. Freedman, M. The Sociology of Race Relations in Southeast Asia with Special Reference to British Malaya. Master's thesis: London School of Economics, 1948.

6393. Gaudart, Hyacinth M. A Descriptive Study of Bilingual Education in Malaysia. Doctoral dissertation: University of Hawaii, 1985.

6394. Haron, Nadzan. "Colonial Defence and British Approach to the Problems in Malaya 1874-1918." Modern Asian Studies 24 (May 1990): 275-295.

6395. Hashim, Wan. Race Relations in Malaysia. Kuala Lumpur: Heinemann Educational Books (Asia), 1983.

486 WORLD RACISM AND RELATED INHUMANITIES

6396. Hirschman, Charles. "Labor Markets and Ethnic Inequality in Peninsular Malaysia, 1970." Journal of Developing Areas 18 (October 1983)

6397. Hirschman, Charles. "The Meaning and Measurement of Ethnicity in Malaysia: An Analysis of Census Classifications." Journal of Asian Studies 46 (August 1987): 555-582.

6398. Hua Wu Yin. Class and Communalism in Malaysia: Politics in a Dependent Capitalist State. London: Zed Press, 1983.

6399. Hussin, Mutalib. Islam and Ethnicity in Malay Politics. New York: Oxford University Press, 1990.

6400. Ikemoto, Yukio. "Income Distribution in Malaysia, 1957- 1980." Developing Economies 23 (December 1985)

6401. Islam, M. Nazrul. "The 1948 Emergency and Racial Integration in Malaysia." Journal of the Asiatic Society of Bangladesh 31 (1986): 37-48.

6402. Jain, Prakash C. "Exploitation and Reproduction of Migrant Indian Labour in Colonial Guyana and Malaysia." Journal of Contemporary Asia 18 (1988): 189-206.

6403. Jain, Ravindra K. Migrants, Proletarians or Malayans? South Indians on the Plantation in Malaya. 2 vols. Doctoral dissertation: Australian National University, 1965.

6404. Jomo. "Estates of Poverty." Inside Asia No. 6 (November- December 1985): 18-19. [Workers on Malaysian rubber estates and plantations.]

6405. Jomo Kwame Sundaram. A Question of Class: Capital, the State, and Uneven Development in Malaya. New York: Oxford University Press, 1986.

6406. Kalimuthu, K. The Politics of Language Education: A Case Study of West Malaysia 1930-1971. Master's thesis: University of British Columbia, 1978.

6407. Kasim, Mustapa Bin. Preferential Policy in Higher Education in Malaysia: A Case Study of Malay Graduates at the University of Science, Malaysia. Doctoral dissertation: University of Wisconsin, 1989. UMO # 9006887.

6408. King, Dwight Y. "Human Rights, Social Structure and Indonesia's New Order." Journal of Contemporary Asia 16 (1986): 342-350.

6409. Kok, Loy F. "Chinese Mining Labour in Ampang, 1900-1914." Malaysia Hist. 20 (1983): 51-59.

6410. Krenn, Heliena. Conrad's Lingard Trilogy: Empire, Race, and Women in the Malay Novels. New York: Garland, 1990.

6411. Lee, Raymond L. M. and R. Rajoo. "Sanskritization and Indian Ethnicity." Modern Asian Studies 21 (April 1987): 389-415.

6412. Lim, Julian. "Social Problems of Chinese Female Immigrants in Malaya 1925-1940." Malaysia Hist. 23 (1980): 101-109.

6413. Lim, Mah Hui. "Affirmative Action, Ethnicity and Integration: The Case of Malaysia." Ethnic and Racial Studies 8 (1985): 250-276.

6414. Lim, Teck Ghee. "British Colonial Administration and the Ethnic Division of Labour in Malaya." Kajian Malaysia 2 (1984): 28-66.

6415. Linn, H. T. "Public Library Services in Malaysia: An Analysis." Library Review 36 (Spring 1986): 5-12.

6416. McGee, T. G. "Proletarianization, Industrialization and Urbanization in Asia: A Case Study of Malaysia." Akademika 23 (July 1983): 3-20.

6417. Means, Gordon P. "The Orang Asli: Aboriginal Policies in Malaysia." Pacific Affairs 58 (1985-1986): 637-652.

6418. Means, Gordon P. "'Special Rights' as a Strategy for Development: The Case of Malaysia." Comparative Politics 5 (1972): 29-61. [Affirmative action.]

6419. Mehmet, Ozay. Development in Malaysia: Poverty, Wealth, and Trusteeship. Dover, NH: Croom Helm, 1986.

6420. Milne, R. S. and Diane K. Mauzy. Malaysia: Tradition, Modernity, and Islam. Boulder, CO: Westview, 1986.

6421. Milner, A. C. "Colonial Records History: British Malaya." Modern Asian Studies 21 (1987): 773-792.

6422. Mohammad Haji Yusuf. "Ethnicity or Social Class: An Analysis of Equality and Integration Attitudinal Scales among Malaysians." Akademika 24 (January 1984): 97-133.

6423. Mohd Noor, Sharifah. Streaming in the Malaysian Primary Schools. Doctoral dissertation: University of Wisconsin, 1985. UMO # 8601845.

6424. Naipaul, V. S. Among the Believers: An Islamic Journey. New York: 1981. [pp. 270-274.]

6425. Nam, Tae Y. Racism, Nationalism, and Nation-building in Malaysia and Singapore. Meerut: Sadhna Prakashan, 1973.

6426. Narayanan, Suresh. "Equity Aspects of the Malaysian Tax System: Some Observations and Suggestions." Kajian Malaysia 2 (1984): 23-37.

6427. Nogata, Judith. "In Defense of Ethnic Boundaries: The Changing Myth and Charters of Malay Identity." In Ethnic Change, edited by Charles Keyes. Seattle: University of Washington Press, 1981.

6428. Ongkili, James P. Nation-building in Malaysia 1946-1974. New York: Oxford University Press, 1985.

6429. Parmer, J. Norman. "Health and Health Services in British Malaya in the 1920's." Modern Asian Studies 23 (Feb. 1989): 49-71.

6430. Rabushka, Alvin. "Racial Stereotypes in Malaya." Asian Survey (July 1971)

6431. Roff, William R. The Origins of Malay Nationalism, 1900- 1941. Doctoral dissertation: Australian National University, 1965.

6432. Salleh, Halim. "Exploitation and Control of Labour Within the Malayan Rubber Industry Up Till 1941." Kajian Malaysia 6 (June 1988): 1-43.

6433. Sandhu, K. S. Indians in Malaya: Immigration and Settlement 1786-1957. London: 1969,

6434. Sani, Rustam A. "The Malay Ruling Elite in the Post- Colonial State of Malays." Solidarity 114 (September- October 1987): 20-28.

6435. Selvaratnam, V. "Ethnicity, Inequality, and Higher Education in Malaysia." Comparative Education Review 32 (May 1988): 173-196.

6436. Simanjuntak, M. "The Malay Language and the World View of Its Speakers." SARI 2 (January 1984): 81-89.

6437. Soltow, Lee. "Literacy and Colonialism in Peninsular Malaysia from 1894-1957." Malaysia Hist. 28 (1985): 1-14.

6438. Soltow, Lee. "Long-run Wealth Inequality in Malaysia." Singapore Economic Review 28 (October 1983)

6439. Soltow, Lee. "Malaysia's Goal: Wealth Equity." Kajian Ekonomi Malaysia 19 (December 1982): 85-99.

6440. Stanson, Michael. Class, Race, and Colonialism in West Malaysia: The Indian Case. Vancouver: University of British Columbia Press, 1980.

6441. Stockwell, A. J. "Insurgency and Decolonization During the Malayan Emergency." Journal of Commonwealth & Comparative Politics 25 (1987): 71-81.

6442. Stockwell, A. J. "The White Man's Burden and Brown Humanity: Colonialism and Ethnicity in British Malaysia." South East Asin Journal Social Science 10 (1982): 44-68.

6443. Sundaram, J. K. A Question of Class: Capital, the State, and Uneven Development in Malaya. New York: Oxford University Press, 1986.

6444. Syed Arabi Idid and Latiffah Pawanteh. "Media, Ethnicity and National Unity." Media Asia 16 (1989): 78-85.

6445. Tan, Chee-Beng. "Ethnic Relations in Malaysia in Historical and Sociological Perspectives." Kajian Malaysia 5 (1987): 99-119.

6446. Tan, Loong-Hoe. "The State and the Distribution of Wealth within the Malay Society in Peninsular Malaysia." South East Asian Affairs (1981): 217-232.

6447. Thillainathan, R. "Discriminatory Allocation of Public Expenditure Benefits for Reducing Interracial Inequality in Malaysia-An Evaluation." Dev. Ec. 18 (September 1980): 251- 274.

6448. Warren, James F. "Slave Markets and Exchange in the Malay World: The Sulu Sultanate, 1770-1878." Journal of Southeast Asian Studies (1977): 162-175.

6449. Wazir-jahan Karim. "Electronic Woman." Inside Asia No. 6 (November-December 1985): 20-21. [Young women workers in the Malaysian electronics industry.]

6450. Wilbon, Eleanor K. Malaysia and Multinational Corporations: Federalism, Ethnic Cleavage, and Foreign Capital. Doctoral dissertation: University of Southern California, 1984.

6451. Winzeler, Robert H. Ethnic Relations in Kelantan: A Study of the Chinese and Thai as Minority Communities in a Malay State. New York: Oxford University Press, 1986.

6452. Yahaya, N. "Housing in Malaysia, 1955-1990." Habitat International 13 (1989)

6453. Yen Ching-Hwang. A Social History of the Chinese in Singapore and Malaya, 1800-1911. New York: Oxford University Press, 1986.

MALI

6454. Diakite, S. <u>Education, the State and Class Conflict: A Study of Three Education Classes in Mali</u>. Doctoral dissertation: Stanford University, 1985. UMO # 8522128.

6455. Francais, Piere. "Class Struggle in Mali." <u>Review of African Political Economy</u> 24 (December 1982): 22-38.

6456. Roberts, Richard L. <u>Warriors, Merchants, and Slaves: The State and the Economy in the Middle Niger Valley, 1700-1914</u>. Stanford, CA: Stanford University Press, 1987.

6457. Saad, Elias N. <u>Social History of Timbuktu: The Role of Muslim Scholars and Notables, 1400-1900</u>. New York: Cambridge University Press, 1983.

MAURITANIA

6458. Bennoune, Mahfoud. "Mauritania: A Neocolonial Desert." Dialectical Anthropology 3 (1978): 43-66.

6459. Bennoune, Mahfoud. "The Political Economy of Mauritania: Imperialism and Class Struggle." Review of African Political Economy 12 (May-August 1978): 31-52.

6460. Carr, David W. "Difficulty of Restoring Economic Viability with Lopsided Development: The Mauritanian Case." Jr. Dev. Areas 18 (April 1984): 373-386.

6461. Chassey, Francis de. Mauritanie, 1900-1975: facteurs economiques, politiques, ideologiques et educatifs dans la formation d'une societe sous-developpee. Paris: Editions l'Harmattan, 1984.

6462. Gozalbes Cravioto, Enrique. "Consideraciones sobre la esclavitud en las provincas romanas de Mauretania." Cah. Tunisie 27 (1979): 35-67.

6463. Mercer, John. Mauretaniens Sklaven. Die Haratin. Gottingen: Reihe Pogrom, 1982.

6464. Mercer, John. "Slavery in Mauritania Today." Plural Societies 12 (Autumn-Winter 1981): 125-130.

6465. Mercer, John. Slavery in Mauritania Today. Edinburgh: Human Rights Group, 1982.

6466. Noble, Kenneth B. "An African Exodus With Racial Overtones." New York Times (July 22, 1989)

MAURITIUS

6467. Allen, Richard B. "Economic Marginality and the Rise of the Free Population of Colour in Mauritius, 1767-1830." Slavery & Abolition 10 (September 1989): 126-150.

6468. Anderson, Desmond. "The Development of Commercial Education in England, Ireland and Mauritius (Mainly during the 19th and 20th centuries)." Compare 9 (1979): 157-169.

6469. Asgarally, Issa. "Histoire et linguistique: langues, colonialisme et sous-developpement." Journal of Mauritian Studies 1 (1986): 130-147.

6470. Barz, R. K. "Indian Immigration and Hindi Literature in Mauritius." Journal of Mauritian Studies 1 (1986): 57-89.

6471. Benedrit, B. Mauritius: The Problems of a Plural Society. London: Pall Mall Press, 1965.

6472. Carter, Marina. Indian Labor Migration to Mauritius and the Indenture Experience, 1834-1874. Doctoral dissertation: University of Oxford, 1987. [Order No. BRD-86557.]

6473. Eriksen, Thomas H. "Creole Culture and Social Change." Journal of Mauritian Studies 1 (1986): 59-72.

6474. Houbert, Jean. "Mauritius:Independence and Dependence." Journal of Modern African Studies 19 (March 1981): 75-106.

6475. Kalla, Abdool Cader. "Early Concerns for the Education of Indians in Mauritius." Journal of Mauritius Inst. Educ. (October 1987): 37-55.

6476. Liberasyon, Muwman. The Women's Liberation Movement in Mauritius. Port Louis: Ledikasyon pu Travayer, 1988.

6477. Mannick, A. R. Mauritius: The Development of a Plural Society. Nottingham: Spokesman, 1979.

6478. Manrakhan, J. "Mauritius and the Idea of a University (Part 2, Chapter 7: From Parliament to Political Platform)." J. U. Mauritius 1-51 (July-December 1983)

6479. Manrakhan, J. "Mauritius and the Idea of a University: Part Two, Chapters 8-11." J. U. Mauritius 1-229 (January-June 1984)

6480. Minogue, M. "Mauritius: Political, Economic and Social Development in a Small Island." Manchester Pap. Dev. No. 8 (1983): 31-76.

6481. Moore, Jill. "Exporting European Core Values: British and French Influence on Education in Mauritius." European Journal of Education 19 (1984): 39-52.

6482. North-Coombes, M. D. "From Slavery to Indenture: Forced Labour in the Political Economy of Mauritius, 1834-1867." In Indentured Labour in the British Empire, 1834-1920, edited by Kay Saunders. London: Croom Helm, 1984.

6483. Nwulia, Moses D. E. The History of Slavery in Mauritius and the Seychelles, 1810-1875. Rutherford, NJ: Fairleigh Dickenson University Press, 1981.

6484. Parahoo, A. K. A Sociological Analysis of the Organisation, Distribution and Uses of Health Care in Mauritius. Doctoral dissertation: University of Keele, 1985.

6485. Simmons, Adele S. Modern Mauritius: The Politics of Decolonization. Bloomington: Indiana University Press, 1982.

6486. Yahil, Leni. "Mauritius." In Encyclopedia of the Holocaust, III. New York: 1990.

MEXICO

6487. Acosta Saignes, Miguel. "La etnohistoria y el estudio de negro en Mexico." In Acculturation in the Americas, edited by Sol Tax. Chicago: 1952,

6488. Aguirre Beltran, Gonzalo. La poblacion negra de Mexico, 1519-1810. 2d ed. Mexico: Fondo de Cultura Economica, 1972.

6489. Ahrendt, Christina. Franciscan Education and Empire in Sixteenth-century Mexico. Master's thesis: University of Texas, 1978.

6490. Alberno-Semerena, José Luis and Maria Dolores Nieto-Stuarte. "Empirical Estimates of Marxian Categories in Mexico: 1970-1975." Review of Radical Political Economics 18 (Winter 1986): 32-46.

6491. Alonso, Jorge, ed. Los movimientos sociales en el Valle de Mexico. Vol. 3. Mexico City: Centro de Investigaciones y Estudios Superiores en Antropologia Social, 1986.

6492. Anderson, Rodney D. Outcasts in Their Own Land: Mexican Industrial Workers, 1906-1911. DeKalb: Northern Illinois University Press, 1976.

6493. Anderson, Rodney D. "Race and Social Stratification: A Comparison of Working-Class Spaniards, Indians, and Castas in Guadalajara, Mexico in 1821." Hispanic American Historical Review 68 (May 1988): 209-244.

6494. Arnold, Marigene. Mexican Women: The Anatomy of a Stereotype in a Mestizo Village. Doctoral dissertation: University of Florida, 1973.

6495. Arriola Woog, Carlos. Los empresarios y el Estado, 1970-1982. 2d ed., rev. and enl. Mexico City: Grupo Editorial Miguel Angel Porrua, 1988.

6496. Barrera Bassols, Dalia. Condiciones de vida de los trabajadores de Tijuana, 1970-1978. Mexico City: Instituto Nacional de Antropologia e Historia, 1987.

6497. Basanez, Miguel. La lucha por la hegemonia en Mexico, 1968-1980. Mexico City: Siglo Veintiuno Editores, 1981.

6498. Basurto, Jorge. El proletariado industrial en Mexico, 1850-1930. Mexico City: UNAM, 1975.

6499. Batra, Roger. "Capitalism and the Peasantry in Mexico." Latin American Perspectives 9 (Winter 1982)

6500. Beezley, William H. Judas at the Jockey Club and other Episodes of Porfirian Mexico. Lincoln: University of Nebraska Press, 1987.

6501. Bejar Navarro, R. "Prejudicio y discriminación racial en Mexico." R. Mexico Sociol. 31 (1969): 417-433.

6502. Beneria, Lourdes and Martha Roldan. The Crossroads of Class & Gender: Industrial Homework, Subcontracting and Household Dynamics in Mexico City. Chicago, IL: University of Chicago Press, 1987.

6503. Benitez, Fernando. Las indios de Mexico. 4 vols. Mexico City: Era, 1972.

6504. Borah, Woodrow. Justice by Insurance: The General Indian Court of Colonial Mexico and the Legal Aides of the Half Real. Berkeley: University of California Press, 1983.

6505. Borah, Woodrow. "Race and Class in Mexico." Pacific Historical Review 23 (1954): 331-342.

6506. Boyd-Bourman, Peter. "Negro Slaves in Early Colonial Mexico." Americas 26 (October 1969): 134-153.

6507. Brack, Gene M. "La opinion mexicana, el racismo norteamericano y la guerra de 1846." Anglia (1971)

6508. Brady, Robert L. "The Domestic Slave Trade in Sixteenth- Century Mexico." The Americas 24, 3 (1968): 281-289.

6509. Brady, Robert L. The Emergence of a Negro Class in Mexico, 1542-1640. PhD dissertation: University of Iowa, 1965.

6510. Buendia, Manuel. La CIA en Mexico. Mexico City: Ediciones Oceano, 1983.

6511. Cantú Corro, José. La esclavitud en el mundo y en México. Mexico: 1926.

6512. Cardoso, Ciro F. S., ed. Formación y desarrollo de la burguesia en Mexico, siglo XIX. Mexico City: Siglo XXI, 1978.

6513. Carlsen, Laura. "Mexican Grassroots Social Movements." Radical America 22 (July-August 1988): 34-51.

6514. Carr, Barry, ed. The Mexican Left, the Popular Movement, and the Politics of Austerity. La Jolla, CA: Center for U.S.- Mexican Studies, UC San Diego, 1986.

6515. Carrasco, Rosalba and Enrique Provencio. "La politica social 1983-1988 y sus principales consecuencies." Investigacion Economica 47 (April-June 1988): 91-110.

6516. Carroll, Patrick J. "Mandinga: The Evolution of a Mexican Runaway Slave Community, 1735-1827." Comparative Studies in Society and History 19 (October 1977): 489-505.

6517. Chacon, Ramon D. "Rural Educational Reform in Yucatan: From the Porfiriato to the Era of Salvador Alvarado, 1910-1918." The Americas 42 (October 1985): 207-228.

6518. Chance, John K. Race and Class in Colonial Oaxaco. Stanford, CA: Stanford University Press, 1978.

6519. Chowning, M. "The Management of Church Wealth in Michoacan, Mexico, 1810-1856: Economic Motivations and Political Implications." Journal of Latin American Studies 22 (October 1990)

6520. Cockcroft, James D. "Immiseration, Not Marginalization. The Case of Mexico." Latin American Perspectives 10 (Spring- Summer 1983): 86-107.

6521. Cope, Robert D. The Limits of Racial Domination: Plebian Society in Colonial Mexico City, 1660-1720. Doctoral dissertation: University of Wisconsin, 1987. UMO # 8800702.

6522. Cordera, Rolando and Carlos Tello, eds. La desigualdad en Mexico. Mexico City: Siglo Veintiuno Editores, 1984.

6523. Cordero H., Salvador and Ricardo Tirado, eds. Clases dominantes y Estado en Mexico. Mexico City: Universidad Nacional Autonoma de Mexico, 1984.

6524. Cornelius, Wayne. Politics and the Migrant Poor in Mexico City. Stanford, CA: Stanford University Press, 1975.

6525. Cornelius, Wayne and others, eds. Mexico's Alternative Political Futures. La Jolla, CA: Center for U.S.-Mexican Studies, University of California, San Diego, 1989.

6526. Cuello, José. "The Persistence of Indian Slavery and Encomienda in the Northeast of Colonial Mexico, 1577-1723." Journal of Social History 21 (Summer 1988): 683-700.

6527. Davidson, David M. Negroes in Colonial Mexico, 1519-1650. MA thesis: University of Wisconsin, 1965.

6528. Davis, Diane E. "Divided Over Democracy: The Embeddedness of State and Class Conflicts in Contemporary Mexico." Politics & Society 17 (September 1989): 247-280.

6529. De La Peña, Sergio. La formacion del capitalismo en Mexico. Mexico City: Siglo XXI, 1975.

6530. Dennis, Philip A. "The Anti-Chinese Campaigns in Sonora, Mexico." Ethnohistory 26 (Winter 1979): 65-80.

6531. DiTella, Torcuato. "The Dangerous Classes in early Nineteenth Century Mexico." Latin American Studies 7 (1973): 79-105.

6532. Doolittle, William E. Canal Irrigation in Prehistoric Mexico: The Sequence of Technological Change. Austin: University of Texas Press, 1989.

6533. Dusenberry, William H. "Discriminatory Aspects of Legislation in Colonial Mexico." Journal of Negro History 33 (July 1948): 284-302.

6534. Elazar, Daniel J. "Mexican Jewry: Some Persistent Issues." Forum 36 (1979): 123-129.

6535. Fernandez, Gabriela T. and others, eds. Case Studies of Educational Needs among Refugees: I. Mexico and Costa Rica. Cambridge, England: International Extension College, 1984.

6536. Figueroa, Manuel. Methodological Explorations on Schooling and the Reproduction of the Social Division of Labor: A Case Study in Mexico City, Mexico. Doctoral dissertation: Stanford University, 1987. UMO # 8720385.

6537. Frost, Elsa C. and others, eds. Labor and Laborers through Mexican History. Tuscon: University of Arizona Press, 1979.

6538. Fuentes Molinor, Olac. Educación y politica en Mexico. Mexico City: Nueva Imagen, 1981.

6539. Gojman de Backal, Alicia. "La accion revolucionaria mexicanista y el fascismo en Mexico: los Dorados." Jahrbuch für Geschichte von Staat, Wirtschaft und Gesellschaft Lateinamerikas 25 (1988): 291-302.

6540. Gojman de Backal, Alicia. "El antisemitismo y la xenofobia en la prensa de derecha en Mexico." Rumbos 20 (1987): 101-115.

6541. González Navarro, Moisés. La Pobreza en Mexico. Mexico City: El Colegio de Mexico, 1985. [18th century to the present.]

6542. Gonzalez Casanova, Pablo, ed. La clase obrera en la historia de Mexico. Mexico City: Siglo XXI, 1980-1983.

6543. Gonzalez Casanova, Pablo. "Dynamics of Class Structure." In Comparative Perspectives on Stratification: Mexico, Great Britain, Japan, edited by Joseph A. Kahl. Boston, MA: Little Brown, 1968.

6544. Gosner, Kevin. "Las élites indigenas en los Altos de Chiapas (1524-1714)." Hist. Mex. 33 (April-June 1984): 405- 424.

6545. Greenleaf, Richard E. Inquisicion y sociedad en el México colonial. Madrid: Ediciones J. Porrua Turanzas, 1985.

6546. Greenleaf, Richard E. "The Inquisition in Eighteenth- Century Mexico." New Mexico Hist. Rev. 60 (January 1985): 29-60.

6547. Greenwood, Michael J. and Jerry R. Lodman. "Intertemporal and Intersectional Aspects of Income Distribution in Mexico." Review of Social Economy 45 (April 1987): 48-63.

6548. Gregory, Peter. The Myth of Market Failure: Employment and the Labor Market in Mexico. Baltimore, MD: Johns Hopkins University Press, 1986.

6549. Grunberg, Bernard. "Les premiers juifs mexicains (1521- 1571)." Revue des Etudes Juives 145 (1986): 359-382.

6550. Gruzinski, Serge, The Net Torn Apart: Ethnic Identities and Westernization in Colonial Mexico, Sixteenth-Nineteenth Century. in Ethnicities and Nations Remo Guidieri and others. Houston, Texas: The Rothko Chapel, 1988.

6551. Guzman Gomez, Alba. Indigenous Voices Assess the Bilingual Bicultural Education Program in Mexico: An Action-Research Study and Its Effects on Policy Issues. Doctoral dissertation: Harvard University, 1985.

6552. Hamel, R. "Socio-cultural Conflict and Bilingual Education: The Case of the Otomi Indians in Mexico." International Social Science Journal 36 (1984): 113-128.

6553. Harding, Timothy F. and Nora Hamilton, eds. Modern Mexico-State, Economy, and Social Conflict. Beverly Hills, CA: Sage, 1985.

6554. Haslag, J. H. and others. "A Study of the Relationship between Economic Growth and Inequality: The Case of Mexico." Federal Reserve Bank of Dallas Economic Review (May 1988)

6555. Hernandez, E. and J. Cordoba. La Distribucion del Ingreso en Mexico. Mexico, D.F.: Centro de Investigacion para la Integracion Social, 1982.

6556. Hicks, Frederic. "Dependent Labor in Prehispanic Mexico." Estudios de Cultra Náhuatl 11 (1974): 243-266.

6557. Hordes, Stanley M. The Crypto-Jewish Community of New Spain, 1620-1649. A Collective Biography. Doctoral dissertation: Tulane University, 1980.

6558. Hordes, Stanley M. "Historiographical Problems in the Study of the Inquisition and the Mexican Crypto-Jews in the Seventeenth Century." American Jewish Archives 34 (November 1982): 138-152.

6559. Hordes, Stanley M. "The Inquisition as Economic and Political Agent: The Campaign of the Mexican Holy Office against the Crypto-Jews in the Mid-Seventeenth Century." The Americas 39 (July 1982): 23-38.

6560. Hovell, Melbourne F. and others. "Occupational Health Risks for Mexican Women: The Case of the Maquiladora along the Mexican-United States Border." International Journal of Health Services 18 (1989)

6561. Hu-Dehart, Evelyn. "Racism and Anti-Chinese Persecution in Sonora, Mexico, 1876-1932." Amerasia Journal 9 (1982): 1- 28.

6562. Israel, Jonathan I. Race, Class, and Politics in Colonial Mexico, 1610-1670. London: Oxford University Press, 1975.

6563. Jacques, Leo M. D. The Anti-Chinese Campaign in Sonora, Mexico, 1900-1931. Doctoral dissertation: University of Arizona, 1974.

6564. Jacques, Leo M. D. "The Anti-Chinese Legislative and Press Campaign in Sonora, Mexico, 1916-1921." Immigrants & Minorities 5 (July 1986): 167-180.

6565. Jones, Grant D. Maya Resistance to Spanish Rule: Time and History On a Colonial Frontier. Albuquerque: University of New Mexico Press, 1989.

6566. Kantz, Barbara Less. A Social History of the Urban Working Class in Mexico City, 1882-1910. Doctoral dissertation: State University of New York at Stony Brook, 1988. UMO # 8926282.

6567. Kicza, John E. Colonial Entrepreneurs: Families and Business in Bourbon Mexico City. Albuquerque: University of New Mexico Press, 1983.

6568. Kicza, John E. "The Great Families of Mexico: Elite Maintenance and Business Practices in Late Colonial Mexico City." Hispanic American Historical Review 62 (August 1982): 429-457.

6569. Kiessling, Wolfgang. "V. Lombardo Toledano an der Seite der deutschen Antifaschisten." Beitrage zur Geschichte der Arbeiterbewegung 27 (1985): 644-653.

6570. Knight, Alan. "Mexican Peonage: What Was it and Why Was It? " Journal of Latin American Studies 18 (May 1986): 41-74.

6571. Knight, Alan. The Mexican Revolution. 2 vols. New York: Cambridge University Press, 1986.

6572. Kolack, Shirley and Kolack, Sol. "The Ambiguous Status of Jews in Mexico." Conservative Judaism 33 (Fall-Winter, 1976-1977): 78-85.

6573. Krause, Corinne A. The Jews in Mexico: A History with Special Emphasis on the Period from 1857 to 1930. Doctoral dissertation: University of Pittsburgh, 1970. Order No. 71- 8418.

6574. Krause, Corrine A. Los Judios en Mexico: Una Historia con Enfasis Especial en el Periodo de 1857 a 1930. Mexico City: U. Iberamericana, 1987.

6575. Krutz, Gordan V. "Chinese Labor, Development and Social Reaction." Ethnohistory 18 (1971): 321-334. [Sonora.]

6576. Lerner, Victoria. La educacion socialista. Mexico, D.F.: El Colegio de Mexico, 1979.

6577. Lesser, Harriet Sara. A History of the Jewish Community of Mexico City, 1912 to 1970. Doctoral dissertation: New York University, 1972.

6578. Liebman, Seymour. The Jews in New Spain: Faith, Flame, and the Inquisition. Coral Gables, Florida: University of Miami Press, 1975.

6579. Logan, Kathleen. "Getting by with Less: Economic Strategies of Lower Income Households in Guadalajara." Urban Anthropology 10 (1981): 231-246.

6580. López Camara, Francisco. La clase media en la era del populismo. Mexico City: Grupo Editorial Miguel Angel Porrua, 1988. [1970-1982.]

6581. Lopez Monjardin, Adriana. La lucha por los ayuntamientos: una utopia viable. Mexico City: Siglo Veintiuno Editores, 1986.

6582. Love, Edgar F. "Legal Restrictions on Afro-Indian Relations in Colonial Mexico." Journal of Negro History 55, 2 (1970): 131-139.

6583. Love, Edgar F. "Negro Resistance to Spanish Rule in Colonial Mexico." Journal of Negro History 52,2 (1967): 89- 103.

6584. Lustig, N. "Economic Crisis Adustment and Living Standards in Mexico, 1982-1985." World Development 18 (October 1990)

6585. Macias, Anna. Against All Odds: The Feminist Movement in Mexico to 1940. Westport, CT: Greenwood, 1982.

6586. Marion, Marie-Odile. "Desigualdad social y minorias etnicas de Mexico." Cuad. am. 250 (September-October 1983): 43-54.

6587. McGinn, N. and S. Street. "Has Mexican Education Generated Human or Political Capital?" Comparative Education 20 (1984): 323-338.

6588. Medina Hernandez, Andres. "La cuestion etnica en Mexico: una reconsideration historica." Bol. Antropol. Am. 16 (December 1987): 5-20.

6589. Mejia Pineros, Maria C. and Sergio Sarmiento Silva. La lucha indigena: un reto a la ortodoxia. Mexico City: Siglo Veintiuno Editores,

6590. Miller, R. "Mexican Literacy Education Today." Journal of Reading 29 (1985): 132-134.

6591. Morales-Gomez, Daniel A. and Alberto Torres. The State, Corporatist Politics and Educational Policy Making in Mexico. Westport, CT: Praeger, 1990.

6592. Morton, Ward M. Woman Suffrage in Mexico. Gainesville, FL: University of Florida Press, 1962.

6593. Nash, June. "The Aztecs and the Ideology of Male Dominance." Signs 4 (Winter 1978): 349-362.

6594. Nazario, Bejar. "Prejuicio y Discriminacion Racial en Mejico." Revista Mexicana de Sociologia 31 (1969)

6595. Nutini, Hugo G. and others. "Historical Development of the Mexican Aristocracy: 1519-1940." L'Uomo (Rome) 6 (1982): 3-37.

6596. Oliveira, Orlandina de. Trabajo, poder y sexualidad. Mexico City: El Colegio de Mexico, 1989.

6597. Olson, Wayne. "Crisis and Social Change in Mexico's Political Economy." Latin American Perspectives 12 (Summer 1985): 7-28.

6598. Palmer, Colin A. Slaves of the White God: Blacks in Mexico, 1570-1650. Cambridge, MA: Cambridge, MA, Harvard University Press.

6599. Pare, L. El Proletariado Agricula de Mexico. Mexico City: Siglio 21, 1977.

6600. Pena, Sergio de la. La formacion del capitalismo en Mexico. Mexico: Siglo Veintiuno Editores, 1975.

6601. Pi-Sunyer, Oriol. "Historical Background to the Negro in Mexico." Journal of Negro History 42 (October 1957): 239- 242.

6602. Poston, Dudley L., Jr. and others. "Modernization and Childlessness in the States of Mexico." Economic Development Cultural Change 34 (April 1985): 503-520.

6603. Poulton, David W. Public Policy and Rural Poverty in Mexico. Master's thesis: University of Calgary, 1985.

6604. Pozas, Ricardo and Isabel H. de Pozas. Los indios en las clases sociales de Mexico. Mexico City: Siglio 21, 1971.

6605. Querol y Roso, Luis. "Negros y mulatos de Nueva Espana, historia de su alzamiento de 1612." Anales de la Universidad de Valenica Ano XII, cuaderno 90 (1935): 121-162.

6606. Raby, David. Educación y revolución social en Mexico. Mexico, D.F.: Sepsetentes, 1974.

6607. Ramos Escandón, Carmen, ed. Presencia y Transparencia: La Mujer en la Historia de Mexico. Mexico City: El Colegio de Mexico, 1987.

6608. Reina, Leticia, ed. Historia de la cuestion agraria mexicana: Estado de Oaxaca. 2 vols. Mexico City: Juan Pablos Editor, 1988.

6609. Richmond, Douglas W. "Nationalism and Class Conflict in Mexico, 1910-1920." The Americas 43 (January 1987): 279- 304.

6610. Robles, Martha. Educación y sociedad en la historia de Mexico. Mexico City: Siglo XXI, 1977.

6611. Rohter, Larry. "Mexico Feels Squeeze of Years of Austerity." New York Times, (July 25, 1989)

6612. Romero Aceves, Ricardo. La mujer en la historia de México. Mexico City: Costa-Amic Editores, 1982.

6613. Roncal, Joaqim. "The Negro Race in Mexico." Hispanic American Historical Review 24, 3 (1944): 530-540.

6614. Ruz Ménendez, Rodolfo. La emancipacion de los esclavos en Yucatan. Merida: 1970.

6615. Salvucci, Richard J. Textiles and Capitalism in Mexico, An Economic History of the Obrajes, 1539-1840. Princeton, NJ: Princeton University Press, 1987.

6616. Schryer, Frans J. Ethnicity and Class Conflict in Rural Mexico. Princeton, NJ: Princeton University Press, 1990.

6617. Seed, Patricia. "Social Dimensions of Race: Mexico City 1753." Hispanic American Historical Review 62 (1982): 569- 606.

6618. Semo, Enrique. Historia mexicana: economia y lucha de clases. Mexico City: Era, 1978.

6619. Smith, Michael E. "The Role of Social Stratification in the Aztec Empire: A View from the Provinces." American Anthropologist 88 (1986): 70-91.

6620. Sullivan, Paul. Unfinished Conversations: Mayas and Foreigners Between Two Wars. New York: Knopf, 1990. [The Mayan Caste War of 1847.]

6621. Testimonios de las esclavitud en la Nueva Galicia. Guadalajara, Jalisco, Mexico: Gobierno de Jalisco, Secretria General, Unidad Editorial, 1985.

6622. Tyler, Ronnie C. "Fugitive Slaves in Mexico." Journal of Negro History 57 (January 1972): 1-12. [Escaped slaves from Texas.]

6623. Valdés, Dennis N. "The Decline of Slavery in Mexico." The Americas 44 (October 1987): 167-194.

6624. Vanachere, M. "Conditions of Agricultural Day-Labourers in Mexico." International Labour Review 127 (1988)

6625. Vaughn, Mary Kay, Women, Class, and Education in Mexico: 1880-1928. in Modern Mexico, edited by Nora Hamilton and Timothy F. Harding. Newbury Park, CA: Sage, 1986.

6626. Vaughn, Mary Kay. The State, Education, and Social Class in Mexico, 1880-1928. DeKalb: Northern Illinois University Press, 1982.

6627. Vejar, Jesus R. and Lisa W. Larkin. "Abating Migration of Mexico's Rural Poor: A Legal, Practical, and Technical Examination." Arizona Journal of International and Comparative Law (1988): 105-137.

6628. Ward, Peter M. Welfare Politics in Mexico. Papering Over the Cracks. Winchester, MA: Allen & Unwin, 1986.

6629. Wasserman, Mark. Capitalists, Caciques, and Revolution. The Native Elite and Foreign Enterprise in Chihuahua, Mexico, 1854-1911. Chapel Hill: University of North Carolina Press, 1984.

6630. Weiss, Eduard. Schule zwischen Staat and Gesellschaft: Mexiko, 1920-1976. Munich: Wilhelm Fink, 1983.

6631. Wobeser, Gisela von. "Los esclavos negros en el Mexico colonial: las haciendas de Cuernavaca-Cuautla." Jahrbuch für Geschichte von Staat, Wirtschaft und Gesellschaft Lateinamerikas 23 (1986): 145-171.

6632. Zavala, Silvio A. El servicio personal de los indios en la Nueva España. 2 vols. Mexico: El Colegio de Mexico and El Colegio Nacional, 1984-1985. [1521-1575.]

6633. Zavala, Silvio A. "Servidumbre natural y libertad cristiana, según los tratadistas españoles de los siglos XVI y XVII." Buenos Aires (1944) Publicaciones del Instituto de investigaciones historicas, No. 87.

6634. Zermeño, Sergio. Mexico: una democracia utopica, el movimiento estudiantil del 68. Mexico City: Siglo XXI, 1978.

MONGOLIAN PEOPLE'S REPUBLIC

6635. Academy of Sciences, People's Republic of Mongolia. *Information Mongolia: The Comprehensive Reference Source of the People's Republic of Mongolia (MRP)*. New York: Pergamon Press, 1990.

6636. Bawden, Charles R. *The Modern History of Mongolia*. 2d ed. New York: Kegan Paul, 1989.

6637. Halkovic, Stephen A., Jr. *The Mongols of the West*. Bloomington: Research Institute for Inner Asian Studies, Indiana University, 1985.

6638. Krader, Lawrence. "The Cultural and Historical Position of the Mongols." *Asia Minor* 3 (1953)

6639. Lattimore, Owen. *Nationalism and Revolution in Mongolia*. New York: 1955.

6640. Moses, Larry and Stephen A. Halkovic, Jr. *Introduction to Mongolian History and Culture*. Bloomington: Research Institute for Inner Asian Studies, Indiana University, 1985.

6641. Murphy, George G. S. *Soviet Mongolia. A Study of the Oldest Political Satellite*. Berkeley: University of California Press, 1966.

6642. Rundall, R. A. and R.D. Terrell. "Educational Desert or Oasis? An Educator's Trek to Outer Mongolia." *Adolescence* 21 (1986): 185-189.

6643. Rupen, Robert A. *How Mongolia Is Really Ruled: A Political History of the Mongolian People's Republic, 1900-1978*. Stanford, CA: Hoover Institution Press, 1979.

6644. Rupen, Robert A. "Mongolian Nationalism." *Royal Central Asian Journal* 45 (1958)

6645. Rupen, Robert A. *Outer Mongolian Nationalism, 1900-1919*. Doctoral dissertation: University of Washington, 1954.

6646. Sanders, Alan J. K. Mongolia: Politics, Economics and Society. Boulder, Co: Lynne Rienner, 1987.

6647. Sanjdorj M. Manchu Chinese Colonial Rule in Northern Mongolia. Translated by N. Onon. New York: St. Martin's Press, 1980.

6648. Zhubov, Y. M. and others, eds. History of the Mongolian People's Republic. Moscow: Nauka Publishing House, 1973.

MOROCCO

6649. Abitbol, Michel. "Morocco." In Encyclopedia of the Holocaust, pp. 991-995. New York: Macmillan, 1990.

6650. Baron, A. M. "La femme dans le proletariat morocain." Masses Ouvrieres No. 118 (1956): 84-91.

6651. Belguendouz, Abdelkrim. "Les determinants de la colonisation du Maroc, le devenir du secteur agraire colonial, et la gauche marocaine." Revue Juridique, Politique et Economique du Maroc (1982): 207-307.

6652. Bennani, Boubker. L'islamisme et les droits de l'homme. Lausanne: Editions de l'Aire, 1984.

6653. Bidwell, Robin. Morocco Under Colonial Rule: French Administration of Tribal Areas, 1912-1956. London: Cass, 1973.

6654. Davis, Susan S. The Determinants of Social Position Among Rural Moroccan Women. Trenton, NJ: 1975.

6655. Davis, Susan S. Patience and Power: The Lives of Moroccan Village Women. Cambridge, MA: Schenkman, 1983.

6656. Dwyer, Daisy H. Images and Self-Images: Male and Female in Morocco. New York: Columbia University Press, 1978.

6657. Dwyer, Daisy H. "Values about Self and Other: Fields of Stereotypes and Political Cognition." In The Content of Culture: Constants and Variants, edited by Ralph Bolton. New Haven, CT: Human Relations Area Files P, 1989.

6658. Enmaji, M. "What Future for Morocco's Poor?" Ceres 19 (1986): 42-45.

6659. Goldberg, Harvey E. "The Mimuna and the Minority Status of Moroccan Jews." Ethnology 17 75-88 (January 1978)

6660. Hamman, A. L'Influence de la penetration francaise sur la situation economique et politique du Maroc de 1830 a 1880. These de IIIe cycle: University of Toulouse, 1987.

6661. Hoffman, Bernard G. The Structure of Traditional Moroccan Rural Society. The Hague: Mouton, 1967.

6662. Juifs de Maroc. Grenoble: 1981,

6663. Kenbib, Mohammed. "Les juifs de Tetouan entre la chronique et l'histoire." Hesperis-Tamuda 24 (1986): 273-299.

6664. Kenbib, Mohammed. "Les relations entre musulmans et juifs au Maroc, 1859-1945." Hesperis Tamuda 23 (1985): 83-104.

6665. Laskier, Michael M. "Jewish Emancipation from Morocco to Israel: Government Policies and the Position of International Jewish Organizations, 1949-1956." Middle Eastern Studies 25 (July 1989)

6666. Laskier, Michael M. "Zionism and the Jewish Communities of Morocco: 1956-1962." Studies in Zionism 6 (1985): 119-138.

6667. Mernissi, Fatima. Beyond the Veil: Male-Female Dynamics in a Modern Muslim State. New York: Halsted Press, 1975.

6668. Mernissi, Fatima. "The Degrading Effect of Capitalism on Female Economy." Peuples mediterranean (January-March 1979): 41-57.

6669. Mourad, K. E. "The Origins of the Moroccan Bourgeoisie." International Journal of Politics (Fall 1977): 88-99.

6670. Mrabet, Mohammed. Look and Move On: An Autobiography As Told to Paul Bowles. Translated by Paul Bowles. London: Peter Owen, 1989.

6671. Munson, Henry. "The Social Base of Islamic Militancy in Morocco." Middle East Journal 40 (Spring 1986): 267-284.

6672. Oved, Georges. La gauche francaise et le nationalisme marocain, 1905-1955. 2 vols. Paris: Editions l'Harmattan, 1984.

6673. Oved, Georges. "Luttes de class et privileges nationaux dans les dernieres annees du Protectorat Marocain." R. fr. hist. outre-mer 70 (1983): 151-178.

6674. Park, Thomas. "Essaouira: The Formation of the New Elite, 1940-1980." African Studies Review 31 (December 1988): 111- 132.

6675. Pennell, C. R. "Women and Resistance to Colonialism in Morocco: The Rif 1916-1926." Journal of African History 28 (1987): 107-118.

6676. Romanelli, Samuel A. Travail In An Arab Land. Translated by Yedida K. Stillman and Norman A. Stillman. Tuscaloosa: University of Alabama, 1989. [Jews in Morocco, early 19th century.]

6677. Salmi, Jamil. "Language and Schooling in Morocco." International Journal of Educational Development 7 (1987): 21-31.

6678. Sundiata, I. K. "Beyond Race and Colour in Islam." Journal of Ethnic Studies, edited by 6 (Spring 1978): 1-23.

6679. Zartman, I. William, ed. The Political Economy of Morocco. New York: Praeger, 1987.

MOZAMBIQUE

6680. Arnfeld, Signe. "Women in Mozambique: Gender Struggle and Politics." R. Afric. Pol. Ec. (September 1988): 5-16.

6681. Azvedo, Mario J. "The Legacy of Colonial Education in Mozambique (1876-1976)." A Current Bibliography on African Affairs 11 (1978-1979): 3-16.

6682. Braganca, Aquino de and Jacques Depelchin. "From the Idealization of Frelimo to the Understanding of Mozambique Recent History." Review 11 (Winter 1988): 95-117.

6683. Cahen, Michel. Mozambique: la révolution implosée: études sur 12 ans d'independence (1975-1987). Paris: Editions l'Harmattan, 1987.

6684. Campbell, Gwyn. "The East African Slave Trade, 1861-1895: The 'Southern' Complex." International Journal African Historical Studies 22 (1989): 1-26.

6685. Cliff, Julie and others. "Mozambique Health Holding the Line." Review of Radical Political Economy 7-23 (September 1986)

6686. Correia, Alamir A. "Education as a Factor in the Process of National Consciousness in Mozambique." Lusophone Area Studies Journal 100-115 (June 1985)

6687. Cross, Michael. "The Political Economy of Colonial Education: Mozambique, 1930-1975." Comparative Education Review 31 (November 1987): 550-569.

6688. Demele, Isolde. "Bildung und Gesellschaft in Mosambik. Koloniale und nachkoloniale Strukturen." Afrika Spectrum 20 (1985): 67-82.

6689. Egero, Bertil. *Mozambique: A Dream Undone: The Political Economy of Democracy, 1975-1984*. Uppsala, Sweden: Nordiska Afrikainstitetet, 1987.

6690. First, Ruth. *Black God: The Mozambique Miner, Proletarian and Peasant*. New York: St. Martin's Press, 1983.

6691. Friedland, Elaine. "Mozambique National Resistance, 1920- 1940." *Transafrica Journal History* 8 (1979): 117-128.

6692. Hall, Margaret. "The Mozambican National Resistance Movement (RENAMO): A Study in the Destruction of an African Country." *Africa* 60 (1990)

6693. Hermele, Kenneth. *Land Struggles and Social Differentiation in Southern Mozambique: A Case Study of Chokwe, Limpopo, 1950-1987*. Uppsala: Scandanavian Institute of African Studies, 1988.

6694. Isaacman, Allen. "Colonial Mozambique, an Inside View: The Life History of Raul Honwana." *Cah Ét. Afric.* 28 (1988): 59-88.

6695. Issacman, Allen and Barbara Issacman. *Mozambique: From Colonialism to Revolution, 1900-1982*. Boulder, CO: Westview, 1983.

6696. Magaia, Lina. *Dumba Nengue: Run for Your Life-Peasant Tales of Tragedy in Mozambique*. Trenton, NJ: Africa World Press, 1988.

6697. Mondlane, Eduardo C. "Race Relations and Portuguese Colonial Policy, with Special Reference to Mozambique." *Objective: Justice* 1 (1969)

6698. Searle, Chris. "École nouvelle au Mozambique: le changement au quotidian." *Environment Afric. Ser. Et. Rech.* (October 1984): 3-103.

6699. Urdang, Stephanie. "Concerning Women in Mozambique." *Ufahamu* 11 (Spring 1982): 40-48.

6700. Vail, Leroy and Landeg White. *Capitalism in Mozambique*. Minneapolis: University of Minnesota Press, 1984. [Quelimane District.]

6701. Verschuur, Christine and others. *Mozambique, dix ans de solitude*. Paris: Editions l'Harmattan, 1986.

MYANMAR

6702. Aung-Thwin, Michael. "The British 'Pacification' of Burma: Order without Meaning." Journal of Southeast Asian Studies 16 (1985): 245-261.

6703. Aung-Thwin, Michael. "Hierarchy and Order in Pre-Colonial Burma." Journal South East Asian Studies 15 (September 1984): 224-232.

6704. Boucaud, Andre and Louis Boucaud. Birmanie: sur la piste des seigneurs de la guerre. Paris: Editions l'Harmattan, 1985. [Minority insurgents in Burma.]

6705. Clifford, Robert L. "The Rise and Fall of British Investment in Burma." Asian Affairs 62 (1975): 196-203.

6706. Crossette, Barbara. "Long-Running Revolt Is Being Run Out of Burma." New York Times, (November 8, 1985)

6707. Dettmer, K. M. Christianizing the Karen and Karenizing Christianity: The Political Economy of Colonial Burma. Master's thesis: Arizona State University, Tempe, 1987.

6708. Kanbawza Win. "Education in the Socialist Republic of the Union of Burma." Asian Pac. 2 16 (Spring 1984): 52-59.

6709. Khaing, Mi Mi. The World of Burmese Women. London: Zed, 1984.

6710. Lehman, F. K. "Freedom and Bondage in Traditional Burma and Thailand." Journal South East Asian Studies 15 (September 1984): 233-244.

6711. Lieberman, Victor B. "Reinterpreting Burmese History." Comparative Studies in Society and History 29 (1987): 162- 194.

6712. Ling, Trevor. "Religious Minorities in Burma in the Contemporary Period." Ethnic Studies Report (Sri Lanka) 3 (July 1985)

6713. Lissak, Moshe. "The Class Structure of Burma: Continuity and Change." Journal of Southeast Asian Studies 1 (1970): 60-73.

6714. Marks, Thomas A. "The Karen Revolt in Burma." Issues and Studies 14 (1978): 48-84.

6715. Maung, Mya. "The Burma Road to Poverty: A Socio-political Analysis." Fletcher Forum of World Affairs 13 (Summer 1989): 271-294.

6716. Mirante, E. T. "The Victim Zone: Recent Accounts of Burmese Military Human Rights Abuse in the Shan State." Contemporary Crises 13 (September 1989)

6717. Mya Sein, Daw. "Towards Independence in Burma: The Role of Women." Asian Affairs 59 (1972): 288-299.

6718. Myint, Ni Ni. Burma's Struggle Against British Imperialism. Rangoon: Universities Press, 1983.

6719. Razvi, Mujtaba. "The Problem of the Burmese Muslims." Pakistan Horizon 31 (1978): 82-93. [Western Burma.]

6720. Selth, Andrew. "Race and Resistance in Burma, 1942-1945." Modern Asian Studies 20 (July 1986): 483-507. [Japanese occupation during World War II.]

6721. Silverstein, Josef. Burmese Politics: The Dilemma of National Unity. New Brunswick, NJ: Rutgers University Press, 1980.

6722. Silverstein, Josef, ed. Independent Burma at Forty Years: Six Assessments. Ithaca, NY: Southeast Asia Program, 1989.

6723. Sulak, Sivaraksa. "The Minorities of Siam and Burma." Solidarity 121 (January-March 1989): 65-74.

6724. Taylor, Robert H. "Party, Class and Power in British Burma." Journal of Commonwealth and Comparative Politics 19 (1981)

6725. Taylor, Robert H. "Perceptions of Ethnicity in the Politics of Burma." Southeast Asian Journal of Social Science 10 (1982): 7-22.

6726. Taylor, Robert H. The State in Burma. Honolulu: University of Hawaii Press, 1987.

NAMIBIA

6727. Andersson, Neil and Shula Marks. "Work and Health in Namibia: Preliminary Notes." Journal of Southern African Studies 13 (1987): 274-292.

6728. Berat, Lynn. Walvis Bay and the Decolonization of International Law. Doctoral dissertation: Yale University, 1988. UMO # 9009399.

6729. Booh, Jacques-Roger. La decolonisation de la Nambie: un mandat usurpe. Paris: Les Publications universitaires, 1982.

6730. Campaign Against the Namibian Uranium Contracts Group. Namibia- A Contract to Kill. London: 1986.

6731. Cassidy, Bryan. "A Transition to Fairness." Times Educational Supplement, (October 25, 1985)

6732. Coslett, C. "The Economics of 'Illegal' Development: International Law and Natural Resource Exploitation in Namibia, 1966-1986." Journal of International Affairs 41 (Summer-Fall, 1987): 165-192.

6733. Cronje, Gillian and Suzanne Cronje. The Workers of Namibia. London: International Defence and Aid Fund, 1979.

6734. Dale, Richard. "African Resistance to German and South African Rule in Namibia, 1904-1907 and 1922: Its Significance for Subsequent African Nationalism and Protracted Guerilla War." Africana Journal 14 (1987): 302-322.

6735. Drechsler, H. Let Us Die Fighting. Chicago, IL: Imported Publications, Inc., [History of German colonialism in South West Africa in late 19th century.]

6736. First, Ruth. South West Africa. Baltimore,MD: Penguin, 1963.

6737. Fraenkel, Peter and Roger Murray. The Namibians. new ed. London: Minority Rights Group, 1985.

6738. Gottschalk, Keith. "The Political Economy of Health Care: Colonial Namibia, 1915-1961." Social Science Medicine 26 (1988): 577-582.

6739. Gottschalk, Keith. "South African Labour Policy in Namibia 1915-1975." South African Labour Bulletin 4 (1978)

6740. Green, Reginald H. and others, eds. Namibia, the Last Colony. New York: Longman, 1981.

6741. Grovogui, Siba N'Zatioula. Conflicting Selves in International Law: An Analysis of Colonialism and Decolonization in Namibia. Doctoral dissertation: University of Wisconsin, 1988. UMO # 8901166.

6742. Haarhoff, Dorian. "Fighting and Writing: The Origins of Indigenous Namibian Literature." Current Writing: Text and Reception in Southern Africa 1 (October 1989): 89-101.

6743. Harneit-Sievers, Axel. SWAPO of Namibia: Entwicklung, Programatik und Politik seit 1959. Hamburg: Institut fur Afrikakunde, 1985.

6744. Katjavivi, Peter H. A History of Resistance in Namibia. London: James Currey, 1988.

6745. Khalifa, Ahmad M. Adverse Consequences for the Enjoyment of Human Rights of Political, Military, Economic, and Other Forms of Assistance Given to the Racist and Colonialist Regime of South Africa. New York: 1985.

6746. Lau, Brigitte. "Conflict and Power in Nineteenth-century Namibia." Journal of African History 27 (1986): 29-40.

6747. Mbuende, Kaire. Namibia, the Broken Shield: Anatomy of Imperialism and Revolution. Malmo, Sweden: Liber Forlag, 1986.

6748. Mbumba, Nangolo and Norbert H. Noisset. Namibia in History, Junior Secondary History Book. London: Zed Books, 1989.

6749. Melber, Henning, ed. Our Namibia. A Social Studies Textbook. London: Zed, 1986.

6750. Moorehead, Caroline. Namibia, Apartheid's Forgotten Children. Oxford, England: Oxfam Publications, 1988.

6751. Moorson, R. G. B. The Political Economy of Namibia to 1945. Master's thesis: University of Sussex, 1973.

6752. Nambala, Shekutaamba V. "From Colonialism to Nationalism in Namibia." Lutheran Quarterly 2 (1988): 391-418.

6753. Nambala, Shekutaamba V. "Namibia." Lutheran Quarterly 1 (1987): 249-306, 513-569. [2 parts.]

6754. Nambala, Shekutaamba V. "Namibian Churches under Colonialism." Lutheran Quarterly 2 (1988): 245-269.

6755. Namibia Support Committee, ed. Namibia 1884-1984: Readings on Namibia's History and Society. New York: United Nations, 1988.

6756. "Namibia: die Aktualität des Kolonialen Verhältnisses." Diskurs (Bremen) No. 6 (August 1982): 5-276.

6757. "A Nation in Peril: Health in Apartheid." Fact Pop. S. Africa (May 1985): 1-35.

6758. O'Callaghan, Marion. Namibia: The Effects of Apartheid on Culture and Education. Paris: UNESCO, 1977.

6759. Pfouts, Anita. "Changing Times: Women in Namibia." Ufahamee 11 (Spring 1982): 49-60.

6760. Pickering, A. Law, State and Social Control in Contemporary Namibia. L L.M. thesis: University of Warwick, 1983.

6761. Pierard, Richard V. "The Transportation of White Women to German Southwest Africa, 1898-1914." Race 12 (January 1971): 317-322.

6762. Plunder of Namibian Uranium: Major Findings of the Hearings on Namibian Uranium held by the United Nations Council for Namibia in July 1980. New York: United Nations, 1982.

6763. Sparks, Donald L. Namibia's Future: The Economy at Independence. London: Economist Intelligence Unit, 1985.

6764. Sudholt, Gert. Die deutsche Eingeborenenpolitik in Südwestafrika. Hildesheim: Olms, 1975.

6765. SWAPO Women's Solidarity Campaign. "Class, Gender & Race: Women in Namibia." Journal of African Marxists (January 1986): 43-74.

6766. Totemeyer, G. and others, eds. Namibia in Perspective. Windhoek: Angelus Press, 1987.

6767. Ulenga, Ben and Barnabas Tjizu. "Namibia: Economics and Racism- The Workers' Perspective." PCR Information (World Council of Churches) No. 24 (1987): 19-23. [Interview by Eva Militz.]

6768. Veiter, Theodor. "Die heutige Lage der deutschen Volksgruppe in Südwestafrika/Namibia." Europa Ethnica 43 (1986): 139-141.

6769. Voeltz, Richard A. German Colonialism and the South West Africa Company, 1884-1914. Athens: Ohio University Press, 1988.

6770. Wallace, Marion. Namibia: Women in War. Atlantic Highlands, NJ: Zed Books, 1990.

6771. Working under South African Occupation- Labour in Namibia. London: International Defence and Aid, 1987.

6772. "Working Under South African Occupation: Labour in Namibia." Fact Pap. S. Africa No. 14 (1987): 5-56.

6773. Ya Otto, J. Battlefront Namibia- An Autobiogrpahy. London: Heinemann, 1981.

NEPAL

6774. Ansar, Tahir A. "The Muslim Minority in Nepal: A Socio-Historical Perspective." Jr. Inst. Muslim Minority Affairs 9 (January 1988): 159-166.

6775. Ashby, Jacqueline A. "Equity and Discrimination among Children: Schooling Decisions in Rural Nepal." Comparative Education Review 29 (February 1985): 68-79.

6776. Crossette, Barbara. "A Town So Old, Commmunism Is Hope of Future." New York Times, (January 19, 1991) [Bungamati, Nepal.]

6777. Jamison, D. T. and M.E. Lockheed. "Participation in Schooling: Determinants and Learning Outcomes in Nepal." Economic Development and Cultural Change 35 (January 1987)

6778. Moock, P. R. and J. Leslie. "Childhood Malnutrition and Schooling in the Terai Region of Nepal." Journal of Development Economics 20 (January-February 1986)

6779. Sharma, P. R. "Nepali Culture and Society: A Historical Perspective." Contrib. Nepalese Studies 10 (December 1982- June 1983): 1-20.

6780. Shrestha, Gajendra M. and others. "Determinants of Educational Participation in Rural Nepal." Comparative Educational Review 30 (November 1986): 508-522.

6781. Upodhyay, Ram Raj. Socio-economic and Background Factors and Educational Opportunity: An Educational Case Study of Birganj, Nepal. Doctoral dissertatioon: University of Connecticut, 1987. UMO # 8728907.

NETHERLANDS

6782. Aalberts, Monique M. J. *The Police between Discretion and Discrimination: Internal Immigration Controls in the Netherlands*. Doctoral dissertation: University of Rotterdam, 1990. [In Dutch.]

6783. Amersfoort, Hans van and Surie Boudewijn. "Reluctant Hosts: Immigration into Dutch Society 1970-1985." *Ethnic and Racial Studies* 10 (1987): 169-185.

6784. Aymard, Maurice, ed. *Dutch Capitalism and World Capitalism*. New York: Cambridge University Press, 1982.

6785. Bakker, A. M. van der and R.W. Boesjes-Hommes. "Woman and Education in the Netherlands." *Society and Leisure* 6 (1974): 7-28.

6786. Bakvis, Herman. "Toward a Political Economy of Consociationalism: A Commentary on Marxist Views of Pillarization in the Netherlands." *Comp. Pol.* 16 (1984): 315-334.

6787. Barbour, Violet. *Capitalism in Amsterdam in the Seventeenth Century*. Baltimore: Johns Hopkins University Press, 1950.

6788. Barker, Ralph. *Not Here, But in Another Place*. New York: St. Martin's Press, 1980. [South Moluccans in the Netherlands.]

6789. Bartels, Dieter. "Can the Train Ever be Stopped Again? Developments in the Moluccan Community in the Netherlands before and after the Hijackings." *Indonesia* 41 (April 1986): 23-45.

6790. Bax, Erik H. *Modernization and Cleavage in Dutch Society*. Avebury: 1990.

6791. Bleich, Anet and others. *Nederlands racisme*. Amsterdam: Van Gennep, 1984.

NETHERLANDS 519

6792. Blom, J. C. H. "The Persecution of the Jews in the Netherlands: A Comparative Western European Perspective." Eur. Hist. Quarterly 19 (1989): 333-351.

6793. Boas, Jacob H. Boulevard des Miseres. The Story of Transit Camp Westerbork. Hamden, CT: Archon Books/The Shoe String Press, 1985. [Jews in World War II Netherlands.]

6794. Boissevain, Jeremy and Hanneke Grotenberg. "Culture, Structure and Ethnic Enterprise: The Surinamese of Amsterdam." Ethnic & Racial Studies 9 (1986): 1-23.

6795. Boogaart, Ernst van den. "Colour Prejudice and the Yardstick of Civility: The Initial Dutch Confrontation with Black Africans, 1590-1635." In Racism and Colonialism Robert Ross (ed.). The Hague: Martimus Nyhoff, 1982.

6796. Bovenkerk, Frank. "The Netherlands As a Multi-Racial Society. A Bibliography." Translated by Peter McCaffery. Sage Race Relations Abstracts 2 (March 1977): 1-9.

6797. Brock, Colin, ed. The Caribbean in Europe: Aspects of the West Indian Experience in Britain, France, and the Netherlands. Totowa, NJ: Frank Cass, 1987.

6798. Crone, Michael. Hilversum unter dem Hakenkreuz: die Rundfunkpolitik der Nationalsozialisten in den besetzten Niederlanden, 1940-1945. Munich: K.G. Saur, 1983.

6799. Crone, Michael. Die Rundfunkpolitik der Nationalsozialisten in den besetzten Niederlanden in den Jahren 1940- 1945. Doctoral dissertation: University of Münster, 1983.

6800. Cross, Malcolm and Hans Entzinger, eds. Lost Illusions: Caribbean Minorities in Britain and the Netherlands. London: Routledge, 1988.

6801. Custers, Martin. "Muslims in the Netherlands: Newcomers in an Established Society." Journal of the Institute of Muslim Minority Affairs 6 (1985): 167-180.

6802. Daalder, H. "Dutch Jews in a Segmented Society." Acta Hist. Neerlandica 10 (1978): 175-194.

6803. De Jong, Louis. The Netherlands and Nazi Germany. Cambridge, MA: Harvard University Press, 1990.

6804. De Jong, Mart-Jan. "Ethnic Origin and Educational Careers in Holland." Netherlands Journal of Sociology 24 (1988): 65-75.

6805. De Jongh, R. J. "Solidarity in Exchange for Adaptation: Dutch Trade Unionism and Immigrant Workers." International Migration Review 19 (1985): 760-767.

6806. De Vries, Petra. "Feminism in the Netherlands." In The Women's Liberation Movement, edited by Jan Bradshaw. 389-407. New York: Pergamon Press, 1982.

6807. Domingo, Vernon A. The Underdevelopment of Ex-Colonial Immigrants in Metropolitan Society: A Study of Surinamers in the Netherlands. Doctoral dissertation: Clark University, 1980. UMO # 8027961.

6808. Driehuis, W. "Unemployment in the Netherlands, 1960-1983." Economica 53 (1986): Supplement.

6809. No entry

6810. Eisinga, R. and others. "Church Involvement, Prejudice and Nationalism: A Research on the Curvilinear Relationship between Church Involvement and Ethnocentrism in the Netherlands." Review of Religious Research 31 (June 1990)

6811. Elich, Joed H. "Netherlands." In International Handbook on Race and Race Relations, edited by Jay A. Sigler. Westport, CT: Greenwood, 1987.

6812. Ellemers, J. E. "Minorities and Policy-Making in the Netherlands: South Moluccans and Other Aliens in Comparative Perspective." Netherlands Journal of Socialism 15 (1979): 97-122.

6813. Ellen, Roy F. "The Development of Anthropology and Colonial Policy in the Netherlands, 1880-1960." Journal of the History of Behavioral Sciences 12 (1976): 303-324.

6814. Entzinger, H. B. "Race, Class and the Shaping of a Policy for Immigrants: The Case of the Netherlands." International Migration 25 (March 1987): 5-20.

6815. Essed, Philomena. "Black Women in White Women's Organizations: Ethnic Differentiation and Problems of Racism in the Netherlands." Resources for Feminist Research 18 (December 1989): 10-15.

6816. Essed, Philomena. Everyday Racism: Reports from Women of Two Cultures. Claremont, CA: Hunder House, 1989. [Netherlands and USA.]

6817. Ester, P. and A.P.N. Nauta. "A Decade of Social and Cultural Reports on the Netherlands." Netherlands Journal of Sociology 22 (1986): 72-86.

6818. Fishman, Joel S. "The Jewish Community in Postwar Netherlands." Midstream 22 (1976): 42-54.

6819. Fishman, Joel S. "The Reconstruction of the Dutch Jewish Community and Its Implications for the Writing of Contemporary Jewish History." In *American Academy for Jewish Research Proceedings* (1978) 67-101. 1978.

6820. Franke, H. "Dutch Tolerance-Facts and Fables." *British Journal of Criminology* 30 (Winter 1990)

6821. Friedhoff, Herman. *Requiem for the Resistance: The Civilian Struggle against Nazism in Holland and Germany*. London: Bloomsbury, 1989.

6822. Geurts, P. A. T.M. and G.P.A. Braam. "Changes in Occupational Stratification in the Netherlands." *Netherlands Journal of Sociology* 20 (1984): 150-167.

6823. Goslinga, C. C. *The Dutch in the Caribbean and in the Guianas, 1680-1791*. Wolfeboro, NH: Longwood, 1985.

6824. Goudsblom, Johan. *Dutch Society*. New York: Random House, 1967.

6825. Goudswaard, Keej and P. De Jong. "The Distributional Impact of Current Income Transfer Policies in the Netherlands." *Journal of Social Policy* 14 (1985): 367-383.

6826. Graaf, Paul M. de and Harry B.G. Ganzeboom. "Intergenerational Educational Mobility in the Netherlands for Birth Cohorts from 1891-1960." *Netherlands Journal of Social Science* 26 (April 1990)

6827. Hagendoorn, Louk and J. Hanssen. "Right Wing Views among Dutch School Pupils." *Netherlands Journal of Sociology* 22 (1986): 87-91.

6828. Hagendorn, Louk and Joseph Hraba. "Social Distance toward Holland's Minorities: Discrimination against and among Ethnic Outgroups." *Ethnic and Racial Studies* 10 (1987): 317-333.

6829. Haleber, Ron. "L'alienation croissante du migrant marocain dans la societe hollandaise." *Economie et Socialisme* No. 8 (1988): 65-89.

6830. Hansen, Erick. "Fascism and Nazism in the Netherlands, 1929-1939." *European Studies Review* 11 (1981): 355-385.

6831. Hingstman, L. and H. Boon. "Regional Dispersion of Independent Professionals in Primary Health Care in the Netherlands." *Social Science Medicine* 28 (1989): 121-129.

6832. Hirschfeld, Gerhard. *Nazi Rule and Dutch Collaboration. The Netherlands under German Occupation*. Translated by Louise Wilmont. New York: St. Martin's Press, 1987.

6833. Hogeweg de Haart, H. P. "The History of the Women's Movement in the Netherlands." *Netherlands Journal of Sociology* 14 (1978): 19-40.

6834. Hondius, Dienke. Antisemitisme in Nederland vlak na de bevrijding. Doctoral dissertation: University of Amsterdam, 1988.

6835. Hooghoff, Hans. "Government Policy and Curriculum Development with an Intercultural Perspective: The Netherlands, a Multi-Ethnic Society." In Education for Democratic Citizenship. A Challenge for Multi-Ethnic Societies, edited by Roberta S. Sigel and Marilyn Hoskin. Hillsdale, NJ: Lawrence Erlbaum Assoiates, 1990.

6836. Hooghoff, Hans. "Social and Political Education in the Netherlands." International Schulbuchforschung 8 (1986): 47-59.

6837. Hraba, Joseph and others. "The Ethnic Hierarchy in the Netherlands: Social Distance and Social Representation." British Journal of Social Psychology 28 (March 1989): 57- 69.

6838. Huijsman, R. and others. "An Empirical Analysis of College Enrollment in the Netherlands." De Economist 134 (1986)

6839. James, Estelle. "Benefits and Costs of Privatized Services: Lessons from the Dutch Educational System." Comparative Education Review 28 (1984): 605-624.

6840. Jong, Wiebe de. "The Development of Inter-Ethnic Relations in an Old District of Rotterdam between 1970 and 1985." Ethnic and Racial Studies 12 (April 1989): 257-278.

6841. Jungbluth, Paul. "Covert Sex Role Socialization in Dutch Education. A Survey among Teachers." Netherlands Journal of Sociology 20 (1984): 43-57.

6842. Junger, Marianne. "Intergroup Bullying and Racial Harassment in the Netherlands." Sociology and Social Research 74 (1990): 65-72.

6843. Karsten, Sjoerd and Y. Leeman. "Holland in Surinam, Surinamese in Holland." Compare 18 (1988): 63-77.

6844. Keller, Wouter J. and others. "Real Income Changes of Households in the Netherlands, 1977-1983." Review of Income and Wealth 33 (September 1987): 257-271.

6845. Khleif, Bud B. "Issues of Theory and Methodology in the Study of Ethnolinguistic Movements: The Case of Frisian Nationalism in the Netherlands." In New Nationalisms of the Developed West: Toward Explanation, edited by Edward A. Tiryakian and Ronald Ragowski. Boston: Allen & Unwin, 1985.

6846. Koot, William C. J. and others. "Processes of Ethnic Identification among Surinamese Children in the Netherlands." In The Caribbean in Europe, edited by Colin Brock. London: Frank Cass, 1986.

6847. Koot, William C. J. and others. Surinaanse kinderen op school. Muiderberg, Netherlands: Coutinho, 1986.

6848. Kornalijnslijper, Nora and Wasif Shadid. "Immigrants and Housing in the Netherlands." New Community 13 (1987): 421- 430.

6849. Kriesi, Hanspeter. "New Social Movements and the New Class in the Netherlands." American Journal of Sociology 94 (1989): 1078-1116.

6850. Kuietenbromer, Maarten. The Netherlands and the Rise of Modern Imperialism. Colonies and Foreign Policy, 1870-1902. Translated by High Beyer: Berg, 1991.

6851. Kwiet, Konrad. "Zur Geschichte der Mussertbewegung." Vierteljahreshefte fur Zeitgeschichte 18 (1970): 165-195. [Native fascist movement in Netherlands, 1918-1945.]

6852. Maassen, Gerard and Martijnde Golde. "Public Opinion About Unemployed People in the Period 1975-1985; the Case of the Netherlands." The Netherlands Journal of Social Sciences 25 (October 1989)

6853. Mackenboch, J. P. "Health Care Policy and Regional Epidemiology: International Comparison and a Case-Study from the Netherlands." Soc. Sci. Med. 24 (1987): 247-253.

6854. Marshall, A. The Import of Labour: The Case of the Netherlands. Rotterdam: Rotterdam University Press, 1973.

6855. Mason, Henry L. The Purge of Dutch Quislings: Emergency Justice in the Netherlands. The Hague: 1952.

6856. Mason, Henry L. "Testing Human Bonds within Nations: Jews in the Occupied Netherlands." Political Science Quarterly 99 (1984): 315-343.

6857. Michman, Joseph. "The Controversy Surrounding the Jewish Council of Amsterdam." In Patterns of Jewish Leadership in Nazi Europe, 1933-1945, edited by Y. Gutman and C.J. Haft. Jerusalem: 1979.

6858. Michman, Joseph, ed. Dutch Jewish History. Vol. 2. Jerusalem: Institute for Research on Dutch Jewry, 1989.

6859. Michman, Joseph. "Joodse Raad." In Encyclopedia of the Holocaust. New York: Macmillan, 1990.

6860. Michman, Joseph. "The Netherlands." In Encyclopedia of the Holocaust. 1045-1057. New York: Macmillan, 1990.

6861. Michman, Joseph. "Planning for the Final Solution against the Background of Developments in Holland in 1941." Yad Vashem Studies 17 (1986): 145-180.

6862. Michman, Joseph. "Some Reflections on the Dutch Churches and the Jews." In Judaism and Christianity under the Impact of National Socialism, 1919-1945, edited by Otto Dov Kulka and Paul R. Mendes-Flohr. Jerusalem: Historical Society of Israel, 1987.

6863. Moore, Bob. "Nazism and German Nationals in the Netherlands, 1933-1940." Journal of Contemporary History 22 (1987): 45-70.

6864. Muus, P. J. Migration, Minorities and Policy in the Netherlands: Recent Trends and Developments. Amsterdam: Institute for Social Geography, University of Amsterdam, November 1986.

6865. Netherlands Scientific Council for Government Policy (WRR). Ethnic Minorities. The Hague: State Publishing Office, 1979. [Report No. 17.]

6866. Oomens, C. A. and T. Palthe. "The Distribution of Income between Socio-Economic Groups in the Netherlands." Review of Income and Wealth 16 (December 1970): 353-362.

6867. Paape, A. H. "Le mouvement national-socialiste en Hollande: aspects politiques et historiques." R. d'Hist. de la Deuxieme Guerre Mondiale 17 (1967): 31-60.

6868. Paldiel, Mordecai. "Douwes, Arnold." In Encyclopedia of the Holocaust, I. 401-402. New York: Macmillan, 1990.

6869. Pen, Jan. "A Clear Case of Leveling: Income Equalization in the Netherlands." Social Research 46 (Winter 1979)

6870. Penninx, Rinus. "Ethnic Groups in the Netherlands- Emancipation or Minority Group-Formation." Ethnic and Racial Studies 12 (January 1989)

6871. Penninx, Rinus. Ethnic Minorities, a Report to the Government and Towards and Overall Ethnic Minorities Policy. Netherlands Scientific Council for Government Policy, 1979.

6872. Penninx, Rinus. Migration, Minorities and Policy in the Netherlands: Recent Trends and Developments. Rijswijk: Social Research Bureau, 1983.

6873. Pennix, M. J. A. "The Contours of a General Minorities Policy." Planning and Development in the Netherlands 13 (1981): 5-25.

6874. Presser, J. Downfall: The Persecution and Extermination of the Dutch Jewish Community 1940-1945. Hague, Netherlands: National Institute of War Archives, 1965.

6875. Priemus, Hugo. "Housing Policy and Economic Stagnation: The Case of the Netherlands." In Housing and Neighborhoods, edited by William van Vliet and others. Westport, CT: Greenwood, 1987.

6876. Rath, Jan. "Political Action of Immigrants in the Netherlands: Class or Ethnicity?" European Journal of Policy Research 16 (1988): 623-544.

6877. Rietveld, P. and H. Ouwersloot. "Intraregional Income Distribution and Poverty: Some Investigations for the Netherlands, 1960-1981." Environment and Planning A 21 (July 1989)

6878. Rijk, Tineke. "Women at Work in Holland." In Working Women, An International Survey, edited by Marilyn J. Davidson and Cary L. Cooper. 83-102. New York: Wiley, 1984.

6879. Rupps, J. C. C. and A.A. Wesselingh. "Education, Social Inequality and Citizenship: An Overview of 25 Years of Research and Theoretical Development in The Netherlands." Netherlands Journal of Social Science 26 (October 1990)

6880. Scheepers, Peer and others. "Ethnocentrism in the Netherlands: A Typological Analysis." Ethnic and Racial Studies 12 (1989): 289-308.

6881. Schenk, Magdalena G. Women in the Netherlands Past and Present. Bearn, Holland: World's Window Ltd., 1956.

6882. Schoffer, I. "The Jews in the Netherlands: The Position of a Minority through Three Centuries." Studia Rosenthaliana 15 (1981)

6883. Schoonboom, I. J. and H. M. Int. Veld-Langeveld. "Values Affecting Women's Position in Society." Planning and Development in the Netherlands 8 (1976): 17-33.

6884. Schutte, Gerritt J. "The Netherlands, Cradle of Apartheid?" Ethnic Racial Studies 10 (1987): 392-414.

6885. Sijes, B. A. "The Position of the Jews During the German Occupation of the Netherlands: Some Observations." Acta Historiae Neerlandicae 11 (1976): 170-192.

6886. Stein, Andre. Quiet Heroes, True Stories of the Rescue of the Jews by Christians in Nazi-Occupied Holland. New York: New York University Press, 1989.

6887. Stein, Richard A. "Antisemitism in the Netherlands-Past and Present." Patterns of Prejudice 19 (January 1985): 17-24.

6888. Steingart-Hollander, Rachel. "A Dutch Lesson." Jerusalem Post, (June 28, 1983) [Resistance to Nazi Policy on Jews in the Netherlands.]

6889. Stokes, L. D. "Anton Mussert and the Nationaal- Socialistische Beweging der Nederlanden, 1931-1945." History 56 (1971): 387-407.

6890. Strikwerda, Carl. "Language and Class Consciousness: Netherlandic Culture and the Flemish Working Class." In Papers from the First Interdisciplinary Conference on Netherlandic Studies, edited by William H. Fletcher. London: 1985.

6891. Szirmai, Adam. Inequality Observed. A Study of Attitudes Towards Income Inequality. Brookfield, Vt.: Gower, 1988.

6892. Tash, Robert C. Verzuiling and Its Social Implications for Dutch Society. Doctoral dissertation: New School for Social Research, 1985. UMO # 8602001.

6893. Tribalat, Michele. "L'Immigration des etrangers aux Pays- Bas." Population 40 (1985): 299-334.

6894. Vallen, Ton and Sjef Stijnen. "Language and Educational Success of Indigenous and Non-indigenous Minority Students in the Netherlands." Language & Education 1 (1987): 109-124.

6895. Van Amersfoort, J. M. M. Immigration and the Formation of Minority Groups. The Dutch Experience 1945-1975. New York: Cambridge Univesity Press, 1982.

6896. Van Dijk, Tenn A. "Elite Discourse and Racism." In Poetics and Psychiatry, edited by Iris M. Zavala and others. Amsterdam: Benjamins, 1987.

6897. Van Dorsten, Jan. "Authority and Tolerance: The Dutch Experience." In High Technology and Human Freedom, edited by Lewis H. Lapham. Washington, D.C.: Smithsoniam Institution, 1986.

6898. Van Hoorn, F. J. J. H. and J.A. Van Ginkel. "Racial Leapfrogging in a Controlled Housing Market. The Case of the Mediteranean Minority in Utrecht, the Netherlands." TESG 77 (1986): 187-196.

6899. Van Mierlo, Hands J. G.A. "Depillarisation and the Decline of Consociationalism in the Netherlands: 1970-1985." W. Eur. Pol. 9 (1986): 97-119.

6900. Van Otterloo, Annekke H. "Foreign Immigrants and the Dutch at Table, 1945-1985. Bridging or Widening the Gap." Netherlands Journal of Sociology 23 (1987): 126-144.

6901. van Roon, Ger. "The Dutch Protestants, The Third Reich and the Persecution of the Jews." In Judaism and Christianity under the Impact of National Socialism, 1919-1945, edited by Otto Dov Kulka and Paul R. Mendes Flohr. Jerusalem: Historical Society of Israel, 1987.

6902. Vanderplank, P. H. "L'ethnicite dans une province peripherique: la Frise." Rech. social. 16 (1985): 129-141.

6903. Veld-Langeveld, H. M. In't. "Woman-Job-Society: An Analysis of a Retarded Emancipation." Sociologia Neerlandica 8 (1972): 64-81.

6904. Verdoner-Sluizer, Hilde and Francisca Verdoner, eds. Signs of Life: The Letters of Hilde Verdoner-Sluizer: From Westerbork Nazi Transit Camp, 1942 to 1944. Washington, D.C.: Acropolis Books, 1990.

6905. Verwey-Jonker, H. "Poverty in the Past and Poverty Today." Neth. J. Sociol. 21 (1985): 99-109.

6906. Voet, J. "Holland's Record vis-a-vis the Jews." Jerusalem Post, (December 26, 1986)

6907. Warmbrunn, Werner. The Dutch under German Occupation: 1940-1945. Stanford, CA.: Stanford University Press, 1963.

6908. Wesseling, H. L. "The Giant That Was a Dwarf, or the Strange History of Dutch Imperialism." In Theory and Practice in the History of European Expansion Overseas, edited by Andrew Porter and Robert Holland. Totowa, NJ: Frank Cass, 1988.

6909. Willems, Fredericus. "Manifestations of Discrimination in the Netherlands." In Foreigners in Our Community, edited by Hans van Houte and Willy Melgert. Amsterdam: Keesing, 1972.

6910. Wilterdink, N. "Property Relations and Wealth Distribution in the Netherlands: Main Developments since the Nineteenth Century." Netherlands Journal of Sociology 21 (1985): 83-98.

6911. With, J. and J. M. Rabbie. "Racist Attitudes about Intimate Relationships between Blacks and Whites in the Netherlands." Gedrag: Tijdschrift voor Psychologie 13 (1985): 10-28.

6912. Wolfson, Dirk Jr. "Controlling the Welfare State: A Case Study of Retrenchment in the Netherlands." Public Finance 42 (1987): 165-180.

NEW ZEALAND

6913. Anderson, Atholl J. "Maori Settlement in the Interior of Southern New Zealand from the Early 18th to the Late 19th Centuries." Journal of the Polynesian Society 91 (1982): 53-80.

6914. Anderson, Christopher. "Aborigines and Tin Mining in north Queensland: A Case Study in the Anthropology of Contact History." Mainland (Sydney) 13 (1983): 473-498.

6915. Armstrong, M. J. "Interethnic Conflict in New Zealand." In Ethnic Conflict. International Perspectives, edited by Jerry Boucher and others. Newbury Park, CA: Sage, 1987.

6916. Armstrong, Warwick. "New Zealand: Imperialism, Class and Uneven Development." Australian and New Zealand Journal of Sociology 14, part 2 (1978): 297-303.

6917. Awatere, Donna. Maori Sovereignty. Auckland: Broadsheet, 1984.

6918. Ballara, Angela. Proud to be White? A Survey of Pakeha Prejudice in New Zealand. Auckland: 1986.

6919. Barrington, J. M. "Maori Schools Policy: A View from the Schools." New Zealand Journal of Educational Studies 20 (1985): 151-164.

6920. Barrington, J. M. and T.H. Beaglehole. Maori Schools in a Changing Society: An Historical Review. Wellington: New Zealand Council for Educational Research, 1974.

6921. Bedggood, David. Rich and Poor in New Zealand: A Critique of Class, Politics, and Ideology. Boston, MA: Allen & Unwin, 1980.

6922. Belich, James. "The Victorian Interpretation of Racial Conflict and the New Zealand Wars: An Approach to the Problem of One-sided Evidence." Journal of Imperial and Commonwealth History 15 (January 1987): 123-147.

6923. Belich, James. The Victorian Interpretation of Racial Conflict: The Maori, the British, and the New Zealand Wars. Montreal: McGill-Queen's University Press, 1989.

6924. Bender, B. Linguistic Factors in Maori Education. Wellington: New Zealand Council for Educational Research, 1971.

6925. Bethune, N. and K.D. Ballard. "Interviews with 50 Young Job Seekers on their Experience of Unemployment." New Zealand Journal of Educational Studies 21 (November 1986)

6926. Binney, Judith. "Some Observations on the Status of Maori Women." New Zealand Journal of History 23 (April 1989): 22- 31.

6927. Blackburn, Alan. Race Against Time. Wellington: Human Rights Commission, 1982. [Maori in New Zealand society.]

6928. Blythe, Martin J. From Maoriland to Aotearoa: Images of the Maori in New Zealand Film and Television. Doctoral dissertation: University of California, Los Angeles, 1988. UMO # 8907579.

6929. Boyd, Mary. "Racial Attitudes of New Zealand Officials in Western Samoa." New Zealand Journal of History 21 (1987): 139-155.

6930. Bray, D. and C. Hill, eds. Polynesian and Pakeha in New Zealand Education. 2 vols. Auckland, NZ: Heinemann, 1973- 1974.

6931. Brosman, Peter and Craig Hill. "New Zealand Maori/Non-Maori Labour Force Income Differentials." Journal of Industrial Relations 25 (September 1983): 327-338.

6932. Buchanan, Anne. "150 Years of White Domination in New Zealand." Race & Class 31 (April-June 1990): 73-80.

6933. Cazden, Courtney B. "Differential Treatment in New Zealand: Reflections on Research in Minority Education." Teaching and Teacher Education 6 (1990)

6934. Cleave, Peter. "Tribal and State-like Political Formations in New Zealand Maori Society, 1750-1900." Journal of Polynesian Society 92 (1983): 51-92.

6935. Courie, J. A. The Effect of Civilization on the Maori Race, with Special Reference to Health and Disease. Doctoral dissertation: University of Glasgow, 1913.

6936. Dale, William S. J. The Maori of New Zealand. A Socio- Educational Study in Race Relations. Doctoral dissertation: Yale University, 1936. UMO # 7002288.

6937. Fairburn, Miles. The Ideal Society and Its Enemy: The Foundations of Modern New Zealand Society, 1850-1900. Auckland University Press: 1989,

6938. Firth, Raymond. Economics of New Zealand Maori. Wellington: Government Printer, 1959.

6939. Fleras, Augie. "Aboriginality as a Language Issue: The Politicization of 'Te Reo Maori' in New Zealand." Plural Societies 17 (September 1987): 25-51.

6940. Fleras, Augie. "From Social Control towards Political Self Determination? Maori Seats and the Politics of Separate Maori Representation in New Zealand." Canadian Journal of Political Science 18 (September 1985): 551-576.

6941. Forster, John. "Maori-White Relations in New Zealand." In Politics of Race-Comparative Studies, edited by Donald G. Baker. Saxon House: D.C. Heath, 1975.

6942. Francis, Elizabeth J. The Residential Location and Mobility of Ethnic Minorities in Auckland. Master's thesis: University of Auckland, 1969.

6943. Frazer, Ian L. Pitcairn Islanders in New Zealand. Master's thesis: University of Otago, 1970.

6944. Gibson, Katherine D. "Political Economy and International Labour Migration: The Case of Polynesians in New Zealand." New Zealand Geographer 39 (April 1983): 29-42.

6945. Goldie, Terry. Fear and Temptation: The Image of the Indigene in Canadian, Australian, and New Zealand Literature. Kingston: McGill-Queen's University Press, 1989.

6946. Gould, John. The Rake's Progress: The New Zealand Economy Since 1945. Auckland: Hodder and Stoughton, 1982. [Chapter on Maori.]

6947. Hamilton, Linda G. The Political Integration of Samoan Immigrants in New Zealand. Master's thesis: University of Canterbury, 1974.

6948. Hanson, Allan. "Making of the Maori: Culture Invention and its Logic." American Anthropologist 91 (1989): 890-902.

6949. Hazelhurst, Kayleen M. Racial Conflict and Resolution in New Zealand: The Haka Party Incident and Its Aftermath 1979- 1980. Canberra: Peace Research Centre, Australian National University.

6950. Higham, Charles. The Maoris. New York: Cambridge University Press, 1981.

6951. Howe, K. R. "On Aborigines and Maoris in Australian and New Zealand Historiography." Int. Hist. Rev. 10 (November 1988): 594-610.

6952. Huttenback, Robert A. Racism and Empire. White Settlers and Colored Immigrants in the British Self-governing Colonies, 1830-1910. Ithaca, New York: Cornell University Press, 1976.

6953. Imhoff, Arthur E. "Der Vorzeitige Tod in Australien und Neuseeland: kein Mysterium, sondern ein Anlass zum Nachdenken." Zeitschrift fur die Bevolkerungswissenschaft: Demographie 12 (1986): 53-97.

6954. "Indian Women in New Zealand." In Learning About Sexism in New Zealand. Wellington: Learmouth Publishers, 1976.

6955. Jackson, Moana. "Criminality and the Exclusion of Maori." Victoria University of Wellington Law Review 20 (February 1990): 23-34.

6956. Jesson, Bruce and others. Revival of the Right: New Zealand Politics in the 1980's. Auckland: Heinemann Reed, 1988.

6957. Kelsey, Jane. "Decolonizing in the First World-Indigenous Peoples' Struggles for Justice and Self-Determination." Windsor Yearbook of Access to Justice 5 (1985): 102-141.

6958. Kelsey, Jane. "Economic Libertarianism versus Maori Self- determination: Aotearoa/New Zealand in Crisis." International Journal of the Sociology of the Law 18 (August 1990): 239- 258.

6959. Kenderdine, Shonagh. "Legal Implications of Treaty Jurisprudence." Victoria University of Wellington Law Review 19 (November 1989): 347-383. [Treaty of Waitangi, New Zealand.]

6960. Kolig, Erich. "Andreas Reischek and the Maori: Villany of the Nineteenth-century Scientific Ethos?" Pacific Studies 10 (November 1986): 55-78.

6961. Laomis, Terrence. Fresh Off the Boat: Pacific Migrant Labour, Class, and Racism in New Zealand. Brookfield, Vt.: Gower, 1990.

6962. Leckie, Jacqueline. "In Defence of Race and Empire: The White New Zealand League at Pukekohe." New Zealand Journal of History 20 (October 1985): 103-129.

6963. Lian, Kwen Fee. "Interpreting Maori History: A Case for Historical Sociology." Journal of the Polynesian Society 96 (1987): 445-471.

6964. Lian, Kwen Fee. "The Sociopolitical Process of Identity Formation in an Ethnic Community: The Chinese in New Zealand." Ethnic and Racial Studies 11 (November 1988): 506-532.

6965. McCulloch G. "Secondary Education without Selection? School Zoning Policy in Auckland since 1945." New Zealand Journal of Educational Studies 21 (November 1986)

6966. MacDonald, Robert. The Maori of New Zealand. London: Minority Rights Group, 1985.

6967. McHugh, P. G. "Aboriginal Servitudes and the Land Transfer Act 1952." Victoria University of Wellington Law Review 16 (1986): 313-335.

6968. McLeay, E. M. "Political Arguments About Representation: The Case of the Maori Seats." Political Studies 28 (March 1980): 43-62.

6969. McRobie, Alan. "Ethnic Representation: The New Zealand Experience." Occasional Paper-University of Waikato, Center for Maori Studies and Research No. 14 (1981): 2-17.

6970. Miller, John. Early Victorian New Zealand: A Study of Racial Tension and Social Attitudes, 1839-1812. Westport, Ct: Greenwood, 1986 (orig. 1958).

6971. Nicolson, Malcolm. "Medicine and Racial Politics: Changing Images of the New Zealand Maori in the Nineteenth Century." In Imperial Medicine and Indigenous Societies, edited by David Arnold. New York: Manchester University Press, 1988.

6972. O'Connor, P. S. "Keeping New Zealand White, 1908-1920." New Zealand Journal of History 2 (April 1968): 41-65.

6973. O'Malley, Patrick. "The Amplification of Maori Crime: Cultural and Economic Barriers to Equal Justice in New Zealand." Race 15 (July 1973): 47-57.

6974. Older, Jules. "Reducing Racial Imbalances in New Zealand Universities and Professions." Australian and New Zealand Journal of Sociology 20 (1984): 243-256.

6975. Orange, Claudia. "An Exercise in Maori Autonomy: The Rise and Demise of the Maori War Effort Organization." New Zealand Journal of History 21 (1987): 156-172.

6976. Orange, Claudia. The Treaty of Waitangi. Wellington: 1987.

6977. Palmer, Kenneth A. "Law, Land, and Maori Issues." Canterbury Law Review 3 (1988): 322-346.

6978. Pearson, David. "From Communality to Ethnicity: Some Theoretical Considerations on the Maori Ethnic Revival." Ethnic and Racial Studies 11 (1988): 168-191.

6979. Ritchie, James E. "The Evidence for Anti-Maori Prejudice." Victoria University of Wellington Publications in Psychology 16 (1964): 85-99.

6980. Schaniel, William C. The Maori and the Economic Frontier: An Economic History of the Maori of New Zealand, 1769-1840. Doctoral dissertation: University of Tennessee, 1985. UMO # 8608290.

6981. Shadbolt, Maurice. Season of the Jew. New York: Norton, 1987. [Novel about Maori revolt against British in 1868- 1869.]

6982. Shafer, S. "Bilingual/Bicultural Education for Maori Cultural Preservation in New Zealand." Journal of Multilingual and Multicultural Development 9 (1988): 487- 502.

6983. Simmons, D. R. Whakairo: Maori Tribal Art. New York: Oxford University Press, 1985.

6984. Simms, Norman. "The Literary Situation in New Zealand, II: Maor/Third World Literature and European Culture." South Asian Review of English (Kuala Lumpur Malaysia) 2 (August 1981): 28-39.

6985. Simpson, Tony. Te Riri Pakeha: The White Man's Anger. Wellington: 1979.

6986. Sinclair, Keith. "The Maoris in New Zealand History." History Today 30 (July 1980): 39-44.

6987. Sorrenson, M. P. K., ed. Na To Hoa Aroha: From Your Dear Friend: The Correspondence Between Sir Apirana Ngata and Sir Peter Buck 1925-1950. Vol. 1. New York: Oxford University Press, 1987. [Maori life.]

6988. Spolsky, B. "Maori Bilingual Education and Language Revitalization." Journal of Multilingual and Multicultural Development 10 (1989)

6989. Spoonley, Paul. The Politics of Nostalgia: Racism and the Extreme Right in New Zealand. Palmerston North: Dunmore Press, 1987.

6990. Spoonley, Paul. The Polynesian and Educational Inequality in New Zealand. December 2, 1981. [ERic Ed 225 774.]

6991. Spoonley, Paul. "The Renegotiation of Ethnic Relations in New Zealand." New Community 15 (July 1989): 577-589.

6992. Spoonley, Paul and others. Taviwi: Racism and Ethnicity in New Zealand. Palmerston North, New Zealand: Dunmore Press, 1984.

6993. St. George, Ross. "Racial Intolerance in New Zealand: A Review of Studies." in Schools in New Zealand Society, edited by C.H. Robinson and B.T. O'Rourke. Sydney: Wiley, 1973.

6994. Sutherland, O. R. W. and others. "Justice and Race: A Monocultural System in a Multicultural Society." Hamilton: New Zealand Race Relations Council, 1973.

6995. Taylor, Nan. "Human Rights in World War II in New Zealand." New Zealand Journal of History 23 (October 1989): 109-123.

6996. Thompson, Richard. Race Discrimination in Sport- A New Zealand Controversy. National Council of Churches in New Zealand, 1969.

6997. Trlin, Andrew D. "The New Zealand Race Relations Act: Conciliators, Conciliation and Complaints (1972-1981)." Political Science 34 (December 1982): 170-193.

6998. Trlin, Andrew D. and Paul Spoonley. "New Zealand." In International Handbook on Race and Race Relations, edited by Jay A. Sigler. Westport, CT: Greenwood, 1987.

6999. van Mowrik, A. and others. "Trends in Occupational Segregation of Women and Men in New Zealand: Some New Evidence." New Zealand Economic Papers 23 (1989)

7000. Vaughn, Graham M., ed. Racial Issues in New Zealand. Auckland: Akarana Press, 1972.

7001. Vowles, Jack. "Liberal Ideology: Pakeha Political Ideology." New Zealand Journal of History 21 (1987): 215- 227.

7002. Waldergrave, Charles and Rosalyn Coventry. Poor New Zealand: An Open Letter on Poverty. Wellington: 1987.

7003. Ward, Alan D. A Show of Justice: Racial 'Amalgamation' in Nineteenth Century New Zealand. Toronto: University of Toronto Press, 1974.

7004. Ward, Alan D. Towards One New Zealand: The Government and the Maori People, 1861-1893. Doctoral dissertation: Australian National University, 1967.

7005. Ward, J. T. "Compensation for Maori Land Rights. A Case Study of the Otago Tenths." New Zealand Economic Papers 20 (1986)

7006. Willer, Harold G. Race Conflict in New Zealand, 1814-1865. Westport, Ct: Greenwood Press, 1982. [reprint.]

7007. Williams, David V. "Aboriginal Rights in Aotearoa (New Zealand)." Law and Anthropology 2 (1987): 423-440.

7008. Williams, David V. "The Constitutional Status of Treaty of Waitangi: An Historical Perspective." New Zealand Universities Law Review 14 (June 1990): 9-36.

7009. Williams, John A. Maori Society and Politics 1891-1909. Doctoral dissertation: University of Wisconsin, 1963. UMO # 6400678.

7010. Williams, John A. Politics of the New Zealand Maori: Protest and Cooperation, 1891-1909. Seattle: University of Washington Press, 1969.

7011. Yensen, Helen and others. Honouring the Treaty. Auckland: 1989.

NICARAGUA

GENERAL

7012. Arnove, Robert F. Education and Revolution in Nicaragua. New York: Praeger, 1986.

7013. Austin, J. and others. "The Role of the Revolutionary State in the Nicaraguan Food System." World Development 13 (January 1985)

7014. Behrman, J. R. and others. "Human Capital and Earnings Distribution in a Developing Country: The Case of Prerevolutionary Nicaragua." Economic Development and Cultural Change 34 (October 1985)

7015. Berman, Paul. "Double Reality. People's Revolution versus Sandinista Revolution." Village Voice (December 5, 1989)

7016. Bermann, Karl. "Nicaraguans'Book-Buying Habits Astounding." National Catholic Reporter (September 8, 1989)

7017. Biderman, Jaime. "The Development of Capitalism in Nicaragua: A Political Economic History." Latin American Perspective 10 (Winter 1983): 7-32.

7018. Blau, D. M. "Fertility, Child Nutrition, and Child Mortality in Nicaragua: An Economic Analysis of Interrelationships." Journal of Developing Areas 20 (January 1986)

7019. No entry

7020. Cody, Edward. "Managua's Jews Reject Anti-Semitism Charge." Washington Post, (August 29, 1983)

7021. Colburn, Forrest D. Post-Revolutionary Nicaragua: State, Class, and the Dilemmas of Agrarian Policy. Berkeley: University of California Press, 1986.

7022. Congress, Rick. The Afro-Nicaraguans. Atlanta, GA: 1987.

NICARAGUA - GENERAL

7023. Darke, Roy. "Housing in Nicaragua." *International Journal of Urban Regional Research* 11 (March 1987): 100-114.

7024. Donahue, John M. *The Nicaraguan Revolution in Health: From Somoza to the Sandinistas*. South Hadley, MA: Bergin & Garvey, 1986.

7025. Donahue, John M. "Politics of Health Care in Nicaragua Before and After the Revolution of 1979." *Human Organization* 42 (1983): 264-272.

7026. Garcia, Victoria L. *Adult Education and Political Development: Case Study Based on the Nicaraguan Literacy Campaign and Adult Education Program*. Doctoral dissertation: Princeton University, 1987. UMO # 8709205.

7027. Garfield, Richard and Glen Williams. *Health and Revolution. The Nicaraguan Experience*. Oxford, England: Oxfam Publications, 1989.

7028. Glickman, Paul and Ilana De Bare. "Charges of Sandinista Anti-Semitism Unfounded." *In These Times*, (October 5, 1983)

7029. Gould, Jeffrey L. *To Lead as Equals: Rural Protest and Political Consciousness in Chinandega, Nicaragua, 1912-1979*. Chapel Hill: University of North Carolina Press, 1990.

7030. Hirshom, Sheryl. "'Contra'-vention Slows Change." *Guardian (NYC)*, (January 15, 1986): [Literacy crusade in Nicaragua.]

7031. Kinzer, Stephen. "Nicaragua's Economic Crisis Is Seen as Worsening." *New York Times*, (October 16, 1988)

7032. Kleinbach, Russell. "Nicaraguan Literacy Campaign: Its Democratic Essence." *Monthly Review* 37 (July-August 1985): 75-84.

7033. Kraft, Richard J. *Nicaragua: The Values, Attitudes and Beliefs of its Educated Youth*. 1977. [ERIC ED 182-220.]

7034. McArthur, Harvey. "Challenges Facing Nicaraguan Gov't on Corn Island." *Militant* (May 15, 1987): [Creole area on Atlantic Coast.]

7035. Muravachik, Joshua and others. "Sandinista Anti-Semitism and Its Apologists." *Commentary* 82 (September 1986): 25-29.

7036. Núñez Soto, Orlando. "Social Movements in the Struggle for Democracy, Revolution, and Socialism." Translated by Lawrence J. Gillooly. *Rethinking Marxism* 2 (Spring 1989): 7-22.

7037. Núñez Soto, Orlando. *Transición y lucha de clases en Nicaragua (1979-1986)*. Buenos Aires: Siglo Veintiuno Editores, 1987.

7038. Palumbo, Gene. "U.S. Embassy Agrees as Sandinistas Deny Anti-Semitism Charges." National Catholic Reporter (February 3, 1984)

7039. Rosenthal, Morton M. and others. "[On charges of antisemitism in] Nicaragua- An Exchange." Present Tense 14 (March-April 1987): 3-7.

7040. Ruby, Walter. "NJA Investigates Allegations of Anti- Semitism in Nicaragua." Jewish World (August 31, 1984): [New Jewish Agenda.]

7041. "Sandinista Anti-Semitism (an exchange of letters)." Commentary (January 1987)

7042. "Sandinistas Are Anti-semitic." Jerusalem Post, (May 28, 1986): [Charge by seven Jews who left Nicaragua in 1979.]

7043. Sandino, Augusto C. Sandino. The Testimony of a Nicaraguan Patriot, 1921-1934. Princeton, NJ Translated by Robert Edgar Conrad: Princeton University Press, 1990.

7044. Vargas, Oscar Rene. "El Desarrollo del Capitalismo en Nicaragua (1900-1912)." Estudios Sociales Centroamericanos 20 (1978)

7045. Vilas, Carlos M. "Nicaragua: The Fifth Year-Transformations and Tensions in the Economy." Capital & Class 28 (Spring 1986): 105-138.

7046. Winson, Anthony. "Nicaragua's Private Sector and the Sandinista Revolution." Studies in Political Economy No. 17 (Summer 1985): 71-106.

7047. Zalkin, M. "Food Policy and Class Transformation in Revolutionary Nicaragua, 1979-1986." World Development 15 (July 1987)

NICARAGUA - MISKITOS

7048. Adams, Richard. "The Sandinistas and the Indians: The New Indian 'Problems'." Caribbean Review 10 (Winter 1981): 22-25.

7049. Anaya, Jim. "Brooklyn Rivera: Peace With Justice...The Reunification of the Indian Family." Akwesasne Notes 16 (Early Winter 1984)

7050. Barreiro, Jose. "Miskito/Sandinista War. Brooklyn Rivera Conducts Peace Initiative." Akwesasne Notes 16 (Early Winter 1984)

7051. Barreiro, Jose. "Thoughts on Reconciliation. An Interview with Miskito Pastor Norman Bent." Akwesasne Notes 16 (Early Spring 1984): 14-15.

7052. Bates, Eric. "Putting Autonomy into Practice on Nicaragua's Atlantic Coast." In These Times (October 21, 1987)

7053. Borge, Tomas. "The Indigenous Peoples of the Americas. 500 years of Struggle Against Colonialism." International Socialist Review (August 1988): [Text of speech of February 11, 1988 to World Council of Indigenous Peoples seminar.]

7054. Borge, Tomas. "We Had Difficulty Grasping the Ethnic Character of the Miskito Problem." In Nicaragua, The Sandinista People's Revolution: Speeches by Sandinista Leaders, edited by Bruce Marcus, 348-351.

7055. Borge, Tomas. "Tomas Borge Talks About the Revolution." In These Times (September 18, 1985)

7056. Bourgois, Philippe. "Class, Ethnicity, and the State Among the Miskitu Amerindians of Northeastern Nicaragua." Latin American Perspectives 2 (Spring 1981): 22-39.

7057. Bourgois, Philippe. "Miskito Indians of Nicaragua." Anthropology Today 2 (April 1986): 4-9.

7058. Bourgois, Philippe. "The Miskitu Conflict: CIA Incompetence Matched by Sandinista Reforms and Indian Pragmatism." Jr. Soc. Americans 74 (1988): 209-212.

7059. Bourgois, Philippe. "Nicaragua's Ethnic Minorities in the Revolution." Monthly Review 36 (January 1985): 22-44.

7060. Bourgois, Philippe. "The Problematic of Nicaragua's Indigenous Minorities." in Nicaragua in Revolution, edited by Thomas Walker. 303-318. New York: Praeger, 1982.

7061. Brooks, David C. "U. S. Marines, Miskitos and the Hunt for Sandino: The Rio Coco Patrol in 1928." Journal of Latin American Studies 21 (May 1989): 311-342.

7062. Butler, Judy. "Charting a Rocky Atlantic Coast." Guardian Nicaragua Anniversary Supplement (July 19, 1989)

7063. Buvollen, Hans P. "The Miskitu-Sandinista Conflict: International Concerns and Outside Actors." Bulletin of Peace Proposals (Norway) 18 (1987): 591-601.

7064. Calderon, Manuel. "Sandinistas Address Problems of Atlantic Coast." Militant (July 3, 1981)

7065. Carrigan, Ann. "Ending the Other War in Nicaragua." Nation (February 6, 1988)

7066. Centro de Investigaciones y Documentacion de la Costa Atlantica. "The Atlantic Coast: A Policy of Genocide?" Envio 3 (June 1984)

7067. Clarke, Graham. "Briefing: Peace Our of Grasp of Misurasatas and Sandinistas." In These Times (January 23, 1985)

7068. Colhoun, Jack. "Miskito Ways and Means." Guardian (NYC) (November 27, 1985)

7069. Congress, Rick. The Afro-Nicaraguans. The Nicaraguan Revolution and the Meaning of Autonomy on the Atlantic Coast. Atlanta, GA: Atlanta Committee on Latin America, 1988.

7070. Congress, Rick. "Hard Road to Self-determination for Coast's Black Community." Guardian Nicaragua Anniversary Supplement (July 19, 1989): [Atlantic Coast.]

7071. Constable, Pamela. "Nicaraguan Indians Move to Honduras." Boston Globe, (April 7, 1986)

7072. Conzemius, Eduard. "Ethnic Survey of the Miskito and Sumu Indians of Honduras and Nicaragua." Bureau of American Ethnology Bulletin 106 (1932): Washington, D.C., Smithsonian Institution.

7073. D.H. "Borge Meets Indian Rebels on Atlantic Coast." Guardian (NYC) (June 4, 1986)

7074. Diaz Polanco, Hector and Gilberto López y Rivas, eds. Nicaragua: autonomia y revolución. Mexico City: Juan Pablos Editor, 1986.

7075. Dinges, John. "Nicaraguan Troops Uproot Indians After Rebel Forays." Washington Post, (February 5, 1982)

7076. Diskin, Martin. "Ethnic Autonomy in Nicaragua- The Second Nicaraguan Revolution." Canadian Dimension 19 (1985): 23- 25, 31.

7077. Dozier, Craig L. Nicaragua's Mosquito Shore: The Years of British and American Presence. University of Alabama Press, 1985.

7078. Dunbar Ortiz, Roxanne. La cuestión miskita en la revolución nicaraguense. Mexico City: Editorial Linea, 1986.

7079. Dunbar Ortiz, Roxanne. Indians of the Americas: Self- Determination and International Human Rights. New York: Praeger, 1984.

7080. Dunbar Ortiz, Roxanne. "[Letter on Miskito Indians]." Akwesasne Notes 14 (Late Summer 1982): 29.

7081. Dunbar Ortiz, Roxanne. The Miskito Indians of Nicaragua. London: Minority Rights Group, 1988.

7082. Dunbar Ortiz, Roxanne. "Miskitus in Nicaragua: Who is Violating Human Rights?" In Revolution in Central America, edited by Stanford Central American Action Network. Boulder, Co: Westview, 1983.

7083. Dunbar Ortiz, Roxanne. "Miskitus Victims of U.S. Intervention." Indigenous World 2 (1983): 7-12.

7084. Dunbar Ortiz, Roxanne and Penny Lernoux. "The Sandinistas and the Miskitos." Nation (January 11, 1986): [Exchange of letters.]

7085. Epstein, Jack and James H. Evans. "Indians Sandinistas Vie for Control in Nicaragua." National Catholic Reporter (October 22, 1982)

7086. Evans, James H. and Jack Epstein. "Miskitos Arm for Move on Nicaragua." In These Times (November 3, 1982)

7087. Evans, James H. and Jack Epstein. "Nicaragua's Miskito Move Based on False Allegations." National Catholic Reporter (December 24, 1982)

7088. Floyd, Troy S. The Anglo-Spanish Struggle for Mosquitos. Aluquerque: University of New Mexico Press, 1967.

7089. Frawley, Joan. "Among the Miskitos: Bluefields, Nicaragua, Under the Sandinista Harrow." Policy Review 28 (Spring 1984): 50-54.

7090. Freeland, Jane. "Nationalist Revolution and Ethnic Rights: The Miskitu Indians of Nicaragua's Atlantic Coast." Third World Quarterly 11 (October 1989): 166-190.

7091. Gander, Cathy. "Miskito Villages." Akwesasne Notes (Early Summer 1982): 20-22.

7092. Gasperini, William. "First Miskito Group Returns to Homeland." In These Times (August 7, 1985)

7093. Gasperini, William. "Miskito Exodus II: Refugees Endure a Violent Sequel." In These Times (May 14, 1986)

7094. Glickman, Paul. "MISURA Forced Recruitment Steps Up in the Border Region." In These Times (February 27, 1985)

7095. Goins, Lori L. The Miskito Tragedy: The Crime of U.S. British and Nicaraguan Power. Master's thesis: University of Texas, El Paso, 1987.

7096. Gordon Gitt, Edmundo. "Aproximación teóretica a la problematica de la costa atlantica nicaragüense." Bol. antropol. am. 9 (July 1984): 109-114.

7097. Gordon Gitt, Edmundo. "La Labor del CIDCA y Aproximacion Teorica a la Problematica de la Costa Atlantica de Nicaragua." In Memoria del Seminario Costa Atlantica de Centroamerica, edited by Carmen Murrillo and David Smith. San Jose, Costa Rica: Confederacion Universitaria Centroamerica, 1983.

7098. Hale, Charles. "Ethnopolitics, Regional War, and a Revolution's Quest for Survival: An Assessment of the Miskitu Question in Nicaragua." Alternative Newsletter (Committee on Native American Struggles of the National Lawyers Guild) (June 1984)

7099. Harpo, Nan and Kees van Swinden. De Ontgoocheling: Miskito Indianen en Solidaiteit met Nicaragua. Amsterdam: Raket en Loont, 1985.

7100. Helms, Mary W. Asang: Adaptations to Culture Contact in a Miskito Community. Gainesville: University of Florida Press, 1971.

7101. Helms, Mary W. "Miskito Slaving and Culture Contact: Ethnicity and Opportunity in an Expanding Population." Journal of Anthropological Research 39 (1983): 179-197.

NICARAGUA - MISKITOS

7102. "Historic Program of the FSLN." In Sandinistas Speak Tomas Borge and others. 13-22. New York: 1982.

7103. Holland, L. "The 'Undeclared War': Indians and the Revolution in Nicaragua." Survival International Review NO. 44 (1985): 74-90.

7104. Huss, Doug. "Autonomy Plan Beckons to Exiled Miskitos." Guardian (NYC) (December 10, 1986)

7105. Huss, Doug. "Autonomy Plan: New Beginning." Guardian (NYC) (June 3, 1987): [Agreement between Indian rebels and Nicaraguan government.]

7106. Huss, Doug. "Miskito Autonomy Talks, and the War, Go On." Guardian (May 7, 1986)

7107. Indians in the Crossfire. The Miskito, Sumo and Rama People. Cambridge, MA: Cultural Survival Inc.: Akwesasne Notes, 1987.

7108. INRA. La Mosquitia en la Revolution. Managua: 1981.

7109. Inter-American Commission on Human Rights. Report on the Situation of Human Rights in the Republic of Nicaragua. Washington, D.C.: Organization of American States, 1981.

7110. Inter-American Commission on Human Rights. Report on the Situation of Human Rights of a Segment of the Nicaraguan Population of Miskito Origin. Washington, D.C.: Organization of American States, 1984.

7111. Ismaelillo. "Colonialism and Revolution. Nicaraguan Sandisism and the Liberation of the Miskito, Suma and Rama Peoples." Akwesasne Notes 13 (Late Autumn 1981): 4-15. [Interview with Armstrong Wiggins.]

7112. Jaquith, Cindy. "Nicaragua's Indian Contras Take Amnesty." Militant (Otober 23, 1987)

7113. Jenkins, Loren. "Accounts by Indians Differ on Miskito- Sandinista Class." Washington Post, (April 30, 1982)

7114. Kemmerle, Peter. "Sandinistas Mend Fences in Miskito Territory." Guardian (NYC) (August 8, 1984)

7115. Kinzer, Stephen. "For Nicaraguan Indians, A Shaky Cease- Fire Hold." New York Times, (July 29, 1985)

7116. Kinzer, Stephen. "Indians Struggle with Regime to keep Traditional Way of Life." Boston Globe, (July 19, 1980)

7117. Kinzer, Stephen. "Nicaraguan Indians Called 'Innocent'." Boston Globe, (February 25, 1981)

544 WORLD RACISM AND RELATED INHUMANITIES

7118. Kinzer, Stephen. "The Way Home Is Hard for Indians of Nicaragua." New York Times, (August 22, 1985)

7119. Knell, Michael F. "Miskito Doctor Recalls Attack." In These Times (February 16, 1983)

7120. Kruckewitt, Joan. "Hope, Fear and Wariness as Miskitos Head Home." Guardian (NYC) (August 7, 1985)

7121. Kruckewitt, Joan. "Return to the Rio Coco." Guardian (NYC) (October 2, 1985)

7122. Kuttner, Bob. "Another Force in the Nicaragua Struggle." Boston Globe, (April 18, 1988): [Miskito and other Indians.]

7123. Law Blanco, Hazel. "Indigenous Rights and the Autonomy Project in Nicaragua." Bulletin Peace Proposal 18 (1986): 613-622.

7124. Le Moyne, James. "Anti-Sandinista Indians Reported Getting Battle." New York Times, (April 9, 1985)

7125. Le Moyne, James. "Miskitos Are Arguing With Themselves." New York Times, (August 3, 1986)

7126. Le Moyne, James. "Nicaragua Indians Fail to Heal Split." New York Times, (July 5, 1986)

7127. Le Moyne, James. "U.S. Hopes Miskito Indian Parley Will Bolster Fight against Sandinistas." New York Times, (June 7, 1987)

7128. Le Moyne, James. "U.S. Program in Honduras Helps Families of Nicaraguan Guerillas." New York Times, (April 19, 1985)

7129. Lernoux, Penny. "The Indians and the Comandantes." Nation (September 28, 1985)

7130. Lernoux, Penny. "Strangers in a Familiar Land (Part 1)." Nation (September 14, 1985)

7131. Lernoux, Penny. "Sandinista Treatment of Miskitos a Betrayal of Revolution Ideals." National Catholic Reporter (April 26, 1985)

7132. Lopez y Rivas, Gilberto and Exkart Bolge. "Los Miskitos y la cuestion nacional en Nicaragua." Boletin de Antropologica Americana No. 9 (1984): 99-107.

7133. MacDonald, Theodore Jr. "Advances Toward a Miskito- Sandinista Cease-Fire." Cultural Survival Quarterly 9 (1985): 38-39.

7134. MacDonald, Theodore Jr. "The Moral Economy of the Miskito Indians: Local Roots of a Geopolitical Conflict." In Ethnicities and Nations, edited by Remo Guidiere and others. Houston, TX: The Rothko Chapel, 1988.

7135. MacDonald, Theodore Jr. "On Nicaraguan Indians." New York Times, (March 30, 1982)

7136. MacLean, Robert C. The Economy of Atlantic Nicaragua in Historical Perspective. Master's thesis: Dalhousie University, 1987.

7137. Manuel, Anne. "Nicaraguan Indians Caught in the Middle." New York Times, (October 23, 1982)

7138. McArthur, Harvey. "Armed Miskito Indian Group Makes Peace with Sandinistas." Militant (October 28, 1988)

7139. McArthur, Harvey. "Indians and Blacks Celebrate Nicaragua's Autonomy Plan." Militant (May 8, 1987)

7140. McArthur, Harvey. "Nicaragua's Atlantic Coast Autonomy Process." Militant (June 12, 1987): [Multiethnic Assembly, Puerto Cabezas, Nicaragua, April 22- 24, 1987.]

7141. McArthur, Harvey and Judy White. "Peace and Autonomy in Nicaragua's North Atlantic Region." Militant (November 11, 1988): [First of four articles.]

7142. McArthur, Harvey. "Peasants Make Gains on Nicaragua's Atlantic Coast." Militant (April 29, 1988)

7143. McArthur, Harvey and Judy White. "Revolution Comes to the Atlantic Coast." Militant (November 18, 1988): [Second of four articles.]

7144. McArthur, Harvey and Judy White. "Sandinistas Champion Autonomy Process." Militant (November 25, 1988): [Third of a series of four articles.]

7145. McArthur, Harvey. "Thousands of Miskitos Return to Nicaragua's Atlantic Coast." Militant (July 22, 1988)

7146. Meisler, Stanley. "In Nicaragua, Relocated Miskitos Dream of Returning to Homeland." Boston Globe, (March 19, 1982)

7147. "Miskito Indians of Nicaragua." In World Directory of Minorities, edited by Minority Rights Group. 61-62. Harlow: Longman, 1990.

7148. "Miskitos Are Part of Sandinista Revolution." Navajo Times (January 26, 1984)

7149. The Miskitos in Nicaragua, 1981-1984. New York: Americas Watch Committee, 1984. [36 W. 44th St., NY, NY 10036.]

7150. Mohawk, John. "Nicaragua: Deceptions Cloud the Issues." Akwesasne Notes (Late Winter 1983)

7151. Moore, John H. "The Miskitu National Question in Nicaragua: Background to a Misunderstanding." Science & Society 50 (Summer 1986): 132-147.

7152. Nelson, Craig. "U.S. Wages a Secret War in Nicaragua." In These Times (April 28, 1982)

7153. Newson, Linda A. Indian Survival in Colonial Nicaragua. Norman: University of Oklahoma Press, 1987.

7154. "Nicaragua's Indian War: A Mistake of Tragic Proportions." Akwesasne Notes 14 (Early Winter 1982): 14.

7155. "Nicaragua: More than 100 Dead in Miskito-Sandinista Clashes in July." Akwesasne Notes 14 (Late Summer 1982): 17.

7156. Nietschmann, Bernard. Between Land and Water: The Subsistence Ecology of the Miskito Indians, Eastern Nicaragua. New York: Seminar Press, 1973.

7157. Nietschmann, Bernard. "The Indian Resistance in Nicaragua." Akwesasne Notes 16 (Early Spring 1984): 12-13.

7158. Nietschmann, Bernard. "Nicaragua Indians' Struggle." New York Times, (December 31, 1983)

7159. Nietschmann, Bernard. The Unknown War: The Miskito Nation, Nicaragua, and the United States. Lanham, MD: University Press of America, 1989.

7160. Noveck, Daniel. "Class, Culture and the Miskito Indians: A Historical Perspective." Dialectical Anthropology 13 (1988): 17-29.

7161. Ohland, Klandine and Robin Schneider, eds. National Revolution and Indigenous Identity: The Conflict between Sandinista and Miskito Indians on Nicaragua's Atlantic Coast. Copenhagen: International Work Group for Indigenous Affairs, 1982.

7162. Olier, Michael D. "Miskito Kings and the Line of Succession." Journal of Anthropological Research 39 (1983): 198-241.

7163. Ortega Hegg, Manuel. "The Ethnic Question in Nicaragua: Indigenous Autonomy and Ethnic Plurality." Bull. Peace Proposals 18 (1986): 603-612.

7164. Ortega, Manuel. "The Ethnic Question and the Autonomy Project." Annual Review of Nicaraguan Sociology 1 (1988): 35-39.

7165. Potthast, Barbara. Die Mosquitokuste in Spannungsfeld Britischer und Spanischer Politik 1502-1821. Cologne: Bohlau Verlag, 1988.

7166. Quintana, Jorge. "Indian Identity Is Future for Nicaragua." Daybreak (Highland, MD) Vol. 1, issue No. 1 (Autumn 1987): 32.

7167. Ramirez, William. "The Imperialist Threat and the Indigenous Problem in Nicaragua." Akwesasne Notes 14 (Spring 1982): 13-17.

7168. Rediske, Michael and Robin Schneider. "The Indians of Nicaragua: Between Colonialism and Revolution." Newsletter, International Work Group for Indigenous Affairs 30 (1982): 29-36.

7169. "Religiones en las Costa Atlantica." Nicarauc 8 (October 1982): 133-145.

7170. Riding, Alan. "Latin Border Area Becomes Volatile." New York Times, (February 21, 1982)

7171. Rivera, Brooklyn. "Miskito Nation. Some Further Words. Interview with Brooklyn Rivera." Akwesasne Notes (Early Summer 1982): 18-20.

7172. Rivera, Brooklyn. "Respect for Indian Rights Needed in Nicaragua." New York Times, (June 20, 1988): [letter.]

7173. Rohmer, Harriet. "I Have No Trouble With Uncle Sam. Miskitos Tell Why They Don't Like the Sandinistas." In These Times (June 13, 1984)

7174. Rooper, Alison and Hazel Smith. "From Nationalism to Autonomy: The Ethnic Question in the Nicaraguan Revolution." Race & Class 27 (Spring 1986): 1-20.

7175. Russell, George. "Indians Caught in the Middle." Time (August 20, 1984)

7176. Ryan, Randolph. "Indians, Sandinistas Inch Toward Accord." Boston Globe, (April 28, 1985)

7177. Ryan, Randolph. "Miskitos the Victims of Political Game?" Boston Globe, (May 16, 1982)

7178. Seigle, Larry. "Sandinistas Win Over Indian Contras to Peace and Coast Autonomy." Militant (November 6, 1987)

7179. Shapiro, Michael. "Bilingual-Bicultural Education in Nicaragua's Atlantic Coast Region." Latin American Perspectives 14 (Winter 1987): 67-86.

7180. Sollis, Peter. "The Atlantic Coast of Nicaragua: Development and Autonomy." Journal of Latin American Studies 21 (October 1989): 481-520.

7181. Sosa, Macarena. "Miskitos and Managua: Closer to an Understanding." Guardian (NYC) (May 15, 1985)

7182. Stephen, David. "Miskitos Bite the Sandinista Regime." New Society (June 17, 1982)

7183. Struggle over Autonomy: A Report on the Atlantic Coast of Nicaragua. American Friends Service Committee,

7184. Taylor, Jerome E. The Political Geography of Indian War in Nicaragua. Master's thesis: University of California, Berkeley, 1985.

7185. Trabil Nani: Historical Background and Current Situation on the Atlantic Coast of Nicaragua. Managua: Center for Research and Documentation of the Atlantic Coast (C.DCA), 1984.

7186. Trahant, M. N. "Nicaragua: Miskito Indians Face Celebration and Terror (Part 1)." Navajo Times (January 26, 1984)

7187. Trahant, M. N. "Political Hurricane-Eye of the Storm is War [Part 2]." Navajo Times (February 9, 1984)

7188. Vilas, Carlos M. State, Class and Ethnicity in Nicaragua: Capitalist Modernization and Revolutionary Change on the Atlantic Coast. London: Eurospan, 1989.

7189. Wallace, Scott. "Miskito Coast." Nation (December 27, 1986)

7190. Wallace, Scott. "The Real Miskito Coast." Newsweek (December 15, 1986)

7191. Wheelock, Jaime R. Raices Indigenas de la Lucha Anti- colonialista en Nicaragua. Mexico City: Siglio Veintiuno, 1974.

7192. White, Judy. "Nicaragua's Atlantic Coast: How Miskito Indian Women Organize, Make Gains." Militant (December 9, 1988)

7193. Wilson, David B. "An American Indian Finds a New War to Fight, Far From the Reservation." Boston Globe, (July 1, 1986) [Russell Means, Oglala-Lakota Sioux and Miskitos in Nicaragua.]

7194. Wood, David. "Obscure Nicaragua Tribe Focus of a Global Furor." Los Angleles Times, (March 12, 1982)

7195. Yih, Katherine. "Nicaragua's Atlantic Coast Dialogue: Autonomy & Revolution." Against the Current 2 (November- December 1987): 41-46.

NIGERIA

7196. Aba, E. O., Jr. Regional Socio-economic Disparities in Nigeria: Policy Implications. Doctoral dissertation: Texas A & M University, 1987. UMO # 8720853.

7197. Abudu, F. "Personal Income Distribution in the Modern Sector: The Western States of Nigeria." Aman 1 (June 1982): 14-27.

7198. Achebe, Chinua. The Trouble with Nigeria. Lagos: Heinemann, 1983.

7199. Afigbo, A. E. "The Eclipse of the Aro Slaving Oligarchy of South-eastern Nigeria, 1901-1927." Journal of the Historical Society of Nigeria 6 (1971): 3-24.

7200. Aforka Nweke, G. "Inequality and Instability in Nigeria: The Political Economy of Neo-Colonial Development." Nigerian Journal Development Studies 1 (April 1981): 47-60.

7201. Agbon, Solomon G. Class and Economic Development in Nigeria, 1900-1980. Doctoral dissertation: University of Texas, 1985. UMO # 8527509.

7202. Ahire, P. T. "Re-writing the Distorted History of Policing in Colonial Nigeria." International Journal of the Sociology of Law 18 (February 1990)

7203. Aigbokhan, B. E. "Size Distribution of Income in Nigeria: Decomposition Analysis." Scandanvian Journal of Development Alternatives 5 (December 1986): 25-33.

7204. Ajayi, J. F. Ade. Evolution of Political Culture in Nigeria. Ibaden: 1985.

7205. Akin Aina, Tade. "Class Structure and the Economic Development Process in Nigeria, 1946-1975." Odu (January 1986): 17-36.

550 WORLD RACISM AND RELATED INHUMANITIES

7206. Alubo, S. O. "State Violence and Health in Nigeria." Social Science & Medicine 31 (1990)

7207. Anusionwu, E. C. "The Distribution of Farm Income and Wealth among Nigerian Rural Households." Nigerian Journal Economic Social Studies 26 (July 1984): 145-158.

7208. No entry

7209. Aribiah, Oberu. "Prolegomenon to the Evolution of Housing Policy in Nigeria." Journal of Business Social Studies 6 (December 1983): 22-36.

7210. Asobie, Assisi. "Indigenization, Class Formation and Class Struggle in Nigeria: An Analysis." Africa Development 13 (1988): 29-76.

7211. Atanda, J. A. "A Historical Perspective to Intellectual Life in Yoruba Society up to c. 1900." Journal of the Historical Society of Nigeria 11 (December 1982-June 1983): 49-65.

7212. Awoniji, T. A. "Yoruba Language and the Schools System: A Study in Colonial Language Policy in Nigeria 1882-1952." International Journal of African Historical Studies 8 (1975)

7213. Ayandele, E. A. "Observations on Some Social and Economic Aspects of Slavery in Pre-Colonial Northern Nigeria." In Nigerian Historical Studies. London: Cass, 1979.

7214. Bamgbose, Ayo. "Mother-Tongue Medium and Scholastic Attainment in Nigeria." Prospects 14 (1984): 87-94.

7215. Bashir, Ibrahim L. "Classism Conflict and Socio-Economic Transition in a Changing Society." Kano Studies 2 (1982- 1985): 120-137.

7216. Blench, Roger. "A Revision of the Index of Nigerian Language." Nigerian Field 52 (October 1987): 77-84.

7217. Bonat, Z. A. "Colonialism and the Destruction of the Local Industrial System: A Case Study of Zaria Province, 1902- 1945." Savanna 9 (December 1988): 6-23.

7218. Brooke, James. "Ethnic Quota for Nigerians Is Challenged." New York Times, (November 6, 1988): [Affirmative Action.]

7219. Brown, Carolyn A. "The Dialectics of Colonial Labour Control: Class Struggles in the Nigerian Coal Industry, 1914- 1949." Journal Asian African Studies 27 (January-April 1988): 32-59.

7220. Callaway, Helen. Gender, Culture and Empire: European Women in Colonial Nigeria. London: Macmillan, 1987.

7221. Chukwudum, A. M. Nigeria: The Country in a Hurry. Lagos: John West Publications, 1981.

7222. Cole, Bankole A. Police Power and Accountability in the Nigerian Criminal Process. Doctoral dissertation: University of Keele, 1988. [Order No. BRDX 89951.]

7223. Diamond, Larry J. "Class, Ethnicity, and the Democratic State: Nigeria, 1950-1966." Comparative Studies in Society and History 25 (July 1983): 457-489.

7224. Diamond, Larry J. Class, Ethnicity, and Democracy in Nigeria. Syracuse, NY: Syracuse University Press, 1988.

7225. Diamond, Larry J. The Social Foundations of Democracy: The Case of Nigeria. Doctoral dissertation: Stanford University, 1980. UMO # 8103503.

7226. Din, Isaac U. Educational Expansion and Equality of Opportunity in Secondary Schools in Imo State of Nigeria. Doctoral dissertation: State University of New York at Buffalo, 1985. UMO # 8528247.

7227. Ejimofor, Cornelius Ogu. British Colonial Objectives and Policies in Nigeria. Onitsha, Nigeria: 1987.

7228. Ekong, Elsong E. "The Fictiveness of Class Analysis in Contemporary Nigerian Society." West African Journal ofSociology and Political Science 2 (1976-1977)

7229. Enaohwo, J. O. "Planning for the Development and Supply of Educated Manpower for National Economic Development: The Nigerian experience, 1960-1974." Compare 8 (1978): 159-165.

7230. Esedebe, P. O. "The Educated Elite in Nigeria Reconsidered." Journal of the Historical Society of Nigeria 10 (December 1980): 111-132.

7231. Esiemokhai, E. O. The Colonial Legal Heritage in Nigeria. Akure, Nigeria: 1986.

7232. Fajana, Ade. "Colonial Control and Education: The Development of Higher Education in Nigeria, 1900-1950." Journal of the Historical Society of Nigeria 6 (1972): 323-340.

7233. Falola, Toyin. "Power Relations and Social Interventions among Ibadan Slaves, 1800-1900." African Economic History 16 (1987): 95-114.

7234. Forest, Tom. "The Political Economy of Civil Rule and the Economic Crisis in Nigeria, 1979-1984." Review of African Political Economy 4-26 (May 1986)

7235. Gana, Aaron T. "Local Government and Class Domination in Nigeria: A Historical Sketch." Nigerian Journal of Economic and Social Studies 27 (July 1985): 133-146.

7236. Gana, Aaron T. "On the Political Economy of Crime in Nigeria: Social Polarization in Peripheral Capitalism." Nigerian Journal of Political Science 4 (1985): 172-184.

7237. Gboyega, Alex. "Local Government and Democracy in Nigeria." Nigerian Journal of Economic Social Studies 16 (July 1984): 173-184.

7238. Goke-Pariola, A. "The Political Content of Language Education in Nigeria." Odu 54-65 (January 1985)

7239. Harber, Clive. "Schooling for Bureaucracy in Nigeria." International Journal of Education Development 4 (1984): 145-154.

7240. Heinecke, P. Divided Truths: A Probe into Myths and Fallacies of Nigerian Social Science. Okpella, Gendel State, Nigeria: S.Asekome, 1988.

7241. Hill, Polly. Population, Prosperity and Poverty. Rural Kano, 1900-1970. New York: Cambridge University Press, 1977. [Slavery.]

7242. Hubbard, James P. Education Under Colonial Rule: A History of Katsina College, 1921-1942. Doctoral dissertation: University of Wisconsin, 1973.

7243. Ibegbu, C. U. Regional Disparities and Social Inequalities in Nigerian Universities: A Study of Educational Expansion and Selection. Doctoral dissertation: State University of New York at Buffalo, 1989. UMO # 8921547.

7244. Ihonvbere, J. O. and Toyin Falola. "Hegemony, Neo- Colonialism and Political Instability in Contemporary Nigeria." Africa Review 11 (1984): 41-62.

7245. Ikiddeh, Ime. "English, Bilingualism and a Language Policy for Nigeria." Ibadan Journal of Humanistic Studies (October 1983): 65-79.

7246. Iliffe, John. "Poverty in Nineteenth-century Yoruba-land." Journal of African History 25 (1984): 43-57.

7247. Imoagene, O. Social Mobility in Emergent Society: The New Elite in Western Nigeria. Canberra: Australian National University, 1976.

7248. Ityavyar, Dennis A. "The State, Class and Health Services in Nigeria." Afrika Spectrum No. 3 (1987): 285-314.

7249. Iwe, N. S. S. Socio-ethical Issues in Nigeria. New York: 1987.

7250. Izeogu, Chukudi V. "Who Benefits from the Government Land Serving Programmes for Urban Housing Development in Nigeria?" African Urban Quarterly 1 (May 1986): 117-130.

7251. Jaja, S. O. "Enugu Colliery Massacre in Retrospect: An Episode in British Administration of Nigeria." Journal, Historical Society of Nigeria 11 (1982-1983): 86-106.

7252. Jinadu, L. Adele. Federalism, Ethnicity, and Affirmative Action in Nigeria. May 1984. [ERIC ED 249 300.]

7253. Kolinsky, Martin. "The Growth of Nigerian Universities 1948-1980: The British Share." Minerva 23 (Spring 1985): 29-61.

7254. Lawal, A. A. "Anatomy of Corruption in the British Colonial Service in Nigeria." Odu 31 (January 1987): 92- 103.

7255. Lerche, Charles O. "Development and Social Strife: A Case Study of Nigeria." Scandanavian Journal of Development Alternatives 4 (March 1985): 1-24.

7256. Lovejoy, Paul E. "Concubinage and the Status of Women Slaves in Early Colonial Northern Nigeria." Journal of African History 29 (1988): 245-266.

7257. Lubeck, Paul M., ed. The African Bourgeoisie: Capitalist Development in Nigeria, Kenya, and the Ivory Coast. Boulder, CO: Rienner, 1987.

7258. Madunagu, Edwin. The Tragedy of the Nigerian Socialist Movement. Calabar, Nigeria: Centaur Press, 1980.

7259. Mohammed, Abubakr Bala. "European Imperialism and African Cultural Legacy: The Case of a Plundered Past." Nigeria Magazine 53 (January-March 1985): 69-76.

7260. Mordi, A. A. "A Socio-Historical Reconstruction of Ethnicism in Nigeria." Odu (January 1984): 83-92.

7261. National Conference of the Urban Poor. The Urban Poor in Nigeria. Ibadan: 1987.

7262. Noble, Kenneth B. "Nigeria's Leader to Seek Slavery Reparations." New York Times, (December 24, 1990)

7263. Nolutshungu, S. C. "Fragments of a Democracy. Reflections on Class and Politics in Nigeria." Third World Quarterly 12 (January 1990)

7264. Northrup, David. "Nineteenth Century Patterns of Slavery and Economic Growth in Southeastern Nigeria." Journal of African Historical Studies 12, 1 (1979): 1-16.

7265. Nwagbaraocha, Victor I. "Vocational and Technical Education in Eastern Nigeria during the Colonial Period." Proc. Fr. Colonial Historical Society 8 (1982): 124-136.

7266. Nwagwu, N. A. "The Politics of Universal Primary Education in Nigeria, 1955-1977." Compare 8 (1978): 149-157.

7267. Nwaka, Geoffrey I. "The Civil Rights Movement in Colonial Igboland." International Journal of African Historical Studies 18 (1985): 473-485. [Osu and Ohu.]

7268. Nziuriro, Francis I. "Feudalism in Nigeria." In Toward a Marxist Anthropology. The Hague: Mouton, 1979.

7269. Oduleye, S. Q. "Decline in Nigerian Universities." Higher Education 14 (1985): 17-40.

7270. Okoh, S. E. N. "Poverty as a Socio-Economic Problem in Nigeria." Aman 4 (December 1984): 129-148.

7271. Okpoko, John. The Biafran Nightmare: The Controversial Role of International Relief Agencies in a War of Genocide. Enegu, Nigeria: Delta of Nigeria, 1986.

7272. Okpu, U. Ethnic Minority Problems in Nigerian Politics, 1960-1965. Uppsala: Scandanavian Institute of African Studies, 1977.

7273. Okubadejo, Adebola K. Capitalism in Nigeria. Master's thesis: Brooklyn College, 1980.

7274. Omolewa, Michael. "The First Year of Nigeria's Mass Literacy Campaign and New Prospects for the Future." Convergence 17 (1984): 55-62.

7275. Onabadejo, Martins A. Class and Ethnicity in a Changing Nigeria. Doctoral dissertation: Temple University, 1987. UMO # 8711387.

7276. Onimode, Bade. Imperialism and Underdevelopment in Nigeria: The Dialectics of Mass Poverty. London: Zed Press, 1983.

7277. Oputa, C. A. Human Rights in the Political and Legal Culture of Nigeria. Lagos: Nigerian Law Publications, 1988.

7278. Oriji, J. N. "The Slave Trade, Warfare and Aro Expansion in the Igbo Hinterland." Transafrican Journal of History 16 (1987): 151-166.

7279. Osoba, Segun. "The Nigerian Power Elite, 1952-1965." In African Social Studies: A Radical Reader, edited by P.Gutkind and P. Waterman. London: Heinemann, 1977.

7280. Pittin, Renee. "Gender and Class in Nigeria." Review of African Political Economy (December 1984): 71-81.

7281. Pritchett, Willis. Slavery and the Economy of Kano Emirate, 1810-1903. Master's thesis: Southern Connecticut State University, 1990.

7282. Raheem, T. A. and A. Olukoshi. "The Left in Nigerian Politics and the Struggle for Socialism." Review of African Political Economy (December 1986): 64-80.

7283. Rogers, Cyril A. "A Study of Race Attitudes in Nigeria." Rhodes-Livingstone Journal 26 (1959): 51-64.

7284. Rural Underdevelopment in Nigeria, 1900-1980. Zaria, Nigeria: Department of Political Science, Ahmadu Bello University, 1985.

7285. Salamone, Frank A. "Colonialism and the Emergence of Fulani Identity." Journal of Asian and African Studies 20 (1985): 193-202.

7286. Shenton, Robert W. The Development of Capitalism in Northern Nigeria. Toronto: University of Toronto Press, 1986.

7287. Siddique Mohammed, Abubakar and Tony Edoh, eds. Nigeria, a Republic in Ruins. Zaria, Nigeria: Department of Political Science, Ahmadu Bello University, 1986.

7288. Smith, S. "Colonialism in Economic Theroy: The Experience of Nigeria." Journal of Development Studies 15 (April 1979)

7289. Sule, R. A. Olu. "The Future of the Nigerian Housing Subsidy: The Unanswered Question." Nigerian Journal Economic Social Studies 23 (March 1981): 109-128.

7290. Taylor, William H. "The Presbyterian Educational Impact in Eastern Nigeria." Journal of Religion Africa 14 (1983): 223-245.

7291. Thiessen, William. Schooling and Socio-cultural Change in Middle Belt Nigeria. Master's thesis: University of Saskatchewan, 1981.

7292. Tibenderana, Peter K. "The Beginnings of Girls' Education in the Native Administration Schools in Northern Nigeria, 1930-1945." Journal of African History 26 (1985): 93-110.

7293. Tibenderana, Peter K. "The Irony of Indirect Rule in the Sokoto Emirate, Nigeria, 1903-1944." African Studies Review 31 (1988): 67-92.

7294. Tibenderana, Peter K. Sokoto Province under British Rule, 1903-1939: A Study in Institutional Adaptation and Culturalization of a Colonial Society in Northern Nigeria. Zaria: Ahmadu Bello University Press, 1988.

7295. Tyoden, S. G. "Spatial Inequalities and Social Equity: The Political Economy of Resource Distribution in Nigeria." Nigerian Journal Political Economy 1 (1983): 106-127.

7296. Ubawike, Eugene U. Income Distribution in Nigeria. Master's thesis: Long Island University, 1980.

7297. Uche, L. U. "Broadcasting in Nigeria and Cultural Identity in an Era of Media Imperialism." Third Channel 2 (1986): 346-364.

7298. Ukpak, Akpan N. Educational Expansion in Nigeria: A Case Study. Doctoral dissertation: New School for Social Research, 1985. UMO # 8607156.

7299. Umo, Joe U. "Educational-Employment Connection: The Nigerian Experience." Nigerian Journal of Economic and Social Studies 27 (March 1985): 23-38.

7300. Urevbu, Andrew O. "Vocational Education in Nigeria: A Preliminary Appraisal." International Journal Education Development 4 (1984): 223-230.

7301. Usman, Yusufu Bala. The Manipulation of Religion in Nigeria, 1977-1987. Kaduna, Nigeria: Vanguard, 1987.

7302. Usman, Yusufu Bala, ed. Political Repression in Nigeria. Kano, Nigeria: Bala Mohammed Memorial Committee, 1982.

7303. Watkins, William H. The Political Sociology of Postcolonial Social Studies Curriculum Development: The Case of Nigeria, 1960-1980. Doctoral dissertation: University of Illinois at Chicago, 1986. UMO # 8705197.

7304. Watts, Michael. Silent Violence: Food, Famine and Peasantry in Northern Nigeria. Berkeley: University of California Press, 1983.

7305. Williams, G. "The Social Stratification of a Neo-Colonial Economy: Western Nigeria." In African Perspectives, edited by C. Allen and R.W. Johnson. London: Cambridge University Press, 1970.

7306. Williams, G. State and Society in Nigeria. Idanre: Afrografika, 1980.

NORWAY

7307. Abrahamsen, Samuel. "The Destruction of Jews in Norway (1942-1943)." World Congress of Jewish Studies 9 (1986): 173-180.

7308. Abrahamsen, Samuel. "The Exclusion Clause of Jews in the Norwegian Constitution of May 17, 1814." Jewish Social Studies 30 (1968): 67-88.

7309. Andenaes, J. and others. Norway and the Second World War. Lillehammer, Norway: 1983.

7310. Brown, Ross. "Norway Keeps the Gypsies Moving." Race Today 4 (July 1972): 248.

7311. Brown, Ross. "Norway-Reserved Xenophobic?" Race Today 4 (March 1972): 92.

7312. Christenson, Bruce A. Modernization and Inequality of Schooling in Norway: A Comparison of the Educational Careers of Males from Privileged, Modern, and Traditional Social Origins. Doctoral dissertation: University of Wisconsin, 1986. UMO # 8613385.

7313. Dahl, Tove S. Child Welfare and Social Defence. Oslo, Norway: Norwegian University Press, 1986.

7314. Derry, T. K. "Norway." In Fascism in Europe, edited by S.J. Woolf. London: Methuen, 1982.

7315. Eidheim, Harold. Aspects of the Lappish Minority Situation. Oslo: Universitetsforlaget, 1974.

7316. Fagerberg, Jan and others. "The Decline of Social- Democratic State Capitalism in Norway." New Left Review No. 181 (May-June 1990): 60-94.

7317. Gjelsvik, Tore. Norwegian Resistance, 1940-1945. London: C. Hurst, 1979.

7318. Gordon, Gerd S. The Norwegian Resistance During the German Occupation 1940-1945: Repression, Terror, and Resistance: The West Country of Norway. Doctoral dissertation: University of Pittsburgh, 1978. UMO # 7902755.

7319. Hodne, Fritz and Bjorn Basberg. "Public Infrastructure, Its Indispensability for Economic Growth: The Case of Norwegian Public Health Measures, 1850-1940." Scandanavian Economic History REview 35 (1987): 1145-169.

7320. Hoidal, O. K. Quisling: A Study in Treason. New York: 1989.

7321. Kierulf, Hakon. "Linguistic and Cultural Differences Encountered by Indigenous People in Court." Canadian Native Law Reporter (Spring 1990): 1-8. [Sami in Norway.]

7322. Lic, Suzanne S. Immigrant Women in Norway. Hong Kong: Asian Research Service, 1986. [P.O. Box 2232 G.P.O., Hong Kong.]

7323. Mendelsohn, Oskar. "Actions against the Jews in Norway during the War." Nord. Judaistik 3 (1981): 27-35.

7324. Milward, Alan S. The Fascist Economy in Norway. 1972.

7325. Myhre, Jan E. "Research into Norwegian Living Conditions in the Period 1750-1914." Scandanavian Economic Historical Review 34 (1986): 159-166.

7326. Petrow, R. The Bitter Years: The Invasion and Occupation of Denmark and Norway, April 1940-May 1945. New York: 1974.

7327. Rian, Oystein. "State and Society in Seventeenth-century Norway." Scandanavian Journal of History 10 (1985): 337- 363.

7328. Riste, O. and B. Nokleby. Norway, 1940-1945: The Resistance Movement. Oslo: 1970.

7329. Rokhsar, Jacqueline and Samuel Abrahamsen. "Norway." In Encyclopedia of the Holocaust. New York: Macmillan, 1990.

7330. Sanders, Douglas. "The Sami Parliament in Norway." Canadian Native Law Reporter (Winter 1990): 7-8.

7331. Soltow, Lee. Toward Income Equality in Norway. Madison, WI: 1965.

7332. Spencer, Arthur. The Lapps. New York: Crane, Russak, 1978.

PAKISTAN

7333. Ahmed, Emajuddin. "Development Strategy: Class and Regional Interests of the Ruling Elites in Pakistan." Indian Economic and Social History Review 15 (1978): 421-449.

7334. Alavi, Hamza. "Nationhood and the Nationalists in Pakistan." Economic and Political Weekly 24 (July 8, 1989)

7335. Bilquees, F. and S. Hamid. "Employment Situation and Economic Exploitation of Poor Earning Women in Raivalpindi." Pakistan Development Review 27 (Winter 1988)

7336. Bouma, Cees. "Non-Muslims in Pakistan: A Question of Justice and Equality." Journal of the Institute of Muslim Minority Affairs 9 (January 1988): 35-42.

7337. Chandra, Nirmal K. "The Class Character of the Pakistani State." International Journal of Politics 4 (1974): 26-70.

7338. de Kruijk, H. "Sources of Income Inequality in Pakistan." Pakistan Development Review 26 (Winter 1987)

7339. Ercelawn, A. "Income Inequality in Rural Pakistan: A Study of Sample Villages." Pakistan Journal of Applied Economics 3 (Summer 1984)

7340. Iqbal, Justice Javid. "Crimes Against Women in Pakistan." Journal of South Asian and Middle Eastern Studies 13 (Spring 1990): 37-48.

7341. Islam, M. N. "Communalism and Contradiction in the Birth of Pakistan: An Historical and Ideological Background." Journal of the Asiatic Society of Bangladesh 30 (June 1985): 125-140.

7342. Jalal, Ayesha. The State of Martial Rule: The Origins of Pakistan's Political Economy of Defence. New York: Cambridge University Press, 1990.

7343. Kazi, Aftab A. "Ethnic Nationalities, Education, and Problems of National Integration in Pakistan." Asian Profile 16 (1988): 147-161.

7344. Kazi, S. and Z.A. Sathar. "Difference in Household Characteristics by Income Distribution in Pakistan." Pakistan Development Review 24 (Autumn-Winter 1985)

7345. Kemal, A. R. "Changes in Poverty and Income Inequality in Pakistan during the 1970s: Comments." Pakistan Development Review 24 (Autumn-Winter 1985)

7346. Kennedy, Charles H. "Policies of Ethnic Preference in Pakistan." Asian Survey 24 (June 1984): 688-703.

7347. Khan, M. A., ed. Islam, Politics, and the State: The Pakistan Experience. Totowa, NJ: Zed Books, 1985.

7348. Khan, S. R. and others. "An Assessment of the Distribution of Public-Sector Educational Investment in Pakistan: 1970-71- -1982-83." Pakistan Development Review 25 (Summer 1986)

7349. Krotki, K. J. "Differences in Household Characteristics by Income Distribution in Pakistan: Comments." Pakistan Development Review 24 (Autumn-Winter 1985)

7350. No entry

7351. Mahmood, Z. "Income Inequality in Pakistan: An Analysis of Existing Evidence." Pakistan Development Review 23 (Summer- Autumn 1984): [See Tahir, below.]

7352. Malik, M. H. and Majam-us-Saqib. "Tax Incidence by Income Classes in Pakistan." Pakistan Development Review 28 (Spring 1989)

7353. Mumtaz, Khawar and Farida Shaheed. Women of Pakistan. London: Zed Press, 1987.

7354. Noman, Omar. The Political Economy of Pakistan 1947-1985. New York: KPI, 1988.

7355. Parveen Shaukat Ali. Status of Women in the Muslim World: A Study in the Feminist Movements in Turkey, Egypt, Iran, and Pakistan. Lahore: Aziz Publishers, 1975.

7356. Rashid, A. The Islamization of Laws in Pakistan, with Special Reference to the Status of Women. Doctoral dissertation: School of Oriental and African Studies, University of London, 1987.

7357. Sharma, B. K. "From Communalism to Separation: Politico- Economic Basis for the Origin of Pakistan." South Asian Studies 21 (January-June 1986): 23-45.

7358. Tahir, S. "Income Inequality in Pakistan: An Analysis of Existing Evidence: Comment." Pakistan Development Review 23 (Summer-Autumn 1984): [See Mahmood, above.]

7359. Weiss, Anita M. Culture, Class, and Development in Pakistan: The Emergence of a Industrial Bourgeoisie in Punjab. Boulder, CO: Westview Press, 1990.

7360. Woodsmall, Ruth F. "Women in Pakistan." In Women and the New East Ruth F. Woodsmall. 99-148. Washington, D.C.: Middle East Institute, 1960.

7361. Zaidi, S. Akbar. "Religious Minorities in Pakistan Today." Journal of Contemporary Asia 18 (1988): 444-457.

7362. Ziring, Lawrence. "Public Policy Dilemmas and Pakistan's Nationality Problem: The Legacy of Zia ul-Haq." Asian Survey 28 (August 1988): 795-812.

PANAMA

7363. Biesanz, John and Luke Smith. "Race Relations in Panama and the Canal Zone: A Comparative Analysis." American Journal of Sociology 57 (1951): 7-14.

7364. Burkhauser, Richard V. "Social Security in Panama: A Multiperiod Analysis of Income Distribution." Journal of Development Economics 21 (April 1986): 53-64.

7365. Castillero Calvo, Alfredo. "Subsistencias y economia an la sociedad colonial. El caso del istmo de Panama,Siglos XVI y XVII." R. Hist. (Costa Rica) 18 (July-December 1988): 23- 92.

7366. Chavira, Ricardo. "Meanwhile, Back in Panama." Time (November 26, 1990)

7367. Conniff, Michael L. Black Labor on a White Canal. Panama, 1904-1981. Pittsburgh, PA: University of Pittsburgh Press, 1985.

7368. Escobar Bethancourt, Rómulo. Torrijos: colonia americana, no! Bogota: Carlos Valencia Editores, 1981.

7369. Figueroa Navarro, Alfredo. Los Grupos Populares de la Ciudad de Panama a Fines del Siglo Diecinueve. Panama City: University of Santa Maria la Antigua, 1987.

7370. Gellhorn, Martha. "The Invasion of Panama." Granta 32 (Spring 1990): 203-229.

7371. Gjording, Chris N. The Cerro Colorado Copper Project: Panama Multinational Corporations and the Guaymi Indians. Doctoral dissertation: New School for Social Research, 1985. UMO # 8607154.

7372. Herlihy, Peter H. "Panama's Quiet Revolution: Comarca Homelands and Indian Rights." Cultural Survival Quarterly 13 (1989)

7373. Howell, Bing P. The Anatomy of Discrimination in the Canal Zone vis-a-vis Stated United States Policy from 1940-1977. Doctoral dissertation: University of California Los Angeles, 1979. UMO # 8002486.

7374. James, Joy. "US Policy in Panama." Race & Class 32 (July- September 1990): 17-32.

7375. Joly, Luz Gracie. "Notes on the Historical, Ethnographical and Social Status of the Negro in Panama." Notes in Antropology 13 (1968): 5-18.

7376. Koster, R. M. and Guillermo Sanchez Borhon. In the Times of the Tyrants: Panama, 1968-1989. New York: Norton, 1990.

7377. Kuhn, Gary. "Liberian Contract Labor in Panama, 1887- 1897." Liberian Studies Journal 6 (1975): 43-52.

7378. Lewis, Lancelot S. The West Indian in Panama: Black Labor in Panama, 1850-1914. Washington, D.C.: University Press of America, 1980.

7379. Lipski, John. "The Negros Congos of Panama: Afro-Hispanic Creole Language and Culture." Journal of Black Studies 16 (June 1986): 409-428.

7380. López Tirone, Humberto. Panamá: una revolución democrática. Mexico City: Praxis, grafica editorial, 1986. [In re: Omar Torrijos.]

7381. Madrid, Elsie A. and others. Situación de la mujer en Panamá, 1989. Departamento de Sociologia, Universidad de Panama: 1989.

7382. Massaquoi, Hans J. "Panama, It's Much More Than Just a Canal." Ebony 33 (July 1978): 44-56.

7383. Meisler, Stanley. "The Blacks of Panama." Nation (June 22, 1974)

7384. Newton, Velma. The Silver Men: West Indian Labour Migration to Panama, 1850-1914. Mona, Kingston, Jamaica: Institute of Social and Economic Research, University of the West Indies, 1984.

7385. Paz B., Sadith. The Status of West Indian Immigrants in Panama from 1850-1941. Master's thesis: University of Massachusetts, Amherst, 1978.

7386. Pinnock, Roberto and Charlotte Elton. La evolución de la pobreza rural en Panama. Santiago de Chile: International Labour Office, Programa Regional del Empleo para America Latina y el Caribe, 1983.

7387. Poehner, W. Mark. "Influence of Imperialist Slavery Policy on the Labor Policy of the United States in Building the Panama Canal." California Anthropologist 15 (1988): 27-37.

7388. Rohter, Larry. "America's Blind Eye." New York Times Magazine, (May 29, 1988)

564 WORLD RACISM AND RELATED INHUMANITIES

7389. Sahota, Gian S. "The Distribution of the Benefits of Public-Expenditure in Panama." Public Finance Quarterly 5 (April 1977)

7390. Sahota, Gian S. Poverty Theory and Policy: A Study of Panama. Baltimore, MD: Johns Hopkins University Press, 1990.

7391. Soler, Ricaurte. Panama: Historia de una crisis. Mexico City: Siglo Veintiuno Editores, 1989.

7392. Westerman, George W. "Gold vs. Silver Workers in the Canal Zone." Common Ground 8 (Winter 1948): 92-95. [Discrimination]

PAPUA-NEW GUINEA

7393. Ashton, C. P. M. The Study of European Colonial and Ruling Minorities, with Special Reference to the Australians in Papua-New Guinea. B. Litt. thesis: Oxford University, 1968.

7394. Bricknell, Nancy J. The Problems of Inequalities of Educational Opportunity in Papua-New Guinea. Master's thesis: University of Sydney, 1973.

7395. Chowning, Ann. "The Development of Ethnic Identity and Ethnic Stereotypes on Papua New-Guinea Plantations." Journal de la Societe Oceanistes 42 (1986): 153-162.

7396. Codell, Joan C. New Guinea Race Relations to 1942. B.A. (Hons.) thesis: Monash University, 1970.

7397. Donaldson, M. "Class Formation in Papua New-Guinea: The Indigenous Bourgeoisie." Journal of Australian Political Economy No. 7 (April 1980): 63-85.

7398. Fitzpatrick, Peter. "Law, Labour and Resistance in Papua New Guinea." Melanesian Law Journal 14 (December 1986): 111-152.

7399. Good, Kenneth. Papua New Guinea. A False Economy. London: Anti-Slavery Society, 1986.

7400. Gordon, Robert, ed. The Plight of Peripheral People in Papua New Guinea. Vol.I, The Inland Situation. Cambridge, MA: Cultural Survival Inc., 1981.

7401. Nelson, Hyland N. Black, White and Gold. Gold Mining in Papua New Guinea 1878-1930. Doctoral dissertation: University of Papua New-Guinea, 1975.

7402. Nelson, Hyland N. "From Kanaka to Fuzzy Wuzzy Angel: Race and Labour Relations in Australian New Guinea." In Who Are Our Enemies? Racism and the Australian Working Class, edited by Ann Curthoys and Andrew Markus. Canberra: Australian Society for the Study of Labour History, 1978.

7403. Nelson, Hyland N. Papua New Guinea: Black Unity or Black Chaos. Ringwood, Victoria: Penguin, 1972.

7404. Perkins, John. "Nazi Colonial Revisionism and Australia's New Guinea Mandate." Journal of Pacific History 24 (1989)

7405. Perry, D. W. "Papua New Guinea, the Political Economy of Education." In Education, Recession and the World Village, edited by Frederick M. Wirt and Grant Harman. Philadelphia, PA: Falmer Press, 1986.

7406. Rowley, Charles D. The New Guinea Villager: The Impact of Colonial Rule on Primitive Society and Economy. New York: Praeger, 1966.

7407. Strathern, A., ed. Inequality in New Guinea Highlands Societies. New York: Cambridge University Press, 1982.

7408. Torrey, Barbara B. "Australian Imperialism in Papua New Guinea." Bulletin of Concerned Asian Scholars 6 (September- October 1974): 2-6.

7409. Turner, Mark M. "Plantations, Politics and Policy-making in Papua New Guinea, 1965-1986." Journal de la Societe des Oceanistes 42 (1986): 129-138.

7410. Ward, R. Gerard. "Contract Labor Recruitment from the Highlands of Papua New Guinea, 1950-1974." International Migration Review 24 (Summer 1990)

7411. Weisbrot, David. "Papua New Guinea's Indigenous Jurisprudence and the Legacy of Colonialism." University of Hawaii Law Review 10 (Summer 1988): 1-45.

7412. Wesley-Smith, Terence. "Pre-Capitalist Mode of Production in Papua New Guinea." Dialectical Anthropology 14 (1989)

7413. Wolfers, Edward P. Race, Law and Colonial Rule in Papua New Guinea. Doctoral dissertation: University of Papua New Guinea, 1975.

7414. Wolfers, Edward P. Race Relations and Colonial Rule in Papua New Guinea. Sydney: Australia and New Zealand Book Company, 1975.

7415. Young, R. E. "Papua New Guinea: A New Paternalism." Australian Journal of Education 20 (June 1976): 149-159.

7416. Zable, Arnold. "Neo-Colonialism and Race Relations: New Guinea and the Pacific Rim." Race 14 (April 1973): 393-441.

PARAGUAY

7417. Abente, Diego. "Foreign Capital, Economic Elites and the State in Paraguay during the Liberal Republic (1870-1936)." Journal of Latin American Studies 21 (1989): 61-88.

7418. "The Aché Indians: Genocide in Paraguay." Akwasasne Notes 5 (Early Winter 1973): 26-27.

7419. Arens, Richard, ed. Genocide in Paraguay. Philadelphia, PA: Temple University Press, 1976.

7420. Chase-Sardi, M. and O. Vysokolán. "El etnocidio en el pensamiento paraguayo." Suplemento Anropologico 19 (1984): 109-119.

7421. Cooney, Jarry W. "Abolition in the Republic of Paraguay, 1840-1870." Jahrbuch für Geschichte von Staat, Wirtschaft, und Gesellschaft Lateinamerikas 11 (1974): 149-166.

7422. Maybury-Lewis, David and James Howe. The Indian Peoples of Paraguay: Their Plight and Their Prospects. Cambridge, MA: Cultural Survival Inc., 1980.

7423. Muenzel, Mark. The Aché Indians: Genocide in Paraguay. Copenhagen: International Work Group for Indigenous Affairs, 1973.

7424. Pla, Josefina. Hermano negro. La esclavitud en el Paraguay. Madrid: 1972.

7425. Schvartzman, M. "El 'indio' y la sociedad: los prejucios étnicos en la Paraguay." Suplemento Anropologico 18 (1983): 179-243.

7426. Seiferheld, Alfredo M. Nazismo y fascismo en el Paraguay. 2 vols. Asunción: Histórica, 1986.

7427. La sociedad nacional y las comunidades indigenas: estudio de la educacion y las salud en cuatro communidades indigenas del alto Paraguay y actitudes de la poblacion nacional hacia los indigenas. Asuncion: Instituto Paraguayan del Indigena, 1985.

PERU

7428. Amat y Léon, Carlos and Hector Léon. <u>Niveles de vida y grupos sociales en el Peru</u>. Lima: Centro de Investigacion, Universidad del Pacifico, 1983.

7429. Amith, Gavin. "The Long Memory of a Forgotten People: The Struggle of Peru's Highland Peasants." <u>Candian Dimension</u> 19 (1985): 32-36.

7430. Balb, Florence. <u>The Development of Sexual Inequality in Vicos, Peru</u>. Buffalo: Council on International Studies, State University of New York at Buffalo, 1976.

7431. Ballon Aguirre, Francisco. <u>Etnia y represión penal</u>. Lima: Editora Ital-Peru, 1980.

7432. Beauclerk, John and Jeremy Narby. <u>Lessons from the Peruvian Amazon. A Fieldguide to Indigenous Peoples and Development</u>. Oxford: Oxfam Publications, 1987.

7433. Blanco, Hugo. <u>Land or Death</u>. New York: Pathfinder Press, 1973.

7434. Bonner, Raymond. "Peru's War." <u>New Yorker</u> (January 4, 1988)

7435. Bourque, Susan C. <u>Peru: Affirmative Action for the Majority</u>. May, 1984. ERIC ED 249 304.

7436. Bowser, Frederick P. <u>The African Slave in Colonial Peru, 1524-1650</u>. Stanford, CA: Stanford University Press, 1973.

7437. Bradley, Barbara. "'Resistance to Capitalism' in the Peruvian Andes." <u>Cambridge Studies in Social Anthropology</u> 41 (1982): 97-122.

7438. Campbell, Leon G. "Crime and Punishment in the Tupacamaru Rebellion in Peru." <u>Criminal Justice History</u> 5 (1984): 57- 89.

7439. Center of Studies and Promotion of Development (DESCO). Violencia politica en el Peru 1980-1988. Lima, Peru: DESCO, 1989.

7440. Cerron-Palomino, Rodolfo. "Language Policy in Peru: A Historical Overview." International Journal of the Sociology of Language 77 (1989): 11-33.

7441. Charney, Paul J. The Destruction and Reorganization of Indian Society in the Lima Valley, Peru, 1532-1824. Doctoral dissertation: University of Texas, 1989. UMO # 9016860.

7442. Cornell, A. and K. Roberts. "Democracy, Counterinsurgency, and Human Rights: The Case of Peru." Human Rights Quarterly 12 (November 1990)

7443. Cotler, Julio. "The Mechanisms of Internal Domination and Social Change in Peru." In Masses in Latin America, edited by J.L. Horowitz. New York: Oxford University Press, 1970.

7444. Cotler, Julio. "The Political Radicalization of Working- class Youth in Peru." Cepal Review No. 29 (August 1986): 107-118.

7445. Davies, Thomas M., Jr. "Indian Integration in Peru, 1820- 1948: An Overview." Americas 30 (1973): 184-208.

7446. Davies, Thomas M., Jr. Indian Integration in Peru: A Half Century of Experience, 1900-1948. Lincoln: University of Nebraska Press, 1974.

7447. DeWind, Josh. Peasants Become Miners: The Evolution of Industrial Mining Systems in Peru, 1902-1974. New York: Garland, 1987.

7448. Dietz, H. "Peru's Sendero Luminoso as a Revolutionary Movement." Journal of Political and Military Sociology 18 (Summer 1990)

7449. Doughty, Paul L. "Peace, Food and Equity in Peru." Urban Anthropology 15 (Spring-Summer 1986): 45-60.

7450. Epstein, Erwin H. "Education and Peruanidad: 'Internal' Colonialism in the Peruvian Highlands." Comparative Education Review 15 (June 1971): 188-201.

7451. Gilbert, Dennis L. The Oligarchy and the Old Regime in Peru. Doctoral dissertation: Cornell University, 1977. UMO # 7728351 [ca. 1850-1968.]

7452. Glewwe, Paul and Dennis de Tray. The Poor in Latin America during Adjustment: A Case Study of Peru. Washington, D.C.: World Bank, 1989.

7453. Gonzalez, Michael M. "Chinese Plantation Workers and Social Conflict in Peru in the Late Nineteenth Century." Journal of Latin American Studies 21 (1989): 385-424.

7454. Gonzalez, Michael M. "Neo-colonialism and Indian Unrest in Southern Peru, 1867-1989." Bulletin of Latin American Research 6 (1987): 1-26.

7455. Gonzalez, Raúl. "Ayachucho: por los caminos de Sendero [Luminoso]." QueHacer No. 19 (October 1982): 36-77.

7456. Gonzalez, Raúl. "Especial sobre Sendero." QueHacer No. 30 (August 1984): 6-29.

7457. Gras, Pierre. L'autre Pérou: l'integration des indiens, mythe ou réalité? Lyons: Editions Federop, 1981.

7458. Guerra Garcia, Francisco. Velasco: del Estado oligárquico al capitalismo de Estado. Lima: Centro de Estudios para el Desarrollo y la Participación, 1983.

7459. Harding, Colin. "Antonio Diaz Martinez and the Ideology of Sendero Luminoso." Bulletin of Latin American Research 7 (1988): 65-73.

7460. Harth-Terré, Emilio. Negros e Indios: un estamento social ignorado de Perú colonial. Lima: 1973.

7461. Hornberger, Nancy H. Bilingual Education and Quechua Language Maintenance in Highland Puno, Peru. Doctoral dissertation: University of Wisconsin, 1985. UMO # 8512303.

7462. Izquierda Unida, Comision de Plan de Gobierno Comision de Educacion. Plan de educacion de Izquierda Unida. Lima: Izquierda Unida, 1987.

7463. Kapsoli E., Wilfredo. Sublevaciones de esclavos en el Perú, s. XVIII. Lima: 1975,

7464. Lipp, Solomon. "Racial and Ethnic Problems: Peru." International Journal of Group Tensions 19 (Winter 1989): 339-348.

7465. Lopez de Romaña, Guillermo and others. "Health and Growth of Infants and Young Children in Huáscar, Peru." Ecology Food & Nutrition 19 (1987): 213-229.

7466. López Soria, José I., ed. El pensamiento fascista (1930- 1945). Lima: Mosca Azul Editores, 1981.

7467. Malcomson, Scott. "Alan Garcia and the Crisis of Populist Rule in Peru." Against the Current 2 (November-December 1987): 11-16.

7468. Mallon, Florencia E. The Defense of Community in Peru's Central Highlands: Peasant Struggle and Capitalist Transition, 1860-1940. Princeton, NJ: Princeton University Press, 1984.

7469. Mallon, Florencia E. "Patriarchy in the Transition to Capitalism: Central Peru, 1830-1950." Feminist Studies 13 (Summer 1987): 379-407.

7470. Malpica Silva Santisteban, Carlos. El poder económico en el Peru. Vol. 1, Lima: Mosca Azul Editores, 1989.

7471. Mariategui, Juan. La reforma agraria peruana: antecedentes historicos. Lima: Editorial Horizonte, 1985.

7472. Maude, H. E. The Peruvian Slave Trade in Polynesia, 1862-1864. Stanford, CA: Stanford University Press, 1981.

7473. McCormick, Gordon H. "The Shining Path and Peruvian Terrorism." Journal of Strategic Studies 10 (1987): 109-126.

7474. Mellafe, Rolando. La esclavitud en Hispanoamérica. Buenos Aires: 1964. [Esp. Peru.]

7475. Millones, Luis. Minorias etnicas en el Peru. Lima: Pontificia Universidad Catolica del Peru, 1973.

7476. Nunn, Audrey M. The Peruvian Educational Reform of 1972 and Its Implementation in Ayacucho. Doctoral dissertation: University of Sussex, 1987. [Order No. BRD-80189.]

7477. Palmer, David Scott. "Rebellion in Rural Peru: The Origins and Evolution of Sendero Luminoso." Comparative Politics 18 (1986): 127-146.

7478. Pastor, Manuel. "Peru's Failed Experiment." Dollars & Sense No. 148 (July-August 1989): 12-15, 21.

7479. Portugal Catacora, José. El niño indigena. Lima: Artex Editores, 1988.

7480. Post, David M. The Social Demand for Education in Peru: A Study of the Niero-Foundations. Doctoral dissertation: University of Chicago, 1987.

7481. Quiroz, Alfonso W. "Financial Leadership and the Formation of Peruvian Elite Groups, 1884-1930." Journal of Latin-American Studies 20 (May 1988): 49-81.

7482. Ramirez, Susan E. Provincial Patriarchy: Land Tenure and the Economics of Power in Colonial Peru. Albuquerque: University of New Mexico Press, 1985.

7483. Riding, Alan. "In the Incas' Land, a War for the People's Hearts." New York Times, (November 18, 1986)

7484. "Sendero en los Andes centrales." QueHacer (August-September 1989): 62-89.

7485. Smith, Gavin. Livelihood and Resistance. Peasants and the Politics of Land in Peru. Berkeley: University of California Press, 1990.

7486. Smith, Richard Chase. The Dialectics of Domination in Peru: Native Communities and the Myth of the Vast Amazonian Emptiness. Cambridge, MA: Cultural Survival Inc., 1982.

7487. Stewart, Watt. Chinese Bondage in Peru. A History of the Chinese Coolie in Peru, 1849-1874. Durham, NA: Duke University Press, 1951.

7488. Trahtenberg, Leon. "Antisemitism in the Peruvian Press." Latin American Jewish Studies Newsletter (Ann Arbor) (January 1988)

7489. Trahtenberg, Leon. Vida Judia en Lima y en las Provincias del Peru. Lima: Union Israelita del Peru, 1989.

7490. U. S. Congress, 99th 1st session, House of Representatives, Committee on Foreign Affairs, Subcommittee on Human Rights and International Organization. Human Rights in Peru: Hearing... Washington, D.C.: GPO, 1986.

7491. Valencias Quintanilla, Felix. Luchas campesinas en el contexto semifeudal del Oriente de Lucanas. Lima: Liberia Editorial Minerva-Miraflores, 1984. [Ayacucho department.]

7492. Varon Gabai, Rafael and A.P. Jacobs. "Peruvian Wealth and Spanish Investments: The Pizzaro Family during the Sixteenth Century." Hispanic American Historical Review 67 (1987): 657-696.

7493. Wachtel, Natan. The Vision of the Vanquished: The Spanish Conquest of Peru through Indian Eyes, 1530-1570. London: Harvester Press, 1977.

7494. Webb, Richard C. Government Policy and the Distribution of Income in Peru, 1963-1973. Cambridge, MA: Harvard University Press, 1977.

7495. Weeks, John. Limits to Capitalist Development: The Industrialization of Peru, 1950-1980. Boulder, CO: Westview Press, 1984.

7496. Wheat, A. "Shining Path's Fourth Sword Ideology." Journal of Political & Military Sociology 18 (Summer 1990)

7497. Wolff, Inge. "Negersklaverei und Negerhandel in Hochperu, 1540-1640." In Jahrbuch für Geschichte von Staat, Wirtschaft und Gesellschaft Lateinamerikas, 157-186. 1964.

7498. Zuckerman, Sam. "Peru on the Brink." Guardian (NYC) (October 8, 1986)
7499. No entry

PHILIPPINES

7500. Abubabar, Carmen A. "Muslim-Christian Relation: a Moro Perception." Solidarity 110 (January-February): 130-135.

7501. Abuso, Julian E. "Ethnicity and Education: Gaps and Links." Dansalan Quarterly 8 (April 1987): 10273.

7502. Ahmad, Aijaz. "Class and Colony in Mindanao." S.E. Asian Chronicle 82 (February 1982): 4-14.

7503. Alzona, Encarnacion. History of Education in the Philippines, 1565-1930. Manila: University of the Phillippines Press, 1932.

7504. Anderson, Benedict. "Cacique Democracy in the Philippines: Origins and Dreams." New Left Review 169 (May-June 1988): 3-31.

7505. Arce, Wilfredo and Ricardo Abad. "Social Situation." Marcos Era and Beyond, edited by John Bresnan. Princeton, 1986.

7506. Bagadion, Benjamin C., Jr. Trees, Monies, Rebels and Cronies: the Case of the Cellophil Resources Corporation. Doctoral dissertation, Cornell University, 1990.

7507. Beattie, Helen P. "American Teachers and the Filipinos (1904)." Bulletin of the American History Collection (Manila) (July-September 1984): 70-81.

7508. Bernad, Miguel A. "Structure and Culture of Philippine Society before the Spanish Conquest." Asian Pacific Quarterly (Summer 1972)

7509. Berry, Albert. "Income and Consumption Distribution Trends in the Philippines, 1950-1970." Review of Income and Wealth 24 (September 1978): 313-331.

7510. Brown, Elaine C. "Pundasyon Hanunoo Mangyan School - Participatory Education in the Philippines." Cultural Survival Quarterly 9, 2 (1985): 6-9.

7511. Buruma, Ian. "Saint Cory and the Yellow Revolution." New York Review of Books (November 6, 1986)

7512. Cantas, M. and others. Land, Poverty, and Politics in the Philippines. London: Catholic Institute for International Relations,

7513. Caoili, Manuel A. "Quezon and His Business Friends: Notes on the Origins of Philippine National Capitalism." Philippine Journal of Public Administration 31 (January 1987): 65-106.

7514. Carino, Theresa. "Chinese in the Philippines: a Survey of the Literature." Journal of South Seas Society 43 (1988): 43- 54.

7515. Casino, E. S. "Interethnic Conflict in the Philippine Archipelago." Ethnic Conflict: International Perspectives, edited by Jerry Boucher and others. Newbury Park, CA: Sage, 1987.

7516. Chapman, William. Inside the Philippine Revolution. New York: Norton, 1987.

7517. Clymer, Kenton J. Protestant Missionaries in the Philippines 1898-1916: An Inquiry into the American Colonial Mentality. Urbana: University of Illinois Press, 1986.

7518. Constantino, Renato. "Miseducation of the Filipino." Journal of Contemporary Asia (Autumn 1970)

7519. Constantino, Renato. Miseducation of the Filipino. Manila: Foundation for Nationalist Studies, 1982.

7520. Constantino, Renato. Neocolonial Identity and Counterconsciousness: Essays on Cultural Decolonization. White Plains, NY: Sharpe, 1979.

7521. Corpuz, Onofre D. "Education and Socio-economic Change in the Philippines, 1870-1960." Philippine Social Science and Humanities Review 32 (1967): 193-268.

7522. Corpuz, Onofre D. "Western Colonization and the Filipino Response." Journal of Southeast Asia History 3 (March 1962): 1-23.

7523. Cortes, Josefina R. "Education, Politics and Social Equity in the Philippines." S.E. Asian Journal of Education Studies 24 (1987): 1-37.

7524. Cruz, Romeo V. "America's Colonial Desk and the Philippines, 1898-1934." Philippine Social Service and Humanities Review 37 (1972): 267-514.

7525. Cullinane, Michael. <u>Illustrado Politics: the Response of the Filipino Educated Elite to American Colonial Rule, 1898- 1907</u>. University of Michigan, 1989. Doctoral dissertation.

7526. David, Randolph G., ed. <u>Marxism in the Philippines</u>. Quezon City, 1984.

7527. De los Reyes, Romana P. <u>Claims to Land: Lessons from Haciendas in Negros Occidental</u>. Quezon City, Philippines: Institute of Philippines Culture, 1989.

7528. DeBevoise, Ken. <u>Compromised Host: the Epidemiological Context of the Philippine-American War</u>. University of Oregon, 1986.

7529. Del Rosario, Virginia O. "Child Labor Phenomenon in the Philippines: Problems and Policy Thrusts." <u>Philippine Journal of Industrial Relations</u> 8 (1986): 37-52.

7530. Deoppers, D. T. <u>Manila, 1900-1941: Social Change in a Late Colonial Metropolis</u>. New Haven, CT: Yale University Southeast Asian Studies, 1984.

7531. Eder, James F. "Deforestation and Detribalization in the Philippines: the Palaevan Case." <u>Population and Environment</u> 12 (Winter 1990)

7532. Eder, James F. <u>On the Road to Tribal Extinction: Depopulation, Deculturation, and Adaptive Well-Being among the Batak of the Philippines</u>. Berkeley: University of California Press, 1987.

7533. Enriquez, Virgilio G. "Decolonizing the Filipino Psyche: Philippine Psychology in the Seventies." <u>Philippine Social Science Humanities Review</u> 45 (January-December 1981): 191- 216.

7534. Escultura, Edgar E. "Roots of Backwardness: an Analysis of the Philippine Condition." <u>Science and Society</u> 38 (Spring 1974): 49-76.

7535. Felix, Alfonso L., Jr. "Colonial Society in the Philippines." <u>Bulletin of American History Collections (Manila)</u> 6 (January-March 1978): 30-51.

7536. Foley, Douglas E. "Colonialism and Schooling in the Philippines from 1898 to 1970." <u>Education and Colonialism</u>, edited by Philip G. Altbach and Gail P. Kelly. New York: Longman, 1978.

7537. Francisco, Juan R. "Islamic Literature in the Philippines." <u>Mindando Journal</u> 11 (1976): 6-45.

7538. Friend, Theodore. <u>Blue-Eyed Enemy: Japan against the West in Java and Luzon, 1942-1945</u>. Princeton, New Jersey: Princton University Press, 1988.

7539. George, T. J. S. Revolt in Mindanao: the Rise of Islam in Philippine Politics. Oxford, 1980.

7540. Gibson, Katherine and Julie Graham. "Situating Migrants in Theory: the Case of Filipino Migrant Contract Construction Workers." Capital and Class 29 (Summer 1986): 130-149.

7541. Gluck, Lewis E. Jr. "American Planters and the Tribes in Mindanao." Bulletin of the American History Collection (Manila) 17 (April-June 1989): 42-55.

7542. Gonzalez, Michael M. "Philippine Railroads: Ideology of Progress in an American Colony." Philippine Social Science and Humanities Review 45 (January-December 1981): 271-283.

7543. Gowing, P. S. Muslim-Filipinos - Heritage and Horizon. Quezon City, 1979.

7544. Graff, H. F. American Imperialism and the Philippine Insurrection. Boston, MA: 1969.

7545. Grossman, Zoltan. "Inside the Philippine Resistance." Race and Class 28 (Autumn 1986): 1-29.

7546. Hart, Charles D. "American Teacher in Paragua." Bulletin of the American History Collection (Manila) 12 (July-September 1984): 82-103.

7547. Horton, S. "Child Nutrition and Family Size in the Philippines." Journal of Development Economics 23 (September 1986)

7548. Hunt, Chester L. "Education and Economic Development in the Early American Period in the Philippines." Philippine Studies 36 (1988): 352-364.

7549. Imperial, Reynaldo H. "Spanish and American Colonization Processes in Samar." Asian Studies (Quezon City) 22-24 (1984- 1986): 28-51.

7550. Javier, Ernesto O. "Deterioration in Philippine Education." Kinaadman 8 (1986): 5-8.

7551. Jones, Gregg R. "On Fertile Negros: Filipinos Die of Malnutrition." Boston Globe (September 7, 1986)

7552. Jones, Gregg R. Red Revolution: Inside the Philippine Guerrilla Movement. Boulder, CO: Westview, 1989.

7553. Jose, Vivencio R. "Contemporary Education and Culture: Basic Problems and Perspectives." Philippine Social Science and Humanities Review 44 (January-December 1980): 21-56.

7554. Jose, Vivencio R. "Workers' Response to Early American Rule, 1900-1935." Philippine Social Science and Humanities Review 45 (January-December 1981): 285-311.

7555. Kerkvliet, Benedict J. T. "Everyday Resistance to Injustice in a Philippine Village." Journal of Peasant Studies 13 (January 1986): 107-123.

7556. Khan, M. H. and J.A. Zerby. "Socioeconomic Position of the Philippines in the Third World." Philippine Economic Journal 23 (1984)

7557. Koike, Kenji. "Reorganization of Zaibatsu Groups under the Marcos and Aquino Regimes." East Asian Cultural Studies 28 (March 1989): 127-143.

7558. Kowalewski, David. "Vigilante Counterinsurgency and Human Rights in the Philippines: a Statistical Analysis." Human Rights Quarterly 12 (May 1990): 246-264.

7559. Lacer, Luis Q. "Neglected Dimensions in the Development of Filipino Muslims." Solidarity 113 (July-August 1987): 8-16.

7560. Lallana, Emmanuel C. "Alternative Conception of Philippine Class Structure: a Critique of Orthodox Understanding." Philippine Journal of Public Administration 31 (July 1987): 309-350.

7561. An Lim, Jaime L. Literature and Politics: the Colonial Experience in the Philippine Novel. Doctoral dissertation, Indiana University, 1989. UMO # 8925123.

7562. Lopez-Gonzaga, Violeta. "Roots of Agrarian Unrest in Negros, 1850-1890." Philippines Studies 36 (1988): 151-165.

7563. Maceda, Marcelino N. "'Cultural Minorities': A Suggested Approach to their Development." Philippine Political Science Journal 15-16 (June-December 1982): 32-44.

7564. Majul, Cesar A. Contemporary Muslim Movement in the Philippines. Berkeley, CA: Mizan Press, 1985.

7565. Manasan, Rosario G. "Tax Evasion in the Philippines, 1981- 1985." Journal of Philippine Development 15 (1988): 167-190.

7566. Mangalres, M. "What Happened to the Poor on the Way to the Next Development Plan?" Philippine Economic Journal 21 (1982)

7567. May, Glenn A. Social Engineering in the Philippines: the Aims, Execution and Impact of American Colonial Policy, 1900- 1913. Westport, CT: Greenwood, 1980.

7568. May, Glenn A. "Why the United States Won the Philippine- American War, 1899-1902." Bulletin of American History Collection (Manila) 13 (January-March 1985): 67-90.

7569. McCoy, Alfred W. "Philippines: Independence without Decolonization." Asia - the Winning of Independence: the Philippines, India, Indonesia, Vietnam, Malaya, edited by Robin Jeffrey. New York: St. Martin's Press, 1981.

7570. Miller, Stuart C. "Benevolent Assimilation": the American Conquest of the Philippines, 1899-1903. New Haven, CT: Yale University Press, 1982.

7571. Mojares, Resil B. "Worcester in Cebu: Filipine Response to American Business, 1915-1924." Philippine Quarterly Culture Society 13 (March 1985): 1-13.

7572. Molloy, Ivan. "Decline of the Moro National Liberation Front in the Southern Philippines." Journal of Contemporary Asia 18 (1988): 59-76.

7573. Munro, Ross H. "New Khmer Rouge." Commentary 80 (December 1985): 19-38.

7574. Mydans, Seth. "In the Big Manila Land Plan, Steps Are Small." New York Times (October 18, 1987)

7575. Nagano, Yoshiko. "Agrarian Reform under Aquino: A Macro- view from Negros." Solidarity 120 (October-December 1988): 83-90.

7576. Oadea, Rizalino. Social and Economic Background of Philippine Nationalism, 1830-1892. Doctoral dissertation, University of Hawaii, 1974.

7577. Ofreno, Rene E. "Structure of the Economy during the American Colonial Period." Journal of History (Philippine National Historical Society) 27 (January-December 1982): 1- 39.

7578. Ortiz, Alan T. Towards a Theory of Ethnic Separatism: a Case Study of Muslims in the Philippines. University of Pennsylvania, 1986. UMO# 8614846.

7579. Oshima, H. T. "Changes in Philippine Income Distribution in the 1970's." Philippine Review of Economics and Business 20 (September-December 1983)

7580. Owen, Norman G. Comprador Colonialism: Studies on the Philippines under American Rule. Ann Arbor: University of Michigan Papers on South and Southeast Asia, 1971.

7581. Pablo, Renato Y. and Richard C. Gardner. "Ethnic Stereotypes of Filipino Children and their Parents." Philippine Studies 31 (1987): 332-347.

7582. Palanea, Ellen H. "Transfer of Socioeconomic Status Across Generations in Filipino Families." Philippine Economic Journal 21 (1982): 60-94.

7583. Paredes, Ruby R. Partido Federal, 1900-1907: Political Collaboration in Colonial Manila. 2 vols. Doctoral dissertation, University of Michigan, 1989. UMO# 9023614.

7584. Parpan, Alfredo G. "Japanese and the Philippine Church, 1942-1945." Philippine Studies 37 (1989): 451-466.

7585. Phelan, John L. Hispanization of the Philippines: Spanish Arms and Filipino Responses, 1505-1700. Madison: University of Wisconsin Press, 1959.

7586. Philippines - Authoritarian Government, Multinationals and Ancestral Lands. London: Anti-Slavery Society, 1983.

7587. Pomeroy, William J. American Neo-colonialism: Its Emergence in the Philippines and Asia. NY, 1970.

7588. Quirino, Carlos. "Spanish Colonial Army: 1878-1898." Philippine Studies 36 (1988): 381-386.

7589. Quisumbing, Agnes R. "Agrarian Reform and Rural Poverty in the Philippines." Philippine Economic Journal 27 (1988): 149- 168.

7590. Ragsdale, Jane S. Coping with the Yankees: the Filipino Elite, 1898-1903. Doctoral dissertation, University of Wisconsin, 1975. UMO# 759994.

7591. Ramos, Elias T. "Labor Conflict and Recent Trends in Philippine Industrial Relations." Philippine Quarterly Cultural Society 15 (September 1987): 173-197.

7592. Ramos-Jimenez, Pilar and others. "Poor in Philippine Cities: A Situation Analysis." Sojourn 3 (February 1988): 79- 89.

7593. Razon, Felix and Richard Hensman. Oppression of the Indigenous Peoples of the Philippines. Copenhagen: IWGIA, 1976.

7594. Regalado, Basilia M. "Distribution Impacts of Selected Food Policies on Human Nutrition in the Philippines." Philippine Economic Journal 24 (1985): 143-180.

7595. Reid, Anthony. "Islamization and Colonial Rule in Moroland." Solidarity 100 (1984): 64-74.

7596. Remotique, Fe. "Lowlanders Need to Learn of Tribal Filipinos." PCR Information 22 (1986): 27-32.

7597. Reyes, Renato B. "American Jesuit Missionaries and the Rise of Catholic Schools in Northern Mindanao." Kinaadman 7 (1985): 51-71.

7598. Rivera, Roselle L. K. "Children at Work: The Labor Scene through the Eyes of Filipino Children." Philippine Sociological Review 33 (January-June 1985): 11-17.

7599. Rosca, Ninotchka. Endgame: the Fall of Marcos. NY: Watts, 1988.

7600. Salanga, Alfredo and Esther M. Pacheco, eds. Versus: Philippine Protest Poetry, 1983-1986. Seattle: University of Washington Press, 1987.

7601. Saleeby, Najeeb M. "Moro Problem: An Academic Discussion of the History and Solution of the Problem of the Government of the Moros of the Philippine Islands." Danoalan 2 5 (October 1983): 7-48.

7602. "Salvaging" Democracy: Human Rights in the Philippines. NY: Lawyers Committee for Human Rights, 1985.

7603. San Juan, Epifanio. Crisis in the Philippines: the Making of a Revolution. South Hadley, MA: Bergin & Garvey, 1986.

7604. San Juan, Epifanio. Towards a People's Literature: Essays in the Dialectics and Contradiction in Philippine Writing. Quezon City: University of the Philippines Press, 1984.

7605. Santiago, Domingo C. History of Philippine Education During the Japanese Occupation. Master's thesis. University of the Philippines, 1951.

7606. Sates, John M. Schoolbooks and Krags: the United States Army in the Philippines, 1989-1902. Westport, CT: Greenwood, 1973.

7607. Schirmer, Daniel B. and Stephen R. Shalom, eds. Philippines Reader: a History of Colonialism, Neo-colonialism, Dictatorship, and Resistance. Boston, MA: South End Press, 1986.

7608. Scott, William Henry. "Class Structure in the Unhispanized Philippines." Philippine Studies 27 (1979): 137-159.

7609. Scott, William Henry. "Filipino Class Structure in the Sixteenth Century." Cracks in the Parchment Curtain and Other Essays in Philippine History. Quezon City: New Day Publishers, 1982.

7610. Serrano, Josephine B. "Poor Little City of Manila: 1942- 1945." Unitas 44 (1971): 95-108.

7611. Shalom, Stephen R. United States and the Philippines: a Study of Neocolonialism. Philadelphia, PA: Institute for the Study of Human Issues, 1982.

7612. Shaplen, Robert. "Thin Edge II." New Yorker (September 28, 1987)

7613. Shinzo, Hayase. "Tribes on the Davao Frontier, 1899-1941." Philippine Studies 33 (1985): 139-150.

7614. Sicat, Gerardo P. "Historical and Current Perspective of Philippine Economic Problems." Philippine Economic Journal 24 (1985): 24-63.

7615. Simbulan, Dante C. Study of the Socio-economic Elite in Philippine Politics and Government, 1946-1963. Doctoral dissertation, Australian National University, 1966.

7616. Simons, Lewis M. Worth Dying For. NY: Morrow, 1987.

7617. Sison, Jose Maria. "Revolutionary Prospects in the Philippines." Monthly Review 40 (December 1988): 1-9.

7618. Smith, D. H. "American Atrocities in the Philippines: Some New Evidence." Pacific Historical Review 55 (May 1986): 281-283.

7619. Smith, H. L. and P.P.L. Cheung. "Trends in the Effects of Family Background on Educational Attainment in the Philippines." American Journal of Sociology 91 (1986): 1387-1408.

7620. Solon, F. S. and others. "Bulacan Nutrition and Health Study: Part 1. Baseline Socioeconomic and Related Characteristics of Subject Families and Their Impact on the Nutritional Health of Infants." Ecology Food Nutrition 16 (1985): 299-315.

7621. Solon, F. S. and others. "Bulacan Nutrition and Health Study: Part 2. Food, Immunization, Sanitation, and Education as Intervention to Improve the Growth of Infants. Part 3. The Cost of Nutrition and Health Interventions and Their Combinaions in Relation to Their Effectiveness." Ecology Food Nutrition 17 (1985): 65-85, 87-99.

7622. Solon, Orville. "Urban Poor: Their Case from Selected Communities in Metro Manila, Cebu, and Davao, Philippines." Philippine Economic Journal 27 (1988): 169-187.

7623. Sta. Romana, E. R. "Philippines State's Hegemony and Fiscal Base, 1950-1985." Development Economies 27 (June 1989): 185-205.

7624. Stanley, Peter W., ed. Reappraising an Empire: New Perspectives on Philippine-American History. Cambridge, MA: 1984.

7625. Steinberg, David J. Philippines: a Singular and Plural Place. Boulder, CO: Westview Press, 1982.

7626. Tan, Antonio S. "Chinese Mestizos and the Formation of the Filipine Nationality." Archipel 32 (1986): 141-162.

7627. Tawagon, Manuel R. "Moro Struggle for Self-Determination: A Fourth Alternative." Dansalan Quarterly 9 (January-April 1988): 65-85.

7628. Terasaki, Y. "Income Distribution and Development Policies in the Philippines." Developing Economies 23 (December 1985)

7629. Utrecht, Ernst. "Separatist Movement in the Southern Philippines." Race and Class 16 (April 1975): 387-403.

7630. Villegas, Edberto M. "Foreign Investments and the Multinational Corporations in the Philippines." Philippine Social Sciences and Humanities Review 42 (January-December 1978): 27-55.

7631. Villegas, Edberto M. "Philippine Labor Code and the Industrial Workers." Philippine Social Science and Humanities Review 44 (January-December 1980): 75-101.

7632. Walters, W. G. "Rise and Fall of Provincial Elites in the Philippines: "Nueva Ecija" from the 1880's to the Present Day." Sojourn 4 (1989): 54-74.

7633. Warren, Charles P. "Black Asians in the Philippines: the 'Negrito Problem' Revisited." Pilipinas (Fall 1985): 53-67.

7634. Watkins, David and others. "Antecedents of Affective and Cognitive Learning: Outcome in Privileged and Depressed Areas of the Philippines." Journal of Developing Societies 2 (April 1986): 103-118.

7635. Weeks, Priscilla. "Appropriation of Social Science by the Rural Elite: Knowledge or Power." Philippine Quarterly Cultural Society 16 (March 1988): 3-18.

7636. Weightman, George R. "Anti-sinicism in the Philippines." Asian Studies 5 (April 1967): 220-231.

7637. Weightman, George R. "Philippine Sociology and Its Colonial Past." Solidarity 102 (1985): 104-118.

7638. Wickberg, Edgar B. Chinese in Philippine Life, 1850-1898. New Haven, CT: Yale University Press, 1965.

7639. Williams, Vernon L. U.S. Navy in the Philippine Insurrection and Subsequent Native Unrest, 1898-1906. Doctoral dissertation, Texas A & M University, 1985. UMO# 8528397.

7640. Zwick, Jim. Militarism and Repression in the Philippines. McGill University Centre for Developing Area Studies, 1983.

POLAND

7641. Andreski, S. "Poland." In Fascism in Europe. 2d ed., edited by S.J. Woolf. London: Methuen, 1982.

7642. Banas, Josef. The Scapegoats: The Exodus of the Remnants of Polish Jewry. New York Translated by Tadeusz Szafar: Holmes & Meier, 1979.

7643. Bartoszewski, Wladyslaw. "Polish-Jewish Relations in Occupied Poland, 1939-1945." The Jews of Poland (1986): 147- 160.

7644. Baske, Siegfried, ed. Bildungspolitik in der Volksrepublik Polen, 1944-1986. Wiesbaden: Otto Harrassowitz, 1987.

7645. Bauman, Zygmunt. "Officialdom and Class: Bases of Inequality in Socialist Society." In The Social Analysis of Class Structure, edited by Frank Parkin. London: Tavistock, 1974.

7646. "Belorussians in the Eyes of the Poles, 1918-1939." Acta Poloniae Historica (Poland) No. 51 (1985): 101-122. Translated by Jerzy Tomaszewski and Phillip G. Smith.

7647. Bielasiak, Jack. "Social Confrontation and Contrived Crisis: March 1968 in Poland." East European Quarterly 22 (1988): 81-105.

7648. Blit, Lucjan. The Anti-Jewish Campaign in Present-Day Poland, 2nd ed. London: Institute of Jewish Affairs, 1968.

7649. Bloch, Andrzei J. "The Private Sector in Poland." Telos No. 66 (Winter 1985-86): 128-133.

7650. Bobinska, Celina &. Adam Galos. "Poland: Land of Mass Migration (19th and 20th Centuries)." In Poland at the 14th International Congress of Historical Sciences in San Francisco. Wroclaw: 1975.

7651. Bohdanowicz, L. "The Muslims in Poland- Their Origin, History, and Cultural Life." Journal of the Royal Asiatic Society (October 1942)

7652. Borwicz, Michel. "La Pologne et les survivants." Espirit 6 (1986): 53-62. [Polish Jewry since 1945.]

7653. Breyer, Richard. "Die deutsche Bevölkerung in Polen 1933- 1939." Schriftenreihe Georg-Eckert-Inst. int. Schulbuchforsch. 22 (1986): 71-83.

7654. Brumberg, Abraham. "The Troubling Trends in Poland." Boston Globe, (January 5, 1991): [Authoritarianism, clericalism, and antisemitism.]

7655. Cala, Alina. "Die Anfänge des Antisemitismus im Königreich Polen in der zweiten Hälfte des neunzehnten Jahrhunderts." International Review of Social History 30 (1985): 342-373.

7656. Central Commission for Investigation of German Crimes in Poland. German Crimes in Poland. 2 vols. New York: Fertig, 1982.

7657. Clark, Joanna and Abraham Brumberg. "Jews in Poland." New York Times Book Review (November 23, 1986): [Exchange of letters, relating to 1930s and 1940s.]

7658. Cooper, Lolek. "Poland's Guilt." Jerusalem Post, (April 13, 1987): [Polish antisemitism.]

7659. Corrsin, Stephen D. "Language Use in Cultural and Political Change in Pre-1914 Warsaw: Poles, Jews, and Russification." Slavonic and East European Review 68 (January 1990): 69- 90.

7660. Corrsin, Stephen D. Warsaw before the First World War: Poles and Jews in the Third City of the Russian Empire, 1880- 1914. Boulder, CO: East European Monographs, 1989.

7661. Czubinski, A. "Poland's Place in Nazi Plans for a New Order in Europe in the Years 1934-1940." Polish Western Affairs 21 (1980): 19-46.

7662. Dangschat, Jens and J. Blasius. "Social and Spatial Disparities in Warsaw in 1978: An Application of Correspondence Analysis to a 'Socialist' City." Urban Studies 24 (June 1987)

7663. Dangschat, Jens. Soziale und raumliche Ungleichheit in Warschau. Hamburg: Hans Christians Druckerei und Verlag, 1985.

7664. Daniel, Krystyna. "The Image of Jews in the Consciousness of Polish Youth." Europa Ethnica 47 (1990): 1-12. [May 1988.]

7665. Diehl, Jackson. "Poorest Poles Fall Below Reach of Statist Welfare." Washington Post, (January 24, 1986)

7666. Drozdowski, Marian M. "The Attitude of Sikorski's Government to the Tragedy of the Polish Jews (1939-1944)." Acta Poloniae hist. 52 (1985): 147-170.

7667. Drozdowski, Marian M. "The National Minorities in Poland 1918-1939." Acta Poloniae Historica 22 (1970)

7668. Druker, Abraham. "Fight Against Ghetto Benches in Polish Universities and Ghettos for Jewish Students in Warsaw Colleges." School and Society 46 (1937): 502, 591.

7669. Dubnov, Simon M. History of the Jews in Russia and Poland from the Earliest Times Until the Present Day. Philadelphia: Jewish Publication Sociology of America, 1916-1946.

7670. Dunin-Wasowicz, Krzysztof and Israel Gutman. "Warsaw." In Encyclopedia of the Holocaust,IV, pp. 1598-1625. New York: Macmillan, 1990.

7671. Edelman, Marek. The Ghetto Fights: Warsaw 1941-1943. London: Bookmarks, 1990.

7672. Engel, David. In the Shadow of Auschwitz. The Polish Government-in-Exile and the Jews, 1939-1942. Chapel Hill: University of North Carolina Press, 1987.

7673. Feffer, John. "Eastern Economic Outlook." Z Magazine 3 (July-August 1990): 27-31. [Transition to capitalism in Poland.]

7674. Fiedor, Karol. "The Attitude of German Right-wing Organizations to Poland in the Years 1918-1933." Polish Western Affairs 14 (1973): 247-269.

7675. Flakierski, Henryk. "Economic Reform and Income Distribution: A Case study of Hungary and Poland." Eastern European Economics 24 (Fall-Winter 1985-1986)

7676. Flakierski, Henryk. Economic Reform and Income Distribution. A Case Study of Hungary and Poland. Armonk, New York: Sharpe, 1986.

7677. Franklin, James L. "Poland's Ukrainian Culture Faces Eradication." Boston Globe, (August 31, 1986)

7678. Gitman, Joseph. The Jews and Jewish Problems in the Polish Parliament, 1919-1939. Doctoral dissertation: Yale University, 1963. UMO # 67-10,345.

7679. Golczewski, Frank. Polnisch-judische Beziehungen 1881-1922: eine Studie zur Geschichte d. Antisemitismus in Osteuropa. Doctoral dissertation: University of Cologne, 1981.

7680. Goldberg, Jacob. "Poles and Jews in the 17th and 18th Centuries, Rejections or Acceptance." Jahrbucher fur Geschichte Osteuropas 22 (1974): 248-282.

7681. Green, Warren. "The Karaite Community in Interwar Poland." Nationalities Papers 14 (1986): 101-109.

7682. Gross, Feliks. "Tolerance and Intolerance in Poland: The Two Political Traditions." Polish Review 20 (1975): 65-69.

7683. Gross, Jan T. Polish Society under German Occupation: The Generalgouvernement, 1939-1944. Princeton, NJ: Princeton University Press, 1979.

7684. Gross, Jan T. "Polish-Jewish Relations During the War: An Interpretation." Dissent 34 (Winter 1987): 73-81. [W.W.II.]

7685. Gross, Jan T. and Irena Gross. War through Children's Eyes: The Soviet Occupation of Poland and the Deportation, 1939- 1941. Stanford, CA: Hoover Institution, 1981.

7686. Groth, Alexander J. "Dimoski, Pilsudski, and Ethnic Conflict in Pre-1939 Poland." Canadian Slavic Studies (Spring 1969)

7687. Grulich, Rudolf. "Die nationalen Minderheiten in Polen." Europa Ethnica 32 (1975): 177-181. [English summary, p.181.]

7688. Grynberg, Henryk. "Is Polish Anti-Semitism Special?" Midstream 29 (August-September 1983): 19-23.

7689. Gutman, Israel. The Jews of Warsaw, 1939-1943: Ghetto, Underground, Revolt. Translated by Ina Friedman. Bloomington, IN: Indiana University Press, 1982.

7690. Gutman, Israel. "Polish Responses to the Liquidation of Warsaw Jewry." Jerusalem Quarterly 17 (1980): 40-55.

7691. Gutman, Israel. "Warsaw Ghetto Uprising." In Encylopedia of the Holocaust, IV. 1625-1632. New York: Macmillan, 1990.

7692. Gutman, Israel and others, eds. The Jews of Poland Between Two World Wars. Hanover, N.H.: University Press of New England, 1989.

7693. Gutman, Israel and Shmuel Krakowski. Unequal Victims. Poles and Jews During World War Two. New York Translated by Ted Gorelick and Witold Jedlicki: Holocaust Library, 1986.

7694. Hann, C. M. A Village without Solidarity: Polish Peasants in Years of Crisis. New Haven, CT: Yale University Press, 1985. [Ukrainians.]

7695. Hauser, Przemyslaw. "Die deutsche Minderheit in Polen 1918- 1933." Schriftenreihe Georg-Eckert-Inst. int. Schulbuchforsch. 22 (1985): 67-88.

7696. Heller, Celia S. On the Edge of Destruction: The Jews of Poland Between the 2 World Wars. New York: Columbia University Press, 1976.

7697. Hertz, Aleksander. The Jews in Polish Culture. Evanston, IL Translated by Richard Lowrie: Northwestern University Press, 1988.

7698. Hertz, Aleksander. "The Social Background of the Pre-war Polish Political Structure." Journal of Central European Affairs 146-161 (July 1942): 2.

7699. High Commission for Research into Nazi Crimes in Poland. Crimes Against Polish Children, 1939-1945. Warsaw: Polish Scientific Publishers, 1973.

7700. Hillel, Marc. Le massacre des survivants: En Pologne apres l'holocauste (1945-1947). Paris: Plon, 1985.

7701. Horak, Stephan. Poland and Her National Minorities, 1919- 1939. New York: Vantage, 1961.

7702. Hundert, Gershon D. "The Role of the Jews in Commerce in Early Modern Poland-Lithuania." Journal of European Economic History 16 (1987): 245-275.

7703. Imbrogno, Salvatore. "Social Policy Planning and Social Work Practices in Poland." Social Work 35 (July 1990): 302- 306.

7704. Irwin-Zarecka, Iwona. "After the Holocaust: National Attitudes to Jews: Catholics and Jews in Poland Today." Holocaust and Genocide Studies 4 (1989): 27-40.

7705. Irwin-Zarecka, Iwona. Neutralizing Memory: The Jew in Contemporary Poland. New Brunswick, NJ: Transaction, 1989.

7706. Jedruszak, Tadeusz. "Anti-Nazi Organizations of the Resistance Movement in Poland (1939-1945)." Polish World Affairs 2 (1975): 168-204.

7707. Jivonen, Jyrki K. Independence or Incorporation? The Idea of Poland's National Self-determination and Independence within the Russian and Soviet Socialism from the 1870s to the 1920s. Helsinki: Finnish Institute of International Affairs, 1990.

7708. Jobert, Ambroise. "Religious Tolerance in Sixteenth-century Poland." In Poland in Christian Civilization, edited by Jerry Braun. London: Veritas Foundation, 1985.

7709. Kaufman, Michael T. "Trip by Pope Stirring Issue of Ukrainians." New York Times, (June 5, 1987)

7710. Kloczowski, Jerzy. "The Religious Orders and the Jews in Nazi-occupied Poland." Polin 3 (1988): 238-243.

7711. Kloskowska, Antonina. "The Negroes as Seen by Polish Children." International Journal of Comparative Sociology 3 (1962): 189-199.

7712. Korzec, Pawel. "Polen und der Minderheitenschutzvertrag (1919-1934)." Jahrbucher fur Geschichte Osteuropas 22 (1974): 515-555.

7713. Kozlowski, Maciej. "Poles and Ukrainians: Troubled History." Polish Review 23 (1988): 271-293.

7714. Krajewski, Stanislaw. "Jewish Identity in a Non-Jewish World." Christian Jewish Relations 20 (Autumn 1987): 8-25.

7715. Labuda, Gerard. "The Polish Western Frontier in the Thousand Year History of the Polish State and Nation." Polish Western Affairs 26 (1985): 3-28.

7716. Lipski, Jan J. KOR: A History of the Workers' Defense Committee in Poland, 1976-1981. Translated by Olga Amsterdamska and Gene M. Moore. Berkeley: University of California Press, 1986.

7717. Lipton, D. and J. Sachs. "Creating Market Economy in Eastern Europe. The Case of Poland." Brookings Papers on Economic Activity No. 1 (1990)

7718. Lukas, Richard C. Forgotten Holocaust. Poles under German Occupation 1939-1944. Lexington: University Press of Kentucky, 1987.

7719. Lukas, Richard C. Out of the Inferno. Poles Remember the Holocaust. Lexington: University Press of Kentucky, 1989.

7720. Maczak, Antoni. "Vicissitudes of Feudalism in Modern Poland." In The Power of the Past: Essays for Eric Hobsbawm, edited by Pat Thane and others. New York: Cambridge University Press, 1984.

7721. Madajcayk, Czeslaw and Israel Gutman. "Poland." In Encyclopedia of the Holocaust, III. New York: Macmillan, 1990.

7722. Mahler, Raphael. "Anti-semitism in Poland." In Essays in Antisemitism, edited by K.S. Pinson. New York: 1942.

7723. Marcus, Joseph. Social and Political History of the Jews in Poland, 1919-1939. Berlin: Mouton, 1983.

7724. Mauersberg, Stanislaw. "The Educational System and Democratization of Society in Poland (1918-1939)." Acta Poloniae Hist. 55 (1987): 133-158.

7725. Micgiel, John and others, ed. Poles and Jews: Myth and Reality in the Historical Context. New York: Institute on East Central Europe, Columbia University, 1986.

7726. Miskiewicz, Benon. "The Development of Higher Education in the Recovered Territories during the Forty Years of People's Poland." Polish World Affairs 26 (1985): 303-316.

7727. Modras, Ronald. "Pope John Paul II, St. Maximilian Kolbe, and Antisemitism: Some Current Problems and Perceptions Affecting Catholic-Jewish Relations." Journal of Ecumenical Studies 20 (Fall 1983): 630-639.

7728. Motzkin, Leo. La campagne antisemite en Pologne. Paris: Rousseau, 1932.

7729. Mushkat, Marion. "Antisemitism Without Jews: The Case of Communist Poland." International Problems (Tel Aviv) Nos. 1-4 (1983): 1-138.

7730. Niezabitowska, Malgorzata. Remnants. The Last Jews of Poland. Translated by William Brand and Hanna Dobosiewicz. New York: Friendly Press, 1986.

7731. Olszewski, Henryk. "The Essence and Legal Foundations of the Magnate Oligarchy in Poland." Acta Poloniae Hist. 56 (1987): 29-49.

7732. Pinchuk, Ben-Cion. "Cultural Sovietization in a Multi- ethnic Environment: Jewish Culture in Soviet Poland, 1939- 1941." Jewish Social Studies 48 (1986): 63-174.

7733. "A Polish Pastoral Letter on the Jews." New York Times, (January 20, 1991): [Read to masses in all Roman Catholic churches in Poland in January 20, 1991.]

7734. Polonsky, Antony, ed. My Brother's Keeper. Recent Polish Debates on the Holocaust. New York: Routledge, 1990.

7735. Prekerowa, Teresa. "Zegota." In Encyclopedia of the Holocaust, IV. New York: Macmillan, 1990.

7736. Radziejowski, Janusz. "Ukrainians and Poles, the Shaping of Reciprocal Images and Stereotypes." Acta Poloniae Historica No. 50 (1984): 115-140.

7737. Resnick, Sid. "Polish Jewry and Socialist 'Renewal': Anti-Semitism, a Weapon against Solidarity." Jewish Currents 35 (1981): 4-9, 31-33.

7738. Ringelblum, Emmanuel. Polish-Jewish Relations During the Second World War. New York: Howard Featig, 1976.

7739. Rosman, M. J. "Reflections on the State of Polish-Jewish Historical Study." Jewish History 3 (Fall 1988): 115-130.

7740. Rozenbaum, Wlodzimierz. "The Anti-Zionist Campaign in Poland, June-December 1967." Canadian Slavonic Papers 20 (1978): 218-236.

7741. Ryszka, Franciszck. "Anti-Semitism: Ideas-Attitudes- Genocides." Acta Poloniae Historica No. 50 (1984): 57-80.

7742. Schatz, Jaff. "At the End of the Road: The Ethnic Identity of the Former Jewish Communists in Poland." Nordisk Judaistik (Finland) 9 (1988): 32-50.

7743. Schatz, Jaff. The Generation. The Rise and Fall of the Generation of Jewish Communists of Poland. Doctoral dissertation: University of Lund, Sweden, 1989.

7744. Siemienska, Renata. "Women and Social Movements in Poland." Women & Politics 6 (1986): 5-35.

7745. Sliwowski, Z. Polish-Ukrainian Relations, 1919-1939. B. Phil. dissertation: Oxford University, 1947.

7746. Smolar, Aleksander. "Jews as a Polish Problem." Daedalus 116 (1987): 31-73.

7747. Sobelman, Michael. "Polish Socialism and Jewish Nationality: The View of Kazimierz Kelles-Krauz." Soviet Jewish Affairs 20 (Spring 1990): 47-55.

7748. Somczynski, K. M. and Tadeusz K. Krauze, eds. Social Stratification in Poland: Eight Empirical Studies. Armonk, New York: M.E. Sharpe, 1986.

7749. Staniszkius, Jadwiga. "The Obsolescence of Solidarity." Telos No. 80 (Summer 1989): 37-50.

7750. Sysyn, Frank E. Between Poland and the Ukraine: The Dilemma of Adam Kysil, 1600-1653. Cambridge, MA: Harvard Ukrainian Research Institute, 1986.

7751. Szarota, Tomasz. "Germans in the Eyes of Poles during the World War II." Acta Poloniae Hist. 47 (1983): 151-195.

7752. Szarota, Tomasz. "La vie culturelle en Pologne pendant l'occupation allemande." Acta Poloniae Hist. 55 (1987): 159-202.

7753. Tighe, Carl. "Render Unto Caesar: Church and State in Poland." Monthly Review 38 (December 1986): 20-30.

7754. Tims, R. W. Germanizing Prussian Poland. New York: Columbia University Press, 1941.

7755. Toranska, Teresa. ONI-Stalin's Polish Puppets. London: Collins-Harvill, 1987.

7756. Trendowski, Thomas. Ukrainian Minority in Poland, 1920- 1932. Master's thesis: Wayne State University, 1938.

7757. Tuwim, Julian. "Prewar Polish Anti-Semitism." Jewish Currents 29 28-30 (February 1975)

7758. Wat, Aleksander. My Century, The Odyssey of a Polish Intellectual. Edited and translated by Richard Levine. Berkeley: University of California Press, 1988.

7759. Wnuklipinski, E. "The Polish Country Profile: Economic Crisis and Inequalities in Health." Social Science & Medicine 31 (1990)

7760. Wozniak, Peter. The Habsburg Middle School Reform, 1849- 1860: With Special Reference to West Galicia. Doctoral dissertation: Indiana University, 1987. UMO # 8727557.

7761. Wynot, Edward D., Jr. "A Necessary Cruelty: The Emergence of Official Anti-Semitism in Poland; 1936-1939." American Historical Review (October 1971): 1035-1058.

7762. Wynot, Edward D., Jr. "Poland's Christian Minorities, 1919- 1939." Nationalities Papers 13 (1985): 209-246. Ukrainians, Belorussians, and Germans.]

7763. Wynot, Edward D., Jr. "The Polish Germans, 1919-1939: National Minority in a Multinational State." Polish Review 17 (1972): 23-64.

7764. Wynot, Edward D., Jr. "The Polish Peasant Movement and the Jews, 1918-1939." Nationalities Papers 15 (1987): 71-89.

7765. Wynot, Edward D., Jr. "The Ukrainians and the Polish Regime 1937-1939." Ukrains'kyi Istoryk 7 (1970): 44-60.

7766. Wynot, Edward D., Jr. "World of Delusions and Disillusions: The National Minorities of Poland During World War II." Nationalities Papers 7 (Fall 1979): 177-196.

7767. Zaniewski, Kazimierz J. Housing Inequalities under Socialism. Doctoral dissertation: University of Wisconsin, Milwaukee, 1987.

7768. Zarnowski, Janusz. "The Evolution of Polish Society Since 1918." East European Quarterly 24 (June 1990): 227-236.

7769. Zukowski, Ryszard. "Standards of Living Compared: France- Poland (1983)." R. Et. comp Est-Ouest 18 (Sept. 1987): 73- 122.

PORTUGAL

7770. Boxer, Charles R. "S.R. Welch and His History of the Portuguese in Africa 1495-1806." Journal of African History 1 (1960): 55-63. [On the alleged absence of racial prejudice among the Portuguese.]

7771. Boxer, Charles R. Women in Iberian Expansion Overseas, 1415-1815: Some Facts, Fancies and Personalities. New York: Oxford University Press, 1975.

7772. Heleno, Manuel. Os escravos em Portugal. Vol.I. Lisboa: 1933.

7773. Herculano, A. History of the Origin and Establishment of the Inquisition in Portugal. Stanford: 1926.

7774. Machado, Diamantino P. The Structure of Portuguese Society During the Period 1926-1976. Doctoral dissertation: Temple University, 1989. UMO # 9007368.

7775. Oliveira, Mario A. F. do and others. A descolonização portuguesa, Vol. 2. Lisbon: Instituto Amaro da Costa, 1983.

7776. Pereira, João. "Equity Objectives in Portuguese Health Policy." Social Science & Medicine 31 (1990)

7777. Raby, Dawn L. Fascism and Resistance in Portugal: Communists, Liberals and Military Dissidents in the Opposition to Salazar, 1941-1974. New York: St. Martin's Press, 1988.

7778. Roditi, E. "The Making of Jews, or the Inquisition in Portugal." Judaism 19 (Fall 1970): 435-443.

7779. Russell-Wood, A. J. R. "Iberian Expansion and the Issue of Black Slavery: Changing Portuguese Attitudes, 1440-1770." American Historical Review 83 (February 1978): 16-42.

7780. Salomon, Herman P. "The Portuguese Inquisition and Its Victims in the Light of Recent Polemics." Journal of the American Portuguese Cultural Society 5 (Summer-Fall 1971)

7781. Saunders, A. C. de C.M. A Social History of Black Slaves and Freedmen in Portugal, 1441-1555. New York: Cambridge University Press, 1982.

7782. Saunders, A. C. de C.M. A Social History of Black Slaves and Freedmen in Portugal, 1441-1555. Doctoral dissertation: Oxford University, 1978.

7783. Schwartzman, Kathleen C. "Portugal at the Neocolonial Fringe of the British Empire." In Rethinking the Nineteenth Century: Contradictions and Movements, edited by Francis O. Ramirez. Westport, CT: Greenwood, 1988.

7784. Vilar, Enriquetta Vila. "Los asientos portugueses y el contrabando de negros." Anuario de estudios americanos 30 (1973): 557-609.

7785. Yerushalmi, Yosef H. The Lisbon Massacre of 1506 and the Royal Image in the Shebet Yehudah. Cincinnati, Ohio: Hebrew Union College, Jewish Institute of Religion, 1976.

RUMANIA

7786. Amnesty International. Romania: Human Rights Violations in the Eighties. New York: Amnesty International, 1987.

7787. Ancel, Jean. "Bukovina." In Encyclopedia of the Holocaust. 261-263. New York: Macmillan, 1990.

7788. Ancel, Jean, ed. Documents Concerning the Fate of Romanian Jewry During the Holocaust. New York: The Beate Klarsfeld Foundation, 1986. [12 volumes; 7, 361 pages.]

7789. Ancel, Jean. "The Romanian Way of Solving the 'Jewish Problem' in Bessarabia and Bukovina, June-July 1941." Yad Vashem Studies 19 (1988): 187-232.

7790. Ancel, Jean. Romania. Jerusalem: 1989.

7791. Armon, Teodor. "'Enemies' and 'Traitors': Aspects of the Antisemitism of the Iron Guard." Romanian Jewish Studies 1 (1987): 67-76.

7792. Barbu, Zev. "Rumania." In Fascism in Europe, edited by S.J. Woolf. London: Methuen, 1982.

7793. Beek, Sam. "The Origins of Gypsy Slavery in Romania." Dialectical Anthropology 14 (1989)

7794. Bobango, Gerald J. Religion and Politics: Bishop Valerian Trifa and His Times. New York: Columbia University Press, 1981.

7795. Bodea, Cornelia and Virgil Candea. Transylvania in the History of the Romanians. Boulder, CO: East European Monogrpahs, 1983.

7796. Boia, Lucian. Relationships between Romanians, Czechs and Slovaks, 1848-1914. Translated by Sanda Michailescu. Bucharest : Editura Academei Republicii Socialist, Romania, 1977.

7797. Boteni, Viorica. Les minorites en Transylvanie. Doctoral dissertation: University of Paris, 1938.

7798. Braham, R.L. Genocide and Retribution. Hingham, MA: Kluwer/Nijhoff, 1984. [Jews in Rumania during Holocaust.]

7799. Cabot, J. M. The Rumanian Claims in Hungary before the Peace Conference. B. Litt. dissertation: Oxford University, 1924.

7800. Cadzow, John F. and others, eds. Transylvania: The Roots of Ethnic Conflict. Kent, Ohio: Kent Ohio University Press, 1983.

7801. Ceausescu, Ilie. Transylvania: An Ancient Romanian Land. 2d ed. Bucharest: Military Publishing House, 1989.

7802. Cohen, Lloyd A. "The Jewish Question during the Period of the Romanian National Renaissance and the Unification of the Two Principalities of Moldavia and Wallachia, 1848-1866." In Romania between East and West, edited by Stephen Fischer-Galati and others. Boulder, CO: East European Monographs, 1982.

7803. Cole, John W., ed. Economy, Society and Culture in Contemporary Romania. Amherst: University of Massachusetts Press, 1984.

7804. Crowther, William E. The Political Economy of Romanian Socialism. Doctoral dissertation: University of California, Los Angeles, 1986. UMO # 8621050.

7805. Dascalu, Nicolae. "The Economic and Political-Cultural Life of the Coinhabiting Nationalities in Romania between the Two World Wars." In Nouvelles etudes d'histoire, publiees a l'occasions du XV congres international des sciences historiques. 2 vols., edited by Stephan Pascu and others. Bucharest: Editura Academiei Republicii Socialiste Romania, 1980.

7806. Dascalu, Nicolae. "La presse des minorites nationales dans la Roumanie d'entre les deux guerres (1919-1939). Analyse statistique." R. Roumaine hist. 1 (1981): 111-135.

7807. De Jong, Frederick. "The Turks and Tatars in Romania. Materials Relative to their History and Notes on their Present Condition." Turcica (France) 18, 165-189.

7808. Elteto, Louis J. "Anti-Magyar Propaganda in Rumania and the Hungarian Minority in Transylvania." Hungarian Studies Review 26 (1989): 121-135.

7809. Florer, Edward J. Hitler's Impact Upon the German Community in Romania, 1933-1945. Master's thesis: California State University, Fullerton, 1979. UMO # 1312645.

7810. Fur, Lajos. Report on the Situation of the Hungarian Minority in Rumania. Budapest: Prepared for the Hungarian Democratic Forum, n.d.

7811. Gelber, N. M. "The Problem of the Rumanian Jews at the Bucharest Peace Conference." Jewish Social Studies 12 (April 1950): 223-246.

7812. Georgescu, Vlad, ed. Romania: 40 Years (1944-1984). New York: Praeger, 1985.

7813. Gilberg, Trond. "Ethnic Minorities in Romania under Socialism." East European Quarterly 7 (1973): 435-458.

7814. Gyemant, Ladislau. "School as a Link between the Intelligentsia and the People: Regarding the Romanians in Transylvania in the First Half of the Nineteenth Century." In Academie des Sciences Sociales et Politiques, Nouvelles etudes d'historire. Bucharest: Editura Academici Republicii Socialiste Romania, 1985.

7815. Haraszti, Endre. The Ethnic History of Transylvania. Astor Park, FL: Danubian Press, 1971.

7816. Heinen, Armin. Die Legion "Erzengel Michael" in Rumanien: Soziale Bewegung und politische Organisation: Ein Beitrag zum Problem des internationalen Faschismus. Munchen: R. Oldenbourg, 1986.

7817. Hilbeln, Ewald. Codreanu und die Eiserne Garde. Siegen: J.G. Herder-Bibliothek Siegerland, 1984.

7818. Hitchins, Keith. The Idea of Nation: The Romanian of Transylvania, 1691-1849. Bucharest: Editura Stuntifica si Enciclopedica, 1985.

7819. Hockenos, Paul. "Free Speech Unleashes Hitlerism in Romania." In These Times (December 19, 1990): [The Roma (Gypsies).]

7820. Hockenos, Paul. "The Winter of Our Discontent." Nation (January 7, 1991): [Some possibilities of fascism in Romania largely at the expense of Jews, Gypsies, and Hungarians.]

7821. "Hungarians of Romania." In World Directory of Minorities. 108-114. Harlow: Longman, 1990.

7822. Illyes, Elemer. Ethnic Continuity in the Carpatho-Danubian. Boulder, CO: East European Monographs, 1988. [Romanians and Hungarians in Transylvania.]

7823. Illyes, Elemer. National Minorities in Romania: Change in Transylvania. New York: Columbia University Press, 1982.

7824. Ioanid, Radu. The Sword of the Archangel. Fascist Ideology in Romania. Boulder, CO: East European Monographs, 1990.

7825. Jagendorf, Siegfried. Jagendorf's Foundry. A Memoir of the Romanian Holocaust, 1941-1944. New York: Harper Collins, 1991. [Edited by Aron Hirt-Manheimer.]

7826. Kamm, Henry. "Cold Days Are Back in Rumania." New York Times, (January 4, 1987): [Levels of living.]

7827. Kamm, Henry. "The Hungarians of Rumania: A Debate Dispute." New York Times, (December 27, 1986)

7828. Kenedi, Janos. "To Be a Democrat: Yes, But Why?" Across Frontiers 3 (Fall 1986): 19-20, 46-47. [On discrimination against the Hungarian minority in Rumania.]

7829. Kohler, Max J. and Simon Wolf. Jewish Disabilities in the Balkan States. Philadelphia: American Jewish Historical Society, 1916. [Esp. Romania.]

7830. Kurti, Laszlo. "Transylvania, Land Beyond Reason: Toward an Anthropological Analysis of a Contested Terrain." Dialectical Anthropology 14 (1989)

7831. Lazar, Gyorgy, pseud. "Die rumänische Nationalitätenpolitik." Zeitschrift für Donauraumforschung 25 (1980): 137-182.

7832. Lemny, Stefan. "L'Ecole Transilvaine et l'idee de la patrie." R. Roumaine Hist. 23 (1984): 157-164.

7833. Lipcsey, Ildiko. "Hungarians in Rumania: 1945-1987." New Hungarian Quarterly 29 (1988): 125-140.

7834. Livezeanu, Irina. The Politics of Culture in Greater Romania: Nation-building and Student Nationalism 1918-1927. Doctoral dissertation: University of Michigan, 1986. UMO # 8702781.

7835. Lustig, Oliver. "Horthyst Terror in Transylvania- Increasingly Ruthless Methods and Means in the Service of the Same Inhumane Purposes." In 1918: The Triumph of a Great Ideal: The Making of a Unitary National State, edited by Ilie Ceausescu. Bucharest: Military Publishing House, 1988.

7836. Malaparte, Curzio. Kaputt. Marlboro, VT: Marlboro Press, 1986. [The fate of the Jews in Rumania during World War II.]

7837. Maneacu, M. "Forty Years of Outstanding Successes in the Socio-economic Development of Romania, 1944-1984." Economic Computation and Economic Cybernetics Studies and Research 19 (1984)

7838. Mertens, Lothar. "Die Lage des rumänischen Judentums." Südosteuropa 37 (1988): 1-7.

7839. Moses, Jennifer. "The Age of [Rabbi David Moses] Rosen." Present Tense 52-54 (Summer 1986)

7840. Moskoff, William. "Sex Discrimination, Community, and the Role of Women in Rumanian Development." Slavic Review 37 (1978): 440-456.

7841. Nagy-Talavera, Miklos. The Green Shirts and the Others: A History of Fascism in Hungary and Rumania. Doctoral dissertation: University of California at Berkeley, 1967.

7842. Nancy, Julia. Transylvania: The Hungarian Minority in Rumania. Astor, FL: Danubian Press, 1976.

7843. Natanson, Ephriam. "Romanian Governments and the Legal Status of Jews between the Two World Wars." Romanian Jewish Studies 1 (1987): 51-66.

7844. Nelson, Daniel N. "Conflict, Management and the Institutions of Communist Rule in Rumania." Crossroads No. 22 (1986): 49-59.

7845. Popisteanu, Cristian and Jean Ancel. "Romania." In Encyclopedia of the Holocaust. 1289-1300. New York: Macmillan, 1990.

7846. Remember: 40 Years Since the Massacre of the Jews from Northern Transylvania under Horthyist Occupation. Bucharest: Federation of Jewish Communities in the Socialist Republic of Romania of Romania, Documentary Section, 1985.

7847. Ronnas, P. J. Urbanization in Romania: A Geography of Social and Economic Change since Independence. EFI, Box 6501, S-113 83 Stockholm, Sweden: 1984.

7848. Safran, A. Resisting the Storm-Romania, 1940-1947: Memoirs. Jerusalem: 1987.

7849. Sampson, Steven L. "Romania: House of Cards." Telos No. 79 (Spring 1989): 217-224.

7850. Schneider, J. S. The Jewish Problem in Romania prior to the First World War. Doctoral dissertation: University of Southampton, 1982.

7851. Schopflin, George. The Hungarians of Rumania. London: Minority Rights Groups, 1978.

7852. Schopflin, George. "Hungarians under Romanian Rule." In The Hungarians: A Divided Nation, edited by Stephen Borsody. New Haven: Yale Center for International and Area Studies, 1988.

7853. Shafir, Michael. "From Eminescu to Goga via Corneliu Vadim Tudor: A New Round of Anti-semitism in Romanian Cultural Life." Soviet Jewish Affairs 14 (November 1984): 3-14.

7854. Shafir, Michael. "The Men of the Archangel Revisited: Anti- Semitic Formations among Communist Romania's Intellectuals." Studies in Comparative Communism 16 (1983): 223-243.

7855. Sozan, Michael. "Ethnocide in Rumania." Current Anthropology 18 (December 1977): 781-782. [The Hungarian Szekrlers of Transylvania.]

7856. Stankovich, Victor de. "The Way the Hungarians University School of Marosvasarhely (Tirgu-Mures) Is Made to Disappear." Europa Ethnica 40 (1983): 77-79.

7857. Steigerwald, Jacob. Tracing Romania's Heterogeneous German Minority from Its Origin to the Diaspora. Winona, MN: Winona State University Press, 1985.

7858. Szasz, Zsombor. The Minorities in Roumanian Transylvania. London: Richards Press, 1927.

7859. Transylvanian World Federation and the Danubian Research and Information Center. Genocide in Transylvania: Nation on the Death Row: A Documentary. Astor, FL: Danubian Press, 1985. [Minorities in Rumania.]

7860. Turdeanu, L. and N. Marcu. "Romania's Wealth Estimations before the Second World War." Review of Income and Wealth 31 (March 1985)

7861. Turnock, David. The Romanian Economy in the Twentieth Century. New York: St. Martin's Press, 1986.

7862. Ussoskin, Moshe. Struggle for Survival. Jerusalem: Academic Press, 1975. [Jews in Romania, 1910-1950.]

7863. Vago, Bela. "Postwar Rumanian Jewry." European Judaism 34-38 (1968): 3.

7864. Vago, Raphael. The Grandchildren of Trianon: Hungary and the Hungarian Minority in the Communist State. Boulder, CO: East European Monographs, 1989.

7865. Verdery, Katherine. Transylvanian Villagers: Political, Economic, and Ethnic Change, 1700-1980. Berkeley: University of California Press, 1983.

7866. Volgyes, Ivan. "The Treatment of Minority Nationalities in Romania: The Case of Ceausescu's Hungarians." Nationalities Papers 5 (Spring 1977): 79-90.

7867. Zach, Krista. "Rumäniens kleine Minderheitengruppen nach 1945." Europa Ethnica 39 (1982): 49-62.

7868. Zaharia, G. "Quelques donnees concernant la terreur fasciste en Roumanie (1940-1944)." In La Roumanie pendant la Deuxieme Guerre Mondiale: Etudes, 9-36. Bucharest: 1964.

7869. Zolcsak, Istvan. Rumania's Violations of Helsinki Final Act Provisions. Forced Assimilation of the Minorities in Rumania. Sao Paulo, Brazil: Transylvanian World Federation, June 1980.

RWANDA

7870. Botte, Roger. "Rwanda and Burundi, 1889-1930: Chronology of a Slow-Assimilation (2 parts)." International Journal African Historical Studies 18 (1985): 53-91 and 289-314.

7871. Cotanegre, Jean-Francois. "Contribution a la connaissance de la malnutrition au Rwanda." Cah. Outre-Mer. 41 (April- June 1988): 179-196.

7872. Kuper, Leo. The Pity of It All: Polarization of Racial and Ethnic Relations. London: Duckworth, 1977.

7873. Newbury, Catherine. The Cohesion of Oppression: Clientships and Ethnicity in Rwanda, 1860-1960. New York: Columbia University Press, 1988.

7874. Ntampaka, C. "L'evolution des droits de la femme au Rwanda." Penant 98 (January-May 1988): 43-74.

7875. Nyagahene, Antoine. "L'Histoire du Rwanda: problemes, controverses, perspectives." Educ. Sci. Cult. (April-June 1986): 87-136.

7876. Rutayisire, Paul. La christianisation du Rwanda (1900- 1945). Fribourg, Switzerland: 1987.

7877. Vidal, C. "Colonisation et decolonisation du Rwanda la question tutsi-luitu." Revue Francaise d'Etudes Politiques Africaines 91 (1973): 32-47.

SAUDI ARABIA

7878. Abir, M. "Consolidations of the Ruling Class and the New Elite in Saudi Arabia." Mid. E. Stud. 23 (April 1987): 150- 171.

7879. Aleissa, Ibrahim M. The Political Economy of Saudi Arabia: Investment in Human Capital and the Economics of Higher Education. Doctoral dissertation: University of Denver, 1989. UMO # 9012618.

7880. Al-Baadi, Howard M. Social Change, Education, and the Roles of Women in Arabia. Doctoral dissertation: Stanford University, 1982. UMO # 8220420.

7881. Islami, A. Reza S. and R.M. Kavoussi. The Political Economy of Saudi Arabia. Seattle: University of Washington Press, 1984.

7882. Lackner, Helen. A House Built on Sand-A Political Economy of Saudi Arabia. London: Ithaca Press, 1978.

7883. Newby, Gordon D. A History of the Jews of Arabia. Columbia: University of South Carolina Press, 1988.

7884. Salameh, Ghassane. "Political Power and the Saudi State." Merip Reports 91 (October 1980): 5-22.

7885. Al-Sultan, Ali A. Class Structure in Saudi Arabia. 2 vols. Doctoral dissertation: Michigan State University, 1988. UMO # 8912545.

7886. Zarea, A. R. A. Petroleum and Socio-cultural Changes in Saudi Arabia 1973-1988. Master's thesis: University of Salford, 1989.

SENEGAL

7887. Ba, Sylvie Washington. *The Concert of Negritude in the Poetry of Leopold Sedar Senghor*. Princeton, NJ: Princeton University Press, 1973.

7888. Bathily, Abdoulaye. "Senegal's Fraudulent 'Democratic Opening'." In *Africa's Crisis*, edited by Nzongola-Ntalaja. London: Institute for African Alternatives, 1987.

7889. Boone, C. "The Making of a Rentier Class, Wealth Accumulation and Political Control in Senegal." *Journal of Development Studies* 26 (April 1990)

7890. Crowder, Michael. *Senegal-A Study of French Assimilation*. rev. ed. London: 1967.

7891. Diane, Bakary. *French Presence in Senegalese Education, 1958-1968: Has Senegal Educated the Black Frenchman During that Decade?* Master's thesis: University of California, Los Angeles, 1972.

7892. Fatton, Robert Jr. *The Making of a Liberal Democracy: Senegal's Passive Revolution, 1975-1985*. Boulder, CO: Rienner, 1987.

7893. Founow-Tchnugoua, Bernard. *Fondements de l'economie de traite au Senegal (la surexploitation d'une colonie de 1880 a 1960)*. Paris: Editions Silex, 1981.

7894. Hyman, Jacques L. *Leopold Sedar Senghor: An Intellectual Biography*. Edinburgh: Edinburgh University Press, 1971.

7895. Keita, M. A. *The Political Economy of Health Care in Senegal*. Doctoral dissertation: Howard University, 1988. UMO # 8827300.

7896. Mackintosh, Maureen. *Gender, Class, and Rural Transition: Agribusiness and the Food Crisis in Senegal*. Atlantic Highlands, NJ: Zed Books, 1989.

7897. Moitt, Bernard. "Slavery and Emancipation in Sengal's Peanut Basin: The Nineteenth and Twentieth Centuries." Int. Jr. Hist. Studies 22 (1989): 27-50.

7898. Obichere, Boniface I. "Colonial Education Policy in Senegal: A Structural Analysis." Black Academy Review 1 (Winter 1970): 17-24.

7899. Renault, Francois. L'Abolition de l'esclavage au Senegal: l'attitude de l'administration francaise, 1848-1905. Paris: 1972.

7900. Robinson, David. "French 'Islamic' Policy and Practice in Late Nineteenth-Century Senegal." Journal of African History 29 (1988): 415-436.

7901. Shattuck, Roger and Samba Ka. "Born Again African." New York Review of Books, (December 20, 1990): [Review essay on Leopold Sedar Senghor.]

7902. Snyder, Francis G. "Colonialism and Legal Form: The Creation of 'Customary Law' in Senegal." Journal of Legal Pluralism No. 19 (1981): 49-90.

7903. Vaillant, Janet G. Black, French, and African. A Life of Leopold Sedar Senghor. Cambridge, MA: Harvard University Press, 1990.

SIERRA LEONE

7904. Abraham, Arthur. "The Institution of "Slavery" in Sierra Leone." Geneve-Afrique 14, 2 (1975): 46-57.

7905. Ekobo, A. E. "Strategic-Imperial Factor in British Expansion in Sierra-Leone, 1882-1899." Journal, Historical Society of Nigeria 11 (1981-1982): 138-152.

7906. Fanusie, Yaya. Social Class, the State and Public Policy in the Republic of Sierra Leone: 1968-1980. Doctoral dissertation: University of California, Riverside, 1981. UMO # 8119570.

7907. Frenkel, Stephen and John Western. "Pretext or Prophylaxis? Racial Segregation and Malaria Mosquitos in a British Tropical Colony: Sierre Leone." Annals of the Association of American Geographers 78 (1988): 211-228.

7908. Ketkar, Kusum W. Tax Burden Distribution in Sierra Leone. Master's thesis: Cleveland State University, 1977.

7909. Last, Murray and Paul Richards, eds. Sierre Leone, 1787- 1987: Two Centuries of Intellectual Life. New York: Manchester University Press, 1988.

7910. Mukonoweshuro, E. G. "Underdevelopment and Class Formation in Sierra Leone: A Neglected Analytical Theme." Journal of Asian and African Studies 21 (1986): 159-170.

7911. Nowak, Bronislaw. "The Slave Rebellion in Sierra Leone in 1785-1796." Hemisphere (Poland) 3 (1986): 151-169.

7912. Porter, Arthur T. Creoledom. New York: Oxford University Press, 1963.

7913. Riddell, J. Barry. "Internal and External Forces Acting Upon Disparities in Sierra Leone." Journal of Modern African Studies 23 (1985): 389-406.

7914. Spitzer, Leo. The Creoles of Sierra Leone: Responses to Colonialisim, 1870-1945. Madison: University of Wisconsin, 1974.

7915. Timbo, A. B. Human Rights in Sierre Leone. Doctoral dissertation: University of London, 1979.

SINGAPORE

7916. Chen, Peter S. J. "The Power Elite in Singapore." In *Studies in ASEAN Sociology*. 73-82. Singapore: Chopmen Enterprises, 1978.

7917. Ching-Hwang, Yen. "Class Structure and Social Mobility in the Chinese Community in Singapore and Malaya 1800-1911." *Modern Asian Studies* 21 (July 1987): 417-445.

7918. Clammer, John. "Singapore." In *International Handbook on Race and Race Relations*, edited by Jay A. Sigler. Westport, CT: Greenwood, 1987.

7919. Erlanger, Steven. "Chinese-Malay Relations Turn Sour in Singapore." *New York Times*, (May 13, 1990)

7920. Field, Brian. "Public Housing in Singapore." *Land Use Policy* 4 (April 1987): 147-156.

7921. Fong, Pang Eng. "Growth, Inequality and Race in Singapore." *International Labour Review* 111 (January 1975): 15-28.

7922. Foon, Chew Sock. *Ethnicity and Nationality in Singapore*. Athens: Ohio University Center for International Studies, 1987.

7923. George, T. J. S. *Lee Kuan Yew's Singapore*. London: Andre Deutsch, 1974.

7924. Gook, Aik guan. "Singapore: A Third World Fascist State." *Journal of Contemporary Asia* 11 (1981): 244-254.

7925. Leung, Ywen Sang. "Employment, Earning and Expenditure: Daily Life of the Chinese Labourers in Singapore (1870- 1900)." *Journal of Humanities and Social Sciences* 5 (1986): 103-121.

7926. Liaw, Yoch F. "Minority Literature Among the Ethnic Chinese." *Solidarity* No. 101 (1984): 33-36.

7927. MacDougall, John A. Shared Burdens: A Study of Communal Discrimination by the Political Parties of Malaysia and Singapore. Doctoral dissertation: Harvard University, 1968. UMO # 6813449.

7928. Martland, Nicholas. "Library Services to Ethnic Groups: The Singapore Experience." Singapore Lib. 17 (1987): 3-11.

7929. Nam, Tae Y. Racism, Nationalism, and Nation-Building in Malaysia and Singapore. Meerut: Sadhna Prakashan, 1973.

7930. Pitt, K. W. "Chinese Coolie Immigrants in Nineteenth Century Singapore." Review of S.E. Asian Studies 14 (June 1984): 31-59.

7931. Salaff, Janet W. State and Family in Singapore: Restructuring a Developing Society. Ithaca, NY: Cornell University Press, 1988.

7932. Sheng-Yi, Lee. "Income Distribution, Taxation, and Social Benefits of Singapore." Journal of Developing Areas 14 (October 1980): 71-98.

7933. Song Ong Siang. One Hundred Years' History of the Chinese in Singapore. New York: Oxford University Press, 1984 orig. 1923.

7934. Trocki, Carl A. Opium and Empire. Chinese Society in Colonial Singapore, 1800-1910. Ithaca, New York: Cornell University Press, 1990.

7935. Trocki, Carl A. "The Rise of Singapore's Great Opium Syndicate, 1840-1886." Journal of South East Asian Studies 18 (March 1987): 58-80.

7936. Turnbull, Constance M. A History of Singapore, 1819-1988. rev. ed. New York: Oxford University Press, 1989.

7937. Wan Hussin Zoohri. "Socio-Economic Problems of the Malays in Singapore." Fajar Islam 1 (1988): 1-23.

7938. Wimalasiri, Jayantha. "Values and Modernism: The Case of the Chinese in Singapore." Asian Thought Society 12 (Nov. 1987): 227-251.

7939. Wong, E. Women, Equality and Education in Singapore from the 19th Century to the Present Day. Doctoral dissertation: University of Bath, 1986.

7940. Yen, Ching-Hwang. "Class Structure and Social Mobility in the Chinese Community in Singapore and Malaysia, 1800-1911." Modern Asian Studies 21 (July 1987): 417-445.

7941. Yen Ching-Hwang. A Social History of the Chinese in Singapore and Malaya, 1800-1911. New York: Oxford University Press, 1986.

7942. Yong, C. F. "Some Thoughts on the Creation of a Singaporean Identity among the Chinese: The Pre-PAP Phase, 1945-1959." R. S.E. Asian Studies 15 (June 1985): 52-60.

SOMALIA

7943. Bulhan, H. A. "The Captive Intelligentsia of Somalia." <u>Horn of Africa</u> 3 (January-March 1980): 25-37.

7944. Jamal, V. "Somalia: Survival in a 'Doomed' Economy." <u>International Labour Review</u> 127 (1988).

7945. Laitin, David D. and Said S. Samatar. <u>Somalia: Nation in Search of a State</u>. Boulder, CO: Westview, 1987.

7946. Lewis, Ian M. <u>A Modern History of Somalia</u>. London: Longman, 1980.

7947. <u>Somalia: A Government at War With Its Own People</u>. New York: Human Rights Watch, 1990.

SOUTH AFRICA

7948. Abedian, Iraj and B. Standish. "Poor Whites and the Role of the State: The Evidence." South African Journal of Economics 53 (June 1985): 141-165.

7949. Abedian, Iraj. "The Public Sector and Income Distribution in South Africa during the Period 1970-1982." Social Dynamics 10 (June 1984): 49-60.

7950. Academic Freedom Committee, University of Cape Town. The Open Universities in South Africa and Academic Freedom, 1957- 1974. Cape Town: 1974.

7951. Adam, Heribert. "Racist Capitalism versus Capitalist Non- racialism in South Africa." Ethnic and Racial Studies 7 (1984)

7952. Adam, Heribert and K. Moodley. "The Ultraright in South Africa and Ethnic Nationalism." Canadian Review of Studies in Nationalism 14 (1987): 83-92.

7953. Adelberg, Martyn. "The Future of the Jewish Community in South Africa." South Africa International 13 (1982): 445- 456.

7954. Ajam, M. "Muslim Educational Effort in South Africa: A Report." Jr. Inst. Muslim Minority Aff. 5 (July 1984): 468- 473.

7955. Allison, J. "In Search of Revolutionary Justice in South Africa." International Journal of the Sociology of Law 14 (November 1990)

7956. Anderson, Muff. Music in the Mix: The Story of South African Popular Music. New York: Harper and Row, 1987.

7957. Anderson, Neil. "Tuberculosis and Social Stratification in South Africa." International Journal of Health Services 20 (1990)

7958. The Anti-Jewish Movements in South Africa. The Need for Action. Johannesburg: South African Jewish Board of Deputies, 1936.

7959. Anti-semitism in South Africa. Johannesburg: South African Jewish Board of Deputies, January 1986.

7960. "Antisemitic Irritations in South Africa." Patterns of Prejudice 10 (1976): 2o-22, 33.

7961. "Antisemitism in South Africa During World War II: A Documentation." Simon Wiesenthal Center Annual 4 (1987): 263-303. Translated by Albrecht Hagermann and others.

7962. Appel, Stephen W. "'Outstanding Individuals Do Not Arise from Ancestrally 'Poor Stock': Racial Science and the Education of Black South Africans." Journal of Negro Education 58 (Autumn 1989)

7963. Arkin, A. J. "The Relative Contribution of the Indian to the South African Economy, 1860-1970." J. U. Durban-Westville 4 (1983): 164-175.

7964. Armstrong, James C. "The Slaves, 1652-1795." In The Shaping of South African Society 1652-1820, edited by Richard Elphick and Hermann Giliomee. New York: Longman, 1979.

7965. Ashley, M. J. "African Education and Society in the 19th Century Eastern Cape." In Beyond the Cape Frontier, edited by C. Saunders and R. Derricourt, 119-211. London: 1974.

7966. Atkins, Keletso E. "Kaffir Time: Preindustrial Temporal Concepts and Labour Discipline in Nineteenth-Century Colonial Natal." Journal of African History No. 29 (1988): 229-244.

7967. Auerbach, F. E. South African School Enrollment Patterns (1920-1970) and Problems of Early Learning in African Coloured and Indian Schools. Doctoral dissertation: University of Natal-Pietemaritzburg, 1977.

7968. Avineri, Shlomo. "The Jewish Predicament." Jerusalem Post, (August 30, 1985) [Jews in South Africa]

7969. Baker, Julie J. The Silent Crisis: Black Labour, Disease, and the Economics and Politics of Health on the South African Gold Mines, 1902-1930. Doctoral dissertation: Queen's University at Kingston (Canada), 1989.

7970. Barkat, Anwar. "Combating Racism in South Africa." Journal of International Affairs 36 (Winter 1983)

7971. Barlow, Edna. Immigration to the Union, 1910-1948: Policies and Attitudes. 4 vols. Doctoral dissertation: University of Cape Town, 1978. [Restrictions on immigration of Jews, vol. 2, pp.186-342.]

7972. Battersby, John D. "Liberal Universities Battle for Survival in South Africa." New York Times, (October 18, 1987)

7973. Behr, A. L. New Perspectives in South African Education: A Review of Education in South Africa, 1652-1984. 2d ed. Durban: Butterworth, 1984.

7974. Behr, A. L. Three Centuries of Coloured Education: Historical and Comparative Studies of the Education of the Coloured People in the Cape and Transvaal 1652-1952. Doctoral dissertation: University of Potchefstroom, 1952.

7975. Beinart, William. "The Politics of Colonial Conservation." Journal of Southern African Studies 15 (1989): 143-162.

7976. Bellon, Cynthia. "Jewish Rebels with a Cause." Jerusalem Post, (July 7, 1986): [South African Jews and the defense of Republican Spain.]

7977. Berkman, Joyce A. The Healing Imagination of Olive Schreiner. Beyond South African Colonialism. Amherst: University of Massachusetts, 1990.

7978. Bhana, S. and B. Pachai, eds. A Documentary History of Indian South Africans 1860-1982. Stanford, CA: Hoover Institution Press, 1984.

7979. Biko, Steve. "White Racism and Black Consciousness." In Student Perspectives on South Africa, edited by H. W. van der Merwe and D. Welsh. Cape Town: 1972.

7980. No entry

7981. Bloch, H. The Psychological Effects of Detention with Particular Reference to the South African Detainee. Master's thesis: University of Cape Town, 1986.

7982. Bonner, Philip. Kings, Commoners, and Concessionaires. Johannesburg: Ravan Press, 1984.

7983. Bozzoli, Belinda, ed. History Workshop 2-Town and Countryside in the Transvaal. Capitalist Production and Popular Responses. Johannesburg: Ravan Press, 1983.

7984. Bozzoli, Belinda and Peter Delius, eds. "History from South Africa." Radical History Review Nos. 46-47 (Winter 1990): 1-456.

7985. Bradlow, Frank R. "A Jewish View of the Just Society in South Africa." Patterns of Prejudice 12 12 (July-August 1978): 20-24, 29.

7986. Bristow, A. P. "Libraries and Library Services in Venda." Mousaion 3 (1985): 49-61.

7987. Brookes, E. H. The History of Native Policy in South Africa from 1830 to the Present. Cape Town: 1924.

7988. Bundy, Colin. "Street Sociology and Politics: Aspects of Youth and Student Resistance in Cape Town." Journal of Modern African Studies 25 (March 1987): 303-330.

7989. Burawoy, M. "The Capitalist State in South Africa: Marxist and Sociological Perspectives on Race and Class." Political Power and Social Theory 2 (1981): 279-335.

7990. Burchell, D. E. "The Emergence and Growth of Student Militancy at the University College of Fort Hare in the 1940s and 1950s." Journal of the University of Durban-Westville 3 (1986): 149-167.

7991. Burman, Sandra and Wilfried Scharf. "Creating People's Justice: Street Committees and People's Courts in a South African City." Law & Society Review 24 (August 1990): 693- 744.

7992. Burton, Sandra. "The New Black Middle Class." Time (February 29, 1988)

7993. Cameron, M. The Transformation of "Native Education" into "Bantu Education" with Special Resistance in the Western Cape during the Period 1948-1955. Master's thesis: University of Cape Town, 1986.

7994. Cartwright, J. O. and others. "A Survey of Learning Problems in Black Primary School Children." SA Medical Journal 59 (March 1981): 488-490.

7995. Chandramohan, B. The Writings of Alex La Guma: A Study in Transethnicity. Doctoral dissertation: University of Sheffield, 1988.

7996. Chanock, Martin. "Writing South African Legal History: A Prospectus." Jr. African Hist. 30 (1989): 265-288.

7997. Charney, Craig. "Graduate of Apartheid Takes Charge." Times Higher Education Supplement, (June 13, 1986) University of the Western Cape.]

7998. Charney, Craig. "Thinking of Revolution: The New South African Intelligentsia." Monthly Review 38 (December 1986): 10-19. [Left groups in white South African universities.]

7999. Chick, J. Keith. "The Interactional Accomplishment of Discrimination in South Africa." Language in Society 14 (September 1985): 299-326.

8000. The Child Is Not Dead- Youth Resistance in South Africa 1976-1986. London: IDAF and Inner London Education Authority, 1986.

8001. Christie, Pam. "Reforming the Racial Curriculum: Curriculum Change in Desegregated Schools in South Africa." British Journal of Sociology of Education 11 (1990)

8002. Christie, Pam. The Right to Learn: The Struggle for Education in South Africa. Braamfontein, South Africa: Ravan Press, 1985.

8003. Christopher, A. J. "Apartheid within Apartheid: An Assessment of Official Intra-Black Segregation on the Witwatersrand, South Africa." Professional Geographer 41 (August 1989)

8004. Cobley, Alan G. Class and Consciousness. The Black Petty Bourgeoisie in South Africa, 1924-1950. Westport, CT: Greenwood, 1990.

8005. Cock, Jacklyn. "Hidden Consequences of State Violence: Spinal Cord Injuries in Soweto, South Africa." Social Science & Medicine 29 (1989)

8006. Cock, Jacklyn and others. "Childcare and the Working Mother." Africa Perspective No.26 (1985): 29-60.

8007. Coetzee, C. G. "Bantu and the Study of History." Historia 11 (June 1966): 96-105.

8008. Comaroff, Jean and John L. Comaroff. "The Colonization of Consciousness in South Africa." Economy and Society 18 (1989): 267-296.

8009. Comaroff, John L. "Images of Empire, Contests of Conscience: Models of Colonial Domination in South Africa." American Ethnologist 16 (1989): 661-685.

8010. Cope, N. "The Zulu Petit Bourgeoisie and Zulu Nationalism in the 1920s: Origins of Inkatha." Journal of Southern African Studies 16 (September 1990)

8011. Cornevin, Marianne. Apartheid: Power and Historical Falsification. Paris: UNESCO, 1980.

8012. Cowell, Alan. "School Crisis on Apartheid Blights Hopes." New York Times, (December 1, 1985)

8013. Crankshaw, O. "Theories of Class and the African 'Middle Class' in South Africa, 1969-1983." Africa Perspectives N.S.I (1986): 3-33.

8014. Cross, Michael. "The Foundations of a Segregated Schooling System in the Transvaal 1900-1924." History of Education (England) 16 (1987): 259-274.

8015. Cross, Michael. "A Historical Review of Education in South Africa: Towards an Assessment." Comparative Education 22 (1986): 185-200.

8016. Curtis, Fred. "'Cheap' African Labor-power and South African Capitalism: 1948-1978." In Research in Political Economy, vol. 7, edited by Paul Zarembka, 185-235. Greenwich, CT: JAI Press, 1984.

8017. Curtis, Fred. "Class, Race and Income Distribution: Analyzing 'White' South Africa." In Research in Political Economy, vol. 9, edited by Paul Zarembka. Greenwich, CT: JAI Press, 1986.

8018. Curtis, Fred. "The Value of African Labour-Power in South Africa, 1948-1978." Africa Perspective 1 (1987): 63-91.

8019. Cuthbertson, G. C. "Jewish Immigration as an Issue in South African Politics, 1937-1939." Historia 26 (September 1981): 119-133.

8020. Daniels, Rudolph. "The Agrarian Land Question in South Africa in Its Historical Context, 1652-1988." American Journal of Economics and Sociology 48 (July 1989): 327-338.

8021. Daniels, Rudolph. "The Structure of the South African Labor Market, 1970-1983." Review of Black Political Economy 15 (Spring 1987): 63-78.

8022. Davies, A. R. L. "Security Laws and Children in Prison: The Issue of Psychological Impact." Psychology in Society 8 (1987): 27-47.

8023. Davies, John. "U.S. Foreign Policy and the Education of Black South Africans." Comparative Education Review 29 (May 1985): 171-188.

8024. Davies, Robert and David Kaplan. "Capitalist Development and the Evolution of Racial Policy in South Africa." Tarikh 6 (1979): 46-62.

8025. Davies, Robert and others. "Class Struggle and the Periodization of the South African State." Review of African Political Economy 7 (1976)

8026. Davis, John. "United States Foreign Policy and the Education of Black South Africans." African Perspective No. 26 (1985): 61-79.

8027. Davis, R. Hunt, Jr. Bantu Education and the Education of Africans in South Africa. Athens, Ohio: 1972.

8028. de Beer, Cedric. The South African Disease. Apartheid Health and Health Services. London: Catholic Institute for International Relations, 1986.

8029. De Gregori, T. R. and William A. Darity, Jr. "Surplus People and Expendable Children: The Structure of Apartheid and the Mortality Crisis in South Africa." Review of Black Political Economy 15 (Spring 1987)

8030. De Villiers. F.J. The Financing of Bantu Education. Johannesburg: South African Institute of Race Relations, 1964.

8031. Dean, Elizabeth and others. History in Black and White: An Analysis of South African School History Textbooks. New York: UNIPUB, 1983.

8032. DeKock, Victor. *Those in Bondage: An Account of the Life of the Slave at the Cape in the Days of the Dutch East India Company*. Part Washington, N.Y.: 1971.

8033. *Divided Campus: Universities in South Africa*. London: World University Service, 1986.

8034. Dlamini, C. R. M. "The Influence of Race on the Administration of Justice in South Africa." *South African Journal of Human Rights* 4 (March 1988): 37-54.

8035. Dreyer, Lynette. *The Modern African Elite of South Africa*. London: Macmillan, 1989.

8036. Du Pleissis, A. "Revolutionary Strategy and Intra-Societal Division in South Africa: Select Theoretical Perspectives and Practical Implications." *Strategic Review South Africa* 10 (May 1988): 63-90.

8037. Du Preez, J. N. *The Educational System of Transkei: A System Description and Needs Assessment*. Bloemfontein: Research Unit for Education System Planning, University of the Orange Free State, 1980.

8038. Dubb, A. A. "Johannesburg and Jerusalem: An Inquiry into the Problem of 'Dual Loyalty' among South African Jews." *Proceedings of the Sixth World Congress of Jewish Studies* 265-277.

8039. Dube, E. F. "Racism in South Africa: Are There One or Two Categories of Victims?" *Philosophical Forum* (Winter-Spring 1986-1987) [Reprinted in *Militant*, May 1, 1987.]

8040. Dube, Thandi. "The Fighting Youth of South Africa." *African Communist* No. 3 (1985): 21-31.

8041. Dubnow, S. "Holding a 'Just Balance between White and Black': The Native Affairs Department in South Africa, c. 1920-1933." *Journal South African Studies* 12 (April 1986): 217-239.

8042. Durbach, Elaine. "Warnings and Portents." *Present Tense* 14 (May/June 1987): 47-50. [Jews in South Africa.]

8043. Dyasi, H. M. *The History of the Problems of Bantu Urban Secondary Education in the Eastern Cape, 1937-1954 (Ciskei Region)*. Master's thesis: UNISA, 1962.

8044. Eberstadt, Nicolas. "Poverty in South Africa." *Optima* 36 (March 1988): 20-33.

8045. Eckert, J. B. and D. Mullins. "Income Redistribution and Its Effects on the South African Economy." *Journal for Studies in Economics and Econometrics* 13 (November 1989)

8046. Edgecombe, Ruth and Bill Guest. "The Coal Miners' Way of Death: Safety in the Natal Colieries, 1910-1953." Journal of Natal Zulu History 8 (1985): 63-83.

8047. Edwards, I. E. Towards Emancipation: A Study in South African Slavery. Cardiff: 1942.

8048. Elphick, Richard. Khoikhoi and the Founding of White South Africa. Johannesburg: Ravan, 1985.

8049. Elphick, Richard and Hermann Giliomee, eds. The Shaping of South African Society, 1652-1820. Cape Town: Longman, 1979.

8050. Emanuelson, O. E. A History of Native Education in Natal between 1835 and 1927. Master's thesis: University of Natal, 1927.

8051. Enklaar, Ido H. Life and Work of Dr. J. Th. van der Kemp, 1747-1811: Missionary Pioneer and Protagonist of Racial Equality in South Africa. Cape Town: A.A. Balkema, 1988.

8052. "Eskia Mphahele." African Commentary 2-3, # 8 (December 1990-January 1991): 57-61.

8053. "The Fate and Future of South African Jewry." Jewish Quarterly, London No. 4 (1986): 18-27. [Symposium]

8054. Feit, Ewald. "Community in a Quandary: The South African Jewish Community and Apartheid." Race 8 (April 1967)

8055. Finnegan, William. Crossing the Line, A Year in the Land of Apartheid. New York: Harper & Row, 1986. [Teaching at Grassy Park Senior Secondary School, a "colored" school in Cape Town, 1980-1981.]

8056. Finnegan, William. "Getting the Story- II." New Yorker (July 20, 1987): [Black journalists in South Africa.]

8057. Finnegan, William. "A Reporter at Large. Getting the Story- I." New Yorker (July 13, 1987): [Black journalists in South Africa, 1986.]

8058. Foster, D. H. "The Development of Racial Orientation in Children: A Review of South African Research." In Growing Up in a Divided Society, edited by S. Burman and P. Reynolds, 158- 183. Johannesburg: Ravan Press, 1986.

8059. Foster, D. H. "Justice and the Critique of Pure Psychology." Psychology in Society 5 (1986): 144-150.

8060. Foster, D. H. and others. Detention and Torture in South Africa: Psychological, Legal and Historical Studies. London: James Currey, 1987.

8061. Foster, D. H. and others. "Detention, Torture and the Criminal Justice Process in South Africa." International Journal of the Sociology of Law 15 (1987): 105-120.

8062. Franks, P. E. "White Resistance to Black Advancement: Empirical Findings." South African Journal of Labour Relations 11 (March 1987): 30-39.

8063. Fransman, M. and R. Davies. "The South African Social Formation in the Early Capitalist Period, circa 1870-1939. Some Views on the Question of Hegemony." In Perspectives on South Africa, edited by T. Adler. Johannesburg: African Studies Institute, University of Witwatersrand, 1977.

8064. Freedman, Samuel G. "Winning the Minds of South Africans." New York Times Education Life, (January 4, 1987): [South African students in American higher education.]

8065. Freund, W. M. "Race in the Social Structure of South Africa, 1652-1836." Race and Class 18 (Summer 1976): 53-67.

8066. A Fund for Free Expression. Human Rights in the Homelands: South Africa's Delegation of Repression. New York: A Fund for Free Expression, 1984.

8067. Furlong, Patrick J. Between Crown and Swastika: The Impact of the Radical Right on the Afrikaner Nationalist Movement in the Fascist Era. Middletown, CT: Wesleyan University Press, 1990.

8068. Furlong, Patrick J. National Socialism, the National Party and the Radical Right in South Africa, 1934-1948. Doctoral dissertation: University of California, Santa Barbara, 1987. UMO # 8803278.

8069. Furlong, Patrick J. "Pro-Nazi Subversion in South Africa." Ufahama 16 (Fall 1987-1988): 26-40.

8070. Garbers, Johan G. "The Education Crisis in South Africa." Business and Society Review (Fall 1986): 51-55.

8071. Ghozali, N. E. "L'opposition aux violations des droits de l'homme et plus particulierement a l'apartheid et au racisme et le droit international general." Revue Algerienne des Sciences Juridiques, Economique et Politiques 21 (1984): 131-168.

8072. Gibson, K. The Effects of Civil Unrest on Children: A Guide to Research. Master's thesis: University of Cape Town, 1986.

8073. Giliomee, H. "The Emergence and Early Development of Afrikaner Nationalism, 1870-1915." South African Historical Journal 19 (November 1987)

8074. Ginwala, Irene. Indian South Africans. new ed. London: Minority Rights Group, 1985.

8075. Goldin, Ian. Making Race: the Politics and Economics of Coloured Identity in South Africa. Cape Town: 1987.

8076. Goldreich, Arthur. "Stranger Than Fiction (interview)." New Outlook 33 (April 1990): 32-34. [South African Jews and the anti-apartheid movement.]

8077. Gonzalez, Carmen. "The South African Black Working Class." R. Africa Medio Oriente (1989): 37-88.

8078. Gool, S. Y. Mining Capitalism and Black Labour in the Early Industrial Period in South Africa- A Critique of the New Historiography. Doctoral dissertation: Lunds University, 1983.

8079. Gordon, A. "Environmental Constraints and their Effect on the Academic Achievement of Urban Black Children in South Africa." South African Journal of Education 6 (1986): 70- 74.

8080. Gordon, Robert. "The White Man's Burden: Ersatz Customary Law and Internal Pacification in South Africa." Journal of Historical Sociology 2 (1989): 41-65.

8081. Gordon, Suzanne. Under the Harrow: Lives of White South Africans Today. London: Heinemann, 1988.

8082. "Green Pastures." New Yorker (December 2, 1985): [St. Barbabas College, interracial school in Joahnnesburg.]

8083. Guelke, Leonard. "The Origin of White Supremacy in South Africa: An Interpretation." Social Dynamics 15 (1989): 40- 45.

8084. Guy, Jeff. The Destruction of the Zulu Kingdom. Johannesburg: Ravan Press, 1979.

8085. Haarlov, Jens. Labour Regulation and Black Workers' Struggles in South Africa. Uppsala: Scandanavian Institute of African Studies, 1983.

8086. Hageman, Albrecht. "Antisemitism in South Africa during World War II: A Documentation." Simon Wiesenthal Center Annual 4 (1987): 303.

8087. Harinck, Gerrit. "Interaction between Xhosa and Khoi: Emphasis on the Period 1620-1750." In African Societies in Southern Africa, edited by Leonard Thompson. London: 1969.

8088. Harries, Ann and others. The Child Is Not Dead. London: ILEA/British Defence and Aid Fund for Southern Africa, 1986. [Black youth resistance in South Africa during past decade.]

8089. Harries, Patrick. "Plantations, Passes and Proletarians: Labour and the Colonial State in 19th Century Natal." Journal of Modern African Studies 25 (March 1987): 372-399.

8090. Hart, Deborah M. Master Plans: The South African Government's Razing of Sophiatown, Cato Mano and District Six. Doctoral dissertation: Syracuse University, 1990. UMO # 9024387.

8091. Hatton, J. D. Race and Racism in the Union of South Africa. Master's thesis: National University of Ireland, 1948.

8092. Hazlett, T. W. "Economic Origins of Apartheid." Contemporary Policy Issues 6 (October 1988)

8093. Hellig, Jocelyn. "Anti-Semitism in South Africa Today." Jewish Affairs (Johannesburg) (March-April 1989): 37-39.

8094. Hellmann, Ellen and Henry Lever, eds. Race Relations in South Africa 1929-1979. New York: St. Martin's Press, 1980.

8095. Herrmann, Louis. A History of the Jews in South Africa, from the Earliest Times to 1895. reprint of 1935 ed. Westport, CT: Greenwood, 1975.

8096. Higginbotham, A. Leon, Jr. "Racism in American and South African Courts: Similarities and Differences." New York University Law Review 65 (June 1990): 479-588.

8097. Hirschmann, D. "The Black Consciousness Movement in South Africa." Journal of Modern African Studies 28 (March 1990)

8098. Holiday, Tony. "The South African Legal Press: Self- censored, Biased, Bound by Legislation." Sechaba (April 1987): 7-11.

8099. Holmes, Colin. Antisemitism and British Society 1876-1939. London: 1979. [Deals also with South Africa.]

8100. Holt, Nathan V., Jr. "Human Rights and Capital Punishment: The Case of South Africa." Virginia Journal of International Law 30 (Fall 1989): 273-318.

8101. Horrell, Muriel. A Decade of Bantu Education. Johannesburg: South African Institute of Race Relations, 1964.

8102. Horrell, Muriel. The Education of the Coloured Community in South Africa 1652-1970. Johannesburg: South African Institute of Race Relations, 1970.

8103. Hull, Richard W. American Enterprises in South Africa: Historical Dimensions of Engagement and Disengagement. New York: New York University Press, 1990.

8104. Human, L. and H. Pringle. "The Attitudes of White Workers to the Vertical Occupation Mobility of Blacks: An Introductory Study." South African Journal of Labour Relations 10 (September-December 1986): 21-34.

8105. Human, L. and M.J. Greenacre. "Labor Market Discrimination in the Manufacturing Sector: The Impact of Race, Gender, Education and Age on Income." South African Journal of Economics 55 (June 1987)

8106. Human, P. and L. Human. "Silver Spoons and Black Mobility: The White South African Elite and Its Implications for the Upward Mobility of Blacks." South African Journal of Business Management 18 (1987): 65-73.

8107. Hyslop, Jonathan. "The Concepts of Reproduction and Resistance in the Sociology of Education: The Case of the Transition from 'Missionary' to 'Bantu' Education 1940-1955." Perspectives Education 9 (September 1987): 3-24.

8108. Hyslop, Jonathan. "Food, Authority, and Politics: Student Riots in South Africa, 1945-1976." Africa Perspective 3-41 (1987)

8109. Hyslop, Jonathan. "State Education Policy and the Social Reproduction of the Urban African Working Class: The Case of the Southern Transvaal, 1955-1976." Jr. So. African Studies 14 (April 1988): 446-476.

8110. "Interview with Lauretta Ngcobo." Gen 3 (1985): 3-9. [South African teacher of course, "Images of Black Women in Literature".]

8111. Isaacs, Henry. Struggles within the Struggle. An Inside View of the PAC of South Africa. London: Zed Press, 1986. [Pan African Congress.]

8112. Jabavu, D. D. T. The Life of John Tengo Jabavu. Lovedale: 1922.

8113. Jacobs, J. U. "The Colonial Mind in a State of Fear: The Psychosis of Terror in the Contemporary South African Novel." North Dakota Quarterly 57 (Summer 1989): 24-43.

8114. Jacobs, S. V. The Development of Post-Primary Education for the Coloured Child in the Cape Province, Union of South Africa. Master's thesis: Syracuse University, 1949.

8115. Jacobson, Dan and Ronald Segal. "Apartheid and South African Jewry: An Exchange." Commentary 24 (November 1957)

8116. Jacobson, Keith and others. "Thoughts on Racism in My Country." Amherst Student (October 14, 1982)

8117. James, W. and L. Loot. "Class and Income Inequality, South Africa, 1980." Social Dynamics 11 (1985): 74-83.

8118. The Jews of South Africa: What Future? Johannesburg: Southern Book Publishers, 1988. [Interview by Tzippi Hoffman and Alan Fischer.]

8119. Johnstone, F. "White Prosperity and White Supremacy in South Africa." African Affairs 69 (1970): 124-140.

8120. Joseph, Helen. Side by Side. London: Zed Books, 1986. [Autobiography of a white participant in struggle against apartheid.]

8121. Kadalie, Clements. My Life and the I.C.U.: The Autobiography of a Black Trade Unionist in South Africa. London, New York: Cass, Humanities Press, 1960, 1970.

8122. Kallaway, Peter, ed. Apartheid and Education: The Education of Black South Africans. Johannesburg: Ravan Press, 1984.

8123. Kane-Berman, John. Soweto, Black Revolt, White Reaction. Johannesburg: Ravan Press, 1978.

8124. Kannemeyer, H. D. A Critical Survey of Indian Education in Natal, 1860-1937. Master's thesis: University of Witwatersrand, 1943.

8125. Kaplan, D. "Capitalist Development in South Africa: Class Conflict and the State." In Perspectives on South Africa, edited by T. Adler. Johannesburg: African Studies Institute, University of Witwatersrand, 1977.

8126. Katiya, N. The Development of Bantu Rural Secondary Education in the Ciskei, 1941-1968, a Historical Survey. Fort Hare: 1973.

8127. Keegan, Timothy. "Crisis and Catharsis in the Development of Capitalism in South African Agriculture." Afric. Aff. (London) 84 (July 1985): 371-398.

8128. Keenan, Jeremy and Mike Sarakinsky. "Poverty in South Africa." South African Labour Bulletin 12 (May-June 1987): 108-117.

8129. Kerr, A. Fort Hare, 1915-1948. The Evolution of an African College. London: 1968.

8130. Kgware, W. M. Bantu Education in the Province of the OFS during the 20th Century: 1900-1953: An Historical Study. Master's thesis: UNISA, 1955.

8131. Kinkead-Weekes, B. Africans in Cape Town: The Origins and Development of State Policy and Popular Resistance to 1936. Master's thesis: University of Cape Town, 1985.

8132. Kirk, Joyce F. The African Middle Class, Cape Liberalism, and Resistance to Residential Segregation at Port Elizabeth, South Africa, 1880-1910. Doctoral dissertation: University of Wisconsin-Madison, 1987. UMO # 8712422.

8133. Kline, Benjamin. "The National Union of South African Students: A Case Study of the Plight of Liberalism, 1924- 1977." J. Mod. Afric. Studies 23 (March 1985): 139-146.

8134. Knight, J. B. and M.B. McGrath. "An Analysis of Racial Wage Discrimination in South Africa." Oxford Bulletin of Economics and Statistics (November 1977): 245-271.

8135. Kreindler, Joshua D. "South Africa, Jewish Palestine and Israel: The Growing Relationship, 1919-1974." Africa Quarterly 20 (1980): 48-87.

8136. Kuppusami, C. Indian Education in Natal, 1860-1946. Master's thesis: UNISA, 1946.

8137. Kuppusami, C. Pioneer Footprints: Growth of Indian Education in South Africa, 1860-1977. Nasou Limited, 1978.

8138. Kuzwayo, Ellen. Call Me Woman. London: Women's Press Ltd., 1985. [Growing up in Soweto, and more.]

8139. Lapchick, Richard E. and Stephanie Urdang. Oppression and Resistance: The Struggle of Women in Southern Africa. Westport, CT: Greenwood, 1982.

8140. Laurence, Patrick. "White Capitalism and Black Rage." Johannesburg Weekly Mail (September 13-19, 1985)

8141. Lazerson, Joshua N. The Communist Party of South Africa, the Springbok Legion and the South African Congress of Democrats: "Democratic Whites" in the South African Liberation Movement, 1942-1964. Doctoral dissertation: Northwestern University, 1990. UMO # 9031953.

8142. Lekhela, E. P. The Development of Bantu Education in the North-Western Cape 1840-1947 (A Historical Survey). Master's thesis: UNISA, 1958.

8143. Leonie, A. The Development of Bantu Education in South Africa: 1652 to 1954. Doctoral dissertation: Montana State University, 1965.

8144. Levin, R. "Black Education, Class Struggle and the Dynamics of Change in South Africa since 1946." Africa Perspective 17 (Spring 1980): 17-41.

8145. Lewis, Gavin. Between the Wire and the Wall: A History of South African "Coloured" Politics. Cape Town: 1987.

8146. Lindfors, Bernt, ed. Contemporary Black South African Literature: A Symposium. Washington, D.C.: Three Continents Press, 1985. [Revised and enlarged.]

8147. Lingle, C. "Apartheid as Racial Socialism." Kyklos 43 (1990)

8148. Lipton, Merle. *Capitalism and Apartheid: South Africa, 1910-1984*. Brookfield, VT: Gower, 1985.

8149. Lombard, B. Urban. "Employment Discrimination in South Africa: Towards a Solution." *South African Journal of Labour Relations* 10 (September-December 1986): 61-84.

8150. Loubser, J. A. *The Apartheid Bible: A Critical Review of Racial Theology in South Africa*. Cape Town: Maskew Miller Longman, 1987.

8151. Louw, S. J. H. "The Economics of Education in Bophathatswana." *Dev. S. Afric.* 1 (1984): 359-368.

8152. Lynch, I. R. *The Financing of State Education in the Union of South Africa, 1910-1935*. Master's thesis: University of Pretoria, 1935.

8153. Mabin, Alan. "Labour, Capital, Class Struggle and the Origins of Residential Segregation in Kimberley, 1880-1920." *Journal of Historical Geography* 12 (January 1986): 4-26.

8154. Magida, Arthur J. "What Are South Africa's Jews Doing about Apartheid?" *Baltimore Jewish Times* (February 20, 1987): 30- 32, 35.

8155. Magubane, Bernard. "Social Inequality: The South Africa Case." In *Social Inequality*. 257-276. New York: Academic Press, 1981.

8156. Malherbe, E. G. *Education in South Africa 1925-1976*. 2 vols. Cape Town.

8157. Mantzaris, E. A. "The Fight against Anti-Semitism and the 'Labour Front': The Cape Town Poalei Zion, 1940-1948." *Jr. U. Durban-Westville* No.4 (1987): 37-47.

8158. Maphai, V. T. "Affirmative Action in South Africa a Genuine Option?" *Social Dynamics* 15 (December 1989)

8159. Maphalala, S. J. "Zulu Relations with the Whites During the 19th Century: A Broad Perspective." *Historia* 25 (May 1980): 19-27.

8160. Marais, J. S. *The Cape Coloured People 1652 to 1937*. London: 1939.

8161. Marais, M. A. "The Allocation of Resources to Education in South Africa." *South African Journal of Economics* 52 (March 1984)

8162. Maree, Johann. "The Emergence, Struggles and Achievements of Black Trade Unions in South Africa from 1973 to 1984." *Labour, Capital, & Society* 18 (November 1985): 278-303.

8163. Marks, Shula. *The Ambiguities of Dependence in South Africa. Class, Nationalism, and the State in Twentieth Century Natal*. Baltimore, MD: Johns Hopkins University Press, 1985.

8164. Marks, Shula. "Khoisan Resistance to the Dutch in the Seventeenth and Eighteenth Centuries." Journal of African History 11 (1971): 517-530.

8165. Marks, Shula. "Natal, the Zulu Royal Family and the Ideology of Segregation." Journal of Southern African Studies 4 (1978): 172-194.

8166. Marks, Shula and Stanley Trapido, eds. The Politics of Race, Class and Nationalism in Twentieth Century South Africa. London: 1987.

8167. Mashinini, Emma. Strikes Have Followed Me All My Life: A South African Autobiography. London: Women's Press, 1989.

8168. Mathabane, Mark. Kaffir Boy: The True Story of a Black Youth Coming of Age in Apartheid South Africa. New York: Macmillan, 1986.

8169. Matthews, Z. K. Freedom for My People...Southern Africa 1901-1968. Cape Town: 1981.

8170. Maurice, E. L. The Development of Policy in Regard to the Education of Coloured Pupils at the Cape, 1880-1940. Doctoral dissertation: University of Cape Town, 1966.

8171. Maurice, E. L. The History and Administration of the Coloured Peoples of the Cape 1652-1910. Bachelor's thesis: University of Cape Town, 1946. [2 vols.]

8172. Mbali, Zolile. The Churches and Racism: A Black South African Perspective. London: SCM Press, 1987.

8173. McGrath, Mike. "Economic Growth and the Distribution of Racial Incomes in the South African Economy." So. Africa Int. 15 (April 1985): 223-232.

8174. McGrath, Mike. "Global Poverty in the South African Economy." Social Dynamics 10 (June 1984): 38-48.

8175. Meer, Fatima. "Indians within Apartheid: Indentured Labor and Group Formation in South Africa." Studies in Third World Societies 39 (1987): 49-68.

8176. Meer, Fatima. Portrait of Indian South Africans. Durban: Avon House, 1969.

8177. Meillassoux, Claude, ed. Verrouillage ethnique en Afrique du Sud. Paris: Presses Universitaires de France, 1988.

8178. Meli, Francis. A History of the ANC: South Africa Belongs To Us. London: James Currey, 1989.

8179. Merrett, Christopher. "In a State of Emergency: Libraries and Government Control in South Africa." Library Quarterly 60 (January 1990)

8180. Mertz, Elizabeth. "The Uses of History: Language Ideology, and Law in the United States and South Africa." Law & Society Review 22 (November 1988): 661-685.

8181. Miller, P. R. "The Jury System in Early Natal (1846-1874)." Journal of Legal History 8 (1987): 129-147.

8182. Mivaga, D. Z. The Crime of Apartheid. Dar es Salaam: Dar es Salaam University Press, 1985.

8183. Moeti, Sello. "Ten Years of Soweto Uprising." Sechaba (June 1986): 2-10.

8184. Mohan, Jitenaha. "Southern Africa: Imperialism, Racism and Neo-colonialism." Review of African Political Economy 11 (January-April 1978): 31-39.

8185. Mokgatle, D. D. "The Exclusion of Blacks from the South African Judicial System." South African Journal of Human Rights 3 (March 1987): 44-51.

8186. Moloisi, Thapelo. "June 16 [1976]- A Turning Point." Sechaba (June 1986): 11-18. [Personal reminiscence.]

8187. Morris, M. "The Development of Capitalism in South Africa." Journal of Development Studies (1976)

8188. Mphahlele, Ezekiel. Africa My Music: An Autobiography, 1957-1983. Johannesburg: Ravan Press, 1986.

8189. Muller, A. L. "Slavery and the Development of South Africa." South African Journal of Economics 49 (June 1981)

8190. Muller, Neil. "The Dynamics of Rural Poverty in the Transkei." Africanus 14 (1984): 53-64.

8191. Murray, Martin J. "The Triumph of Marxist Approaches in South African Social and Labour History." Jr. Asian Afric. Studies 27 (January-April 1988): 79-101.

8192. Mzimela, Sipo E. Apartheid, South African Naziism. Nairobi, Kenya: Evangel Pub. House, 1983.

8193. Nasson, Bill. "Ambiguous Hope: Education and Poverty." Social Dynamics 10 (June 1984): 1-19.

8194. National Union of South African Students. NUSAS Talks to the ANC: Report on a Meeting Held from 31 March-2 April in Harare. Johannesburg: NUSAS, 1986.

8195. Ncube, Don. The Influence of Apartheid and Capitalism on the Development of Black Trade Unions in South Africa. Johannesburg: 1985.

8196. Neevbury, C. W. *The Diamond Ring: Business, Politics, and Precious Stones in South Africa, 1867-1947*. New York: Oxford University Press, 1989.

8197. Neichardt, L. "National Socialism in South Africa." *Fascist Quarterly* 2 (1936): 557-570.

8198. Nkabinde, A. C. "Crisis in South Africa." *Times Higher Education Supplement*, (June 27, 1986): [The black universities.]

8199. Nkomo, Mokubung O. "Apartheid Education in Crisis." *Transafrica Forum* 3 (Fall 1985): 71-84.

8200. O'Leary, John. "Instruments of Apartheid or Vehicles of Change?" *Times Higher Education Supplement*, (November 14, 1986): [Five South African universities open to multiracial enrollment.]

8201. O'Meara, Dan. *Volkskapitalisme: Class, Capital, and Ideology in the Development of Afrikaner Nationalism*. New York: Cambridge University Press, 1983.

8202. Odendaal, Andre. *Vakuni Bantu! The Beginnings of Black Protest Politics in South Africa to 1912*. Capetown: David Phillip, 1984.

8203. Okafor, C. G. "Of Spooks and Virile Men: Patterns of Response to Imperialism." In *Sizwe Dansi Is Dead and The Trial of Dedan Kimathi. Commonwealth Essays & Studies* 12 (Autumn 1989): 87-94.

8204. Omond, Roger. *The Apartheid Handbook. A Guide to South Afrika's Everyday Racial Policies*. Penguin: 1986.

8205. Onselen, Charles van. *New Babylon, New Nineveh*. Johannesburg: Ravan Press, 1982.

8206. Onselen, Charles van. *Studies in the Social and Economic History of the Witwatersrand, 1886-1914*. 2 vols. New York: Longman, 1982.

8207. Packard, Randall M. *White Plague, Black Labor. Tuberculosis and the Political Economy of Health and Disease in South Africa*. Berkeley: University of California Press, 1990.

8208. Pallister, David and others. *South Africa, Inc.: The Oppenheimer Empire*. rev. and updated ed. New Haven: Yale University Press, 1988.

8209. Parnell, S. "Shaping a Racially Divided Society: State Housing Policy in South Africa, 1920-1950." *Environment & Planning* 7 (August 1989)

8210. Peires, J. B. *The House of Phalo: A History of the Xhosa People in the Days of their Independence*. Berkeley: University of California Press, 1982.

8211. Pete, Steve. "Punishment and Race: The Emergence of Racially Defined Punishment in Colonial Natal." Natal Univ. Law Soc. Review 1 (Nov. 1986): 99-114.

8212. Peterson, Kirsten H., ed. Criticism and Ideology: Second African Writers' Conference. Uppsala: Sweden: Scandanavian Institute of African Studies, 1988.

8213. Pirie, G. H. "Racial Segregation on Johannesburg Trams. Procedures and Protest, 1904-1927." African Studies 48 (1989)

8214. Pitts, Joe W. "Public Interest Law in South Africa." Stanford Journal of International Law 22 (Spring 1986): 153-182.

8215. Poinsette, C. L. "Black Women under Apartheid: An Introduction." Harvard Women's Law Journal 8 (1985): 91- 119.

8216. Quinlan, Tim. "The Perpetuation of Myths: A Case Study on 'Tribe' and 'Chief' in South Africa." Journal of Legal Pluralism and Unofficial Law (1988): 79-115.

8217. Racism in Southern Africa: The Commonwealth Stand. London: Commonwealth Secretariat, 1989.

8218. Ramphele, M. A. and E.A. Boonzaier. "The Position of African Women: Race and Gender in South Africa." In South African Keywords, edited by E.A. Boonzaier and J.S. Sharp. Cape Town: David Philip, 1988.

8219. Ray, J. J. "Racism and Personal Adjustment: Testing the Bagley Hypothesis in Germany and South Africa." Personality & Individual Differences 9 (1988): 685-686.

8220. Rhoodie, Nic J. and A.D. Louw. "Black Attitudes towards the Desegregation of Public Amenities in a White Satellite city of Johannesurg." International Social Science Review 107- 122 (Summer 1986)

8221. Richardson, David and Roy Issacowitz. "The Reds and the Blacks." Jerusalem Post Magazine (April 5, 1985): [South African Jewish involvement in struggle against apartheid.]

8222. Roberts, M. and A.E.G. Trollip. The South African Opposition, 1939-1945. London: 1947.

8223. Robertson, H. M. "150 Years of Economic Contact Between Black and White." South African Journal of Economics 2, 3 (1934, 1935): 403-425, 3-25.

8224. Robertson, Michael. "Land Reform: South African Options." Columbia Human Rights Law Review 21 (Fall): 193-209.

8225. Ross, Robert. Cape of Torments: Slavery and Resistance in South Africa. Boston, MA: Routledge & Kegan Paul, 1983.

8226. Russel, M. Intellectual and Academic Apartheid 1950-1965. Edited by Pierre van de Berghe. London: 1979.

8227. Russell, Margo. "Slaves or Workers? Relations between Bushman, Tswana, and Boers in the Kalahari." Journal of South African Studies 2 (1976): 178-197.

8228. Saron, Gustav. Combating Anti-Semitism in South Africa. Johannesburg: 1945.

8229. Saul, John. "South Africa: The Question of Strategy." New Left Review No.160 (November-December 1986): 3-22.

8230. Savage, M. T. D. "An Anatomy of the South African Corporate Economy: Ownership, Control and the Interlocking Directorate." Industrial Relations Journal of South Africa 7 (1987): 4-29.

8231. Savage, M. T. D. "An Anatomy of South African Health Services." Energos (November 1987)

8232. Schoombee, G. F. "Some Crucial Social Variables which Hamper the Development of Sound Intergroup Relations in South Africa." S. Afric. J. Sociol. 13 (1982): 54-61.

8233. Schwarz, Harry. "South African Jews in the 1980s." Jewish Affairs 35 (1980): 23-27.

8234. Scully, Malcolm G. and others. "South Africa: The Crisis, the Campuses, and Some Messages for Americans." Chronicle of Higher Education (June 11, 1986): [Number of articles on black higher education in South Africa.]

8235. Seboni, M. O. M. The South African Native College, Fort Hare, 1903-1954: A Historical-Critical Survey. Doctoral dissertation: UNISA, 1958.

8236. Segar, Julia and Caroline White. "Constructing Gender: Discrimination and the Law in South Africa." Agenda (1989): 95-113.

8237. Shain, Milton. "Diamonds, Pogroms, and Undesirables: Anti- Alienism and Legislation in the Cape Colony, 1898-1910." S. Afric. Hist. J. (November 1980): 13-28.

8238. Shain, Milton. "From Pariah to Parvenu: The Anti-Jewish Stereotype in South Africa, 1880-1910." Jewish Journal of Sociology 26 (1984): 111-127.

8239. Shain, Milton. "The History of South African Jewry-1800 to Contemporary Times." In Contemporary Jewish Civilization, edited by Shimoni. New

York: International Centre for University Teaching of Jewish Civilization, 1985.

8240. Shain, Milton. "The Open Ghetto: Growing Up Jewish in South Africa." In Growing Up In a Divided Society: The Contexts of Childhood in South Africa, edited by Sandra Burman and P. Reynolds. 208-225. Johannesburg: Ravan Press, 1986.

8241. Shain, Milton. "South Africa." In Encyclopedia of the Holocaust, IV. 1382-1383. New York: Macmillan, 1990.

8242. Shava, Piniel. A People's Voice: Black South African Writing in the 20th Century. Athens: Ohio University Press, 1989.

8243. Shell, Robert C. H. Slavery at the Cape of Good Hope, 1680 to 1731. Doctoral dissertation: Yale University, 1986. UMO # 8701086.

8244. Shillington, Kevin. The Colonisation of the Southern Tswana, 1870-1900. Johannesburg: Ravan Press, 1985.

8245. Shindler, Colin. "South Africa's Nazi Record." New Zealand Jewish Chronicle 36 (1980): 7-9.

8246. Shute, Jenefer P. "A Separate Development." Boston Globe, Magazine (January 10, 1988): [Growing up white in South Africa.]

8247. Sidzumo-Sanders, Ruth A. N. The Bantu Education System: Impact on Black Women in South Africa. Doctoral dissertation: Wayne State University, 1989. UMO # 8922782.

8248. Simkins, Charles E. W. What Has Been Happening to Income Distribution and Poverty in the Homelands? Cape Town: University of Cape Town, Conference Paper No. 7, Second Carnegie Inquiry into Poverty and Development in Southern Africa, 1988.

8249. Simson, Howard. The Social Origins of Afrikaner Fascism and Its Apartheid Policy. Atlantic Highlands, NJ: Humanities Press, 1981.

8250. Slovo, Joe. "The Working Class and Nation Building." In The National Question in South Africa, edited by Marie van Diepen. London: 1988.

8251. Smollan, Roy, ed. Black Advancement in the South African Economy. New York: St. Martin's Press, 1986.

8252. Sokolsky, Joel J. "South African Jewry, Apartheid and American Attitudes." Judaism 29 (1980): 404-417.

8253. Sole, Kelwyn. "Working Class Culture." S. Afric. Labour Bulletin 10 (June 1985): 43-56.

8254. Sookdeo, Anil. "Ethnic Myths from South Africa: Bigoted Boer and Liberal Briton." Journal of Ethnic Studies 18 (Winter 1991): 29-45.

8255. South African Jewish Board of Deputies. The Anti-Jewish Movements in South Africa. The Need for Action. Johannesburg: L.E. Joseph & Co., 1936.

8256. South African Research Service. South African Review, One and Two. Johannesburg: Ravan Press, 1983-1984.

8257. South Africa's Impending Socialist Revolution. Perspectives of the Marxist Workers' Tendency of the African National Congress. London: Inqaba ya Basebenzi, 1982.

8258. Southall, Roger. "African Capitalism in Contemporary South Africa." Journal of Southern African Studies 7 (October 1980): 38-70.

8259. Stasiulis, Daiva K. "Pluralist and Marxist Perspectives on Racial Discrimination in South Africa." British Journal of Sociology 31 (1980): 463-490.

8260. Stevens, B. "Struggle for Life. Health in a Liberated South Africa." Sechaba (March 1986): 28-31.

8261. Suttner, Raymond and others. 30 Years of the Freedom Charter. Johannesburg: Ravan Press, 1986.

8262. Swanson, Maynard W. "The Asiatic Menace: Creating Segregation in Durban-1870-1900." Int. Jr. Afric. Hist. Studies 16 (1983): 401-422.

8263. Switzer, Les. Media and Dependency in South Africa. A Case Study of the Press and the Ciskei "Homeland". Athens: Ohio University Monographs in International Studies, 1985.

8264. Thabe, G. A. L. It's a Goal! 50 Years of Sweat, Tears, and Drama in Black Soccer. Johannesburg: Skotaville Publishers, 1983.

8265. Theron, J. H. "The Student Conference of April 1985: The Need for White/Black Liaison Reaffirmed." Journal of Contemporary History 10 (1985): 68-83. [Bloemfontein.]

8266. Tomaselli, Keyan G. The Cinema of Apartheid: Race and Class in South African Films. New York/Smyrna: Lakeview Press, 1988.

8267. Tripathy, J. T. "Plight of Black Women in South Africa: Feminism Reinforced sans Humanism." Africa Quarterly 24 (1985): 52-71.

8268. Tsotsi, W. M. From Chattel to Wage Slavery. Maseru: 1981.

8269. Turshen, Meredith. "Health and Human Rights in a South African Bantustan." Social Science Medicine 22 (1986): 887-892.

8270. Turton, R. W. and B.E. Chalmers. "Apartheid, Stress and Illness: The Demographic Context of Distress Reported by South African Africans." Social Science & Medicine 31 (1990)

8271. Two Dogs and Freedom: Black Children of South Africa Speak Out/from the Open School. New York. Rosset & Co.: 1987.

8272. Ucko, Peter. Academic Freedom and Apartheid: The Story of the World Archeological Conference. London: Duckworth, 1988.

8273. Unterhalter, Elaine. "The Struggle for People's Education." Sechaba (September 1986): 2-7.

8274. Uran, Steven. "Le judaisme sud-africain entre conflits ethniques et dilemmes moraux." Yod No. 22 (1986): 109-128.

8275. Van der Vyver, J. D. "State-Sponsored Terror Violence." South African Journal of Human Rights 4 (March 1988): 55-75.

8276. van der Berg, S. "On Interracial Income Distribution in South Africa to the End of the Century." South African Journal of Economics 57 (March 1989)

8277. Van der Horst, Sheila T., ed. Race Discrimination in South Africa: A Review. Cape Town: David Philip, 1982.

8278. Van Duin, P. "Black Trade Unionism in South Africa, 1917-1948." Leidschrift No. 3 (1988): 58-73.

8279. van Dyk, D. F. The Education of the Griquas, Coloureds and Bantu in E. Griqiraland- A Historical Survey, 1863-1892. Doctoral dissertation: University of the Orange Free State, 1964.

8280. van Eyssen, J. F. The Supervision and Aministration of Education in the Cape Province and Natal from 1652-1945. Master's thesis: UNISA, 1946.

8281. van Niekerk, Phillip. "Pretoria's Black Schools Threatened." Boston Globe, (December 22, 1985)

8282. Van Staden, F. J. "White South Africans' Attitudes Toward the Desegregation of Public Amenities." Journal of Social Psychology 127 (1987): 163-173.

8283. Van Zyl Smit, Dirk. "Adopting and Adapting Criminological Ideas: Criminology and Afrikaner Nationalism in South Africa." Contemporary Crises 13 (September 1989): 227-251.

8284. Van Zyl Smit, Dirk. "Public Policy and the Punishment of Crime in a Divided Society: A Historical Perspective on the South African Penal System." Natal University Law and Society Review 1 (November 1985): 54-67.

8285. VanderRoss, R. E. The Rise and Decline of Apartheid. A Study of Political Movements among the Coloured People of South Africa, 1880-1985. Cape Town: Tafelberg, 1986.

8286. Verbeek, Jennifer. "Racially Segregated School Libraries in Kwa Zulu/Natal,South Africa." Journal of Librarianship 18 (1986): 23-46.

8287. Voss, Tony. "The Image of the Bushman in South African English Writing of the Nineteenth and Twentieth Centuries." Eng. Africa 21-40 (May 1987)

8288. Vukani Makhosikazi Collective. South African Women on the Move. London: Zed Press, 1986.

8289. The War against Children: South Africa's Youngest Victims. New York: Lawyers Committee for Human Rights, 1986.

8290. Wasburn, Philo C. "The Counter-Propaganda of Radio RSA: The Voice of South Africa." Journal of Broadcasting & Electronic Media 33 (1989): 117-138.

8291. Watkinson, E. J. A Decade of Progress in Native Secondary Education in the Cape Province, 1933-1942. Master's thesis: UNISA, 1942.

8292. Watson, Richard L. The Slave Question: Liberty and Property in South Africa. Middletown, CT: Wesleyan University Press, 1990.

8293. Webster, David J. "The Political Economy of Food Production and Nutrition in Southern Africa in Historical Perspective." Journal of Modern African Studies 24 (1986): 447-463.

8294. Webster, Edward. Cast in a Racial Mold. Johannesburg: Ravan Press, 1985.

8295. Weisbord, R. G. "The Dilemma of South African Jewry." Journal of Modern African Studies 5 (1967)

8296. Welsh, David. The Roots of Segregation 1845-1910. 2d ed. Cape Town: Oxford, 1973.

8297. Welsh, David. "South Africa's Ultra Right- Part Two." Patterns of Prejudice 23 (Spring 1989): 3-15.

8298. West, Michael. "Indian Politics in South Africa: 1860 to the Present." South Asia Bulletin 7 (1987): 97-111.

8299. Westcott, Gill and Francis Wilson, eds. Economics of Health in South Africa. Johannesburg: Ravan Press, 1977, 1980. [2 vols.]

8300. Western, John. Outcast Cape Town. Minneapolis: University of Minnesota Press, 1981. [From integration to segregation.]

8301. White, D. R. and J. H. Kiely. "The Drop-Out Phenomenon of Senior Secondary Pupils in Black Schools." South African Journal of Education 5 (1985): 162-166. [Bafokeng High School, Phokeng, Bophutatswana.]

8302. Wilkinson, Peter. "The South African State and the Resolution of the African Housing Crisis 1948-1954." In Working Papers in Southern African Studies, edited by Doug Hindson. Johannesburg: Raven Press, 1983.

8303. Willan, Brian. Sol Plaatje: a Biography. Johannesburg: 1984.

8304. Wilson, Francis and M. Ramphele. Uprooting Poverty: The South African Challenge. New York: Norton, 1989. [Black poverty in resource-rich South Africa.]

8305. Wolpe, Harold. "The Changing Class Structure of South Africa: The African Petit-Bougeoisie." In Research in Political Economy, Vol. 1, edited by Paul Zarembka. Greenwich, Ct: JAI Press, 1977.

8306. Wolpe, Harold. Race, Class & the Apartheid State. London: 1988.

8307. Wolpe, Harold. "The Theory of Internal Colonialism: The South African Case." Bulletin of the Conference of Socialist Economists 9 (Autumn 1974)

8308. Wolpe, Harold. "The Theory of Internal Colonialism: The South African Case." In The Sociology of Development, edited by Ivar Oxaal and others. London: 1975.

8309. Worden, Nigel. Slavery in Dutch South Africa. New York: Cambridge University Press, 1985. [1652-1795.]

8310. Worger, William H. South Africa's City of Diamonds. Mine Workers and Monopoly Capitalism in Kimberley, 1867-1895. New Haven, CT: Yale University Press, 1987.

8311. Wren, Christopher S. "Rumblings On the Right." New York Times Magazine (October 7, 1990): [Extreme right-wing groups in South Africa.]

8312. Zilke, Helen. "5 Student Leaders Surrender in South Africa: Police Agree to Withdraw from their Campus." Chronicle of Higher Education (August 13, 1986): [Predominantly Indian University of Durban-Westville.]

SPAIN

8313. Abella, Rafael. *La vida cotidiana en España bajo el régimen de Franco*. Barcelona: Editorial Argos Vergara, 1985. [1939- 1975.]

8314. Alcala, Angel, ed. *The Spanish Inquisition and the Inquisitorial Mind*. Boulder, CO: Atlantic Research and Publications, 1987.

8315. Alcalde, Carmen. *La mujer en la guerra civil espanola*. Madrid: Editorial Cambio 16, 1976.

8316. Arnau, J. and H. Boada. "Languages and School in Catalonia." *Journal of Multilingual and Multicultural Development* 7 (1986): 107-123.

8317. Aronsfeld, C. C. *The Ghosts of 1492: Jewish Aspects of the Struggle for Religious Freedom in Spain, 1848-1976*. New York: Columbia University Press, 1979.

8318. Aronsfeld, C. C. "Right-wing Subversion: Spain's 'National Revolutionaries'." *Patterns of Prejudice* 8 (1974): 9-12. [1970s.]

8319. Aronsfeld, C. C. "Spain's Returning Jews." *History Today* 37 (1987): 38-43.

8320. Ashtor, Eliyahu. *The Jews of Moslem Spain*. Philadelphia Translated by Aaron Klein and Jenny M. Klein: Jewish Publication Society of America, 1974, 1984.

8321. Avni, Haim and Stanley G. Payne. "Spain." In *Encyclopedia of the Holocaust, IV*. 1390-1395. New York: Macmillan, 1990.

8322. Avni, Haim. *Spain, the Jews and Franco*. Philadelphia, PA Translated by Emanuel Shimoni: Jewish Publication Society of America, 1983.

8323. Bachrach, Bernard S. "A Reassessment of Visigothic Jewish Policy, 589-711." *American Historical Review* 78 (1973): 20- 22.

8324. Baer, Yitzhak. History of the Jews in Christian Spain. Philadelphia, PA Translated by Louis Schoffman: Jewish Publication Society of America, 1961.

8325. Bentwich, N. "Jewish Reinstatement in Spain and Portugal." Wiener Library Bulletin 23 (Winter 1968-1969): 24-28.

8326. Berneriá, Lourdes. Mujer, economia y patriarcado durante la Espana franquista. Barcelona: Anagrama, 1977.

8327. Cámara Villar, Gregoria. Nacional-catolicismo y escuela: la socializacion politica del franquissmo (1936-1951). Jaen, Spain: Editorial Hesperia, 1984.

8328. Camiller, Patrick. "Spanish Socialism in the Atlantic Order." New Left Review No. 156 (March-April 1986): 5-36.

8329. Capel Martinez, Roza Maria. La Mujer española en el mundo del trabajo 1900-1930. Madrid: Fundación Juan March, 1980.

8330. Caro Baroja, Julio. El laberinto vasco. San Sebastian, Spain: Editorial Txertoa, 1984. [Basque people.]

8331. Caro Baroja, Julio. Los Judios en la Espana Moderna y Contemporánea. 3 vols. Madrid: Edicions Arion, Artes Gráficas Benzal, 1961-2.

8332. Carpenter, Dwayne E. Alfonso X and the Jews... Berkeley: University of California, 1986.

8333. Cazorla Perez, Jose. "Desigualdad e intolerancia en la evolucion politica española." Revista de Estudios Politicos No. 44 (1985): 9-24.

8334. Chaffee, Lyman. "Social Conflict and Alternative Mass Communications: Public Art and Politics in the Service of Spanish-Basque Nationalism." European Journal of Policy Research 16 (1988): 545-572.

8335. Charnes, Gloria L. "The Re-emergence of Spanish Jewry." Christian Century 706-708 (August 3-10, 1988)

8336. Clark, Robert P. The Basque Insurgents: ETA, 1952-1980. Madison: University of Wisconsin Press, 1984.

8337. Collins, Roger. The Basques. Cambridge, MA: Blackwell, 1990.

8338. Cortes, Vicenta. La enclavitud en Valencia durante el reinado de los Reyes Católicos, 1479-1516. Valencia: 1964. [Black slaves in Spain, pp. 56-59.]

8339. DeFebo, Giuliana. Resistancia y movimento de mujeres en España, 1936-1976. Madrid: Icaria, 1979.

8340. Delaney, Paul. "In the Schools, a Quieter Basque War." New York Times, (June 1, 1987)

8341. Delaney, Paul. "'Real Racists', Black Asserts of Spaniards." New York Times, (September 10, 1987)

8342. Diego Aguirre, José R. Historia del Sahara Español. Madrid: Kaydeda Ediciones, 1988.

8343. Díez Medrano, Juan. Nationalism and Independence in Spain: Basques and Catalans. Doctoral dissertation: University of Michigan, 1989. UMO # 9001618.

8344. Dominguez Ortiz, Antonio. "La esclavitud en Castilla durante la edad moderna." In Estudios de historia social de España. Vol II, 369-428. Madrid: 1952.

8345. Douglass, William A. Basque Politics: A Case Study in Ethnic Nationalism. Tarrytown, New York: Associated Faculty Press, 1985.

8346. Dumas, Claude and Jacqueline Covo, eds. Minorités et marginalités en Espagne et en Amérique latine au XIXeme siècle. Villeneuve-d'Ascq: Presses universitaires de Lille, 1990.

8347. Duran, Maria A. Dominación, sexo y cambio social. Madrid: Editorial, 1977.

8348. Ellwood, Sheelagh M. Spanish Fascism in the Franco Era. London: Macmillan, 1987.

8349. "Ethnic Minority Groups and Self determination: The Case of the Basques." Columbia Journal of Law and Social Problems 20 (1986): 55-87.

8350. Fernandez Vargas, Valentina. La resistencia interior en la España de Franco. Madrid: Ediciones Istmo, 1981.

8351. Fishman, Robert M. Working Class Organization and the Return to Democracy in Spain. Ithaca, New York: Cornell University Press, 1990.

8352. Franco Silva, Alfonso. Los esclavos de Sevilla. Sevilla: Diputación Provincial de Sevilla, 1980.

8353. Friedman, Jerome. "Jewish Conversion. The Spanish Pure Blood Laws and Reformation: a Revisionist View of Radical and Religious Antisemitism." Sixteenth Century Journal 18 (1987): 3-30.

8354. Gampel, Benjamin R. "The Decline of Iberian Jewries: Pogroms, Inquisition and Expulsion." The Sephardim (1987): 36-57.

8355. Gampel, Benjamin R. The Last Jews on Iberian Soil: Navarrese Jewry 1479-1498. Berkeley: University of California Press, 1989.

8356. Garcia Delgado, Jose L. Origines y Desarrollo del Capitalismo en Espana. Madrid: 1975.

8357. Giner, Salvador and Eduardo Sevilla. "The Latifundio As a Local Mode of Class Domination: The Spanish Case." Iberian Studies 6 (1977): 47-58.

8358. Goldberg, Harriet. "Two Parallel Medival Commonplaces: Antifeminism and Antisemitism in the Hispanic Literary Tradition." In Aspects of Jewish Culture in the Middle Ages, edited by Paul E. Szarmach. Albany: State of New York University Press, 1979.

8359. Gonzalez, Anabel and others. Los Orígenes del feminismo en Espana. Madrid: Zero, 1980.

8360. Gonzalez Garcia, Isidro. "El problema del racismo y los judios en el fascismo ialiano y su incidencia en el govierno de Burgos en el año 1938." Hispania 47 (1987): 309-335.

8361. Gonzalez Garcia, Isidoro. "Los intelectuales españoles y la cuestion judia en la Europa de final del siglo 19." El Olivo 21 (1985): 87-110.

8362. Haliczer, Stephen H. "The First Holocaust: The Inquisition and the Converted Jews of Spain and Portugal." Inquisition and Society in Early Modern Europe (1987): 7-18.

8363. Haliczer, Stephen H. Inquisition and Society in the Kingdom of Valencia, 1478-1834. Berkeley: University of California Press, 1990.

8364. Harrison, J. "Big Business and the Rise of Basque Nationalism." European Studies Review 7 (October 1977): 371-391.

8365. Hebbert, M. "Regional Autonomy and Economic Action in the First Catalan Government, 1980-1984." Regional Studies 19 (October 1985)

8366. Heiberg, Marianne. The Making of the Basque Nation. New York: Cambridge University Press, 1990.

8367. Hernandez, Francesc and Francese Mercade, eds. Estructuras sociales y cuestión nacional en España. Barcelona: Editorial Ariel, 1986.

8368. Kamen, Henry. "The Mediterranean and the Expulsion of Spanish Jews in 1492." Past & Present 119 (May 1988): 30- 55.

8369. Katz, Solomon. The Jews in the Visigothic and Frankish Kingdoms of Spain and Gaul. Cambridge, MA: Medieval Academy of America, 1937.

8370. Lacave, José L. "España y los Judios españoles." R. ét juives 144 (1985): 7-25.

8371. Laitin, David D. "Linguistic Revival: Politics and Culture in Catalonia." Comparative Studies in Society and History 31 (April 1989): 297-317.

8372. Lannon, Frances and Paul Preston, eds. Elites and Power in Twentieth-century Spain: Essays in Honor of Sir Raymond Carr. New York: Oxford University Press, 1990.

8373. Lawrence, J. N. H. "The Spread of Lay Literacy in Late Medieval Castile." Bull. Hisp. Stud. 62 (January 1985): 79- 94.

8374. Legarreta, Dorothy. The Guernica Generation: Basque Refugee Children of the Spanish Civil War. Reno: University of Nevada Press, 1984.

8375. Lipschitz, Chaim U. Franco, Spain, the Jews, and the Holocaust. New York: KTAV, 1984. [Ed. by Ira Axelrod.]

8376. Lopez Garrido, Diego. El aparato policial en España: historia, sociologia e ideologia. Barcelona: Editorial Ariel, 1987.

8377. Lopez Rodo, Laureano. Las autonomias, encrucijada de España. Madrid: Ediciones Aguilar, 1980.

8378. MacKay, Ruth. "Workers' Children Boycott University." Guardian (NYC) (March 11, 1987)

8379. Manjarre, J. M. Esclavos y libertos en la Espana Romana. Salamanca: University of Salamanca, 1971.

8380. Marcus, Ivan G. "Jewish Minority Experience in Medieval Spain." Response 40 (1981): 59-71.

8381. Martinez Carreras, J. U. "La abolición de la esclavitud en España durante el siglo XIX, segun la reciente bibliografía y estado de cuestiones." Revista de Indias 45 (1985): 263- 274.

8382. McDonogh, Gary W., ed. Conflict in Catalonia. Gainesville: Monographs in Social Science, University of Florida, 1986.

8383. McDonogh, Gary W. Good Families of Barcelona: A Social History of Power in the Industrial Era. Princeton, NJ: Princeton University Press, 1986.

8384. McDonogh, Gary W. "Lenguaje, historia y poder: Uso del lenguaje de la elite en la Barcelona industrial." R. int. Sociol. 45 (1987): 217-243.

8385. McGrath Grubb, E. E. "Attitudes towards Black Africans in Imperial Spain." Legon J. Humanities 1 (1974): 68-90.

8386. Medhurst, Kenneth. The Basques and Catalans. new ed. London: Minority Rights Groups, 1977.

8387. Meyerson, Mark D. *The Muslims of Valencia in the Age of Fernando and Isabel. Between Co-existence and Crusade*. Berkeley: University of California Press, 1991.

8388. Monter, E. William. *Frontiers of Heresy: The Spanish Inquisition from the Basque Lands to Sicily*. New York: Cambridge University Press, 1990.

8389. Morán, Gregorio. *Los españoles que dejaron de serio: Euskadi, 1937-1981*. Barcelona: Editorial Planeta, 1982.

8390. Mulcahy, F. David. "Gypsy-Non-Gypsy Conflict in Spain." *International Journal of Group Tensions* 19 (Winter 1989): 349-363.

8391. Payne, Stanley G. "Catalan and Basque Nationalism." *Journal of Contemporary History* 6 (1971): 15-51.

8392. Payne, Stanley G. "Spanish Fascism." *Salmagundi* Nos. 76- 77 (1987-1988): 101-112.

8393. Penafiel Ramon, Antonio. "Gitanos en Murcia en la primera mitad del siglo XVIII: Integracion o extincion?" *Anales de Historia Contemporanea* 4 (1985): 7-34.

8394. Pescatello, Ann M. *Power and Pawn: The Female in Iberian Families, Societies, and Culture*. Westport, CT: Greenwood, 1976.

8395. Petras, James. "The Road to Marbella." *Against the Currents* 5 (September/October 1990): 15-23. [Spanish society and politics.]

8396. Pi-Sunyer, Oriol. "Catalan Nationalism: Some Theoretical and Historical Considerations." In *New Nationalisms of the Developed West: Toward Explanation*, edited by Edward A. Tiryakian and Ronald Ragowski. Boston: Allen & Unwin, 1985.

8397. *La pobreza en la España de los 80*. Madrid: Editorial Aceb, 1989.

8398. Preston, Paul. "Persecuted and Persecutors: Modern Spanish Catholicism." *European History Quarterly* 20 (April 1990): 285-292. [Review article.]

8399. Preston, Paul. "Spain." In *Fascism in Europe*, edited by S.J. Woolf. London: Methuen, 1982.

8400. Quintana, Bertha B. and Lois G. Floyd. *Que Gitano. Gypsies of Southern Spain*. New York: Holt, 1972.

8401. Rambaum, J. E. "Medieval Christianity Confronts Talmudic Judaism." *Judaism* 34 (Summer 1985): 373-384.

8402. Read, Jan. *The Catalans*. London: Faber and Faber, 1978.

8403. Robinson, N. The Spain of Franco and Its Policies toward the Jews. New York: 1944.

8404. San Roman, Teresa. Gitanos de Madrid y Barcelona: ensayos sobre aculturacion y ethnicidad. Barcelona: Publicaciones, Universidad Autónoma de Barcelona, 1984.

8405. Scanlon, Geraldine M. La polemica feminista en la españa contemporanea (1868-1974). Madrid: Siglo XXI de España Editores, 1976.

8406. Schumacher, Edward. "In the Land of the Moors, New Trouble for Spain." New York Times, (February 12, 1987): [Melilla.]

8407. Simon, Larry J. "Jews, Visigoths, and the Muslim Conquest of Spain." UCLA Hist. Jr. 4 (1983): 5-33.

8408. Sullivan, John. ETA and Basque Nationalism: The Fight for Euskadi 1890-1986. London: Routledge, 1988.

8409. Tamames, Ramon. The Spanish Economy: An Introduction. New York: St. Martin's Press, 1986.

8410. Tardieu, Jean-Pierre. "Les Noirs en Espagne aux XVe, XVIe, et XVIIe siècles." Langues néo-latines 77 (1983): 27-44.

8411. Todd, Jay L. Franco and the Jews: Spain's Role in Saving Sephardim during World War II. Master's thesis: Purdue University, 1986.

8412. Urla, Jacqueline. Being Basque, Speaking Basque: The Politics of Language and Identity in the Basque Country. Doctoral dissertation: University of California, Berkeley, 1987. UMO # 8726394.

8413. Vazquez, Jesus M., ed. Los gitanos en Murcia hoy, 1980. Murcia, Spain: Departamento de Etica y Sociologia, Universidad de Murcia, 1981.

8414. Vigil, Ralph H. "Negro Slaves and Rebels in the Spanish Possessions, 1503-1558." Historian 33 (1971): 637-655.

8415. Vila, I. "Bilingual Education in the Basque Country." Journal of Multilingual and Multicultural Development 7 (1986): 123-145.

8416. Vilar, Pierre. "Spain and Catalonia." Review 3 (Spring 1980)

8417. Woolard, K. A. and T. J. Gahng. "Changing Language Policies and Attitudes in Autonomous Catalonia." Language in Society 19 (September 1990)

8418. Yerushalmi, Yosef H. Assimilation and Racial Anti-Semitism: the Iberian and the German Models. New York: Leo Baeck Institute, 1982.

8419. Yerushalmi, Yosef H. *From Spanish Court to Italian Ghetto- Isaac Cardoso. A Study in Sevententh-Century Marranism and Jewish Apologetics*. 2d ed. Seattle: University of Washington Press, 1981.

SRI LANKA

8420. Akram-Lodhi, A. Haroon. "Class and Chauvinism in Sri Lanka." Journal of Contemporary Asia 17 (1987): 160-186.

8421. Alailima, Patricia J. The Impact of Public Policy on the Poor in Sri Lanka: A Study of Policies Relating to Incomes, Assets and Living Standards and their Effects on the Poor, 1970-1984. Doctoral dissertation: University of Bradford (U.K.), 1988.

8422. Ali, Ameer. "The 1915 Racial Riots in Ceylon (Sri Lanka): A Reappraisal of Its Causes." S. Asia 4 (December 1981): 1- 20.

8423. Arasaratnam, S. "Sinhala-Tamil Relations in Modern Sri Lanka (Ceylon)." In Ethnic Conflict. International Perspectives, edited by Jerry Boucher and others. Sage, 1987.

8424. Bandarage, Asoka. Colonialism in Sri Lanka: The Political Economy of the Kandyan Highlands, 1833-1886. New york: Mouton, 1983.

8425. Bavnick, Maarten. Small Fry: The Economy of Petty Fisherman in Northern Sri Lanka. Amsterdam: VU Uitgevery Free University Press, 1984.

8426. Burger, Angela S. "Policing a Communal Society: The Case of Sri Lanka." Asian Survey 27 (July 1987): 822-833.

8427. Campaign for Social Democracy. "Sri Lanka: The Choice of Two Terrors." Race & Class 30 (1989): 57-71.

8428. Canagaretna, Sugit M. "Nation Building in a Multiethnic Setting: The Sri Lanka Case." Asian Affairs 14 (Spring 1987): 1-19.

8429. Colmey, John. "Sri Lanka: The Eye of the Storm." In These Times (May 23, 1990)

8430. De Silva, Kingsley M. A History of Sri Lanka. Berkeley: University of California Press, 1981.

8431. De Silva, Kingsley M. Managing Ethnic Tensions in Multi- Ethnic Societies: Sri Lanka, 1880-1985. Lanham, MD: University Press of America, 1986.

8432. Dissanayaka, T. D. S.S. The Agony of Sri Lanka: An In-Depth Account of the Racial Riots of 1983. Colombo: Swastika, 1983.

8433. Divisekera, S. and B.S. Felmingham. "Growth and Equity in Sri Lanka, 1963-1982." Economic Letters 28 (1988)

8434. Edirisinghe, Neville. The Food Stamps Scheme in Sri Lanka: Costs, Benefits, and Options for Modification. Washington, D.C.: International Food Policy Research Center, 1987.

8435. Ellison, Christopher G. "Elites, Competition, and Ethnic Mobilization: Tamil Politics in Sri Lanka, 1947-1977." Journal of Political and Military Sociology 15 (1987): 213-228.

8436. Fries, Yvonne and Thomas Bibin. The Undesirables: The Expatriation of the Tamil People "Of Recent Indian Origin" from the Plantations of Sri Lanka to India. Calcutta: K.P. Bagchi, 1985.

8437. Glewwe, Paul. "The Distribution of Income in Sri Lanka in 1969-1970 and 1980-1981." Journal of Development Economics 24 (December 1986): 255-274.

8438. Gooneraine, D. D. M. The Sinhalese in Ceylon: A Study in Historical and Social Geography. Master's thesis: University of Liverpool, 1930.

8439. Gooneratne, Yasmine. Relative Merits: A Personal Memoir of the Bandaranaike Family of Sri Lanka. New York: St. Martin's Press, 1986.

8440. Gopal, Krishan. "Ethnic Problem in Sri Lanka: The Historical Perspective." S. Asian Studies 22 (July-December 1987): 62-77.

8441. Greenberg, Richard. "Sri Lanka Lurches Toward Civil War." Nation (November 30, 1985)

8442. Grossholtz, Jean. Forging Capitalist Patriarchy: The Economic and Social Transformation of Feudal Sri Lanka and Its Impact on Women. Durham, NC: Duke University Press, 1984.

8443. Hillier, Stella and Lynne Gerlach. Whose Paradise? Tea and Plantation Tamils of Sri Lanka. London: Minority Rights Groups, 1987.

8444. Jayanntha, D. The Economic and Social Bases of Political Allegiance in Sri Lanka, 1947-1982. Doctoral dissertation: University of Cambridge, 1982.

8445. Jayasundera, Punchi B. Economic Growth, Income Distribution, and Welfare Expenditure: The Case of Sri Lanka. Doctoral dissertation: Boston University, 1986. UMO # 8602737.

8446. Jayawardena, V. K. "Origins of the Left Movement in Ceylon." MCS 2 (1971): 195-221.

8447. Jayewardene, C. H. S. and Hilda Jayewardene. Tea for Two, Ethnic Violence in Sri Lanka. Ottawa: Crincare, 1984.

8448. Kadirgamer, Silan. "Sri Lanka: The Elam Tamil's Struggle for Justice." PCR Information No. 22 (1986): 44-55.

8449. Kakwani, N. "Income Inequality, Welfare and Poverty in a Developing Economy with Applications to Sri Lanka." Social Choice and Welfare 5 (1988)

8450. Kannangara, A. P. "The Riots of 1915 in Sri Lanka: A Study in the Roots of Communal Violence." Past and Present 102 (February 1984): 130-165.

8451. Kearney, Robert N. "Language and the Rise of Tamil Separatism in Sri Lanka." Asian Survey 18 (May 1978): 521- 534.

8452. Kearney, Robert N. "Territorial Elements of Tamil Separatism in Sri Lanka." Pacific Affairs 60 (Winter 1987- 1988): 561-577.

8453. Kunanayakam, Tamara. "The Tamil Scapegoat: The Roots of Racism in Sri Lanka." PCR Information (World Council of Churches) 15 (1982): 43-48.

8454. Kurian, R. Women Workers in the Sri Lanka Plantation Sector: An Historical and Contemporary Analysis. London: International Labour Office, 1983.

8455. Lamballe, Alain. Le probleme Tamoul a Sri Lanka. Paris: L'Harmattan, 1985.

8456. Leary, Virginia A. Ethnic Conflict and Violence in Sri Lanka. Geneva: International Commission of Jurists, 1983.

8457. Ludowyk, E. F. C. Those Long Afternoons: Childhood in Colonial Ceylon. Columbo, Sri Lanka: Lake House Bookshop, 1989.

8458. Mahroof, M. M. M. "An Educational and Sociological Perspective of the Muslims of Sri Lanka, 1902-1914." Islamic Cult. 61 (April 1987): 84-113.

8459. Manogaran, C. Ethnic Conflict and Reconciliation in Sri Lanka. Honolulu: University of Hawaii Press, 1987.

8460. Marasinghe, M. L. "Ethnic Politics and Constitutional Reform: The Indo-Sri Lankan Accord." International and Comparative Law Quarterly 37 (July 1988): 551-587.

648 WORLD RACISM AND RELATED INHUMANITIES

8461. Marino, Eduardo. Political Killings in Southern Sri Lanka: On the Brink of Civil War. London: International Alert, 1989.

8462. McGowan, William. "India's Quagmire in Sri Lanka." Nation (June 25, 1988)

8463. Meyer, E. "Aspects of the Sinhalese-Tamil Relations in the Plantation Areas of Sri Lanka under the British Raj." Indian Economic and Social History Review 27 (April-June 1990)

8464. Mohan, V. "The Ethnic Tangle in Sri Lanka." Asian Profile 13 (December 1985): 523-540.

8465. Moore, M. "Economic Liberalization versus Political Pluralism in Sri Lanka." Modern Asian Studies 24 (May 1990)

8466. "The National Question in Sri Lanka." South Asian Bulletin (Fall 1986): entire issue.

8467. O'Ballance, Edgar. The Cyanide War: Tamil Insurrection in Sri Lanka, 1973-1988. Washington, D.C.: Brassey's, 1990.

8468. Oberst, Robert. "Democracy and the Persistence of Westernized Elite Dominance in Sri Lanka." Asian Survey 25 (July 1985): 760-772.

8469. Omvedt, Gail. "The Tamil National Question." Bulletin of Concerned Asian Scholars 16 (January-March 1984): 23-26.

8470. Peebles, Patrick. "Colonization and Ethnic Conflict in the Dry Zone of Sri Lanka." Journal of Asina Studies 49 (February 1990): 30-55.

8471. Peiris, G. L. "Continuing Ethnic Conflict in Sri Lanka: Current Constitutional Dimensions." Public Law, (Winter 1988): 515-523.

8472. Pfaffenberger, Bryan. "The Harsh Facts of Hydraulics: Technology and Society in Sri Lanka's Colonization Scheme." Technology and Culture 31 (July 1990): 361-397.

8473. Pieris, P. R. The Sociological Consequences of Imperialism, with Special Reference to Ceylon. Doctoral dissertation: London School of Economics, 1950.

8474. Piyadasa, L. Sri Lanka: The Holocaust and After. London: Marram Books, 1984.

8475. Ponnambalam, Satchi. Dependent Capitalism in Crisis: The Sri Lankan Economy, 1948-1980. London: 1980.

8476. Ponnambalam, Satchi. Sri Lanka: The National Question and the Tamil Liberation Struggle. London: Zed Books, 1983.

8477. Premdas, Ralph R. and S.W.R. De A. Samarasinghe. "Sri Lanka's Ethnic Conflict: The Indo-Lanka Peace Accord." Asian Survey 28 (June 1988): 676-690.

8478. Prinz, Thomas. "Kolonialismus-nationalismus-Rassismus: Uber vernachlassigte Zusammenhange am Beispiel Sri Lankas." Asien No. 27 (1988): 16-37.

8479. Roberts, Michael. "Elite Formations and Elites, 1832-1931." In University of Ceylon History of Ceylon, Vol.3, edited by K.M. da Silva, 263-284. Colombo: 1973.

8480. Roberts, Michael. "Ethnic Conflict in Sri Lanka and Sinhalese Perspectives: Barriers to Accomodation." Modern Asian Studies 12 (July 1978): 353-376.

8481. Roberts, Michael. "A Tale of Resistance: The Story of the Arrival of the Portuguese in Sri Lanka." Ethnos 54 (1989): 69-82.

8482. Rogers, John D. Crime, Justice, and Society in Colonial Sri Lanka. Riverdale, MD: Riverdale and Curzon, 1987.

8483. Sabaratnam, Lakshmanan. Colonial Rule and Its Consequences: The Social Bases of the Modern State and Nation in Sri Lanka, 16th to 18th Centuries. Doctoral dissertation: University of Washington, 1984. UMO # 8501090.

8484. Sabaratnam, Lakshmanan. "Intra-ethnic Stratification and Ethno-Nationalism." Journal of Developing Societies 5 (January-April 1989): 15-29.

8485. Sahn, D. E. "Changes in the Living Standards of the Poor in Sri Lanka during a Period of Macroeconomic Restructuring." World Development 15 (June 1987)

8486. Samaraweera, Vijaya. "Land, Labour, Capital, and Sectional Interests in the National Politics of Sri Lanka." Modern Asian Studies 15 (1981): 127-162.

8487. Sanders, Claire. "Chronicle of Deaths Untold." New Statesman and Society (November 18, 1988): [Sinhalese violence against Tamils.]

8488. Sanmugathasan, N. Political Memoirs of an Unrepentant Communist. Colombo, Sri Lanka: Lake House, 1989.

8489. Schwarz, Walter. The Family of Sri Lanka. 3d ed. London: Minority Rights Group, 1986.

8490. Scott, Bob. "Profile [on Sri Lanka]." LINK (World Council of Churches) No.4 (1990)

650 WORLD RACISM AND RELATED INHUMANITIES

8491. Shanmugaratnam, N. "Anti-Muslim Violence in Sri Lanka." Economic and Political Weekly 25 (October 13, 1990): [letter.]

8492. Shanmugaratnam, N. "Seven Days in Jaffna: Life Under Indian Occupation." Race & Class 31 (October-December 1989): 1-15. [June 23-30, 1989.]

8493. Shastri, Amita. "The Material Basis for Separatism: The Tamil Eelam Movement in Sri Lanka." Journal of Asian Studies 49 (February 1990): 56-77.

8494. Sivanandan, S. "Sri Lanka: Racism and the Politics of Underdevelopment." Race & Class 26 (Summer 1984)

8495. Sivarajah, A. The Strategy of an Ethnic Minority Party in Government and in Opposition: The Tamil Federal Party of Sri Lanka (1956-1970). Master's thesis: University of New Brunswick, 1977.

8496. Skjonsberg, Else. A Special Caste? Village Women in Sri Lanka Today. Westport, CT: Hill, 1982.

8497. Spencer, Jonathan. "Writing Within: Anthropology, Nationalism and Culture in Sri Lanka." Current Anthropology 31 (June 1990)

8498. Sri Lanka: "Disappearances". New York: Amnesty International, September 1986.

8499. "Sri Lanka: Racism and the Authoritarian State." Race & Class, series of articles (Summer 1984)

8500. Tambiah, Stanley J. "Ethnic Fratricide in Sri Lanka: An Update." In Ethnicities and Nations, edited by Remo Guidieri and others. Houston, TX: The Rothko Chapel, 1988.

8501. Tambiah, Stanley J. Sri Lanka- Ethnic Fratricide and the Dismantling of Democracy. Chicago, IL: University of Chicago Press, 1986.

8502. Thornton, E. M. and R. Niththyanathan. Sri Lanka: Island of Terror: An Indictment. London: Eelam Research Organization, 1984.

8503. Venkateshwar Rao, P. "Ethnic Conflict in Sri Lanka: India's Role and Perception." Asian Survey 28 (April 1988): 419- 436.

8504. Waters, Judy. "Origins of the Ethnic Conflict in Sri Lanka: The Colonial Experience." South Asia Bulletin 6 (1986): 3-8.

8505. Weisman, Steven R. "Sri Lanka. A Nation Disintegrates." New York Times Magazine (December 13, 1987)

8506. Wilson, A. Jeyaratnam. The Break-up of Sri Lanka: The Sinhalese-Tamil Conflict. Honolulu: University of Hawaii Press, 1989.

8507. World Solidarity Forum for Sri Lanka. "Highlighting the Priorities of the Struggle for Democracy and Justice in Sri Lanka: 1990." PCR Information No.27 (1990): 95-106.

SUDAN

8508. Abu Affan, Bodour O. "The New Economic Policies and the Structural Imbalances of the Sudan Economy." Sudan Jr. Dev. Res. 3 (December 1979): 1-45.

8509. Ahmed, Samira Amin. "The Changing Position of Arab Women." Ahfad Journal 5 (June 1988): 30-38.

8510. Ali, Ali A. G., ed. The Sudan Economy in Disarray: Essays on the IMF Model. London: Ithaca Press, 1985.

8511. Anti-Slavery Society. "Slavery in Sudan." Cultural Survival Quarterly 12 (1988): 41-42.

8512. Babiker, Abdel B. A.G. "Probleme der nationalen und regionalen Identitat im Sudan." Verfassung und Recht in Ubersee 15 (1982): 421-432.

8513. Badal, R. K. "The Rise and Fall of Separatism in Southern Sudan." African Affairs 75 (1976): 463-474.

8514. Balamoan, G. Ayoub. Peoples and Economics in the Sudan, 1884 to 1956. Rev. ed. Edited by J.B. Wyon.Cambridge, MA: Harvard University Center for Population Studies, 1981.

8515. Bedri, N. S. and L.G. Burchival. "Educational Attainment as an Indicator of the Status of Women in the Sudan." Ahfad Journal 2 (1985): 30-38.

8516. Benoist, Joseph-Roger de. Eglise et pouvoir colonial au Soudan francais de 1885 a 1945. Bamako: Centre Djoliba, 1988.

8517. Beshir, M. O. "Ethnicity, Regionalism and National Cohesion in the Sudan." Sudan Notes Rec. 61 (1980): 1-14.

8518. Collins, Robert O. and Francis M. Deng, eds. The British in the Sudan, 1898-1956. London: Macmillan, 1985.

8519. Collins, Robert O. Shadows in the Grass: Britain in the Southern Sudan, 1918-1956. New Haven, CT: Yale University Press, 1983.

8520. El-Amin, Mohammed N. The Emergence and Development of the Leftist Movement in the Sudan during the 1930s and 1940s. Khartoum: 1984.

8521. El-Khawas, Mohammed A. "The Problems of Southern Sudan." Afric. Stud. 4 (1975): 21-41.

8522. Fluehr-Lobban, Carolyn. Islamic Law and Society in the Sudan. Totowa, NJ: Frank Cass, 1986.

8523. Grandin, Nicole. Le Soudan nilotique et l'administration britannique (1896-1956):elements d'interpretation socio- historique d'une experience coloniale. Leiden, Netherlands: E.J. Brill, 1982.

8524. Johnson, Douglas H. The Southern Sudan. London: Minority Rights Group, 1988.

8525. Khalafalla, Elfatih S. D. "Capital Accumulation and the Consolidation of a Bourgeois Dependent State in Sudan, 1898- 1978." In Research in Political Economy, vol. 4, edited by Paul Zarembka, 29-80. Greenwich, CT: JAI Press, 1981.

8526. Khalid, Mansour. The Government They Deserve: The Role of the Elite in Sudan's Political Evolution. New York: Routledge, 1990.

8527. Khalid, Mansour, ed. John Garang Speaks. New York: Methuen, 1987.

8528. Lesch, Ann. "Sudan." In International Handbook on Race and Race Relations, edited by Jay A. Sigler. Westport, CT: Greenwood, 1987.

8529. Mawson, Andrew. "Southern Sudan: A Growing Conflict." World Today 40 (December 1984): 520-527.

8530. McLoughlin, P. F. M. "Economic Development and the Heritage of Slavery in the Sudan Republic." Africa (October 1962)

8531. Mohammed, Adam A. Regional Resource Allocations in the Sudan: 1971-1980. Doctoral dissertation: Florida State University, 1981. UMO # 8205734.

8532. Morrison, Godfrey. The Southern Sudan and Eritrea: Aspects of Wider African Problems. London: Minority Rights Group, 1971.

8533. Niblock, Trin. Class and Power in Sudan: The Dynamics of Sudanese Politics, 1898-1985. Albany, New York: SUNY Press, 1987.

8534. Oduho, Joseph and William Deng. The Problem of the Southern Sudan. London: Oxford University Press, 1963.

8535. O'Neill, Norman. "Imperialism and Class Struggle in Sudan." Race and Class 20 (Summer 1978): 1-19.

8536. Osman, A. A. M. The Political and Ideological Development of the Muslim Brotherhood in Sudan, 1945-1986. Doctoral dissertation: University of Reading, 1989. Order No. BRDX88539.

8537. Osman, M. K. "The Rise and Decline of the People's ('Ahlia') Education in the Northern Sudan (1927-1957)." Paedagog. Hist. (1979): 355-371.

8538. Prunier, Gerard. From Peace to War: The Southern Sudan 1972-1984. Hull: Department of Sociology and Social Anthropology, University of Hull, 1986.

8539. Rosenberg, Diana, ed. Role of Southern Sudanese People in the Building of Modern Sudan. Khartoum University of Juba: 1985,

8540. Rushwan, Hamid. "Maternal and Child Health and Family Planning Services in the Sudan." Ahfad Journal (June 1987): 5-11.

8541. Salah el-Din el-Zain el-Tayeb. The Student Movement in Sudan, 1940-1970. Khartoum: Khartoum University Press, 1971.

8542. Salih, K. O. "British Policy and the Accentuation of Inter-ethnic Divisions: The Case of the Nuba Mountains Region of Sudan, 1920-1940." African Affairs 89 (July 1990)

8543. Salih, K. O. "The Sudan, 1985-1989: The Fading Democracy." Journal of Modern African Studies 28 (June 1990)

8544. Sanderson, Lilian. "Some Aspects of Development of Girls' Education in Northern Sudan." Sudan Notes and Records 42 (1961): 91-101.

8545. Shaked, Haim. "Charles George Gordon and the Problem of Slavery in the Sudan." Slavery & Abolition 1 (December 1980): 276-291.

8546. Sherman, S. C. "Shari'a Law in the Sudan: Why It Does Not Work under the Sudanese Constitutions of 1973 and 1985." Dickinson Journal of International Law 7 (Winter 1989): 277-299.

8547. Spaulding, Jay. "Slavery, Land Tenure, and Social Class in Northern Turkish Sudan." Int. J. Afric. Hist. Stud. 15 (1982): 1-20.

8548. Starratt, Priscilla Ellen. "Tuareg Slavery and Slave Trade." Slavery & Abolition 2 (September 1981): 83-113.

8549. Sudan: Denying the Honor of Living. New York: Human Rights Watch,

8550. Tosh, J. "The Economy of the Southern Sudan 1898-1955." Journal of Imperial Commonwealth History 9 (1981): 275- 288.

8551. Voll, John O. and Sarah P. Voll. The Sudan: Unity and Diversity in a Multicultural State. Boulder, CO: Westview Press, 1985.

8552. Warburg, Gabriel R. "Democracy in the Sudan: Trial and Error." Northeast Afric. Stud. (1986): 77-94.

8553. Warburg, Gabriel R. "Slavery and Labour in the Anglo-Egyptian Sudan." Asian and African Studies 12 (1978): 221-245.

8554. Wolfers, Michael. "Race and Class in Sudan." Race and Class 23 (Summer 1981): 65-79.

SURINAME

8555. Chin, Henk E. and Hans Buddingh. Surinam. Politics, Economics, and Society. Pinter, 1987.

8556. Dew, Edward. The Difficult Flowering of Surinam: Ethnicity and Politics in a Plural Society. The Hague: Martinus Nijhoff, 1978.

8557. Franszoon, Adiante. "Suriname Maroon Crisis." Cultural Survival Quarterly 12 (1988): 32-35.

8558. Hoefte, Rosemarijn A. "Control and Resistance: Indentured Labor in Suriname." Nieume West-Indische Gids 61 (1987): 1- 22. [1880-1940.]

8559. Hoefte, Rosemarijn A. Plantation Labor after the Abolition of Slavery: The Case of Plantation Marienburg (Suriname), 1880-1940. Doctoral dissertation: University of Florida, 1987. UMO # 8724916.

8560. Kom, Anton de. We Slaves of Surinam. Translated by Arnold J. Pomerans. London: Zed Press, 1987 (orig. 1934).

8561. Lamur, Humphrey E. The Production of Sugar and the Reproduction of Slaves at Vossenburg (Suriname), 1705-1863. Amsterdam: Amsterdam Centre for Caribbean Studies, 1987.

8562. Lenoir, J. D. "Surinam National Development and Maroon Cultural Autonomy." Social and Economic Studies 24 (September 1975): 308-319.

8563. Lier, Rudolf A. J. van. "Negro Slavery in Surinam." Caribbean Historical Review (1954): 108-148.

8564. Price, Richard. Alabi's World: Conversion, Colonialism, and Resistance on an Afro-American Frontier. Baltimore, MD: Johns Hopkins University Press, 1990.

8565. Thompson, Alvin. "Dutch Society in Guyana in the Eighteenth-Century." Journal of Caribbean History 20 (1985- 1986): 169-191.

SWAZILAND

8566. Kuper, H. <u>The Uniform of Color: A Study of White-Black Relationships in Swaziland</u>. Johannesburg: Witwatersrand University Press, 1947.

8567. Macmillan, Hugh. "Swaziland: Decolonization and the Triumph of 'Tradition'." <u>Journal of Modern African Studies</u> 23 (1985): 643-666.

SWEDEN

8568. Ahlmark, Pen. "Old-New Anti-Semitism." New York Times, (November 12, 1989)

8569. Ball, Stephen J. and Staffan Larsson, eds. The Struggle for Democratic Education. New York: Falmer Press, 1989.

8570. Beach, Hugh. "Three Complementary Processes that Alienate the Sami from Their Land in Sweden." Nomadic People 20 (1986): 11-20.

8571. Boje, Per. "The Standard of Living in Scandanavia 1750- 1914." Scand. Ec. Hist. Review 34 (1986): 73-75.

8572. Bradley, David. "Perspectives on Sexual Equality in Sweden." Modern Law Review 53 (May 1990): 283-303.

8573. Cramer, Tomas. "Sami Land Rights in Sweden." Europa Ethnica 38 (1981)

8574. Diderichsen, Finn and Gudrun Lindberg. "Better Health-But Not For All: The Swedish Public Health Report." International Journal of Health Services 19 (1989): 221-255.

8575. Ehn, Billy. Det otydliga Kulturmotet: Om invandrare och svenskar pa ett daghem. Malmo: Liber Forlag, 1986. [Interethnic relations in a multi-national nursery school in Stockholm suburb.]

8576. Engelbrektsson, Ulla-Britt. "Ethnicity in the Local Context: Italians and Greeks in a Swedish Town." Ethnos 51 (1986): 148-172.

8577. Ericsson, Tom. "The Mittelstand in Swedish Class Society 1870-1914." Scandanavian Journal of History 9 (1984): 313- 328.

8578. Erikson, Robert and Rune Aberg, eds. Welfare in Transition: Living Conditions in Sweden, 1968 to 1981. New York: Oxford University Press, 1986.

8579. Fulcher, James. "Class Conflict in Sweden." Sociology 7 (1973): 49-70.

8580. Gesser, Bengt. "From Robinsonade to Marionette-Sociology of Education in Sweden." In The Multiparadigmatic Trend in Sociology. A Swedish Perspective, edited by Ulf Himmelstrand. Stockholm Acta Univ. Ups., Studia Sociologica Upsaliensia 25: Almquist & Wiksell, 1987.

8581. Grossman, J. B. "The Occupational Attainment of Immigrant Women in Sweden." Scandanavian Journal of Economics 86 (1984)

8582. Gustafsson, Bjorn. "International Migration and Falling into the Income 'Safety Net': Social Assistance among Foreign Citizens in Sweden." International Migration 24 (1986): 461-483.

8583. Gustafsson, Bjorn and A. Uusitabo. "The Welfare State and Poverty in Finland and Sweden from the Mid-1960s to the Mid-1980s." Review of Income and Wealth (September 1990)

8584. Gustavson, Carl G. The Small Giant: Sweden Enters the Industrial Era. Athens: Ohio University Press, 1986.

8585. Haavio-Mannila E. "Social Adjustment of Finns in Sweden." Surtolaisuus-Migration, 1974-1984 Volume 3 25-53.

8586. Hufford, Larry. Sweden's Power Elite. Washington, D.C.: University Press of America, 1977.

8587. Jahreskog, B. The Sami National Minority in Sweden. Atlantic Highlands, NJ Translated by A. Nordin and L. Schanck: Humanities Press, 1981.

8588. Karras, Ruth M. Slavery in Medieval Scandanavia. Doctoral dissertation: Yale University, 1985. UMO # 8601070.

8589. Karras, Ruth M. Slavery and Society in Medieval Scandanavia. New Haven, CT: Yale University Press, 1988.

8590. Koblik, Steven. "'No Truck with Himmler': the Politics of Rescue and the Swedish Red Cross Mission, March-May 1945." Scandia 51 (1985): 173-195.

8591. Koblik, Steven. Om Vi Teg, Skulle Stenarna Ropa. 1987. [The Stones Cry Out: Sweden and the Jewish Problem.]

8592. Koblik, Steven. "Sweden's Attempts to Aid Jews, 1939-1945." Scand. Studies 56 (1984): 89-113.

8593. Lind, Joan D. "The Ending of Slavery in Sweden: Social Structure and Decision Making." Scandanavian Studies 50 (Winter 1978): 51-71.

8594. Lind, Martin. "Church and National Socialism in Sweden, 1933-1945." Kyrkohistorisk Arsskrift 77 (1977): 303-308.

8595. Lindquist, M. Classmates. On Industrial Work and Culture Formation, 1882-1920. Malmo, Sweden: Liber Forlag, 1987. [Working-class culture in Svedala.]

8596. Lundbergh, B. Remember that You Are Inferior. Education for Swedish Middle-class Girls in the 1880s (In Swedish). Doctoral dissertation: University of Lund, 1986.

8597. Madsen, M. "Class Power & Participatory Equality: Attitudes Towards Economic Democracy in Denmark & Sweden." Scandanvian Political Studies 3 (1980): 277-298.

8598. McNab, Christine. "Minority Education in the Swedish Comprehensive School." In The Struggle for Democratic Education. Equality and Participation in Sweden, edited by Stephen J. Ball and Staffan Larsson, 67-87. New York: Falmer Press, 1989.

8599. Mecus, Bandewijn. "Politico-Linguistic Analysis of the Situation of the Finnish-speaking Minority in Tornedalem." Europa Ethnica 33 (1976): 162-169. [Northern Sweden.]

8600. Meyer, Donald. Sex and Power: The Rise of Women in America, Russia, Sweden, and Italy. Middletown, CT: Wesleyan University Press, 1987.

8601. Mussener, Helmut. Exil in Schweden: Politische und Kulturelle Emigration nach 1933. Munich: Carl Hanser Verlag, 1974. [German anti-Nazi emigration to Sweden.]

8602. Olsson, Ulf. "Recent Research in Sweden on the Standard of Living during the Eighteenth and Nineteenth Century." Scand. E. Hist. Review 34 (1986): 153-158.

8603. Persson, Gunner. "Social Mobility in Sweden 1925-1945." Economy and History 17 (1974): 83-94.

8604. Politt, Gunther. "Rassismus und Einwandererfeindlichkeit im gegenwärtigen Schweden." In Ausländerfeindschaft im 19. und 20. Jahrhundert-Ursachen, Erscheinungen, Konsequenzen. Rostock: Wilhelm Pieck-Universität Rostock, Sektion Geschichte, 1989.

8605. Prokesch, Steven. "In a Haven for Refugees, Hate Makes an Entrance." New York Times, (June 20, 1990)

8606. "Racialism in Sweden." Patterns of Prejudice 14 (July 1980): 11-14.

662 WORLD RACISM AND RELATED INHUMANITIES

8607. Ross, Carl. "The Utopian Vision of Finnish Immigrants: 1900-1930." Scandanavian Studies 60 (1988): 481-496.

8608. Rothstein, B. "Marxism, Institutional Analysis, and Working-class Power: The Swedish Case." Politics & Society 18 (September 1990)

8609. Rothstein, B. The Social Democratic State. Reforms and Administration in Swedish Labour Market and School Policy. Doctoral dissertation: University of Lund, 1986. [In Swedish.]

8610. Sandberg, Lars G. and R. H. Steckel. "Overpopulation and Malnutrition Rediscovered: Hard Times in 19th Century Sweden." Explorations in Economic History 25 (1988): 1-19.

8611. Sandin, Bengt. The Family, the Street, the Factory or the School. Popular Education and Childcare in Swedish Cities, 1600-1850. Lund, Sweden: Askivs forlag, 1986.

8612. Scase, Richard, ed. Swedish Class Structure. New York: Pergamon, 1976.

8613. Schierup, C. U. Do They Dance to Keep Up Tradition? Analysis of a Social Situation among Yugoslav Immigrants in Scandanavia. Umea, Sweden: University of Umea, 1984.

8614. Shlaes, Amity. "Swedish Schools Threaten to Create a Tower of Babel." Wall Street Journal, (July 9, 1986): [Bilingual program in Swedish schools.]

8615. Sjoholm, Tommy. "Women in the Swedish Class Structure." Acta Sociologica 26 (1983): 299-311.

8616. Soderberg, Johan and Arne Jansson. "Corn-Price Rises and Equalisation: Real Wages in Stockholm 1650-1719." Scandanavian Economic History Review 36 (1988): 62-47.

8617. Soltow, Lee. "The Rich and the Destitute in Sweden, 1805- 1855: A Test of Tocqueville's Inequality Hypothesis." Economic History Review 42 (February 1989): 43-63.

8618. Soltow, Lee. "The Swedish Census of Wealth at the Beginning of the 19th Century." Scandanavian Economic History Review 33 (1985): 1-24.

8619. Spant, Roland. "The Development of the Distribution of Wealth in Sweden." Review of Income and Wealth 27 (March 1981): 65-74.

8620. SPRINS Group. Immigrants Pupils at the Senior Level of Compulsory School and in Upper Secondary School. Stockholm: Swedish National Board of Education, November-December 1985. [Deals with linguistic development of immigrant children in Sweden.]

8621. Stillschweig, Kurt. "Legislative Proposals Against Anti-semitic Propaganda in Sweden." Historia Judaica 6 (October 1944): 139-146.

8622. Stjarne, Kerstin. "A Report from Sweden." Interracial Books for Children 5 (1974): 15. [Racism in Swedish children's literature.]

8623. "Sweden: Racists Organize through Groups." Searchlight No. 108 (June 1984): 14-15.

8624. "Swedish Authorities' Action?" Patterns of Prejudice 13 (March-June 1979): 25-26. [Neo-Nazis in Sweden.]

8625. Takman, John with Lars Lindgren. The Gypsies in Sweden. A Socio-Medical Study. Stockholm: Liber Forlag, 1976.

8626. Tingbjorn, Gunnar. "Immigrant Pupils at the Senior Level of Compulsory School and in Upper Secondary School." School Research Newsletter (Swedish National Board of Education) (November-December 1985)

8627. Trankell, Arne and Ingrid Trankell. "Problems of the Swedish Gypsies." Scandanavian Journal of Educational Research (1968): 141-214.

8628. Tung, Ko-Chih R. "Voting Rights for Alien Residents-Who Wants It?" International Migration Review 19 (Fall 1985): 451-467.

8629. Verba, Sidney and others. Elites and the Idea of Equality. A Comparison of Japan, Sweden, and the United States. Cambridge, MA: Harvard University Press, 1987.

8630. Wernersson, Inga. "Gender Equality-Ideology and Reality." In The Struggle for Democratic Education. Equality and Participation in Sweden, edited by Stephen J. Ball and Staffan Larsson. New York: Falmer Press, 1989.

8631. Westin, Charles. Majoritet om Minoritet: En Studie i Etnisk Tolerans i 80-Talets Sverige. Stockholm: Liberforlag, 1984.

8632. Wheelersburg, Robert P. The Effects of Scandanavian Society on Sami (Lapp) Land-use, Economic Behavior and Settlemtn in Northern Sweden, 1600-1986. Doctoral dissertation: Brown University, 1987. UMO # 8822612.

8633. Yahil, Leni. "Sweden." In Encyclopedia of the Holocaust, IV, 1430-1440. New York: Macmillan, 1990.

8634. Zimbalist, Sidney E. "A Welfare State against the Economic Current: Sweden and the United States as Contrasting Cases." International Social Work 30 (January 1987): 15-30.

8635. Zimbalist, Sidney E. "Winning the War on Poverty: The Swedish Strategy." Social Work 33 (January-February 1988): 46-49.

8636. Zitomersky, Joseph. "Assimilation or Particularity? Approaches to the Study of Jews as an Historical Minority in Sweden." Scandanavian Journal of History 12 (1987): 245- 271.

SWITZERLAND

8637. Amman, H. Die Italiener in der Schweiz. Basel: 1917.

8638. "Antisemitism in Switzerland." Patterns of Prejudice 13 (July-August 1979): 14-15.

8639. Arlettaz, Gerald. "Demographie et identite nationale (1850- 1914): La Suisse et 'La question des etrangers'." Stud. U. Quel. 11 (1985): 83-180.

8640. Billigmeier, Robert H. A Crisis in Swiss Pluralism: The Romanasch and their Relations with the German and Italian Swiss. The Hague: Mouton, 1979.

8641. Bory, Valerie. Dehors! de la chasse aux Italiens a la peur des refugies, 1896-1986. Paris: Pierre-Marcel Favre, 1987. [Xenophobia in Switzerland against foreign workers and other immigrants.]

8642. Boscardin, Lucio. Die italienische Einwanderung in die Schweiz mit besonderer Berucksichtgung der Jahre 1946-1959. Doctoral dissertation: University of Basle, 1962.

8643. Buhrig, Marga and Anny Schmid-Affolter. Die Frau in der Schweiz. Bern: Haupt, 1969.

8644. Catrina, Werner. Die Ratoromanen zwischen Resignation und Aufbruch. Zurich: Orell Fussli Verlag, 1983. [Romanisch-speaking people in Switzerland elsewhere.]

8645. Cattani, Alfred and Alfred A. Hasler, eds. Minderheiten in der Schweiz: Toleranz auf dem Prüfstand. Zurich: Verlag Neue Zurcher Zeitung, 1984.

8646. Cerutti, Mauro. "Mussolini bailleur de fonds des fascistes suisses: les relations entre le colonel Arthur Fonjallaz et le duce, a la lumiere de nouveaux documents italiens." Schweizerische Zeitschrift fur Geschichte 35 (1985): 25- 46.

8647. Cushman, Richard O. Anti-Fascist, Satirical Publications in Switzerland from 1939-1945. Master's thesis: University of South Carolina, 1988.

8648. Donneur, Andre. "Un nationalisme suisse romand est-il possible?" Revue Canadienne des Etudes sur le Nationalisme 9 (1982): 201-224.

8649. Glardon, Marie-Jo. Les pauvres dans la ville: a la recherche des familles sous-proletariennes a Geneve. Lausanne: Editions d'En Bas, 1984.

8650. Glaus, Beat. Die Nationale Front. Eine Schweizer Faschistische Bewegung 1930-1940. Doctoral dissertation: University of Basel, 1968.

8651. Guggenheim, Willy. "A Drama in Black and White." Jerusalem Post Supplement, (June 15, 1982): [History of Jews in Switzerland, 1918-1945.]

8652. Hassler, A. H. The Lifeboat Is Full: Switzerland and the Refugees, 1933-1945. New York: 1969.

8653. Hoffman-Nowotny, H. J. "Immigrant Minorities in Switzerland: Sociological, Legal and Political Aspects." In Current Research in Sociology, edited by M. Archer. The Hague: Mouton, 1974.

8654. Humbel, Kurt. Nationalsozialistischen Propaganda in der Schweiz 1931-1939. Doctoral dissertation: University of Zurich, 1976.

8655. Jeffries, Vincent and others. "Values, Authoritarianism, and Antagonism toward Ethnic Minorities: A Swiss Replication." Pacific Sociological Review 16 (1973): 357- 376. [Italian workers.]

8656. Jenkins, John R. G. Jura Separatism in Switzerland. New York: Oxford University press, 1986.

8657. Krahenbuhl, Hans-Ulrich. "Diskriminierung der Frauenarbeit in der Schweiz." Industrielle Organisation 41 (1972): 37- 42.

8658. Kriesi, Hanspeter. Entscheidungsstrukturen und Entscheidungsprozesse in der Schweizer Politik. Frankfurt: Campus Verlag, 1980.

8659. Kulling, Friedrich. Bei Uns wie überall? Antisemitismus in der Schweiz 1866-1900. Zurich: SIG, 1977.

8660. Leu, R. E. and others. "Die personelle Einkommens-und Vermögensverteilung der Schweiz 1982." Schweizerische Zeitschrift für Volkswirtschaft und Statistik 122 (June 1986)

8661. Ludwig, Carl. Die Flüchtlingspolitik der Schweiz seit 1933 bis zur Gegenwart (1957). Berne: Verlag Herbert Lang & Cie, 1966.

8662. McRae, Kenneth D. Conflict and Compromise in Multilingual Societies, Vol. I: Switzerland. Waterloo, Ontario: Wilfrid Laurier University Press, 1984.

8663. Pilet, Jacques. Le Crime nazi de Payerne. Paris: Editions Pierre Marcel Fevre, 1977. [Antisemitism in Canton of Vaud.]

8664. Schmid, Carol. "Switzerland." In International Handbook on Race and Race Relations, edited by Jay A. Sigler. Westport, Ct: Greenwood Press, 1987.

8665. Schmid, Max, ed. Schalom! Wir Werden Euch Töten! Texte und Dokumente zum Antisemitismus in der Schweiz 1930-1980. Zurich: Eco-Verlag, 1979.

8666. Thode-Studer, Sylvia. Les Tsiganes suisses: la marche vers la reconaissance. Lausanne: Editions Realites Sociales, 1987.

8667. Vuilleumier, M. Immigres et Refugies en Suisse. Apercu historique. Zurich: Pro Helvetia, 1987.

8668. Wandel, Lee P. Always Among Us. Images of the Poor in Zwingli's Zurich. New York: Cambridge University Press, 1990.

8669. Wandel, Lee P. Images of the Poor in Reformation Zurich. Doctoral dissertation: University of Michigan, 1985. UMO # 8521005.

8670. Watts, Richard J. "Language, Dialect and National Identity in Switzerland." Multilingua 7 (1988): 313-334.

8671. Wecker, Regina, ed. Frauen in der Schweiz: von den Problemen einer Mehrheit. Zug: Klett und Balmer, 1983.

8672. Yahil, Leni. "Switzerland." In Encyclopedia of the Holocaust, 1441-1444. New York: Macmillan, 1990.

8673. Zoeberlein, Klaus D. Die Anfänge des deutschschweizerischen Frontismus. Die Entwicklung der politischen Vereinigung 'Neue Front' und 'Nationale Front' bis zu ihrem Zusammenschluss im Frühjahr 1933. Doctoral dissertation: University of Marburg, 1969.

SYRIA

8674. Abrabba, S. "Sex Division of Labour in Syrian School Textbooks." International Review of Education 31 (1985): 335-348.

8675. Abramski-Bligh, Irit, Syria and Lebanon. in Encyclopedia of the Holocaust, IV. 1444-1446. New York: Macmillan, 1990.

8676. Ahsan, S. A. -al. "Economic Policy and Class Structure in Syria: 1958-1980." Int. Jr. Middle E. Studies 16 (1984): 301-323.

8677. Baron, Salo W. "The Jews and the Syrian Massacres of 1860." American Academy for Jewish Research Proceedings 4 (1932- 1933)

8678. Batatu, Hanna. "Some Observations on the Social Roots of Syria's Ruling Military Group and the Causes for Its Dominance." Middle East Journal 25 (Summer 1981): 331-344.

8679. Bouchair, Noureddine. The Merchant and Moneylending Class of Syria under the French Mandate, 1920-1946. Doctoral dissertation: Georgetown University, 1986. UMO # 9027664.

8680. Dan, Nikolaos van. The Struggle for Power in Syria: Sectarianism, Regionalism, and Tribalism in Politics, 1961- 1978. New york: St. Martin's Press, 1979.

8681. Friedman, Saul S. "The Anguish of Syrian Jewry." Midstream 21 (1975): 14-22.

8682. Friedman, Saul S. Without Future. The Plight of Syrian Jewry. Westport, CT: Praeger, 1989.

8683. Haddad, Robert M. Syrian Christians in Muslim Society: An Interpretation. Princeton, NJ: Princeton University Press, 1970.

8684. Hyamson, Albert M. "The Damascus Affair-1840." Transactions of the Jewish Historical Society of England 16 (1945-1951): 47-70.

8685. Ibish, Y. K. H. The Problem of Minorities in Syria. Master's thesis: American University of Beirut, 1951.

8686. Maoz, Moshe and Avner Yaniv, eds. Syria under Assad. New York: St. Martin's Press, 1986.

8687. Mayer, T. "The Islamic Opposition in Syria, 1961-1982." Orient 24 (December 1983): 589-629.

8688. Nazdar, Mustafa. "The Kurds in Syria." In People Without a Country, The Kurds and Kurdistan, edited by Gerard Chaliand. 211- 219. London Translated by Michael Pallis: Zed Press, 1980.

8689. Philipp. T. "The Farhi Family and the Changing Position of the Jews in Syria, 1750-1860." Mid. E. Studies 20 (Oct. 1984): 37-52.

8690. Rabinovich, I. "The Compact Minorities and the Syrian State, 1918-1945." Journal of Contemporary History 14 (October 1979): 693-712.

8691. Sakakini, Widad. "The Evolution of Syrian Women." United Asian Journal 1 (1949): 531-533.

8692. Salkin, Yves. "La minorite druze en Syrie de 1920 a 1955." Guerres Mondiales et Conflits Contemporains 38 (1988): 93- 102.

8693. Sanjian, Avedis K. The Armenian Communities in Syria under Ottoman Dominion. Cambridge, MA: Howard University Press, 1965.

8694. Shestack, Jerome. "Persecution of Syrian Jews." Bulletin of International League for the Rights of Man (September 1974)

8695. Swedenburg, Theodore R. The Development of Capitalism in Greater Syria, 1830-1914: An Historico-geographical Approach. Master's thesis: University of Texas, 1980.

8696. Viorst, Milton. "A Reporter at Large, The View from the Mustansiriyah." New Yorker (October 19, 1987)

TANZANIA

8697. Ahmed, M. "The Education Revolution in Tanzania." Assignment Children 65/68 (1984): 225-245.

8698. Bryceson, Deborah F. Food Insecurity and the Social Division of Labour in Tanzania, 1919-1985. New York: St. Martin's Press, 1990.

8699. Collier, Paul and others. Labour and Poverty in Rural Tanzania: Ujamoa and Rural Development in the United Republic of Tanzania. New York: Oxford University Press, 1986.

8700. Cooper, Frederick. From Slaves to Squatters: Plantation Labour and Agriculture in Zanzibar and Coastal Kenya 1890- 1925. New Haven, CT: Yale University Press, 1980.

8701. Giblin, J. "Famine and Social Change during the Transition to Colonial Rule in Northeastern Tanzania, 1880-1986." African Economic HIstory 15 (1986)

8702. Gould, W. T. S. "Patterns of School Provision in Colonial East Africa." Et. hist. afric. 8 (1976): 131-148.

8703. Herzog, Jurgen. Geschichte Tansanias: von Beginn des 19. Jahrhunderts bis zur Gegenwart. East Berlin: VEB Deutschen Verlag der Wissenschaften, 1986.

8704. Juma, M. S. Self-determination, The Experience of Zanzibar. Dar es Salaam: Centre for Foreign Relations, 1981.

8705. Kagan, Alfred. "Literacy, Libraries and Underdevelopment- With Special Attention to Tanzania." Afric. Jr. 13 (1982): 1-23.

8706. Kaniki, M. H. Y., ed. Tanzania Under Colonial Rule. London: Longman, 1980.

8707. Little, M. "Imperialism, Colonialism and the New Science of Nutrition: The Tanganyika Experience, 1925-1945." Social Science & Medicine 32 (1991)

8708. Mbilinyi, Marjorie J. "Agribusiness and Casual Labor in Tanzania." African Economic History 15 (1986): 107-141.

8709. Mbilinyi, Marjorie J. "Education, Stratification, and Sexism in Tanzania: Policy Implications." African Review 3 (June 1973): 327-340.

8710. Mbunda, D. Education and "Ujamaa": An Examination of their Relationship in Traditional and Contemporary Society in Tanzania. Doctoral dissertation: University of Southampton, 1985.

8711. Mbwiliza, J. F. "Class, Class Struggle and the State During the Transition to Socialism in Tanzania." Taamuli 12 (December 1982): 11-28.

8712. McCarthy, D. M. P. "Language Manipulation in Colonial Tanganyika, 1919-1940." Journal of African Studies 6 (Spring 1979): 9-16.

8713. Mueller, Susanne D. "Barriers to the Further Development of Capitalism in Tanzania: The Case of Tobacco." Capital & Class No.15 (Autumn 1981): 23-54.

8714. Mueller, Susanne D. "The Historical Origins of Tanzania's Ruling Class." Canadian Journal of African Studies 15 (1981): 459-496.

8715. Oluyemi-Kusa, Dayo. "The Theory and Practice of Socialism in Tanzania: A Critique." Nigerian Forum 8 (July-August 1988): 129-139.

8716. Ong'wamuhana, K. "Human Rights in Tanzania: A Constitutional Overview." E. Africa Law Review 11-14 (1977- 1981): 240-280.

8717. Raa, Eric T. "Malnutrition and Social Organization: A Central Tanzanian Perspective." Paideuma 29 (1983): 121- 140.

8718. Rodney, Walter. "Class Contradictions in Tanzania." Panafricanist 6 (1975): 15-29.

8719. Rubagumya, C. M. "Language Planning in the Tanzanian Educational System: Problems and Prospects." Journal of Multilingual and Multicultural Development 7 (1986): 283- 300.

8720. Samoff, Joel. "Bureaucrats, Politicians, and Power in Tanzania: The Institutional Context of Class Struggle." Journal of African Studies 10 (Fall 1983): 84-96.

8721. Samoff, Joel. "Pluralism and Conflict in Africa: Ethnicity, Institutions and Class in Tanzania." Civilzations 32, 33 (1982, 1983): 97-134.

8722. Semboja, J. "Inflation, Progressive Taxation and Equity in Tanzania." Zimbabwe Journal of Economics 1 (January 1987): 36-47.

8723. Sheriff, Abdul. Slaves, Spices & Ivory in Zanzibar: Integration of an East African Commercial Empire into the World Economy, 1770-1873. Athens: Ohio University Press, 1987.

8724. Shivji, Issa G. Class Struggles in Tanzania. New York: Monthly Review Press, 1976.

8725. Shivji, Issa G. "Law and Conditions of Child Labour in Colonial Tanganyika, 1920-1940." International Journal of the Sociology of Law 13 (August 1985): 221-236.

8726. Shivji, Issa G. Law, State, and the Working Class in Tanzania, c. 1920-1964. Portsmouth, NH: 1986,

8727. Shivji, Issa G. "Working Class Struggles and Organizations in Tanzania: 1939-1975." Mawazo 5 (December 1983): 3-24.

8728. Tanzania, Twenty Years of Independence, (1961-1981): A Review of Political and Economic Performance. Dar es Salaam: Bank of Tanzania, 1983.

8729. Teacher, Freda and Teacher, Anna. "The Solomon Mahlangu Freedom College: Door of Learning and Culture." Sechaba (April 1987): 12-17. [ANC school in Mazimbu, Tanzania.]

8730. Turki, Benyan S. British Policy and Education in Zanzibar, 1890-1945. Doctoral dissertation: University of Exeter, 1987. Order No. BRDX81225.

8731. Turshen, M. "The Impact of Colonialism on Health and Health Services in Tanzania." Int. Jr. Health Services 7 (1977): 7-35.

8732. Van den Berg, Leo. "On the Measurement of Regional Inequality." G. Geog. Assoc. Tanzania (June 1979): 87-99.

8733. Wayne, Jack. "Colonialism and Underdevelopment in Kigoma Region, Tanzania: A Social Structural View." Canadian Review of Sociology and Anthropology 12 (1975): 316-2332.

THAILAND

8734. Bruneau, Michel. "Class Formation in the Northern Thai Peasantry, 1966-1976." J. Contemp. Asia 14 (1984): 343-359.

8735. Chulikavit, Yotin. Capitalism in Thailand. Master's thesis: Brooklyn College, 1982.

8736. Coughlin, Richard J. Double Identity: The Chinese in Modern Thailand. Hong Kong: University of Hong Kong Press, 1960.

8737. Cruikshank, R. B. "Slavery in Nineteenth Century Siam." Journal of the Siam Society 63 (July 1975): 315-333.

8738. Elliott, David. "The Socio-economic Formation of Modern Thailand." Journal of Contemporary Asia 8 (1978): 21-50. [Since 1767.]

8739. Farouk, Omar. "The Muslims of Thailand: A Survey." S.E. Asian Review 13 (January-December 1988): 1-30.

8740. Feeny, David. "The Decline of Property Rights in Man in Thailand, 1800-1913." Journal of Economic History 49 (June 1989): 285-296.

8741. Forbes, Andrew D. W. "Thailand's Muslim Minorities: Assimilation, Secession or Coexistence?" Asian Survey 22 (November 1982): 1056-1073.

8742. Girling, John. "Hegemony and Domination in Third World Countries: A Case Study of Thailand." Alternatives 10 (Winter 1984-1985): 435-452.

8743. Hong, Lysa. Thailand in the Nineteenth Century: Evolution of the Economy and Society. Singapore: Institute of Southeast Asian Studies, 1984.

8744. Hossain, Zakir. "Assimilation of Indian Minorities in Thailand." Eastern Anthropol. 40 (October-December 1987): 321-330.

8745. Ikemoto, Yukio and Kitti Limskul. "Income Inequality and Regional Disparity in Thailand, 1962-1981." Dev. Ec. 25 (Sept. 1987): 249-269.

8746. Krongkaew, M. "Agricultural Development, Rural Poverty, and Income Distribution in Thailand." Developing Economies 23 (December 1985)

8747. Landon, K. P. The Chinese in Thailand. London: Oxford University Press, 1941.

8748. Laothamatas, Anek. "Business and Politics in Thailand: New Patterns of Influence." Asian Survey 28 (1988): 451-470.

8749. Lehman, F. K. "Freedom and Bondage in Traditional Burma and Thailand." J.S.E. Asian Stud. 15 (September 1984): 233-244.

8750. Nakornthap, S. Educational Policy and Politics in Thailand: A Case Study of Education Reform, 1973-1977. Doctoral dissertation: Florida State University, 1986. UMO # 8708187.

8751. Panananon, Chatchai. Siamese "Slavery": The Institution and its Abolition. Doctoral dissertation: University of Michigan, 1982. UMO # 8210611.

8752. Pholwaddhana, Niyaphan. Ethnic Relations in Thailand: The Mon-Thai Relationship. Doctoral dissertation: University of Kansas, 1986. UMO # 8619935.

8753. Pitsuwan, Surin. Islam and Malay Nationalism: A Case Study of the Malay-Muslims in Southern Thailand. Bangkok: Thai Khadi Research Institute, Thammasat University, 1985.

8754. Prasert Yamklinfung. "Economic Development and Rural-Urban Disparities in Thailand." S.E. Asian Studies 25 (December 1987): 342-362.

8755. Punyaratabandhu-Bhakdi, Suchitra and Juree Vichit-Vadakdan. "Thailand." In International Handbook on Race and Race Relations, edited by Jay A. Sigler. Westport, Ct: Greenwood, 1987.

8756. Rachatatanun, Witit. Disparities in the Distribution of Qualified Public Secondary School Teachers in Thailand. Doctoral dissertation: Harvard University, 1989. UMO # 9000878.

8757. Rangson Prasertsri and W.R. Ball. "A Multi-level Cost Effectiveness Analysis of Educational Allocations in Thailand." Thai Journal of Dev. Adm. 25 (July 1985): 406- 433.

8758. Sulak, Sivaraksa. "The Minorities of Siam and Burma." Solidarity 121 (January-March 1989): 65-74.

8759. Suthasasna, A. Ruling Elite, Higher Education, and Thai Society. Doctoral dissertation: University of Illinois, 1973. UMO # 7412205.

8760. Tan, Edita A. and W. Naiyavitit. "The Distribution Flow of Education in the Formal School System: An Analysis of Distribution of Education Attainment." J. Nat. Res. Council Thailand 16 (July-December 1984): 19-43.

8761. Tapp, Nicholas. The Hmong of Thailand. Cambridge, MA: Cultural Survival, 1986.

8762. Tapp, Nicholas. Sovereignty and Rebellion: The Hmong of Northern Thailand. New York: Oxford University Press, 1989.

8763. Terwiel, B. J. "Bondage and Slavery in Early Nineteenth Century Siam." In Slavery, Bondage and Dependency in Southeast Asia, edited by Anthony Reid. St. Lucia: 1983.

8764. Thomson, Curtis N. Political Unity and Ethnic Diversity: A Study of the Chinese in Thailand in the Nineteen Seventies. Master's thesis: University of Utah, 1983.

8765. Vimille, A. "Lutte de classes en Thailande." Critique de l'economie politique 12-14 (1973): 188-229.

8766. Wongyai, Prasan. Elites and Power Structure in Thailand. Doctoral dissertation: Florida State University, 1974. UMO # 7500983.

TOGO

8767. Cornevin, Robert. Histoire du Togo. 3d ed. Paris: Berger-Leurault, 1969.

8768. Decalo, S. Historical Dictionary of Togo. Metuchen, NJ: Scarecrow, 1976.

8769. Decalo, S. "The Politics of Military Rule in Togo." Geneve- Afrique 12 (1973): 62-96.

8770. Delval, R. Les musulmans au Togo. Paris: Publications orientalistes de France, 1981.

8771. Knoll, A.-J. Togo under Imperial Germany. Stanford, CA: Hoover Institution Press, 1979.

8772. Stoecker, H., ed. German Imperialism in Africa. Atlantic Highlands, NJ: Humanities Press, 1986.

TUNISIA

8773. Abitbol, Michel. "Tunisia." In Encyclopedia of the Holocaust. 1520-1523. New York: Macmillan, 1990.

8774. Anderson, Lisa. The State and Social Transformation in Tunisia and Libya, 1830-1980. Princeton, NJ: Princeton University Press, 1986.

8775. Attal, Robert. "Tunisian Jewry During the Last Twenty Years." Jewish Journal of Sociology 2 (1960): 4-15.

8776. Fitouri, Chadly. "Biculturalism, Bilingualism, and Scholastic Achievement in Tunisia." Prospects 14 (1984): 75-86.

8777. Fozzard, A. Tribesmen and the Colonial Encounter: Southern Tunisia during the French Protectorate 1882-1940. Doctoral dissertation: University of Durham, 1988.

8778. Hagege, Claude. "Communautes juive de Tunisie a la veille du Protectorat français." Mouvement social 110 (January 1980): 35-50.

8779. Jones, Marie T. "Regional Disparities and Public Policy in Tunisian Education." Comparative Education 22 (1986): 201- 220.

8780. Kraiem, Mustapha. Le mouvement social en Tunisie dans les années trente. Tunis: Centre d'études et de recherches économiques et sociales, 1984.

8781. Macken, Richard A. The Indigenous Reaction to French Protectorate in Tunisia, 1881-1900. Doctoral dissertation: Princeton University, 1973. UMO # 7318767.

8782. Mahfoudh, Dor (ra). "Politique scolaire et mobilisation des compétences pour le système productif tunisien." R. Tunisienne Sci. Sociales 19 (1982): 35-80.

8783. Neumann, Gudrun. "The Formation of the Tunisian Working Class." <u>Asien, Afrika, Lateinam</u> 15 (1987): 367-374.

8784. Perkins, Kenneth J. <u>Tunisia: Crossroads of the Islamic and European Worlds</u>. Boulder, CO: Westview Press, 1986.

8785. Pignon, Jean. "L'esclavage en Tunisie de 1590 à 1620." <u>Cahiers de Tunisie</u> 93-94 (1976): 143-165.

8786. Sabille, Jacques. <u>Les Juifs de Tunisie sous Vichy et l'occupation</u>. Paris: 1954.

TURKEY

8787. Abadan-Unat, Nermin and others, eds. Women in Turkish Society. Leiden: E.J. Brill, 1981.

8788. Ahmad, Feroz. The Turkish Experiment in Democracy, 1950- 1975. Boulder, CO: Westview, 1977.

8789. Allen, W. E. D. "The Turkish Mirror." Asiatic Review 24 (October 1928): 576-596. [Minorities in Turkey.]

8790. Andreades, A. "The Greek Minority in Constantinople." Contemporary Review 132 (January 1927): 34-40.

8791. Artinian, Vartan. A Study of the Historical Development of the Armenian Constitutional System in the Ottoman Empire, 1839-1863. Doctoral dissertation: Brandeis University, 1970.

8792. Bardakjian, Kevork B. Hitler and the Armenian Genocide. Cambridge, MA: Joryan Institute for Contemporary Armenian Research and Documentation, 1985.

8793. Belli, Mihri. Eine Analyse der turkischen Linken (Selbstkritik). 2d ed. Munich: Verlag Das Freie Buch, 1982.

8794. Berberoglu, B. Turkey in Crisis: From State Capitalism to Neo-Colonialism. Westport, CT: HIll, 1982.

8795. Besikci, Ismail. "State Ideology and the Kurds." Translated by Lale Yalcin. Middle East Report No.153 (July-August 1988): 43.

8796. Bezalel, Itzhak, ed. Pe'amim: Studies in the Cultural Heritage of Oriental Jewry. Jerusalem: Ben-Zvi Institute for the Study of Jewish Communities in the East, 1982. [Jews in Turkey, 16th-20th centuries.]

8797. Blair, Susan K. "Excuses for Inhumanity: The Official German Response to the 1915 Armenian Genocide." Armenian Review 37 (Winter 1984): 14-30.

8798. Boyajian, Dickran H. Armenia: The Case for a Forgotten Genocide. Westwood, NJ: Educational Book Crafters, 1972.

8799. Bozarslan, Hamit. "Les revoltes kurdes en Turquie kemaliste (quelques aspects)." Guerres Mondiales et Conflits Contemporains 38 (1988): 121-136.

8800. Bruinessen, Martin van. "Between Guerrilla War and Political Murder: The Workers' Party of Kurdistan." Middle East Report No.153 (July-August 1988): 40-42,44-46.

8801. Celasun, M. "Income Distribution and Domestic Terms of Trade in Turkey, 1978-1983: Estimated Measures of Inequality and Poverty." Middle East Technical University Studies in Development 13 (1986)

8802. Chaliand, Gerard and Yves Ternon. The Armenians, From Genocide to Resistance. Translated by Tony Berrett. London: Zed Press, 1983.

8803. Cicek, Y. "Turkey: Politics of Human Rights." Zeta Magazine 2 (November 1989): 93-96.

8804. Cohen, Amnon. "Ritual Murder Accusations against the Jews during the Days of Suleiman the Magnificent." Journal of Turkish Studies 10 (1986): 73-78.

8805. Cohen, Israel. The Turkish Persecution of the Jews. London: 1918.

8806. Commins, David D. Islamic Reform: Politics and Social Change in Late Ottoman Syria. New York: Oxford University Press, 1990.

8807. Couzinos, Efthimios N. Twenty-three Years in Asia Minor (1899-1922). New York: Vantage Press, 1969.

8808. Cowell, Alan. "Feuds of Turkish Kurds Spilling Over Into Europe." New York Times, (June 14, 1987)

8809. Cowell, Alan. "In Turkey, Springtime Brings Revival of Kurds' Insurgency." New York Times, (May 17, 1987)

8810. Dadrian, Vahakn N. "The Circumstances Surrounding the 1909 Adana Holocaust." Armenian Review 1-16 (Winter 1988)

8811. Dadrian, Vahakn N. "Genocide as a Problem of National and International Law: The World War I Armenian Case and Its Contemporary Legal Ramifications." Yale Journal of International Law 14 (Summer 1989): 221-334.

8812. Dadrian, Vahakn N. "A Theoretical Model of Genocide, With Particular Reference to the Armenian Case." Sociologia Internationalis 14 (1976): 99-126.

8813. Dahlberg, Robin L. and others. "Torture in Turkey." The Record of the Association of the Bar of the City of New York 45 (January-February 1990): 6-131.

8814. Daniel, Robert L. "The Armenian Question and American Turkish Relations, 1914-1927." Journal of American History 46 (September 1959): 252-275.

8815. Davis, Leslie A. The Slaughterhouse Province: An American Diplomat's Report on the Armenian Genocide, 1915-1917. Edited by Susan L. Blair: Aristide D. Karatzas, 1990.

8816. Dodd, C. H. Crisis of Turkish Democracy. Atlantic Highlands, NJ: Humanities Press, 1983.

8817. Drumont, Paul. "La condition juive en Turquie a la fin du XIXe siecle." Nouveaux Cahiers 57 (1979): 25-38.

8818. Drumont, Paul. "Jewish Communities in Turkey during the Last Decade of the Nineteenth Century in the Light of the Archives of the Alliance Israelite Universelle." In Christians and Jews in the Ottoman Empire, the Functioning of a Plural Society, edited by Benjamin Braude and Bernard Lewis. 209-242. New York: Holmes & Meier, 1982.

8819. Epstein, Mark A. The Ottoman Jewish Communities and their Role in the Fifteenth and Sixteenth Centuries. Doctoral dissertation: University of Washington, 1979.

8820. Fisher, Alan. "Chattel Slavery in the Ottoman Empire." Slavery and Abolition 1 (May 1980): 25-45.

8821. Galante, Abraham. Historie des Juifs d'Anatolie. 2 vols. Istanbul: 1937, 1939.

8822. Galante, Abraham. Historie des Juifs de Turquie. 9 vols. Istanbul: Editions Isis, 1985.

8823. Gerber, Haim. "Jews and Money-Lending in the Ottoman Empire." Jewish Quarterly Review 72 (October 1982): 101-118.

8824. Gunter, Michael M. "The Historical Origins of Contemporary Armenian Terrorism." Jr S. Asian and Mid. E. Stud. 9 (Fall 1985): 77-96.

8825. Gunter, Michael M. "The Kurdish Problem in Turkey." Mid. E. Journal 42 (Summer 1988): 389-406.

8826. Gunter, Michael M. "Kurdish Military in Turkey: The Case of PKK." Crossroads No.29 (1989): 43-59.

8827. Gunter, Michael M. The Kurds in Turkey: A Political Dilemma. Boulder, CO: Westview Press, 1990.

8828. Gunter, Michael M. Pursuing the Just Cause of their People: A Study of Contemporary Armenian Terrorism. Westport, CT: Greenwood, 1986.

8829. Gurun, Kamuran. The Armenian File: The Myth of Innocence Exposed. New York: St. Martin's Press, 1986. [Turkish view denying anti-Armenian genocide or massacres.]

8830. Hoffman, Tessa and Gerayer Koutcharian. "The History of Armenian-Kurdish Relations in the Ottoman Empire." Armenian Review 39 (Winter 1986)

8831. Hovannisian, Richard G. Armenia on the Road to Independence. Berkeley: University of California Press, 1967.

8832. Hovannisian, Richard G., ed. The Armenian Genocide in Perspective. New Brunswick, NJ: Transaction Books, 1986.

8833. Hovannisian, Richard G., ed. The Armenian Genocide. New York: St, Martin's Press, 1991.

8834. Hovannisian, Richard G. The Republic of Armenia. 2 vols. Berkeley: University of California Press, 1971, 1982.

8835. Hussein, Fuad M. The Legal Concept of Self-Determination and the Kurdish Question. Amsterdam: Luna, 1985.

8836. Inalick, Halil. "Servile Labor in the Ottoman Empire." In The Mutual Effects of the Islamic and Judeo-Christian Worlds: The East European Pattern, edited by Abraham Ascher and others. Brooklyn, N.Y.: Brooklyn College Press, 1979.

8837. Jernazian, Ephriam K. Judgment Unto Truth: Witnessing the Armenian Genocide. New Brunswick, NJ Translated by Alice Haig: Transaction, 1990.

8838. Karasapan, Omer. "Democracy and the Kurds." Middle East Report No. 153 (July-August 1988): 45.

8839. Karmi, Ilan. The Transformation of the Jewish Community of Istanbul in the Nineteenth Century: The Impact of the Ottoman Reforms (Tanzimat) upon the Legal, Political, Social And Economic Status of Istanbul Jewry: 1839-1878. Doctoral dissertation: University of Wisconsin, 1990. UMO # 9027505.

8840. Kasparian, Vartan S. The Historical Roots of the Armenian Question, 1878-1897. Doctoral dissertation: University of Utah, 1977.

8841. Katz, Y. "Pathos of Zionist Political Activity in Turkey, 1882-1914." International Journal of Turkish Studies 4 (1987): 115-135.

8842. Kazarian, H. "The Turkish Genocide of the Armenians: A Premeditated and Official Assault." Armenian Review 30 (Spring 1977): 3-25.

8843. Kendal. "Kurdistan in Turkey." In People Without a Country. The Kurds and Kurdistan, edited by Gerard Chaliand. London: Zed Press, 1980.

8844. Keyder, Coglar. Turkey. The Ottoman Legacy. New York: Verso, 1987.

8845. Klein, C. L. "Jews, Christians, Muslims under Turkish Rule in 1860-1907." Patterns of Prejudice 12 (July-August 1978): 25-28.

8846. "Kurds, Kurdistan." The Encyclopedia of Islam. new ed. vol. 5 (1981): 438-486.

8847. Kushner, David. "The Ottoman Government of Palestine, 1864- 1914." Middle Eastern Studies 23 (July 1987): 274-290.

8848. Kushner, David. "Turkish Secularists and Islam." Jerusalem Quarterly No. 38 (1986): 89-106.

8849. Laber, Jeri. "Turkey's Nonpeople." New York Review of Books (February 4, 1988): [The Kurds.]

8850. Laizer, Sheri. Into Kurdistan. Frontiers Under Fire. London: Zed Books, 1990.

8851. Libardian, Gerard J. "The Ultimate Repression: The Genocide of the Armenians, 1915-1917." In Genocide and the Modern Age: Etiology and Case Studies of Mass Death, edited by Isidor Wallimann and Michael N. Dobkowski. Westport, Ct: Greenwood, 1987.

8852. Marcus, ALiza. "Hearts and Minds in Kurdistan." Middle East Report No. 163 (March-April 1990): 41,42,44. [Sirnak, Turkey.]

8853. Margulis, Ronnie and Ergin Yildizoglu. "The Political Uses of Islam in Turkey." Middle East Report No. 153 (July- August 1988): 12-17, 50.

8854. McCarthy, Justin. Muslims and Minorities. The Population of Ottoman Anatolia and the End of the Empire. New York: New York University Press, 1983.

8855. McDowall, David. The Kurds. London: Minority Rights Group, 1985.

8856. More, Christiane. Les Kurdes d'aujourdhui. Mouvement national et partis politiques. Paris: L'Harmattan, 1984.

8857. Munir, O. Minderheiten in osmanischen Reich und in der neuen Turkei. Doctoral dissertation: University of Cologne, 1937.

8858. Nalbandian, Louise. The Armenian Revolutionary Movement. Berkeley: University of California Press, 1963.

8859. Olds, Sharon. "Silenced Voices: Turkey-Ismail Besikci." American Poetry Review 15 (July-August 1986): 29-30.

8860. Olson, Robert. "The Young Turks and the Jews: A Historiographical Revision." Turcica (France) 18 (1986): 219-235.

8861. Othman, S. "Historical Observations on the Genesis of the Kurdish National Movement." Stud. Kurdica 1 (January 1984): 20-32.

8862. Pamuk, Sevket. The Ottoman Empire and European Capitalism, 1820-1913. New York: Cambridge University Press, 1988.

8863. Papadopoulos, T. M. The History of the Greek Church and People Under Turkish Domination. Brussels: Demeester, 1952.

8864. Parveen Shaukat Ali. Status of Women in the Muslim World: A Study in the Feminist Movements in Turkey, Egypt, Iran, and Pakistan. Lahore: Aziz Publishers, 1975.

8865. Peeters, Yvo J. D. "The Rights of Minorities in Present-Day Turkey." Europa Ethnica 44 (1987): 131-138.

8866. Permanent Peoples' Tribunal. A Crime of Silence: The Armenian Genocide. London: Zed Press, 1985.

8867. Price, Claire. "Mustafa Kemal and the Christians." Current History 16 (September 1922): 985-993.

8868. Renda, Gunsel and C. Kortepeter, eds. The Transformation of Turkish Culture: The Ataturk Legacy. Princeton, N.J.: Kingston Press, 1986.

8869. Roditi, Edouard. "Ritual Murder Charges in the Ottoman Empire." Midstream 34 (January 1988): 19-23.

8870. Rodrique, Aron. French Jews, Turkish Jews. The Alliance Israelite Universelle and the Politics of Jewish Schooling in Turkey, 1860-1925. Bloomington: Indiana University Press, 1990.

8871. Rost, Yuri. Armenian Tragedy. New York Translated by Elizabeth Roberts: St. Martin's Press, 1990.

8872. Rustem, Ahmed. "La situation des chretiens en Turquie." Orient et Occident 1 (March 1922): 331-356.

8873. Salamone, S. D. "The Dialectics of Turkish National Identity: Ethnic Boundary Maintenance and State Ideology." East European Quarterly 23 (1989): 33-61, 225-248.

8874. Schnick, Irvin C. and E.A. Touak, eds. Turkey in Transition: New Perspectives. New York: Oxford University Press, 1987.

8875. Smith, Roger W. "Genocide and Denial: The Armenian Case and Its Implications." Armenian Review 42 (Spring 1989): 1-38.

8876. Sonyel, S. The Ottoman Armenians. London: Rustum, 1987.

8877. Suakjian, Kevork Y. Genocide in Trebijond: A Case Study of Armeno-Turkish Relations during the First World War. Doctoral dissertation: University of Nebraska, 1981.

8878. Suakjian, Kevork Y. "The Preconditions of the Armeno-Turkish Case of Genocide." Armenian Review 34 (December 1981): 403-411.

8879. Ternon, Yves. The Armenians: History of a Genocide. Translated by Rouben C. Cholakian. Delmar, New York: Caravan Books, 1990.

8880. Theodore, Demetrios E. The Sacrificials. Part of an Autobiography Depicting the Life of Minorities in a War-Torn Country. Boston, MA: Branden Press, 1970. [Greeks in Turkey.]

8881. Toledano, Ehud R. The Ottoman Slave Trade and Its Suppression. Princeton, N.J.: Princeton University Press, 1983.

8882. Tonjoroff, S. J. "Kurds Would Destroy Turkish Republic." Christian Register 444-465 (May 7, 1925)

8883. Weil, Chalva. "Programmed for the Working Classes." Times Educational Supplement, (August 8, 1986): [Early childhood education in Turkey.]

8884. Wheeless, Carl M. Turkey's Policy Toward Her Minorities, 1922-1952. Doctoral dissertation: Georgetown University, 1957.

8885. Yildizoglu, Ergin and Ronnie Margulies. Crisis and Transformation in Turkey. London: Saqi Books, 1988.

8886. Yonan, G. "Ein vergessener Holocaust: die Vernichtung der christlichen Assyrer in der Türkei." Pogrom 148/149 (1989): 1-422.

8887. Yorgun, Pembenaz. "The Women's Question and Difficulties of Feminism in Turkey." Khamsin No. 11 (1984)

8888. Zubaida, Sami. "Report from Paris: The Kurdish Conference." Middle East Report No. 163 (March-April 1990): 40-41.

UGANDA

8889. Bass, James D. British Colonial Policy in Uganda. Doctoral dissertation: University of Virginia, 1975. UMO # 7526090.

8890. Brittain, Victoria. "The Liberation of Kampala." New Left Review No. 156 (March-April 1986): 51-61.

8891. Bwengye, F. A. W. The Agony of Uganda from Idi Amin to Obote: Repressive Rule and Bloodshed: Causes, Effects and the Cure. London: Regency Press, 1985.

8892. Fuller, Thomas. "African Labor and Training in the Uganda Colonial Economy." Int. Journal of African Historical Studies 10 (1977): 77-95.

8893. Hansen, Bernt. Mission, Church and State in a Colonial Setting: Uganda, 1890-1925. London: Heinemann, 1984.

8894. Harden, Blaine. "Political Violence Has Left Psychic Scars on Ugandan Children." Washington Post, (July 15, 1986)

8895. Hooper, Ed. Uganda. London: Minority Rights Group, 1989.

8896. Jamal, Vali. "Taxation and Inequality in Uganda, 1900- 1964." Journal of Economic History 38 (June 1978): 418-438.

8897. Jorgensen, Jan J. Uganda: A Modern History. New York: St. Martin's Press, 1981.

8898. Kabwegyere, Tarsis B. "The Dynamics of Colonial Violence: The Inductive System in Uganda." Journal of Peace Research 9 (1972): 303-314.

8899. Kasozi, A. B. K. "The Process of Islamisation in Uganda, 1854-1927." Uganda Journal 38 (1976): 83-108.

8900. Kiwanuka, M. S. M.S. Amin and the Tragedy of Uganda. Munich: Weltforum, 1979.

8901. Mamdani, Mahmood. Imperialism and Fascism in Uganda. Trenton, NJ: Africa World Press, 1984.

8902. Mamdani, Mahmood. Politics and Class Formation in Uganda. New York: Monthly Review Press, 1976.

8903. Morris, H. S. The Indians in Uganda. London: Weidenfeld and Nicolson, 1968.

8904. Mukherjee, Ramkrishna. Uganda, an Historical Accident? Class, Nation, State Formation. Trenton, NJ: Africa World Press, 1985.

8905. Nsibambi, Apolo. "Corruption in Uganda." Ufahamu 15 (1986-1987): 109-118.

8906. Nyeko, Balam. "The Background to the Political Instability in Uganda." Ufahamu 15 (1986-1987): 11-32.

8907. Oloka-Onyango, Joe. "Race, Class, and Imperialism in Uganda." Transafrica Forum 5 (Fall 1987): 13-28.

8908. Patel, H. H. Race, Class and Citizenship in Uganda. The Indian Minority, 1900-1972. Berkeley: University of Calfornia Press, 1977.

8909. Perlez, Jane. "The Land Amin Seized Now Preoccupies Uganda." New York Times, (June 12, 1990): [Asian property confiscated by Idi Amin.]

8910. Tandon, Yash. "Fascism, War and Revolution in Uganda." Jr. Afric. Marxists (March 1984): 75-101.

8911. Twaddle, Michael. "Decentralized Violence and Collaboration in Early Colonial Uganda." Journal of Imperial and Commonwealth History 16 (1988): 71-85.

8912. Twaddle, Michael, ed. Expulsion of a Minority: Essays on Ugandan Asians. London: Athlone Press, 1975.

8913. Uganda and Sudan. London: Minority Rights Group, 1984.

URUGUAY

8914. Carvalho-Neto, Paulo de. El Negro Uraguayo (hasta la abolicion). Quito, Ecuador: Editorial Universitaria, 1965.

8915. Errandones, Alfredo. "Conflicto de clases." Cuad. CLAEH 13 (1988): 175-191.

8916. Gillespie, Charles and others, eds. Uruguay y la democracia. 3 vols. Montevideo: Ediciones de la Bonda Oriental, 1984-1985.

8917. Isola, Ema. La esclavitud en el Uruguay desde sus comienzos hasta su extinctión, 1743-1852. Montevideo: 1975.

8918. Merino Burghi, Francisco M. El negro en la sociedad montevideana. Montevideo: Ediciones de la Banda Oriental, 1982.

8919. Pereda, Valdes I. El Negro en el Uruguay: Pasado y Presente. Montevideo: Revista del Instituto Histórico y Geografico del Uruguay, 1965.

8920. Pobreza y nutrición infantil. 2 vols. Montevideo: Latinoamericano de Economia Humana, 1985.

8921. Rama, Carlos M. Los Afro-Uruguayos. Montevideo: El Sigo Instrado, 1967.

8922. Rama, Germán W. "La démocratie en Uruguay: un essai d'interpretation." Notes et Etudes Documentaires (Série Problèmes d'Amerique Latine) No. 4796 (Fourth Quarter 1985): 3-49.

8923. Servicio Paz y Justicia. Uruguay nunca más: informe sobre la violación a los derechos humanos (1972-1985). 1989. [Joaquín Requena 1642, Montevideo, Uruguay.]

8924. Terra, Juan P. and Mabel Hopenhaym. La infancia en el Uruguay (1973-1984): effectos sociales de la recesión y los politicas de ajuste. Montevideo: Ediciones de la Banda Oriental SRL, 1986.

8925. Winn, D. E. Uruguay and British Economic Expansion, 1880-93. Doctoral dissertation: University of Cambridge, 1971.

U.S.S.R.

8926. Abramsky, Chimen. "The Birobidzhan Project, 1927-1959." In *The Jews in Russia since 1917*, edited by Lionel Kochan, 62-75. Oxford: 1970.

8927. Aganbegyan, Abel. "New Directions in Soviet Economics." *New Left Review* No. 169 (May-June 1988): 89-95.

8928. Agursky, Mikhail. "The Jewish Problem in the Russian Religious Radical Right: The Case of Metropolitan Antonii (Kerapovitskii)." *Ostkirchliche Studien* 36 (1987): 39-44.

8929. Agursky, Mikhail. *The Third Rome: National Bolshevism in the USSR*. Boulder, CO: Westview Press, 1987.

8930. Ahlberg, Rene. "De Mythos der sozialen Gleichheit im Sozialismus." *Osteuropa* 31 (1981): 963-984.

8931. Ainsztein, R. "Soviet Jewry in the Second World War." In *The Jews in Soviet Russia since 1917*, edited by Lionel Kochan, 269-287. New York: 1972.

8932. Alexeyeva, Ludmilla. "Nationalist Movements in the USSR." *New Politics* 1 (Winter 1988): 133-147.

8933. Allen, W. E. D. *A History of the Georgian People from the Beginning Down to the Russian Conquest in the Nineteenth Century*. London: 1932.

8934. Allworth, Edward A. *The Modern Uzbeks: From the Fourteenth Century to the Present: A Cultural History*. Stanford, CA: Hoover Institution Press, 1990.

8935. Allworth, Edward A. "The Search for Group Identity in Turkistan March 1917-September 1922." *Canadian-American Slavic Studies* 17 (1983): 487-502.

8936. Allworth, Edward A., ed. Tatars of the Crimea. Their Struggle for Survival. Durham, NC: Duke University Press, 1988.

8937. Altschuler, Mordechai. "The Jewish Antifascist Committee in the USSR in the Right of New Documentation." Studies in Contemporary Jewry 1 (1984): 253-291.

8938. Altschuler, Mordechai. "The Attitude of the Communist Party of Russia to Jewish National Survival." YIVO Annual of Jewish Social Science 14 (1969): 68-86.

8939. Altschuler, Mordechai. Soviet Jewry Since the Second World War: Population and Social Structure. Westport, CT: Greenwood, 1987.

8940. Altschuler, Mordechai. "Soviet Union." In Encyclopedia of the Holocaust, IV. 1383-1390. New York: Macmillan, 1990.

8941. Altstadt, Audrey L. "Azerbaijani Turks' Response to Russian Conquest." Stud. Comp. Communism 19 (1986): 267-286.

8942. Altstadt, Audrey L. "Negorno-Karabagh: 'Apple of Discord' in the Azerbaijan SSR." Central Asian Survey 7 (1988): 63-78.

8943. Altstadt-Mirhadi, Audrey L. The Azerbaijani Turkish Community of Baku before World War I. Doctoral dissertation: University of Chicago, 1983.

8944. Anderson, B. A. and B.D. Silver. "Infant Mortality in the Soviet Union: Regional Differences and Measurement Issues." Population and Development Review 12 (December 1986)

8945. Andreyev, C. Vlasov and the Russian Liberation Movement: Soviet Reality and Emigre Theories. New York: 1988.

8946. Anweiler, Oskar. "Die sowjetische Schul-und Berufsbildungsreform von 1984." Osteuropa 34 (1984): 839-860.

8947. "Appeal by Pamyat Patriotic Asociation to the Russian People and to Patriots of All Countries and Nations." Soviet Jewish Affairs 18 (Spring 1988): 60-71.

8948. Armstrong, John A. "Acculturation to the Russian Bureaucratic Elite: The Case of the Baltic Germans." Journal of Baltic Studies 15 (1984): 119-129.

8949. Armstrong, John A. Ukrainian Nationalism. 3d ed. Englewood, CO: Ukrainian Academic Press, 1989.

8950. Arnovitz, Benton. "Zion in Siberia." Survey 29 (1985): 129-152. [Birobidzhan.]

8951. Aronson, Gregor and others, eds. Russian Jewry, 1917- 1967. Translated by Joel Carmichael. New York : Yoseloff, 1969.

8952. Aronson, I. Michael. Troubled Waters. The Origins of the 1881 Anti-Jewish Pogroms in Russia. Pittsburgh, PA: University of Pittsburgh Press, 1990.

8953. Aster, Howard and Peter J. Potichniyj. Jewish Ukrainian Relations: Two Solitudes. Oakville, Ont: Mosaic Press, 1983.

8954. Atkin, Muriel. "The Survival of Islam in Soviet Tajikistan." Mid. E. Journal 43 (Autumn 1989): 605-618.

8955. Azarenko, Jury. The Russian Liberation Movement during World War II- Historical Accounts. Doctoral dissertation: Georgetown University, 1984. UMO # 8527449 ["Vlasov Movement".]

8956. Babchin-Herzenberg, Tatyana. "Solzhenitsyn and the Jews." Jerusalem Post, (August 22, 1975)

8957. Bacon, Elizabeth E. Central Asia under Russian Rule: A Study in Cultural Change. Ithaca, New York: Cornell University Press, 1966.

8958. Bagdassarin, Greg, ed. The Right to Struggle: Selected Writings of Monte Melkonian on the Armenian National Question. San Francsico, CA: Sadarabad Press, 1990.

8959. Bahry, Donna. Outside Moscow. Power, Politics, and Budgetary Policy in the Soviet Republics. New York: Columbia University Press, 1987.

8960. Baker, Janice. "The Position of Women in Kazakhstan in the Interwar Years." Central Asian Survey 4 (1985): 75-114.

8961. Balzer, M. and others. "The Soviet Multiethnic State: Trends and Debates." Soviet Anthropology and Archeology 28 (Winter 1990): entire issue.

8962. Baron, Salo W. The Russian Jew Under Tsars and Soviets. 2d ed. New York: Macmillan, 1975.

8963. Barringer, Felicity. "Tartars Stage Noisy Protest in Moscow." New York Times, (July 26, 1987)

8964. Bassin, Mark. "Expansion and Colonialism on the Eastern Frontier: Views of Siberia and the Far East in Pre-Petrine Russia." Journal of Historical Geography 14 (1988): 3-21.

8965. Baumann, Robert F. "Subject Nationalities in the Military Service of Imperial Russia: The Case of the Bashkirs." Slavic Review 46 (1987): 489-502.

8966. Beaudry, Lucille. "The Causes of the Black Market Phenomenon in the USSR." Translated by Barbara Nield. Studies in Political Economy No. 13 (Spring 1984): 83-108.

8967. Becker, Eduard. "Germans in Russia and in the USSR." Russia No. 11 (1985): 7-18.

8968. Belkindas, M. V. and M.J. Sagers. "A Preliminary Analysis of Economic Relations among Union Republics of the USSR, 1970-1988." Soviet Geography 31 (November 1990)

8969. Belstserkovsky, Vadin. "What is Russian Anti-Semitism?" Midstream 33 (April 1987): 6-10.

8970. Bennigsen, Alexandre. "Mullahs, Mujahadin, and Soviet Muslims." Problems of Communism 33 (November-December 1984): 28-44.

8971. Bennigsen, Alexandre and S. Enders Wimbush. Muslims of the Soviet Empire: A Guide. Bloomington, IN: Indiana University Press, 1986.

8972. Bergson, Abram. "Income Inequality Under Soviet Socialism." Journal of Economic Literature 22 (September 1984): 1052- 1099.

8973. Berk, Stephen M. Year of Crisis, Year of Hope: Russian Jewry and the Pogroms of 1881-1881. Westport, CT: Greenwood, 1985.

8974. Bigelow, Poultney. "The Russian and His Jew." In The Borderland of Czar and Kaiser. 98-130. New York: Harper, 1895.

8975. Bihl, Wolfdieter. "Ukrainer als Teil der Streitkrafte des Deutschen Reiches im Zweiten Weltkrieg." Osterr. Osth. 29 (1987): 28-55.

8976. Bilinsky, Yaroslav. "Nationality Policy in Gorbachev's First Year." Orbis 30 (1986): 331-342.

8977. Bilinsky, Yaroslav and Tonu Parming. Helsinki Watch Committees in the Soviet Union: Implications for the Soviet Nationality Question. Final Report to the National Council for Soviet and East European Research, 1980.

8978. Birch, Julian. "Border Disputes and Disputed Borders in the Soviet Federal System." Nationalities Papers 15 (1987): 43- 70.

8979. Birch, Julian. The Ukrainian Nationalist Movement in the USSR since 1956. London: Ukrainian Publishers, 1971.

8980. Birnbaum, Henrik. "On Some Evidence of Jewish Life and Anti-Jewish Sentiments in Medieval Russia." Viator 4 (1973): 225-255.

694 WORLD RACISM AND RELATED INHUMANITIES

8981. Blakely, Allison. Russia and the Negro: Blacks in Russian History and Thought. Washington, D.C.: Howard University Press, 1986.

8982. Bland-Spitz, Daniela. Die Lage der Juden und die judische Opposition in der Sowjetunion, 1967-1977. Thurgau, Switzerland: Verlag Ruegger, 1980.

8983. Blank, Stephen J. "National Education, Church and State in Tsarist Nationality Policy: The Il'minskii System." Canadian- American Slavic Studies 17 (1983): 466-486.

8984. Blank, Stephen J. "The Origins of Soviet Language Policy 1917-1921." Russian History 15 (1988): 71-92.

8985. Blank, Stephen J. "Soviet Nationality Policy and Soviet Foreign Policy: The Polish Case 1917-1921." Int. Hist. Review 7 (1985): 103-128.

8986. Blum, A. and A. Monnier. "Recent Mortality Trends in the USSR." Population Studies 43 (July 1989)

8987. Blum, Jakub, pseud. and Vera Rich. The Image of the Jew in Soviet Literature: The Post-Stalin Period. Translated by P.S. Falla. London: Institute of Jewish Affairs, 1985.

8988. Bociwrkiw, Bohdan R. "The Soviet Destruction of the Ukrainian Orthodox Church, 1929-1936." Journal of Ukrainian Studies 12 (1987): 3-21.

8989. Bohac, Rodney. "Everyday Forms of Resistance: Serf Opposition to Gentry Exactions, 1800-1861." In Peasant Economy, Culture and Politics of European Russia, 1800-1921, edited by E. Kingston-Mann and T. Mixter. Princeton, NJ: Princeton University Press, 1990.

8990. Bojcun, Jaromyr M. The Working Class and the National Question in Ukraine, 1880-1920. Doctoral dissertation: York University (Canada), 1985.

8991. Bonner, Elena. "The Shame of Armenia." New York Review of Books, (October 11, 1990)

8992. Borys, Jury. The Sovietization of Ukraine, 1917-1923. Toronto: University of Toronto Press,

8993. Boshyk, Yury, ed. Ukraine during World War II: History and Its Aftermath: a Symposium. Edmonton: Canadian Institute of Ukrainian Studies, University of Alberta, 1986.

8994. Bourdeaux, Michael and others. Religious Minorities in the Soviet Union. rev. 4th ed. London: Minority Rights Group, 1984.

8995. Bourret, Jean-Francois. Les Allemands de la Volga: Historie culturelle d'une minorite, 1763-1941. Lyon: Presses Universitaires de Lyon and Centre Nationale de Recherche Scientifique, 1986.

8996. Brackman, Rowan S. Anti-semitism of Joseph Stalin. Doctoral dissertation: New York University, 1980. UMO # 8027869.

8997. Bradley, Joseph. Muzhik and Muscovite. Urbanization in Late Imperial Russia. Berkeley: University of California Press, 1985.

8998. Brandt, Joseph C. "Economic Reform and the Soviet National Question." Telos No. 84 (Summer 1990): 58-68.

8999. Bromley, Julian and Viktor Kozlov. "The Theory of Ethnos and Ethnic Processes in Soviet Social Sciences." Comparative Studies in Society and History 31 (July 1989): 425-438.

9000. Brucan, Silviu. "Historical Evolution of Classes and Class Policy in the USSR." Review 13 (Summer 1990): 299-328.

9001. Bruchis, Michael. "The Language Policy of the Soviet Communist Party: Comments and Observations." East European Quarterly 21 (1987): 231-257.

9002. Bugayenko, Yevgeni. On the Bank of the Amur, 50th Anniversary of the Jewish Autonomous Region. Moscow: Novosti, 1984.

9003. Burston, Bradley. "Anti-Semitism and Ukrainians." Jerusalem Post, (January 29, 1987): [About the work of Shimon Redlich.]

9004. Campbell, Kurt. "Glasnost and Godfathers." Boston Globe Magazine, (January 6, 1991): [Organized crime in the USSR.]

9005. Campeanu, Pavel. The Genesis of the Stalinist Social Order. New York: M.E. Sharpe, 1989.

9006. Carlisle, Donald S. "The Uzbek Power Elite: Politburo and Secretariat (1938-1983)." Central Asian Survey 5 (1986): 91-132.

9007. Caroe, Olaf. Soviet Empire: The Turks of Central Asia, and Stalinism. London: 1953.

9008. Carrere d'Encausse, Helene. The Great Challenge. Nationalities and the Bolshevik State, 1917-1930. New York Translated by Nancy Festinger: Holmes & Meier, 1990.

9009. Carrere d'Encausse, Helene. Islam and the Russian Empire. Reform and Revolution in Central Asia. Berkeley Translated by Quintin Hoare: University of California Press, 1989.

9010. Chase, William J. Workers, Society, and the Soviet State. Labor and Life in Moscow, 1918-1929. Urbana: University of Illinois Press, 1987.

9011. Chertok, Shimon. "Jewish Themes in the Soviet Cinema." Soviet Jewish Affairs 16 (November 1986): 29-42.

9012. Choseed, Bernard J. "The Soviet Jew in Literature." Jewish Social Studies 11 (1949): 259-282.

9013. Cleary, James W. Politics and Administration in Soviet Kazakhstan, 1955-1964. Doctoral dissertation: Australian National University, 1967.

9014. Clines, Francis X. "Lost Colony of Koreans Strives for New Dignity." New York Times, (October 21, 1990): [Sakhalin Island.]

9015. Coffman, Edward M. "The Intervention in Russia, 1918-1921." Military Review 58 (1988): 60-71.

9016. Colbias, Karen A. Heroes and Patriots: The Ethnic Integration of Youth in the Soviet Union during the Brezhnev Era, 1965-1982. Doctoral dissertation: Columbia University, 1987. UMO # 9020507 [Uzbekistan.]

9017. Cole, Lester. "Russian Anti-Semitism (letter)." Nation (November 29, 1980): [See reply by Peggy Dennis, same issue.]

9018. Conquest, Robert. The Harvest of Sorrow. Soviet Collectivization and the Terror Famine. New York: Oxford University Press, 1986. [1929-1933.]

9019. Conquest, Robert, ed. The Last Empire: Nationality and the Soviet Future. Stanford, Ca: Hoover Institution Press, 1986.

9020. Coogan, Kevin. "Specter of Dying Aral Sea Haunts USSR." Guardian (NYC), (May 23, 1990)

9021. Crisp, Olga and Linda Edmondson. Civil Rights in Imperial Russia. New York: Oxford University Press, 1989.

9022. Critchlow, James. "'Corruption,' Nationalism, and the Native Elites in Soviet Central Asia." Journal of Communist Studies 4 (1988): 142-161.

9023. Dallin, David J. The Rise of Russia in Asia. New Haven, CT: Yale University Press, 1949.

9024. Davies, R. W. The Soviet Economy in Turmoil 1929-1930: The Industrialization of Soviet Russia. London: Macmillan, 1988.

9025. Demko, George J. The Russian Colonization of Kazakhstan, 1896-1916. Bloomington: Research Center for the Language Sciences, Indiana University, 1969.

9026. Deyneka, Peter Jr. "The Problems and Victories of Russian- Germans in Siberia." Journal of the American Historical Society of Germany from Russia 8 (1985): 41-45.

9027. Dienes, Leslie. "Economic and Strategic Position of the Soviet Far East." Sov. Ec. 1 (1985): 146-176.

9028. Dienes, Leslie. Soviet Asia: Economic Development and National Policy Choices. Boulder, CO: Westview Press, 1987.

9029. Dinstein, Yoram. "The Cultural Rights of Soviet Jews under International Law." In Vision Confronts Reality, edited by Ruth Kozodoy and others. New York: Herzl Press, 1989.

9030. "Discrimination of Lithuanians in the Belorussian SSR." Lituanus 21 (1975): 70-74. [1945-1972.]

9031. Dmytryshyn, Basil and others, eds. Russia's Conquest of Siberia, 1558-1770: A Documentary Record. Translated by editors. Portland: Western Imprints, The Press of the Oregon Historical Society, 1985.

9032. Dneprov, E. D. "The Autocracy and Public Education in Postreform Russia." Sov. Studies in History 25 (1986-1987): 31-77. [Pre-1917.]

9033. Dobson, Richard B. "Georgia and the Georgians." In Handbook of Major Soviet Nationalities, edited by Zev Katz. New York: 1975.

9034. Domalskii, I. "New Developments in Anti-Semitism. A Social Essay." In Anti-Semitism in the Soviet Union. Its Roots and Consequences. Vol. I. Jerusalem: The Centre for Research and Documentation of East-European Jewry, Hebrew University, 1979.

9035. Dreifelds, Juris. "Social Inequalities in the Baltics: The Case of Occupational Hierarchy and Upward Mobility." Journal of Baltic Studies 19 (1988): 67-88.

9036. Dreizin, Felix. The Russian Soul and the Jew: Essays in Literary Ethno-criticism. Lanham, MD: University Press of America, 1990.

9037. Dudwick, Nora. "The Karabagh Movement: An Old Scenario Gets Rewritten." Armenian Review 42 (Autumn 1989): 63-70.

9038. Dunlop, John B. The Faces of Contemporary Russian Nationalism. Princeton, NJ: Princeton University Press, 1984.

9039. Dunston, John. "Soviet Schools and the Road of Reform." Journal of Russian Studies 49 (1985): 27-36.

9040. Dutter, L. E. "Theoretical Perspectives on Ethnic Political Behavior in the Soviet Union." Journal of Conflict Resolution 34 (June 1990)

9041. Dymerskaya-Tsigelman, L. "L. Korneev as a Phenomenon of Soviet Anti-Semitism in the 1970s-1980s." Jews and Jewish Topics in Soviet and East European Publications 2/3 (1986): 8-27.

9042. Ehrenburg, Ilya and Vasily Grossman, eds. The Black Book: the Ruthless Murder of Jews by German-Fascist Invaders Throughout the Temporarily-Occupied Regions of the Soviet Union and in the Death Camps of Poland During the War of 1941-1945. Translated by John Glad and James S. Levine. New York: Schocken, 1981.

9043. Eklof, Ben. Russian Peasant Schools: Officialdom, Village Culture, and Popular Pedagogy, 1864-1914. Berkeley: University of California Press, 1986.

9044. Ellman, Michael. "A note on the Distribution of Income in the USSR Under Gorbachev." Soviet Studies 42 (January 1990)

9045. Enteen, George and others. Soviet Historians and the Study of Russian Imperialism. University Park: Pennsylvania State University Press, 1979.

9046. Epstein, Erwin H. "Ideological Factors in Soviet Educational Policy Toward Jews." Education and Urban Society 10 (February 1978): 223-254.

9047. Ettinger, Shmuel. "The Position of Jews in Soviet Culture: A Historical Survey." In Jews in Soviet Culture, edited by Jack Miller. New Brunswick, NJ: Transaction, 1984.

9048. Ettinger, Shmuel. "The Roots of Soviet Anti-Semitism and the Struggle of the Jews." Dispersion and Unity 12 (1971): 101-113.

9049. Ezergailis, Andrew. "Latvia." In Encyclopedia of the Holocaust, III. 849-852. New York: Macmillan, 1990.

9050. Farmer, Kenneth C. Ukrainian Nationalism in the Post-Stalin Era: Myth, Symbols, and Ideology in the Soviet Nationalities Policy. Boston, MA: Marturnus Nijhoff, 1980.

9051. Fein, Esther B. "Glasnost Is Opening the Door on Poverty." New York Times, (January 29, 1989)

9052. Fein, Esther B. "In Soviet Asia Backwater, Infancy's a Rite of Survival." New York Times, (August 14, 1989)

9053. Field, Mark G. "In Sickness and in Health." Wilson Quarterly 9 (1985): 47-60.

9054. Fierman, William. "Cultural Nationalism in Soviet Uzbekistan: A Case Study of The Immortal Cliffs." Soviet Union 12 (1985): 1-41.

9055. Finkelstein, Eitan. "Jewish Revival in the Baltics: Problems and Perspectives." Soviet Jewish Affairs 20 (Spring 1990): 3-13.

9056. Firstenberg, Barbara. An Aspect of Soviet Jewry: Anti-Semitism and Birobidzhan. Master's thesis: Adelphi University, 1972.

9057. Fish, Daniel, pseud. "The Jews in Syllabuses of World and Russian History: What Soviet School Children Read About Jewish History" Soviet Jewish Affairs 8 (Spring 1978)

9058. Fisher, Alan W. The Crimean Tatars. Stanford, Ca: Hoover Institution Press, 1978.

9059. Flaherty, Patrick. "Class Power in Soviet Society." New Politics 2 (Winter 1990): 157-177.

9060. Flaherty, Patrick. "Perestroika and the Soviet Working Class." Studies in Political Economy No. 29 (Summer 1989): 39-61.

9061. Fleischauer, Ingeborg. Das Dritte Reich und die Deutschen in der Sowejetunion. Stuttgart: Deutsche Verlags-Anstalt, 1983.

9062. Fleischauer, Ingeborg and Benjamin Pinkus. The Soviet Germans: Past and Present. London Edited by Edith R. Frankel: C. Hurst, 1986.

9063. Forgus, Silvia P. "Manifestations of Nationalism in the Baltic Republics." Nationalities Papers 7 (Fall 1979): 197- 211.

9064. Franklin, Simon. "Literacy and Documentation in Early Medieval Russia." Speculum 60 (January 1985): 1-38.

9065. Fraser, N. M. and others. "A Conflict Analysis of the Armenian-Azerbaijani Dispute." Journal of Conflict Resolution 34 (December 1990)

9066. Freiman, Grigori. It Seems I Am a Jew. A Samizdat Essay on Soviet Mathematics. Translated by Melvyn B. Nathanson. Carbondale: Southern Illinois University Press, 1980.

9067. Friedberg, Maurice. "Anti-Semitism as a Policy Tool in the Soviet Union." New Politics 9 (Fall 1971): 61-79.

9068. Friedgut, Theodore H. "Soviet Anti-Zionism and Antisemitism- Another Cycle." Soviet Jewish Affairs 3-22 (February 1984): 14.

9069. Friedgut, Theodore H. and Lewis Siegelbaum. "Perestroika from Below: The Soviet Miners' Strike and Its Aftermath." New Left Review No. 181 (May-June 1990): 5-32.

9070. Friedman, Philip. "Ukrainian-Jewish Relations During the Occupation." In Roads to Extinction: Essays on the Holocaust Philip Friedman. Philadelphia, PA: Jewish Publications Society, 1980.

9071. Friedman, Philip. "Ukrainian-Jewish Relations During the Nazi Occupation." YIVO Annual of Social Science 12 (1958- 1959): 259-296.

9072. Fuller, Elizabeth. "The Azeris in Georgia and the Ingilos: Ethnic Minorities in the Limelight." Central Asian Survey 3 (1984): 75-85.

9073. Galuzo, Peter G. "Das Kolonialsystem der russischen Imperialismus am Vorabend der Oktoberrevolution." Zeitschrift fur Geschichtswissenschaft 15 (1967): 997-1014.

9074. Garrard, John and Carol Garrard. "Soviet Book Hunger." Problems of Communism 34 (Sept.-Oct. 1985): 72-81.

9075. Gergel, N. "The Pogroms in the Ukraine in 1918-1921." YIVO Annual of Jewish Social Sciences 6 (1951): 237-252.

9076. Gilboa, Jehoshua A. A Language Silenced: The Suppression of Hebrew Literature and Culture in the Soviet Union. Rutherford, N.J.: Fairleigh Dickinson University Press, 1982.

9077. Ginaite, Sara. "Access to Advanced Education in the U.S.S.R." Nationalities Papers 15 (1987): 158-183.

9078. Gitelman, Zvi. "The Abridgement of the Rights of Jews in the Fields of Nationality, Culture and Religion." Soviet Jewish Affairs 15 (February 1985): 79-87.

9079. Gitelman, Zvi. A Century of Ambivalence. The Jews in Russia and the Soviet Union, 1881 to the Present. New York: Schocken, 1988.

9080. Gitelman, Zvi. "History, Memory and Politics: The Holocaust in the Soviet Union." Holocaust and Genocide Studies 5 (1990): 23-37.

9081. Gitelman, Zvi. Jewish Nationality and Soviet Politics. The Jewish Sections of the CPSU, 1917-1930. Princeton, NJ: Princeton University Press, 1972.

9082. Gitelman, Zvi. "Shaping Jewish Identity in the U.S.S.R. and Eastern Europe: The State as Social Engineer." Midstream 36 (April 1990): 16-21.

9083. "Glasnost and the New Russian Anti-semitism." Soviet Jewish Affairs 17 (1987): 53068. [Translation of three Soviet commentaries critical of Pamyat, an antisemitic association based in Moscow; annotated by Howard Spier.]

9084. Goldberg, Anatol. Ilya Ehrenburg. New York: Viking, 1984.

9085. Goldberg, Marilyn P. "Women in the Soviet Economy." Review of Radical Political Economy 4 (1972): 60-74.

9086. Goldman, Philip. "Perestroika: End or Beginning of Soviet Federalism?" Telos No. 84 (Summer 1990): 69-87.

9087. Greenbaum, Alfred A. Jewish Scholarship and Scholarly Institutions in Soviet Russia 1918-1953. Jerusalem: Hebrew University Centre for Research and Documentation of East European Jewry, 1978.

9088. Gregory, Paul R. "Russian Living Standards During the Industrialization Era, 1885-1913." Review of Income and Wealth 26 (March 1980): 87-103.

9089. Gregory, Paul R. and I. L. Colbier, Jr. "Unemployment in the Soviet Union: Evidence from the Soviet Interview Project." American Economic Review 78 (September 1988)

9090. Guthier, Steven L. "The Belorussians: National Identification and Assimilation, 1897-1970." Soviet Studies 29 (1970): 270-283.

9091. Haimson, Leopold. "The Problem of Social Stability in Urban Russia, 1905-1914." Slavic Review 23,24 (1964, 1965): 619- 642, 1-22.

9092. Hajda, Lubomyr and Mark Berssinger, eds. The Nationalities Factor in Soviet Politics and Society. Buolder, CO: Westview, 1990.

9093. Halevy, Zvi. Jewish Schools Under Czarism and Communism: A Struggle for Cultural Identity. New York: Springer, 1976.

9094. Harap, Louis. "Stalinism and the Jewish Question: Lenin's Basic Principles Violated." Jewish Currents 33 (1979): 4-9, 38-42.

9095. Harris, David A. and Izrail Rabinovich. The Jokes of Oppression: The Humour of Soviet Jews. Northvale, NJ: Jason Aronson, 1988.

9096. Heinen, Jacqueline. "Inequalities at Work: The Gender Division of Labour in the Soviet Union and Eastern Europe." Studies in Political Economy No. 33 (Autumn 1990): 39-61.

9097. Heinzig, Dieter. "Russia and the Soviet Union in Asia: Aspects of Colonialism and Expansionism." Contemp. S.E. Asia 4 (March 1983): 417-450.

9098. Heitlinger, Alena. Women and State Socialism: Sex Inequality in the Soviet Union and Czechoslovakia. London: Macmillan, 1979.

9099. Heitman, Sidney. "Jews in the 1989 USSR Census." Soviet Jewish Affairs 20 (Spring 1990): 23-30.

9100. Hellie, Richard. "Muscovite Slavery in Comparative Perspective." Russian History 6, part 2 (1979): 133-209.

9101. Hellie, Richard. "Recent Soviet Historiography on Medieval to Early Modern Russian Slavery." Russian Review 1-32 (January 1976)

9102. Hellie, Richard. "Reply [to Herbert Leventer]." Russian Review 36 (January 1977): 68-75.

9103. Hellie, Richard. Slavery in Russia, 1450-1725. Chicago: University of Chicago Press, 1982.

9104. Hellie, Richard. "Slavery among the Early Modern Peoples on the Territory of the USSR." Canadian American Slavic Studies 17 (1983): 454-465.

9105. Herzstein, Robert E. "Anti-Jewish Propaganda in the Orel Region of Great Russia, 1942-1943: The German Army and Its Russian Collaborators." Simon Wiesenthal Center Annual 6 (1989): 33-55.

9106. Hinshaw, Christine R. "A Source of the Social History of Late Imperial Russia: the 1895 Primary School Survey Conducted by the Free Economic Society." Cah. monde russe sovietique 25 (1984): 455-462.

9107. Hirszowicz, Lukasz. "Anti-Jewish Discrimination in Education and Employment." Soviet Jewish Affairs 15 (February 1985): 25-30.

9108. Hoch, Steven L. Serfdom and Social Control in Russia: Petrovskoe, a Village in Tambov. Chicago, Il: University of Chicago Press, 1986.

9109. Holland, Barbara, ed. Soviet Sisterhood. Bloomington: Indiana University Press, 1985.

9110. Holt, Alix. "The First Soviet Feminists." In Soviet Sisterhood, edited by B. Holland. London: 1986.

9111. Hosking, Geoffrey. The First Socialist Society. A History of the Soviet Union from Within. Cambridge, MA: Harvard University Press, 1985.

9112. Hunczak, Taras. "Ukrainian-Jewish Relations during the Soviet and Nazi Occupations." In Ukraine during World War II: History and Its Aftermath. A Symposium, edited by Yury Boshyk. Edmonton: Canadian Institute of Ukrainian Studies, University of Alberta, 1986.

9113. Hunt, Albert. "Bitter in Yorkshire." New Society (November 21, 1986) [Ukrainians in Britain.]

9114. Hutton, Marcelline J. Russian and Soviet Women, 1897-1939: Dreams, Struggles, and Nightmares. Doctoral dissertation: University of Iowa, 1986. UMO # 8622775.

9115. Iakovlev, Aleksandr. "Constitutional Socialist Democracy: Dream or Reality." Columbia Journal of Transnational Law 28 (Fall 1990): 117-132.

9116. Imart, G. G. "Kirgizia-Kazakhstan: A Hinge or a Faultline?" Problems of Communism 39 (September-October 1990)

9117. Jews and Jewish Topics in the Soviet Union and Eastern Europe. Jerusalem: Centre for Research and Documentation of East European Jewry, Hebrew University, 1989.

9118. Johanson, Christine. Women's Struggle for Higher Education in Russia, 1855-1900. McGill-Queen's University Press, 1986.

9119. Johnson. Robert E. Peasant and Proletarian: The Working Class of Moscow in the Late Nineteenth Century. New Brunswick, NJ: 1979.

9120. Jones, Ellen. Red Army and Society: A Sociology of the Soviet Military. Boston, MA: Allen & Unwin, 1984.

9121. Jones, Ellen and Fred W. Grupp. "Modernization and Traditionality in a Multiethnic Society: The Soviet Case." American Political Science Review 79 (June 1985): 474-490.

9122. Jones, Stephen. "The Establishment of Soviet Power in Transcaucasia: The Case of Georgia 1921-1928." Soviet Studies 40 (1988): 616-639.

9123. Journal of Soviet Nationalities (Published by Duke University, beginning in 1990)

9124. Jurgila, C. Lithuania: The Outpost of Racedom. St. Petersburg, FL: 1976.

9125. Kabuzan, V. M. "Zahl und Siedlungsgebiete der Deutschen im Russischen Reich (1796-1917)." Z. Geschichtswiss 32 (1984): 866-874.

9126. Kagarlitsky, Boris. "The Intelligentsia and the Changes [in the USSR]." New Left Review No. 164 (July-August 1987): 5-16.

9127. Kagarlitsky, Boris. "Perestroika: The Dialectic of Change." New Left Review No. 169 (May-June 1988): 63-83.

9128. Kagedan, Allan L. The Formation of Soviet Jewish Territorial Units, 1924-1937. Doctoral dissertation: Columbia University, 1985. UMO # 8809370.

9129. Kahan, Stuart. The Wolf of the Kremlin: The First Biography of L.M. Kaganovich, the Soviet Union's Architect of Fear. New York: Morrow, 1988.

9130. Kaiser, Daniel H., ed. The Workers' Revolution in Russia, 1917. The View from Below. New York: Cambridge University Press, 1987.

9131. Kamentsky, Ihor. Hitler's Occupation of Ukraine, 1941-1944: A Study of Totalitarian Imperialism. Milwaukee, WI: Marquette University Press, 1956.

9132. Kanatchikov, Semen I. A Radical Worker in Tsarist Russia. The Autobiography of Semen Ivanovich Kanatchikov. Stanford, CA Translated and edited by Reginald E. Zelnik: Stanford University Press, 1986.

9133. Karklins, Rasma. Ethnic Relations in the U.S.S.R.: The Perspective from Below. London: 1988.

9134. Karpat, Kemal H. "Elites and the Transmission of Nationality and Identity." Central Asian Survey 5 (1986): 5-24.

9135. Kasbarian-Bricout, Beatrice. Les armeniens au XXe siecle. Paris: Editions l'Harmattan, 1984.

9136. Kasimovskii, E. "Social Justice and the Improvement of Distribution Relations in the USSR." Problems of Economics 30 (September 1987)

9137. Kassow, Samuel D. "Should Soviet Jews Leave?" Tikkun 5 (September-October 1990): 27-30, 99-101.

9138. Kassow, Samuel D. Students, Professors, and the State in Tsarist Russia. Berkeley: University of California Press, 1987.

9139. Kaszeta, Daniel J. "Lithuanian Resistance to Foreign Occupation, 1940-1952." Lituanus 34 (1988): 5-32.

9140. Katz, Alyssa. "Soviet Jews under Soviet Law: A Practical Guide." Loyola of Los Angeles International and Comparative Law Journal 9 (Summer 1987): 711-750.

9141. Kaufman, Deborah. "Moscow Diary." Tikkun 5 (July-August 1990): 19-21. [Jewish Film Festival in Moscow.]

9142. Kazesnzadeh, Firuz. The Struggle for Transcaucasia (1917- 1921). New York: 1951.

9143. Keller, Bill. "Allah and Gorbachev Mixing in Central Asia." New York Times, (February 12, 1988)

9144. Keller, Bill. "For a Soviet Military Editor, Battling Changes, Even Hitler Serves the Cause." New York Times, (January 7, 1991): [Major General Viktor I. Filatov.]

9145. Keller, Bill. "Riot's Legacy of Distrust Quietly Stalks a Soviet City." New York Times, (August 31, 1988): [Riot in February 1988 against Armenians in Azerbaijan city of Sumgait.]

9146. Keller, Bill. "Russia's Restless Youth." New York Times Magazine, (July 26, 1987)

9147. Kelman, Jacob M., ed. Anti-semitism in the Soviet Union. Its Roots and Consequences 2 vols. Jerusalem: The Centre for Research and Documentation of East-European Jewry, 1979-1980.

9148. Khoderkovsky, Michael. *Where Two Worlds Meet: The Russian State and the Kalmyk Nomads in the Seventeenth and Eighteenth Centuries*. Doctoral dissertation: University of Chicago, 1987.

9149. Khromov, S. S. "Social Development of the Working Class of the USSR between the Wars (1918-1939)." *East European Quarterly* 24 (June 1990): 185-199.

9150. Kingston-Mann, Esther and Timothy Mixter, eds. *Peasant Economy, Culture, and Politics of European Russia, 1800-1921*. Princeton, NJ: Princeton University Press, 1990.

9151. Kirimli, Hakan. "Soviet Educational and Cultural Policies Toward the Crimean Tatars in Exile (1944-1987)." *Central Asian Survey* 8 (1989): 69-88.

9152. Klier, John D. "1855-1894 Censorship of the Press in Russia and the Jewish Question." *Jewish Social Studies* 48 (Summer- Fall 1986): 257-268.

9153. Klier, John. *Russia Gathers Her Jews. The Origins of the "Jewish Question" in Russia, 1772-1825*. De Kalb: Northern Illinois University Press, 1986.

9154. Knothe, Tomasz. "The Strategy of the Informal Empire and 'New' Imperialism in Tsarist Russia's Policy Toward the Far East and Persia from the 1890s to 1914." *Hemisphere (Poland)* 2 (1986): 129-160.

9155. Kochan, Lionel, ed. *The Jews in Soviet Russia Since 1917*. 3d ed. New York: Oxford University Press, 1978.

9156. Kohut, Zenon E. *Russian Centralism and Ukrainian Autonomy. Imperial Absorption of the Hetmanae, 1760s-1830s*. Cambridge, MA: Harvard University Press, 1988.

9157. Kolarz, Walter. *Russia and Her Colonies*. London: 1952.

9158. Kolchin, Peter. *Unfree Labor: American Slavery and Russian Serfdom*. Cambridge, MA: Belknap Press of Harvard University Press, 1987.

9159. Korey, William. "Anti-Semitic Quotas in the Soviet Union." *Reform Judaism* (February 1978)

9160. Korey, William. "The Legal Position of Soviet Jewry: A Historical Inquiry." in *The Jews in Soviet Russia Since 1917* 3d ed., edited by Lionel Kochan. New York: Oxford University Press, 1978.

9161. Korey, William. "Legitimizing Antisemitism: The Role of the Soviet Academy of Sciences." *Israel Yearbook on Human Rights* 9 (1979)

9162. Korey, William. "The Origins and Development of Soviet Anti-Semitism: An Analysis." *Slavic Review* 31 (1972): 111- 135.

9163. Korey, William. The Soviet Cage. Anti-Semitism in Russia. New York: Viking, 1973.

9164. Korey, William. "Teaching Anti-Semitism in the Soviet Army: The Politburo's 'Protocols'." Hadassah Magazine (May 1981)

9165. Kosyk, Volodymyr. L'Allemagne national-socialiste et l'Ukraine. Paris: Publications de l'Est europeen, 1986.

9166. Kosyk, Volodymyr. "The Ukrainian National Resistance Movement, 1941-1944." Ukrainian Review 33 (1985): 17-30.

9167. Kowalewski, David A. "The Crimean Tartars: Ten Years of Rehabilitation." Ethnic Groups 2 (1980): 323-358.

9168. Kowalewski, David A. "The Structure of Soviet Jewish Protest 1965-1978." Europa Ethnica 41 (1984): 7-14.

9169. Kozlov, V. The Peoples of the Soviet Union. London: 1987.

9170. Krader, Lawrence. Peoples of Central Asia. 2d ed. Bloomington: Indiana University Publications, 1966.

9171. Krawchenko, Bohdan. Social Change and National Consciousness in Twentieth-Century Ukraine. London: Macmillan, 1985.

9172. Kreindler, Isabelle T. "The Mordvinians: A Doomed Soviet Nationality?" Cah. monde russe sovietique 26 (1985): 43-62.

9173. Kreindler, Isabelle T. "The Soviet Departed Nationalities: A Summary and an Update." Soviet Studies 38 (1986): 387- 405.

9174. Kritsman, L. N. "Class Stratification of the Soviet Countryside." Journal of Peasant Studies 11 (1984): 85-149.

9175. Krivickas, Vladas. "The Polish Minority in Lithuania, 1918- 1926." Slavonic and East European Review 53 (1975): 78-91.

9176. Kuoljok, Kerstin E. The Revolution in the North: Soviet Ethnography and Nationality Policy. Stockholm: 1985.

9177. Kurnosov, Y. A. "The Ukrainian Intelligentsia: The Process of Formation and Development." East European Quarterly 24 (June 1990): 201-218.

9178. Kutzik, Alfred J. "Anti-Semitism and Anti-Sovietism." Jewish Affairs 20 (March-April 1990): 4, 16-17, 23.

9179. Kuzio, Taras. "Nationalist Riots in Kazakhstan." Central Asian Survey 7 (1988): 79-100.

9180. Laber, Jeri. "Stalin's Dumping Ground." New York Review of Books, (October 11, 1990): [Kazakhstan.]

9181. Lambroza, Shlomo. The Pogrom Movement in Tsarist Russia, 1903-1906. Doctoral dissertation: Rutgers University, 1981. UMO # 8204224.

9182. Lambroza, Shlomo. "The Tsarist Government and the Pogroms of 1903-1906." Modern Judaism 7 (1987): 287-296.

9183. Lane, David S. "Ethnic and Class Stratification in Soviet Kazakhstan, 1917-1939." Comparative Studies in Society and History 17 (April 1975): 165-189.

9184. Lang, D. M. A Modern History of Soviet Georgia. New York: 1962.

9185. Lansky, Aaron. "Yiddish in the Soviet Union. A First Person Report by Aaron Lansky." The Book Peddlar No. 13 (Summer 1990): 6-57.

9186. Lapidus, Gail W. "The Soviet Nationality Question." In The Gorbachev Era, edited by Alexander Dallin and Condoleezza Rice. Stanford, CA: Stanford Alumni Association, 1986.

9187. Latsis, Otto. "Farewell to the Communist Party in Latvia." New Left Review No. 182 (July-August 1990): 152-160. [Translated by Cathy Porter from Izvestiya, April 18, 1990.]

9188. Latvia Writes: One Hundred Poems from the Ethnic Diversity of the Soviet Republic, Vol.I. West Menlo Park, CA: Echo Publishers, 1985.

9189. Law, Alfred D. Soviet Jewry and Soviet Policy. Boulder, CO: East European Monogrpahs, 1990.

9190. Lee, David C. The People's Universities in the USSR: A Description and Analysis of a Large-scale Nonformal Educational Program. Doctoral dissertation: University of Massachusetts, 1985. UMO # 8602657.

9191. Lenin, V. I. The Development of Capitalism in Russia. 2d rev. ed. Moscow: Progress Publishers, 1974.

9192. Leskov, Nikolai S. The Jews in Russia: Some Notes on the Jewish Question. Translated by Harold K. Schefski. Princeton, NJ: Kingston Press. [Written 1884.]

9193. Levenberg, S. "Jewish Culture Re-emerges in Baltic States." Soviet Jewish Affairs 20 (Spring 1990): 15-21.

9194. Leventer, Herbert. "Comments on Richard Hellie's 'Recent Russian Historiography on Medieval & Early Modern Russian Slavery'." Russian Review 36 (January 1977): 64-67. [See Hellie, above.]

9195. Levin, Dov. "Estonian Jews in the USSR, 1941-1945." Yad Vashem Studies 11 (1976): 273-297.

9196. Levin, Dov. "Estonia." In Encyclopedia of the Holocaust, II. 448-450. New York: Macmillan, 1990.

9197. Levin, Dov. "Lithuania." In Encyclopedia of the Holocaust. 895-899. New York: Macmillan, 1990.

9198. Levin, Dov. "On the Relations between the Baltic Peoples and Their Jewish Neighbors Before, During and After World War II." Holocaust and Genocide Studies 5 (1990): 53-66.

9199. Levin, Nora. The Jews in the Soviet Union. A History from 1917 to the Present. 2 vols. New York: New York University Press, 1988.

9200. Levine, Norman. "Lenin on Jewish Nationalism." Wiener Library Bulletin 33 (1980): 42-55.

9201. Levitats, Isaac. The Jewish Community in Russia, 1844-1917. Jerusalem: Posner & Sons, 1985.

9202. Lewytzkyj, Borys. Politics and Society in Soviet Ukraine, 1953-1980. Edmonton, Alberta: Canadian Institute of Ukrainian Studies, University of Alberta, 1984.

9203. Libardian, Gerard J., ed. The Karabagh File: Documents and Facts on the Question of Mountainous Karabagh, 1918-1988. Cambridge, MA: The Zoryan Institute, 1988.

9204. Liber, George O. The Urban Harvest: Ethnic Policy, Legitimation, and the Unintended Consequences of Social Change in the Ukrainian SSR, 1923-1933. Doctoral dissertation: Columbia University, 1986. UMO # 8610788.

9205. Liebowitz, Ronald D. The Spatial and Ethnic Dimensions of Soviet Regional Investment: 1956-1975. Doctoral dissertation: Columbia University, 1985. UMO # 8523195.

9206. Linz, Susan J., ed. The Impact of World War II on the Soviet Union. Totowa, NJ: 1985.

9207. Lipset, Harry. Jewish Schools in the Soviet Union, 1917- 1947: An Aspect of Soviet Minorities Policy. Doctoral dissertation: Columbia University, 1966.

9208. Littlejohn, Gary. "Agrarian Marxist Research in Its Political Context: State Policy and the Development of the Soviet Rural Class Structures in the 1920s." Journal of Peasant Studies 11 (1984): 61-84.

9209. Long, James W. From Privileged to Dispossessed. The Volga Germans, 1860-1917. Lincoln: University of Nebraska Press, 1989.

9210. Lossowski, P. "National Minorities in the Baltic States, 1919-1940." Acta Poloniae Historica 25 (1972)

9211. Lubachko, Ivan S. Byelorussia Under Soviet Rule, 1917-1957. Lexington: University of Kentucky Press, 1972.

9212. Lubin, Nancy. "Uzbekistan: The Challenge Ahead." Mid. East. Jr. 43 (Autumn 1989): 619-634.

9213. Lubin, Nancy. "Women in Soviet Central Asia. Progress and Contradictions." Soviet Studies 182-203 (April 1981)

9214. Luzhnytskyi, G. "The Russian Persecution of the Ukrainian Orthodox Church." Ukrainian Review 36 (1988): 47-58.

9215. Mace, James E. Communism and the Dilemmas of National Liberation: National Communism in Soviet Ukraine, 1918-1933. Cambridge, MA: Harvard Ukrainian Research Institute and the Ukrainian Academy of Arts and Sciences in the U.S., 1983.

9216. Magocsi, Paul R. The Shaping of a National Identity: Subcarpathian Rus', 1848-1948. Cambridge, MA: Harvard University Press, 1978.

9217. Mandel, David. "A Market without Thorns: The Ideological Struggle for the Soviet Working Class." Studies in Political Economy No.33 (Autumn 1990): 7-38.

9218. Mandel, David. "Soviet Workers and Gorbachev's Reforms." Against the Current 5 (September-December 1990)

9219. Mandel, David. "Why Soviet Workers Resist." Against the Current 5 (September/October 1990): 24-28.

9220. Manz, Beatrice F. "Central Asian Uprisings in the Nineteenth Century: Ferghana under the Russians." Russian Review 46 (1987): 267-281.

9221. Mars, Gerald and Yochanan Altman. "The Cultural Bases of Soviet Georgia's Second Economy." Soviet Studies 25 (October 1983)

9222. Massel, G. The Surrogate Proletariat: Moslem Women and Revolutionary Strategies in Soviet Central Asia 1919-1920. Princeton, NJ: Princeton University Press, 1974.

9223. Masters, Peter, ed. Remember the Prisoners. Chicago, Il: Moody Press, 1986. [Persecution of Baptists in USSR.]

9224. Matossian, Mary A. The Impact of Soviet Policies in Armenia. Leiden: Brill, 1962.

9225. Matthews, Mervyn. Patterns of Deprivation in the Soviet Union under Brezhnev and Gorbachev. Stanford, CA: Hoover Institution Press, 1989.

9226. Matthews, Mervyn. "Poverty in the Soviet Union." Wilson Quarterly 9 (1985): 75-84.

9227. Matthews, Mervyn. Poverty in the Soviet Union. New York: Cambridge University Press, 1986.

9228. Matthews, Mervyn. Privilege in the Soviet Union: A Study of Elite Life-Styles Under Communism. Boston, MA: Allen & Unwin, 1978.

9229. Matysiak, A. "The Decay of Economic Stalinsim." Eastern European Economics 28 (Spring 1990)

9230. McAuley, Alistair. "Economic Development and Political Nationalism in Uzbekistan." Central Asian Survey 5 (1986): 161-182.

9231. McAuley, Alistair. Women's Work and Wages in the USSR. London: 1981.

9232. McClelland, James C. "Proletarianizing the Student Body: The Soviet Experience during the New Economic Policy." Past and Present No. 80 (1978): 122-146. [1921-1928.]

9233. McDaniel, Tim. Autocracy, Capitalism and Revolution in Russia. Berkeley: University of California, 1988. [Radical labor movement.]

9234. Mehta, Vinod. Soviet Economy: Development of Azerbaijan. New Delhi: Sterling, 1984.

9235. Meissner, Boris. "The Change in the Social Structure of Estonia." Journal of Baltic Studies 18 (1987): 301-322.

9236. Mendelsohn, Ezra. Class Struggle in the Pale: The Formative Years of the Jewish Workers Movement in Tsarist Russia. London: Cambridge University Press, 1970.

9237. Meyer, Donald. Sex and Power: The Rise of Women in America, Russia, Sweden, and Italy. Middletown, Ct: Wesleyan University Press, 1987.

9238. Mezentseva, E. and N. Rinachevskaya. "The Soviet Country Profile: Health of the USSR Population in the 70s and 80s: An Approach to a Comprehensive Analysis." Social Science & Medicine 31 (1990)

9239. Mironov, B. N. "Literacy in Russia, 1797-1917." Sov. Stud. Hist. 25 (1986-1987): 89-117.

9240. Misiunas, Romuald J. and Rein Taagepera. The Baltic States, Years of Dependence, 1940-1980. Berkeley: University of California Press, 1984.

9241. Misiunas, Romuald J. and Rein Taagepera. "The Baltic States: Years of Dependence, 1980-1986." Journal of Baltic Studies 20 (1989): 65-88.

9242. Missman, David B. The Soviet Union and Iranian Azerbaijan: The Use of Nationalism for Political Penetration. Boulder, CO: 1987.

9243. Molyneux, Maxine. "The 'Woman Question' in the Age of Perestroika." New Left Review No. 183 (September-October 1990): 23-49. [The USSR and Eastern Europe.]

9244. Morris, L. P. "The Subjugation of the Turcomans." Middle Eastern Studies 15 (May 1979): 193-210.

9245. Morton, Henry W. "The Housing Game." Wilson Quarterly 9 (1985): 61-74.

9246. Morton, Henry W. "Housing in a Collectivist Economy: The USSR." In Housing and Neighborhoods, edited by Wilhem van Vliet and others. Westport, CT: Greenwood, 1987.

9247. Moses, Joel C. The Politics of Women and Work in the Soviet Union and the United States: Alternative Work Schedules and Sex Discrimination. Berkeley: Institute of International Studies, University of California, Berkeley, 1982.

9248. Moskoff, William. "Soviet Higher Education Policy During World War II." Soviet Studies 38 (1986): 406-415.

9249. Motyl, Alexander J. Will the Non-Russians Rebel? State, Ethnicity, and Stability in the USSR. Ithaca, New York: Cornell University Press, 1987. [Esp. Ukrainian SSR.]

9250. Motzkin, L., ed. Die Judenpogrome in Russland. 2 vols. Cologne: 1910.

9251. Mouradian, Claire S. L'Armenie sovietique depuis le mort de Staline. Doctoral dissertation: Ecole des Hautes Etudes en Sciences Sociales, 1982.

9252. Mouradian, Claire S. De Staline a Gorbatchev: histoire d'une republique sovietique, l'Armenie. Paris: Ramsay, 1990.

9253. Mukhachev, Yuri. Classes and the Class Struggle in the USSR, 1920s-1930s. Translated by Galina Glagoleva and Alery Podkolzin. Moscow: Progress.

9254. Mulligan, Timothy P. The Politics of Illusion and Empire. German Occupation Policy in the Soviet Union, 1942-1943. Westport, CT: Greenwood, 1988.

9255. Mykula, Volodymyr. "Soviet Nationality Policy in Ukraine, 1920-1930." Ukrainian Review 18 (1971): 2-23.

9256. Nahaylo, Bohdan and Victor Swoboda. Soviet Disunion. A History of the Nationalities Problem in the USSR. New York: Free Press, 1990.

9257. Nahaylo, Bohdan and C.J. Peters. The Ukrainians and Georgians. London: Minority Rights Group, 1981.

9258. Navrozov, Lev. "Solzhenitsyn-Stalin's Victim. A Study in Totalitarianism." Midstream 32 (January 1986): 21-31. [Antisemitism in the USSR.]

9259. Nazarov, Kh KH. "Contemporary Ethnic Development of the Central Asian Gypsies (Liuli)." Soviet Anthropology and Archeology 21 (1982-1983): 3-28.

9260. Newland, Samuel J. Cossacks in the German Army, 1941-1945. Savage, MD: Frank Cass, 1989.

9261. Nolan, J. P. "An Army Without a State: The Ukrainian Army (UPA) and the National Resistance During and After the Second World War." Ukrainian Review 35 (1987): 16-24, 41-50.

9262. Nove, Alec. "The Class Nature of the Soviet Union Revisited." Soviet Studies 35 (1983): 298-312.

9263. Nove, Alec and J.A. Newth. The Soviet Middle East- A Model for Development. London: George Allen & Unwin, 1967.

9264. Ofer, Gur. "Soviet Economic Growth: 1928-1985." Journal of Economic Literature 25 (December 1987): 1767-1833.

9265. Okenfuss, Max J. "From School Class to Social Caste. The Divisiveness of Early-Modern Russian Education." Jb. Gesch. Osteur. 33 (1985): 321-344.

9266. Okladnikov, A. P. Yakutia: Before Its Incorporation Into the Russian State. McGill-Queen's University Press: 1970.

9267. Olcott, Martha B. "The Emergence of National Identity in Kazakhstan." Canadian Review of Studies of Nationalism 8 (Fall 1981): 285-300.

9268. Olcott, Martha B. The Kazakhs. Stanford, CA: Hoover Institution Press, 1987.

9269. Olcott, Martha B. and William Fierman. "The Challenge of Integration: Soviet Nationality Policy and the Muslim Conscript." Soviet Union 14 (1987): 65-101.

9270. Oleszczuk, Thomas A. Political Justice in the USSR: Dissent and Repression in Lithuania, 1969-1987. New York: East European Monographs, 1988.

9271. Oliner, Samuel P. "Union of Soviet Socialist Republics." In International Handbook on Race and Race Relations, edited by Jay A. Sigler. Westport, CT: Greenwood, 1987.

9272. "An Open Letter on Anti-Armenian Pogroms in the Soviet Union." New York Review of Books, (September 27, 1990)

9273. Orbach, W. "The Destruction of the Jews in the Nazi- Occupied Territories of the USSR." Soviet Jewish Affairs No. 2 (1976): 14-51.

9274. Ostrowski, Wiktor, ed. Anti-semitism in Byelorussia and Its Origin. London: Byelorussian Central Council, 1960.

9275. Padmore, George. How Russia Transformed her Colonial Empire. London: Dennis Dobson, 1946.

9276. Paksoy, H. B. ALPAMYSH: Central Asian Identity under Russian Rule. Hartford, CT: AACAR, 1989. [Association for the Advancement of Central Asian Research.]

9277. Parsons, J. W. R. The Emergence and Development of the National Question in Georgia, 1801-1921. Doctoral dissertation: University of Glasgow, 1987.

9278. Peled, Yoav. Class and Ethnicity in the Pale. The Political Economy of Jewish Workers' Nationalism in Late Imperial Russia. New York: St. Martin's Press, 1989.

9279. Peled, Yoav and Gershon Shafir. "From Caste to Exclusion: The Dynamics of Modernization in the Russian Pale of Settlement." Stud. Contemp. Jewry 3 (1987): 98-114.

9280. Perfecky, George A. "The Status of the Ukrainian Language in the Ukrainian SSR." E. Eur. Quarterly 21 (1987): 207- 230.

9281. Pierce, Richard A. Russian Central Asia, 1867-1917. Berkeley: University of California Press, 1957.

9282. Pignon, Dominique, ed. "La discrimination contre les Juifs a l'entree de l'Universite Moscou, 1979." Les Temps Modernes 406 (1980)

9283. Pinkus, Benjamin. The Soviet Government and the Jews, 1948- 1967. New York: Cambridge University Press, 1988.

9284. Pinkus, Benjamin. "Soviet Campaigns Against Jewish Nationalism and 'Cosmopolitism', 1946-1953." Soviet Jewish Affairs 4 (1974): 53-72.

9285. Porket, J. L. "Social Deprivation under Soviet Full Employment." In The Soviet Union: Party and Society, edited by Peter J. Potichuyj. New York: Cambridge University Press, 1988.

9286. Pospielovsky, Dmitry V. Soviet Antireligious Campaign and Persecutions. New York: St. Martin's Press, 1988.

9287. Possony, Stefan S. "The Ukrainian-Jewish Problem: A Historical Retrospect." Ukrainian Quarterly 31 (1975): 139- 151.

9288. Poujol, Catherine. "Les juifs de Buhara: ou la permanence d'une communaute." Cahiers du Monde Russe et Sovietique 27 (1986): 111-123.

9289. Praisman, Leonid. "Pogroms and Jewish Self-defence." Soviet Jewry 1 (1986): 64-81.

9290. Pritsak, Omeljan. "The Pogroms of 1881." Harvard Ukrainian Studies 11 (1987): 8-43.

9291. Pritsak, Omeljan. "Prolegomena to the National Awakening of the Ukranians during the Nineteenth Century." In Culture and Nationalism in Nineteenth-Century Eastern Europe, edited by Roland Sussex and J.C. Eade. Columbus, Ohio: Slavica, 1984.

9292. Procyk, Oksana and others. Famine in the Soviet Ukraine 1932-1933. Cambridge, MA: Harvard University Press, 1986.

9293. Rakowska-Harmstone, Teresa. Russia and Nationalism in Central Asia. The Case of Tadzhikistan. Baltimore, MD: Johns Hopkins University Press, 1970.

9294. Rapoport, Louis. Stalin's War Against the Jews: The Doctors' Plot and the Soviet Solution. New York: Free Press, 1990.

9295. Rapoport, Yakov L. The Doctors' Plot of 1953. Cambridge, MA: Harvard University Press, 1991.

9296. Raun, Toivo U. Estonia and the Estonians. Stanford, CA: Hoover Institution Press, 1987.

9297. Raun, Toivo U. "The Latvian and Estonian National Movements, 1860-1914." Slavonic E. Eur. R. 64 (1986): 6-80.

9298. Redlich, Shimon. "Metropolitan Andrei Sheptyts'kyi, Ukrainians and Jews During and After the Holocaust." Holocaust and Genocide Studies 5 (1990): 39-51.

9299. Redlich, Shimon. Propaganda and Nationalism in Wartime Russia: The Jewish Anti-Fascist Committee in the USSR, 1941- 1948. New York: Columbia University Press, 1982.

9300. Resnick, Sid. "Birobidjan, Soviet Jews and Anti-Semitism." Jewish Currents 33 (July-August 1979): 5-11.

9301. Rhinelander, Laurens H., Jr. The Incorporation of the Caucasus into the Russian Empire: The Case of Georgia, 1801- 1854. Doctoral dissertation: Columbia University, 1972.

9302. Ro'i, Yaacov. "The Historical Link between Soviet Domestic Developments and Jewish Emigration." Jerusalem Quarterly 53 (Winter 1990): 137-144.

9303. Ro'i, Yaacov and Avi Beker, eds. Jewish Currents and Identity in the Soviet Union. New York: New York University Press, 1990.

9304. Ro'i, Yaacov. "The Islamic Influence on Nationalism in Soviet Central Asia." Problems of Communism 39 (July-August 1990)

9305. Robeson, Paul Jr. "How My Father Last Met Itzik Feffer." Jewish Currents 35 (November 1981): 4-8.

9306. Rockett, Rocky L. Ethnic Nationalities in the Soviet Union: Sociological Perspectives on a Historical Problem. New York: Praeger, 1981.

9307. Rogers, James A. "Racism and Russian Revolutionists." Race 14 (January 1973): 279-289.

9308. Rogger, Hans. Jewish Policies and Right-Wing Politics in Imperial Russia. Berkeley: University of California Press, 1986.

9309. Rorlich, Azade-Ayse. The Volga Tatars: A Profile in National Resilience. Stanford, CA: Hoover Institution Press, 1986.

9310. Rosefielde, Steven. "An Assessment of the Sources and Uses of Gulag Forced Labor 1929-1956." Soviet Studies 33 (January 1981): 51-87.

9311. Rosefielde, Steven. "Incriminating Evidence: Excess Deaths and Forced Labour under Stalin: A Final Reply to Critics." Soviet Studies 39 (1987): 292-313. [1929-1953.]

9312. Rosenthal-Shneiderman, Esther. Birobidghan fun der Noent. Tel Aviv, Israel: H. Leivik, 1983. [Close-up on Birobidzhan.]

9313. Rost, Yuri. Armenian Tragedy. An Eye-Witness Account of Human Conflict and Natural Disaster in Armenia and Azerbaijan. New York Translated by ELizabeth Roberts: St. Martin's Press, 1990. [Nagorny Karabakh.]

9314. Rudden, Bernard. "A New Law for Birobidzhan." Soviet Jewish Affairs 13 (February 1983): 51-55.

9315. Rudnytsky, Ivan L. "Carpatho-Ukraine: A People in Search of their Identity." E. Eur. Q. 19 (1985): 139-159.

9316. Rumer, Boris Z. Soviet Central Asia: "A Tragic Experiment". Boston, MA: Unwin Hyman, 1989.

9317. Rummel, Rudolph J. Lethal Politics: Soviet Genocides and Mass Murders Since 1917. New Brunswick, NJ: Transaction, 1990.

9318. Rywkin, Michael. "Cadre Competition in Uzbekistan: The Ethnic Aspect." Central Asian Survey 5 (1986): 183-194.

9319. Rywkin, Michael. Moscow's Muslim Challenge. Soviet Central Asia. rev. ed. Armonk, New York: Sharpe, 1990.

9320. Rywkin, Michael, ed. Russian Colonial Expansion. London: Institute of Muslim Minority Affairs, 1985.

9321. Rywkin, Michael, ed. Russian Colonial Expansion to 1917. New York: Mansell, 1988.

9322. Sabalinas, L. Lithuania in Crisis: Nationalism to Communism, 1939-1940. Bloomington: Indiana University Press, 1972.

9323. Sakalys, Jurate A. "Higher Education in Lithuania: An Historical Analysis." Lituanus 31 (1985): 5-22.

9324. Salitan, Laurie P. "Domestic Pressures and the Politics of Exit: Trends in Soviet Emigration." Political Science Quarterly (Winter 1989-1990): 671-687.

9325. Sarkisyanz, Manuel. A Modern History of Transcaucasian Armenia: Social, Cultural and Polticial. Leiden: E. J. Brill, 1975.

9326. Saroyan, M. "The Karabakh Syndrome and Azerbaijani Politics." Problems of Communism 39 (September-October 1990)

9327. Scharff, Roland. "Jugendsoziologische Forschung." Osteuropa 36 (1986): 417-432.

9328. Schechtman, Joseph B. Star in Eclipse: Russian Jewry Revisited. New York: 1961.

9329. Schulte, Theo. The German Army and Nazi Policies in Occupied Russia. Oxford: Berg, 1989.

9330. Schwartz, Solomon. "Birobidzhan: An Experiment in Jewish Colonization." In Russian Jewry, edited by Gregory Aronson and others. 342-395. New York: Thomas Yoseloff, 1969.

9331. Shanin, Teodor. "Ethnicity in the Soviet Union: Analytical Perceptions and Political Strategy." Comparative Studies in Society and History 31 (July 1989): 409-424.

9332. Shanin, Teodor. The Roots of Otherness: Russia's Turn of Century. 2 vols. London: Macmillan, 1986.

9333. Shanin, Teodor. "Soviet Theories of Ethnicity: The Case of a Missing Term." New Left Review No. 158 (July-August 1986): 113-122.

9334. Sharma, R. R. A Marxist Model of Social Change: Soviet Central Asia: 1917-1940. Atlantic Highlands, NJ: Humanities Press, 1980.

9335. Sheehy, Ann. "The Case of the Crimean Tatars." East Europe 20 (1971): 23-32.

9336. Sheehy, Ann. "Recent Events in Abkhazia Mirror the Compexities of National Relations in the USSR." Radio Liberty Research RL 141 (June 26, 1978)

9337. Sheehy, Ann and Bohdan Nahaylo. The Crimean Tatars, Volga Germans and Meskhetians: Soviet Treatment of Some National Minorities. 2d rev. ed. London: Minority Rights Group, 1980.

9338. Shlapentokh, Vladimir E. The Politics of Sociology in the Soviet Union. Boulder, CO: Westview Press, 1987.

9339. Shmelev, N. and V. Popov. The Turning Point, Revitalizing the Soviet Economy. New York: Doubleday, 1989.

9340. Shochat, Azriel. "The Beginnings of Anti-Semitism in Independent Lithuania." Yad Vashem Studies on the European Catastrophe and Resistance 2 (1958): 7-48.

9341. Shoykhet, Roman. "Birobidzhan: Behind the Facade." Soviet Jewish Affairs 18 (Spring 1988): 71-75.

9342. Shtromas, Alexander. "Soviet Occupation of the Baltic States and Their Incorporation into the USSR: Political and Legal Aspects (2 parts)." E. Eur. Quarterly 19 (1985): 289- 304, 459-467.

9343. Shtromas, Alexander and Morton A. Kaplan, eds. The Soviet Union and the Challenge of the Future. 4 vols. Paragon House, 1990.

9344. Sidorova, M. "Reducing Difference in the Living Standards of the Urban and Rural Population." Problems of Economics 28 (September 1985)

9345. Slezkine, Yuri. Russia's Small Peoples: The Policies and Attitudes Towards the Native Northerners, 17th Century-1938. Doctoral dissertation: University of Texas, 1989. UMO # 8920842.

9346. Slider, Darrell. "Crisis and Response in Soviet Nationality Policy: The Case of Abkhazia." Central Asian Survey 4 (1985): 51-68.

9347. Slider, Darrell. "A Note on the Class Structure of Soviet Nationalities." Soviet Studies 37 (1985): 535-540.

9348. Smith, Graham E. "Administering Ethnoregional Stability: The Soviet State and the Nationalities Question." In *Community Conflict, Partition and Nationalism*, edited by Colin H. Williams and Eleonore Kofman. New York: Routledge, 1989.

9349. Smith, Graham E. "Ethnic Nationalism in the Soviet Union: Territory, Cleavage, and Control." *Environment and Planning C* 3 (1985)

9350. Snitow, Alan. "Soviet Prospects, Jewish Fears." *Tikkun* 5 (July-August 1990): 15-18, 80-84.

9351. Solchanyk, Roman and Ann Sheehy. "Kapitanov on Nationality Relations in Georgia." *Radio Liberty Research* RL 125/178 (June 1, 1978)

9352. Solomon, Susan G. and John F. Hutchinson, eds. *Health and Society in Revolutionary Russia*. Bloomington: Indiana University Press, 1990.

9353. Sorokowsky, Andrew. "National Discrimination in Ukraine." *Ukrainian Quarterly* 41 (1985): 184-195.

9354. "Soviet Paper Offers Glimpse of Prejudice Encountered by Blacks." *Boston Globe*, (August 20, 1989)

9355. Spector, Shmuel. "Ukraine." In *Encyclopedia of the Holocaust, IV*. 1525-1530. New York: Macmillan, 1990.

9356. Spier, Howard. "Russian Chauvinists and the Thesis of a Jewish World Conspiracy: Three Case Studies." *Research Report (Institute of Jewish Affairs)* No.6 (August 1987)

9357. Spier, Howard. "Soviet Antisemitism Unchained: The Rise of the 'Historical and Patriotic Association 'Pamyat'.'" *Research Report (Institute of Jewish Affairs)* No. 3 (July 1987)

9358. Stanislawski, Michael. *For Whom Do I Toil? Judah Leib Gordon and the Crisis of Russian Jewry*. New York: Oxford University Press, 1988.

9359. Stanislawski, Michael. *Tsar Nicholas I and the Jews: The Transformation of Jewish Society in Russia, 1825-1855*. Philadelphia, Pa: Jewish Publication Society, 1983.

9360. Stetski, Slava. "National Persecution in the USSR." *Ukrainian Review* (1976): 31-55.

9361. Stillman, Gerald. "The Yiddish Culture that Was Destroyed." *Jewish Currents* 35 (June 1981): 4-8. [In the context of events of 1930s and 1940s.]

9362. Stites, Richard. *The Women's Liberation Movement in Russia. Feminism, Nihilism, and Bolshevism, 1860-1930*. Princeton, NJ: Princeton University Press, 1991.

U.S.S.R. **719**

9363. Stites, Richard. "Women's Liberation Movements in Russia, 1900-1930." Canadian-American Slavic Studies 7 (1973): 460- 474.

9364. Stovall, Don Owen. The Role of the Soviet Army as an Instrument of National Integration. 2 vols. Doctoral dissertation: Georgetown University, 1988. UMO # 8923224.

9365. Strokata, Nina. "The Ukrainian National Front: A Look at Its Activity, 1962-1967." Ukrainian Review 34 (1986): 21- 29.

9366. Suh, Dae-Sook, ed. Koreans in the Soviet Union. Honolulu: University of Hawaii Press, 1987.

9367. Suny, Ronald G. The Baku Commune, 1917-1918: Political Strategy in a Social Revolution. Doctoral dissertation: Columbia University, 1968.

9368. Suny, Ronald G. The Baku Commune, 1917-1918: Class and Nationality in the Russian Revolution. Princeton, NJ: Princeton University Press, 1972.

9369. Suny, Ronald G. "The Emergence of Political Society in Georgia." In Transcaucasia, Nationalism and Social Changes, edited by Ronald G. Suny. Ann Arbor: University of Michigan Press, 1983.

9370. Suny, Ronald G. The Making of the Georgian Nation. Bloomington: Indiana University Press, 1988.

9371. Suny, Ronald G. "Return to Ararat: Armenia in the Cold War." Armenian Review 42 (Autumn 1989): 1-19.

9372. Suny, Ronald G. "The Revenge of the Past: Socialism and Ethnic Conflict in Transcaucasia." New Left Review No. 184 (November-December 1990): 5-34.

9373. Suny, Ronald G., ed. Transcaucasia: Nationalism and Social Change: Essays in the History of Armenia, Azerbazian, and Georgia. Ann Arbor: Michigan Slavic Publications, University of Michigan, 1983.

9374. Suny, Ronald G. "What Happened in Soviet Armenia?" Middle East Report No. 153 (July-August 1988): 37-40.

9375. Swietochowski, Tadeusz. Russian Azerbaijan, 1905-1920: The Shaping of National Identity in a Muslim Community. New York: Cambridge University Press, 1985.

9376. Sword, Keith, ed. The Soviet Takeover of the Polish Eastern Provinces, 1939-1941. New York: St. Martin's Press, 1991.

9377. Szajkowski, Zosa. An Illustrated Sourcebook of Russian Antisemitism, 1881-1978. Vol. I. New York: Ktav Publishing House, 1979.

9378. Taheri, Amir. Crescent in a Red Sky. The Future of Islam in the Soviet Union. London: Hutchinson, 1989.

9379. Taubman, Philip. "Chopped Liver and Yiddish, but Where's the Soul?" New York Times, (September 23, 1987): [Birobidzhan, the Jewish Autonomous Region.]

9380. Teczarowska, Danuta. Deportation into the Unknown. Brauton, Devon, England: Merlin Books, 1987. [Autobiographical novel about Polish author's deportation to USSR during World War II.]

9381. Thaden, Edward C., ed. Russification in the Baltic Provinces and Finland, 1855-1914. Princeton, NJ: Princeton University Press, 1980.

9382. Thurston, Robert. "Developing Education in Late Imperial Russia: The Concerns of State, 'Society,' and People in Moscow, 1906-1914." Russian Hist./Hist. Russe 11 (1984): 53-82.

9383. Tillett, Lowell. The Great Friendship: Soviet Historians on the Non-Russian Nationalities. Chapel Hill: University of North Carolina Press, 1969.

9384. Tottle, Douglas. Fraud, Famine and Fascism: The Ukrainian Genocide Myth from Hitler to Harvard. Toronto: Progress, 1987.

9385. Toumanoff, Cyril. Studies in Christian Caucasian History. Washington, D.C.: 1963.

9386. Trapans, Janis A. The Emergence of a Modern Latvian Nation: 1764-1914. Doctoral dissertation: University of California, Berkeley, 1979. UMO # 800548.

9387. Trehub, Aaron. "Social and Economic Rights in the Soviet Union." Survey 29 (August 1987): 6-42.

9388. Tsipko, A. "The Sources of Stalinism." Soviet Law and Government 29 (Autumn 1990)

9389. Tuzmukhamedov, R. How the National Question Was Solved in Soviet Central Asia. Moscow: Progress Publishers, 1973.

9390. Ul'masov, A. and M. Sharifkhodzhaev. "Formation and Development of the Socialist Economy in the Central Asian Republics." Problems of Economics 28 (October 1985)

9391. Urban, G. R. and others. "Social and Economic Rights in the Soviet Bloc." Survey 29 (August 1987): 1-244. [Symposium.]

9392. "USSR." In World Directory of Minorities Minority Rights Group. 141-175. Harlow: Longman, 1990.

9393. Vali, A. Revolutionary Movements in Azerbaijan. Master's thesis: University of Keele, 1976.

9394. Vernadsky, G. "Serfdom in Russia." X Congresso Internazionale di Scienze Storiche, Relazioni III (Florence, 1955): 247-272. [Slavery in Russia.]

9395. Vihavainen, Timo. "The Status of the East-Karelian Ethnical Group during the Soviet Rule." Europa Ethnica 41 (1984): 129-134.

9396. Vijnar, Bohdan. "The Establishment of Soviet Economic Colonialism in Ukraine." Ukrainian Quarterly 13 (1957): 23- 35.

9397. Vishniak, Mark. "Anti-Semitism in Tsarist Russia." In Essays on Anti-Semitism, edited by Koppel Pinson. New York: 1946.

9398. Vizulis, I. Joseph. Nations under Duress: The Baltic States. Port Washington, New York: Associated Faculty Press, 1985. [1941-1944.]

9399. von Rauch, George. The Baltic States: Estonia Latvia, Lithuania. The Years of Independence, 1917-1940. Berkeley: University of California Press, 1974.

9400. Voslensky, Michael. Nomenklatura: The Soviet Ruling Class. Garden City, New York Translated by Eric Mosbacher: Doubleday, 1984.

9401. Walker, Christopher J. Armenia. The Survival of a Nation. new ed. London: Routledge, 1990.

9402. Walker, Franklin A. "Patriotic Rhetoric, Public Education, and Language Choice in the Russia of Tsar Alexander I (1801- 1825)." Canadian Review of Studies of Nationalism 12 (Fall 1985): 261-271.

9403. Wang, Yu-Ling. "Jewish Autonomous Region of Birobidjan." Plural Societies 19 (1989): 73-91.

9404. Weinberg, Robert. "Workers, Pogroms, and the 1905 Revolution in Odessa." Russian Review 46 (1987): 53-75.

9405. Weiner, Richard E. "70 Languages Equal and Free? the Legal Status of Minority Languages in the Soviet Union." Arizona Journal of International and Comparative Law 6 (Spring 1989): 73-87.

9406. Weinryb, Bernard D. "A Note on Anti-Semitism in Soviet Russia." Slavic Review 25 (1966)

9407. Wheeler, Geoffrey E. Racial Problems in Soviet Muslim Asia. London: Oxford University Press, 1960.

9408. Willis, David K. Klass: Status and Privilege in the Soviet State. New York: Empire Books, 1982.

9409. Wimbush, S. Enders. "Soviet Muslims in the 1980s." Institute of Muslim Minority Affairs Journal 6 (1985)

9410. Wimbush, S. Enders and Alex Alexiev. The Ethnic Factor in the Soviet Armed Forces. Santa Monica, CA: Rand Corp., 1982.

9411. Winawer, H. M. The Jewish Question in the District of Wilno in 1880-1914. B. Phil. dissertation: Oxford University, 1948.

9412. Wishnevsky, Julia. "The Origins of Pamyat." Survey 30 (1988): 79-91.

9413. Witts, Noel. "Iron Curtain Calls." Times Higher Education Supplement (August 29, 1986): [People's theater in Estonia.]

9414. Wixman, Ronald. "Ethno-Linguistic Data in Soviet Censuses: Some Problems and Methodologies." Canadian-American Slavic Studies 17 (1983): 545-558.

9415. Wolf, Lucien, ed. The Legal Sufferings of the Jews in Russia,. A Survey of the Present Situation and An Appendix of Laws. London: Fisher-Unwin, 1912.

9416. Woll, Josephine. "Russia and 'Russiaphobes': Antisemitism on the Russian Literary Scene." Soviet Jewish Affairs 19 (Winter 1989): 3-21.

9417. Wood, Alan and R.A. French, eds. The Development of Siberia: People and Resources. New York: St. Martin's Press, 1989.

9418. Worobec, Christine D. Peasant Russia. Family and Community in the Post-emancipation Period. Princeton, NJ: Princeton University Press, 1991.

9419. Wynn, Charters S. Russian Labor in Revolution and Reaction: The Donbass Working Class, 1870-1905. Doctoral dissertation: Stanford University, 1987. UMO # 8801061.

9420. Yanowitch, Murray, ed. The Social Structure of the USSR: Recent Soviet Studies. Armonk, New York: M.E. Sharpe, 1986.

9421. Yaroshevski, Dov B. "Russian Regionalism in Turkestan." Slavonic and East Euorpean Review 65 (1987): 77-100.

9422. Zaionchkovoskii, P. A. The Abolition of Serfdom in Russia, 1855-1861. Gulf Breeze, FL: 1978.

9423. Zakharova, Larisa G. "Autocracy and the Abolition of Serfdom in Russia, 1856-1861." Sov. Stud. Hist. 26 (1987): 12-115.

9424. Zakharova, Larisa G. and others, eds. The Great Reforms in Russia. Bloomington: Indiana University Press, 1991. [Emancipation of the serfs.]

9425. Zamascikov, Sergei. "Soviet Methods and Instrumentalities of Maintaining Control over the Balts." Journal of Baltic Studies 18 (1987): 221-234.

9426. Zaslavsky, Victor. "Ethnic Groups Divided: Social Stratification and Nationality Policy in the Soviet Union." In The Soviet Union: Party and Society, edited by Peter J. Potichnyi. New York: Cambridge University Press, 1988.

9427. Zaslavsky, Viktor. The Neo-Stalinist State: Class, Ethicity, and Consensus in Soviet Society. Armonk, New York: Sharpe, 1982.

9428. Zelnick, Reginald E., ed. A Radical Worker in Tsarist Russia: The Autobiography of Semen Ivanovich Kanatchikov. Stanford, CA: Stanford University Press, 1986.

9429. Zenushkina, I. Soviet Nationalities Policy and Bourgeois Historians. The Formation of the Soviet Multinational State (1917-1922) in Contemporary American Historiography. Moscow Translated by Keith Hammond: Progress Publishers, 1976. [Soviet Central Asia.]

9430. Zevelev, A. How the National Question Was Solved in the USSR. Moscow: Novisto Press Agency Publishing House, 1977.

USA

9431. Acuna, Rodolfo. *Occupied America: A History of Chicanos*. 3d ed. New York: Harper & Row, 1988.

9432. Alexander, Charles C. *The Ku Klux Klan in the Southwest*. Lexington: University of Kentucky Press, 1965.

9433. Allen, Charles R. *Nazi War Criminals in America: Facts- Action: The Basic Handbook*. New York: Highgate House, 1985. [180 Cabrini Blvd., New York, NY 10033.]

9434. Almaguer, Tomas. "Historical Notes on Chicano Oppression: The Dialectics of Racial and Class Domination in North America." *Aztlan* 5 (Spring and Fall 1972): 27-56.

9435. Anderson, James D. *The Education of Blacks in the South, 1860-1935*. Chapel Hill: University of North Carolina Press, 1988.

9436. Anti-Defamation League, Civil Rights Division. *The Campaign Against the U. S. Justice Department's Prosecution of Suspected Nazi War Criminals*. New York: Anti-Defamation League, June 1985.

9437. *Anti-Semitism in America, 1878-1939*. New York: Arno, 1977.

9438. Appel, John and Selma Appel. "Anti-Semitism in American Caricature." *Society* 24 (Nov.-Dec. 1986): 78-83.

9439. Aptheker, Herbert, ed. *The Complete Published Works of W.E.B. DuBois*. 37 vols. White Plains, New York: Kraus International Publications, 1986.

9440. Aptheker, Herbert. "The History of Anti-Racism in the United States." *Black Scholar* 6 (January-February 1975): 16-22.

9441. Aptheker, Herbert. "Racism, Anti-Semitism and Affirmative Action." Jewish Affairs 8 (January- February 1978): 6-9.

9442. Aptheker, Herbert. "U.S. Imperialism and Racism: A History." Political Affairs 52 (July 1973): 75-85.

9443. Ashe, Arthur Jr. and others. A Hard Road to Glory. 3 vols. New York: Warner, 1988. [History of black athletes in the U.S.]

9444. Athans, Mary C. "A New Perspective on Father Charles E. Coughlin." Church History 56 (June 1987): 224-235.

9445. Averkieva, I. Pablovna. Slavery Among the Indians of North America. Victoria, B.C. Translated by G.R. Elliott: 1966.

9446. Bailey, L. R. Indian Slave Trade in the Southwest. Los Angeles: Western Lore Press, 1966.

9447. Baker, David B. Race, Racism, and the Death Penalty in the United States: An Historical, Theoretical, and Empirical Analysis. Doctoral dissertation: University of California, Riverside, 1987. UMO # 8808633.

9448. Ballard, A. B. The Education of Black Folk. New York: Harper & Row, 1973.

9449. Banton, Michael. "What Do We Mean by Racism?" New Society (April 10, 1969)

9450. Baron, Harold M., ed. The Racial Aspects of Urban Planning. Chicago, IL: Chicago Urban League, 1968.

9451. Barrera, Mario. Race and Class in the Southwest: A Theory of Racial Inequality. Notre Dame, IN: University of Notre Dame Press, 1979.

9452. Bayer, Ronald and others, eds. In Search of Equity: Health Needs and the Health Care System. New York: Plenum, 1983.

9453. Bell, Derrick A., Jr. "Preferential Affirmative Action." Harvard Civil Rights-Civil Liberties Law Review 16 (Winter 1982): 855-873.

9454. Bell, Derrick A., Jr. Race, Racism, and American Law. Boston, MA: Little Brown.

9455. Berghahn, Volker R. and Hanna Schessler, eds. Perceptions of History: International Textbook Research on Britain, Germany, and the United States. New York: Berg, 1987.

9456. Berlin, Ira. Slaves Without Masters. The Free Negro in the Antebellum South. New York: Pantheon, 1974.

9457. Berlin, Ira and Ronald Hoffman, eds. Slavery and Freedom in the Age of the American Revolution. Charlottesville: University Press of Virginia, 1983.

9458. Berlowitz, Marvin J. "Multicultural Education: Fallacies and Alternatives." In Racism and the Denial of Human Rights: Beyond Ethnicity, edited by Berlowitz and Ronald S. Edari. Minneapolis, MN: MEP Publications, 1984.

9459. Berman, Aaron. Nazism, the Jews and American Zionism: 1933- 1948. Detroit, MI: Wayne State University Press, 1990.

9460. Berman, Myron. The Attitude of American Jewry towards East European Jewish Immigration, 1881-1914. New York: Arno Press, 1980.

9461. Berman, Sanford. "Racism and Library Science." Library Journal (February 1969)

9462. Berrol, Selma C. "Julia Richman and the German Jewish Establishment: Passion, Arrogance, and the Americanization of the Ostjuden." American Jewish Archives 38 (November 1986): 137-177.

9463. Black, Isabella. "Race and Unreason: Anti-Negro Opinion in Professional and Scientific Literature Since 1954." Phylon (Spring 1965)

9464. Blassingame, John W. The Slave Community: Plantation Life in the Antebellum South. 2d ed. New York: Oxford University Press, 1979.

9465. Blum, Howard. Wanted! The Search for Nazis in America. New York: Simon & Schuster, 1989.

9466. Bond, Horace Mann. "Intelligence Tests and Propaganda." Crisis 28 (June 1924): 61-64.

9467. Bond, Horace Mann. "What the Army 'Intelligence Tests' Measure." Opportunity (July 1924)

9468. Boorstein, Edward and Regula. Counterrevolution: The Worldwide U.S. Campaign. New York: International Publishers, 1990.

9469. Boskin, Joseph. Into Slavery: Racial Decisions in the Virginia Colony. Philadelphia: 1976.

9470. Boskin, Joseph. Sambo: The Rise and Decline of an American Jester. New York: Oxford University Press, 1986.

9471. Boston, Thomas B. Race, Class and Conservatism. Winchester, MA: Unwin Hyman, 1988.

9472. Bracey, John and others, eds. Black Nationalism in America. Indianapolis, IN: Bobbs-Merrill, 1970.

9473. Braddock, J. H. and J.M. McPartland. "How Minorities Continue to Be Excluded from Equal Employment Opportunities: Research on Labor Market and Institutional Barriers." Journal of Social Issues 43 (1987): 5-39.

9474. Breitman, Richard and Alan M. Kraut. American Refugee Policy and European Jewry, 1933-1945. Bloomington, IN: Indiana University Press, 1987.

9475. Brenner, Lenni. Jews in America Today. Secaucus, NJ: L. Stuart, 1986.

9476. Brown, David. "The White Man's Problem." African Methodist Episcopal Zion Quarterly 4 (April 1894): 268-274.

9477. Bruening, William H. "Racism: A Philosophical Analysis of a Concept." Journal of Black Studies 5 (September 1974): 3- 17.

9478. Brumberg, Stephen F. "Going to America, Going to School: The Immigrant-Public School Encounter in Turn-of-the-Century New York City." American Jewish Arch. 36 (November 1984): 86-135.

9479. Bullock, Charles S., III. "Defiance of the Law: School Discrimination Before and After Desegregation." Urban Education 11 (October 1976): 239-262.

9480. Bullock, Charles S., III and C. Lamb, eds. Implementation of Civil Rights Policy. Monterey, CA: Brooks/Cole Publishing Co., 1984.

9481. Burns, Haywood. "Racism and American Law." In Law Against the People: Essays to Demystify Law, Order and the Courts, edited by Robert Lefcourt. New York: Vintage, 1971.

9482. Butcher, P., ed. The Ethnic Image in Modern American Literature, 1900-1950. 2 vols. Washington, D.C.: Howard University Press, 1984.

9483. Campos, R. and F. Bonilla. La economia politica de la relacion colonial: la experiencia puertorriquena. New York: Centro de Estudios Puertorriquenos, CUNY, 1979.

9484. Chalmers, David M. Hooded Americanism. The History of the Ku Klux Klan. 2d ed. New York: Watts, 1980.

9485. Chan, Sucheng. The Asian Americans: An Interpretive History. Boston, MA: Hall/Twayne, 1990.

9486. Cherry, Robert. "Black Youth Employment Problems." In The Imperiled Economy. Vol. 3, edited by Cherry and others. New York: Union for Radical Political Economics, 1988.

9487. Chrisman, Robert. "Blacks, Racism and Bourgeois Culture." Black Scholar 7 (January-February 1976): 2-10.

9488. Churchill, Ward. "Indigenous Peoples of the United States: A Struggle Against Internal Colonialism." Black Scholar 16 (January-February 1985): 29-35.

9489. Churchill, Ward. "White Studies: The Intellectual Imperialism of Contemporary U.S. Education." Integrateducation 19 (January-April 1981): 51-57.

9490. Clark, Kenneth B. "The Black Plight. Race or Class?" New York Times Magazine, (October 5, 1980)

9491. Clark, Kenneth B. Dark Ghetto. An Analysis of the Dilemma of Social Power. New York: Harper & Row, 1965.

9492. Coles, Robert. "Understanding White Racists." New York Review of Books, 18 (December 1971): 12-15.

9493. Cornelius, Janet. "We Slipped and Learned to Read: Slave Accounts of the Literacy Process, 1830-1865." Phylon 44 (September 1983): 171-186.

9494. Crockett, N. L. The Black Towns. Lawrence: University Press of Kansas.

9495. Cruse, Harold. Plural but Equal: A Critical Study of Blacks and Minorities and the American Plural Society. New York: Morrow, 1986.

9496. Cummins, Jim. "Psychological Assessment of Minority Students: Out of Context, Out of Focus, Out of Control?" Journal of Reading, Writing, and Learning Disabilities International 2 (1986): 9-19.

9497. Curry, L. P. The Free Black in Urban America, 1800-1850: The Shadow of the Dream. Chicago, IL: University of Chicago Press, 1981.

9498. Daniel, P. The Shadow of Slavery: Peonage in the South 1901-1969. Urbana: University of Illinois Press, 1972.

9499. Daniels, Roger. "Change in Immigration Law and Nativism since 1924." American Jewish History 76 (December 1986): 159-180.

9500. Daniels, Roger and others. Japanese Americans from Relocation to Redress. Salt Lake City: University of Utah Press, 1986.

9501. Darity, William A., Jr. "Equal Opportunity, Equal Results, and Social Hierarchy." Praxis International 7 (July 1987): 174-185.

9502. Davies, Alan. Infected Christianity: A Study of Modern Racism. Montreal: McGill-Queens University Press, 1988.

9503. Davis, F. "Problems of Economic Growth in the Black Community: Some Alternative Hypotheses." Review of Black Political Economy 1 (1971): 75-107.

9504. Degler, Carl N. "Slavery and the Genesis of American Race Prejudice." Comparative Studies in Society and History 2 (1959): 49-66. [Reprinted in Making of Black America, edited by Meier and Rudwick, 91-108.]

9505. Dillard, Joey Lee. Black English: Its History and Usage in the United States. New York: Random House, 1972.

9506. Dinnerstein, Leonard. Uneasy at Home. Antisemitism and the American Jewish Experience. New York: Columbia University Press, 1987.

9507. Dobkowski, Michael N. "American Antisemitism and American Historians: A Critique." Patterns of Prejudice 14 (April 1980): 33-43.

9508. Domhoff, G. William. Who Rules America Now? A View for the '80s. New York: Simon & Schuster, 1986.

9509. Douglass, Frederick. "Citizenship of Colored Americans." Douglass Monthly (February 1863)

9510. Douglass, Frederick. "The Color Line." North American Review 132 (1881)

9511. Douglass, Frederick. Life and Times of Frederick Douglass. Hartford, CT: Park Publishing CO., 1882.

9512. Drake, St. Clair. "The Ghettoization of Negro Life." In Negroes and Jobs, edited by Louis A. Ferman and others. Ann Arbor: University of Michigan Press, 1968.

9513. Du Bois, W. E. B. The Autobiography of W.E.B. Du Bois. New York: International Publications, 1968.

9514. Du Bois, W. E. B. "An Essay Toward a History of the Black Man in the Great War." Crisis 18 (June 1919): 63-87.

9515. Du Bois, W. E. B. "Socialism and the Negro Problem." New Review 1 (February 1, 1913): 138-141.

9516. Edelman, M. W. Families in Peril: An Agenda for Social Change. Cambridge, MA: Harvard University Press, 1987.

9517. Edwards, Harry. The Revolt of the Black Athlete. New York: Free Press, 1969.

9518. Ehrlich, Judith R. and Barry J. Rehfeld. The New Crowd. The Changing of the Jewish Guard on Wall Street. Boston, MA: Little, Brown, 1989.

9519. Elsasser, Nan and others. La Mujeres: Conversations from a Hispanic Community. Old Westbury, New York: Feminist Press, 1981.

9520. England, R. E. and D.R. Morgan. Desegregating Big City Schools: Strategies, Outcomes, and Impacts. New York: Associated Faculty Press, 1986.

9521. Erens, Patricia. The Jew in American Cinema. Bloomington: Indiana University Press, 1984.

9522. Estrada, L. F. and others. "Chicanos in the United States: A History of Exploitation and Resistance." Daedalus 110 (Spring 1981): 103-131.

9523. Farley, Reynolds and W.R. Allen. The Color Line and the Quality of Life: Problem for the Twenty-first Century. New York: Russell Sage Foundation, 1987.

9524. Feagin, J. R. Discrimination American Style. Englewood Cliffs, NJ: Prentice-Hall, 1984.

9525. Fein, Helen. "Toleration of Genocide." Patterns of Prejudice 7 (September-October 1973): 22-28. [Attitudes in U.S., 1933-1945.]

9526. Feingold, Henry L. "United States of America." In Encyclopedia of the Holocaust, IV. 1546-1549. New York: Macmillan, 1990.

9527. Feuer, Lewis S. "America's First Jewish Professor: James Joseph Sylvester at the University of Viginia." American Jewish Arch. 36 (November 1984): 151-201.

9528. Feuer, Lewis S. "The Stages in the Social History of Jewish Professors in American Colleges and Universities." American Jewish History 71 (June 1982)

9529. Filippelli, Ronald L., ed. Labor Conflict in the United States. New York: Garland, 1990.

9530. Finkelman, Paul. An Imperfect Union: Slavery, Federalism, and Comity. Chapel Hill: University of North Carolina Press, 1980. [Slaves in free states.]

9531. Flynn, Kevin and Gary Gerhardt. The Silent Brotherhood, Inside America's Racist Underground. New York: Free Press, 1989.

9532. Foner, Philip S. American Socialism and Black Americans: From the Age of Jackson to World War II. Westport, CT: Greenwood, 1978.

9533. Forman, James. The Making of Black Revolutionaries: A Personal Account. New York: Macmillan, 1972.

9534. Franklin, Vincent P. "Black Social Scientists and the Mental Testing Movement, 1920-1940." In Black Psychology, edited by Reginald L. Jones. New York: Harper & Row, 1980.

9535. Franklin, Stephen D. and J.D. Smith. "Black-White Differences in Income and Wealth." American Economic Review (1977): 405-409.

9536. Franklin, Vincent P. Black Self-Determination. A Cultural History of the Faith of the Fathers. Westport, CT: Lawrence Hill and Co., 1986.

9537. Freedman, Francesca. "The Internal Structure of the American Proletariat: A Marxist Analysis." Socialist Review 20 (October-December 1975)

9538. Friedman, Lawrence J. "The Search for Docility: Racial Thought in the White South, 1861-1917." Phylon 31 (Fall 1970): 313-323.

9539. Gabriel, John G. and G. Ben-Tovin. "Marxism and the Concept of Racism." Economy and Society 7 (May 1978): 118-154.

9540. Genovese, Eugene D. From Rebellion to Revolution: Afro- American Slave Revolts in the Making of the Modern World. Baton Rouge: Louisiana State University Press, 1979.

9541. Genovese, Eugene D. Roll, Jordan, Roll: The World the Slaves Made. New York: Random House, 1974.

9542. Gerber, David A., ed. Antisemitism in American History. Urbana: University of Illinois Press, 1986.

9543. Gibbs, Jewelle T. Young, Black and Male in America. Dover, MA: Auburn House, 1988.

9544. Gill, Flora. Economics and the Black Exodus. New York: Garland, 1979. [1910-1970.]

9545. Gimbel, John. "U.S. Policy and German Scientists: The Early Cold War." Political Science Quarterly 101 (1986): 433-451.

9546. Glasgow, Douglas G. The Black Underclass: Poverty, Unemployment and Entrapment for Ghetto Youth. London: Jossey- Bass, 1980.

9547. Greer, E. "Racial Biases in the Property Tax System." Review of Radical Political Economics 7 (1975): 22-31.

9548. Guillemin, J. "American Indian Resistance and Protest." In Violence in America. Vol. II, edited by Ted R. Gurr. Newbury Park, CA: Sage, 1989.

9549. Gutierrez, Jose Angel. "Chicanos and Mexicans Under Surveillance: 1940-1980." Renato Rosaldo Lecture Series Monograph 2 (Spring 1986): 29-58.

9550. Hall, Patricia A. "'Yassuh! Ise the Reference Librarian'." American Libraries (November 1988): 900-901.

9551. Handlin, Oscar. "Anti-Semitism: 1890-1941." In Adventure on Freedom. 174-210. New York: McGraw-Hill, 1954.

9552. Harlan, Louis R. Separate and Unequal Public School Campaigns and Racism in the Southern Seaboard States, 1901- 1915. Chapel Hill: University of North Carolina Press, 1958.

9553. Harley, Sharon and Rosalyn Terborg-Penn, eds. The Afro- American Women: Struggles and Images. Port Washington, New York: Kennikat Press, 1978.

9554. Harris, Abram L. "The Economic Foundation of American Race Division." Social Forces 5 (1927): 468-478.

9555. Harris, Abram L. The Negro as Capitalist: A Study of Banking and Business Among American Negroes. New York: 1936.

9556. Harris, William H. The Harder We Run. Black Workers Since the Civil War. New York: Oxford University Press, 1981.

9557. Hearden, Patrick J. Roosevelt Confronts Hitler. America's Entry into World War II. DeKalb: Northern Illinois University Press, 1988.

9558. Helper, Rose. Racial Policies and Practices of Real Estate Brokers. Minneapolis: University of Minnesota Press, 1969.

9559. "Henry Ford Defends Klan as a Body of Patriots." New York Times, (August 27, 1924)

9560. Higginbotham, A. Leon, Jr. "Racism and the Early American Legal Process, 1619-1896." Annals 407 (May 1973): 1-17.

9561. Higham, Charles. American Swastika. Garden City, New York: Doubleday, 1985.

9562. Hill, Herbert. "Race and Ethnicity in Organized Labor: The Historical Sources of Resistance to Affirmative Action." Journal of Intergroup Relations 12 (1984): 5-49.

9563. Hirsch, Herbert and Jack D. Spiro, eds. Persistent Prejudice: Perspectives on Anti-Semitism. Fairfax, VA: George Mason University Press, 1988.

9564. History Task Force, Centro. Labor Migration under Capitalism: The Puerto Rican Experience. New York: Monthly Review Press, 1979.

9565. Hodge, John L. Cultural Bases of Racism and Group Oppression. Berkeley, CA: Two Riders Press, 1975.

9566. Hogan, Lloyd. Principles of Black Political Economy. Boston, MA: Routledge & Kegan Paul, 1984.

9567. Hooks, Bell. "Black Women and Feminism." Zeta Magazine 1 (July-August 1988): 39-42.

9568. Huggins, Nathan Irvin. Black Oddessy. The Afro-American Ideal in Slavery. New York: Pantheon, 1977.

9569. Institute of Medicine. Health Care in a Context of Civil Rights. Washington, D.C.: National Academy Press, 1981.

9570. Iyeki, M. H. "The Japanese American Coram Nobis Cases: Exposing the Myth of Disoyalty." Review of Law and Social Change 13 (1984-1985): 199-221.

9571. Jackson, Kenneth T. The Ku Klux Klan in the City, 1915- 1930. New York: Oxford University Press, 1967.

9572. Jacobs, Wilbur R. Dispossessing the American Indian: Indians and Whites on the Colonial Froniers. New York: Scribner's, 1972.

9573. Jeansome, Glen. Gerald L.K. Smith. Minister of Hate. New Haven: Yale University Press, 1988.

9574. Jiobu, Robert M. Ethnicity and Inequality. Albany: State University of New York Press, 1990.

9575. Joint Center for Political Studies. Black Business Enterprise: A Statistical Portrait. Washington, D.C.: The Center, 1983.

9576. Jones, Rhett S. "Black and Native American Relations before 1800." Western Journal of Black Studies 1 (September 1977): 151-163.

9577. Jorgensen, J. G. "A Century of Political Economic Effects on American Indian Society 1880-1980." Journal of Ethnic Studies 6 (Fall 1978): 1-82.

9578. Josey, E. J. "Black Aspirations, White Racism, and Libraries." Wilson Library Bulletin 44 (1970): 736-742.

9579. Katz, Phyllis A. and Dalmes A. Taylor, eds. Eliminating Racism: Profiles in Controversy. New York: Plenum Press, 1988.

9580. Katz, Phyllis A., ed. Towards the Elimination of Racism. New York: Pergamon, 1976.

9581. Kaufman, Allan. Capitalism, Slavery, and Republican Values: Antebellum Political Economists, 1819-1848. Austin: University of Texas Press, 1982.

9582. Kettner, J. H. The Development of American Citizenship, 1608-1870. Chapel Hill: University of North Caolina Press, 1978.

9583. Kilson, Martin. "Black Social Classes and Intergenerational Poverty." Public Interest 64 (Summer 1981): 58-78.

9584. King, Mel. Chain of Change, Struggles for Black Community Development. Boston, MA: South End Press, 1981.

9585. King, Wayne. "Neo-Nazis' Dream of a Racist Territory in a Pacific Northwest Refuses to Die." New York Times, (July 5, 1986)

9586. Kluger, Richard. Simple Justice: The History of Brown v. Board of Education and Black America's Struggle for Equality. New York: Knopf, 1975.

9587. Knowles, Louis and Kenneth Prewitt, eds. Institutional Racism in America. Englewood Cliffs, NJ: Prentice-Hall, 1969.

9588. Koehler, David H. and Margaret T. Wrightson. "Inequality in the Delivery of Urban Services: A Reconsideration of the Chicago Parks." Journal of Politics 49 (February 1987): 80- 99.

9589. Kushner, James A. Apartheid in America: An Historical and Legal Analysis of Contemporary Racial Segregation in the United States. Port Washington, New York: Associated Faculty Press, 1982.

9590. "The LaRouche Network: A Political Cult." ADL Facts (Spring 1982): 1-14.

9591. Lauter, Paul. "Race and Gender in the Shaping of the American Literary Canon: A Case Study from the Twenties." Feminist Studies 9 (Fall 1983): 435-463.

9592. Lawrence, Charles R., III. "The Id, the Ego, and Equal Protection: Reckoning with Unconscious Racism." Stanford Law Review 39 (January 1987): 317-388.

9593. Leab, Daniel J. From Sambo to Superspade: The Black Experience in Motion Pictures. Boston, MA: Houghton Mifflin, 1975.

9594. Lipstadt, Deborah E. Beyond Belief, The American Press and the Coming of the Holocaust, 1933-1945. New York: Free Press, 1985.

9595. Littlefield, Daniel F., Jr. & Underhill. "Slave Revolt in the Cherokee Nation." American Indian Quarterly 3 (Summer 1977): 121-131.

9596. Litwack, Leon F. North of Slavery: The Negro in the Free States. Chicago, IL: University of Chicago Press, 1961.

9597. Longres, J. F., Jr. "Racism and Its Effects on Puerto Rican Continentals." Social Casework 55 (February 1974): 67-75.

9598. Lookstein, Haskel. Were We Our Brothers' Keepers? The Public Response of American Jews to the Holocaust, 1938-1944. New York: Hartmore House, 1985.

9599. MacDonald, J. Fred. Blacks and White TV: Afro-Americans in Television Since 1948. Chicago, IL: Nelson-Hall, 1983.

9600. MacGregor, Morris J. Integration of the Armed Forces, 1940- 1965. Washington, D.C.: Government Printing Office, 1981.

9601. Maga, Timothy P. America, France, and the European Refugee Problem, 1933-1947. New York: Garland, 1985.

9602. Magdol, Edward. A Right to Land: Essays on the Freedmen's Community. Westport, CT: Greenwood, 1977.

9603. Mangum, Garth L. and Stephen F. Seninger. Coming of Age in the Ghetto: A Dilemma of Youth Unemployment. Baltimore, MD: Johns Hopkins University Press, 1978.

9604. Manning, Kenneth R. Black Apollo of Science: The Life of Ernest Everett Just. New York: Oxford University Press, 1983.

9605. Marable, Manning. Race, Reform, and Rebellion. The Second Reconstruction in Black America, 1. Jackson: University Press of Mississippi, 1984.

9606. Marketti, Jim. "Black Equity in the Slave Industry." Review of Black Political Economy, 2, 1 (1972): 22-42.

9607. Marshall, Thurgood. "Those the Constitution Left Out." Judges Journal 26 (Summer 1987)

9608. McAdoo, H. P. and J.L. McAdoo, eds. Black Children, Social, Educational and Parental Environments. Newbury Park, CA: Sage, 1985.

9609. McAdoo, William. The Settler State: Immigration Policy and the Rise of Institutional Racism in Nineteenth-century Michigan. 2 vols. Doctoral dissertation: University of Michigan, 1983. UMO # 8324245.

9610. McDougald, Elsie J. "The Double Talk: The Struggle of Negro Women for Sex and Race Emancipation." Survey Graphic 6 (March 1925)

9611. McKnight, Gerald D. "A Harvest of Hate: The FBI's War Against Black Youth-Domestic Intelligence in Memphis, Tennessee." South Atlantic Quarterly 86 (Winter 1987): 1- 19.

9612. McWilliams, Carey. A Mask for Privilege: Anti-Semitism in America. Boston, MA: Little, Brown, 1948.

9613. Mercer, Jane R. "Ethnic Differences in IQ Scores: What Do They Mean?" Hispanic Journal of Behavioral Sciences 10 (September 1988): 199-218.

9614. Meyer, Donald. Sex and Power: The Rise of Women in America, Russia, Sweden, and Italy. Middletown, CT: Wesleyan University Press, 1987.

9615. Miller, Judith. One, By One, By One. New York: Simon & Schuster, 1990. [How the U.S., West Germany, Austria, France, the Netherlands, and the USSR have dealt with the memory of the Holocaust.]

9616. Mirikatani, Janice, ed. Third World Women. San Francisco, CA: Third World Communications Press, 1973.

9617. Moeller, James W. "United States Treatment of Alleged Nazi War Criminals: International Law Immigration Law, and the Need for International Cooperation." Virginia Journal of International Law 25 (1985)

9618. Moore, R. L. "Flawed Fraternity-American Socialist Response to the Negro, 1901-1912." Historian 32 (November 1969): 1- 18.

9619. Morgan, Edmund S. American Slavery American Freedom: The Ordeal of Colonial Virginia. New York: Norton, 1975.

9620. Murgia, E. Assimilation, Colonialism and the Mexican American People. Austin: University of Texas Press, 1975.

9621. Myers, Samuel L., Jr. "Statistical Tests of Discrimination in Punishment." Journal of Quantitative Criminology 1 (June 1985): 191-218.

9622. Nalty, Bernard C. Strength for the Fight. A History of Black Americans in the Military. New York: Free Press, 1986.

9623. Nash, Gary. Red, White and Black: Peoples of Early America. 2d ed. Englewood Cliffs, NJ: Prentice-Hall, 1982.

9624. Noonan, John T., Jr. The Antelope: The Ordeal of Recaptured Africans in the Administrations of James Monroe and John Quincy Adams. Berkeley: 1977.

9625. Novak, D. A. The Wheel of Servitude: Black Forced Labor After Slavery. Lexington: University of Kentucky Press, 1978.

9626. Novick, Peter. That Noble Dream: The "Objectivity Question" and the American Historical Profession. New York: Cambridge University Press, 1988.

9627. O'Hare, William P. Wealth and Economic Status: A Perspective on Racial Inequality. Washington, D.C.: Joint Center for Political Studies, 1983.

9628. O'Reilly, Kenneth. "Racial Matters." The FBI's Secret File on Black America, 1960-1972. New York: Free Press, 1989.

9629. Okihiro, G. Y. "Japanese Resistance in America's Concentration Camps: A Reevaluation." Amerasia Journal 2 (Fall 1973): 20-34.

9630. Okolo, C. B. Racism-A Philosophic Probe. New York: Exposition Press, 1974.

9631. Olexer, Barbara. The Enslavement of the American Indian. Monroe, New york: Library Research Associates, 1982.

9632. Orfield, Gary. Must We Bus? Segregated Schools and National Policy. Washington, D.C.: Brookings, 1978.

9633. Pagden, Anthony. The Fall of Natural Man: The American Indian and the Origins of Comparative Ethnology. New York: Cambridge University Press, 1983.

9634. Painter, Nell Irvin. Exodusters: Black Migration to Kansas after Reconstruction. New York: Knopf, 1977.

9635. Pamphlets Printed and Distributed by the Women's Anti- Suffrage Association of the Third Judicial District of the State of New York. Littleton, CO.: F.B. Rothman, 1990, orig. 1905.

9636. Parker, James R. "Paternalism and Racism: Senator John C. Spooner and American Minorities, 1897-1907." Wisconsin Magazine of History 57 (Spring 1974): 195-200.

9637. Patterson, William L. Adolf Hitler in the American Press, 1922-1933. Master's thesis: Middle Tennessee State University, 1979.

9638. Patterson, William L., ed. We Charge Genocide: The Crime of Government Against the Negro People. New York: 1951.

9639. Payne, Charles. M. Getting What We Ask For: The Ambiguity of Success and Failure in Urban Education. Westport, CT: Greenwood, 1984.

9640. Payne, Charles M. "Multicultural Education and Racism in American Schools." Theory Into Practice 23 (1984): 124-131.

9641. Pearson, Willie Jr. Black Scientists, White Society, and Colorless Science: A Study of Universalism in American Science. Associated Faculty Press, 1985.

9642. Pessen, Edward. "Wealth in America Before 1865." In Wealth and the Wealthy in the Modern World, edited by W.D. Rubenstein. 167-188. London: Croom Helm, 1980.

9643. Pierce, Paulette. "The Roots of the Rainbow Coalition." Black Scholar 19 (March-April 1988): 2-16.

9644. Pinderhughes, Dianne. Race and Ethnicity in Chicago Politics: A Reexamination of Pluralist Theory. Urbana: University of Illinois Press, 1987.

9645. Pinkney, A. The Myth of Black Progress. New York: Cambridge University Press, 1984.

9646. Porter, Kenneth W. The Negro on the American Frontier. New York: Arno, 1976 (orig. 1971). [Blacks and Indians.]

9647. Prager, Jeffrey. "White Racial Privilege and Social Change: An Exploration of Theories of Racism." Berkeley Journal of Sociology 17 (1972): 117-150.

9648. Prager, Jeffrey and others. School Desegregation Research: New Directions in Situational Analysis. New York: Plenum Press, 1986.

9649. Preston, Michael B. and others, eds. The New Black Politics: The Search for Political Power. New York: Longman, 1982.

9650. Raboteau, Albert J. Slave Religion: The "Invisible Institution" in the Antebellum South. New York: Oxford University Press, 1978.

9651. Raines, H. My Soul Is Rested. Movement Days in the Deep South Remembered. Penguin, 1983.

9652. Rawick, George, ed. The American Slave. 41 vols. Westport, CT: Greenwood, 1972-1979. [Interviews with over 2, 000 ex-slaves.]

9653. Reed, L. The Southern Conference for Human Welfare and the Southern Conference Educational Fund 1938-1963. Doctoral dissertation: Indiana University, 1986. UMO # 8617789.

9654. "A Reexamination of a Classic Work in American Jewish History: John Higham's Strangers in the Land." American Jewish History 107-226 (December 1986)

9655. Rich, Evelyn. Ku Klux Klan Ideology, 1954-1988. 2 vols. Doctoral dissertation: Boston University, 1988. UMO # 8814385.

9656. Richards, J. G. The Southern Negro Youth Congress: A History. Doctoral dissertation: University of Cincinnati, 1987. UMO # 8722073.

9657. Ringer, B. B. "We the People" and Others: Duality and America's Treatment of Its Racial Minorities. New York: Methuen, 1983.

9658. Robinson, Forrest G. In Bad Faith: The Dynamics of Deception in Mark Twain's America. Cambridge, MA: Harvard University Press, 1986.

9659. Roof, W. Clark. Race and Residence in American Cities. Philadelphia, PA: American Academy of Political and Social Science, 1979.

9660. Rose, Harold M. The Black Ghetto: A Spatial Behavioral Perspective. New York: McGraw-Hill, 1971.

9661. Rosenberg, Neil V. Stereotypes and Tradition: White Folklore about Blacks. 2 vols. Doctoral dissertation: Indiana University, 1970.

9662. Ross, Robert, ed. Racism and Colonialism. The Hague: Martinus Nijhoff, 1982.

9663. Rubenstein, Judith A. "Confronting the Perpetrators-Anti-Semitism at Syracuse University." Lilith (Fall 1987)

9664. Rupp, Leila J. and Verta Taylor. Survival in the Doldrums: The American Women's Rights Movement 1945 to the 1960s. Columbus: Ohio State University Press, 1990.

9665. Sachs, Albert L. and Joan H. Wilson. Sexism and the Law: A Study of Male Beliefs and Legal Bias in Britain and the United States. New York: Free Press, 1979.

9666. Saidel, Rochelle G. The Outraged Conscience: Seekers of Justice for Nazi War Criminals in America. Albany: State University of New York Press, 1984.

9667. Santiago Santiago, Isaura. A Community's Struggle for Equal Educational Opportunity: Aspira v. Board of Education. Princeton, NJ: Office for Minority Education, Educational Testing Service, 1978.

9668. Schappes, Morris U., ed. A Documentary History of the Jews in the US, 1654-1875. 3d ed.

9669. Schonbach, Morris. Native American Fascism during the 1930s and 1940s: A Study of Its Roots, Its Growth, and its Decline. New York: Garland, 1985.

9670. Schuman, Howard and others. Racial Attitudes in America. Trends and Interpretations. Cambridge, MA: Harvard University Press, 1985. [1940s-1980s.]

9671. Scott, James F. "White Racism Explanation or Anathema?" Journal of Social and Behavioral Sciences 18 (Fall-Winter 1971-1972): 27-34.

9672. Sedler, R. A. "Beyond Bakke: The Constitution and Redressing the Social History of Racism." Harvard Civil Rights-Civil Liberties Law Review 14 (Spring 1979): 133- 171.

9673. Shapiro, Herbert. White Violence and Black Response. From Reconstruction to Montgomery. Amherst: University of Massachusetts Press, 1988.

9674. Shaw, Van B. "The Concept of Institutional Racism." Journal of Intergroup Relations 5 (November 1976): 3-12.

9675. Simon, Rita J. Public Opinion and the Immigrant: Mass Media Coverage, 1880-1980. Lexington, MA: Lexington Books, 1985.

9676. Simpson, Christopher. Blowback: America's Recruitment of Nazis and Its Effect on the Cold War. New York: Weidenfeld and Nicolson, 1988.

9677. Singer, David G. "Has God Truly Abrogated the Mosaic Covenant? American Catholic Attitudes toward Judaism as Reflected in Catholic Thought, 1945-1977." Jewish Social Studies 47 (Fall 1985): 243-254.

9678. Sivanandan, A. "RAT [Racism Awareness Training] and the Degradation of Black Struggle." Race and Class 26 (Spring 1985)

9679. Smith, Graham. When Jim Crow Met John Bull. Black American Soldiers in World War II Britain. New York: St. Martin's Press, 1988.

9680. Smith, H. Shelton. In His Image, But...Racism in Southern Religion, 1780-1910. Durham, NC: Duke University Press, 1972.

9681. Smith, Jesse Carney. Images of Blacks in American Culture. Westport, CT: Greenwood, 1988.

9682. Smitherman-Donaldson, Geneva and Teun A. van Dijk, eds. Discourse and Discrimination. Detroit, MI: Wayne State University Press, 1988.

9683. Sobel, Mechal. Trabelin 'On: The Slave Journey to an Afro- Baptist Faith. Westport, CT: Greenwood, 1979.

9684. Sollors, Werner. "Literature and Ethnicity." In Harvard Encyclopedia of American Ethnic Groups, edited by Stephan Thernstrom. 647-665. Cambridge, MA: Harvard University Press, 1980.

9685. Stafford, Walter and Joyce Ladner. "Comprehensive Planning and Racism." Journal of the American Institute of Planners (March 1969)

9686. Stamps, Spurgeon M. and M.B. Stamps. "Race, Class and Leisure Activities of Urban Residents." Journal of Leisure Research 17 (1985): 40-56.

9687. Stanback, Howard J. Racism, Black Labor, and the Giant Corporation. Doctoral dissertation: University of Massachusetts, 1980. UMO # 8101399.

9688. Stedman, Raymond W. Shadows of the Indian: Stereotypes in American Culture. Norman: University of Oklahoma Press, 1982.

9689. Stepick, Alex. Haitian Refugees in the U.S. London: Minority Rights Group, 1982.

9690. Sterling, Dorothy, ed. We Are Your Sisters: Black Women in the 19th Century. New York: Norton, 1984.

9691. Streater, J. B. Jr. The National Negro Congress: 1936-1947. Doctoral dissertation: University of Cincinnati, 1981.

9692. Stuckey, Sterling. Slave Culture, Nationalist Theory and the Foundation of Black America. New York: Oxford University Press, 1987.

9693. Sutton, Imre, ed. Irredeemable America: The Indians' Estate and Land Claims. Albuquerque: University of New Mexico Press, 1985.

9694. Swan, James H. Racism in Labor Markets. 2 vols. Doctoral dissertation: Northwestern University, 1981. UMO # 8125020.

9695. Takagi, P. "Tracing Racism in U.S. National Policies." Journal of Intergroup Relations 3 (September 1974): 14-30.

9696. Terrell, Henry S. "Wealth Accumulation of Black and White Families: The Empirical Evidence." Journal of Finance 26 (May 1971): 363-377.

9697. Thornton, Russell. American Indian Holocaust and Survival: A Population History Since 1492. Norman: University of Oklahoma Press, 1987.

9698. Trelease, Allen W. White Terror, The Ku Klux Conspiracy and Southern Reconstruction. New York: Harper & Row, 1971.

9699. Turner, Jonathan H. and others. Oppression: A Socio-History of Black-White Relations in America. Chicago, IL: Nelson-Hall, 1984.

9700. Turner, T. S. "Anthropology and the Politics of Indigenous Peoples' Struggles." Cambridge Anthropology 5 (1979): 1-43.

9701. Vachon, Robert. "The Fight Against Racism. Could Our Assumptions Be Racist?" Rikka 7 (Summer 1980): 18-25.

9702. Van Deburg, William L. "Elite Slave Behaviour during the Civil War: Black Drivers and Foremen in Historiographical Perspective." Southern Studies 16 (1977): 253-270.

9703. Van Der Zee, J. *Bound Over: Indentured Servitude and American Conscience*. New York: Simon and Schuster, 1986.

9704. van Dijk, Teun A. *Communication Racism. Ethnic Prejudice in Thought and Talk*. Newbury Park, CA: Sage, 1987.

9705. Vander Zanden, James W. "The Ideology of White Supremacy." *Journal of the History of Ideas* 20 (1959): 385-402.

9706. La Vega, M. I. de. *El racismo en los Estados Unidos-una vision latinamericana del problema*. Bogota: Ediciones Centro de Estudios Colombianos, 1970.

9707. Victorisz, T. and B. Harrison. *The Economic Development of Harlem*. New York: Praeger, 1970.

9708. Vivo, Paquita, ed. *Forum on the Status of Hispanic Health*. Rockville, MD: Public Health Service, 1979.

9709. Wagenheim, Kal and Leslie Dunbar. *Puerto Ricans in the US*. London: Minority Rights Group, 1983.

9710. Walker, Nancy and Zita Dresner, eds. *Redressing the Balance. American Women's Literary Humor from Colonial Times to the 1980s*. Jackson: University Press of Mississippi, 1988.

9711. Walton, Hanes Jr. *Invisible Politics: Black Political Behavior*. Albany: State University of New York Press, 1985.

9712. Ware, Gilbert, ed. *From the Black Bar. Voices for Equal Justice*. New York: Putnam's, 1976.

9713. Washburn, Wilcomb E. *History of Indian-White Relations*. Washington, D.C.: Smithsonian Institution, 1988.

9714. Washington, Johnny. *Alain Locke and Philosophy: A Quest for Cultural Pluralism*. Westport, CT: Greenwood, 1986.

9715. Watson, Bernard C. "The Social Consequences of Testing: Another View." *New Directions for Testing and Measurement* 9 (1981): 39-51.

9716. Weaver, Jerry L. and Sharon D. Garrett. "Sexism and Racism in the American Health Industry: A Comparative Analysis." *International Journal of Health Services* 8 (1978): 677- 703.

9717. Wechsler, James. "The Coughlin Terror." *Nation* (July 22, 1939)

9718. Weigel, Russell H. and Paul W. Howes. "Conceptions of Racial Prejudice." *Journal of Social Issues* 41 (Fall 1985): 117-138.

9719. Weinberg, Meyer. A Chance to Learn. A History of Race and Schools. New York: Cambridge University Press, 1977.

9720. Weisbord, R. G. and A. Stein. Bittersweet Encounter: The Afro-American and the American Jew. Westport, CT: Negro Universities Press.

9721. Werner, John M. "Reaping the Bloody Harvest": Race Riots in the United States during the Age of Jackson, 1824-1849. New York: Garland, 1987.

9722. Weston, Rubin F. Racism in U.S. Imperialism: The Influence of Racial Assumptions on American Foreign Policy, 1893-1946. Columbia: University of South Carolina Press, 1972.

9723. White, J. and J.S. Frideres. "Race Prejudice and Racism: A Distinction." Canadian Review of Sociology and Anthropology 14 (February 1977)

9724. White, Philip V. "Race Against Time: The Role of Racism in U.S. Foreign Relations." In Impacts of Racism on White Americans, edited by Benjamin P. Bowser and Raymond G. Hunt. 177- 189. Beverly Hills, CA: Sage, 1981.

9725. Wiecek, Wm. M. "The Statutory Law of Slavery and Race in the Thirteen Mainland Colonies of British America." William and Mary Quarterly 34 (Spring 1977): 258-280.

9726. Wilhelm, Sidney H. "Equality: America's Racist ideology." In Radical Sociology, edited by J. David Colfax and Jack L. Roach. 246-262. New York: Basic Books, 1971.

9727. Williams, Jenny. "Redefining Institutional Racism." Ethnic and Racial Studies 8 (1985)

9728. Willie, Charles V. The Family Life of Black People. Columbus, Ohio: Merrill, 1970.

9729. Willie, Charles V. and others, eds. Racism and Mental Health: Essays. Pittsburgh, PA: University of Pittsburgh Press, 1972.

9730. Willis, William S., Jr. "Divide and Rule: Red, White and Black in the Southeast." Journal of Negro History 48 (July 1963): 157-176.

9731. Willis, William S., Jr. "Skeletons in the Anthropological Closet." In Re-inventing Anthropology, edited by Dell Hymes, 121- 152. New York: Vintage.

9732. Wilson, Clint C., II and Felix Gutierrez. Minorities and Media. Diversity and the End of Mass Communication. Beverly Hills, CA: Sage, 1985.

9733. Wilson, W. Forced Labor in the United States. New York: AMS Press, 1971, orig. 1933.

9734. Wilson, William Julius. The Declining Significance of Race: Blacks and Changing American Institutions. 2d ed. Chicago, IL: University of Chicago Press, 1980.

9735. Winston, Michael R. "Racial Consciousness and the Evolution of Mass Communications in the United States." Daedalus (Fall 1982): 171-182.

9736. Wong, M. G. "The Cost of Being Chinese, Japanese, and Filipino in the United States: 1960, 1970, and 1976." Pacific Sociological Review 25 (January 1982): 58-78.

9737. Wood, Forrest B. Black Scare. The Racist Response to Emancipation and Reconstruction. Berkeley: University of California Press, 1968.

9738. Wright, Bruce. Black Robes, White Justice. Lyle Stuart: 1987.

9739. Wright, James D. and others. "Survey Research." In Harvard Encyclopedia of American Ethnic Groups, edited by Stephan Thernstrom. 954-971. Cambridge, MA: Harvard University Press, 1980.

9740. Zangrando, Robert L. The NAACP Crusade against Lynching, 1909-1950. Philadelphia, PA: Temple University Press, 1980.

VENEZUELA

9741. Acosta Saignes, Miguel. *Vida de los esclavos negros en Venezuela*. Caracas: Hespiredes, 1967.

9742. Aizenberg, Isidoro. "'Die or Leave': An Anti-Jewish Riot in Nineteenth Century Venezuela." *American Jewish History* 69 (1980): 478-487.

9743. Aizenberg, Isidoro. "The 1855 Expulsion of the Curacoan Jews from Coro, Venezuela." *American Jewish History* 72 (June 1983): 495-507.

9744. Briceño Perozo, Mario. *Temas de Historia Colonial Venezolana*. Caracas: Acod. Nac. de la Hist., 1981.

9745. Brito Figueroa, Federico. *El problema tierra y esclavos en la historia de Venezuela*. Caracas: 1973.

9746. Brooke, James. "Ex-Rebel in a Muumuu Becomes a Potent Force." *New York Times* (September 24, 1990): [Argelia Laya, Africans Latino head of Venezuelan left-wing party, Movement Toward Socialism.]

9747. de la Plaza, Salvador. "La formacion de las clases sociales en Venezuela." *Cultura Universitaria* 87 (1965)

9748. *Diccionario de la corrupcion en Venezuela, Vol.I, 1959-1979*. Caracas: Consorcio de Ediciones Capriles, 1989.

9749. Levine, Daniel H. "Venezuela: The Origins, Nature and Prospects of Democracy." In *Democracy in Developing Countries*, edited by S. Lyset and others. pp. 246-289. Boulder, CO: Rienner, 1989.

9750. Lizarralde, Roberto and others. *Indigenous Survival Among the Bari and Arhuaco, Strategies and Perspectives*. Copenhagen: International Work Groups for Indigenous Affairs (IWGIA), 1987. [Venezuela and Columbia.]

9751. Lombardi, John. "Manumission, manumisos, and aprendizaje in Republican Venezuela." Hispanic American Historical Review 49, 4 (1969): 656-678.

9752. Megenney, William W. "Themes of Socio-ethnic Awareness in the Oral Literature of Venezuelan Blacks." Afro-Hispanic Review 8 (January-May 1989): 3-8.

9753. Nuñez Ponte, J. M. Estudio histórico acerca de la esclavitud y de su abolición en Venezuela. Caracas: 1911.

9754. Pazmino-Farias, Carlos. University Reform, Stratification and Social Reproduction in Venezuela. Doctoral dissertation: Stanford University, 1986. UMO # 861780.

9755. Pollak-Eltz, Angelina. "El negro en Venezuela." Boletin- Musoe de Hombre Dominicano 9 (1980)

9756. Reiss, Spencer. "The Last Days of Eden." Newsweek (December 3, 1990): [Yanomama people in Venezuela.]

9757. Roseberry, William. Coffee and Capitalism in the Venezuelan Andes. Austin: University of Texas Press, 1983.

9758. Serbin, Andres. "Estado, indigenismo e indianidad en Venezuela, 1946-1979." Boletin de Estudios Latinoamericanos y del Caribe 20 (September-December 1983): 59-81.

9759. Slibe, M. A. J. de. Indian Slavery in Venezuela and Brazil in the Sixteenth Century. Master thesis: University of Liverpool, 1977.

9760. Whitehead, N. L. "Carib Ethnic Soldiering in Venezuela, the Guianas, and the Antilles, 1492-1820." Ethnohistory 37 (Autumn 1990)

9761. Wright, Winthrop R. "Elitist Attitudes toward Race in Twentieth-century Venezuela." In Slavery and Race Relations in Latin America, edited by Robert B. Toplin. pp. 325-347. Westport, CT: Greenwood, 1974.

9762. Wright, Winthrop R. "Race, Nationality and Immigration in Venezuelan Thought, 1890-1937." Canadian Review of Studies in Nationalism 6 (Spring 1979): 1-12.

9763. Wright, Winthrop R. "The Todd Duncan Affair: Acción Democratica and the Myth of Racial Democracy in Venezuela." Americas 44 (1988): 441-459. [Incident of 1945.]

VIETNAM

9764. "Amerasians in Vietnam: New Climate of Hope, but Problems Remain."
Refugee Reports 9 (August 12, 1988): 1-17.

9765. Crossette, Barbara. "Regional Rivalry in Vietnam: Marxists against Pragmatists." New York Times, (August 23, 1987)

9766. DeFrancis, John F. Colonialism and Language Policy in Vietnam. The Hague: Mouton, 1977.

9767. Dournes, Jacques. Minorities of Central Vietnam: Autochtonous Indochinese Peoples. London: Minority Rights Group, 1980.

9768. Gunn, Geoffrey C. "Minority Manipulation in Colonial Indochina: Lessons and Legacies." Bulletin of the Concerned Asian Scholars 19 (July-September 1987): 20-28.

9769. Johnston, Howard J. "The Tribal Soldier: A Study of the Manipulation of Ethnic Minorities." Naval War College Review 19 (January 1967): 98-143.

9770. Kahin, George M. "Minorities in the Democratic Republic of Vietnam." Asian Survey 12 (1972): 580-586.

9771. Kelly, Gail P. "Colonial Schools in Vietnam: Policy and Practice." In Education and Colonialism, edited by Philip G. Altbach and Gail P. Kelly. 96-121. New York: Longman, 1978.

9772. Klenner, Uwe. "Zur ökonomischen Entwicklung und sozialen Struktur der Gesellschaft in Nordvietnam (1945 bis 1975)." Jahrbuch für Wirtschaftsgeschichte No.4 (1987): 29-51.

9773. Ky, Luong Nhi. The Chinese in Vietnam: A Study of Vietnamese-Chinese Relations with Special Attention to the Period 1862-1961. Doctoral dissertation: University of Michigan, 1963. UMO # 6304983.

9774. Laffey, John F. "Racism in Tonkin before 1914: The Colons' View of the Vietnamese." French Colonial Studies 1 (Spring 1977): 65-81.

9775. Marr, David G. Vietnamese Anticolonialism, 1885-1925. Berkeley: University of California Press, 1971.

9776. The Montagnards of South Vietnam. London: Minority Rights Group, 1974.

9777. Munholland, J. Kim. "'Collaboration Strategy' and the French Pacification of Tonkin, 1883-1897." Historical Journal 24 (1981): 629-650.

9778. Murray, Martin J. The Development of Capitalism in Colonial Indochina (1870-1940). Berkeley: University of California Press, 1980.

9779. Nitz, Kiyoko K. "Japanese Policy towards French Indochina during the Second World War: The Road to the Meigo Sakusen (9 March 1945)." Journal of South East Asian Studies (September 1983): 328-353.

9780. Pao Min Chang. "The Sino-Vietnamese Conflict Over the Ethnic Chinese." China Quarterly 90 (1982)

9781. Porter, Gareth. "Vietnam's Ethnic Chinese and the Sino- Vietnamese Conflict." Bulletin of Concerned Asian Scholars 12 (October-December 1980): 55-60.

9782. Stern, Lewis M. "The Overseas Chinese in the Socialist Republic of Vietnam, 1979-1982." Asian Survey 25 (May 1985): 521-536.

9783. Stern, Lewis M. Vietnamese Comunist Policy Toward the Overseas Chinese, 1930-1982. Doctoral dissertation: University of Pittsburgh, 1984. UMO # 8421309.

9784. Stern, Lewis M. "The Vietnamese Communist Policy Toward the Overseas Chinese, 1983-1986." Asian Profile 16 (April 1988): 141-146.

9785. Ta Van Tai. "Ethnic Minorities and the Law in Traditional Vietnam." Vietnam Forum 5 (Winter-Spring 1985): 22-36.

9786. The, Au Duong. Die politische Entwicklung in Gesamtvietnam 1975 bis 1982: Anspruch und Wirklichkeit. Munich: Tuduv Verlagsgesellschaft, 1987.

9787. Ungar, E. S. "The Struggle Over the Chinese Community in Vietnam, 1946-1986." Pacific Affairs 60 (Winter 1987-1988): 596-614.

9788. Wiegersma, Nancy. "Women in the Transition to Capitalism: Nineteenth to Mid-Twentieth Century Vietnam." In Research in Political Economy. Vol. 4, edited by Paul Zarembka. Greenwich, CT: JAI Press, 1981.

9789. Woodside, ALexander. "Vietnamese History: Confucianism, Colonialism and the Struggle for Independence." Vietnam Forum 11 (Winter-Spring 1988): 21-48.

YEMEN

9790. Abu-Amr, Ziad M. *The People's Democratic Republic of Yemen: The Transformation of Society*. Doctoral dissertation: Georgetown University, 1986. UMO# 8726450.

9791. Bidwell, Robin. *The Two Yemens*. London: Longman Westview Press, 1983.

9792. Burrowes, Robert D. *The Yemen Arab Republic: The Politics of Development, 1962-1986*. Boulder, CO: Westview, 1987.

9793. Halliday, Fred. "North Yemen Today." *Merip Reports* 130 (February 1985): 3-9.

9794. Ismael, Tarez Y. and Jacqueline S. Ismael. *The People's Democratic Republic of Yemen: Politics, Economics, and Society: The Politics of Socialist Transformation*. Boulder, CO: L.Rienner, 1986.

9795. Labourne, Patrick. "Democratic tribale et systeme politique en Republique Arabe du Yemen." *Revue Francaise de Science Politique* 31 (1981): 745-768.

9796. Lackner, Helen. *PDR Yemen: Outpost of Socialist Development in Arabia*. London: Ithaca Press, 1985.

9797. Makhlouf, Carla. *Changing Veils: Women and Modernization in North Yemen*. London: Croom Helm, 1979.

9798. El Mallakh, Ragaei. *The Economic Development of the Yemen Arab Republic*. London: Croom Helm, 1986.

9799. Molyneux, Maxine. "Legal Reform and Socialist Revolution in Democratic Yemen: Women and the Family." *International Journal of the Sociology of Law* No.13 (1985): 147-172.

9800. Molyneux, Maxine. State Policies and the Position of Women Workers in the People's Democratic Republic of Yemen between 1967 and 1977. London: International Labour Office, 1983.

9801. Pridham, B. R., ed. Economy, Society, and Culture in Contemporary Yemen. London: Croom Helm, 1985. [South Yemen.]

9802. Stookey, Robert W. South Yemen: A Marxist Republican Arabia. Boulder, CO: Westview Press, 1982.

YUGOSLAVIA

9803. Alexander, Stella. "Croatia: The Catholic Church and the Clergy, 1919-1945." In Catholics, the State, and the European Radical Right, 1919-1945, edited by Richard J. Wolff and Jorg K. Hoensch. Boulder, CO: Social Science Monographs, 1987.

9804. Beljo, Ante. Yugoslavia Genocide: A Documented Analysis. Translated by D. Sladojevic-Sola. Sudbury, Ontario: Croation Folklore Federation of Canada, 1985.

9805. Beloff, Nora. Tito's Flawed Legacy: Yugoslavia and the West Since 1939. Boulder, CO: Westview, 1986.

9806. Biberaj, Elez. "The Conflict in Kosovo." Survey 28 (Autumn 1984): 39-57.

9807. Binder, David. "In Yugoslavia, Rising Ethnic Strife Brings Fears of Worse Civil Conflict." New York Times, (November 1, 1987): [The role of ethnic Albanians.]

9808. Browning, Christopher R. "The Final Solution in Serbia: The Semlin Judenlager-A Case Study." Yad Vashem Studies 15 (1983): 55-90.

9809. Browning, Christopher R. "Wehrmacht Reprisal Policy and the Mass Murder of Jews in Serbia." Militargesch. Mitt. 33 (1983): 31-47.

9810. Burg, Steven L. "Ethnic Conflict and the Federalization of Socialist Yugoslavia: The Serbo-Croat Conflict." Publius 7 (Fall 1977): 119-143.

9811. Carpi, D. "The Rescue of Jews in the Italian Zone of Occupied Croatia." In Rescue Attempts during the Holocaust, edited by Y. Gutman and E. Zuroff. 465-526. Jerusalem: 1977.

9812. Clark, Cal and Janet Clark. "The Gender Gap in Yugoslavia: Elite versus Mass Levels." Political Psychology 8 (September 1987): 411-426. [Political activity.]

9813. Clissold, Stephen. "Croat Separatism: Nationalism, Dissidence and Terrorism." Conflict Studies No. 103 (January 1979)

9814. Cohen, Lenard J. The Socialist Pyramid: Elites and Power in Yugoslavia. Oakville: Mosaic Press, 1989.

9815. Cowell, Alan. "A Land of Serbs and Albanians and Trouble." New York Times, (April 29, 1987)

9816. Cuvalo, Ante. The Croatian National Movement, 1966-1972. Doctoral dissertation: Ohio State University, 1987. UMO # 8717615.

9817. Dedic, Abdullah. "The Muslim Predicament in Yugoslavia: An Impression." Journal (Institute of Muslim Minority Affairs) 8 (1987): 121-131.

9818. Dedijer, Vladimir. Jasenovac-das jugoslawische Auschwitz. Edited by Gottfried Niemietz. Translated by Durdica Durkovic. Freiburg: Ahriman-Verlag, 1988.

9819. Devetak, Silvo. "The Equality of Nations and Nationalities in Yugoslavia." Europa Ethnica 42 (1985): 99-105.

9820. Devetak, Silvo. "National Minorities and Cultural- Educational Cooperation between Yugoslavia and Its Neighbors." Europa Ethnica 45 (1988)

9821. Diehl, Jackson. "Ethnic Rivalries Cause Unrest in Yugoslav Region." Washington Post, (November 29, 1986)

9822. Djilas, Aleksa. The Contested Country. Yugoslav Unity and Communist Revolution, 1919-1953. Cambridge, MA: Harvard University Press, 1991.

9823. Djilas, Aleksa. "The Foundations of Croatian Identity: A Sketch for Historical Reinterpretation." S. Slav J 8 (1985): 1-12.

9824. Dragnich, Alex N. "The Rise and Fall of Yugoslavia: The Omen of the Upsurge of Serbian Nationalism." East European Quarterly 23 (June 1989): 183-198.

9825. Dragnich, Alex N. and Slavko Todorovich. The Saga of Kosovo. Focus of Serbian-Albanian Relations. New York: East European Monographs, 1985.

9826. Falconi, Carlo. The Silence of Pius XII. Boston, MA Translated by Bernard Wall: Little, Brown, 1970. [See pp. 259-351.]

754 WORLD RACISM AND RELATED INHUMANITIES

9827. Flakierski, Henryk. The Economic System and Income Distribution in Yugoslavia. Armonk, New York: Sharpe, 1989.

9828. Flakierski, Henryk. "The Economic System and Income Distribution in Yugoslavia." Eastern European Economics 27 (Summer 1989)

9829. Franolic, Branko. "Language Policy in Yugoslavia with Special Reference to Croatian." Journal of Croatian Studies 25-26 (1984-1985): 126-152.

9830. Freidenreich, Harriet P. The Jews of Yugoslavia: A Quest for Community. Philadelphia, PA: Jewish Publication Society of America, 1979.

9831. Gross, Mirjana. "Croatian National-Integrational Ideologies from the End of Illyrism to the Creation of Yugoslavia." Austrian History Yearbook 15-16 (1979-1980): 3-33.

9832. Grothusen, Klaus-Detlev, ed. Jugoslawien-Yugoslavia. Gottingen: Vandenhoeck and Ruprecht, 1975.

9833. Gruenwald, Oskar and Karen Rosenblum-Cale, eds. Human Rights in Yugoslavia. Irvington Publishers, 1990.

9834. Haboucha, Reginette. "Type and Motif Index of Tales of the Sephardic Jews in Macedonia." Macedonian Review 19 (1989): 57-87.

9835. Harriman, Helga H. Slovenia Under Nazi Occupation, 1941- 1945. New York: Studia Slovenica, 1977.

9836. Hocevar, Toussaint. "Linguistic Minorities of Yugoslavia and Adjacent Areas During the Interwar Period: An Economic Perspective." Nationalities Papers 12 (1984): 209-221.

9837. Hockenos, Paul. "Albanians and Serbians On the Brink of Civil War." In These Times, (February 28, 1990)

9838. Hor, Ladislaus and Martin Broszat. "Der kroatische Ustascha-Staat 1941-1945." Vierteljahrshefte fur Zeitgeschichte 8 (1964)

9839. Indjic, Tirvo. Affirmative Action: The Yugoslav Case. May 1984. [ERIC ED 249 303.]

9840. Irwin, Zachary. "The Islamic Revival and the Muslims of Bosnia-Hercegovina." East European Quarterly 17 (1983): 437-458.

9841. Jancar, Barbara. "Neofeminism in Yugoslavia: A Closer Look." Women & Politics 8 (1988): 1-30.

9842. Jelavich, Charles. South Slav Nationalisms-Textbooks and Yugoslav Union Before 1914. Columbus: Ohio State University Press, 1990.

9843. Jonic, Koca. Nationalities in Yugoslavia. Belgrade: Jugoslavenska Stvarnost-Medjunarodna Politika, 1982.

9844. Kaiser, R. J. "The Equalization Dilemma in Yugoslavia." Geoforum 21 (1990)

9845. Kamm, Henry. "Minorities Are Uneasy in Yugoslav Province." New York Times, (July 27, 1986): [Kosovo Antonomous Province.]

9846. Kamm, Henry. "Slovenes of Yugoslavia Speak Freely and Thrive Financially." New York Times, (June 17, 1987)

9847. Kamm, Henry. "Yugoslavia Unglued: How Unrest Grew." New York Times, (October 11, 1988)

9848. Karlovic, N. L. "Internal Colonialism in a Marxist Society: The Case of Croatia." Ethnic and Racial Studies 5 (1982): 276-299.

9849. Al-Khalidi, Abdullah. The Moslem Community in the Country of Nations- The Soviet Federal Republic of Yugoslavia. Master's thesis: Eastern Michigan University, 1986.

9850. Kovac, Miha. "The Slovene Spring (interview)." New Left Review No. 171 (Sept.- Oct. 1988): 115-128.

9851. Lederer, Z., ed. The Crimes of the Germans and their Collaborators against the Jews of Yugoslavia. Belgrade: 1953.

9852. Lee, Michele. "Kosovo Between Yugoslavia and Albania." New Left Review No. 140 (July-August 1983): 62-91.

9853. Levntal, Z., ed. The Crimes of the Fascist Occupiers and their Assistants Against the Jews in Yugoslavia. Belgrade: Savez jevrejskih opstina Jugoslavige, 1952. [In Serbo- Croatian with English summary.]

9854. Licht, Sonja. "The Yugoslav Experience: The Failure of Reform Without Democracy." New Politics 2 (Summer 1989): 152-165.

9855. Littlefield, Frank C. Germany and Yugoslavia, 1933-1941: The German Conquest of Yugoslavia. Boulder, CO: East European Monographs, 1988.

9856. Logoreci, Anton. "The Albanians of Yugoslavia." Encounter (July-August 1988)

9857. Ludanyi, Andrew. "The Hungarians of Vojvodina under Yugoslav Rule." In The Hungarians: A Divided Nation, edited by Stephen Borsody. New Haven, CT.: Yale Center for International and Areas Studies, 1988.

9858. Magas, Branka. "Yugoslavia: The Spectre of Balkanization." New Left Review No. 174 (March-April 1989): 3-31.

9859. Magner, Thomas F. "Language and Nationality in the Balkans: The Case of Yugoslavia." Geolinguistics 14 (1988): 108-124.

9860. Magnusson, Kjell. "The Serbian Reaction: Kosovo and Ethnic Mobilization among the Serbs." Nordic Journal of Soviet and East European Studies (Sweden) 4 (1987): 3-30.

9861. Markovic, Mihailo. "Tragedy of National Conflict in 'Real Socialism'- The Case of the Yugoslav Autonomous Province of Kosovo." Praxis International (January 4, 1990): 408-424.

9862. Milanovic, B. "Patterns of Regional Growth in Yugoslavia, 1952-1983." Journal of Development Economics 25 (February 1987)

9863. Milazzo, M. The Chetnik Movement and the Yugoslav Resistance. Baltimore, MD: 1975.

9864. Neal, Fred Warner. "Yugoslav Approaches to the Nationalities Problem: The Politics of Circumvention." E. Eur. Q. 18 (1984): 327-334.

9865. Nystrom, Kerstin. "Regional Identity and Ethnic Conflict: Croatia's Dilemma." In Regions in Upheaval: Ethnic Conflict and Political Mobilization, edited by S. Tagil. Stockholm: Esselte Studium, 1984.

9866. Nystrom, Kerstin. "The Serbs in Croatia: A Dual Identity?" Nordic Journal of Soviet and East European Studies (Sweden) 4 (1987): 31-52.

9867. Ott, Andre. Dangers serbes sur la Croatie. Paris: Nouvelles Editions Latines, 1982.

9868. Palmer, S. and R. King. Yugoslav Communism and the Macedonian Question. London: Archon Books, 1971.

9869. Paris, Edmond. Genocide in Satellite Croatia, 1941-1945: A Record of Racial and Religious Persecutions. Chicago, IL Translated by Lois Perkins: American Institute for Balkan Affairs,

9870. Pavlowitch, Steven K. The Improbable Survivor: Yugoslavia and Its Problems, 1918-1988. Columbus: Ohio State University Press, 1990.

9871. Pavlowitch, Steven K. Unconventioanl Perceptions of Yugoslavia, 1940-1945. New York: East European Monographs, 1985.

9872. Pecujlic, Miroslav. The University of the Future. The Yugoslav Experience. Westport, CT Translated by Tanja Lorkovic: Greenwood, 1987.

9873. Perry, Duncan M. The Politics of Terror. The Macedonian Revolutionary Movements, 1893-1903. Durham, NC: Duke University Press, 1988.

9874. Pipa, Arshi. "The Political Situation of the Albanians in Yugoslavia, with Particular Attention to the Kosovo Problem: A Critical Approach." East European Quarterly 23 (June 1989): 159-181.

9875. Pipa, Arshi. "Serbian Apologetics: Markovic on Kosovo." Telos No. 83 (Spring 1990): 168-176.

9876. Pipa, Arshi and Sami Repishti, eds. Studies on Kosova. Boulder, CO: East European Monogrpahs, 1984.

9877. Plestina, Dijana M. Politics and Inequality: A Study of Regional Disparities in Yugoslavia. Doctoral dissertation: University of California, Berkeley, 1987. UMO # 8814020.

9878. Pomeragn, Frank. "The Holocaust in Macedonia." Soviet Jewish Affairs 17 (Winter 1987): 75-78. [Yugoslav Macdeonia, Review of Z. Kolonomos & V. Veskovic- Vangeli, The Jews in Macedonia During the Second World War, 1941-1945: A Collection of Documents, in Macedonian; introduction in English.]

9879. Prcela, Ivan and Stanko Guldescu, eds. Operation Slaughterhouse: The Massacre of the Croatian Armed Forces and Civilian Population, 1945-1947. Philadelphia, PA: Dorrance, 1970.

9880. Primorac, Igro. "Yugoslav Jewry in World War II." Soviet Jewish Affairs 12 (1982)

9881. Puxon, Grattan. "Romanes and Language Policy in Yugoslavia." International Journal of the Sociology of Language 19 (1979): 83-90. [Gypsies.]

9882. Rabinovich, Abraham. "Rescue, Italian Style." Jerusalem Post, (March 9, 1984): [Rescue of Yugoslav Jews during World War II by Italians.]

9883. Ramet, Pedro. "From Strossmayer to Stepinac: Croatian National Ideology and Catholicism." Can. R. Stud. Nationalism 12 (Spring 1985): 123-139.

9884. Ramet, Pedro. "Kosovo and the Limits of Yugoslav Socialist Patriotism." Can. R. Stud. Nationalism 16 (1989): 227-250.

9885. Ramet, Pedro. Nationalism and Federalism in Yugoslavia, 1963-1983. Bloomington: Indiana University Press, 1984. [Part 3, on Croatian crisis, 1967-1972.]

9886. Ramet, Pedro. "Primordial Ethnicity or Modern Nationalism: The Case of Yugoslavia's Muslims." Nationalities Papers 13 (1985): 165-187.

9887. Ramet, Pedro. "Problems of Albanian Nationalism in Yugoslavia." Orbis 25 (1981): 369-388.

9888. Reinhartz, Dennis. "Aryanism in the Independent State of Croatia, 1941-1945: The Historical Basis and Cultural Questions." South Slavic Journal 9 (1986): 19-25.

9889. Reuter, Jens. "Der Bd K J [Bund der Kommunisten Jugoslawien] und das Kosovo Problem: Massnahmen zur Bekämpfung einer staatsgefahrenden Krise." Wissenschaftlicher Dienst Südosteuropa 30 (1981): 191-197.

9890. Reuter, Jens. Die Albaner in Jugoslawien. Munich: R. Oldenbourg, 1982.

9891. Reuter, Jens. "Die albanische Minderheit in Mazedonien: der separatistische Kosovo-Bazillus." Südosteuropa 36 (1987): 587-597.

9892. Robinson, Gertrude J. "Mass Media and Ethnic Strife in Multinational Yugoslavia." Journalism Quarterly 51 (Autumn 1974): 490-497.

9893. Romano, Jasha. The Jews of Yugoslavia 1941-1945: Victims of Genocide and Participants in the War of National Liberation. Belgrade: The Federation of Jewish Communities and Its Historical Museum in Belgrade, 1981.

9894. Sadkovich, James J. "The Use of Political Trials to Repress Croatian Dissent, 1929-1934." Journal of Croatian Studies 28-29 (1987-1988): 103-140.

9895. Scammell, Michael. "The New Yugoslavia." New York Review of Books, (July 19, 1990)

9896. Scammell, Michael. "Yugoslavia: The Awakening." New York Review of Books, (June 28, 1990)

9897. Schlarp, Karl Heinz. Wirtschaft und Besatzung in Serbien 1941-1944: Ein Beitrag zur nationalsozialistischen Wirtschaftspolitik in Sudosteuropa. Stuttgart: Franz Steiner, 1986.

9898. Schopflin, George. "Croatian Nationalism." Survey 19 (Winter 1973)

9899. Sekelj, Laslo. "Anti-Semitism in Yugoslavia, 1918-1945." East European Quarterly 22 (1988): 159-172.

9900. Shelah, Menachem. "The Catholic Church in Croatia, the Vatican and the Murder of Croatian Jews." Holocaust and Genocide Studies 4 (1989)

9901. Shelah, Menachem. "Chetniks." In Encyclopedia of the Holocaust. 288-289. New York: Macmillan, 1990.

9902. Shelah, Menachem. "Croatia." In Encyclopedia of the Holocaust, I. New York: Macmillan, 1990.

9903. Shelah, Menachem. "Sajmiste: An Extermination Camp in Serbia." Holocaust & Genocide Studies 2 (1987): 243-260.

9904. Shelah, Menachem. "Serbia." In Encyclopedia of the Holocaust, IV. 1340-1342. New York: Macmillan, 1990.

9905. Shelah, Menachem. "Ustasa." In Encyclopedia of the Holocaust, IV. New York: Macmillan, 1990.

9906. Shelah, Menachem. "Yugoslavia." In Encyclopedia of the Holocaust. 1716-1722. New York: Macmillan, 1990.

9907. Siljegovic, Blagoje. Nationalism: Yugoslavia's Insoluble Problem. Master's thesis: Niagara University, 1979.

9908. Sirc, Ljubo. Betwen Hitler and Tito: Nazi Occupation and Communist Oppression. London: Andre Deutsch, 1990.

9909. Stankovic, Slobodan. Titos Erbe: die Hypothek der alten Richtungskampfe ideologischer und nationaler Fraktionen. Munich: R. Oldenbourg Verlag, 1981.

9910. Steinberg, Jonathan. All or Nothing: The Axis and the Holocaust. Routledge, 1990. [Jews under Italian and German occupation in Yugoslavia, Greece, and France, 1941-1943.]

9911. Tashkovski, Dragan. "The Macedonian Nation." Macedonian Review 8 (1978): 275-295.

9912. Tolstoy, Nikolai. The Minister and the Massacres. London: Hutchinson, 1986. [Enforced repatriation of Chetniks to Yugoslavia at end of World War II.]

9913. Tomasevich, J. The Chetniks: War and Revolution in Yugoslavia, 1941-1945. Stanford: 1975.

9914. Tonnes, Bernhard. "Kosovo und die jugoslawisch-albanischen Beziehungen." Europaische Rundschau 10 (1982): 55-65.

9915. Verna, Frank P. Yugoslavia under Italian Rule, 1941-1943: Civil and Military Aspects of the Italian Occupation. 2 vols. Doctoral dissertation: University of California, Santa Barbara, 1985. UMO # 8605960.

9916. Vinski, I. "The Distribution of Yugoslavia's National Income by Social Classes in 1938." Review of Income and Wealth 13 (Sept. 1967): 259-281.

9917. Vinskovic, Boris. "Social Inequality in Yugoslavia." New Left Review 95 (January-February 1976): 26-44.

9918. Yugoslavia: Prisoners of Conscience. Amnesty International, 1990.

ZAIRE

9919. Brown, Judith E. and Richard C. Brown. Finding the Causes of Child Malnutrition: A Community Handbook. 2d ed. Kangu-Mayombe, Zaire: Bureau of Study and Research for the Promotion of Health, 1984.

9920. Celis, Georges and I. Maothea. "Sur une Réforme Authentique de l'Enseisgnement au Zaire." R. Afric. Sci. Educ. 5 (1983): 37-58.

9921. Fabian, Johannes. Language and Colonial Power: The Appropriation of Swahili in the Former Belgian Congo, 1880- 1938. New York: Cambridge University Press, 1986.

9922. Gazi, Losso. "Culture, Litterature et Enseignement au Zaire: Essai de Bilan." Cah. CEDAF No.8 (1984): 1-116.

9923. Gould, David J. Bureaucratic Corruption and Underdevelopment in the Third World: The Case of Zaire. New York: Pergamon Press, 1990.

9924. Harms, Robert W. River of Wealth, River of Sorrow: The Central Zaire Basin in the Era of the Slave and Ivory Trade, 1500-1891. New Haven, CT: Yale University Press, 1981.

9925. Higginson, John. "Bringing the Workers Back In: Worker Protest and Popular Intervention in Katanga, 1931-1941." Canadian Journal of African Studies 22 (1988): 199-223.

9926. Higginson, John. A Working Class in the Making, Belgian Colonial Labor Policy, Private Enterprise, and the African Mineworker, 1907-1951. Madison: University of Wisconsin Press, 1989.

9927. Jewsiewicki, B. "Raison d'etat ou raison du capital: l'accumulation primitive au Congo belge." African Economic History No. 12 (1983): 157-182.

9928. Kabarhuza, H. B. "Christian Intellectuals in Zaire." *Pro mundi vita dossiers* Nos. 30-31 (1984): 1-47.

9929. Kasa-Vubu, Z. J. M'Poyo. "L'évolution de la femme congolaise sous le régime colonial belge." *Civilisations* 37 (1987): 159-190.

9930. Kasangana, Mwalaba. "L'Economie Zairoise." *Cah. Éc. Sociaux* 20 (September-December 1982): 204-259.

9931. Kivilu, Sabakinu. "Population and Health in Zaire during the Colonial Period from the End of the 19th Century to 1960." *Transafric. Jr. Hist.* 13 (1984): 92-109.

9932. Lyons, Maryinez. *The Colonial Disease: Sleeping Sickness in the Social History of Northern Zaire, 1903-1930*. Doctoral dissertation: University of California, Los Angeles, 1987. UMO # 8719966.

9933. MacGaffey, Janet. *Entrepreneurs and Parasites. The Struggle for Indigenous Capitalism in Zaire*. New York: Cambridge University Press, 1988.

9934. MacGaffey, W. "Religion, Class, and Social Pluralism in Zaire." *Canadian Journal of African Studies* 24 (1990)

9935. Muteba-Tshitenge. *Zaire: combat pour la deuxième independance*. Paris: Editions l'Harmattan, 1985.

9936. Ndoma, Ungina. "Belgian Politics and Linguistic Policy in Congolese Schools, 1885-1914." *Transafric. Jr. Hist.* 13 (1984): 146-156.

9937. Pachter, Elise F. *Our Man in Kinshasa: U.S. Relations with Mobutu, 1970-1983: Patron-Client Relations in the International Sphere*. Doctoral dissertation: Johns Hopkins University, 1987. UMO # 8716678.

9938. "Réforme du systeme éducatif au Zaire." *R. afric. sci. éduc.* (May 1982): 1-88.

9939. Schatzberg, Michael. *The Dialectics of Oppression in Zaire*. Bloomington: Indiana University Press, 1988.

9940. Schmitz, Erich. "Stabilisierende und destabilisierende Faktoren eines Systems im wirtschaftlichen Niedergang: der Fall Zaire." *Afrika Spektrum* 18 (1983): 49-70.

9941. Streiffeler, Friedhelm. *Sozialpsychologie des Neokolonialismus: Intergruppenbeziehungen in Zaire*. Frankfurt: Campus Verlag, 1982.

9942. Tiker-Tiker. "Inégal Développement des Régions Zaïroises." *Cah. Ec. Sociaux* 20 (January-June 1982): 71-119.

9943. Turner, Margaret A. Housing in Zaire: How the System Works and How the People Cope. Doctoral dissertation: University of Wisconsin, 1985. UMO # 8522541.

9944. Winternitz, Helen. East Along the Equator. A Journey Up the Congo and Into Zaire. Boston, MA: Atlantic Monthly Press, 1987.

9945. Yates, Barbara A. "White Views of Black Minds: Schooling in King Leopold's Congo." History of Education Quarterly 20 (Spring 1980): 27-50.

9946. Zajaczkowski, A. "Belgian Congo: Between Indirect and Direct Rule." Hemispheres (1985): 259-270.

ZAMBIA

9947. Clark, John and Caroline Allison. Zambia. Debt and Poverty. Oxford, England: Oxfam Publications, 1989.

9948. Foster, G. M. "Colonial Administration in Northern Rhodesia in 1962." Human Organization 46 (1987): 359-368.

9949. Hall, R. Zambia 1890-1964: The Colonial Period. London: 1976.

9950. Henderson, Ian. "The Limits of Colonial Power: Race and Labour Problems in Colonial Zambia, 1900-1953." Imperial Commonwealth History 2 (May 1974): 294-307.

9951. Henderson, Ian. "Pre-Nationalist Resistance to Colonial Rule in Zambia." African Social Research No.9 (1970): 669- 680.

9952. Honeybone, R. and A. Marter, eds. Poverty and Wealth in Zambia. Lusaka: Institute of African Studies, 1979.

9953. Kaluba, L. H. "Education in Zambia: The Problem of Access to Schooling and the Paradox of the Private School Solution." Comparative Education 22 (1986): 159-170.

9954. Lungu, G. F. "Elites, Incrementalism and Educational Policy-making in Post-Independence Zambia." Comparative Education 22 (1985): 287-296.

9955. Meebelo, Henry S. African Proletarians and Colonial Capitalism: The Origins, Growth and Struggles of the Zambian Labour Movement to 1964. Lusaka, Zambia: Kenneth Kaunda Foundation, 1986.

9956. Meebelo, Henry S. Reaction to Colonialism. Manchester, England: Manchester University Press, 1973.

9957. Mufune, P. "The Formation of Dominant Classes in Zambia: Critical Notes." Africa Today 35 (1988): 5-20.

9958. Ragsdale, John P. Protestant Mission Education in Zambia, 1880-1954. Selinsgrove, PA: Susquhenna University Press, 1986.

9959. Turok, Ben. "Zambia's System of State Capitalism." Development & Change 11 (July 1980): 455-478.

9960. Vickery, Kenneth P. Black and White in Southern Zambia: The Tonga Plateau Economy and British Imperialism, 1890-1939. Westport, CT: Greenwood, 1986.

ZIMBABWE

9961. Arrighi, G. "Labour Supplies in Historical Perspective: A Study of Proletarianization of the African Peasantry in Rhodesia." In Essays on the Political Economy of Africa G. Arrighi and J. Saul. London: Monthly Review Press, 1973.

9962. Beach, D. N. The Shona and Zimbabwe, 900-1850. London: Heinemann Educational, 1981.

9963. Berger, Elena L. Labour, Race and Colonial Rule: The Copperbelt from 1924 to Independence. Oxford, England: Clarendon Press, 1974.

9964. Bond-Stewart, Kathy. Independence Is Not Only for One Sex. Harare, Zimbabwe: 1987.

9965. Bourdillon, M. F. C. "Christianity and Wealth in Rural Communities in Zimabwe." Zambezia 11 (1983): 37-54.

9966. Caute, David. Under the Skin: The Death of White Rhodesia. Evanston, IL: Northwestern University Press, 1983.

9967. Charlton, Michael. The Last Colony in Africa: Diplomacy and the Independence of Rhodesia. Cambridge, MA: Blackwell, 1990.

9968. Cheater, Angela P. "The Role and Position of Women in Colonial and Pre-Colonial Zimbabwe." Zambia 13 (1986): 65-80.

9969. Choate, S. L. Aspects of the Economic Development of Southern Rhodesia, 1923-1953. Doctoral dissertation: University of Bristol, 1985.

9970. Clarke, D. G. The Distribution of Income and Wealth in Rhodesia. Gwelo: Mambo Press, 1977.

9971. Clarke, D. G. "Land Inequality and Income Distribution." African Studies Review 18 (1975): 1-8.

9972. Clarke, D. G. "Settler Ideology and African Underdevelopment in Postwar Rhodesia." Rhodesian Journal of Economics 8 (March 1974): 17-38.

9973. Foley, S. "The Myth of Early African Indifference to Education in Zimbabwe." Zimbabwean History 11 (1980): 44- 55.

9974. Gargan, Edward A. "Whites Who Left Zimbabwe, Fearful of Future Drift Back." New York Times, (May 18, 1986)

9975. Gilmurray, John. The Struggle for Health. Gwelo, Zimbabwe: 1979.

9976. Grant, George C. The Africans' Predicament in Rhodesia. London: Minority Rights Group, 1972.

9977. Gray, Richard. The Two Nations-Aspects of the Development of Race Relations in the Rhodesias and Nyasaland. London: Oxford University Press, 1960.

9978. Hawkins, Tony. "Zimbabwe's Socialist Transformation." Optima 35 (December 1987): 184-195.

9979. Herbst, Jeffrey. "Racial Reconciliation in Southern Africa." International Affairs (Great Britain) 65 (1988- 1989): 43-54.

9980. Hitchens, Christopher and David Stephen. Inequalities in Zimbabwe. rev. ed. London: Minority Rights Group, 1981.

9981. International Labour Office. Labour Conditions and Discrimination in Southern Rhodesia (Zimbabwe). London: ILO, 1977.

9982. International Commission of Jurists. Racial Discrimination and Repression in Southern Rhodesia: A Legal Study. London: Catholic Institute for International Relations, 1976.

9983. Kazembe, J. and M. Mol. "The Changing Legal Status of Women in Zimbabwe since Independence." Canadian Women Stud. 7 (1986): 53-59.

9984. Kennedy, Dane K. Islands of White: Settler Society and Culture in Kenya and Southern Rhodesia, 1890-1939. Durham, NA: Duke University Press, 1987.

9985. Keppel-Jones, Arthur. Rhodes and Rhodesia: The White Conquest of Zimbabwe, 1884-1902. Buffalo, New York: McGill- Queen's University Press, 1983.

9986. Kinloch, Graham C. "Changing Black Reaction to White Domination." Rhodesian History 5 (1974): 67-78.

ZIMBABWE 767

9987. Klostris, C. The Effects of Multinational Corporations on the Zimbabwe Economy. Doctoral dissertation: University of Strathclyde, 1987.

9988. Kosmin, Barry A. Majuta. A History of the Jewish Community in Zimbabwe. Gwelo: Mambo Press, 1982. [Zimbabwe Independent, P.O. Box 5, Salisbury, Zimbabwe.]

9989. Lacy, Creighton. "'Christian' Racism in Rhodesia." Christian Century (March 15, 1972)

9990. Lemon, David M. H. Ivory Madness. Harare: College Press, 1983.

9991. Loney, Martin. Rhodesia, White Racism and Imperial Response. Harmondsworth: Penguin, 1975.

9992. Mackenzie, Clayton G. "Zimbabwe's Educational Miracle and the Problems It Has Created." International Review of Education 34 (1988): 337-354.

9993. Mahoso, T. P. Between Two Nationalisms: A Study in Liberal Activism and Western Domination, Zimbabwe, 1920-1980. 2 vols. Doctoral dissertation: Temple University, 1987. UMO # 8711371.

9994. Makambe, E. P. "The Asian Labour Solution in Zimbabwe, 1898-1904: Labour Practice and Racial Attitudes in a Colonial Society." Transafric. Jr. Hist. 13 (1984): 110-145.

9995. Mayana, Henry. The Political Economy of Land in Zimbabwe. Gweru, Zimbabwe: 1984.

9996. McGregor, R. Native Segregation in Southern Rhodesia: A Study of Social Policy. Doctoral dissertation: University of London, external degree, 1940.

9997. Mombeshora, S. "The Salience of Ethnicity in Political Development: The Case of Zimbabwe." International Sociology 5 (December 1990)

9998. Mosley, Paul. The Settler Economies: Studies in the Economic History of Kenya and Southern Rhodesia, 1900-1963. New York: Cambridge University Press, 1983.

9999. Mungazi, Dickson A. "The Educational Policy of the British South African Company in Zimbabwe: A Dilemma of Choice, 1899- 1923." Afric. Urban Quarterly 2 (February 1987): 3-12.

10000. Mutambirwa, James A. C. The Rise of Settler Power in Southern Rhodesia (Zimbabwe), 1898-1923. Rutherford, NJ: Fairleigh Dickinson University Press, 1980.

10001. Mutiti, M. Aaron Benjamin. "Rhodesia and Her Four Discriminatory Constitutions." African Review 4 (1974): 259-278.

10002. Nzenza, Sekai. Zimbabwean Women: My Own Story. London: Karia Press, 1988.

10003. Palley, Claire. "Law and the Unequal Society: Discriminatory Legislation in Rhodesia under the Rhodesian Front from 1963-1969 (2 parts)." Race 12 (July and October 1970): 15-47, 139-167.

10004. Palley, Claire. "A Note on the Development of Legal Inequality in Rhodesia: 1890-1962." Race 12 (July 1970): 87-93.

10005. Palmer, Robin. Land and Racial Domination in Rhodesia. London: Heinemann Educational, 1977.

10006. Pankhurst, D. T. The Dynamics of the Social Relations of Production and Reproduction in Zimbabwean Communal Areas. Doctoral dissertation: University of Liverpool, 1989.

10007. Phimister, Ian R. "The Combined and Contradictory Inheritance of the Struggle against Colonialism." In Zimbabwe's Prospects. London: Macmillan, 1988.

10008. Phimister, Ian R. An Economic and Social History of Zimbabwe, 1890-1948: Capital Accumulation and Class Struggle. New York: Longman, 1988.

10009. Phimister, Ian R. "Pasi Ne (Down With) Class Struggle? The New History for Schools in Zimbabwe." History in Africa 11 (1984): 367-374.

10010. Phimister, Ian R. "Zimbabwe: The Inheritance of the Anti- Colonial Struggle." Transformation 5 (1987): 51-59.

10011. Ranger, T. O. Revolt in Southern Rhodesia 1896-1897. London: Heinemann, 1979.

10012. Rogers, Cyril A. and Charles Frantz. Racial Themes in Southern Rhodesia: The Attitudes and Behavior of the White Population. New Haven, CT: Yale University Press, 1962.

10013. Rule, Sheila. "Zimbabwe Schools Are Swamped by High Hopes." New York Times, (March 11, 1986)

10014. Skalnes, Tor. "Group Interests and the State: An Explanation of Zimbabwe's Agricultural Policies." Journal of Modern African Studies 27 (March 1989): 85-108.

10015. Skelton, Kenneth. Bishop in Smith's Rhodesia: Notes from a Turbulent Octave, 1962-1970. Gweru, Zimbabwe: Mambo Press, 1985.

10016. Stoneman, Colin, ed. Zimbabwe's Inheritance. New York: St. Martin's Press, 1982.

10017. Stoneman, Colin and Lionel Cliffe. Zimbabwe: Politics, Economics, and Society. New York: Pinter, 1989.

10018. Tamarkin, M. The Making of Zimbabwe: Decolonization in Regional and International Politics. Savage, MD: Frank Cass, 1990.

10019. Vambe, Lawrence. An Ill-Fated People: Zimbabwe Before and After Rhodes. Pittsburgh, PA: University of Pittsburgh Press, 1973.

10020. van Onselen, Charles. Chivaro: African Mine Labour in Southern Rhodesia, 1900-1933. London: Pluto Press, 1976.

10021. Verrier, Anthony. The Road to Zimbabwe 1890-1980. London: Jonathan Cape, 1986.

10022. Vickery, Kenneth P. "The Second World War Revival of Forced Labor in the Rhodesias." International Journal of African Historical Studies 22 (1989): 423-438.

10023. Warhurst, P. R. "The History of Race Relations in Rhodesia." Zambezia 3 (1973): 15-19.

10024. Weiner, D. "Socialist Transition in the Capitalist Periphery: A Case Study of Agriculture in Zimbabwe." Political Geography Quarterly 10 (January 1991)

10025. Weinrich, A. K. H. Black and White Elites in Rival Rhodesia. Manchester, England: Manchester University Press, 1973.

10026. ZANU, Department of Education and Culture. The New Teacher: Decolonizing the Classroom. Harare: Zimbabwe Foundation for Education with Production, 1987.

10027. Zimbabwe: A Break With The Past. New York: Human Rights Watch, 1990.

10028. Zvogbo, C. J. "Aspects of Interaction between Christianity and African Culture in Colonial Zimbabwe." Zambezia 13 (1986): 43-57.

AFRICA

10029. Abanime, Emeka P. "Ideologies of Race and Sex in Literature: Racism and Antiracism in the African Francophone Novel." CLA Journal 30 (1986): 125-143.

10030. Abitbol, Michel. The Jews of North Africa during the Second World War. Detroit, MI: Wayne State University Press, 1989.

10031. Abitbol, Michel, ed. Judaisme d'Afrique du Nord aux XIX- XXe siecles. Histoire, société, culture. Leiden: Brill, 1980.

10032. Abun-Nasr, Jamil M. A History of the Maghrib in the Islamic Period. New York: Cambridge University Press, 1987.

10033. Africa and the Africans: as Seen by Classical Writers: The Leo William Hansberry African History Notebook. 2d ed. Edited by J.E. Harris. Washington, D.C., 1977.

10034. African Reactions to Colonization in Central Africa. Ruhengeri: Faculte des Lettres de l'Universite Nationale du Rwanda, 1986. [In French and English.]

10035. Afshar, Haleh, ed. Women, State, and Ideology: Studies from Africa and Asia. Basingstoke, Hampshire: Macmillan, 1987.

10036. Ahmed-An-Na'lm, Abdullahi and Francis M. Deng, eds. Human Rights in Africa: Cross-Cultural Perspectives. Washington, D.C.: Brookings Books, 1990.

10037. Akiwowo, Akinsola. "Racialism and Shifts in the Mental Orientation of Black People in West Africa and the Americas, 1856-1956." Phylon 31 (1970): 256-264.

10038. Alpers, Edward A. The East African Slave Trade. Nairobi: East Africa Publishing House, 1967.

10039. Alpers, Edward A. Ivory and Slaves in East Central Africa. Berkeley: University of California Press, 1974.

10040. Amadi, Adolphe O. African Libraries: Western Tradition and Colonial Brainwashing. Metuchen, NJ: Scarecrow Press, 1981.

10041. Amin, Samir. Neo-Colonialism in West Africa. Translated by Francis McDonagh. New York: Monthly Review Press, 1973.

10042. Amin, Samir. "Underdevelopment and Dependence in Black Africa-Origins and Contemporary Forms." Journal of Modern African Studies 10 (1972): 503-524.

10043. Andersson, Neil and Shula Marks. "The State, Class and the Allocation of Health Resources in Southern Africa." Social Science and Medicine 28 (1989): 515-530.

10044. Andreyev, I. L. "Petty-Bourgeois and Pauper-Lumpen Strata in the Liberation Movement in African Countries." Africa Soviet Stud. (1985): 72-92.

10045. Apedaile, L. P. "An Exploration of the Role of Education in Rural-to-Urban Migration in Africa." E. Afric. J. Rural Dev. 12 (1979): 66-84.

10046. Austen, Ralph A. African Economic History: Internal Development and External Dependency. Portsmouth, NH: Heinemann, 1987.

10047. Bartlett, B. R. "Capitalism in Africa: A Survey." Journal of Developing Areas 24 (1990)

10048. Bay, Edna G. Women and Work in Africa. Boulder, CO: Westview Press, 1982.

10049. Baylies, Carolyn. "The Meaning of Health in Africa." Review of African Political Economy (September 1986): 62-72.

10050. Beachey, R. W., ed. A Collection of Documents on the Slave Trade of Eastern Africa. New York: Barnes & Noble, 1976.

10051. Bellagamba, A. "Preferential Option for the Poor: African Perspective." Afric. Christian Studies 3 (September 1987): 19-48.

10052. Bennett, Norman R. "Christian & Negro Slavery in Eighteenth-Century North Africa." Jr. of African History 1 (1960): 65-82.

10053. Berg, Wilfried. "The Neo-Colonialist Strategy of World Bank and IDA in the Eighties." Asien, Afrika, Lateinam. 15 (1987): 604-617.

772 WORLD RACISM AND RELATED INHUMANITIES

10054. Berman, Edward H. African Reactions to Missionary Education. New York: Teachers College Press, 1975.

10055. Bernard, Claude. "Aux origines du discours scolaire en pays capitaliste et colonialiste." Psych. Educ. (July 1982): 31-140.

10056. Bingham, Marjorie W. and Susan H. Gross. Women In Africa of the Sub-Sahara. 2 vols. Hudson, WI: Gem Publishers, 1982.

10057. Binsbergen, Wim van and Peter Geschiere, eds. Old Mode of Production and Capitalist Encroachment: Anthropological Explorations in Africa. Boston: Kegan Paul, 1985.

10058. Boahen, A. Adu. African Perspectives on Colonialism. Baltimore, MD: Johns Hopkins University Press, 1989.

10059. Boahen, A. Adu, ed. The UNESCO General History of Africa. Vol. VII, Africa Under Domination 1880-1935. Berkeley: University of California Press, 1985.

10060. Borruso, Paolo. "Le Missioni cattoliche italiane nella politica imperiale del fascismo (1936-1940)." Africa (Rome) 44 (March 1989): 50-78.

10061. Boxer, Charles R. Race Relations in the Portuguese Colonial Empire, 1415-1825. Oxford, England: Clarendon Press, 1963.

10062. Braginsky, M. I. "New Phenomena in the Emergence of the African Proletariat." Africa Soviet Studies (1983): 90-103.

10063. Bray, M. and others. Education and Society in Africa. London: Edward Arnold, 1986.

10064. Brillon, Yves. Ethnocriminologie de l'Afrique Noire. Montreal: Les Presses de l'Université de Montreal, 1980.

10065. Brinkman, Ronald J. Racism and Political Development in British Equatorial Africa 1880-1920. Doctoral dissertation: University of Denver, 1972. UMO # 8101696.

10066. Brokensha, David. "Inequality in Rural Africa: Fallers Reconsidered." Manchester Pop. Dev. 3 (1987): 1-21.

10067. Buettner, Thea. "Ideological Aspects of the Early Anticolonial Struggle in Subsaharan Africa." Asien, Afrika, Lateinam 15 (1987): 477-489.

10068. Campbell, Gwyn. "The East African Slave Trade, 1861-1895: The 'Southern' Complex." International Journal of African Historical Studies 22 (1989): 1-26.

10069. Cell, John W. "Anglo-Indian Medical Theory and the Origins of Segregation in West Africa." American Historical Review 91 (April 1986): 307-335.

10070. Champion, Jacques. "Linguistic and Cultural Diversities within Unitary Education Systems in French-speaking African Countries since Independence." Compare 8 (1978): 113-117.

10071. Chandhoke, N. "The Nature of the Dominant Elite in Africa." India Quarterly 35 (April-June 1984): 165-184.

10072. Chipman, John. The French in Africa. New York: Blackwell, 1989.

10073. Chouraqui, Andre. Between East and West: A History of the Jews of North Africa. Translated by Michael M. Bernet. Philadelphia, PA: Jewish Publication Society of America, 1968.

10074. Chouraqui, Andre. A Man in Three Worlds. Translated by Kenton Kilmer, Lanham, MD: University Press of America, 1984.

10075. Christopher, A. J. Colonial Africa. Totowa, NJ: Barnes & Noble, 1984.

10076. Clarke, John Henrik. "Pan-Africanism: A Brief History of an Idea in the African World." Presence Africaine (1988): 26- 56.

10077. Les classes moyennes au Maghreb. Paris: Editions du Centre Nationale de la Recherche Scientifique, 1980.

10078. Clegg, Legrand H., II. "Black Rulers of the Golden Age." Journal of African Civil. 6 (November 1985): 47-68.

10079. Clissold, Stephen. The Barbary Slaves. Totowa, NJ: Rowman and Littlefield, 1977. [ca. 1500-1800.]

10080. Cohen, Robin, ed. Forced Labour in Colonial Africa. London: Zed Press, 1979.

10081. Cohen, Ronald. "Slavery in Africa." Trans-action (Jan-Feb 1967)

10082. Conklin, Alice L. A Mission to Civilize: Ideology and Imperialism in French West Africa, 1895-1930. Doctoral dissertation: Princeton University, 1989. UMO # 9007150.

10083. Constantin, Francois. "Social Stratification on the Swahili Coast: From Race to Class?" Africa (London) 59 (1989): 145-160.

10084. Cooper, Frederick. "From Free Labor to Family Allowances: Labor and African Society in Colonial Discourse." American Ethnologist 16 (1989): 745-765.

10085. Cooper, Frederick. Plantation Slavery on the East Coast of Africa. New Haven, Conn.: Yale University Press, 1977.

10086. Cooper, Frederick. "The Problem of Slavery in African Studies." Journal of African History 20 (1979): 103-125.

10087. Cooper, Frederick and Ann L. Stoler. "Tensions of Empire: Colonial Control and Visions of Rule." American Ethnologist 16 (1989): 609-621.

10088. Coquery-Vidrovitch, Catherine. L'Histoire des femmes en Afrique. Paris: 1987.

10089. Cordell, Dennis D. and Joel W. Gregory, eds. African Population and Capitalism: Historical Perspectives. Beverly Hills, CA: Sage, 1986.

10090. Costa, Emilia V. da. "The Portuguese-African Slave Trade: A Lesson in Colonialism." Latin-Am. Perspectives 12 (1985): 41-62.

10091. Crocker, Chester A. "Military Dependence: The Colonial Legacy in Africa." Journal of Modern African Studies 12 (1974): 265-286.

10092. Crummey, Donald, ed. Banditry, Rebellion, and Social Protest in Africa. Portsmouth, NH: Heinemann, 1986.

10093. Curtin, Philip D., ed. Africa Remembered: Narratives by West Africans From the Era of the Slave Trade. Madison: Univerity of Wisconsin, 1967.

10094. Curtin, Philip D. "The End of the White Man's Grave: 19th Century Mortality in West Africa." Journal of Interdisciplinary History 21 (Summer 1990)

10095. Curtin, Philip D. "Nutrition in African History." In Hunger and History, edited by Robert I. Rotberg and Theodore K. Rabb. New York: Cambridge University Press, 1985.

10096. Daaku, K. Y. "The Slave Trade and African Society." In Emerging Themes of African History, edited by T.O. Ranger. 134- 140. Dar-Es-Salaam: East African Publishing House, 1965.

10097. Davidson, Basil. The People's Cause: A History of Guerrillas in Africa. Harlow: Longman, 1981.

10098. De Felice, Renzo. Ebrei in paese arabo: Gli ebrei nella Libia contemporanea tra colonialismo, nazionalismo arabo esionismo (1835-1970). Bologna: Il Mulino, 1978. [Jews in North Africa and their relation to the Arabs.]

10099. La décolonisation de l'Afrique vue par des Africains. Paris: Editions l'Harmattan, 1987.

10100. DeMarco, Roland R. Italianization of African Natives: Government Native Education in the Italian Colonies, 1890- 1937. New York: Teachers College Press, 1943.

10101. Diamond, Larry J. "Class Formation in the Swollen African State." Journal of Modern African Studies 25 (1987): 567- 596.

10102. Diamond, Larry J. "Ethnicity and Ethnic Conflict." Jr. Mod. African Studies 25 (March 1987): 117-128.

10103. Digre, Brian K. Imperialism's New Clothes: The Repartition of Tropical Africa, 1914-1919. New York: P. Lang, 1990.

10104. Diop, Cheikh Anta. The African Origin of Civilization: Myth or Reality. Translated by Mercer Cook. Westport, CT: 1974.

10105. Dobrska, Z. "General Trends of Income Distribution in Africa." Afr. Bulletin 35 (1988): 105-114.

10106. Donkov, Rumen. "National Revolution and the Church in the African South." Bulgarian Historical Review 14 (1986): 18- 29.

10107. Drake, St Clair. "The Black Diaspora in Pan-African Perspective." Black Scholar 7 (1975): 2-13.

10108. Ekeh, Peter P. "Social Anthropology and Two Contrasting Uses of Tribalism in Africa." Comparative Studies in Society and History 32 (October 1990): 660-700.

10109. Fage, J. D. "African Societies and the Atlantic Slave Trade." Past & Present No. 125 (November 1989)

10110. Fage, J. D. "Slavery and the Slave Trade in the Context of West African History." Journal of African History 10 (1969): 393-404.

10111. Fasi, M. El, ed. The UNESCO History of Africa. Vol. III, Africa from the Seventh to Eleventh Century. Berkeley: University of California Press, 1988.

10112. Fatton, Robert. "Bringing the Ruling Class Back: Class, State, and Hegemony in Africa." Comparative Politics 20 (April 1988): 253-264.

10113. Feierman, Steven. Health and Society in Africa. Waltham, MA: 1979.

10114. Feuser, Willfried and Isa M. Simoes. "The Emergence of African Literature in Portuguese." NSUKKA Stud. Afric. Lit. 4 (1986): 73-99.

10115. Feuerstein, R. and M. Richelle. Children of the Mellah. Jerusalem: Jewish Agency and Szold Foundation, 1953. [Jewish children of North Africa.]

10116. Fieldhouse, David. Black Africa, 1945-1980. London: 1986.

10117. Fieldhouse, David. Colonialism, 1875-1940. New York: 1981.

10118. Fieldhouse, Roger. "Cold War and Colonial Conflicts in British West African Adult Education, 1947-1953." History of Education Quarterly 24 (Fall 1984): 359-372.

10119. Fields, Karen E. Revival and Rebellion in Colonial Central Africa. Princeton, NJ: Princeton University Press, 1985.

10120. Friedman, Ellen G. Spanish Captives in North Africa in the Early Modern Age. Madison: University of Wisconsin Press, 1983.

10121. Gardinier, David E. "Education in French Equatorial Africa, 1945-1960." Cult. et Dev. (Louvain) 16 (1984): 303- 334.

10122. Gardinier, David E. "Vocational and Technical Education in French Equatorial Africa, 1842-1960." Proc. French Colonial Hist. Soc. 8 (1982): 113-123.

10123. Gerber, Jane S. Jewish Society in Fez: Studies in Communal and Economic Life. Doctoral dissertation: Columbia Univ., 1972.

10124. Gesheketer, Charles L. "Anti-colonialism and Class Formation: The Eastern Horn of Africa before 1950." Int. Jr. Afric. Hist. Stud. 18 (1985): 1-32.

10125. Ghai, Dharam and Samir Radwan, eds. Agrarian Policies and Rural Poverty in Africa. Geneva: International Labour Office, 1983.

10126. Ghai, Yash and Dharam Ghai. The Asian Minorities of East and Central Africa. London: Minority Rights Group, 1971.

10127. Ghebre-Ab, Habtu. World War II and the Disposal of "Africa orientale italiana" (a Comparative Study). Doctoral dissertation: Miami University, 1990. UMO # 9029383 [Eritrea, Libya, and Somaliland.]

10128. Gifford, Prosser and Timothy Weiskel. "African Education in a Colonial Context: French and British Styles." In France and Britain in Africa, edited by Gifford and W. Roger Louis. New Haven, CT: 1971.

10129. Gifford, Prosser and William R. Louis, eds. The Transfer of Power in Africa: Decolonization 1940-1960. New Haven, CT: Yale University Press, 1982.

10130. Githige, R. M. "The Issue of Slavery: Relations between the CMS and the State on the East African Coast Prior to 1895." Journal of Religion in Africa 16 (1986): 209-225.

10131. Haile-Mariam, Y. "Legal and Other Justifications for Writing-Off the Debts of the Poor Third World Countries: The Case of Africa South of the Sahara." Journal of World Trade 24 (February 1990): February 1990.

10132. Hair, P. E. H. The Atlantic Slave Trade and Black Africa. Liverpool: Liverpool University Press, 1988.

10133. Harries, Patrick. "Slavery, Social Incorporation and Surplus Extraction: The Nature of Free and Unfree Labour in South-East Africa." Journal of African History 22 (1981): 309-330.

10134. Haseeb, Khair El-Din, ed. The Arabs and Africa. Dover, NH: Croom Helm,

10135. Headrick, Rita. The Impact of Colonialism on Health in French Equatorial Africa: 1880-1934. Doctoral dissertation: University of Chicago, 1987.

10136. Hinchliffe, Keith. Higher Education in sub-Saharan Africa. Wolfeboro, NH: Croom Helm, 1987.

10137. Hirschberg, Joachim W. A History of the Jews in North Africa. 2d rev. ed. Leiden: E.J. Brill, 1981. [Vol. 2: From the Ottoman Conquests to the Present Time.]

10138. Ho, David Y. F. "Prejudice, Colonialism and Interethnic Relations: An East-West Dialogue." Journal of Asian and African Studies 20 (July-October 1985): 218-231.

10139. Hodges, Tony. Jehovah's Witnesses in Central Africa. London: Minority Rights Group, 1976.

10140. Hodges, Tony. The Western Saharans. London: Minority Rights Group, 1984.

10141. Howard, Rhoda E. Human Rights in Commonwealth Africa. Totowa, NJ: Rowman & Littlefield, 1986.

10142. Iliffe, John. The African Poor. A History. New York: Cambridge University Press, 1988.

10143. Iliffe, John. The Emergence of African Capitalism. Minneapolis: University of Minnesota Press, 1984.

10144. Inikori, J. E., ed. Forced Migration. The Impact of the Export Slave Trade on African Societies. London: Hutchinson, 1983.

10145. Institute for Advanced Study and the Academic Committee of the World Jewish Congress. Proceedings of the Seminar on Muslim-Jewish Relations in North Africa. New York: Waldon Press, 1975.

10146. Ismagilova, R. N. "Ethnic Stereotypes and Problems of National Integration in Contemporary Tropical Africa." Africa (Rome) 41 (December 1986): 545-559.

10147. Israel, Jonathan. "The Jews of Spanish North Africa, 1600- 1669." In The Jewish Historical Society of England, Transactions Sessions 1974-1978,

Vol. 26 and Miscellanies Part II. London: Jewish Historical Society of England, 1979.

10148. Ivan-Smith, Edda and others. Women in Sub-Saharan Africa. London: Minority Rights Group, 1988.

10149. Jaffe, Hosea. A History of Africa. Totowa, NJ: Zed Books, 1985.

10150. James, Lawrence. The Savage Wars: British Campaigns in Africa, 1870-1920. London: R. Hale, 1985.

10151. Jeijifo, Biodun. "Class Perspectives in the Analysis of Contemporary African Culture and Literature: The Issues Involved (part I)." Odu (January 1983): 1-16.

10152. Jeijifo, Biodun. "Class Perspectives in the Analysis of Contemporary African Culture and Literature: The Issues Involved [Part 3]." Odu (July 1983): 3-9.

10153. Johnson, D. H. "The Structure of a Legacy: Military Slavery in Northeast Africa." Ethnohistory 36 (1989): 72- 88.

10154. Jones, Adam. "Kolonialherrschaft und Geschichtsbewusstsein. Zur Rekonstruktion der Vergangenheit in Schwarzafrika 1865-1965." Historische Zeitschrift 250 (February 1990): 73-92.

10155. Jones, E. The Elizabethan Image of Africa. Charlottesville: University Press of Virginia, 1971.

10156. Kelly, Gail P. "Interwar Schools and the Development of African History in French West Africa." History in Africa 10 (1983): 163-185.

10157. Kelly, Gail P. "Learning To Be Marginal: Schooling in Interwar French West Africa." Journal of Asian and African Studies 21 (July-October 1986): 171-184.

10158. Kelly, Gail P. "Learning to Be Marginal: Schooling in Interwar French West Africa." Proc. Fr. Colonial Historical Society 11 (1987): 299-312.

10159. Kennedy, James H. "Political Liberalization, Black Consciousness and Recent Afro-Brazilian Literary Production." Presence Afric. (1987): 148-162.

10160. Kennedy, Paul. African Capitalism: The Struggle for Ascendancy. New York: Cambridge University Press, 1988.

10161. Kerr, David. "An Approach to Pre-Colonial African Theatre." African Theatre Review 1 (April 1986): 1-20.

10162. Killingray, David. "Labour Exploitation for Military Campaigns in British Colonial Africa, 1870-1945." Journal of Contemporary History 24 (July 1989): 483-502.

10163. Killingray, David. "'A Swift Agent of Government': Air Power in British Colonial Africa, 1916-1939." Journal of African History 25 (1984): 429-444.

10164. Kirk, Greene Anthony. "Imperial Administration and the Athletic Imperative." In Sport in Africa: Essays in Social History, edited by William J. Baker and James A.Mangan. New York: Africana Pub. Co., 1987.

10165. Kiwanuka, Richard N. "Some Reflections on the Problems of Human Rights Education in Africa." Verfassung Recht Übersee 20 (1987): 81-98.

10166. Koehn, Peter. "Political Access and Capital Accumulation: An Analysis of State Land Allocation Processes and Beneficiaries." African Development 12 (1987): 163-186.

10167. Kofele-Kale, N. "Our Colonial Mentality: Europe's Legacy to Africa." Pan-Africanism (December 1971)

10168. Kosukhin, N. D. Revolutionary Democracy in Africa: Its Ideology and Policy. Translated by Glenys Kozlov. Moscow: Progress Publishers, 1985.

10169. Kunze, Jurgen. "The Formation of the Bureaucratic Bourgeoisie in Sub-Saharan Africa." Economic Quarterly 22 (1987): 50-70.

10170. Laffin, John. The Arabs as Master Slaves. Englewood, NJ: SBS Publishing, Inc., 1983.

10171. Law, Robin. "Human Sacrifice in Pre-colonial West Africa." African Affairs 84 (1985): 53-87.

10172. Law, Robin. "Slaves, Trade and Taxes: The Material Basis of Political Power in Pre-Colonial West Africa." In Research in Economic Anthropology, edited by George Dalton. Greenwich, CT: JAI Press, 1978.

10173. Lazarus, Neil. Resistance in Postcolonial African Fiction. New Haven, CT: Yale University Press, 1990.

10174. Letnev, A. B. "The Shaping of Social Aspirations of West African evolues (late 1930s-early 1940s)." Africa Sov. Stud. (1985): 93-106.

10175. Leys, Norman. The Colour Bar in East Africa. London: Hogarth, 1941.

10176. Littman, David. "Quelques aspects de la condition de dhimmi: Juifs d'Afrique du Nord avant la colonisation..." Yod 2 (1976): 23-52.

10177. London, Bette. "Reading Race and Gender in Conrad's Dark Continent." Criticism 31 (Summer 1989): 235-252.

10178. Lovejoy, Paul E., ed. The Ideology of Slavery in Africa. Beverly Hills, Calif.: Sage, 1981.

10179. Lovejoy, Paul E. "The Impact of the Atlantic Slave Trade on Africa: A Review of the Literature." Journal of African History 30 (1989): 365-397.

10180. Lovejoy, Paul E. "Indigenous African Slavery." Historical Reflections/Reflexions historique 6 (1979)

10181. Lubeck, Paul M., ed. The African Bourgeoisie: Capitalist Development in Nigeria, Kenya, and the Ivory Coast. Boulder, CO: L. Rienner, 1986.

10182. Lumenga-Neso, Kiobe. "La Révolution américaine et la question de l'esclavage au 18e siècle." Zaïre-Afrique 16 (1976): 327-336.

10183. M'buyinga, E. Pan Africanism or Neo-Colonialism: The Bankruptcy of the OAU 1975-1982. London.

10184. Madu, Oliver V. Models of Class Domination in Plural Societies of Central Africa. Washington, D.C.: University Press of America, 1978.

10185. Maestri Filho, Mario J. História da Africa negra pré-colonial. Porto Alegre-RS: Mercado Alberto, 1988.

10186. Mafejo, A. "The Ideology of Tribalism." Journal of Modern African Studies 9 (1971): 253-261.

10187. Mahmoud, Fatima B. "Capitalism, Racism, Patriarchy, and the Women Question." In Africa's Crisis, edited by Nzongola-Ntalaja. London: Institute for African Alternatives, 1987.

10188. Mamdani, Mahmood. "Peasants and Democracy in Africa." New Left Review No. 156 (March-April 1986): 37-49.

10189. Manchuelle, Francois. "Emancipation and Labour Migration in West Africa: The Case of the Soninke." Journal of African History 30 (1989): 89-106.

10190. Manning, Patrick. "The Enslavement of Africans: A Demographic Model." Canadian Journal of African Studies 15 (1981): 499-526.

10191. Manning, Patrick. Slavery and African Life. Occidental, Oriental and African Slave Trade. New York: Cambridge University Press, 1990.

10192. Manny, Raymond. "Le Judaisme. Les Juifs et l'Afrique Occidentale." Bulletin de l'Institut français d'Afrique Noire 11 (July-August 1949)

10193. Markakis, John. National and Class Conflict in the Horn of Africa. New York: Cambridge University Press, 1988.

10194. Marnham, Patrick. Nomads of the Sahel. London: Minority Rights Group, 1977.

10195. Mazrui, Ali A. "The Afro-Saxons." Society 12 (1975): 14-21.

10196. Meebelo, Henry S. African Proletarians and Colonial Capitalism. Lusaka, Zambia: 1986.

10197. Meillassoux, C., ed. L'Esclavage en Afrique précoloniale. Paris: 1974.

10198. Melo, Joao de, ed. Os Anos da Guerra 1961-1975: Os Portugueses em Africa-Crónica, Ficção e Historia. Lisbon: Circulo de Leitores, 1988.

10199. Mercer, John. The Sahrawis of Western Sahara. London: Minority Rights Group, 1979.

10200. Mesa-Lago, Carmelo and June S. Belkin, eds. Cuba in Africa. Pittsburgh, PA: Center for Latin American Studies, University Center for International Studies, University of Pittsburgh, 1982.

10201. Miers, Suzanne and Igor Kopytoff, eds. Slavery in Africa. Historical and Anthropological Perspectives. Madison: University of Wisconsin Press, 1977.

10202. Miers, Suzanne and Richard Roberts, eds. The End of Slavery in Africa. Madison: University of Wisconsin Press, 1988.

10203. Miller, Christopher L. "Ethnicity and Ethics in the Criticism of Black African Literature." South Atlantic Quarterly 87 (Winter 1988): 75-108.

10204. Miller, John. "Class Collaboration for the Sake of Religion: Elite Control and Social Mobility in a Nineteenth- century Colonial Mission." Journal for the Scientific Study of Religion 29 (March 1990): 35-53.

10205. Mokhtar, G., ed. The UNESCO History of Africa, Vol II, Ancient Africa. Berkeley: University of California Press, 1980.

10206. Moreau, René Luc. Africains musulmans: des communautés en mouvement. Dakar, Senegal: Éditions Présence Africaine, 1982.

10207. Morikawa, Jun. "The Myth and Reality of Japan's Relations with Colonial Africa- 1885-1960." Journal of African Studies 12 (1985): 39-46.

10208. Mosha, Herme J. "The Role of African Universities in National Development: A Critical Analysis." Comparative Education 22 (1986): 93-110.

10209. Mowe, Isaac J. and Richard Bjornson, eds. Africa and the West: The Legacies of Empire. Westport, CT: Greenwood, 1988.

10210. Mpakati, Attati. "Problems and Nature of Anti-colonial Struggle in Africa." Pan-African Journal 5 (1972): 239-252.

10211. Mudenda, Gilbert. "Problems and Prospects of Class Analysis in the Study of African Social Formations." J. Afric. Marxists (November 1981): 65-80.

10212. Mudimbe, V. Y. The Invention of Africa. Bloomington: Indiana University Press, 1988.

10213. Nafziger, E. Wayne. Inequality in Africa: Political Elites, Proletariat, Peasants and the Poor. New York: Cambridge University Press, 1988.

10214. "Nation, Tribe and Ethnic Group in Africa." Cultural Survival Quarterly 9 (1985)

10215. Needham, D. E., E.K. Mashingaidze, and N. Bhebe. From Iron Age to Independence: A History of Central Africa. new ed. Harlow, Essex, England: Longman, 1984.

10216. Niane, D. T., ed. The UNESCO General History of Africa. Vol. IV, Africa from the XIIth to the XVIth Century. Berkeley: University of California Press, 1984.

10217. Nzula, A. T. and others. Forced Labour in Colonial Africa. Translated by Hugh Jenkins. London: Zed Press, 1979.

10218. Obbo, Christine. African Women: Their Struggle for Economic Independence. London: Zed Press, 1980.

10219. Obiechina, Emmanuel N. "Africa in the Soul of Dispersed Children: West African Literature from the Era of the Slave Trade." NSUKKA Stud. Afric. Lit. (1986): 101-160.

10220. Obiechina, Emmanuel N. "Perceptions of Colonialism in West African Literature." Ufahamu 5 (1974): 45-70.

10221. Obudho, R. A. and Constance C. Mhlanga, eds. Slum and Squatter Settlements in SubSaharan Africa: Towards a Planning Strategy. New York: Praeger, 1988.

10222. Ochai, A. "The Purpose of the Library in Colonial Tropical Africa: An Historical Survey." Int. Lib. Review 16 (1984): 309-315.

10223. Offiong, Daniel A. "The Cheerful School and the Myth of the Civilizing Mission of Colonial Imperialism." Pan-African Journal 9 (1976): 35-54.

10224. Ofosu-Appiah, L. H. Slavery: A Brief Survey. Accra: 1969.

10225. Ogunbameru, O. A. "The African Proletariat in Industrial Employment: A Reappraisal." International Social Science Journal 36 (1984): 341-354.

10226. Okojie, Paul. "Africa and Poverty." Journal of African Marxists (February 1989): 33-53.

10227. Okpaku, Joseph O. and others, eds. The Arts and Civilization of Black and African Peoples. 10 vols. Nigeria: Centre for Black and African Arts and Civilization, 1986.

10228. Omissi, David E. Air Power and Colonial Control. The Royal Air Force 1919-1939. Manchester University Press, 1990.

10229. Onimode, Bade. A Political Economy of the African Crisis. London: Zed Press,

10230. Osa, O. "The Rise of African Children's Literature." Reading Teacher 38 (April 1985): 750-754.

10231. Parpart, Jane L. and Kathleen A. Standt, eds. Women and the State in Africa. Boulder, CO: Rienner, 1989.

10232. Peel, J. D. Y. and Charles C. Stewart, eds. Popular Islam South of the Sahara. Wolfeboro, NH: Manchester University Press, 1987.

10233. Phillips, Anne. The Enigma of Colonialism: British Policy in West Africa. London: Currey, 1989.

10234. Rathbone, Richard. "Slavery in Pre-colonial Africa." In People's History and Socialist Theory, edited by Raphael Samuel. London: Routledge & Kegan Paul, 1980.

10235. Ray, Donald I. Dictionary of the African Left: Parties, Movements, and Groups. Brookfield, VT: Dartmouth, 1989.

10236. Reed, John N. Mercenary Activity in Africa Since 1960. 1982.

10237. Les relations entre Juifs et Musulmans en Afrique du Nord, XIXe-XXe siecles. Paris: Editions du CNRS, 1980.

10238. Renault, Francois. "The Structure of the Slave Trade in Central Africa in the 19th Century." Slavery & Abolition 9 (1988): 146-165.

10239. Roberts, Andrew, ed. The Colonial Moment in Africa. Essays on the Movement of Minds and Materials, 1900-1940. New York: Cambridge University Press, 1990.

10240. Robertson, Claire C. "A Growing Dilemma: Women and Change in African Primary Education, 1950-1980." Journal of African Research and Development 15 (1985): 17-35.

10241. Robertson, Claire C. and Martin A. Klein, eds. Women and Slavery in Africa. Madison: University of Wisconsin Press, 1983.

10242. Robertson, Claire C. and Iris Berger, eds. Women and Class in Africa. New York: Africana Publishing of Holmes and Meier, 1986.

10243. Rodney, Walter. "African Slavery and Other Forms of Social Oppression in the Context of the Atlantic Slave-Trade." Journal of African History 7 (1966): 431-443.

10244. Rodney, Walter. How Europe Underdeveloped Africa. Washington, D.C.: Howard University Press, 1972.

10245. Romero, Patricia W., ed. Life Histories of African Women. Atlantic Highlands, NJ: Ashfield, 1988.

10246. Rosenblum, Mort and Doug Williamson. Squandering Eden: Africa at the Edge. San Diego, CA: Harcourt Brace Jovanovich, 1987.

10247. Rotberg, Robert I., ed. Imperialism, Colonialism, and Hunger: East and Central Africa. Lexington, MA: Lexington Books, 1983.

10248. Rothchild, Donald and Naomi Chazan, eds. The Precarious Balance: State and Society in Africa. Boulder, CO: Westview Press, 1988.

10249. Rummelt, Peter. Sport im Kolonialismus, Kolonialismus im Sport: zur Genese und Funktion des Sports in Kolonial-Afrika von 1870 bis 1918. Koln: Pahl-Rugenstein, 1986.

10250. Samarin, William J. The Black Man's Burden: African Colonial Labor on the Congo and Ubangi Rivers, 1880-1900. Boulder, CO: Westview Press, 1989.

10251. Samuel-Mbaekwe, Iheanyi J. "Colonialism and Social Structure." Transafrican Journal of History 15 (1986): 81- 95.

10252. Sandbrook, Richard with Judith Parker. The Politics of Africa's Economic Stagnation. New York: Cambridge University Press, 1986.

10253. Schulte-Althoff, Franz-Josef. "Rassenmischung im kolonialen System: Zur deutschen Kolonialpolitik im letzten Jahrzehnt vor dem Ersten Weltkrieg." Hist. Jr. 105 (1985): 52-94.

10254. Seidman, Ann W. Transnationals in Southern Africa. Harare, Zimbabwe: 1986.

10255. Sender, John and Sheila Smith. The Development of Capitalism in Africa. New York: Methuen, 1986.

10256. "Shelter and Homelessness in Africa." African Urban Quarterly 2 (August 1987): entire issue.

10257. Sifuna, Daniel N. "Indigenous Education in Nomadic Communities." Presence africain (1984): 66-88.

10258. Sifuna, Daniel N. "Universal Education and Social Class Formation." Ufahamu 15 (1986): 164-181.

10259. Sithole, Ndabaningi. African Nationalism. 2d ed. Oxford: 1968.

10260. Sivan, E. "Stéréotypes antijuifs dans la mentalite pied- noir." In Les relations entre Juifs et Musulmans en Afrique du Nord, XIXe-XXe siècles. Paris: Centre National de la Recherche Scientifique, 1980.

10261. Sklar, Richard L. "The Colonial Imprint on African Political Thought." In African Independence: The First Twenty-Five Years, edited by Gwendolen M. Carter and Patrick O'Meara. 1-30. Bloomington: Indiana University Press, 1985.

10262. Sklar, Richard L. "Democracy in Africa." In Political Domination in Africa: Reflections on the Limits of Power, edited by Patrick Chabal. New York: Cambridge University Press, 1986.

10263. Sklar, Richard L. "The Nature of Class Domination in Africa." Journal of Modern African Studies 17 (December 1979): 531-552.

10264. Slouschz, Nahum. The Jews of North Africa. Philadelphia: 1944.

10265. Soff, Harvey G. "British Colonial Attitudes towards Indians in East Africa." Journal of Indian History 50 (1972): 573-596.

10266. Sogolo, Godwin. "On a Socio-Cultural Conception of Health and Disease in Africa." Africa (Rome) 41 (September 1986): 390-404.

10267. Staniland, Martin. "Democracy and Ethnocentrism." In Political Domination in Africa: Reflections on the Limits of Power, edited by Patrick Chabal. New York: Cambridge University Press, 1986.

10268. Stoecker, Helmut. German Imperialism in Africa: From the Beginnning until the Second World War. Atlantic Highlands, NJ: Humanities, 1986.

10269. "Sub-Saharan Africa." In World Directory of Minorities, edited by Minority Rights Group. 216-283. Harlow: Longman, 1990.

10270. Suliman, Hassan S. The Nationalist Movements in the Maghrib: A Comparative Approach. Uppsala: Scandanavian Institute of African Studies, 1987. [Algeria, Morocco, and Tunisia.]

10271. Syagga, Paul M. "Myths and Realities in Low Income Housing in Africa." Afric. Urban Quarterly 2 (August 1987): 202- 212.

10272. Tandon, Yashpal and Arnold Raphael. The New Position of East Africa's Asians: Problems of a Displaced Minority. 2d rev. ed. Minority Rights Group, 1984.

10273. Tuden, Arthur and Leonard Plotincov, eds. Social Stratification in Africa. New York: Free Press, 1970.

10274. Turner, Victor, ed. Colonialism in Africa, 1870-1960. Vol. 3, Profiles of Change: African Society and Colonial Rule. New York: Cambridge University Press, 1971.

10275. Turshen, Meredith. "Workers' Health in Africa." Review of African Political Economy (September 1986): 24-29.

10276. Ukadike, N. F. Black African Cinema. Doctoral dissertation: New York University, 1989. UMO # 9016318.

10277. Vail, Leroy, ed. Creation of Tribalism in Southern Africa. Berkeley: University of California Press, 1989.

10278. Van den Berghe, Pierre L. "Class, Race and Ethnicity in Africa." Ethnic and Racial Studies 6 (1983): 221-236.

10279. Veiter, Theodor. "Die Berber, Volk ohne Staat, Volksgruppen ohne Volksgruppenrecht." Europa Ethnica 40 (1983): 129-138.

10280. Vengroff, Richard. "Neo-colonialism and Policy Outputs in Africa." Comparative Political Studies 8 (1975): 234-250.

10281. Wa Thiong'o, N. "The Commitment of the Intellectual." R. Afric. Pol. Ec. (April 1985): 18-24.

10282. Wansborough, John. "The Decolonization of North African History." Journal of African History 10 (1968): 643-650.

10283. Ware, Helen, ed. Women, Education, and Modernization of the Family in West Africa. Canberra: Australian National University Press, 1981.

10284. Waters, Harold A. "Research Problems in Black Francophone Literature: The Case of Theater." Fr. Rev. 61 (October 1987): 71-78.

10285. Watson, James L., ed. Asian and African Systems of Slavery. Oxford: 1980.

10286. Whyte, Robert O. and Pauline Whyte. The Women of Rural Asia. Boulder, CO: Westview Press, 1982.

10287. Willis, John Ralph, ed. Slaves and Slavery in Muslim Africa. 2 vols. Totowa, NJ: Frank Cass, 1985.

10288. "Women and Development in Africa." African Urban Quarterly 4 (November 1989): entire issue.

10289. World Jewish Congress. Muslim-Jewish Relations in North Africa. New York: 1975.

10290. Wylie, Diana. "The Changing Face of Hunger in Southern African History 1880-1980." Past & Present No. 122 (February 1989): 159-199.

10291. Yimam, Arega. Social Development in Africa, 1950-1985: Historical and Methodological Perspectives and Indications for Future Orientations. 2 vols. Doctoral dissertation: University of Bristol (U.K.), 1988. [BRDX 85257.]

10292. Yoloye, E. A. "The Relevance of Educational Content to National Needs in Africa." International Review of Education 32 (1986): 149-174.

10293. Young, M. Crawford. "Nationalism, Ethnicity, and Class in Africa: A Retrospective." Cah. et afric. 26 (1986): 421- 496.

10294. Zell, Hans M. "Publishing in Africa Yesterday and Today." Geneve-Afrique 22 (1984): 173-182.

ASIA

10295. Brown, D. "The State of Ethnicity and the Ethnicity of the State- Ethnic Politics in Southeast Asia." Ethnic and Racial Studies 12 (January 1989)

10296. Brown, Ian. "Rural Distress in Southeast Asia during the World Depression in the Early 1930s: A Preliminary Reexamination." Journal of Asian Studies 45 (1986): 995- 1025.

10297. Crossette, Barbara. "Prejudice Is One of Asia's More Common Afflictions." New York Times, (December 29, 1985)

10298. Deyo, Frederick C. Beneath the Miracle: Labor Subordination in the New Asian Industrialism. Berkeley: University of California Press, 1989.

10299. Dirks, N. B. "The Original Caste: Power, History and Hierarchy in South-Asia." Contributions to Indian Sociology 23 (Jan.-June 1989)

10300. Dowling, J. M. and others. "Income Distribution, Poverty and Economic Growth in Developing Asian Countries." Singapore Economic Review 30 (April 1985)

10301. Gokhale, B. G. "Slavery in South and Southeast Asia in the 17th Century." J. Asiatic Soc. Bombay 47-48 (1972-1973): 108-117.

10302. Goodman, Grant K., ed. Japanese Cultural Policies in Southeast Asia during World War II. New York: St. Martin's Press, 1991.

10303. Griffin, Keith. "Growth and Impoverishment in the Rural Areas of Asia." Regional Development Dialogue 2 (1981): 30- 66.

10304. Griffin, Keith and A. R. Khan, eds. Poverty and Landlessness in Rural Asia. Geneva: International Labor Organization, 1977.

10305. Harris, J. E. The African Presence in Asia: Consequences of the East African Slave Trade. Evanston, IL: Northwestern University Press, 1971.

10306. "Hear the Downtrodden Speak. Reports of PCR Team Visits in Asia." PCR Information No. 27 (1990): entire issue. [Programme to Combat Racism of the World Council of Churches.]

10307. Hsiung, James C., ed. Human Rights in East Asia: A Cultural Perspective. New York: Paragon House, 1986.

10308. Jahan, Rounaq. Women in Asia. rev. ed. London: Minority Rights Group, 1982.

10309. Juwoso Sudarsono. "Religious, Ethnic and Ideological Dissension in the ASEAN Status." In Internal and External Security Issues in Asia, edited by Robert Scalapino and others. Berkeley, CA: Institute of East Asian Studies, 1986.

10310. Kirkpatrick, V. J. and G.T. Harris. "A Note on Trends in Poverty and Inequality in Rural Asia, 1950-1985." Journal of Contemporary Asia 19 (1989)

10311. Lasker, Bruno. Human Bondage in Southeast Asia. 1950.

10312. Lin, Vivian. "Health and Welfare and the Labour Process; Reproduction and Compliance in the Electronics Industry in Southeast Asia." Journal of Contemporary Asia 16 (1986): 456-474.

10313. Matsui, Y. Women's Asia. London: Zed, 1989.

10314. McCarthy, F. E. and S. Feldman. "Human Rights as Class Conflict: A Reconceptualization of the Issues." South Asia Bulletin 7 (1987): 64-67.

10315. Oshima, H. T. "Why Monsoon Asia Fell Behind the West since the 16th Century: Conjectures." Philippine Review of Economics and Business 20 (June 1983)

10316. Papanek, Hannah. "Women in South and Southeast Asia: Issues and Research." Signs 1 (1975): 193-214.

10317. Pinches, Michael and Salim Lahka, eds. Wage Labour and Social Change: The Proletariat in Asia and the Pacific. Clayton, Victoria: Centre of Southeast Asian Studies Monash University, 1987.

10318. Rao, V. V. B. "Income Distribution in East Asian Developing Countries." Asian-Pacific Economic Literature 2 (March 1988)

10319. Reid, Anthony. Slavery, Bondage, and Dependency in Southeast Asia. New York: St. Martin's Press, 1983.

10320. Reid, Anthony. Southeast Asia in the Age of Commerce, 1450-1680. Vol. I, The Lands Below the Winds. New Haven, CT: Yale University Press, 1988.

10321. Rhim, Soon Man. Women of Asia: Yesterday and Today. New York: Friendship Press, 1983.

10322. Schulten, C. M. "Tactics of the Dutch Colonial Army in the Netherlands East Indies." R. int. Hist. mil. No. 70 (1988): 59-66.

10323. Scobie, Harry M. and Laurie S. Wiseberg, eds. Access to Justice: Human Rights Struggles in South East Asia. London: Zed Books, 1985.

10324. Sharma, Basu. "Multinational Corporations and Industrialization in Southeast and East Asia." Contemp. S.E. Asia 6 (September 1984): 159-171.

10325. Shosh, Partha. "Ethnic and Religious Conflicts in South Asia." Conflict Studies No. 178 (1985): 1-19.

10326. "South Asia and South-East Asia." In World Directory of Minorities, edited by Minority Rights Group. 284-358. Harlow: Longman, 1990.

10327. Southeast Asian Tribal Groups and Ethnic Minorities. Cambridge, MA: Cultural Survival, Inc., 1987.

10328. Srinivasan, T. N. and P.K. Barhan, eds. Rural Poverty in South Asia. New York: Columbia University Press, 1988.

10329. Tharpar, Romila. "The History of Female Emancipation in Southern Asia." In Women in the New Asia: The Changing Social Roles of Men and Women in South and South-east Asia, edited by Barbara E. Ward. 473-499. Paris: UNESCO, 1963.

10330. Truong, Thanh-Dam. Sex, Money, and Morality: Prostitution and Tourism in Southeast Asia. Atlantic Highlands, NJ: Zed Books, 1990. [Philippines and Thailand.]

10331. Velinkar, J. "Jesuit Educational Style in Sixteenth Century Goa." Indica 21 (March 1984): 17-27.

10332. Visaria, Pravin M. Poverty and Living Standards in Asia. Washington, D.C.: World Books, 1986.

10333. Visser, H. K. A. and J. G. Bindels, eds. Child Nutrition in South East Asia. Boston, MA: Kluwer Academic, 1990.

10334. Watson, James L., ed. Asian and African Systems of Slavery. Berkeley: University of California Press, 1980.

10335. Watson, Keith. "Dependence or Independence in Education? Two Cases from Post-colonial South-East Asia." International Journal of Educational Development 5 (1985): 83-94.

10336. Whitney, Craig R. "For Asia's Children, Hard Knocks in an Alien Land." New York Times, (September 19, 1989)

10337. Yong, D. G., ed. "Ethnic Chinese in Southeast Asia." Jr. S. E. Asian Studies 12 (March 1981): entire issue.

CARIBBEAN

10338. Abrahams, Roger D. and John F. Szwed, eds. After Africa: Extracts from British Travel Accounts and Journals of the Seventeenth, Eighteenth, and Nineteenth Centuries Concerning the Slaves, Their Manners, and Customs in the British West Indies. New Haven, CT: Yale University Press, 1983.

10339. Alleyne, Mervyn C. Roots of Jamaican Culture. London: Pluto Press, 1988.

10340. Bacchus, M. K. Utilization, Misuse, and Development of Human Resources in the Early West Indian Colonies. Wilfrid Laurier University Press, 1990.

10341. Backles, Hilary McD. "Plantation Production and White Protoslavery: White Indentured Servants and the Colonisation of the English West Indies, 1624-1645." The Americas 41 (January 1985): 21-45.

10342. Bakan, Abigal B. Ideology and Class Conflict in Jamaica. The Politics of Rebellion. McGill-Queen's University Press, 1990.

10343. Barrow, Christine. "Ownership and Control of Resources in Barbados: 1834 to the Present." Social and Economic Studies 32 (September 1983): 83-120.

10344. Bebel-Gisler, Dany. Les enfants de la Guadeloupe. Paris: Editions l'Harmattan, 1985.

10345. Beckles, Hilary McD. A History of Barbados: From Amerindian Society to Nation State. New York: Cambridge University Press, 1990.

10346. Beckles, Hilary McD. Natural Rebels: A Social History of Enslaved Black Women in Barbados. London: Zed Press, 1989.

10347. Bell, Howard H., ed. Black September and the Caribbean, 1860. Ann Arbor, MI: 1970.

10348. Bernhard, Virginia. "Beyond the Chesapeake: The Contrastive Status of Blacks in Bermuda, 1616-1663." Journal of Southern History 54 (November 1988): 545-564.

10349. Besson, W. and J. Besson. Caribbean Reflections: The Life and Times of a Trinidad Scholar (1902-1986). London: Karia Press, 1989.

10350. Birbalsingh, Frank, ed. Indenture and Exile: The Indo- Caribbean Experience. Toronto: TSAR, 1989.

10351. Blérald, Alain-Philippe. Histoire economique de la Guadeloupe et de la Martinique du XVIIe siecle a nos jours. Paris: Editions Karthala, 1986.

10352. Blérald, Alain-Philippe. La question nationale en Guadeloupe et en Martinique: Essai sur l'historie politique. Paris: Editions l'Harmattan, 1988.

10353. Bogues, Tony. "Raza y clase social en la sociedad jamaicana." Nueva Sociedad 63 (December 1982): 113-126.

10354. Boyd, Derick. Economic Management, Income Distribution, and Poverty in Jamaica. Westport, CT: Greenwood, 1987.

10355. Brathwaite, Edward. Folk Culture of the Slaves in Jamaica. New Beacon Books, 1970.

10356. Brereton, Bridget and W. Dockeran, eds. Indians in the Caribbean: Colonialism and the Struggle for Identity. New York: Kraus International Publications, 1982.

10357. Brizan, George. Grenada: Island of Conflict: From Amerindians to People's Revolution, 1498-1979. London: Zed Press, 1984.

10358. Brock, Colin. "Contemporary Educational Issues in the Commonwealth Caribbean." In Dual Legacies in the Contemporary Caribbean: Continuing Aspects of British and French Domination, edited by Paul Sutton. London: Frank Cass, 1986.

10359. Buckley, Roger Norman. Slaves in Red Coats: The British West India Regiments, 1795-1815. New Haven: Yale University Press, 1979.

10360. Burn, W. L. Emancipation and Apprenticeship in the British West Indies. London: 1937.

10361. Burpee, C. Gaye and James N. Morgan. 1985 Household Survey of Grenada... Ann Arbor: Survey Research Center, Institute for Social Research, University of Michigan, 1986.

10362. Bush, Barbara. "Defiance or Submission? The Role of the Slave Woman in Slave Resistance in the British Caribbean." Immigrants and Minorities 1 (1982): 16-38.

10363. Bush, Barbara. Lost Daughters of Afrik: Black Women in British West Indian Society, 1650-1832. Ormskirk: 1982.

10364. Cabort-Masson, Guy. Les puissances d'argent en Martinique. 2d ed. Labatoire de recherches de l'A.M.E.P., 1987.

10365. Camejo, Acton. "Racial Discrimination in Employment in the Private Sector in Trinidad and Tobago: A Study of the Business Elite and the Social Structure." Social and Economic Studies 20 (1971): 294-318.

10366. Campbell, Mavis C. The Dynamics of Change in a Slave Society: A Sociopolitical History of the Free Coloreds of Jamaica 1800-1865. Canbury, N.J.: Associated University Presses, 1976.

10367. Carew, Jan. "Fulcrums of Change." Race and Class 26 (Autumn 1984): 1-13. [Destruction of indigenous Americans in Caribbean.]

10368. Chevannes, Barry. Social Origins of the Rastafari Movement. Mona, Kingston, Jamaica: 1978.

10369. Clarke, Colin G. East Indians in a West Indian Town: San Fernando, Trinidad, 1930-1970. Winchester, MA: Allen & Unwin, 1986.

10370. Colloque d'histoire antillaise (1969). Le passage de la société esclavagiste à la société post-esclavagiste aux Antilles au XIXe siècle. 2 vols. Pointe-à-pitre: 1971.

10371. Craig, Susan, ed. Contemporary Caribbean: A Sociological Reader. 2 vols. Maracas Trinidad and Tobago: College Press, 1981.

10372. Craton, Michael. Searching for the Invisible Man: Slaves and Plantation Life in Jamaica. Cambridge, Mass: Harvard University Press, 1978.

10373. Craton, Michael. "Slave Culture, Resistance, and the Achievement of Emancipation in the British West Indies, 1783- 1838." In Slavery and British Society, 1776-1846, edited by James Walvin. Baton Rouge: Louisiana State University Press, 1982.

10374. Craton, Michael. Testing the Chains: Resistance to Slavery in the British West Indies. Ithaca, New York: Cornell University Press, 1982.

10375. Craton, Michael and J. Walvin. A Jamaican Plantation: The History of Worthy Park, 1670-1970. Toronto: 1970.

10376. Dabien, G. Les Esclaves aux Antilles françaises. Basse- Terre et Fort-de-France: 1974.

10377. Dabydeen, David and Brinsley Samaroo, eds. India in the Caribbean. London: Hansib, 1987. [East Indians.]

10378. Dadzie, Stella. "Searching for the Invisible Woman: Slavery and Resistance in Jamaica." Race & Class 32 (October-December 1990): 21-38.

10379. Dathorne, O. R. Dark Ancestor: The Literature of the Black Man in the Caribbean. Baton Rouge: Louisiana State University Press, 1981.

10380. Davis, Donna D. Gender Inequality in Grenada. Master's thesis: University of New Brunswick, 1986.

10381. Debbasch, Yvan. "Le marronage: essai sur la desertion de l'esclave antillais." L'Anné Sociologique (1961, 1962): 1- 112, 117-195.

10382. Deosaran, Ramesh. "The Social Psychology of Cultural Pluralism: Updating the Old." Plural Societies 17 (1987): 54-77.

10383. Dookeran, Winston. "The Distribution of Income in Trinidad and Tobago, 1957-1976." Review of Income and Wealth 27 (June 1981): 195-206.

10384. Downes, A. S. "The Distribution of Household Income in Barbados." Social and Economic Studies 36 (December 1987)

10385. Downie, Winsome A. Democratic Socialism: The Jamaican Experiment. Doctoral dissertation: Columbia University, 1985. UMO # 8604615.

10386. Elkins, W. F. Black Power in the Caribbean: The Beginnings of the Modern National Movement. New York: Revisionist Press, 1977.

10387. Ellise, Pat, ed. Women of the Caribbean. London: Zed Press, 1987.

10388. Emmanuel, Patrick and others. Political Change and Public Opinion in Grenada 1979-1984. Cave Hill, Barbados: Institute of Social and Economic Research (Eastern Caribbean) University of the West Indies, 1986.

10389. Ennew, Judith and Pansy Young. Child Labour in Jamaica: A General Review. London: Anti-Slavery Society, 1981.

10390. Erickson, E. L. "The Introduction of East Indian Coolies Into the British West Indies." Journal of Modern History (June 1934)

10391. Ferguson, James. Far from Paradise: An Introduction to Caribbean Development. London: Latin American Bureau, 1990.

10392. Ferguson, James. Grenada: Revolution in Reverse. London: 1990.

10393. Forsythe, Dennis. "Race, Color, and Class in the British West Indies." Journal of Social and Behavioral Sciences 20 (Fall 1974): 58-68.

10394. Fraser, H. Aubrey. "Constitutional Protection Against Racism in the Commonwealth Caribbean." Caribbean Affairs (Trinidad) 1 (1988): 128-141. [12 nations.]

10395. Gibson, Margaret A. "Ethnicity and Schooling: West Indian Immigrants in the United States Virgin Islands." Ethnic Groups 5 (1983): 173-197.

10396. Glazier, Stephen D. "Trinidad." In International Handbook on Race and Race Relations, edited by Jay A. Sigler. Westport, CT: Greenwood, 1987.

10397. Glissant, Edouard. Caribbean Discourse: Selected Essays. Translated by J. Michael Dash Charlottesville: University Press of Virginia, 1989.

10398. Graham, Margaret E. and Franklin W. Knight, ed. Africa and the Caribbean: The Legacies of a Link. Baltimore, MD: Johns Hopkins University Press, 1979.

10399. No entry

10400. Gullick, Charles J. M.R. Myths of a Minority. The Changing Traditions of the Vincentian Caribs. Assen: Van Gorcum, 1985.

10401. Harewood, Jack and Ralph Henry. Inequality in a Post-colonial Society: Trinidad and Tobago, 1965-1981. St. Augustine, Trinidad: ISER, UWI, 1986.

10402. Harrison, Alferdteen. Institutional Racism Against the French West Indian People of African Descent 1789-1802: A Legislative Case Study. Doctoral dissertation: University of Kansas, 1971. UMO # 7211751.

10403. Hart, Richard. Rise and Organise: The Birth of the Workers and National Movements in Jamaica (1936-1939). London: Karia, 1989.

10404. Henry, Paget. Peripheral Capitalism and Underdevelopment in Antigua. New Brunswick, NJ: Transaction Books, 1984.

10405. Herold, Marc W. "Development in a Peripheral Socialist Economy: Grenada, 1979-1983." In Economic Processes and Political Conflicts, edited by Richard W. England. New York: Praeger, 1986.

10406. Higman, B. W. Slave Populations of the British Caribbean, 1807-1834. Baltimore, MD: Johns Hopkins University Press, 1984.

10407. Ho, Christine. "'Hold the Chow Mein Gimme Soca': Creolization of the Chinese in Guyana, Trinidad and Jamaica." Amerasia 15 (1989): 3-25.

10408. Hoenisch, Michael. "Symbolic Politics: Perceptions of the Early Rastafari Movement." Massachusetts Review 29 (1988): 432-449.

10409. Hoetink, H. "'Race' and Color in the Caribbean." In Carribean Contours, edited by Sidney W. Mintz and Sally Price. Baltimore, MD: Johns Hopkins University Press, 1985.

10410. Holder, C. and R. Prescod. "The Distribution of Personal Income in Barbados." Social and Economic Studies 38 (March 1989)

10411. Hulme, Peter. Colonial Encounters: Europe and the Native Caribbean, 1492-1797. New York: Methuen, 1987.

10412. James, Ariel. "La United Fruit Company y la penetracion imperialista en el area del Caribe." Santiago (Cuba) No. 15 (1974): 69-80.

10413. James, C. L. R. "Race Relations in the Caribbean." Newsletter of the Institute of Racial Relations (March 1964): 19-23.

10414. James-Bryan, M. "Youth in the English-speaking Caribbean: The High Cost of Dependent Development." Cepal Review No. 29 (August 1986)

10415. Johnson, Howard. "The Anti-Chinese Riots of 1918 in Jamaica." Immigrants and Minorities 2 (March 1983): 50-63.

10416. Johnson, Howard. "The Chinese in Trinidad in the Late Nineteenth Century." Ethnic and Racial Studies 10 (January 1987): 82-95.

10417. Joseph, Gloria I. "Caribbean Women: The Impact of Race, Sex and Class." In Perspectives of Third World Women: The Impact of Race, Sex, and Class, edited by Beverly Lindsay. New York: Praeger, 1980.

10418. Kaufman, Michael. Jamaica Under Manley-Dilemmas of Socialism and Democracy. London: Zed Books, 1985.

10419. Kincaid, Jamaica. A Small Place. New York: Farrar, Straus & Giroux, 1988. [Antigua.]

10420. King, Ruby and Mika Morrissey. Images in Print: Bias and Prejudice in Caribbean Textbooks. Kingston 7, Jamaica, West Indies: Publications Section, Institute of Social and Economic Research, University of the West Indies,

10421. Knight, Franklin W. The Caribbean, the Genesis of a Fragmented Nationalism. 2d ed. New York: Oxford University Press, 1990.

10422. Lai, Wally Look. "Chinese Indentured Labor: Migrations to the British West Indies in the Nineteenth Century." Amerasia Journal 15 (1989): 117-138.

10423. Lewis, Gordon K. Grenada: The Jewel Despoiled. Baltimore, MD: Johns Hopkins University Press, 1987.

10424. Lewis, Gordon K. Main Currents in Caribbean Thought. The Historical Evolution of Caribbean Society in its Ideological Aspects, 1492-1900. Baltimore, MD: Johns Hopkins University Press, 1983.

10425. Liebman, S. B. "Anti-Semitism in Martinique in the 17th Century." Tradition 10 (Fall 1969): 40-47.

10426. Lowenthal, David. "Black Power in the Caribbean Context." Economic Geography 48 (January 1972): 116-134.

10427. Mahabir, Noor K. The Still Cry: Personal Accounts of East Indians in Trinidad and Tobago during Indentureship, 1845- 1917. Tacarigua, Trinidad: Cataloux Publications, 1985.

10428. Mair, L. M. A Historical Study of Women in Jamaica from 1655 to 1844. Doctoral dissertation: University of West Indies, 1974.

10429. Mandle, Jay R. Big Revolution, Small Planning. The Rise and Fall of the Grenada Revolution. Lanham, MD: North-South Pub. Co., 1985. [P.O. Box 610, Lanham, MD 20706.]

10430. Martin, Tony. "Race as a Continuing Function of Slavery, Colonialism and Capitalism in the West Indies- an Overview." Journal of Human Relations 19 (1971): 300-310.

10431. McCloy, Shelby T. The Negro in the French West Indies. Lexington: University of Kentucky Press, 1966.

10432. Millette, Robert E. and M. Gosine. The Grenada Revolution: Why It Failed. New York: African Research Publications, 1985.

10433. Mintz, Sidney W. and Richard Price. An Anthropological Approach to the Afro-American Past: A Caribbean Perspective. Philadelphia, PA: Institute for the Study of Human Issues, 1976.

10434. Mumford, Clarence. "Slavery in the French Caribbean 1625- 1715. A Marxist Analysis." Journal of Black Studies 17 (September 1986): 49-70.

10435. Munroe, Trevor. "Marxism in the Caribbean." Studies in Political Economy No. 31 (Spring 1990): 9-29.

10436. Murch, Arvin. Black Frenchmen: The Political Integration of the French Antilles. Cambridge, MA: Schenkman, 1971.

10437. Nelson, Gersham A. The Peasantry and Working Class in the Jamaican Political Process, 1838-1980. Doctoral dissertation: University of Illinois, Chicago, 1987. UMO # 8726096.

10438. Nettleford, Rex. "Cultivating a Caribbean Sensibility. Media, Education and Culture." Caribbean Review 15 (Winter 1987): 4-8, 28.

10439. Newark, John W. Economic Development and the Peasant Economy in Jamaica. Doctoral dissertation: University of Toronto, 1988.

10440. Oakes, Elizabeth. "Grenada under Occupation: U.S. Economic Policy, 1983-1987." Rethinking Marxism 1 (Fall 1988): 131- 157.

10441. Panneflek, Aignald J. Academic Achievement among Sixth- graders in Curacao, Netherlands Antilles. Doctoral dissertation: Loma Linda University, 1986. UMO # 8702191.

10442. Parris, C. "Power and Privilege in Trinidad and Tobago." Social and Economic Studies 34 (June 1985)

10443. Payne, A. J. and P.K. Sutton, eds. Dependency Under Challenge: The Political Economy of the Commonwealth Caribbean. Dover, NH: Manchester University Press, 1984.

10444. Perotindumon, A. "Ambiguous Revolution in the Caribbean: The White Jacobins, 1789-1800." Historical Reflections 13 (Summer-Fall 1986): 499-516.

10445. Persand, Naraine. The Development of Underdevelopment in Grenada. Doctoral dissertation: Florida State University, 1985. UMO # 85528709.

10446. Pope, Polly. "Danish Colonialism in the West Indies." In War, Its Causes and Correlates, edited by Martin A. Netteship and others. Chicago, IL: Aldine, 1975.

10447. Poplin, Moulton G. Education and Inequality in Jamaica. Doctoral dissertation: City University of New York, 1988. UMO # 8821113.

10448. El Proceso Abolicionista en Puerto Rico: Documentos Para Su Estudia, Volumen I, La institucion de la esclavitud y sa crisis (1823-1873). Rio Piedras, P.R.: Editorial Edil, 1974.

10449. Pryor, Frederic L. Revolutionary Grenada: A Study in Political Economy. New York: Praeger, 1986.

10450. Purcell, Trevor. "Structural Transformation and Social Inequality in a Plural Society: The Case of Limon." West Indian Law Journal 11 (May 1987): 119-142.

10451. Pyde, Peter H. Stratification in the Carribbean: Anthropological Literature Review. Master's thesis: University of Toronto, 1987.

10452. Ragoonath, Bishnu. "Race and Class in Caribbean Politics." Plural Societies 18 (July 1988): 71-101.

10453. Richardson, Ronald K. Moral Imperium: Afro-Caribbeans and the Transformation of British Rule, 1776-1838. Westport, Ct: Greenwood, 1987.

10454. Riviere, Bill. *Oppression and Resistance: The Black Condition in the Caribbean*. Ithaca, New York: Africana Studies and Research Center, Cornell University, 1976.

10455. Rooke, P. T. "Planters and Pedagogues: The Social and Political Implications of Education in British West Indian Slave Society." *Alberta Journal of Educational Research* 24 (March 1978): 37-52.

10456. Safa, Helen I. "Popular Culture, National Identity, and Race in the Caribbean." *Niewe West-Indische Gids* 61 (1987): 115-126.

10457. Sandiford, Keith A. P. and Brian Stoddart. "The Elite Schools and Cricket in Barbados: A Study in Colonial Continuity." *International Journal of the History of SPort* 4 (1987): 333-350.

10458. Sandy, Cleve P. *The Democratization of Secondary Education in Trinidad and Tobago and Socio-Economic Effects*. Doctoral dissertation: University of Toronto, 1986.

10459. Saskana, Amon S. *The Colonial Legacy in Caribbean Literature*. London: 1987.

10460. Searle, Chris. *Grenada Morning: A Memoir of the Revo*. London: Karia, 1989.

10461. Shepherd, Verene A. "The Dynamics of Afro-Jamaican-East Indian Relations in Jamaica, 1845-1945: A Preliminary Analysis." *Caribbean Quarterly* 32 (1986): 14-26.

10462. Sheridan, Richard B. *Doctors and Slaves: A Medical and Demographic History of Slavery in the British West Indies, 1680-1834*. New York: Cambridge University Press, 1985.

10463. Smith, M. G. *Culture, Race and Class in the Commonwealth Caribbean*. Moma Jamaica: Department of Extra-Mural Studies, University of the West Indies, 1984.

10464. Smith, M. G. *The Plural Society in the British West Indies*. Berkeley: University of California Press, 1965.

10465. Solow, Barbara L. and Stanley L. Engerman, eds. *British Capitalism and Caribbean Slavery, The Legacy of Eric Williams*. New York: Cambridge University Press, 1988.

10466. Solow, Barbara L. "Caribbean Slavery and British Growth: The Eric Williams Hypothesis." *Journal of Development Economics* 17 (January-February 1985)

10467. Solow, Barbara L. and others. "Caribbean Slavery and British Capitalism (symposium)." Journal of Interdisciplinary History 17 (Spring 1987): 707-870.

10468. St. Pierre, Maurice. "The 1938 Jamaican Disturbances: A Portrait of Mass Reaction against Colonialism." Social and Economic Studies 27 (1978): 171-196.

10469. Steel, Mark J. Power, Prejudice and Profit: The World View of the Jamaican Slaveowning Elite, 1788-1834. Doctoral dissertation: University of Liverpool, 1988. [Order No. BRDX 88754.]

10470. Stone, Carl. "Race and Economic Power in Jamaica: Toward the Creation of a Black Bourgeoisie." Caribbean Review 16 (Spring 1988): 10-14.

10471. Sutton, Paul, ed. Dual Legacies in the Contemporary Caribbean: Continuing Aspects of British and French Dominion. Totowa, NJ: Frank Cass, 1986.

10472. Thomas, Clive. "Black Exploitation in the Caribbean." In Is Massa Day Done?, edited by Orde Coombs. Garden City, NY: Anchor Books, 1974.

10473. Thomas-Hope, Elizabeth M. "Caribbean Diaspora- The Inheritance of Slavery: Migration from the Commonwealth Caribbean." In The Caribbean in Europe: Aspects of the West Indian Experience in Britain, France, and the Netherlands, edited by Colin Brock. London: Frank Cass, 1986.

10474. Tomich, Dale W. Slavery in the Circuit of Sugar, Martinique and the World Economy, 1830-1848. Baltimore, MD: Johns Hopkins University Press, 1990.

10475. Trotman, Donald A. B. and Keith Friday. Report on Human Rights in Grenada: A Survey of Political and Civil Rights in Grenada during the Period of 1970-1983. Bustamante Institute of Public and International Affairs.

10476. Turner, Mary. Slaves and Missionaries: The Disintegration of Jamaican Slave Society, 1787-1834. Urbana: University of Illinois Press, 1982.

10477. Ward, J. R. Poverty and Progress in the Caribbean, 1800- 1960. Basingtoke, Hamps: Macmillan, 1985.

10478. Webb, Oliver R. Jewel, New Jewel, the Grenada Revolution: Its Crisis and Collapse. Doctoral dissertation: American University, 1989. UMO # 9006686.

10479. Whitelock, Otto V. St. "Social and Cultural Pluralism in the Caribbean." Annals of the New York Academy of Sciences 83 (January 20, 1960): 761-916.

802 WORLD RACISM AND RELATED INHUMANITIES

10480. Williams, Eric. From Columbus to Castro: The History of the Caribbean 1492-1969. New York: Harper & Row, 1970.

10481. Wood, Donald. Trinidad in Transition: The Years After Slavery. New York: Oxford University Press, 1986.

10482. Woolcock, J. "Class Conflict and Class Reproduction: An Historical Analysis of the Jamaican Educational Reforms of 1957 and 1962." Social and Economic Studies 33 (December 1984)

10483. Wright, Ernest. French Politics in the West Indies: A Study of the Assimilation Policy in the History of Martinique and Guadeloupe, 1789-1900. Doctoral dissertation: Howard University, 1976. UMO # 7805454.

EUROPE

10484. Adler, Karen. "Council of Europe Report on the Integration of Immigrant and Ethnic Minority Communities." Patterns of Prejudice 48 (Winter 1989-1990): 23.

10485. Adler, Karen. "European Inquiry into Racism and Xenophobia Publishes Report." Patterns of Prejudice 24 (Summer 1990): 47-51.

10486. Ainsztein, R. Jewish Resistance in Nazi- Occupied Eastern Europe. New York: Barnes and Noble, 1974.

10487. Allardt, Erik. Implications of the Ethnic Revival in Modern, Industrialized Society. A Comparative Study of the Linguistic Minorities in Western Europe. Helsinki: Societas Scientiarusm Fennica, 1979.

10488. Allardt, Erik and others. Nordic Democracy, Ideas, Issues, and Institutions in Politics, Economy, Education, Social and Cultural Affairs of Denmark, Finland, Iceland, Norway and Sweden. Copenhagen: Det Danske Selskab, 1981.

10489. Almog, Shmuel, ed. Antisemitism through the Ages. Oxford: 1988.

10490. Almog, Shmuel. Nationalism and Antisemitism in Europe, 1815-1945. New York: Pergamon Press, 1989.

10491. Amersfoort, Hans van and others. "International Migration, the Economic Crisis and the State: An Analysis of Mediterranean Migration to Western Europe." Ethnic and Racial Studies 7 (1984): 238-268.

10492. Ammarate, Pablo de. The League of Nations and National Minorities. Translated by Eileen E. Brooke. Washington, D.C.: 1945.

10493. Andreski, S. "An Economic Interpretation of Anti-Semitism in Eastern Europe." Jewish Journal of Sociology 5 (1963): 201-213.

804 WORLD RACISM AND RELATED INHUMANITIES

10494. Anne Frank Stichtung. Fascisme, Neo-Fascisme, Rechts extremisme in West-Europa. Voorburg: Protestantse Stichting Bibliotheckwezen, 1977.

10495. Anti-Defamation League of B'nai B'rith. "Jewish-Christian Relations in Western Europe." Face to Face (Summer 1980): 1- 26.

10496. Anwar, Muhammad and Roger Garaudy. Social and Cultural Perspectives on Muslims in Western Europe. Birmingham: Centre for the Study of Islam and Christian-Muslim Relations, Selby Oakes Colleges, 1984.

10497. Arad, Yitzhak. Belzce Sobibor Treblinka. The Operation Reinhard Death Camps. Bloomington: Indiana University Press, 1987.

10498. Aronsfeld, C. C. "The Christian Mission to the Jews." Jewish Quarterly 34 (1987): 21-22.

10499. Ascher, Abraham and others, eds. The Mutual Effects of the Islamic and Judeo-Christian Worlds: The East European Pattern. Brooklyn, New York: Brooklyn College Press, 1979.

10500. Bachrach, Bernard S. Jews in Barbarian Europe. Lawrence, KS: Coronado Press, 1977.

10501. Baechler, Jean and others, eds. Europe and the Rise of Capitalism. New York: Blackwell, 1987.

10502. Balic, Smail. "Muslims in Eastern and South-Eastern Europe." Institute of Muslim Minority Affairs Journal 6 (1985)

10503. Banac, I. and F.E. Sysyn, eds. "Concepts of Nationhood in Early Modern Eastern Europe." Harvard Ukranian Studies 10 (1986): entire issue.

10504. Banton, Michael. "The Classification of Races in Europe and North America: 1700-1850." International Social Science Journal 39 (1987): 45-60.

10505. Barber, Malcolm. "Lepers, Jews and Moslems: The Plot to Overthrow Christendom in 1321." History 66 (February 1981): 1-17.

10506. Barber, P. The League of Nations and National Minorities. Master's thesis: University of Wales, 1924.

10507. Barnard, Patrick. "Does Tomorrow Belong to Them?" Nation (July 30, 1990) [Antisemitism and extreme right wing in West and East Europe.]

10508. Basgoz, Ilhan and Norman Furniss, eds. Turkish Workers in Europe. An Interdisciplinary Study. Bloomington: 1985. [Turkish Studies, 143 Goodbody Hall, Indiana University.]

10509. Bauer, Yehuda. "Gypsies." In Encyclopedia of the Holocaust, II. pp. 634-38. New York: Macmillan, 1990.

10510. Bauer, Yehuda. "On the Place of the Holocaust in History." Holocaust and Genocide Studies 2 (1987): 209-222.

10511. Bauman, Zygmunt. Modernity and the Holocaust. Oxford: Polity Press, 1989.

10512. Bauman, Zygmunt. "Sociology After the Holocaust." British Journal of Sociology 39 (1988): 469-497.

10513. Beach, H. "After the Fallout: Chernobyl and the Sami." Cultural Survival Quarterly 13 (1989): 72-75.

10514. Bell, Andrew. Against Racism and Fascism in Europe. Brussels: Socialist Group, European Parliament, 1986.

10515. Bell, Raley H. Woman from Bondage to Freedom. New York: The Critic and Guide Company, 1921.

10516. Bentil, J. Kodmo. "Educational Discrimination in the EEC." Solicitor's Journal 129 (November 1, 1985): 744-747.

10517. Berger, John. A Seventh Man: Migrant Workers in Europe. New York: Viking, 1975.

10518. Bernadac, Christian. L'holocauste oublié: le massacre des Tsiganes. Paris: France-Empire, 1979.

10519. Berov, Ljudben. "Trends in the Level and Structure of the Incomes of the Working People in the Balkan Countries in the 18th and 19th Centuries up to 1912." Bulgarian Historical Review 15 (1987): 65-83.

10520. Beyme, Klaus von. "Right-wing Extremism in Post-war Europe." West European Politics 11 (1988): 1-18.

10521. Biddiss, Michael D. "Myths of the Blood: European Racist Ideology, 1850-1945." Patterns of Prejudice 9 (September- October 1975): 11-19.

10522. Binder, David. "A Vital Shadow Society: East Bloc Breadwinner." New York Times, (January 6, 1988): [Economic life in Eastern Europe.]

10523. Blackbourn, David. "Economic Crises and the Petite Bourgeoisie in Europe during the Nineteenth and Twentieth Centuries." Social History 10 (January 1985): 95-104.

10524. Blaha, Jaroslav and others. "Les principales minorités nationales en Europe de l'Est." Notes et Etudes Documentaires No. 18 (1985): 41-79.

10525. Blaschke, Jochen, ed. Handbuch der westeuropäischen Regionalbewegungen. Frankfurt am Main: Berliner Institut für vergleichende Sozialforschung, 1980.

806 WORLD RACISM AND RELATED INHUMANITIES

10526. Bloch, Marc. "L'Esclavage dans l'Europe médiévale." Annales d'histoire sociale (1939)

10527. Bloch, Marc. Slavery and Serfdom in the Middle Ages. Selected Papers by Marc Bloch. Translated by Wm R. Beer. Berkeley, Calif.: University of California Press, 1975.

10528. Boase, Roger. "The Disputed Heritage: Europe's Cultural Debt to the Arabs." Bulletin of Hispanic Studies 66 (April 1989): 155-159.

10529. Bohlen, Celestine. "Ethnic Rivalries Revive in East Europe." New York Times, (November 12, 1990)

10530. Bornstein, Stephen and others. The State in Capitalist Europe. London: Allen & Unwin,

10531. Bovenkerk, Frank and others. "Racism, Migration and the State in Western Europe: A Case for Comparative Analysis." International Sociology 5 (December 1990)

10532. Braga, Michael. Völker zur Freiheit! vom Kampf europäischer Volksgruppen um Selbstbestimmung. Kiel: Arndt-Verlag, 1982.

10533. Braham, R.L., ed. Jewish Leadership During the Nazi Era. New York: Columbia University Press, 1985.

10534. Breitman, Richard. "The Allied War Effort and the Jews 1942-1943." Journal of Contemporary History 20 (January 1985): 135-156.

10535. Bremer, Thomas, ed. Europäische Literatur gegen den Faschismus 1922-1945. Munich: Beck, 1986.

10536. Bridenthal, Renate and Claudia Koonz, eds. Becoming Visible: Women in European History. Boston, MA: Houghton Mifflin, 1977.

10537. Brink, Jean R. and others, eds. The Politics of Gender in Early Modern Europe. Kirksville, MO: Sixteenth Century Journal Publishers, 1989.

10538. Brownlow, William R. B. Lectures on Slavery and Serfdom in Europe. New York: Negro Universities Press, 1969.

10539. Buchheim, Christoph. "Die besetzten Länder im Dienste der deutschen Kriegswirtschaft während des zweiten Weltkriegs." Vierteljahrsch. Zeitgesch. 34 (1986): 117-145.

10540. Burns, Michael and others, eds. From East and West: The Jewish Experience in a Changing Europe, 1750-1870. Oxford: Blackwell, 1990.

10541. Carsten, Francis L. The Rise of Fascism. 2d ed. Berkeley: University of California Press, 1980.

10542. Castells, M. "Immigrant Workers and Class Struggles in Advanced Capitalism: The Western European Experience." Politics and Society 5 (1975): 33-66.

10543. Castles, Stephen. "The Guest Worker in Western Europe-An Obituary." International Migration Review 20 (Winter 1986): 761-778.

10544. Castles, Stephen and others. Here for Good: Western Europe's New Ethnic Minorities. London: Pluto Press, 1984.

10545. Ceplair, Larry. Under the Shadow of War. Fascism, Anti- Fascism, and Marxists, 1918-1939. New York: Columbia University Press, 1987.

10546. Chairoff, P. Dossier Néo-nazisme. Paris: J.P. Ramsey, 1977.

10547. Chazan, Robert. European Jewry and the First Crusade. Berkeley: University of California Press, 1987.

10548. Chirot, Daniel, ed. The Origins of Backwardness in Eastern Europe. Economics and Politics from the Middle Ages until the Early Twentieth Century. Berkeley: University of California Press, 1989.

10549. "Church Protests Regarding Antisemitism in Europe." Christian Jewish Relations 23 (Summer 1990): 41-42.

10550. Clebert, Jean-Paul. The Gypsies. Translated by Charles Duff. London: Vista Books, 1963.

10551. Clough, Patricia. "The Neo-Nazi Network." Contemporary Affairs Briefing (London) (May 1982)

10552. Co-existence in Some Plural European Societies. London: Minority Rights Group, 1986.

10553. Coakley, J. "National Minorities and the Government of Divided Societies- A Comparative Analysis of Some European Evidence." European Journal of Political Research 18 (July 1990)

10554. Cohen, Asher. "La politique antijuive en Europe (Allemagne exclue), 1938-1941." Guerres Mondiales et Conflits Contemporains 38 (1988): 45-59.

10555. Cole, John W. "Culture and Economy in Peripheral Europe." Ethnologie Europaea 15 (1985): 3-26.

10556. Cole, John W. "Studies in the Political Economy of Peripheral Europe." Dialectical Anthropology 6 (1981): 81- 101.

10557. Collinder, Bjorn. The Lapps. New York: Oxford University Press, 1949.

808 WORLD RACISM AND RELATED INHUMANITIES

10558. Commission of the European Communities. Xenophobia and Intolerance: Human Rights and Immigration in the European Community. November 1989.

10559. Conway, John S., Franklin H. Littell, and Israel Gutman. "Christian Churches." In Encyclopedia of the Holocaust, I, 291-299. New York: Macmillian, 1990.

10560. Council of Europe. Human Rights of Aliens in Europe. Boston, MA: Martinus Nijhoff, 1985.

10561. Courtney, Daria Treat. "The Minorities Treaties: The Post- World War I Quest for Stability in East Central Europe." Maryland Historian 14 (Spring-Summer 1983): 23-41.

10562. Crespi, Gabrielle. The Arabs in Europe. New York: Rizzoli, 1986.

10563. Crossick, Geoffrey. "The Petite Bourgeoisie in Nineteenth- century Europe: Problems and Research." Historische Zeitschrift special issue (1986): 227-277.

10564. Dabene, Louise and others, eds. Status of Migrants' Mother Tongues. Le Statut des Langues d'Origine des Migrants. Strasbourg: European Science Foundation, 1983.

10565. Daman, Gilbert, ed. Les Juifs au regard de l'histoire. Paris: Picard, 1985. [Articles by 30 scholars on France, Germany, Britain, and Italy.]

10566. De Marchi, Bruna and Anna Maria Boilieu, eds. Boundaries and Minorities in the Western World. Milan: Franco Angeli Editore, 1982.

10567. Debrunner, Hans W. Presence and Prestige: Africans in Europe: A History of Africans in Europe before 1918. Basel: Basler Afrika Bibliographien, 1979.

10568. Derville, Alain. "L'alphabetisation du peuple a la fin du Moyen Age." R. Nord 66 (April-September 1984): 761-776.

10569. Dicker, Herman. Piety and Perserverance. Jews from the Carpathian Mountains. New York: Sepher-Wiesel, 1981.

10570. Dinstein, Yoram. Models of Antonomy. New Brunswick, NJ: Transaction Books, 1981.

10571. Dockès, Pierre. Medieval Slavery and Liberation. Translated by Arthur Goldhammer Chicago, II.: University of Chicago Press, 1982.

10572. Don, Yehudah and Victor Karady, eds. A Social and Economic History of Central European Jewry. New Brunswick, NJ: Transaction, 1989. [Includes Austria.]

10573. Drescher, Seymour. "The Ending of the Slave Trade and the Evolution of European Scientific Racism." Social Science History 14 (Autumn 1990)

10574. Droz, Jacques. Histoire de l'antifascisme en Europe, 1923- 1939. Paris: Éditions La Découverte, 1985. [Austria, France, Germany, Great Britain, Italy, and Spain.]

10575. Druks, Herbert. Jewish Resistance during the Holocaust. New York: Irvington, 1983.

10576. Dunstan, G. R. and R.F. Hobson. "A Note on an Early Ingredient of Racial Prejudice in Western Europe." Race 6 (1965): 322-332.

10577. Dyer, Christopher. Standards of Living in the Later Middle Ages. New York: Cambridge University Press, 1989.

10578. Ebels-Dolanova, Vera. The Extreme Right in Europe and the United States. Amsterdam: 1988.

10579. Edelheit, Abraham J. "Historiography of the Holocaust." In Encyclopedia of the Holocaust, II, 666-672. New York: Macmillan, 1990.

10580. Edwards, John. The Jews in Christian Europe 1400-1700. New York: Routledge and Kegan Paul, 1988.

10581. Eichholtz, Dietrich and Klaus Mammach, eds. Studien zur Geschichte des Faschismus und des antifaschistischen Widerstandes. E. Berlin: Akademie-Verlag, 1983.

10582. Elklit, Jorgen and Ole Tonsgaard. "Elements for a Structured Theory of Ethnic Segregation and Assimilation." European Journal of Political Research 12 (March 1984): 89-100.

10583. Engelstein, Laura. "Gender and the Juridical Subject: Prostitution and Rape in Nineteenth-Century Criminal Codes." Journal of Modern History 60 (1988): 458-495.

10584. Epstein, Simon. Cry of Cassandra: The Resurgence of European Antisemitism. Translated by Norman S. Posel Bethesda, MD: National Press, 1985.

10585. "Estimated Jewish Losses in the Holocaust." In Encyclopedia of the Holocaust, IV, 1797-1802. New York: Macmillan, 1990.

10586. Eyal, J. "Eastern Europe- What About the Minorities?" World Today 45 (December 1989)

10587. Falconi, C. The Silence of Pius XII. Boston: 1970.

10588. Falter, Jurgen W. and Siegfried Schumann. "Affinity Towards Right-wing Extremism in Western Europe." West European Politics 11 (1988): 96-110.

10589. Fein, Helen. Accounting for Genocide: National Responses and Jewish Victimization during the Holocaust. New York: Free Press, 1979.

10590. Fejto, François. Les juifs et l'antisemitisme dans les pays communistes. Paris: Plon, 1960.

10591. Ferencz, Benjamin B. Less Than Slaves: Jewish Forced Labor and the Quest for Compensation. Cambridge, Ma: Harvard University Press, 1979.

10592. Fikes, Robert Jr. "Confirming Intellectual Capacity: Black Scholars in Europe During the Renaissance and the Enlightenment." Presence Africaine 2 (1980): 120-131.

10593. "Flash sur la droite." Raison Présente (1988): 1-124. [Deals with right wing extremism in Belgium as well as other countries.]

10594. Flint, Valerie I. J. "Anti-Jewish Literature and Attitudes in the 12th Century." Journal of Jewish Studies 37 (1986): 39-57, 183-205.

10595. Fox, Genovese Elizabeth and Eugene D. Genovese. Fruits of Merchant Capital, Slavery and Bourgeois Property in the Rise and Expansion of Capitalism. New York: Oxford University Press, 1983.

10596. Fox, J., ed. Health Inequalities in Europe. London: 1988.

10597. Fox, John P., Elly Din, Sharon Gillerman, and Chaim Schatzker. "Education on the Holocaust." In Encyclopedia of the Holocaust, II, 418-425. New York: Macmillan, 1990.

10598. Fox, John P. "German and European Jewish Refugees, 1933- 1945: Reflections on the Jewish Condition under Hitler and the Western World's Response to Their Expulsion and Flight." In Refugees in the Age of Total War, edited by Anna C. Bramwell. Boston, MA: Unwin Hyman, 1988.

10599. Frankel, Jonathan. "The Paradoxical Politics of Marginality: Thoughts on the Jewish Situation during the Years 1914-1921." Stud. Contemp. Jewry 4 (1988): 3-21.

10600. Frankel, Jonathan, ed. Studies in Contemporary Jewry. Vol. IV: The Jews and the European Crisis, 1914-1921. New York: Oxford University Press, 1987.

10601. Fried, Johannes, ed. Schulen und Studium im sozialen Wandel des hohen und späten Mittelalters. Sigmaringen: Jan Thorbecke, 1986.

10602. Friedman, Ina R. The Other Victims: Stories of Non-Jews Persecuted by the Nazis. Boston, MA.: Houghton Mifflin, 1990. [Written for young people.]

10603. Frijhoff, Willem. "L'État et l'education (XVIe-XVIIe siècles): Une perspective globale." In Culture et ideologie dans la genèse de l'Etat Moderne. Rome: École Française de Rome with cooperation of the Centre Nationalo de la Recherche Scientifique, 1985.

10604. Geiss, Imanuel. Geschichte des Rassismus. Frankfurt am Main: Suhrkamp, 1988.

10605. Gella, Aleksander. Development of Class Structures in Eastern-Europe: Poland and Her Southern Neighbors. Albany: State University of New York Press, 1988. [Poland, Czechoslovakia, Hungary, and Rumania.]

10606. Gellner, Ernest. "Ethnicity and Faith in Eastern Europe." Daedalus 119 (Winter 1990)

10607. Genn, Rowel and Anthony Lerman. "Fascism and Racism in Europe: The Report of the European Parliament's Committee of Inquiry." Patterns of Prejudice (April 1986): 13-26.

10608. George, Vic and Roger Lawson, eds. Poverty and Inequality in Common Market Countries. London: Routledge & Kegan Paul, 1980.

10609. Glebe, Gunther and John O'Loughlin, eds. Foreign Minorities in Continental European Cities. Stuttgart: Franz Steiner Verlag Wiesbaden, 1987.

10610. Gliozzi, Giuliano. Adamo el il nuova mondo: la nascita dell' antropologia come ideologia coloniale. Florence: 1977.

10611. Goldthorpe, John H., ed. Order and Conflict in Contemporary Capitalism. Studies in the Political Economy of Western European Nations. New York: Oxford University Press, 1984.

10612. Gould, J. D. "European Inter-Continental Emigration 1815- 1914; Patterns and Causes." Journal of European Economic History 8 (Winter 1979)

10613. Grahl-Madsen, Atle and Tore Modeen, eds. "The Small Nations of the North in International and Constitutional Law." Nordisk Tidsskrift for International Ret-Acta scandinavica juris gentium Nos. 1-2 (1982): entire issue.

10614. Greenbaum, Avraham, ed. Minority Problems in Eastern Europe between the World Wars, with Emphasis on the Jewish Minority. Jerusalem, Israel: Institute of Advanced Studies, Hebrew University, 1988.

10615. Greussing, Fritz. "Die Vertreibung der 'fahrenden' Roma und ihre Heimatlosigkeit in Westeuropa." Pogrom 13 (September 1982): 6-20.

10616. Gronemeyer, Reimer, ed. Eigensinn und Hilfe: Zigeuner in der Sozialpolitik heutiger Leistungsgesellschaften. Giessen: Focus-Verlag, 1983.

10617. Groth, Alexander J. "The Politics of Xenophobia and the Salience of Anti-Semitism." Comparative Politics 4 (1971): 89-108.

10618. Guha, Amalendu and others, eds. Immigrant Women and Children in Industrial Europe. Hong Kong: Asian Research Service, 1986. [P.O. Box 2232 G.P.O. Hong-Kong.]

10619. Guha, Amalendu. LDC-Immigrants in Nordic Countries. Hong Kong: Asian Research Service, 1986. [P.O. Box 2232 G.P.O. Hong Kong.]

10620. Gunn, Simon. Revolution of the Right: Europe's New Conservatives. London: Pluto Press, 1989.

10621. Gutman, Israel. "Antisemitism." In Encyclopedia of the Holocaust, I, 55-74. New York: Macmillan, 1990.

10622. Gutman, Israel (editor in chief). Encyclopedia of the Holocaust. 4 vols. New York: Macmillan, 1990.

10623. Gutman, Israel. "Holocaust, Denial of the." In Encyclopedia of the Holocaust, II, 681-687. New York: Macmillan, 1990.

10624. Gutman, Israel and others. "Partisans." In Encyclopedia of the Holocaust. 1108-1122. New York: Macmillan, 1990.

10625. Gutman, Israel and others. "Youth Movements." In Encyclopedia of the Holocaust, IV, 1697-1716. New York: Macmillan, 1990.

10626. Gutman, Y. [Israel] and G. Greif, eds. The Historiography of the Holocaust Period. Jerusalem: 1988.

10627. Gutman, Y. [Israel] and C. J. Haft, eds. Patterns of Jewish Leadership in Nazi Europe, 1933-1945. Jerusalem: 1979.

10628. Hagen, William W. "Capitalism and the Countryside in Early Modern Europe: Interpretations, Models, Debates." Agricultural History 62 (1988): 13-47.

10629. Hagenaars, Aldi J. M. The Perception of Poverty. Amsterdam, North Holland: 1986.

10630. Haller, Max, ed. Class Structure in Europe: New Findings from East-West Companions of Social Structure and Mobility. Armonk, NY: M. E. Sharpe, 1990.

10631. Halpern, Joel. "Yugoslav Migration Process and Employment in Western Europe. A Historical Perspective." In Migrants in Europe: The Role of

Family, Labor, and Politics, edited by Hans Christian Buechler and Judith Maria Buechler. Westport, CT: Greenwood, 1987.

10632. Hammar, Tomas, ed. *European Immigration Policy: A Comparative Study*. New York: Cambridge University Press, 1985.

10633. Hancock, Ian. "Gypsies, Jews, and the Holocaust." *Shmate* No. 17 (Winter 1987): 8-15.

10634. Harman, Chris. *Class Struggles in Eastern Europe 1945-1983*. London: Pluto Press, 1984.

10635. Harris, Geoffrey. *The Dark Side of Europe. The Extreme Right Today*. Savage, MD: Rowman & Littlefield, 1990.

10636. Hay, Malcolm. *The Foot of Pride: The Pressure of Christendom on the People of Israel for 1,900 Years*. Boston: Beacon Press, 1960.

10637. "Health Inequities in Europe." *Social Science & Medicine* 31 (1990): entire issue.

10638. Heilke, Thomas W. *Voegelin on the Idea of Race. An Analysis of Modern European Racism*. Baton Rouge: Louisiana State University Press, 1990.

10639. Heisler, Barbara S. "Immigrant Settlement and the Structure of Emergent Immigrant Communities in Western Europe." *Annals of the American Academy of Political and Social Science* (May 1986): 485.

10640. Hertzberg, Arthur. "United States of Europe." *Tikkun* 5 (September-October 1990): 44-46. [Antisemitism in Europe.]

10641. Hilberg, Raul. *The Destruction of the European Jews*. 3 vols. Rev. and definitive ed. New York: Holmes & Meier, 1985.

10642. Hill, Ray with Andrew Bell. *The Other Face of Terror: Inside Europe's Neo-Nazi Network*. London: Grafton Books, 1988. [The first author is a former leading British Nazi who, in 1980, secretly changed his views and operated as a spy in neo-Nazi groups.]

10643. Hirschfeld, Gerhard, ed. *The Policies of Genocide*. London: Allen & Unwin, 1986. [Fate of Jewish and Soviet captives in Nazi hands during World War II.]

10644. Hirszowicz, Lukasz. "Antisemitism in the Communist World." *Soviet Jewish Affairs* 9 (1979)

10645. The Historical Society of Israel. *Judaism and Christianity under the Impact of National Socialism*. Jerusalem: Zalman Shazar Center for Jewish History, 1987.

10646. Hobsbawm, Eric J. Nations and Nationalism since 1780: Programme, Myth, Reality. New York: Cambridge University Press, 1990.

10647. Hockenos, Paul. "Refugees from Former East Bloc Confront Europe's New Walls." In These Times (September 26, 1990)

10648. Hodos, George H. Show Trials. Stalinist Purges in Eastern Europe. Westport, Ct: Praeger, 1987.

10649. Hoffman, Bruce. "Right-wing Terrorism in Europe." Conflict 5 (1984): 185-210.

10650. Hohenberg, Paul M. and Lynn Hollen Lees. The Making of Urban Europe, 1000-1950. Cambridge, MA: Harvard University Press, 1985.

10651. Holzer, Willibald I., ed. Zwischen Selbstfindung und Identitätsverlust: ethnische Minderheiten in Europa. Vienna: Verlag für Gesellschaftskritik,

10652. Horak, Stephen M., ed. Eastern European National Minorities, 1919-1980. A Handbook. Littleton, CO: Libraries Unlimited, 1985.

10653. Horch, Hans O. and Horst Denkler, eds. Conditio Judaica: Judentum, Antisemitismus und deutschsprachige Literatur vom 18. Jahrhundert bis zum Ersten Weltkrieg. Tubingen: Niemeyer, 1989.

10654. Hroch, Miroslav. Social Preconditions of National Revival in Europe: A Comparative Analysis of the Social Composition of Patriotic Groups among the Smaller European Nations. Translated by Ben Fowkes New York: Cambridge University Press, 1985.

10655. Hudson, Ray and Jim Lewis, eds. Uneven Development in Southern Europe: Studies of Accumulation, Class Migration and the State. London: Methuen, 1985.

10656. Hune, Shirley. "Drafting an International Convention on the Protection of the Rights of All Migrant Workers and Their Families." International Migration Review 19 (Fall 1985): 570-615.

10657. Husbands, Christopher T. "Contemporary Right-wing Extremism in Western European Democracies." European Journal of Political Research 9 (1981): 75-99.

10658. Husbands, Christopher T. "The Dynamics of Racial Exclusion and Expulsion: Racist Politics in Western Europe." European Journal of Political Research 16 (1988): 701-720.

10659. Institut historiques de la Résistance en Vallée d'Aoste, ed. Les Minorités ethniques européennes vis-a-vis du nazisme et du fascisme. Aoste: Musumeci, 1985.

10660. Israel, Jonathan I. European Jewry in the Age of Mercantilism, 1550-1750. 2d rev. ed. New York: Oxford University Press, 1989.

10661. Janowsky, Oscar J. The Jews and Minority Rights, 1898-1918. Columbia University Press, 1933.

10662. Janowsky, Oscar. People at Bay: The Jewish Problem in East Central Europe. London: 1938.

10663. Joes, Anthony J. Fascism in the Contemporary World: Ideology, Evolution, Resurgence. Boulder, CO: Westview, 1978.

10664. Jonassen, C. T. "Some Historical and Theoretical Bases of Racism in Northwestern Europe." Social Forces 30 (1951)

10665. Jones, Mervyn. The Sami of Lapland. London: Minority Rights Group, 1982.

10666. Kaelble, Hartmut. "Arbeiter und soziale Ungleichheit in Westeuropa, 1850-1930." Historische Zeitschrift special issue (1986): 137-178.

10667. Kaelble, Hartmut. Auf dem Weg zu einer europäischen Gesellschaft: Eine Sozialgeschichte Westeuropas 1880-1980. Munich: C.H. Beck, 1987.

10668. Kaelble, Hartmut. Historical Research on Social Mobility: Western Europe and the USA in the Nineteenth and Twentieth Centuries. Translated by Ingrid Noakes New York: Columbia University Press, 1981.

10669. Kaelble, Hartmut. Industrialization and Social Inequality in 19th Century Europe. New York: St. Martin's Press, 1986.

10670. Kaelble, Hartmut. A Social History of Western Europe, 1880-1980. Savage, MD: Barnes & Noble, 1990.

10671. Karras, Ruth M. Slavery and Society in Medieval Scandanavia. New Haven, CT: Yale University Press, 1988.

10672. Katz, Jacob. From Prejudice to Destruction. Anti-Semitism, 1700-1933. Cambridge, Mass.: Harvard University Press, 1980.

10673. Katz, Jacob. Jewish Emancipation and Self-emancipation. Philadelphia, PA: Jewish Publication Society, 1986.

10674. Katz, Jacob. Out of the Ghetto. The Social Background of Jewish Emancipation, 1770-1870. Cambridge, MA: Harvard University Press, 1973.

10675. Kaufman, Debra. "Gypsies Ponder Who Counts." In These Times (June 6, 1990): [Gypsies and the Holocaust.]

10676. Kautsky, Karl. Are the Jews a Race? New York: International, 1927.

10677. Kedward, H. R. Fascism in Western Europe, 1900-1945. Glasgow: Blackie, 1973.

10678. Kende, Pierre and Zdenek Strimeska, eds. Égalité et inegalités en Europe de l'Est. Paris: Presses de la Fondation Nationale des Sciences Politiques, 1984.

10679. Kenrick, Donald and Grattan Puxon. The Destiny of Europe's Gypsies. London: Heinemann, 1972.

10680. Kenrick, Donald and others. Die Zigeuner. Verkannt- Verachtet-Verfolgt. Hannover: Niederländische Landeszentrale für politische Bildung, 1980.

10681. King, Robert R. Minorities under Communism: Nationalities as a Source of Tension among Balkan Communist States. Cambridge, MA: Harvard University Press, 1973.

10682. Kisch, Guido. "Jewry-Law in Central Europe-Past and Present." Journal of Central European Affairs 2 (January 1943): 396-422.

10683. Kisch, Guido. "The Yellow Badge in History." Historia Judaica 4 (October 1942): 95-144. [See also appendix and references.]

10684. Klein, George and Milan J. Reban, eds. The Politics of Ethnicity in Eastern Europe. Boulder, CO: East European Monographs, 1981.

10685. Kombs, John. "Patterns of Children's Growth in East- Central Europe in the Eighteenth Century." Annals of Human Biology 13 (January-February 1986): 33-48.

10686. Korey, William. "Judaism in East Europe. Decay and Disintegration." Present Tense 10 (Spring 1983): 41-44.

10687. Koshar, Rudy, ed. Splintered Classes: Politics and the Lower Middle Classes in Interwar Europe. New York: Holmes & Meier, 1990.

10688. Koval, B. I. "Colonial Plantation Slavery and Primary Capital Accumulation in Western Europe." In Soviet Historians on Latin America: Recent Scholarly Contributions Russell H. Bartley (ed. and trans.). University of Wisconsin Press, 89- 108.

10689. Kozminski, Maciej. "Nationalism, National Minorities and Dictatorial Regimes in East-Central Europe in the Years 1918- 1939." In Dictatorships in East-Central Europe, 1918-1939, edited by Janusz Zarnowski. Wroclaw: Ossolineum, 1983.

10690. Kreici, Jaroslaw and V. Velimsky. Ethnic and Political Nations in Europe. London: Croom Helm, 1981.

10691. Kulka, Otto Dov and Paul R. Mendes-Flohr, eds. Judaism and Christianity under the Impact of National Socialism. Jerusalem: Historical Society of Israel and the Zalman Shazar Center for Jewish History, 1987.

10692. Land, Hilary. "The Changing Place of Women in Europe." Daedalus 108 (Spring 1979): 73-94.

10693. Lang, Michel R., ed. "Strasse frei": die neue Nazi- Internationale. W. Berlin: Rotation-Verlag Juergen Vetter, 1982. [Western Europe.]

10694. Large, David C. The Politics of Law and Order: Counter- revolutionary "Self-Defence" Organizations in Central Europe, 1918-1923. Doctoral dissertation: University of California at Berkeley, 1974.

10695. Larsen, Stein N. and others, eds. Who Were the Fascists? Social Roots of European Fascism. Bergen, Norway: Universitetsforlaget, 1980.

10696. Lavsky, Hagit and Leonard Dinnerstein. "Displaced Persons, Jewish." In Encyclopedia of the Holocaust, I, 377-390. New York: Macmillan, 1990.

10697. Layton-Henry, Zig, ed. The Political Rights of Migrant Workers in Western Europe. Newbury Park, CA: Sage, 1989.

10698. Lee, Martin and Kevin Coogan. "Killers on the Right: Inside Europe's Fascist Underground." Mother Jones (May 1987): 40-46, 52-54.

10699. Lee, Stephen J. The European Dictatorships 1918-1945. New York: Methuen, 1987.

10700. Lendvai, Paul. Anti-Semitism Without Jews. Communist Eastern Europe. Garden City, NJ: Doubleday, 1971.

10701. Lesse, S. "The Political and Economic Change in Central and Eastern Europe. Possible Macro-Psychosociologic Implications." American Journal of Psychotherapy 44 (April 1990)

10702. Limage, L. J. "Policy Aspects of Educational Provision for Children of Migrants in Western European Schools." International Migration 23 (June 1985): 251-262.

10703. Lin, Ming-yih. "New Aspects of the Chinese Communists in Europe in the Last Ten Years." Issues & Studies (Taiwan) 22 (1986): 101-116.

10704. Linden, Marcel van der. "The National Integration of European Working Classes (1871-1914): Exploring the Causal Configuration." International Review of Social History 33 (1988): 285-311.

10705. Lis, Catharina &. Hugo Saly. Poverty and Capitalism in Pre-Industrial Europe. Atlantic Highlands, NJ: Humanities, 1979.

818 WORLD RACISM AND RELATED INHUMANITIES

10706. Littell, Franklin H. "Christian Antisemitism and the Holocaust." In Judaism and Christianity under the Impact of National Socialism, 1919-1945, edited by Otto Dov Kulka and Paul R. Mendes-Flohr. Jerusalem: Historical Society of Israel, 1987.

10707. Lloyd, David. "Genet's Genealogy: European Minorities and the Ends of the Canon." Cultural Critique No.6 (Spring 1987)

10708. Lowenthal, Marvin. "Anti-Semitism in European Universities." Nation 117 (November 14, 1923): 547.

10709. Lucassen, Jan. Migrant Labour in Europe, 1700-1900. Wolfeboro, NH: Croom Helms, 1986.

10710. MacLean, Pam. "Control and Cleanliness: German-Jewish Relations in Occupied Eastern Europe during the First World War." War and Society 6 (September 1988): 47-69.

10711. Mahler, Raphael. A History of Modern Jewry, 1780-1815. New York: Schocken Books, 1971.

10712. "The Making of a Righteous Gentile." Jerusalem Post, (January 24, 1987): [Nearly 7,000 "righteous gentiles".]

10713. Marcolungo, Ezio and Mirella Karpati, eds. Chi sono gli zingari? Turin: Edizioni Gruppo Abele, 1985. [Gypsies.]

10714. Margolin, Arnold D. The Jews of Eastern Europe. New York: Seltzer, 1926.

10715. Markham, James M. "Minorities in Western Europe: Hearing 'Not Welcome' in Several Languages." New York Times, (August 5, 1986)

10716. Markham, James M. "Old World Fearful of Third World's 'silent Invasion'." New York Times, (February 14, 1988): [Immigrants in Western Europe.]

10717. Markham, James M. "Rightist Parties Forming in Europe." New York Times, (November 22, 1987)

10718. Marrus, Michael R. "European Jewry and the Politics of Assimilation: Assessment and Reassessment." Journal of Modern History 49 (March 1977): 89-109.

10719. Marrus, Michael. "Jewish Leaders and the Holocaust." French Historical Studies 15 (Fall 1987): 316-331.

10720. Marrus, Michael R., ed. The Nazi Holocaust, No. 5: Public Opinion and Relations to the Jews in Nazi Europe. 2 vols. Westport, CT: Meckler, 1989.

10721. Marrus, Michael R. The Unwanted European Refugees in the Twentieth Century. New York: Oxford University Press, 1985.

10722. Masurovsky, Marc J. The Safehaven Program: The Allied Response to Nazi Post-defeat Planning, 1944-1948. Master's thesis: American University, 1990. [Nazi influences in wartime neutral countries.]

10723. Mayer, Arno J. Why Did the Heavens Not Darken? The "Final Solution" in History. New York: Pantheon, 1988.

10724. Mazian, Florence. Why Genocide? The Armenian and Jewish Experiences in Perspective. Ames: Iowa State University Press, 1990.

10725. McEachern, Douglas. The Expanding State: Class and Economy in Europe Since 1945. New York: St. Martin's Press, 1990.

10726. Mendelsohn, Ezra. "Jewish Leadership between the Two World Wars." In Patterns of Jewish Leadership in Nazi Europe, 1933- 1945, edited by Yisrael Gutman and Cynthia Haft. Jerusalem: 1979.

10727. Mendelsohn, Ezra. The Jews of East Central Europe Between the World Wars. Bloomington: Indiana University Press, 1983.

10728. Meulen, Hans W. Eurofaschismus und der Zweite Weltkrieg: Europas verratene Söhne. W. Berlin: Universitäs-Verlag Dr. Klaus Schweitzer, 1980.

10729. Meyer, Ernie. "The Making of a Righteous Gentile." Jerusalem Post Magazine, (January 16, 1987): [How Yad Vashem selects candidates for the designation.]

10730. Micksch, Jürgen. Kulturelle Vielfalt statt nationaler Einfalt. Eine Strategie gegen Nationalismus und Rassismus. Frankfurt: Verlag Otto Lembeck, 1989.

10731. Miles, Robert. "Labour Migration, Racism and Capital Accumulation in Western Europe since 1945: An Overview." Capital & Class No. 28 (Spring 1986): 49-86.

10732. Miller, Judith. One, By One, By One. New York: Simon & Schuster, 1990. [How the U.S., West Germany, Austria, France, The Netherlands, and the USSR have dealt with the memory of the Holocaust.]

10733. Minderheitenschutz in Europa. Heidelberg: C.F. Müller Juristischer Verlag, 1985.

10734. Mollat, Michel. The Poor in the Middle Ages. An Essay in Social History. Translated by Arthur Goldhammer New Haven, CT: Yale University Press, 1986. [5th to 15th centuries.]

10735. Monroe, K. R. and others. "Altruism and the Theory of Rational Action:Rescuers of Jews in Nazi Europe." Ethics 101 (October 1990)

10736. Moore, R. J. The Formation of a Persecuting Society. Power and Deviance in Western Europe 950-1250. New York: Blackwell, 1987.

10737. Morley, J. F. Vatican Diplomacy and the Jews during the Holocaust, 1939-1943. New York: 1980.

10738. Morrisson, C. "Income Distribution in East European and Western Countries." Journal of Comparative Economics 8 (June 1984)

10739. Mosse, George L. Masses and Man: Nationalist and Fascist Perceptions of Reality. Detroit, MI: Wayne State University Press, 1980.

10740. Mosse, George L. "Racism." In Encyclopedia of the Holocaust. 1206-1217. New York: Macmillan, 1990.

10741. Mosse, George L. Toward the Final Solution: A History of European Racism. New York: Fertig, 1979.

10742. Moulier-Boutang, Yann. "Resistance to the Political Representation of Alien Populations: The European Paradox." International Migration Review 19 (Fall 1985): 485-492.

10743. Muhlberger, Detlef, ed. The Social Basis of European Fascist Movements. London: Croom Helm, 1987.

10744. Muller, Detlef and others. The Rise of the Modern Educational System. Structural Change and Social Reproduction 1870-1920. New York: Cambridge University Press, 1989.

10745. Mushkat, Marian and others. "Trials of War Criminals." Encyclopedia of the Holocaust, IV, 1488-1518. New York: Macmillan, 1990.

10746. Narkiewicz, Olga. Eastern Europe 1968 to 1984. Totowa, New Jersey: Barnes and Noble, 1986.

10747. Nelson, Daniel N. "Socioeconomic and Political Change in Communist Europe." International Studies Quarterly 21 (June 1977): 359-388.

10748. Niederhauser, Emil. The Rise of Nationality in Eastern Europe. Budapest: Corvina Kiado, 1982.

10749. Nordic Council. Level of Living and Inequality in the Nordic Countries. Stockholm: The Nordic Council, 1984.

10750. Oberman, Heiko A. The Roots of Antisemitism in the Age of Renaissance and Reformation. Translated by James J. Porter Philadelphia, PA: Fortress Press, 1984.

10751. Okey, Robin. Eastern Europe 1740-1985. Feudalism to Communism. 2d ed. Minneapolis: University of Minnesota Press, 1987.

10752. Olson, J. S., ed. Historical Dictionary of European Imperialism. Westport, CT: Greenwood, 1991.

10753. Palley, Claire and others. Co-existence in Some European Plural Societies. London: Minority Rights Groups, 1986.

10754. Payne, Stanley G. Fascism: Comparison and Definition. Madison: University of Wisconsin Press, 1980.

10755. Pearson, Raymond. National Minorities in Eastern Europe, 1843-1944. New York: St. Martin's Press, 1984.

10756. Penninx, Rinus. Immigrant Populations and Demographic Development in the Member States of the Council of Europe. 3 parts. Strasbourg: Council of Europe, 1984.

10757. Penninx, Rinus. "International Migration in Western Europe since 1973: Developments, Mechanisms and Controls." International Migration Review 20 (Winter 1986): 951-972.

10758. Pilat, J. F. "Euroright Extremism." Wiener Library Bulletin 53-54 (1981): 48-64.

10759. Pilbeam, Pamela. The Middle Classes in Europe, 1789-1914: France, Germany, Italy, and Russia. Chicago, Il: Lyceum Books, 1990.

10760. Poliakov, Leon. The Aryan Myth: A History of Racist and Nationalist Ideas in Europe. Translated by Edmund Howard New York: New American Library, 1977.

10761. Poliakov, Leon. Suicidal Europe, 1870-1933. Vol.4 of The History of Antisemitism. New York: 1985.

10762. Pollard, Sidney. Peaceful Conquest: The Industrialization of Europe 1760-1970. New York: Oxford University Press, 1981.

10763. Popovic, Alexandre. L'Islam balkanique: les musulmans du sud-est européen dans la période post Ottomane. Wiesbaden: Otto Harrassowitz, 1986.

10764. Pott, A. F. Die Zigeuner in Europa und Asien. 2 vols. Leipzig: Edition Leipzig, 1964.

10765. Poulton, Hugh. Minorities in the Balkans. London: Minority Rights Group, October 1989. [Report No. 82.]

10766. Powell, James M., ed. Muslims under Latin Rule, 1100- 1300. Princeton, NJ: Princeton University Press, 1990. [Muslim minorities in Christian lands.]

10767. Power, Jonathan and Anna Hardman. Western Europe's Migrant Workers. rev. ed. London: Minority Rights Group, 1984.

10768. Prager, L. "The Impoverished Rich and the Well-to-Do Poor (Investigations Concerning Personal Income)." Eastern European Economics 23 (Winter 1984-1985)

10769. Prechal, Sacha and Noreen Burrows. European Community Law Relating to Gender Discrimination. Brookfield, VT: Gower, 1990.

10770. Pullan, Brian S. The Jews of Europe and the Inquisition of Venice, 1550-1670. Totowa, NJ: Barnes & Noble, 1983.

10771. Puxon, Grattan. Roma: Europe's Gypsies. 4th ed. London: Minority Rights Groups, 1987.

10772. Ramet, Pedro. Cross and Commissar: The Politics of Religion in Eastern Europe and the USSR. Bloomington: Indiana University Press, 1987.

10773. Rassinier, Paul. Debunking the Genocide Myth. A Study of the Nazi Concentration Camps and the Alleged Extermination of European Jewry. Translated by Adam Robbins Torrance, CA: Institute for Historical Review, 1978. [Denies 6,000,000 Jews were killed in a Holocaust; see Pierre Vidal-Naquet, below.]

10774. Rassinier, Paul. Drama of the European Jews. Translated by Harry Elmer Barnes Silver Springs, MD: Steppingstones Publications, 1975. [Denies 6,000,000 Jews were killed in a Holocaust.]

10775. Rawley, James A. The Transatlantic Slave Trade: A History. London: Norton, 1982.

10776. Reddy, William. Money and Liberty in Modern Europe. New York: 1987.

10777. Reich, Emil. "The Jew-Baiting on the Continent." Nineteenth Century 40 (1896): 422-438.

10778. Rhode, Gotthold, ed. Juden in Ostmitteleuropa: Von der Emanzipation bis zum Ersten Weltkrieg. Marburg/Lahn: Johann- Gottfried-Herder Institut, 1989.

10779. "Right-Radical Round Up [in Europe]." Patterns of Prejudice 17 (April 1983): 36-44.

10780. "Right-Wing Extremism in Western Europe." West European Politics 11 (April 1988): entire issue.

10781. "The Righteous Among the Nations- The Few Who Defied Tyranny." Center for Holocaust Studies Newsletter 3 (1988)

10782. Robertson, Priscilla. An Experience of Women, Pattern and Change in Nineteenth-Century Europe. Philadelphia, PA: Temple University Press, 1982.

10783. Robinson, Jacob and others. Were the Minorities Treaties a Failure? New York: Institute of Jewish Affairs of the American Jewish Committee and the World Jewish Congress, 1943.

10784. Rogers, Rosemarie, ed. Guests Come to Stay. The Effects of European Labor Migration on Sending And Receiving Countries. New York: Praeger, 1985.

10785. "Roma in Eastern Europe." In World Directory of Minorities, edited by Minority Rights Group. Harlow: Longman, 1990.

10786. "Roma in Western Europe." In World Directory of Minorities, edited by Minority Rights Group. 93-95. Harlow: Longman, 1990.

10787. Roniger, Luis. "Social Stratification in Southern Europe." In Centre Formation, Protest Movements and Class Structure in Europe and the United States, edited by S.N. Eisenstadt and others. New York: New York University Press, 1987.

10788. Rosenfeld, Stephen S. "Eastern Europe's Nasty Side." Present Tense 17 (March-April 1990): 14-15. [Antisemitism.]

10789. Rosoli, Gianfausto. "Italian Migration to European Countries from Political Unification to World War I." In Labor Migration in the Atlantic Economies, edited by Dirk Hoerder. Westport, CT: Greenwood, 1985.

10790. Roth, Stephen J. "CSCE Outlaws Antisemitism." Research Report (Institute of Jewish Affairs) No. 6 (1990): [Conference on Security and Cooperation in Europe.]

10791. Roth, Stephen J. "Ten Years After Helsinki and the Ottawa Human Rights Stalemate." Research Report (Institute of Jewish Affairs) No. 6 (September 1985)

10792. Rozett, Robert and Shmuel Krakowski. "Resistance, Jewish." In Encyclopedia of the Holocaust, III. New York: Macmillan, 1990.

10793. Ruether, Rosemary R. Faith and Fratricide: The Theological Roots of Anti-Semitism. New York: 1974.

10794. "Saami." In World Directory of Minorities, edited by Minority Rights Group. Harlow: Longman, 1990.

10795. Salvi, Sergio. Le nazioni proibite. Florence: Ed. Vallechi, 1973.

10796. Sampson, Steven. "The Informal Sector in Eastern Europe." Telos No. 66 (Winter 1985-1986): 44-66.

10797. Saueressig-Schreuder, Yda. "Education and the Decline of Traditional Industries in Mid-Nineteenth Century Europe." Immigration Hist. Newsletter 17 (May 1985): 8-10.

10798. Scardigli, Victor. L'Europe des modes de vie. Paris: Editions du Centre Nationale de la Recherche Scientifique, 1987.

10799. Schmugge, Ludwig. "Über nationale Vorurteile im Mittelalter." Deutsches Archiv für Erforschung des Mittelalters 38 (1982)

10800. Schönfeld, Roland. Nationalitätenprobleme in Südosteuropa. Munich: R. Oldenbourg, 1987.

10801. Schöpflin, George. "The Stalinist Experience in Eastern Europe." Survey 30 (1988): 124-147.

10802. Scobie, Edward. "African Women in Early Europe (2 parts)." Journal of African Civilizations 6, 7 (April 1984, November 1985): 135-154, 203-222.

10803. Scott, Hilda. Does Socialism Liberate Women? Experiences from Eastern Europe. Boston: Beacon, 1974.

10804. Seidel, Gill. The Holocaust Denial: Antisemitism, Racism and the New Right. Leeds: Beyond the Pale Collective, 1986.

10805. Self-Determination and Indigenous Peoples: Sami Rights and Northern Perspectives. Copenhagen: IWGIA, 1987.

10806. Shoup, Paul S., ed. Problems of Balkan Security: Southeastern Europe in the 1990's. Wilson Center Press, 1990.

10807. Sierpowski, S. "Dilemma der Minderheiten im Völkerbund." Polnische Weststud 3 (1984): 211-237.

10808. Silbermann, Alphons and Julius Schoeps, eds. Antisemitismus nach dem Holocaust: Bestandaufnahme und Erscheinungsformen in deutschsprachigen Ländern. Cologne: Verlag Wissenschaft und Politik, 1986.

10809. Simons, Marlise. "East Europe's Gypsies: Unwanted Refugees." New York Times, (July 30, 1990)

10810. Sivanandan, A. "The New Racism." New Statesman & Society (November 4, 1988)

10811. Sivanandan, A. "Racism 1992." Race & Class 30 (1989): 85-90.

10812. Skyum-Nielson, Niels. "Nordic Slavery in an International Setting." Med. Scand. 11 (1978-1979): 126-148.

10813. Slomp, Hans. Labor Relations in Europe: A History of Issues and Developments. New York: Greenwood Press, 1990.

10814. Smith, Alan. "Higher Education Cooperation 1975-1985: Creating a Basis for Growth in an Adverse Economic Climate." European Journal of Education 20 (1985): 267-292.

10815. Soulis, George C. "The Gypsies in the Byzantine Empire and the Balkans in the Late Middle Ages." Dumbarton Oaks Papers 15 (1961)

10816. Sparks, Colin. Never Again! The Hows and Whys of Stopping Fascism. London: Bookmarks, 1980.

10817. Steinherr, A. "Income Distribution and Employment in the European Communities 1960-1982." Zeitschrift fur Wirtschafts- und Sozialwissenschaften (1985): 105.

10818. Stephens, Meic. Linguistic Minorities in Western Europe. Gomer Press, 1976.

10819. Sternhell, Zeev. "Fascism." In Encyclopedia of the Holocaust. 472-479. New York: Macmillan, 1990.

10820. Strom, Yale. The Last Jews of Eastern Europe. New York: Philosophical Library, 1986.

10821. Sugar, Peter F., ed. Ethnic Diversity and Conflict in Eastern Europe. Santa Barbara, CA: ABC-Clio, 1980.

10822. Sugar, Peter F., ed. Native Fascism in the Successor States, 1918-1945. Santa Barbara, CA: American Bibliographical Center, 1971.

10823. Sukiennicki, Wiktor. East Central Europe in World War I: From Foreign Domination to National Freedom. 2 vols. New York: Columbia University Press, 1984.

10824. Sutherland, N. M. "Persecution and Toleration in Reformation Europe." Stud. Church Hist. 21 (1984): 153-164.

10825. Svensson, Per-Gunnar. "Health and Social Policy Responses to Unemployment in Europe." Journal of Social Issues 44 (1988): 173-191.

10826. Svensson, Tom G. "Patterns of Transformation and Local Self-determination: Ethnopower and the Larger Society in the North, the Sami Case." Nomadic Peoples 24 (1987): 1-13.

10827. Taguieff, Pierre-Andre. "L'heritage nazi: Des Nouvelles Droites europeennes a la litterature niant le genocide." Nouveaux Cahiers 64 (1981): 3-22.

826 WORLD RACISM AND RELATED INHUMANITIES

10828. Teichova, Alive &. others. "Economic Concepts and European Thoughts in Historical Perspective." History of European Ideas 9 (1988): 123-255.

10829. Thurlow, Richard C. "Fascism and Nazism- No Siamese Twins, II." Patterns of Prejudice 14 (April 1980): 15-23.

10830. Todorov, Nikolai. "Social Structures in the Balkans During the Eighteenth and Nineteenth Centuries." Etudes Balkaniques 21 (1985): 48-71.

10831. Tomaszewski, Jerzy. The Socialist Regimes of East Central Europe: Their Establishment and Consolidation 1944-1967. Translated by Jolanta Krauze London: Routledge and Kegan Paul, 1989.

10832. Trunk, Isaiah E. Judenrat. New York: Stein and Day, 1978.

10833. Tudjman, Frenjo. Nationalism in Contemporary Europe. Boulder, CO: East European Monographs, 1981.

10834. Vaggi, Gianni. "Social Classes and Income Distribution in Eighteenth-Century Economies." History of European Ideas 9 (1988): 171-182.

10835. Vago, Bela. The Shadow of the Swastika: The Rise of Fascism and Anti-Semitism in the Danube Basin, 1936-1939. Farnborough, Hants: Saxon House for the Institute of Jewish Affairs, 1975.

10836. Vago, Bela and George L. Mosse, eds. Jews and Non-Jews in Eastern Europe, 1918-1945. New York: Wiley, 1975.

10837. Valdes, Mario. "The Black Wiseman in European Symbolism." Journal of African Civilization 3 (April 1981): 67-85.

10838. Valentin, H. "Rescue and Relief Activities in Behalf of Jewish Victims of Nazism in Scandanavia." YIVO Annual of Jewish Social Science 8 (1953): 224-251.

10839. Vali, Ference A. "International Minority Protection from the League of Nations to the United Nations." In The Hungarians: A Divided Nation, edited by Stephen Borsody. New Haven, CT: Yale Center for International and Area Studies, 1988.

10840. Valkeapoa, Nils-Aslak. Greetings from Lappland. The Sami- Europe's Forgotten People. London: Zed Books, 1983.

10841. Van Amersfoor, H. and others. "International Migration, the Economic Crisis and the State: An Analysis of Mediterranean Migration to Western Europe." Ethnic & Racial Studies 7 (1984): 238-268.

10842. Van Arkel, D. "Racism in Europe." In Racism and Colonialism, edited by R. Ross. Boston, MA: Nijhoff, 1982.

10843. van Weeren, H. and B.M.S. van Praag. "The Inequality of Actual Incomes and Earning Capacities between Households in Europe." European Economic Review 24 (March 1984)

10844. Vassaf, Gunduz. Wir haben unsere Stimme noch nicht laut gemacht: Türkische Arbeiterkinder in Europa. Istanbul, Turkey: Felsburg Istanbul, 1985.

10845. Venn-Brown, Janet, ed. For a Palestinian: A Memorial to Wael Zuaiter. Boston, MA: Keegan Paul International, 1984. [Anti-Islamic prejudice in Europe.]

10846. Verlinden, Charles. L'Esclavage en Europe médiévale. Vol. 1. Péninsule Iberique, France. Bruges, 1955.

10847. Verlinden, Charles. L'Esclavage dans l'Europe Médiévale. Vol.2. Italie-Colonies italiennes du Levant-Levant latin- Empire byzantin. Ghent: Rijksuniversiteit te Gent, 1977.

10848. Verlinden, Charles. "Medieval "Slavers"." Explorations in Economic History 7 (1970): 1-14.

10849. Verlinden, Charles. "Précedénts et perallèles européens de l'esclavage colonial." O Instituto de Coimbra 113 (1949): 1-41.

10850. Vermeulen, H. and J. Boissevain, eds. Ethnic Challenge: The Politics of Ethnicity in Europe. Gottingen: Edition Herodet, 1984.

10851. Vidal-Naquet, Pierre. Les Assassins de la Mémoire. Un Eichmann de papier et autres essais sur le revisionnisme. Paris: Editions la Decouverte, 1987. [On those writers who deny the reality of the Holocaust; see Rassinier, above.]

10852. Wardi, Charlotte and others, Literature on the Holocaust. In Encyclopedia of the Holocaust, III. 877-895. New York: Macmillan, 1990.

10853. "Was There 'Another Europe'? New Light on Rescue and Rescuers." Dimensions (ADL International Center for Holocaust Studies 3 (No. 3) (1988): 1-29 (entire issue).

10854. Washington, Booker T. and Robert E. Park. The Man Farthest Down. A Record of Observation and Study of Europe. New Brunswick, NJ: Transaction Publishers, 1983 (orig. 1910).

10855. Wayne, Jack. "Capitalism and Colonialism in Late Nineteenth Century Europe." Studies in Political Economy No.5 (Spring 1981): 79-106.

10856. Weinstock, Nathan. Le pain de misère: Histoire du mouvement ouvrier juif en Europe. 3 vols. Paris: Découverte, 1984, 1986.

10857. Weisbord, Robert G. "Scandanavia: A Racial Utopia?" Journal of Black Studies 2 (June 1972): 471-488.

10858. Weiss, Aahron. "Judenrat." In Encyclopedia of the Holocaust, II, 762-771. New York: Macmillan, 1990.

10859. Wergeland, A. M. Slavery in Germanic Society During the Middle Ages. Chicago: 1916.

10860. Whitehouse, S. Youth Unemployment in the European Community. Doctoral dissertation: University of Bath, UK, 1986.

10861. Wiesner, Merry E. "Making Ends Meet: The Working Poor in Early Modern Europe." In Pietas et Societas: New Trends in Reformation Social History, edited by Kyle C. Sessions and Phillip N. Bebb. Kirksville, MO: Sixteenth-Century Journal, 1985.

10862. Wilcox, C. "The Causes and Consequences of Feminist Consciousness among Western European Women." Comparative Political Studies 23 (January 1991)

10863. Wippermann, Wolfgang. Europäischer Faschismus im Vergleich (1922-1982). Frankfurt: Sukrkamp Verlag, 1983.

10864. Witt, Peter-Christian, ed. Wealth and Taxation in Central Europe. The History and Sociology of Public Finance. New York: St. Martin's Press, 1987. [Late Middle Ages to 20th Century.]

10865. Wolchik, Sharon L. "Ideology and Equality: The Status of Women in Eastern and Western Europe." Comparative Political Studies 13 (January 1981): 445-477.

10866. Wolchik, Sharon L. and Alfred G. Meyer, eds. Women, State, and Party in Eastern Europe. Durham, NC: Duke University Press, 1985.

10867. Wolf, Eric R. Europe and the People Without History. Berkeley: University of California Press, 1982.

10868. Wolff, Richard J. and Jorg K. Hoensch, eds. Catholics, the State, and the European Radical Right, 1919-1945. New York: Columbia University Press, 1987.

10869. Woolf, Stuart. The Poor in Western Europe in the 18th and 19th Centuries. London: Methuen, 1986.

10870. Wyman, Mark. DQ: Europe's Displaced Persons, 1945-1951. Philadelphia, PA: Balch Institute, 1989.

10871. Yardeni, Myrian. Anti-Jewish Mentalities in Early Modern Europe. Lanham, MD: University Press of America, 1989.

10872. Yunker, J. A. "The Distribution of Lifetime Capital Property Income under Capitalism and Market Socialism." ACES Bulletin (Association for Comparative Economic Studies) 26 (Summer-Fall 1984)

10873. Zagorin, Perez. Ways of Living: Dissimulation, Persecution, and Conformity in Early Modern Europe. Cambridge, MA: Harvard University Press, 1990.

10874. Zisenevine, David W., ed. Anti-Semitism in Europe: Sources of the Holocaust. New York: Behrman House, 1976.

10875. Zulch, T. ed. In Auschwitz vergast; bis heute verfolgt. Hamburg: 1979. [Gypsies.]

LATIN AMERICA

10876. Abel, Christopher and Colin M. Lewis, eds. Latin America, Economic Imperialism, and the State: The Political Economy of the External Connection from Independence to the Present. Dover, NH: Athlone, 1985.

10877. Acker, Alison. Children of the Volcano. London: Zed Press, 1986. [Guatemala, El Salvador, Honduras, and Nicaragua.]

10878. Adams, Richard N. "The Conquest Tradition of Mesoamerica." The Americas 46 (October 1989): 119-136. [Colonial period.]

10879. Altimir, O. "Income Distribution Statistics in Latin America and Their Reliability." Review of Income and Statistics 33 (June 1987): 111-155.

10880. Altimir, O. and Juan Sourrouille. Measuring Levels of Living in Latin America. Washington, D.C.: World Bank, 1986 (orig. 1980).

10881. Alvarez, Sonia E. The Politics of Gender in Latin America. Doctoral dissertation: Yale University, 1986.

10882. "Antisemitism in South America." Patterns of Prejudice 13 (November-December 1979): 12-13.

10883. Aricó, José. Marx y América Latina. Lima: CEDEP, 1980.

10884. Arner, David and Patrick Costello. Literacy and Power: The Latin America Battleground. London: Earthscan, 1990.

10885. Aronsfeld, C. C. "Jews, Arabs and Antisemites in Latin America." Research Report (Institute of Jewish Affairs) No. 16 (September 1983)

10886. Avery, William P. "Collective Self-reliance in Latin America: Evaluating Counterdependency." Journal of Developing Societies 4 (1988): 149-165.

10887. Banuri, Tariq, ed. The Limits of Economic Liberalization: No Panacea: The Experiences of Latin America and East Asia. New York: Oxford University Press, 1990.

10888. Barros, Robert. "The Left and Democracy: Recent Debates in Latin America." Telos No. 68 (Summer 1986): 49-70.

10889. Barry, Tom. Roots of Rebellion: Land and Hunger in Central America. Boston, MA: South End Press, 1987.

10890. Batalla, G. B. Utopia y Revolucion. El Pensamiento Politico Contemporaneo de los Indios en America Latina. Mexico: Editorial Nueva Imagen, 1981.

10891. Bauer, Arnold J. "Rural Workers in Spanish America: Problems of Peonage and Oppression." Hispanic American Historical Review 59 (February 1979): 34-63.

10892. Behrman, J. R. "Schooling in Latin America: What are the Patterns and What is the Impact?" Jr. Interam. Stud. World Aff. 27 (Winter 1985-1986): 21-36.

10893. Beller, Jacob. Jews in Latin America. New York: 1969.

10894. Bergiust, Charles. Labor in Latin America: Comparative Essays in Chile, Argentina, Venezuela, and Columbia. Stanford, CA: Stanford University Press, 1986.

10895. Bergmann, Emilie and others. Women, Culture, and Politics in Latin America. Seminar on Feminism and Culture in Latin America. Berkeley: University of California Press, 1990.

10896. Berry, Albert. "Poverty and Inequality in Latin America." Latin American Research Review 22 (1987): 202-214.

10897. Beyhaut, Gustavo. Raices de América Latina. Buenos Aires, Argentina: Eudeba Editorial Universitariá de Buenos Aires, 1964.

10898. Boff, Leonardo. Ecclesiogenesis: The Base Communities Reinvent the Church. Maryknoll, NY: Orbis Books, 1986.

10899. Booth, John A. "Igualdad socioeconomica en Centroamerica: tendencias recientes y futuras." Annuario de Estudios Centroaméricas: historia, sociedad, conocimiento 13 (1987): 93-115.

10900. Braithwaite, Stanley N. "Real Income Levels in Latin America." Review of Income and Wealth 14 (June 1968): 113-182.

10901. Brockett, Charles D. Land, Power, and Poverty: Agrarian Transformation and Political Conflict in Central America. rev. ed. Boston, MA: Unwin Hyman, 1990.

10902. Brooke, James. "Blacks of South America Fight ' a Terrible Silence'." New York Times, (September 28, 1989)

10903. Bruleaux, Anne-Marie and others, eds. Deux Siècles d'Esclavage en Guyane Francaise 1652-1848. Cayenne, French Guiana: Centre Guyanais d'Etudes et de Recherches, 1986.

10904. Bulmer, Thomas. "Economic Development Over the Long Run- Central America since 1920." Journal of Latin American Studies 15 (1983): 269-294.

10905. Burns, E. Bradford. The Poverty of Progress. Latin America in the Nineteenth Century. Berkeley: University of California Press, 1980.

10906. Cardoso, Fernando H. "Democracy in Latin America." Politics and Society 15 (1986-1987): 23-42.

10907. Chilcote, Ronald H. "Post-Marxism: The Retreat from Class in Latin America." Latin American Perspective 17 (Spring 1990)

10908. Clay, Jason W. Indigenous Peoples and Tropical Forests. Models of Land Use and Management from Latin America. Cambridge, MA: Cultural Survival, Inc., 1988.

10909. Cleary, Edward L., ed. Born of the Poor: The Latin American Church since Medellin. Notre Dame, IN: University of Notre Dame Press, 1990.

10910. Clementi, Hebe. Las abolición de la esclavitud en America Latina. Buenos Aires: 1974,

10911. Cohen, Jacob Xenab. Jewish Life in South America. New York: Bloch, 1941.

10912. Cohen, Martin A., ed. The Jewish Experience in Latin America. 2 vols. New York: Ktav Publishing House, 1971.

10913. Comas, Juan. "Fray Bartoleme, la esclavitud y el racismo." Historiografia y bibliografia americanistas 19-20 (1975- 76): 1-10.

10914. Comas, Juan. "Interracial Relations in Latin America." International Social Science Journal 13 (1961): 271-299.

10915. Couriel, Alberto. "Poverty and Unemployment in Latin America." CEPAL Review 24 (December 1984): 39-62.

10916. Cueva, Agustin. El desarollo del capitalismo en America Latina. Mexico: 1977.

10917. Cueva-Jaramillo, Juan. "Ethnocentrism and Cultural Conflicts: The Anthropology of Acculturation." Cultures (France) 5 (1978): 19-31.

10918. Davis, Shelton H. Land Rights and Indigenous Peoples. The Role of the Inter-American Commission on Human Rights. Cambridge, MA: Cultural Survival, Inc., 1988.

10919. de Carvalho-Neto, Paulo. "Folklore of the Black Struggle in Latin America." Latin American Perspective 5 (Spring 1978): 53-88.

10920. Diaz-Polanco, Hector. Etnia, nación y politica. Mexico City: Juan Pablos Editor, 1987. [Indians in Latin America.]

10921. Diggs, Irene. "Color in Colonial Spanish America." Journal of Negro History 38 (October 1953): 403-427.

10922. Dix, Robert H. "Populism: Authoritarian and Democratic." Latin Am. Res. R. 20 (1985): 29-52.

10923. Dixon, William J. "Progress in the Provision of Basic Human Needs: Latin America, 1960-1980." Journal of Developing Areas 21 (January 1987): 129-140.

10924. Drussel, Enrique. A History of the Church in Latin America: Colonialism to Liberation (1492-1979). Translated by Alan Neely Grand Rapids, MI: Erdmans, 1983.

10925. Duncan, Kenneth &. others, eds. Land and Labour in Latin America. Essays on the Development of Agrarian Capitalism in the 19th and 20th Centuries. New York: Cambridge University Press, 1977.

10926. Eckstein, Susan. Power and Popular Protest: Latin American Social Movements. Berkeley: University of California Press, 1989.

10927. Eisenberg, Warren. "Latin America: A Lingering Presence." B'nai B'rith International Jewish Monthly (October 1989): [Jews in Latin America.]

10928. Elkin, Judith L. Jews of the Latin American Republics. Chapel Hill: University of North Carolina Press, 1980.

10929. Elkin, Judith L. Latin American Jewish Studies. Cincinnati: American Jewish Archives, 1980.

10930. Elkin, Judith L. "Latin America's Jews: A Review of Sources." Latin American Research Review 20 (1985): 124- 141.

10931. Elkin, Judith L., ed. Resources for Latin American Jewish Studies. Ann Arbor, MI: Latin American Jewish Studies Association, 1984.

10932. Elkin, Judith L. "Thinking Latin." Forum on the Jewish People, Zionism and Israel Nos. 42/43 (Winter 1981): 33-45. [Jews in Latin America.]

10933. Elkin, Judith L. and Gilbert W. Merkx, eds. The Jewish Presence in Latin America. Winchester, MA: Allen & Unwin, 1988.

10934. La emigración europea a la América Latina. Fuentes y estado de investigación: Informes presentados a la IV. Reunión de Historiades Latin-americanistas Europeos. Berlin: 1979.

10935. Escobar, Alberto. Lenguaje y Discriminacion Social en America Latina. Lima, Peru: Milla Batres, 1972.

10936. Esteinou Madrid, Javier. Los medios de comunicación y la construcción de la hegemonia. Mexico City: Editorial Nueva Imagen, 1983.

10937. Faber, Daniel R. Imperialism and the Crisis of Nature in Central America. Doctoral dissertation: University of California, Santa Cruz, 1989. UMO # 9021407.

10938. Fals Borda, Orlando. "Social Movements and Political Power: Evolution in Latin America." International Sociology 5 (June 1990)

10939. Favre, Henri. "Bolivar y los indios." Histórica (Peru) 10 (1986): 1-18.

10940. Felix, David. "Income Distribution and the Quality of Life in Latin America: Patterns, Trends, and Policy Implications." Latin American Research Review 18 (1983): 3-33.

10941. Fernandez, Retamar Roberto. "Caliban: Notes Toward a Discussion of Culture in Our America." Massachusetts Review 15 (1974): 7-72.

10942. Fiehrer, Thomas. "Slaves and Freedman in Colonial Central America: Rediscovering a Forgotten Black Past." Journal of Negro History 64 (Winter 1979): 39-58.

10943. Fontaine, Pierre-Michel. "Research in the Political Economy of Afro-America." Latin American Research Review 15 (1980): 111-141.

10944. Franco, José L. La diaspora africana en el nuevo mundo. Havana: Editorial de Ciencias Sociales, 1975.

10945. Franco, José L. "La Prescencia Negra en el Nuevo Mundo." Casa de las Americas 7 (1968): 7-135.

10946. Fried, Jacob. Jews in Latin America. New York: 1949.

10947. Frucht, Richard, ed. Black Society in the New World. New York: 1971.

10948. Frye, A. Nazi Germany and the American Hemisphere, 1933- 1941. New Haven, CT: 1967.

10949. Gayet, Denis. "Le racisme en Guyane francaise." Les Temps Modernes 23 (1968): 1671-1700.

10950. Gledhill, Sabrina. "The Latin Model of Race Relations." In Castro, the Blacks, and Africa Carlos Moore. Los Angeles: Center for Afro-American Studies, University of California, Los Angeles, 1988.

10951. González, Casanova Pablo. Le hegemonia del pueblo y la lucha centroamericana. San Jose: Editorial Universitaria Centroamericana, 1984.

10952. González Casanova, Pablo. Historia politica de los campesinos latinoamericanos. 4 vols. Mexico City: 1984-1985.

10953. González Casanova, Pablo. Las Minorias Etnicas en America Latina. Mexico City: Instituto de Investigaciones Sociales, UNAM, 1978.

10954. González Casanova, Pablo. "Sociedad plural, colonialismo interno y desarrollo." América Latina 6 (1963)

10955. González, Vinicio. "The History of Ethnic Classification in Central America: 1700-1950." International Social Science Journal 39 (1987): 61-84.

10956. Göthner, Karl-Christian. "Genesis, Entwicklung und Krise des Kapitalismus in Lateinamericka. Einige theoretisch- methodologische Überlegen." Asien, Afrika, Lateinamerika 6 (1984): 1095-1105.

10957. Gotlieb, Yosef. "Latin American Jewry: Can They Weather the Storm?" Israel Horizons (January 1980): 10-13.

10958. Gräbener, Jürgen, ed. Zur Marginalisierung des Afro-Amerikaners in Lateinamerika. Dusseldorf: Bertelsmann- Universitätsverlag, 1971.

10959. Graham, Richard, ed. The Idea of Race in Latin America, 1870-1940. Austin: University of Texas Press, 1990.

10960. Gray, Andrew. The Amerindians of South America. rev. ed. London: Minority Rights Group, 1987.

10961. Green, David. "Paternalism and Profits: The Ideology of U.S. Aid to Latin America, 1943-1971." Canadian Historical Association Historical Papers (1972): 335-367.

10962. Gutierrez, Gustavo. Power of the Poor in History. Maryknoll, NY: Orbis Books, 1983.

10963. "Guyane, Réunion: sociétés pluriculturelles." Les Dossiers de l'Outre-mer 16 (1986): 3-79.

10964. Haggard, Stephan. "Political Economy of Foreign Direct Investment in Latin America." Latin American Research Review 24 (1989): 184-208.

10965. Harris, Olivia, ed. Latin American Women. London: Minority Rights Group, 1983.

10966. Harwood, Alan, ed. "The Political Economy of Primary Health Care in Costa Rica, Guatemala, Nicaragua, and El Salvador." Medical Anthrop. Quarterly 3 (1989): entire issue.

10967. Haubert, M. "Adult Education and Grass-Roots Organizations in Latin America: The Contribution of the International Cooperative University." International Labour Review 125 (March-April 1986)

10968. Hengstenberg, Peter, ed. Profundización de la democracia: estrategias en América Latina y Europa. Caracas, Venezuela: Editorial Nueva Sociedad, 1989.

10969. Herbert, Jean-Loup and others. Indianité et lutte des classes. Paris: Union General d'Editions, 1972.

10970. Heuman, Gad and others. "Out of the House of Bondage: Runaways, Resistance and Marronage in Africa and the New World." Slavery & Abolition 6 (December 1985): 1-184.

10971. Hoberman, Louisa S. and Susan M. Socolow, eds. Cities and Society in Colonial Latin America. Alburquerque: University of New Mexico Press, 1986.

10972. Hoetink, H. Slavery and Race Relations in the Americas: Comparative Notes on their Nature and Nexus. New York: Harper & Row, 1973.

10973. Horowitz, Donald L. "Color Differentiation in the American Systems of Slavery." Journal of Interdisciplinary History 3 (1973): 509-541.

10974. Horowitz, Paul. "Jews in Latin America: Past and Present." Jewish Currents 35 (September 1981): 5-9, 27-30.

10975. Hudson, Randall O. "The Status of the Negro in Northern South America, 1820-1860." Journal of Negro History 49 (1964): 225-239.

10976. Indianité, ethnocide, indigenisme en Amerique Latine. Paris: Editions du Centre National de las Recherche Scientifique, 1982.

10977. Inman, Samuel Guy. "The Feminist Movement in Latin America." Bulletin of the Pan American Union 54 (1922): 353-362.

10978. Italaander, Rolf, ed. Juden in Lateinamerika. Tel Aviv: 1971.

10979. Itsigsohn, Jose A. "The Jewish Communities of Latin America." Olam (Spring 1976)

10980. Jackson, Richard L. Black Literature and Humanism in Latin America. Athens: University of Georgia Press, 1988.

10981. Jackson, Richard L. Black Writers in Latin America. Albuquerque: University of New Mexico Press, 1980.

10982. Jelin, Elizabeth, ed. Citizenship and Identity: Women and Social Change in Latin America. Translated by Marilyn Thomson Atlantic Highlands, NJ: Zed Books, 1990.

10983. Kaplan, Fredy H. "Combatting Political Torture in Latin America: An Analysis of the Organization of American States Inter-American Convention to Prevent and Punish Torture." Brooklyn Journal of International Law 15 (March 1989): 399-430.

10984. Kaplan, Marcos. Estado y sociedad en America Latina. Oaxaca: Editorial Oasis, 1984.

10985. Kicaz, John E. "The Social and Ethnic Historiography of Colonial Latin America: The Last Twenty Years." William and Mary Quarterly 45 (July 1988): 453-488.

10986. Kirsch, H. "University Youth as Social Protagonist in Latin America." Cepal Review No. 29 (August 1986)

10987. Klein, Herbert S. African Slavery in Latin America and the Caribbean. New York: Oxford University Press, 1986.

10988. Klich, Ignacio. "Latin America and the Palestinian Question." Research Report (Institute of Jewish Affairs) Nos. 2-3 (January 1986)

10989. Knight, Alan. "Debt Bondage in Latin America." In Slavery and Other Forms of Unfree Labour, edited by Leonie J. Archer. New York: Routledge, 1988.

10990. Knight, Franklin W. The African Dimension in Latin American Societies. New York: Macmillan, 1974.

10991. Knudsen, Jerry W. "Antisemitism in Latin America: Barometer of Social Change." Patterns of Prejudice 6 (1972): 1-11,22-30.

10992. Labrousse, Alain. Le réveil indien en Amérique andine. Paris: Pierre-Marcel Favre, 1985.

10993. Laclau, Ernesto. "Feudalism and Capitalism in Latin America." New Left Review No. 67 (May-June 1971)

10994. Landazabal Reyes, Fernando. Conflicto social. Medellin: Editorial Bedout, 1982.

10995. Langer, Erick D. "Debt Peonage and Paternalism in Latin America." Peasant Studies 13 (Winter 1986): 121-128.

10996. Langley, Lester. The Banana Wars: An Inner History of American Empire 1900-1924. Lexington: University Press of Kentucky, 1983.

10997. "Latin American Jewry Today-The Past, the Politics, the Problems." Jewish Frontier (March 1981): 8-17, 22-27.

10998. Laurell, Asa C. "Social Analysis of Collective Health in Latin America." Social Science Medicine 28 (1989): 1183-1192.

10999. Lavrin, Asuncion. The Ideology of Feminism in the Southern Cone, 1900-1940. Washington, D.C.: Wilson Center, 1986.

11000. Lavrin, Asuncion. "Women and Religion in Spanish America." In Women and Religion in America, II, edited by Rosemary Radford Ruether and Rosemary Skinner Keller. 42-78. San Francisco, CA: Harper & Row, 1983.

11001. Lavrin, Asuncion. "Women in Spanish American Colonial Society." In The Cambridge History of Latin America, edited by Leslie Bethell. 321-355. New York: Cambridge University Press, 1984.

11002. Leon, Magdalena, ed. Debate sobre la mujer en America Latina y el Caribe: discusion acerca de la unidad produccion- reproduccion. 3 vols. Bogota: Asociación Colombiana para el Estudio de la Poblacion, 1982.

11003. Levine, Robert M., ed. Race and Ethnic Relations in Latin America and the Caribbean: An Historical Dictionary and Bibliography. Metuchen, NJ: Scarecrow Press, 1980.

11004. Levy, Daniel C. Higher Education and the State in Latin America. Chicago, IL: University of Chicago Press, 1986.

11005. Liebman, Seymour B. New World Jewry 1493-1825: Requiem for the Forgotten. New York: Ktav Publishing House, 1982.

11006. Lindenberg, M. "Central America: Crisis and Economic Strategy 1930-1985. Lessons from History." Journal of Developing Areas 22 (Jan. 1988)

11007. Luciano Franco, José. Afro-américa. Havana: 1961.

11008. Luis, William, ed. Voices from Under: The Black Narrative in Latin America and the Caribbean. Westport, CT: Greenwood Press, 1984.

11009. MacEoin, Gary. "Letter from Central America. I. Economic Setting." National Catholic Reporter (May 8, 1987)

LATIN AMERICA 839

11010. Mainwaring, S. and A. Wilde. The Progressive Church in Latin America. Notre Dame, IN: University of Notre Dame Press, 1989.

11011. Martinez-Fernandez, Luis. The Hispanic Caribbean between Empires, 1840-1868. Doctoral dissertation: Duke University, 1990. UMO # 9028224 [Cuba, Puerto Rico, and Dominican Republic.]

11012. McKenzie, H. "The Educational Experiences of Caribbean Women." Social and Economic Studies 35 (September 1986)

11013. Melgar Bao, Ricardo. El movimiento obrero latinoamericano: historia de una clase subalterna. Madrid: Abianza Editorial, 1988.

11014. Mellafe, Rolando. Negro Slavery in Latin America. Berkeley: University of California Press, 1975.

11015. Mendez, Juan E. and Jose M. Vivanco. "Disappearances and the Inter-American Court: Reflections on a Litigation Experience." Hamline Law Review 13 (Summer 1990): 507-577.

11016. Meso-Lago, Carmelo. "Social Security and Extreme Poverty in Latin America." Journal of Developing Economics 12 (February-April 1983): 83-110.

11017. Midlarsky, Manus I. "Rulers and the Ruled: Patterned Inequality and the Onset of Mass Political Violence." American Political Science Review 82 (1988): 491-509.

11018. Moreno Fraginals, Manuel, ed. Africa in Latin America: Essays on History, Culture, and Socialization. Translated by Leonor Blum New York: Holmes and Meier, 1984.

11019. Mörner, Magnus, ed. Race and Class in Latin America. New York: Columbia University Press, 1969.

11020. Mörner, Magnus. Race Mixture in the History of Latin America. Boston, MA: Little, Brown, 1967.

11021. Moss, Joyce and George Wilson, eds. Peoples of the World: Latin America. Detroit, MI: Gale, 1989.

11022. Movimientos populares en la historia de Mexico y América Latina. Mexico City: Universidad Nacional Autonoma de Mexico, 1987.

11023. Murra, John V. and others, eds. Anthropological History of Andean Politics. New York: Cambridge University Press, 1986.

11024. Murra, John V. "High Altitude Andean Societies and Their Economies." In Geographic Perspectives in History, edited by Eugene D. Genovese and Leonard Hochberg. New York: Blackwell, 1989.

840 WORLD RACISM AND RELATED INHUMANITIES

11025. Musgrove, Philip. "Food Heads and Absolute Poverty in Latin America." Review of Income and Wealth 31 (March 1985): 63-83.

11026. Nash, June and Helen Safa, eds. Sex and Class in Latin America. South Hadley, MA: Bergin and Garvey, 1980.

11027. Nash, June and Helen Safa, eds. Women and Change in Latin America. South Hadley, MA: Bergin and Garvey, 1985.

11028. Nissan, E. and R. Caveny. "Quality of Life Indicators for Selected South American Nations." Atlantic Economic Journal 13 (September 1985)

11029. O'Shaughnessy, Hugh. What Future for the Amerindians of South America? London: Minority Rights Group, 1973.

11030. Olivera, Carlos E. "Is Education in Latin America Dependent?" Prospects 15 (1985): 227-238.

11031. Pagden, Anthony. Spanish Imperialism and the Political Imagination: Studies in European and Spanish-American Social and Political Theory, 1513-1830. New Haven, CT: Yale University Press, 1990.

11032. Pastor, Manuel Jr. "Capital Flight from Latin America." World Development 18 (January 1990): 1-18.

11033. Pastor, Manuel Jr. The International Monetary Fund and Latin America: Stabilization and Class Conflict. Boulder, CO: Westview, 1987.

11034. Pederson, Duncan and V. Baruffati. "Health and Traditional Medicine Cultures in Latin America and the Caribbean." Social Science Medicine 21 (1985): 5-12.

11035. Pescatello, Ann M., ed. The African in Latin America. New York: Knopf, 1975.

11036. Pescatello, Ann M., ed. Old Roots in New Lands: Historical and Anthropological Perspectives on Black Experiences in the Americas. Westport, Conn: Greenwood Press, 1977.

11037. Pfefferman, G. "Economic Crisis and the Poor in Some Latin American Countries." Finance and Development 24 (June 1987)

11038. Pitt-Rivers, Julian. "Race in Latin America: The Concept of 'Raza'." Arch. Europeennes de Sociologie 14 (1973): 3- 31.

11039. Pitt-Rivers, Julian. "Race, Color, and Class in Central America and the Andes." Daedalus (Spring 1967)

11040. Piuggros, Adriana. Imperialismo y Educacion en Latin America. Mexico, D.F.: Editorial Nueva Imagen, 1980.

11041. Porpora, Douglas V. How Holocausts Happen. The United States in Central America. Philadelphia, PA: Temple University Press, 1990.

11042. Porter, Alejandro. "Latin American Class Structures: Their Composition and Change during the Last Decades." Latin American Research Review 20 (1985): 7-40.

11043. Prebisch, Raul. "The Latin American Periphery in the Global Crisis of Capitalism." Cepal Review No. 26 (August 1985)

11044. Price, Richard, ed. Maroon Societies: Rebel Slave Communities in the Americas. 2d ed. Baltimore, MD: Johns Hopkins University Press, 1979.

11045. Prieto Rozos, Alberto. Crisis burguesa e imperialista en América Latina. Havana: Editorial de Ciencias Sociales, 1988.

11046. Psacharopoulos, G. "Poverty Alleviation in Latin America." Finance and Development 27 (March 1990)

11047. Rama, German W. "Éducation et société en Amérique latine." Probl. Am. latine 77 (1985): 83-101.

11048. Reich, Peter. "Measuring U.S. Government Perception of the 'Communist Menace' in Latin America, 1947-1976." In Statistical Abstract of Latin America 1978, edited by James W. Wilkie. Los Angeles: Latin American Center, University of California, 1978.

11049. Remmer, Karen L. Military Rule in Latin America. Boston, MA: Unwin Hyman, 1989.

11050. Richard, Pablo and Guillermo Melendez, eds. La Iglesia de los pobres en América Central: un analisis socio-politico y teologico de la Iglesia centroamericana (1960-1982). San Jose, Costa Rica: Departamento Eucuménico de Investigaciones, 1982.

11051. Roemer, Milton I. "Medical Care and Social Class in Latin America." Milbank Memorial Fund Quarterly 42 (July 1964): 54-64.

11052. Rohter, Larry. "Central American Plight is People in Abundance." New York Times, (September 6, 1987)

11053. Romero Ibarra, Maria E. "La clase obrera en la estructura de América Latina, 1950-1980." Investigación Economica 47 (July-September 1988): 199-219.

11054. Rosenthal, Morton M. and Elliot Welles. "Latin America: Safe Haven for Nazis." ADL Bulletin 1, 10, 12-14 (May 1983)

11055. Rout, Leslie B., Jr. The African Experience in Spanish America, 1502 to the Present Day. New York: Cambridge University Press, 1976.

842 WORLD RACISM AND RELATED INHUMANITIES

11056. Royle, S. A. "The Falkland Islands, 1833-1876: The Establishment of a Colony." Geographical Journal 151, Part 2 (1985)

11057. Russell-Wood, A. J. R. "The Black Family in the Americas." Societas 8 (Winter 1978): 1-38.

11058. Sable, Martin H., comp. Latin American Jewry: A Research Guide. Cincinnati, Ohio: Hebrew Union College Press, 1978.

11059. Saeger, James S., ed. Essays on Eighteenth-century Race Relations in the Americas. Bethleham, PA: 1987.

11060. Safa, Helen J. "Urbanization and Poverty in Latin America: A Dependency Perspective." Urban Anthropology 15 (Spring- Summer 1986): 135-164.

11061. Sanchez, Rodrigo. "The Andean Economic System and Capitalism." Cambridge Studies in Social Anthropology 41 (1982): 157-190.

11062. Schers, David. "Anti-semitism in Latin America." In Violence and Defense in the Jewish Experience, edited by Salo W. Baron and George S. Wise. Philadelphia, PA: Jewish Publication Society, 1977.

11063. Schers, David and Hadassa Singer. "The Jewish Communities of Latin America: External and Internal Factors in Their Development." Jewish Social Studies (Summer 1977): 241-258.

11064. Sheahan, John. Patterns of Development in Latin America. Poverty, Repression, and Economic Strategy. Princeton, NJ: Princeton University Press, 1987.

11065. Sherman, William L. Forced Native Labor in Sixteenth- Century Central America. Lincoln: University of Nebraska Press, 1979.

11066. Solaun, Mauricio and Sidney. Discrimination Without Violence: Miscegenation and Racial Conflict in Latin America. New York: Wiley, 1973.

11067. Stavenhagen, Rodolfo. Derecho indigena y derechos humanos en America Latina. Mexico City: El Colegio de Mexico, 1988.

11068. Stavenhagen, Rodolfo. "Indians in Latin America." Development 3 (1984): 30-35.

11069. Stephen, David and Philip Wearne. Central America's Indians. London: Minority Rights Group, 1984.

11070. Stephens, E. H. "Capitalist Development and Democracy in South-America." Politics and Society 17 (1989)

LATIN AMERICA 843

11071. Stephens, Thomas M. <u>Dictionary of Latin American Racial and Ethnic Terminology: pt. 1:Spanish-American Terms; pt.2; Brazilian Portuguese Terms</u>. University Press of Florida, 1990.

11072. Stone, Samuel Z. <u>The Heritage of the Conquistadors: Ruling Classes in Central America from the Conquest to the Sandanistas</u>. Lincoln: University of Nebraska Press, 1990.

11073. Tolentino, Hugo. <u>Origenes du préjugé racial aux Amériques</u>. Translated by Valerie Pannier and Claude Couffon Paris: Éditions Robert Laffont, 1984.

11074. Toplin, Robert B., ed. <u>Slavery and Race Relations in Latin America</u>. Westport, CT: Greenwood, 1974.

11075. Torres-Rivas, Edelberto. <u>Repression and Resistance: The Struggle for Democracy in Central America</u>. Boulder, CO: Westview, 1989.

11076. Trindade, Helgio. "La cuestion del fascismo en América Latina." <u>Desarrollo Economico</u> 23 (October-December 1983)

11077. Trindade, Helgio. "La question du fascisme en Amérique Latine." <u>Revue Française de Science Politique</u> 33 (1983): 281-312.

11078. Tyler, S. Lyman, ed. <u>Human Rights and the Native Peoples of the Americas</u>. Salt Lake City: American West Center, University of Utah, 1979.

11079. Wade, Peter. "Race and Class: The Case of South American Blacks." <u>Ethnic and Racial Studies</u> 8 (April 1985): 233-249.

11080. Wade, Peter. "Raza y clase: los negros de América Latina." <u>Revista de Antropología, Universidad de los Andes</u> 3 (1987): 33-50.

11081. Watson, Alan. <u>Slave Law in the Americas</u>. Athens: University of Georgia Press, 1989.

11082. Webb, Michael A. "Economic Opportunity and Labor Markets in Central America." In <u>The Central American Crisis</u>, edited by Kenneth M. Coleman and George C. Herring. Wilmington, DE: Scholarly Resources, 1985.

11083. Weil, Connie, ed. <u>Lucha: The Struggles of Latin American Women</u>. Minneapolis, MN: Prisma Institute, 1988.

11084. Weinberg, G. "A Historical Perspective of Latin American Education." <u>Cepal Review</u> No. 21 (Dec. 1983)

11085. Weinfeld, Eduardo. <u>El antisemitismo en la America Latina</u>. Mexico: Edicion "Or", 1939.

11086. Weisskopf, Thomas and Adolfo Figueros. "Traversing the Social Pyramid: A Comparative Review of Income Distribution in Latin America." Latin American Research Review 11 (1976): 71-112.

11087. Winkler, Donald R. Higher Education in Latin America: Issues of Efficiency and Equity. Washington, D.C.: World Bank, 1990.

11088. Winson, Anthony. "Class Structure and Agrarian Transition in Central America." Latin American Perspectives 5 (1978)

11089. Wright, Richard. "Negro Companions of the Spanish Explorers." American Anthropologist 4, 2 (1902): 217-228.

11090. Zavala A, Lauro. "Humor in Precolombian and Contemporary Mesoamerican Languages." Latin American Indian Literature Journal 5 (Spring 1989): 81-91.

11091. Zelinsky, Wilbur. "The Historical Geography of the Negro Population of Latin America." Journal of Negro History 34 (April 1949): 153-221.

11092. Zschock, Dieter K. "Medical Care under Social Insurance in Latin America." Latin American Research Review 21 (1986): 99-122.

MIDDLE EAST

11093. Abu Izzedin, Nejla. <u>The Druze: A New Study of their History, Faith and Society</u>. Leiden: E.J. Brill, 1984.

11094. Abusulayman, Abdul H. "Al-dhimmah and Related Concepts in Historical Perspective." <u>Jr. Inst. Muslim Minority Affairs</u> No. 9 (1988): 8-29.

11095. Ahmad, Barakat. <u>Muhammad and the Jews: A Re-examination</u>. New Delhi: Vikas, 1979.

11096. Ajami, Fouad. "The Question of Authenticity and Collaboration." In <u>The Arab Predicament</u> Fouad Ajami. New York: Cambridge University Press, 1981.

11097. Al-Faruqi, Lamia. "Women's Rights and the Muslim Women." <u>Islam and the Modern Age</u> 3 (1972): 76-99.

11098. al-Mismad, Sheikha. <u>The Development of Modern Education in the Gulf</u>. Atlantic Highlands, NJ: Humanities Press, 1985.

11099. Alawiye, J. H. <u>Ibn al-Jawjo's Apologia on Behalf of the Black People and their Status in Islam: A Critical Edition and Translation of Kitab Tanwir al-Ghabash fi Fadl'l-Sudan wa'i-Habash</u>. Doctoral dissertation: School of Oriental and African Studies, 1985.

11100. Allen, Calvin H., Jr. <u>Oman: The Modernization of the Sultanate</u>. Boulder, CO: Westview, 1987.

11101. An-Na'im, Abdullahi A. "Religious Minorities under Islamic Law and the Limits of Cultural Relativism." <u>Human Rights Quarterly</u> 9 (February 1987): 1-18.

11102. Arnold, Fred and Nasra Shah. <u>Asian Labor Migration: Pipeline to the Middle East</u>. Boulder, CO: Westview, 1985.

846 WORLD RACISM AND RELATED INHUMANITIES

11103. Awang, A. B. B. The Status of the Dhimmi in Islamic Law. Doctoral dissertation: University of Edinburgh, 1988.

11104. Bacharach, Jere L. "African Military Slaves in the Medieval Middle East: The Cases of Iraq (869-955) and Egypt (868-1171)." International Journal of Middle East Studies 13 (November 1981): 471-495.

11105. Badram, Margot and Miriam Cooke, eds. Opening the Gates: A Century of Arab Feminist Writing. Bloomington: Indiana University Press, 1990.

11106. Baumgart, Marion. Wie Frauen Frauen sehen: westliche Forscherinnen bei arabischen Frauen. Frankfurt/Main: Brandes und Apsel Verlag, 1989.

11107. Baylson, Joshua C. Territorial Allocation by Imperial Rivalry: The Human Legacy in the Near East. Doctoral dissertation: University of Chicago, 1985.

11108. Beck, Lois G. and Nikki Keddie, eds. Beyond the Veil: Women in the Middle East. Cambridge, MA: Harvard University Press, 1976.

11109. Beck, Lois G. and Keddie, Nikki, eds. Women in the Muslim World. Cambridge, MA: Harvard University Press, 1978.

11110. Ben-Zvi, Itzhak. "Eretz Yisrael under Ottoman Rule, 1517- 1917." In The Jews: Their History, Culture and Religion, 3d ed., vol. 1 and 4th ed., edited by Louis Finkelstein. 602-689, 399- 486. New York: 1960.

11111. Brand, Laurie A. Building the Bridge of Return: Palestinian Corporate Mobilization in Egypt, Kuwait and Jordan. Doctoral dissertation: Columbia University, 1985. UMO # 8604599.

11112. Brunschvig, N. "Abd." Encyclopedia of Islam, 2nd ed. Vol. I, pp. 26-31. Leiden, 1960.

11113. Caploe, David. "Discrimination by Law." Middle East International (July 1974)

11114. Chabry, Laurent and Annie Chabry. Politique et minorites au Proche-Orient: les raisons d'une explosion. Paris: Editions G.P. Maisonneuve et Larose, 1984.

11115. Chalala, Elie. "Central Issues in the Debate on Arab Nationalism in the Nineteenth and Twentieth Centuries." Jusur: The UCLA Journal of Middle Eastern Studies 2 (1986): 25-62.

11116. Chaszar, Edward. "International Protection of Minorities in the Middle East: A Status Report." Mid. E. Review 18 (Spring 1986): 37-48.

11117. Cizakca, Murat. "Incorporation of the Middle East into the European World-Economy." Review (F. Braudel Center) 8 (Winter 1985): 353-377.

11118. Cohen, M. "Islam and the Jews: Myth, Counter-Myth, History." Jerusalem Quarterly 38 (1986): 125-137.

11119. Crystal, Jill. Oil and Politics in the Gulf: Rulers and Merchants in Kuwait and Qatar. New York: Cambridge University Press, 1990.

11120. Dearden, Ann. Arab Women. rev. ed. London: Minority Rights Group, 1983.

11121. El Saadawi, Nawal. The Hidden Face of Eve: Women in the Arab World. London: Zed Press, 1980.

11122. Entessar, Nader. "The Kurdish Mosaic of Discord." Third World Quarterly 11 (October 1989): 83-100.

11123. Epstein, Edward Jay. "Secrets from the CIA Archive in Tehran." Orbis 31 (1987): 33-41.

11124. Feiler, Gil. "Peace and Egyptian Labor Migration to the Arab Oil Countries." New Outlook 30 (November-December 1987): 22-23.

11125. Fernea, Elizabeth and Basima Bezirgan, eds. Middle Eastern Women Speak. Austin: University of Texas Press, 1977.

11126. Firrom, K. "Political Behaviour of the Druze as a Minority in the Middle East: An Historical Perspective." Orient (Opladen) 27 (1986): 463-470.

11127. Freund, W. S. "Judisches Erbe arabischer Lander: Ein 'vergessenes' Thema der zeitgenossischen Orientforschung." Orient 27 (1986): 104-126, 170.

11128. Gabay, Z. "Arab Intolerance to Minorities: The Record." Forum (Jerusalem) 57-58 (1985-1986): 73-81.

11129. Gerber, Haim. The Social Origins of the Modern Middle East. Boulder, CO: Rienner, 1987.

11130. Gerber, Jane S. Jewish Society in Fez, 1450-1700. Studies in Communal and Economic Life. Leiden: E.J. Brill, 1980.

11131. Ghaussy, S. "The Role of Minorities in the Middle East: The Case of the Kurdish Question." An. Japan Association for Mid. E. Stud. 1 (1986): 287-309.

11132. Ghoussoub, Mai. "Feminism- or the Eternal Masculine-in the Arab World." New Left Review No. 161 (1987): 3-18.

11133. Gotlieb, Yosef. Self-Determination in the Middle East. New York: Praeger, 1982.

11134. Graziani, J. "The Momentum of the Feminist Movement in the Arab World." Middle East Review 7 (1974): 26-33.

848 WORLD RACISM AND RELATED INHUMANITIES

11135. Gruen, George E. "Militant Islam. The Jewish Communities of the Middle East, and Prospects for Arab-Israel Peace." Jewish Frontier 57 (May-June 1990): 9-12.

11136. Hennerbichler, Ferdinand, ed. Die fur die Freiheit sterben: Geschichte des kurdischen Volkes. Vienna: Edition S., Verlag der Osterreichischen Staatsdruckerei, 1988.

11137. Hilal, Jamil. "The Management of Male Dominance in 'Traditional' Arab Culture: a Tentative Model." Civilization 21 (1971): 85-95.

11138. Hofmann, Tessa and G. Koutcharian. "The History of Armenian-Kurdish Relations in the Ottoman Empire." Armenian Review 39 (Winter 1986): 1-45.

11139. Hourani, Albert. A History of the Arab People. Cambridge, MA: Harvard University Press, 1991.

11140. "Human Rights in the Arab World." Journal of Arab Affairs 9 (Spring 1990): entire issue.

11141. "Human Rights in the Middle East." MERIP No. 149 (November-December 1987): entire issue.

11142. International Organization for the Elimination of All Forms of Racial Discrimination (Eaford) and American Jewish Alternatives to Zionism (Ajaz). Judaism or Zionism: What Difference for the Middle East? London: Eaford and Zed/Third World Books, 1986.

11143. Ja'far, Mohammed. "The Arab Ruling Classes in the 1970s." Khamsin 7 (1980): 73-85.

11144. Janzen, Jorg. Nomads in the Sultanate of Oman: Tradition and Development in Dhofar. Boulder, CO: Westview Press, 1986.

11145. "Jews of Arab Lands." Jews of Arab Lands 1 (1977): entire issue.

11146. Keddie, Nikki. "Problems in the Study of Middle Eastern Women." International Journal of Middle East Studies 10 (1979): 225-240.

11147. Kushner, D. "Intercommunal Strife in Palestine during the Late Ottoman Period." Asian and African Studies 18 (July 1984): 187-204.

11148. Lara, Oruno D. "Esclavage et revoltes negro-africaines dans l'Empire musulman du Haut Moyen Age." Presence africaine No. 2 (1976): 50-103.

11149. Levy, Reuben. Social Structure of Islam. New York: Cambridge University Press, 1967.

11150. Lewis, Bernard. "Race and Colour in Islam." Encounter 35 (1970): 18-36.

11151. Lewis, Bernard. Race and Slavery in the Middle East. An Historical Enquiry. 2d ed. New York: Oxford University Press, 1990.

11152. Luca, Costa, pseud. "Legal Discrimination among Arabs." Patterns of Prejudice 10 (July-August 1976): 1-14.

11153. MacDonald, Charles G. "The Kurdish Question in the 1980s." In Ethnicity, Pluralism and the State in the Middle East, edited by Milton J. Esman and Itamar Rabinovich. Ithaca, New York: Cornell University Press, 1988.

11154. Makhlouf, Carla. Changing Veils: A Study of Women in South Arabia. Austin: University of Texas Press, 1979.

11155. Malika, Cirrine. "Islam and the Emancipation of Women." Islamic Review (November-December 1965): 34-69.

11156. Mann, F. A. "The Unlawful Exercise of Rights in the Civil Codes of the Arab Countries of the Middle East." International and Comparative Law Quarterly 39 (April 1990): 396-412.

11157. Margo, Andrew. "Minorities and Majorities [in the Middle East]." Middle Eastern Studies 23 (1987): 512-528.

11158. McCarthy, Justin. The Population of Palestine: Population History and Statistics of the Late Ottoman Period and the Mandate. New York: Columbia University Press, 1990.

11159. McDowall, David. The Kurds. London: Minority Rights Group, 1990. [Report No. 23.]

11160. McLaurin, R. D., ed. The Political Role of Minority Groups in the Middle East. New York: 1979.

11161. Michalak, Laurence O. and Jeswald W. Salacuse, eds. Social Legislation in the Contemporary Middle East. Berkeley, CA: Institute of International Studies, 1986.

11162. "Middle East and North Africa." In World Directory of Minorities, edited by Minority Rights Group. Harlow: Longman, 1990.

11163. Minces, Juliette. The House of Obedience: Women in Arab Society. London: Zed Press, 1980.

11164. Mukamel, Susan. "Jews in Arab Lands: The Current Situation." Intercom (Canadian Jewish Congress) 1-2 (July- August 1987)

11165. Mustaffa-Kedah, Omar. "The Education of Women in the Arab States." Literacy Discussion 6 (Winter 1975-1976): 119-139.

850 WORLD RACISM AND RELATED INHUMANITIES

11166. Nasman, Abdallah. Les Levantins: une race; essai d'analyse sociale. Jounieh, Lebanon: Maison Naaman pour la culture, 1984.

11167. Nevo, Joseph. "The Attitude of Arab Palestinian Historiography Toward the Germans and the Holocaust." Remembering for the Future: Theme II. The Impact of the Holocaust on the Contemporary World. 2241-2250. Oxford, England: Pergamon Press, 1988.

11168. O'Shaughnessy, Thomas J. "Growth in Educational Opportunity for Muslim Women, 1950-1973." Anthropos 73 (1978): 887-901.

11169. Okyar, Osman. "A New Look at the Problem of Economic Growth in the Ottoman Empire (1800-1914)." Journal of European Economic History 16 (Spring 1987): 7-49.

11170. Othman, Siyamend. "Kurdish Nationalism: Instigators and Historical Influences." Armenian Review 42 (Spring 1989): 39-59.

11171. Owen, Edward R. J. Migrant Workers in the Gulf. London: Minority Rights Group, 1985.

11172. Pelletiere, Stephen C. The Kurds: An Unstable Element in the Gulf. Boulder, CO: Westview, 1984.

11173. Ponko, Vincent Jr , comp. Britain in the Middle East, 1921-1956. New York: Garland, 1990.

11174. Porat, D. "Al-Domi: Palestinian Intellectuals and the Holocaust." Studies in Zionism 5 (Spring 1984): 92-124.

11175. "The 'Protocols' among Arabs." Patterns of Prejudice 9 (1975): 17-19. [Protocols of the Elders of Zion.]

11176. Ricks, Thomas M. "Slaves and Slave Traders in the Persian Gulf, 18th and 19th Centuries: An Assessment." Slavery & Abolition 9 (1988): 60-70.

11177. Robinson, Nehemiah. The Arab Countries of the Near East and their Jewish Communities. New York: Institute of Jewish Affairs, 1951.

11178. Rondot, Pierre. "Les minorites dans le proche-orient (3 parts)." Afrique et l'Asie Modernes No. 151; No. 152; No. 153 (1986-87; 1987; 1987): 14-27; 16-29; 85-101.

11179. Rondot, Pierre. "Note sur le caractere des relations entre les Musulmans, Chretiens et Juifs du Proche-Orient." L'Afrique et L'Asie Moderns No. 142 (Fall 1984): 3-13.

11180. Roshwald, Aviel. Estranged Bedfellows: Britain and France in the Middle East During the Second World War. New York: Oxford University Press, 1990.

11181. Roth, Cecil. "Jews in Arab Lands." Near East Report (August 1967)

11182. Saeed, S. "The Legal Status of Muslim Women." Islamic Quarterly 24 (1980): 13-21.

11183. Schatkowski Schilcher, Linda. "The Lore and Reality of Middle Eastern Patriarchy." Welt des Islams 28 (1988): 496- 512.

11184. Seib, Gerald F. "Born Yesterday: Oman Finally Has a College of Its Own." Wall Street Journal (November 10, 1986)

11185. Selwyn, P. Causes of Poverty among the Rural Populations of the Arab States. B. Litt. dissertation: Oxford University, 1947.

11186. Siddiqui, M. M. Women in Islam. New York: Orientalia, 1969.

11187. Thobie, Jacques. Ali et les 40 voleurs: imperialisme et moyen-orient de 1914 a nos jours. Paris: Messidor/Temps Actuels, 1985.

11188. Tibi, Bassam. Arab Nationalism. A Critical Enquiry. 2d ed. New York: St. Martin's Press, 1990.

11189. Tuma, Elias H. "The Rich and the Poor in the Middle East." Middle East Journal 34 (Autumn 1980): 413-433.

11190. Turner, Bryan S. Capitalism and Class in the Middle East: Theories of Social Change and Economic Development. London: Heinemann, 1984.

11191. Van Nieuwenhuijze, C. A. O. Social Stratification in the Middle East. Leiden: E.J. Brill, 1965.

11192. Van Nieuwenhuijze, C. A. O. Sociology of the Middle East. Leiden: E.J.Brill, 1971.

11193. Viennot, Jean-Pierre. La tragedie kurde. 2 vols. Paris: Ecole pratique des hautes etudes, 1969.

11194. Wild, Stefan. "National Socialism in the Arab Near East Between 1933 and 1939." Welt des Islams 25 (1985): 126-173.

11195. Woodsmall, Ruth Frances. A Study of the Role of Women in Lebanon, Egypt, Iraq, Jordan and Syria. Woodstock, NY: Elm Tree Press, 1956.

11196. Young, Elise G. The Judeo-Arabic Heritage. A Historical Analysis and Teaching Curriculum. Doctoral dissertation: University of Massachusetts, Amherst, 1988.

OCEANIA

11197. Abbey, Robert A. Race Relations in Rabaul, 1921-1931. B.A.(hons.) thesis: Flinders University, 1974.

11198. Abe, Goh. An Ethnohistory of Palau under the Japanese Colonial Administration. Doctoral dissertation: University of Kansas, 1986. UMO # 8619874.

11199. Abeysinghe, Ariya and Franklin Vivekananda. "Economics of South Pacific Countries: Colonial Hangovers-Dependency and Challenges to Economic Development." Scandanavian Journal of Dev. Alternatives 8 (March 1989): 167-206.

11200. Agostini, Eric. "Aboriginal Rights in New Caledonia." Law and Anthropology 2 (1987): 337-346.

11201. Albinski, Henry S. and others. The South Pacific: Political, Economic, and Military Trends. Washington, D.C.: Pergamon-Brassey's International Defense Publishers, 1989.

11202. Aldrich, Robert. The French Presence in the South Pacific, 1842-1940. Honolulu: University of Hawaii Press, 1989.

11203. Aldrich, Robert. "Le lobby colonial de l'Oceanie francaise." R. fr. Hist. Outre Mer 284-285 (1989): 411-424.

11204. Aldrich, Robert. "New Caledonia: The Current Crisis in Historical Perspective." Contemporary French Civilization 10 (1986): 175-209.

11205. Ali, Ahmed. Fiji and the Franchise: A History of Political Representation, 1900-1937. Doctoral dissertation: Australian National University, 1974.

11206. Alkire, WIlliam H. An Introduction to the Peoples and Cultures of Micronesia. 2d ed. Menlo Park, CA: Cummings, 1977.

11207. Benguigul, Georges. "The Middle Classes in Tonga." Journal of the Polynesian Society 98 (December 1989)

11208. Bennett, Judith A. Wealth of the Solomons: A History of Pacific Archipelago, 1800-1978. Honolulu: University of Hawaii Press, 1986.

11209. Bensa, Alban. "Colonialisme, racisme et ethnologie en Nouvelle-Caledonie." Ethnologie francaise 18 (1988): 188- 197.

11210. Biddick, T. V. "Diplomatic Rivalry in the South Pacific." Asian Survey 29 (1989): 800-815.

11211. Boutilier, J. A. "Hungry Sharks: Japanese Economic Activity in Melanesia, 1960-1980." Pacific Studies 8 (Fall 1984): 71-94.

11212. Bretania-Shafer, Nerissa. A Theoretical Analysis of Paulo Freire's Literary Model In View of the Chamorro Socio- Cultural Context. Doctoral dissertation: University of Oregon, 1989. UMO # 9010098.

11213. Browne, Christopher. Economic Development in Seven Pacific Countries. Washington, D.C.: International Monetary Fund, 1989. [Fiji, Kiribati, Papua New Guinea, Solomon Islands, Tonga, Vanuatu, and Western Samoa.]

11214. Bullivant, Brian M. "Cultural Reproduction in Fiji: Who Controls Knowledge/Power?" Comparative Education Review 27 (1983)

11215. Byrt, Neville. Labour Regulation in the Solomon Islands, 1904-1932. Master's thesis: University of Auckland, 1975.

11216. Campbell, J. C. A History of the Pacific Islands. Berkeley: University of California Press, 1990.

11217. Campbell, J. C. "Race Relations in the pre-Colonial Pacific Islands: A Case of Prejudice and Pragmatism." Pacific Studies 8 (Spring 1985): 61-80.

11218. Chand, G. "Race and Regionalism in Fiji, Pacific and India-Some Generally-Held Misconceptions." Economic and Political Change 25 (January 20, 1990)

11219. Chapman, M., ed. "Mobility and Identity in the Island Pacific." Pacific Viewpoint 26 (April 1985): entire issue.

11220. Chappele, A. J. "The Fijian Voice in Fiji's Colonial History." Journal of Pacific Studies 1 (1975)

11221. Christnacht, Alain. "La Nouvelle Caledonie." Notes et Etudes Documentaires No. 14 (1987): 1-143.

11222. Clark, Alan. "Constitutional Dynamic, Political Risk: Self-determination in New Caledonia, 1986-1987." Pacific Studies 12 (1988): 5-22.

11223. Clark, Roger and Sue Rabbitt Roff. Micronesia: The Problem of Palau. London: Minority Rights Group, 1985.

11224. Cochrane, D. G. "Racialism in the Pacific: A Descriptive Analysis." Oceania 40 (September 1969): 1-12. [Solomon Islands.]

11225. Cohen, Herbert. Class and Land Tenure in Micronesia. Master's thesis: University of Chicago, 1952.

11226. Colt, Elizabeth. "Poverty in an Island Paradise." Boston Globe, (September 14, 1986): [Marshall Islands.]

11227. Cooper, Matthew. "On the Beginnings of Colonialism in Melanesia." In Association for Social Anthropology in Oceania Monograph Series. 25-41. Honolulu: University Press of Hawaii, 1979.

11228. Corban, B. P. N. Law and Order in Melanesia. A Case Study: The Pacification of the British Solomon Islands, 1893-1900 and 1913-1930. Master's thesis: University of Auckland, 1972.

11229. Cordy, Ross H. "Relationships between the Extent of Social Stratification and Population in Micronesian Politics at European Contact." American Anthropologist 88 (March 1986): 136-142.

11230. Cordy, Ross H. "Social Stratification in the Mariana Islands." Oceania 53 (1983): 272-276.

11231. Corris, Peter R. Passage, Port and Plantation: A History of Solomon Islands Labour Migration, 1870-1914. Doctoral dissertation: Australian National University, 1970.

11232. Coutau-Begarie, Herve. Geostrategie du Pacifique. Paris: Editions Economica, 1987.

11233. Davidson, James W. European Penetration of the South Pacific 1779-1842. Doctoral dissertation: Cambridge University, 1942.

11234. Delius, Ulrich. Tahiti, Französisch-Polynesien: Südseepardies unter dem Atompilz. Göttingen: Gesellschaft für Bedrohte Völker, 1982.

11235. Dibblin, Jane. Day of Two Suns: U.S. Nuclear Testing and the Pacific Islanders. London: Virago, 1988.

11236. Dorrance, John C. Oceania and the United States: An Analysis of U.S. Interests and Policy in the South Pacific. Washington, D.C.: GPO, 1980.

11237. Dorrance, John C. and others, eds. South Pacific: Emerging Security Issues and U.S. Policy. London: Brassey's Defense Publishers, 1990.

11238. Drost, Richard. Forced Labor in the South Pacific, 1850-1914. Doctoral dissertation: State University of Iowa, 1934.

11239. Durutalo, Simione. Internal Colonialism and Unequal Regional Development: The Case of Western Viti Levu, Fiji. Master's thesis: University of South Pacific, 1985.

11240. Epstein, Joshua L. Dependency and Affluence as Challenges to National Development in Palau. Doctoral dissertation: University of Hawaii, 1986. UMO # 8622097.

11241. Farrell, William. Prelude to American Imperialism: United States Involvement in Samoa, 1869-1878. Master's thesis: Stetson University, 1981.

11242. Fine, J. David. "Micronesian Legal History: Legacies of German and Japanese Law and Administration." University of Hawaii Law Review 12 (Fall 1990): 321-338.

11243. Firth, Raymond. Primitive Polynesian Economy. New York: Norton, 1975.

11244. Firth, Stewart. "The Nuclear Issue in the Pacific Islands." Journal of Pacific History 21 (1986): 202-216.

11245. Fisk, E. K. Fiji: A Developing Australian Colony. North Fitzroy, Victoria, Australia: 1973.

11246. France, Peter. The Charter of the Land: A Study in the Cross-fertilization of Fijian Tradition and British Colonial Policy. Doctoral dissertation: Australian National University, 1966.

11247. Gabriel, Claude and Vincent Kermel. Nouvelle-Calédonie: la revolte Kanake. Paris: Editions la Breche, 1985.

11248. Gale, Roger W. The Americanization of Micronesia. Washington, D.C.: 1979.

11249. Gibson, Robert E. "State of the Art of Pacific Bilingual Education." Bilingual Education Paper Series 4 (May 1981)

11250. Gillion, K. L. The Fiji Indians: Challenge to European Dominance 1920-1940. Canberra: Australian National University Press, 1977.

11251. Gillion, K. L. Fiji's Indian Migrants. Melbourne: Oxford University Press, 1962.

11252. Gilson, Richard P. Samoa 1830-1900: The Politics of a Multi-Cultural Community. New York: 1970.

11253. Gold, Jerry. Modern Human Migration and the Emergence of a Class System in American Samoa. Doctoral dissertation: University of Washington, 1988. UMO # 8906900.

11254. Graves, Adrian. "Colonialism and Indentured Labour Migration in the Western Pacific, 1840-1915." In Colonialization and Migration: Indentured Labour before and after Slavery, edited by P.C. Emmer. Dordecht: Martinus Nijhoff, 1986.

11255. Gray, J. A. C. Amerika Samoa: A History of American Samoa and Its U.S. Naval Administration. Annapolis, MD: U.S. Naval Institute, 1960.

11256. "Guyane, Reunion: societes pluriculturelles." Les Dossiers de l'Outre-mer 16 (1986): 3-79.

11257. Hagan, Stephanie. "Race, Politics, and the Coup in Fiji." Bulletin of Concerned Asian Scholars 19 (October-December 1987)

11258. Hammett, Michael P. and others, eds. Pacific Island Studies: A Survey of the Literature. Westport, CT: Greenwood, 1986.

11259. Hampenstall, Peter and Noel Rutherford. Protest and Dissent in the Colonial Pacific. Suva: University of the South Pacific, 1984.

11260. Hanlon, David. "Micronesia: Writing and Rewriting the Histories of a Nonentity." Pacific Studies 12 (March 1989): 1-21.

11261. Hassall, Graham H. Religion and Nation-state Formation in Melanesia: 1945 to Independence. Doctoral dissertation: Australian National University, 1990. UMO # 9029091. [Christian missions.]

11262. Hayes, Peter and others. American Lake: Nuclear Peril in the Pacific. Ringwood, Australia: Penguin, 1986.

11263. Hempenstall, Peter J. Indigenous Resistance to German Rule in the Pacific Colonies of Samoa, Ponape and New Guinea, 1884-1914. Doctoral dissertation: Oxford University, 1973.

11264. Henningham, Stephan. "Keeping the Tricolor Flying: The French Pacific into the 1990s." Contemporary Pacific 1 (1989): 97-132.

11265. Hezel, F. X. and M. G. Driver. "From Conquest to Colonisation: Spain in the Mariana Islands 1690-1740." Journal of Pacific History 23 (1988): 137-155.

11266. Hill, Adrian V. S. and Susan W. Serjeantson, eds. The Colonization of the Pacific: A Genetic Trail. New York: Oxford University Press, 1989.

11267. Hirayasu, Naomi. "The Process of Self-determination and Micronesia's Future Political Status under International Law." University of Hawaii Law Review 9 (Fall 1987): 487- 532.

11268. Hogbin, Herbert J. P. The Maintenance of Order in Oceania. Doctoral dissertation: University of London, 1931.

11269. Hooper, Antony, ed. Class and Culture in the South Pacific. Suva; Fiji: University of the South Pacific, 1987.

11270. Horrocks, Linley. European Massacres in Late Eighteenth Century Polynesia. Master's (Qual.) thesis: 1975.

11271. Houbert, Jean. "France in the Indian Ocean: Decolonizing without Disengaging." Round Table No.298 (1986): 145-166. [Reunion.]

11272. Howe, K. R. Where the Waves Fell: A South Sea Islands History from First Settlement to Colonial Rule. Honolulu: University of Hawaii Press, 1984.

11273. Indigenous Struggle in the Pacific. Canberra: National Aboriginal Conference, 1984.

11274. Islam, M. R. "The Recent Self-Determination Referendum in New Caledonia: Terms Mitigating Against Its Validity." Melanesian Law Journal 15 (1987): 136-153.

11275. Jackson, Miles M. and others, eds. Pacific Island Studies: A Survey of the Literature. Westport, CT: Greenwood, 1986.

11276. Johnstone, Diana. "New Caledonia Killings Upset Self- Rule." In These Times (May 24, 1989)

11277. Jolly, E. and M. MacIntyre, eds. Family and Gender in the Pacific. New York: Cambridge University Press, 1989.

11278. Joralemon, Victoria. "Development and Inequity: The Case of Tubuai a Welfare Economy in Rural French Polynesia." Human Organization 45 (Winter 1986): 283-295.

11279. "Kanaks of New Caledonia." In World Directory of Minorities, edited by Minority Rights Group. 369-372. Harlow: Longman, 1990.

11280. Kanost, Richard F. "The American Performance in Micronesia: A Retrospective Appraisal." Amerasia Journal 12 (1985-1986): 57-82.

11281. Kaplan, Martha. "Coups in Fiji: Colonial Contradictions and the Post-colonial Crisis." Critique of Anthropology 8 (1988): 93-116.

11282. Keesing, Felix. Modern Samoa. London: 1934.

11283. Kelly, John D. "Fear of Culture: British Regulation of Indian Marriage in Post-indenture Fiji." Ethnohistory 36 (1989): 372-391.

11284. Kelly, John D. "Fiji Indians and Political Discourse in Fiji: From the Pacific Romance to the Coups." Journal of Historical Sociology 1 (1988): 399-422.

11285. Kerr, George H. Okinawa: The History of an Island People. Tokyo: 1958.

11286. Kircher, Ingrid A. The Kanaks of New Caledonia. London: Minority Rights Group, 1986.

11287. Knapman, Bruce. "Aid and the Dependent Development of Pacific Island States." Journal of Pacific History 21 (July 1986): 139-152.

11288. Knapman, Bruce. Capitalism and Colonial Development: Studies in the Economic History of Fiji, 1874-1939. Doctoral dissertation: Australian National University, 1984.

11289. Knapman, Bruce. "Capitalism's Economic Impact in Colonial Fiji 1874-1939: Development or Underdevelopment?" Journal of Pacific History 20 (1985): 66-83.

11290. Knapman, Bruce. Fiji's Economic History, 1874-1939: Studies of Capitalist Colonial Development. Canberra, Australia: Australian National University, 1987.

11291. Knapman, Bruce. "The Rise and Fall of the White Sugar Planter in Fiji, 1880-1925." Pacific Studies 9 (November 1985): 53-82.

11292. Knapman, C. "The White Child in Colonial Fiji, 1895-1930." Journal of Pacific History 23 (1988): 206-213.

11293. Koskinen, Aarne A. Missionary Influence as a Political Factor in the Pacific Islands. Doctoral dissertation: Helsingfors Universitet, 1953.

11294. Kristof, Nicholas D. "In a South Seas Eden, a First Taste of Race Strife." New York Times, (May 1, 1987): [Fiji.]

11295. Kuschel, R. "Twenty-four Generations of Intergroup Conflicts on Bellona Island (Solomon Islands)." In Ethnic Conflict International Perspectives, edited by Jerry Boucher and others. Newbury Park, CA: Sage, 1987.

11296. Lal, Brij Victor. Fiji: Coups in Paradise, Race, Politics and Military Intervention. London: Zed Press, 1987.

11297. Lal, Brij Victor, ed. Politics in Fiji. North Sydney: Allen and Unwin, 1986.

11298. Langer, Odette. "Nouveau Pacifique sud: donnees statistiques." Journal, Societe des oceanistes 87 (1988): 89-123.

11299. Larmor, Peter. "Alienated Land and Independence in Melanesia." Pac. Stud. 8 (Fall 1984): 1-47.

11300. Lawson, Stephanie. "The Myth of Cultural Homogeneity and Its Implications for Chiefly Power and Politics in Fiji." Comparative Studies in Society and History 32 (October 1990): 795-821.

11301. Levine, Stephen and others. "Political Change in the Pacific." Pacific Studies 12 (November 1988): 1-51.

11302. Linnekin, Jocelyn and Lin Poyer. Cultural Identity and Ethnicity in the Pacific. Honolulu: University of Hawaii Press, 1990.

11303. Lockwood, Victoria S. "Development, French Neocolonialism, and the Structure of the Tubuai Economy." Oceania 58 (1988): 176-192.

11304. Low-Hang, K. Colour and Class Inequality in Seychelles. Doctoral dissertation: University of Bristol, 1985.

11305. Lutz, Catherine, ed. Micronesia as Strategic Colony: The Impact of U.S. Policy on Micronesian Health and Culture. Cambridge, MA: Cultural Survival Inc., 1984.

11306. MacDonald, Barrie K. "Decolonization and Beyond: The Framework for Post-Colonial Relationships in Oceania." Journal of Pacific History 21 (July 1986): 115-126.

11307. Macdonald, Barrie K. Policy and Practice in an Atoll Territory: British Rule in the Gilbert and Ellise Islands 1892-1970. Doctoral dissertation: Australian National University, 1971.

11308. Macnaught, Timothy J. The Fijian Colonial Experience: A Study of the Neotraditional Order under British Colonial Rule Prior to World War II. Canberra: Australian National University Press, 1982.

11309. Mamak, Alexander and others. Race, Class and Rebellion in the South Pacific. Boston, MA: G. Allen & Unwin, 1979.

11310. Marshall, Leslie B., ed. Infant Care and Feeding in the South Pacific. New York: Gordon and Breach, 1985.

11311. Mason, Leonard. "Marshallese Nation Emerges from the Political Fragmentation of American Micronesia." Pacific Studies 13 (1989): 1-46.

11312. Matheson, Trevor D. P. Aid in An Island Microstate: The Case of Niue. Doctoral dissertation: Australian National University, 1986.

11313. McHenry, Donald. Micronesia: Trust Betrayed. New York: 1975.

11314. McKibben, Lizabeth A. "The Political Relationship between the United States and Pacific Islands Entities: The Path to Self-government in the Northern Mariana Islands, Palau, and Guam." Harvard International Law Journal 31 (Winter 1990): 257-293.

11315. McKinney, Robert J. Micronesia under German Rule, 1885- 1914. Master's thesis: Stanford University, 1947.

11316. Meller, Norman. Constitutionalism in Micronesia. Honolulu: University of Hawaii Press, 1986.

11317. Milford, Sereisa. "Imperialism and Samoan National Identity." Amerasia Journal 12 (1985-1986): 49-56.

11318. ""Militarization and Indigenous Peoples"." Cultural Survival Quarterly 11 (1987): entire issue.

11319. "Mobility and Identity in the Island Pacific." Pacific Viewpoint 26 (April 1985): entire issue.

11320. Morton, Keith L. "The Atomization of Tongan Society." Pacific Studies 10 (March 1987): 47-72.

11321. Negrin, J. P. "La Republique des Seychelles: 1976-1980." An. Pays Ocean Indien 10 (1984-1985): 263-290.

11322. Nevin, David. The American Touch in Micronesia. New York: 1977.

11323. Newbury, Colin W. The Administration of French Oceania, 1842-1906. Doctoral dissertation: Australian National University, 1956.

11324. Norton, Robert E. Race and Politics in Fiji. New York: St. Martin's Press, 1978.

11325. "Oceania." In World Directory of Minorities, edited by Minority Rights Group. 359-386. Harlow: Longman, 1990.

11326. Oliver, Douglas L. The Pacific Islands. 3d ed. Honolulu: University of Hawaii Press, 1989.

11327. Oliver, Douglas L., ed. Planning Micronesia's Future, A Summary of the United States Commercial Company's Economic Survey of Micronesia. Honolulu: 1971.

11328. Parry, T. G. "Foreign Investment and Industry in the Pacific Islands." Journal of Developing Areas 22 (April 1988)

11329. Paxman, John T. "Minority Indigenous Populations and Their Claims for Self-determination." Case Western Reserve Journal of International Law 21 (Summer 1989): 185-202. [Fiji.]

11330. Peacock, Karen M. The Maze of Schools: Education in Micronesia, 1951-1964: The Gibson Years. Doctoral dissertation: University of Hawaii, 1990. UMO # 9030575.

11331. Peattie, Mark R. Nan'yo: The Rise and Fall of the Japanese in Micronesia, 1885-1945. Honolulu: University of Hawaii Press, 1987.

11332. Peterson, Glenn. "The Ponapean Culture of Resistance." Radical History Review Nos. 28-30 (1984): 347-366. [Eastern Caroline Island.]

11333. Peterson, Glenn. "Redistribution in a Micronesian Commercial Economy [Pohnpei]." Oceania 57 (December 1986): 83-98.

11334. Pollard, S. "Pacific Atoll Economies." Asian-Pacific Economic Literature 3 (March 1989)

11335. Premdas, Ralph R. "Fiji." In International Handbook on Race and Race Relations, edited by Jay A. Sigler. Westport, CT: Greenwood, 1987.

11336. Premdas, Ralph R. "Fiji: Anatomy of a Revolution." Pacifica 1 (January 1989): 67-110.

11337. Premdas, Ralph R. "Melanesian Socialism: Vanuatu's Quest for Self-Definition and Problems of Implementation." Pacific Studies 11 (November 1987): 107-129.

11338. Price, J. "A Note on Mental Retardation in the Cook Islands." Australian Journal of Developmental Disabilities 6 (March 1980): 35-38.

11339. Pritchard, George. The Aggressions of the French at Tahiti and Other Islands of the Pacific. Edited by Paul de Dekker New York: Oxford University Press, 1983.

11340. Puckhov, P. J. "Policy on the National Question and Interethnic Relations in Oceania." In Ethnocultural Processes and National Problems in the Modern World, edited by J.R. Grigulevich and S. Ya Koztov. Moscow: Progress Publications, 1981.

11341. Reeves, Peter and others. "The Maritime Peoples of the Indian Ocean Region since 1800." Mariner's Mirror 74 (1988): 241-254.

11342. Robertson, R. T. and A. Tamanisau. "Fiji: Race, Class and the Military." Development and Change 20 (April 1989): 203- 234.

11343. Robie, David. Blood on their Banner. Nationalist Struggles in the South Pacific. London: Zed Books, 1989.

11344. Rodman, Margaret and Matthew Cooper, eds. The Pacification of Melanesia. Lanham, MD: University Press of America, 1983.

11345. Rogers, Robert F. "Guam's Quest for Political Identity." Pacific Studies 12 (November 1988): 49-70.

11346. Rollat, Alain. Tjibaou le Kanak. Lyons: Le Manufacture, 1989. [New Caledonia.]

11347. Ross, Angus ed. New Zealand's Record in the Pacific Islands in the Twentieth Century. New York: Humanities Press, 1969.

11348. Routledge, David. Matanitu: The Struggle for Power in Early Fiji. Suva: Institute of Pacific Studies, 1985.

11349. Sage, Yves-Louis. "French Courts in Tahiti and Its Dependencies: 1842-1927." Victory Univ. Wellington Law Review 19 (August 1989): 295-328.

11350. Sahlins, Marshall. Islands of History. Chicago: University of Chicago Press, 1985.

11351. Sahlins, Marshall. Social Stratification in Polynesia. Seattle: 1958.

11352. "Sanctity and Power: Gender in Polynesian History." Journal of Pacific History 22 (1987): entire issue.

11353. Scarlott, Jennifer. "U.S. Offers Palau Dollars or Democracy." Bulletin of the Atomic Scientists 44 (1988): 31-35.

11354. Scarr, Deryck. Fiji: A Short History. Honolulu: University of Hawaii Press, 1984.

11355. Scarr, Deryck. Fiji: The Politics of Illusion: The Military Coups in Fiji. Kensington: New South Wales University Press, 1988.

11356. Simms, Norman. Writers from the South Pacific. Washington, D.C.: Three Continents Press, 1989.

11357. Small, Cathy A. Women's Associations and their Pursuit of Wealth in Tonga: A Study in Social Change. 2 vols. Doctoral dissertation: Temple University, 1987. UMo # 8716395.

11358. Smith, Steven C. The Federated States of Micronesia: An Emerging Nation. Columbia, MD: Development through Self-Reliance, Inc., 1986.

11359. Smith, Steven C. The Republic of the Marshall Islands; An Emerging Nation. Columbia, MD: Development through Self-Reliance, INc., 1986.

11360. Spate, O. H. K. The Pacific Since Magellan. Vol. 2, Monopolists and Freebooters. Minneapolis: University of Minnesota Press, 1983.

11361. Spencer, Michael and others, eds. New Caledonia: Essays in Nationalism and Dependency. New York: University of Queensland Press, 1988.

11362. Stover, Mary L. The Individualization of Land in American Samoa. Doctoral dissertation: University of Hawaii, 1990. UMO # 9030584.

11363. Tagupa, William E. Politics in French Polynesia, 1945- 1975. Wellington: New Zealand Institute for International Affairs, 1976.

11364. Tanuvasa, Alofa. United States in Micronesia: What Went Wrong? Master's thesis: Brigham Young University, 1983.

11365. Tate, Merze and Fidele Foy. "Slavery and Racism in South Pacific Annexations." Journal of Negro History 50 (January 1965): 1-21.

11366. Tawake, S. "South Pacific Literature in English Education." Journal of Reading 34 (November 1990)

11367. Thomas, Nicholas. "Blood and Purity: a Comment on the Interpretation of Polynesian Culture." Journal of the Polynesian Society 98 (June 1989)

11368. Thomas, Nicholas. Marquesan Societies: Inequality and Political Transformation in Eastern Polynesia. New York: Oxford University Press, 1990.

11369. Thomas, Nicholas. "Material Culture and Colonial Power: Ethnological Collecting and the Establishment of Colonial Rule in Fiji." Man 24 (1989): 41-56.

11370. Thompson, Roger C. Australian Imperialism and the New Hebrides, 1862-1922. 2 vols. Doctoral dissertation: Australian National University, 1970.

11371. Tinker, Hugh and others. Fiji. London: Minority Rights Group, 1987.

11372. Tolstedt, Mark A. Micronesian Broadcasting and U.S. Strategic Interests: The Evolution of a Dependency. Doctoral dissertation: Northwestern University, 1986. UMO # 8621876.

11373. Toulellan, Pierre-Yves. "Le colonialisme triomphant: Tahiti et la IIIe Republique." R. fr. Hist. Outre-Mer 284- 285 (1989): 425-454.

11374. Trask, Haunani-Kay. "Politics in the Pacific Islands: Imperialism and Native Self-Determination." Amerasia Journal 16 (1990): 1-19.

11375. Trumbull, Robert. Paradise in Trust, A Report on Americans in Micronesia 1946-1958. New York: 1959.

11376. Underwood, Robert A. American Education and the Acculturation of the Chamorros of Guam. Doctoral dissertation: University of Southern California, 1987.

11377. Underwood, Robert A. "Language Survival, the Ideology of English and Education in Guam." Educational Research Quarterly 8 (1984): 72-81.

11378. Underwood, Robert A. and Laura Souder, eds. Chamorro Self-Determination. Agana, Guam: Micronesia Area Research Center, 1987.

11379. Wacquant, Loic J. D. "The Dark Side of the Classroom in New Caledonia: Ethnic and Class Segregation in Noumea's Primary School System." Comparative Education Review 33 (May 1989): 194-212.

11380. Watanabe, Akio. Japanese Attitudes towards the Okinawa Problem: 1945-1965. 2 vols. Doctoral dissertation: Australian National University, 1966.

11381. Weeks, Charles J., Jr. "The United States Occupation of Tonga 1942-1945: The Social and Economic Impact." Pacific Historical Review 50 (August 1987): 399-426.

11382. Weisgall, Jonathan M. "Micronesia and the Nuclear Pacific since Hiroshima." SAIS Review 5 (1985): 41-56.

11383. West, Dalton. "Ethnic Strife in Paradise-Fiji 1987." Conflict 8 (1988): 217-235.

11384. White, Geoffrey M. and John Kirkpatrick, eds. Person, Self, and Experience: Exploring Pacific Ethnopsychologies. Berkeley: University of California Press, 1985.

11385. Wong, J. A. M. The Distribution and Role of the Chinese in Fiji: A Geographical Study of an Imigrant Group in the Plural Society of Fiji. Master's thesis: University of Sydney, 1964.

11386. Woodworth, Stephen C. A History of American Anthropology in Micronesia: Applied Social Science in a Neocolonial Setting. Master's thesis: State University of New York, Binghamton, 1980.

11387. Yusuf, Shahid and R. Kyle Peters. Western Samoa: The Experience of Slow Growth and Resource Imbalance. Washington, D.C.: World Books, 1985.

ELSEWHERE

11388. Abraham, Sameer Y. Race, Class, and the World System. New York: 1987.

11389. Adam, Michel. "Racisme et catégories du genre humain." Homme 24 (April-June): 77-96.

11390. Adas, Michael. Science, Technology, and Ideologies of Western Dominance. Ithaca, New York: Cornell University Press,

11391. Aglietta, Michel. "World Capitalism in the Eighties." New Left Review 136 (November-December 1982): 5-41.

11392. Aglitzin, L. and R. Ross, eds. Women in the World: A Comparative Study. Santa Barbara, CA: ABC Clio, 1976.

11393. Agnelli, Susanna. Street Children: A Growing Urban Tragedy. London: Weidenfeld and Nicolson, 1986.

11394. Ahmad, Eqbal. "Neo-Fascist State: Notes on the Pathology of Power in the Third World." International Foundation for Development Alternatives 19 (1980): 15-26.

11395. Al-Hardallo, Abrahim. Antisemitism: A Changing Concept. Khartoum, 1970.

11396. Alachar, A. and W.J. Serow. "Socioeconomic Determinants of Mortality: An International Comparison." Genus 44 (1988): 131-151.

11397. Alexander, Paul. "Religious Persecution and Resistance in the Byzantine Empire of the Eighth and Ninth Centuries." Speculum 52 (1977): 238-264.

11398. Alfredsson, Gudmundur. "International Discussion of the Concerns of Indigenous Peoples." Current Anthropology 30 (April 1989): 255-259.

866 WORLD RACISM AND RELATED INHUMANITIES

11399. Altschiller, Donald. "Third World Racism." African Commentary 1 (June 1990): 30-31.

11400. Ambert, Alba N. "Language Minorities in an International Context: Many Countries, One Theme." In Bilingual Education and English as a Second Language: A Research Handbook, 1986- 1987. New York: Garland, 1988.

11401. Amin, Samir. "Colonialism and the Rise of Capitalism: A Comment." Science & Society 53 (Fall 1989): 67-72. [See Blaut, below.]

11402. Andersen, C. "Social Responsibility of Foreign Investors in Developing Countries." Bull. Seane Academy Roy. Sci Outre- Mer 33 (1987): 327-343. [In Flemish; summary in English.]

11403. Anderson, Scott. Inside the League: The Shocking Expose of How Terrorists, Nazis and Latin American Death Squads Have Infiltrated the World Anti-Communist League. New York: Dodd Mead, 1986.

11404. Andrew, Cristopher M. and Sidney Kanya-Forstner. "Centre and Periphery in the Making of the Second French Colonial Empire, 1815-1920." Journal of Imperial Commonealth History 16 (1988): 9-34.

11405. Anker, Richard and others, eds. Women's Roles and Population Trends in the Third World. London: Croom Helm, 1982.

11406. Archer, Leonie. Slavery and Other Forms of Unfree Labor. New York: 1988.

11407. Arendt, Hannah. Burden of Our Time. London: Lecker and Warburg, 1951.

11408. Arnold, David. Imperial Medicine and Indigenous Societies. Manchester: Manchester University Press, 1988.

11409. Aronsfeld, C. C. "First Anti-Semitic International 1882- 1883." Immigrants and Minorities 4 (March 1985): 64-75.

11410. Asad Talal, ed. Anthropology and the Colonial Encounter. London: Ithaca Press, 1974.

11411. Ashworth, G., ed. World Minorities. 2 vols. Sunbury, Middlesex: Quartermaine House, 1977-1978.

11412. Ashworth, G., ed. World Minorities in the Eighties. Sunbury, Middlesex: 1980.

11413. Badian, E. "Bitter History of Slave History." New York Review of Books (October 22, 1981)

11414. Bahl, Vinay. "Women in the Third World: Problems in Proletarianization and Class Consciousness." Sage Race Relations Abstracts 14 (May 1989): 3-27.

11415. Barry, Kathleen and others, eds. International Feminism: Networking Against Female Sexual Slavery. New York: International Women's Tribune Centre, 1984.

11416. Barsh, Russel L. "Advocate's Guide to the Convention on Indigenous and Tribal Peoples." Oklahoma City University Law Review 15 (Spring 1990): 209-253. [Includes text of the Convention.]

11417. Barsh, Russel L. "Ethnic Factor in Security and Development: Perceptions of United Nations Human-Rights Bodies." Acta Sociologica 31 (1988): 333-341.

11418. Bauer, Yehuda, ed. Present-Day Antisemitism. Jerusalem: Vidal Sassoon International Center for the Study of Antisemitism, 1988.

11419. Beauvoir, Simone de. "Concerning Half the Human Race." International Educators 1 (1972): 15-22.

11420. Beck, Norman A. Mature Christianity: The Recognition and Repudiation of the Anti-Jewish Polemic of the New Testament. Cranbury, NJ: Susquehanna University Press, 1987.

11421. Becker, George. "Racism in Children's and Young People's Literature in the Western World." Journal of Peach Research 10 (1973): 295-304.

11422. Beetham, David. Marxists in Face of Fascism: Writings by Marxists on Fascism from the Interwar Period. Manchester: Manchester University Press, 1985.

11423. Bein, Alex. Jewish Question: Biography of a World Problem. translated by Harry Zohn, Rutherford NJ: Fairleigh Dickenson University Press, 1989.

11424. Bein, Alex. "Modern Anti-Semitism and Its Place in the History of the Jewish Question." In Between East and West A. Altmann. London: East & West Library, 1958.

11425. Belotti, Elena Gianini. What Are Little Girls Made Of? The Roots of Feminine Stereotypes. New York: Schocken Books, 1976.

11426. Benewick, Robert. "Study of Antisemitism." Jewish Journal of Sociology 29 (December 1987)

11427. Bennett, Anne McGrew. "Overcoming the Biblical and Traditional Subordination of Women." Radical Religion 1 (Spring 1974): 26-33.

11428. Berberoglu, B. Internationalization of Capital: Imperialism and Capitalist Development on a World Scale. New York: Praeger, 1987.

11429. Beres, Louis R. "Genocide, State and Self." Denver Journal of International Law and Policy 18 (Fall 1989): 37-57.

868 WORLD RACISM AND RELATED INHUMANITIES

11430. Bergman, Shlomo. "Some Methodological Errors in the Study of Antisemitism." Jewish Social Studies 5 (1943): 43-60.

11431. Berry, Albert. "On Trends in the Gap Between Rich and Poor in Less Developed Countries: Why We Know So Little." Review of Income and Wealth 31 (December 1985): 337-354.

11432. Betts, Raymond F. Uncertain Dimensions: Western Overseas Empires in the Twentieth Century. Minneapolis: University of Minnesota Press, 1985.

11433. Bhola, Harbrams S. "Policy Analysis of Adult Literacy Promotion in the Third World: An Accounting of Promises Made and Promises Fulfilled." International Review of Education 30 (1984): 249-264.

11434. Billig, Michael. L'Internationale Raciste. Paris: Editions Maspero, 1981.

11435. Billig, Michael. "Extreme Right: Continuities in the Antisemitic Conspiracy Tradition." In Nature of the Right, edited by R. Eatwell and N.O. O'Sullivan. London: 1989.

11436. Billig, Michael. "Psychological Aspects of Fascism." Patterns of Prejudice 24 (Summer 1990): 19-31.

11437. Bills, Scott L. Empire and Cold War: The Roots of U.S. - Third World Antagonism, 1945-1947. New York: St. Martin's Press, 1990.

11438. Bjorkman, J. W. "Comparative Health Policies: A World of Difference." Pakistan Development Review 27 (Winter 1988)

11439. Black, Naomi and Ann Baker Cothell, eds. Women and World Change: Equity Issues in Development. Beverly Hills, CA: Sage, 1981.

11440. Blaut, J. M. "Colonialism and the Rise of Capitalism." Science & Society 53 (Fall 1989): 260-296. [See Amin, above.]

11441. Blick, Jeffrey P. "Genocidal Warfare in Tribal Societies as a Result of European-induced Culture Conflict." Man 23 (1988): 654-670.

11442. Blinkhorn, Martin, ed. Fascists and Conservatives. Boston, MA: Unwin Hyman, 1990.

11443. Bodrova, V. and Richard Anker. Working Women in Socialist Countries: The Fertility Connection. Geneva: 1985.

11444. Bollen, Kenneth A. "Political Rights and Political Liberties in Nation: An Evaluation of Human Rights Measures, 1950 to 1984." Human Rights Quarterly 8 (November 1986): 567- 591.

11445. Bongie, Christopher L. Rewriting Colonialism: Allegories of the 'New Imperialism', 1876-1914. Stanford University, 1988. [Doctoral dissertation.]

11446. Boucher, Jerry and others, eds. Ethnic Conflict International Perspectives. Newbury Park, CA: Sage, 1987.

11447. Boulding, Elise and others. Handbook of International Data on Women. New York: John Wiley and Sons, 1976.

11448. Bowen, Huw V. "Investment and Empire in the Later Enlightenment Century: East India Stockholding, 1756-1791." Economic History Review 42 (1989): 186-206.

11449. Braham, R.L., ed. Origins of the Holocaust: Christian Anti-Semitism. New York: East European Monographs, 1986.

11450. Brakelmann, Gunter and Martin Rosowski, eds. Antisemitismus: Von religiöser Judenfeindschaft zur Rassenideologie. Göttingen: Vandenhoeck & Ruprecht, 1989.

11451. Bray, M. "High School Selection in Less Developed Countries and the Quest for Equity: Conflicting Objectives and Opposing Pressures." Comparative Education Review 29 (May 1985): 216-231.

11452. Brennan, Tim, ed. "Narratives of Colonial Resistance." Modern Fiction Studies 35 (Spring 1989): entire issue.

11453. Brock, Colin and W. Tulasiewicz, eds. Cultural Identity and Educational Policy. New York: St. Martin's Press, 1985.

11454. Brown, Paul. "This Thing of Darkness I Acknowledge Mine: "The Tempest" and the Discourse of Colonialism." In Political Shakespeare: New Essays in Cultural Materialism Dollimore and Alan Sinfield. Ithaca, NY: Cornell University Press, 1985.

11455. Brownfeld, Allan. "Anti-Semitism: Its Changing Meaning." Journal of Palestine Studies 16 (Spring 1987): 53-67.

11456. Brydon, L. and S. Chant. Women in the Third World. Aldershot: Edward Edgar, 1989.

11457. Buger, Julian. Report from the Frontier: The State of the World's Indigenous Peoples. London: Zed, 1987.

11458. Bullock, Bradley P. Basic Needs Fulfillment among Less Developed Countries, 1960-1980: Social Progress over Two Decades of Economic Growth. Vanderbilt University, 1986. [Doctoral dissertation.]

11459. Bunzl, John. Klassenkampf in der Diaspora. Vienna: Europaverlag, 1975.

11460. Burn, Barbara B. "Access to Higher Education." In International Encyclopedia of Education: Research and Studies, edited by T. Husen and T. Neville Postlethwaite. Oxford, England: Pergamon Press, 1985.

11461. Bussard, Robert L. "'Lumpenproletariat' in Leftist Thought: The Marxist and Bakuninist Tradition." E.C. Barksdale Student Lectures 1985-1986 (9): 7-33.

11462. Cahnman, Werner J. "Socio-economic Causes of Antisemitism." Social Problems 5 (July 1957)

11463. Campbell, Persia C. Chinese Coolie Emigration to Countries within the British Empire. London: Cass, 1923.

11464. Canny, Nicolas and Anthony Pagden, eds. Colonial Identity in the Atlantic World, 1500-1800. Princeton, NJ: Princeton University Press, 1987.

11465. Carboni, Carlo. "Advanced Capitalist Countries' Class Composition: A Comparative Analysis." Economia e Lavoro 17 (April-June 1983)

11466. Carnoy, Martin and others. Education and Social Transition in the Third World. Princeton, NJ: Princeton University Press, 1990.

11467. Cartelli, Thomas. "Prospero in Africa: "The Tempest" as Colonial Text and Pretext." In Shakespeare Reproduced: The Text in History and Ideology, edited by Jean E. Howard and Marion F. O'Connor. Routledge, 1988.

11468. Castles, Stephen. Migrant Workers and the Transformation of Western Societies. Ithaca, NY: Center for International Studies, Cornell University, 1989.

11469. Chahnazarian, A. and J. L. deMeyer. "La racisme, mythes et sciences: un essai critique." Revue de l'Institut de Sociologie (1982): 527-540.

11470. Chaliand, Gerard, ed. Minority Peoples in the Age of Nation-states. Translated by Tony Berrett, London: Pluto Press, 1989.

11471. Chalk, Frank and Kurt Jonassohn. History and Sociology of Genocide: Analysis and Case Studies. New Haven, CT: Yale University Press, 1990.

11472. Charney, Israel W., ed. Toward the Understanding and Prevention of Genocide: Proceedings of the International Conference on the Holocaust and Genocide. Boulder, CO: 1984.

11473. Chattierjee, Partha. Nationalist Thought and the Colonial World. London: Zed Books, 1986.

11474. Cheema, G. Shabbir, ed. Reaching the Urban Poor: Project Implementation in Developing Countries. Boulder, CO: Westview, 1986.

11475. Chernyak, Y. Advocates of Colonialism. Translated by Roger Silverman. Moscow: Progress Publishers, 1968.

11476. Child, Lydia Marie. History of the Condition of Women in Various Ages and Nations. 2 vols. Boston: J. Allen, 1835.

11477. Christodoulou, Demetrios. Unpromised Land: Agrarian Reform and Conflict Worldwide. London: Zed, 1990.

11478. Clarence-Smith, W. Gervase. "Economics of the Indian Ocean and Red Sea Trades in the 19th Century: An Overview." Slavery & Abolition 9 (1988): 1-20.

11479. Clark, Lorenne M. G. and Lynda Lange, eds. Sexism of Social and Political Theory: Women and Reproduction from Plato to Nietzsche. Toronto: University of Toronto Press, 1979.

11480. Clarke, Colin G. and others, eds. Geography and Ethnic Pluralism. Winchester, MA: Allen and Unwin, 1984.

11481. Cohen, Ronald. "Human Rights and Cultural Relativism: The Need for a New Approach." American Anthropologist 91 (1989): 1014-1017.

11482. Cohen, Ronald. "Servility in Social Evolution." In Migration and Anthropology American Ethnological Society. Seattle: University of Washington Press, 1972.

11483. Cohn, Norman. Warrant for Genocide: The Myth of the Jewish World-Conspiracy and the Protocols of the Elders of Zion. London: Eyre & Spottiswoode, 1967.

11484. Comaroff, Jean and John Komaroff. "Through the Looking-glass: Colonial Encounters of the First Kind." Journal of Historical Sociology 1 (1988): 6-32. [Cultural as well as political and economic factors in colonialism.]

11485. Conway, John S. "Anti-semitism and the Conflict in the Churches since 1945." Christian Jewish Relations 16 (March 1983): 21-37.

11486. Cornell, R. W. "Class Formation on a World Scale." Review 7 (Winter 1984): 407-440.

11487. Corner, T., ed. Education in Multicultural Societies. London: Croom Helm, 1984.

11488. Craton, Michael, ed. Roots and Branches: Current Directions in Slave Studies. New York: Pergamon Press, 1979.

11489. Craton, Michael, James Walvin, and David Wright, eds. Slavery, Abolition and Emancipation: Black Slaves and the British Empire: A Thematic Documentary. London: Longman, 1976.

11490. Cromwell, Jerry. "Size Distribution of Income: An International Comparison." Review of Income and Wealth 23 (September 1977): 291-308.

11491. Crow, Ben and Alan Thomas. Third World Atlas. Philadelphia, PA: Open University Press, 1985.

11492. Curtin, Leslie B. Status of Women: A Comparative Analysis of Twenty Developing Countries. ERIC ED 224 630, June 1982.

11493. Curtin, Philip D. "Black Experience of Colonialism and Imperialism." Daedalus 103 (Spring 1974): 17-29.

11494. Dahmani, Mohamed. L'occidentalisation des pays du Tiers Monde: Mythes et réalités. Paris: Editions Economica, 1983.

11495. Dasgupta, P. "Well-being and the Extent of Its Realism in Poor Countries." Economic Journal 100, Supplement (1990)

11496. Davenport, Manuel M. "Moral Paternalism of Albert Schweitzer." Ethics 84 (January 1974): 116-127.

11497. Davidson, Basil. "Was Colonialism Really Useless?" Scandanavian Economic History Review 37 (1989): 60-64. [Review article.]

11498. Dawidowicz, Lucy S. "Holocaust and the Textbooks." Social Studies Review No. 4 (Spring 1990): 10-11.

11499. De Vaus, David and Ian McAllister. "Changing Politics of Women: Gender and Political Alignment in 11 Nations." European Journal of Political Research 17 (1989): 241-262.

11500. DelBoca, Angelo and Mario Giovana. Fascism Today. New York: Pantheon, 1968.

11501. Denis, Pierre. Les derniers nomades. Paris: Editions l'Harmattan, 1989.

11502. DeRosa, Peter. Vicars of Christ: The Dark Side of the Papacy. London: Bantam Press, 1988.

11503. Devalle, S. B. C. "Clandestine Culture of Protest in Colonial Situations." Canberra Anthropology 8 (1985): 32-57.

11504. DeVillefosse, L. Geographie de la Liberte. Les Droits de l'Homme dans le Monde, 1953-1964. Paris: R. Laffont, 1965.

11505. "Dimensions of the Racial Situations." International Social Science Journal 23 (1971): 507-625. [Worldwide survey of discrimination.]

11506. Dmitriev, Ivan. "System of Neocolonialist Exploitation." Social Sciences (USSR) 17 (1986): 160-173.

11507. Dnoon, Donald. Settler Capitalism: The Dynamics of Dependent Development in the Southern Hemisphere. New York: Oxford University Press, 1983. [South America, South Africa, Australia, and New Zealand.]

11508. Dofny, Jacques and Abinsola A. Abiwowo, eds. National and Ethnic Movements. Beverly Hills, CA: Sage, 1980.

11509. Donnelly, Jack. "Human Rights at the United Nations 1955- 1985." International Studies Quarterly 32 (September 1988): 275-303.

11510. Downing, Theodore E. and Gilbert Kushner, eds. Human Rights and Anthropology. Cambridge, MA: Cultural Survival, Inc., 1988.

11511. Dubnov, Semen M. History of the Jews. 5 vols. South Brunswick: Joseloff, 1967-1973.

11512. Dubnov-Erlich, Sophie. Life and Work of S.M. Dubnov: Diaspora Nationalism and Jewish History. Translated by Judith Vowles and edited by Jeffrey Shandler, Bloomdington: Indiana University Press, 1991.

11513. Durand-Lasserve, Alain. L'exclusion des pauvres dans les villes du Tiers-Monde acces au sol et au logement. Paris: Editions l'Harmattan, 1986.

11514. Eagleton, Terry and others. Nationalism, Colonialism, and Literature. Minneapolis: University of Minnesota Press, 1990.

11515. Eberstadt, Nick. Poverty of Communism. New Brunswick, NJ: Transaction, 1989.

11516. Einstein, Albert. "Why Do They Hate Jews?" Colliers 102 (November 26, 1936): 3-10,38.

11517. Eitinger, Leo, ed. Anti-Semitism In Our Time: A Threat Against Us All. Forlaget Norvatel A/S, Gamie Torgata bad, N- 0181 OSLO 1, Norway.

11518. Ellerin, Milton and others. "How to Combat Antisemitism." Patterns of Prejudice 17 (October 1983): 3-18.

11519. Elling, Ray H. "Comparison of Health Systems in World- System Perspective." Research in the Sociology of Health Care 8 (1989): 207-226.

11520. Elson, Diane, ed. Male Bias in the Development Process. Manchester: 1990.

11521. Emmer, P. C., ed. Colonialism and Migration: Indentured Labour before and after Slavery. Dordrecht, Netherlands: Nijhoff, 1986.

11522. Ennew, Judith. Debt Bondage: A Survey. London: Anti- Slavery Society, 1981.

11523. Ermacora, Felix. *Protection of Minorities before the United Nations*. Hague: Marinus Nijoff, 1984.

11524. Esman, Milton J. *Ethnic Conflict in the Western World*. Ithica, NY: Cornell University Press, 1977.

11525. Etienne, Mona and Eleanor Leacock, eds. *Women and Colonization: Anthropological Perspectives*. New York: Praeger, 1980.

11526. Evans, William McKee. "From the Land of Canaan to the Land of Guinea: The Strange Odyssey to the 'Sons of Ham'." *American Historical Review* 85 (February 1980): 15-43.

11527. Fanon, Frantz. *Black Skin, White Masks*. Translated by Charles Lam Markmann, New York: Grove Press, 1967. [Colonialism.]

11528. Fawcett, James. *International Protection of Minorities*. London: Minorities Rights Group, 1979.

11529. Fergison, Russell and others, eds. *Out There: Marginalization and Contemporary Cultures*. Cambridge, MA: MIT Press, 1990.

11530. Fernandez, Retamar Roberto. *Caliban and Other Essays*. Minneapolis: University of Minnesota Press, 1989. [Colonialism.]

11531. Fiala, Robert and Andri G. Lanford. "Educational Ideology and the World Educational Revolution, 1950-1970." *Comparative Education Review* 31 (August 1987): 315-32.

11532. Finley, Moses J. "Slavery." *International Encyclopedia of Social Sciences* (1968)

11533. Fishman, Joshua A. *Language and Ethnicity in Minority Sociolinguistic Perspective*. Clevedon: Multilingual Matters, 1989.

11534. Flint, V. I. J. "Anti-Jewish Literature and Attitudes in the Twelfth Century." *Journal of Jewish Studies* 37 (Spring 1986): 39-57.

11535. Fox-Genovese, Elizabeth and Eugene D. Genovese. "Social Classes and Class Struggle in Geographic Perspective." In *Geographic Perspectives in History*, edited by Eugene D. Genovese and Leonard Hochberg. New York: Blackwell, 1989.

11536. Freeman, Marsha A. "Measuring Equality: A Comparative Perspective on Women's Legal Capacity and Constitutional Rights in Five Commonwealth Countries." *Berkeley Women's Law Journal* 5 (1990): 110-138.

11537. Fried, C., ed. *Minorities: Community and Identity*. New York: Springer-Verlag, 1983.

11538. Friedman, Robert and others, eds. Modern Welfare States: A Comparative View of Trends and Prospects. New York: New York University Press, 1987.

11539. Friedman, Milton. Capitalism and Freedom. Chicago: University of Chicago, 1962. [See C.B. MacPherson, below.]

11540. Fuller, Bruce. "Is Primary School Quality Eroding in the Third World?" Comparative Education Review 30 (Novemeber 1986): 491-507.

11541. Furedi, Frank. "Britain's Colonial Wars: Playing the Ethnic Card." Journal of Commonwealth & Comparative Politics 28 (March 1990)

11542. Furnivall, J. S. Colonial Policy and Practice. Cambridge: Cambridge University Press, 1948.

11543. Gamble, Eiza B. Sexes in Science and History: An Inquiry into the Dogma of Woman's Inferiority to Man. New York: Putnam's, 1916.

11544. Gantzel, Klaus J. and Jorg Meyer-Stamer. Die Kriege nach dem Zweiten Weltkrieg bis 1984: Daten und erste Analysen. Cologne: Weltforum Verlagsgesellschaft, 1986.

11545. Ganzeboom, Harry B. G. and others. "Intergenerational Class Mobility in Comparative Perspective." Research in Social Stratification and Mobility 8 (1989): 3-84. [Men in 35 countries.]

11546. Geiger, Roger L. Private Sectors in Higher Education: Structure, Function, and Change in Eight Countries. Ann Arbor: University of Michigan Press, 1986.

11547. Genocide. Moscow: Progress Publishers, 1985. [S.Korea, N.Ireland, Kampuchea, Israel, U.S.A., Guatemala, El Salvador, Nazi Germany.]

11548. Genovese, Eugene D. "Treatment of Slaves in Different Countries: Problems in the Applications of the Comparative Method." In Slavery in the New World, edited by Laura Foner and Eugene D. Genovese. Englewood Cliffs, NJ: Prentice-Hall, 1969.

11549. Gilbert, Geoff. "Criminal Responsibility." International and Comparative Law Quarterly 39 (April 1990): 345-369. [Crimes against humanity.]

11550. Gilman, Sander L. "Medical Colonialism and Disease." In Disease and Representation: Images of Illness from Madness to AIDS Sander L. Gilman. Ithaca, NY: Cornell University Press, 1988.

11551. Gimernez, Martha E. "Minorities and the World System: Theoretical and Political Implications of the Internationalization of Minorities." In Racism, Sexism and the World System, edited by Joan Smith and others. Westport, CT: Greenwood, 1988.

11552. Giraud, Michel. "Distracted Look: Ethnocentrism, Xenophobia, or Racism?" Dialectical Anthropology 12 (1987): 413-419.

11553. Gist, Noel and Anthony Dworkin, eds. Blending of Roses: Marginality and Identity in World Perspective. New York: Interscience, 1972.

11554. Glaser, Kurt and Stefan T. Possony. Victims of Politics: The State of Human Rights. New York: Columbia Unversity Press, 1979.

11555. Goldberg, Gertrude S. and Eleanor Kremen. Feminization of Poverty: Only in America? Westport, CT: Greenwood, 1990.

11556. Good, K. "Class Formation in Colonial Situations." Australian and New Zealand Journal of Sociology 12 (1976)

11557. Goodman, David and Michael Redclift. From Peasant to Proletarian: Capitalist Development and Agrarian Transition. New York: St. Martin's Press, 1982.

11558. Gorter, Durk and others, eds. "Special Issue on Fourth International Conference on Minority Languages." Journal of Multilingual and Multi-Cultural Development 11 (1990)

11559. Graff, Harvey J. Legacies of Literacy: Continuities and Contradictions in Western Culture and Society. Bloomington: Indiana University Press, 1986.

11560. Greenberg, Jack. Affirmative Action in Other Lands: A Summary. ERIC ED 249 306, May 1984.

11561. Greenblatt, Stephen J. "Learning to Curse: Aspects of Linguistic Colonialism in the Sixteenth Century." In First Images of America, II, edited by Fredi Chiapelli. Berkeley: University of California Press, 1976.

11562. Griffin, Keith and John Gurley. "Radical Analyses of Imperialism, The Third World, and the Transition to Socialism: A Survey Article." Journal of Economic Literature 23 (September 1985): 1089-1143.

11563. Griffin, Larry J. and others. "National Variation in the Context of Struggle: Post-War Class Conflict and Market Distribution in the Capitalist Democracies." Canadian Review of Sociology & Anthropology 26 (1989): 37-68.

11564. Grimal, Pierre, ed. Histoire Mondiale de la Femme. 4 vols. Paris: Nouvelle Librairie de France, 1967.

11565. Grosh, M. E. and E. W. Nafziger. "Computation of World Income Distribution." Economic Development and Cultural Change 34 (January 1986)

11566. Grunfeld, F. V. "Cultural Persecution: The First Step towards Genocide." UNESCO Courier 38 (May 1985): 6-7.

11567. Guidieri, Remo and others, eds. Ethnicities and Nations: Processes of Inter-ethnic Relations in Latin America, Southeast Asia, and the Pacific. Houston, TX: Rothko Chapel, 1988.

11568. Haas, Ernest B. "What Is Nationalism?" International Organization 40 (1986): 707-745.

11569. Hall, Raymond L., ed. Ethnic Autonomy-Comparative Dynamics the Americas, Europe and Developing World. New York: Pergamon Press, 1979.

11570. Halliday, Fred. "Terrorism in Historical Perspective." Arab Studies Quarterly 9 (1987): 139-148.

11571. Halloran, James D. and others. Race as News. Paris: UNESCO, 1974.

11572. Halpern, Ben. "What Is Anti-Semitism?" Modern Judaism 1 (December 1981): 251-262.

11573. Hamerow, Theodore S. "Hidden Holocaust." Commentary 79 (1985): 32-42.

11574. Hammond, Dorothy and Alta Jablow. Women in Cultures of the World. Reading, MA: Addison-Wesley, 1976.

11575. Hancock, Ian. Pariah Syndrome: An Account of Gypsy Slavery and Persecution. Ann Arbor, MI: Karoma Publishers, 1987.

11576. Handwerker, W. P. "Fiscal Corruption and the Moral Economy of Resource Acquisition." Res. Econ. Anthropology 9 (1987): 307-353.

11577. Hanson, John R., II. "Third World Incomes before World War I: Some Comparisons." Explorations in Economic History 25 (July 1988): 323-336.

11578. Harap, Louis. "On the Meaning of Marx's Essay 'On the Jewish Question'." Journal of Ethnic Studies 7 (1979)

11579. Harff, Barbara and Ted R. Gurr. "Genocide and Politicides Since 1945: Evidence and Anticipation." Internet on the Holocaust and Genocide No.13 (December 1987)

11580. Harris, Richard. "Residential Segregation and Class Formation in the Capitalist City: A Review and Directions for Research." Progress in Human Geography 11 (1984): 26-49.

11581. Harrison, A. Distribution of Wealth in Ten Countries. London: Royal Commission on the Distribution of Income and Wealth, 1979.

11582. Hawkins, J. N. and T.J. LaBelle, eds. Education and Intergroup Relations: An International Perspective. New York: Praeger, 1985.

11583. Hepburn, A. C., ed. Minorities in History. New York: St. Martin's Press, 1979.

11584. Hertzberg, Arthur. "Anti-Semitism and Jewish Uniqueness." Encyclopedia Judaica (Yearbook 1975-1976): 211-218.

11585. Hess, P. N. "Military Burden, Economic Growth and the Human Suffering Index: Evidence from the LDCs." Cambridge Journal of Economics 13 (December 1989)

11586. Hicks, Alexander and Duane H. Swank. "Governmental Redistribution in Rich Capitalistic Democracies." Policy Studies Journal 13 (December 1984): 265-286.

11587. Hill, K. and A.R. Pebley. "Child Mortality in the Developing World." Population and Development Review 15 (December 1989)

11588. Hladczuk, John and others, comps. Literacy/ Illiteracy in the World: A Bibliography. New York: Greenwood, 1989.

11589. Ho, D. Yau-fai. "Prejudice, Colonialism, and Inter-ethnic Relations: An East-West Dialogue." Journal of Asian and African Studies 20 (1985): 218-231.

11590. Hobsbawm, Eric J. "Are We Entering a New Era of Anti- Semitism?" New Society (December 11, 1980)

11591. Hobsbawm, Eric J. Nations and Nationalism Since 1780: Programme, Myth, Reality. New York: Cambridge University Press, 1990.

11592. "Holocaust: At the Edge of Comprehension." Origins: CNS Documentary Service 19 (February 15, 1990): 601-605. [Published by the Catholic News Service, Washington D.C.]

11593. Hopkins, Philip G. H. Workers' Education: An International Perspective. Philadelphia, PA: Open University Press, 1985.

11594. Horowitz, Donald L. Ethnic Groups in Conflict. Berkeley: University of California Press, 1985.

11595. Horowitz, Irving Louis. "Jews, Anti-Semitism, and Sociology." Congress Monthly (November-December 1986): 4-7.

11596. How Nations Serve Young Children: Profiles of Child Care and Education in 14 Countries. Ypsilanti, MI: High/Scope Educational Research Foundation, October 1990.

11597. Hugill, Peter J. "Structural Changes in the Core Regions of the World-Economy, 1830-1945." Journal of Historical Geography 14 (April 1988): 111-127.

11598. Hyam, Ronald. "Empire and Sexual Opportunity." Journal of Imperial and Commonwealth History 14 (1986): 34-90.

11599. "Identity and Education." Cultural Survival Quarterly 9, 2 (1985): entire issue.

11600. Image of the Black in Western Art. Cambridge MA: Harvard University Press, 1976. [As of 1990, vols. 1, 2, and 4 were published.]

11601. Independent Commission on International Humanitarian Issues. Indigenous Peoples: A Global Quest for Justice. London: Zed Press, 1987.

11602. Irwin, Graham W., ed. Africans Abroad: A Documentary History of the Black Diaspora in Asia, Latin America, and the Caribbean in the Age of Slavery. New York: Columbia University Press, 1977.

11603. Isaac, Jules. Teaching of Contempt, Christian Roots of Anti-Semitism. New York: Holt, Rinehart & Winston, 1964.

11604. Ismaelillo, S. and R. Wright. Native Peoples in Struggle: Cases from the Fourth Russell Tribunal and Other International Forums. Bombay: E.R.I.N. Publications, 1982.

11605. Jackman, Robert W. "Political Democracy and Social Equality: A Comparative Analysis." American Sociological Review 39 (1974): 29-45.

11606. Jackson, James Walvin. Slavery and the Slave Trade: A Short Illustrated History. Jackson: University Press of Mississippi, 1983.

11607. Jackson, P. "Social Geography: Race and Racism." Progress in Human Geography 9 (1985): 99-108.

11608. Jacobs, Jack. "Marxism and Anti-Semitism: Kautsky's Perspective." International Social History 30 (1985): 401- 430.

11609. Jacobson, John R., ed. Territorial Rights of Peoples. Lewiston, New York: E. Mellen Press, 1989.

11610. Jain, P. C. Colonialism, Class and Race Relations: The Case of Overseas Indians. Doctoral dissertation: Carleton University, Canada, 1985. [Guyana, Kenya, and Malaysia.]

11611. Janssen-Jurreit, Marielouise. Sexism: The Male Monopoly on History and Thought. New York: Farrar Strauss & Giroux, 1982.

11612. Jayawardena, Kumari. Feminism and Nationalism in the Third World. London: Zed Press, 1986. [12 Asian and Middle Eastern countries.]

11613. Jeffrey, Keith. "Colonial Warfare, 1900-39." In Warfare in the Twentieth Century: Theory and Practice, edited by Colin McInnes and G.D. Sheffield. Boston, MA: Unwin Hyman, 1988.

11614. Johansson, S. Ryan. "Status Anxiety and Demographic Contradiction of Privileged Populations." Population and Development Reveiw 13 (1987): 439-470.

11615. Joseph, John Earl. "Cultural and Linguistic Imperialism." In Studies in Modern and Classical Language, edited by Fidel Lopez Criado. Madrid: Origenes, 1988.

11616. Junquera, Carlos. "Antropología frente a dos realidades historico-sociales: el racismo y la xenofobia." RS. Cuadernos de Realidades Sociales Nos. 25-26 (January 1985): 49-68.

11617. Kandil, Fuad. Nativismus in der Dritten Welt: Wiederentdeckung der Tradition als Modell für die Gegenwart. Sankt Michael, Austria: J.B. Blaschke Verlag, 1983.

11618. Karni, Michael G., ed. Finnish Diaspora I: Canada, South America, Africa, Australia and Sweden; Finnish Diaspora II: United States. Toronto: 1981.

11619. Katz, Jacob. "State Within a State, the History of an Anti-Semitic Slogan." Proceedings of the Israel Academy of Sciences and Humanities 4 (1971)

11620. Katz, Steven T. "'Unique' Intentionality of the Holocaust." Modern Judaism (September 1981): 161-183.

11621. Kelly, Gail P. and Carolyn M. Elliott, eds. Women's Education in the Third World. Albany: State University of New York Press, 1982.

11622. Kettani, M. Ali. Muslim Minorities in the World Today. London: Mansell, 1986.

11623. Khoury, A. T. Islamische Minderheiten in der Diaspora. Mainz/ Munich: Matthias-Grünewald Verlag/ Chr. Kaiser Verlag, 1985.

11624. Kiernan, V. S. Lords of Human Kind: Black Man, Yellow Man, and White Man in an Age of Empire. New York: Columbia University Press, 1984.

11625. Kiple, Kenneth F. "Survey of Recent Literature on the Biological Past of the Black." Social Science History 10 (1986): 343-368.

11626. Kliot, N. "Accommodation and Adjustment to Ethnic Demands: The Mediterranean Framework." Journal of Ethnic Studies 17 (1989): 45-70. [18 countries.]

11627. Kliot, N. "Mediterranean Potential for Ethnic Conflict- Some Generalization." Tijdschrift voor Economische en Sociale Geografie 80 (1989)

11628. Klitgaard, Robert. Elitism and Meritocracy in Developing Countries: Selection Policies for Higher Education. Baltimore, MD: Johns Hopkins University Press, 1986. [China, Indonesia, Pakistan, and the Philippines.]

11629. Kloss, Heinz. Grundfragen der Ethnopolitik in 20 Jahrhundert. Die Sprachgemeinschaften zwischen Recht und Gewalt. Stuttgart: Braumüller, 1966.

11630. Kraas-Schneider, Frauke. Bevölkerungsgruppen und Minoritäten. Handbuch der ethnischen, sprachlichen und religiösen Bevölkerungsgruppen der Welt. Wiesbaden: Franz Steiner Verlag, 1989.

11631. Kukreja, Sunil and James D. Miley. "Government Repression: A Test of the Conflict, World-System Position, and Modernization Hypotheses." International Journal of Contemporary Sociology 26 (1989): 147-157.

11632. Kuper, Leo. Genocide: Its Political Use in the Twentieth Century. New Haven, CT: Yale University Press, 1982.

11633. Kuper, Leo. International Action against Genocide. London: Minority Rights Group, 1982.

11634. Kuper, Leo. "Prevention of Genocide: Cultural and Structural Indicators of Genocidal Threat." Ethnic and Racial Studies 12 (April 1989): 157-173.

11635. Kurian, George T. Encyclopedia of the Third World. 3 vols. 3d ed. New York: Facts on File, 1987.

11636. Kurian, George and Ratna Ghosh, eds. Women in the Family and the Economy: An International Comparative Survey. Westport, CT: Greenwood, 1981.

11637. Laska, Vera, ed. Women in the Resistance and in the Holocaust: The Voices of Eyewitnesses. Westport, CT: Greenwood, 1983.

11638. Lang, David M. and Christopher J. Walker. Armenians, Revised edition. London: Minority Rights Group, 1978.

11639. Langmuir, Gavin I. History, Religion, and Antisemitism. Berkeley: University of California Press, 1990.

11640. Langmuir, Gavin I. "Medieval Anti-Semitism." In The Holocaust, edited by Henry Friedlander and Sybil Milton. Millwood, NY: 1980.

11641. Langmuir, Gavin I. "Prolegomena to Any Present Analysis of Hostility against Jews." Social Science Information 15 (1976): 689-727.

882 WORLD RACISM AND RELATED INHUMANITIES

11642. Langmuir, Gavin I. Toward a Definition of Antisemitism. Berkeley: University of California Press, 1990.

11643. Lauren, Paul G. Power and Prejudice: The Politics and Diplomacy of Racial Discrimination. Boulder, CO: Westview, 1988.

11644. Lawson, Edward H., ed. Encyclopedia of Human Rights. Bristol, PA: Taylor & Francis, 1991.

11645. Lea, Edward and R.E.L. Masters. Anti-Sex: The Belief in the Natural Inferiority of Women. New York: Julian Press, 1964.

11646. Lemerle, Paul. Byzantine Humanism: The First Phase: Notes and Remarks on Education and Culture in Byzantium from Its Origins to the Tenth Century. Translated by Helen Linday and Ann Moffat, Canberra: Australian Association for Byzantine Studies, 1986.

11647. Leon-Portilla, Miguel. Endangered Cultures. Translated by Julie Goodson-Lawes: Southern Methodist University Press, 1990.

11648. Lerman, Anthony, ed. Jewish Communities of the World: A Contemporary Guide 4th edition. New York: Facts on File, 1989.

11649. Levy, Richard S. Antisemitism in Modern Times: An Anthology of Texts. Lexington, MA: D.C. Heath, 1990.

11650. Lewis, Rupert. Marcus Garvey, Anti-Colonial Champion. Trenton, NJ: Africa World Press, 1988.

11651. Liebscher, Gertraud. Der kollektive Neokolonialismus. East Berlin: Insitut fur Internationale Beziehungen of the Akademie fur Staats-und Rechtswissenschaften der Deutschen Demokratischen Republik, 1987.

11652. Liegeois, Jean-Pierre. Gypsies: An Illustrated History. London: Al Saqi Books, 1986.

11653. Limage, Leslie J. "Adult Literacy Policy in Industrialized Countries." Comparative Education Review 30 (February 1986): 50-72.

11654. Lovenderski, Joni and Jill Hills, eds. Politics of the Second Electorate: Women and Public Participation. London: Routledge & Kegan Paul, 1981.

11655. Luster, Robert E. Amelioration of the Slaves in the British Empire, 1790-1833. New York University, 1988. [Doctoral dissertation.]

11656. Lipson, Charles. Standing Guard, Protection Foreign Capital in the Nineteenth and Twentieth Centuries. Berkeley: University of California Press, 1985.

11657. Macpherson, C. B. "Elegant Tombstones: A Note on Friedman's Freedom." In Democratic Theory. London: Oxford University Press, 1973.

11658. Maderspacher, Florian and Peter E. Stuben, eds. Bodenschätze contra Menschenrechte: Vernichtung der letzten Stammesvölker und die zerstörung der Erde in Zeichen des 'Fortschritts'. Hamburg: Junius Verlag, 1984. [Genocide.]

11659. Mahler, Vincent A. and Claudio J. Katz. "Social Benefits in Advanced Capitalist Countries: A Cross-National Assessment." Comparative Politics 21 (1988): 37-51.

11660. Mangan, J. A., ed. Making Imperial Mentalities, Socialisation and British Imperialism. Manchester University Press, 1990.

11661. Mann, Michael. "Ruling Class Strategies and Citizenship." Sociology 21 (1987): 339-354.

11662. Manning, Patrick. Slavery, Colonialism, and Economic Growth. New York: Cambridge University Press, 1982.

11663. Mannoni, Octave. Propero and Caliban: The Psychology of Colonialization. Translated by Pamela Powesland, New York: Praeger, 1956.

11664. Maolain, Ciaran O. Radical Right: A World Directory. London: Longman, 1987.

11665. Marger, Martin M. Race and Ethnic Relations: American and Global Perspective. Belmont, CA: Wadsworth, 1985.

11666. Marglin, Frederique A. and Stephen A. Marglin, eds. Dominating Knowledge. Oxford: Clarendon Press, 1990.

11667. Marglin, Stephen A. "Sustainable Development: A Systems of Knowledge Approach." Black Scholar 21 (January-March 1990): 35-42.

11668. Maritain, Jacques. Antisemitism. London: New Century Press, 1939.

11669. Martinez Carreras, José U. Historia de la descolonización (1919-1986): las independencias de Asia y Africa. Madrid: Edicines Istmo, 1989.

11670. Maxwell, J. F. Slavery and the Catholic Church: The History of Catholic Teaching Concerning the Moral Legitimacy of the Institution of Slavery. Chichester/London: 1975.

11671. Mayall, James and Anthony Payne. Fallacies of Hope: The Post-Colonial Record of the Commonwealth Third World. Manchester University Press, 1991.

11672. Mayer, Tamar. "Consensus and Invisibility: The Representation of Women in Human Geography Textbooks." Professional Geographer 41 (November 1989): 397-409.

11673. Mayer, Thomas. "UN Resolution Equating Zionism with Racism: Genesis and Repercussions." Research Report (Institute of Jewish Affairs) No. 1 (April 1985)

11674. Mazza, Mario. "Poveri e poverta nel mondo bizantino (IV - VII secolo)." Studi Stor. 23 (April-June 1982): 283-315.

11675. McNeil, William H. Poly-ethnicity and National Unity in World History. Toronto: University of Toronto Press, 1986.

11676. Meade, J. E. "Inheritance of Inequalities: Some Biological, Demographic, Social, and Economic Factors." Proceedings of the British Academy No. 59 (1973): 355-381.

11677. Meillassoux, Claude. Anthropologie de l'esclavage: le ventre de fer et d'argent. Paris: Presses Universitaires de France, 1986.

11678. Meinardus, Marc. Marginalitat: theoretische Aspekte und entwicklungspolitische Konsequenzen. Saarbrucken: Verlag Breitenbach Publishers, 1982.

11679. Melrose, Dianna. Bitter Pills: Medicines and the Third World Poor. Oxford, England: OXFAM, 1982.

11680. Memmi, Albert. Colonizer and the Colonized. Translated by Howard Greenfield, New York: Orion Press, 1965.

11681. Metzer, M. Slavery from the Rise of Western Civilization to the Renaissance. Chicago: 1971.

11682. Michaelis, Meir. "Fascism, Totalitarianism and the Holocaust: Reflections on Current Interpretations of National Socialist Anti-Semitism." European History Quarterly 19 (1989): 85-103.

11683. Miles, Robert. Anomaly or Necessity? Capitalism and Unfree Labour. University of Glasgow, 1986. [Doctoral dissertation.]

11684. Miles, Robert and V. Satzewich. "Migration, Racism and Postmodern Capitalism." Economy and Society 19 (August 1990)

11685. Miliband, Ralph. Divided Societies: Class Struggle in Contemporary Capitalism. New York: Oxford University Press, 1990.

11686. Miller, Richard Roscoe. Slavery and Catholicism. Durham: 1957.

11687. Mingat, A. and J.P. Tan. "On Equity in Education Again: An International Comparison." Journal of Human Resources 20 (Spring 1985)

11688. Minority Rights Group, ed. World Directory of Minorities. Harlow: Longman, 1990.

11689. Momsen, Janet H. and Janet Townsend, eds. Geography of Gender in the Third World. Albany: State University of New York Press, 1987.

11690. Montville, Joseph V., ed. Conflict and Peacemaking in Multi-ethnic Societies. Lexington, MA: Lexington Books, 1989.

11691. Morgan, Robin, ed. Sisterhood Is Global. Garden City, New York: Anchor Press, Doubleday, 1984.

11692. Morner, Magnus and Thommy Svenson. History of the Third World in Nordic Research. Goteborg: Kungl. Vetenskaps - och Vitterhets - Samhallet, 1986.

11693. Mosley, W. Henry and Lincoln C. Chen, eds. Child Survival. New York: Cambridge University Press, 1984.

11694. Mosse, George L., ed. International Fascism: New Research and New Methodologies. Beverly Hills, CA: Sage, 1980.

11695. Mullen, K. "Le chômage et la santé: une perspective internationale." Rev. Inst. Sociol. Brux. (1985): 523-555.

11696. Munslow, B. and H. Finch, eds. Proletarianisation in the Third World. Dover, NH: Croom Helm, 1984.

11697. Murphy, A. B. "Historical Justifications for Territorial Claims." Annals of the Association of American Geographers 80 (December 1990)

11698. Nadel, George H. and Perry Curtis, eds. Imperialism and Colonialism. New York: Macmillan, 1964.

11699. Naipaul, V. S. "Our Universal Civilization." New York Review of Books (January 31, 1991)

11700. Najafizadeh, M. and L.A. Mennerick. "Worldwide Educational Expansion from 1950 to 1980: The Failure of the Expansion of Schooling in Developing Countries." Journal of Developing Areas 22 (April 1988)

11701. Nash, June. "Ethnographic Aspects of the World Capitalist System." Annual Review of Anthropology 10 (1981): 393-423.

11702. Newby, H. "Rural Sociology of Advanced Capitalist Societies." In International Perspectives in Rural Sociology, edited by H. Newby. New York: 1978.

11703. Newland, Kathleen. Women in Politics: A Global Review. Washington D.C.: Worldwatch Institute, 1975.

11704. Newman, Lucile F. and others, eds. Hunger in History: Food Storage, Poverty, and Deprivation. Cambridge, MA: Blackwell, 1990.

886 WORLD RACISM AND RELATED INHUMANITIES

11705. Nkrumah, Kwame. Neo-Colonialism: The Last Stage of Imperialism. New York: International Publishers, 1966.

11706. Nuss, S. and others. Women in the World of Work: Statistical Analysis and Projections to the Year 2000. Albany, NY: ILO Publications Center, 1989.

11707. O'Brien, Patrick K. "Costs and Benefits of British Imperialism 1864-1914." Past & Present No. 120 (1988): 163- 200.

11708. O'Higgins, Michael. "Income Distribution and Redistribution: A Microdata Analysis for Seven Countries." Review of Income and Wealth 35 (June 1989): 107-131.

11709. Okin, Susan M. Women in Western Political Thought. Princeton, NJ: Princeton University Press, 1979.

11710. Padgug, Robert S. "Problems in the Theory of Slavery and Slave Society." Science and Society 40 (Spring 1976): 3-27.

11711. Padmore, George. Life and Struggles of Negro Toilers. San Bernardino, CA: Borgo Press, 1985, orig. 1971.

11712. Paloheimso, H. "Distributive Struggle and Economic Development in the 1970's in Developed Capitalist Countries." European Journal of Political Res. 12 (1984): 171-190.

11713. Paquot, Élisabeth, ed. Terre des femmes: panorama de la situation des femmes dans le monde. Montreal: Editions du Boréal Express, 1982.

11714. Paraf, Pierre. Racisme dans le monde. New ed., rev. and updated. Paris: Payot, 1981.

11715. Patai, Raphael, ed. Women in the Modern World. Toronto, Canada: Free Press, 1967.

11716. Patte, Daniel. "Anti-semitism in the New Testament: Confronting the Dark Side of Paul's and Matthew's Teaching." Chicago Theological Seminary Register 78 (Winter 1988): 31- 52.

11717. Patterson, Orlando. Freedom. Vol. I, Freedom in the Making of Western Culture. New York: Basic Books, 1991.

11718. Patterson, Orlando. "On Slavery and Slave Formations." New Left Review No. 117 (September-October 1979): 31-67.

11719. Patterson, Orlando. "Slavery." Annual Review of Sociology 3 (1977): 407-449.

11720. Patterson, Orlando. Slavery and Social Death: A Comparative Study. Cambridge, MA: Harvard University Press, 1982.

11721. Paulston, Christina B., ed. International Handbook of Bilingual Education. Westport, CT: Greenwood, 1988.

11722. Peretz, Don. "Semantics of Zionism, Anti-Zionism, and Anti-Semitism." In Judaism or Zionism? What Difference for the Middle East, edited by EAFORD and AJAZ. London: Zed Books, 1986.

11723. Phadnis, Urmila, ed. Women of the World: Illusion and Reality. Columbia, MO: South Asia Books, 1978.

11724. Phillips, William D. Jr. Slavery from Roman Times to the Early Transatlantic Trade. Minneapolis: University of Minnesota Press, 1985.

11725. Pinkney, Robert. Right-wing Military Government. Boston, MA: Twayne Publishers, 1990.

11726. Plumb, J. H. "Slavery, Race, and the Poor." In In the Light of History. 102-113. London: Penguin, 1972.

11727. "Policy Issues in the Education of Minorities: A Worldwide View." Education and Urban Society (May 1986): entire issue.

11728. Pollaud-Dulian, Marcel. Aujourd'hui esclavage: Servitude et esclavage contemporains. Paris: 1967.

11729. Porter, A. N. and A.J. Stockwell. British Imperial Policy and Decolonization, 1938-64. Vol. 2, 1951-64. New York: St. Martin's Press, 1989.

11730. Potts, Lydia. World Labour Market: A History of Migration. Translated by Terry Bond, Atlantic Highlands, NJ: Zed Books, 1990.

11731. Price, David H. Atlas of World Cultures: A Geographical Guide to Ethnographic Literature. Newbury Park, CA: Sage, 1989.

11732. Price, Richard, ed. Maroon Societies: Rebel Slave Communities in the Americas. New York: 1973.

11733. Pryor, Frederic L. "Comparative Study of Slave Societies." Journal of Comparative Economics 1, 1 (1977): 25- 49.

11734. Ravenholt, R. T. "Tobacco's Global Death March." Population and Development Review 16 (June 1990)

11735. Ray, John J. and Michael Billig. "Research on Fascism: A Debate." Ethnic and Racial Studies 8 (1985): 441-449.

11736. Rees, Philip. Biographical Dictionary of the Extreme Right Since 1890. New York: Simon & Schuster, 1990.

11737. Reinharz, Jehuda, ed. Living with Antisemitism: Modern Jewish Response. Hanover, NH: University Press of New England, 1987.

11738. Reiter, Rayna R., ed. Toward an Anthropology of Women. New York: Monthly Review Press, 1975.

11739. Rhoodie, Eschel M. Discrimination Against Women: A Global Survey of the Economic, Educational, Social, and Political Status of Women. Jefferson, NC: McFarland, 1989.

11740. Robinson, J. W. "Migrant Labor and Minority Communities: Class, Ethnicity, Age, and Gender as Social Barriers to Health Care." Journal of Health Politics, Policy and Law 1 (1987): 514-522.

11741. Rodison, Maxime. "Few Simple Thoughts on Anti-Semitism." In Cult, Ghetto, and the State. 172-191. London: Al-Saqi Books, 1983.

11742. Rogers, Spencer L. Colors of Mankind: The Range and Role of Human Pigmentation. Springfield, IL: Thomas, 1990.

11743. Roht-Arriaza, Naomi. "State Responsibility to Investigate and Prosecute Grave Human Rights Violations in International Law." California Law Review 78 (March 1990): 449-513.

11744. Rojahn, J. "Contributions on Anti-Semitism." International Review of Social History 30 (1985): 265-443. [Symposium.]

11745. Rosenbaum, H. Jon and Peter C. Sederberg. "Vigilantism: An Analysis of Establishment of Violence." Comparative Politics 6 (1974): 541-570.

11746. Ross, Robert J. S. and Kent C. Trachte. Global Capitalism: The New Leviathan. Albany: State University of New York Press, 1990.

11747. Roth, Stephen J. "Antisemitism and International Law." Israel Yearbook of Human Rights (1983): 208-225.

11748. Rothermund, Dietman and John Simon, eds. Education and the Integration of Ethnic Minorities. New York: St. Martin's Press, 1986.

11749. Rotter, Gernot. Die Stellung des Negers in der islamisch - arabischen Gesellschaft bis XVI Jahrhundert. Rheinische: Friedrich-Wilhelms Universität, Bonn, 1967. [Doctoral dissertation.]

11750. Rowan, Patricia. "Passion and Pragmatism in Painful Times." Times Educational Supplement (November 8, 1985): [Schooling in Zimbabwe.]

11751. Rowbotham, Sheila. Hidden from History: 300 Years of Women's Oppression and the Fight Against It. London: Pluto Press, 1973.

11752. Rowse, Tim. "Paternalism's Changing Reputation." Mankind 18 (1988): 57-73.

11753. Rubenstein, Richard L. and others. "After the Holocaust: National Attitudes to Jews." Holocaust & Genocide Studies 4 (1989): 1-88. [Symposium.]

11754. Rubenstein, W. D. "Introduction." In Wealth and the Wealthy in the Modern World, edited by W. D. Rubenstein, 9-45. London: Croom Helm, 1980.

11755. Ruether, Rosemary. "Anti-Semitism in Christian Theology." In Auschwitz, Beginning of a New Era?, edited by Eva Fleischner. New York: Ktav, 1977.

11756. Ruether, Rosemary, ed. Religion and Sexism: Images of Women in the Jewish and Christian Tradition. New York: Simon & Schuster, 1974.

11757. Ruether, Rosemary. "Theological Roots of Misogynism and the Prospects of Liberation Today." In Women and Religion. Ann Arbor: University of Michigan, Office of Religious Affairs, 1972.

11758. Rule, Sheila. "British Group Finds Slavery Is Flourishing." New York Times (July 5, 1989): [World.]

11759. Russell, James W. Modes of Production in World History. New York: Routledge, 1989.

11760. Ruzie, David. "Procès de Nuremberg et les persécutions raciales." Yod 21 (1985): 33-64.

11761. Ryan, Stephen. Ethnic Conflicts and International Relations. Brookfield, VT: Gower, 1990.

11762. Ryan, Stephen. "Ethnic Conflict and the United Nations." Ethnic and Racial Studies 13 (January 1990)

11763. Samuel-Mbaekwe, Ieanyi J. "Colonialism and Social Structure." Transafrican Journal of History 15 (1986): 81-95.

11764. Sangmeister, Hartmut and Peter Abel. "Grundbedürfnisbefriedigung in arabischen Ländern." Orient 24 (1983): 656-676. [20 Arab countries.]

11765. Sawyer, Roger. Children Enslaved. New York: Routledge, 1988.

11766. Sawyer, Roger. Slavery in the Twentieth Century. Boston: Routledge & Kegan Paul, 1986.

11767. Schlegel, Alice. Sexual Stratification: A Cross-Cultural View. New York: Columbia University Press, 1977.

11768. Schmelz, U. O. World Jewish Population: Estimates and Projections. Jerusalem: Institute of Contemporary Jewry, Hebrew University, 1981.

11769. Schott, Kerry. Policy, Power and Order: The Persistence of Economic Problems in Capitalist States. New Haven, CT: Yale University Press, 1984.

11770. Schutz, Barry M. and Robert O. Slater, eds. Revolution and Political Change in the Third World. Boulder, CO: Reinner, 1990.

11771. Science (La) face au racisme. Bruxelles: Editions Complexe, 1984.

11772. Seager, J. and A. Olson. Women in the World: An International Atlas. London: Pluto Press, 1986.

11773. Seligson, Mitchell A., ed. Gap Between Rich and Poor: Contending Perspectives on the Political Economy of Development. boulder, CO: Westview, 1984.

11774. Sen, Amartya. "More Than 100 Million Women Are Missing." New York Review of Books (December 20, 1990)

11775. Shahak, Israel. "History Remembered, History Distorted, History Denied." Race and Class 30 (April and June 1989): 80-86. [Anti-Arabism and antisemitism.]

11776. Shatzmiller, Joseph. Shylock Reconsidered: Jews, Moneylending, and the Medieval Society. Berkeley: University of California Press, 1989.

11777. Shaw, A. G. L., ed. Great Britain and the Colonies, 1815-1865. London: 1970.

11778. Sigler, Jay A., ed. International Handbook on Race and Race Relations. Westport, CT: Greenwood, 1987.

11779. Simmel, Ernst, ed. Anti-Semitism: A Social Disease. New York: International Universities Press, 1946.

11780. Skutnabb-Kangas, Tove and J. Cummins, eds. Minority Education: From Shame to Struggle. Clevedon, England: Multilingual Matters, 1988.

11781. Skutnabb-Kangas, Tove and Robert Phillipson. Wanted! Linguistic Human Rights. Roskilde: Roskilde Universitetscenter, 1989.

11782. Skyhawk, Hugh van, ed. 'Minorities' on Themselves. Stuttgart: Franz Steiner, 1985.

11783. Smallman-Raynor, M. R. and A.D. Cliff. "Acquired Immune Deficiency Syndrome (AIDS): Literature, Geography Origins and Global Patterns." Progress in Human Geography 14 (June 1990): 157-213.

11784. Smith, Anthony D. Ethnic Origins of Nations. New York: Origins of Nations, 1986.

11785. Smith, Anthony D. "Supersession of Nationalism." International Journal of Comparative Sociology 31 (January- April 1990)

11786. Smith, Joan and others, eds. Racism, Sexism, and the World System. Westport, CT: Greenwood, 1988.

11787. Smith, Susan J. "Social Geography: Patriarchy, Racism, Nationalism." Progress in Human Geography 14 (June 1990): 261-271.

11788. Snyder, Louis L. Encyclopedia of Nationalism. New York: Peragon House, 1990.

11789. Stein, L. "Third World Poverty, Economic Growth and Income Distribution." Canadian Journal of Development Studies 10 (1989)

11790. Stern, Sheldon M. Black Response to Enslavement. Washington D.C.: University Press of America, 1976.

11791. Stoler, Ann L. "Making Empire Respectable: The Politics of Race and Sexual Morality in 20th Century Colonial Cultures." American Ethnology 16 (November 1989): 634-660.

11792. Stone, John. Racial Conflict in Contemporary Society. Cambridge, MA: Harvard University Press, 1986.

11793. Stromquist, Nelly P. "Women and Illiteracy: The Interplay of Gender Subordination and Poverty." Comparative Education Review 34 (February 1990): 95-111.

11794. Summers, R. and others. "Changes in the World Income Distribution." Journal of Policy Modeling 6 (May 1984)

11795. Sundrum, R. M. Income Distribution in Less Developed Countries. New York: Routledge, 1990.

11796. Suret-Canal, Jean. "Dead Ends of Neo-colonialism." World Marxist Review 17 (1974): 111-120.

11797. Swepaton, L. and R. Plant. "International Standards and the Protection of the Land Rights of Indigenous and Tribal Populations." International Labour Review 124 (January- February 1985)

892 WORLD RACISM AND RELATED INHUMANITIES

11798. Talmon, Jacob. "Mission and Testimony: The Universal Significance of Modern Anti-Semitism." In Essays on Human Rights, edited by David Sidorsky. Philadelphia, PA: Jewish Publication Society, 1979.

11799. Tambiah. "Ethnic Conflict in the World Today." American Ethnologist 16 (May 1989)

11800. Taylor, Charles &. David Jodice. World Handbook of Political and Social Indicators. New Haven, CT: Yale University Press, 1983.

11801. Temperley, Howard. "Capitalism, Slavery, and Ideology." Past and Present 75 (1977): 94-118.

11802. "Tensions of Empire." American Ethnologist 16 (November 1989): special section.

11803. Therborn, Goran. "Prospects of Labour and the Transformation of Advanced Capitalism." New Left Review No. 145 (May-June 1984): 5-38.

11804. Thornberry, Patrick. International Law and the Rights of Minorities. New York: Oxford University Press, 1990.

11805. Thornberry, Patrick. Minorities and Human Rights Law. London: Minority Rights Group, 1987.

11806. Thornberry, Patrick. Rights of Ethnic, Religious and Linguistic Minority Groups and their Members in Modern International Law. University of Keele, 1985. [Doctoral dissertation.]

11807. Thornberry, Patrick. "Self-determination, Minorities, Human Rights: A Review of International Instruments." International and Comparative Law Quarterly 38 (October 1989): 867-889.

11808. Thornton, A. P. Imperialism in the Twentieth Century. Minneapolis: University of Minnesota Press, 1978.

11809. Tinker, Hugh. Export of Indian Labour Overseas, 1830-1920. London: Oxford University Press, 1974.

11810. Tinker, Irene, ed. Persistent Inequalities: Women and World Development. New York: Oxford University Press, 1990.

11811. Tiryakian, Edward A. and Ronald Rogowski, eds. New Nationalisms of the Developed West: Toward Explanation. Boston: Allen & Unwin, 1985.

11812. Tonkin, Elizabeth and others, eds. History and Ethnicity. New York: Routledge, 1989.

11813. Torney-Pinta, Judith and John Schwille. "Civic Values Learned in School: Policy and Practice in Industrial Nations." Comparative Education Review 30 (February 1986): 30-49.

11814. UN, Department of International Economic and Social Affairs. Selected Demographic and Social Characteristics of the World's Children and Youth. New York: United Nations, 1986.

11815. United Nations Development Programme. Human Development Report 1990. New York: Oxford University Press, 1990. [Contains a human development index.]

11816. van Arkel, Dirk. "Growth of the Anti-Jewish Stereotype: An Attempt at a Hypothetical-deductive Method of Historical Research." International Review of Social History 30 (1985)

11817. Van den Berghe, Pierre L. Race and Racism: A Comparative Perspective, 2nd edition. New York: Wiley, 1978.

11818. van den Berghe, Pierre L., ed. State Violence and Ethnicity. Niwot, CO: University of Colorado Press, 1990.

11819. van der Heven, R. and P.J. Richards, eds. World Recession and Global Interdependence: Effects on Employment, Poverty and Policy Formation in Developing Countries. Washington D.C.: International Labour Office, 1987.

11820. Vanhanen, Tatu. Process of Democratization: A Comparative Study of 147 States, 1980-88. New York: Crane, Russak, 1990.

11821. Vidal-Naquet, P. Assassins de la memoire. Paris: 1987. [Critique of those who deny the reality of the Holocaust.]

11822. Waldron, Ingrid. "Role of Genetic and Biological Factors in Sex Differences in Mortality." In Sex Differences in Mortality, edited by A. D. Lopez and L.T. Ruzicka. Lopez. Canberra: Australian National University, Department of Demography, 1983.

11823. Wallace, Iain. Global Economic System. London: Unwin Hyman, 1990.

11824. Wallace, Tina and Candida March, eds. Our Work Is Just Beginning: A Reader on Gender and Development. Oxford, England: Oxfam Publications, 1990.

11825. Wallerstein, Immanuel. Historical Capitalism. New York: Schocken, 1983.

11826. Wallerstein, Immanuel. "Ideological Tensions of Capitalism: Universalism versus Racism and Sexism." In Racism, Sexism, and the World System, edited by Joan Smith and others. Westport, CT: Greenwood, 1988.

894 WORLD RACISM AND RELATED INHUMANITIES

11827. Walvin, James. Slavery and the Slave Trade: A Short Illustrated History. London: Macmillan, 1983.

11828. Weil, Frederick D. "Variable Effects of Education on Liberal Attitudes: A Comparative Historical Analysis of Anti- Semitism Using Public Opinion Survey Data." American Sociological Review (August 1985): 458-474. [Austria, France, West Germany & U.S.]

11829. Wesseling, H. L. "Giant That Was a Dwarf, or the Strange History of Dutch Imperialism." Journal of Imperial and Commonwealth History 16 (1988): 58-70.

11830. Whalley, John. "Worldwide Income Distribution: Some Speculative Calculations." Review of Income and Wealth 25 (September 1979): 261-276.

11831. Whitaker, Ben, ed. Fourth World: Victims of Group Oppression. New York: Schocken Books, 1973.

11832. Whiteside, Noel. "Unemployment and Health: An Historical Perspective." Journal of Social Policy 17 (April 1988): 177- 194.

11833. Whitfield, Stephen J. "Jewish History and the Torment of Totalitarianism." Judaism 36 (Summer 1987): 304-319.

11834. Whitlam, E. G. "International Law-making." Monash University Law Review 15 (September-December 1989): 176-200. [Crimes against humanity.]

11835. Wigoder, Geoffrey. Jewish-Christian Relations Since the Second World War. New York: St. Martin's Press, 1988.

11836. Wilkinson, Paul. New Fascists. London: Pan, 1984.

11837. Willcos, Walter and Imre Ferenczi, eds. International Migrations. 2 vols. New York: 1929, 1931.

11838. Williams, Colin H., ed. National Separatism. Vancouver: University of British Columbia Press, 1982.

11839. Wilmsen, Edwin N., ed. We Are Here: Politics of Aboriginal Land Tenure. Berkeley: University of California Press, 1989.

11840. Wistrich, Robert S., ed. Anti-Zionism and Antisemitism in the Contemporary World. New York: New York University Press, 1990.

11841. Wolpin, Miles D. "Third World Repression: Parameters and Prospects." Peace and Change 11 (1986): 95-124.

11842. "Women and Development in Africa." African Urban Quarterly 4 (November 1989): entire issue.

11843. Worboys, Michael. "Discovery of Colonial Malnutrition between the Wars." In <u>Imperial Medicine and Indigenous Societies</u>, edited by David Arnold. New York: Manchester University Press, 1988.

11844. World Council of Churches. <u>Sexism in the 1970's: Discrimination against Women: A Report of a World Council of Churches Consultation, West Berlin, 1974</u>. Geneva: World Council of Churches, 1975.

11845. Yotopoulos, Pan A. "'World' Distribution of Income and of Real Poverty and Affluence." <u>Pakistan Development Review</u> 26 (Autumn 1987). [See comments by Cornelisse, Khan and Malik.]

11846. Yotopoulos, Pan A. "Distributions of Real Income: Within Countries and By World Income Classes." <u>Review of Income and Wealth</u> 35 (December 1989): 357-376.

11847. Young, Kate and others, eds. <u>Of Marriage and Market: Women's Subordination Internationally and Its Lessons</u>. London: Routledge & Kegan Paul, 1984.

11848. Zachariah, Mathew. "Lumps of Clay and Growing Plants: Dominant Metaphors of the Role of Education in the Third World, 1950-1980." <u>Comparative Education Review</u> 29 (February 1985): 1-21.

11849. Zuckerman, Nathan, ed. <u>Wine of Violence: An Anthology of Anti-Semitism</u>. New York: Association Press, 1947.

ANCIENT HISTORY

11850. Abel, E. L. "Myth of Jewish Slavery in Ptolemaic Egypt." Revue des Etudes Juives 127 (1968): 253-258.

11851. Abel, E. L. "Were the Jews Banished from Rome in 19 A.D.?" Revue des Etudes Juives 127 (1968): 383-386.

11852. Bakir, Abd el-Mohson. Slavery in Pharanoic Egypt. 1952.

11853. Baldry, H. C. Unity of Mankind in Greek Thought. England: Cambridge, 1965.

11854. Balsdon, John P. V. Romans and Aliens. Chapel Hill: University of North Carolina Press, 1979.

11855. Barrow, Reginald H. Slavery in the Roman Empire. New York: Barnes & Noble, 1968, orig. 1928.

11856. Bastomsky, S. J. "Rich and Poor: The Great Divide in Ancient Rome and Victorian England." Greece & Rome 37 (1990): 37-43.

11857. Beardsley, S. H. Negro in Greek and Roman Civilization: A Study of the Ethiopian Type. New York: Arno Press, 1979, orig. 1929.

11858. Bellen, Heinz. Studien zur Sklavenflucht im römischen Kaiserreich. Wiesbaden, 1971. [Bd. 4: Forschungen zur antiken Sklaverei.]

11859. Bernal, Martin. "Black Athena: the African and Levantine Roots of Greece." African Presence in Early Europe, Journal of African Civilization 7 (1985): 66-82.

11860. Bernal, Martin. Black Athena: The Afroasiatic Roots of Western Civilization. Vol. II, Greece: Aryan or Mediterranean? The Archeological and

Documentary Evidence. New Brunswick, NJ: Rutgers University Press, 1990.

11861. Biezunska-Malowist, Iza. L'Esclavage dans l'Egypte gréco-romaine. 2 vols. Warsaw, 1974, 1977.

11862. Bomer, F. Untersuchungen über die Religion der Sklaven in Griechenland und Rom. 4 vols. Wiesbaden: F. Steiner, 1957- 1968.

11863. Booth, Alan D. "Schooling of Slaves in First-Century Rome." Trans. American Philosophy Association 109 (1979): 11- 19.

11864. Boulvert, Gérard. Domestique et fonctionnaire sous le haut-empire romain: la condition de l'affranchi et de l'esclave du prince. Paris: 1974.

11865. Bradley, Keith R. "Seneca and Slavery." Class. at Med. 37 (1986): 161-172.

11866. Bradley, Keith R. Slavery and Rebellion in the Roman World, 140 B.C. - 70 B.C. Bloomington: Indiana University Press, 1989.

11867. Brinkmen, J. A. "Forced Laborers in the Middle Babylonian Period." Journal of Cuneiform Studies 32 (1980): 17-22.

11868. Brockmeyer, Nobert. Antike Sklaverei. Darmstadt: Wissenschaftliche Buchgesellschaft, 1979.

11869. Brunt, P. A. "Romanization of the Local Ruling Classes in the Roman Empire." In Assimilation et Resistance à la culture Gréco-Romaine dans le monde ancien, edited by D. M. Peppidi. Paris: Les Belles Lettres, 1976.

11870. Brunt, P. A. Social Conflict in the Roman Republic. London: Chatto & Windus, 1971.

11871. Burford, Alison. Craftsmen in Greek & Roman Society. Ithaca, NY: Cornell University Press, 1972.

11872. Callinicos, Alex. "Note on Racism in the Ancient World." International Socialism 37 (Winter 1988): 133-138. [see Carlin, below.]

11873. Carlin, Norah. "Reply to Callinicos [:"A Note on Racism in the Ancient World"]." International Socialism 40 (Autumn 1988): 129-136. [See Callinicos, above.]

11874. Carlin, Norah. "Was There Racism in Ancient Society?" International Socialism 36 (Autumn 1987): 90-104. [See Callinicos, above.]

11875. Cracco Ruggini, Lellia. "Intolerance: Equal and Less Equal in the Roman World." Classical Philology 82 (1987): 187-205.

11876. D'iakonov, L. M. "Slaves, Helots, and Serfs in Early Antiquity." Soviet Antropol. Archael. 15 (1976-1977): 50-102.

11877. Dandamayev, Muhammad A. Slavery in Babylonia: From Nabopolassar to Alexander the Great (626 -331 B.C.). DeKalb: Northern Illinois University Press, 1984.

11878. Dandamayev, Muhammad A. "Social Stratification in Babylonia (7th - 4th Centuries B.C.)." Acta Antiqua (Budapest) 22 (1974): 433-444.

11879. Daniel, J. L. "Anti-Semitism in the Hellenistic-Roman Period." Journal of Biblical Literature 98 (March 1979): 45- 65.

11880. Daube, David. Civil Disobedience in Antiquity. Edinburgh: Edinburgh University Press, 1972.

11881. Davis, S. Race-Relations in Ancient Egypt: Greek, Egyptian, Hebrew, Roman. London: 1953 repr.

11882. Delacampagne, Christiane. L'invention du racisme: antiquité et moyen-age. Paris: Fayard, 1983.

11883. Desanges, J. "L'Afrique noire et le monde méditerranéen dans l'Antiquité (Ethiopiens et Greco-romains)." Revue française d'histoire d'outre-mer 62 (1975)

11884. Desanges, J. "L'Antiquité gréco-romaine et l'homme noir." Revue des études latines 48 (1970)

11885. Diakonoff, L. M. "Slaves, Helots, & Serfs in Early Antiquity." Acta Antiqua (Budapest) 22 (1974): 45-78.

11886. Diller, A. Race Mixture Among the Greeks Before Alexander. Urbana: University of Illinois Press, 1937.

11887. Du Bois, W. E. B. "Slavery in Greece and Rome." Voice of the Negro 2 (May 1905): 320-323.

11888. Finley, Moses J. "Extent of Slavery." In Slavery: A Comparative Perspective: Readings from Ancient Times to the Present Robin W. Winks. New York: New York University Press, 1972.

11889. Finley, Moses J. "Servile Status of Ancient Greece." Revue internationale des droits de l'antique 3d ser., 7 (1960): 167-189.

11890. Finley, Moses J., ed. Slavery in Classical Antiquity: Views and Controversies. England: Cambridge, 1960.

11891. Finley, Moses J. "Was Greek Civilization Based on Slave Labour?" Historia 8 (1959)

11892. Flory, Marteen B. "Family in Familia. Kinship and Community in Slavery." American Journal of Ancient History 3, 1 (1978): 78-95.

11893. Forbes, C. A. "Education and Training of Slaves in Antiquity." <u>Transactions and Proceedings of the American Philological Association</u> 86 (1955): 321-360.

11894. Fryatt, Diane Terry. <u>Slavery in the Ancient Near East: 3000 - 1000 B.C.</u> Master's thesis. Fullerton: California State University, 1978.

11895. Gagé, J. <u>Les Classes Sociales dans l'Empire romain</u>. Paris: Payot, 1964.

11896. Gager, John G. <u>Origins of Antisemitism: Attitudes toward Judaism in Pagan and Christian Antiquity</u>. New York: Oxford University Press, 1983.

11897. Garlan, Yvon. <u>Les esclaves en grèce ancienne</u>. Paris: Francois Maspero, 1982.

11898. Garlan, Yvon. <u>Slavery in Ancient Greece</u>. Translated by Janet Lloyd. Ithaca, NY: Cornell University Press, 1988.

11899. Garnsey, Peter and C.R. Whittaker, eds. <u>Imperialism in the Ancient World</u>. New York: Cambridge University Press, 1978.

11900. Gordon, Mary L. "Nationality of Slaves Under the Early Roman Empire." In <u>Slavery in Classical Antiquity</u>, edited by M. J. Finley. Heffer, 1960.

11901. Graindor, P. <u>Un Milliardaire antique</u>. Cairo: 1930.

11902. Gülzow, H. <u>Christentum und Sklaverei in den ersten drei Jahrhunderten</u>. Bonn: 1969.

11903. Hamel, Gildas H. <u>Poverty and Charity in Roman Palestine, First Three Centuries C.E.</u> Berkeley: University of California Press, 1990.

11904. Harrington, J. Drew. "Classical Antiquity and the Proslavery Argument." <u>Slavery & Abolition</u> 10 (1989): 60-72.

11905. Heinen, Heinz. "Zur Sklaverei in der hellenistischen Welt." <u>Ancient Society</u> 7 (1976): 127-149.

11906. Hertzberg, Arthur. "Anti-Semitism and Jewish Uniqueness: Ancient and Contemporary." <u>Tradition and Change in Jewish Experience</u> (1978)

11907. Hopkins, Keith. <u>Conquerors and Slaves</u>. New York: Cambridge University Press, 1978. [Slavery in Rome.]

11908. Imbert, J. "Réflexions sur le christianisme et l'esclavage en droit romain." <u>Revue internationale des droits de l'antiquité</u> 2 (1949): 445-476.

11909. Jackson, Alastar Hurlstone. <u>Plundering in War and Other Depredations in Greek History from 800 B.C. to 146 B.C.</u> Doctoral dissertation, University of Cambridge, 1970.

11910. Jameson, Michael H. "Agriculture and Slavery in Classical Athens." Classical Journal 73 (1977-1978): 122-145.

11911. Jones, A. H. M. "Caste System in the Later Roman Empire." Eirene 8 (1970): 79-96.

11912. Karageorghis, Vassos. Blacks in Ancient Cypriot Art. Houston TX: Merril Foundation, 1988.

11913. Kasher, A. "Some Comments on the Jewish Uprising in Egypt in the Time of Trajan." Journal of Jewish Studies 27 (1976): 147-158.

11914. Lauffer, S. Die Bergwerkssklaven von Laureion. Vol. 2. Academie der Wissenschaft und der Literatur (Mainz): Abhandlungen der Geistes-und sozialwissenschaftlichen Klause, 1956.

11915. Macmillen, Ramsay. Changes in the Roman Empire, Essays in the Ordinary. Princeton, NJ: Princeton University Press, 1990.

11916. MacMillen, Ramsay. Roman Social Relations, 50 B.C. to A.D. 284. New Haven: Yale University, 1976.

11917. Melikishvili, G. A. "Some Aspects of the Question of the Socioeconomic Structure of Ancient Near Eastern Societies." Soviet Antropo. Archael. 17, 1 (1978): 25-72.

11918. Mendelsohn, I. "State Slavery in Ancient Palestine." Bulletin of the American School of Oriental Research 85 (1942): 14-17.

11919. Miles, Gary B. "Roman and Modern Imperialism: A Reassessment." Comparative Studies in Society and History 32 (October 1990): 629-659.

11920. Mohler, S. L. "Slave Education in the Roman Empire." Transactions and Proceedings of the American Philological Association 71 (1940): 262-280.

11921. Momigliano, Arnaldo. "Religion in Athens, Rome and Jerusalem in the First Century B.C." Approaches to Ancient Judaism 5 (1985): 1-18.

11922. Morris, Jenny. "Jews and Judaism in the Ancient World." History Today 31 (1981): 9-13.

11923. Oppenheim, A. L. "New Look at the Structure of Mesopotamian Society." JESHO 10 (1967): 1-16.

11924. Padgug, R. "Clan Structures of Classical Greece." Arethusa (Spring 1975)

11925. Parain, Charles. "La Lutte des classes dans l'Antique classique." La Pensee 108 (1963)

ANCIENT HISTORY 901

11926. Randers-Pehrson, Justine D. Barbarians and Romans: The Birth Struggle of Europe, A.D. 400-700. Norman: University of Oklahoma Press, 1983.

11927. Rogers, Anne. "Roots of Racism." Socialist Worker Review 82 (December 1985)

11928. Saddinton, D. B. "Race Relations in the Early Roman Empire." In Aufsteig und Niedergang der römischen Welt, vol. 2, part 3, edited by H. Temporini and W. Hasse. New York: Walter de Gruyter, 1975.

11929. Schaifer, R. "Greek Theories of Slavery from Homer to Aristotle." Harvard Studies in Classical Philology 47 (1936): 184 ff.

11930. Schtajerman, E. M. (Staerman). Die Krise der Sklavenhalterordnung im Westen des römischen Reiches. Berlin: 1964.

11931. Seilbert, Ilse. Women in the Ancient Near East. London: G. Prior Associated Publishers, 1975.

11932. Senghor, Léopold Sédar. "Les noir dans l'antiquite romaine." Et. Class 45, 3 (1977): 202-216.

11933. Sevenster, J. N. Roots of Pagan Antisemitism in the Ancient World. Leiden: E.J. Brill, 1975.

11934. Sherwin-White, S. N. Racial Prejudice in Imperial Rome. New York: Cambridge University Press, 1967.

11935. Snowden, Frank M. Before Color Prejudice: The Ancient View of Blacks. Cambridge, MA: Harvard University Press, 1983.

11936. Snowden, Frank M., Jr. "Bernal's 'Blacks', Herodotus, and Other Classical Evidence." Arethusa (Fall 1989): 83-95.

11937. Snowden, Frank M., Jr. Blacks in Antiquity: Ethiopians in the Greco-Roman Experience. Cambridge, MA: 1970.

11938. Snowden, Frank M., Jr. "Negro in Classical Italy." American Journal of Philology (July 1947)

11939. Ste. Croix, G. E. M de. Class Struggle in the Ancient Greek World from the Archaic Age to the Arab Conquests. Ithaca, NY: Cornell University Press, 1981.

11940. Ste. Croix, G. E. M. de. "Early Christian Attitudes to Property and Slavery." Studies in Church History 12 (1975): 1-38.

11941. Syme, Ronald. "Human Rights and Social Status at Rome." Classical Outlook 64 (1986-1987): 37-41.

11942. Syme, Ronald. Colonial Elites: Rome, Spain and the Americas. London: Oxford University Press, 1970.

11943. Thompson, E. A. "Peasant Revolts in Late Roman Empire, Gaul and Spain." Past and Present 2 (1952): [Central role of slaves in revolts.]

11944. Thompson, L. A. "Observations on the Perception of "Race" in Imperial Rome." Proc. Afric. Class. Assoc. 17 (1983): 1- 21.

11945. Thompson, L. A. Rome and Race. Ibadan, 1987.

11946. Urdahl. L.B. "Jews in Attrea." Symbolae Osloenses 43 (1968): 39-56.

11947. Vercoutter, J. and others. Image of the Black in Western Art, I: From the Pharaohs to the Fall of the Roman Empire. New York: 1976.

11948. Walbank, F. W. "Nationality as a Factor in Roman History." Harvard Studies in Classical Philology 76 (1972): 145-171.

11949. Watts, W. J. "Race Prejudice in the Satires of Juvenal." Acta Classica 19 (1976): 83-104.

11950. Wegner, Judith R. Chattel or Person? The Status of Women in the Mishnah. New York: Oxford University Press, 1988.

11951. Westermann, W. L. "Industrial Slavery in Roman Italy." Journal of Economic History 2 (1942): 149-163.

11952. Wiedemann, Thomas, ed. Greek and Roman Slavery: A Sourcebook. Baltimore, MD: Johns Hopkins University Press, 1981.

11953. Wiesen, D. S. "Juvenal and the Blacks." Classica et Mediaevalia 31 (1970): 132-150.

11954. Williams, Margaret H. "Expulsion of the Jews from Rome in A.D. 19." Latomus 48 (1989): 765-784.

BIBLIOGRAPHY

11955. Abbink G. Jon , comp. "Bibliography on the Ethiopian Jews, 1958-1984." Studies in Bibliographical Booklore 16 (1986): 37-38.

11956. al-Qazzaz, Ayad, comp. Women in the Middle East and North Africa: An Annotated Bibliography. Austin: Center for Middle Eastern Studies, University of Texas, 1977.

11957. Alman, S. B., comp. Select Bibliography of S.A. Native Life and Problems: Modern Status and Conditions, 1964-1970. Cape Town: University of Cape Town, 1973.

11958. Anant, Suchitra and others, comps. Women at Work in India: A Bibliography. Newbury Park, CA: Sage, 1986.

11959. Attal, Robert, comp. "Bibliographic Annotée sur les Juifs d'Afrique du Nord: 1974-1979." Pa' ame Ma'arav (1983): 305- 357. [Algeria.]

11960. Ballou, Patricia K., comp. Women: A Bibliography of Bibliographies. Boston, MA: Hall, 1986.

11961. Banuazizi, Ali, comp. Social Stratification in the Middle- East and North Africa: A Bibliographic Survey. New York: Mansell, 1984.

11962. Barnard, Henry, ed. Slavery: a Bibliography and Union List of the Microform Collection. Vol. 1. Sanford, N.C.: Microfilming Corporation of America, 1980.

11963. Bibliografia de temas afrocubanos. Havana: 1985.

11964. Bjorling, Joel, comp. Baha'i Faith: An Historical Bibliography. New York: Garland, 1985.

11965. Black, George F., comp. Gypsy Bibliography. Ann Arbor, MI: Gryphon Books, 1971, orig. 1914.

11966. Braham, R.L., comp. Hungarian Jewish Catastrophe: A Selected and Annotated Bibliography. 2d ed., rev. and enlarged. New York: Columbia University Press, 1984.

11967. Brockmeyer, Norbert, comp. Bibliographie zur antiken sklaverei. Bochum, 1971. [Ed. J. Vogt.]

11968. Bryan, Gordon, comp. Scottish Nationalism and Cultural Identity in the Twentieth Century: An Annotated Bibliography of Secondary Sources. Westford, CT: Greenwood, 1984.

11969. Bullwinkle, Davis A., comp. African Women: A General Bibliography, 1976-1985. Westport, CT: Greenwood, 1989.

11970. Bullwinkle, Davis A., comp. Women of Eastern and Southern Africa: A Bibliography, 1976-1985. New York: Greenwood, 1989.

11971. Burnett, John and others, comps. Autobiography of the Working Class. Vol.1: 1790-1900. New York: New York University Press, 1985. [England, Scotland and Wales.]

11972. Buvinic, Mayra, comp. Women and World Development: An Annotated Bibliography. Washington D.C.: Overseas Development Council, 1976.

11973. Byrne, Pamela R. and S.R. Ontiveros, eds. Women in the Third World: A Historical Bibliography. Santa Barbara, CA: ABC-Clio Information Services, 1985.

11974. Canadian Women's Indexing Group. Canadian Feminist Periodical Index (1972-1985). OISE Press, 1989.

11975. Cargas, Harry J., comp. Holocaust: An Annotated Bibliography. Chicago, IL: American Library Association, 1985.

11976. Cheng, Lucie and others, comps. Women in China: Bibliography of Available English Language Materials. Berkeley: Institute of East Asian Studies, Center for Chinese Studies, University of California, 1984.

11977. Coetzee, J. C., comp. Annotated Bibliography of Research in Education, Five parts. Pretoria: Human Sciences Research Council, 1970-1976.

11978. Cohen, Sarah, comp. Antisemitism: An Annotated Bibliography. New York: Garland, 1987.

11979. Conrad, Robert E., comp. Brazilian Slavery: An Annotated Research Bibliography. Boston: G.K. Hall, 1977.

BIBLIOGRAPHY 905

11980. Currie, J. C. Bibliography of Material Published during the Period 1946-1956 on the Indian Question in SA. Cape Town: University of Cape Town, 1957.

11981. Dasgupta, Kalpana, ed. Women on the Indian Scene: An Annotated Bibliography. New Delhi: Abhinav Publications, 1976.

11982. Davis, Lenwood G., comp. Black-Jewish Relations in the United States, 1752-1984: A Selected Bibliography. Westport, CT: Greenwood,

11983. Deletant, Andrea and D. Deletant. Romania. Santa Barbara, CA: Clio, 1985.

11984. Descan, J. P. and Y.J.D. Peeters, comp. "Ethnic Processes and Interethnic Relations in Socialist Countries: A Select Bibliography (1975-1988)." Plural Societies 18 (1989): 120-141.

11985. Deutscher Bundestag, comp. "Ausländer in der Bundesrepublik Deutschland: Auswahlbibliographie mit Annotationen." Wissenschaftliche Dienste Bibliographien 53 (1982)

11986. Divekar, V. D., ed. Annotated Bibliography on the Economic History of India (1500 A.D. - 1947 A.D.). 5 vols. Calcutta: K.P. Bagchi,

11987. Douyon, Emerson and Andre Normandeau, comps. "Justice and Ethnic Minorities: An International Selective Bibliography." Canadian Journal of Criminology 32 (October 1990): 661-668.

11988. Downing, Theodore E. and Gilbert Kushner, eds. Human Rights and Anthropology. Cambridge, MA: Cultural Survival, 1988. [Contains bibliography of more than 1,000 entries.]

11989. Dyer, Aldrich J., comp. Indian, Metis and Inuit of Canada in Theses and Dissertations 1892-1987. University of Saskatchewan, 1989.

11990. Edelheit, Abraham J. and Hershel Edelheit, comps. Bibliography on Holocaust Literature. Boulder, CO: Westview, 1990.

11991. Edelheit, Abraham J. and Hershel Edelheit, comps. Bibliography on Holocaust Literature Supplement. Boulder, CO: Westview, 1990.

11992. Edelheit, Abraham J. and Hershel Edelheit, comps. Jewish World in Modern Times: A Selected, Annotated Bibliography. London: Mansell, 1988.

11993. Edwards, E. and others (comps.). Urban Riots and Public Order: A Selected Bibliography 1975-1985. London: Greater London Council Research Library, 1985.

11994. Engleman, Uriah Zevi. Jewish Education in Europe 1914- 1962: Annotated Bibliography. Jerusalem: Hebrew University, 1965.

11995. Eriksen, Tore L. with Richard Moorson, comps. Political Economy of Namibia: An Annotated Critical Bibliography. 2d ed. Uppsala, Sweden: Scandanavian Institute of African Studies, 1989.

11996. Fluk, Louis R., comp. Jews in the Soviet Union. Revised edition. New York: American Jewish Committee, 1975.

11997. Frey, Linda and others, comp. Women in Western European History: A Select Chronological, Geographical, and Topical Bibliography. Westport, CT: Greenwood, 1982.

11998. Gaudier, Maryse, comp. Le Progrès social pour une solidarité mondiale: orientation bibliographie. Geneva, Switzerland: International Labour Organization, Institut international d'etudes sociales, 1983. [Social justice.]

11999. Giffen, R., comp. Select Bibliography of SA Native Life and Problems: Modern Status and Conditions 1950-1958. Cape Town: University of Cape Town, 1958.

12000. Gilbert, Victor F. and D.S. Tatla, comps. Immigrants, Minorities and Race Relations: A Bibliography of Theses and Dissertations Presented at British and Irish Universities, 1900-1981. New York: Mansell, 1984.

12001. Gilbert, Victor F. and D.S. Tatla, comp. Women's Studies: A Bibliography of Dissertations 1870-1982. New York: Blackwell, 1985.

12002. Ginsberg, E. S. and M. Schwarts, comps. Medical Research on the Bantu in SA 1920-1952. Cape Town: University of Cape Town, 1952.

12003. Goetzfridt, Nicholas J. and William L. Wuerch, comps. Micronesia 1975-1978: A Social Science Bibliography. New York: Greenwood, 1989.

12004. Goodwater, Leanna, comp. Women in Antiquity: An Annotated Bibliography. Metuchen, NJ: Scarecrow Press, 1975.

12005. Goonetileke, H. A. I., comp. "July 1983 and the National Question in Sri Lanka: A Bibliographical Guide." Race and Class 26 (1984)

12006. Gordon, Paul, comp. Race in Britain: A Research and Information Guide. London: Runnymede Trust, 1988.

12007. Gordon, Paul and Francesco Klug, comps. Racism and Discrimination in Britain: A Select Bibliography, 1970-1983. London: Runnymede Trust, 1984.

12008. Gorman, G. E. and J.J. Mills. Guide to Current Bibliographies in the Third World. 2d rev. ed. New York: H. Zell, 1987.

12009. Govia, Francine, comp. Blacks in Canada: In Search of the Promise: A Bibliographical Guide to the History of Blacks in Canada. Edmonton: Harambee Centres Canada, 1988.

12010. Greyling J.J.C. and J. Miskin, comps. Bibliography on Indians in South Africa. Durban: Institute for Social and Economic Research, University of Durban-Westville, 1976.

12011. Gronemeyer, Reimer, comp. Zigeuner in Osteuropa: eine Bibliographie zu den Landern Polen, Tsechoslowakei und Ungarn.... Munich: K.G. Saur, 1983.

12012. Hackett, Nan, comp. Nineteenth-Century British Working-Class Autobiographies: An Annotated Bibliography. New York: AMS, 1985.

12013. Harrison, Gail G. and others, comps. Food and Nutrition in the Middle East, 1970-1986: An Annotated Bibliography. Westport CT: Greenwood, 1988.

12014. Herand, Guy and M. van Halgendoren, comps. "Bibliography of European Ethnic Groups." Plural Societies 12 (1981): 167-187.

12015. Herman, Elisa Beth, comp. Bibliographie zur antiken Sklaverei. 2 vols. Bochum, FGR: N. Brockmeyer, 1983.

12016. Hetzer, Armin and Viorel S. Roman, comps. Albanien.... Munich: K.G. Saur, Verlag, 1983. [Comprehensive bibliography of Albania.]

12017. Hillebrecht, Werner, comp. Namibia in Theses and Dissertations: A Bibliography on All Aspects of Namibian Concern Including German Colonial Policy and International Law 1851-1984. Basel: Basler Afrika Bibliographien, 1985.

12018. Hladczuk, John and others, comps. Literacy/Illiteracy in the World: A Bibliography. Westport, CT: Greenwood, 1990.

12019. Hoffmann, Johannes, comp. Sterotypen-Vorurteile- Völkerbilder in Ost und West in Wissenschaft und Unterricht. Eine Bibliographie. Wiesbaden: Otto Harrassowitz, 1986.

12020. Holocaust in Books and Films. New York: Anti-Defamation League, 1982.

12021. Horn, Charles, comp. Native North Americans: Crime, Conflict and Criminal Justice: A Research Bibliography. Burnaby: Simon Fraser University - Northern Justice Society, 1989.

12022. Hovannisian, Richard G. "Armenian Genocide." In Genocide: A Critical Bibliographic Review, edited by Israel W. Charney. London: Mansell, 1988.

908 WORLD RACISM AND RELATED INHUMANITIES

12023. Hovannisian, Richard G., comp. "Deportation and Massacres of the Armenian Population of the Ottoman Empire, 1915-1922." Armenian Review 28 (1975): 180-192.

12024. Hundert, Gershon D. and Gershon C. Bacon, comps. Jews in Poland and Russia. Bibliographical Essays. Bloomington: Indiana University Press, 1984.

12025. Iatrides, John O., comp. Greece in the 1940's: A Bibliographic Companion. Hanover, NH: University Press of New England, 1981. [See material on Jews.]

12026. Jewish Experience in America: A Historical Bibliography. Santa Barbara, CA: ABC-Clio, 1983.

12027. Kallaway, P. and others. Bibliography of Education for Black South Africans. Cape Town: University of Cape Town, 1986.

12028. Kalley, Jacqueline A., comp. Bophuthatswana Politics and the Economy: A Select and Annotated Bibliography. Johannesburg: South African Institute of Race Relations, 1978.

12029. Kalley, Jacqueline A., comp. South African under Apartheid: A Select and Annotated Bibliography. Westport, CT: Meckler, 1989.

12030. Kalley, Jacqueline A., comp. Transkei Region of Southern Africa 1877-1978: An Annotated Bibliography. Boston: Hall, 1980.

12031. Kanner, Barbara, ed. Women of England from Anglo-Saxon Times to the Present: Interpretive Bibliographical Essays. Hamden, CT: Archor, 1979.

12032. Kehr, Helen and Janet Langmaid, comps. Nazi Era, 1919- 1945: A Select Bibliography of Published Works from the Early Roots to 1980. London: Mansell, 1983.

12033. Khalidi, Walid compiler. Palestine and the Arab-Israeli Conflict: An Annotated Bibliography. Box 329, R.D. 1, Oxford, PA 19363: Institute for Palestine Studies, 1974.

12034. Knaster, Meri, comp. Women in Spanish America: An Annotated Bibliography from Pre-Conquest to Contemporary Times. Boston: G.K. Hall, 1977.

12035. Knell, Robert and Leo Eitinger, comps. Psychological and Medical Effects of Concentration Camps and Related Persecutions of Survivors of the Holocaust: A Research Bibliography. Vancouver: University of British Columbia, 1985.

BIBLIOGRAPHY 909

12036. Krichmar, Albert, comp. Women's Movement in the Seventies: An International English-Language Bibliography. Metuchen, NJ: Scarecrow Press, 1977.

12037. Lambert, Ronald D., comp. Sociology of Contemporary Quebec Nationalism: An Annotated Bibliography and Review. New York: Garland,

12038. Laska, Vera, comp. Nazism, Resistance & Holocaust in World War II: A Bibliography. Metuchen, NJ: Scarecrow Press, 1985.

12039. Lefall, Dolores C., comp. "Black Experience in Africa, Latin America, and the Caribbean: A Selected Bibliography of Articles Appearing in Periodicals 1973-1974." Journal of Negro History 59 (1974): 312-395.

12040. Lehmann, Ruth P., comp. Nova bibliotheca Anglo-Judaica: A Bibliographic Guide to Anglo-Jewish History, 1937-1960. London: Jewish History Society of England, 1961.

12041. Lerski, Jerzy J. and Halina T. Lerski, comps. Jewish-Polish Coexistence, 1772-1939: A Topical Bibliography. Westport, CT: Greenwood, 1986.

12042. Lowenthal, Rudolph, comp. "Jews in China: An Annotated Bibliography." Chinese Social and Political Science Review 24 (1940): 113-234.

12043. Magocsi, Paul R., comp. Galicia: A Historical and Bibliographical Guide. Toronto: University of Toronto Press, 1983.

12044. Marcus, Ralph, comp. "Selected Bibliography (1920-1945) of the Jews in the Hellenistic-Roman Period." American Academy for Jewish Research Proceedings 16 (1947)

12045. Marie, Jacquelyn, comp. "Resources on Women of Color." Women's Studies 17 (November 1989): 149-151.

12046. Matzozky, Eliyo, comp. From Shtetl to Destruction: The Jewish Experience in Eastern Europe. Monticello, IL: Council of Planning Librarians, 1977.

12047. Mazur, Carol and Sheila Pepper, comps. Women in Canada: A Bibliography 1965-1983. OISE Press, 1984.

12048. Meghdessian, Samira Rafidi and others, comps. Status of the Arab Woman: A Select Bibliography. Westport, CT: Greenwood, 1980.

12049. Meiklejohn, C. and D.A. Rokala, comps. Native Peoples of Canada: An Annotated Bibliography of Population Biology, Health, and Illness. Canadian Museum of Civilization, 1986.

12050. Meinhardt, Olav, ed. Generalindex, Europa Ethnica 1958-1988. Vienna: Universitäts-Verlagsbuchhandlung, 1989.

910 WORLD RACISM AND RELATED INHUMANITIES

12051. Merritt, Anna J. and Richard L. Merritt, comp. Politics, Economics, and Society in the Two Germanies, 1945-1975: A Bibliography of English-Language Works. Urbana: University of Illinois Press, 1978.

12052. Michelucci, Alessandro, comp. Select Bibliography on Ethnic Minorities of Western and Northern Europe 1970/1987. Firenze: Published by the compiler, October 1987.

12053. Milano, Attilio, comp. Bibliotheca Historica Italo- Judaica. Firenza: Sansoni, 1954. [Supplemento 1954-1963 (Sansoni, 1964).]

12054. Muffs, Judith H. and Dennis B. Klein, eds. Holocaust in Books and Films. New York: Anti-Defamation League of B'nai B'rith, 1986.

12055. Muneles, Otto, comp. Bibliographical Survey of Jewish Prague. Prague: 1952.

12056. Musiker, Naomi, comp. South African History: A Bibliographical Guide with Special Reference to Territorial Expansion and Colonization. New York: Garland, 1984.

12057. Narby, Jeremy and Shelton Davis, comps. Resource Development and Indigenous Peoples: A Comparative Bibliography. Cambridge MA: Anthropology Resource Center, 1983.

12058. National Library of Canada, comp. Indian-Inuit Authors: An Annotated Bibliography. Canadian Government, 1974.

12059. Nenberg, Assia compiler. State of Israel, 1946-1968. An Annotated Bibliography. Jerusalem: Graduate Library School, Hebrew University, 1970.

12060. Newenham, E. A., comp. South African Bibliographies: A Survey of Bibliographies and Bibliographical Works: Supplement 1970-1976. Johannesburg: University of the Witwatersrand, 1977.

12061. Newton, Jennifer L. and Carol Zavitz, comps. Women: A Bibliography of Special Periodical Issuess. 2 vols. 152 Bllor St. West, Toronto: OISE, Resources for Feminist Research,

12062. Nicaraguan National Bibliography, 1800-1978. 3 vols. Redlands, CA: Latin American Bibliographic Foundation, 1987.

12063. Nicolas, Suzanne, comp. Bibliography on Women Workers....(1861-1965). Geneva: Central Library and Documentation Branch, International Labour Office, 1977.

12064. Ofcansky, Thomas P., comp. British East Africa, 1850- 1963: An Annotated Bibliography. New York: Garland, 1986.

12065. Offen, Karen M., comp. "Women Question as a Social Issue in Nineteenth-century France: A Bibliographical Essay." Third Republic 3-4 (1977): 238-299.

12066. Olson, James S. Slave Life in America: A Historiography and Selected Bibliography. Lanham, MD: University Press of America, 1983.

12067. Paco, Delfina and Virginia Piérola, comps. Bibliografia de cultura popular y educacion en América Latina. La Paz: Centro Boliviano de Investigacion y Acción Educativas, 1986.

12068. Peters, E., comp. Aboriginal Self-Government in Canada: A Bibliography, 1986. Kingston, Ontario: Institute of Intergovernmental Relations, Queen's University, 1987.

12069. Pogarell, Reiner, comp. Minority Languages in Europe: A Classified Bibliography. New York: Mouton, 1983.

12070. Potgieter, L., comp. Bibliography of Bantu Education in the Union of South Africa, 1949-1959. Cape Town: University of Cape Town, 1965.

12071. Potgieter, P. J. J.S. Index to Literature on Race Relations in South Africa, 1910-1955. Boston: Hall, 1979.

12072. Pyatt, Sherman E., comp. Apartheid: A Selective Annotated Bibliography, 1979-1987. New York: Garland, 1989.

12073. Raaflaub, Kurt A. and others, eds. Social Struggles in Archaic Rome: New Perspectives on the Conflict of the Orders. Berkeley: University of California Press, 1986.

12074. Raccagni, Michelle, comp. Modern Arab Woman: A Bibliography. Metuchen, NJ: Scarecrow Press, 1978.

12075. Ramos Guedez, Jose M., comp. El negro en Venezuela: aporte bibliografico, 2nd edition. Caracas: Instituto Autonomo Biblioteca Nacional y de Servicios de Bibliotecas, 1985.

12076. Rees, Philip. Fascism and Pre-Fascism in Europe, 1890- 1945: A Bibliography of the Extreme Right. Totowa, NY: Barnes and Noble, 1984.

12077. Robinson, Jacob and Philip Friedman, comps. Guide to Jewish History under Nazi Impact. New York: Ktar Publishing House, 1973.

12078. Rodger, D. J., comp. University College of Fort Hare, 1905-1959. Cape Town: University of Cape Town, 1960.

12079. Rome, David and others, comps. Les Juifs du Québec: Bibliographie retrospective annotée. Montreal: Institut Québecois de Recherche sur la Culture, 1984.

12080. Rosenberg, Louise Renee, comp. Jews in the Soviet Union: An Annotated Bibliography, 1967-1971. New York: American Jewish Committee, 1971.

12081. Rothenberg, Joshua, comp. Judaica Reference Materials: A Selective Annotated Bibliography. Waltham, MA: Brandeis Univsersity, Library, 1971. [Preliminary edition.]

12082. Rousseau, M. H., comp. Bibliography of African Education in the Federation of Rhodesia and Nyasaland, 1890-1958. Cape Town: University of Cape Town, 1958.

12083. Sakala, Carol, comp. Women of South Asia: A Guide to Resources. Millwood, NY: Kraus, 1980.

12084. Salzmann, Zdenek, comp. "Bibliography of Sources Concerning the Czechs and Slovaks in Romania." East European Quarterly 13 (1979): 465-488.

12085. Sarti, Roland, comp. Select Bibliography of English- Language Books on Modern Italian History. Amherst: University of Massachusetts, Western European Studies Program, 1990.

12086. Schapera, I., comp. Select Bibliography of SA Native Life and Problems. London: Oxford University Press, 1941.

12087. Scholtz, P. L. and others, comps. Select Bibliography on Race Relations at the Cape, 1652-1795: A Guide for Historical Research. Bellville: University of the Western Cape, 1976.

12088. Select Bibliography on Indian Women. Hyderabad: Indian Council of Social Science Research, Southern Regional Center, Osmania University Library, 1982.

12089. Shulman, Frank J., comp. Doctoral Dissertations in Jewish Studies and Related Subjects, 1945-1975.

12090. Sim, Fan Kok, comp. Women in Southeast Asia: A Bibliography. Boston: Hall, 1982.

12091. Simmons, Donita V. and Sin Joan Yce, comps. Women in the South Pacific: A Bibliography. Suva, Fiji: Library, University of the South Pacific, 1982.

12092. Singerman, Robert, comp. Antisemitic Propaganda: An Annotated Bibliography and Research Guide. New York: Garland, 1982.

12093. Singerman, Robert, comp. Jewish Serials of the World: A Research Bibliography of Secondary Sources. Westport, CT: Greenwood, 1986.

12094. Singerman, Robert, comp. Jews in Spain and Portugal: A Bibliography. New York: Garland, 1975.

12095. Skirball, Sheba F. Films of the Holocaust: An Annotated Filmography of the Collections in Israel. New York: Garland, 1990.

12096. Smith, John D., comp. Black Slavery in the Americas: An Interdisciplinary Bibliography, 1865-1980. 2 vols. Westport, CT: Greenwood, 1982.

12097. Smooha, S., comp. Social Research on Arabs in Israel, 1977-1982: A Bibliography. Haifa: University of Haifa, 1984.

12098. Sparks, Linda, comp. Institutions of Higher Education: An International Bibliography. Westport, CT: Greenwood, 1990.

12099. Stock, Karl F. and others, eds. Bibliographie österreichischer Bibliographien und Nachschlagewerke.... Vol. 7, Tirol. Graz, Austria: Karl F. Stock, 1981.

12100. Stokes, Gale, comp. Nationalism in the Balkans: An Annotated Bibliography. New York: Garland, 1983.

12101. Stultz, Newell M., comp. South Africa: An Annotated Bibliography with Analytical Introduction. Ann Arbor, MI: Pierian Press, 1989.

12102. Suryandinata, L. Ethnic Chinese in the ASEAN State: Bibliographic Essays.

12103. Suzuki, Peter T. French, German and Swiss University Dissertations on Twentieth Century Turkey.... Wiesbaden, 1970.

12104. Taylor, C. J., comp. Coloured Education: A Bibliography. Cape Town: University of Cape Town, 1970.

12105. Thompson, Edgar T., comp. Plantation: An International Bibliography. Boston, MA: Hall/Twayne, 1983.

12106. Tutorow, Norman E., comp. War Crimes, War Criminals and War Crimes Trials: An Annotated Bibliography and Source Book. Westport, CT: Greenwood, 1986.

12107. United Nations: Dag Hammarskjöld Library. Status of Women: A Select Bibliography. White Planes, New York: UNIFO Publishers, 1976.

12108. Valdes, Nelson P., comp. "Bibliography of Cuban Women in the 20th Century." Cuban Studies 4 (1974): 1-31.

12109. van Dijk, Teun, comp. Select Bibliography on Racism and the Press. Amsterdam: Department of General Literary Studies, University of Amsterdam, 1989.

12110. Vanden, Harry E., comp. Latin American Marxism: A Bibliography. New York: Garland.

12111. Veiter, Theodor, comp. Bibliographie zur Südtirolfrage 1945-1983. Vienna: Braumuller, 1986.

12112. Verrall, Catherine and others, comps. Resources/Reading List: Annotated Bibliography of Resources By and About Native People, 3rd edition. Toronto: Canadian Association in Solidarity with the Native Peoples, 1989.

12113. Vincent Davios, Diana, comp. "Occupied Territories of Israel and International Law: A Research Guide." New York University Journal of International Law and Politics 21 (Spring 1989): 575-665. [Bibliography.]

12114. Vogt, J., comp. Bibliographie zur antiken Sklaverei. Bochum, n.d.

12115. Wai, L., comp. Native Peoples of Canada in Contemporary Society: A Demographic and Socioeconomic Bibliography.

12116. Wei, Karen T., comp. Women in China: A Selected and Annotated Bibliography. Westport, CT: Greenwood Press, 1984.

12117. Weil, Bernard, comp. Faschismustheorie: eine vergleichende Übersicht mit Bibliographie. Frankfurt: Rita G. Fischer Verlag, 1984.

12118. Weinberg, Meyer, comp. Racism in the United States: A Comprehensive Classified Bibliography. Westport, CT: Greenwood Press, 1990.

12119. Weitz, Margaret C., comp. Femmes: Recent Writings on French Women. Boston, MA: Hall, 1985.

12120. Whiteside (Sin-a-Paw), Don, comp. Aboriginal People: A Selected Bibliography Concerning Canada's First People. Ottawa: National Indian Brotherhood, 1973.

12121. Women Studies Abstracts. Rush, New York: Rush Publishing, 1972.

12122. Woods, Richard D., comp. Mexican Autobiography / La Auto-Biografia Mexicana. Translated by Josephina Cruz-Melendez. Westport, CT: Greenwood, 1988.

12123. Zafoni, Yigal, comp. "Bibliography of the Holocaust for those Regions of the Soviet Union Occupied by German Forces from June 1941 - Part 1." Journal of the Academic Proceedings of Soviet Jewry 1 (1986)

AUTHOR INDEX

Numbers refer to entries not page numbers.

A'si, Murad, 5334
Aalberts, Monique M.J., 6782
Aalen, F. H. A., 5169
Aarons, Mark, 163
Aaronvitch, S., 3675
Aba, E.O., Jr., 7196
Abacchi, Alberto, 2266
Abad, Ricardo, 7505
Abadan-Unat, Nermin, 8787
Aballea, Francois, 2372
Abanime, Emeka P., 2373, 10029
Abbas, Rogeb, 5603
Abbay, Frehiwot, 4611
Abbey, Robert A., 11197
Abbink, G. Jon, 2151, 2267, 5205-5207
Abdalla, Ahmed, 2151
Abdel Kadel, Soha, 2152
Abdel-Khalek, Gouda, 2153
Abdo-Zubi, Nahla, 5335
Abdulhadi, Rami S., 5336
Abdus Shukur, 3353
Abe, Goh, 11198
Abe, Kazuhiro, 6030, 6031
Abed, George T., 5337, 5338
Abedian, Iraj, 7948, 7949
Abega, Prosper, 981
Abel, Christopher, 10876
Abel, E. L., 2154, 4612, 11850, 11851
Abel, Peter, 11764
Abele, F., 1325
Abella, Irving, 1005-1007
Abella, Rafael, 8313
Abente, Diego, 7417

Aberg, Rune, 8578
Abeysinghe, Ariya, 11199
Abir, M., 7878
Abitbol, Michel, 25, 6331, 6649, 8773, 10030, 10031
Abiwowo, Abinsola A., 11508
Abog Loko, J., 4361
Abouchar, A., 2268
Abowitz, Deborah A., 1326
Abrabba, S., 8674
Abraham, Arthur, 7904
Abraham, Ascher, 8836
Abraham, C.E.R., 6370, 6371
Abraham, Margaret, 4613
Abraham, Sameer Y., 11388
Abrahams, Roger D., 10338
Abrahamsen, Samuel, 7307, 7308, 7329
Abramov, S. Zalman, 5339
Abramski-Bligh, Irit, 5133, 6331, 8675
Abramsky, Chimen, 8926
Abray, Jane, 2374
Abu Affan, Bodour O., 8508
Abu-Amr, Ziad M., 9790
Abu-El-Assal, Riah, 5343
Abu-El-Haj, Jawdat Ahed, 731
Abu Izzedin, Nejla, 11093
Abu Khalaf, Nader A.M., 5340
Abu-Laban, B., 5345
Abu-Lughod, Ibrahim, 5344, 5345
Abu-Lughod, Janet L., 5346, 5347
Abu Shakrah, Jan, 5341, 5342
Abubabar, Carmen A., 7500
Abucar, Mohmed, 1120

AUTHOR INDEX

Abudu, F., 7197
Abun-Nasr, Jamil M., 10032
Abuso, Julian E., 7501
Abusulayman, Abdul H., 11094
Acer, 3327
Achebe, Chinua, 7198
Acheson, T.W., 1327
Achiezra, A., 5889
Achio, Mayra, 1827
Achyuthan, K.R., 4614
Acker, Alison, 4509, 10877
Acosta Saignes, Miguel, 6487, 9741
Acuña de Chacon, Angela, 1828
Acuña, Rodolfo, 9431
Adam, Heribert, 7951, 7952
Adam, Magda, 1973
Adam, Michel, 11389
Adam, Ruth, 3676
Adamo, Sam C., 732
Adams, Howard, 1174
Adams, Richard, 7048
Adams, Richard H., Jr., 2155, 2156
Adams, Richard N., 4387, 10878
Adamson, Nancy, 1329
Adas, Michael, 11390
Adebola, A.S., 6167
Adelberg, Martyn, 7953
Aditjondro, George J., 5013
Adler, Chaim, 5208
Adler, Jacques, 2375
Adler, Karen, 2376, 10484, 10485
Adler, M., 3677
Adler, T., 8063, 8125
Adler, Winfried, 5896
Adolphe, Robin W., 1330
Adolphs, Lotte, 2782
Adorno, Theodor W., 2783
Adriance, Madelaine, 733
Afigbo, A.E., 7199
Aforka Nweke, G., 7200
Afshar, Haleh, 10035
Aganbegyan, Abel, 8927
Agbon, Solomon G., 7201
Ageron, Charles-Robert, 2377, 2378
Aglietta, Michel, 11391
Aglitzin, L., 11392
Agnelli, Susanna, 11393
Agnew, Vijay, 4615
Agocs, Carol, 1331
Agostini, Eric, 11200

Aguilera Peña, Mario, 1785
Aguilera Peralta, Gabriel, 4388
Aguirre Beltran, Gonzalo, 6488
Agursky, Mikhail, 5209, 8928, 8929
Ahamed Kutty, E.K., 4616
Aharon, Shmuel, 5825
Ahearn, Clare, 655
Ahire, P.T., 7202
Ahlberg, Rene, 8930
Ahlmark, Pen, 8568
Ahmad, Abdussamod H., 2269
Ahmad, Aijaz, 7502
Ahmad, Barakat, 11095
Ahmad, Eqbal, 1, 11394
Ahmad, Feroz, 8788
Ahmad, Syed Nesar, 4617, 4618
Ahmed, Abu I.M.U., 1062
Ahmed-An-Na'lm, Abdullahi, 10036
Ahmed, Emajuddin, 7333
Ahmed, M., 8697
Ahmed, Nahleen, 609
Ahmed, Samira Amin, 8509
Ahmed, Sharma , 3328
Ahmed, Zaheda, 4619
Ahrendt, Christina, 6489
Ahsan, S.A.-al, 8676
Aidoo, Agnes A., 3252
Aigbokhan, B.E., 7203
Aiken, Rebecca B., 1063
Aikio, Pekka, 2366
Aimes, Hubert H.S., 1848
Aimi, A., 5897
Ainsworth, Martha, 6018
Ainsztein, R., 8931, 10486
Aitchison, J. W., 3652, 3653
Aizenberg, Isidoro, 9742, 9743
Ajam, M., 7954
Ajami, Fouad, 11096
Ajayi, J.F. Ade, 7204
Akbari, A.H., 1332
Akelaguelo, A., 2777
Akenson, Donald H., 5170
Akhtar, S., 3329, 3678
Akin Aina, Tade, 7205
Akir, Oki, 5057
Akiwowo, Akinsola, 10037
Akpa, E.K., 6302
Akpan, Monday B., 6303, 6304
Akram-Lodhi, A. Haroon, 8420
Al-Asmar, Fouzi, 5349

Al-Assal, Riah Abu, 5351
Al-Azmeh, Aziz, 6281
Al-Baadi, Howard M., 7880
Al-Faruqi, Lamia, 11097
Al-Haj, Majid, 5349, 5351-5354
Al-Hardallo, Abrahim, 11395
Al-Mismad, Sheikha, 11098
Al-Ostad, Ameer B., 6267
Al-Qazzaz, Ayad, 11956
Al-Sultan, Ali A., 7885
Alachar, A., 11396
Alailima, Patricia J., 8421
Alam, Sultana, 610
Alavi, Hamza, 4620, 7734
Alawiye, J.H., 11099
Alberno-Semerena, José Luis, 6490
Albert, Robert, 2157
Albinski, Henry S., 164, 11201
Albistur, Maité, 2379
Albrecht, Richard, 2784
Albright, Joseph, 5608
Alcala, Angel, 8314
Alcalay, Ammiel, 5356
Alcalde, Carmen, 8315
Alcantara Almanzar, José, 2109
Alcock, Anthony E., 5898, 5899
Alden, Dauril, 734
Alderman, Geoffrey, 165, 3270-3271, 3679
Aldrich, Howard, 3330
Aldrich, Robert, 11202, 11203, 11204
Aleissa, Ibrahim M., 7879
Alestalo, M., 2336
Alexander, Charles C., 9432
Alexander, Christian, 334
Alexander, E., 1121
Alexander, Jennifer, 5014
Alexander, K. C., 4621
Alexander, Paul, 5014, 11397
Alexander, Peter, 3680
Alexander, Stella, 9803
Alexander, Tamar, 5210
Alexeyeva, Ludmilla, 8932
Alexiev, Alex, 9410
Alfieri, Paola, 5900
Alfieri, Vittorio E., 5901
Alfredsson, Gudmundur, 11398
Algazy, Joseph, 2380, 2381
Algini, Maria L., 5902
Algranti, Leila M., 735

Ali, A.K.M. Y., 4622
Ali, Ahmed, 11205
Ali, Ali A.G., 8510
Ali, Ameer, 6372, 8422
Ali, Imran, 4623
Alibhai, Yasmin, 1333, 3331, 3332
Alkire, William H., 11206
Alladina, S., 3333
Allardt, Erik, 10487-10488
Allen, C., 7305
Allen, Calvin H., Jr., 11100
Allen, Charles R., 9433
Allen, David, 217
Allen, Harry, 335
Allen, Paul D., 5082
Allen, Richard B., 6467
Allen, Robert B., 2382
Allen, S., 3681
Allen, W.E.D., 8789, 8933
Allen, W.R., 9523
Alleyne, Mervyn C., 10339
Allison, Caroline, 9947
Allison, J., 7955
Allsobrook, David, 3683
Allworth, Edward A., 8936-8935
Almaguer, Tomas, 9434
Alman, S.B., 11957
Almog, Shmuel, 3272, 10489-10490
Alnasrawi, Abbas, 5357
Alonso, Jorge, 6491
Aloula, Malek, 26
Alpers, Edward A., 10038, 10039
Alschuler, Alfred, 2270
Altbach, Philip G., 7536, 9771
Altimir, O., 93, 10879-10880
Altman, Jon C., 336
Altman, Yochanan, 9221
Altmann, A., 11424
Altner, Günter, 2785
Altschiller, Donald, 11399
Altschuler, Mordechai, 8937-8940
Altstadt, Audrey L., 8942, 8943
Altstadt-Mirhadi, Audrey, 8941
Alubo, S.O., 7206
Alvarez, Sonia E., 736, 10881
Aly, G., 2786, 2787
Alzona, Encarnacion, 7503
Amadi, Adolphe O., 10040
Aman, Reinhold, 166
Amanat, Abbas, 5083

Amare, Girma, 5211
Amat y Léon, Carlos, 7428
Amayo, Gershom N., 2158
Ambedkar, B.R., 4624
Ambert, Alba N., 11400
Ambrosini, G., 5900
Ameringer, Charles D., 1829
Amersfoort, Hans van, 6783, 10491
Amilat, 1854
Amin, Mohammad, 6373
Amin, Samir, 6019, 10041-10042, 11401
Amin, Shahid, 4625
Amipaz-silber, Gitta, 27
Amitay, Yossi, 5359
Amith, Gavin, 7429
Amman, H., 8637
Ammarate, Pablo de, 10492
Ammassari, Paolo, 5903
Amolo, Milcah, 6168
Amondji, Marcel, 6020
Amos, Valerie, 3334
Amouyal, Barbara, 5212
Amtouche, Fadhma A.M., 28
Amun, Hasan, 5362
An-Na'im, Abdullahi A., 11101
An-Na'M, A., 2159
Anabtaw, Samir N., 5363
Anand, Sudhir, 6374
Anand, V.S., 3684
Anant, Suchitra, 11958
Anawati, George C., 2160
Anaya, Jim, 7049
Ancel, Jean, 7787-7790, 7845
Anctil, Pierre, 1008, 1009
Andenaes, J., 7309
Ander Egg, Ezequil, 94
Andereggen, Anton, 2788
Andersen, C., 11402
Anderson, Atholl J., 6913
Anderson, B.A., 8944
Anderson, Benedict, 5015, 7504
Anderson, Christopher, 6914
Anderson, Desmond, 6468
Anderson, Don S., 167
Anderson, Ellen M., 1334
Anderson, J.G., 2090
Anderson, James D., 9435
Anderson, Kay J., 1064, 1065
Anderson, Ken, 2250, 4389
Anderson, Lisa, 6332, 8774

Anderson, Muff, 7956
Anderson, Neil, 7957
Anderson, Richard, 2250
Anderson, Robert D., 3612-3614
Anderson, Rodney D., 6492, 6493
Anderson, Scott, 11403
Andersson, Neil, 6727, 10043
Andiappan, Palaniappan, 1335
Andics, Hellmut, 484
Andorka, Rudolf, 4579
Andors, Phyllis, 1661
Andreades, A., 8790
Andreski, S., 7641, 10493
Andrew, Cristopher M., 11404
Andrews, George R., 95, 737
Andreyev, C., 8945
Andreyev, I.L., 10044
Angenot, Marc, 1010
Angress, Ruth K., 2789
Angress, Werner T., 2790
Anis Kassim, 5855
Anker, Richard, 11405, 11443
Anne Frank Stichting, 2383
Anri Assa, 918
Ansah-Koi, K., 3253
Ansar, Tahir A., 6774
Ansari, Hamried, 2161
Ansbach, Tatjana, 2791
Ansky, Michel, 29
Antler, Steven, 1336
Antonelli, Judith, 2271
Antweiler, Phillip L., 2384, 3654
Anusionwu, E.C., 7207
Anwar, Muhammad, 3686-3687, 10496
Anwar, Raja, 2,
Anweiler, Oskar, 8946
Anyang' Nyong'o P., 6169
Apana, A.B., 4626
Apedaile, L.P., 10045
Appel, John, 9438
Appel, Selma, 9438
Appel, Stephen W., 7962
Applebey, G., 3533
Appleby, Andrew B., 3688
Apps, Eric P., 1337
Aptheker, Herbert, 9439-9442
Aqil, Mahmoud, A., 5364
Arad, Yitzhak, 10497
Arango M., Francisco, 1786
Arasaratnam, S., 8423

AUTHOR INDEX

Araya, M., 2272
Arbim, Kwame, 3254
Arce, Wilfredo, 7505
Archer, John H., 1175
Archer, Leonie, 10989, 11406
Archer, M., 8653
Archibald, Bruce P., 1338
Arendt, Hannah, 11407
Arendt, Hans-Jürgen, 2793
Arens, Moshe, 5367
Arens, Richard, 7419
Arias, Arturo, 4390, 4391
Aribiah, Oberu, 7209
Aricó, José, 10883
Aristide, Jean-Bertrand, 4465
Arkin, A.J., 7963
Arlettaz, Gerald, 8639
Armen, Hartoune K., 6286
Armitage, Peter, 1339
Armogathe, Daniel, 2379
Armon, Teodor, 7791
Armstrong, Bruce, 6032
Armstrong, James C., 7964
Armstrong, John A., 8948, 8949
Armstrong, M.J., 6915
Armstrong, Warwick, 6916
Arnal, Oscar L., 2385
Arnau, J., 8316
Arndt, Ino, 2794
Arner, David, 10884
Arnfeld, Signe, 6680
Arnold, B., 2795
Arnold, David, 4627-4628, 11408, 11843
Arnold, David, 6971
Arnold, Fred, 11102
Arnold, Marigene, 6494
Arnold, W. Vincent, 5904
Arnove, Robert F., 7012
Arnovitz, Benton, 8950
Arns, Paulo Evaristo, 738
Arocha, Jaime, 1797
Aron, Raymond, 2386
Aronsfeld, C.C., 2796-2797, 3273, 3689, 8317-8319, 10498, 10885, 11409
Aronson, Dori, 5368
Aronson, Geoffrey, 5369
Aronson, Gregor, 8951
Aronson, Gregory, 9330

Aronson, I. Michael, 8952
Arrabal, Fernando, 1849
Arrighi, G., 9961
Arriola Woog, Carlos, 6495
Artingstoll, Trevor, 3690
Artinian, Vartan, 8791
Asad Talal, 11410
Asamoa, Anoa, 3255
Asche, Michael, 1176
Ascher, Abraham, 10499
Ascoli, G., 5905
Asgarally, Issa, 6469
Ash, Mitchell G., 2929
Ashbrook, Tom, 1662
Ashby, Jacqueline A., 6775
Ashe, Arthur, Jr., 9443
Ashkenazi, Abraham, 5213, 5370
Ashkenazi, Michael, 5214, 5215
Ashley, M.J., 7965
Ashmore, Robert B., 5371
Ashton, C.P.M., 7393
Ashtor, Eliyahu, 8320
Ashworth, Brandon, 4303
Ashworth, G., 11411, 11412
Asobie, Assisi, 7210
Asp, Erkki, 2337
Asra, Abuzar, 5016
Assad, Maurice, 2162
Assu, Harry, 1177
Aster, Howard, 1035, 1011, 1012, 8953
Asthana, Pratima, 4629
Astroff, Roberta J., 3655
Astrom, Sven-Erik, 2338
Asturias, M. Angel, 4392
Ata, Ibrahim W., 5373
Atanda, J.A., 7211
Atash, Farhad, 5084
Athans, Mary C., 9444
Athnias, Floya, 1967
Atieni-Odhiambi, E.J., 6170, 6171
Atkin, Muriel, 8954
Atkins, Keletso E., 7966
Atkinson, A.B., 3692, 3693, 3694
Atkinson, Alan, 337
Atlas, Yedidya, 5216
Atran, Scott, 5218, 5374
Attal, Robert, 8775, 11959
Attar, K.A-R., 5134
Aubenos-Bastie, Jaqueline, 640
Aubert, Roger, 641

Auerbach, F.E., 7967
Aulestia, Juan A., 2130
Aung-Thwin, Michael, 6702, 6703
Aurora, G.S., 3695
Austen, Ralph A., 10046
Austin, Diane J., 170
Austin, J., 7013
Austin, Roger, 2387
Avedon, John, 1582
Averkieva, I. Pablovna, 9445
Avery, D., 1340
Avery, William P., 10886
Avineri, Shlomo, 7968
Avnery, Uri, 5375
Avni, Jaim, 98, 8321-8322
Avraham, Shmuel, 2300
Awang, A.B.B., 11103
Awatere, Donna, 6917
Awoniji, T.A., 7212
Axelgard, Frederick W., 5135
Ayab, Ahmad Y., 6375
Ayalon, Ami, 2163
Ayalon, Hanna, 5219
Ayandele, E.A., 7213
Aymard, Maurice, 5906, 5907, 6784
Ayoun, Richard, 30
Ayres, Ron, 1967
Azarenko, Jury, 8955
Azariah, M., 4630
Azevedo, Aluisio, 739
Azicri, Max, 1850
Aziz, M.A., 5018
Aziz, Philippe, 2388
Azizah, Kassim, 6376
Azvedo, Mario J., 6681

Ba, Sylvie Washington, 7887
Babchin-Herzenberg, Tatyana, 8956
Baber, Colin, 4457
Babiker, Abdel B.A.G., 8512
Babington, Anthony, 3696
Babu, Yuko, 6033
Bacchus, M.K., 10340
Bacchus, Wilfred A., 740
Bacharach, Jere L., 11104
Bacher, John C., 1341
Bachmaier, Peter, 907
Bachmann, Kurt, 2850
Bachrach, Bernard S., 8323, 10500
Backes, Uwe, 2799-2803

Backes-Gellner, Uschi, 2804
Backles, Hilary McD., 10341
Bacon, Elizabeth E., 8957
Bacon, Gershon C., 12024
Badal, R.K., 8513
Badawi, Z., 3336
Badcock, William T., 1178
Bade, Klaus J., 2805, 2806, 2807
Badian, E., 11413
Badram, Margot, 11105
Baechler, Jean, 10501
Baer, Douglas E., 1342
Baer, Gabriel, 2164, 2165
Baer, Yitzhak, 8324
Baest, Torsten F., 908
Báez Evertsz, Franc, 2110, 4466
Bagadion, Benjamin C., Jr., 7506
Bagdassarin, Greg, 8958
Bah, Khalifah S. el-, 6333
Bahcheli, Tozun, 4362
Bahiri, Simcha, 5220, 5376
Bahl, Vinay, 11414
Bahry, Donna, 8959
Baig, Tara Ali, 4631
Bailey, Clinton, 6158
Bailey, L.R., 9446
Bailey, Susan F., 3697
Bains, H.S., 3779
Baiocchi, Mari de Nasare, 741
Bairagi, R., 611
Bajohr, Frank, 3107
Bajumid, Ibrahim A., 6377
Bakan, Abigal B., 10342
Baker, Ahmed M., 5377-5378
Baker, C., 3656
Baker, D. P., 2808
Baker, David B., 9447
Baker, Donald G., 288, 6941, 1156
Baker, Janice, 8960
Baker, Julie J., 7969
Baker, Marilyn, 1179
Baker, Nick, 3337
Baker, Stephanie, 1974
Baker, William J., 10164
Bakhash, Shaul, 5085, 5086, 5087
Bakir, Abd el-Mohson, 11852
Bakker, A.M. van der, 6785
Bakker, H., 5019
Bakker, Isabella, 1343
Bakri, Muhammad, 5379

Bakvis, Herman, 6786
Balachandran, G., 4632
Balamoan, G. Ayoub, 8514
Balasubramanuam, V.N., 4633
Balb, Florence, 7430
Baldouf, R.B. Jr., 455
Baldry, H.C., 11853
Balic, Smail, 10502
Balinska, Maria, 2389-2390, 3698-3699
Ball, Stephen J., 8569, 8598, 8630
Ball, W.R., 8757
Ballara, Angela, 6918
Ballard, A.B., 9448
Ballard, K.D., 6925
Ballhatchet, Kenneth, 4634
Ballon Aguirre, Francisco, 7431
Ballou, Patricia K., 11960
Balogh, Eva S., 4515
Balsdon, John P.V., 11854
Balzer, M., 8961
Bamberger, Ib Nathan, 2079, 2080
Bamford, Calire, 3802
Bamgbose, Ayo, 7214
Banac, I., 10503
Banaji, D.R., 4635
Banas, Josef, 7642
Bandarage, Asoka, 8424
Bandler, Kenneth, 5380, 5381
Bandyopadhyay, Sekhar, 4636
Baneijee, A.C., 4637
Banerjee, B. 4638
Banerjee, H. N., 4639
Banerjee, Nirmala, 4640
Banerjee, Sanjoy, 4641
Banerjee, Sumanta, 4642
Bankiers, David, 2809
Banting, Keith, 1344
Banton, Michael, 3700, 3701, 9449, 10504
Banuazizi, Ali, 11961
Banuri, Tariq, 10887
Bar, Luc-Henri de, 6282
Bar-On, Mordechai, 5221, 5382
Barakat, Halim, 6283
Baramki, Gabi, 5383
Baranski, Zygmunt G., 5908
Barash, Liora, 5384
Barbara, Susan B., 173
Barbe, Dominique, 742
Barber, Malcolm, 10505

Barber, P., 10506
Barber, Sarah, 3517
Barbosa, Luiz C., 743
Barbour, Violet, 6787
Barbu, Zev, 7792
Bard, Mitchell, 5222
Bardakjian, Kevork B., 8792
Bardham, Pranab, 4643, 4644
Bare, Ilana De, 7028
Barfuss, Karl M., 2810
Barhan, P.K., 10328
Barie, Ottavio, 2273
Barillas, Edgar, 4393
Barkai, Abraham, 2811
Barkat, Anwar, 7970
Barker, F., 5173
Barker, M., 3702
Barker, Ralph, 6788
Barker, Thomas M., 486,487
Barkin, Kenneth, 2812
Barlett, Richard H., 1180
Barlow, Edna, 7971
Barman, Jean, 1181, 1182
Barnard, Henry, 11962
Barnard, Patrick, 10507
Barnes, Ian R., 2391, 2392
Barnet, Richard J., 1,
Barnett, Don S., 5223
Barnett, John, 3703
Barney, Louis, 4516
Barnouw, Dagmar, 2813
Baron, A.M., 6650
Baron, Alan A., 4394
Baron, Harold M., 9450
Baron, Salo W., 8677, 8962, 11062
Barontine, C., 2393
Barou, Pierre, 2394
Barouh, Ida S., 2395
Barreda, Pedro, 1851
Barreiro, José, 7050, 7051
Barrera Bassols, Dalia, 6496
Barrera, Mario, 1622, 9451
Barreto, M.A., 4430
Barrett, Michele, 3704
Barrett, Stanley R., 1013, 1183, 1345, 1346
Barringer, Felicity, 8963
Barringer, H.R., 6230
Barrington, J.M., 6919, 6920
Barrios de Chungara, Domitila, 702

AUTHOR INDEX

Barron, R.D., 3705
Barros, Robert, 10888
Barrow, Christine, 10343
Barrow, Jocelyn, 3392
Barrow, Reginald H., 11855
Barrows, Carl P., 6305
Barry, Kathleen, 11415
Barry, Tom, 10889
Bärsch, Claus-E., 2814
Barsh, Russel L., 11416, 11417
Barta, Tony, 338
Bartels, Dennis A., 4444-4446
Bartels, Dieter, 6789
Barthe, Marie-Annick, 2396
Barthelemy, Anthony S., 3338
Bartlett, B.R., 10047
Bartlett, Eleanor A., 1347
Bartley, Russell H., 10688
Bartolome, Miguel A., 99
Bartoszewski, Wladyslaw, 7643
Bartov, Owen, 2815
Baruah, Sanjib, 4645, 4646
Baruffati, V., 11034
Barz, R.K., 6470
Basanez, Miguel, 6497
Basavarajappa, K.G., 1066
Basberg, Bjorn, 7319
Basgoz, Ilhan, 10508
Basham, Richard D., 6378
Bashir, Ibrahim L., 7215
Bashour, Munir, 6284
Basisu, Mu'in, 5385
Baske, Siegfried, 7644
Basran, G.S., 1348
Bass, James D., 8889
Bassin, Mark, 8964
Bastenier, Albert, 642, 643
Bastide, Roger, 744
Bastomsky, S.J., 11856
Basu, Alaka, 4647
Basurto, Jorge, 6498
Batalla, G.B., 10890
Batatu, Hanna, 5136, 8678
Bates, Eric, 7052
Bathily, Abdoulaye, 7888
Batra, Roger, 6499
Batta, L.D., 3422
Battersby, John D., 7972
Baubock, Rainer, 488
Bauer, Arnold J., 10891

Bauer, Yehuda, 10509, 10510, 11418
Baum, Karl, 1975
Baum, R. C., 489
Bauman, Zygmunt, 7645, 10511, 10512
Baumann, Robert F., 8965
Baumgart, Marion, 11106
Baureiss, Gunter, 1067
Bauschinger, Sigrid, 2959
Bavnick, Maarten, 8425
Bawden, Charles R., 6636
Bax, Erik, H., 6790
Baxendale, Michael S., 1253
Baxter, Carol, 3706
Baxter, David, 3706
Baxter, J. H. , 174
Bay, Edna G., 10048
Bayer, Ronald, 9452
Baylies, Carolyn, 10049
Baylson, Joshua C., 11107
Bayly, C.A., 4648-4651
Bayly, Susan, 4652
Bayme, Steven Gilbert, 3274
Bayoudh, Edma, 6285
Beach, D.N., 9962
Beach, H., 10513
Beach, Hugh, 8570
Beachey, R.W., 10050
Beaglehole, T.H., 6919
Bearden, Jim, 1122
Beardsley, S.H., 11857
Bearfield, Lev, 5386, 5387
Bearman, Jonathan, 6334
Beattie, Helen P., 7507
Beaucage, P., 4510
Beauclerk, John, 7432
Beaud, Paul, 2397
Beaude, H., 1306
Beaudry, Lucille, 8966
Beaumont, J., 4447
Beauvilain, Alain, 982
Beauvoir, Simone de, 11419
Bebb, Phillip N., 10861
Bébel-Gisler, Dany, 10344
Beck, Lois G., 11108, 11109
Beck, Norman A., 11420
Becker, Eduard, 8967
Becker, George, 11421
Becker, Jean-Jacques, 2398
Becker, Jorg, 2816, 2817
Becker, Josef, 3161

Beckett, J. V., 3707
Beckett, Jeremy R., 339
Beckles, Hilary McD., 10345, 10346
Beckman, Evelyn T., 2818
Beckmann, Klaus-Martin, 2785
Beckwith, Christopher I., 1583
Bedein, David S., 5224
Bedford, Judith B., 1349
Bedggood, David, 6921
Bedri, N.S., 8515
Bee, M., 3708
Beek, Sam, 7793
Beeman, Mark A., 6379
Beeman, William O., 5088
Beer, William R., 2399, 2400
Beetham, David, 11422
Beezley, William H., 6500
Begag, Azouz, 2401
Begum, S., 612
Behlmer, George K., 3709
Behnken, Renate, 2819
Behr, A.L., 7973, 7974
Behrman, J. R., 7014, 10892
Beier, A.L., 3710
Bein, Alex, 11423, 11424
Beinart, William, 7975
Beinin, Joel, 2166, 5225, 5388
Beit-Hallahmi, Benjamin, 5226
Beit-Ishoo, B., 5165
Bejar Navarro, R., 6501
Bejarano, Jesús A., 1787
Bejarano, Margalit, 1852, 1853, 1854
Bejin, A., 2402, 2741
Beker, Avi, 9303
Belbahri, Abdelkader, 2403
Belfer, Ella, 5227
Belguendouz, Abdelkrim, 6651
Belich, James, 6922, 6923
Beljo, Ante, 9804
Belkin, June S., 10200
Belkindas, M.V., 8968
Bell, Andrew, 3721, 10514, 10642
Bell, D., 340
Bell, Derrick A., Jr., 9453, 9454
Bell, Donald H., 5909, 5910
Bell, Howard H., 10347
Bell, J.H., 175
Bell, Raley H., 10515
Bellagamba, A., 10051
Bellamy, Joan, 3711

Bellardi, Marta, 100
Bellen, Heinz, 11858
Beller, Jacob, 10893
Beller, Steven, 490
Belli, Mihri, 8793
Bellon, Cynthia, 7976
Bellos, Susan, 5389
Beloff, Nora, 9805
Belorgey, Jean-Michel, 2404
Belotti, Elena Gianini, 11425
Belstserkovsky, Vadin, 8969
Ben-Aharon, Yitzak, 5391
Ben-Dror, Graciela, 101
Ben, Eyal, 909
Ben-Ezer, G., 5229
Ben, Gershom E., 2821
Ben Jelloun, Tahar, 2405
Ben, Joseph, 4363
Ben-Porat, Amir, 5230, 5231
Ben-Porath, Yoram, 5232, 5390
Ben Shaul, D'vora, 5228
Ben-Tovim, Gideon, 3712-3714, 9539
Ben-Yakov, Avraham, 910
Ben-Yehuda, Nachman, 5233
Ben-Zadok, Efraim, 5260
Ben-Zvi, Itzhak, 11110
Benard, Cheryl, 491
Bendelow, Paul, 2822
Bender, B., 6924
Bender, Gerald J., 80
Benedikter, Rudolf, 5911
Benedrit, B., 6471
Beneria, Lourdes, 6502
Benewick, Robert, 11426
Bengelsdorf, Carollee, 1855
Benguigul, Georges, 11207
Benhassine, M.L., 31
Benitez, Fernando, 6503
Benjamin, A., 5392
Benjamin, Jesse, 5393
Bennani, Boubker, 6652
Bennell, Paul, 3257
Bennett, Anne McGrew, 11427
Bennett, Judith A., 11208
Bennett, Norman R., 10052
Bennett, Scott C., 341
Bennigsen, Alexandre, 8970, 8971
Bennoune, Mahfoud, 32, 33, 6458-6459
Benoist, Joseph-Roger de, 8516
Bensa, Alban, 11209

BenShaul, D'vora, 5237
Bensimon, Doris, 2406, 2407
Benson, John , 3490, 3715
Benson, Linda, 1584
Benthan, G., 3491
Bentil, J. Kodmo, 10516
Bentwich, N., 8325
Benvenisti, Eyal, 5394
Benvenisti, Meron, 5235-5236, 5395-5407
Benvenisty, David, 911, 912
Benyon, John , 3716
Benziger, Marguerite M., 492
Berat, Lynn, 6728
Berberoglu, B., 8794, 11428
Bercuson, David Jay, 1014
Bercusson, Brian, 3717
Berend, Ivan R., 4517
Berentsen, William H., 2823
Beres, Louis R., 11429
Berg, Wilfried, 10053
Bergad, Laird W., 1856
Bergen, Barry H., 2408
Berger, Elena L., 9963
Berger, Iris, 10242
Berger, John, 10517
Berghahn, Volker R., 2824, 3718, 9455
Bergiust, Charles, 10894
Bergman, Arlene E., 1857
Bergman, Shlomo, 11430
Bergmann, Emilie, 10895
Bergmann, Werner, 2825
Bergson, Abram, 8972
Berhrman, J.R., 4653
Bering, Dietz, 2826
Berk, Stephen M., 8973
Berkeley, Bill, 6306
Berkin, A. G. K., 2827
Berkman, Joyce A., 7977
Berlanstein, Lenard R., 2409
Berlin, Ira, 9456, 9457
Berlowitz, Marvin, J., 9458
Berman, Aaron, 9459
Berman, Edward H., 10054
Berman, Myron, 9460
Berman, Paul, 7015
Berman, Peter, 5021
Berman, Sanford, 9461
Bermann, Karl, 7016
Bermudez, Fernando, 4395

Bernad, Miguel A., 7508
Bernadac, Christian, 10518
Bernal, Martin, 11859, 11860
Bernard, Claude, 10055
Bernard, L. Faber, 2025
Bernard, Rene, 2410
Bernardini, Gene, 5912
Bernat, Tivadar , 4518
Berndt, Ronald M., 342
Berneriá, Lourdes, 8326
Berney, Louis, 1976
Bernhard, Virginia, 10348
Bernstein, Deborah, 5238
Bernstein, Irving, 5239
Bernstein, Richard, 2411, 2412
Berov, Ljudben, 10519
Berridge, Virginia, 3339
Berrol, Selma C., 9462
Berry, A., 1788
Berry, Albert, 7509, 10896, 11431
Berssinger, Mark, 9092
Berstein, S., 2398
Bertelsmann, Klaus, 3108
Bertley, Leo W., 1123
Bertrand, Marc, 2728
Beshir, M. O., 8517
Besikci, Ismail, 8795
Besson, J., 10349
Besson, W., 10349
Bestor, Jane F., 5089
Betancourt Bencomo, Juan Rene, 1858, 1859, 1860, 1861
Betarces Medina, Emelio K., 2111
Betcherman, Lita-Rose, 1015
Beteille, Andre, 4654
Bethell, Leslie, 11001
Bethune, N., 6925
Bettelheim, Charles, 1664
Betts, Raymond F., 2413, 11432
Betz, Hans-Georg, 2828, 2829
Beyan, Amos J., 6307
Beyer, Lisa, 2414
Beyerchen, A. D., 2830
Beyhaut, Gustavo, 10897
Beyme, Klaus von, 10520
Bezalel, Itzhak, 8796
Bezirgan, Basima, 11125
Bhachu, Parminder, 3340-3341, 3393
Bhadra, B.K., 4655
Bhagavan, M.R., 81, 4656

Bhagwati, J. N., 2831
Bhana, S., 7978
Bharti, I., 4657
Bhaskar, Manu, 4658
Bhat, Ashok, 3342
Bhattacharya, S., 4659
Bhebe, N., 10215
Bhola, Harbrams S., 11433
Bianco, Janis R., 745
Biarnes, Jean, 2415
Biberaj, Elez, 15, 9806
Bibin, Thomas, 8436
Bickenbach, Jerome E., 1350
Bickerton, James, 1351
Biddick, T.V., 11210
Biddiss, Michael D., 10521
Biderman, Jaime, 7017
Bidouze, Henriette, 2416
Bidwell, Robin, 6653, 9791
Bidwell, Sydney, J., 3719
Bielasiak, Jack, 7647
Bienvenue, Rita M., 1307
Bier, Jean-Paul, 2832
Bierck, Harold A., Jr., 1789
Biesanz, John, 7363
Biezunska-Malowist, Iza, 11861
Biffot, Laurent, 2778
Big Flame, 3720
Bigelow, Poultney, 8974
Bigler, Robert M., 4519
Bigsten, Arne, 6172, 6173, 6174
Bihl, Wolfdieter, 8975
Biko, Steve, 7979
Biles, D., 343
Bilinsky, Yaroslav, 8976, 8977
Billig, Michael, 3721-3722, 11434-11436
Billigmeier, Robert H., 8640
Bills, David B., 746
Bills, Scott L., 11437
Bilquees, F., 7335
Bilu, Yoram, 5408
Bin-Sallik, Mary Ann, 344
Bindels, J.G., 10333
Binder, David, 913, 9807, 10522
Binder-Wehberg, Friedelind, 2833
Bingham, Marjorie W., 10056
Binney, Judith, 6926
Binsbergen, Wim van, 10057
Binur, Yusuf K., 5409

Birbalsingh, Frank, 10350
Birch, Julian, 8978, 8979
Birdsell, Nancy, 747
Birkas, Maria, 4520
Birkbeck, Rosie, 2274
Birnbaum, Henrik, 8980
Birnbaum, Lucia C., 5913
Birnbaum, Norman, 1585
Birrell, R., 176
Bisharat, Carol, 5411
Bisharat, George E., 5412, 5413
Biskup, Peter, 345, 346, 347
Bister, Feliks J., 493
Bitton, Livia, 4521
Bix, Herbert, 1665
Bjerke, Kjeld, 2081
Bjorkman, J.W., 11438
Bjorling, Joel, 11964
Bjornsons, Richard, 10209
Black, George, 1862, 4396
Black, George F., 11965
Black, Ian, 5414
Black, Isabella, 9463
Black, John, 3723
Black, Naomi, 11439
Blackaby, D.H., 3724
Blackbeney, Michael, 177
Blackbourn, David, 2834, 10523
Blackburn, Alan, 6927
Blackburn, Gilmer W., 2835
Blackman, Trin, 3534
Blackmore, Jillian A., 178
Blaha, Jaroslav, 10524
Blair, Susan K., 8797
Blaise, Clark, 4660
Blakely, Allison, 8981
Blanco, Hugo, 7433
Bland-Spitz, Daniela, 8982
Blank, Stephen J., 8983-8985
Blaschke, Jochen, 10525
Blasius, J., 7662
Blassingame, John W., 9464
Blau, D.M., 7018
Blaupain, Roger, 645
Blaut, J.M., 11440
Blecher, Marc, 1666, 1667
Bleich, Anet, 6791
Blench, Roger, 7216
Blérald, Alain-Philippe, 10351, 10352
Blewett, Neal, 3725

AUTHOR INDEX

Blick, Jeffrey P., 11441
Blin, Louis, 34
Blinkhorn, Martin, 11442
Blit, Lucjan, 7648
Bloch, Andrzei J., 7649
Bloch, H., 7981
Bloch, Marc, 10526, 10527
Bloch-Michel, Jean, 2417
Blom, J.C.H., 6792
Blossfeld, H.P., 3182
Blum, A., 8986
Blum, Howard, 9465
Blum, Jakub, 8987
Blum, Leonor, 102, 1863
Blume, H.S.B., 3275
Blusse, L., 6237
Blust, Robert, 6380
Blythe, Martin J., 6928
Boada, H., 8316
Boahen, A. Adu, 10058, 10059
Boas, Jacob H., 6793
Boase, Roger, 10528
Boast, R.P., 348
Bobango, Gerald J., 7794
Bobinska, Celina, 7650
Bocca, Giorgio, 5914
Bociwrkiw, Bohdan R., 8988
Bock, Gisela, 2836
Bodea, Cornelia, 7795
Boder, Menachem, 1977
Bodrova, V., 11443
Boesjes-Ho, R.W., 6785
Boff, Leonardo, 10898
Bogonko, S.N., 6175
Bogues, Tony, 3346, 10353
Bohac, Rodney, 8989
Bohdanowicz, L., 7651
Bohlen, Celestine, 10529
Boia, Lucian, 7796
Boilieu, Anna Maria, 10566
Boissevain, J., 6794, 10850
Boisvert, Collette C., 2418
Boisvert, David, 1184
Boivin, Michelle, 1352
Bojcun, Jaromyr M., 8990
Boje, Per, 2082, 8571
Bolaria, B.Singh, 1353
Bolchover, R.L., 3276
Boldt, Menno, 1185, 1247
Bolge, Exkart, 7127

Bolin-Hoit, Per, 3727
Bolland, O. Nigel, 689, 690
Bolle, Pierre, 2419
Bollen, Kenneth A., 11444
Bollig, Michael, 6176
Bolton, Ralph, 6657
Bomer, F., 11862
Bonaparte, T.H., 6308
Bonat, Z.A., 7217
Bond, Horace Mann, 3481, 9466-9467
Bond-Stewart, Kathy, 9964
Bondyova, J., 1978
Bone, David, S., 6359
Bongie, Christopher L., 11445
Bongonki, S.N., 6177
Bonilla, F., 9483
Bonner, Arthur, 4661
Bonner, Elena, 8991
Bonner, Philip, 7982
Bonner, Raymond, 7434
Bonnett, A., 3728
Boogaart, Ernst van den, 6795
Booh, Jacques-Roger, 6729
Booker, Roger, 3729
Bookmiller, Robrt J., 5241
Boon, H., 6831
Boone, C., 7889
Boonzaier, E.A., 8218
Boorstein, Edward, 9468
Booth, Alan D., 11863
Booth, Anne, 5022
Booth, David, 1864
Booth, H., 2837
Booth, John A., 10899
Borah, Woodrow, 6504, 6505
Borale, P.T., 4662
Borchsensius, Paul, 2083
Bordewich, Fergus M., 5090
Borge, Tomas, 7053-7055, 7102
Borhon, Guillermo Sanchez, 7376
Bornstein, Stephen, 10530
Borooah, V.K., 3730
Borruso, Paolo, 10060
Borsody, Stephen, 1999, 2075, 4522, 7852, 9857, 10839
Borwicz, Michel, 7652
Bory, Valerie, 8641
Borys, Jury, 8992
Bosanguet, N., 3731, 3811
Boscardin, Lucio, 8642

Bose, Nemai S., 4663
Boshyk, Yury, 494, 1187, 8993, 9112
Boskin, Joseph, 9469, 9470
Boskoff, A., 6067
Bossen, Laurel, 4397
Boston, Thomas B., 9471
Boteni, Viorica, 7797
Botman, Selma, 2167, 2168
Botte, Roger, 7870
Bottos, Dino, 1188
Bottourley, Gill, 179
Botz, Gerhard, 495,496
Boucaud, Andre, 6704
Boucaud, Louis, 6704
Bouchair, Noureddine, 8679
Boucher, Jerry, 1649, 3481, 6915, 7515, 8423, 11295, 11446
Boucher, Michel, 1308
Boudewijn, Surie, 6783
Bouillon, Antoine, 6350
Boulding, Elise, 11447
Boulle, Pierre, 2420
Boulot, Serge, 2421
Boulvert, Gérard, 11864
Bouma, Cees, 7336
Bourdeaux, Michael, 8994
Bourdieu, Pierre, 35
Bourdillon, M.F.C., 9965
Bourgeault, Ron, 1189
Bourgeois, Donald J., 1190
Bourgois, Philippe, 7056-7060
Bourne, Jenny, 3732, 3732
Bourque, Susan C., 7435
Bourret, Jean-Françoise, 8995
Boutilier, J.A., 11211
Bovenkerk, Frank, 6796, 10531
Bowen, Huw V., 4664, 11448
Bowen, Kurt, 5171
Bower, Tom, 2422, 2838
Bowers, Stephen R., 16
Bowes, A.M., 3615-3616
Bowling, B., 3733
Bowman, Steven B., 4364-4366
Bowser, Benjamin P., 9724
Bowser, Frederick P., 7436
Boxer, Charles R., 7770, 7771, 10061
Boyadjjieff, Christo, 914
Boyajian, Dickran H., 8798
Boyce, Robert, 3734
Boyd, Derick, 10354

Boyd, Herb, 1124
Boyd, Mary, 6929
Boyd-Bourman, Peter, 6506
Boyer, George R., 3735
Boyer, Jefferson C., 4511
Boyer, John W., 497
Boyns, T., 3657
Boyzon-Fradet, Danielle, 2421
Bozarslan, Hamit, 8799
Bozhinov, Voin, 915
Bozzoli, Belinda, 7983, 7984
Braam, G.P.A., 6822
Bracey, John, 9472
Brachmann, Hans-Jürgen, 2839
Brack, Gene M., 6507
Brackman, Rowan S., 8996
Bradbury, Bruce, 180
Braddock, J.H., 9473
Bradley, Barbara, 7437
Bradley, Carol, 349
Bradley, David, 8572
Bradley, Joseph, 8997
Bradley, K. R., 11865, 11866
Bradlow, Frank R., 7985
Bradshaw, Jan, 6806
Bradsher, Henry S., 3,
Brady, Ciaran, 5172
Brady, Robert L., 6508, 6509
Braeckman, C., 646
Braga, Michael, 10532
Braganca, Aquino de, 6682
Braginsky, M.I., 10062
Braham, P., 3347
Braham, R.L., 3123, 4523-4524, 4571, 7798, 6087, 10533, 11449, 11966
Braithwaite, Stanley N., 10900
Brake, Mike, 3736
Brakelmann, Gunter, 11450
Bramble, Linda, 1125
Bramwell, Anna C., 494, 10598
Brand, Jack A., 3617
Brand, Laurie A., 11111
Brandt, Joseph C., 8998
Brankack, Jan, 2840
Braslavsky, Cecilia, 103,104
Brass, Paul, 4665
Brathwaite, Edward, 10355
Bratton, J. S., 3737
Braude, Benjamin, 8818
Braun, Jerry, 7708

Braun, Sidney D., 36
Bray, D., 6930
Bray, M., 10063, 11451
Breen, Richard, 3739, 3740
Breezer, A., 3702
Brehmer, Ilse , 2841
Breitman, Richard, 9474, 10534
Breman, Jan, 4666, 4667
Bremer, Thomas, 10535
Brennan, Martin, 6381
Brennan, Tim, 3741, 11452
Brenner, Lenni, 9475
Brenner, Rachel F., 1016
Brereton, Bridget, 10356
Bresnan, John, 7505
Bresser Pereira, Luiz, 748
Bretania-Shafer, Nerissa, 11212
Breton, Raymond, 1354
Brett, Michael, 37
Brewer, John D., 3277, 3742
Brewer, R.J., 3743
Brewster, Jennifer, 977
Breyer, Richard, 7653
Briceño Perozo, Mario, 9744
Bricknell, Nancy J., 7394
Bridenthal, Renate, 3082, 10536
Bridges, Lee, 3492
Briey, Philippe de, 647
Brilliant, Joshua, 5580
Brillon, Yves, 10064
Brink, Jean R., 10537
Brinkley, Joel, 5416
Brinkman, Ronald J., 10065
Brinkmen, J.A., 11867
Brinner, William H., 5417, 5418
Bristow, A.P., 7986
Brito Figueroa, Federico, 9745
Britschgi-Schimmer, I., 2842
Brittain, Victoria, 8890
Brizan, George, 10357
Broadfoot, Barry, 1068
Broadfoot, P., 3744
Brock, Colin , 2423, 3349, 3556, 6846, 6979, 10358, 10473, 11453
Brockett, Charles D., 10901
Brockmeyer, Nobert, 11868, 11967
Broddason, Thorbjorn, 4603
Brodersen, Soren, 2081
Brodie, Janine, 1355
Brodribb, Somer, 1191

Brokensha, David, 10066
Bromley, Julianj, 8999
Brooke, James, 105, 2131, 2275, 7218, 9746, 10902
Brookes, E.H., 7987
Brookman, Alison, 380
Brooks, David C., 7061
Broome, Richard, 350
Brosman, Peter, 6931
Bross, Paul, 652
Broszat, Martin, 9838
Broune, Dallas L., 6178
Brourberg, E.J., 3658
Brousek, Karl M., 498
Brown, Andrew, 3746, 3750
Brown, C.V., 3747
Brown, Carolyn A., 7219
Brown, Colin, 3748, 3749
Brown, D., 10295
Brown, David, 3258, 9476
Brown, Elaine C., 7510
Brown, Ian, 10296
Brown, Jennifer S. H., 1266
Brown, Judith E., 9919
Brown, Kevin M., 351, 3750
Brown, Malcolm, 3278
Brown, Michael, 1017
Brown, Paul, 11454
Brown, Richard C., 9919
Brown, Ross, 7310, 7311
Brown, Susan E., 1790, 2112
Browne, Christopher, 11213
Brownfeld, Allan, 11455
Browning, Christopher R., 9808, 9809
Brownlow, William R.B., 10538
Brubaker, W.R., 2424, 2843
Brucan, Silviu, 9000
Bruchis, Michael, 9001
Brudnoy, David, 6231
Bruegel, Irene, 3751
Bruening, William H., 9477
Bruinessen, Martin van, 5091-5093, 5137, 8800
Bruleaux, Anne-Marie, 10903
Brumbaugh, Charles S., 1830
Brumberg, Abraham, 7654, 7654
Brumberg, Stephen F., 9478
Brumby, E., 385
Brumlich, Micha , 2844
Bruneau, Michel, 8734

Brunschvig, N., 11112
Brunt, P.A., 11869, 11870
Brustein, William, 648, 2425, 5915
Bryan, Beverley, 3350
Bryan, Gordon, 11968
Bryan Keon-Cohen, 391
Bryce, Jennifer W., 6286
Bryceson, Deborah F., 8698
Brydon, L., 11456
Brym, Robert J., 1356-1358
Bryn, R.J., 1336
Bryson, Lois, 181
Bryson, Philip J., 2845
Bucek, Josef, 512
Buch-Hanson, M., 6179
Buchanan, Anne, 6932
Buchanan, George, 6034
Buchanan, Keith, 3752, 6180
Buchheim, Christoph, 10539
Buchignani, Norman, 1359, 1360
Buckley, Ken, 182, 224, 322, 323
Buckley, Roger Norman, 10359
Buddingh, Hans, 8555
Budeiri, Musa, 5419
Budiardjo, Carmel, 5023
Buechler, Hans Christian, 10631
Buechler, Judith Maria, 2394, 2418, 3246, 10631
Buenaventura-Posso, Elisa, 1790
Buendia, Manuel, 6510
Bueno, Salvador, 1865
Bueso, Julio A., 4512
Buettner, Thea, 10067
Bugayenko, Yevgeni, 9002
Buger, Julian, 11457
Buhrig, Marga, 8643
Bulhan, H.A., 7943
Bullen, John, 1361
Bullivant, Brian M., 11214
Bullock, Bradley P., 11458
Bullock, Charles S., III, 9479, 9480
Bullwinkle, Davis A., 11969, 11970
Bulmer, Thomas, 10904
Bulnes A., Gonzalo, 1547
Bundy, Colin, 7988
Bunheang Ung, 964
Bunker, Stephen G., 749
Bunleigh, ELizabeth, 4398
Bunyan, Tony, 3753
Bunzl, John, 499, 500, 11459

Burawoy, M., 7989
Burchell, D.E., 7990
Burchival, L.G., 8515
Burder, Dieter A., 501
Burford, Alison, 11871
Burg, Steven L., 9810
Burger, Angela S., 8426
Burger, Julian, 352
Burke, A., 3473
Burke, B. Meredith, 6035
Burkhauser, Richard V., 7364
Burkshardt, William R., 6036
Burleigh, Michael, 2846
Burman, Sandra, 7991, 8240
Burn, Barbara B., 11460
Burn, W.L., 10360
Burnett, John, 3493, 11971
Burns, E. Bradford, 10905
Burns, Haywood, 9481
Burns, John F., 1126, 1668
Burns, Michael, 10540
Burpee, C. Gaye, 10361
Burrell, Leon F., 1362
Burrian, Peter, 502
Burrowes, Carl P., 6309
Burrowes, Robert D., 9792
Burrows, Noreen, 10769
Burston, Bradley, 9003
Burstyn, Joan N., 3754
Burt, R.A., 3755
Burton, Antoinette M., 4668
Burton, Margaret Ernestine, 1669
Burton, Sandra, 7992
Burtonwood, Neil, 3756
Buruma, Ian, 7511
Buscher, Frank M., 2847
Bush, Barbara, 10362, 10363
Bush, Rod, 1942
Busi, Frederick, 2426, 2427
Bussard, Robert L., 11461
Buszko, Jozef, 2848
Butcher, John G., 6382
Butcher, P., 9482
Butler, Judy, 7062
Butler, Linda Jean, 1122
Butlin, N.G., 183, 353
Butterfield, Fox, 1586
Buvinic, Mayra, 11972
Buvollen, Hans P., 7063
Bwengye, F.A.W., 8891

Byock, Jesse L., 4604
Byram, Michael, 2084, 2103
Byrne, Pamela R., 11973
Byrnes, Robert F., 2428
Byrt, Neville, 11215

Cabort-Masson, Guy, 10364
Cabot, J.M., 7799
Caciagli, Mario, 5916
Cadzow, John F., 4525, 7800
Caffaz, Ugo, 5917
Cage, R.A. , 3618
Cahen, Michel, 6683
Cahndra, Bipan, 4669
Cahnmann, W.J., 6067, 11462
Caicedo, Edgar, 1791
Cain, P.J., 3757, 3758
Cainkar, Louise, 5420, 5421, 5797
Cairns, Edmund, 3535-3538, 3571, 3602, 3607
Cala, Alina, 7655
Calderon, Manuel, 7064
Calderwood, William, 1363, 1364, 1365
Caldwell, Gary, 1309
Caldwell, J. C., 4670
Caldwell, Malcolm, 6373
Callan, T., 5191
Callaway, Helen, 7220
Callinicos, Alex, 3619, 3759, 11872
Calliste, Agnes, 1127, 1128
Calman, Leslie J., 4671, 4672
Calvert, Hildegund M., 2849
Cámara Villar, Gregoria, 8327
Cambranes, J.C., 4399
Camejo, Acton, 10365
Cameron, M., 7993
Camiller, Patrick, 8328
Campbell, Gwyn, 6351, 6684, 10068
Campbell, J.C., 11216, 11217
Campbell, Judy, 354
Campbell, Kurt, 9004
Campbell, Leon G., 7438
Campbell, Mavis C., 10366
Campbell, Mike, 3761
Campbell, Persia C., 11463
Campbell, Tom , 3762
Campeanu, Pavel, 9005
Campion, Joan, 1979
Campos, R., 9483
Canagaretna, Sugit M., 8428

Candau, Pierre, 1310
Candea, Virgil, 7795
Canepa, Andrew M., 5918
Canestrini, Sandro, 5919
Cannon, Terry, 1866
Canny, Nicolas, 11464
Cantan, M. Maurice, 2429
Cantas, M., 7512
Cantú Corro, José, 6511
Caoili, Manuel A., 7513
Capel Martinez, Roza Maria, 8329
Caplan, Neil, 5422
Caploe, David, 11113
Caprile, Jean, 1539
Caputo, G., 5920
Caraffe, Marc de, 1311, 1312
Carboni, Carlo, 5921, 5922, 11465
Cardinal, Linda, 2430
Cardoso, Ciro F.S., 6512
Cardoso, Fernando H., 10906
Cardoso, Gerald, 750
Carew, Jan, 10367
Carey, Iskandar, 6383
Carey, Miriam R., 1193
Carey, Sean, 3352, 3353, 4106
Cargas, Harry J., 11975
Carino, Theresa, 7514
Carlebach, Emil, 2850
Carlin, Norah, 5173, 11873, 11874
Carlisle, Donald S., 9006
Carlsen, Laura, 6513
Carlson, Marifran, 106
Carmack, R., 4400
Carmi, Shulamit, 5242
Carmichael, Kay, 3354
Carneado, José F., 1867
Carneiro, Maria L.T., 751
Carney, Robert, 1368
Carnoy, Martin, 11466
Caro Baroja, Julio, 8330, 8331
Caroe, Olaf, 9007
Carpenter, Dwayne E., 8332
Carpi, D., 4367, 5923, 5969, 9811
Carpinelli, Giovanni, 649, 650
Carr, Barry, 6514
Carr, David W., 6460
Carr-Hill, Ray A., 2431
Carrasco, Rosalba, 6515
Carreira, Antonio, 1535
Carrera, Nicolás, 107

Carrere d'Encausse, Helene, 9008, 9009
Carrigan, Ann, 7065
Carrington, Bruce, 3355, 3356, 3764
Carroll, Patrick J., 6516
Carroll, William K., 1369-1372
Carson, Penelope, 4673
Carsten, Francis L., 503, 10541
Carswell, L., 3540
Cartelli, Thomas, 11467
Carter, B., 3963
Carter, Barbara Lynn, 2169
Carter, Bob, 3357
Carter, Gwendolen M., 10261
Carter, H., 3653
Carter, M., 184
Carter, Marina, 6472
Carter, Trevor, 3358
Carter, Velma, 1129
Cartwright, J.O., 7994
Carvajal, M.J., 1831
Carvalho-Neto, Paulo de, 8914
Casal, L., 1868, 1878
Case, Frederic I., 1373
Casey, B., 2851
Cashmore, Ernest Ellis, 3765-3767
Casino, E.S., 7515
Casper, Ronald L., 1414
Cassa, Roberto, 2113
Cassidy, Bryan, 6731
Cassidy, Frank, 1194
Cassidy, Julie, 355,356
Cassilly, Thomas A., 2432
Castell, Pablo, 108
Castellano, Isabel, 1869, 1870
Castellanos, Jorge, 1869, 1870
Castells, M., 10542
Castillero Calvo, Alfredo, 7365
Castillo, Hugo P., 109
Castillo-Cardenas, Gonzalo, 1792
Castles, S., 185, 2852, 2853, 10543, 10544, 11468
Castor, Elie, 2433
Castro, Donald S., 110
Castro, Max J., 2114
Catley, R., 186
Catrice, Paul, 2434
Catrina, Werner, 8644
Cattani, Alfred, 8645
Caudrey, Adriana, 3359

Caute, David, 9966
Caveny, R., 11028
Cazden, Courtney B., 6933
Cazorla Pérez, José, 8333
Ceausescu, Ilie, 7801, 7835
Celasun, M., 8801
Celis, Georges, 9920
Cell, John W., 10069
Ceplair, Larry, 10545
Cerny, Philip G., 2548
Cerron-Palomino, Rodolfo, 7440
Cerutti, Mauro, 8646
Cervinka, Frantisek, 1980
Cesarani, David, 3279-3281
Cha, Jongchun, 6232
Chabal, Patrick, 4431, 4432, 10262, 10267
Chabry, Annie, 11114
Chabry, Laurent, 11114
Chacón, Ramon D., 6517
Chae-Jin Lae, 1587
Chafets, Ze'ev, 5424
Chafetz, Gary, 5243
Chaffee, John W., 1670
Chaffee, Lyman, 8334
Chagnollaud, Jean-Paul, 5425
Chahnazarian, A., 11469
Chairoff, P., 2435, 10546
Chakrabarti, R., 4675
Chakrabarty, Dipesh, 4674
Chakravarti, Ranabir, 4676
Chakravarti, U., 4677
Chalala, Elie, 11115
Chalam, K.S., 4678
Chaliand, Gerard, 5168, 8688, 8802, 8843, 11470
Chalk, Frank, 1019, 6310, 11471
Chalmers, B.E., 8270
Chalmers, David M., 9484
Cham, B.N., 6384
Chamie, J., 6287
Champion, Jacques, 10070
Champion, Marc, 916
Chan, Kwok, B., 1069-1072
Chan, Sucheng, 9485
Chance, John K., 6518
Chand, G., 11218
Chandhoke, N., 10071
Chandler, David L., 1793, 2132
Chandler, David P., 965

Chandra, Kanamur V., 1073
Chandra, Nirmal K., 4679, 7337
Chandramohan, B., 7995
Chandrasekhar, S., 1074, 1075
Chang, Hajji Yusuf, 1588
Chang-Yun-Shik, 6230
Chanock, Martin, 7996
Chant, S., 11456
Chao, Arnold, 1725
Chao, Wei Wang, 1589
Chape, A., 3769
Chapman, M., 11219
Chapman, William, 7516
Chappele, A.J., 11220
Charlot, Monica, 2436
Charlton, Michael, 9967
Charnes, Gloria L., 8335
Charney, Craig, 7997, 7998
Charney, Israel W., 11472, 12022
Charney, Paul J., 7441
Chartrand, J.P., 1269
Chary, Frederick B., 917
Chase-Sardi, M., 7420
Chase, William J., 9010
Chasin, Barbara, 4730
Chassey, Francis de, 6461
Chaszar, Edward, 11116
Chatain, Jean, 2437
Chatel, Nicole, 2438
Chater, A., 3770
Chatterjee, A.K., 4680
Chatterjee, Partha, 4681, 4682, 11473
Chattopadhyay, Amal Kumar, 4683, 4684
Chattopadhyay, D.K., 4685
Chattopadhyay, M., 4686, 4687
Chatworthy, Stewart J., 1195
Chaudhary, N., 4688
Chaudhury, R.H., 613
Chauduri, Buddhabed, 4689
Chauveau, Jean-Pierre, 6021
Chavira, Ricardo, 7366
Chazan, Naomi, 10248
Chazan, Robert, 10547
Chea Urruela, José Luis, 4401
Cheater, Angela P., 9968
Chebel d'Appollonia, Ariane, 2439
Cheema, G. Shabbir, 11474
Chen, Ching-chi, 1671
Chen, Lincoln C., 614, 11693

Chen, Martha A., 615
Chen, Peter S.J., 7916
Chen Qiuping, 1672
Chen Xiao, 1673
Cheng, Joseph Y.S., 3482
Cheng, Lucie, 11976
Chernichovsky, Dov., 716, 717, 5024
Chernyak, Y., 11475
Cherry, Robert, 9486
Chertok, Shimon, 9011
Cheruiyot, Ruth C., 6181
Cherwinski, W.J.C., 1426
Cheung, P.P.L., 7619
Chevannes, Barry, 10368
Chevannes, Mel, 3442, 3478
Chianese, Gloria, 5924
Chiang, Yung-Chen, 1674
Chiao, Chien, 1590
Chiapelli, Fredi, 11561
Chick, J. Keith, 7999
Chien Lin, Sharon, 1675
Chiesi, Antonio M., 5925
Chilcote, Ronald H., 752, 10907
Child, Lydia Marie, 11476
Chin, Henk E., 8555
Ching-Hwang, Yen, 7917
Chinn, Carl, 3773
Chiplin, Brian, 3774
Chipman, John, 10072
Chira, Susan, 6037, 6038, 6233
Chirot, Daniel, 10548
Chisick, Harvey, 2440, 2441
Chitham, E.J., 2170
Choate, S.L., 9969
Choe, Won Hyung, 6234
Chokay, J., 5094
Choksi Mithan, 4741
Chomsky, Noam, 5426
Choseed, Bernard J., 9012
Chossudovsky, Michel, 1676
Chouraqui, André, 38, 10073, 10074
Chowdhury, Bazlul M., 616
Chowning, Ann, 7395
Chowning, M., 6519
Chrisman, Robert, 1871, 9487
Christelow, Allan, 39
Christens, Carole P., 1362
Christenson, Bruce A., 7312
Christian, Hans, 2394, 2418, 3246
Christie, Pam, 8001, 8002

AUTHOR INDEX 933

Christison, Kathleen M., 5427
Christnacht, Alain, 11221
Christodoulou, Demetrios, 11477
Christophe, Marc A., 2442
Christopher, A.J., 8003, 10075
Chua, Yee Yen, 6385
Chuchryk, Patricia, 1549
Chukwudum, A.M., 7221
Chulikavit, Yotin, 8735
Chung, Chin-Sung, 6039
Churchill, Ward, 1196, 9488, 9489
Cicek, Y., 8803
Cizakca, Murat, 11117
Claiborne, Louis, 3775
Clammer, John, 7918
Clapham, John H., 3518
Clarence-Smith, W. Genvase, 82-85, 11478
Clarimont, Donald H., 1130
Clark, Alan, 11222
Clark, B.A., 1197
Clark, C.M.H., 187
Clark, Cal, 9812
Clark, Janet, 9812
Clark, Joanna, 7657
Clark, John, 9947
Clark, Kenneth B., 9490, 9491
Clark, Linda L., 2443, 2444
Clark, Lorenne M.G., 11479
Clark, Mari H., 6182
Clark, Martin, 5926
Clark, Paul, 1593
Clark, Peter, 1374
Clark, Robert P., 8336
Clark, Roger, 11223
Clark, Samuel, 651
Clarke, Colin G., 10369, 11480
Clarke, D.G., 9970, 9971, 9972
Clarke, Graham, 7067
Clarke, John Henrik, 10076
Clary, Norman J., 2445
Clay, Jason W., 10908
Cleary, David, 753
Cleary, Edward L., 10909
Cleary, James W., 9013
Cleave, Peter, 6934
Clebert, Jean-Paul, 10550
Clegg, Legrand H., II, 10078
Clemens, Bärbel, 2854
Clement, W., 1325, 1375

Clementi, Hebe, 10910
Cliff, A.D., 11783
Cliff, Julie, 6685
Cliffe, Lionel, 2276, 10017
Clifford P., 3914
Clifford, Robert L., 6705
Clines, Francis X., 3541, 9014
Clissold, Stephen, 9813, 10079
Closets, Francois de, 2446
Clough, Patricia, 10551
Clow, Michael, 1376
Clymer, Kenton J., 7517
Clytus, John, 1872
Coakley, J., 10553
Coates, David, 3776
Coates, Kenneth S., 1198, 1199, 1377
Cobbett, Deborah, 5138
Cobley, Alan G., 8004
Cochran, Judith, 2171
Cochrane, D.G., 11224
Cochrane, Raymond, 3456, 3457
Cock, Jacklyn, 8005, 8006
Cockcroft, James D., 6520
Codell, Joan C., 7396
Cody, Edward, 7020
Coetzee, C.G., 8007
Coetzee, J.C., 11977
Coffman, Edward M., 9015
Cohen, Albert, 918
Cohen, Amnon, 8804
Cohen, Asher, 10554
Cohen, Avraham, 5428
Cohen, Cary B., 1981
Cohen, David, 3777
Cohen, Hayyim J., 5139
Cohen, Herbert, 11225
Cohen, Israel, 8805
Cohen, J., 40
Cohen, Jack J., 5429
Cohen, Jacob Xenab, 10911
Cohen, Jerome Alan, 1734
Cohen, Jim, 2447
Cohen, John M., 2277
Cohen, Lenard J., 9814
Cohen, Lloyd A., 7802
Cohen, M., 11118
Cohen, M.J., 3282
Cohen, Martin A, 10912
Cohen, Mitchell J., 5244
Cohen, Nava, 2855

Cohen, Paul, 3778
Cohen, Philip, 3779
Cohen, R. J., 2448
Cohen, Robin, 10080
Cohen, Ronald, 10081, 11481, 11482
Cohen, Sarah, 11978
Cohen, Stanley, 5430
Cohen, Steve, 3283, 3284
Cohen, Stuart A., 5140
Cohen, William B., 2449, 2450
Cohen, Youssef, 754
Cohn, Norman, 11483
Cohn, Werner, 1020
Coker, Olumide, 1873
Colakis, Marianthe, 4368
Colbenson, Peter D., 3285
Colbias, Karen A., 9016
Colbier, I.L., Jr., 9089
Colburn, Forrest D., 7021
Cole, Bankole A., 7222
Cole, Hubert, 4467
Cole, Jeffrey A., 703
Cole, John W., 7803, 10555, 10556
Cole, Johnnetta B., 1866, 1874
Cole, Juan Ricardo I., 2172
Cole, Lester, 9017
Cole, Mike, 357, 3781
Coleman, Alice, 3494
Coleman, Kenneth M., 11082
Coleman, William, 2451
Coleman, William D., 1313
Coles, Robert, 9492
Colfax, J. David, 9726
Colhoun, Jack, 7068
Collatz, Jürgen, 2856
Colletta, N.J., 6386
Colley, Linda, 3782
Collier, J., 3473
Collier, Paul, 6183, 6184, 8699
Collinder, Bjorn, 10557
Collins, Frank, 5431
Collins, Jeffrey G., 2173
Collins, Robert O., 8518, 8519
Collins, Roger, 8337
Colmey, John, 8429
Colonna, Fanny, 41, 42
Colt, Elizabeth, 11226
Comaroff, Jean, 8008, 11484
Comaroff, John L., 8008, 8009
Comas, Juan, 10913, 10914

Commins, David D., 8806
Compton, R., 3783
Con, Harry, 1076
Congress, Rick, 7022, 7069, 7070
Conklin, Alice L., 10082
Conklin, Margaret, 112
Connell, R.W., 188,189
Connelly, M. Patricia, 1378
Conniff, Michael L., 755, 756, 7367
Connock, Michael, 3784
Conquest, Robert, 9018, 9019
Conrad, Christoph, 2857
Conrad, Robert E., 757, 758, 759, 11979
Constable, Pamela, 1550, 4468, 7071
Constantin, Francois, 10083
Constantine, L., 3785
Constantino, Renato, 7518-7520
Conway, A.G., 3542
Conway, John S., 1982, 2858, 10559, 11485
Cony, Stella, 113
Conzemius, Eduard, 7072
Coogan, Kevin, 9020, 10698
Cook, J., 3786
Cook, Lindsey, 5432
Cook, Ramsey, 1379
Cooke, James L., 43
Cooke, Miriam, 11105
Coombe, Vivienne, 3787
Coombs, H. C., 359,360,361
Coombs, Orde, 10472
Cooney, Jarry W., 7421
Cooper, Adrienne E., 4691, 4692
Cooper, Anna Julia, 2452
Cooper, Cary L., 6878
Cooper, Frederick, 6185, 6186, 8700, 10084-10087
Cooper, Lolek, 7658
Cooper, Mark, 2174
Cooper, Matthew, 11227, 11344
Cooper, Richard, 3788
Cooper, Roger, 5095
Cooper, Stephanie, 3496
Cope, N., 8010
Cope, Robert D., 6521
Copp, T., 1314
Coppel, Charles A., 5025, 5026
Copper, John F., 1677
Coquery-Vidrovitch, Catherine, 10088

Corban, B.P.N., 11228
Corbitt, Duvon C., 1875
Cordell, Dennis D., 948, 10089
Cordera, Rolando, 6522
Cordero H., Salvador, 6523
Cordoba, J., 6555
Cordy, Ross H., 11229, 11230
Cormack, R.J., 3549, 3587, 3591
Cornelius, Janet, 9493
Cornelius, Wayne, 6524, 6525
Cornell, A., 7442
Cornell, R.W., 11486
Corner, Lorraine, 6387
Corner, T., 11487
Cornevin, Marianne, 8011
Cornevin, Robert, 694, 8767
Corpuz, Onofre D., 7521, 7522
Corradi, Juan E., 114, 115, 116
Correia, Alamir A., 6686
Corrett, J.A., 2278
Corris, Peter R., 11231
Corrsin, Stephen D., 7659, 7660
Cortes, Josefina R., 7523
Cortes, Pedro, 1795
Cortes, Vicenta, 8338
Corwin, Arthur F., 760
Coslett, C., 6732
Cossali, Paul, 5754
Costa, Emilia V. da, 10090
Costa-Lascou, Jacqueline, 2453, 2454
Costello, Patrick, 10884
Costelloe, Kevin, 2859
Costisella, Joseph, 1200
Cotanegre, Jean-François, 7871
Cothell, Ann Baker, 11439
Cotic, Meir, 1983
Cotler, Julio, 7443, 7444
Cotton, Richard W,, 5096
Coughlin, Richard J., 8736
Coulet, N., 2455
Couper, K., 4203
Courbet, A., 2503
Courie, J.A., 6935
Couriel, Alberto, 10915
Court, Andy, 5433
Courtney, Daria Treat, 10561
Courtois, Stephane, 2457
Courtwon, Isabelle de, 2604
Cousins, David, 362
Coutau-Begarie, Herve, 11232

Couzinos, Efthimios N., 8807
Covell, Maureen, 652
Coventry, Rosalyn, 7002
Covo, Jacqueline, 8346
Cowburn, Will, 3789
Cowell, Alan, 5434, 8012, 8808, 8809, 9815
Cowlishaw, Gillian, 190
Cox, Bruce A., 1201
Cox, Donald, 2458
Coyle, Angela, 3790
Crabtree, Michael F., 3791
Cracco Ruggini, Lellia, 11875
Craig, Gordon A., 2860
Craig, Susan, 10371
Craig, Terrence, 1380
Cramer, Tomas, 8573
Crankshaw, O., 8013
Craton, Michael, 10372-10375, 11488, 11489
Crawfford, James, 363
Crawford, E. Margaret, 5174
Creery, Ian, 1202
Creese, Gillian L., 1381
Cresciani, Gianfranco, 191
Crespi, Gabrielle, 10562
Creveld, M. van, 5928
Criado, Fidel Lopez, 11615
Crisp, Olga, 9021
Critchlow, James, 9022
Crocker, Chester A., 10091
Crockett, G., 192
Crockett, N.L., 9494
Croll, Elisabeth, 1678
Cromer, Gerald, 5435-5437
Crompton, R., 3793
Cromwell, Jerry, 11490
Crone, Michael, 6798, 6799
Cronje, Gillian, 6733
Cronje, Suzanne, 6733
Crook, David, 1595
Cross, Colin, 3794, 3795
Cross, Malcolm, 3796, 4448, 6800
Cross, Michael, 6687, 8014, 8015
Crossette, Barbara, 4693, 6706, 6776, 9765, 10297
Crossick, Geoffrey, 3797, 3798, 10563
Crossley, David W., 4132
Crossley, John E., 1203
Crossley, Pamela Kyle, 1679, 1680

Crotty, Raymond D., 5175
Croucher, Richard, 3799
Crow, Ben, 11491
Crow, Gain, 3362
Crowder, Michael, 718, 7890
Crowley, F.K., 193
Crowther, William E., 7804
Cruikshank, R.B., 8737
Crummey, Donald, 10092
Cruse, Harold, 9495
Cruz, Romeo V., 7524
Crystal, Jill, 11119
Cuello, José, 6526
Cueva, Agustin, 2133, 10916
Cueva-Jaramillo, Juan, 10917
Cullen, Kevin, 3543
Cullen, Stephen, 3800
Cullinane, Michael, 7525
Cummins, Jim, 1382, 9496, 11780
Cunard, Nancy, 1961
Cuneo, Carl J., 1383
Cunningham, Hugh, 3801
Cunningham, James, 4433
Curran, P.S., 3544
Curran, Thomas D., 1681
Currie, C., 4694
Currie, J.C., 11980
Currie, Kate, 6187
Curry, L.P., 9497
Curry, R.L., Jr., 719, 720
Curthoys, Ann, 194, 195, 7401
Curthoys, M., 3932
Curtin, Leslie B., 11492
Curtin, Philip D., 10093-10095, 11493
Curtis, Bruce, 1384, 1385
Curtis, Fred, 8016, 8017, 8018
Curtis, Liz, 3519
Curtis, Perry, 11698
Curtius, Mary, 5438-5441
Cushman, Richard O., 8647
Custers, Martin, 6801
Cuthbertson, G.C., 8019
Cutler, P., 4695
Cuvalo, Ante, 9816
Cyz, Beno, 2861
Czubinski, A., 7661

D.H., 7073
D'Azevedo, Mario, 1542
D'iakonov, L.M., 11876

D'Orsay, John V., 1386
D'Oyley, Vincent, 1131
D'Souza, Henry J., 4696
da Valle Silva, Nelson, 793
Daaku, K.Y., 10096
Daalder, H., 6802
Dabbak, Ibrahim, 5442, 5443
Dabene, Louise, 10564
Dabien, G., 10376
Dabydeen, D., 3363, 3364, 10377
Dadrian, Vahakn N., 8810-8812
Dadzie, Stella, 10378
Dagis, Janis, 2862
Dahl, Robert, 669
Dahl, Tove S., 7313
Dahlberg, Robin L., 8813
Dahlie, Jorgen, 1387
Dahmani, Mohamed, 11494
Dai Yannian, 1682
Daikun, Yue, 1780
Dalal, Agit K., 4697
Dale, A., 3523, 3802
Dale, Richard, 6734
Dale, William S.J., 6936
Dallal, Sahw J., 5444
Dallin, Alexander, 9186
Dallin, David J., 9023
Dalton, George, 10172
Daman, Gilbert, 10565
Dan, Nikolaos van, 8680
Danda, A.K., 4698
Dandamayev, M.A., 11877, 11878
Dange, Shripad A., 4699
Dangschat, Jens, 7662, 7663
Daniel, J.L., 11879
Daniel, Krystyna, 7664
Daniel, P., 9498
Daniel, Robert L., 8814
Daniels, Harry, 1204
Daniels, Roger, 1077, 9499, 9500
Daniels, Rudolph, 8020, 8021
Daniels, Therese, 3365
Daninos, Guy, 1822
Dann, Uriel, 2163
Danner, Mark D., 4469
Dantas Júnior, Altino, 761
Daphne Davidson, 112
Dar, Y., 5245
Darbari, I., 4700
Darby, John, 3545-3550

Darity, William A., Jr., 8029, 9501
Darke, Roy, 7023
Darko, Samuel F., 3259
Das, Amal, 4701
Das Gupta, Monica, 4704
Das, N.R., 4702
Das, Suranjan, 4703
Dascalu, Nicolae, 7805, 7806
Daschke, John W., 1984
Dasgupta, Kalpana, 11981
Dasgupta, P., 11495
Dashwood, A., 3803
Dassetto, Felice, 642, 643
Dassin, Joan, 762
Dathorne, O.R., 10379
Datta, Kalinkar, 4705
Datta, N.K., 4706
Datta, P., 4707
Datta, R.C., 4708
Datta-Ray, S.K., 4709
Daube, David, 11880
Daud, Fatimah, 6388
Daumard, Adeline, 2459-2461
Daunton, M.J., 3497
Dauril Alden, 867
Daus, Timothy D., 2175
Davenport, Manuel M., 11496
David, Helen, 5246
David, Peggy A., 4449
David, Randolph G., 7526
David, Zdenek V., 536
Davidova, Eva, 1985
Davidson, Andrew P., 4710
Davidson, Basil, 1536, 2279, 4434, 10097, 11497
Davidson, David M., 6527
Davidson, James W., 11233
Davidson, Marilyn J., 6878
Davidson, Nicolas, 5929
Davies, A.R.L., 8022
Davies, Alan, 1021, 1022, 9502
Davies, Alan T., 2462, 2863
Davies, Bernard, 3804
Davies, C., 3659
Davies, J.B., 1388
Davies, Janet, 3551
Davies, John, 8023
Davies, R., 8063
Davies, R.R., 3620, 3660, 5176
Davies, R.W., 9024

Davies, Robert, 8024, 8025
Davies, Susanne, 364
Davies, Thomas M., Jr., 7445, 7446
Davis, Anthony, 1374
Davis, Deborah, 1683
Davis, Diane E., 6528
Davis, Donna D., 10380
Davis, F., 9503
Davis-Friedman, Deborah, 1684
Davis, Horace B., 1596
Davis, Jennifer, 3805
Davis, John, 8026
Davis, Lenwood, 6311, 11982
Davis, Leslie A., 8815
Davis, Michael C., 3483
Davis, Peter, 238
Davis, R. Hunt, Jr., 8027
Davis, Robert, 1205
Davis, S., 2176, 11881
Davis, Shelton H., 4402, 10918, 12057
Davis, Susan S., 6654, 6655
Davis, Uri, 5446, 5447, 5448
Davosta, Cornel, 3366
Dawidowicz, Lucy S., 11498
Dawson, James, 365
Dayal, E., 4711
Daye, S.G., 3367
de Beer, Cedric, 8028
de Carvalho-Neto, Paulo, 10919
de Cillia, Rudolf, 520
De Comarmond, P., 2463
de Czege Geza W., 4574
De Felice, Renzo, 10098
De Francis, John, 1685
De Gregori, T.R., 8029
De Jong, Frederick, 7807
De Jong, Louis, 6803
De Jong, Mart-Jan, 6804
De Jong, P., 6825
De Jongh, R.J., 6805
de Kruijk, H., 7338
De La Peña, Sergio, 6529
de la Plaza, Salvador, 9747
De Lepervanche, Marie M., 196
De los Reyes, Romana P., 7527
De Marchi, Bruna, 10566
De Silva, Kingsley M., 8430, 8431
De Souza, Alfred, 4952
De Vaus, David, 11499
De Villiers. F.J., 8030

De Vos, George A., 6040, 6041
De Vries, Petra, 6806
Deak, Istvan, 4528-4530
Deakin, S., 3806
Deal, David, 1597
Dean, D.W., 3368
Dean, Elizabeth, 8031
Dean, Macabee, 6042
Deane, Hugh, 1686
Dearden, Ann, 11120
Debbasch, Yvan, 10381
DeBevoise, Ken, 7528
Debrunner, H.W., 3807, 10567
Decalo, S., 8768, 8769
DeConchy, Jean P., 2464
Dedic, Abdullah, 9817
Dedijer, Vladimir, 9818
Deeb, Marius K., 2177, 6335
Deeb, Mary Jane 6335
Deepak, Lal, 6183, 6184
DeFebo, Giuliana, 8339
DeFelice, Renzo, 6336
DeFrancis, John F., 9766
Degler, Carl N., 9504
Dehter, Aaron, 5449
DeKock, Victor, 8032
Del Castillo, José, 2115
Del Rosario, Virginia O., 7529
Delacampagne, Christiane, 11882
Delamont, Sara, 3808
DeLancey, Mark W., 983
Delaney, Paul, 8340, 8341
Delapina, Thomas, 504
DelBoca, Angelo, 11500
Deleeck, Herman, 653
Deleris, Ferdinand, 6352
Deletant, Andrea, 11983
Deletant, D., 11983
Delius, Peter, 7984
Delius, Ulrich, 11234
Delval, R., 8770
DeMarco, Roland R., 10100
Demarest, William, 4422
Demele, Isolde, 6688
deMeyer, J.L., 11469
Demko, George J., 9025
Dempster, Carolyn, 2339
Dench, Geoff, 3809
Deng, Francis M., 8518, 10036
Deng, William, 8535

Denis, Ann B., 1389
Denis, Pierre, 11501
Denkler, Horst, 10653
Dennis, Ferdinand, 3369
Dennis, John A., 2465
Dennis, Philip A., 6530
Dennis, Richard, 3498
Denslow, D., Jr., 763
Denton, C., 1832
Deolalikar, A.B., 4653
Deoppers, D.T., 7530
Deosaran, Ramesh, 10382
Depelchi, Jacques, 6682
Dermenjian, Genevieve, 44, 45
Dern, Ann L., 2085
DeRosa, Peter, 11502
Derricourt, R., 7965
Derry, T.K., 7314
Dersa, 46
Derville, Alain, 10568
Desai, A.R., 4712, 4713
Desai, L.P., 4714
Desai, Niera, 4715
Desanges, J., 11883, 11884
Descan, J.P., 11984
Désert, Gabriel, 2466
Désir, Harlem, 2467
Desir, Lucia M., 1796
Desmangles, L.G., 4470
Dessart, Francis, 5931
Dettmer, K.M., 6707
Deutsch, Sandra M., 117,118
Devalle, S.B.C., 11503
DeVanzo, J., 6389
Devens, Carol, 1206
Deverell, J., 1474
Devetak, Silvo, 9819, 9820
DeVillefosse, L., 11504
Devine, T.M., 3621, 3622, 3647
Devitt, Richard B., 4716
Dew, Edward, 8556
Dewald, Jonathan, 2468
Dewey, Clive, 4717
DeWind, Josh, 7447
Dewitte, Philippe, 2469
Dex, Shirley, 3370, 3371, 3372
Deyneka, Peter, Jr., 9026
Deyo, Frederick C., 10298
Dham, Najwa S., 6288
Dhavan, Rajeev, 4718

AUTHOR INDEX

Dhesi, A., 3810
Dhofier, A., 5027
Dhoquois, Régine, 2470
di Nola, Alfonso M., 5932, 5933
Diakite, S., 6454
Diakonoff, L.M., 11885
Diamant, Alfred, 505
Diamond, Larry J., 7223, 7224, 7225, 10101, 10102
Diamond, Norma, 1598
Diane, Bakary, 7891
Diao, Richard, 1599
Dias, J.R., 86
Diawara, Bakary, 6022
Diaz Polanco, Hector, 7074, 10920
Diaz Santana, Arismendi, 4471
Dibblin, Jane, 11235
Dick, Howard W., 5028, 5029
Dickason, Olive P., 1207
Dicker, Herman, 10569
Dickey, Sara, 4719
Dickinson, Tony, 3623, 3624
Diderichsen, Finn, 8574
Diefendorf, Barbara, 2471
Diego Aguirre, José R., 8342
Diehl, Jackson, 7665, 9821
Diekmann, Andreas, 506
Dienes, Leslie, 9027, 9028
Diepen, Marie van, 8250
Dietrich, Donald J., 2865
Dietz, H., 7448
Dietz, Ton, 5030
Díez Medrano, Juan, 8343
Digby, Anne, 3811
Diggs, Irene, 10921
Dighe, Anita, 4807
Digre, Brian K., 10103
Dikotter, F., 1687
Dillard, Joey Lee, 9505
Diller, A., 11886
Dillman, Jeffrey D., 5450
Dilnot, A.W., 197, 3812, 3813
Din, Elly, 10597
Din, Isaac U., 7226
Dinges, John, 7075
Dingwaney, M. , 4885
Dinnerstein, Leonard, 9506, 10696
Dinstein, Yoram, 9029, 10570
Diogo, Junior, Alfredo, 87
Diop, Cheikh Anta, 2178, 10104

Dippmann, Klaus J., 2866
Dirks, N.B., 10299
Diskin, Martin, 7076
Dissanayaka, T.D. S.S., 8432
DiTella, Torcuato, 6531
Ditton, P., 340
Divekar, V.D., 11986
Divisekera, S., 8433
Dix, Robert H., 10922
Dixey, R.A., 721
Dixon, Heriberto, 1876
Dixon, Marlene, 1942
Dixon, P.B., 424
Dixon, Peter B., 263
Dixon, William J., 10923
Djilas, Aleksa, 9822, 9823
Djursaa, Malene, 2086
Dlamini, C.R.M., 8034
Dmitriev, Ivan, 11506
Dmytryshyn, Basil, 9031
Dneprov, E.D., 9032
Dnoon, Donald, 11507
Dobkowski, Michael N., 8851, 9507
Dobrska, Z., 10105
Dobson, R.B., 3286, 9033
Dockeran, W., 10356
Dockès, Pierre, 10571
Dodd, C.H., 8816
Doeringer, P.B., 3731
Dofny, Jacques, 1315, 11508
Dogra, B., 4720
Dohse, Knuth, 2867, 2868, 2869
Dollimore, 11454
Dolton, P.J., 3708
Domalskii, I., 9034
Domb, Yocheved, 5247
Domergue-Cloaree, Camille, 6023
Domhoff, G. William, 9508
Dominelli, Lena, 3814, 3815
Domingo, Vernon A., 6807
Dominguez, Jorge J., 1877
Dominguez Ortiz, Antonio, 8344
Don, Yehuda, 4531, 10572
Donad, Patrick C., 1208
Donahue, John M., 7024, 7025
Donaldson, M., 7397
Dong, Wonmo, 6235
Donkov, Rumen, 10106
Donnelly, Jack, 11509
Donneur, Andre, 8648

AUTHOR INDEX

Donovan, Jenny, 3374, 3835
Donovan, Kenneth, 1390
Doobov, A.L., 198
Dookeran, Winston, 10383
Dooley, Martin D., 1391
Doolittle, William E., 6532
Dor, Milo, 507
Dorais, Louis-Jacques, 1078
Doré y Cabral, Carlos, 2116
Doring, J. J., 2870
Dörner, K., 2871
Doron, Abraham, 5248
Dorrance, John C., 11236, 11237
Dos Santos, Eliana P. L., 766
Dos Santos, Pe. A. F., 767
Doskow, Ambrose, 2872
Dostal, W., 508
Dothan, T., 5249
Doug Hindson, 8302
Doughan, David, 3816
Doughty, Paul L., 7449
Douglass, Frederick, 9509-9511
Douglass, William A., 8345
Dournes, Jacques, 9767
Douyon, Emerson, 11987
Dowd, Lynette Toni, 367
Dowdle, Nancy B., 1600
Dowe, Dieter, 2660, 5981
Dowling, J.M., 10300
Downes, A.S., 10384
Downie, Winsome A., 10385
Downing, Theodore E., 11510, 11988
Dowty, Alan, 5097
Dozier, Craig L., 7077
Dozon, Jean-Pierre, 6021
Drabek, Anna M., 509
Drache, Daniel, 1392
Dragnich, Alex N., 9824, 9825
Drago, R., 199
Drake, Christine, 5031
Drake, St. Clair, J. G., 3817, 9512, 10107
Drake-Terry, Joanne, 1209
Dramaliev, K., 919
Dray, Julien, 2473
Drechsler, H., 6735
Dreifelds, Juris, 9035
Dreifuss, Rene A., 768
Dreizin, Felix, 9036
Drescher, Seymour, 769, 10573

Dresner, Zita, 9710
Drew, D., 3375
Dreyer, June T., 1601
Dreyer, Lynette, 8035
Dreyfus, Francois-Georges, 2474
Driehuis, W., 6808
Driver, Edwin D., 4722, 4723
Driver, M.G., 11265
Drost, Richard, 11238
Drover, G., 1456
Droz, Jacques, 10574
Drozdowski, Marian M., 7666, 7667
Druker, Abraham, 7668
Druks, Herbert, 10575
Drumont, Edouard, 2475
Drumont, Paul, 8817, 8818
Drury, David A., 4724
Drussel, Enrique, 10924
Du Bois, W.E.B., 9513, 9514, 9515, 11887
Du Pleissis, A., 8036
Du Preez, J.N., 8037
Dubar, Claude, 6289
Dubb, A.A., 8038
Dube, E.F., 8039
Dube, Thandi, 8040
Dubet, Francois, 1551
Dubnov, Simon M., 7669, 8041, 11511
Dubnov-Erlich, Sophie, 11512
Dubuch, Claude, 949
Dubuisson, Wilfrid, 1132
Duchen, Calire, 2476
Duchet, C., 2463
Dudek, Peter, 2873
Dudwick, Nora, 9037
Duff, S.G., 1986
Duffield, Ian, 200
Dugas, Clermont, 1394
Duggan, Christopher, 5934
Duguid, Charles, 366
Duke, Vic, 3818
Dumas, Claude, 8346
Dumasy, E.A.H., 5032
Dummett, Ann, 3819, 3820
Dumont, Fernand, 1316
Dumont, Serge, 2477
Dunbar, Leslie, 9709
Dunbar Ortiz, Roxanne, 7078-7084
Duncan, Kenneth, 10925
Duncan, Wendy A., 722

Dundes, Alan, 2874, 2875, 3060
Dunin-Wasowicz, Krzysztof,7670
Dunkerley, James, 704
Dunlop, Anne, 3636
Dunlop, John B., 9038
Dunn, Seamus, 3550, 3552-3560
Dunstan, G.R., 10576
Dunston, John, 9039
Dupuy, Alex, 4472
Duran, Maria A., 8347
Durand-Lasserve, Alain, 11513
Durbach, Elaine, 8042
Dures, A., 3821
Dures, K., 3821
Durica, Milan S., 1987
Duriez, B., 3537
Durrenberger, E. Paul, 4605
Durutalo, Simione, 11239
Dusenberry, William H., 6533
Dutt, A.K., 4725
Dutt, Romesh, 4726
Dutta, Ranjana, 4927
Dutter, L.E., 9040
Dutton, Alan, 1395
Duus, Peter, 1688, 1692
Dwight, Alan, 201
Dwork, Deborah, 3822
Dworkin, Anthony, 11553
Dwyer, Daisy H., 6656, 6657
Dwyer, Jeffrey W., 897
Dyasi, H. M., 8043
Dyer, Aldrich J., 11989
Dyer, Christopher, 10577
Dymerskaya-Tsigelman, L., 9041
Dzidzienyo, Anani, 770, 771, 1878

Eade, John, 3376, 9291
Eagles, Munroe, 3625
Eagleton, Terry, 11514
Eakin, Marshall C., 772
Eashman, Green Fay, 5250
Eatwell, R., 11435
Ebels-Dolanova, Vera, 10578
Eberstadt, Nicolas, 8044, 11515
Eble, Roland H., 4403
Echenberg, Myron, 2478
Echeverria, Rafael, 1552
Eckermann, Anne-Katrin, 367
Eckert, Carter J., 6236
Eckert, J.B., 8045

Eckert, Rainer, 4369
Eckstein, Susan, 1879, 10926
Edari, Ronald S., 9458
Edelheit, Abraham J., 10579, 11990-11992
Edelheit, Hershel, 11990-11992
Edelman, M.W., 9516
Edelman, Marek, 7671
Edelman, Martin, 5451
Eder, James F., 7531, 7532
Edgecombe, Ruth, 8046
Edgell, Stephen, 3818
Edirisinghe, Neville, 8434
Edmondson, C. Earl, 510
Edmondson, Linda, 9021
Edoh, Tony, 7287
Edwards, E., 11993
Edwards, G. E., 2876
Edwards, Harry, 9517
Edwards, I. E., 8047
Edwards, John, 655, 10580
Edwards, Judith, 3825, 3826
Edwards, N. R., 368
Edwards, R. Randle, 1689
Edwards, Susan, 3827
Edwards, Viv, 3377, 3378
Edyvean, Janine E., 202
Efrat, Elisha, 5452, 5692
Egero, Bertil, 6689
Egger, Vernon, 2179
Eggleston, John, 3828
Egner, E.B., 723
Ehn, Billy, 8575
Ehrenburg, Ilya, 9042
Ehrenreich, Jeffrey D., 2134
Ehrlich, Judith R., 9518
Ehrlich, Konrad, 2877
Eichholtz, Dietrich, 10581
Eidheim, Harold, 2340, 7315
Einhorn, Barbara, 2878
Einstein, Albert, 11516
Eisenberg, Warren, 10927
Eisenstadt, S.N., 5251, 10787
Eisikovits, R.A., 5252
Eisinga, R., 6810
Eitinger, Leo, 11517, 12035
Ejimofor, Cornelius Ogu, 7227
Ekeh, Peter P., 10108
Eklof, Ben, 9043
Ekoko, A.E., 3260, 7905

Ekong, Elsong E., 7228
El-Amin, Mohammed N., 8520
El-Asmar, Fouzi, 5453
El Batrawi, A.M., 2180
El Bushra, Judy, 2280
El-Garid, El, 6337
El-Khawas, M.A., 6338, 8521
El-Khazen, Farid E., 6290
El Saadawi, Nawal, 11121
El-Sayed, Mustapha, 2181
El Tayeb, Salah El Din El, 47
Elango, Lovett Z., 984
Elazar, Daniel J., 6534
Eley, Geoff, 2879-2882
Elich, Joed H., 6811
Eliraz, Giora, 2182
Elkin, Judith L., 10928-10933
Elkins, W.F., 10386
Elklit, Jorgen, 10582
Ellain, Judith, 3829
Ellemers, J. E., 6812
Ellen, Roy F., 6813
Ellerin, Milton, 11518
Elling, Hanna, 2883
Elling, Ray H., 11519
Ellingson, Lloyd S., 2281
Elliot, D.R., 1023
Elliott, Carolyn M., 11621
Elliott, David, 8738
Ellis, Alex, 3830
Ellis, C.J., 203
Ellis, Evelyn, 3561
Ellis, S., 369
Ellise, Pat, 10387
Ellison, Christopher G., 8435
Ellman, M., 17, 9044
Ellwood, Sheelagh M., 8348
Elman, Bruce P., 1024
Eloy Martinez, Tomas, 119
Elpeleg, Zvi, 5454
Elphick, Richard, 7964, 8048, 8049
Elrazik, Adnan A., 5455
Elsasser, Nan, 9519
Elsehans, Theodor, 2884
Elsie, Robert, 18
Elsner, Eva-Maria, 2885
Elsner, Lothar, 2885, 2886
Elson, Diane, 11520
Elteto, Louis J., 7808
Elton, Charlotte, 7386

Emanuelson, O.E., 8050
Emmanuel, Patrick, 10388
Emmer, P.C., 11254, 11521
Enaohwo, J. O., 7229
Encel, Sol, 204-207
Endelman, Todd M., 3287
Endruweit, Gunter, 2887
Engel, David, 7672
Engelbrektsson, Ulla-Britt, 8576
Engelmann, Bernt, 2888
Engelstein, Laura, 10583
Engerman, Stanley L., 10465
Engineer, A.A., 4727
England, R.E., 9520
England, Richard W., 10405
Engleman, Uriah Zevi, 11994
Engo, P.D., 985
Enklaar, Ido H., 8051
Enmaji, M., 6658
Ennab, Wa'el Rif'at M. Ali, 5456
Ennals, David, 617
Ennew, Judith, 10389, 11522
Enriquez, Eugène, 2479
Enriquez, Virgilio G., 7533
Ens, Gerhard J., 1210
Enssle, Manfred J., 2889
Enteen, George, 9045
Entelis, John P., 48
Entessar, Nader, 5098, 11122
Entzinger, Hans, 6800, 6814
Epale, Simon J., 986
Epstein, Edward Jay, 11123
Epstein, Erwin H., 1880, 1881, 7450, 9046
Epstein, Jack, 7085, 7086, 7087
Epstein, Joshua L., 11240
Epstein, Mark A., 8819
Epstein, Simon, 2480, 10584
Epstein, Yitzak, 5458
Erbslöh, Barbara, 2890
Ercelawn, A., 7339
Erdmann-Degenhardt, Dan, 656
Erens, Patricia, 9521
Erez, Manny, 5786
Erickson, E.L., 10390
Ericsson, Tom, 8577
Eriksen, Thomas H., 6473
Eriksen, Tore L., 11995
Erikson, Robert, 8578
Erkes, E., 1690

Erlanger, Steven, 7919
Erlich, Haggai, 2283
Ermacora, Felix, 11523
Eros, J., 4532
Errandones, Alfredo, 8915
Eschwege, H. , 2891
Escobar, Alberto, 10935
Escobar Bethancourt, Romulo, 7368
Escultura, Edgar E., 7534
Esedebe, P.O., 3831, 7230
Esh, S., 2892
Esiemokhai, E.O., 7231
Eskandaramy, Ya'acoub D., 2183
Esmailzadeh, Nadir, 5099
Esman, Milton J., 11153, 11524
Espaces 89, 2481
Espinal, R.F., 2117
Espinoza Esquivel, Juan R., 1833
Essed, Philomena, 6815, 6816
Esser, H., 2893
Estebe, Jean, 2482
Esteinou Madrid, Javier, 10936
Ester, P., 6817
Estrada, L.F., 9522
Eteki-Otabela, Marie-Louise, 987
Etienne, Mona, 1790, 11525
Eto, Skinkichi, 6237
Ettinger, Shmuel, 9047, 9048
Evans, Grant, 5033, 6274
Evans, James H., 7085, 7086, 7087
Evans, M.D.R., 208
Evans, Neil, 3379, 3661, 3832
Evans, R. , 209
Evans, Richard J., 2894
Evans, William McKee, 11526
Even, Herbert, 2975
Everett, Jana G.M., 4728
Everitt, Alan, 3833
Everitt, J.C., 691
Eyal, J., 10586
Eyles, John, 3834, 3834
Ezergailis, Andrew, 9049

Faber, Daniel R., 10937
Fabian, Johannes, 9921
Fabian, Suzanne, 210
Fage, J.D., 10109, 10110
Fagerberg, Jan, 7316
Fairburn, Miles, 6937
Fairley, Bryant D., 1396

Faith, K. , 1211
Faizi, Ghazala, 3380
Fajana, Ade, 7232
Falah, Ghazi, 5459-5462
Falconi, Carlo, 9826, 10587
Faller, Kurt, 2895, 2896
Fallick, Arthur L., 1397
Falloon, Virgil, 5463
Falola, Toyin, 88, 7233, 7244
Fals Borda, Orlando, 10938
Falter, Jürgen W., 10588
Falus-Szikra, K., 4533
Fan Wenlan, 1602
Fan Yew Teng, 6390
Fanon, Frantz, 11527
Fanoudh-Siefer, Leon, 2483
Fanusie, Yaya, 7906
Farah, Nadia R., 2184
Fargion, Libana P., 5935
Farky, Ben-Zion, 5464
Farley, Reynolds, 9523
Farmer, Kenneth C., 9050
Farouk, Omar, 8739
Farouk-Sluglett, Marion, 5142, 5143, 5144
Farrar, Max, 3381
Farrell, Joseph P., 1553
Farrell, William, 11241
Fasheh, Munir J., 5465, 5466
Fasi, M. El, 10111
Fatton, Robert, Jr., 7892, 10112
Faust, James P., 5034
Faustino-Santos, Ronald, 1079
Favre, Henri, 10939
Fawcett, James, 11528
Feagin, J.R., 9524
Federspiel, Howard M., 5035
Feeny, David, 8740
Feffer, John, 7673
Feheney, J. Matthew, 3520
Fei Hsiao Tung, 1603
Feierman, Steven, 10113
Feil, C., 2899
Feiler, Gil, 11124
Fein, Esther B., 9051, 9052
Fein, Helen, 9525, 10589
Feingold, Henry L., 9526
Feinsilver, Julie M., 1883
Feit, Ewald, 8054
Feit, Margret, 2900

Feitag, Sandria B., 4729
Feitelson, Dina, 5145
Fejto, François, 10590
Fekete, Liz, 3839, 3840
Felak, James R., 1988
Felden, Klemens, 2901
Feldman, S., 10314
Felix, Alfonso L., Jr., 7535
Felix, David, 10940
Fellah, A., 5467
Fellner, Gunther, 511
Fells, Kenneth, 1133
Felmingham, B.S., 8433
Fenet, Alain, 2484
Fennal, Alan, 2430
Fennema, Meindert, 2118
Fenton, James, 966
Ferdinand, Klaus, 67
Ferencz, Benjamin, 2902, 10591
Ferenczi, Imre, 11837
Fergison, Russell, 11529
Ferguson, James A., 4473, 4474, 10391, 10392
Ferguson, Ted, 1080, 1398
Ferman, Louis A., 9512
Fermoselle-Lopez, Rafael, 1884, 1885
Fernandes, Florestan, 773, 774
Fernandez, Gabriela T., 1834, 6535
Fernandez, Retamar Roberto, 10941, 11530
Fernandez Vargas, Valentina, 8350
Fernando, Tissa, 1387
Fernea, Elizabeth, 11125
Fernea, Robert, 2185
Ferrer, Ada, 775
Fetscher, Irving, 2903
Feuchtwang, Stephen, 1691
Feuer, Lewis S., 9527, 9528
Feuerstein, R., 10115
Feuerwerker, Albert, 1692
Feuser, Willfried, 10114
Fiala, Robert, 11531
Fick, Carolyn E., 4475
Fiddick, P., 4244
Fiedor, Karol, 7674
Fiehrer, Thomas, 4476, 10942
Field, Brian, 7920
Field, Frank, 3841
Field, Geoffrey G., 2904, 3288
Field, Mark G., 9053

Field, S., 3842
Fieldhouse, David, 10116, 10117
Fieldhouse, Roger, 10118
Fields, Karen E., 10119
Fields, Rona M., 3562
Fien, John, 370
Fierman, William, 9054, 9269
Figueroa Ibarra, Carlos, 4404
Figueroa, John J., 3383
Figueroa, Manuel, 6536
Figueroa Navarro, Alfredo, 7369
Figueroa, Peter M.E., 3384
Figueroa Salazar, Amilcar, 2251
Figueros, Adolfo, 11086
Fijalkowski, Jürgen, 2905
Fikes, Robert, Jr., 10592
File, N., 3385
Filippelli, Ronald L., 9529
Filmer, Werner, 2906
Finch, H., 11696
Fine, J. David, 11242
Finebrace, James, 2301
Finestein, Israel, 3289, 3290
Fink, Carole K., 2907
Finkel, Alvin, 1399
Finkelman, Paul, 9530
Finkelstein, Eitan, 9055
Finkelstein, Louis, 11110
Finlay, John L., 1400
Finley, Moses J., 11532, 11891, 11900
Finn, Geraldine, 1452
Finnegan, Richard B., 5177
Finnegan, William, 8055, 8056, 8057
Firrom, K., 11126
First, Ruth, 6339, 6690, 6736
Firstenberg, Babara, 9056
Firth, Raymond, 6938, 11243
Firth, Stewart, 11244
Fischel, Walter J., 5100
Fischer, C., 2908
Fischer, Fritz, 2909
Fischer, R., 513
Fischer, Rolf, 4534
Fischer-Galati, Stephen, 7802
Fischer-Kowalski, Marina, 512
Fiscian, C.E., 3386
Fish, Arthur, 1212
Fish, Daniel, 9057
Fisher, Alan, 8820, 9058
Fisher, Robin, 1213

Fishman, Joel S., 6818, 6819
Fishman, Joshua A., 11533
Fishman, Robert M., 8351
Fishman, Sterling, 2910
Fisk, E.K., 371, 6391, 11245
Fitouri, Chadly, 8776
Fitz, J., 3843
Fitzgerald, Marian, 3387
FitzHerbert, K., 3388
Fitzpatrick, Brian, 211
Fitzpatrick, Peter, 3844, 7398
Flaherty, Patrick, 9059, 9060
Flakierski, Henryk, 4535, 7675, 7676, 9827, 9828
Flamand, Jean-Paul, 2485
Flambeau Ngayap, Pierre, 988
Flanagan, Thomas, 1214, 1215
Flapan, Simha, 5468
Fleischauer, Ingeborg, 9061, 9062
Fleischner, Eva, 11755
Flem, Lydia, 2486
Flender, Harold, 2087
Fleras, Augie, 1216, 6939, 6940
Fletcher, Elaine R., 5469, 5470
Fletcher, Frank, 212
Fletcher, William H., 6890
Fleuret, Anne, 6188
Fleuret, Patrick, 6188
Flint, James, 3845
Flint, Valerie I.J., 10594, 11534
Florer, Edward J., 7809
Flory, Marteen B., 11892
Flory, Thomas, 776
Floyd, Lois G., 8400
Floyd, Troy S., 7088
Fluehr-Lobban, Carolyn, 8522
Fluk, Louis R., 11996
Flushe, Della M., 1554
Flynn, Kevin, 9531
Folayan, Kola, 6340, 6341
Folds, R., 372
Foley, Douglas E., 7536
Foley, S., 9973
Foner, Laura, 11548
Foner, Philip S., 9532
Fong, Pang Eng, 7921
Fontaine, Pierre-Michel, 777-780, 894, 10943
Foon, Chew Sock, 7922
Foot, Paul, 3846

Foracchi, Marialice M., 781
Foran, John F., 5101
Forbes, Andrew D.W., 1604, 8741
Forbes, C.A., 11893
Forest, Tom, 7234
Forgacs, David, 5936
Forgus, Silvia P., 9063
Forman, James, 9533
Forrer, Stephen E., 6044
Forrest, Alan, 2487
Forrest, Joshua B., 4435
Forster, Imogen, 3389
Forster, John, 6941
Forster, Robert, 2488
Forsythe Dennis, 1134, 10393
Forte, Janette, 4450
Forycki, P. Edmund, 2911
Fossett, Mark, 3847
Foster, Charles R., 5991
Foster, D.H., 8058, 8059, 8060, 8061
Foster, G.M., 9948
Foster, Margaret, 3848
Foster, Peter M., 3849
Foster-Carter, Olivia, 3390, 3850, 3851
Fouad, Ajami, 11096
Founow-Tchuigoua, Bernard, 7893
Fouquet, A., 2489
Fournier, M. H., 679
Foweraker, Joe, 782
Fox, Alan, 3852
Fox, Bonnie J., 1356
Fox, Geoffrey E., 1886, 1887
Fox, Irene, 3853
Fox, John P., 6045, 10596-10598
Fox-Genovese, Elizabeth, 10595, 11535
Foxley Rioseco, Felipe, 1555
Foy, Colm, 1537
Foy, Fidele, 11365
Fozzard, A., 8777
Fraenkel, Josef, 514, 579
Fraenkel, Peter, 6737
Fraiman, Y., 5483
Framar, Lindsay, 3854
Francais, Pierre, 6455
France, Peter, 11246
Francis, Elizabeth J., 6942
Francisco, Juan R., 7537
Franco, José L., 10944, 10945
Franco Silva, Alfonso, 8352
Frangieh, Rizk T., 6291

Franke, H., 6820
Franke, Richard, 4730
Frankel, David, 5471
Frankel, Jonathan, 10599, 10600
Franklin, A. E., 373
Franklin, Bob, 3855
Franklin, James L., 7677
Franklin, Simon, 9064
Franklin, Stephen D., 9534
Franklin, Vincent P., 9535, 9536
Franks, C.E.S., 1217
Franks, P.E., 8062
Franolic, Branko, 9829
Fransman, M., 8063
Franszoon, Adiante, 8557
Frantz, Charles, 10012
Fraser, David, 1401
Fraser, H. Aubrey, 10394
Fraser, N.M., 9065
Fraser, Stewart E., 374
Frawley, Joan, 7089
Frayha, Nemer M., 6292
Frazer, Ian L., 6943
Fredericks, Marcel, 4451
Freedman, Francesca, 9537
Freedman, M., 6392
Freedman, Samuel G., 8064
Freeland, Jane, 7090
Freeman, Gary P., 2493
Freeman, Marsha A., 11536
Freese, C., 2912
Freid, Yochanan, 5253
Freidenreich, Harriet P., 515, 9830
Freiman, Grigori, 9066
Freindly, Alfred, 5254
Fremgen, Gisela, 2913
Fremigacci, Jean, 6353
French, R.A., 9417
Frenkel, Shlomo, 5255
Frenkel, Stephen, 7907
Freris, A.F., 4370
Fresco, Nadine, 2494
Freund, J., 2402, 2741
Freund, W.M., 8065
Freund, W.S., 11127
Frevert, Ute, 2914
Frey, Linda, 11997
Frick, Bernd, 2804
Friday, Keith, 10475

Frideres, James S., 1218, 1402, 1403, 9723
Fried, C., 11537
Fried, Jacob, 10946
Fried, Johannes, 10601
Friedberg, Maurice, 9067
Friedgut, Theodore H., 9068, 9069
Friedhoff, Herman, 6821
Friedland, Elaine, 6691
Friedlander, Henry, 2915, 11639
Friedlander, Judith, 2495
Friedler, Ya'acov, 5256, 5472
Friedman, Alice T., 3856
Friedman, E., 49
Friedman, Ellen G., 10120
Friedman, Gerald, 2496
Friedman, I, 516
Friedman, Ina R., 10602
Friedman, Jean-Pierre, 2497
Friedman, Jerome, 8353
Friedman, Lawrence J., 9538
Friedman, Philip, 9070, 9071, 12077
Friedman, Regine M., 2916
Friedman, Robert, 11538
Friedman, Robert J., 5472
Friedman, Saul S., 8681, 8682
Friedman, Thomas L., 5474-5482
Friedman, Wilton, 11539
Friedmann, D., 5257
Friedmann, Nina S. de, 1797
Friend, Theodore, 7538
Fries, Yvonne, 8436
Friesen, J., 1105
Frieson, Kate, 967
Frigessi, Delia, 5937
Frijhoff, Willem, 10603
Frisch, Hiller, 5483
Frost, Elsa C., 6537
Frost, Richard A., 6189
Frucht, Richard, 10947
Fruhling Ehrlich, Hugo, 1556
Fry, E.C., 213
Fry, V.C., 3859
Fryatt, Diane Terry, 11894
Frye, A., 10948
Frykenberg, Robert E., 4731-4733
Fuchs, Abraham, 1989
Fuchs, Rachel G., 2499
Fuentes, Carlos, 1806
Fuentes Molinor, Olac, 6538

Fujiyoshi, Ronald Susumu, 6046
Fukuda, Masa-aki, 6047
Fulcher, James, 8579
Fuller, Bruce, 11540
Fuller, Elizabeth, 9072
Fuller, Thomas, 8892
Fullerton, Madeline, 3860
Funcke, L., 2917
Fung, Edmund S.K., 1620, 1731
Funke, Hajo, 2918
Fur, Lajos, 7810
Furedi, Frank, 11541
Furet, F., 2500
Furlong, Patrick J., 8067-8069
Furnham, Adrian, 3861, 4153
Furniss, Norman, 10508
Furnivall, J.S., 11542

Gabay, Z., 11128
Gabbai, Sheli, 5484
Gabriel, Claude, 11247
Gabriel, John, 3712
Gabriel, John G., 9539
Gabriel, Judith, 5485
Gabriel, S.A., 5486
Gacs, E., 4536
Gaddi, Giuseppe, 5938
Gadgil Madhav, 4755
Gadolin, Axel von, 2341
Gaffney, John, 3862
Gagé, J., 11895
Gager, John G., 11896
Gagnier, Regina, 3863
Gagnon, Nathaly, 1404
Gahug, T.J., 8417
Gaiha, R., 4734
Gaine, Chris, 3864
Galanis, Georgios N., 2919
Galante, Abraham, 8821, 8822
Galanter, Marc, 4735-4737
Galbo, Joseph, 5939
Gale, Fay, 375-382
Gale, Roger W., 11248
Galli, Rosemary E., 4436, 4437
Gallie, Duncan, 2501
Gallin, Alice, 2920
Gallissot, Rene, 50
Gallou, J. Y., 2502
Galos, Adam, 7650
Galtung, Johan, 5487

Galuzo, Peter G., 9073
Gama, Katherine de, 4074
Gambier, Yves, 2342
Gamble, Eiza B., 11543
Gampel, Benjamin R., 8354, 8355
Gana, Aaron T., 7235, 7236
Gander, Cathy, 7091
Gandhi, Raj S., 4739
Gandhi, Rajmohan, 4738
Gankovsky, Yu. V., 4,
Gantzel, Klaus J., 11544
Ganzeboom, Harry B.G., 6826, 11545
Gao Yuan, 1693
Garai, George, 4537
Garaud, X., 2503
Garaudy, Roger, 10496
Garbers, Johan G., 8070
Garcia Delgado, José L., 8356
Garcia H., Alvaro, 1557
Garcia, Lue, 695
Garcia, Victoria L., 7026
Gardinier, David E., 989, 1543, 10121, 10122
Gardner, John, 214, 3865
Gardner, Richard C., 7581
Garfield, Richard, 7027
Garfinkels, B., 657
Gargan, Edward A., 1605, 1694, 9974
Garlan, Yvon, 11897, 11898
Garnsey, Peter, 11899
Garrard, Carol, 9074
Garrard, John, 9074
Garrett, Sharon D., 9716
Garriqus, John, 4477
Garside, W.R., 3866
Gasiorowski, Mark, 5102
Gaskell, A., 1695
Gasperini, William, 7092, 7093
Gat, Moshe, 5146
Gates, Henry Louis, Jr., 3391
Gatz, Karen L., 2921
Gaudart, Hyacinth M., 6393
Gaudier, Maryse, 11998
Gauri, Viswanathan, 4740
Gayet, Denis, 10949
Gazi, Losso, 9922
Gboyega, Alex, 7237
Gearing, Brian, 3867
Gebru Tareke, 2285
Gedge, Evelyn S., 4741

Geggus, David, 2504
Gehmacher, Ernst, 542
Geiger, Roger L., 11546
Geiser, Peter, 6048
Geiss, Imanuel, 10604
Geissler, Rainer, 2922, 2923
Geithman, D.T., 1831
Gelber, Mark H., 2924, 3291
Gelber, N.M., 7811
Gella, Aleksander, 10605
Gellately, Robert, 2925, 2926
Gellhorn, Martha, 7370
Gellner, Ernest, 51, 10606
Genders, Elaine, 3868
Gendler, Everett, 1888
Genn, Rowel, 10607
Genovese, Eugene D., 9540, 9541, 10595, 11024, 11535, 11548
Geoffroy, Claude, 2505
George, Alan, 6346
George, Alexander, 4742
George, T.J.S., 7539, 7923
George, Vic, 10608
Georgeoff, John, 920
Georgescu, Vlad, 7812
Gerard Pierre-Charles, 2127
Gerber, David A., 9542
Gerber, Haim, 8823, 11129
Gerber, Jane S., 10123, 11130
Gergel, N., 9075
Gergere, Marie-Claire, 1696
Gerhardi Bon, Silvia, 5940
Gerhardt, Gary, 9531
Gerlach, Lynne, 8443
Gerner, Deborah J., 5488
Gershoni, Israel, 2186, 2187
Gershoni, Yekutiel, 6312, 6313
Gerson, Jane, 3365
Gertzel, Cherry, 4438
Geschiere, Peter, 10057
Gesheketer, Charles L., 10124
Gesser, Bengt, 8580
Getzler, Israel, 215, 216
Geurts, P.A.T.M., 6822
Geuter, Ulfried, 2928, 2929
Geva, Ahron, 5489
Ghai, Dharam, 10125, 10126
Ghai, Yash, 10126
Ghareeb, Edmund A., 5147
Gharpure, J. R., 4743

Ghaussy, S., 11131
Ghebre-Ab, Habtu, 10127
Ghorayyib, Rose, 6285
Ghose, A.K., 2286
Ghosh, P., 4744
Ghosh, Ratna, 4745, 11636
Ghostkeeper, Elmer, 1219
Ghoussoub, Mai, 11132
Ghozali, N.E., 8071
Giacaman, Rita, 5490
Giacomini, Sonia Maria, 783
Giannone, A., 5941
Giannou, Chris, 5491
Giarizzo, Guiseppi, 5907
Gibbs, Jewelle T., 9543
Giblin, Beatrice, 2506, 2507
Giblin, J., 8701
Gibson, Ashton, 3392
Gibson, John, 217
Gibson, Katherine D., 6944, 7540, 8072
Gibson, Margaret A., 3393, 10395
Gibson, Robert E., 11249
Giddings, Jeff, 218
Giele, Janet Z., 636
Gietzelt, Dale, 5036
Giffen, R., 11999
Gifford, Lord, 3869
Gifford, Prosser, 10128, 10129
Gil, Germán R., 120
Gilam, Abraham, 3292
Gilberg, Trond, 7813
Gilbert, Dennis L., 7451
Gilbert, Geoff, 11549
Gilbert, V.F., 3870, 12000, 12001
Gilboa, Jehoshua A., 9076
Giles, Geoffrey J., 2930, 2931
Giliomee, Hermann, 7964, 8049, 8073
Gill, Flora, 9544
Gillerman, Sharon, 10597
Gillespie, Charles, 8916
Gillespie, Raymond, 5172
Gilley, Sheridan, 3521
Gilliat, Penelope, 3871
Gillie, Donna A., 1161
Gillingham, John, 5178
Gillion, K.L., 11250, 11251
Gilman, Sander L., 2932, 2933, 11550
Gilmurray, John, 9975
Gilroy, Paul, 3872
Gilson, Richard P., 11252

Gimbel, John, 2934, 9545
Gimernez, Martha E., 11551
Ginaite, Sara, 9077
Ginat, Joseph, 5492, 5493
Giner, Salvador, 8357
Gini, Corrado, 5942
Ginor, Fanny, 5258
Ginsberg, E.S., 12002
Gintzburder, Alphonse, 6354
Ginwala, Irene, 8074
Giorgetti, G., 5943
Giovana, Mario, 11500
Gipoulon, Catherine, 1697
Girard, Andre, 921
Giraud, M., 1220, 2508, 2509, 1152
Girling, John, 8742
Gislason, Ingolfur V., 4607
Gisli, Palsson, 4605
Gist, Noel, 11553
Gitelman, Zvi, 9078-9082
Githige, R.M., 10130
Gitman, Joseph, 7678
Giudice, Fausto, 2510
Giullon, Michelle, 2511
Giura, Vincenzo, 5944
Gjelsvik, Tore, 7317
Gjording, Chris N., 7371
Glardon, Marie-Jo, 8649
Glaser, Kurt, 1221, 11554
Glasgow, Douglas G., 9546
Glasgow, Roy W., 4452
Glass, Bentley, 2935
Glass, Ruth, 4746
Glassman, Bernard, 3293
Glaus, Beat, 8650
Glazier, Stephen D., 10396
Glebe, Gunther, 10609
Gledhill, Sabrina, 10950
Gleijeses, Piero, 4405, 4406
Glettler, Monika, 517,518
Glewwe, Paul, 7452, 8437
Glickman, Paul, 7028, 7094
Gliozzi, Giuliano, 10610
Glissant, Edouard, 10397
Gluck, Lewis E. Jr., 7541
Go, G.T., 5037
Goddard, H.P., 2188
Godfrey, Brian J., 784
Godt, Paul, 2694
Goell, Yosef, 5494-5499

Goetzfridt, Nicholas J., 12003
Goglia, Luigi, 5945
Gohl, Gerhard, 6049
Goins, Lori L., 7095
Gojman de Backal, Alicia, 6539, 6540
Goke-Pariola, A., 7238
Gokhale, B.G., 10301
Golb, Norman, 2512
Golczewski, Frank, 7679
Gold, Jerry, 11253
Goldberg, Albert I., 5259
Goldberg, Anatol, 9084
Goldberg, Ellis, 2189
Goldberg, Faye J., 6050
Goldberg, Gertrude S., 11555
Goldberg, Giora, 5260
Goldberg, H.E., 5261, 6342, 6343, 6659
Goldberg, Harriet, 8358
Goldberg, Jacob, 7680
Goldberg, Marilyn P., 9085
Goldberger, Leo, 2088
Golde, Martijnde, 6852
Golden, M.A., 5946
Goldenberg, Paulette, 785
Goldie, Terry, 383, 1222, 6945
Goldin, Ian, 8075
Goldkorn, Isaac, 2513
Goldlust, J., 219
Goldman, A., 3294
Goldman, Philip, 9086
Goldreich, Arthur, 8076
Goldschmidt, Arthur, Jr., 2190
Goldstein, Eric, 5501, 5502
Goldstein, James, 2252
Goldstein, Melvyn C., 1606
Goldstrom, J. M., 3873
Goldthorpe, J. H., 3874
Goldthorpe, John H., 10611
Gomes, Gustavo M., 786
Gomes, Joaquim, 4439
Gomes, Mercio P., 787
Gonzalez, Anabel, 8359
Gonzalez, Carmen, 8077
Gonzalez, Michael M., 7542, 7453, 7454
González, Raúl, 7455, 7456
González, Vinicio, 10955
González Arzac, Alberto Ricardo, 121
González Casanova, Pablo, 6542, 6543, 10952-10954

González Garcia, Isidro, 8360, 8361
González Navarro, Moisés, 6541
González-Suarez, Mirta, 1835
Good, Kenneth, 7399, 11556
Goodman, David, 6051, 11557
Goodman, Grant K., 10302
Goodwater, Leanna, 12004
Gook, Aik guan, 7924
Gool, S. Y., 8078
Goonatilake, S., 4747
Gooneraine, D.D.M., 8438
Gooneratne, Yasmine, 8439
Goonetileke, H.A.I., 12005
Gopal, Krishan, 8440
Gordon, A., 8079
Gordon, Alec, 5038
Gordon, Bertram M., 2514
Gordon, David C., 52
Gordon, Gerd S., 7318
Gordon, Haim, 5503
Gordon, Jean, 5504
Gordon, Mary L., 11900
Gordon, Paul, 3394-3397, 3875-3883, 3980, 12006, 12007
Gordon, Richard K., Jr., 4748
Gordon, Robert, 7400, 8080
Gordon, Suzanne, 8081
Gordon Gitt, Edmundo, 7097
Gordon Gitt, Edmundo, 7096, 7097
Gorenberg, Gerahom, 5505, 5506
Gorman, G.E., 12008
Gormley, Daniel J., 1223
Gorny, Yosef, 5507
Gorter, Durk, 11558
Goschler, Constantin, 2936
Gosine, M., 10432
Goslinga, C.C., 6823
Gosner, Kevin, 6544
Gosschalk, Brian, 3777
Göthner, Karl-Christian, 10956
Gotlieb, Yosef, 10957, 11133
Gotovitch, José, 658
Gott, K.D., 220
Gottman, Yosef, 5643
Gottschalk, Keith, 6738, 6739
Goudsblom, Johan, 6824
Goudswaard, Keej, 6825
Gough, Kathleen, 4749, 4750
Goulbourne, Harry, 3398
Gould, David J., 9923

Gould, J.D., 10612
Gould, Jeffrey L., 7029
Gould, John, 6946
Gould, W.T.S., 6190, 8702
Gourgey, Perey S., 4751
Gover, Yerach, 5508
Govia, Francine, 12009
Gowing, P.S., 7543
Goyal, B.R., 4752
Gozalbes Cravioto, Enrique, 6462
Graaf, Paul M. de, 6826
Gräbener, Jürgen, 10958
Grabosky, Peter N., 384
Grabowski, R., 2191
Graces, Pamela M., 3884
Graetz, Brian, 221
Graf, P., 3076
Graff, H. F., 7544
Graff, Harvey J., 11559
Graham, Julie, 7540
Graham, Margaret E., 10398
Graham, Richard, 10959
Grahl-Madsen, Atle
Graindor, P., 11901
Gran, Peter, 2192
Grand, Alexander de, 5947
Grandin, Nicole, 8523
Grant, George C., 9976
Gras, Pierre, 7457
Grassby, Albert J., 222, 385, 386
Grassby, Richard, 3885, 3886
Grassi, Corrado, 5948
Grassi, Fabio, 5945
Graves, Adrian, 11254
Gray, Andrew, 10960
Gray, Beverly Ann, 6314
Gray, J., 3375
Gray, J.A.C., 11255
Gray, M., 3545, 3563
Gray, M.W., 5510
Gray, Nigel, 3887
Gray, Pat, 3749
Gray, R., 3888
Gray, Richard, 9977
Grayson, J. Paul, 1405, 1470
Graziani, J., 11134
Greaney, V., 5179
Grebing, Helga, 2938
Green, A.E., 3894
Green, David, 10961

AUTHOR INDEX 951

Green, December, 990
Green, Duncan, 788
Green, Elliot A., 53
Green, Geoffrey, 3295
Green, Jeffrey P., 3400
Green, John, 3564
Green, Leslie C., 1224, 1317
Green, Mary Jean, 2516
Green, Nancy, 2517
Green, Reginald H., 6740
Green, Warren, 7681
Greenacre, M.J., 8105
Greenbaum, Alfred A., 9087
Greenbaum, Avraham, 10614
Greenbaum, Linda, 789
Greenberg, Jack, 11560
Greenberg, Joel, 5511-5516
Greenberg, Richard, 8441
Greenberg, Susan, 5517
Greenberger, A.J., 4753
Greenblatt, Stephen J., 11561
Greenleaf, Richard E., 6545, 6546
Greenwood, Michael J., 6547
Greer, Allan, 1406
Greer, E., 9547
Greer, John, 3565
Gregg, W., 3544
Gregory, Joel W., 10089
Gregory, Paul R., 9088, 9089
Gregory, Peter, 6548
Gregory, Robert G., 4754
Greif, G., 10626
Greiner, C., 2939
Gress, Franz, 2940
Greussing, Fritz, 10615
Grew, Raymond, 2518-2520
Greyling J.J.C., 12010
Grieshaber, Erwin P., 705
Griffin, Keith, 10303, 10304, 11562
Griffin, Larry J., 11563
Griffith, Albert R., 1889
Griffiths, Curt T., 1225
Griffiths, Richard, 2521
Griggin, Keith, 1698
Griggs, Clive, 3895
Grigulevich, J.R., 11340
Grillo, R.D., 2522, 2523
Grillo Saez, David, 1890
Grimal, Pierre, 11564
Grimm, Reinhold, 2941

Gritti, Jules, 2524
Gronemeyer, Reimer, 10616, 12011
Groote, Jacqueline de, 659
Grosh, M.E., 11565
Gross, Feliks, 5949, 7682
Gross, Irena, 7685
Gross, Jan T., 7683, 7684, 7685
Gross, Mirjana, 9831
Gross, R., 790
Gross, Susan H., 10056
Grossholtz, Jean, 8442
Grossman, David, 5518, 5519
Grossman, Edward, 5520, 5521
Grossman, J.B., 8581
Grossman, Vasily, 9042
Grossman, Zoltan, 7545
Grotenber, Hanneke, 6794
Groth, Alexander J., 7686, 10617
Grothaus, M., 519
Grothusen, Klaus-Detlev, 9832
Grove, Lloyd, 2942
Grovogui, Siba N'Zatioula, 6741
Gruat, J.V., 2779, 2780
Gruber, Alfons, 5950
Gruber, Helmut, 520
Gruber, Ruth, 2287
Gruen, George E., 11135
Gruenwald, Oskar, 9833
Gruessing, Kurt, 5093
Grugel, Jean, 1558
Grugeon, E., 4351
Grulich, Rudolf, 7687
Grunberg, Bernard, 6549
Grunfeld, A. Tom, 1607
Grunfeld, F.V., 11566
Grupp, Fred W., 9121
Gruson, Lindsey, 2253, 2254
Gruzinski, Serge, 6550
Grynberg, Henryk, 7688
Guan, Shijie, 1699
Gucht, A.-M. van der, 2525
Gudeta, Mammo, 2288
Gudmundson, Lowell, 122, 1836, 1837
Guelke, Leonard, 8083
Guerra Garcia, Francisco, 7458
Guerre, J., 10399
Guerry, Louis, 5951
Guest, Bill, 8046
Guggenheim, Willy, 8651
Guha, Amalendu, 10618, 10619

Guha, R., 4755
Guidiere, Remo, 6550, 7129, 8500
Guidieri, Remo, 11567
Guillaumin, Colette, 2526, 2527
Guillemin, J., 9548
Guir, Roger, 1310
Guiral, Pierre, 2528
Guisso, Richard W., 1700
Guldescu, Stanko, 9879
Gullick, Charles J.M.R., 10400
Gülzow, H., 11902
Gumbert, Marc, 387
Gunn, Geoffrey C., 6275, 9768
Gunn, Simon, 10620
Gunnarsson, Thorsteinn V., 4608
Gunter, Michael M., 8824, 8825, 8826, 8827, 8828
Gupta, A.R., 4756
Gupta, Devendra B., 4757
Gupta, Dipankar, 1407
Gupta, S.K., 4758
Gurley, John, 11562
Gurnah, Ahmed, 3896
Gurr, Ted Robert, 388, 389, 9548, 11579
Gurun, Kamuran, 8829
Gustaffson, B., 2343, 8582, 8583
Gustavson, Carl G., 8584
Gut, Israel, 7670
Guthier, Steven L., 9090
Gutierrez, Felix, 9732
Gutierrez, Gustavo, 10962
Gutierrez, José Angel, 9549
Gutkind, P., 7279
Gutman, Israel, 6857, 7689-7693, 7721, 9811, 10559, 10621-10627, 10726
Gutteridge, Richard J., 2943
Gutto, S.B.O., 6191
Guy, D.E., 1985
Guy, Jeff, 8084
Guzman Gomez, Alba, 6551
Gyemant, Ladislau, 7814

Haarhoff, Dorian, 6742
Haarlov, Jens, 8085
Haarman, Ulrich W., 2193
Haas, Ernest B., 11568
Haas, Hanna, 5952
Haas, Sandra K., 390
Haavio-Mannila E., 8585

Habbe, Christian, 2944
Haberer, Rose B., 5522
Haberly, David, 791
Haberman, Clyde, 922, 923, 6052, 6053
Habermas, Jürgen, 2945
Habib, Irfan, 4759, 4760
Habib, Jack, 5262
Habiby, Emile, 5523
Habicht, J.P., 6389
Haboucha, Reginette, 9834
Hackett, Nan, 12012
Hackett, Rick 1416
Hadawi, Sami, 5524
Haddad, Robert M., 8683
Haddad, Subhy, 5148
Haddock, Mike, 521
Hadjor, Kofi B., 3261
Haestrup, Jorgen, 2089
Haft, C.J., 6857, 10627, 10726
Hagan, Stephanie, 11257
Hagege, Claude, 8778
Hageman, Albrecht, 8086
Hagen, William W., 2946, 10628
Hagenaars, Aldi J.M., 10629
Hagendoorn, Louk, 6827, 6828
Hager, Mark M., 1701
Haggard, Stephan, 10964
Haggis, Jane, 3897
Hahn, Fred, 1990
Hahner, June E., 792
Haidar, Aziz, 5525-5528
Haig-Brown, Celia, 1226
Haile-Mariam, Y., 10131
Haim, Sylvia G., 5149
Haim, Yehoyada, 5529
Haimson, Leopold, 9091
Hainsworth, Paul, 2529
Hair, P.E.H., 10132
Haj, Samira, 5150
Hajda, Jan, 1991
Hajda, Lubomyr, 9092
Hale, C.A., 1408
Hale, Charles, 7098
Haleber, Ron, 6829
Halevy, Zvi, 9093
Halgendoren, M. van, 12014
Haliczer, Stephen H., 8362, 8363
Halkovic, Stephen A., Jr., 6637, 6640
Hall, Anthony J., 1227
Hall, D.J., 1228

Hall, Margaret, 6692
Hall, Patricia A., 9550
Hall, R., 9949
Hall, Raymond L., 11569
Hall, Stuart, 3898, 3899
Hallaj, Muhammad, 5530, 5531
Haller, A. O., 746
Haller, Max, 522, 2947, 10630
Halliday, Fred, 5, 2289, 9793, 11570
Halliday, Jon, 6238, 6239
Halloran, James D., 11571
Halper, J., 5263
Halperin, Jean, 2948
Halpern, Ben, 11572
Halpern, Joel, 10631
Halsey, A.H., 3900, 3911
Halstead, J. M., 3401
Halstead, Mark, 3901
Hamarneh, Mustafa B., 6159
Hamel, Gildas H., 11903
Hamel, R., 6552
Hamerow, Theodore S., 11573
Hamid, S., 7335
Hamilton, Clive, 6240
Hamilton, Linda G., 6947
Hamilton, Nora, 6553, 6625
Hamilton, Roberta, 1409
Hamish, Ernst, 523
Hamman, A., 6660
Hammar, Tomas, 10632
Hammett, Michael P., 11258
Hammond, Dorothy, 11574
Hamnett, C., 3499, 3902
Hamoumou, Mohand, 54, 2530
Hampenstall, Peter, 11259
Hampton, Francesca, 4761
Hampton, Ken, 421
Hanak, Peter, 4538
Hanawalt, Barbara A., 3903
Hancock, Ian F., 2949, 2950, 10633, 11575
Handlin, Oscar, 9551
Handwerker, W.P., 11576
Handy, Jim, 4408, 4409
Hanke, Lewis, 757
Hanks, Peter, 391
Hanley, S.B., 6054
Hanlon, David, 11260
Hann, C.M., 7694
Hanna, Martha T., 2531

Hannoun, Michel, 2532
Hannum, Hurst, 968
Hansen, Bernt, 8893
Hansen, David O., 5039
Hansen, Erick, 6830
Hanson, Allan, 6948
Hanson, John R., II, 11577
Hanssen, J., 6827
Haq, E., 4762
Haque, Mozammel, 4763, 4764
Haque, S.A., 4765
Haraguchi, Koichi, 6055
Harap, Louis, 9094, 11578
Haraszti, Endre, 7815
Harber, Clive, 7239
Harbison, J. and J., 3536, 3566
Harbury, C.D., 3904
Harcourt, David, 223
Hardach, Karl, 2951
Harden, Blaine, 8894
Harding, Colin, 7459
Harding, Jim, 1229
Harding, Timothy F., 6553, 6625
Hardman, Anna, 10767
Hares, Abdullatif K., 6293
Harewood, Jack, 10401
Harff, Barbara, 11579
Harfouche, Jamal K., 6294
Harik, Elsa M., 55, 6192
Harinck, Gerrit, 8087
Harkabi, Yehoshafat, 5532, 5533
Harkness, David, 3567
Harlan, Louis R., 9552
Harley, Sharon, 9553
Harlow, Barbara, 5534
Harman, Chris, 3759, 10634
Harman, Grant, 3488, 7405
Harms, Robert W., 9924
Harneit-Sievers, Axel, 6743
Haroda, Tomobiko, 6056
Haron, Nadzan, 6394
Harouel, Jean-Louis, 2533
Harper, Carol A., 3905
Harpo, Nan, 7099
Harries, Ann, 8088
Harries, Patrick, 8089, 10133
Harrigan, Patrick, 2519
Harriman, Ed, 3500
Harriman, Helga H., 9835
Harrington, J. Drew, 11904

Harris, A.H., 3626
Harris, Abram L., 9554, 9555
Harris, Barbara J., 136
Harris, C.C., 3662
Harris, David A., 6057, 9095
Harris, G.T., 10310
Harris, Geoffrey, 10635
Harris, J., 5071
Harris, J.E., 10305
Harris, John, 6315
Harris, Olivia, 10965
Harris, Richard, 11580
Harris-Schenz, B., 2952
Harris, Sydney, 3906
Harris, William H., 9556
Harrison, A., 11581
Harrison, A.J., 3691, 3694
Harrison, Alferdteen, 10402
Harrison, B., 9707
Harrison, Brian, 3907
Harrison, Gail G., 12013
Harrison, J., 1230, 8364
Harrison, Paul, 3908
Harriss, John, 4766
Hart, Charles D., 7546
Hart, Deborah M., 8090
Hart, Nicky, 3909
Hart, Richard, 10403
Harth-Terré, Emilio, 7460
Hartmann, P., 3910
Hartnaek, Christiane, 4767
Hartung, Gunter, 2953
Hartwig, M.C., 224
Harvey, Ruth A., 2954
Harviainen, Tapani, 2344
Harvie, Dominique, 4084, 4085
Harwood, Alan, 10966
Hasan, Mishirul, 4768
Haseeb, Khair El-Din, 10134
Haselsteiner, Horst, 4539
Hasenbalg, Carlos A., 793, 794
Hashemi, Syed, 619
Hashim, Wan, 6395
Hashmi, Tajul-Islam, 4769
Haslag, J.H., 6554
Hasler, Alfred A., 8645
Haslinger, M., 524
Haslum, 3743
Hassall, Graham H., 11261
Hassan, Amira, 5535

Hassan, M.K., 4770
Hassan, Sana, 5536
Hasse, W., 11928
Hasselblatt, Gunnar, 2290
Hassell, K. L., 392
Hassen, Mohammed, 2291
Hassim, Yael, 5537
Hassler, A.H., 8652
Hastie, R. M., 393
Hatch, S., 3402
Hate, Chandrakala Anandrao, 4771
Hatem, Michael, 2194
Hatton, J.D., 8091
Haubert, M., 10967
Hauschild, Thomas, 2874, 2875
Hause, Steven C., 2534
Hauser, Przemyslaw, 7695
Hausmann, Bernd, 2955
Havelange, Pierre, 660
Hawkins, Alun, 3912
Hawkins, J.N.,
Hawkins, Tony, 9978
Hawthorne, Lasleeyanne, 225
Haxthausen, Charles W., 3198
Hay, Malcolm, 10636
Hayes, M., 3568
Hayes, Peter, 2956, 11262
Haynes, Aaron, 3403
Hazarika, Sanjoy, 4772
Hazelhurst, Kayleen M., 6949
Hazlett, T.W., 8092
He Dougchang, 1702
Heacock, Roger, 5538
Head, Wilson A., 1135
Headrick, Rita, 10135
Healy, John J., 394
Hearden, Patrick J., 9557
Hearn, Francis, 3913
Heath, A.F., 3914
Heaton, William R., Jr., 1608
Hebbert, M., 8365
Heberer, Thomas, 1609-1611
Hebert, John R., 123
Hebert, Yvonne M., 1283
Hedrich, Kurt, 2957
Hedva Ben-Israel, Coli, 3326
Heffernan, Michael J., 56
Hegarty, Seamus, 3461, 4270
Heggoy, Alf A., 57, 58, 59
Heiberg, Marianne, 8366

Heikkinen, Sakari, 2345
Heilke, Thomas W., 10638
Heimer, Franz-Wilhelm, 4440
Heinecke, P., 7240
Heinemann, L., 1231
Heinemann, M., 2958
Heinen, Armin, 7816
Heinen, Heinz, 11905
Heinen, Jacqueline, 9096
Heinrich, Hans-Georg, 4540
Heinrichs, Terry, 1025
Heintz, Hans-Joachim, 2791
Heinzig, Dieter, 9097
Heisler, Barbara S., 10639
Heitlinger, Alena, 9098
Heitman, Sidney, 9099
Heleno, Manuel, 7772
Hell, Jürgen, 795
Heller, Celia S., 7696
Heller, Milton I., 796
Heller, Peter, 2959
Hellfeld, Matthias von, 2960
Hellie, Richard, 9100-9104
Hellig, Jocelyn, 8093
Hellmann, Ellen, 8094
Hellwig, David J., 797
Hellwing, I. A., 525
Helly, Denise, 1070, 1612
Helms, Mary W., 7100, 7101
Helper, Rose, 9558
Hémery, Daniel, 2535
Hemming, John, 798-800
Hempenstall, Peter J., 11263
Henderson, Ian, 9950, 9951
Henderson, Toni, 3627
Hendrickson, Carol, 4410
Henfrey, J., 3989
Hengstenberg, Peter, 10968
Henke, Klaus-Dietmar, 2961
Henker, Reinhold, 526
Hennerbichler, Ferdinand, 11136
Hennig, Eike, 2962
Henningham, Stephan, 11264
Henningsen, Manfred, 2963
Henouda, A., 60
Henriques, U. R. G., 3296
Henry, Frances, 1136, 1410
Henry, Franklin J., 1081
Henry, Keith S., 1137
Henry, Paget, 10404

Henry, Ralph, 10401
Hensman, Richard, 7593
Hentoff, Nat, 5539, 5540
Henze, Paul, 2292
Hepburn, A.C., 3569, 11583
Heppell, M., 395
Hepple, B., 3570, 3915
Herand, Guy, 12014
Herberg, Edward N., 1411
Herbert, Jean-Loup, 10969
Herbert, Ulrich, 2964, 2965
Herbst, Jeffrey, 9979
Herculano, A., 7773
Hercus, Luise, 396
Herde, Georg, 2966
Herliky, Peter H., 7372
Herman, Elisa Beth, 12015
Herman, Karel, 1992
Hermann-Pillath, Carsten, 1703
Hermele, Kenneth, 6693
Hernandez, E., 6555
Hernandez, Francesca, 8367
Hernández, Isabel, 124, 125
Herold, Marc W., 10405
Heron, Craig, 1392
Herring, George C., 11082
Herrmann, Louis, 8095
Hersch, J., 2536
Hershatter, Gail, 1704
Herte, Robert de, 2537
Hertz, Aleksander, 7697, 7698
Hertzberg, Arthur, 10640, 11584, 11906
Hertzog, Stephen, 1412
Herzig, Arno, 2967
Herzog, Ferencz, 4541
Herzog, Jürgen, 8703
Herzstein, Robert Edwin, 2538, 9105
Hess, P.N., 11585
Hetzer, Armin, 12016
Heuman, Gad, 10970
Hever, Hannan, 5264
Hewitt, Roger, 3916
Hewitt, W.E., 801, 802
Hewton, Eric, 3917
Heyck, Thomas W., 3474
Heye, Uwe-Karsten, 2968
Heywood, Colin, 2539
Heywood, Linda M., 89
Hezel, F.X., 11265
Hicks, Alexander, 11586

956 AUTHOR INDEX

Hicks, Frederic, 6556
Hicks, George L., 714
Hifi, Belkacem, 2540
Higginbotham, A. Leon, Jr., 8096, 9560
Higginson, John, 9925, 9926
Higham, Charles, 6950, 9561
Higley, John, 226
Higman, B.W., 10406
Hijab, Nadia, 5666
Hilal, Jamil, 11137
Hilbeln, Ewald, 7817
Hilberg, Raul, 10641
Hill, Adrian V.S., 11266
Hill, Arlette C., 2969
Hill, Craig, 3918, 6930, 6931
Hill, Daniel G., 1138
Hill, Dave, 3919
Hill, Donna, 1139
Hill, Herbert, 9562
Hill, J.S., 1140
Hill, K., 11587
Hill, Leonides E., 1026
Hill, M., 386
Hill, Polly, 7241
Hill, R.G.P., 2346, 2347
Hill, Ray, 10642
Hillebrecht, Werner, 12017
Hillel, Marc, 7700
Hillel, Shlomo, 5151
Hillier, Stella, 8443
Hills, Jill, 11655
Hillson, Jon, 1891
Hiltermann, Joost R., 5541-5548
Hilton, Stanley E., 803
Himka, John-Paul, 527
Himmelstrand, Ulf, 8580
Hinchliffe, Keith, 10136
Hind, Robert J., 3920
Hingstman, L., 6831
Hinnebusch, R., 2195
Hinshaw, Christine R., 9106
Hinton, William H., 1705, 1706, 1707
Hintze, Susana, 126
Hintzer, Percy C., 4453
Hirasawa, Yasumasa, 6058, 6059
Hirayasu, Naomi, 11267
Hiro, Dilip, 4773
Hirsch, Herbert, 9563
Hirsch, Kurt, 2970
Hirschberg, Joachim W., 10137

Hirschfeld, Gerhard, 2541, 6832, 10643
Hirschman, Charles, 6396, 6397
Hirschmann, D., 8097
Hirshom, Sheryl, 7030
Hirst, John, 227
Hirszowicz, Lukasz, 9107, 10644
Hirway, Inira, 4774
Histor, Manfred, 2971
Hitchens, Christopher, 5549, 9980
Hitchins, Keith, 528, 7818
Hjejle, Benedicte, 4775
Hladczuk, John, 11588, 12018
Hlophe, S.S., 6316
Ho, Christine, 4454, 10407
Ho, David Y.F., 10138, 11589
Hoapala, Pertti, 2348
Hobart, Charles W., 1232
Hoberman, J.M., 2542
Hoberman, Louisa S., 10971
Hobsbawm, Eric J., 1798, 3921, 10646, 11590, 11591
Hobson, Dorothy, 3922
Hobson, R.F., 10576
Hocevar, Toussaint, 9836
Hoch, Marie-Therese, 2543
Hoch, Steven L., 9108
Hochberg, Leonard, 11024, 11535
Hochmaulova, D., 1993
Hockenos, Paul, 2972, 2973, 7819, 7820, 9837, 10647
Hodge, John E., 127
Hodge, John L., 9565
Hodge, Robert W., 5601
Hodges, Tony, 10139, 10140
Hodges-Betts, Bobbie, 804
Hodne, Fritz, 7319
Hodos, George H., 1994, 10648
Hoefte, Rosemarijn A., 8558, 8559
Hoenisch, Michael, 10408
Hoensch, Jorg K., 9803, 10868
Hoerder, Dirk, 517, 2886, 3020, 10789
Hoetink, Harry, 2119, 10409, 10972
Hoff, Jens, 2090
Hoffman, Bernard G., 6661
Hoffman, Bruce, 10649
Hoffman, Charles, 5265, 5266, 5267
Hoffman, G.H., 1027
Hoffman, Ronald, 9457
Hoffman, Tessa, 8830
Hoffman-Nowotny, H. J., 8653

Hoffmann, Barbara, 2974
Hoffmann, Johannes, 12019
Hoffmann, Lutz, 2975
Hoffmann, Peter, 4371
Hofman, John E., 5550
Hofmann, Tessa, 11138
Hofwiler, R., 924
Hogan, J., 3923
Hogan, Lloyd, 9566
Hogbin, Herbert, J. P., 11268
Hogeweg de Haart, H.P., 6833
Hoggart, Keith, 3924
Hohenberg, Paul M., 10650
Hohmann, Joachim S., 2976, 2977
Hoidal, O.K., 7320
Holder, C., 10410
Holdesheimer, Esriel, 3037
Holgate, Geoff, 3925
Holiday, Tony, 8098
Holland, B., 9109, 9110
Holland, L., 7103
Holland, Robert, 6908
Holliday, Jon, 19
Hollifield, James F., 2544, 2545
Hollingsworth, P., 228
Hollows, Fred, 397
Hollstein, Dorothea, 2978
Holmes, Colin, 3297, 3298, 3522, 3926-3928, 8099
Holmes, Colin, 3521
Holmstrom, Mark, 4776
Holsinger, Donald, 61
Holt, A. E., 2196
Holt, Alix, 9110
Holt, Nathan V., Jr., 8100
Holt-Seeland, Inger, 1892
Holter, Age, 2197
Holtfrerich, Carl-Ludwig, 2979
Holton, J.E., 3404
Holzer, Willibald, 529, 10651
Holzner, Lutz, 2980
Hondius, Dienke, 6834
Honeybone, R., 9952
Hong, D.S., 6246
Hong, Lysa, 8743
Honig, Emile, 1613, 1614, 1708
Hooghoff, Hans, 6835, 6836
Hooks, Bell, 9567
Hooper, Antony, 11269
Hooper, Beverley J., 229, 1709

Hooper, Ed, 8895
Hopenhaym, Mabel, 8924
Hopken, Wolfgang, 925, 926, 927
Hopkins, A.G., 3757, 3758
Hopkins, Dwight N., 1893
Hopkins, Eric, 3501
Hopkins, Keith, 11907
Hopkins, Philip G.H., 11593
Hopkins, Sean, 5180
Hoppe, Hans-Joachim, 4372
Horak, Stephen M., 7701, 10652
Horch, Hans O., 10653
Horchem, Hans Josef, 2981
Hordes, Stanley M., 6557, 6558, 6559
Horn, Charles, 12021
Hornberger, Nancy H., 7461
Horne, Gerald C., 1894
Horne, John, 2546
Hornsby-Smith, Michael P., 3523
Horowitz, Aron, 1028
Horowitz, Donald L., 10973, 11594
Horowitz, Irving Louis, 1886, 1887, 11595
Horowitz, J.L., 7443
Horowitz, Paul, 10974
Horowitz, Tamar R., 5268
Horrell, Muriel, 8101, 8102
Horrocks, Linley, 11270
Horsman, Reginald, 3929
Horta, Korinna, 5045
Horton, S., 7547
Hory, Ladislaus, 9838
Hosin, A., 3571
Hoskin, Marilyn, 2893, 6835
Hosking, Geoffrey, 9111
Hossain, Zakir, 8744
Hoston, Germaine A., 6060
Houbert, Jean, 6474, 11271
Houlton, David, 3930
Hounkpatin, Philippe, 696
Hourani, Albert, 2198, 11139
Houston, J.E., 3572
Houston, R.A., 3628, 3629
Hout, M., 5201
Hout, Michael, 3573, 5181
Hovannisian, Richard G., 8831-8834, 12022, 12023
Hovell, Melbourne F., 6560
Howard, Jean E., 11467
Howard, Michael C., 398, 399

AUTHOR INDEX

Howard, Pat, 1710, 1711
Howard, Rhoda E., 10141
Howard, Roger, 1711
Howarth, Janet, 3932
Howe, Darcus, 2547, 3405
Howe, James, 7422
Howe, K.R., 400, 6951, 11272
Howe, Marvine, 20
Howell, Bing P., 7373
Howes, Paul W., 9718
Howorth, Jolyon, 2529, 2548
Hraba, Joseph, 6837, 6828
Hradilek, Tomas, 1995
Hroch, Miroslav, 10654
Hsia, R. Po-chia, 2982
Hsiao, Wey, 1712
Hsiung, James C., 10307
Hu-Dehart, Evelyn, 6561
Hu Jimkai, 1713
Hua Wu Yin, 6398
Huang Shoubao, 1615
Hubbard, James P., 7242
Hudson, Kenneth, 3933
Hudson, Randall O., 10975
Hudson, Ray, 10655
Hufford, Larry, 8586
Huggins, Martha K., 805
Huggins, Nathan Irvin, 9568
Hughes, David R., 1413
Hugill, Barry, 3934
Hugill, Peter J., 11597
Huhn, Anne, 2983
Huijsman, R., 6838
Hulchanski, J. David, 1341
Hull, Jeremy, 1195
Hull, Richard W., 8103
Hulme, Peter, 10411
Human, L., 8104-8106
Human, P., 8106
Humbel, Kurt, 8654
Hume, John C., Jr., 4777
Humes, Walter M., 3630
Humphrey, D., 3935
Humphries, Jane, 3936
Hunczak, Taras, 9112
Hundert, Gershon D., 7702, 12024
Hune, Shirley, 10656
Hunecke, Volken, 5953
Hunt, Albert, 9113
Hunt, Chester L., 7548

Hunt, David, 2549
Hunt, Paul, 5552
Hunt, Raymond G., 9724
Hunting, Claudine, 2550
Huntington, Guellen, 794
Hurtado, Oswaldo, 2135
Husayni, Faysal, 5553
Husband, C., 3910
Husband, Charles, 3937, 3938
Husbands, Christopher T., 3939, 3940, 10657, 10658
Husen, T., 11460
Huss, Doug, 7104, 7105, 7106
Hussain, Athar, 1691, 1714
Hussain, Monirul, 4778
Hussein, Fuad M., 8835
Hussin, Mutalib, 6399
Hutchinson, John F., 9352
Huttenback, Robert A., 401, 6952
Hutton, Marcelline J., 9114
Hwaletz, Otto, 530
Hwang, K.C., 6095
Hyam, Ronald, 11598
Hyamson, Albert M., 8684
Hyland, Aine, 5182
Hyman, Anthony, 6,
Hyman, Jacques L., 7894
Hymes, Dell, 9731
Hyslop, Jonathan, 8107-8109

Iakovlev, Aleksandr, 9115
Iatrides, John O., 12025
Iatridis, Demetrius S., 1895
Ibarra Illannez, Alicia, 2136
Ibegbu, C.U., 7243
Ibish, Y.K.H., 8685
Ibrahim, Ferhad, 5152
Ibrahim, Fouad N., 2199
Ichiro, Ono, 6061
Ichiyo, Muto, 6062
Iggers, Wilma, 1996, 1997
Ihonvbere, J. O., 7244
Ijaz, Mian A., 1082
Ikemoto, Yukio, 6400, 8745
Ikiddeh, Ime, 7245
Ilam, Yigal, 5269
Iliffe, John, 7246, 10142, 10143
Illyes, Elemer, 7822, 7823
Imart, G.G., 9116
Imbert, J., 11908

AUTHOR INDEX 959

Imbrogno, Salvatore, 7703
Imhoff, Arthur E., 402, 6953
Imoagene, O., 7247
Imonti, Felix, 6063
Imperial, Reynaldo H., 7549
Inalick, Halil, 8836
Inamina, Odida T., 4455
Incerti Delmonte, Maria G., 5955
Inden, R., 4779
Inder, Pal S., 4780
Indjic, Tirvo, 9839
Indra, D.M., 1072, 1083
Inglis, C.B., 231
Inigo Carrera, Nicolos, 128
Inikori, Joseph E., 3941, 3942, 10144
Inman, Samuel Guy, 10977
Insdorf, Annette, 531
Insh, G.P., 3631
Ioanid, Radu, 7824
Iqbal, Justice Javid, 7340
Iram, Yaacov, 2986
Iredale, R.R., 232
Irschick, Eugene F., 4782
Irving, Ronald E.M., 661
Irwin, Graham W., 11602
Irwin, Philippe B., 1838
Irwin, Zachary, 9840
Irwin-Zarecka, Iwona, 7704, 7705
Isaac, Jad, 5556
Isaac, Jules, 11603
Isaacman, Allen, 6694
Isaacs, Henry, 8111
Isenberg, Shirley B., 4783
Isenburg, Luisa, 5956
Isherwood, H. B., 3944
Ishida, Hiroshi, 6064, 6065
Ishow, Habib, 6268
Islam, Iyanatul, 5040, 5041
Islam, J., 620
Islam, M. Nazrul, 6401, 7341
Islam, M.R., 11274
Islam, Rizwanul, 621
Islami, A. Reza S., 7881
Ismae, Jacqueline S., 9794
Ismael, Jacqueline S., 6269, 6270
Ismael, Tarez Y., 9794
Ismaelillo, 7111, 11604
Ismagilova, R.N., 10146
Isola, Ema, 8917
Israel, Jonathan I., 6562, 10147, 10660

Israel, Rosha, 3423
Israeli, Rafi, 5562
Issacman, Allen, 6695
Issacman, Barbara, 6695
Issacowitz, Roy, 8221
Italaander, Rolf, 2987, 10978
Itani, Francis, 1084
Itsigsohn, Jose A., 10979
Ityavyar, Dennis A., 7248
Iutub, Ishaq, 6160
Ivan-Smith, Edda, 10148
Ivanitz, M.J., 1233
Ivorra, Pierre, 2553
Iwaasa, David B., 1085
Iwassawa, Yuji, 6066
Iwe, N.S.S., 7249
Iyeki, M.H., 9570
Iyengar, N.S., 4784
Iyer, V.R.K., 4785
Izeogu, Chukudi V., 7250

Ja'far, Mohammed, 11143
Jabavu, D.D.T., 8112
Jabbra, Nancy W., 1414
Jaber, Kamel Abu, 6161
Jablow, Alta, 11574
Jackman, Robert W., 11605
Jackson, Alastar Hurlstone, 11909
Jackson, Harold, 3574
Jackson, James H., 2988
Jackson, James Walvin, 11606
Jackson, Karl D., 969
Jackson, Kenneth T., 9571
Jackson, Michael, 1234
Jackson, Miles M., 11275
Jackson, Moana, 6955
Jackson, P., 11607
Jackson, Richard L., 10980, 10981
Jackson, Sandra C., 1896
Jacob, James B., 2554
Jacobs, A.P., 7492
Jacobs, Brian D., 3945
Jacobs, Brian E., 3407
Jacobs, J.U., 8113
Jacobs, Jack, 11608
Jacobs, N., 6067
Jacobs, S.V., 8114
Jacobs, Wilbur R., 9572
Jacobson, Dan, 8115
Jacobson, John R., 11609

Jacobson, Keith, 8116
Jacoby, Sidney B., 2872
Jacquard, A., 2555
Jacquemin, J-M, 663
Jacquemyns, J., 662
Jacques, Leo M.D., 6563, 6564
Jaffe, Eliezer D., 5271, 5272
Jaffe, Hosea, 10149
Jagendorf, Siegfried, 7825
Jahan, Rounaq, 10308
Jahoda, Marie, 533
Jahreskog, B., 8587
Jain, Devaki , 4786
Jain, Harish C., 1415, 1416, 1417
Jain, L. R., 4973
Jain, P.C., 11610
Jain, Prakash C., 4456, 6402
Jain, Ravindra K., 6403
Jainj, Anrudh K., 4787
Jaja, S.O., 7251
Jakubowicz, A.M. , 233, 234
Jalal, Ayesha, 7342
Jalali, Rita, 4788
Jalata, Asafa, 2293
Jamal, V., 7944, 8896
Jamard, Jean-Luc, 2508
James, Ariel, 10412
James, C.L.R., 3946, 10413
James, Estelle, 6839
James, John A., 3947
James, Joy, 7374
James, Lawrence, 10150
James, W., 8117
James, Winston, 3408
James-Bryan, M., 10414
Jameson, Michael H., 11910
Jamison, D.T., 1715, 6777
Jancar, Barbara, 9841
Janics, Kalman, 1998, 1999, 2000
Jankowski, James P., 2186
Janner, Greville, 3299
Janos, Andrew C., 4543
Janowsky, Oscar J., 10661, 10662
Janssen-Jurreit, Marielouise, 11611
Jansson, Arne, 8616
Janzen, Jorg, 11144
Jaquith, Cindy, 7112
Jaramillo Uribe, Jaime, 1799
Jarausch, Konrad H., 2989
Jaschke, Hans Gerd, 2940

Jatin, 5566
Jauhianen, Marjatta, 2349
Javier, Ernesto O., 7550
Jawad, Sa'ad N., 5153
Jay, Martin, 2990, 2991
Jayanntha, D., 8444
Jayaraman, Raja, 4789
Jayasundera, Punchi B., 8445
Jayawardena, Kumari, 11612
Jayawardena, V.K., 8446
Jayewardene, C.H.S., 8447
Jayewardene, Hilda, 8447
Jazouli, Adil, 2556
Jeansome, Glen, 9573
Jedlicka, Ludwig, 534
Jedlicki, Witold, 5567
Jedruszak, Tadeusz, 7706
Jedwab, Jack, 1029
Jefferson, Tony, 3948
Jeffery, Roger, 4790
Jeffrey, Henry B., 4457
Jeffrey, Keith, 11613
Jeffrey, Robin, 4791, 7569
Jeffries, Vincent, 8655
Jeijifo, Biodun, 10151, 10152
Jelavich, Charles, 9842
Jelin, Elizabeth, 10982
Jelinek, Yeshayahu A., 2001-2010
Jenkins, John R.G., 8656
Jenkins, Loren, 7113
Jenkins, Richard, 3410, 3951, 3952
Jenkinson, Jacqueline, 3409, 3949, 3950
Jenks, Manfred, 2992
Jennings, Ronald C., 1968
Jenson, Jane, 2557
Jeong Ho Lee, 6073
Jernazian, Ephriam K., 8837
Jersch-Wenzel, Stefi, 2993
Jesse, Eckhard, 2799, 2801, 2802
Jesson, Bruce, 6956
Jewsiewicki, B., 9927
Jimenez, E., 1800
Jimenez Pastrana, Juan, 1897
Jinadu, L. Adele, 7252
Jiobu, Robert M., 9574
Jirava, M., 2012
Jivonen, Jyrki K., 7707
Jo, Moon Hwan, 6074
Jobert, Ambroise, 7708
Joby, Gertrude, 6295

Jochmann, W., 2994
Jodice, David, 11800
Joei, Bernard T.K., 1221
Joes, Anthony J., 10663
Joffe, E.G.H., 6344
Johan, Kwesi, 3262
Johannese, Stanley, 1700
Johansen, Hans C., 2091
Johanson, Christine, 9118
Johansson, S. Ryan, 11614
John, Angela V., 3953
John, Gus, 3411
John, Michael, 2995
Johnson, Charles S., 6317
Johnson, D., 235
Johnson, D.H., 10153
Johnson, Dana, 1418
Johnson, Douglas H., 8524
Johnson, Herschel, 1898
Johnson, Howard, 10415, 10416
Johnson, Kay Ann, 1716
Johnson, Leo, 1419, 1420
Johnson, Linton Kwesi, 3412
Johnson, Lyman L, 129
Johnson, Mark, 3954
Johnson, Owen V., 2013
Johnson, P., 3955
Johnson, Paul, 3956
Johnson, Penny, 5569-5577
Johnson, Phyllis J., 1086
Johnson, R.W., 7305
Johnson, Robert E., 9119
Johnson, Thomas, 1421
Johnson-Krojzal, Clare, 2996
Johnston, Darlene, 1235
Johnston, Eric, 1236
Johnston, Gerald L., 236
Johnston, Howard J., 9769
Johnston, Hugh J.M., 1087
Johnstone, Diana, 11276
Johnstone, F., 8119
Join-Lambert, P., 2558
Jolivet, Marie-José, 2559
Jolliffe, Jill, 5042
Jolly, E., 11277
Joly, Daniele S., 3413, 3414
Joly, Luz Gracie, 7375
Jomo, 6404
Jonas, Serge, 5273
Jonassen, C.T., 10664

Jonassohn, Kurt, 11471
Jones, A.H.M., 11911
Jones, Adam, 10154
Jones, C., 3957
Jones, E., 10155
Jones, Ellen, 9120, 9121
Jones, Frank E., 1422
Jones, Frank L., 237,238
Jones, Gareth Stedman, 3958
Jones, Grant D., 4411, 6565
Jones, Gregg R., 7551, 7552
Jones, Greta, 3959
Jones, Jocelyn, 4437
Jones, Jock, 3960
Jones, Marie T., 8779
Jones, Mervyn, 10665
Jones, P.N., 2997
Jones, Peter D., 403
Jones, Randall S., 6242
Jones, Reginald L., 9535
Jones, Rhett S., 9576
Jones, Stephen, 9122
Jones, W. Glyn, 2092
Jong, Wiebe de, 6840
Jonic, Koca, 9843
Joralemon, Victoria, 11278
Jordan, D.F., 420
Jordan, Deirdre F., 404,405
Jordan, Ellen, 3961
Jordan, Thomas E., 3962
Jordan, William, 2560, 2561
Jorge, Antonio, 1899
Jorgensen, J.G., 9577
Jorgensen, Jan J., 8897
José, Oiliam, 806
José, Vivencio R., 7553, 7554
Joseph, Gloria I., 10417
Joseph, Helen, 8120
Joseph, John Earl, 11615
Josephs, Bernard, 5579
Josephs, J., 2562
Josey, E.J., 9578
Joshi, Barbara, 4792
Joshi, Rama, 4820, 4821
Joshi, S., 3963
Jost, Herman, 2941
Jouanna, Arlette, 2563
Journard, Ron, 5580
Jowell, Roger, 3964
Jubb, Michael, 3965

Judd, Carol, 1237
Juergensmeyer, Mark, 4793
Juhasz, Gyula, 4544
Juma, M.S., 8704
Jungbluth, Paul, 6841
Junger, M., 3966
Junger, Marianne, 6842
Junker, H., 2200
Junquera, Carlos, 11616
Jupp, Peter J., 3967
Jureidini, Paul A., 6162
Jürgensen, Kurt, 2998
Jurgila, C., 9124
Jurich, Marilyn, 406
Jutikkala, Eino, 2350
Juwoso Sudarsono, 10309

Ka, Samba, 7901
Kaarsted, Tage, 2093
Kabarhuza, H.B., 9928
Kabeer, Naila, 622
Kaberry, P. M., 407
Kabir, Muhammad G., 623-625
Kabuzan, V.M., 9125
Kabwegyere, Tarsis B., 8898
Kadalie, Clements, 8121
Kadirgamer, Silan, 8448
Kadish, A., 3968
Kaelble, Hartmut, 10666-10670
Kafer, Istvan, 4545
Kagan, Alfred, 8705
Kagarlitsky, Boris, 9126, 9127
Kagedan, Allan L., 9128
Kahan, David, 5582
Kahan, Stuart, 9129
Kahane, Reuven, 5274
Kahin, George M., 9770
Kahl, Joseph A., 6543
Kahn, Siegbert, 2999
Kaiser, Daniel H., 9130
Kaiser, R.J., 9844
Kakwani, Nanak, 239, 291, 8449
Kalantzis, Mary, 240
Kalela, Jorma, 2351
Kalimuthu, K., 6406
Kalinga, Owen J. M., 6360
Kalippan, V.R, 4911
Kalirajam, K. P., 4794
Kalla, Abdool Cader, 6475
Kalla, Moise, 2564

Kallaway, Peter, 8122, 12027
Kalleberg, L., 3182
Kallen, Evelyn, 1413, 1423, 1424
Kalley, Jacqueline A., 12028, 12029, 12030
Kalmanovitz, Salomon, 1801
Kaluba, L.H., 9953
Kalvoda, Josef, 2014
Kamble, N.D., 4795
Kamen, Charles S., 5583-5585
Kamen, Henry, 8368
Kamenec, Ivan, 2015
Kamentsky, Ihor, 9131
Kamil, Jill, 2201
Kamm, Henry, 970, 4546, 7826, 7827, 9845-9847
Kampe, Norbert, 3000
Kanatchikov, Semen I., 9132
Kanbawza Win, 6708
Kandil, Fuad, 11617
Kane-Berman, John, 8123
Kang, Chong-Sook, 3001
Kaniki, M.H.Y., 8706
Kann, Robert A., 535,536
Kannangara, A.P., 8450
Kannemeyer, H.D., 8124
Kanner, Barbara, 12031
Kanost, Richard F., 11280
Kantz, Barbara Less, 6566
Kanya-Forstner, Sidney, 11404
Kapeliouk, Amnon, 5586
Kaplan, Alice Y., 2565
Kaplan, D., 8125
Kaplan, David, 8024
Kaplan, Fredy H., 10983
Kaplan, John, 5275
Kaplan, Karel, 2016
Kaplan, M. A., 3002
Kaplan, Marcos, 10984
Kaplan, Martha, 11281
Kaplan, Morton A., 9343
Kaplan, Patricia, 4796
Kaplan, Steve L., 2566
Kapoor, B.L., 4797
Kapoor, M.P., 4798
Kappel, Robert, 6318
Kapsoli E., Wilfredo, 7463
Karady, Victor, 4547, 10572
Karageorghis, Vassos, 1969, 11912
Karasapan, Omer, 928, 8838

Karasch, Mary C., 807
Karasek, Erika, 3003
Karbach, Oskar, 537
Karim, Abdul, 4799
Karklins, Rasma, 9133
Karlovic, N.L., 9848
Karmel, Peter, 241, 242
Karmi, Ilan, 8839
Karn, Valerie, 3969
Karni, Michael G., 11618
Karp, Judith, 5276
Karpat, Kemal H., 9134
Karpati, Mirella, 10713
Karran, T.J., 4097
Karras, Ruth M., 8588, 8589, 10671
Karst, Inge, 3187
Karsten, Sjoerd, 6843
Karuppaiyan, E., 4800
Kasa-Vubu, Z.J. M'Poyo, 9929
Kasangana, Mwalaba, 9930
Kasbarian-Bricout, Beatrice, 9135
Kasher, A., 11913
Kashif, Lonnie, 1900
Kasim, Mustapa Bin, 6407
Kasimovskii, E., 9136
Kasozi, A.B.K., 1141, 8899
Kasparian, Vartan S., 8840
Kasper, Martin, 3004
Kass, David, 5277
Kassim, Anis, F. , 5587
Kassow, Samuel D., 9137, 9138
Kastoryano, Riva, 2567
Kaszeta, Daniel J., 9139
Kater, Michael H., 3005, 3006
Katiya, N., 8126
Katjavivi, Peter H., 6744
Kato, Hiroaki, 1238
Katouzian, Homa, 5103
Katz, Alyssa, 9140
Katz, Claudio J., 11659
Katz, Jacob, 3007, 10672-10674, 11619
Katz, Phyllis A., 9579, 9580
Katz, Solomon, 8369
Katz, Steven T., 11620
Katz, Wendy R., 3970
Katz, Y., 8841
Katz, Y.J., 5278
Katz, Zev, 9033
Katzburg, Nathaniel, 4548, 4549, 4550
Katzenstein, M.F., 4801

Katzer, Bruce, 1239
Kaufman, Allan, 9581
Kaufman, Deborah, 9141
Kaufman, Debra, 10675
Kaufman, Edy, 5588, 5589
Kaufman, Michael T., 7709, 10418
Kautsky, Karl, 10676
Kavale, Kenneth A., 3971
Kavoussi, R.M., 7881
Kay, J.A., 3972
Kay, Reginald, 955
Kaya, Ural, 3008
Kayfetz, Ben, 1030
Kazarian, H., 8842
Kazembe, J., 9983
Kazesnzadeh, Firuz, 9142
Kazi, Aftab A., 7343
Kazi, S., 7344
Kazuhiro, Tanimoto, 6075
Kealey, Gregory S., 1425, 1426
Keane, M., 3575
Kearney, Robert N., 8451, 8452
Keddie, Nikki, 5104, 11108, 11109, 11146
Kedourie, E., 5154
Kedward, H.R., 10677
Kedward, Roderick, 238
Keeffe, Kevin, 408
Keegan, Timothy, 8127
Keen, Ian, 409
Keenan, Jeremy, 8128
Keesing, Felix, 11282
Kehr, Helen, 12032
Keiler, J., 6179
Keita, G., 6024
Keita, M.A., 7895
Keitaro, O., 6076
Kelby, J., 3526
Kelidar, Abbas , 5155
Kelker, S.V., 4802
Kellaghan, T., 5179
Kelleher, Patricia, 5183
Keller, Bill, 9143-9146
Keller, Edmond J., 2294-2296
Keller, Rosemary Skinner, 11000
Keller, Wouter J., 6844
Kelley, J., 208
Kelley, Jonathan, 243, 706, 707
Kelling, George H., 1970
Kelly, David D., 1240

Kelly, Gail P., 7536, 9771, 10156-10158, 11621
Kelly, John D., 11283, 11284
Kelman, Jacob M., 9147
Kelsey, Jane, 6957, 6958
Kemal, A.R., 7345
Kemmerle, Peter, 7114
Kenan, Amos, 5279
Kenbib, Mohammed, 6663, 6664
Kendal, 8843
Kende, Pierre, 4551, 10678
Kenderdine, Shonagh, 6959
Keneally, Thomas, 2297
Kenedi, Janos, 7828
Kenneally, Christopher, 3577
Kennedy, Charles H., 7346
Kennedy, Dane K., 6195, 9984
Kennedy, James H., 808, 10159
Kennedy, John C., 1339
Kennedy, Liam, 3578
Kennedy, Paul, 3009, 3973, 3974, 10160
Kenney, Anne R., 2534
Kenny, Jamie, 3975
Kenrick, Donald, 3010, 10679, 10680
Kent, Bruce, 3011
Kent, Susan K., 3976
Kepel, Gilles, 2457
Keppel-Jones, Arthur, 9985
Kerkvliet, Benedict J. T., 7555
Kermel, Vincent, 11247
Kerr, A., 8129
Kerr, David, 10161
Kerr, George H., 11285
Kershaw, Ian, 3012
Kessler, David, 2298, 2299, 2317
Kestenberg-Amighi, Janet T., 5105
Kestenberg-Gladstein, Ruth, 2017
Ketkar, Kusum W., 7908
Kettani, M. Ali, 11622
Kettner, J. H., 9582
Keunings, Lue, 664
Keyder, Coglar, 8844
Keyes, Charles, 6427
Keyserlink, Robert H., 539
Kgware, W.M., 8130
Khadduri, W., 5156
Khafre, Kadallah, 6319
Khaing, Mi Mi, 6709
Khalafalla, Elfatih S.D., 8525

Khalid, Mansour, 8526, 8527
Khalidi, Abdullah, 9849
Khalidi, Raja, 5590, 5591
Khalidi, Walid, 12033
Khalifa, Ahmad M., 6745
Khalifeh, Sahar, 5592
Khan, A.A., 626
Khan, A.R., 10304
Khan, H., 620, 5040, 5041
Khan, M.A., 7347, 7556
Khan, S.R., 7348
Khandriche, Mohammed, 2568
Khare, R.S., 4803
Khazoum, E., 5157
Khleif, Bud B., 6845
Khoderkovsky, Michael, 9148
Khoury, A.T., 11623
Khromov, S.S., 9149
Kicza, John E., 6567, 6568, 10985
Kiely, J.H., 8301
Kiernan, Ben, 965, 971, 972
Kiernan, V.S., 11624
Kierulf, Hakon, 7321
Kiessling, Wolfgang, 6569
Kieval, Hillel J., 2018
Kifner, John, 2202, 5593
Kil, Jeong Woo, 6243
Kilian, Crawford, 1142
Kiljunen, Kimmo, 973
Killingray, David, 3977, 10162, 10163
Kilson, Martin, 9583
Kim Dong Hoon, 6078
Kim, S.K., 6244
Kim, Yoon Shin, 6077
Kimche, Jon, 5594
Kimmerling, Baruch, 5280, 5595, 5798
Kimura, Mitsuhiko, 6245
Kincaid, Jamaica, 10419
King, Dwight Y., 6408
King, Mel, 9584
King, R., 9868
King, Robert R., 10681
King, Ronald, 3978
King, Ruby, 10420
King, Wayne, 9585
Kingston-Mann, E., 8989, 9150
Kingston, Paul J., 2569
Kinkead-Weekes, B., 8131
Kinloch, Graham C., 9986
Kintanar, Thelma B., 5043

AUTHOR INDEX

Kinzer, Stephen, 4412, 7031, 7116-7118
Kinzer, Stephen, 7115
Kinzley, W. Dean, 6079
Kiple, Dalila de S., 809
Kiple, Kenneth F., 1901, 11625
Kircher, Ingrid A., 11286
Kirimli, Hakan, 9151
Kirk, Greene Anthony, 10164
Kirk, Joyce F., 8132
Kirk, Neville, 3979
Kirkby, Dianne, 410
Kirkpatrick, John, 11384
Kirkpatrick, V.J., 10310
Kirsch, H., 10986
Kirschbaum, Stanislav J., 2019, 2020, 2043
Kirschenbaum, Alan, 5259
Kirsner, D., 290
Kirst, Michael, 3488
Kisch, Guido, 3013, 10682, 10683
Kitahara, Michio, 6080
Kitakamal, Taro, 6081
Kitchen, Martin, 540
Kitching, G.N., 6196
Kitroeff, Alexander, 2203, 4373
Kivilu, Sabakinu, 9931
Kivo, E.M., 991
Kiwanuka, M.S.M.S., 8900
Kiwanuka, Richard N., 10165
Kiyoshige, Naohuro, 6082
Klanberg, Frank, 3014
Klarsfeld, Serge, 2570, 2571, 3015
Klassen, John, 2021
Klatt, W., 1616
Klaus-Erich, Gerth, 2572
Klausen, A., 723
Klawiter, Richard F., 2256
Kleber, Wolfgang, 3016
Klee, Ernst, 3017, 3018
Kleff, Hans-Gunter, 3019
Klein, Bernard, 4552
Klein, C.L., 3300, 8845
Klein, Dennis B., 12054
Klein, Gabriella, 5957
Klein, George, 920, 10684
Klein, Herbert S., 707, 10987
Klein, Martin A., 10241
Kleinbach, Russell, 7032
Klemperer, Klemens von, 541
Klenner, Uwe, 9772

Kless, Schlomo, 665
Klessmann, Christoph, 3020, 3021
Klich, Ignacio, 10988
Klier, John D., 3022, 9152, 9153
Klima, Otakar, 5106
Kline, Benjamin, 8133
Klinge, Matti, 2352
Kliot, N., 5596, 5597, 11626, 11627
Klitgaard, Robert, 11628
Kloczowski, Jerzy, 7710
Klönne, Arno, 3023
Kloskowska, Antonina, 7711
Kloss, Heinz, 11629
Klostris, C., 9987
Klug, Francesca, 3877, 3980, 12007
Kluger, Richard, 9586
Kly, Y.N., 4804
Knapman, Bruce, 11287-11291
Knapman, C., 11292
Knaster, Meri, 12034
Knauss, Peter R., 62
Knell, Michael F., 7119
Knell, Robert, 12035
Knibbs, G.H., 244
Knight, Alan, 6570, 6571, 10989
Knight, Franklin W., 1902, 10398, 10421, 10990
Knight, J.B., 4638, 8134
Knipping, Franz, 3161
Knoll, A.-J., 8771
Knothe, Tomasz, 9154
Knowles, Louis, 9587
Knudsen, Jerry W., 130, 708, 10991
Knutter, Hans-Helmuth, 3024
Kobayashi, A., 1427
Kobayashi, Cassandra, 1088
Koblik, Steven, 8590-8592
Koch, Erich, 1031
Kochan, Lionel, 8926, 8931, 9155, 9160
Kocka, Jürgen, 3025
Koehler, David H., 9588
Koehn, Peter, 10166
Koepp, Cynthia J., 2566
Kofele-Kale, N., 10167
Kofman, Eleonore, 3924, 9348
Kofman, Ilana, 5598
Kofos, Evangelos, 4374
Kohler, Max J., 7829
Kohli, Stul, 4805
Kohno, Testsu, 6083

Kohut, Zenon E., 9156
Koike, Kenji, 7557
Kok, Loy F., 6409
Kolack, Shirley, 6572
Kolack, Sol, 6572
Kolarz, Walter, 9157
Kolchin, Peter, 9158
Kolff, D.H.A., 4651, 5020
Kolig, Erich, 6960
Kolinsky, Eva, 3026
Kolinsky, Martin, 3026, 5599, 7253
Koltringer, Richard, 542
Kom, Anton de, 8560
Komarek, V., 2022
Komaroff, John, 11484
Kombs, John, 10685
Kondert, Reinhard, 543
Konrad, Helmut, 544
Koo, Hagen, 6246, 6247
Koolmatrie, Janis, 411
Koonz, Claudia, 10536
Koot, William C.J., 6846, 6847
Kop, Yaakov, 5281, 5282
Kopytoff, Igor, 10201
Korey, William, 9159-9164, 10686
Korn, David A., 5158
Kornai, Janos, 4553
Kornalijnslijper, Nora, 6848
Kortepeter, C., 8868
Korth, Eugene H., 1554
Korzec, Pawel, 7712
Kosambi, Meere, 4806
Koshar, Rudy, 10687
Koskinen, Aarne A., 11293
Kosmin, Barry A., 3301, 9988
Kossaifi, G., 5600
Kostelancik, D.J., 2023
Koster, R.M., 7376
Kosukhin, N.D., 10168
Kosyk, Volodymyr, 9165, 9166
Kothari, Sunitu, 4937
Kottak, Conrad P., 6355
Kourvetaris, Yorgos A., 2204
Koutcharian, Gerayer, 8830, 11138
Kovac, Miha, 9850
Kovacs, Andras, 4554
Kovacs, I., 4555
Kovago, Laszlo, 4556
Koval, B.I., 10688
Kovalcheck, Kassian A., 3579

Kovaly, Heda, 2024
Kowalewski, David A., 7558, 9167, 9168
Kozel, Valerie, 6025
Kozenski, Jerzy, 545
Kozig, Jan, 546
Kozlov, V., 8999, 9169
Kozlowski, Maciej, 7713
Kozminski, Maciej, 4557, 10689
Kozodoy, Ruth, 9029
Koztov, S. Ya, 11340
Kraas-Schneider, Frauke, 11630
Krader, Lawrence, 6638, 9170
Kraft, Richard J., 7033
Krahenbuhl, Hans-Ulrich, 8657
Kraiem, Mustapha, 8780
Krajewski, Stanislaw, 7714
Krajzman, Maurice, 666
Krakowski, Shmuel, 7693, 10792
Kramer, Gudrun, 2205
Kramer, Jane, 810, 2573
Kramer, Martin, 5085
Krane, Dale A., 2259
Krantz, Frederick, 2420
Kranzler, David, 6084-6087
Krasnowolski, Andrzej, 697
Kraus, Birgitta, 3028
Kraus, Vered, 5601
Krause, Corinne A., 6573, 6574
Krauss, Clifford, 1903
Kraut, Alan M., 9474
Krauze, Tadensz K., 7748
Krawchenko, Bohdan, 9171
Krayem, Hassan H., 6296
Kreici, Jaroslaw, 10690
Kreimer, Sarah, 5602, 5603
Kreindler, Isabelle T., 9172, 9173
Kreindler, Joshua D., 8135
Krejci, Jaroslav, 2025
Kremen, Eleanor, 11555
Krenn, Heliena, 6410
Kressel, Gideon M., 5604
Kretzmer, David, 5605
Krichmar, Albert, 12036
Krieger-Krynicki, Anne, 2574
Kriesi, Hanspeter, 6849, 8658
Krishna, Raj, 4808
Krishnam, Prakha, 4807
Krisjjanson, Lowell G., 1839
Kristof, Nicholas D., 11294

Kritsman, L.N., 9174
Krivickas, Vladas, 9175
Krivine, David, 5606, 5607
Kroll, Robert E., 4558
Krongkaew, M., 8746
Krotki, K.J., 7349
Krotz, Larry, 1241
Kruckewitt, Joan, 7120, 7121
Kruks , Sonia, 2878
Krutz, Gordan V., 6575
Kubayanda, Joseph B., 1904
Kuber, Waman N., 4809
Kublin, Hyman, 6088
Kuczynski, Jürgen, 3029, 3030
Kuehn, Thomas James, 5958
Kuhlmann, Michael, 3031
Kuhn, Gary, 7377
Kuhnert, Hanno, 3032
Kuhnrich, Heinz, 3033
Kuhuke, La Verne, 2206
Kuietenbromer, Maarten, 6850
Kujala, Antti V., 2353
Kukovecz, Gyorgy, 1905
Kukreja, Sunil, 11631
Kulczycki, John J., 3034, 3035
Kulka, Erich, 2026
Kulka, Otto Dov, 598, 2054, 3036-3039, 6862, 6901, 10691, 10706
Kulling, Friedrich, 8659
Kumar, Dharma, 4810, 4811
Kumar, Ikram Ali, 4812
Kumar, Pramod, 4813
Kumar, Radha, 4814
Kunanayakam, Tamara, 8453
Kundu, A., 4815
Kunst, J., 4413
Kunstadter, Peter, 1599
Kunstel, Marcia, 5608
Kunze, Jürgen, 10169
Kuo Mo-jo, 1717
Kuoljok, Kerstin E., 9176
Kuper, H., 8566
Kuper, Leo, 7872, 11632-11634
Kupferman, Fred, 2575
Kupferschmidt, Uri M., 5609
Kuppusami, C., 8136, 8137
Kurian, George T., 11635, 11636
Kurian, R., 8454
Kurkansky, Mark, 2120
Kurnosov, Y.A., 9177

Kurti, Laszlo, 7830
Kuschel, R., 11295
Kushner, Arlene, 2300
Kushner, D., 5610, 11147
Kushner, David, 8847, 8848
Kushner, Gilbert, 11510, 11988
Kushner, James A., 9589
Kushner, Tony, 3302, 3303, 3981
Kushnick, Louis, 3982, 3983
Kutschera, C., 2576
Kuttab, Daoud, 5611-5613
Kuttab, Jonathan, 5614-5616
Kuttner, Bob, 7122
Kutzik, Alfred J., 9178
Kuzio, Taras, 9179
Kuzwayo, Ellen, 8138
Kwamdela, Odimumba, 3984
Kwan, Chan Wai, 3484
Kwaniewski, K., 3040
Kwasnik-Rabinowicz, Kurt A.M., 2027
Kwiet, K., 245, 6851
Kwon, J.K., 6266
Kwon, Manhak, 6248
Kwong, J., 1617, 1618
Ky, Luong Nhi, 9773
Kyba, Patrick, 1428
Kyle, Keith, 1971
Kynch, Jocelyn, 4932

Laacher, Smain, 63
Labarca, Guillermo, 1560
Labarca Huberston, Amanda, 1559
Labelle, Micheline, 4478
LaBelle, T.J., 11582
Laber, Jeri, 7, 929, 8849, 9180
Labourne, Patrick, 9795
Labrousse, Alain, 10992
Labuda, Gerard, 7715
Labumore, Elsie R., 412
Lacave, José L., 8370
Lacer, Luis Q., 7559
Lachantanere, Romulo, 1906
Lackner, Helen, 7882, 9796
Lacko, M., 4559
Laclau, Ernesto, 10993
Lacy, Creighton, 9989
Ladanyi, Janos, 4560
Ladner, Joyce, 9685
Lador-Lederer, J.J., 547, 5617
Ladurie, Emmanuel Le Roy, 2579

Laferriere, M., 1143, 1429, 1430
Laffey, John F., 2580, 9774
Laffin, John, 10170
Lahka, Salim, 10317
Lai, David C., 1431
Lai, Wally Look, 10422
Laing, Stuart, 3985
Laitin, David D., 7945, 8371
Laizer, Sheri, 8850
Lal, A.K., 4816
Lal, Brij Victor, 11296, 11297
Lal, Deepak, 4817
Lallana, Emmanuel C., 7560
Lam, Lawrence, 1069
Lamb, C., 9480
Lamba, I.C., 6361
Lamballe, Alain, 8455
Lambert, John, 4172
Lambert, Ronald D., 12037
Lambroza, Shlomo, 9181, 9182
Lamming, George, 3415
Lamontagne, Jacques, 1718, 1719
LaMonte, Ruth B., 5618
Lamore, Jean, 1907
Lamur, Humphrey E., 8561
Land, Hilary, 10692
Landau, Dov, 5619
Landau, Lazare, 2581
Landau, Nick, 3986
Landazabal Reyes, Fernando, 10994
Landis, Jean M., 5314
Landon, K.P., 8747
Landsberger, Michael, 5283
Lane, David S., 9183
Lanford, Andri G., 11531
Lang, D.M., 9184, 11637
Lang, Michel R., 10693
Langdon, John W., 2582
Langellier, Jean-Pierre, 5620
Langenmayr, Arnold, 3042
Langer, Erick D., 10995
Langer, Felicia, 5621, 5622
Langer, Jo, 2028
Langer, Odette, 11298
Langes, Lynda, 11479
Langlais, Joeques, 1032
Langley, Lester D., 1908, 10996
Langmaid, Janet, 12032
Langmuir, Gavin I., 11638-11641
Langton, Marcia, 440

Lannon, Frances, 8372
Lansky, Aaron, 9185
Laomis, Terrence, 6961
Laothamatas, Anek, 8748
Lapchick, Richard E., 8139
Lapham, Lewis H., 6897
Lapidus, Gail W., 9186
Laponce, J.A., 1033
LaPrairie, Carol, 1242, 1243
Laqueur, Thomas, 3987
Lara, Oruno D., 11148
Lardinois, Roland, 4818
Large, David C., 3043, 10694
Larkin, Lisa W., 6627
Larmor, Peter, 11299
Larsen, K., 413
Larsen, Stein N., 10695
Larson, Brooke, 709
Larsson, Staffan, 8569, 8598, 8630
Lashley, Horace, 3416, 3988
Laska, Vera, 11642, 12038
Lasker, Bruno, 10311
Laskier, Michael, 2207, 6665, 6666
Last, Murray, 7909
Laszlo, Leslie, 4561
Latortue, Paul, 2121
Latsis, Otto, 9187
Lattas, Andrew, 414
Lattimore, Owen, 6639
Lattuado, Mario J., 131
Lau, Brigitte, 6746
Lauffer, S., 11914
Laurell, Asa C., 10998
Lauren, C., 2354
Lauren, Paul G., 11643
Laurence, Patrick, 8140
Lauter, Paul, 9591
Lautmann, Rudiger, 3044
Lavrijsen, J. S. G., 6197
Lavrin, Asuncion, 10999-11001
Lavsky, Hagit, 10696
Law, Alfred D., 9189
Law Blanco, Hazel, 7123
Law, Howard, 1144
Law, I., 3989
Law, Robin, 698-699, 10171, 10172
Lawal, A.A., 7254
Lawrence, Anne, 3990
Lawrence, Charles R., III, 9592
Lawrence, Daniel, 3991

Lawrence, Dina, 5624
Lawrence, J. N.H., 8373
Lawson, Edward H., 11644
Lawson, Fred, 6271
Lawson, Roger, 10608
Lawson, Stephanie, 11300
Layton-Henry, Zig, 3417, 3992, 3993, 10697
Layton, Robert, 415
Lazar, Gyorgy, 7831
Lazarus, Neil, 10173
Lazer, Arnold, 2029
Lazerson, Joshua N., 8141
Lazniekova, A., 2030
Le Moyne, James, 7124-7128
Lea, Edward, 11645
Leab, Daniel J., 9593
Leacock, Eleanor, 1790, 11525
Leacock, Ruth, 811
Leadbeater, David T.L., 1432
Leal Buitrago, Francisco, 1802
Leal, Juan F., 1909
Leary, Virginia A., 8456
Lebzelter, Gisela C., 3304, 3305
Leckie, Jacqueline, 6962
Ledeen, Michael A., 5959, 5960
Lederer, Z., 9851
Lee, A.M., 3995
Lee, Chae-Jin, 1619
Lee, Changsoo, 6089-6091
Lee, David C., 9190
Lee, Eddy, 2223
Lee, Eric, 5284, 5625
Lee, Gil Sang, 6249
Lee, Jeri, 1135
Lee, Martin, 10698
Lee, Mi-Na, 6250
Lee, Michele, 9852
Lee, Raymond L.M., 6411
Lee, Robert Stuart, 1720
Lee, Stephen B.S., 1721
Lee, Stephen J., 10699
Lee, W. R., 3045
Lee, W.M., 1089
Leech, Kenneth, 3418, 3996
Leeman, Y., 6843
Leepile, M., 724
Lees, Lynn H., 3524, 10650
Lefall, Dolores C., 12039
Lefcourt, Robert, 9481

Lefebvre, M-C, 659
Leff, Carol S., 2031
Legarreta, Dorothy, 8374
Legendre, Camille, 1318
Leggewie, Claus, 3046
Legros, D., 1244
Legum, Colin, 2301
Lehman, F.K., 6710, 8749
Lehmann, André, 2583
Lehmann, Ruth P., 12040
Lehn, Walter, 5448
Leibel, Aaron, 5626
Leibfried, Stephan, 3947
Leigh, L. H., 3997
Leis, Hector R., 132
Leis, Philip E., 714
Leiser, E., 3048
Leitman, Spencer L., 812
Lekhela, E.P., 8142
Lemarchand, René, 956-958
Lemerle, Paul, 11646
Lemny, Stefan, 7832
Lemoine, Maurice, 2122
Lemon, David M.H., 9990
Lencho, Tumtu, 2302
Lendvai, Paul, 10700
Lenin, V.I., 9191
Lenoir, J.D., 8562
Leo, Christopher, 6198
León de Leal, Magdalena, 1803, 1804
Léon, Hector, 7428
Leon, Magdalena, 11002
Leon, P., 2584
Leon-Portilla, Miguel, 11647
Leonet, Isabelle T., 2511
Leong, S.T., 1620
Leonie, A., 8143
Leopold, Joan, 4819
Lepervanche, Marie M. de, 246
Lepsius, M. Ranier, 3049
Lerche, Charles O., 7255
Lerman, Anthony, 10607, 11648
Lerner, Natan, 5285
Lerner, Victoria, 6576
Lernoux, Penny, 7084, 7129-7131
Lersch, Paul , 3050
Lerski, Halina T., 12041
Lerski, Jerzy J., 12041
Leruez, Jacques, 3632
Lesch, Ann M., 5627, 5628, 8528

Leschinski, Achim, 3051
Leser, Norbert, 551
Leskov, Nikolai S., 9192
Leslie, J., 6778
Lesse, S., 10701
Lesser, Harriet Sara, 6577
Lesser, Jeffrey H., 813, 814
Lesser, M., 2137
Lessmann, R., 4414
Lethtinen, Erkki, 2355
Letnev, A.B., 10174
Leu, R.E., 8660
Leung, Benjamin K.P., 3485
Leung, Trini, 1722
Leung, Ywen Sang, 7925
Levai, E., 4562, 4563
Levenberg, S., 9193
Leventer, Herbert, 9194
Lever, Henry, 8094
Lever, William, 3633
Levey, Richard, 1723
Levi, Abraham, 5286
Levin, Dov, 9195-9198
Levin, Jerry, 5629
Levin, Nora, 9199
Levin, R., 8144
Levine, Daniel H., 9749
Levine, David, 3998
Levine, H. S., 3052
Levine, Kenneth, 3999
Levine, Marc V., 1319
Levine, Norman, 9200
Levine, Robert M., 815, 11003
Levine, Stephen, 11301
Levitats, Isaac, 9201
Levitt, Cyril, 1034, 1433
Levntal, Z., 9853
Levy, Daniel C., 11004
Levy, Deborah R., 2585
Levy, E.D., 3306
Levy, Reuben, 11149
Levy, Richard Simon, 3053, 11649
Levy, Victor, 2208
Lewando-Hundt, G.A., 5630
Lewin-Epstein, Noah, 5631, 5632, 5793
Lewis, Bernard, 8818, 11150, 11151
Lewis, Colin M., 10876
Lewis, D.S., 4000
Lewis, Debra J., 1434
Lewis, Flora, 2586

Lewis, G., 4001
Lewis, Gavin, 8145
Lewis, Gordon K., 10423, 10424
Lewis, Ian M., 7946
Lewis, J., 4002
Lewis, J. M., 2303
Lewis, Jill, 548
Lewis, Jim, 10655
Lewis, Lancelot S., 7378
Lewis, Milton, 247
Lewis, Paul, 1245, 6163
Lewis, Paul H., 133
Lewis, Rand C., 3054
Lewis, Robert D., 1412
Lewis, Rupert, 11650
Lewy, Guenter, 3055
Lewytzkyj, Borys, 9202
Ley, David, 1435
Leyburn, James G., 4479
Leys, Norman, 10175
Li Maoguan, 1724
Li, Peter S., 1090, 1091, 1348, 1436
Liakos, Anthony, 4375
Lian, Kwen Fee, 6963, 6964
Liang, Hsi-Huey, 3056
Liao, H. S., 1621
Liaw, Yoch F., 7926
Libardian, Gerard J., 8851, 9203
Liber, George O., 9204
Liberasyon, Muwman, 6476
Liberman, Kenneth, 416
Lic, Suzanne S., 7322
Licht, Sonja, 9854
Lichtenberger, Elizabeth, 549
Liddle, Joanna, 4820, 4821
Lie, John, 6092
Lieberman, Victor B., 6711
Liebkind, Karmela, 2356
Liebman, Marcel, 667
Liebman, Seymour, 6578, 10425, 11005
Liebmann, Maximilian, 550, 551
Liebowitz, Ronald D., 9205
Liebscher, Gertrand, 11651
Liegeois, Jean-Pierre, 11652
Lier, Rudolf A.J. van, 8563
Lifschultz, Lawrence, 627
Lifton, R. J., 3057
Lilienthal, Georg, 3058
Lim, Byung O., 6251
Lim, Jaime L., 7561

Lim, Julian, 6412
Lim, Mah Hui, 6413
Lim, Teck Ghee, 6414
Limage, L.J., 10702, 11653
Limskul, Kitti, 8745
Lin, Ming-yih, 10703
Lin, T-b., 3486
Lin, Vivian, 10312
Lin Wei, 1725
Lind, Joan D., 8593
Lind, Martin, 8594
Lindberg, Gudrun, 8574
Lindblad, J. Thomas, 5044
Linden, Marcel van der, 10704
Lindenberg, M., 11006
Lindert, Peter H., 4003, 4004
Lindfors, Bernt, 8146
Lindgren, Lars, 8625
Lindo-Fuentes, Hector, 2257
Lindquist, M., 8595
Lindsay, Beverly, 10417
Lindsay Jonathan M., 4748
Lindstrom, Ulf, 2094
Ling, Trevor, 6712
Lingle, C., 8147
Linhart-Fischer, Ruth, 6093
Linke, R.D. , 248
Linke, Uli H., 3059, 3060
Linn, H. T., 6415
Linnekin, Jocelyn, 11302
Linz, Juan, 156
Linz, Susan J., 9206
Lion, Antoine, 2587
Liong, L.S., 5023
Lipcsey, Ildiko, 7833
Lipman, Vivian D., 3307, 3308
Lipp, Solomon, 7464
Lippman, Lorna, 249, 250, 417, 418
Lipscher, Ladislav, 2032
Lipschitz, Chaim U., 8375
Lipset, Harry, 9207
Lipsey, David, 4006
Lipski, Jan J., 7716
Lipski, John, 7379
Lipson, Charles, 11654
Lipstadt, Deborah E., 9594
Lipton, D., 7717
Lipton, Merle, 8148
Lis, Catharina, 668, 10705
Liss, Sheldon B., 1910

Lissak, Moshe, 6713
Lister, I., 4007
Lister, Ruth, 4008
Litani, Yehuda, 5633, 5634
Littell, Franklin H., 10559, 10706
Little, Alan, 3787, 4009
Little Bear, Leroy, 1185
Little, John Irvine, 1437
Little, Kenneth L., 4010
Little, M., 8707
Littlefield, Daniel F., Jr., 9595
Littlefield, Frank C., 9855
Littlejohn, Gary, 9208
Littlewood, R., 4011
Littman, David, 10176
Litwack, Leon F., 9596
Liu Chia-yi, 1726
Liu Jianjun, 1727
Liu Suinian, 1728
Liu Xiaojun, 1729
Liu Zonghe, 1615
Livada, Alexander, 4376
Livezeanu, Irina, 7834
Lizarralde, Roberto, 9750
Llata, Richard, 1622
Lloyd, Cathie, 2588
Lloyd, David, 10707
Lloyd-Jones, Robin, 1805
Lo Giudice, Maria R., 5961
Lo, S.H., 3487
Lobb, John, 4480
Locke, Richard, 5635
Lockheed, M.E., 6777
Lockman, Zachary, 2209, 2166
Locksley, Gareth, 4039
Lockwood, Victoria S., 11303
Lodma, Jerry R., 6547
Loeb, Laurence D., 5107, 5108
Loebl, Eugene, 2033
Loewenstein, Kurt, 3061
Loewenthal, Troetje, 2118
Loft, Frances, 959
Lofton, Joseph Evans, Jr., 2095
Logan, Kathleen, 6579
Logan, Rayford, 4481
Logoreci, Anton, 9856
Loh, Jeanette Morag, 210
Lohmann, Klaus, 552
Lohr, Steve, 2357, 3580
Loiskandl, H., 6153

Lombard, B.Urban, 8149
Lombardi, John, 9751
London, Bette, 10177
Loney, Martin, 9991
Long, J. Anthony, 1185, 1246, 1247
Long, James W., 9209
Longboat, Diane, 1236
Longres, J.F., Jr., 9597
Lonnqvist, Bo, 2358
Lookstein, Haskel, 9598
Loomba, Amia, 4012
Loot, L., 8117
Lopes, Carlos, 4441
Lopes, Jorge E. G., 816
Lopez, A.D., 11822
López Camara, Francisco, 6580
López de Romaña, Guillermo, 7465
López Garrido, Diego, 8376
López-Gonzaga, Violeta, 7562
López Monjardin, Adriana, 6581
López Rodo, Laureano, 8377
López Soria, José I., 7466
López Tirone, Humberto, 7380
López Valdez, Rafael, 1911, 1912
López y Rivas, Gilberto, 7074, 7132
Lorch, Netanel, 5636
Lorimer, Douglas A., 4013, 4014
Lorwin, Val R., 669, 670
Losang Chenlei, 1730
Lossowski, P., 9210
Lottman, Herbert R., 2589
Lotz, Rainer E., 3419
Loubser, J.A., 8150
Loughran, Maria C., 3581
Louis, Roger W., 10128, 10129
Louw, A.D., 8220
Louw, S.J.H., 8151
Love, Edgar F., 6582, 6583
Lovejoy, Paul E., 7256, 10178-10180
Lovell, Peggy Ann, 817
Lovell, William George, 4415-4417
Loveman, Brian, 1561
Lovenderski, Joni, 11655
Low, Frances, 4015
Low-Hang, K., 11304
Lowe, W. J., 3525
Lowenthal, David, 10426
Lowenthal, Marvin, 10708
Lowenthal, Richard, 3147, 3251
Lowenthal, Rudolph, 12042

Lu Yun, 1623, 1624
Luazza, Guido, 5962
Lubac, Henri de, 2590
Lubachko, Ivan S., 9211
Lubeck, Paul M., 7257, 10181
Lubin, Nancy, 9212, 9213
Luca, Costa, 11152
Lucas, Martin, 1249
Lucas, Rex A., 1438
Lucassen, Jan, 10709
Luciano Franco, José, 11007
Luciuk, Lubomyr Y., 1439, 1440
Ludanyi, Andrew, 9857
Ludowyk, E.F.C., 8457
Lüdtke, Alf, 3062
Ludwig, Carl, 8661
Ludwig, Klemens, 5045
Ludzev, Ditimar, 930
Luebke, Frederick C., 818
Luis, William, 1913, 11008
Lukas, Richard C., 7718, 7719
Luks, H. P., 5159
Lumenga-Neso, Kiobe, 10182
Lund, Jens, 2096
Lundahl, Mats, 4482
Lundbergh, B., 8596
Lundgreen, P. , 3063
Lungo U., Mario, 2258
Lungu, G.F., 9954
Lunn, Kenneth, 3981, 4016-4018
Luostarinen, Heikki, 2359
Lupul, Manoly R., 1035
Luraghi, Raimondo, 5963
Lussier, Antoine S., 1250
Luster, Robert E., 11656
Lustgarten, Laurence, 4019
Lustick, Ian, 64, 5637-5640
Lustig, N., 6584
Lustig, Oliver, 7835
Lutz, Catherine, 11305
Luza, Radomir V., 553
Luzhnytskyi, G., 9214
Luzon, Jose L., 1914
Lynch, I. R., 8152
Lynch, K., 5184
Lynk, Michael, 5641
Lyon, Judson M., 4442
Lyons, Maryinez, 9932
Lyons, Patrick M., 5185
Lyotard, Jean-Francois, 3064

Lyset, S., 9749
Lyttelton, Adrian, 5964

M'buyinga, E., 10183
Ma Yin, 1625
Ma'oz, Moshe, 5642
Maassen, Gerard, 6852
Mababe, Tomoko, 1092
Mabey, Christine, 3420
Mabin, Alan, 8153
Mac an Ghaill, Mairtin, 3421
Macciocchi, Maria-Antonietta, 640
Maccurtain, Margaret, 5186
MacDona, Martha, 1378
MacDonald, Barrie K., 11306, 11307
MacDonald, Charles G., 11153
Macdonald, J., 4020
MacDonald, J. Fred, 9599
MacDonald, John A., 1251
MacDonald, Neil, 819
MacDonald, Robert, 6966
MacDonald, Theodore, Jr., 7133-7135
MacDougall, Hugh A., 4021
MacDougall, John A., 7927
Mace, James E., 9215
Maceda, Marcelino N., 7563
MacEoin, Gary, 11009
Macey, M., 3681
Macfarlane, Alan, 4022
MacGaffey, Janet, 9933
MacGaffey, W., 9934
MacGregor, Morris J., 9600
Macgregor, Roy, 1252
Machado, Diamantino P., 7774
Machann, Clinton, 2034
Macharia, K., 6200
Macias, Anna, 6585
MacIntyre, M., 11277
Macintyre, S., 4023
Mack-Kit, Samuel, 2591
MacKay, Ruth, 8378
Macken, Richard A., 8781
Mackenboch, J.P., 6853
Mackenzie, Clayton G., 9992
MacKenzie, John M., 4024, 4025
Mackerras, Colin, 1731
MacKinnon, Catharine A., 1441
MacKintosh, Gordon H., 1442
Mackintosh, Maureen, 7896
Maclachlan, Colin, 820

MacLaine, Craig S., 1253
MacLaren, A. Allan , 3634
MacLean, Pa,, 10710
MacLean, Robert C., 7136
Maclennan, D., 3503
MacLeod, Roy A., 247
Maclouf, Pierre, 2587
Macmillan, Hugh, 8567
Macmillen, Ramsay, 11915, 11916
Macnaught, Timothy J., 11308
Macnicol, John, 4026, 4027
Macpherson, C.B., 1443, 11657
MacRitchie, David, 4028
MacShane, Denis, 2592
Macu, Pavel, 2035
Maczak, Antoni, 7720
Madajcayk, Czeslaw, 7721
Madden, Richard R., 1915
Maddison, Angus, 5046
Maddock, R., 184
Maderspacher, Florian, 11658
Madhok, Balraj, 4822
Madrian, Jean, 2593
Madrid, Elsie A., 7381
Madsen, M., 8597
Madu, Oliver V., 10184
Madunagu, Edwin, 7258
Maestri Filho, M. J., 821, 10185
Mafei, Maristela, 822
Mafejo, A., 10186
Maga, Timothy P., 9601
Magaia, Lina, 6696
Magas, Branka, 9858
Magdol, Edward, 9602
Magida, Arthur J., 8154
Magill, Dennis, 1130
Magner, Thomas F., 9859
Magno de Carvalho, José, 903
Magnusson, Kjell, 9860
Magocsi, Paul R., 2036, 9216, 12043
Magubane, Bernard, 8155
Maguran, H.C., 671
Mahabir, Noor K., 10427
Mahajani, Usha, 4823
Mahameed, Hashem, 5643
Mahamid, Muhamid, 5644
Mahar, J. Michael , 4824
Mahfoudh, D., 8782
Mahler, Raphael, 7722, 10711
Mahler, Vincent A., 11659

Mahlmann, Peter, 6201
Mahmood, Z., 7351
Mahmoud, Fatima B., 10187
Mahoso, T.P., 9993
Mahroof, M.M.M., 8458
Mahshi, K., 5645
Maier, Charles S., 3065
Mainwaring, S., 11010
Mair, L.M., 10428
Majam-us-Saqib, 7352
Majewska-Peyre, U., 2594
Majid, M.G., 5109
Majjar, Fauzi M., 2210
Majul, Cesar A., 7564
Makambe, E.P., 9994
Makhlouf, Carla, 9797, 11154
Makhul, Makram Khuri, 5646
Makihara, Kumiko, 6095
Malaparte, Curzio, 7836
Malausséna, Paul-Louis, 2595
Malcomson, Scott, 7467
Male, George A., 4029-4031
Malherbe, E.G., 8156
Malhotra, M. K., 3066
Malik, Iftikhar H., 1093
Malik, M.H., 7352
Malika, Cirrine, 11155
Malin, Merridy A., 419
Malinvaud, E., 2596
Mallakh, Ragaei, 9798
Mallison, Sally V., 5647
Mallison, W. Thomas, 5647
Mallon, Florencia E., 7468, 7469
Malone, John, 3582
Malova, A.O., 6202
Malpica Silva Santisteban, Carlos, 7470
Mamak, Alexander, 11309
Mambo, Robert M., 6203
Mamdani, Mahmood, 8901, 8902, 10188
Mammach, Klaus, 10581
Mampouya, Joseph, 1823
Manasan, Rosario G., 7565
Manchuelle, Edouard F., 2597
Manchuelle, Francois, 10189
Mancorps, P.H., 2598
Mandala, Elias, 6362
Mandel, David, 9217-9219
Mandel, Ernest, 672
Mandel, Neville J., 5648
Mandell, Joan, 5649

Mandle, Jay R., 10429
Maneacu, M., 7837
Mangalres, M., 7566
Mangan, J.A., 4033, 5047, 10164, 11660
Mango, A., 931
Mangru, Basdeo, 4458
Mangum, Garth L., 9603
Manjarre, J. M., 8379
Manmohan, Kaur, 4825
Mann, F.A., 11156
Mann, J., 3793
Mann, Michael, 11661
Manne, Robert, 251
Mannette, Joy Anne, 1145
Mannick, A.R., 6477
Manning, Kenneth R., 9604
Manning, Patrick, 10190, 10191, 11662
Mannock, Robin, 6297
Mannoni, Octave, 11663
Manny, Raymond, 10192
Manogaran, C., 8459
Manor, Yohanan, 2599
Manorama, Ruth Austen Brandt, 6096
Manrakhan, J., 6478, 6479
Mansour, Atallah, 5650
Mantegra, G., 823
Mantle, Goontatlhe, 725
Mantzaris, E.A., 8157
Manuel, Anne, 7137
Manz, Beatrice F., 9220
Maolain, Giaran O., 11664
Maothea, I., 9920
Maoz, Moshe, 8686
Maphai, V.T., 8158
Maphalala, S.J., 8159
Mar'i, Mariam Mahmoud, 5651, 5652
Mar'i, Sami K., 5653
Marable, Manning, 9605
Marais, J.S., 8160
Marais, M.A., 8161
Maran, Rita R., 65, 66
Marasinghe, M.L., 8460
March, Candida, 11824
Marchant, Alexander, 824
Marcil-Lacoste, Louise, 1320
Marcolungo, Ezio, 10713
Marcu, N., 7860
Marcus, Aliza, 8852
Marcus, Bruce, 7054

Marcus, Harold G., 2304
Marcus, Ivan G., 8380
Marcus, Joseph, 7723
Marcus, Ralph, 12044
Marcuse, Peter, 3067
Mardle, W. F., 345
Maree, Johann, 8162
Maretzki, T. W., 3068
Margalit, Avishai, 5654
Marger, Martin M., 11665
Marglin, Frederique A., 11666
Marglin, Stephen A., 11661, 11667
Margo, Andrew, 11157
Margolin, Arnold D., 10714
Margulies, Ronnie, 8853, 8885
Mariategui, Juan, 7471
Marie, Gillian, 1094
Marie, Jacquelyn, 12045
Marin, Bernd, 554
Mariñez, Pablo A., 2123
Marino, Eduardo, 8461
Marion, Marie-Odile, 6586
Maritain, Jacques, 11668
Marjoribanks, Kevin, 420
Markakis, John, 2305, 10193
Marke, Ernest, 4034
Marketti, Jim, 9606
Markham, James M., 2600-2601, 3069, 10715-10717
Markoff, John, 2602, 2603
Markova, Dagmar, 4826
Markovic, Mihailo, 9861
Markovits, Andrie S., 555
Markovits, Claude, 4827
Markovitz, Irving L., 6019
Markovsky, B., 5915
Marks, Elaine, 2604
Marks, Frederick W., III, 4418
Marks, Gary N., 252
Marks, Sally, 3070
Marks, Shannee, 5655
Marks, Shula, 6727, 8163-8166, 10043
Marks, Thomas A., 6714
Markus, Andrew, 195, 253, 7401
Marnham, Patrick, 10194
Maron, S., 5656
Marquez, Robert, 1916
Marr, David G., 9775
Marriott, Stuart, 4035

Marrus, Michael R., 2605-2609, 10718-10721
Mars, Gerald, 9221
Marsden, William E., 4036, 4037
Marseille, Jacques, 2610
Marsh, Alan, 4038
Marsh, David, 3220
Marsh, David, 4039
Marsh, Patrick, 2541
Marshall, A., 6854
Marshall, Adriana, 134
Marshall, Gordon, 4040, 4041, 4042
Marshall, Leslie B., 11310
Marshall, P. J., 4828
Marshall, Phil, 5657
Marshall, Thurgood, 9607
Marter, A., 9952
Marti, Jorge L., 1917
Martin, Benjamin F., 2611
Martin, C.J., 6204
Martin, David, 958
Martin, Douglas, 5110, 5111
Martin, Gregory, 4829
Martin, J., 4043
Martin, John E., 4044
Martin, Juan Luis, 1918
Martin, Lothar, 2910
Martin, Michael F., 1732
Martin, Phillip, 825
Martin, Ron, 4045
Martin, Tony, 10430
Martinez, Carreras, J. U., 8381, 1169
Martinez, Elizabeth Sutherland, 1919
Martinez-Fernandez, Luis, 11011
Martinez Heredia, Fernando, 1920
Martinez, Javier, 1562
Martinez, Luciano, 2139
Martinka, K., 2037
Martins-Heuss, Kirsten, 3071
Martland, Nicholas, 7928
Martnis, José de Souza, 826
Martos, Fernando, 2612
Masalha, Nur-eldeen, 5658
Masferrer, Marianne, 1921
Mashingaidze, E.K., 10215
Mashinini, Emma, 8167
Maskiell, Michelle, 4830
Masliyah, Sadok H., 5160
Maslujak, S., 5112
Mason, D.M., 3635

Mason, Henry L., 6855, 6856
Mason, Leonard, 11311
Mason, T. David, 2259
Mason, Tim, 3072, 3073
Massaquoi, Hans J., 7382
Massel, G., 9222
Massey, James, 4831
Massing, Michael, 4483
Massing, Paul W., 3074
Masson, Jack K., 1095
Masters, Peter, 9223
Masters, R.E.L., 11645
Mastuy, V., 2038
Masurovsky, Marc J., 10722
Matar, N.J., 3309
Mathabane, Mark, 8168
Matheson, Gwen, 1445
Matheson, Trevor D.P., 11312
Mathew, A., 4832
Mathiesen, Anders, 2097
Mathur, S.C., 4833, 4834
Mathur, Y. B., 4835
Matkovski, A., 932
Matossian, Mary A., 9224
Matsui, Y., 10313
Mattelart, Armand, 1563
Mattelart, Michele, 1563
Mattes, Hanspeter, 6345
Matthew, Zachariah, 4745
Matthews, D., 3918
Matthews, Glen, 4046
Matthews, Mervyn, 9225-9228
Matthews, P.W, 254
Matthews, Z.K., 8169
Mattingley, Christobel, 421
Mattoso, Katia M deIueros, 827
Matysiak, A., 9229
Matza, Michael, 2613
Matzozky, Eliyo, 12046
Mauco, Georges, 2614
Maude, H.E., 7472
Mauersberg, Stanislaw, 7724
Maughan-Brown, David, 6205
Maung, Mya, 6715
Maurice, E.L., 8170, 8171
Maurice, Galton, 3808
Mauzy, Diane K., 6420
Mawassi, Idris, 5659
Mawby, R.L., 3422
Mawhiney, Anne-Marie, 1254

Mawson, Andrew, 8529
Maxon, Robert M., 6206
Maxwell, J.F., 11670
Maxwell, Neville G.A., 4836
May, Glenn A., 7567, 7568
May, Laurie J., 828
Mayall, David, 4047
Mayall, James, 11671
Mayana, Henry, 9995
Maybury-Lewis, David, 7422
Mayda, Giuseppe, 5965
Mayer, Arno J., 10723
Mayer, Nonna, 2615
Mayer, T., 8687
Mayer, Tamar, 11672
Mayer, Thomas, 11673
Mayerson, Philip, 2211
Mayled, John, 4048
Mazian, Florence, 10724
Mazrui, Ali A., 10195
Mazur, Carol, 12047
Mazza, Mario, 11674
Mbali, Zolile, 8172
Mbilinyi, Marjorie J., 8708, 8709
Mboukou, Alexandre, 1824
Mbu, A.N.T., 992
Mbuende, Kaire, 6747
Mbumba, Nangolo, 6748
Mbunda, D., 8710
Mbwiliza, J.F., 8711
McAdoo, H.P., 9608
McAdoo, J.L., 9608
McAdoo, William, 9609
McAllister, I., 3576
McAllister, Ian, 243, 11499
McArthur, Harvey, 7034, 7138-7145
McAuley, Alistair, 9230, 9231
McAuley, P., 3583
McBryde, Isabel, 465
McCaffrey, Vivian E., 1321
McCagg, William O. Jr., 4564
McCallum, Margaret C., 1446
McCandless, Robert, 1255
McCann, Frank D., 755, 756
McCann, James, 2306
McCarthy, D.M.P., 8712
McCarthy, F.E., 10314
McCarthy, Justin, 8854, 11158
McCarthy, M., 4049
McCarthy, Patrick, 2699

McCarthy, Tim, 4484
McCaskie, T.C., 3263
McClelland, Charles E., 3075
McClelland, James C., 9232
McCloy, Shelby T., 2616, 10431
McConnell, Bernie Scott, 2617, 2618
McCormack, A.R., 1106
McCormack, Gavan, 974
McCormick, B., 4050, 4051
McCormick, Gordon H., 7473
McCoy, Alfred W., 7569
McCready, William C., 6378
McCreery, David, 4419, 4420
McCulloch G., 6965
McDaniel, Tim, 9233
McDermott, Joseph P., 1733
McDermott, Patricia C., 1447
McDonald, J.R., 2619
McDonald, Maryon, 2620
McDonall, David, 6298
McDonogh, Gary W., 8382, 8383, 8384
McDougald, Elsie J., 9610
McDougall, David, 1448
McDowall, David, 8855, 11159
McEachern, Douglas, 10725
McEvoy, F.J., 1096
McFarlane, B., 186
McGee Deutsch, Sandra M., 135, 136
McGee, T.G., 6416
McGill, Stuart C., 255
McGinn, N., 6587
McGlyne, John, 3663
McGowan, William, 8462
McGrady, Richard, 4052
McGrath Grubb, E.E., 8385
McGrath, M.B., 8134
McGrath, Mike, 8173, 8174
McGrath, Tom, 1922
McGregor, R., 9996
McHenry, Donald, 11313
McHugh, P.G., 6967
McInnes, Colin, 11613
McIvor, A.J., 4053
McKenzie, Eric F., 1626
McKenzie, H., 11012
McKibben, Lizabeth A., 11314
McKibbin, Rose, 4054
McKinney, Robert J., 11315
McKnight, Gerald D., 9611
McLachlan, K.S., 6344

McLaughlin, B., 3076
McLaurin, R.D., 6162, 11160
McLean, Donald G., 1256
McLean, Jan, 256
McLean, M., 4055
McLeay, E.M., 6968
McLoughlin, P.F.M., 8530
McMichael, A.J., 257
McMichael, Philip, 258, 259, 260
McMillan, Alan D., 1257
McMillan, James, 2621
McMillen, Donald H., 1627
McNab, Christine, 8598
McNamara, Dennis L., 6252
McNamara, Jo Ann, 136
McNeil, William H., 11675
McPartland, J.M., 9473
McPherson, Dan, 1106
McQueen, Humphrey, 261-262, 422-423
McRae, Kenneth D., 8662
McRoberts, Kenneth, 1322
McRobie, Alan, 6969
McWilliams, Carey, 9612
Meacham, Standish, 4056
Mead, Richard, 6346
Meade, J.E., 11676
Meade, Teresa, 829
Meagher, G.A., 263, 424
Mealing, Stanley R., 1449
Means, Gordon P., 6417, 6418
Mecus, Bandewijn, 8599
Medding, Peter Y., 5287
Medhurst, Kenneth, 8386
Medina Hernandez, Andres, 6588
Medina, Laurie K., 692
Medzini, A., 5594
Meebelo, Henry S., 9955, 9956, 10196
Meer, Fatima, 8175, 8176
Meesook, O.A., 5024
Megenney, William W., 9752
Meghdessian, Samira Rafidic, 12048
Meghji, Alnasir, 1450
Mehlman, Jeffrey, 2622
Mehmet, Ozay, 6419
Mehta, J. L., 4837
Mehta, Vinod, 9234
Meijer, Marinus J., 1734
Meiklejohn, C., 12049
Meillassoux, Claude, 8177, 10197, 11677

AUTHOR INDEX

Meinardus, Marc, 11678
Meinhardt, Olav, 12050
Meinhardt, Rolf, 3077
Meinicke, Wolfgang, 3078
Meintel, Deidre, 1538
Meisler, Stanley, 7146, 7383
Meissner, Boris, 9235
Mejia Piñeros, Maria C., 6589
Melasuo, Tuomo, 67
Melber, Henning, 6749
Melendez, Guillermo, 11050
Melgar Bao, Ricardo, 11013
Melgert, Willy, 6909
Meli, Francis, 8178
Melikishvili, G.A., 11917
Mellafe, Rollando, 1564, 7474, 11014
Meller, Norman, 11316
Melo, Joao de, 10198
Melrose, Dianna, 11679
Melville, Joy, 3423
Memmi, Albert, 11680
Menache, Sophia, 3310
Menard, Larry, 1296
Mendelsohn, Ezra, 9236, 10726, 10727
Mendelsohn, I., 11918
Mendelsohn, Oskar, 7323
Mendelsohn, Ronald, 265
Mendes-Flohr, Paul R., 598, 2054, 5660, 6862, 6901, 10691, 10706
Mendez, Juan E., 11015
Mendiola, Haydee M., 1840
Menezes, Mary N., 4459
Menjivar, Rafael, 2260
Mennerick, L.A., 11700
Mentor, Ian, 4057
Menzies, A.C.C, 266
Mercade, Francese, 8367
Mercer, David, 425
Mercer, Jane R., 9613
Mercer, John, 6463-6465, 10199
Mercer, Patricia M., 267,268
Mergui, Raphael, 5661
Merhav, Meir, 3079
Merino Burghi, Francisco M., 8918
Merive, H. W. van der, 7979
Merkx, Gilbert W., 10933
Merlan, Francesca, 426
Mernissi, Fatima, 6667, 6668
Merrett, Christopher, 8179
Merritt, Anna J., 12051

Merritt, Richard L., 12051
Mertens, Lothar, 7838
Mertz, Elizabeth, 8180
Mesa-Lago, Carmelo, 1841, 1921, 10200, 11016
Meserve, Ruth I., 1628
Meserve, Walter J., 1628
Mesghenna, Yemane, 2307
Messina, Anthony M., 4059-4063
Messinger, Hans, 1451
Metcalf, Thomas R., 4838
Metsk, Frido, 2840
Mettam, Roger, 2623
Metzer, M., 11681
Metzger, Jan, 5662
Meulen, Hans W., 10728
Meumann, Gudrun, 8783
Mey, Wolfgang, 628
Meyer, Alfred G., 3133, 10866
Meyer, Alwin, 2983, 3031
Meyer, Donald, 5966, 8600, 9237, 9614
Meyer, E., 8463
Meyer, Ernie, 6097, 10729
Meyer, Gertrud, 3250
Meyer-Stamer, Jorg, 11544
Meyerson, Mark D., 8387
Mezentseva, E., 9238
Mezoff, Richard, 1469
Mgadla, Part T., 726
Mhlanga, Constance C., 10221
Mi'Ari, Mahmoud, 5663
Miari, Samir M., 5664
Miccoli Giovanni, 5967
Micgiel, John, 7725
Michael, Robert, 3080
Michaelis, Meir, 5968, 5969, 11682
Michalak, Laurence O., 11161
Michelucci, Alessandro, 12052
Michman, Dan, 673, 674, 675
Michman, Joseph, 6857-6862
Micksch, Jürgen, 10730
Middleton, Hannah, 427
Midlarsky, Manus I., 11017
Mieder, Wolfgang, 3081
Miers, Suzanne, 10201, 10202
Mignone, Emilio F., 137
Mihovilovic Eterovic, Milenko, 1565
Mikell, Gwendolyn, 3264
Miklos, Locko, 4572
Mikus, Joseph A., 2039

Milano, Attilio, 12053
Milano, Serge, 2624, 2625
Milanovic, B., 9862
Milazzo, M., 9863
Miles, Angela, 1452
Miles, Gary B., 11919
Miles, Robert, 3636, 4064-4071, 10731, 11683, 11684
Miley, James D., 11631
Milford, Sereisa, 11317
Miliband, Ralph, 11685
Miller, Barbara, 4839
Miller, Charles, 428
Miller, Christopher L., 10203
Miller, David, 1453
Miller, Jack, 9047
Miller, James Rodger, 1258, 1259
Miller, John, 6970, 10204
Miller, Joseph C., 90, 734
Miller, Judith, 4565, 9615, 10732
Miller, M.L., 933
Miller, P.R., 8181
Miller, Paul W., 270, 429
Miller, Paula, 269
Miller, R., 6590
Miller, Richard Roscoe, 11686
Miller, Stuart C., 7570
Miller, Ylana N., 5288
Millette, Robert E.
Millner, R., 4072
Millones, Luis, 7475
Mills, Dennis R., 4073
Mills, J.J., 12008
Milman, David, 4074
Milne, R.S., 6420
Milner, A.C., 6421
Milner, Henry, 1323
Milner, Joseph O., 406
Milner, Sheilagh H., 1323
Milson, Menahem, 5665
Milton, Sybil, 3082, 11639
Milward, Alan S., 7324
Milza, Pierre, 2626, 2627
Minayo, Maria C. de Souza, 830
Minc, R., 2628
Minces, Juliette, 11163
Miner, Kathleen N., 4075
Minev, D., 934
Ming Chan, 3488
Ming Yin, 1629

Mingat, A., 11687
Minglhi, Julian V., 1110
Minns, Amina, 5666
Mino Grijalva, Manuel, 2140
Minogue, M., 6480
Mintz, Sidney W., 10409, 10433
Mirante, E.T., 6716
Mirelman, Victor A., 138,139
Mirikatani, Janice, 9616
Miron, Louis F., 1842
Mironov, B.N., 9239
Mirza, Z., 3424
Misiunas, Romuald J., 9240, 9241
Miskiewicz, Benon, 7726
Miskin, J., 12010
Misra, B.B., 4840, 4841
Misra, Sailendra, 4842
Missman, David B., 9242
Mitch, David F., 4076
Mitchell, Allan, 2630
Mitchell, Richard H., 6098
Mitchell, Timothy, 2212
Mitchinson, Wendy, 1379
Mitchison, Rosalind, 3637, 3647
Mitra, Asok, 4843
Mitra, Subrata, 2631, 4844
Mittar, V., 4845
Mitter, Swasti, 3425, 4077
Mivaga, D.Z., 8182
Mixter, T., 8989, 9150
Miyazawa, Masanoti, 6099
Mize, D., 5667
Mizrahi, Maurice, 2213
Mizuno, Takaaki, 6100
Mlynar, Zdenek, 2040
Mock, Karen R., 1454
Modeens, Tore, 10613
Moderegger, Silvia, 556
Modi, B.M., 4846
Modras, Ronald, 7727
Moeckel, Margot J., 430
Moeller, James W., 9617
Moeti, Sello, 8183
Moghadam, Val, 8,
Mohamed-Salih, M.A., 2360
Mohammad Haji Yusuf, 6422
Mohammed, Abubakr Bala, 7259
Mohammed, Adam A., 8531
Mohan, Jitenaha, 8184
Mohan, V., 8464

AUTHOR INDEX

Mohanti, Prafulla, 3426
Mohanty, S.P., 4078
Mohawk, John, 7150
Mohd Aris Hj Othman, 5048
Mohd Noor, Sharifah, 6423
Mohler, S.L., 11920
Mohtadi, H., 5113
Moitt, Bernard, 7897
Mojares, Resil B., 7571
Mokgatle, D.D., 8185
Mokhtar, G., 10205
Mokhtar, Hermine, 2214
Mokyr, Joel, 4079, 4080, 5187
Mol, M., 9983
Molamu, Louis, 727
Molden, Fritz, 557
Molesworth, B.H., 271
Molet, Louis, 6356
Molho, Michael, 4377
Molho, Rena, 4378, 4379
Mollat, Michel, 10734
Molloy, Ivan, 7572
Moloisi, Thapelo, 8186
Molutsi, Patrick P., 728
Molyneux, Maxine, 2289, 9243, 9799, 9800
Mombeshora, S., 9997
Momigliano, Arnaldo, 11921
Momsen, Janet H., 11689
Moncan, Patrice de, 2632
Mondlane, Eduardo C., 6697
Monnesland, Svein, 935
Monnier, A., 8986
Monroe, K.R., 10735
Monroe, Sylvester, 3427
Montagnon, Pierre, 2633
Montejo, Esteban, 1923
Montejo, Victor, 4421
Monter, E. William, 8388
Monture, Patricia A., 1260
Montville, Joseph V., 11690
Moock, P.R., 6778
Moodley, K., 7952
Moodley, Ronnie, 4081
Moore, Andrew, 272
Moore, Bob, 6863
Moore, Brian L., 4460
Moore, C.R., 268
Moore, Carlos, 10950
Moore, Carlos, 1924-1926

Moore, Chris, 3633
Moore, Clive, 273
Moore, G., 5188
Moore, Jill, 6481
Moore, John H., 7151
Moore, M., 8465
Moore, R.J., 4461, 10736
Moore, R.L., 9618
Moore, Robert, 4082, 5189
Moore, Robin James, 4847
Moore, Zelbert L., 831, 832
Moorehead, Caroline, 6750
Moorson, R.G.B., 6751
Moorson, Richard, 11995
Moraes, Evaristo de., 833
Moraes Farias, P. F., 858
Moraes, M. 823
Morales Anaya, Rolando, 710
Morales-Gomez, Daniel A., 6591
Morales, Rolando, 704
Moralig, Gilead, 5668
Morán, Gregorio, 8389
Moran, Theodore H., 1566
Mordi, A.A., 7260
More, Christiane, 8856
Moreau, René Luc, 10206
Moreau de Saint-Mery, Mederic L. E., 4485
Moreen, Vera B., 5114, 5115, 5116
Moreira Alves, Maria H., 834
Morel, Bernard, 2634
Morelli, Anne, 677
Moreno Fraginals, Manuel, 1927, 11018
Morgan, D.R., 9520
Morgan, Edmund S., 9619
Morgan, James N., 10361
Morgan, Robin, 491, 11691
Morgan, Sally, 431
Mori, G., 5970
Moriel, Liora, 5289
Morikawa, Jun, 10207
Moris-Suzuki, Tessa, 6101
Morishima, Michio, 6102
Morley, J.F., 10737
Morner, Magnus, 11019, 11020, 11692
Morony, Michael G., 5161
Morris, Barry, 432
Morris, Benny, 5669-5675
Morris, G.M., 3705
Morris, H.S., 8903

Morris, Jenny, 11922
Morris, L.P., 9244
Morris, M., 8187
Morrison, Godfrey, 8532
Morrison, William R., 1261
Morrissey, Mika, 10420
Morrisson, C., 10738
Morrock, Lucy F., 406
Morrow, A.M.M., 1455
Morsbach, G., 3424
Morton, Henry W., 9245, 9246
Morton, James, 4083-4085
Morton, John, 274
Morton, Keith L., 11320
Morton, Rodger Frederic, 6207
Morton, Ward M., 6592
Mosca, Libiana, 6357
Moscatelli, Luigi, 835
Moscovitch, Allan, 1456, 1457
Moseley, George Van Horn, III, 1630
Moser, Leo J., 1735
Moser, Mary Theresa, 2635
Moses, Jennifer, 7839
Moses, Joel C., 9247
Moses, Larry, 6640
Mosha, Herme J., 10208
Moskin, J. Robert, 5676
Moskoff, William, 7840, 9248
Moskovitch, Wolf, 5290
Moskowitz, Moses, 2041
Moskowitz, Stuart B., 5291
Mosley, Paul, 9998
Mosley, W. Henry, 11693
Moss, Joyce, 11021
Mosse, George L., 2636, 10739-10741, 10835, 11694
Mosse, W. E., 3083
Motley, Mark E., 2637
Motyl, Alexander J., 9249
Motzkin, Leo, 7728, 9250
Moughrabi, Fouad, 5677
Moulier-Boutang, Yann, 10742
Moulton, Muriel, 5678
Moura, Clóvis, 836, 837
Mourad, K.E., 6669
Mouradian, Claire S., 9251, 9252
Mowe, Isaac J., 10209
Mozaffari, Mehdi, 67
Mozzoni, Anna Mana, 5971
Mpakati, Attati, 6363, 10210

Mphahlele, Ezekiel, 8188
Mpuyi-Buatu, Th., 2638
Mrabet, Mohammed, 6670
Muchembled, Robert, 2639
Mucke, Karl-Heinz, 3084
Mudenda, Gilbert, 10211
Mudimbe, V.Y., 10212
Mueller, Susanne D., 8713, 8714
Muenzel, Mark, 7423
Muffs, Judith H., 12054
Mufune, P., 9957
Muhareb, M., 5679
Muhlberger, Detlef, 10743
Mukamel, Susan, 11164
Mukhachev, Yuri, 9253
Mukherjee, Bharati, 4660
Mukherjee, Ila, 4848
Mukherjee, R., 629
Mukherjee, Ramkrishna, 8904
Mukherji, R., 4849
Mukhopadhyay, Maitrayee, 4850
Mukonoweshuro, E.G., 7910
Mukonoweshuro, Eliphas, 6208
Mulat, T., 2308
Mulcahy, F. David, 8390
Mullard, Chris, 4086, 4087
Mullen, K., 11695
Muller, A.L., 8189
Müller, Detlef K., 2640, 3085, 4088, 10744
Müller, Hermann, 3086
Müller, Ingo, 3087
Muller, Neil, 8190
Müller-Hill, Berno, 3088
Mulley, Klaus-Dieter, 558
Mulligan, Timothy P., 9254
Mullin, Chris, 1631
Mullins, D., 8045
Mumford, Clarence, 10434
Mumtaz, Khawar, 7353
Munck, Ronaldo, 140, 3584
Mundy, Yosef, 5680
Muneles, Otto, 12055
Mungawa Fasl, Eve, 275
Mungazi, Dickson A., 9999
Munholland, J. Kim, 9777
Munir, O., 8857
Munn, G.H., 4089
Munoz, Juan, 6018
Munro, Ross H., 7573

982 AUTHOR INDEX

Munroe, Trevor, 10435
Munslow, B., 11696
Munson, Henry, 6671
Muqtada, M., 621
Muraleedharan, V.R., 4851
Murati, Antoine, 2641
Muravachik, Joshua, 7035
Murch, Arvin, 10436
Murgia, E., 9620
Murphey, Elizabeth H., 68
Murphy, A.B., 11697
Murphy, George G.S., 6641
Murphy, J., 4091
Murphy, Martin F., 2115
Murphy, P.L., 1458
Murphy, Robert T., 2215
Murra, John V., 11023, 11024
Murray, Charles, 4092
Murray, Davis, 276
Murray, Dominic, 3585
Murray, Martin J., 8191, 9778
Murray, Nancy, 4093, 5681
Murray, Roger, 6737
Murrillo, Carmen, 7097
Musgrove, Philip, 11025
Mushkat, Marion, 7729, 10745
Musiker, Naomi, 12056
Muslih, Muhammad Y., 5682, 5683
Mussener, Helmut, 8601
Mustaffa-Kedah, Omar, 11165
Mutambirwa, James A.C., 10000
Muteba-Tshitenge, 9935
Muthiah, S. , 4852
Mutiti, M. Aaron Benjamin, 10001
Muus, P.J., 6864
Mwabu, G.M., 6209
Mwangi, W.M., 6209
Mya Sein, Daw, 6717
Mydans, Seth, 7574
Myeng, Ayi M., 993
Myers, Charles R., 3664
Myers, Gustavus, 1459
Myers, Ramon H., 6103
Myers, Samuel L., Jr., 9621
Myhre, Jan E., 7325
Myint, Ni Ni, 6718
Mykula, Volodymyr, 9255
Mysliwiec, Eva, 975
Myung, Park Moon, 6104
Mzimela, Sipo E., 8192

N'Gakegni, Prosper, 1825
Nadel, George H., 11698
Nadel, Ira Bruce, 5190
Nafziger, E. Wayne, 10213, 11565
Nagano, Yoshiko, 7575
Nagel, Joane, 678, 3598
Nagy, Karoly, 2042
Nagy, Peter, 4566
Nagy-Talavera, Miklos, 4567, 7841
Nahaylo, Bohdan, 9256, 9257, 9336
Nahm, Andrew C. , 6253
Naidir, Mark, 4854
Naidoo, Josephine C., 1097, 1098
Naipaul, V.S., 6424, 11699
Nair, D.P., 4855
Nairn, Allan, 5684
Naiyavitit, W., 8760
Najafizadeh, M., 11700
Najmabadi, Afsaneh , 5117
Nakano, Leatrice 1099
Nakano, Takeo Uyo,1099
Nakatsuru, Shaun, 1262
Nakhaie, Mahmoud R., 5118
Nakleh, Emile A,, 5685
Nakornthap, S., 8750
Nalbandian, Louise, 8858
Nalty, Bernard C., 9622
Nam, Jung H., 1632
Nam, Tae Y., 6425, 7929
Nambala, Shekutaamba V., 6752-6754
Nana-Fabu, Stella, 994
Nanavati, M.B., 4856
Nancy, Julia, 7842
Nandy, Ashis, 4857
Naranjo, Consuelo, 1928
Narayan, T., 4858
Narayanan, Suresh, 6426
Narby, Jeremy, 7432, 12057
Narendranathan, W., 4094
Narkiewicz, Olga, 10746
Nascimento, Abdias do, 764, 765, 838
Nascimento, Elisa Larkin, 839
Nash, Gary, 9623
Nash, Geoffrey, 5119
Nash, June, 711, 6593, 11027, 11701
Nashat, Guity , 5120
Nasman, Abdallah, 11166
Nasr, Kamel, 5624
Nassar, Jamal, 5538, 5686
Nasse, Simone, 2643

Nasser, Munir H., 5162
Nasson, Bill, 8193
Natanson, Ephriam, 7843
Nathan, Andrew, 1736
Natsume, Ryo, 4859
Naumann, Uwe, 3089
Nauta, A.P.N., 6817
Navrozov, Lev, 9258
Nawawi, M.A., 5049
Nayak, J. L., 4860
Naylor, Robert A., 693
Nazar, Ek, 3428
Nazario, Bejar, 6594
Nazarov, Kh KH., 9259
Nazdar, Mustafa, 8688
Nazzal, Nafez, 5688
Nazzari, Muriel, 1929
Ncube, Don, 8195
Ndoma, Ungina, 9936
Ndongko, W.A., 995
Neal, Fred Warner, 9864
Neary, Peter, 1460
Neatby, Hilda, 1461
Neave, Guy R., 3475
Nebe, J. M., 3090
Nedale, A.R., 277
Needham, D.E., 6364, 10215
Neevbury, C.W., 8196
Negash, Lemlem, 2309
Negash, Tekeste, 2310
Negrin, J.P., 11321
Neichardt, L., 8197
Neild, N., 4095
Neira de Fonseca, Cristina, 1806
Neis, Barbara, 1462
Nelhama, Joseph, 4377
Nellemann, George, 2098
Nelson, Craig, 7152
Nelson, Cynthia, 2216
Nelson, Daniel N., 7844, 10747
Nelson do Valle Silva, 882
Nelson, Gersham A., 10437
Nelson, Hyland N., 7401-7403
Nelson, Wade, W., 4096
Nenberg, Assia, 12059
Nestler, Ludwig, 578, 2064
Nesvisky, Matthew, 5292
Neto, Felix, 2644
Netteship, Martin A., 10446
Nettheim, Garth, 433-435

Nettleford, Rex, 10438
Netzer, Amnon, 5121
Neugebauer, Wolfgang, 544, 561
Neumann, Franz, 3091
Neumann, Gerd, 91
Neumann, Kurt K., 2043
Neumann, Yermeyahu Oscar, 2044
Neveux, Hugues, 2645
Nevile, J.W., 278
Nevin, David, 11322
Nevo, Joseph, 11167
Nevo, Ofra, 5689
Newark, John W., 10439
Newbury, Catherine, 7873
Newbury, Colin W., 11323
Newby, Gordon D., 7883
Newby, H., 11702
Newby, Laura J., 1633
Newell, Richard S., 9,
Newenham, E.A., 12060
Newham, Anne, 3878
Newland, Kathleen, 11703
Newland, Samuel J., 9260
Newman, A., 2045
Newman, Aubrey, 3311
Newman, Lucile F., 11704
Newman, Peter C., 1463
Newnham, Anne, 3429
Newson, Linda, 4514, 7153
Newth, J.A., 9263
Newton, Jennifer L., 12061
Newton, K., 4097
Newton, Velma, 7384
Ng'Ong'Ola, Clement, 6365
Niane, D.T., 10216
Niani, 840
Niblock, Trin, 8533
Nicholas, Joe, 4098
Nicholas, S., 3437
Nicholls, Anthony, 3009, 3974
Nichols, Roger L., 1263
Nichols, Stephen, 279
Nickerson, Colin, 6105, 6106, 6107, 6254
Nickul, K., 2347, 2361
Nicol, Andrew, 3819
Nicolas, Suzanne, 12063
Nicolson, Malcolm, 6971
Nicosia, Francis R., 3092
Niederhauser, Emil, 10748

Nielsen, F., 678
Nielsen, Jorgen S., 3430
Niemöller, Martin, 3093
Nieto-Stuarte, Maria Dolores, 6490
Nietschmann, Bernard, 7156-7159
Nieuwenhuysen, John P., 336, 362
Niezabitowska, Malgorzata, 7730
Nimrod, Yoram, 5690
Niosi, Jorge, 1464
Niranjana, T., 4861, 4862
Nissan, E., 11028
Niththyanathan, R., 8502
Nitz, Kiyoko K., 9779
Nixon, Anne, 5691
Nkabinde, A.C., 8198
Nkomo, Mokubung O., 8199
Nkrumah, Kwame, 11705
Noakes, Jeremy, 3094
Noble, Allen G., 5692
Noble, Kenneth B., 6466, 7262
Nodal, Roberto, 1930
Nogata, Judith, 6427
Noggo, Y., 5293
Noirel, Gérard, 2646, 2647
Noisi, Jorge, 1465
Noisset, Norbert H., 6748
Nokleby, B., 7328
Nolan, B., 5191, 5192
Nolan, J.P., 9261
Nolan, Mary, 3095
Noll, Hans, 3096
Nolutshungu, S.C., 7263
Noman, Omar, 7354
Noonan, John T., Jr., 9624
Noonan, Kathleen M., 3526
Norberg, Kathryn, 2648
Norbu, Dawa, 1634, 1635
Nordheimer, Jon, 1931, 5193
Nordic Council, 10749
Normandeau, Andre, 1466, 11987
North-Coombes, M.D., 6482
North, Joseph, 1932
North, Lusa L., 2261
Northam, Gerry, 4099
Northrup, David, 7264
Norton, Robert E., 11324
Nossiter, T.J., 4863
Notle, Detlef, 1567
Nouschi, André, 2649
Novak, D.A., 9625

Nove, Alec, 9262, 9263
Noveck, Daniel, 7160
Novick, Peter, 9626
Novogrodsky, Charles, 4277
Nowak, Bronislaw, 7911
Nqcobo, Lauretta, 3431
Nsibambi, Apolo, 8905
Ntampaka, C., 7874
Ntoko, Samuel N., 996
Numa, Guy, 2650
Nundi-Izrael, Dafna, 5294
Núñez Ponte, J. M., 9753
Núñez Soto, Orlando, 7036, 7037
Nunn, Audrey M., 7476
Nura, Resh, 5245
Nuss, S., 11706
Nutini, Hugo G., 6595
Nwagbaraocha, Victor I., 7265
Nwagwu, N.A., 7266
Nwaka, Geoffrey I., 7267
Nwulia, Moses D.E., 6483
Nyagahene, Antoine, 7875
Nyasani, Joseph M., 6210
Nye, John V., 2458
Nyeko, Balam, 8906
Nystrom, Kerstin, 9865, 9866
Nzenza, Sekai, 10002
Nzibo, Y.A., 6211
Nziuriro, Francis I., 7268
Nzongola-Ntalaja, 7888, 10187
Nzula, A.T., 10217

O'Ballance, Edgar, 8467
O'Brien, Anne, 280
O'Brien, Jack, 5194
O'Brien, Lee, 5693
O'Brien, Patrick K., 3973, 4100-4102, 11707
O'Brien, T.F., 1568
O'Callaghan, Marion, 6758
O'Connell, John, 5195
O'Connor, Marion F., 11467
O'Connor, P.S., 6972
O'Corra, Douncha, 5186
O'Donnell, Charles P., 630
O'Donnell, Guillermo, 142
O'Donnell, Mike, 4103
O'Dowd, Anne, 5196
O'Driscoll, E., 4104
O'Farrell, Patrick, 281

O'Hanlon, Rosalind, 4864
O'Hara, P., 3542
O'Hare, William P., 9627
O'Higgins, Michael, 4105, 11708
O'Leary, John, 8200
O'Loughlin, J., 3097, 10609
O'Malley, Patrick, 6973
O'Meara, Dan, 8201
O'Meara, Patrick, 10261
O'Neil, Bernard J., 436
O'Neil, Daniel J., 1101, 5197
O'Neill, Norman, 8535
O'Reilly, Kenneth, 9628
O'Riordan, Manus, 5198
O'Rourke, B.T., 6993
O'Shaughnessy, Hugh, 11029
O'Shaughnessy, Thomas J., 11168
O'Sullivan, A.J., 3503
O'Sullivan, N.O., 11435
O'Toole, Thomas, 1540
Oadea, Rizalino, 7576
Oakes, Elizabeth, 10440
Oakley, Robin, 4106
Oba, Kaoru Y., 6108
Obbo, Christine, 10218
Oberkofler, Gerhard, 3118
Oberman, Heiko A., 10750
Oberst, Robert, 8468
Obichere, Boniface I., 700, 7898
Obiechina, E.N., 10219, 10220
Obudho, R.A., 10221
Occhiogrosso, Paul F., 5694
Ochai, A., 10222
Ochieng, William R., 6212
Oculi, Okello, 6213
Oddie, G.A., 282
Odendaal, Andre, 8202
Oduho, Joseph, 8534
Oduleye, S.Q., 7269
Oertel, Joachim, 3098
Ofcansky, Thomas P., 12064
Ofer, Gur, 9264
Offen, Karen M., 2651, 12065
Offiong, Daniel A., 10223
Ofosu-Appiah, L.H., 10224
Ofreno, Rene E., 7577
Ogden, P., 2652
Ogunbameru, O.A., 10225
Ohland, Klandine, 7161
Ohnuki-Tierney, Emiko, 6109

Ohwae, Kenichi, 6110
Oiwa, K., 1467
Okafor, C.G., 8203
Okely, Judith, 4107
Okenfuss, Max J., 9265
Okey, Robin, 10751
Okihiro, G.Y., 9629
Okin, Susan M., 11709
Okladnikov, A.P., 9266
Okoh, S.E.N., 7270
Okojie, Paul, 10226
Okolo, C.B., 9630
Okpaku, Joseph O., 10227
Okpoko, John, 7271
Okpu, U., 7272
Oksenburg, Michael, 1647
Okubadejo, Adebola K., 7273
Okyar, Osman, 11169
Olaniyan, Richard, 4443
Olav Riste, 2939
Olcott, Martha B., 9267-9269
Older, Jules, 6974
Oldfield, John R., 6321
Oldham, James, 3432
Olds, Sharon, 8859
Oleszczuk, Thomas A., 9270
Olexer, Barbara, 9631
Olier, Michael D., 7162
Oliner, Samuel P., 9271
Oliveira, Mario A.F. do, 7775
Oliveira, Orlandina de, 6596
Oliver, Douglas L., 11326, 11327
Oliver, Haim D., 936
Olivera, Carlos E., 11030
Ollerenshaw, Philip, 3578
Olliz-Boyd, Antonio, 1933
Olmert, Yossi, 6299
Olmi, Massimo, 5972
Oloka-Onyango, Joe, 8907
Olson, A., 11772
Olson, J.S., 10752, 12066
Olson, Robert, 8860
Olson, Wayne, 6597
Olsson, Ulf, 8602
Olszewski, Henryk, 7731
Olukoshi, A., 7282
Oluyemi-Kusa, Dayo, 8715
Olzak, Susan, 678, 3598
Omissi, David E., 10228
Ommen, T.K., 4865

Omolewa, Michael, 7274
Omond, Roger, 8204
Omvedt, Gail, 4866-4869, 8469
Onabadejo, Martins A., 7275
Ong'wamuhana, K., 8716
Ongkili, James P., 6428
Onimode, Bade, 7276, 10229
Ono, Dawn K., 1102
Ono Kazuko, 1737
Onselen, Charles van, 8205, 8206
Ontiveross, S.R., 11973
Oomen, T.K., 4870
Oomens, C.A., 6866
Opekokew, Delia, 1264
Ophir, Adi, 5695
Oppenheim, A.L., 11923
Oppolzer, Alfred, 3099
Oputa, C.A., 7277
Orange, Claudia, 6975, 6976
Orbach, W., 9273
Orchard, G.E., 535
Oren, N., 937
Orent, Wendy, 5295
Orfield, Gary, 9632
Oriedger, Leo, 1469
Origo, Iris, 5973
Oriji, J.N., 7278
Oriol, Paul, 2653
Ornstein, Michael, 1470, 1471
Orobator, S.E., 1544
Orosz, E., 4568
Orpaz, Yitzhak, 5696
Orr, Akiva, 5296
Ortega Hegg, Manuel, 7163
Ortega, Manuel, 7164
Ortiz, Alan T., 7578
Ortiz, Fernando, 1934
Orwell, George, 3312
Ory, Pascal, 2654
Orywal, Erwin, 10,
Osa, O., 10230
Osborne, G., 345
Osborne, Milton E., 976
Osborne, P. D., 437
Osborne, R.D., 3549, 3550, 3586-3591
Oschlies, Wolf, 938
Oshane, R.K., 69
Oshima, H.T., 7579, 10315
Osman, A.A.M., 4108, 8536
Osman, M.K., 8537

Osman-Rani, H., 6391
Osoba, Segun, 7279
Ossman-Dorent, Susan, 2655
Ostenc, Michel, 5974, 5975
Ostergaard, Geoffrey, 4871
Ostow, Robin, 3100
Ostrowski, Wiktor, 9274
Othily, Georges, 2433
Othman, S., 8861, 11170
Ott, Andre, 9867
Ott, Thomas O., 4486
Ottaway, Marina , 2311
Otten, Mariel, 5050
Ouwersloot, H., 6877
Oved, Georges, 6672, 6673
Overton, John, 6214, 6215
Ovrut, Barnett D., 3313
Oweiss, Ibrahim M., 5697
Owen, Edward R.J., 11171
Owen, Norman G., 7580
Owen, R., 6281
Owusu, Kwesi, 3433, 3434
Oxaal, Ivar , 562, 8308
Oyatek, René, 950
Ozouf, J., 2500

Paape, A.H., 6867
Paasivirta, Juhani, 2362
Pablo, Renato Y., 7581
Pachai, Bridglal, 1146-1148, 6366, 7978
Pacheco, Esther M., 7600
Pachter, Elise F., 9937
Paci, Massimo, 5976, 5977
Pacione, M., 3638
Packard, Randall M., 8207
Paco, Delfina, 12067
Padgug, R., 11710, 11924
Padmanabhan, C.B., 4872
Padmore, George, 9275, 11711
Padula, Alfred, 1935
Pagden, Anthony, 9633, 11031, 11464
Pagliaro, Harold E., 1461
Pahl, Jan, 4110
Painter, Nell Irvin, 9634
Pakrasi, Kanti B., 4873
Paksoy, H.B., 9276
Pal, P., 4874
Palanea, Ellen H., 7582
Paldiel, Mordecai, 6868
Pallemaerte, Marc, 842

Palley, Claire, 10003, 10004, 10753
Pallister, David, 8208
Palloni A., 3923
Palmer, Bryan, 1472
Palmer, Colin A., 6598
Palmer, David Scott, 7477
Palmer, Frank, 4111
Palmer, H., 1103, 1265, 1473
Palmer, Ian, 438
Palmer, Kenneth A., 6977
Palmer, Robin, 10005
Palmer, S., 9868
Palmer, Stanley, 4112
Paloheimso, H., 11712
Palthe, T., 6866
Palumbo, Gene, 7038
Palumbo, Michael, 5701
Pamphile, Léon D., 4487, 4488
Pamuk, Elsie R., 4113, 4114
Pamuk, Sevket, 8862
Panahi, Bodi, 3101
Panananon, Chatchai, 8751
Panandikar, S.G., 4875
Panda, M.K., 4876
Pandey, R.N., 4877
Pandey, U.S., 175
Pandey, V.N., 4878
Paniagua, Carlos G., 1843
Panigrahi, Lalita, 4879
Panitch, Leo, 1503
Pankhurst, D.T., 10006
Pankhurst, Richard, 2312-2315, 5978
Pankhurst, Rita, 2316
Panneflek, Aignald J., 10441
Pannikar, K. M., 4880
Pao Min Chang, 9780
Papadopoulos, T.M., 8863
Papanek, Hannah, 2217, 10316
Pape, Marc, 6026
Papp, N.S., 4569
Paquette, Robert L., 1936
Paquot, Élisabeth, 11713
Paraf, Pierre, 2656, 11714
Parahoo, A.K., 6484
Parain, Charles, 11925
Pare, L., 6599
Paredes, Ruby R., 7583
Parekh, Bhikhu, 3476, 4115, 4116, 4881
Parfitt, Tudor, 2299, 2317, 2318
Parikh, S., 4882

Paris, Edmond, 9869
Park, Henry, 1738
Park, Philip, 6111
Park, Robert E., 10854
Park, Soon-chul, 6112
Park, Thomas, 6674
Parker, James R., 9636
Parker, Judith, 10252
Parker, R.S., 283
Parker, Sara, 4117
Parkin, Frank, 7645
Parkins, Geoffrey, 1636
Parkinson, Dilworth B., 2218
Parkinson, Loraine, 6113
Parkinson, Michael, 4118
Parlin, Timothy B., 3489
Parmenter, Barbara M., 5702
Parmer, J. Norman, 6429
Parming, Tonu, 8977
Parnell, S., 8209
Parpan, Alfredo G., 7584
Parpart, Jane L., 10231
Parra Sandoval, Rodrigo, 1807
Parris, C., 10442
Parry, T.G., 11328
Parson, J.D., 729
Parsons, J.W.R., 9277
Partnoy, Alicia, 143
Parvathamma, C., 4883
Parveen Shaukat, Ali, 2219, 5122, 7355, 8864
Pascu, Stephan, 7805
Passelecq, G., 679
Passerini, Luisa, 5979
Pastor, Manuel, 7478, 11032, 11033
Pastore, Jose, 843
Patai, Raphael, 5703, 11715
Patel, H.H., 8908
Pateman, R., 2319
Pathy, Joganath, 4884
Patnaik, Utsa, 4885
Paton, L., 1474
Patricio Dooner D., 1577
Patte, Daniel, 11716
Pattee, Richard, 4489
Patterson, Orlando, 11717-11720
Patterson, William L., 9637, 9638
Pattman, Jan, 439
Patton, Adell, 3265
Patwardham, S.P., 4886

Patzold, Kurt, 3102
Paucker, Arnold, 3103
Paul, Benjamin, D., 4422
Paul, David, W., 4570
Paula, Aldo de, 100
Pauley, Bruce F., 563,564
Paulin, Adjai, 997
Paulston, Christina B., 11721
Paupst, K., 1104
Pavier, Barry, 4887
Pavlat, Leo, 2046
Pavlov, V.I., 4888
Pavlowitch, Steven K., 9870, 9871
Pavy, David, 1808
Pawanteh, Latiffah, 6444
Pawelka, Peter, 2220
Paxman, John T., 11329
Paxton, Robert O., 2609
Payen, Geoff, 4119
Payne, A.J., 10443
Payne, Anthony, 11671
Payne, Charles M., 9639, 9640
Payne, Stanley G., 8321, 8391, 8392, 10754
Paz B., Sadith, 7385
Paz, D.G., 3527
Paz Gomez, Enelia, 1809
Pazmino-Farias, Carlos, 9754
Peach, Ceri, 4120
Peacock, Karen M., 11330
Pearson, David, 6978
Pearson, Karland N. Moul, 4121
Pearson, Raymond, 10755
Pearson, Willie, Jr., 9641
Peattle, Mark R., 6103, 11331
Pebley, A.R., 11587
Pecujlic, Miroslav, 9872
Pedatella, R. Anthony, 5980
Pederson, Duncan, 11034
Peebles, Patrick, 8470
Peek, M., 2047
Peek, Peter, 2141
Peel, J.D.Y., 10232
Peeters, Yvo J.D., 8865, 11984
Pehle, Walter H., 3104
Peires, J. B., 8210
Peiris, G.L., 8471
Peitchinis, Stephen G., 1475
Peled, Yoav, 5297, 5298, 9278, 9279
Peleg, Ilan, 5704

Peleg, R., 5392
Pelinka, Anton, 565
Pelissier, Rene, 92
Pelletiere, Stephen C., 11172
Pellow, Deborah, 3266
Pelteret, David A.E., 4122
Pemberton, John, 5051
Pen, Jan, 6869
Peña, Sergio de la, 6600
Penafiel Ramon, Antonio, 8393
Penders, C.L.M., 5052, 5053
Pennant, Thomas, 6367
Pennell, C.R., 6675
Pennington, J.D., 2221
Penninx, Rinus, 6870-6872, 10756-10757
Pennix, M.J.A., 6873
Penny, David H., 5054
Penrose, Janet M., 2363
Pentland, H. Clare, 1476, 1477
Pepper, Sheila, 12047
Peppidi, D.M., 11869
Pereda, Valdes, I., 8919
Pereira, Joao, 7776
Peres, Yochanan, 5705
Peretz, Don, 5706, 5707, 5820, 11722
Pérez de la Riva, Juan, 1940
Perez, Louis A., Jr., 1937, 1938, 1939
Perfecky, George A., 9280
Perkin, Harold, 4123
Perkins, John, 7404
Perkins, Kenneth J., 8784
Perlez, Jane, 960, 8909
Perotindumon, A., 10444
Perrineaux, Pascal, 2615
Perrott, Roy, 4124
Perry, D.W., 7405
Perry, Duncan M., 9873
Perry, Glenn E. , 5708
Persand, Naraine, 10445
Persson, Gunner, 8603
Perville, Guy, 2658
Pescatello, Ann M., 4889, 8394, 11035, 11036
Pess, Flavia, 5709
Pessen, Edward, 9642
Pete, Steve, 8211
Peters, Annie, 2659
Peters, C.J., 9257
Peters, E., 12068

Peters, Kyle R., 11387
Petersen, Jens, 5981
Peterson, Brian, 3105
Peterson, Glenn, 11332, 11333
Peterson, Jacqueline, 1266
Peterson, James W., 2048
Peterson, Kirsten H., 8212
Peterson, Nicolas, 440
Petras, James, 8395
Petraskova, V., 1978
Petrone, Penny, 1267
Petrow, R., 2099, 7326
Pettman, J., 284
Peukert, Detlev J. K., 3106, 3107
Peyronnie, Didier, 2660
Pezzati, Sergio, 5982
Pfaffenberger, Bryan, 8472
Pfarr, Heide M., 3108
Pfefferman, Guy, 844 , 11037
Pfeifer, Karen, 70
Pfouts, Anita, 6759
Phadnis, Urmila, 11723
Pharr, Susan J., 6114
Phelan, John L., 7585
Philip, Alan Butt, 3665
Philipp, Thomas, 2222, 8689
Phillip, Robert, 11781
Phillipps, K.C., 4125
Phillips, Anne, 10233
Phillips, David, 4152, 4184
Phillips, R., 4126
Phillips, W.M., Jr., 1941, 11724
Phimister, Ian R., 10007-10010
Phizacklea, A., 4065, 4071
Phlipponneau, Michel, 2661
Pholwaddhana, Niyaphan, 8752
Pi-Sunyer, Oriol, 6601, 8396
Piachaud, David, 4127
Piazza, Alan L., 1739
Picadou, Nadine, 5710
Picard, Louis A., 730
Pichetto, Maria Teresa, 5983
Pickering, A., 6760
Pien, F.K., 1638
Pierard, Richard V., 6761
Pierce, Paulette, 9643
Pierce, Richard A., 9281
Pierenkemper, Toni, 3109
Pieris, P.R., 8473
Pierola, Virginia, 12067

Pieroni Bortolotti, Franca, 5984
Pierre-Charles, Gerard, 2124, 4490
Pierson, Donald, 845
Piggott, John, 285,286,287
Pignon, Dominique, 9282
Pignon, Jean, 8785
Pilat, J.F., 10758
Pilbeam, Pamela, 10759
Pilet, Jacques, 8663
Pilger, John, 441
Pilkington, Edward, 4128
Pillsbury, Barbara L.K., 1639
Pinches, Michael, 10317
Pinchuk, Ben-Cion, 7732
Pinderhughes, Dianne, 9644
Pinkney, A., 9645
Pinkney, Robert, 11725
Pinkus, Benjamin, 2407, 9062, 9283, 9284
Pinn, Irmgard, 3110
Pinnock, Roberto, 7386
Pinson, K.S., 7722
Pinson, Koppel, 9397
Pinto, Antonio C., 2662
Pinto, Marina R., 4890
Pinto Vallejos, Julio, 846
Pipa, Arshi, 21, 22, 9874, 9875, 9876
Pirie, G. H., 8213
Pirio, G. A., 829
Pirrotta, R.A., 5985
Piscitelli, E., 5986
Pitsuwan, Surin, 8753
Pitt, K.W., 7930
Pitt-Rivers, Julian, 11038, 11039
Pittau, Franco, 5987
Pittin, Renee, 7280
Pittock, Barrie A., 288, 289, 442
Pitts, Joe W., 8214
Piuggros, Adriana, 11040
Pivato, Stefano, 5988
Piyadasa, L., 8474
Pizzaro, C., 1569
Pla, Josefina, 7424
Plant, D. N., 847
Plant, R., 11797
Plant, Roger, 2125, 4491
Plascov, Avi, 6164
Platek, Yizak , 5644
Platt, Steve, 4129, 4130
Player, Elaine, 3868

AUTHOR INDEX

Playfair, Emma, 5711, 5712
Playford, J., 290
Plenel, E., 2663
Plestina, Dijana M., 9877
Plewis, G., 4131
Plocker, Sever I., 5713
Plotincov, Leonard, 10273
Pluchon, Pierre, 2664
Plumb, J.H., 11726
Plummer, Brenda G., 4492-4496
Podder, N., 291
Podoluk, J.R., 1478
Poehner, W. Mark, 7387
Poer, C., 292
Pogarell, Reiner, 12069
Poinsette, C. L., 8215
Pokora, Timoteus, 1740
Poliakov, Leon, 2665, 10760, 10761
Policar, Alain, 2666
Politt, Gunther, 8604
Pollak-Eltz, Angelina, 9755
Pollard, David, 443
Pollard, Sidney, 4132, 10762, 11334
Pollaud-Dulian, Marcel, 11728
Pollins, Harold, 3314
Polonsky, Antony, 3315, 7734
Polyzoi, E., 1479
Pomeragn, Frank, 9878
Pomerantz, Marsha, 5715
Pomery, William J., 7587
Pommerin, Reiner, 3111, 3112
Pong, David, 1620, 1731
Ponger, Anna, 5716
Ponko, Vincent, Jr., 11173
Ponnambalam, Satchi, 8475, 8476
Ponting, J. Rick, 1268
Pooley, C.G., 3504
Pope, Alan, 444
Pope, Polly, 10446
Pope, Rex, 4133
Popisteanu, Cristian, 7845
Popkess, A., 4134
Poplin, Moulton G., 10447
Popov, V., 9339
Popovic, Alexandre, 940, 5163, 10763
Popplewell, Richard, 4135
Porat, Dina, 5299, 11174
Porket, J.L., 9285
Porpora, Douglas V., 11041
Porter, A.N., 11729

Porter, Alejandro, 11042
Porter, Andrew, 6908
Porter, Arthur T., 7912
Porter, Bernard, 4136
Porter, Gareth, 9781
Porter, Kenneth W., 9646
Portugal Catacora, José, 7479
Portugali, J., 5717
Poskonina, L. S., 848
Pospielovsky, Dmitry V., 9286
Possony, Stefan S., 9287, 11554
Post, David M., 7480
Posten, D.L., Jr., 1640
Postlethwaite, T. Neville, 11460
Poston, Dudley L., Jr., 6602
Potgieter, L., 12070
Potgieter, P.J.J.S., 12071
Potichuyj, Peter J., 1035, 9285, 9426, 8953
Pototsching, Franz, 566
Pott, A.F., 10764
Potter, Anne L., 144
Potter, Harold H., 1149
Potthast, Barbara, 7165
Potts, Lydia, 11730
Poujol, Catherine, 9288
Poulter, Sebastian M., 3436, 4137
Poulton, David W., 6603
Poulton, Hugh, 10765
Powell, James M., 10766
Power, C., 3385, 4138
Power, Jonathan, 10767
Powers, David S., 71
Poyer, Lin, 11302
Pozas, Isabel H. de, 6604
Pozas, Ricardo, 6604
Poznanski, Renee, 2667
Prabhakar, M.E., 4891, 4892
Prager, Jeffrey, 9647, 9648
Prager, L., 10768
Praisman, Leonid, 9289
Prakash, Gyan, 4893
Prakash, Nirupawa, 4894
Prantner, Robert, 567
Prasa, L., 2065
Prasert Yamklinfung, 8754
Prasertsri, Rangson, 8757
Prashar, U., 3437
Pratt, Geraldine, 1480
Pratt, L.R., 1489

Prattis, J. Ian, 1269
Prcela, Ivan, 9879
Prebisch, Raul, 11043
Prechal, Sacha, 10769
Prekerowa, Teresa, 7735
Premdas, Ralph R., 8477, 11335-11337
Prentice, Alison, 1481
Prescod, R., 10410
Pressburg, Gail, 5718
Presser, J., 6874
Prest, Mike, 4139
Preston, Barbara, 4140
Preston, Michael B., 9649
Preston, Paul, 8372, 8398, 8399
Preti, Luigi, 5990
Prewitt, Kenneth, 9587
Price, Claire, 8867
Price, David, 850
Price, David H., 11731
Price, J., 11338
Price, Richard, 8564, 10433, 11044, 11732
Price, Roger, 2668
Price, Sally, 10409
Pridham, B.R., 9801
Priemus, Hugo, 6875
Prieto Rozos, Alberto, 11045
Prifiti, Peter, 23
Primorac, Igro, 9880
Prince, Graham J., 3438
Pringle, H., 8104
Prinz, Thomas, 8478
Pristinger, Flavia, 5991
Pritchard, George, 11339
Pritchard, Rosalind M. O., 3113
Pritchett, Willis, 7281
Pritsak, Omeljan, 9290, 9291
Prochaska, David, 72
Proctor, Robert N., 3114
Procyk, Oksana, 9292
Prokesch, Steven, 8605
Promuihane, K., 6276
Pronay, Inge, 568
Pronay, Nicholas, 2998
Prost, Antoine, 2670
Proudfoot, Lindsay J., 5199
Provencio, Enrique, 6515
Prunier, Gerard, 8538
Pryce, Ken, 3439
Pryor, Frederic L., 10449, 11733

Przeworski, Adam, 2671
Przeworski, Joanne F., 1570
Psacharopoulos, G., 11046
Puanamaki, Raija-Leena, 5719
Pucci, Bruno, 851
Puckhov, P.J., 11340
Pugh, Terry, 1483
Pullan, Brian S., 10770
Pulleyblank, E.G., 1741
Pulzer, Peter, 569, 3115
Punamaki, Raija-Leena, 5720
Punyaratabandhu-Bhakdi, Suchitra, 8755
Purcell, Trevor, 10450
Purs, Jaroslav, 2049
Pusch, Luise F., 3116
Puxon, Grattan, 3010, 3117, 9881, 10679, 10771
Pyatt, Sherman E., 12072
Pyde, Peter H., 10451
Pyle, Jean L., 5200

Queirós Mattoso, Katia M. De, 852
Queiroz, S. R. R., 853
Quenneville, Ginette, 1036
Querol y Roso, Luis, 6605
Quigley, John, 5722
Quinlan, Tim, 8216
Quinn, Frederick, 998
Quinney, Valerie, 2672
Quintana, Bertha B., 8400
Quintana, Jorge, 7166
Quirino, Carlos, 7588
Quiroga, Hugo, 145
Quiroz, Alfonso W., 7481
Quisumbing, Agnes R., 7589

Raa, Eric T., 8717
Raaflaub, Kurt A., 12073
Rabb, Theodore K., 10095
Rabbani, Mouin, 5723
Rabbie, J.M., 6911
Rabenau, Kurt von, 6255
Rabin, Roni C., 5724
Rabinovich, Abraham, 5725, 6115, 9882
Rabinovich, I., 8690, 9095, 11153
Rabofsky, Eduard, 3118
Raboteau, Albert J., 9650
Rabushka, Alvin, 6430
Raby, David, 6606
Raby, Dawn, L., 7777

AUTHOR INDEX

Raccagni, Michelle, 12074
Rachatatanun, Witit, 8756
Raday, Frances, 5300
Radden, Viki, 6116
Radhakrishnan, P., 4895, 4896
Radwan, Samir M., 2223, 10125
Radziejowski, Janusz, 7736
Raftery, A.E., 5201
Ragoonath, Bishnu, 10452
Ragowski, Ronald, 2752, 3617, 3666, 3674, 6845, 8396
Ragsdale, Jane S., 7590
Ragsdale, John P., 9958
Rahav, Michael, 5301
Raheem, T.A., 7282
Rahim, Aminur, 631, 1485
Rahman, Anika, 4897
Rahman, Atiur, 632, 633, 634
Rahman, P.M.M., 635
Rahmato, Dessalegn, 2320
Rai, Kauleshwar, 6217
Raines, Howell, 3592, 9651
Rainger, Ronald, 4148
Raizada, Ajit, 4898
Raj Chanana, Dev, 4899
Rajagopal, Indhu, 4900
Rajewsky, Christiane, 3119
Rajoo, R., 6411
Rajshekar, Shetty, V.T., 4901
Rakindo, Adil, 5055
Rakowska-Harmstone, Teresa, 9293
Ralaton, H.K., 1105
Ralston, Richard D., 1942
Rama, Carlos M., 8921
Rama, Germán W., 8922, 11047
Ramachandran, V.K., 4902
Ramanujam, G., 4903
Ramaswamy, V., 4904
Rambaum, J.E., 8401
Ramcharan, Subhar, 1486
Ramdin, Ron, 3441
Ramet, Pedro, 9883-9887, 10772
Ramirez, Francis O., 7783
Ramirez, Susan E., 7482
Ramirez, William, 7167
Ramos, Artur, 854
Ramos, Elias T., 7591
Ramos Escandón, Carmen, 6607
Ramos Guedez, José M., 12075
Ramos-Horta, José, 5056

Ramos-Jimenez, Pilar, 7592
Ramphele, M. A., 8218, 8304
Ramras-Rauch, Gila, 5726
Ramsland, John, 293
Randa, Ernest W., 5727
Randal, Jonathan C., 6300
Randall, Steve, 4149
Randers-Pehrson, Justine D., 11926
Ranger, T.O., 10011, 10096
Rangiah, Darryl, 445
Ranki, G., 4517, 4571-4572
Rao, V.V.B., 10318
Rapaport, C., 5728
Rapaport, Louis, 2321
Raphael, Arnold, 10272
Raphael, Samuel, 10234
Rapoport, Louis, 5302, 5303, 9294
Rapoport, Yakov L., 9295
Rapp, Uri, 5729
Rappaport, Joanne, 1810
Rappaport, Steve, 4150
Rashid, A., 7356
Rasmussen, R., 253
Rassinier, Paul, 10773, 10774
Rasson, Lue, 2674
Ratcliffe, Peter, 4151
Rath, Jan, 6876
Rathbone, Richard, 10234
Rathkolb, Oliver, 570
Rathwell, Thomas, 4152
Raun, Toivo U., 9296, 9297
Rautkallio, Hannu, 2364
Rav, Shudha, 4905, 4906
Rav, T.D., 4907
Ravenholt, R.T., 11734
Ravitsky, Aviezer, 5730
Rawick, George, 9652
Rawkins, Phillip, 3666
Rawley, James A., 10775
Rawson, J.L., 4908
Ray, Arthur J., 1270
Ray, Donald I., 10235
Ray, John J., 294, 295, 446, 3120, 4153, 8219, 11735
Ray, Krishnalal, 4909
Ray, Larry, 6187
Ray, R., 4154
Raychaudhury, Rakhi, 4910
Razafimahatratra, F.Y., 6358
Razon, Felix, 7593

Razvi, Mujtaba, 6719
Read, Jan, 8402
Read, Peter, 447,448
Reban, Milan J., 920, 10684
Rebatet, Lucien, 2675
Recabarron, Maria E., 146
Reches (Rekhess), Elie, 5733-5739
Redclift, Michael, 11557
Reddy, T. Chandramohan, 4911
Reddy, William M., 2676, 10776
Redford, James W., 1271
Rediske, Michael, 7168
Redley, M.G., 6218
Redlich, Shimon, 9298, 9299
Reed, John N., 10236
Reed, L., 9653
Reed, Michael C., 2781, 4155, 4156
Rees, Alwyn D., 3667
Rees, H., 3509
Rees, Philip, 11736, 12076
Reeves, Frank, 3442, 3478, 4157
Reeves, Peter, 11341
Reeves, William J., 1402
Regalado, Basilia M., 7594
Regev, Menachem, 5741
Regula, 9468
Regular, William K., 1272
Rehfeld, Barry J., 9518
Reich, Emil, 10777
Reich, Peter, 11048
Reicher Madeira, Felicia, 855
Reichhold, Ludwig, 571
Reicin, Cheryl V., 5742
Reid, Anthony, 977, 5057-5058, 7595, 8763, 10319-10320
Reina, Leticia, 6608
Reinders, Robert, 3121
Reinfeld, Barbara, 2050
Reinhardt, O., 245
Reinhartz, Dennis, 9888
Reinharz, Jehuda, 3122, 11737
Reis, Elisa P., 856
Reis, João José, 857, 858
Reiss, Nira, 5743
Reiss, Spencer, 9756
Reissner, Will, 5471
Reiter, Rayna R., 1813, 11738
Reitz, J.G., 1487
Rejwan, Nissim, 5164
Remmer, Karen L., 11049

Remotique, Fe, 7596
Renaud, L., 1488
Renault, Francois, 7899, 10238
Renda, Gunsel, 8868
Rendall, Jane, 4158
Rendell, M.P., 296
Renn, Walter F., 3124, 3123
Repishti, Sami, 9876
Resnick, Sid, 7737, 9300
Retallack, James N., 3125, 3126
Retboll, Torben, 5059, 5060
Reuter, Jens, 9889-9891
Reuveni, Sari, 4573
Revell, J.R.S., 4159
Rex, John, 4160
Reyes Posada, Alvaro, 1811
Reyes, Renato B., 7597
Reyna, S.P., 1545
Reynolds, Henry, 449-451
Reynolds, P., 8060, 8240
Rhee, Ma-Ji, 6256
Rhim, Soon Man, 10321
Rhinelander, Laurens H., Jr., 9301
Rhoades, Robert E., 3127
Rhode, Gotthold, 10778
Rhoodie, Eschel M., 11739
Rhoodie, Nic J., 8220
Rian, Oystein, 7327
Rice, Condoleezza, 9186
Rice, Francis J., 3639
Rice, P.G., 4161
Rich, Evelyn, 9655
Rich, Paul B., 3443-3444, 3993, 4162-4167
Rich, Vera, 8987
Richard, Pablo, 11050
Richards, Alan R., 2224
Richards, Eric, 4169
Richards, J.G., 9656
Richards, Jeffrey, 4170
Richards, John, 1489
Richards, P.J., 11819
Richards, Paul, 7909
Richards, Thomas, 4171
Richardson, David, 8221
Richardson, John, 4172
Richardson, Ronald K., 10453
Richardson, Ruth, 4173
Richardson, Sue, 256
Richarz, Monika, 3128

Richelle, M., 10115
Richmond, Douglas W., 6609
Ricks, Thomas M., 5749, 11176
Ricoeur, Paul, 2677
Riddell, J. Barry, 7913
Riddell, William R., 1150
Riding, Alan, 859, 2678, 7170, 7483
Ridley, F., 3684
Riedlsperger, Max E., 572
Riel, Louis, 1273
Riendeau, Roger, 1151
Rietveld, P., 6877
Riff, Michael A., 2051, 2052
Rihan, R., 5645
Riis, Thomas, 943
Rijk, Tineke, 6878
Rinachevskaya, N., 9238
Ring, Harvey, 1943
Ringelblum, Emmanuel, 7738
Ringer, B.B., 9657
Rinser, Luise, 3129
Rios, José A., 860
Rischin, Moses, 1005, 5418
Rishmawi, Mona, 5750
Riskin, Carl, 1742
Riste, O., 7328
Ritchie, Harry, 3640
Ritchie, James E., 6979
Rivas Munoz, Mercedes, 1944
Rivera, Brooklyn, 7171, 7172
Rivera, Roselle L.K., 7598
Rivera Sierra, Jairo, 1812
Rivers, Richard, 861
Riviere, Bill, 10454
Ro'i, Yaacov, 9302-9304
Roach, Jack L., 9726
Robb, Peter, 4913
Robbins, Diana, 4009
Robert, Michael, 8479
Roberts, Adam, 5751, 5752
Roberts, Andrew, 10239
Roberts, B., 1490
Roberts, Barbara, 1453
Roberts, Elizabeth, 4174, 4175
Roberts, Hugh J. R., 73
Roberts, J. P., 4914
Roberts, K., 7442
Roberts, M., 8223
Roberts, Michael, 8480, 8481
Roberts, R., 4320

Roberts, Richard L., 6456, 10202
Robertson, Claire C., 10240-10242
Robertson, Esmonde M., 5994
Robertson, F., 292
Robertson, H. M., 8222
Robertson, Michael, 8224
Robertson, Priscilla, 10782
Robertson, R.T., 11342
Robeson, Paul, Jr., 9305
Robie, David, 11343
Robins, E.A., 5753
Robinson, Alan, 3593, 3594
Robinson, C.H., 6993
Robinson, Cedric, 6322
Robinson, David, 7900
Robinson, Forrest G., 9658
Robinson, Gertrude J., 9892
Robinson, J.W., 11740
Robinson, Jacob, 10783, 12077
Robinson, Jean C., 1744
Robinson, Kathryn M., 5061
Robinson, N., 8403
Robinson, Nehemiah, 11177
Robinson, Vaughan, 3445, 3446
Robinson, Walter S. Jr., 2679
Robison, Dick, 5062
Robles, Martha, 6610
Robson, A. H., 4176
Robson, Clive, 5754
Robson, M., 4177
Roche, Daniel, 2680
Rock, David, 147, 148
Rockett, Rocky L., 9306
Roderick, Gordon W., 3668, 4178
Rodger, D.J., 12078
Rodger, Richard, 3506, 3507
Rodison, Maxime, 5755, 11741
Roditi, E., 7778, 8869
Rodman, Margaret, 11344
Rodney, Walter, 4462, 4463, 8718, 10243, 10244
Rodrique, Aron, 8870
Rodriquez Grossi, Jorge, 1555, 1571
Rodriquez, José L., 1945
Rodriquez, Nemesio J., 149
Roebuck, Peter, 3637
Roemer, Milton I., 11051
Rofel, Lisa B., 1745
Roff, Sue Rabbitt, 11223
Roff, William R., 6431

Rogers, Anne, 11927
Rogers, Cyril A., 7283, 10012
Rogers, James A., 9307
Rogers, John D., 8482
Rogers, Rick, 4179
Rogers, Robert F., 11345
Rogers, Rosemarie, 10784
Rogers, Spencer L., 11742
Roggenkamp, Gerhard H. W., 3130, 3131
Rogger, Hans, 9308
Rogowski, Ronald, 1315, 11811
Rohmer, Harriet, 7173
Roht-Arriaza, Naomi, 11743
Rohter, Larry, 6611, 7388, 11052
Rojahn, J., 11744
Rokala, D.A., 12049
Rokhsar, Jacqueline, 7329
Roland, Joan G., 4915
Roldan, Martha, 6502
Rolef, Susan Hattis, 5756
Rollat, Alain, 2663, 2681, 11346
Rolsten, Bill, 3595
Roman, Anne C.R., 2019, 2043
Roman, Michael, 5757
Roman, Viorel S., 12016
Romanelli, Samuel A., 6676
Romann, Michael, 5758
Romano, Jasha, 9893
Rome, David, 1038-1044, 12079
Romero Aceves, Ricardo, 6612
Romero Ibarra, Maria E., 11053
Romero, Patricia W., 10245
Roncal, Joaqim, 6613
Rondot, Pierre, 11178, 11179
Rone, Jerema, 2252
Ronel, Eti, 5759
Ronen, Dov, 701
Roniger, Luis, 10787
Ronnas, P.J., 7847
Roof, W. Clark, 9659
Rooke, P.T., 10455
Rooney, Barney, 4180
Rooper, Alison, 7174
Roosen, William, 2727
Roosens, Eugeen, 680, 681
Rorlich, Azade-Ayse, 9309
Rosario, Esteban, 2126
Rosca, Ninotchka, 7599
Rose, David, 1032, 4041

Rose Green-Williams, C., 1946
Rose, Harold M., 9660
Rose, Lionel, 4181
Rose, Madhuri, 4916
Rose, Michael E., 4182, 4183
Rose, Paul L., 3132
Roseberry, William, 9757
Rosefielde, Steven, 9310, 9311
Rosen, Miriam, 5760
Rosen, Stanley, 1746, 1747
Rosenaft, Menachem Z., 573
Rosenbaum, H. Jon, 11745
Rosenberg, David, 3397
Rosenberg, Diana, 8539
Rosenberg, Dorothy, 3133
Rosenberg, Emily S., 6323
Rosenberg, Louise Renee, 12080
Rosenberg, Neil V., 9661
Rosenberg, Tina, 1573
Rosenblum, Mort, 10246
Rosenblum-Cale, Karen, 9833
Rosenbluth, David, 1491
Rosenfeld, Henry, 5242
Rosenfeld, Stephen S., 10788
Rosenfield, Leonora C., 2682
Rosenhaft, Eve, 3134
Rosenkranz, Herbert, 574,575
Rosenthal, Morton M., 7039, 11054
Rosenthal-Shneiderman, Esther, 9312
Roshwald, Aviel, 11180
Roslyng-Jensen, Palle, 2100
Rosman, M.J., 7739
Rosoli, Gianfausto, 10789
Rosowski, Martin, 11450
Ross, Angus, 11347
Ross, Carl, 8607
Ross, David, 11,
Ross, David P., 1492
Ross, George, 2529
Ross, Jacobi, 3433
Ross, Malcolm, 1045
Ross, R., 10842
Ross, Robert, 2413, 6795, 8225, 9662, 11392
Ross, Robert H., III, 5995
Ross, Robert J.S., 11746
Rossi, Amato, 5996
Rossiter, Margaret L., 2683
Rost, Yuri, 8871, 9313

Rotberg, Robert I., 4497, 4498, 10095, 10247
Rotermundt, Rainer, 3135
Roth, Cecil, 5997, 11181
Roth, Jürgen, 3136
Roth, Stephen, 5202, 10790-10791, 11747
Rothbarth, Maria, 3137
Rothchild, Donald, 6219, 10248
Rothenberg, Joshua, 12081
Rothenberg, Julie, 2309
Rothenhofer, D., 3138
Rothermund, Dietman, 11748
Rothkirchen, Livia, 2053-2058
Rothschild, Walter, 3316
Rothstein, B., 8608, 8609
Rothwell, Tom, 4184
Rotter, Gernot, 11749
Rouanet, Gustave, 74
Rouhana, Kate, 5761
Rouhana, Nadim, 5762, 5763
Roumani, Maurice M., 5304, 5305, 6347
Rouquie, Alain, 150
Rousseau, M.H., 12082
Roussel, Eric, 2684
Rousso, Henri, 2685
Rout, Leslie B., Jr., 862, 11055
Routledge, David, 11348
Rovan, Joseph, 2686
Rowan, Patricia, 11750
Rowbotham, Sheila, 1947, 11751
Rowe, David E., 3139
Rowley, A.R., 576, 5998
Rowley, C.D., 452, 453, 7406
Rowney, D., 535
Rowse, Tim, 454, 11752
Roy, M.N., 4917
Roy, Olivier, 2687
Roy, Patricia E., 1105-1108
Roy, Sara, 5764, 5765, 5766
Roy, Sudipta, 1109
Royle, S.A., 11056
Rozenbaum, Wlodzimierz, 7740
Rozett, Robert, 2009, 10792
Rubagumya, C.M., 8719
Rubbo, Anna, 1813
Rubenberg, Cheryl A., 5767
Rubenstein, Danny, 5768, 5769, 5808
Rubenstein, Judith A., 9663

Rubenstein, Richard L., 11753
Rubenstein, W.D., 297-298, 2461, 3317, 4185-4196, 6015, 9642, 11754
Rubin, Miri, 4197
Ruby, Walter, 7040
Ruck, Calvin W., 1152, 1153
Rudd, E., 3479
Rudden, Bernard, 9314
Rudge, David, 5770-5773
Rudnytsky, Ivan L., 9315
Rudra, A., 4918
Rudra, Ashok Utsa Patnaik, 4919
Ruether, Rosemary, 5774, 10793, 11000, 11755-11757
Ruhela, Satya Pal, 4920
Rule, John, 4198
Rule, Sheila, 10013, 11758
Rumer, Boris Z., 9316
Rummel, Rudolph J., 9317
Rummelt, Peter, 10249
Rumpf, Roger, 6277
Runciman, W.G., 4199
Rundall, R.A., 6642
Runge, C., 884
Rupen, Robert A., 6643-6645
Rupp, Leila J., 9664
Rupps, J. C.C., 6879
Rürüp, Reinhard, 3140
Ruscio, Alain, 2688
Rushwan, Hamid, 8540
Russel, M., 8226
Russell, Bob, 1493
Russell, Emily, 3447
Russell, George, 7175
Russell, J., 3596, 3597
Russell, James W., 11759
Russell, Margo, 8227
Russell-Wood, A.J.R., 863, 7779, 11057
Russo, C., 455
Rustant, Maurice, 2689
Rustem, Ahmed, 8872
Rutayisire, Paul, 7876
Rutherford, Noel, 11259
Rutkoff, Peter M., 2690
Rutland, Suzanne D., 299
Ruyle, Eugene E., 6117, 6118
Ruz Ménendez, Rodolfo, 6614
Ruzicka, L.T., 11822
Ruzickova, Z., 2059
Ruzie, David, 11760

Ryan, Donna F., 2691
Ryan, Lyndall, 456
Ryan, Randolph, 7176, 7177
Ryan, Sheila, 5878
Ryan, Stephen, 11761, 11762
Ryerson, Stanley B., 1494-1499
Ryszka, Franciszck, 7741
Ryu, Sanghee, 6119
Rywkin, Michael, 9318-9321

Saad, Elias N., 6457
Sabahi, Houshang, 5123
Sabak, Constantine, 2060
Sabalinas, L., 9322
Sabaratnam, Lakshmanan, 8483, 8484
Sabatello, E.F., 5486
Saber, Mostafa, 5124
Sabille, Jacques, 8786
Sable, Martin H., 11058
Sachs, Albert L., 4200, 9665
Sachs, J., 7717
Sacouman, R. James, 1500
Saddinton, D.B., 11928
Sadji, Uta, 3141
Sadkovich, James J., 9894
Sadoun, Marc, 2692
Saeed, S., 11182
Saeger, James S., 11059
Safa, Helen I., 10456, 11026, 11027, 11060
Safran, A., 7848
Safran, William, 2693, 2694
Sage, Yves-Louis, 11349
Sagers, M.J., 8968
Saggar, Shamit, 3448
Saha, Suranjit K., 4921
Sahlins, Marshall, 11350, 11351
Sahliyah, Emile, 5775
Sahn, D.E., 8485
Sahota, Gian S., 7389, 7390
Said, Edward W., 5776-5779
Saidel, Rochelle G., 9666
Saignes, Thierry, 712
Saini, Krishan G., 4922
Saith, Ashwani, 2322
Sakakini, Widad, 8691
Sakala, Carol, 12083
Sakalys, Jurate A., 9323
Sala, Garry C., 6120
Sala-Molins, Louis, 2695

Salacuse, Jeswald W., 11161
Salaff, Janet W., 7931
Salah el-Din el-Zain el-Tayeb, 8541
Salah, Rima Y., 6165
Salameh, Ghassane, 7884
Salamone, Frank A., 7285
Salamone, S.D., 8873
Salanga, Alfredo, 7600
Saleeby, Najeeb M., 7601
Saleh, Abdul A., 5063
Saleh, Abdul Jawad, 5780, 5781
Salhab, A.A.S., 5780
Salih, K.O., 8542, 8543
Salitan, Laurie P., 9324
Salkin, Yves, 8692
Salleh, Halim, 6432
Sallen, H.A., 3174
Saller, K., 3142
Salmi, Jamil, 6677
Salomon, Herman P., 7780
Salt, J., 3143
Salter, Brian, 4201
Saltman, Jack, 577
Salvatore, Ricardo D., 151
Salvi, Sergio, 10795
Salvucci, Richard J., 6615
Saly, Hugo, 10705
Salzman, Mark, 1748
Salzmann, Zdenek, 2061-2062, 12084
Samara, Adel, 5782, 5783, 5784
Samarasinghe, S.W.R., De A., 8477
Samaraweera, Vijaya, 8486
Samarin, William J., 1541, 10250
Samaroo, Brinsley, 10377
Samatar, Said S., 7945
Samatas, Minces, 4380
Samoff, Joel, 8720, 8721
Sampson, Steven L., 7849, 10796
Samuel, M., 2696
Samuel-Mbaekwe, Iheanyi J., 10251, 11763
Samuels, S., 682
San Gupta, Bhabani, 12,
San Juan, Epifanio, 7603, 7604
San Roman, Teresa, 8404
Sanasarian, Eliz, 5125
Sanborn, Anne F., 4574
Sánchez, Juan, 1948
Sánchez, Rodrigo, 11061
Sandberg, Lars G., 8610

Sandbrook, Richard, 10252
Sanders, Alan J.K., 6646
Sanders, Andrew, 4464
Sanders, Claire, 8487
Sanders, Douglas, 7330
Sanders, Ivan, 4575
Sanders, Margaret, 1826
Sanderson, Barbara M., 2697
Sanderson, Lilian, 8544
Sanderson, M., 4202
Sandhu, K.S., 1110, 6433
Sandiford, Keith A.P., 10457
Sandin, Bengt, 8611
Sandino, Augusto C., 7043
Sandy, Cleve P., 10458
Sang Ye, 1783
Sangari, Kumkum, 4923
Sangmeister, Hartmut, 11764
Sangster, Joan, 1501
Sangwan, Satparl, 4924
Sani, Rustam A., 6434
Sanjdorj M., 6647
Sanjian, Avedis K., 8693
Sanjorj, M., 1642
Sanmarco, Philippe, 2634
Sanmugathasan, N., 8488
Sant Cassia, Paul, 1972
Santamaria, U., 4203, 5257
Santana, Roberto, 2143
Santana, S.M., 1949
Santiago, Domingo C., 7605
Santiago Santiago, Isaura, 9667
Santos, E., 2144
Santos, Paula, 864
Santos, Silvio C. dos, 865
Sapounas, G., 4381
Saradamoni, K., 4925
Sarakinsky, Mike, 8128
Sarasivathi, S., 4926, 4927
Sargius, Francis, 5165
Sarigiania, Steven M., 4499
Sarkar, B.N., 4928
Sarkar, S., 4929
Sarkisyanz, Manuel, 9325
Saron, Gustav, 8228
Saroyan, M., 9326
Sarpellon, Giovanni, 5999
Sarre, P., 4204
Sarti, Roland, 5990, 6000, 12085
Saskana, Amon S., 10459

Sates, John M., 7606
Sathar, Z.A., 7344
Sato, Kazuo, 6121
Sattin, Anthony, 2225
Satzewich, Vic, 1111, 1154, 1502, 11684
Saueressig-Schreuder, Yda, 10797
Saul, Amir, 2226
Saul, John, 1392, 8229, 9961
Saunders, A.C. de C.M., 7781, 7782
Saunders, C., 7965
Saunders, D., 3449
Saunders, K., 300
Saunders, Kay, 6482
Sauners, Barbara, 4205
Savage, M.T.D., 8230, 8231
Saville, Richard, 3641
Sawchuk, Joe, 1274
Sawer, Marian, 457
Sawh, Roy, 3450
Sawyer, Amos, 6324
Sawyer, Roger, 11765, 11766
Sayigh, Yusif A., 5785
Sayler, Wilhelmine M., 3144
Sbacchi, Alberto, 2323
Scalapino, Robert, 10309
Scammell, Michael, 9895, 9896
Scanlon, Geraldine M., 8405
Scarantino, Anna, 2227
Scardigli, Victor, 10798
Scarlott, Jennifer, 11353
Scarman, Lord, 4206
Scarr, Deryck, 11354, 11355
Scase, Richard, 8612
Schaeffer, Herman, 3145
Schaifer, R., 11929
Schain, Martin A., 2698, 2699
Schaller, Helmut W., 3146
Scham, Alan M., 2700
Schaniel, William C,, 6980
Schapera, I., 12086
Schappes, Morris U., 9668
Scharf, Wilfried, 7991
Scharff, Roland, 9327
Schatkowski Schilcher, Linda, 11183
Schatz, Jaff, 7742, 7743
Schatzberg, Michael G., 999, 6220, 9939
Schatzker, Chaim, 10597
Schechtman, Joseph B., 9328

AUTHOR INDEX 999

Schecter, Stephen, 1503
Scheepers, Peer, 6880
Schenk, Magdalena G., 6881
Schenker, Hillel, 5786, 5787
Schermerhorn, R.S., 1643
Schers, David, 11062, 11063
Schessler, Hanna, 9455
Scheuch, Erwin K., 3147
Schickert, Klaus, 4576
Schiel, Tilman, 5064
Schierup, C.U., 8613
Schiff, Michel, 2701
Schifferes, Steve, 4207
Schilling, Donald G., 55, 6192
Schire, Robert, 962
Schirmer, Daniel B., 7607
Schissler, Hanna, 2824, 3718
Schlaffer, Edit, 491
Schlarp, Karl Heinz, 9897
Schlegel, Alice, 11767
Schleunes, Karl A., 3148, 3149
Schlicht, Alfred, 2228
Schlotzhauer, Inge, 3150
Schmalz, Peter S., 1275
Schmelz, U.O., 11768
Schmerl, Christiane, 3151
Schmid-Affolter, Anny, 8643
Schmid, Carol, 8664
Schmid, Max, 8665
Schmidt, Maria, 2063
Schmitter, B., 3152
Schmitz, Adelheid, 3119
Schmitz, Erich, 9940
Schmugge, Ludwig, 10799
Schnapper, Dominique, 2702
Schneider, J.S., 7850
Schneider, Pablo R., 4426
Schneider, Robin, 7161, 7168
Schneider, Rudolf, 3153
Schneider, Stanley, 5247
Schneider, Ullrich, 3154, 3155
Schneider, William, 2703
Schneller, R., 5306
Schnick, Irvin C., 8874
Schober-Brinkmann, K., 3156
Schoenberg, Ulrike, 3157
Schoeps, Julius H., 3173, 10808
Schoffer, I., 6882
Scholch, A. , 5788
Scholder, Klaus, 3158

Scholtz-Klink, Gertrud, 3159
Scholtz, P.L., 12087
Schonbach, Morris, 9669
Schonfeld, Roland, 10800
Schooler, C., 6122
Schoombee, G.F., 8232
Schoonboom, I.J., 6883
Schoonover, Thomas, 2262
Schöpflin, George, 7851, 7852, 9898, 10801
Schor, Ralph, 2704
Schott, Kerry, 11769
Schrag, Carl, 5308
Schreter, S.M., 1046
Schröder, Hannelore , 3160
Schröder, Hans-Jürgen, 3161
Schryer, Frans J., 6616
Schtajerman, E. M. (Staerman), 11930
Schubert, Grace, 2145
Schudrick, Michael J., 6123
Schuler, Hans, 3162
Schulte, Axel, 3163
Schulte, Theo, 9329
Schulte-Althoff, Franz-Josef, 10253
Schulten, C.M., 5065, 10322
Schultz, John, 1155
Schumacher, Edward, 8406
Schuman, Howard, 9670
Schumann, Siegfried, 10588
Schumann, Wolfgang, 578, 2064
Schutt, Peter, 3164
Schutte, Gerritt J., 6884
Schütte, Wolfgang, 3165
Schutz, Barry M., 11770
Schvartzman, M., 7425
Schvarzer, Jorge, 152
Schwab, Peter, 5309
Schwan, Heribert, 2906
Schwarts, M., 12002
Schwartz, Jonathan M., 2101
Schwartz, Kessel, 153
Schwartz, Nathan H., 3508
Schwartz, Robert M., 2705
Schwartz, Ronald, D., 1644
Schwartz, Rosalie, 1950
Schwartz, Solomon, 9330
Schwartz, Stuart B., 866-869,
Schwartz, Thomas A., 3166
Schwartzman, Kathleen C., 7783
Schwarz, Hans-Peter 3147

Schwarz, Harry, 8233
Schwarz, Henry G., 1645, 1646, 1647
Schwarz, L.D., 4208
Schwarz, Robert, 579,580
Schwarz, Walter, 8489
Schweizer, Thomas, 5066
Schwille, John, 11813
Scitovsky, Tibor, 1749, 6257
Scjaky, Leon, 4382
Scobie, Edward, 10802
Scobie, Harry M., 10323
Scott, Bob, 8490
Scott, Hilda, 4209, 10803
Scott, James F., 9671
Scott, Nobert P., Jr., 1156, 1157
Scott, Rebecca, 870
Scott, Rebecca J., 870, 1951-1954
Scott, William Henry, 7608, 7609
Scott-Brown, Joan, 1276
Scouloudi, I., 4211
Scraton, Phil, 4212
Scully, Malcolm G., 8234
Seabrook, Jeremy, 4213
Seager, J., 11772
Sealey, D. Bruce, 1250
Searle, Chris, 4214-4217, 6698, 10460
Sears, Alan, 1504
Sears, William, 5126
Seboni, M.O.M., 8235
Sebstad, Jennefer, 4930
Secher, Knud, 2102
Sederberg, Peter C., 11745
Sedler, R.A., 9672
See, K.O., 3598
Seed, Patricia, 6617
Seetharamu, A.S., 4931
Seewann, Gerhard, 4577
Segal, Mark, 5789, 5790
Segal, Ronald, 8115
Segar, Julia, 8236
Segev, Tom, 5791
Segre, Claudio G., 6348
Seib, Gerald F., 11184
Seidel, Gill, 3167, 3318, 10804
Seidl, V., 2059, 2065
Seidman, Ann W., 10254
Seiferheld, Alfredo M., 7426
Seigle, Larry, 7178
Seilbert, Ilse, 11931
Seitz, A., 176

Seiyama Takuro, 6101
Sekelj, Laslo, 9899
Selby, M., 6124
Seligson, Mitchell A., 11773
Seliktar, Ofira, 5704
Selth, Andrew, 6720
Selvaratnam, V., 6435
Selwyn, P., 11185
Semboja, J., 8722
Semo, Enrique, 6618
Semyonov, Moshe, 5632, 5792-5794
Sen, Amartya, 4932, 11774
Sen, Jahar, 4933
Sen, R., 4934
Sen, Sunil K., 4935
Sender, John, 10255
Senghor, Léopold Sédar, 11932
Seninger, Stephen F., 9603
Senkman, Leonardo, 154
Sennett, R., 3524
Serbia, Ken, 871, 872,
Serbin, Andres, 9758
Serjeants, Susan W., 11266
Serow, W.J., 11396
Serrano, Josephine B., 7610
Serviat, Pedro, 1955
Seshadari, K., 4936
Sessions, Kyle C., 10861
Sethi, Harsh, 4937
Sevenster, J.N., 11933
Sevilla, Eduardo, 8357
Sevillias, Errikos, 4383
Sewell, William H., 2706
Sexton, Robert D., 4219
Seydewitz, M., 3168
Seydewitz, R., 3168
Seyhan, Azade, 3169
Seyon, Patrick L.N., 6325
Shadbolt, Maurice, 6981
Shafer, S., 6982
Shaffer, Harry, 3170
Shaffer, William, 1433
Shaffir, W., 1034
Shafir, Gershon, 9279
Shafir, Michael, 7853, 7854
Shah, A., 3509, 4220, 4221
Shah, Mohammad, 4938
Shah, Nasra M., 6272, 11102
Shah, S. Shamim, 4939
Shah, Sneh, 4222

Shahak, Israel, 5795-5797, 11775
Shaheed, Farida, 7353
Shaikh, A.U., 4940
Shain, Milton, 8237-8241
Shakabpa, Tsepon W.D., 1654
Shaked, Haim, 8545
Shakur, Assata, 1956
Shalev, Michael, 5798
Shalom, Stephen R., 7607, 7611
Shamai, S., 5799
Shammas, Anton, 5800
Shand, R.T., 4794
Shanin, Teodor, 9331-9333
Shankar, K., 4941
Shanmugaratnam, N., 8491, 8492
Shannon, Elizabeth, 3599
Shapir, Gershon, 5298
Shapira, Amos, 5310
Shapiro, Amos, 5801
Shapiro, Ann-Louise, 2707
Shapiro, D.M., 1324
Shapiro, Herbert, 9673
Shapiro, Michael, 7179
Shapiro, Shelby, 4223
Shaplen, Robert, 7612
Sharaf, Shamil, 5802
Sharansky, Natan, 5311
Sharfman, Glenn R., 3171
Sharifkhodzhaev, M., 9390
Sharkansky, I., 5312
Sharma, A.K., 4942
Sharma, B.K., 7357
Sharma, Basu, 10324
Sharma, Monica, 4943, 4944
Sharma, P.R., 6779
Sharma, R.R., 9334
Sharma, Rawa, 4945
Sharma, Satish K., 4946
Sharp, Gene, 5803
Sharp, J.S., 8218
Sharp, Robin, 951
Sharp, William J., 1814
Sharpe, D.R., 3730
Sharpe, L.J., 4224
Shashi, S.S., 4947
Shastri, Amita, 8493
Shati, P.M., 6221
Shattty, V.T.R., 4948
Shattuck, Roger, 7901
Shatzmiller, Joseph, 11776

Shava, Piniel, 8242
Shaver, Sheila, 301
Shavit, Yossi, 5804
Shaw, A.G.L., 11777
Shaw, Frederick, 3510
Shaw, R.P., 1505, 1506
Shaw, Van B., 9674
Shaw, William, 6258
Shawana, Perry, 1277
Sheahan, John, 11064
Shedel, James, 581
Sheean, Edward R.F., 4423
Sheehan, Elizabeth A., 5203
Sheehy, Ann, 9335-9337, 9351
Sheffield, G.D., 11613
Shehadeh, Raja, 5805-5807
Shehim, Kassim, 2324
Shelah, Menachem, 9900-9906
Shell, Robert C.H., 8243
Shen Che, 1648
Sheng-Yi, Lee, 7932
Shenker, Barry, 5127
Shenton, Robert W., 7286
Shepard, R. Bruce, 1158-1160
Shepherd, Verene A., 10461
Sheridan, Gilley, 3529, 3530
Sheridan, Richard B., 10462
Sheriff, Abdul, 8723
Sherman, Richard, 2325
Sherman, S.C., 8546
Sherman, William L., 11065
Sherwin-White, S.N., 11934
Sherwood, Marika, 4225
Shestack, Jerome, 8694
Shiblak, Abbas, 5166
Shick, Tom W., 6326, 6327
Shidlo, Gil, 873
Shields, James G., 2708
Shifu, Z., 1649
Shillington, Kevin, 8244
Shillony, Ben Ami, 6125
Shimahara, Nobuo, 6126
Shimoni, 8239
Shin, Yoon Hwan, 5067
Shinar, Dov, 5808
Shindler, Colin, 8245
Shinichiro, Tahakura, 6127
Shinzo, Hayase, 7613
Shipler, David K., 5809-5811
Shipley, Peter, 4226

Shivji, Issa G., 8724-8727
Shkilmyk, Anastasia M., 1278
Shlaes, Amity, 8614
Shlaim, Avi, 5812
Shlapentokh, Vladimir E., 9338
Shmelev, N., 9339
Shochat, Azriel, 9340
Shodid, Wasif, 6848
Shoemaker, Adam, 302, 458
Shoji, Tsutomu, 6128
Shor, Yitzhak, 5813, 5814
Short, Brian M., 4073
Short, Geoffrey, 3764, 4227
Shosh, Partha, 10325
Shoup, John A., 6166
Shoup, Paul S., 10806
Shoykhet, Roman, 9341
Shrestha, Gajendra M., 6780
Shrivastava, G., 4949
Shrivastava, Paul, 4950
Shtromas, Alexander, 9342, 9343
Shu, J., 1640, 1650
Shulman, Frank J., 12089
Shute, Jenefer P., 8246
Siagian, T.P., 5068
Sibley, D., 4228
Sicat, Gerardo P., 7614
Sichrovsky, Peter, 3172
Siddiq, Fazley, 1507
Siddique Mohammed, Abubakar, 7287
Siddiqui, M.M., 11186
Siddle, D.J., 2709
Sider, Gerald M., 1508
Sidhom, Samcha, 2229
Sidorova, M., 9344
Sidorsky, DAvid, 11798
Sidzumo-Sanders, Ruth A.N., 8247
Siebold, Heinz, 2896
Siegal, James T., 5069
Siegelba, Lewis, 9068
Siemienska, Renata, 7744
Sierpowski, S., 10807
Sifuna, D.N., 6222, 10257, 10258
Sigel, Roberta S., 2893, 6835
Sigit, Hananto, 5070
Sigler, Jay A., 30, 164, 770, 2980, 6157, 6370, 6811, 6998, 8528, 8664, 8755, 9271, 10396, 11335, 11778
Sijes, B.A., 6885

Siklos, Andras, 4578
Silber, Irwin, 978
Silbermann, Alphons, 3173, 3174, 10808
Silberner, Edmund, 3175, 3176
Siljegovic, Blagoje, 9907
Silva, Aracy Lopes dea, 874
Silva, K.M. da, 8479
Silva, Martiniano José da, 875
Silva, Sergio Sarmiento, 6589
Silveira, Ricardo A. R., 876
Silver, B.D., 8944
Silver, Eric, 5254
Silverberg, M., 1047
Silverman, Carol, 941
Silverman, Jason H., 1161-1163
Silverstein, Josef, 6721, 6722
Sim, Fan Kok, 12090
Sim, Joe, 4229
Simanjuntak, M., 6436
Simbulan, Dante C., 7615
Simkins, Charles E.W., 8248
Simkus, Albert, 4579
Simmel, Ernst, 11779
Simmons, Adele S., 6485
Simmons, Colin, 4951
Simmons, D.R., 6983
Simmons, Donita V., 12091
Simms, Norman, 6984, 11356
Simoes, Isa M., 10114
Simon, Brigette, 713
Simon, Jean-Marie, 4389, 4424
Simon, Larry J., 8407
Simon, Rita J., 5313-5314, 5815, 9675
Simon, Walter B., 582
Simoni, Pierre, 2710
Simonnot, Philippe, 5661
Simonovich, Javier, 155
Simons, John, 11748
Simons, Lewis M., 7616
Simons, Marlise, 877-878, 2711, 10809
Simpson, Christopher, 9676
Simpson, Tony, 6985
Simpson, William W., 3319
Simson, Howard, 8249
Sinclair, Keith, 303, 6986
Sinfield, Alan, 11454
Singer, Daniel, 2712
Singer, David G., 9677
Singer, Hadassa, 11063
Singer, Paul, 879

Singerman, Robert, 12092-12094
Singh, Andrea M., 4952
Singh, Anita I., 4953
Singh, B., 1348
Singh, Bhawani, 4954
Singh, Gian, 4955
Singh, H., 4956
Singh, J.B., 4957, 4958
Singh, K.S. , 4959
Singh, M., 4960
Singh, Rajendra, 4961
Singh, Ram G., 4962
Singleton, Fred, 2365
Sinha, Arun, 4963, 4964
Siniora, Hanna, 5816, 5817
Sink, Christopher, 3971
Sirc, Ljubo, 9908
Siruainen, Eino, 2366
Sison, José Maria, 7617
Sithole, Ndabaningi, 10259
Sitzler, Kathrin, 4580
Sivan, E., 10260
Sivanandan, A., 3451, 4230-4234, 8494, 9678, 10810-10811
Sivarajah, A., 8495
Sivaramayya, B., 4965
Sjoholm, Tommy, 8615
Skalnes, Tor, 10014
Skalnik Leff, Carol, 2066
Skelton, Kenneth, 10015
Skidmore, Thomas E., 880, 881,
Skilbeck, Malcolm, 3600
Skilling, H. Gordon, 2067, 2068
Skirball, Sheba F., 12095
Skjonsberg, Else, 8496
Sklar, Deborah, 6129, 6259
Sklar, Richard L., 10261-10263
Skutnabb-Kangas, T., 1382, 11780, 11781
Skyhawk, Hugh van, 11782
Skyum-Nielson, Niels, 10812
Slack, Paul A., 4235
Slaney, Robert A., 4236
Slapnicka, Harry, 583
Slater, J.R., 3511
Slater, Robert O., 11770
Slezkine, Yuri, 9345
Slibe, M. A. J. de, 9759
Slider, Darrell, 9346, 9347
Sliwowski, Z., 7745

Sloane, P.J., 3774
Slomp, Hans, 10813
Slouschz, Nahum, 10264
Slovo, Joe, 8250
Slugle, Peter, 5142, 5144
Sluglett, Peter, 5167
Small, Cathy A., 11357
Small, Stephen, 4237
Smallman-Raynor, M.R., 11783
Smiley, D.V., 1509
Smith, Alan, 10814
Smith, Anthony D., 11784, 11785
Smith, Arthur Richard, 459
Smith, Colin, 5818
Smith, D.H., 7618
Smith, David, 7097
Smith, David J., 4238
Smith, F.B., 4239
Smith, Gavin, 7485
Smith, Graham E., 9348, 9349, 9679
Smith, H. L., 7619
Smith, H. Shelton, 9680
Smith, Hazel, 7174
Smith, J.D., 9534
Smith, Jesse Carney, 9681
Smith, Joan, 11551, 11786, 11826
Smith, John D., 12096
Smith, Luke, 7363
Smith, M.G., 10463, 10464
Smith, Michael E., 6619
Smith, Peter, 5128
Smith, Peter H., 156
Smith, Richard Chase, 7486
Smith, Richard L., 2713
Smith, Roger W., 8875
Smith, S., 7288
Smith, Sheila, 10255
Smith, Stephen, 4240, 4241, 4242
Smith, Steven C., 11358, 11359
Smith, Susan J., 4243, 11787
Smith, Woodruff D., 3177, 3178
Smitherman-Donaldson, Geneva, 9682
Smithies, B., 4244
Smock, Audrey C., 636
Smolar, Aleksander, 7746
Smolicz, J.J., 304
Smollan, Roy, 8251
Smooha, Sammy, 5819-5824, 12097
Smout, T.C., 3644
Smyth, Alibhe, 5204

Smyth, Rosaleen, 4245
Smyth, W., 3601
Smythe, Hugh, 6130
Snell, K.D. M., 4246
Snitow, Alan, 9350
Snow, Helen Foster, 1750
Snow, Philip, 1751
Snowden, Frank M., 6001, 11935-11938
Snyder, Francis G., 7902
Snyder, Louis L., 11788
Soares, Glaucio, 882
Sobchack, Thomas, 4247
Sobel, Mechal, 9683
Sobelman, Michael, 7747
Sobrinho, José A., 883
Sochatzky, Klaus, 3179
Socolow, Susan M., 10971
Socouman, R.J., 1336
Soderberg, Johan, 8616
Sodi, Risa, 6002
Soen, Dan, 5825
Soff, Harvey G., 10265
Sogolo, Godwin, 10266
Sohlberg, S.C., 5826
Sohn-Rethel, Alfred, 3180
Soikkanen, Hannu, 2367
Sojndergaard, B., 2103
Sokolsky, Joel J., 8252
Solaún, Mauricio, 1815, 11066
Solaun, Sidney, 11066
Solchanyk, Roman, 9351
Sole, Kelwyn, 8253
Soler, Ricaurte, 7391
Soliman, Ahmed M., 2230-2232
Sollis, Peter, 7180
Sollors, Werner, 9684
Solomon, Rovell, P., 1164
Solomon, Susan G., 9352
Solomos, John, 3410, 3452-3453, 4248-4249
Solon, F.S., 7620, 7621
Solon, Orville, 7622
Soloun, Sidney, 11066
Solow, Barbara L., 10465-10467
Solta, Jan, 3181
Soltow, Lee, 305, 6437-6439, 3645, 7331, 8617-8618
Somczynski, K.M., 7748
Somers, David J., 6131
Song, K.S., 6261

Song Ong Siang, 7933
Sonyel, S., 8876
Soo Hae Oh, 6096, 6132
Sookdeo, Anil, 8254
Sorensen, A.B., 3182
Sorlin, Pierre, 2716
Sorokowsky, Andrew, 9353
Soroudi, Sorour, 5129
Sorrenson, M.P.K., 6987
Sosa, Macarena, 7181
Soto Acosta, Willy A., 1844
Soucy, Robert J., 2717
Souder, Laura, 11378
Soulier, Gerard, 2484
Soulis, George C., 10815
Souriau, C., 6349
Sourrouille, Juan, 10880
Southall, Roger, 8258
Southgate, D., 884
Sovik, Anne, 2948
Sozan, Michael, 7855
Spafford, Duff, 1428
Spalding, I., 460
Spangenthal, Max, 3183
Spant, Roland, 8619
Sparks, Colin, 4250, 4251, 10816
Sparks, Donald, L., 6763
Sparks, Linda, 12098
Spate, O.H.K., 11360
Spaulding, Jay, 8547
Speare, A., Jr., 5071
Spector, David, 3320
Spector, Shmuel, 9355
Spence, Jonathan D., 1752
Spenceley, G.F.R., 4252
Spencer, Arthur, 7332
Spencer, Elaine, 3184
Spencer, Jonathan, 8497
Spencer, Michael, 11361
Spender, Dale, 4253
Spidle, Jake W., 4254
Spiegel, Tilly, 584
Spiegler, S., 4425
Spielmann, Miriam, 5827
Spier, Howard, 9356, 9357
Spillmann, Georges, 2718
Spindley, B., 4255
Spira, Leopold, 585
Spira, Thomas, 4581-4585
Spiro, Jack D., 9563

AUTHOR INDEX

Spitta, Arnold, 157
Spitzer, Leo, 586, 7914
Spivak, Gayatri C., 2719
Spivey, Donald, 6328
Spolsky, B., 6988
Spoo, Eckart, 3185
Spoonley, Paul, 6989-6992, 6998
Sprague, D.N., 1280
Spree, Reinhard, 3186
Sprenger, George H., 1281
Sprinzak, Ehud, 5315, 5316, 5828, 5829
Spurr, Russell, 306
Squires, P., 4256
Srinivasan, T.N., 10328
Srivastava, S.N., 4966
Srivastava, Swesh C., 4967
St. George, Ross, 6993
St. Pierre, Maurice, 10468
St.Onge, Nicole J.M., 1282
Sta. Romana, E.R., 7623
Stacey, Judith, 1753, 1754
Stack, John F. Jr., 780
Stadler, Karl R., 587,588
Staeck, Klaus, 3187
Stafford, Walter, 9685
Stallabrass, Julian, 4257
Stamm, Christoph, 24
Stamps, M.B., 9686
Stamps, Spurgeon M., 9686
Stanback, Howard J., 9687
Standish, B., 7948
Standt, Kathleen A., 6223, 10231
Staniland, Martin, 10267
Stanislawski, Michael, 9358, 9359
Staniszkius, Jadwiga, 7749
Stankovic, Slobodan, 9909
Stankovich, Victor de, 7856
Stanley, Peter W., 7624
Stanner, William E. H., 461
Stanson, Michael, 6440
Stapleton, M., 3454
Stariulis, D., 1325
Stark, G.K., 3812, 3955
Stark, Thomas, 4258
Starke, J.S., 307
Starratt, Priscilla Ellen, 8548
Stasiulis, Daiva K., 1510-1512, 8259
Stavenhagen, Rodolfo, 11067, 11068
Stavrianos, L.S., 4384
Ste. Croix, G.E.M. de, 11939, 11940

Steckel, R.H., 8610
Stedman, Raymond W., 9688
Steel, Mark J., 10469
Stefanizzi, Sonia, 6006
Steigerwald, Jacob, 7857
Stein, A., 9720
Stein, Andre, 6886
Stein, Georg, 5830
Stein, Kenneth W., 5831
Stein, L., 11789
Stein, Richard A., 6887
Steinberg, Bernard, 3321, 5832
Steinberg, David J., 7625
Steinberg, Jonathan, 2720, 4385, 9910
Steinberg, M.B., 5317
Steinberg, Maxine, 683
Steingart-Hollander, Rachel, 6888
Steinherr, A., 10817
Steinmetz, Selma, 589
Steins, M., 2721
Stekner, M., 1324
Stepan, Alfred, 156
Stephen, David, 7182, 9980, 11069
Stephens, E.H., 11070
Stephens, Marc, 5833
Stephens, Meic, 10818
Stephens, Michael, 4178
Stephens, Thomas M., 11071
Stephens, W.B., 4259
Stephenson, James, 4260
Stephenson, Jill, 3188
Stepick, Alex, 9689
Sterling, Dorothy, 9690
Sterling, Robert, 1283
Sterman, Kaye, 466
Stern, Lewis M., 9782-9784
Stern, Nicholas, 1714
Stern, Sheldon M., 11790
Sternber, Maxine, 684
Sternhell, Zeev, 2722-2726, 5834, 10819
Stetski, Slava, 9360
Steven, Rob, 6133, 6134
Stevens, B., 8260
Stevens, Frank S., 462-464
Stevens, Meic , 3669
Stevenson, Paul, 1513
Stever, Tammie L., 1574
Steward, Antony, 5635
Stewart, Watt, 7487
Stewarts, Charles C., 10232

Stief, William, 4500
Stiefel, Dieter, 590
Stijnen, Sjef, 6894
Stiller, Michael, 3189
Stilley, Susan A., 3190
Stillman, Andy, 4262
Stillman, Gerald, 9361
Stillschweig, Kurt, 8621
Stipac, Boris, 4586
Stites, Richard, 9362, 9363
Stjarne, Kerstin, 8622
Stock, Karl F., 12099
Stockton, Ronald R., 5835, 5836
Stockwell, A.J., 11729
Stockwell, A.J., 6441, 6442
Stoddart, Brian, 10457
Stoecker, H., 8772, 10268
Stok, Lawrence D., 3092
Stokes, Gale, 12100
Stokes, L.D., 6889
Stokes, Raymond G., 3191
Stolcke, Varena Martinez-Alier, 1957
Stoler, Ann L., 5072, 10087, 11791
Stone, Carl, 10470
Stone, Gerald, 3192
Stone, J.O., 308
Stone, John, 4263, 11792
Stone, Lawrence, 4264
Stone, Maureen, 3455
Stone, Norman, 2026
Stone, Samuel, 1845
Stone, Samuel Z., 11072
Stone, Thomas, 1284
Stoneman, Colin, 10016, 10017
Stookey, Robert W., 9802
Stopes-Roe, Mary, 3456, 3457
Stöss, Richard, 3193, 3194, 3195
Stouffer, Allen P., 1165
Stovall, Don Owen, 9364
Stovall, Tyler, 2727
Stover, Mary L., 11362
Stow, Kenneth R., 6003
Stranzinger, Ernst, 591
Strathern, A., 7407
Strauss, Herbert A., 3196
Strauss-Kohn, D., 2489
Streater, J.B. Jr., 9691
Street, S., 6587
Streeter, Allan, 5318
Streiffeler, Friedhelm, 9941

Strikwerda, Carl, 6890
Stringer, M., 3602
Strmeska, Zdenek, 10678
Stroganov, A. I,, 158
Strokata, Nina, 9365
Strom, Yale, 10820
Stromquist, N.P., 4265, 11793
Stronach, Ian, 3329
Strouhal, Eduard, 2026
Strouhal, Eugen, 2233
Strudel, Sylvie, 2702
Strumingher, Laura S., 2728, 2729
Strunin, Lee, 5319
Strutz, I., 3008
Stuart-Fox, Martin, 6278
Stubbs, Paul, 4266
Stube, Peter E., 11658
Stuckey, Naneen E., 1285
Stuckey, Sterling, 9692
Studlar, Donley T., 3417, 3515, 4325
Stultz, Newell M., 12101
Suakjian, Kevork Y., 8877, 8878
Subrahmanyam, S., 4969
Sudama, Trevor, 1758
Sudholt, Gert, 6764
Sugar, Peter F., 10821, 10822
Suh, Dae-Sook, 9366
Suh, Jae J., 6262
Suh, Sun-Hee, 6263
Suhr, Heidrun, 3197-3198
Sukiennicki, Wiktor, 10823
Sulak, Sivaraksa, 6723, 8758
Sule, R.A. Olu, 7289
Suliman, Hassan S., 10270
Sullivan, Anthony T., 5838, 5839
Sullivan, John, 8408
Sullivan, Paul, 6620
Sullivan, Sharon, 465
Sullivan, Veronica, 1166
Summers, R., 11794
Sunahara, Ann, 1514
Sunahara, Ann G., 1112
Sundaram, J. K., 6443
Sundaram, Jomo Kwame, 6405
Sundberg, J., 2368
Sundiata, I.K., 885, 6329, 6678
Sundrum, R.M., 4970, 11795
Suntharalingham, R., 4971
Suny, Ronald G., 9367-9374
Suppan, Arnold, 592

Supraptong, Seha, 5073
Suret-Canal, Jean, 11796
Surhomme, Michele, 2415
Suro, Roberto, 6004
Suryadinata, Leo, 1759, 12102
Suss, Waldemar, 3165
Sussex, Roland, 9291
Sutcliffe, David, 3458
Suter, Keith, 466, 5074
Suthasasna, A., 8759
Sutherland, A.E., 3604
Sutherland, N.M., 10824
Sutherland, O.R.W., 6994
Suttner, Raymond, 8261
Sutton, Imre, 9693
Sutton, Inez, 3267
Sutton, P.K., 10443
Sutton, Paul, 10358, 10471
Sutton, Peter, 396
Suzuki, Peter T., 12103
Svensson, Per-Gunnar, 10825
Svensson, Thommy, 11692
Svensson, Tom G., 10826
Swainson, Nicola, 6224
Swan, D., 2191
Swan, James H., 9694
Swank, Duane H., 11586
Swank, Emory, 979
Swanson, Maynard W., 8262
Swart, L. Thomas, 4267
Swartz, Mary, 6137
Swedenburg, Theodore R., 8695
Sweets, John F., 2730
Swenarton, Mark, 3512
Swepaton, L., 11797
Swietochowski, Tadeusz, 9375
Swift, Roger, 3528-3530
Swinden, Kees van, 7099
Swirski, Shlomo, 5320
Switzer, Les, 8263
Swoboda, Victor, 9256
Sword, Keith, 9376
Syagga, Paul M., 10271
Syed Arabi Idid, 6444
Syme, Ronald, 11941, 11942
Symonds, Richard, 3480
Syrkin, Marie, 5840
Sysyn, Frank E., 7750, 10503
Szajkowski, Zosa, 2731, 9377
Szaraz, Gyorgy, 4587

Szarka, Laszlo, 2069
Szarmach, Paul E., 8358
Szarota, Tomasz, 7751, 7752
Szasz, Zsombor, 7858
Szelenyi, Ivan, 4588
Szirmai, Adam, 6891
Szollosi-Janze, Marget, 4589
Szucs, Ivan K., 4590
Szwed, John F., 10338
Szymusiak, Molyda, 980

Ta Van Tai, 9785
Ta'a, Tesema, 2327
Taagepera, Rein, 9240, 9241
Tabari, Azar, 5130
Tabili, Laura E., 4268, 4269
Tabory, Ephraim, 75, 5321
Tabory, Mala, 75
Tachibanaki, T., 6135
Tadros, H., 2234
Taggan, Yehuda, 5841
Taggart, Simon, 5842
Tagil, S., 9865
Tagliabue, John, 3199, 6005
Taguieff, Pierre-André, 2732-2744, 10827
Tagupa, William E., 11363
Taheri, Amir, 9378
Tahir, S., 7358
Tajfel, Henri, 3538
Takagi, P., 9695
Takashima, Shizuya, 1113
Takata, Toyo, 1114
Takazato, Suzuyo, 6136
Takman, John, 8625
Tala, Kashim I., 1000
Talbot, Carol, 1167
Taleb, A., 2745
Talmon, Jacob L., 5843, 11798
Talos, Emmerich, 593
Tam, Sui-Mi, 1651
Tamames, Ramon, 8409
Tamanisau, A., 11342
Tamarkin, M., 10018
Tambiah, Stanley J., 8500, 8501, 11799
Tan, Antonio S., 7626
Tan, Chee-Beng, 6445
Tan, Edita A., 8760
Tan, J.P., 1800, 11687
Tan, Loong-Hoe, 6446

Tan, Mily G., 5075
Tandon, Yash, 8910, 10272
Tanner, Adrian, 1286
Tanner, Christopher, 887
Tannous, Izzat, 5844
Tanuvasa, Alofa, 11364
Tapia, Gabriel G., 2263
Tapp, Nicholas, 1590, 6279, 8761-8762
Tapper, Ted, 4201
Tarbush, Mohammad A., 5845
Tarbush, S., 5846
Tardanieo, Richard, 1879
Tardieu, Jean-Pierre, 8410
Tarnopolsky, W.S., 1515
Tarrow, Sidney, 6006
Taryor, Nya K., Jr. , 6330
Tash, Robert C., 6892
Tashkovski, Dragan, 9911
Tate, Merze, 11365
Tatla, D.S., 12000, 12001
Tatz, Colin M., 467-469
Taubman, Philip, 9379
Tawagon, Manuel R., 7627
Tawake, S., 11366
Tax, Sol, 6487
Taylor, C.J., 12104
Taylor, Charles, 11800
Taylor, Dalmes A., 9579
Taylor, Frank F., 1958
Taylor, Jerome E., 7184
Taylor, John Leonard, 1287
Taylor, Monica J., 3459-3461, 4270, 4271
Taylor, Nan, 6995
Taylor, P.M., 6007
Taylor, Quintard, 887
Taylor, Richard, 4272
Taylor, Robert H., 6724-6726
Taylor, Rupert L., 3605, 3606
Taylor, Sandra, 3512
Taylor, Verta, 9664
Taylor, William H., 7290
Teacher, Anna, 8729
Teacher, Freda, 8729
Teczarowska, Danuta, 9380
Teeple, Gary, 1419
Teichova, Alice, 2070, 10828
Teimourian, Hazhir, 5099
Tekiner, Roselle, 5847, 5848
Tello, Carlos, 6522

Temine, Émile, 2528
Temperley, Howard, 11801
Temporini, H., 11928
Tendulkar, S.D., 4973
Tennant, Paul, 1288
Tennstedt, Florian, 3047
Tennyson, Brian D., 1155
Tenorth, Heinz-Elmar, 3200
Teraoka, Arlene A., 3201
Terasaki, Y., 7628
Terborg-Penn, Rosalyn, 9553
Teresa, Mother, 4974
Termine, Emile, 2453
Ternon, Yves, 8802, 8879
Terra, Juan P., 8924
Terrel, H., 2747, 9696
Terrell, R.D., 6642
Terris, Milton, 1959
Terry, Janice, 5849
Terwiel, B.J., 8763
Tesse, Richard, 2748
Tessler, Mark, 5850
Tettey, Charles, 3268
Thabe, G.A.L., 8264
Thaden, C., 2369, 9381
Thakur, D.S., 4975, 4976
Thakur, V.K., 4977
Thalmann, Rita, 3202
Thane, Pat, 4276, 7720
Thapar, Romila, 4978, 10329
Tharamangalam, Joseph, 4979
Thaxton, Ralph, 1652
Thee, Au Duong, 9786
Thee, Kian W., 5076
Theodore, Demetrios E., 8880
Théolleyre, Jean-Marc, 3203
Therborn, Goran, 11803
Thernstrom, Stephan, 3524, 9684, 9739
Theron, J. H., 8265
Thiessen, William, 7291
Thillainathan, R., 6447
Thobie, Jacques, 11187
Thode-Studer, Sylvia, 8666
Thogersen, Stig, 1760
Thomas, Ajamah Asa-Ah, 1001
Thomas, Alan, 11491
Thomas, B., 3670
Thomas, Barb, 4277
Thomas, Clive, 10472
Thomas, David, 3462

Thomas, David N., 4278
Thomas, Hugh, 1960
Thomas, Nicholas, 11367, 11368, 11369
Thomas, V., 888
Thomas-Chevallier, Hubert, 2749
Thomas-Hope, Elizabeth M., 10473
Thompson, Alvin, 8565
Thompson, E.A., 3204, 11943
Thompson, Edgar T., 12105
Thompson, L.A., 11944, 11945
Thompson, Leonard, 8087
Thompson, Richard, 6996
Thompson, Roger C., 11370
Thompson, Stephen I., 714
Thomson, Colin A., 1168
Thomson, Curtis N., 8764
Thomson, Duncan D., 1289
Thomson, Frank, 3646
Thomson, Marilyn, 2264
Thornberry, Patrick, 11804-11807
Thorner, Alice, 4811, 4980
Thorner, Daniel, 4811
Thornton, A.P., 11808
Thornton, E.M., 8502
Thornton, Russell, 9697
Thoumi, Francisco E., 4501
Throup, David, 6225
Thurlow, Richard C., 3322, 4279-4281, 10829
Thurner, Erika, 594
Thurston, Robert, 9382
Tian, Jujian, 1761
Tibawi, A., 5851
Tibebu, Teshale, 2328
Tibenderana, Peter K., 7292-7294
Tibi, Bassam, 11188
Tighe, Carl, 7753
Tignor, Robert, 2153, 2235
Tiker-Tiker, 9942
Tilak, J.B.G., 4981, 4982
Tilkovazky, Lorant, 4591
Tillett, Lowell, 9383
Tilly, Charles, 2750
Tilly, Louise A., 2750
Timbo, A.B., 7915
Tims, R.W., 7754
Tingbjorn, Gunnar, 8626
Tinker, Hugh, 4282, 11371, 11809
Tinker, Irene, 11810
Tirado, Ricardo, 6523

Tirono Barrios, Eugenio, 1575
Tiryakian, Edward A., 1315, 2752, 3617, 3666, 3674, 6845, 8396, 11811
Tiso, Joseph, 2071
Titmuss, Richard, 4283
Tizard, Barbara, 4284
Tjizu, Barnabas, 6767
Tlemcani, Rachid, 76
Tobias, John L., 1290
Todd, Dave, 2329
Todd, Jay L., 8411
Todd, Loreto, 1002
Todorov, Nikolai, 10830
Todorova, Maria, 942, 943
Todorovich, Slavko, 9825
Tokayer, Marien, 6137
Tokei, F., 1762
Toledano, Ehud R., 2236, 2237, 8881
Toledano, Shmuel, 5852
Tolentino, H., 2127, 4502, 11073
Tolstedt, Mark A., 11372
Tolstoy, Nikolai, 9912
Tomasek, P., 2072
Tomaselli, Keyan G., 8266
Tomasevich, J., 9913
Tomasson, Richard F., 1101, 4609
Tomaszewski, Jerzy, 10831
Tomich, Dale W., 10474
Tomlinson, B.R., 4983
Tomlinson, S., 3478, 4238, 4285-4286
Tompson, Keith, 4287
Tonjoroff, S.J., 8882
Tonkin, Elizabeth, 11812
Tonkinson, Robert, 342
Tonnes, Bernhard, 9914
Tonsgaard, Ole, 10582
Toohey, K., 1291
Toplin, Robert B., 760, 889-890, 1902, 1921, 9761, 11074
Toppo, Sita, 4984
Toranska, Teresa, 7755
Torkington, Ntombenhie, P.K., 4288
Torney-Pinta, Judith, 11813
Torres, Alberto, 6591
Torres Giraldo, Ignacio, 1816
Torres-Rivas, Edelberto, 11075
Torres Sanchez, Jaime, 1817
Torrey, Barbara B., 7408
Torri, M., 4985

Toscano, Mario, 6008, 6009
Tosh, J., 8550
Tosi, Arturo, 4289
Totah, Khalil A., 5853
Totemeyer, G., 6766
Tottle, Douglas, 9384
Touak, E.A., 8874
Tough, Frank J., 1292
Toukan, Fadwa, 5854
Toulellan, Pierre-Yves, 11373
Toumanoff, Cyril, 9385
Touraine, Alain, 2751-2752
Toure, Abdou, 6027
Tournier, Michelle, 3205
Townsends, Janet, 11689
Trachte, Kent C., 11746
Trachtenberg, Henry M., 1048, 1049
Trahant, M.N., 7186, 7187
Trahtenberg, Leon, 7488, 7489
Trainor, Catherine H., 1516
Trankell, Arne, 8627
Trankell, Ingrid, 8627
Traore, Fathié, 953
Trapans, Janis A., 9386
Trapido, Stanley, 8166
Trask, Haunani-Kay, 11374
Trautmann, Wolfgang, 77
Tray, Dennis de, 7452
Treadgold, M. L., 470
Treagust, D.F., 393
Treble, J. H., 3647, 4291
Tredinnick, D.A.S., 4292
Trehub, Aaron, 9387
Trelease, Allen W., 9698
Trenard, Louis, 2753
Trendowski, Thomas, 7756
Tribalat, Michele, 6893
Trigger, Bruce G., 1293, 1294
Trigger, David S., 309
Triggs, Pat, 3829
Trindade, Helgio, 11076, 11077
Tripathy, J.T., 8267
Trivedi, Harshad R., 4986
Trlin, Andrew D., 6997-6998
Trochim, Michael, 891
Trocki, Carl A., 7934, 7935
Troebst, S., 944
Trofiurenkoff, S.M., 1363
Trollip, A.E.G., 8223
Trollope, Joanna, 4293

Tronrud, Thorold J., 4294
Troper, Harold, 1007, 1050-1054, 1169
Trotman, Donald A.B., 10475
Trouillot, Michel-Rolph, 4503-4506
Troy, Patrick N., 310
Troyna, Barry, 4295
Trudel, Marcel, 1517
Trumbull, Robert, 11375
Trunk, Isaish E., 10832
Truong, Thanh-Dam, 10330
Tsakloglou, P., 4386
Tsemel, Lea, 5855
Tsiakolos, Georgios, 3206
Tsipko, A., 9388
Tsokhes, Kosmas, 311
Tsotsi, W.M., 8268
Tsurumi, Yoski, 6138
Tuathaigh, M.O.O., 3531
Tucker, Judith, 2238
Tuden, Arthur, 10273
Tudjman, Frenjo, 10833
Tulasiewicz, Witold, 3556, 11453
Tulchin, Joseph S., 109
Tullock, Gordon, 4296
Tuma, Elias H., 11189
Tung, Ko-Chih R., 8628
Tunteng, P. Kiven, 1170
Turcow, Marc, 111
Turdeanu, L., 7860
Turgeon, Lynn, 4592, 4593
Turki, Benyan S., 8730
Turkovic, Robert J., 159
Turnbull, Clive, 471
Turnbull, Constance M., 7936
Turnbull, Keith, 1184
Turner, Barry, 4297
Turner, Bryan S., 11190
Turner, C.J., 2754
Turner, Graeme, 472
Turner, Ian D., 3208, 3236
Turner, Jonathan H., 9699
Turner, Margaret A., 9943
Turner, Mark M., 7409
Turner, Mary, 10476
Turner, T.S., 9700
Turner, Victor, 10274
Turnock, David, 7861
Turok, Ben, 9959
Turshen, Meredith, 8269, 8731, 10275
Turton, R.W., 8270

Tutorow, Norman E., 12106
Tuttle, Carolyn, 4298
Tuwim, Julian, 7757
Tuzmukhamedov, R., 9389
Twaddle, Michael, 8911, 8912
Twitchin, John, 4299
Tworuschka, Monika, 3209
Tyabil, Badr-Ud-Din, 4987
Tyler, Ronnie C., 6622
Tyler, S. Lyman, 11078
Tyler, William, 473, 763
Tynan, James, 1295
Tyoden, S.G., 7295
Tyrnauer, Gabrielle, 3210
Tzannatos, A., 4360
Tzemach, Mina, 5857, 5858
Tzin, Ruth, 5858

Ubawike, Eugene U., 7296
Uche, L.U., 7297
Ucko, Peter, 8272
Ugochukwu, Françoise, 2755
Ujimoto, K. Victor, 1115
Ukadike, N.F., 10276
Ukpak, Akpan N., 7298
Ul'masov, A., 9390
Ulc, Otto, 2073
Ulenga, Ben, 6767
Ulivi, Giuseppe, 5987
Um Nyobé, Ruben, 1003
Umo, Joe U., 7299
Underwood, Robert A., 11376-11378
Ungar, E.S., 9787
Unterhalter, Elaine, 8273
Upadhya, Carol B., 4988
Upham, Frank K., 6139, 6140
Upodhyay, Ram Raj, 6781
Uppal, J.S., 5077, 5078
Upton, A.F., 2370
Uran, Steven, 8274
Urban, G.R., 9391
Urban, Greg, 892
Urdahl. L.B., 11946
Urdang, Stephanie, 6699, 8139
Urevbu, Andrew O., 7300
Urioste Fernandez de Cordova, Miguel, 715
Urla, Jacqueline, 8412
Urrutia, Gustavo E., 1961
Urrutia, Miguel, 1818

Urry, John, 4301
Urzua F., Raul, 1577
Ushadevi, M.D., 4931
Usiskin, Roz, 1055
Usker, Graham, 4302
Usman, Yusufu Bala, 7301, 7302
Ussoskin, Moshe, 7862
Utangi, Takashi, 6141
Utrecht, Ernst, 7629
Uusitabo, A., 8583
Uusitalo, H., 2343
Uval, Beth, 5862

Vacante, Russell A., 6264
Vachel, J., 2074
Vachon, Robert, 9701
Vader, John P., 5131
Vaggi, Gianni, 10834
Vago, Bela, 7863, 10835, 10836
Vago, Raphael, 4594, 7863, 7864
Vaid, Gudesh, 4923
Vail, Leroy, 6700, 10277
Vaile, Michael, 4110
Vaillant, Janet G., 7903
Vaisanen, Maija, 2371
Vakil, A.K., 4989
Vakil, C.N., 4856
Valdes Bunstr, Gustavo, 1579
Valdés, Dennis N., 6623
Valdes, Juan G., 1578
Valdes, Mario, 10837
Valdes, Nelson P., 12108
Valdex-Cruz, Rosa, 1962
Valencias Quintanilla, Felix, 7491
Valentin, H., 10838
Valenzuela, Eduardo, 1562
Vali, A., 9393
Vali, Ference A., 10839
Valkeapoa, Nils-Aslak, 10840
Valle Silva, Nelson do, 893
Vallen, Ton, 6894
Vallerand, Robert J., 1296
Vambe, Lawrence, 10019
Van Amersfoort, H., 10841
Van Amersfoort, J. M.M., 6895
Van Arkel, Dirk, 595, 10842, 11816
Van Beek, Wonter, 1004
van de Berghe, Pierre, 8226
van de Walle, D., 4990
Van Deburg, William L., 9702

Van den Berg, Leo, 8732
Van den Berghe, Pierre L., 10278, 11817, 11818
van der Berg, S., 8276
Van der Hardt, Anya A., 5863
van der Heven, R., 11819
Van der Horst, Sheila T., 8277
Van der Vyver, J.D., 8275
Van Der Zee, J., 9703
Van Dijk, Tenn A., 6896, 9704, 9682, 12109
Van Dorsten, Jan, 6897
Van Duin, P., 8278
van Dyk, D.F., 8279
van Eyssen, J.F., 8280
Van Ginkel, J.A., 6898
van Ginneken, W.K., 1763
Van Hear, Nick, 3269
Van Hoorn, F.J.J.H., 6898
van Houte, Hans, 6909
Van Mierlo, Hands J.G.A., 6899
van Mowrik, A., 6999
Van Ness, Carol, 1963
van Niekerk, Phillijo, 8281
Van Nieuwenhuijze, C.A.O., 11191, 11192
van Onselen, Charles, 10020
Van Otterloo, Annekke H., 6900
van Praag, B.M.S., 10843
van Roon, Ger, 6901
Van Staden, F.J., 8282
Van Vleck, Michael R., 2239
van Vliet, Wilhem, 3503, 9246
Van Vliet, William, 6875
van Weeren, H., 10843
Van Zyl Smit, Dirk, 8283, 8284
Vanachere, M., 6624
Vanaik, Achin, 4991, 4992
Vanden, Harry E., 12110
Vander Zanden, James W., 9705
Vanderplank, P.H., 6902
VanderRoss, R.E., 8285
Vanhanen, Tatu, 11820
Vanly, Ismet S., 5168
Vardy, Steven Bela, 2075
Vargas-Lundius, Rosemary, 2128
Vargas, Oscar Rene, 7044
Varon Gabai, Rafael, 7492
Vassaf, Gunduz, 10844
Vaszolyi, E., 385

Vatin, Jean Claude, 78
Vaughn, Graham M., 7000
Vaughn, Mary Kay, 6625, 6626
Vaughn, Megan, 6368
Vazquez, Jesus M., 8413
Veenhoven, 6090
Vega, M.I. de, 9706
Veiter, Theodor, 596, 6768, 10279, 12111
Vejar, Jesus R., 6627
Vekerdi, Jozsef, 4595
Veld-Langeveld, H.M. Int., 6883, 6903
Velimsky, Vitezslav, 685, 10690
Velinkar, J., 10331
Velis, Jean-Pierre, 2756
Veltman, Calvin, 1518
Vengroff, Richard, 10280
Venkateshwar Rao, P., 8503
Venn-Brown, Janet, 10845
Venner, Mary, 3464
Veras, Ramon A., 2129
Verba, Sidney, 6142, 8629
Verbeek, Jennifer, 8286
Vercellin, Giorio, 13,
Vercoutter, J., 11947
Verdery, Katherine, 597, 4596, 7865
Verdesota, Luis, 2146
Verdoner, Francisca, 6904
Verdoner-Sluizer, Hilde, 6904
Verhaeren, Raphael-Emmanuel, 2757
Verlinden, Charles, 2758, 6010, 10846-10849
Verma, Gajendra, 3465, 4303, 4304
Verma, R.B.P., 1066
Verma, Y.M., 4993
Vermani, R.C., 4994
Vermeulen, H., 10850
Vermund, S.H., 5864
Verna, Frank P., 9915
Vernadsky, G., 9394
Verrall, Catherine, 12112
Verrier, Anthony, 10021
Verschuur, Christine, 6701
Versztovsek, R., 4597
Vervoorn, A. E. 167
Verwey-Jonker, H., 6905
Vichit-Vadakdan, Juree, 8755
Vicinus, Martha, 4306
Vick, Malcolm, 312
Vickers, Adrian, 313

Vickery, Kenneth P., 9960, 10022
Victora, Cesar G., 894, 895,
Victorisz, T., 9707
Vidal, C., 7877
Vidal-Naquet, Pierre, 10851, 11821
Vidal, Virginia, 1580
Vides de Orive, Enna, 4426
Vidyadharan, A., 4995
Viennot, Jean-Pierre, 11193
Vigil, Ralph H., 8414
Vihavainen, Timo, 9395
Vijnar, Bohdan, 9396
Vila, I., 8415
Vilanilam, J., 4996
Vilar, Enriquetta Vila, 7784
Vilar, Pierre, 8416
Vilas, Carlos M., 7045, 7188
Villegas, Edberto M., 7630, 7631
Vimille, A., 8765
Vina, Shirley W., 5908
Vincent Davios, Diana, 12113
Vincentnatham, Lynn, 4997
Vinski, I., 9916
Vinskovic, Boris, 9917
Viorst, Milton, 5322, 5865, 6273, 8696
Viotti da Costa, Emilia, 896
Vipond, Mary, 1519
Visarea, P., 4787
Visaria, Pravin M., 10332
Vishniak, Mark, 9397
Visram, Rozina, 3466
Visser, H.K.A., 10333
Viswanathan, Gauri, 4998
Vittori, Jean-Pierre, 3211
Vitullo, Anita, 5866, 5867
Vivanco, José M., 11015
Vivekanan, Franklin, 11199
Viviani, Nancy, 316
Vivo, Paquita, 9708
Vizulis, I. Joseph, 9398
Voeltz, Richard A., 6769
Voet, J., 6906, 12114
Voigt, Dieter, 3212
Voigt, Klaus, 6011
Volberg, Heinrich, 3213
Volgyes, Ivan, 4598, 7866
Volker, Paul A., 270
Voll, John O., 8551
Voll, Sarah P., 8551
von Rauch, George, 9399

Voorhis, Jerry L., 2104
Vorlaufer, Karl, 6226
Vorst, Jesse, 1520
Voslensky, Michael, 9400
Voss, Tony, 8287
Vouin, R., 2759
Vowles, Jack, 7001
Vuilleumier, M., 8667
Vysokolán, O., 7420

Wa Thiong'o, N., 10281
Wa. Thiong'O, Ngugi, 6227
Wachtel, Natan, 7493
Wacquant, Loic J.D., 11379
Waddell, N., 3607
Wade, Peter, 1819, 1820, 11079, 11080
Wagatsuma, Hiroshi, 6040
Wagaw, Teshome G., 5323
Wagenheim, Kal, 9709
Wagner, Edward W., 6143
Wagner, Francis S., 4599
Wagner, Jonathan F., 1056-1058, 1297
Wagner, Ulrich, 3215
Wahn, M.B., 1298
Wai, L., 12115
Waisman, Carlos H., 160
Wakeford, John, 4301
Wakeman, Carolyn, 1780
Wakin, Edward, 2240
Walbank, F.W., 11948
Walber, Martin, 4307
Walby, Sylvia, 4308
Walder, Andrew, 1764
Waldergrave, Charles, 7002
Waldman, Menachem, 2330
Waldorf, Brigitte, 3216
Waldron, Ingrid, 11822
Walfe, Joel D., 4309
Walkendine, Valene, 4310
Walker, Christopher J., 9401, 11637
Walker, Clive, 3608
Walker, David, 3671
Walker, Franklin A., 9402
Walker, Monica, 4311
Walker, Nancy, 9710
Walker, Thomas, 7060
Walkowisk, Adam, 3467
Wall, Denis V., 1299
Wall, Henry, 5324
Wallace, C., 4312

AUTHOR INDEX

Wallace, David, 6149
Wallace, Iain, 11823
Wallace, Marion, 6770
Wallace, Scott, 7189, 7190
Wallace, Tina, 11824
Wallace-Crabbe, Chris, 317
Wallach, Janet, 5868
Wallach, John, 5868
Wallerstein, I., 4999, 11825-11826
Wallimann, Isidor, 8851
Wallraff, Günter, 3217, 3218
Walsh, Dave, 3648
Walters, W.G., 7632
Walton, David, 3323
Walton, Hanes, Jr., 9711
Walton, Heather, 3468
Walton, Jonathan W., 1171
Walvin, James, 4313, 4314, 10373, 10375, 11489, 11827
Wan Hussin Zoohri, 7937
Wandel, Lee P., 8668, 8669
Wang, I-t'ung, 1765
Wang, Livia A., 1655
Wang Pi-ch'eng, 1770
Wang, Yu-Ling, 9403
Wangyal, Phuntsog, 1631
Wanner, Richard A., 1521
Wansborough, John, 10282
Warburg, Gabriel R., 8552, 8553
Ward, Alan D., 7003, 7004
Ward, Barbara E., 10329
Ward, Colin, 3513
Ward, J.R., 10477
Ward, J.T., 7005
Ward, Jim, 1522
Ward, Kevin, 4272
Ward, Norman, 1428
Ward, Peter M., 6628
Ward, R. Gerard, 7410
Ward, W. Peter, 1116-1118, 1523
Wardi, Charlotte, 10852
Ware, Gilbert, 9712
Ware, Helen, 10283
Warhurst, P.R., 10023
Warmbold, Joachim, 3219
Warmbrunn, Werner, 6907
Warner, G., 2760
Warnock, Kitty, 5869
Warren, C., 1766
Warren, Charles P., 7633

Warren, James F., 6448
Warren, Kay B., 4427
Warren, N.A., 278
Warshawski, Michel, 5870, 5871
Wasburn, Philo C., 8290
Washburn, Wilcomb E., 9713
Washington, Booker T., 10854
Washington, Johnny, 9714
Wasserman, Mark, 6629
Wasserstein, Bernard, 3324
Wasserstrom, Jeffrey, 1767
Wasserstrom, R., 4428
Wat, Aleksander, 7758
Watanabe, Akio, 11380
Waterhouse, Richard, 318
Waterman, P., 7279
Waterman, S., 5597
Waters, Harold A., 10284
Waters, Judy, 8504
Waters, Robert, 4316
Watkins, David, 7634
Watkins, Mel, 1300
Watkins, Steve, 4317
Watkins, William H., 7303
Watkinson, E.J., 8291
Watson, Alan, 11081
Watson, Bernard C., 9715
Watson, Betty L., 319
Watson, Catherine, 961
Watson, Ian, 4318
Watson, J.K.P., 4319
Watson, James L., 1768, 10285, 10334
Watson, K., 4320
Watson, Keith, 10335
Watson, Richard L., 8292
Watt, S., 3786
Watts, Michael, 7304
Watts, Richard J., 8670
Watts, W.J., 11949
Wayne, Jack, 8733, 10855
Waysman, Dvora, 320
Wazir-jahan Karim, 6449
Weakliem, David, 4321
Wearne, Philip, 11069
Weaver, Jerry L., 9716
Weaver, Sally M., 475
Webb, Andrew, 476
Webb, Bill, 2761
Webb, Keith, 4603
Webb, Michael A., 11082

Webb, Oliver R., 10478
Webb, Richard, 844
Webb, Richard C., 7494
Webber, Douglas, 3220
Webber, G.C., 4322
Weber, Eugen, 2762, 2763
Weber, Eva, 3221
Weber, R.G.S., 3222
Webster, Charles, 3514
Webster, David J., 8293
Webster, Edward, 8294
Webster, Peggy L., 897
Wechsler, James, 9717
Weckbecker, Arno, 3223
Wecker, Regina, 8671
Weeks, Alan, 4323
Weeks, Charles J., Jr., 11381
Weeks, John, 7495
Weeks, Priscilla, 7635
Wegner, G. P., 3224
Wegner, Judith R., 11950
Wehler, Hans-Ulrich, 5953
Wehling, Hans-Georg, 3225
Wei, Karen T., 12116
Wei Liming, 1782
Weidig, Rudi, 3226
Weiermair, Klaus, 1524
Weigel, Russell H., 9718
Weightman, George R., 7636, 7637
Weil, Bernard, 12117
Weil, Chalva, 5872, 8883
Weil, Connie, 11083
Weil, Frederick, 3227
Weil, Frederick D., 11828
Weimann, Gabriel, 1059, 1061
Weinberg, David H., 2764, 2765
Weinberg, G., 11084
Weinberg, Henry H., 2766, 2767, 2768
Weinberg, Meyer, 9719, 12118
Weinberg, Robert, 9404
Weindling, Paul, 3228, 3229
Weiner, D., 10024
Weiner, Michael A., 6144, 6145
Weiner, Richard E., 9405
Weinfeld, Eduardo, 11085
Weinfeld, Morton, 1053, 1060, 1525
Weingart, Peter, 3231
Weingarter, J. J., 3230
Weingrod, Alex, 5214, 5215, 5325
Weinraub, Bernard, 3609

Weinrich, A.K.H., 10025
Weinryb, Bernard D., 9406
Weinstein, Brian, 5326
Weinstein, Warren 962
Weinstock, Nathan, 10856
Weinter, Merle H., 4324
Weinzierl, Erika, 598,599,600
Weisbord, R.G., 8295, 9720, 10857
Weisbrot, David, 7411
Weisbrot, Robert, 161
Weisbund, David L., 5327, 5873
Weische, Alexa, 3232
Weisgall, Jonathan M., 11382
Weiskel, Timothy, 10128
Weisman, Steven R., 5000-5002, 6146, 8505
Weismantel, M.J., 2147
Weiss, Aahron, 10858
Weiss, Anita M., 7359
Weiss, Eduard, 6630
Weiss, Hilde, 601
Weiss, John, 2076
Weiss, Sheila F., 3233, 3234
Weisskopf, Thomas, 11086
Weitz, Bernard O., 3235
Weitz, Margaret C., 2769, 2770, 12119
Welch, David, 3236
Welch, Susan, 3515, 4325
Welch, William M., Jr., 2241
Wellen, Aloys I., 898
Wellers, Georges, 2654
Welles, Elliot, 11054
Wells, John, 1557
Wells, Roger, 4156
Welsch, David, 8296
Welsh, D., 7979, 8297
Wergeland, A.M., 10859
Werner, John M., 9721
Wernersson, Inga, 8630
Wertheimer, D., 1014
Wesern, J.S., 321
Wesley-Smith, Terence, 7412
Wesseling, H. L., 6908, 11829
Wesselingh, A.A., 6879
West, Dalton, 11383
West, Michael, 8298
West, Patrick, 3649
Westcott, Gill, 8299
Westerman, George W., 7392
Westermann, W.L., 11951

Western, John, 7907, 8300
Westin, Charles, 8631
Westmüller, Horst, 3237
Weston, Rubin F, 9722
Westwood, Sallie, 4326
Wetherall, William O., 6041
Whalley, John, 11830
Whatley, Christoper A., 3650
Wheat, A., 7496
Wheeler, Geoffrey E., 9407
Wheelersburg, Robert P., 8632
Wheeless, Carl M., 8884
Wheelock, Jaime R., 7191
Wheelwright, E.L., 224, 322, 323
Wheelwright, Ted, 182
Whelan, Christopher T, 3740
Whitaker, Ben, 638, 4327, 11831
Whitaker, Dulce C. A., 899
Whitaker, R., 1526
White, A.T., 2265
White, Caroline, 8236
White, D.R., 8301
White, Elizabeth B., 162
White, Geoffrey M., 11384
White, Isabel, 477
White, J., 9723
White, Jenny, 4328
White, Judy, 7141, 7143, 7144, 7192
White, Landeg, 6369, 6700
White, Lynn T., III, 1769
White, Patrick, 5875
White, Paul, 2771
White, Philip V., 9724
White, Steven F., 6012
Whitehall, William, 6147
Whitehead, N. L., 9760
Whitehouse, S., 10860
Whiteley, Paul, 4329
Whitelock, Otto V.St., 10479
Whiteman, Kaye, 1546
Whiteside, Arthur G., 602,603
Whiteside, Larry, 6148
Whiteside, Noel, 11832
Whiteside (Sin-a-Paw), Don, 12120
Whitfield, Stephen J., 11833
Whitlam, E.G., 11834
Whitney, Craig R., 10336
Whittaber, C.R., 11899
Whittaker, Alan, 478

Whitten, Norman E., Jr., 2145, 2148, 2149
Whyte, I.D., 3629
Whyte, Pauline, 10286
Whyte, Robert O., 10286
Wickberg, Edgar B., 7638
Widgery, David, 4330, 4331
Widlake, Paul, 4332
Wiecek, Wm. M., 9725
Wied-Nebbeling, Suzan, 4242
Wiedemann, Thomas, 11952
Wiegersma, Nancy, 9788
Wieneke, Christine E., 479
Wiens, Mi Chu, 1770
Wieseltier, Leon, 5328
Wiesen, D.S., 11953
Wiesenthal, Simon, 604
Wiesner, Merry E., 10861
Wiggershaus, Renate, 3238
Wignal, Guillermo J., 1846
Wigoder, Geoffrey, 5329, 11835
Wihtol de Wenden, Catherine, 2772
Wikan, Unni, 2242, 2243
Wilbon, Eleanor K., 6450
Wilce, Hilary, 4333
Wilcox, C., 10862
Wild, Stefan, 11194
Wilde, A., 11010
Wilentz, Amy, 4508
Wilhelm, Sidney H., 9726
Wilkie, Curtis, 5876, 5877
Wilkie, James W., 11048
Wilkins, M, 954
Wilkinson, B.W., 1527
Wilkinson, J.P., 4334
Wilkinson, Paul, 11836
Wilkinson, Peter, 8302
Wilkinson, Richard G., 4335-4337
Wilks, Ivor, 3672
Will, Donald S., 5330, 5878
Willan, Brian, 8303
Willard, M., 324
Willcos, Walter, 11837
Willeke, Venantius, 900
Willems, Fredericus, 6909
Willequet, Jacques, 686, 687
Willer, Harold, G., 7006
Williams, Alan W., 325
Williams, C.O., 4610
Williams, Colin H., 9348, 11838

Williams, D.G., 3673
Williams, David V., 7007, 7008
Williams, Dorothy W., 1172
Williams, Eric, 10480
Williams, Fiona, 4338
Williams, G., 1325, 7305, 7306
Williams, Glen, 7027
Williams, Glyn, 3674
Williams, Jenny, 4295, 9272
Williams, John A., 7009, 7010
Williams, Karel, 4341
Williams, Margaret H., 11954
Williams, Mary M, 901
Williams, Maurice, 605
Williams, Nancy A., 480
Williams, Patrick, 2773
Williams, Peter, 6149
Williams, Ross A., 326
Williams, Teresa, 6150
Williams, Vernon L., 7639
Williamson, Doug, 10246
Williamson, Jeffrey G., 3532, 4339
Williamson, John, 4340
Willie, Charles V., 9728, 9729
Willis, David K., 9408
Willis, John Ralph, 10287
Willis, Paul, 4342
Willis, William S., Jr., 9730, 9731
Wilmsen, Edwin N., 11839
Wilson, A. Jeyaratnam, 8506
Wilson, Clint C., II, 9732
Wilson, David B., 7193
Wilson, Dick, 6151
Wilson, Elizabeth, 4343
Wilson, Francis, 8299, 8304
Wilson, George, 11021
Wilson, J. Donald, 1528
Wilson, J.A., 3610, 3611
Wilson, James, 1301
Wilson, Joan H., 4200, 9665
Wilson, K., 5003
Wilson, Keith, 2244, 2998
Wilson, Nelly, 2774
Wilson, Stephen, 2775
Wilson, W., 9733
Wilson, William Julius, 9734
Wilson-Tagoe, Dabydeen David, 3469
Wilterdink, N., 6910
Wiltschegg, Walter, 606
Wimalasiri, Jayantha, 7938

Wimbush, S. Enders, 8971, 9409, 9410
Winawer, H. M., 9411
Winchester, Hilary P.M., 4344
Winchester, N. Brian, 1077
Windschuttle, Elizabeth, 327
Winkler, Arno, 3239
Winkler, Donald R., 11087
Winks, Robin, 1173, 4345, 11888
Winn, Conrad, 1059, 1061, 1529
Winn, D. E., 8925
Winn, Peter, 1581
Winock, Michel, 2776
Winrow, Gareth, 3240
Winson, Anthony, 7046, 11088
Winston, Diane, 2331
Winston, Michael R., 9735
Winter, J. M., 4346, 4347
Winternitz, Helen, 9944
Winyard, Stephen, 4329
Winzeler, Robert H., 6451
Wippermann, Wolfgang, 10863
Wipzycka, Eva, 2245
Wirahodikusumah, Miftah, 5080
Wirt, Frederick M., 3488, 7405
Wise, George S., 11062
Wiseberg, Laurie S., 10323
Wishnevsky, Julia, 9412
Wistrich, Robert S., 607, 608, 11840
With, J., 6911
Witherspoon, Sharon, 3964
Witke, Roxanne, 1772
Witt, Peter-Christian, 10864
Witts, Noel, 9413
Wiu, H.T., 1771
Wixman, Ronald, 9414
Wnuklipinski, E., 7759
Wobeser, Gisela von, 6631
Woehrling, Jose, 1530
Wohl, Anthony S., 4348
Wohlwill, Joachim F., 3241
Wolchik, Sharon L., 3133, 10865, 10866
Wolf, Eric R., 10867
Wolf, Joseph M., 5879
Wolf, Lucien, 9415
Wolf, Margery, 1772
Wolf, Simon, 7829
Wolfe, Lisa, 5880
Wolfee. W.J., 4349
Wolfers, Edward P., 7413, 7414

AUTHOR INDEX

Wolfers, Michael, 8554
Wolff, Egon, 902
Wolff, Frieda, 902
Wolff, Inge, 7497
Wolff, Richard J., 10868
Wolff, Richard J., 6013, 9803
Wolffsohn, Michael, 5881
Wolfson, Dirk Jr., 6912
Wolfson, Michael C., 1531, 1532
Woll, Josephine, 9416
Wolpe, Harold, 8305-8308
Wolpin, Miles D., 11841
Wong, Ansel, 3458
Wong, E., 7939
Wong, J.A.M., 11385
Wong, Kang-Kau B., 1773
Wong, M.G., 9736
Wongyai, Prasan, 8766
Wood, Alan, 9417
Wood, Charles H., 903
Wood, David, 328, 7194
Wood, Dean, 1302
Wood, Deborah A., 4350
Wood, Donald, 10481
Wood, Edward, 3355
Wood, Forrest B., 9737
Wood, Geoffrey D., 639
Wood, John R., 5004
Woods, Dwayne, 6028
Woods, P., 4351
Woods, R. I,, 4352
Woods, Richard D., 12122
Woods, W. Wilson, 3242
Woodside, Alexander, 9789
Woodsmall, Ruth F., 5005, 7360, 11195
Woodward, R.L. Jr., 4429
Woodward, William R. 2929
Woodworth, Stephen C., 11386
Woolard, K.A., 8417
Woolcock, J., 10482
Woolf, S.J., 587, 649, 2086, 2370, 2760, 6014, 7314, 7641, 7792, 8399, 10869
Woolmington, Jean, 481
Worboys, Michael, 11843
Worden, Nigel, 8309
Worger, William H., 8310
Worobec, Christine D., 9418
Worpole, Ken, 4354
Worthmuller, Angelika, 1821

Wortzel, Larry M., 1774
Woss, Fleur, 6093
Wotherspoon, T., 1533
Wozniak, Peter, 7760
Wray, Natalia, 2150
Wren, Christopher S., 8311
Wright, Bruce, 9738
Wright, C.Y., 3470, 3471
Wright, David, 11489
Wright, Ernest, 10483
Wright, J.F., 4355
Wright, James D., 9739
Wright, Judith, 482
Wright, Margaret T., 9588
Wright, R., 11604
Wright, Richard, 11089
Wright, Winthrop R., 9761-9763
Wrzesinski, Wojciech, 3243
Wu, David Y.H., 1649, 1651, 1656
Wu Lungan, 1728
Wu, Michael R., 1657
Wu Naitao, 1658
Wuerch, William L., 12003
Wülfing, Svea, 3244
Wundersitz, J., 377, 379, 382
Wyatt, J.D., 1303
Wyatt, Jiri, 2077
Wylie, Diana, 10290
Wylie, Jonathan, 2105
Wyman, Mark, 10870
Wynn, Charters S., 9419
Wynne, Edward C., 329
Wynot, Edward D., Jr., 3245, 7761-7766

Xia Zhi, 1775
Xiao, H., 1617
Xinyong Liu, 1767

Ya Otto, J., 6773
Ya'ari, Arieh, 5883
Yadlin, Ricka, 2246
Yahaya, N., 6452
Yahil, Leni, 2106-2108, 4600, 6486, 8633, 8672
Yahuda, Michael, 1776
Yan, Chung-Ming, 330
Yang, Anand A., 5006, 5007
Yaniv, Avner, 8686
Yanowitch, Murray, 9420

Yao, Joseph Y., 6029
Yardeni, Myrian, 10871
Yaroshevski, Dov B., 9421
Yarwood, A.T., 331, 483
Yasuba, Yasukichi, 6152
Yates, Barbara A., 9945
Yates, L., 4356
Yawata, Y. F., 6153
Yce, Sin Joan, 12091
Yee, May, 1119
Yeganeh, Nahid, 5130
Yehoshua, Benzion D., 14,
Yehuda, Don, 4601
Yekwai, Dimela, 3472
Yelling, J.A., 3516, 4357
Yen Ching-Hwang, 6453, 7940, 7941
Yensen, Helen, 7011
Yeo, E., 4358
Yeo, S., 4358
Yerushalmi, Yosef H., 7785, 8418, 8419
Yesudas, R.N., 5008
Yetes, Ronald, E., 6154
Yglesias, José, 1964
Yia Lee, Gary, 6280
Yih, Katherine, 7195
Yildizoglu, Ergin, 8853, 8885
Yimam, Arega, 10291
Yimer, Erku, 2332
Yitzchak, Kerem, 4364
Yitzhaki, Ahiya, 5884
Yogev, A., 3478, 5331
Yohannes, Okbazghi, 2333
Yoloye, E.A., 10292
Yonah, Yossi, 5332
Yonan, G., 8886
Yoneda, K., 5081
Yong, C.F., 7942
Yong, D.G., 10337
Yoo, Jong Goo, 6265, 6266
Yorgun, Pembenaz, 8887
York, Geoffrey, 1304
Yoshihisa Moshiko, Asahi Shinbun, 6155
Yoshikazu, Maezuka, 6094
Yoshinami, Takashi, 1777
Yoshino, I. Roger, 6156
Yotopoulos, Pan A., 11845, 11846
Youe, Christopher P., 6228
Young, Elise G., 11196
Young-Hwan Jo, 6157
Young, James D., 3651

Young, John, 1305
Young, Kate, 11847
Young, Lung-chang, 1778
Young, M. Crawford, 10293
Young, Marilyn Blatt, 1779
Young, Pansy, 10389
Young, R.E., 7415
Younger, Coralie, 5009
Younis, Abdullatif, 5885
Younis, Mona, 5886
Yücel, A. Ersan, 3246
Yuchtman-Yaar, Ephriam, 5887
Yunker, J.A., 10872
Yurco, Frank J., 2247
Yurochko, William P., 3247
Yusuf, Shahid, 11387
Yuval-Davies, Nira, 332, 4359, 5888

Zaalouk, Malak, 2248
Zabalza, A., 4360
Zabih, Sepehr, 5132
Zable, Arnold, 7416
Zach, Krista, 7867
Zachariah, Mathew, 11848
Zaffaroni, Irene G., 1534
Zafoni, Yigal, 12123
Zagorin, Perez, 10873
Zaharia, G., 7868
Zaidi, Grace Lilly, 5010
Zaidi, S.A., 5011, 7361
Zaionchkovoskii, P.A., 9422
Zajaczkowski, A., 9946
Zakaria, R.A., 5012
Zakharova, Larisa G., 9423, 9424
Zalkin, M., 7047
Zamagni, Vera, 6015
Zamascikov, Sergei, 9425
Zamir, Meir, 6301
Zang, Ted, Jr., 947
Zangrando, Robert L., 9740
Zaniewski, Kazimierz, J., 7767
Zannis, Mark, 1205
Zapf, Wolfgang, 3248
Zarea, A.R.A., 7886
Zarembka, Paul, 2137, 5030, 8016, 8017, 8305, 8525, 9788
Zarhi, S., 5889
Zarnowski, Janusz, 7768, 7768
Zartman, I. William, 999, 6679
Zaslavsky, Victor, 9426, 9427

Zauzsa, Daniel, 4526, 4527
Zavala A, Lauro, 11090
Zavala, Iris M., 6896
Zavala, Silvio A., 6632, 6633
Zavitzco, Carol, 12061
Zayyad, Tawfiq, 5890, 5891
Zelinsky, Wilbur, 11091
Zell, Hans M., 10294
Zelnick, Reginald E., 9428
Zenie-Ziegler, Wedad, 2249
Zenushkina, I., 9429
Zerby, J.A., 7556
Zermeño, Sergio, 6634
Zevelev, A., 9430
Zewde, Bahru, 2334, 2335
Zhang Shaowen, 1782
Zhang, Tianlu, 1659
Zhang, X., 1781
Zhang Xinxin, 1783
Zhao Yining, 1713
Zhu Li, 1660
Zhuang, Jiaying, 1784
Zhubov, Y. M., 6648
Zilke, Helen, 8312
Zima, Suellen, 5333
Zimbalist, Andrew, 1965, 1966
Zimbalist, Sidney E., 8634, 8635
Zimmermann, Mosche, 3249

Zinoviev, A., 4602
Ziring, Lawrence, 7362
Zisenevine, David W., 10874
Zitomersky, Joseph, 8636
Zoeberlein, Klaus D., 8673
Zogby, J. J., 5892
Zolberg, Aristide, 688
Zolcsak, Istvan, 7869
Zorach, Jonathan, 2078
Zorn, Gerda, 3250
Zouiche, Farida, 79
Zschock, Dieter K., 11092
Zu'bi, E., 5893
Zubaida, Sami, 8888
Zubrzycki, Jerzy, 333
Zucchinali, Monica, 6016Z
Zuccotti, Susan, 6017
Zuckerman, Nathan, 11849
Zuckerman, Sam, 7498
Zukowski, Ryszard, 7769
Zulch, T., 10875
Zur Muhlen, Patrik von 3251
Zureik, Elia, 5526, 5894, 5895
Zuroff, E., 9811
Zvogbo, C.J., 10028
Zwanenberg, R. van, 6229
Zweig, Ronald W., 3325, 3326
Zwick, Jim, 7640

SUBJECT INDEX

Numbers refer to entries not page numbers.

Affirmative action, *Australia*, 328; *Canada*, 1331, 1338, 1415-1417, 1516, 1525, 1529; *Great Britain*, 4009; *India*, 4626, 4678, 4713, 4737, 4746, 4762, 4801, 4815, 4844, 4882, 4890, 4912, 4965, 4989, 5004; *Japan*, 6140; *Malaysia*, 6407, 6413, 6418, 6447; *Nigeria*, 7218, 7252; *Peru*, 7435; *South Africa*, 8158; *USA*, 9441, 9453, 9562; *Yugoslavia*, 9839, 11560. See also ANTI-RACISM.

Anti-racism, *Great Britain*, 3729, 3763, 3764, 3791, 3792, 3896, 4319. See also AFFIRMATIVE ACTION.

Antisemitism, *Afghanistan*, 14; *Algeria*, 27, 29, 30, 36, 38, 44, 52, 73; *Argentina*, 98, 101, 102, 111, 117, 130, 135, 138, 139, 153-155, 157, 160, 161; *Australia*, 165, 168, 172, 177, 204, 212, 215, 216, 219, 229, 264, 294, 295, 297, 299; *Austria*, 484, 489, 490, 496, 499, 500, 501, 509, 511, 514, 515, 520, 525, 530, 533, 537, 542, 552, 554, 556, 562, 566, 569, 573, 579, 583, 585, 595, 600, 601, 603, 604, 607; *Belgium*, 658, 676, 679, 682; *Bolivia*, 708; *Brazil*, 751, 814, 849; *Bulgaria*, 911, 912, 938; *Canada*, 1005-1061; *Chile*, 1573; *Costa Rica*, 1836; *Cuba*, 1852-1854, 1918; *Czechoslovakia*, 1975, 1980, 1981, 1983, 1990, 1995, 1996, 2004, 2011, 2016-2018, 2024, 2026-2028, 2033, 2045-2047, 2051, 2052, 2055, 2068, 2077; *Denmark*, 2079, 2080; *Egypt*, 2205, 2207, 2227, 2246; *Ethiopia*, 2271, 2287, 2298, 2299, 2317, 2331; *Finland*, 2344; *France*, 2382, 2386, 2406, 2407, 2417, 2427, 2428, 2434, 2445, 2455, 2474, 2475, 2480, 2495, 2512, 2517, 2543, 2560, 2569, 2581, 2589, 2605, 2607-2609, 2622, 2691, 2700, 2722, 2731, 2740, 2764-2766, 2768, 2774, 2775; *Germany*, 2783, 2796, 2809, 2811, 2813, 2814, 2822, 2825, 2826, 2844, 2872, 2891, 2901, 2903, 2918, 2924, 2959, 2967, 2982, 2990, 2991, 2994, 2999, 3002, 3007, 3012, 3013, 3022, 3024, 3036, 3038, 3053, 3061, 3064, 3074, 3083, 3096, 3100, 3103, 3115, 3125, 3128, 3132, 3150, 3168, 3173, 3174, 3176, 3223, 3227, 3249; *Great Britain*, 3270-3326, 3780; *Guatemala*, 4425; *Hungary*, 4524, 4531, 4534, 4542, 4544, 4547-4550, 4552, 4554, 4564, 4565, 4573, 4575, 4576, 4583, 4587, 4601; *India*, 4613, 4751, 4783, 4915; *Iran*, 5100, 5107, 5108, 5112, 5114, 5115, 5121, 5127, 5129; *Iraq*, 5145, 5149, 5151, 5154, 5156, 5157, 5159, 5164, 5166; *Ireland*, 5188, 5198; *Israel*, 5210; *Italy*, 5911, 5917, 5918, 5920, 5923, 5929, 5932, 5933, 5935, 5940, 5951,

5954, 5958-5960, 5965, 5968, 5980, 5983, 5992, 5997, 6009, 6011; *Japan*, 6042, 6051, 6053, 6055, 6057, 6063, 6068, 6070, 6072, 6082, 6083, 6086-6088, 6097, 6099, 6115, 6123, 6125, 6137, 6147; *Libya*, 6336, 6342, 6343; *Mexico*, 6535, 6540, 6549, 6557, 6572-6574, 6577; *Morocco*, 6662-6666, 6676; *Netherlands*, 6792, 6793, 6802, 6818, 6819, 6834, 6856, 6882, 6887, 6906; *Nicaragua*, 7020, 7028, 7035, 7038-7042; *Norway*, 7308; *Poland*, 7642, 7647, 7648, 7652, 7654, 7655, 7657, 7658, 7660, 7664, 7668, 7678-7680, 7688, 7692, 7696, 7697, 7704, 7705, 7714, 7722, 7725, 7728, 7729, 7732, 7733, 7737, 7741, 7742, 7746, 7757, 7758, 7761, 7764; *Portugal*, 7785; *Rumania*, 7791, 7802, 7811, 7829, 7838, 7839, 7843, 7850, 7853, 7862, 7863; *South Africa*, 7958-7961, 8019, 8038, 8086, 8093, 8099, 8157, 8228, 8237-8241; *Spain*, 8317, 8320, 8322, 8353-8355, 8361, 8368, 8380, 8401, 8403, 8419; *Sweden*, 8568, 8591, 8621; *Switzerland*, 8638, 8651, 8659, 8663, 8665; *Syria*, 8677, 8681, 8682, 8684, 8689, 8694; *Tunisia*, 8775, 8778, 8786; *Turkey*, 8804, 8805, 8817, 8818, 8821, 8822, 8869; *USSR*, 8931, 8937, 8947, 8951-8953, 8956, 8962, 8969, 8973, 8980, 8982, 8996, 9003, 9017, 9034, 9041, 9046-9048, 9056, 9066, 9067, 9069, 9075, 9079, 9083, 9093, 9105, 9107, 9137, 9147, 9159-9164, 9168, 9178, 9181, 9182, 9189, 9192, 9199, 9201, 9250, 9274, 9279, 9283, 9284, 9287, 9289, 9290, 9294, 9295, 9300, 9302, 9305, 9328, 9340, 9350, 9356, 9357, 9361, 9377, 9397, 9404, 9406, 9409, 9415, 9416; *USA*, 9437, 9438, 9506, 9507, 9542, 9551, 9563, 9612, 9654, 9663, 9668; *Venezuela*, 9742, 9743; *Yugoslavia*, 9830, 9899; *Zimbabwe*, 9988; *Africa*, 10030, 10031, 10073, 10074, 10098, 10115, 10137, 10147, 10176, 10192, 10237, 10260, 10264, 10289; *Caribbean*, 10425; *Europe*, 10489, 10490, 10493, 10495, 10500, 10540, 10547, 10549, 10554, 10565, 10480, 10584, 10590, 10594, 10599, 10600, 10621, 10636, 10640, 10644, 10653, 10660, 10662, 10672-10674, 10676, 10683, 10686, 10700, 10706, 10708, 10714, 10727, 10750, 10761, 10777, 10778, 10788, 10790, 10793, 10808, 10820, 10835, 10871, 10874; *Latin America*, 10882, 10885, 10893, 10911, 10912, 10927, 10928, 10932, 10933, 10946, 10957, 10974, 10978, 10979, 10991, 10997, 11062, 11063, 11085; *Middle East*, 11118, 11145, 11164, 11175, 11177, 11181; *Elsewhere*, 11395, 11409, 11418, 11420, 11423, 11424, 11426, 11430, 11449, 11450, 11455, 11462, 11485, 11516-11518, 11534, 11572, 11578, 11584, 11590, 11595, 11603, 11608, 11619, 11639-11642, 11649, 11668, 11716, 11737, 11741, 11744, 11747, 11755, 11775, 11776, 11779, 11798, 11828, 11833, 11835, 11840, 11849; *Ancient History*, 11879, 11896, 11906, 11933, 11954; *Bibliography*, 11959, 11978, 12026, 12041, 12092. See also HOLOCAUST.

Bilingual education, *France*, 2342, 2354, 2572; *Germany*, 3035, 3076; *Great Britain*, 3656, 3673; *Malaysia*, 6393; *Mexico*, 6551, 6552; *New Zealand*, 6982, 6988; *Nigeria*, 7245; *Peru*, 7461; *Spain*, 8415; *Sweden*, 8614; *Tunisia*, 8776; *USA*, 9667; *Oceania*, 11249; *Elsewhere*, 11721

Blacks, *Algeria*, 34; *Argentina*, 95, 110, 122; *Australia*, 200; *Brazil*, 741, 760, 771, 779, 794, 797, 804, 812, 825, 829, 831, 832, 836, 839, 845, 853, 854, 862, 863, 872, 877, 889, 891; *Canada*, 1120-1173; *China*, 1693, 1751, 1775; *Colombia*, 1808, 1809; *Costa Rica*, 1837, 1846; *Cuba*, 1857, 1858, 1860, 1861, 1864, 1868-1870, 1872, 1876-1890, 1893, 1894, 1901, 1903, 1904, 1906, 1921, 1924-1927, 1930-1932, 1934, 1941, 1950, 1960, 1962; *Cyprus*, 1969; *Egypt*, 2158, 2176, 2178, 2180, 2185, 2200, 2233, 2247; *France*, 2373, 2394, 2423,

2442, 2449, 2450, 2465, 2469, 2547, 2591, 2695, 2696, 2721; *Germany*, 2913, 2933, 2941, 2952, 3070, 3141, 3242; *Great Britain*, 3329, 3342, 3344, 3364, 3369, 3391, 3403, 3404, 3408, 3427; *Haiti*, 4490; *Israel*, 5226, 5240, 5259, 5275, 5289, 5318; *Japan*, 6106, 6107, 6116, 6148, 6150; *Malaysia*, 6383; *Mexico*, 6487, 6488, 6509, 6527, 6601, 6605, 6613; *Nicaragua*, 7022, 7069, 7070, 7179; *Panama*, 7375, 7382, 7383, 7385; *Philippines*, 7633; *Poland*, 7711; *Portugal*, 7781; *Spain*, 8338, 8341, 8385, 8410; *Uruguay*, 8914, 8918, 8919, 8921; *USSR*, 8981, 9354; *Venezuela*, 9755, 9763; *Africa*, 10195; *Caribbean*, 10348, 10432, 10436; *Europe*, 10567, 10592, 10837; *Latin America*, 10902, 10919, 10943-10945, 10947, 10958, 10975, 10981, 10990, 11007, 11008, 11035, 11036, 11055, 11057, 11079, 11080, 11089, 11091; *Middle East*, 11099; *Elsewhere*, 11493, 11600, 11602, 11625, 11650, 11711, 11749; *Ancient History*, 11857, 11883, 11884, 11912, 11932, 11935-11938, 11947, 11953; *Bibliography*, 11963, 12075. See also RACISM.

Bourgeoisie, *Belgium*, 651; *Bulgaria*, 930; *Canada*, 1465; *China*, 1696; *Cuba*, 1935; *Egypt*, 2235, 2248; *Germany*, 3025; *Kenya*, 6196; *Libya*, 6345; *Morocco*, 6669; *Nigeria*, 7257; *Pakistan*, 7359; *Papua-New Guinea*, 7395; *South Africa*, 8004, 8305; *Africa*, 10169, 10181; *Caribbean*, 10470; *Europe*, 10523, 10563. See also CLASS STRUCTURE.

Capitalism, *Argentina*, 109, 133, 158; *Australia*, 182, 186, 259, 260, 322, 323, 334, 479; *Brazil*, 731, 743, 823, 848; *Cameroon*, 986; *Canada*, 1336, 1358, 1371, 1376, 1392, 1395, 1396, 1406, 1464, 1471, 1489, 1496, 1513; *Chile*, 1557, 1561, 1568, 1570, 1579; *Dominican Republic*, 2111, 2113; *Egypt*, 2174, 2192, 2224; *France*, 2468, 2496, 2521; *Germany*, 2879, 3127; *Great Britain*, 3624, 3675, 3734, 3761, 3885, 4020, 4039, 4044, 4339; *Guyana*, 4453; *Honduras*, 4511; *Hungary*, 4538, 4572; *India*, 4620, 4625, 4655, 4667, 4766, 4888, 4919, 4979, 4988, 4999; *Indonesia*, 5062, 5064, 5067, 5072; *Iran*, 5118; *Israel*, 5335; *Italy*, 5906, 5943, 5970, 5977; *Ivory Coast*, 6019; *Japan*, 6067, 6101, 6102, 6179; *Kenya*, 6224; *Korea*, 6236, 6240, 6243, 6248; *Malawi*, 6362; *Malaysia*, 6372; *Mexico*, 6499, 6529, 6600, 6615, 6629; *Morocco*, 6668; *Mozambique*, 6700; *Netherlands*, 6784, 6787; *Nicaragua*, 7017, 7044; *Nigeria*, 7273, 7286; *Norway*, 7316; *Peru*, 7458, 7468, 7469, 7495; *Philippines*, 7513; *Poland*, 7673, 7717; *Senegal*, 7889; *South Africa*, 7951, 7983, 7989, 8024, 8063, 8127, 8140, 8147, 8187, 8230, 8258, 8310; *Spain*, 8356; *Sri Lanka*, 8475; *Syria*, 8695; *Tanzania*, 8713; *Thailand*, 8735; *Turkey*, 8794, 8862; *USSR*, 9191, 9233; *USA*, 9555, 9581; *Venezuela*, 9757; *Vietnam*, 9778; *Zaire*, 9933; *Zambia*, 9955, 9959; *Africa*, 10047, 10057, 10089, 10143, 10160, 10196, 10255; *Caribbean*, 10404, 10445, 10467; *Europe*, 10501, 10530, 10595, 10611, 10628; *Latin America*, 10916, 10925, 10956, 10993, 11043, 11061; *Middle East*, 11190; *Oceania*, 11288-11290; *Elsewhere*, 11391, 11539, 11557, 11657, 11659, 11701, 11746, 11769, 11803, 11825, 11826. See also BOURGEOISIE and ECONOMIC HISTORY.

Caste, *Belgium*, 681; *Ethiopia*, 2329; *India*, 4621, 4624, 4638, 4639, 4654, 4690, 4694, 4697, 4706, 4721, 4758, 4788, 4795, 4864, 4886, 4900, 4934, 4966, 4997, 5003; *Indonesia*, 5048; *Asia*, 10299; *Bibliography*, 11911. See also HARIJANS and UNTOUCHABLES.

Censorship, *Israel*, 5399, 5463

1024 SUBJECT INDEX

Children, *Australia*, 406; *Canada*, 1251, 1361; *Chile*, 1550; *France*, 2401, 2415, 2539, 2628; *Germany*, 2816, 2817, 3111, 3244; *Great Britain*, 3535, 3563, 3566, 3571, 3572, 3583, 3599, 3772, 3801, 3822, 3829, 3830, 3843, 3851, 3855, 3873, 4027, 4078, 4154, 4181, 4227, 4252, 4254, 4298; *Guatemala*, 4398; *India*, 4927; *Israel*, 5408, 5615, 5624, 5641, 5691, 5719, 5761, 5826, 5827, 5858; *Lebanon*, 6286; *Namibia*, 6750; *Norway*, 7313; *Peru*, 7479; *Philippines*, 7529, 7598; *South Africa*, 8022, 8058, 8073, 8271, 8289; *Spain*, 8374; *Sri Lanka*, 8457; *Sweden*, 8622; *Tanzania*, 8725; *Uganda*, 8894; *USA*, 9508; *Asia*, 10336; *Caribbean*, 10344, 10389; *Europe*, 10685, 10844; *Latin America*, 10877; *Oceania*, 11292; *Elsewhere*, 11393, 11421, 11693, 11765, 11814

CIA, *China*, 1582; *Guatemala*, 4418; *Nicaragua*, 7058; *Middle East*, 11123

Citizenship, *France*, 2424, 2454, 2488, 2653; *Germany*, 2843; *Great Britain*, 3489, 3876, 3908, 4040, 4065, 4243; *Israel*, 5885; *Netherlands*, 6879; *Uganda*, 8908; *USA*, 9509, 9582; *Ancient History*, 11854

Civil Rights, *Brazil*, 887; *France*, 2470; *Nigeria*, 7267; *USSR*, 9021; *USA*, 9480, 9607, 9651; *Middle East*, 11156. See also HUMAN RIGHTS.

Class conflict, *Argentina*, 140; *Australia*, 188; *Brazil*, 835; *Canada*, 1405, 1462; *Costa Rica*, 1838; *Dominican Republic*, 2116; *Ecuador*, 2131; *El Salvador*, 2258; *Ethiopia*, 2302; *France*, 2671; *Great Britain*, 3672, 3936, 4155, 4156, 4358; *Guyana*, 4444, 4446; *India*, 4769, 4785, 4818, 4887, 4964; *Israel*, 5293; *Jordan*, 6162; *Kenya*, 6169; *Mali*, 6455; *Mauritania*, 6459; *Mexico*, 6497, 6616, 6618; *Morocco*, 6673; *Nigeria*, 7037, 7210, 7215, 7219, 7235; *South Africa*, 8025, 8125; *Sudan*, 8535; *Sweden*, 8579; *Tanzania*, 8711, 8718, 8720, 8721, 8724; *Thailand*, 8765; *Tunisia*, 8783; *Uruguay*, 8915; *USSR*, 9236, 9253; *Africa*, 10184, 10193, 10263; *Caribbean*, 10342, 10482; *Europe*, 10542, 10634; *Latin America*, 10994, 11033; *Elsewhere*, 11459, 11535, 11563, 11685; *Ancient History*, 11870, 11925, 11939; *Bibliography*, 12073. See also CLASS STRUCTURE.

Class mobility, *Brazil*, 793, 843; *Czechoslovakia*, 2022; *Ecuador*, 2139; *France*, 2706; *Germany*, 2922, 2923, 3182; *Great Britain*, 3445, 3833, 4119, 4150, 4264; *Ireland*, 5181, 5184; *Jordan*, 6064, 6065; *Korea*, 6230; *Libya*, 6337; *Malaysia*, 6386; *Nigeria*, 7247; *Singapore*, 7917; *South Africa*, 8063, 8104, 8251; *Sweden*, 8603; *Africa*, 10174; *Europe*, 10668; *Elsewhere*, 11545

Class structure, *Algeria*, 31, 35; *Angola*, 83; *Australia*, 174, 189, 193, 205, 233, 238, 257, 258, 261, 269; *Austria*, 522; *Bangladesh*, 616, 619, 633, 639; *Belgium*, 672; *Botswana*, 719, 728; *Brazil*, 746, 752, 777, 879, 882; *Canada*, 1062, 1342, 1355, 1357, 1386, 1390, 1419, 1425, 1426, 1449, 1470, 1472, 1500; *China*, 1712, 1758, 1764, 1774, 1784; *Costa Rica*, 1839; *Cuba*, 1909; *Cuba*, 1951; *Cyprus*, 1967; *Denmark*, 2090; *Egypt*, 2166, 2179; *El Salvador*, 2260, 2265; *Finland*, 2336, 2348; *France*, 2612; *Gabon*, 2778; *Germany*, 2788, 2834, 2890, 2905, 3003, 3029, 3180, 3212, 3226; *Ghana*, 3255; *Great Britain*, 3330, 3367, 3425, 3484, 3490, 3573, 3618, 3634, 3651, 3661, 3707, 3740, 3759, 3797, 3798, 3802, 3818, 3841, 3913, 3924, 3958, 3979, 4041, 4042, 4054, 4056, 4095, 4124, 4192, 4193, 4196, 4199, 4204, 4309; *Greece*, 4375; *Guatemala*, 4404, 4429; *Haiti*, 4480; *Iceland*, 4606, 4610; *India*, 4614, 4634, 4641, 4674, 4722, 4723, 4841, 4861, 4895, 4918, 4962, 4980;

SUBJECT INDEX 1025

Indonesia, 5019, 5029, 5038, 5043, 5066; *Iran*, 5104, 5113, 5124; *Iraq*, 5136; *Israel*, 5219, 5230, 5231, 5273; *Italy*, 5903, 5953, 5976; *Ivory Coast*, 6028; *Japan*, 6133; *Jordan*, 6160; *Kenya*, 6178, 6187, 6223; *Korea*, 6232, 6262; *Kuwait*, 6271; *Lebanon*, 6289, 6291, 6296; *Liberia*, 6305; *Malaysia*, 6405, 6443; *Mexico*, 6490, 6498, 6505, 6512, 6531, 6542, 6543, 6566, 6580, 6595, 6604, 6619; *Morocco*, 6650; *Mozambique*, 6690; *Myanmar*, 6713; *Nigeria*, 7205, 7228, 7275; *Pakistan*, 7337; *Philippines*, 7560, 7582, 7608, 7609; *Poland*, 7645, 7748; *Saudi Arabia*, 7885; *Sierra Leone*, 7906, 7910; *Somalia*, 7940; *South Africa*, 7992, 8013, 8077, 8119, 8306; *Spain*, 8357; *Sri Lanka*, 8420, 8484; *Sweden*, 8577, 8612; *Syria*, 8676, 8679; *Tanzania*, 8727; *Thailand*, 8734; *USSR*, 9000, 9059, 9060, 9119, 9149, 9174, 9183, 9208, 9217, 9262, 9347, 9420; *USA*, 9537, 9546; *Venezuela*, 9747; *Vietnam*, 9772; *Zaire*, 9926; *Zambia*, 9957; *Zimbabwe*, 9961; *Africa*, 10044, 10062, 10077, 10083, 10101, 10124, 10211, 10213, 10225, 10273, 10278; *Asia*, 10317; *Caribbean*, 10353, 10403, 10437, 10451, 10452; *Europe*, 10605, 10630, 10687, 10704, 10759, 10787, 10830; *Latin America*, 10907, 11042, 11088; *Middle East*, 11191; *Oceania*, 11207, 11230, 11253, 11304, 11309; *Elsewhere*, 11461, 11465, 11486, 11556, 11696; *Ancient History*, 11878, 11895-11897; *Bibliography*, 11961, 11971. See also CLASS MOBILITY.

Collaborationism, *Belgium*, 686; *France*, 2514, 2541; *Germany*, 3052; *Philippines*, 7583; *Uganda*, 8911; *Vietnam*, 9777; *Middle East*, 11096

Collective self-defense, *South Africa*, 8111, 8178; *Spain*, 8336

Colonial wars, *Malaysia*, 6394; *Myanmar*, 6702; *Nigeria*, 7251. See also WAR.

Colonialism, *Algeria*, 39, 40, 48, 55, 59, 63, 67, 70, 76, 77; *Angola*, 80, 88; *Australia*, 209, 224, 268, 313, 355, 356, 357, 401, 410, 444; *Austria*, 535, 597; *Belize*, 692; *Benin*, 695; *Bolivia*, 709; *Botswana*, 718; *Burkina Faso*, 948; *Cambodia*, 976; *Cameroon*, 984, 991, 993, 998; *Canada*, 1206, 1207, 1299, 1300, 1322, 1377, 1409, 1437; *Cape Verde Islands*, 1538; *China*, 1642, 1671, 1695; *Colombia*, 1785; *Ecuador*, 2140, 2149; *Egypt*, 2209, 2212, 2225, 2241; *Ethiopia*, 2293, 2307, 2310, 2323, 2333; *France*, 2413, 2432, 2433, 2559, 2610, 2633, 2650, 2718; *Germany*, 3177, 3178, 3219; *Ghana*, 3260; *Great Britain*, 3631, 3700, 3757, 3897, 4232; *Guinea-Bissau*, 4433, 4443; *Guyana*, 4449, 4456, 4464; *Haiti*, 4470; *India*, 4623, 4636, 4651, 4668, 4747, 4755, 4759, 4760, 4767, 4782, 4806, 4828, 4838, 4857, 4881, 4889, 4929, 4985, 4994, 5007; *Indonesia*, 5018, 5020, 5023, 5033, 5034, 5036, 5042, 5045, 5049, 5053, 5056, 5060, 5079; *Ireland*, 5172, 5175, 5189, 5203; *Israel*, 5218, 5374, 5445; *Italy*, 5945; *Ivory Coast*, 6023; *Japan*, 6039, 6103; *Kenya*, 6170, 6176, 6189, 6194, 6201, 6206, 6214; *Korea*, 6231, 6235, 6237, 6242, 6245, 6252, 6253; *Liberia*, 6312; *Libya*, 6341, 6348; *Madagascar*, 6350, 6353; *Malawi*, 6360; *Malaysia*, 6371, 6382, 6414, 6421, 6437, 6442, 6647, 6651, 6653; *Morocco*, 6675; *Mozambique*, 6694, 6697; *Myanmar*, 6707; *Namibia*, 6735, 6740, 6741, 6752, 6779; *Netherlands*, 6813; *Nigeria*, 7111, 7168, 7217, 7227, 7254, 7285, 7288, 7294; *Panama*, 7365, 7368; *Papua-New Guinea*, 7393, 7404, 7406, 7411-7414; *Peru*, 7433, 7450; *Philippines*, 7502, 7522, 7524, 7525, 7530, 7534, 7535, 7542,

SUBJECT INDEX

7549, 7554, 7567, 7577, 7580, 7595, 7607, 7637; *Poland*, 7754; *Rwanda*, 7877; *Senegal*, 7893, 7902; *Sierra Leone*, 7912, 7914; *Singapore*, 7934, 7935; *South Africa*, 7975, 7977, 8008, 8009, 8089, 8163, 8244, 8307, 8308; *Sri Lanka*, 8424, 8463, 8470, 8472, 8478, 8483, 8504; *Sudan*, 8516, 8518, 8519, 8523, 8542; *Suriname*, 8564; *Tanzania*, 8701, 8706, 8733; *Tunisia*, 8777; *Uganda*, 8889, 8898; *USSR*, 8957, 8959, 8964, 9026, 9073, 9097, 9157, 9275, 9316, 9319-9321, 9330, 9334, 9381, 9396, 9425; *USA*, 9483, 9488, 9620, 9662; *Venezuela*, 9744; *Vietnam*, 9775, 9789; *Yugoslavia*, 9848; *Zambia*, 9948, 9949, 9956; *Zimbabwe*, 9967, 10007, 10010; *Africa*, 10034, 10058, 10067, 10117, 10119, 10138, 10167, 10210, 10220, 10228, 10233, 10251, 10265, 10274; *Caribbean*, 10356, 10411, 10446, 10459; *Europe*, 10610, 10855; *Latin America*, 10941, 10954, 11056; *Oceania*, 11198, 11199, 11220, 11227, 11245, 11254, 11259, 11266, 11272, 11281, 11303, 11308, 11323, 11369, 11373, 11386; *Elsewhere*, 11401, 11410, 11440, 11445, 11454, 11464, 11467, 11475, 11484, 11497, 11503, 11506, 11521, 11527, 11530, 11542, 11550, 11589, 11610, 11651, 11663, 11680, 11705, 11763, 11777, 11791, 11796; *Bibliography*, 12017. See also NEO-COLONIALISM.

Communalism, *India*, 4617, 4618, 4649, 4669, 4703, 4707, 4729, 4738, 4744, 4938, 4953; *Malaysia*, 6384, 6398; *Pakistan*, 7341, 7357; *Sri Lanka*, 8450; *Middle East*, 11147. See also RELIGION.

Communism, *Czechoslovakia*, 2002, 2005; *Egypt*, 2167, 2168; *Germany*, 3175; *India*, 4671; *Israel*, 5419, 5679, 5733; *Nepal*, 6776; *Poland*, 7743; *Rumania*, 7844; *Sri Lanka*, 8488; *USSR*, 8938, 9081, 9187, 9322; *Latin America*, 11048;

Elsewhere, 11515. See also SOCIALISM.

Conquest, *Algeria*, 58; *Australia*, 337; *Great Britain*, 3620, 3660; *Guatemala*, 4415, 4416; *Honduras*, 4514; *Ireland*, 5176, 5194; *Peru*, 7493; *Philippines*, 7570, 7618, 7639; *Venezuela*, 8941; *USSR*, 9031; *Latin America*, 10878; *Oceania*, 11202, 11265; *Ancient History*, 11926. See also COLONIAL WARS and WAR.

Conservatism, *Germany*, 2945, 2972

Corruption, *Germany*, 2850; *Zaire*, 9923

Crime, *Brazil*, 805; *France*, 2611; *Great Britain*, 3733, 3867, 3923; *India*, 5006; *Israel*, 5537; *Sri Lanka*, 8482; *USSR*, 9004

Decolonization, *Canada*, 1268, 1323; *France*, 2688; *Malaysia*, 6441; *Mauritius*, 6485; *Namibia*, 6728, 6729; *New Zealand*, 6957; *Philippines*, 7533, 7569; *Portugal*, 7775; *Swaziland*, 8567; *Zimbabwe*, 10018; *Africa*, 10099, 10129, 10282; *Oceania*, 11271, 11306; *Elsewhere*, 11669, 11729

Democracy, *Algeria*, 32; *Australia*, 144, 156; *Brazil*, 826; *Cameroon*, 987; *Canada*, 1443, 1495, 1498; *Chile*, 1551; *China*, 1736; *Costa Rica*, 1829, 1833; *Ecuador*, 2143; *Great Britain*, 3482, 3487; *Guatemala*, 4394; *India*, 4713, 4867; *Kenya*, 6193; *Mexico*, 6528, 6634; *Mozambique*, 6689; *Nicaragua*, 7036; *Nigeria*, 7223-7225, 7237, 7263; *Panama*, 7380; *Peru*, 7442; *Philippines*, 7504; *Senegal*, 7888; *Spain*, 8351; *Sri Lanka*, 8501, 8507; *Sudan*, 8543, 8552; *Sweden*, 8597; *Turkey*, 8802, 8816, 8838; *Uruguay*, 8916, 8922; *USSR*, 9115; *Venezuela*, 9749; *Yugoslavia*, 9854; *Africa*, 10168, 10188, 10262, 10267; *Europe*, 10488; *Latin America*, 10888, 10906, 10968, 11070; *Oceania*, 11353; *Elsewhere*, 11605, 11820

SUBJECT INDEX 1027

Denazification, *Austria*, 570, 590; *Germany*, 2838, 2961, 2998, 3006, 3078, 3155, 3208, 3236. See also NAZIS.
Deportation, *Canada*, 1490; *Israel*, 5545, 5600, 5787; *Bibliography*, 12023
Desegregation, *India*, 4662; *South Africa*, 8002, 8220, 8282; *USA*, 9479, 9520, 9586, 9600, 9632, 9648
Dictatorship, *Haiti*, 4474, 4504
Discrimination, *Belgium*, 645, 659; *Brazil*, 767; *Canada*, 1062, 1081, 1089, 1335, 1359, 1367, 1403, 1434, 1475, 1484, 1515; *Colombia*, 1820; *Cuba*, 1859, 1867, 1943, 1955; *France*, 2472; *Germany*, 2804, 2984; *Great Britain*, 3536, 3561, 3570, 3580, 3587, 3592; *Japan*, 6056, 6061, 6069, 6092; *Kenya*, 6181; *Mexico*, 6533; *Netherlands*, 6828, 6909; *New Zealand*, 6996; *Singapore*, 7927; *South Africa*, 7999; *USA*, 9353, 9473, 9524, 9621, 9682; *Zimbabwe*, 9981, 10001; *Asia*, 10365; *Latin America*, 11066; *Middle East*, 11113, 11152; *Elsewhere*, 11643. See also RACISM.

Economic history, *Brazil*, 748; *China*, 1728; *Czechoslovakia*, 2074; *Denmark*, 2091; *Ethiopia*, 2334; *Finland*, 2365; *Great Britain*, 3578, 3641; *Hungary*, 4517; *India*, 4650, 4726, 4817, 4922, 4951; *New Zealand*, 6946, 6980; *Nigeria*, 7201; *Pakistan*, 7354; *Papua-New Guinea*, 7401; *Peru*, 7447; *Rumania*, 7837, 7861; *South Africa*, 7963, 8092, 8223; *Sudan*, 8514, 8525, 8550; *Sweden*, 8584; *Tanzania*, 8723; *USSR*, 9234, 9264; *Zaire*, 9927; *Zimbabwe*, 9969, 9998, 10008; *Africa*, 10046; *Caribbean*, 10351, 10439; *Europe*, 10725; *Latin America*, 10904; *Middle East*, 11169; *Oceania*, 11208; *Elsewhere*, 11597; *Bibliography*, 11986
Education, *Afghanistan*, 7; *Algeria*, 54; *Argentina*, 103, 125, 127; *Australia*, 167, 176, 178, 192, 198, 210, 221, 228, 236, 241, 242, 248, 249, 270, 292, 293, 312, 326, 344, 368, 372, 393, 411, 419, 430, 459; *Austria*, 576; *Bangladesh*, 630; *Botswana*, 716, 721, 722, 725, 726; *Brazil*, 747, 816, 828, 847, 874, 883, 899; *Bulgaria*, 907; *Cameroon*, 981, 989, 996; *Canada*, 1082, 1134, 1135, 1163, 1181, 1182, 1226, 1236, 1240, 1271, 1275, 1276, 1279, 1283, 1296, 1302, 1303, 1305, 1311, 1312, 1334, 1354, 1362, 1368, 1382, 1384, 1385, 1391, 1408, 1418, 1422, 1431, 1454, 1469, 1474, 1503, 1521, 1527, 1528, 1533; *Chad*, 1543; *Chile*, 1552, 1553, 1560; *China*, 1617, 1670, 1672, 1675, 1681, 1713, 1718, 1719, 1731, 1744, 1747, 1748, 1756, 1757, 1760, 1767, 1771, 1773; *Colombia*, 1800; *Costa Rica*, 1834, 1840, 1842, 1843; *Cuba*, 1863, 1880; *Czechoslovakia*, 1993, 2013, 2042; *Denmark*, 2084, 2097; *Ecuador*, 2130; *Egypt*, 2162, 2171, 2202; *Ethiopia*, 2270, 2280, 2308; *Finland*, 2339; *France*, 2408, 2421, 2440, 2441, 2443, 2456, 2518, 2519, 2520, 2525, 2570, 2582, 2617, 2618, 2637, 2690, 2654, 2658, 2670, 2728, 2729, 2748; *Germany*, 2808, 2824, 2835, 2849, 2851, 2880, 2899, 2910, 2920, 2930, 2931, 2937, 2958, 2968, 2970, 2986, 2989, 3000, 3005, 3028, 3051, 3066, 3075, 3084, 3085, 3113, 3139, 3148, 3154, 3190, 3200, 3209, 3222, 3224, 3235, 3247; *Ghana*, 3259; *Great Britain*, 3337, 3340, 3366, 3370, 3372, 3375, 3388, 3389, 3393, 3401, 3402, 3413, 3420, 3421, 3454-3456, 3459-3461, 3465, 3470, 3471, 3473, 3474, 3476-3479, 3488, 3541-3543, 3547, 3550-3560, 3565, 3577, 3582, 3585, 3586, 3588-3590, 3593, 3594, 3596, 3597, 3600, 3601, 3604-3606, 3610, 3611, 3612-3614, 3630, 3635, 3642, 3668, 3670, 3678, 3683, 3698, 3708, 3728, 3743, 3756, 3768, 3781, 3784, 3808, 3826, 3828, 3853, 3856, 3864, 3879, 3892, 3895, 3901,

3914, 3917, 3920, 3930, 3932, 3934, 3951, 3968, 3978, 3987, 3994, 4029-4931, 4035-4037, 4055, 4076, 4088, 4096, 4108, 4115, 4126, 4130, 4131, 4149, 4176, 4179, 4186, 4201, 4202, 4220, 4221, 4238, 4253, 4255, 4262, 4265, 4267, 4270-4273, 4284, 4285, 4295, 4297, 4303, 4304, 4312, 4318, 4323, 4327, 4332, 4350, 4351; *Guinea-Bissau*, 4430, 4440; *Haiti*, 4468, 4487, 4488; *Hungary*, 4539, 4579; *India*, 4616, 4619, 4622, 4670, 4693, 4698, 4702, 4708, 4716, 4724, 4731, 4733, 4745, 4752, 4763-4765, 4791, 4794, 4798, 4802, 4832, 4834, 4846, 4855, 4872, 4883, 4894, 4896, 4905, 4906, 4909, 4924, 4928, 4931, 4939, 4940, 4969, 4972, 4981, 4982, 5002; *Indonesia*, 5024, 5027, 5032, 5039, 5047, 5052, 5063, 5068, 5071, 5073; *Iran*, 5098; *Ireland*, 5170, 5179, 5182, 5201; *Israel*, 5211, 5245, 5252, 5272, 5278, 5286, 5307, 5317, 5319, 5331, 5340, 5348, 5351, 5363, 5371, 5378, 5383, 5389, 5392, 5410, 5429-5432, 5455, 5465-5467, 5472, 5488, 5497, 5499, 5505, 5509, 5510, 5515, 5530, 5531, 5539, 5558, 5559, 5569-5576, 5579, 5614, 5618, 5645, 5653, 5667, 5693, 5699, 5715, 5732, 5738, 5739, 5749, 5751, 5768, 5769, 5799, 5804, 5814, 5832, 5837-5839, 5845, 5851, 5853, 5861, 5880; *Italy*, 5975, 5995, 5998, 6012, 6013; *Ivory Coast*, 6024, 6029; *Jordan*, 6059; *Kenya*, 6167, 6175, 6177, 6180, 6190, 6192, 6203-6204, 6222; *Korea*, 6234, 6249, 6250, 6256, 6264; *Lebanon*, 6284, 6288, 6292, 6293; *Liberia*, 6328; *Libya*, 6333; *Malaysia*, 6377, 6378, 6415, 6423, 6435; *Mali*, 6454; *Mauritius*, 6468, 6475, 6478, 6479, 6481; *Mexico*, 6489, 6517, 6534, 6535, 6538, 6576, 6587, 6590, 6591, 6606, 6610, 6626, 6630; *Mongolian People's Republic*, 6642; *Mozambique*, 6681, 6686-6688, 6698; *Myanmar*, 6708; *Namibia*, 6758; *Nepal*, 6775, 6777, 6780; *Netherlands*, 6881, 6804, 6826,

6827, 6835, 6836, 6838, 6839, 6847; *New Zealand*, 6919, 6920, 6930, 6933, 6965, 6974, 6990; *Nicaragua*, 7012, 7019, 7026, 7030, 7032, 7226, 7229, 7232; *Nigeria*, 7242, 7253, 7265, 7266, 7269, 7274, 7290-7292, 7298-7300, 7303; *Norway*, 7312; *Pakistan*, 7343, 7348; *Papua-New Guinea*, 7394, 7405; *Paraguay*, 7427; *Poland*, 7462, 7476, 7480, 7501, 7503, 7507, 7510, 7518, 7519, 7521, 7523, 7536, 7546, 7548, 7550, 7553, 7597, 7605, 7619, 7634, 7644, 7653, 7724, 7726, 7760; *Rumania*, 7814, 7832, 7856; *Saudi Arabia*, 7879; *Senegal*, 7891, 7898; *Singapore*, 7928; *South Africa*, 7950, 7954, 7965, 7967, 7972-7974, 7990, 7993, 7994, 7997, 7998, 8001, 8012, 8014, 8015, 8023, 8026, 8027, 8030, 8031, 8033, 8043, 8050, 8055, 8064, 8070, 8079, 8082, 8101, 8102, 8107, 8109, 8114, 8122, 8124, 8126, 8129, 8130, 8136, 8137, 8142-8144, 8151, 8152, 8156, 8161, 8170, 8193, 8198-8200, 8226, 8234, 8235, 8247, 8273, 8279-8281, 8291, 8301; *Spain*, 8327, 8340, 8378; *Sri Lanka*, 8458; *Sudan*, 8537, 8544; *Sweden*, 8569, 8580, 8598, 8609, 8620, 8626, 8630; *Tanzania*, 8697, 8702, 8710, 8729, 8730; *Thailand*, 8750, 8756, 8757, 8760; *Tunisia*, 8779, 8870, 8883; *USSR*, 8946, 8983, 9032, 9039, 9043, 9077, 9106, 9138, 9151, 9190, 9207, 9232, 9248, 9265, 9282, 9323, 9382, 9402; *USA*, 9435, 9448, 9455, 9458, 9478, 9496, 9527, 9528, 9552, 9639; *Venezuela*, 9754; *Vietnam*, 9771; *Zaire*, 9920, 9922, 9938, 9945; *Zambia*, 9953, 9958; *Zimbabwe*, 9973, 9992, 9999, 10009, 10013, 10026; *Africa*, 10045, 10054, 10055, 10063, 10070, 10100, 10118, 10121, 10122, 10128, 10136, 10156-10158, 10208, 10257, 10258, 10293; *Asia*, 10331, 10335; *Caribbean*, 10349, 10358, 10395, 10420, 10438, 10441, 10455, 10457, 10458; *Europe*, 10516, 10601, 10603,

SUBJECT INDEX 1029

10702, 10744, 10797, 10814; *Latin America*, 10892, 10967, 11004, 11030, 11041, 11084, 11087; *Middle East*, 11098; *Oceania*, 11330, 11376, 11379; *Elsewhere*, 11453, 11460, 11466, 11487, 11531, 11540, 11546, 11582, 11593, 11596, 11599, 11646, 11687, 11700, 11727, 11750, 11780, 11813, 11848; *Bibliography*, 11977, 11994, 12027, 12067, 12070, 12098. See also STUDENTS.

Elites, *Australia*, 226, 290; *Benin*, 701; *Brazil*, 755, 756, 773; *Canada*, 1327, 1369, 1458; *Costa Rica*, 1844; *Czechoslovakia*, 2025; *Dominican Republic*, 2126; *Egypt*, 2173, 2195, 2214; *El Salvador*, 2263; *Finland*, 2369; *France*, 2548, 2639; *Great Britain*, 3475, 3640; *India*, 4732; *Italy*, 5925; *Ivory Coast*, 6022; *Japan*, 6142; *Liberia*, 6316; *Malaysia*, 6434; *Mexico*, 6495, 6523, 6544, 6567, 6568; *Morocco*, 6674; *Nigeria*, 7230, 7279; *Pakistan*, 7333; *Peru*, 7451, 7481; *Philippines*, 7557, 7590, 7615, 7632, 7635; *Poland*, 7731; *Saudi Arabia*, 7878; *Singapore*, 7916; *South Africa*, 8035, 8106; *Spain*, 8372, 8383; *Sri Lanka*, 8435, 8468, 8479; *Sudan*, 8526; *Sweden*, 8586, 8629; *Tanzania*, 8714; *Thailand*, 8759, 8766; *USSR*, 8948, 9006, 9022, 9134, 9228, 9400, 9408; *USA*, 9508; *Venezuela*, 9761; *Yugoslavia*, 9814; *Zambia*, 9954; *Zimbabwe*, 10025; *Africa*, 10071, 10112, 10204; *Caribbean*, 10442, 10469; *Latin America*, 11017, 11072; *Middle East*, 11143; *Elsewhere*, 11614, 11628, 11661; *Ancient History*, 11869, 11942. See also CLASS CONFLICT.

Emigration, *Iraq*, 5139, 5146
Employment, *Great Britain*, 3717, 3953, 4050, 4077
Equality, *Australia*, 227; *Cuba*, 1874; *Czechoslovakia*, 2072; *Great Britain*, 3944; *Iceland*, 4603
Ethnocide, *Paraguay*, 7420; *Rumania*, 7855. See also GENOCIDE.

Eugenics, *France*, 2603; *Germany*, 2935, 3228, 3229, 3231, 3234
Euthanasia, *Germany*, 2786, 2787, 2871, 3017
Exploitation, *Canada*, 1383, 1453
Expulsion, *Hungary*, 4585

Family, *Algeria*, 53; *Argentina*, 105; *Egypt*, 2234; *France*, 2418; *Germany*, 3172; *Great Britain*, 3464, 4344; *Israel*, 5353, 5354, 5364, 5373, 5516; *Singapore*, 7931; *South Africa*, 8005; *USA*, 9516, 9728
Fascism, *Australia*, 191; *Austria*, 495, 503, 505, 529, 540, 541, 544, 548, 563, 587; *Belgium*, 648-650, 687; *Brazil*, 803; *Canada*, 1013, 1015, 1027; *Chile*, 1558; *Czechoslovakia*, 2076; *Denmark*, 2079, 2086, 2094; *Egypt*, 2163; *Ethiopia*, 2266, 2284, 2315; *Finland*, 2370; *France*, 2381, 2426, 2565, 2636, 2662, 2674, 2675, 2717, 2723, 2725, 2726, 2760, 2776; *Germany*, 2896-2898, 2962, 2969, 2973, 3134, 3179, 3239; *Great Britain*, 3721, 3742, 3778, 3795, 3800, 3838, 3845, 3981, 4000, 4250, 4251, 4279; *Hungary*, 4530, 4532, 4567; *Ireland*, 5177; *Italy*, 5910, 5911, 5915, 5916, 5930, 5934, 5936, 5939, 5950, 5979, 6000, 6014; *Mexico*, 6539; *Netherlands*, 6830, 6851; *Norway*, 7314, 7324; *Peru*, 7466; *Poland*, 7641; *Rumania*, 7792, 7816, 7820, 7824, 7841, 7854, 7868; *Singapore*, 7924; *South Africa*, 8249; *Spain*, 8348, 8392, 8399; *Switzerland*, 8646, 8650; *Uganda*, 8901, 8910; *USSR*, 9384; *USA*, 9669; *Europe*, 10495, 10535, 10541, 10574, 10581, 10607, 10663, 10677, 10695, 10728, 10739, 10743, 10754, 10816, 10819, 10822, 10829, 10836, 10863; *Middle East*, 11076, 11077; *Elsewhere*, 11394, 11422, 11436, 11442, 11500, 11682, 11694, 11735, 11836; *Bibliography*, 12076, 12117. See also RIGHT-WING EXTREMISM.

1030 SUBJECT INDEX

Feudalism, *China*, 1761; *Nigeria*, 7268; *Poland*, 7720; *Europe*, 10751

Forced labor, *Australia*, 300; *China*, 1733; *Germany*, 2936, 3211; *India*, 4816, 4893, 4916; *Mauritius*, 6482; *Myanmar*, 6710; *Peru*, 7487; *Thailand*, 8749; *Turkey*, 8836; *USSR*, 9158, 9310, 9311; *USA*, 9498, 9625, 9703, 9733; *Zimbabwe*, 10022; *Africa*, 10080, 10133, 10217; *Asia*, 10312; *Europe*, 10591; *Latin America*, 10891, 10989, 10995, 11065; *Oceania*, 11238; *Elsewhere*, 11522, 11683; *Ancient History*, 11867. See also SLAVERY.

Genocide, *Bangladesh*, 609, 628, 637; *Brazil*, 764, 841; *Burundi*, 955, 957-960, 964, 968, 969; *Cambodia*, 971, 973, 974, 980; *Canada*, 1205; *Germany*, 3041, 3057, 3058, 3068, 3088, 3104, 3196; *Great Britain*, 3562; *Guatemala*, 4390; *India*, 4853; *Nicaragua*, 7066; *Nigeria*, 7271; *Paraguay*, 7418, 7419, 7423; *Rumania*, 7798, 7859; *Turkey*, 8792, 8797, 8798, 8802, 8811, 8812, 8815, 8829, 8832, 8833, 8837, 8842, 8851, 8866, 8875, 8877-8879; *USSR*, 9317; *USA*, 9525, 9638; *Yugoslavia*, 9804, 9869, 9893; *Europe*, 10589, 10643, 10724, 10773, 10827; *Elsewhere*, 11429, 11441, 11471, 11472, 11483, 11547, 11566, 11579, 11632-11634, 11638; *Bibliography*, 12022. See also ETHNICIDE and HOLOCAUST.

Gypsies, *Austria*, 508, 524, 589, 594; *Bulgaria*, 941; *Czechoslovakia*, 1985, 2023, 2073; *Finland*, 2360; *France*, 2410, 2558, 2773; *Germany*, 2859, 2870, 2912, 2942, 2949, 2950, 2976, 2977, 3010, 3071, 3094, 3117, 3129, 3210; *Great Britain*, 3709, 4047, 4107, 4219; *Hungary*, 4558, 4577, 4593, 4599; *Ireland*, 5193; *Italy*, 6004; *Norway*, 7310; *Rumania*, 7793, 7819; *Spain*, 8390, 8393, 8400, 8404, 8413; *Sweden*, 8625, 8627; *Switzerland*, 8666; *USSR*, 9259; *Yugoslavia*, 9881; *Europe*, 10509, 10518, 10550, 10615, 10616, 10633, 10675, 10679, 10680, 10713, 10764, 10771, 10785, 10786, 10809, 10815, 10875; *Elsewhere*, 11575, 11652; *Bibliography*, 11965, 12011. See also HOLOCAUST.

Harijans, *India*, 4658, 4700, 4860, 4948

Health, *Angola*, 86; *Australia*, 354, 402, 437; *Bangladesh*, 612, 613, 626; *Botswana*, 727, 732; *Brazil*, 785, 790, 809, 886, 894, 895; *Bulgaria*, 934; *Cameroon*, 990; *Canada*, 1179, 1232, 1277, 1298; *China*, 1714, 1715, 1739; *Colombia*, 1806, 1821; *Costa Rica*, 1841; *Cuba*, 1883, 1895, 1949, 1959; *Czechoslovakia*, 2059; *Egypt*, 2206; *Ethiopia*, 2314; *France*, 2372, 2451; *Germany*, 2820, 2821, 2823, 2856, 2889, 3062, 3099, 3186; *Ghana*, 3268; *Great Britain*, 3361, 3374, 3514, 3540, 3568, 3639, 3649, 3657, 3688, 3703, 3706, 3723, 3788, 3811, 3834, 3835, 3959, 3983, 4001, 4011, 4023, 4026, 4053, 4110, 4113, 4114, 4138, 4140, 4152, 4173, 4184, 4236, 4239, 4288, 4317, 4326, 4335-4337, 4352; *Guinea-Bissau*, 4439; *Guyana*, 4451; *Honduras*, 4513; *Hungary*, 4568; *India*, 4627, 4653, 4777, 4787, 4790, 4803, 4851, 4858, 4944, 4950, 5011; *Indonesia*, 5021, 5054; *Ireland*, 5174, 5192; *Israel*, 5212, 5301, 5358, 5372, 5423, 5457, 5490, 5512, 5630, 5743, 5864; *Kenya*, 6188, 6209, 6213; *Malaysia*, 6389, 6429; *Mauritius*, 6484; *Mexico*, 6560; *Mozambique*, 6685; *Namibia*, 6727, 6738, 6757; *Nepal*, 6778; *Netherlands*, 6831, 6853; *New Zealand*, 6935, 6971; *Nicaragua*, 7018, 7024, 7025, 7027; *Nigeria*, 7206, 7248; *Norway*, 7319; *Peru*, 7465; *Philippines*, 7528, 7547, 7551, 7594, 7620, 7621; *Poland*, 7759; *Portugal*, 7776; *Senegal*, 7895; *Sierra Leone*, 7907; *South Africa*, 7957, 7969, 8028, 8029, 8046, 8207, 8231, 8260, 8269, 8270, 8293, 8299; *Sudan*, 8540; *Sweden*, 8574, 8610;

SUBJECT INDEX 1031

Tanzania, 8707, 8717, 8731; Uruguay, 8920; USSR, 8944, 8986, 9052, 9053, 9238, 9352; USA, 9452, 9569, 9708, 9716, 9729; Zaire, 9919, 9931, 9932; Zimbabwe, 9975; Africa, 10043, 10049, 10094, 10095, 10113, 10135, 10266, 10275, 10290; Asia, 10312, 10333; Europe, 10596, 10637, 10825; Latin America, 10966, 10998, 11034, 11051, 11092; Oceania, 11305, 11310, 11338; Elsewhere, 11396, 11438, 11519, 11587, 11679, 11695, 11704, 11734, 11740, 11783, 11822, 11832, 11843; Bibliography, 12002, 12013, 12049. See also HOUSING and LIVING STANDARDS.

History, Afghanistan, 4; Algeria, 33, 49, 50; Argentina, 147, 159; Australia, 187, 273, 335, 345, 350, 373, 396, 415, 454; Austria, 582; Bangladesh, 630; Belgium, 666; Belize, 689; Benin, 694, 698; Cameroon, 1001; Canada, 1076, 1114, 1174, 1270, 1280-1282, 1290, 1293, 1400, 1508; China, 1602, 1604, 1606, 1607, 1639, 1729, 1752; Colombia, 1801, 1810, 1816; Czechoslovakia, 2014, 2021; Denmark, 2092; Egypt, 2161, 2165, 2175, 2190, 2201, 2237; El Salvador, 2251, 2257, 2261; Ethiopia, 2304, 2327, 2328, 2335; France, 2579, 2668; Gabon, 2777; Germany, 2839, 2909; Great Britain, 3379, 3380, 3385, 3400, 3409, 3438, 3529-3531, 3567, 3584, 3644, 3671, 3718, 3887, 3903, 3967, 4021, 4123, 4174; Guatemala, 4408, 4417; Haiti, 4467, 4472, 4485, 4489, 4506; Honduras, 4509; Iceland, 4604, 4609; India, 4648, 4688, 4837, 4862, 4977, 4978; Indonesia, 5057, 5080; Iran, 5103; Iraq, 5161; Ireland, 5173, 5187; Israel, 5802; Jordan, 6159; Kenya, 6205; Kuwait, 6269; Liberia, 6307, 6313, 6317, 6326, 6327; Libya, 6332, 6344; Madagascar, 6355; Malawi, 6364; Malaysia, 6445; Mali, 6457; Mauritius, 6467; Mexico, 6500, 6550, 6562, 6588; Mongolian People's Republic, 6636, 6640, 6648; Morocco, 6661; Mozambique, 6695; Myanmar, 6711; Namibia, 6748; Nepal, 6779; Netherlands, 6858, 6863; New Zealand, 6913, 6934, 6937, 6986, 7003, 7004; Nicaragua, 7043, 7061, 7077, 7088, 7153, 7165; Nigeria, 7211, 7260; Norway, 7327; Panama, 7367, 7376, 7391; Papua-New Guinea, 7396; Paraguay, 7429; Peru, 7441, 7445, 7446, 7460; Philippines, 7508, 7585; Poland, 7669, 7702, 7723, 7739, 7768; Portugal, 7774; Rumania, 7812, 7815; Rwanda, 7875; Saudi Arabia, 7883; Senegal, 7890; Sierra Leone, 7909; Singapore, 7933, 7936, 7941; Somalia, 7946; South Africa, 7984, 8007, 8011, 8048, 8049, 8051, 8084, 8087, 8094, 8159, 8160, 8169, 8206, 8210, 8169; Spain, 8323, 8324, 8331, 8332, 8369, 8387, 8407; Sri Lanka, 8430, 8440; Suriname, 8565; Tanzania, 8703; Thailand, 8738, 8743; Togo, 8767; Turkey, 8791, 8830, 8834, 8861; Uganda, 8897; USSR, 8933-8936, 9057, 9122, 9142, 9148, 9150, 9153, 9155, 9156, 9184, 9240, 9241, 9252, 9277, 9281, 9291, 9306, 9325, 9332, 9359, 9367-9370, 9373, 9375, 9383, 9386, 9399; USA, 9485, 9497, 9522, 9577, 9623, 9624, 9626, 9633, 9656, 9691, 9719, 9721, 9737, 9756; Yugoslavia, 9805, 9822, 9863, 9870, 9873; Zimbabwe, 9962, 9984, 9985, 10019, 10021, 10023; Africa, 10032, 10059, 10078, 10104, 10111, 10116, 10134, 10149, 10154, 10155, 10171, 10185, 10205, 10121, 10215, 10216, 10227, 10239, 10291; Asia, 10315, 10320; Caribbean, 10339, 10345, 10357, 10424, 10433, 10480; Europe, 10528, 10548, 10667, 10670, 10699, 10711, 10736, 10763, 10766, 10846, 10867; Latin America, 10929, 10971, 10985, 11005, 11059, 11093; Middle East, 11094, 11110, 11129, 11130, 11158, 11196; Oceania, 11204, 11216,

11252, 11255, 11260, 11285, 11315, 11350, 11354, 11360, 11380; *Elsewhere*, 11511, 11570, 11697, 11812, 11860, 11922

Holocaust, *Algeria*, 25; *Australia*, 338; *Belgium*, 656, 657, 667, 673-675, 677, 683, 684; *Bulgaria*, 910, 914, 915, 917, 918, 932, 936, 937; *Canada*, 1051; *Czechoslovakia*, 1977, 1979, 1989, 2001, 2003, 2006, 2009, 2010, 2019, 2032, 2041, 2044, 2053, 2056, 2063, 2071; *Denmark*, 2106, 2107; *Finland*, 2364; *France*, 2375, 2448, 2494, 2562, 2571, 2720; *Germany*, 2797, 2832, 2848, 2963, 3015, 3026, 3037, 3079, 3123, 3124, 3167; *Greece*, 3018, 4363-4367, 4369, 4370, 4373, 4377, 4383-4385; *Hungary*, 4523, 4571; *Indonesia*, 5133; *Israel*, 5469, 5489; *Italy*, 5969, 6017; *Japan*, 6084, 6085; *Libya*, 6331; *Mauritius*, 6486; *Morocco*, 6649; *Netherlands*, 6859-6861, 6868, 6874, 6886, 6901, 6904; *Norway*, 7307, 7323, 7329; *Poland*, 7643, 7656, 7666, 7670, 7672, 7691, 7693, 7699, 7700, 7719, 7721, 7734, 7738; *Rumania*, 7787-7789, 7825, 7836, 7845, 7846, 7848; *South Africa*, 8241; *Spain*, 8321, 8362, 8375; *Sri Lanka*, 8474; *Sweden*, 8592, 8636; *Switzerland*, 8652, 8672; *Syria*, 8675; *Tunisia*, 8773; *Turkey*, 8810, 8886; *USSR*, 8940, 8975, 9042, 9049, 9080, 9112, 9196, 9197, 9273, 9355; *USA*, 9526, 9598, 9615; *Yugoslavia*, 9697, 9615, 9808, 9809, 9818, 9838, 9851, 9853, 9878, 9880, 9882, 9903, 9910; *Europe*, 10497, 10510-10512, 10533, 10534, 10579, 10585, 10597, 10622-10624, 10626, 10627, 10641, 10696, 10720, 10723, 10726, 10729, 10732, 10737, 10774, 10804, 10832, 10851, 10852, 10858; *Latin America*, 11040; *Middle East*, 11167, 11174; *Elsewhere*, 11498, 11573, 11592, 11620, 11753, 11821; *Bibliography*, 11975, 11990, 11991, 12020, 12035, 12046, 12054, 12077, 12095, 12123. See also ANTISEMITISM, ETHNICIDE, and GENOCIDE.

Housing, *Australia*, 395; *Brazil*, 873; *Canada*, 1341, 1397, 1412, 1480, 1522; *China*, 1727; *Cuba*, 1914; *Egypt*, 2230, 2231; *France*, 2485, 2707, 2727; *Germany*, 2819, 2988; *Great Britain*, 3492-3497, 3500, 3501, 3503-3513, 3516, 3524, 3534, 3575, 3902, 3969, 4205, 4357; *Hungary*, 4526, 4527, 4560; *India*, 4611, 4757; *Ireland*, 5169; *Israel*, 5265, 5428, 5770; *Kenya*, 6200; *Malawi*, 6367; *Mali*, 6452; *Netherlands*, 6875, 6898; *Nicaragua*, 7023; *Nigeria*, 7209, 7289; *Poland*, 7767; *Singapore*, 7920; *South Africa*, 8209, 8302; *USSR*, 9245, 9246; *Zaire*, 9943; *Zimbabwe*, 10221; *Africa*, 10256, 10271. See also HEALTH and LIVING STANDARDS.

Human Rights, *Argentina*, 112, 132; *Australia*, 390; *Bulgaria*, 905; *Canada*, 1071, 1352, 1402; *Chile*, 1555, 1556, 1576; *China*, 1677, 1689; *Ecuador*, 2138; *El Salvador*, 2250; *Great Britain*, 3762; *Haiti*, 4507; *Indonesia*, 5017; *Iran*, 5082; *Iraq*, 5158; *Israel*, 5444, 5543, 5551, 5687, 5721, 5746-5748, 5815, 5863, 5866, 5882; *Japan*, 6124, 6155; *Korea*, 6241, 6258; *Liberia*, 6320; *Malaysia*, 6408; *Morocco*, 6652; *Myanmar*, 6716; *Namibia*, 6745; *New Zealand*, 6995; *Nigeria*, 7277; *Peru*, 7490; *Philippines*, 7558, 7602; *Rumania*, 7786, 7869; *Sierra Leone*, 7915; *Somalia*, 7947; *South Africa*, 8066, 8071, 8100; *Sudan*, 8549; *Tanzania*, 8716; *Uruguay*, 8923; *USSR*, 8977; *Zaire*, 9833; *Zimbabwe*, 10027; *Africa*, 10036, 10141, 10165; *Asia*, 10307, 10314, 10323; *Caribbean*, 10475; *Europe*, 10560, 10791; *Latin America*, 11067, 11078; *Middle East*, 11140, 11141; *Elsewhere*, 11417, 11444, 11481, 11504, 11509, 11510, 11554, 11644,

SUBJECT INDEX 1033

11658, 11743, 11781, 11807; *Ancient History*, 11941; *Bibliography*, 11988. See also CIVIL RIGHTS.
Humor, *Australia*, 461; *Germany*, 2874, 2875, 3060; *Great Britain*, 3659; *Israel*, 5689; *USSR*, 9095; *USA*, 9470, 9710; *Latin America*, 11090

Immigrants, *Canada*, 1108; *Great Britain*, 3927; *Israel*, 5254; *Netherlands*, 6801
Immigration, *Australia*, 203, 206, 225, 230-232, 243, 306, 314, 316, 324, 331; *Belgium*, 641, 642, 646, 671, 680; *Brazil*, 814; *Canada*, 1007, 1008, 1050, 1066, 1072, 1074, 1075, 1093, 1094, 1096, 1097, 1110, 1132, 1140, 1141, 1169, 1340, 1348, 1399, 1479, 1502, 1526; *China*, 1668; *Cuba*, 1897, 1928; *Denmark*, 2101; *Dominican Republic*, 2114; *France*, 2393, 2403, 2429, 2431, 2453, 2464, 2481, 2491, 2493, 2502, 2505, 2510, 2515, 2523, 2530, 2535, 2537, 2540, 2544-2546, 2551, 2552, 2567, 2568, 2573, 2576, 2594, 2597, 2619, 2627, 2643, 2646, 2647, 2652, 2686, 2687, 2745, 2772; *Germany*, 2798, 2805, 2806, 2810, 2827, 2831, 2837, 2842, 2852, 2867-2869, 2886, 2887, 2893, 2895, 2917, 2921, 2944, 2955, 2965, 2987, 2996, 2997, 3008, 3019, 3056, 3059, 3069, 3097, 3130, 3131, 3143-3145, 3152, 3157, 3163, 3201, 3221, 3225, 3246, 3341, 3349; *Great Britain*, 3357, 3368, 3446, 3518, 3522, 3523, 3526, 3806, 3819, 3820, 3861, 3880, 3926, 3992, 4016, 4043, 4059, 4121, 4166, 4211, 4244, 4281; *Guyana*, 4463; *India*, 4646, 5205-5207, 5209, 5214-5216, 5222-5224, 5228, 5229, 5243, 5246, 5247, 5249, 5257, 5263, 5266, 5268, 5270, 5271, 5274, 5277, 5290-5292, 5302, 5303, 5306, 5309, 5323, 5326, 5333, 5648; *Italy*, 5897, 5987, 5989; *Jordan*, 6158; *Kuwait*, 6272; *Malaysia*, 6376, 6403, 6433; *Mauritius*, 6472; *Netherlands*, 6783, 6807, 6814, 6829, 6843, 6848, 6854, 6893, 6900;

New Zealand, 6944, 6947, 6972; *Singapore*, 7930; *South Africa*, 7971; *Sweden*, 8576, 8601, 8607, 8613; *Switzerland*, 8637, 8641, 8642; *USA*, 9460, 9499, 9609; *Venezuela*, 9762; *Europe*, 10618, 10619, 10631, 10632, 10639, 10656, 10697, 10716, 10756, 10757, 10767, 10784, 10789, 10841; *Latin America*, 10934; *Middle East*, 11171; *Oceania*, 11251; *Elsewhere*, 11463, 11468, 11618, 11837; *Bibliography*, 11985. See also MIGRATION.
Imperialism, *Algeria*, 60; *Angola*, 82, 85; *Australia*, 202, 211; *Belize*, 693; *Cameroon*, 995; *Canada*, 1186; *China*, 1665, 1688, 1692, 1720; *Cuba*, 1938, 1963; *Cyprus*, 1970; *Dominican Republic*, 2123; *Egypt*, 2239, 2244; *Ethiopia*, 2273; *Finland*, 2338; *France*, 2509, 2641, 2649, 2807; *Ghana*, 3262; *Great Britain*, 3480, 3758, 3973, 4024, 4033, 4089, 4101, 4163, 4166, 4170, 4215, 4293; *India*, 4632, 4659, 4664, 4673, 4679, 4847; *Indonesia*, 5028, 5030, 5044, 5046, 5076; *Iran*, 5123; *Ireland*, 5178; *Japan*, 6134; *Kenya*, 6227; *Liberia*, 6304; *Morocco*, 6660; *Myanmar*, 6705, 6718; *Namibia*, 6747; *Netherlands*, 6823, 6850, 6908; *New Zealand*, 6916, 6962; *Nicaragua*, 7167; *Nigeria*, 7259, 7276; *Papua-New Guinea*, 7408; *Paraguay*, 7417; *Peru*, 7454, 7492; *Philippines*, 7538, 7544, 7571, 7624; *Sierra Leone*, 7905; *South Africa*, 8184, 8203; *Sri Lanka*, 8473; *Togo*, 8771, 8772; *Uganda*, 8907; *Uruguay*, 8925; *USSR*, 9007, 9019, 9045, 9154, 9301; *USA*, 9442, 9489, 9722; *Zaire*, 9937; *Zambia*, 9960; *Africa*, 10060, 10082, 10087, 10103, 10127, 10129, 10223, 10244, 10247, 10268; *Asia*, 10302; *Caribbean*, 10412, 10443, 10453, 10471; *Europe*, 10752; *Latin America*, 10876, 10937, 10961, 10964, 10996, 11011, 11031, 11045; *Middle East*, 11107, 11173, 11180, 11187; *Oceania*, 11210,

1034 SUBJECT INDEX

11233, 11236, 11237, 11241, 11250, 11280, 11287, 11307, 11317, 11331, 11347, 11364, 11370, 11375; *Elsewhere*, 11402, 11404, 11408, 11428, 11432, 11437, 11448, 11562, 11598, 11615, 11624, 11656, 11660, 11698, 11797, 11802, 11808, 11829; *Ancient History*, 11899, 11919. See also COLONIALISM.

Imprisonment, *Israel*, 5556, 5566, 5711. See also CRIME.

Income, Distribution of, *Argentina*, 93; *Australia*, 252, 256, 263, 276, 301, 424, 470; *Austria*, 504; *Bangladesh*, 635; *Brazil*, 888; *Canada*, 1326, 1531; *Chile*, 1571, 1572; *China*, 1673, 1682, 1732, 1763; *Colombia*, 1787, 1788, 1811; *Cuba*, 1856; *Denmark*, 2081; *Egypt*, 2153, 2208; *Germany*, 2947; *Great Britain*, 3486, 3491, 3724, 3730, 3812, 3859, 3956, 4051, 4100, 4258, 4259, 4283; *Greece*, 4376, 4381; *Hungary*, 4533, 4535; *India*, 4687, 4780, 4845, 4941, 4970; *Indonesia*, 5040, 5070, 5077, 5078, 5081; *Israel*, 5258, 5312, 5604; *Ivory Coast*, 6025; *Japan*, 6154; *Jordan*, 6161; *Kenya*, 6172; *Korea*, 6246, 6247, 6251, 6255; *Liberia*, 6302; *Malaysia*, 6400; *Mexico*, 6547, 6555; *Netherlands*, 6825, 6844, 6866, 6869, 6877, 6891; *Nicaragua*, 7014; *Nigeria*, 7197, 7203, 7207, 7296; *Norway*, 7331; *Pakistan*, 7338, 7339, 7344, 7345, 7349, 7351, 7358; *Panama*, 7364; *Peru*, 7494; *Philippines*, 7509, 7579, 7628; *Poland*, 7675, 7676; *Singapore*, 7932; *South Africa*, 7949, 8017, 8045, 8173, 8248, 8276; *Sri Lanka*, 8437, 8445, 8449; *Sweden*, 8582; *Switzerland*, 8660; *Thailand*, 8745, 8746; *Turkey*, 8801; *USSR*, 8972, 9044; *Yugoslavia*, 9827, 9828, 9916; *Africa*, 10105; *Asia*, 10300, 10318; *Caribbean*, 10354, 10383, 10384, 10410; *Europe*, 10519, 10738, 10768, 10817, 10834, 10843, 10872; *Latin America*, 10879, 10900, 10940, 11086; *Elsewhere*, 11490, 11565, 11577, 11708, 11789, 11794, 11795, 11830, 11845, 11846. See also WEALTH, DISTRIBUTION OF.

Indigenous people, *Argentina*, 99, 107, 124, 149; *Bolivia*, 705, 706; *Brazil*, 766, 787, 798, 800, 842, 850, 865, 871, 892, 898; *Canada*, 1176, 1184, 1194, 1197, 1201, 1202, 1204, 1208, 1222, 1238, 1239, 1257; *Chile*, 1547, 1548, 1574; *Colombia*, 1786, 1795; *Ecuador*, 2136, 2142, 2150; *Finland*, 2337, 2340, 2346, 2347, 2357, 2361, 2363, 2366; *Guatemala*, 4392, 4410; *Guyana*, 4450, 4459; *India*, 4657, 4689, 4698, 4836, 4884, 4898, 4920, 4921, 4947, 4959, 4984, 4993, 5001; *Jordan*, 6162; *Malawi*, 6369; *Malaysia*, 6417, 6418; *Mexico*, 6503, 6589, 6632; *Namibia*, 6764; *New Zealand*, 6913-6915, 6917, 6919, 6920, 6923, 6924, 6926-6928, 6931-6936, 6938, 6940, 6941, 6948-6951, 6955, 6958-6960, 6963, 6966-6973, 6975-6980, 6982-6988, 7004, 7005, 7007-7011; *Nicaragua*, 7048-7057, 7059, 7060, 7062-7065, 7067, 7068, 7071-7076, 7078-7087, 7089-7100, 7102-7110, 7112-7152, 7154-7164, 7166, 7169-7178, 7180-7195; *Norway*, 7315, 7332; *Panama*, 7372; *Paraguay*, 7422; *Peru*, 7432, 7457; *Philippines*, 7532, 7541, 7593, 7596, 7613; *South Africa*, 7987, 8041; *Sweden*, 8570, 8573, 8587, 8632; *Tunisia*, 8781; *USA*, 9700; *Venezuela*, 9750, 9756; *Vietnam*, 9767; *Africa*, 10279; *Caribbean*, 10367; *Europe*, 10513, 10557, 10665, 10794, 10805, 10826, 10840; *Latin America*, 10890, 10908, 10920, 10939, 10960, 10969, 10976, 10992, 11029, 11068, 11069; *Oceania*, 11200, 11273, 11279; *Elsewhere*, 11398, 11416, 11457, 11601, 11604; *Bibliography*, 11989, 12058, 12068, 12112, 12120. See also COLONIALISM.

SUBJECT INDEX 1035

Inequality, *Australia*, 310, 321; *Austria*, 506, 512, 532; *Brazil*, 903; *Canada*, 1344, 1394, 1436, 1456, 1482, 1491; *China*, 1666, 1684; *Czechoslovakia*, 2030; *France*, 2501, 2533, 2689, 2701; *Germany*, 2812, 3014; *Great Britain*, 3744, 3842, 3847, 4091, 4105, 4356; *India*, 4677, 4734, 4776, 4789, 4956; *Indonesia*, 5016; *Israel*, 5601, 5848; *Kenya*, 6173; *Mexico*, 6522, 6554, 6586; *Nigeria*, 7196, 7243, 7295; *Pakistan*, 7336; *Papua-New Guinea*, 7407; *Poland*, 7663; *Sierra Leone*, 7913; *Singapore*, 7921; *South Africa*, 8155; *Spain*, 8333; *Sudan*, 8508, 8531; *Sweden*, 8617; *Tanzania*, 8732; *Thailand*, 8754; *USSR*, 8930, 9035, 9205; *USA*, 9451, 9588; *Yugoslavia*, 9917; *Zimbabwe*, 9980; *Africa*, 10066; *Caribbean*, 10401, 10447, 10450; *Europe*, 10666, 10669, 10678; *Latin America*, 10899; *Oceania*, 11239, 11278, 11368; *Elsewhere*, 11676; *Ancient History*, 11875
Inquisition, *Mexico*, 6545, 6546, 6558, 6559, 6578; *Portugal*, 7773, 7778, 7780; *Spain*, 8363, 8388; *Europe*, 10770. See also RELIGION.
Internment, *Canada*, 1031, 1068, 1092, 1099, 1100, 1113, 1116, 1439, 1440
Islam, *Iran*, 5085; *Kenya*, 6211; *Malaysia*, 6420, 6424; *Morocco*, 6671; *Philippines*, 7539, 7564; *Yugoslavia*, 9840, 9849. See also RELIGION.

Kahane, Meir, *Israel*, 5279, 5298, 5316, 5324, 5328, 5386, 5435, 5437, 5549, 5661, 5730, 5829, 5840. See also RIGHT-WING EXTREMISM.
Kurds, *Iran*, 5089, 5091-5093, 5099; *Iraq*, 5137, 5147, 5148, 5152, 5153, 5168. See also MINORITIES.

Labor, *Argentina*, 151; *Australia*, 199, 208, 255, 271, 279, 462; *Austria*, 549; *Bolivia*, 703, 713; *Botswana*, 724; *Brazil*, 737, 761, 866; *Canada*, 1121, 1154, 1237, 1330, 1343, 1476, 1477, 1488; *Chile*, 1565, 1569; *China*, 1667, 1676, 1704, 1708, 1711, 1722, 1745; *Costa Rica*, 1827; *Cuba*, 1937; *Dominican Republic*, 2110; *Egypt*, 2191; *France*, 2549, 2566, 2757; *Germany*, 2946, 2964, 3016, 3020, 3034, 3184, 3217, 3218; *Ghana*, 3269; *Great Britain*, 3371, 3441, 3448, 3517, 3532, 3621, 3695, 3715, 3727, 3731, 3870, 3893, 3912, 3921, 3963, 3985, 4017, 4069, 4070, 4082, 4198, 4223, 4268, 4300; *Guatemala*, 4397; *Guyana*, 4458, 4462; *Haiti*, 4466; *India*, 4666, 4686, 4701, 4797, 4892, 4902-4904, 4955, 4963; *Iraq*, 5144; *Ireland*, 5196; *Israel*, 5390, 5414, 5496, 5548, 5606, 5631, 5632, 5664, 5724, 5735, 5792-5794, 5798, 5842, 5867; *Italy*, 5909, 5956, 6001; *Japan*, 6105; *Kenya*, 6168, 6185; *Korea*, 6233; *Kuwait*, 6270; *Liberia*, 6329; *Malaysia*, 6379, 6396, 6402, 6409, 6432; *Mexico*, 6492, 6496, 6537, 6548, 6556, 6575, 6599, 6624; *Namibia*, 6733, 6739, 6771, 6772; *New Zealand*, 6931, 6961; *Panama*, 7377, 7378, 7384; *Papua-New Guinea*, 7410; *Peru*, 7453, 7540; *Philippines*, 7591, 7631; *Poland*, 7716, 7749; *Singapore*, 7925; *South Africa*, 7966, 8016, 8018, 8021, 8078, 8085, 8105, 8121, 8134, 8149, 8162, 8175, 8191, 8195, 8278; *Suriname*, 8558, 8559; *Tanzania*, 8708; *Uganda*, 8892; *USSR*, 9068, 9218, 9419; *USA*, 9529, 9556; *Zaire*, 9925; *Zambia*, 9950; *Zimbabwe*, 9963, 9994, 10020; *Africa*, 10084, 10189, 10250; *Asia*, 10298; *Caribbean*, 10340, 10390, 10422; *Europe*, 10517, 10543, 10709, 10813, 10856; *Latin America*, 10894, 11013, 11053; *Middle East*, 11102, 11124; *Oceania*, 11215, 11231; *Elsewhere*, 11730, 11809; *Bibliography*, 12012. See also CLASS CONFLICT.

1036 SUBJECT INDEX

Land, *Algeria*, 68; *Australia*, 325, 352, 387, 389, 421, 425-427, 438, 440, 449, 465, 478, 480; *Bangladesh*, 632; *Brazil*, 782, 856; *Canada*, 1178, 1196, 1209, 1227, 1235, 1245, 1253, 1274, 1288; *Colombia*, 1812; *Egypt*, 2232; *El Salvador*, 2253, 2256; *Guatemala*, 4405, 4420; *India*, 4643, 4691, 4692, 4800, 4810, 4811, 4913, 4961; *Iran*, 5086, 5109; *Iraq*, 5143; *Ireland*, 5199; *Kenya*, 6198, 6215; *Malawi*, 6365; *Mozambique*, 6693; *New Zealand*, 6967, 6977, 7005; *Nigeria*, 7250; *Peru*, 7482, 7485; *Philippines*, 7512, 7527, 7562, 7574, 7575; *South Africa*, 8020, 8224; *Uganda*, 8909; *USA*, 9572, 9602, 9693; *Zimbabwe*, 9971, 9995, 10005; *Africa*, 10166; *Asia*, 10304; *Latin America*, 10889, 10901, 10918; *Oceania*, 11225, 11246, 11299, 11362; *Elsewhere*, 11477, 11797; *Ancient History*, 11839

Language, *Algeria*, 42, 74; *Australia*, 166, 217, 250, 317, 385, 455; *Austria*, 502, 513; *Belgium*, 644, 655, 670; *Bulgaria*, 942; *Burkina Faso*, 949; *Canada*, 1078, 1291, 1307, 1317, 1319, 1324, 1337, 1430, 1518, 1530; *Cape Verde Islands*, 1539; *Central African Republic*, 1541; *China*, 1685; *Denmark*, 2103; *Egypt*, 2182, 2218; *Finland*, 2352; *France*, 2522, 2623; *Germany*, 2877, 2892; *Great Britain*, 3333, 3377, 3378, 3399, 3424, 3458, 3537, 3646, 3652, 3653, 3663, 3702, 3823, 3916, 4005, 4098, 4125, 4214, 4216, 4289, 4310; *India*, 4725, 4949; *Indonesia*, 5035, 5069; *Iran*, 5088; *Italy*, 5948, 5957, 5972; *Malaysia*, 6380, 6406, 6436; *Mauritius*, 6469; *Morocco*, 6677; *Netherlands*, 6845, 6890, 6894; *New Zealand*, 6924, 6939; *Nigeria*, 7212, 7214, 7216, 7238; *Norway*, 7321; *Panama*, 7379; *Peru*, 7440; *Poland*, 7659; *South Africa*, 8180; *Spain*, 8316, 8371, 8384, 8412, 8417; *Sri Lanka*, 8451; *Sweden*, 8599; *Switzerland*, 8662, 8670; *Tanzania*, 8712, 8719; *USSR*, 8984, 9001, 9076, 9185, 9280, 9405; *USA*, 9505; *Vietnam*, 9766; *Yugoslavia*, 9829, 9859; *Zaire*, 9921, 9936; *Europe*, 10564, 10818; *Latin America*, 10935; *Oceania*, 11378; *Elsewhere*, 11533, 11558, 11561; *Bibliography*, 12069

Law, *Algeria*, 37; *Argentina*, 96; *Australia*, 201, 218, 307, 340, 343, 363, 364, 381, 384, 391, 433-436, 445; *Austria*, 547, 596; *Belgium*, 662; *Canada*, 1047, 1079, 1180, 1185, 1190, 1193, 1212, 1223, 1224, 1228, 1234, 1242, 1243, 1264, 1284, 1287, 1350, 1401, 1427, 1442, 1466; *China*, 1701, 1724, 1726; *Egypt*, 2210; *France*, 2759; *Germany*, 2915, 2995, 3087, 3118, 3140; *Great Britain*, 3332, 3343, 3362, 3394, 3395, 3422, 3447, 3466, 3738, 3775, 3803, 3827, 3844, 3883, 3915, 3925, 3997, 4019, 4072, 4083-4085, 4137, 4141, 4145, 4218, 4305, 4316, 4334, 4360; *India*, 4735, 4736, 4748, 4804, 4878, 5412; *Israel*, 5413, 5451, 5464, 5552, 5555, 5580, 5581, 5587, 5605, 5621, 5622, 5647, 5694, 5805, 5806, 5878, 5879; *Japan*, 6047, 6066, 6081, 6104, 6108, 6113, 6139; *Kenya*, 6191, 6216; *Korea*, 6259; *Mexico*, 6504; *Netherlands*, 6855; *New Zealand*, 6955, 6959, 6973, 6976, 6997, 7007, 7008, 7011; *Nigeria*, 7231; *Papua-New Guinea*, 7398; *Peru*, 7431, 7438; *South Africa*, 7955, 7991, 7996, 8034, 8059, 8061, 8080, 8096, 8098, 8181, 8185, 8211, 8214, 8216, 8283, 8284; *Sudan*, 8522; *Tanzania*, 8726; *USSR*, 9140; *USA*, 9454, 9481, 9560, 9592, 9672, 9712, 9738; *Zimbabwe*, 9982, 10003, 10004; *Europe*, 10613, 10682; *Latin America*, 11015; *Middle East*, 11103; *Oceania*, 11242, 11316, 11349; *Elsewhere*, 11834; *Bibliography*, 11987, 12021

Libraries, *South Africa*, 7986, 8179, 8286; *USA*, 9461, 9550, 9578; *Africa*, 10040, 10222

SUBJECT INDEX 1037

Literacy, *China*, 1636, 1782; *Egypt*, 2245; *Ethiopia*, 2288, 2332; *France*, 2466, 2500, 2602, 2603, 2645, 2709, 2756; *Great Britain*, 3628, 3999; *Haiti*, 4484; *Spain*, 8373; *Tanzania*, 8705; *USSR*, 9064, 9239; *Europe*, 10568; *Latin America*, 10884; *Elsewhere*, 11433, 11559, 11588, 11653; *Bibliography*, 12018. See also EDUCATION.

Literature, *Albania*, 18; *Australia*, 302, 318, 319, 394, 458; *Austria*, 523; *Brazil*, 739, 808; *Cameroon*, 1000, 1002; *Canada*, 1084, 1267, 1380; *Cuba*, 1851, 1865, 1933; *Dominican Republic*, 2109; *France*, 2483, 2531, 2767; *Germany*, 2789, 2932, 2953, 3089, 3133, 3197; *Great Britain*, 3338, 3363, 3419, 3469, 3669, 3970, 4012, 4104, 4354; *Greece*, 4368; *India*, 4615, 4740, 4998; *Israel*, 5264, 5349, 5453, 5475, 5508, 5523, 5619, 5668, 5680, 5702, 5726, 5729, 5741; *Malaysia*, 6410; *Mauritius*, 6470; *Namibia*, 6742; *New Zealand*, 6945, 6984; *Philippines*, 7537, 7561, 7600, 7604; *Senegal*, 7887; *Singapore*, 7926; *South Africa*, 8110, 8113, 8146, 8212, 8242, 8287; *Turkey*, 8859; *USSR*, 8987, 9012, 9036, 9188, 9258; *USA*, 9482, 9591, 9658, 9661, 9684; *Venezuela*, 9752; *Africa*, 10029, 10114, 10151, 10152, 10159, 10161, 10177, 10203, 10219, 10230, 10284, 10294; *Caribbean*, 10379; *Middle East*, 11105; *Oceania*, 11356, 11366; *Elsewhere*, 11514

Living standards, *Argentina*, 126; *Australia*, 184, 213, 247, 265; *Belgium*, 653; *Brazil*, 859; *Canada*, 1347; *Chile*, 1575; *China*, 1616, 1683, 1703, 1710, 1755, 1781; *Congo*, 1826; *Czechoslovakia*, 1978, 2012, 2049, 2065; *Denmark*, 2082; *Finland*, 2345, 2367; *Gabon*, 2779, 2780; *Germany*, 2857, 3109, 3248; *Great Britain*, 3647, 4080, 4175, 4208, 4355; *Hungary*, 4555; *Indonesia*, 5022; *Iran*, 5084; *Ivory Coast*, 6018; *Japan*, 6054, 6152;

Kenya, 6174; *Korea*, 6265, 6266; *Mexico*, 6584; *Norway*, 7325; *Norway*, 7769; *Rumania*, 7826; *Spain*, 8313; *Sri Lanka*, 8433, 8485; *Sweden*, 8571, 8578, 8602, 8629; *USSR*, 9010, 9088, 9344; *USA*, 9471, 9523, 9645; *Asia*, 10332; *Europe*, 10577; *Latin America*, 10880, 10923, 11028; *Elsewhere*, 11458, 11495, 11538

Mass media, *Australia*, 351, 472; *Austria*, 531; *Canada*, 1041, 1061, 1249, 1363; *China*, 1593; *Czechoslovakia*, 2062; *France*, 2516, 2527, 2713, 2716, 2746; *Germany*, 2916, 2919, 2978, 3048, 3151, 3185; *Great Britain*, 3397, 3428, 3546, 3655, 3686, 3836, 3854, 3899, 3910, 3938, 3957, 3995, 4093, 4217, 4245, 4247, 4274; *India*, 4709, 4807, 4996; *Israel*, 5502, 5511, 5535, 5626, 5737, 5760, 5795, 5808; *Italy*, 5988; *Malaysia*, 6444; *Mexico*, 6564; *Netherlands*, 6798; *New Zealand*, 6928; *Nigeria*, 7297; *South Africa*, 8056, 8057, 8263, 8266, 8290; *Spain*, 8334; *Switzerland*, 8647; *USSR*, 9011, 9141, 9152, 9413; *USA*, 9521, 9593, 9594, 9599, 9637, 9675, 9732, 9735; *Yugoslavia*, 9892; *Africa*, 10276; *Latin America*, 10936; *Oceania*, 11372; *Elsewhere*, 11571; *Bibliography*, 12109. See also PUBLIC OPINION.

Migration, *Poland*, 7650; *USA*, 9544, 9564, 9634; *Europe*, 10491. See also IMMIGRATION.

Militarism, *Argentina*, 145, 150, 162; *Australia*, 272; *Austria*, 543, 606; *Brazil*, 740, 796, 811; *Canada*, 1107, 1339; *China*, 1608; *Colombia*, 1791; *Czechoslovakia*, 2078; *France*, 2478; *Germany*, 2815, 2939; *Great Britain*, 3696; *Guatemala*, 4396; *Indonesia*, 5065; *Israel*, 5220, 5242, 5391, 5501; *Japan*, 6149; *Pakistan*, 7342; *Philippines*, 7589, 7606, 7640; *Syria*, 8678; *Togo*, 8769; *USSR*, 8965, 9144; *Africa*, 10091; *Latin America*,

11049; *Oceania*, 11318, 11342; *Elsewhere*, 11585, 11725
Minorities, *Afghanistan*, 9, 10; *Algeria*, 66; *Austria*, 486-488, 493, 498, 517, 518, 521, 526, 581, 592; *Bangladesh*, 617, 623, 624, 638; *Belgium*, 661, 669; *Bolivia*, 714; *Bulgaria*, 904, 906, 908, 913, 916, 920-925, 927-929, 935, 939, 940, 944-947; *Canada*, 1101, 1143, 1203, 1221, 1393, 1423, 1424, 1429, 1510; *Czechoslovakia*, 1973, 1998, 1999, 2000, 2008, 2031, 2034, 2035, 2036, 2048, 2060, 2066, 2067, 2075; *Denmark*, 2098; *Egypt*, 2157, 2177, 2196, 2197, 2198, 2203, 2204, 2215, 2222, 2226, 2240; *Ethiopia*, 2267, 2269, 2278, 2282, 2291; *Finland*, 2341, 2356, 2368; *France*, 2384, 2395, 2399, 2400, 2426, 2488, 2511, 2620, 2629, 2659, 2661; *Germany*, 2840, 2861, 2862, 2866, 2907, 2911, 2993, 3004, 3021, 3137, 3143, 3145, 3146, 3169, 3181, 3192, 3199; *Great Britain*, 3345, 3615, 3809, 3986; *Greece*, 4372, 4374; *Guyana*, 4448; *Haiti*, 4496; *Hungary*, 4541, 4545, 4546, 4551, 4569, 4574, 4580, 4581, 4584, 4590, 4591, 4594, 4596, 4598; *India*, 4612, 4645, 4727, 4761, 4926; *Indonesia*, 5013, 5025, 5026, 5037, 5053, 5075; *Iran*, 5090, 5094, 5095, 5097, 5105, 5110, 5111, 5116, 5119, 5126, 5128, 5131; *Iraq*, 5134, 5162; *Ireland*, 5171, 5195; *Israel*, 5362, 5380, 5617, 5821-5823, 5887, 5889; *Italy*, 5896, 5898, 5899, 5919, 5931, 5944, 5949, 5952, 5991, 6006, 6008; *Japan*, 6030, 6031, 6033, 6034, 6038, 6040, 6041, 6043, 6046, 6048, 6049, 6052, 6058, 6071, 6073-6078, 6089-6091, 6094-6096, 6098, 6100, 6109, 6111, 6112, 6117-6119, 6126, 6127, 6129, 6131, 6132, 6138, 6141, 6143-6145, 6156; *Jordan*, 6163, 6166; *Kenya*, 6171, 6217, 6219, 6221; *Laos*, 6275, 6280; *Lebanon*, 6282, 6298; *Malawi*, 6359; *Malaysia*, 6451, 6453; *Mexico*, 6582; *Morocco*, 6659; *Myanmar*, 6704, 6712, 6714, 6723; *Netherlands*, 6786, 6788-6790, 6794, 6797, 6800, 6812, 6846, 6864, 6865, 6870-6873, 6895, 6899, 6902; *New Zealand*, 6927, 6936, 6942, 6943, 6948, 6950, 6964, 6966, 6969; *Norway*, 7330; *Pakistan*, 7361; *Peru*, 7475; *Philippines*, 7500, 7514, 7559, 7563, 7572, 7578, 7601, 7627, 7638; *Poland*, 7646, 7667, 7677, 7681, 7682, 7686, 7687, 7694, 7695, 7701, 7709, 7712, 7713, 7736, 7745, 7750, 7756, 7762, 7763, 7765, 7766; *Rumania*, 7795, 7797, 7800, 7805-7808, 7810, 7813, 7821, 7823, 7827, 7828, 7830, 7831, 7833, 7842, 7851, 7852, 7857, 7858, 7864-7867; *Singapore*, 7938, 7942; *South Africa*, 8074, 8176; *Spain*, 8337, 8346; *Sri Lanka*, 8431, 8443; *Sweden*, 8631, 8636; *Switzerland*, 8645, 8653, 8655; *Syria*, 8685, 8690, 8692, 8693; *Thailand*, 8736, 8741, 8744, 8747, 8758, 8764; *Yugoslavia*, 8789, 8790, 8795, 8799, 8800, 8825, 8827, 8840, 8843, 8849, 8854-8857, 8865, 8876, 8880, 8884; *Uganda*, 8903, 8912; *USSR*, 8942, 8995, 9037, 9058, 9065, 9072, 9116, 9145, 9167, 9173, 9175, 9203, 9210, 9212, 9220, 9313, 9326, 9337, 9345; *USA*, 9576, 9646, 9730; *Vietnam*, 9768-9770, 9773, 9776, 9780-9785, 9787, 9806, 9807, 9815, 9820, 9821, 9825, 9836, 9845, 9857, 9868, 9886, 9890, 9891, 9909; *Africa*, 10126, 10269, 10272; *Asia*, 10327, 10337; *Caribbean*, 10400; *Europe*, 10487, 10492, 10506, 10508, 10524, 10544, 10552, 10553, 10561, 10566, 10569, 10586, 10609, 10614, 10651, 10652, 10659, 10661, 10681, 10689, 10707, 10715, 10733, 10755, 10765, 10783, 10807, 10839; *Latin America*, 10953; *Middle East*, 11101, 11114, 11116, 11126, 11128, 11131, 11136, 11138, 11153, 11157, 11159, 11160, 11162, 11170, 11172, 11178; *Oceania*, 11329, 11385; *Elsewhere*, 11400, 11411, 11412, 11470, 11523, 11528, 11537, 11551, 11583, 11622, 11623, 11630, 11688,

SUBJECT INDEX 1039

11748, 11782, 11804-11806; *Bibliography*, 11964, 11980, 12050, 12052. See also KURDS.

Multicultural education, *Australia*, 234, 240, 304, 333; *Canada*, 1450, 1485; *Great Britain*, 3746, 3779, 3849, 4007, 4111, 4116, 4222, 4286, 4320; *USA*, 9640

Multinational corporations, *Chile*, 1566; *Liberia*, 6308; *Malaysia*, 6450; *Panama*, 7371; *Philippines*, 7586, 7630; *Zimbabwe*, 9987; *Africa*, 10254; *Asia*, 10324. See also CAPITALISM.

National self-determination, *Afghanistan*, 11; *Austria*, 528; *Canada*, 1313, 1321; *Czechoslovakia*, 2069; *Ethiopia*, 2274, 2276; *Finland*, 2353; *France*, 2669, 2751, 2752; *Great Britain*, 3617, 3619, 3654; *Hungary*, 4515, 4556, 4578; *India*, 4995; *Israel*, 5843; *New Zealand*, 6940, 6958; *Poland*, 7707; *Spain*, 8343, 8349, 8365, 8366; *Sudan*, 8513, 8521, 8527; *Switzerland*, 8656; *Tanzania*, 8704; *Turkey*, 8835; *USA*, 9536; *Yugoslavia*, 9810; *Zaire*, 9819; *Middle East*, 11133, 11193; *Oceania*, 11222, 11267, 11274, 11374, 11377; *Elsewhere*, 11838. See also MINORITIES.

Nationalism, *Algeria*, 43; *Angola*, 89; *Argentina*, 148; *Australia*, 179, 414; *Austria*, 536, 546, 559; *Bulgaria*, 919, *Cameroon*, 1003; *Canada*, 1018, 1036, 1315; *China*, 1596, 1633; *Costa Rica*, 1832; *Czechoslovakia*, 1974, 1984, 1992, 2020, 2050; *Egypt*, 2186; *Ethiopia*, 2303; *Finland*, 2355, 2371; *Gabon*, 2378; *Great Britain*, 3625, 3664, 3665, 3674, 3872, 4068, 4224; *Guinea-Bissau*, 4434, 4442; *Hungary*, 4521, 4525, 4570, 4586; *India*, 4663, 4826, 4857, 4971; *Indonesia*, 5031; *Iran*, 5096; *Israel*, 5213, 5620, 5657, 5683, 5736; *Madagascar*, 6358; *Malaysia*, 6425, 6428, 6431; *Mexico*, 6609; *Mongolian People's Republic*,

6639, 6644, 6645; *Morocco*, 6672; *Pakistan*, 7334, 7362; *Philippines*, 7576, 7626, 7629; *Rumania*, 7818, 7834, 7945; *South Africa*, 8010, 8073, 8201, 8250; *Spain*, 8345, 8364, 8367, 8391, 8396, 8407; *Sri Lanka*, 8466; *Sudan*, 8497; *Switzerland*, 8648; *Thailand*, 8753; *USSR*, 8949, 8979, 9038, 9050, 9054, 9063, 9200, 9230, 9242, 9268, 9278, 9293, 9299, 9389; *USA*, 9472, 9692; *Yugoslavia*, 9816, 9823, 9824, 9842, 9864, 9885, 9887, 9907; *Zimbabwe*, 9993; *Africa*, 10259, 10270, 10293; *Caribbean*, 10352, 10386, 10421; *Europe*, 10503, 10646, 10654, 10690, 10730, 10748, 10795, 10799, 10800, 10833; *Middle East*, 11115, 11188; *Oceania*, 11240, 11311, 11340, 11343, 11358, 11359, 11361; *Elsewhere*, 11473, 11512, 11568, 11591, 11784, 11785, 11788, 11811; *Bibliography*, 11968, 12037, 12100

Nazis, *Australia*, 163, 171; *Austria*, 492, 507, 558, 560, 564, 572, 580, 591, 593, 602, 605; *Germany*, 2956, 3027, 3043, 3135, 3153, 3203; *Hungary*, 4528, 4559, 4582; *USA*, 9465. See also DENAZIFICATION and RIGHT-WING EXTREMISM.

Nazism, *Australia*, 245, 266; *Canada*, 1030, 1034, 1056-1058, 1297; *Czechoslovakia*, 1986; *Denmark*, 2104; *Egypt*, 2213; *France*, 2388, 2422, 2435, 2538; *Germany*, 2855, 2881, 2888, 2906, 2908, 2966, 3091, 3119, 3149; *Hungary*, 4519; *Japan*, 6045; *Netherlands*, 6799, 6803, 6821, 6863, 6867, 6889; *Norway*, 7320; *Paraguay*, 7426; *Poland*, 7661; *Rumania*, 7809; *South Africa*, 8069, 8193, 8197, 8245; *Switzerland*, 8654; *USSR*, 9061, 9165, 9260; *USA*, 9561, 9585, 9676; *Europe*, 10546, 10551, 10642, 10645, 10691, 10693, 10722, 10829; *Latin America*, 10948, 11054; *Middle East*, 11194; *Bibliography*, 12032, 12038

1040 SUBJECT INDEX

Neo-colonialism, *Belize*, 691; *Canada*, 1229; *Congo*, 1824; *Gabon*, 2781; *Haiti*, 4503; *Liberia*, 6323; *Malawi*, 6363; *Malaysia*, 6373; *Mauritania*, 6458; *Nigeria*, 7200, 7244, 7305; *Papua-New Guinea*, 7416; *Peru*, 7454; *Philippines*, 7520, 7587, 7611; *Portugal*, 7783; *Zaire*, 9941; *Africa*, 10041, 10053, 10183, 10280. See also COLONIALISM.

Occupation, military, *Afghanistan*, 6; *Albania*, 24; *Austria*, 578; *Belgium*, 663; *Canada*, 1063; *Czechoslovakia*, 2064; *Denmark*, 2085, 2099, 2100, 2102; *Ethiopia*, 2312; *France*, 2730; *Indonesia*, 5058, 5059, 5074; *Israel*, 5338, 5342, 5357, 5359, 5361, 5377, 5394, 5395, 5398, 5405, 5406, 5411, 5415, 5421, 5425, 5443, 5449, 5452, 5483, 5518, 5538, 5541, 5560, 5564, 5569, 5577, 5591, 5593, 5611, 5627, 5640, 5649, 5656, 5662, 5665, 5676, 5677, 5684, 5685, 5695-5697, 5707, 5708, 5713, 5716-5718, 5725, 5744, 5745, 5752, 5754, 5765, 5766, 5767, 5775, 5781-5786, 5797, 5800, 5807, 5812, 5830, 5833, 5856, 5859, 5868, 5869, 5884, 5886, 5890, 5895; *Korea*, 6261; *Netherlands*, 6822, 6832, 6857, 6885, 6907; *New Zealand*, 6999; *Norway*, 7318, 7326; *Poland*, 7683, 7685, 7718, 7751, 7752; *Sri Lanka*, 8492; *USSR*, 9070, 9071, 9131, 9254, 9329, 9342; *USA*, 9431; *Yugoslavia*, 9835, 9855, 9897, 9908; *Caribbean*, 10440; *Europe*, 10539, 10710, 10823; *Oceania*, 11381; *Bibliography*, 12113. See also WAR.

Oppression, *Rwanda*, 7873; *USA*, 9434, 9699; *Zaire*, 9939; *Elsewhere*, 11831

Pacification, *Oceania*, 11228, 11344
Pan-Africanism, *Great Britain*, 3831; *Africa*, 10076, 10107, 10183
Paternalism, *Papua-New Guinea*, 7415; *Elsewhere*, 11496, 11752
Peonage, *Guatemala*, 4419; *Mexico*, 6571

Planning, *Israel*, 5336, 5346, 5459, 5578, 5750; *USA*, 9450, 9685
Pluralism, *France*, 2490, 2693, 2694; *India*, 4710; *Israel*, 5751; *USA*, 9495; *Caribbean*, 10382, 10464, 10479; *Europe*, 10753; *Latin America*, 10963; *Oceania*, 11256; *Elsewhere*, 11480
Police, *Australia*, 382; *Belgium*, 664; *Brazil*, 735; *Canada*, 1225, 1261; *France*, 2705; *Great Britain*, 3396, 3405, 3434, 3502, 3608, 3753, 3805, 3891, 3935, 3948, 3965, 4099, 4112, 4212, 4229, 4237, 4256, 4292, 4307, 4315; *India*, 4628, 4675, 4842; *Netherlands*, 6782; *Nigeria*, 7202, 7222; *Sri Lanka*, 8426. See also STATE VIOLENCE.
Politics, *Afghanistan*, 12; *Albania*, 19; *Angola*, 81; *Argentina*, 134, 142; *Australia*, 288, 311, 341, 376, 398, 457, 468, 475; *Botswana*, 730; *Brazil*, 768; *Burundi*, 962; *Cambodia*, 967; *Canada*, 1029, 1033, 1286, 1387, 1457, 1493; *China*, 1770; *Colombia*, 1802; *Cuba*, 1850; *Czechoslovakia*, 1988; *Dominican Republic*, 2117; *Ecuador*, 2133, 2135; *Egypt*, 2151, 2169, 2189; *France*, 2411, 2702; *Ghana*, 3258; *Great Britain*, 3348, 3358, 3376, 3387, 3398, 3407, 3412, 3417, 3442, 3515, 3598, 3636, 3684, 3687, 3725, 3846, 3884, 3907, 3909, 3945, 3988, 3993, 4060, 4062, 4063, 4066, 4071, 4157, 4321, 4325; *Guatemala*, 4391; *Guinea-Bissau*, 4435, 4543; *India*, 4663, 4827, 4859, 4863, 4866, 4937, 4954, 5012; *Israel*, 5221, 5305, 5388, 5439, 5480, 5492, 5598, 5663, 5682, 5710; *Ivory Coast*, 6020; *Japan*, 6114; *Kuwait*, 6268; *Liberia*, 6314; *Malawi*, 6366; *Malaysia*, 6381; *Mexico*, 6514, 6515, 6525, 6628; *Mongolian People's Republic*, 6643; *Mozambique*, 6682; *Myanmar*, 6721, 6724-6726; *Namibia*, 6743; *Netherlands*, 6876; *New Zealand*, 6949, 6956, 6968, 7009, 7010; *Nicaragua*, 7021; *Nigeria*, 7204,

SUBJECT INDEX 1041

7272, 7282, 7302; *Pakistan*, 7347; *Papua-New Guinea*, 7409; *Philippines*, 7515; *Poland*, 7698; *Saudi Arabia*, 7884; *South Africa*, 8145, 8166, 8196, 8202, 8222, 8261, 8285, 8298; *Spain*, 8395; *Sri Lanka*, 8444, 8446, 8465, 8486, 8495; *Sudan*, 8520, 8533; *Suriname*, 8555; *Sweden*, 8628; *Syria*, 8680; *Thailand*, 8748; *Turkey*, 8806, 8853; *Uganda*, 8902, 8906; *USSR*, 9013, 9040, 9202, 9331, 9338; *USA*, 9643, 9644, 9649, 9711; *Vietnam*, 9786; *Yemen*, 9792; *Zimbabwe*, 9997, 10017; *Africa*, 10252, 10261; *Asia*, 10295; *Caribbean*, 10408, 10426, 10483; *Europe*, 10684; *Latin America*, 10938, 10952; *Middle East*, 11119; *Oceania*, 11205, 11229, 11284, 11296, 11297, 11300, 11301, 11324, 11355, 11363

Poverty, *Australia*, 235, 280, 443; *Bangladesh*, 610, 620, 634, 636; *Belgium*, 668; *Bolivia*, 710; *Botswana*, 720, 723; *Brazil*, 745, 763, 792, 844; *Bulgaria*, 943; *Cambodia*, 975; *Canada*, 1314, 1349, 1432, 1451, 1492, 1506; *Colombia*, 1794; *Dominican Republic*, 2128; *Ecuador*, 2137, 2141, 2144, 2147; *Egypt*, 2223, 2242, 2243; *El Salvador*, 2254; *Ethiopia*, 2306; *Finland*, 2343; *France*, 2396, 2404, 2487, 2499, 2587, 2624, 2625, 2657, 2755; *Germany*, 3047, 3136, 3165; *Great Britain*, 3609, 3622, 3637, 3638, 3735, 3769, 3821, 4032, 4049, 4127, 4182, 4183, 4209, 4213, 4235, 4246, 4276, 4291, 4294, 4329, 4341; *Greece*, 4386; *Haiti*, 4465, 4482, 4499, 4695; *India*, 4772, 4774, 4784, 4805, 4808, 4833, 4874, 4876, 4908, 4942, 4952, 4973, 4975, 4976, 4983, 4990; *Indonesia*, 5014, 5041; *Ireland*, 5191; *Israel*, 5308; *Italy*, 5999; *Japan*, 6037, 6079, 6146; *Kenya*, 6182-6184, 6197, 6199; *Korea*, 6254; *Lebanon*, 6294; *Madagascar*, 6354; *Malawi*, 6368; *Malaysia*, 6374, 6387, 6404; *Mexico*, 6520, 6524, 6541, 6579, 6603, 6627; *Morocco*, 6658; *Myanmar*, 6715; *Netherlands*, 6905; *New Zealand*, 7002; *Nigeria*, 7241, 7246, 7261, 7270; *Panama*, 7386, 7390; *Peru*, 7452; *Philippines*, 7566, 7589, 7592, 7610, 7622; *Poland*, 7665; *South Africa*, 7948, 8044, 8128, 8174, 8190, 8304; *Spain*, 8397; *Sri Lanka*, 8421, 8434; *Sweden*, 8583, 8635; *Switzerland*, 8649, 8668, 8669; *Tanzania*, 8699; *USSR*, 9051, 9225-9227, 9285, 9583; *Zambia*, 9947; *Africa*, 10125, 10142, 10226; *Asia*, 10296, 10303, 10310, 10328; *Caribbean*, 10477; *Europe*, 10608, 10629, 10705, 10734, 10861, 10869; *Latin America*, 10896, 10905, 11016, 11025, 11037, 11046, 11060, 11064; *Middle East*, 11185, 11189; *Oceania*, 11226; *Elsewhere*, 11474, 11513, 11555, 11674, 11773; *Ancient History*, 11856, 11903. See also INCOME, DISTRIBUTION OF and WEALTH, DISTRIBUTION OF.

Power, *Australia*, 283; *Brazil*, 778, 780; *Canada*, 3261; *India*, 4911

Public opinion, *Canada*, 1020, 1059; *China*, 1663; *Germany*, 2389, 2665; *Israel*, 5857; *Italy*, 5946; *Netherlands*, 6852; *USA*, 9670, 9739; *Caribbean*, 10388. See also MASS MEDIA.

Racial attacks, *Great Britain*, 3889, 3890, 3928, 3943, 3949, 3950, 3991, 4058, 4090, 4128, 4129, 4134, 4143, 4144, 4147

Racism, *Argentina*, 129, 164; *Australia*, 190, 195, 196, 245, 253, 262, 274, 275, 282, 284, 289, 296, 309, 315, 330, 332, 369, 378, 392, 413, 418, 422, 423, 446, 447, 451, 460, 464, 469; *Belgium*, 654, 660; *Brazil*, 744, 765, 772, 806, 817, 838, 840, 860, 875, 880, 881, 885, 890, 893, 896, 897; *Cambodia*, 972; *Canada*, 1065, 1070, 1073, 1077, 1080, 1087, 1090, 1091, 1103-1106, 1111, 1112, 1117, 1118, 1158, 1160, 1170, 1198-1200,

SUBJECT INDEX

1213, 1216, 1259, 1265, 1272, 1289, 1325, 1333, 1346, 1353, 1360, 1365, 1373, 1398, 1407, 1410, 1413, 1421, 1428, 1444, 1461, 1473, 1486, 1487, 1511, 1512, 1514, 1519, 1523, 1534; *China*, 1680, 1687, 1735; *Colombia*, 1819; *Congo*, 1822; *Cuba*, 1849, 1866, 1871, 1873, 1884-1887, 1891, 1900, 1905, 1907, 1911, 1912, 1916, 1917, 1922, 1948, 1956, 1957, 1961; *Dominican Republic*, 2120, 2127; *Ecuador*, 2134, 2145; *Egypt*, 2211; *Ethiopia*, 2290; *France*, 2383, 2390, 2402, 2405, 2412, 2420, 2430, 2447, 2463, 2467, 2473, 2479, 2486, 2497, 2508, 2513, 2524, 2526, 2528, 2532, 2536, 2554, 2555, 2563, 2564, 2575, 2577, 2580, 2586, 2588, 2592, 2593, 2598, 2600, 2601, 2613, 2614, 2638, 2655, 2656, 2664, 2673, 2678, 2710-2712, 2714, 2715, 2724, 2733, 2735-2739, 2741, 2742, 2744, 2749, 2753, 2761; *Germany*, 2784, 2785, 2791, 2853, 2884, 2885, 2904, 2926, 2957, 2975, 3001, 3009, 3032, 3077, 3101, 3102, 3106, 3110, 3114, 3120, 3121, 3142, 3162, 3164, 3206, 3215, 3230, 3233; *Great Britain*, 3265, 3327, 3347, 3351, 3382, 3386, 3410, 3457, 3462, 3472, 3519, 3521, 3527, 3538, 3616, 3643, 3648, 3677, 3679, 3680, 3701, 3711-3714, 3719, 3720, 3749, 3750, 3755, 3765, 3767, 3770, 3771, 3785, 3810, 3817, 3832, 3840, 3865, 3881, 3882, 3898, 3906, 3929, 3931, 3952, 3974, 3980, 3982, 3989, 4010, 4013, 4014, 4038, 4048, 4064, 4075, 4086, 4087, 4103, 4142, 4151, 4153, 4164, 4172, 4225, 4231, 4233, 4234, 4248, 4249, 4263, 4277, 4287, 4290, 4340, 4345, 4349; *Guyana*, 4445; *Haiti*, 4478, 4502; *India*, 4712, 4754, 4819, 4829, 4856, 4880, 5009; *Ireland*, 5180, 5202; *Israel*, 5250, 5284, 5285, 5310, 5321, 5495, 5517, 5625, 5636, 5801, 5847, 5852; *Italy*, 5914, 5928, 5938, 5961, 5978, 5982, 5990, 5994, 6002, 6007; *Japan*, 6032, 6050, 6080, 6130, 6144, 6151, 6153; *Kenya*, 6229; *Malaysia*, 6392, 6395, 6440; *Mexico*, 6493, 6501, 6507, 6518, 6521, 6530, 6561, 6563, 6594, 6617; *Morocco*, 6678; *Netherlands*, 6767, 6791, 6795, 6796, 6815, 6816, 6842, 6880, 6896, 6911; *New Zealand*, 6915, 6918, 6922, 6923, 6929, 6932, 6941, 6952, 6970, 6972-6974, 6979, 7000, 7006; *Nigeria*, 7283; *Norway*, 7311; *Panama*, 7363, 7373, 7392; *Papua-New Guinea*, 7402; *Paraguay*, 7425; *Peru*, 7464; *Philippines*, 7636; *Portugal*, 7770; *Rwanda*, 7872; *Singapore*, 7929; *South Africa*, 7962, 7970, 7979, 8039, 8065, 8075, 8083, 8091, 8116, 8182, 8204, 8217, 8219, 8259, 8277; *Spain*, 8360; *Sri Lanka*, 8422, 8453, 8494, 8499; *Sweden*, 8566, 8604-8606, 8623; *USSR*, 9307, 9407; *USA*, 9432, 9440, 9447, 9449, 9456, 9463, 9466, 9467, 9477, 9484, 9487, 9492, 9510, 9531, 9538, 9539, 9559, 9565, 9571, 9573, 9579, 9580, 9587, 9596, 9597, 9630, 9636, 9647, 9655, 9657, 9671, 9674, 9687, 9694, 9695, 9598, 9701, 9704-9706, 9718, 9723, 9724, 9726, 9727, 9734, 9740; *Vietnam*, 9774; *Zimbabwe*, 9966, 9989, 9991, 10012; *Africa*, 10037, 10061, 10065, 10175, 10253; *Asia*, 10297, 10306; *Caribbean*, 10394, 10402, 10413, 10415; *Europe*, 10485, 10514, 10521, 10531, 10573, 10576, 10604, 10638, 10658, 10664, 10731, 10740, 10741, 10760, 10810, 10811, 10842, 10845, 10857; *Latin America*, 10914, 10921, 10949, 10950, 10955, 10959, 11003, 11019, 11020, 11038, 11039, 11071, 11073; *Middle East*, 11142, 11150, 11151; *Oceania*, 11197, 11209, 11217, 11224, 11257, 11365, 11383; *Elsewhere*, 11388, 11399, 11421, 11434, 11469, 11505, 11524, 11526, 11594, 11607, 11684, 11714, 11771, 11786, 11792, 11799, 11817; *Ancient History*, 11872-11874, 11881, 11882, 11927, 11928, 11934, 11944, 11945, 11949; *Bibliography*, 12006, 12007,

SUBJECT INDEX 1043

12118. See also BLACKS and DISCRIMINATION.

Refugees, *Austria*, 494; *Bangladesh*, 618; *Bulgaria*, 931; *Canada*, 1086; *Denmark*, 2093; *France*, 2771; *Israel*, 5352, 5370, 5456, 5473, 5586, 5670-5675, 5686, 5688, 5701, 5740, 5860, 5865; *Jordan*, 6163; *Switzerland*, 8661, 8667; *USA*, 9474, 9601, 9689; *Europe*, 10598, 10647, 10721, 10870. See also IMMIGRANTS.

Religion, *Argentina*, 137; *Australia*, 481; *Austria*, 551, 567, 598; *Bangladesh*, 625; *Brazil*, 733, 742, 801, 802, 810, 851; *Canada*, 1175, 1364; *Chile*, 1577, 1578; *China*, 1721; *Colombia*, 1792; *Cuba*, 1888, 1920; *Cyprus*, 1972; *Czechoslovakia*, 1982, 2054, 2057, 2058; *Egypt*, 2159, 2160, 2170, 2184, 2188, 2199, 2228; *France*, 2419, 2462, 2574, 2578, 2606, 2635, 2642; *Germany*, 2858, 2863, 2965, 2943, 2948, 3039, 3055, 3080, 3093, 3158; *Great Britain*, 3336, 3406, 3414, 3520, 3533, 3564, 3576, 3579, 3685, 3837, 3888, 3918, 3954, 3996, 4081, 4120; *Hungary*, 4561; *India*, 4630, 4652, 4718, 4987, 5010; *Iran*, 5083; *Israel*, 5227, 5329, 5476; *Italy*, 5967; *Japan*, 6128; *Laos*, 6279; *Liberia*, 6321; *Mexico*, 6519; *Namibia*, 6754; *Netherlands*, 6810, 6862; *Norway*, 7301; *Philippines*, 7517, 7584; *Poland*, 7651, 7708, 7710, 7727, 7753; *Rumania*, 7794; *Rwanda*, 7876; *South Africa*, 8150, 8172; *Spain*, 8314, 8398; *Sweden*, 8594; *Syria*, 8683; *Thailand*, 8739; *Togo*, 8770; *Turkey*, 8867; *Uganda*, 8893, 8899; *USSR*, 8954, 8970, 8971, 8988, 9214, 9223, 9267, 9286, 9298, 9304, 9378, 9409; *USA*, 9504, 9650, 9677, 9680, 9683; *Yugoslavia*, 9803, 9817, 9826, 9883, 9900; *Zaire*, 9934; *Zimbabwe*, 10015, 10028; *Africa*, 10051, 10106, 10139, 10232; *Asia*, 10309, 10325; *Europe*, 10486, 10496, 10499, 10502, 10559, 10587, 10772, 10824; *Latin America*, 10898, 10909, 10924, 10962, 11010, 11050; *Oceania*, 11261, 11293; *Elsewhere*, 11397, 11502, 11670, 11686; *Ancient History*, 11921. See also ISLAM.

Reparations, *Germany*, 2934, 3011, 3240

Repression, *Elsewhere*, 11631, 11841

Rescue, *Belgium*, 665; *Denmark*, 2083, 2087, 2088, 2108; *Ethiopia*, 2318, 2321; *Hungary*, 4601; *Poland*, 7735; *Sweden*, 8590; *Yugoslavia*, 9811; *Europe*, 10712, 10729, 10735, 10781, 10838, 10853. See also ANTISEMITISM and HOLOCAUST.

Resistance, *Algeria*, 41; *Angola*, 92; *Australia*, 386, 403, 417, 450; *Austria*, 550, 553, 557; *Belgium*, 647; *Belize*, 690; *Benin*, 697; *Brazil*, 837; *Bulgaria*, 909; *Czechoslovakia*, 2007, 2015, 2038; *Denmark*, 2089, 2096; *Ethiopia*, 2285, 2292; *France*, 2387, 2590, 2667, 2683, 2692; *Germany*, 2883, 3033, 3092, 3183, 3250, 3251; *Guatemala*, 4411; *India*, 4681, 4719, 4831, 4870, 4891; *Israel*, 5612, 5901; *Italy*, 5962, 5986, 5996; *Japan*, 6120; *Liberia*, 6303; *Libya*, 6340; *Mexico*, 6565, 6583; *Mozambique*, 6691, 6692; *Myanmar*, 6720; *Namibia*, 6734, 6744; *Netherlands*, 6888; *Norway*, 7317, 7328; *Peru*, 7437; *Philippines*, 7545, 7555; *Poland*, 7671, 7689, 7690, 7706; *Portugal*, 7777; *South Africa*, 7988, 8000, 8088, 8123, 8131, 8141, 8164, 8183, 8186; *Spain*, 8350; *Sri Lanka*, 8481; *USSR*, 8989, 9139, 9166, 9219; *USA*, 9629, 9548; *Zambia*, 9951; *Zimbabwe*, 9986; *Africa*, 10173; *Caribbean*, 10374, 10375, 10378, 10454, 10468; *Europe*, 10575, 10742, 10792; *Latin America*, 10970, 11075; *Oceania*, 11263, 11332; *Elsewhere*, 11452, 11637; *Ancient History*, 11880. See also OPPRESSION.

Resource exploitation, *Bolivia*, 711; *Brazil*, 749, 753, 789, 884; *Great Britain*, 3626; *Namibia*, 6732, 6762;

1044 SUBJECT INDEX

Philippines, 7506, 7531; *Saudi Arabia*, 7886; *USSR*, 9417; *Bibliography*, 12057

Revolution, *Afghanistan*, 5; *Algeria*, 47, 75; *Bangladesh*, 627; *Bolivia*, 707; *Burkina Faso*, 950, 952, 954; *Cambodia*, 978; *China*, 1652; *Cuba*, 1910; *Ethiopia*, 2289, 2295, 2305, 2319, 2325; *Guatemala*, 4400, 4406, 4409, 4428; *Guinea-Bissau*, 4431, 4432, 4438; *Haiti*, 4475, 4486; *India*, 4642, 4871, 5008; *Laos*, 6276; *Liberia*, 6330; *Libya*, 6335, 6339; *Mexico*, 6570; *Mozambique*, 6683; *New Zealand*, 6981; *Nicaragua*, 7015, 7046; *Peru*, 7448; *Philippines*, 7516, 7552, 7603, 7617; *Senegal*, 7892; *Turkey*, 8858; *USSR*, 9130, 9176, 9393; *Yemen*, 9790; *Zimbabwe*, 10011; *Africa*, 10097; *Caribbean*, 10429, 10432, 10444, 10449, 10460, 10478; *Oceania*, 11247, 11336; *Elsewhere*, 11770

Right-wing extremism, *Argentina*, 118; *Australia*, 220, 223; *Austria*, 485, 497, 510, 534, 555, 561, 571; *Brazil*, 774; *Canada*, 1183, 1345, 1483; *Finland*, 2351; *France*, 2376, 2380, 2385, 2391, 2436, 2437, 2439, 2477, 2492, 2498, 2503, 2506, 2507, 2529, 2542, 2585, 2615, 2631, 2634, 2663, 2679, 2681, 2684, 2690, 2698, 2699, 2708, 2734, 2743, 2754, 2762; *Germany*, 2792, 2794, 2799-2803, 2828, 2829, 2864, 2873, 2882, 2900, 2940, 2960, 2971, 2974, 2981, 2983, 2985, 2992, 3046, 3050, 3054, 3098, 3107, 3126, 3147, 3189, 3193-3195, 3214; *Great Britain*, 3722, 3794, 3857, 3878, 3939, 4226; *Hungary*, 4566, 4589; *Israel*, 5315, 5436, 5828; *Italy*, 6016; *New Zealand*, 6989; *Rumania*, 7817; *South Africa*, 7952, 8067, 8068, 8297, 8311; *Spain*, 8318; *Switzerland*, 8673; *USSR*, 8928, 9308; *USA*, 9444, 9590, 9717; *Europe*, 10507, 10520, 10578, 10588, 10593, 10620, 10635, 10649, 10657, 10694, 10698, 10717, 10758, 10779, 10780, 10868; *Elsewhere*, 11403, 11435, 11664, 11736. See also NAZISM.

Science, *Canada*, 1166; *Germany*, 2830, 3063; *USA*, 9604, 9641

Segregation, *Canada*, 1064, 1109; *Germany*, 3090, 3216; *Great Britain*, 3498; *South Africa*, 8003, 8132, 8153, 8165, 8213, 8262, 8296, 8300; *USA*, 9589, 9659; *Zimbabwe*, 9996; *Africa*, 10069; *Europe*, 10582; *Elsewhere*, 11580. See also DISCRIMINATION and RACISM.

Self-government, *Canada*, 1217, 1246, 1247, 1254, 1262; *New Zealand*, 6917

Sexism, *Algeria*, 26, 28, 51, 56, 57, 61, 78; *Argentina*, 94, 106, 113, 136, 146; *Australia*, 173, 175, 181, 194, 207, 214, 237, 327, 349, 379, 407, 477; *Austria*, 491, 568, 584, 599; *Bangladesh*, 611, 614, 615, 622; *Belgium*, 640; *Bolivia*, 702; *Brazil*, 736, 864; *Cameroon*, 994; *Canada*, 1098, 1102, 1119, 1189, 1191, 1211, 1260, 1329, 1378, 1379, 1381, 1389, 1404, 1441, 1445, 1446, 1452, 1481, 1501; *Chile*, 1549, 1554, 1559, 1563, 1580; *China*, 1661, 1669, 1678, 1697, 1700, 1716, 1737, 1750, 1753, 1754, 1766, 1772, 1779, 1780; *Colombia*, 1790, 1804, 1813; *Costa Rica*, 1828, 1831; *Cuba*, 1855, 1892, 1896, 1929, 1946, 1947, 1964; *Czechoslovakia*, 1976; *Dominican Republic*, 2112; *Egypt*, 2152, 2172, 2194, 2216, 2217, 2219, 2229, 2238, 2249; *El Salvador*, 2264; *Ethiopia*, 2316, 2326; *Finland*, 2349; *France*, 2374, 2379, 2416, 2438, 2458, 2476, 2534, 2557, 2583, 2604, 2621, 2651, 2682, 2719, 2750, 2769, 2770; *Germany*, 2782, 2793, 2833, 2836, 2841, 2854, 2860, 2878, 2894, 2914, 2954, 3030, 3042, 3072, 3073, 3082, 3105, 3108, 3116, 3159, 3160, 3170, 3188, 3202, 3205, 3207, 3232, 3237, 3238; *Ghana*, 3252, 3264, 3266; *Great Britain*, 3334, 3390, 3431, 3581, 3595, 3627, 3675, 3682, 3697,

SUBJECT INDEX 1045

3704, 3705, 3751, 3754, 3773, 3774, 3783, 3786, 3790, 3793, 3816, 3824, 3848, 3874, 3922, 3933, 3961, 3976, 4002, 4057, 4074, 4200, 4306, 4308, 4313, 4314, 4324, 4343; *India*, 4629, 4631, 4640, 4647, 4672, 4682, 4704, 4705, 4715, 4720, 4728, 4741, 4743, 4756, 4771, 4781, 4786, 4796, 4814, 4820, 4821, 4825, 4830, 4835, 4839, 4843, 4848, 4850, 4869, 4873, 4877, 4879, 4897, 4910, 4917, 4923, 4930, 4932, 4935, 4943, 4967, 4986, 5005; *Iran*, 5117, 5120, 5122, 5125, 5130; *Iraq*, 5138; *Ireland*, 5186, 5200, 5204; *Israel*, 5237, 5238, 5276, 5294, 5300, 5522, 5652, 5709, 5861, 5893; *Italy*, 5900, 5902, 5905, 5908, 5913, 5924, 5927, 5947, 5955, 5966, 5971, 5974, 5984; *Japan*, 6035, 6093, 6136; *Jordan*, 6165; *Korea*, 6239, 6263; *Lebanon*, 6285, 6295; *Libya*, 6346, 6349; *Malawi*, 6361; *Malaysia*, 6385, 6412, 6449; *Mauritius*, 6476; *Mexico*, 6494, 6585, 6592, 6596, 6607, 6612, 6625; *Morocco*, 6654-6656, 6667; *Mozambique*, 6680, 6699; *Myanmar*, 6709, 6717; *Namibia*, 6759, 6761, 6765, 6770; *Netherlands*, 6785, 6806, 6833, 6841, 6878, 6881, 6883, 6903; *New Zealand*, 6926; *Nigeria*, 7220, 7280; *Norway*, 7322; *Pakistan*, 7335, 7340, 7353, 7355, 7356, 7360; *Panama*, 7381; *Peru*, 7430; *Poland*, 7744; *Portugal*, 7771; *Rumania*, 7840; *Rwanda*, 7874; *Saudi Arabia*, 7880; *Singapore*, 7939; *South Africa*, 8138, 8139, 8167, 8215, 8218, 8236, 8267, 8288; *Spain*, 8326, 8329, 8339, 8347, 8358, 8359, 8394, 8405; *Sri Lanka*, 8442, 8454, 8496; *Sudan*, 8509, 8515; *Sweden*, 8572, 8581, 8596, 8600, 8615; *Switzerland*, 8643, 8657, 8671; *Syria*, 8674, 8691; *Tanzania*, 8709; *Turkey*, 8787, 8887; *USSR*, 8960, 9085, 9096, 9098, 9109, 9110, 9114, 9118, 9213, 9222, 9231, 9237, 9243, 9247, 9262, 9263; *USA*, 9519, 9553, 9567, 9610, 9614, 9616, 9635, 9664, 9665, 9690;
Vietnam, 9788; *Yemen*, 9797-9800; *Yugoslavia*, 9812, 9841; *Zaire*, 9929; *Zimbabwe*, 9964, 9968, 9983, 10002; *Africa*, 10035, 10048, 10056, 10088, 10148, 10187, 10218, 10231, 10240, 10242, 10245, 10283, 10286, 10288; *Asia*, 10308, 10313, 10316, 10321, 10329, 10330; *Caribbean*, 10363, 10380, 10387, 10417, 10428; *Europe*, 10515, 10536, 10537, 10583, 10692, 10769, 10782, 10802, 10803, 10862, 10865, 10866; *Latin America*, 10881, 10895, 10965, 10977, 10982, 10999-11002, 11012, 11026, 11027, 11083; *Middle East*, 11097, 11106, 11108, 11109, 11120, 11121, 11125, 11132, 11134, 11137, 11146, 11154, 11155, 11163, 11165, 11168, 11182, 11183, 11186, 11195; *Oceania*, 11277, 11352; *Elsewhere*, 11392, 11405, 11414, 11415, 11427, 11439, 11443, 11447, 11456, 11476, 11479, 11492, 11499, 11520, 11525, 11536, 11543, 11564, 11574, 11611, 11612, 11621, 11636, 11645, 11654, 11672, 11689, 11691, 11703, 11706, 11709, 11713, 11715, 11723, 11738, 11739, 11751, 11756, 11757, 11767, 11772, 11774, 11787, 11793, 11810, 11824, 11842, 11844, 11847; *Ancient History*, 11931; *Bibliography*, 11956, 11958, 11960, 11969, 11970, 11972-11974, 11976, 11981, 11997, 12001, 12004, 12031, 12034, 12036, 12045, 12047, 12048, 12061, 12063, 12065, 12074, 12083, 12088, 12090, 12091, 12107, 12108, 12116, 12119, 12121
Slavery, *Angola*, 84, 87; *Argentina*, 121; *Benin*, 699, 700; *Brazil*, 734, 750, 757-759, 769, 775, 776, 783, 791, 795, 807, 815, 820, 824, 827, 833, 846, 852, 857, 858, 867-870, 900-902; *Cambodia*, 977; *Cameroon*, 997; *Canada*, 1244; *Chad*, 1542; *Chile*, 1564; *China*, 1690, 1717, 1734, 1740, 1741, 1762, 1765, 1768, 1777; *Colombia*, 1789, 1793, 1799, 1814; *Cuba*, 1848, 1882, 1902, 1908, 1913, 1915, 1923, 1936, 1940, 1944, 1952-1954; *Cyprus*, 1968;

Denmark, 2095; *Dominican Republic*, 2122, 2125; *Ecuador*, 2132; *Egypt*, 2154, 2164, 2236; *Ethiopia*, 2313; *France*, 2452, 2504, 2550, 2561, 2595, 2672, 2697, 2758; *Germany*, 3138, 3204; *Ghana*, 3256; *Great Britain*, 3432, 3658, 3941, 3942, 4160; *Guatemala*, 4414; *Guyana*, 4447; *Haiti*, 4491, 4500, 4505; *India*, 4635, 4680, 4683, 4684, 4699, 4775, 4823, 4854, 4885, 4899, 4925, 4933; *Iran*, 5106; *Iraq*, 5163; *Italy*, 5963, 5973, 6010; *Kenya*, 6186, 6207; *Korea*, 6260; *Liberia*, 6315; *Madagascar*, 6351; *Malaysia*, 6448; *Mali*, 6456; *Mauritania*, 6462-6465; *Mauritius*, 6483; *Mexico*, 6506, 6508, 6511, 6516, 6526, 6614, 6621-6623, 6631; *Mozambique*, 6684; *Nicaragua*, 7101; *Nigeria*, 7199, 7213, 7233, 7256, 7262, 7264, 7278, 7281; *Panama*, 7387; *Paraguay*, 7421, 7424; *Peru*, 7436, 7463, 7472, 7474, 7497; *Portugal*, 7772, 7779, 7782, 7784; *Rumania*, 7793; *Senegal*, 7897, 7899; *Sierra Leone*, 7904, 7911; *South Africa*, 7964, 8032, 8047, 8189, 8225, 8227, 8243, 8269, 8292, 8309; *Spain*, 8338, 8344, 8352, 8379, 8381, 8414; *Sudan*, 8511, 8530, 8545, 8547, 8548, 8553; *Suriname*, 8560, 8561, 8563; *Sweden*, 8588, 8589, 8593; *Tanzania*, 8700; *Thailand*, 8737, 8740, 8751, 8763; *Tunisia*, 8785; *Turkey*, 8820, 8881; *Uruguay*, 8917; *USSR*, 9100-9104, 9194, 9394; *USA*, 9445, 9446, 9457, 9464, 9469, 9493, 9504, 9530, 9540, 9541, 9568, 9595, 9619, 9631, 9652, 9696, 9702, 9725; *Venezuela*, 9741, 9745, 9751, 9753, 9759; *Zaire*, 9924; *Africa*, 10038, 10039, 10050, 10052, 10068, 10079, 10081, 10085, 10086, 10090, 10093, 10096, 10109, 10110, 10120, 10130, 10132, 10144, 10153, 10170, 10172, 10178-10180, 10182, 10190, 10191, 10197, 10201, 10202, 10224, 10234, 10238, 10241, 10243, 10285, 10287; *Asia*, 10301, 10305, 10319, 10334; *Caribbean*, 10338, 10346, 10355, 10359, 10362, 10366, 10370, 10373, 10376, 10381, 10406, 10430, 10434, 10448, 10462, 10466, 10473, 10474, 10476; *Europe*, 10526, 10527, 10538, 10571, 10671, 10688, 10775, 10812, 10846-10849, 10859; *Latin America*, 10903, 10910, 10913, 10942, 10972, 10973, 10987, 11014, 11044, 11074, 11081; *Middle East*, 11104, 11112, 11148, 11176; *Elsewhere*, 11406, 11413, 11478, 11488, 11489, 11532, 11548, 11606, 11655, 11662, 11677, 11681, 11710, 11718-11720, 11724, 11726, 11728, 11732, 11733, 11758, 11766, 11790, 11801, 11827; *Ancient History*, 11852, 11855, 11858, 11861-11866, 11868, 11876, 11877, 11885, 11887, 11894, 11897, 11898, 11900, 11902, 11904, 11905, 11907, 11908, 11910, 11918, 11920, 11929, 11930, 11940, 11943, 11951, 11952; *Bibliography*, 11962, 11967, 11979, 12015, 12066, 12096, 12114. See also FORCED LABOR.

Social work, *Great Britain*, 3814, 3815, 3937, 4180, 4266

Socialism, *Albania*, 23; *Benin*, 696; *Brazil*, 834; *Chile*, 1581; *Great Britain*, 3689, 3776, 4347; *Nigeria*, 7258; *Sri Lanka*, 8328; *Tanzania*, 8715; *USA*, 9515, 9532, 9618; *Zimbabwe*, 9978, 10024; *Caribbean*, 10385, 10405, 10418, 10435; *Europe*, 10831; *Oceania*, 11337. See also COMMUNISM.

Sport, *Great Britain*, 3351, 4275; *South Africa*, 8264; *USA*, 9443, 9517; *Africa*, 10164, 10249

Stalinism, *Albania*, 16, 21; *Czechoslovakia*, 1994; *Portugal*, 7755; *USSR*, 9005, 9094, 9180, 9229, 9388; *Europe*, 10648, 10801

State violence, *Brazil*, 738, 762; *China*, 1769; *Colombia*, 1817; *El Salvador*, 2252, 2259; *Germany*, 2925; *India*, 4968; *Israel*, 5360, 5623, 5698, 5720; *Italy*, 5964; *Kenya*, 6210; *Rumania*, 7835; *South Africa*, 7981,

SUBJECT INDEX 1047

8006, 8060, 8090; *Sri Lanka*, 8432, 8461, 8498; *Turkey*, 8813, 8891; *Yugoslavia*, 9879, 9894; *Latin America*, 10983; *Elsewhere*, 11818. See also POLICE.

Stereotypes, *Australia*, 277, 420; *Canada*, 1069, 1083; *China*, 1778; *Costa Rica*, 1835; *France*, 2763; *Germany*, 3040, 3081; *Great Britain*, 3335, 3602; *Hungary*, 4557; *Israel*, 5643, 5754, 5849; *Italy*, 5937; *Malaysia*, 6430; *Morocco*, 6657; *Papua-New Guinea*, 7395; *Philippines*, 7581; *South Africa*, 8238, 8254, 8275; *USA*, 9688; *Africa*, 10146; *Elsewhere*, 11425, 11816, 12019

Students, *South Africa*, 8108, 8133, 8194, 8265, 8312; *Sudan*, 8541. See also EDUCATION.

Surveillance, *Great Britain*, 4135, 4136; *Mexico*, 6510; *USA*, 9549, 9611, 9628. See also POLICE and STATE VIOLENCE.

Taxes, *Canada*, 1332; *Great Britain*, 3748, 3813, 3972, 4097, 4102; *Malaysia*, 6426; *Pakistan*, 7350, 7352; *Philippines*, 7623; *Sierra Leone*, 7908; *Tanzania*, 8722; *Uganda*, 8896; *USA*, 9547

Terrorism, *Guatemala*, 4388; *Israel*, 5855. See also STATE VIOLENCE.

Tribalism, *Congo*, 1823; *Africa*, 10108, 10186, 10277

Unemployment, *Australia*, 308, 429, 432; *Canada*, 1256, 1505, 1524; *France*, 2596; *Great Britain*, 3429, 3453, 3463, 3549, 3591, 3739, 3799, 3858, 3860, 3866, 3894, 4094, 4161, 4177, 4342, 4353; *Netherlands*, 6808; *New Zealand*, 6925; *USSR*, 9089; *USA*, 9603; *Europe*, 10860; *Latin America*, 10915

Unions, *Canada*, 1494; *Chile*, 1567; *Israel*, 5542; *Netherlands*, 6805. See also LABOR.

Untouchables, *India*, 4774, 4792, 4793, 4809, 4824, 4901. See also CASTE and HARIJANS.

Violence, *Algeria*, 64, 65; *Argentina*, 116, 123, 128, 141; *Ghana*, 3253; *Great Britain*, 3352; *Guatemala*, 4402, 4407, 4421, 4422. See also STATE VIOLENCE.

War, *Australia*, 448, 471; *Bulgaria*, 933; *Canada*, 1215; *China*, 1699; *Ethiopia*, 2309; *Great Britain*, 4346; *India*, 4676; *Mexico*, 6620; *New Zealand*, 6979; *Norway*, 7309; *Panama*, 7370; *Philippines*, 7568; *Sri Lanka*, 8467; *Sudan*, 8538; *USSR*, 9015, 9206; *USA*, 9514, 9557; *Africa*, 10150, 10162, 10163, 10198, 10200, 10228, 10236; *Asia*, 10322; *Europe*, 10545; *Oceania*, 11270, 11339; *Elsewhere*, 11541, 11544, 11613; *Ancient History*, 11909. See also COLONIAL WARS and CONQUEST

War crimes, *Germany*, 2847; *Hungary*, 4562, 4563; *Europe*, 10745; *Bibliography*, 12106

War criminals, *Argentina*, 119; *Canada*, 1053, 1187, 1192; *USA*, 9433, 9436, 9617, 9666

Wealth, Distribution of, *Australia*, 197, 239, 244, 278, 285-287, 291, 298, 305; *Canada*, 1388, 1420, 1459, 1478, 1507, 1532; *Finland*, 2350; *France*, 2446, 2459-2461, 2482, 2489, 2553, 2584, 2632, 2648, 2676; *Ghana*, 3263; *Great Britain*, 3645, 3691-3694, 3886, 3904, 3905, 3940, 3947, 3965, 3903, 3904, 3906, 4132, 4159, 4168, 4185, 4187-4191, 4194, 4195, 4207, 4296; *India*, 4711, 4875, 4907; *Ireland*, 5183, 5185; *Israel*, 5262, 5283; *Italy*, 5941, 5942, 5984, 5993, 6015; *Japan*, 6135; *Malaysia*, 6419, 6438, 6439, 6446; *Netherlands*, 6910; *New Zealand*, 6921; *Peru*, 7492; *Rumania*, 7860; *Sweden*, 8618, 8619; *USA*, 9535, 9627, 9642, 9696; *Zambia*, 9952;

Zimbabwe, 9965, 9970; *Europe*, 10864; *Latin America*, 11189; *Oceania*, 11357; *Elsewhere*, 11431, 11581, 11754; *Ancient History*, 11901. See also INCOME, DISTRIBUTION OF and LIVING STANDARDS.

Xenophobia, *Europe*, 10485, 10558, 10617; *Elsewhere*, 11552, 11616

Youth, *Argentina*, 104; *Australia*, 375, 377; *Belgium*, 643; *Brazil*, 855; *Chile*, 1562; *China*, 1709, 1746; *Colombia*, 1805, 1807; *France*, 2556, 2644, 2660; *Germany*, 2790, 3023, 3086, 3156, 3171; *Great Britain*, 3346, 3411, 3545, 3804, 3962, 4106, 4117, 4139, 4269, 4330, 4331; *India*, 4770; *Israel*, 5659, 5728, 5731, 5759; *Italy*, 5981; *Nicaragua*, 7033; *Peru*, 7444; *South Africa*, 8040, 8168; *USSR*, 9016, 9146; *USA*, 9486, 9543; *Caribbean*, 10414; *Europe*, 10625; *Latin America*, 10986. See also STUDENTS and UNEMPLOYMENT.

Zionism, *Austria*, 516; *France*, 2599; *Germany*, 3122; *Hungary*, 4537; *Iraq*, 5160; *Israel*, 5299, 5350, 5446, 5507, 5529; *Libya*, 6347; *Poland*, 7740; *Turkey*, 8841; *USA*, 9459; *Elsewhere*, 11673, 11722. See also ANTISEMITISM and NATIONAL SELF-DETERMINATION.

About the Compiler

MEYER WEINBERG is Professor Emeritus at the W.E.B. DuBois Department of Afro-American Studies at the University of Massachusetts, Amherst. He is the author or compiler of numerous works dealing with education and race/ethnicity issues.